Solutions Manual

Kelli Jade Hammer
John Garlow

Prealgebra &
Introductory Algebra

K. Elayn Martin-Gay

PEARSON
Prentice
Hall

Upper Saddle River, NJ 07458

Editor-in-Chief: Chris Hoag
Senior Acquisitions Editor: Paul Murphy
Associate Editor: Elizabeth Covello
Supplement Editor: Christina Simoneau
Executive Managing Editor: Vince O'Brien
Production Editor: Allyson Kloss
Supplement Cover Manager: Paul Gourhan
Supplement Cover Designer: Joanne Alexandris
Manufacturing Buyer: Ilene Kahn

© 2005 Pearson Education, Inc.
Pearson Prentice Hall
Pearson Education, Inc.
Upper Saddle River, NJ 07458

Printed in the United States of America

10 9 8 7 6 5 4 3 2 1

ISBN 0-13-148491-5

Pearson Education Ltd., *London*
Pearson Education Australia Pty. Ltd., *Sydney*
Pearson Education Singapore, Pte. Ltd.
Pearson Education North Asia Ltd., *Hong Kong*
Pearson Education Canada, Inc., *Toronto*
Pearson Educación de Mexico, S.A. de C.V.
Pearson Education—Japan, *Tokyo*
Pearson Education Malaysia, Pte. Ltd.

Student Solutions Manual

Table of Contents

Chapter 1

Pretest

1. The place value of the 7 in 5732 is hundreds.

2. 23,490 is written as twenty-three thousand, four hundred ninety.

3.
$$
\begin{array}{r}
\overset{1}{5}8 \\
+\ 29 \\
\hline
87
\end{array}
$$

4.
$$
\begin{array}{r}
413 \\
\times\ 9 \\
\hline
3717
\end{array}
$$

5.
$$
\begin{array}{r}
857 \\
-\ 231 \\
\hline
626
\end{array}
$$

   Check:
$$
\begin{array}{r}
626 \\
+\ 231 \\
\hline
857
\end{array}
$$

6.
$$
\begin{array}{r}
51 \\
-\ 19 \\
\hline
32
\end{array}
$$

   Check:
$$
\begin{array}{r}
\overset{1}{3}2 \\
+\ 19 \\
\hline
51
\end{array}
$$

7. To find how many more pages Karen must read, we subtract the number of pages she has read from the number of pages in the book.
$$
\begin{array}{r}
329 \\
-\ 193 \\
\hline
136
\end{array}
$$
   Karen has 136 pages left to read.

8. To round 9045 to the nearest 10, observe that the digit in the ones place is 5. Since this digit is at least 5, we need to add 1 to the digit in the tens place. The number 9045, rounded to the nearest ten is 9050.

9.
$$
\begin{array}{rll}
382 & \text{rounds to} & 400 \\
436 & \text{rounds to} & 400 \\
2084 & \text{rounds to} & 2100 \\
+\ 176 & \text{rounds to} & +\ 200 \\
\hline
& & 3100
\end{array}
$$
   The estimated sum is 3100.

10. $9(3 + 11) = 9 \cdot 3 + 9 \cdot 11$

11. The perimeter is the sum of the lengths of the sides.
$$
\begin{array}{r}
\overset{1}{8} \\
11 \\
+\ 6 \\
\hline
25
\end{array}
$$
   The perimeter is 25 inches.

12. The area of a rectangle is the product of its length and its width.
   (23 yards)(8 yards) = 184 square yards

13. The total number of seats is the product of the number of rows and the number of seats in each row.
   (32 rows)(18 seats per row) = 576 seats

14.
$$
\begin{array}{r}
243 \\
9\overline{)\ 2187} \\
-18 \\
\hline
38 \\
-36 \\
\hline
27 \\
-27 \\
\hline
0
\end{array}
$$
   Check: $243 \cdot 9 = 2187$

15. $\dfrac{5361}{12}$
$$
\begin{array}{r}
446\ \text{R9} \\
12\overline{)\ 5361} \\
-48 \\
\hline
56 \\
-48 \\
\hline
81 \\
-72 \\
\hline
9
\end{array}
$$
   Check: $446 \cdot 12 + 9 = 5361$

16. There are 7 numbers.

$$
\begin{array}{r}
29 \\
36 \\
84 \\
41 \\
6 \\
12 \\
+\ 65 \\
\hline
273
\end{array}
$$

average $= \dfrac{273}{7} = 39$

The average is 39.

17. To find out how much money each nephew is to receive, we divide the total inheritance of $29,640 by the number of nephews which is 3.

$$
\begin{array}{r}
7880 \\
3\overline{)\ 29,640} \\
\underline{-27} \\
26 \\
\underline{-24} \\
24 \\
\underline{-24} \\
00 \\
\underline{-0} \\
0
\end{array}
$$

Each boy receives $7880.

18. There are 7 factors of 9, so $9 \cdot 9 \cdot 9 \cdot 9 \cdot 9 \cdot 9 \cdot 9 = 9^7$.

19. $7^4 = 7 \cdot 7 \cdot 7 \cdot 7 = 2401$

20. $36 + 18 \div 6 = 36 + 3 = 39$

21.

$$
\begin{aligned}
\frac{2x^2 + 3}{y} &= \frac{2(3)^2 + 3}{7} \\
&= \frac{2(9) + 3}{7} \\
&= \frac{18 + 3}{7} \\
&= \frac{21}{7} \\
&= 3
\end{aligned}
$$

22. In words: twice a number and 6
Translate: $2x + 6$

Section 1.1

Exercise Set 1.1

1. Answers may vary.

3. Answers may vary.

5. The video icon tells you that the corresponding exercise may be viewed on the videotape that corresponds to that section.

7. Answers may vary.

9. Answers may vary.

11. Answers may vary.

13. Answers may vary.

15. Yes; answers may vary

17. Answers may vary.

19. Chart will vary.

Section 1.2

Practice Problems

1. The place value of the 7 in 72,589,620 is ten-millions.

2. The place value of the 7 in 67,890 is thousands.

3. The place value of the 7 in 50,722 is hundreds.

4. 395 is written as three hundred ninety-five.

5. 2807 is written as two thousand, eight hundred seven.

6. 321,670,200 is written as three hundred twenty-one million, six hundred seventy thousand, two hundred.

7. Twenty-nine in standard form is 29.

8. Seven hundred ten in standard form is 710.

9. Twenty-six thousand seventy-one in standard form is 26,071.

10. Six thousand, five hundred seven in standard form is 6507.

11. 1,047,608
$= 1,000,000 + 40,000 + 7000 + 600 + 8$

12. **a.** $0 < 19$

  b. $18 < 32$

  c. $107 > 103$

13. **a.** Read from left to right across the line marked Russia until the "Gold" column is reached. We find that Russia has won 32 bronze medals.

    b. No countries shown have won more than 100 gold medals.

Exercise Set 1.2

1. The place value of the 5 in 352 is tens.

3. The place value of the 5 in 5890 is thousands.

5. The place value of the 5 in 62,500,000 is hundred-thousands.

7. The place value of the 5 in 5,070,099 is millions.

9. 5420 is written as five thousand, four hundred twenty.

11. 26,990 is written as twenty-six thousand, nine hundred ninety.

13. 1,620,000 is written as one million, six hundred twenty thousand.

15. 53,520,170 is written as fifty-three million, five hundred twenty thousand, one hundred seventy.

17. 63,960 is written as sixty-three thousand, nine hundred sixty.

19. 1483 is written as one thousand, four hundred eighty-three.

21. 12,662 is written as twelve thousand, six hundred sixty-two.

23. 13,600,000 is written as thirteen million, six hundred thousand.

25. 3893 is written as three thousand, eight hundred ninety-three.

27. Six thousand, five hundred eight in standard form is 6508.

29. Twenty-nine thousand, nine hundred in standard form is 29,900.

31. Six million, five hundred four thousand, nineteen in standard form is 6,504,019.

33. Three million, fourteen in standard form is 3,000,014.

35. Two hundred twenty miles in standard form is 220.

37. Seven hundred fifty-five in standard form is 755.

39. Seventy-three million, five hundred thousand in standard form is 73,500,000.

41. One thousand eight hundred fifteen in standard form is 1815.

43. One thousand two hundred sixty-two in standard form is 1262.

45. Forty-five thousand in standard form is 45,000.

47. $406 = 400 + 6$

49. $5290 = 5000 + 200 + 90$

51. $62,407 = 60,000 + 2000 + 400 + 7$

53. $30,680 = 30,000 + 600 + 80$

55. $39,680,000 = 30,000,000 + 9,000,000 + 600,000 + 80,000$

57. $1006 = 1000 + 6$

59. $3 < 8$

61. $9 > 0$

63. $6 > 2$

65. $22 > 0$

67. 4000 is written as four thousand.

69. $4145 = 4000 + 100 + 40 + 5$

71. The Nile is the longest river in the world.

73. The Labrador Retriever has the most AKC registrations; one hundred sixty-five thousand, nine hundred seventy-three.

75. The Golden Retriever has more dogs registered than the Chihuahua.

77. The largest number is achieved when the largest number available is used for each place value when reading from left to right. Thus, the largest number possible is 7632.

79. Answers may vary.

81. The town is Canton.

Section 1.3

Practice Problems

1. 7235
   + 542
     7777

2. 1 1 1 1
    27,364
   + 92,977
    120,341

3. $11 + 7 + 8 + 9 + 13 = 11 + 9 + 7 + 13 + 8$
$= (11 + 9) + (7 + 13) + 8$
$= 20 + 20 + 8$
$= 40 + 8$
$= 48$

4. 1 1 2
     19
   5042
    638
  + 526
   6225

5. To find the perimeter, add the lengths of the sides.
5 centimeters + 8 centimeters + 10 centimeters + 4 centimeters = 27 centimeters

6. To find the perimeter of the mall, add the lengths of the sides, all three of which have length 532 feet.
   532
   532
+ 532
  1596
The perimeter of the building is 1596 feet.

7. The phrase "more than" suggests we add. The addition statement
"Texas' pecan production + 15 million pounds = Georgia's pecan production" translates to:

   90 million lbs.
+ 15 million lbs.
  105 million lbs.

Georgia produces 105 million lbs. of pecans per year.

8. The number of thimbles that Elham has is the sum of the numbers of different types of thimbles that she has.

               1 3
glass thimbles   42
steel thimbles   17
porcelain thimbles   37
silver thimbles   9
plastic thimbles   + 15
total thimbles   120
Elham has 120 thimbles.

Calculator Explorations

1. Press the keys 89 $\boxed{+}$ 45 $\boxed{= \text{or ENTER}}$. The display will read 134.

2. Press the keys 76 $\boxed{+}$ 97 $\boxed{= \text{or ENTER}}$. The display will read 173.

3. Press the keys 285 $\boxed{+}$ 55 $\boxed{= \text{or ENTER}}$. The display will read 340.

4. Press the keys 8773 $\boxed{+}$ 652 $\boxed{= \text{or Enter}}$. The display will read 9425.

5. Press the keys 985 $\boxed{+}$ 1210 $\boxed{+}$ 562 $\boxed{+}$ 77 $\boxed{= \text{or ENTER}}$. The display will read 2834.

6. Press the keys 465 $\boxed{+}$ 9888 $\boxed{+}$ 620 $\boxed{+}$ 1550 $\boxed{= \text{or Enter}}$. The display will read 12,523.

Mental Math

1. $5 + 7 = 12$

2. $20 + 30 = 50$

3. $5000 + 4000 = 9000$

4. $4300 + 26 = 4326$

5. $1620 + 0 = 1620$

6. Rearranging will make this easier: $6 + 126 + 4 = 126 + (6 + 4) = 126 + 10 = 136$

Exercise Set 1.3

1. 14
  + 22
   36

3.
$$\begin{array}{r} 62 \\ + 30 \\ \hline 92 \end{array}$$

5.
$$\begin{array}{r} 12 \\ 13 \\ + 24 \\ \hline 49 \end{array}$$

7.
$$\begin{array}{r} 5267 \\ + 132 \\ \hline 5399 \end{array}$$

9.
$$\begin{array}{r} \overset{1}{} \\ 53 \\ + 64 \\ \hline 117 \end{array}$$

11.
$$\begin{array}{r} \overset{1}{} \\ 22 \\ + 49 \\ \hline 71 \end{array}$$

13.
$$\begin{array}{r} \overset{11}{} \\ 38 \\ + 79 \\ \hline 117 \end{array}$$

15.
$$\begin{array}{r} \overset{2}{} \\ 8 \\ 9 \\ 2 \\ 5 \\ + 1 \\ \hline 25 \end{array}$$

17.
$$\begin{array}{r} \overset{2}{} \\ 6 \\ 21 \\ 14 \\ 9 \\ + 12 \\ \hline 62 \end{array}$$

19.
$$\begin{array}{r} \overset{22}{} \\ 81 \\ 17 \\ 23 \\ 79 \\ + 12 \\ \hline 212 \end{array}$$

21.
$$\begin{array}{r} \overset{1}{} \\ 62 \\ 18 \\ + 14 \\ \hline 94 \end{array}$$

23.
$$\begin{array}{r} \overset{1}{} \\ 40 \\ 800 \\ + 70 \\ \hline 910 \end{array}$$

25.
$$\begin{array}{r} \overset{111}{} \\ 7542 \\ 49 \\ + 682 \\ \hline 8273 \end{array}$$

27.
$$\begin{array}{r} \overset{112}{} \\ 24 \\ 9006 \\ 489 \\ + 2407 \\ \hline 11,926 \end{array}$$

29.
$$\begin{array}{r} \overset{12}{} \\ 627 \\ 628 \\ + 629 \\ \hline 1884 \end{array}$$

31.
$$\begin{array}{r} \overset{111}{} \\ 6820 \\ 4271 \\ + 5626 \\ \hline 16,717 \end{array}$$

33.
$$\begin{array}{r} \overset{111}{} \\ 507 \\ 593 \\ + 10 \\ \hline 1110 \end{array}$$

35.
$$\begin{array}{r} 4200 \\ 2107 \\ + 2692 \\ \hline 8999 \end{array}$$

37.
$$\begin{array}{r} \overset{1122}{} \\ 49 \\ 628 \\ 5762 \\ + 29,462 \\ \hline 35,901 \end{array}$$

39.
$$
\begin{array}{r}
{\scriptstyle 1\,2\,2\,2\,1} \\
121,742 \\
57,279 \\
6\,586 \\
+\;426,782 \\
\hline
612,389
\end{array}
$$

41. $8 + 3 + 5 + 7 + 5 + 1 = 8 + 1 + 3 + 7 + 5 + 5$
$$
\begin{aligned}
&= 9 + 10 + 10 \\
&= 29
\end{aligned}
$$
The perimeter is 29 inches.

43. $8 + 10 + 7 = 8 + 7 + 10 = 15 + 10 = 25$
The perimeter is 25 feet.

45. Opposite sides of a rectangle have the same length.
$4 + 8 + 4 + 8 = 12 + 12 = 24$
The perimeter is 24 inches.

47. All the sides of a square have the same length.
$2 + 2 + 2 + 2 = 4 + 4 = 8$
The perimeter is 8 yards.

49.
$$
\begin{array}{r}
3560 \\
+3124 \\
\hline
6684
\end{array}
$$
Mount Mitchell is 6684 feet high.

51.
$$
\begin{array}{r}
{\scriptstyle 2\,1} \\
70 \\
78 \\
90 \\
+\;102 \\
\hline
340
\end{array}
$$
He needs 340 feet of wire.

53.
$$
\begin{array}{r}
{\scriptstyle 1} \\
234,500 \\
+29,200 \\
\hline
263,700
\end{array}
$$
There were 263,700 motorcycles shipped.

55.
$$
\begin{array}{r}
15,000 \\
+13,000 \\
\hline
28,000
\end{array}
$$
The newly combined company had 28,000 employees.

57.
$$
\begin{array}{r}
{\scriptstyle 1\,1} \\
7981 \\
+564 \\
\hline
8545
\end{array}
$$
There were 8545 Blockbuster Stores in 2002.

59. Key word: total
$$
\begin{array}{lr}
\text{upper} & 1430 \\
\text{middle} & 675 \\
+\quad\text{lower} & +\;320 \\
\hline
\text{total height} & 2425 \text{ feet}
\end{array}
$$

61.
$$
\begin{array}{r}
1795 \\
+\;11,460 \\
\hline
13,255
\end{array}
$$
The total highway mileage in Alaska is 13,255 miles.

63.
$$
\begin{array}{r}
{\scriptstyle 1} \\
6532 \\
+953 \\
\hline
7485
\end{array}
$$
Cats had staged 7485 performances.

65.
$$
\begin{array}{r}
{\scriptstyle 1\,1} \\
9821 \\
+\;592 \\
\hline
10,413
\end{array}
$$
There were 10,413 kidney transplants in 2002.

67. Texas has the most Wal-Mart stores.

69.
$$
\begin{array}{r}
{\scriptstyle 1} \\
342 \\
182 \\
+154 \\
\hline
678
\end{array}
$$

71.
$$
\begin{array}{r}
{\scriptstyle 2\,3} \\
102 \\
154 \\
182 \\
115 \\
140 \\
112 \\
104 \\
128 \\
116 \\
+342 \\
\hline
1495
\end{array}
$$
The ten stores total 1495.

73. Answers may vary.

75.
$$
\begin{array}{r}
{\scriptstyle 1\,1\;2\;2\,2\,1} \\
78,962 \\
129,968,350 \\
+\;36,462,880 \\
\hline
166,510,192
\end{array}
$$

77. The computation is not correct; answers may vary.

Section 1.4

Practice Problems

1. a. $14 - 9 = 5$ because $5 + 9 = 14$.

   b. $9 - 9 = 0$ because $0 + 9 = 9$.

   c. $4 - 0 = 4$ because $4 + 0 = 4$.

2. a.
$$\begin{array}{r} 4689 \\ -\ 253 \\ \hline 4436 \end{array}$$

Check:
$$\begin{array}{r} 4436 \\ +\ 253 \\ \hline 4689 \end{array}$$

   b.
$$\begin{array}{r} 981 \\ -\ 630 \\ \hline 351 \end{array}$$

Check:
$$\begin{array}{r} 351 \\ +\ 630 \\ \hline 981 \end{array}$$

3. a.
$$\begin{array}{r} 227 \\ -\ 175 \\ \hline 52 \end{array}$$

Check:
$$\begin{array}{r} {}^{1} \\ 52 \\ +\ 175 \\ \hline 227 \end{array}$$

   b.
$$\begin{array}{r} 1136 \\ -\ 914 \\ \hline 222 \end{array}$$

Check:
$$\begin{array}{r} {}^{1} \\ 222 \\ +\ 914 \\ \hline 1136 \end{array}$$

   c.
$$\begin{array}{r} 8627 \\ -\ 4119 \\ \hline 4508 \end{array}$$

Check:
$$\begin{array}{r} {}^{1} \\ 4508 \\ +\ 4119 \\ \hline 8627 \end{array}$$

4. a.
$$\begin{array}{r} 400 \\ -\ 164 \\ \hline 236 \end{array}$$

Check:
$$\begin{array}{r} {}^{11} \\ 236 \\ +\ 164 \\ \hline 400 \end{array}$$

   b.
$$\begin{array}{r} 200 \\ -\ 45 \\ \hline 155 \end{array}$$

Check:
$$\begin{array}{r} {}^{11} \\ 155 \\ +\ 45 \\ \hline 200 \end{array}$$

   c.
$$\begin{array}{r} 1000 \\ -\ 762 \\ \hline 238 \end{array}$$

Check:
$$\begin{array}{r} {}^{11} \\ 238 \\ +\ 762 \\ \hline 1000 \end{array}$$

5.
$$\begin{array}{ll} \text{radius of Earth} & 6378 \\ \underline{\text{less } 2981} & \underline{-\ 2981} \\ \text{radius of Mars} & 3397 \end{array}$$

The radius of Mars is 3397 kilometers.

6.
$$\begin{array}{ll} \text{original price} & 92 \\ \underline{\text{sale price}} & \underline{-\ 47} \\ \text{amount taken off} & 45 \end{array}$$

$45 was taken off the original price.

7. a. NC-17/X had 0 nominees, which is the least number of Best Picture nominees.

   b.
$$\begin{array}{ll} \text{Rated R nominees} & 52 \\ \underline{\text{Rated G nominees}} & \underline{-\ 2} \\ & 50 \end{array}$$

There were 50 more Best Picture nominees rated R than rated G.

Calculator Explorations

1. Press the keys 865 $\boxed{-}$ 95 $\boxed{= \text{or Enter}}$.
   The display will read 770.

2. Press the keys 76 $\boxed{-}$ 27 $\boxed{= \text{or Enter}}$.
   The display will read 49.

3. Press the keys 147 $\boxed{-}$ 38 $\boxed{= \text{or Enter}}$.
   The display will read 109.

4. Press the keys 366 $\boxed{-}$ 87 $\boxed{= \text{or Enter}}$.
   The display will read 279.

5. Press the keys 9625 $\boxed{-}$ 647 $\boxed{= \text{or Enter}}$.
   The display will read 8978.

6. Press the keys 10,711 $\boxed{-}$ 8925 $\boxed{= \text{or Enter}}$.
   The display will read 1786.

Mental Math

1. $9 - 2 = 7$

2. $6 - 6 = 0$

3. $5 - 0 = 5$

4. $44 - 22 = 22$

5. $93 - 93 = 0$

6. $700 - 400 = 300$

7. $700 - 300 = 400$

8. $700 - 700 = 0$

9. $600 - 100 = 500$

10. $600 - 0 = 600$

Exercise Set 1.4

1.
$$\begin{array}{r} 67 \\ -\ 23 \\ \hline 44 \end{array}$$

   Check:
$$\begin{array}{r} 44 \\ +\ 23 \\ \hline 67 \end{array}$$

3.
$$\begin{array}{r} 82 \\ -\ 22 \\ \hline 60 \end{array}$$

   Check:
$$\begin{array}{r} 60 \\ +\ 22 \\ \hline 82 \end{array}$$

5.
$$\begin{array}{r} 389 \\ -\ 124 \\ \hline 265 \end{array}$$

   Check:
$$\begin{array}{r} 265 \\ +\ 124 \\ \hline 389 \end{array}$$

7.
$$\begin{array}{r} 677 \\ -\ 423 \\ \hline 254 \end{array}$$

   Check:
$$\begin{array}{r} 254 \\ +\ 423 \\ \hline 677 \end{array}$$

9.
$$\begin{array}{r} 998 \\ -\ 453 \\ \hline 545 \end{array}$$

   Check:
$$\begin{array}{r} 545 \\ +\ 453 \\ \hline 998 \end{array}$$

11.
$$\begin{array}{r} 749 \\ -\ 149 \\ \hline 600 \end{array}$$

   Check:
$$\begin{array}{r} 600 \\ +\ 149 \\ \hline 749 \end{array}$$

13.
$$\begin{array}{r} 62 \\ -\ 37 \\ \hline 25 \end{array}$$

   Check:
$$\begin{array}{r} \overset{1}{2}5 \\ +\ 37 \\ \hline 62 \end{array}$$

15.
$$
\begin{array}{r}
70 \\
-25 \\
\hline
45
\end{array}
$$

Check:
$$
\begin{array}{r}
{\scriptstyle 1} \\
45 \\
+25 \\
\hline
70
\end{array}
$$

17.
$$
\begin{array}{r}
938 \\
-792 \\
\hline
146
\end{array}
$$

Check:
$$
\begin{array}{r}
{\scriptstyle 1} \\
146 \\
+792 \\
\hline
938
\end{array}
$$

19.
$$
\begin{array}{r}
922 \\
-634 \\
\hline
288
\end{array}
$$

Check:
$$
\begin{array}{r}
{\scriptstyle 11} \\
288 \\
+634 \\
\hline
922
\end{array}
$$

21.
$$
\begin{array}{r}
600 \\
-432 \\
\hline
168
\end{array}
$$

Check:
$$
\begin{array}{r}
{\scriptstyle 11} \\
168 \\
+432 \\
\hline
600
\end{array}
$$

23.
$$
\begin{array}{r}
42 \\
-36 \\
\hline
6
\end{array}
$$

Check:
$$
\begin{array}{r}
{\scriptstyle 1} \\
6 \\
+36 \\
\hline
42
\end{array}
$$

25.
$$
\begin{array}{r}
923 \\
-476 \\
\hline
447
\end{array}
$$

Check:
$$
\begin{array}{r}
{\scriptstyle 11} \\
447 \\
+476 \\
\hline
923
\end{array}
$$

27.
$$
\begin{array}{r}
6283 \\
-560 \\
\hline
5723
\end{array}
$$

Check:
$$
\begin{array}{r}
{\scriptstyle 1} \\
5723 \\
+560 \\
\hline
6283
\end{array}
$$

29.
$$
\begin{array}{r}
533 \\
-29 \\
\hline
504
\end{array}
$$

Check:
$$
\begin{array}{r}
{\scriptstyle 1} \\
504 \\
+29 \\
\hline
533
\end{array}
$$

31.
$$
\begin{array}{r}
200 \\
-111 \\
\hline
89
\end{array}
$$

Check:
$$
\begin{array}{r}
{\scriptstyle 11} \\
89 \\
+111 \\
\hline
200
\end{array}
$$

33.
$$
\begin{array}{r}
1983 \\
-1904 \\
\hline
79
\end{array}
$$

Check:
$$
\begin{array}{r}
{\scriptstyle 1} \\
79 \\
+1904 \\
\hline
1983
\end{array}
$$

35.
$$
\begin{array}{r}
56,422 \\
-16,508 \\
\hline
39,914
\end{array}
$$

Check:
$$
\begin{array}{r}
{\scriptstyle 11 \quad 1} \\
39,914 \\
+16,508 \\
\hline
56,422
\end{array}
$$

37.
$$
\begin{array}{r}
50,000 \\
-17,289 \\
\hline
32,711
\end{array}
$$

Check:
$$
\begin{array}{r}
{\scriptstyle 11 \ 11} \\
32,711 \\
+17,289 \\
\hline
50,000
\end{array}
$$

39.   7020
        − 1979
        5041

Check:
        1 1 1
        5041
    + 1979
        7020

41.   51,111
        − 19,898
        31,213

Check:
        1 1 1 1
        31,2 13
    + 19,898
        51,111

43.   9
        − 5
        4

Check:
        4
    + 5
        9

45.   41
        − 21
        20

Check:
        20
    + 21
        41

47.   63
        − 56
        7

Check:
        1
        7
    + 56
        63

49.   108
        −36
        72

Check:
        72
    +36
        108

51.   100
        −12
        88

Check:
        1
        88
    +12
        100

53.   503
        − 239
        264

Dyllis must read 264 more pages.

55.   25 million sq km
        −21 million sq km
        4 million sq km

The hole in the Earth's ozone has grown by 4 million square kilometers.

57.   20,320
        − 14,255
        6 065

Mt. McKinley is 6065 feet higher than Long's Peak.

59. We need to find the total amount of the checks.
        1
        27
        101
    + 236
        364

The checks total $364.
        539
        − 364
        175

Buhler will have $175 left in his account.

61.   645
        − 287
        358

The distance between Hays and Denver is 358 miles.

63.   971
        −732
        239

Pat will have $239 left in his savings account.

65.   2380
        −2207
        173

Stackhouse scored 173 more points than Iverson.

67.
$$\begin{array}{r} 38,803 \\ -1768 \\ \hline 37,035 \end{array}$$

There were 37,035 boxers registered with the AKC in 2001.

69. The total number of votes cast for Jo was:
$$\begin{array}{r} {\scriptstyle 1\,2\,1} \\ 276 \\ 362 \\ 201 \\ +179 \\ \hline 1018 \end{array}$$

The total number of votes cast for Trudy was:
$$\begin{array}{r} {\scriptstyle 2\,1} \\ 295 \\ 122 \\ 312 \\ +182 \\ \hline 911 \end{array}$$

Since more votes were cast for Jo than for Trudy, Jo won the election.
$$\begin{array}{r} 1018 \\ -\ 911 \\ \hline 107 \end{array}$$
Jo won by 107 votes.

71.
$$\begin{array}{r} 15,982,378 \\ -12,937,926 \\ \hline 3,044,452 \end{array}$$

Florida's population increased by 3,044,452 people.

73.
$$\begin{array}{r} 100,000 \\ -\ 94,080 \\ \hline 5\ 920 \end{array}$$

The Dole Plantation maze is 5920 square feet larger.

75.
$$\begin{array}{r} 28,547 \\ -26,372 \\ \hline 2175 \end{array}$$

The Lake Pontchartrain Bridge is 2175 feet longer.

77. Atlanta, Hartsfield International is busiest.

79.
$$\begin{array}{r} 67,448 \\ -61,606 \\ \hline 5842 \end{array}$$

Chicago O'Hare International Airport has 5842 thousand more passenger arrivals and departures.

81. General Motors Corp. spent more than $3 billion on advertising.

83.
$$\begin{array}{r} 3,374,400,000 \\ -1,985,300,000 \\ \hline 1,389,100,000 \end{array}$$

Daimler Chrysler spent $1,389,100,000 less on advertising.

85.
$$\begin{array}{r} 3,374,400,000 \\ 2,540,600,000 \\ 2,408,200,000 \\ 2,210,400,000 \\ 2,189,500,000 \\ 1,985,300,000 \\ 1,885,300,000 \\ 1,815,700,000 \\ 1,757,300,000 \\ +1,618,100,000 \\ \hline 21,784,800,000 \end{array}$$

These ten companies spent a total of $21,784,800,000 on advertising.

87.
$$\begin{array}{r} 5269 \\ -2385 \\ \hline 2884 \end{array}$$

89. Answers may vary.

Section 1.5

Practice Problems

1. a. To round 46 to the nearest ten, observe that the digit in the ones place is 6. Since this digit is at least 5, we need to add 1 to the digit in the tens place. The number 46 rounded to the nearest ten is 50.

    b. To round 731 to the nearest ten, observe that the digit in the ones place is 1. Since this digit is less than 5, we do not add 1 to the digit in the tens place. The number 731 rounded to the nearest ten is 730.

    c. To round 125 to the nearest ten, observe that the digit in the ones place is 5. Since this digit is at least 5, we need to add 1 to the digit in the tens place. The number 125 rounded to the nearest ten is 130.

2. a. To round 56,702 to the nearest thousand, observe that the digit in the hundreds place is 7. Since this digit is at least 5, we need to add 1 to the digit in the thousands place. The number 56,702 rounded to the nearest thousand is 57,000.

b. To round 7444 to the nearest thousand, observe that the digit in the hundreds place is 4. Since this digit is less than 5, we do not add 1 to the digit in the thousands place. The number 7444 rounded to the nearest thousand is 7000.

c. To round 291,500 to the nearest thousand, observe that the digit in the hundreds place is 5. Since this digit at least 5, we need to add 1 to the digit in the thousands place. The number 291,500 rounded to the nearest thousand is 292,000.

3. a. To round 2777 to the nearest hundred, observe that the digit in the tens place is 7. Since this digit is at least 5, we need to add 1 to the digit in the hundreds place. The number 2777 rounded to the nearest hundred is 2800.

b. To round 38,152 to the nearest hundred, observe that the digit in the tens place is 5. Since this digit is at least 5, we need to add 1 to the digit in the hundreds place. The number 38,152 rounded to the nearest hundred is 38,200.

c. To round 762,955 to the nearest hundred, observe that the digit in the tens place is 5. Since this digit is at least 5, we need to add 1 to the digit in the hundreds place. The number 762,955 rounded to the nearest hundred is 763,000.

4.

79	rounds to	80
35	rounds to	40
42	rounds to	40
21	rounds to	20
+ 98	rounds to	+ 100
		280

The estimated sum is 280. (The exact sum is 275.)

5.

4725	rounds to	5000
− 2879	rounds to	− 3000
		2000

The estimated difference is 2000. (The exact difference is 1846.)

6.

11	rounds to	10
16	rounds to	20
19	rounds to	20
+ 31	rounds to	+ 30
		80

It is approximately 80 miles from Grove to Hays. (The exact distance is 77 miles.)

7.

120,624	rounds to	120,000
22,866	rounds to	20,000
+ 45,970	rounds to	+ 50,000
		190,000

The approximate number of cases reported was 190,000.

Exercise Set 1.5

1. To round 632 to the nearest ten, observe that the digit in the ones place is 2. Since this digit is less than 5, we do not add 1 to the digit in the tens place. The number 632 rounded to the nearest ten is 630.

3. To round 635 to the nearest ten, observe that the digit in the ones place is 5. Since this digit is at least 5, we need to add 1 to the digit in the tens place. The number 635 rounded to the nearest ten is 640.

5. To round 792 to the nearest ten, observe that the digit in the ones place is 2. Since this digit is less than 5, we do not add 1 to the digit in the tens place. The number 792 rounded to the nearest ten is 790.

7. To round 395 to the nearest ten, observe that the digit in the ones place is 5. Since this digit is at least 5, we need to add 1 to the digit in the tens place. The number 395 rounded to the nearest ten is 400.

9. To round 1096 to the nearest ten, observe that the digit in the ones place is 6. Since this digit is at least 5, we need to add 1 to the digit in the tens place. The number 1096 rounded to the nearest ten is 1100.

11. To round 42,682 to the nearest thousand, observe that the digit in the hundreds place is 6. Since this digit is at least 5, we need to add 1 to the digit in the thousands place. The number 42,682 rounded to the nearest thousand is 43,000.

13. To round 248,695 to the nearest hundred, observe that the digit in the tens place is 9. Since this digit is at least 5, we need to add 1 to the digit in the hundreds place. The number 248,695 rounded to the nearest hundred is 248,700.

15. To round 36,499 to the nearest thousand, observe that the digit in the hundreds place is 4. Since this digit is less than 5, we do not add 1 to the digit in the thousands place. The number 36,499 rounded to the nearest thousand is 36,000.

17. To round 99,995 to the nearest ten, observe that the digit in the ones place is 5. Since this digit is at least 5, we need to add 1 to the digit in the tens place. The number 99,995 rounded to the nearest ten is 100,000.

19. To round 59,725,642 to the nearest ten-million, observe that the digit in the millions place is 9. Since this digit is at least 5, we need to add 1 to the digit in the ten-millions place. The number 59,725,642 rounded to the nearest ten-million is 60,000,000.

		Ten	Hundred	Thousand
21.	5281	5280	5300	5000
23.	9444	9440	9400	9000
25.	14,876	14,880	14,900	15,000

27. To round 11,331 to the nearest thousand, observe that the digit in the hundreds place is 3. Since this digit is less than 5, we do not add 1 to the digit in the thousands place. The number 11,331 rounded to the nearest thousand is 11,000.

29. To round 38,387 to the nearest thousand, observe that the digit in the hundreds place is 3. Since this digit is less than 5, we do not add 1 to the digit in the thousands place. The number 38,387 rounded to the nearest thousand is 38,000.

31. Since the digit in the millions place is at least 5, we add 1 to the digit in the ten-millions place. The number 116,856,000 rounded to the nearest ten-million is 120,000,000.

33. Since the digit in the hundreds place is less than 5, we do not add 1 to the digit in the thousands place. 18,188 rounds to 18,000.

35.

29	rounds to	30
35	rounds to	40
42	rounds to	40
+ 16	rounds to	+ 20

130

The estimated sum is 130.

37.

649	rounds to	650
− 272	rounds to	− 270

380

The estimated difference is 380.

39.

1812	rounds to	1800
1776	rounds to	1800
+ 1945	rounds to	+ 1900

5500

The estimated sum is 5500.

41.

1774	rounds to	1800
− 1492	rounds to	− 1500

300

The estimated difference is 300.

43.

2995	rounds to	3000
1649	rounds to	1600
+ 3940	rounds to	+ 3900

8500

The estimated sum is 8500.

45. $362 + 419$ is approximately
$360 + 420 = 780$.
The answer of 781 is correct.

47. $432 + 679 + 198$ is approximately
$400 + 700 + 200 = 1300$.
The answer of 1139 is incorrect.

49. $7806 + 5150$ is approximately
$7800 + 5200 = 13,000$.
The answer of 12,956 is correct.

51. $31,439 + 18,781$ is approximately
$31,000 + 19,000 = 50,000$.
The answer is 50,220 is correct.

53.

799	rounds to	800
1299	rounds to	1300
+ 999	rounds to	+ 1000

3100

The total cost is approximately $3100.

55.

19	rounds to	20
27	rounds to	30
+ 34	rounds to	+ 30

80

The distance from Stockton to LaCrosse is approximately 80 miles.

57. 20,320 rounds to 20,000
−14,410 rounds to −14,000

6000

The difference in elevation is approximately 6,000 feet.

59. 2,896,016 rounds to 2,900,000
−1,517,550 rounds to −1,500,000

1,400,000

Chicago's population is larger by approximately 1,400,000 people.

61. 41,126,233 rounds to 41,000,000
− 27,174,898 rounds to − 27,000,000

14,000,000

Johnson won the election by approximately 14,000,000 votes.

63. 905,235 rounds to 905,000
−750,695 rounds to −751,000

154,000

The Head Start enrollment increased by approximately 154,000 children.

65. 3274 rounds to 3300
−2159 rounds to −2200

1100

The difference in diameter is approximately 1100 miles.

67. 3,374,400,000 rounds to 3,400,000,000. General Motors Corp. spent approximately $3,400,000,000 on advertising.

69. 2,210,400,000 rounds to 2,000,000,000. PepsiCo spent approximately $2,000,000,000 on advertising.

71. The smallest possible number that rounds to 8600 is 8550.

73. The largest possible number that rounds to 1,500,000 is 1,549,999.

75.   7693 rounds to   7700
         8203 rounds to   8200
       +5950 rounds to +6000
                             21,900

  The perimeter is approximately 21,900 miles.

Section 1.6

Practice Problems

1. **a.** $3 \times 0 = 0$

    b. $4(1) = 4$

    c. $(0)(34) = 0$

    d. $1 \cdot 76 = 76$

2. **a.** $5(2 + 3) = 5 \cdot 2 + 5 \cdot 3$

    b. $9(8 + 7) = 9 \cdot 8 + 9 \cdot 7$

    c. $3(6 + 1) = 3 \cdot 6 + 3 \cdot 1$

3. **a.** $\overset{2}{36}$
              $\underline{\times\ 4}$
               144

    b. $\overset{1}{92}$
              $\underline{\times\ 9}$
               828

4. **a.**   594
              $\underline{\times\ 72}$
              1 188
              $\underline{41,580}$
              42,768

    b.   306
              $\underline{\times\ 81}$
                306
              $\underline{24,480}$
              24,786

5. **a.**   726
              $\underline{\times\ 142}$
              1 452
              29,040
              $\underline{72,600}$
              103,092

b.   4
             $\underline{\times\ 288}$
                32
               320
              $\underline{800}$
              1152

6.   360
         $\underline{\times\ 280}$
                  0
             28,800
             $\underline{72,000}$
            100,800

  The area is 100,800 square miles.

7.   240
       $\underline{\times\ 15}$
        1200
        $\underline{2400}$
        3600

  The printer can print 3600 characters in 15 seconds.

8. The cost of 4 plain shirts is $4 \cdot 6 = \$24$.
    The cost of 5 striped shirts is $5 \cdot 7 = \$35$.
    The total cost is $24 + 35 = \$59$.

9.   259   rounds to   300
       $\underline{\times\ 195}$ rounds to $\underline{\times\ 200}$
                                 60,000

  There are approximately 60,000 words on 195 pages.

Calculator Explorations

1. Press the keys 72 $\boxed{\times}$ 48 $\boxed{\text{= or ENTER}}$.
    The display will read 3456.

2. Press the keys 81 $\boxed{\times}$ 92 $\boxed{\text{= or ENTER}}$.
    The display will read 7452.

3. Press the keys 163 $\boxed{\times}$ 94 $\boxed{\text{= or ENTER}}$.
    The display will read 15,322.

4. Press the keys 285 $\boxed{\times}$ 144 $\boxed{\text{= or ENTER}}$.
    The display will read 41,040.

5   Press the keys 983 $\boxed{\times}$ 277 $\boxed{\text{= or ENTER}}$.
    The display will read 272,291.

6. Press the keys 1562 $\times$ 843 = or ENTER .

The display will read 1,316,766.

Mental Math

1. $1 \cdot 24 = 24$

2. $55 \cdot 1 = 55$

3. $0 \cdot 19 = 0$

4. $27 \cdot 0 = 0$

5. $8 \cdot 0 \cdot 9 = 0$

6. $7 \cdot 6 \cdot 0 = 0$

7. $87 \cdot 1 = 87$

8. $1 \cdot 41 = 41$

Exercise Set 1.6

1. $4(3 + 9) = 4 \cdot 3 + 4 \cdot 9$

3. $2(4 + 6) = 2 \cdot 4 + 2 \cdot 6$

5. $10(11 + 7) = 10 \cdot 11 + 10 \cdot 7$

7.
$$\begin{array}{r} 42 \\ \times\ 6 \\ \hline 252 \end{array}$$

9.
$$\begin{array}{r} 624 \\ \times\ 3 \\ \hline 1872 \end{array}$$

11.
$$\begin{array}{r} 277 \\ \times\ 6 \\ \hline 1662 \end{array}$$

13.
$$\begin{array}{r} 1062 \\ \times\ 5 \\ \hline 5310 \end{array}$$

15.
$$\begin{array}{r} 298 \\ \times\ 14 \\ \hline 1192 \\ 2980 \\ \hline 4172 \end{array}$$

17.
$$\begin{array}{r} 231 \\ \times\ 47 \\ \hline 1\ 617 \\ 9\ 240 \\ \hline 10,857 \end{array}$$

19.
$$\begin{array}{r} 809 \\ \times\ 14 \\ \hline 3\,236 \\ 8\,090 \\ \hline 11,326 \end{array}$$

21.
$$\begin{array}{r} 620 \\ \times\ 40 \\ \hline 0 \\ 24,800 \\ \hline 24,800 \end{array}$$

23. $(998)(12)(0) = 0$

25. $(590)(1)(10) = 5900$

27.
$$\begin{array}{r} 1\ 234 \\ \times\ 48 \\ \hline 9\ 872 \\ 49,360 \\ \hline 59,232 \end{array}$$

29.
$$\begin{array}{r} 609 \\ \times\ 234 \\ \hline 2\ 436 \\ 18,270 \\ 121,800 \\ \hline 142,506 \end{array}$$

31.
$$\begin{array}{r} 5621 \\ \times\ 324 \\ \hline 22,484 \\ 112,420 \\ 1,686,300 \\ \hline 1,821,204 \end{array}$$

33.
$$\begin{array}{r} 1941 \\ \times\ 235 \\ \hline 9\ 705 \\ 58,230 \\ 388,200 \\ \hline 456,135 \end{array}$$

35.
$$
\begin{array}{r}
589 \\
\times\ 110 \\
\hline
0 \\
5\ 890 \\
58,900 \\
\hline
64,790
\end{array}
$$

37.
$$
\begin{array}{r}
964 \\
\times\ 207 \\
\hline
6748 \\
00 \\
192,800 \\
\hline
199,548
\end{array}
$$

39.
$$
\begin{array}{rll}
576 & \text{rounds to} & 600 \\
\times\ 354 & \text{rounds to} & \times\ 400 \\
\hline
 & & 240,000
\end{array}
$$

576×354 is approximately 240,000.

41.
$$
\begin{array}{rll}
604 & \text{rounds to} & 600 \\
\times\ 451 & \text{rounds to} & \times\ 500 \\
\hline
 & & 300,000
\end{array}
$$

604×451 is approximately 300,000.

43.
$$
\begin{array}{rll}
872 & \text{rounds to} & 870 \\
\times\ 27 & \text{rounds to} & \times\ 30 \\
\hline
 & & 26,100
\end{array}
$$

872×27 is approximately 26,100

45.
$$
\begin{array}{rll}
36 & \text{rounds to} & 40 \\
\times\ 87 & \text{rounds to} & \times\ 90 \\
\hline
 & & 3600
\end{array}
$$

36×87 is approximately 3600.

47. Area = length · width

       = (9 meters)(7 meters)

       = 63 square meters

The area is 63 square meters.

49. Area = length · width

       = (30 feet)(13 feet)

       = 390 square feet

The area is 390 square feet.

51.
$$
\begin{array}{r}
125 \\
\times\ 3 \\
\hline
375
\end{array}
$$

There are 375 calories in 3 tablespoons of olive oil.

53.
$$
\begin{array}{r}
54 \\
\times\ 35 \\
\hline
270 \\
1620 \\
\hline
1890
\end{array}
$$

The books cost a total of $1890.

55.
$$
\begin{array}{r}
12 \\
\times\ 8 \\
\hline
96
\end{array}
$$

$2 \times 96 = 192$

There are 192 cans in a case.

57.
$$
\begin{array}{r}
90 \\
\times\ 110 \\
\hline
0 \\
900 \\
9000 \\
\hline
9900
\end{array}
$$

The area of the plot is 9900 square feet.

59.
$$
\begin{array}{r}
350 \\
\times\ 160 \\
\hline
0 \\
21,000 \\
35,000 \\
\hline
56,000
\end{array}
$$

The lobby's area is 56,000 square feet.

61.
$$
\begin{array}{r}
62 \\
\times\ 94 \\
\hline
248 \\
5580 \\
\hline
5828
\end{array}
$$

The screen contains a total of 5828 pixels.

63.
$$
\begin{array}{r}
80 \\
\times\ 25 \\
\hline
400 \\
1600 \\
\hline
2000
\end{array}
$$

There are 2000 characters in 25 lines.

65.
$$
\begin{array}{r}
160 \\
\times\ 8 \\
\hline
1280
\end{array}
$$

There are 1280 calories in 8 ounces of peanuts.

67.   7927
          × 9
       ‾‾‾‾‾‾‾
       71,343

Saturn has a diameter of 71,343 miles.

69. $7 \times 2 = 14$ windows
    $4 \times 2 = 8$ windows
    $14 + 8 = 22$ windows
       22
     × 23
     ‾‾‾‾
       66
      440
     ‾‾‾‾
      506
    The building has a total of 506 windows.

71.   700,000
            × 31
        ‾‾‾‾‾‾‾‾‾
          700,000
       21,000,000
       ‾‾‾‾‾‾‾‾‾‾
       21,700,000

21,700,000 quarts of milk would be used in March.

73. 905,235   rounds to   905,000
        × 6,633   rounds to   × 7000
        ‾‾‾‾‾‾‾   ‾‾‾‾‾‾‾‾‾‾‾‾
                            6,335,000,000

The total cost of the Head Start program is approximately $6,335,000,000.

75. $5 \times 10 = 50$
50 students chose grapes as their favorite fruit.

77. The apple (chosen by $9 \times 10 = 90$ students) and the orange (chosen by $7 \times 10 = 70$ students) were the most popular.

79. The result of multiplying 3 by the digit in the first blank is a number ending in 6. Only 2 works. The result of multiplying the digit in the second blank by 42 is 378, so the digit in the second blank is 9.
       4$\underline{2}$
     × 9$\underline{3}$
     ‾‾‾‾‾
      126
     3780
     ‾‾‾‾
     3906

81. Answers may vary.

83. $61 \times 3 = 183$
        $640 \times 2 = 1280$
          183
         1280
       + 475
       ‾‾‾‾‾
         1938

Kobe Bryant scored 1938 points in the 2000-2001 season.

Section 1.7

Practice Problems

1. a. $8\overline{)48} = 6$ because $6 \cdot 8 = 48$.

b. $35 \div 5 = 7$, because $7 \cdot 5 = 35$.

c. $\frac{49}{7} = 7$, because $7 \cdot 7 = 49$.

2. a. $\frac{8}{8} = 1$, because $1 \cdot 8 = 8$.

b. $3 \div 1 = 3$, because $3 \cdot 1 = 3$.

c. $1\overline{)12} = 12$, because $12 \cdot 1 = 12$.

d. $2 \div 1 = 2$, because $2 \cdot 1 = 2$.

e. $\frac{5}{1} = 5$, because $5 \cdot 1 = 5$.

3. a. $\frac{0}{7} = 0$, because $0 \cdot 7 = 0$.

b. $5\overline{)0} = 0$, because $0 \cdot 5 = 0$.

c. $9 \div 0$ is undefined, because any number multiplied by 0 is 0 and not 9.

d. $0 \div 6 = 0$, because $0 \cdot 6 = 0$.

4. a.   897
          6$\overline{)5382}$
           −48
           ‾‾‾
            58
           −54
           ‾‾‾
            42
           −42
           ‾‾‾
             0

Check: $897 \cdot 6 = 5382$

b.
```
        553
    4) 2212
      −20
       21
      −20
       12
      −12
        0
```
Check: 553 · 4 = 2212

5. a.
```
        799
    3) 2397
      −21
       29
      −27
       27
      −27
        0
```
Check: 799 · 3 = 2397

b.
```
        360
    7) 2520
      −21
       42
      −42
       00
       −0
        0
```
Check: 360 · 7 = 2520

6. a.
```
        189  R 4
    5) 949
      −5
       44
      −40
       49
      −45
        4
```
Check: 189 · 5 + 4 = 949

b.
```
        733  R 1
    6) 4399
      −42
       19
      −18
       19
      −18
        1
```
Check: 733 · 6 + 1 = 4399

7. a.
```
         8168  R 1
    5) 40841
      −40
       08
       −5
       34
      −30
       41
      −40
        1
```
Check: 8168 · 5 + 1 = 40,841

b.
```
        3204  R 2
    7) 22430
      −21
       14
      −14
       03
       −0
       30
      −28
        2
```
Check: 3204 · 7 + 2 = 22,430

8.
```
         302  R 2
    19) 5740
       −57
        04
        −0
        40
       −38
         2
```
Check: 302 · 19 + 2 = 5740

9.
```
          67  R 40
    247) 16589
        −1482
         1769
        −1729
           40
```
Check: 67 · 247 + 40 = 16,589

10.
```
        40
    3) 120
      −12
       00
       −0
        0
```
Each person got 40 diskettes.

11.
```
        32  R 3
    6) 195
      −18
       15
      −12
        3
```

195 sandwiches yield 32 full packages, with 3 sandwiches left over.

12.

$$\begin{array}{r} 20 \ \text{R} \ 17 \\ 24\overline{)\ 497} \\ \underline{-48} \\ 17 \\ \underline{-0} \\ 17 \end{array}$$

20 full boxes will be shipped, with 17 calculators left over.

13. Add the scores, then divide by 7, the number of scores.

$$\begin{array}{r} 5 \\ 7 \\ 20 \\ 6 \\ 9 \\ 3 \\ +48 \\ \hline 98 \end{array} \qquad \begin{array}{r} 14 \\ 7\overline{)\ 98} \\ \underline{-7} \\ 28 \\ \underline{-28} \\ 0 \end{array}$$

The average elapsed time is 14 minutes.

Calculator Explorations

1. Press the keys 848 $\boxed{\div}$ 16 $\boxed{= \text{or ENTER}}$. The display will read 53.

2. Press the keys 8564 $\boxed{\div}$ 12 $\boxed{= \text{or ENTER}}$. The display will read 47.

3. Press the keys 5890 $\boxed{\div}$ 95 $\boxed{= \text{or ENTER}}$. The display will read 62.

4. Press the keys 1053 $\boxed{\div}$ 27 $\boxed{= \text{or ENTER}}$. The display will read 39.

5. Press the keys 32,886 $\boxed{\div}$ 126 $\boxed{= \text{or ENTER}}$. The display will read 261.

6. Press the keys 143,088 $\boxed{\div}$ 264 $\boxed{= \text{or ENTER}}$. The display will read 542.

7. Press the keys 0 $\boxed{\div}$ 315 $\boxed{= \text{or ENTER}}$. The display will read 0.

8. Press the keys 315 $\boxed{\div}$ 0 $\boxed{= \text{or ENTER}}$. The display will read *Error.*

Mental Math

1. $40 \div 8 = 5$

2. $72 \div 9 = 8$

3. $45 \div 5 = 9$

4. $24 \div 3 = 8$

5. $0 \div 5 = 0$

6. $0 \div 8 = 0$

7. $9 \div 1 = 9$

8. $12 \div 1 = 12$

9. $\frac{16}{16} = 1$

10. $\frac{49}{49} = 1$

11. $\frac{25}{5} = 5$

12. $\frac{45}{9} = 5$

13. $6 \div 0$ is undefined

14. $\frac{12}{0}$ is undefined

15. $7 \div 1 = 7$

16. $6 \div 6 = 1$

17. $0 \div 4 = 0$

18. $7 \div 0$ is undefined

19. $16 \div 2 = 8$

20. $18 \div 3 = 6$

Exercise Set 1.7

1.
$$\begin{array}{r} 12 \\ 9\overline{)\ 108} \\ \underline{-9} \\ 18 \\ \underline{-18} \\ 0 \end{array}$$
Check: $12 \cdot 9 = 108$

3.
$$\begin{array}{r} 37 \\ 6\overline{)\ 222} \\ \underline{-18} \\ 42 \\ \underline{-42} \\ 0 \end{array}$$

Check: $37 \cdot 6 = 222$

5.
$$
\begin{array}{r}
338 \\
3)\overline{1014} \\
\underline{-9} \\
11 \\
\underline{-9} \\
24 \\
\underline{-24} \\
0
\end{array}
$$

Check: $338 \cdot 3 = 1014$

7.
$$
\begin{array}{r}
16 \ \text{R } 2 \\
6)\overline{98} \\
\underline{-6} \\
38 \\
\underline{-36} \\
2
\end{array}
$$

Check: $16 \cdot 6 + 2 = 98$

9.
$$
\begin{array}{r}
563 \ \text{R } 1 \\
2)\overline{1127} \\
\underline{-10} \\
12 \\
\underline{-12} \\
07 \\
\underline{-6} \\
1
\end{array}
$$

Check: $563 \cdot 2 + 1 = 1127$

11.
$$
\begin{array}{r}
37 \ \text{R } 1 \\
5)\overline{186} \\
\underline{-15} \\
36 \\
\underline{-35} \\
1
\end{array}
$$

Check: $37 \cdot 5 + 1 = 186$

13.
$$
\begin{array}{r}
265 \ \text{R } 1 \\
8)\overline{2121} \\
\underline{-16} \\
52 \\
\underline{-48} \\
41 \\
\underline{-40} \\
1
\end{array}
$$

Check: $265 \cdot 8 + 1 = 2121$

15.
$$
\begin{array}{r}
49 \\
23)\overline{1127} \\
\underline{-92} \\
207 \\
\underline{-207} \\
0
\end{array}
$$

Check: $49 \cdot 23 = 1127$

17.
$$
\begin{array}{r}
13 \\
55)\overline{715} \\
\underline{-55} \\
165 \\
\underline{-165} \\
0
\end{array}
$$

Check: $13 \cdot 55 = 715$

19.
$$
\begin{array}{r}
97 \ \text{R } 40 \\
97)\overline{9449} \\
\underline{-873} \\
719 \\
\underline{-679} \\
40
\end{array}
$$

Check: $97 \cdot 97 + 40 = 9449$

21.
$$
\begin{array}{r}
206 \\
18)\overline{3708} \\
\underline{-36} \\
10 \\
\underline{-0} \\
108 \\
\underline{-108} \\
0
\end{array}
$$

Check: $206 \cdot 18 = 3708$

23.
$$
\begin{array}{r}
506 \\
13)\overline{6578} \\
\underline{-65} \\
07 \\
\underline{-0} \\
78 \\
\underline{-78} \\
0
\end{array}
$$

Check: $506 \cdot 13 = 6578$

25.
$$
\begin{array}{r}
202 \ \text{R } 7 \\
46)\overline{9299} \\
\underline{-92} \\
09 \\
\underline{-0} \\
99 \\
\underline{-92} \\
7
\end{array}
$$

Check: $202 \cdot 46 + 7 = 9299$

27.
$$
\begin{array}{r}
45 \\
236)\overline{10620} \\
\underline{-944} \\
1180 \\
\underline{-1180} \\
0
\end{array}
$$

Check: $45 \cdot 236 = 10620$

29.
$$\begin{array}{r} 98 \text{ R } 100 \\ 103\overline{)\,10194} \\ \underline{-927} \\ 924 \\ \underline{-824} \\ 100 \end{array}$$
Check: $98 \cdot 103 + 100 = 10{,}194$

31.
$$\begin{array}{r} 202 \text{ R } 15 \\ 102\overline{)\,20619} \\ \underline{-204} \\ 21 \\ \underline{-0} \\ 219 \\ \underline{-204} \\ 15 \end{array}$$
Check: $202 \cdot 102 + 15 = 20{,}619$

33.
$$\begin{array}{r} 202 \\ 223\overline{)\,45046} \\ \underline{-446} \\ 44 \\ \underline{-0} \\ 446 \\ \underline{-446} \\ 0 \end{array}$$
Check: $202 \cdot 223 = 45{,}046$

35.
$$\begin{array}{r} 58 \\ 85\overline{)\,4930} \\ \underline{-425} \\ 680 \\ \underline{-680} \\ 0 \end{array}$$
There are 58 students in the group.

37.
$$\begin{array}{r} 252000 \\ 21\overline{)\,5292000} \\ \underline{-42} \\ 109 \\ \underline{-105} \\ 42 \\ \underline{-42} \\ 00 \\ \underline{-0} \\ 00 \\ \underline{-0} \\ 00 \\ \underline{-0} \\ 0 \end{array}$$
Each person receives $252,000.

39.
$$\begin{array}{r} 415 \\ 14\overline{)\,5810} \\ \underline{-56} \\ 21 \\ \underline{-14} \\ 70 \\ \underline{-70} \\ 0 \end{array}$$
The truck hauls 415 bushels each trip.

41.
$$\begin{array}{r} 88 \text{ R } 1 \\ 3\overline{)\,265} \\ \underline{-24} \\ 25 \\ \underline{-24} \\ 1 \end{array}$$
There are 89 bridges in 265 miles.

43.
$$\begin{array}{r} 23 \text{ R } 1 \\ 8\overline{)\,185} \\ \underline{-16} \\ 25 \\ \underline{-24} \\ 1 \end{array}$$
She has enough for 22 students, with another student's worth plus one more foot, or $8 + 1 = 9$ feet extra.

45.
$$\begin{array}{r} 24 \\ 6\overline{)\,144} \\ \underline{-12} \\ 24 \\ \underline{-24} \\ 0 \end{array}$$
He scored 24 touchdowns during 2002.

47.
$$\begin{array}{r} 1760 \\ 3\overline{)\,5280} \\ \underline{-3} \\ 22 \\ \underline{-21} \\ 18 \\ \underline{-18} \\ 00 \\ \underline{-0} \\ 0 \end{array}$$
There are 1760 yards in 1 mile.

49. There are six numbers.

    14
    22
    45
    18
    30
 + 27
  156

$$\begin{array}{r} 26 \\ 6\overline{)\ 156} \\ -12 \\ \hline 36 \\ -36 \\ \hline 0 \end{array}$$

Average $= \dfrac{156}{6} = 26$

51. There are four numbers.

  204
  968
  552
+ 268
 1992

$$\begin{array}{r} 498 \\ 4\overline{)\ 1992} \\ -16 \\ \hline 39 \\ -36 \\ \hline 32 \\ -32 \\ \hline 0 \end{array}$$

Average $= \dfrac{1992}{4} = 498$

53. There are five numbers.

  86
  79
  81
  69
+ 80
 395

$$\begin{array}{r} 79 \\ 5\overline{)\ 395} \\ -35 \\ \hline 45 \\ -45 \\ \hline 0 \end{array}$$

Average $= \dfrac{395}{5} = 79$

55. Add those month's temperatures, then divide by 3, the number of temperatures.

  18
  12
+ 18
  48

$$\begin{array}{r} 16 \\ 3\overline{)\ 48} \\ -3 \\ \hline 18 \\ -18 \\ \hline 0 \end{array}$$

The average temperature is $\dfrac{48}{3} = 16$ degrees.

57. Add the 2 greatest amounts, then divide by 2.

  3,374,400,000
+ 2,540,600,000
  5,915,000,000

$$\begin{array}{r} 2957500000 \\ 2\overline{)\ 5915000000} \\ -4 \\ \hline 19 \\ -18 \\ \hline 11 \\ -10 \\ \hline 15 \\ -14 \\ \hline 10 \\ -10 \\ \hline 00 \\ -0 \\ \hline 00 \\ -0 \\ \hline 00 \\ -0 \\ \hline 00 \\ -0 \\ \hline 00 \\ -0 \\ \hline 0 \end{array}$$

The average amount spent by the top two companies is $2,957,500,000.

59. Increases, because 71 lies below the average, which is 83.

61. No, because all the numbers are greater than 86.

Integrated Review

1. $\overset{1\ 1}{}$
    23
    46
  + 79
   148

2.   7006
  − 451
  6555

3.   36
  × 45
   180
 1440
 1620

4.
$$\begin{array}{r} 562 \\ 8\overline{)\,4496} \\ \underline{-40} \\ 49 \\ \underline{-48} \\ 16 \\ \underline{-16} \\ 0 \end{array}$$

5. $1 \cdot 79 = 79$

6. $\dfrac{36}{0}$ is undefined.

7. $9 \div 1 = 9$

8. $9 \div 9 = 1$

9. $0 \cdot 13 = 0$

10. $7 \cdot 0 \cdot 8 = 0$

11. $0 \div 2 = 0$

12. $12 \div 4 = 3$

13.
$$\begin{array}{r} 4219 \\ -\ 1786 \\ \hline 2433 \end{array}$$

14.
$$\begin{array}{r} {}^{2\,2\,1} \\ 1861 \\ 7965 \\ 199 \\ +\ 2870 \\ \hline 12,895 \end{array}$$

15.
$$\begin{array}{r} 213 \ \text{R } 3 \\ 5\overline{)\,1068} \\ \underline{-10} \\ 06 \\ \underline{-5} \\ 18 \\ \underline{-15} \\ 3 \end{array}$$

16.
$$\begin{array}{r} 1259 \\ \times\ 63 \\ \hline 3\,777 \\ 75,540 \\ \hline 79,317 \end{array}$$

17. $3 \cdot 9 = 27$

18. $45 \div 5 = 9$

19.
$$\begin{array}{r} 207 \\ -\ 69 \\ \hline 138 \end{array}$$

20.
$$\begin{array}{r} {}^{1} \\ 207 \\ +\ 69 \\ \hline 276 \end{array}$$

21.
$$\begin{array}{r} 1099 \ \text{R } 2 \\ 7\overline{)\,7695} \\ \underline{-\ 7} \\ 06 \\ \underline{-\ 0} \\ 69 \\ \underline{-\ 63} \\ 65 \\ \underline{-\ 63} \\ 2 \end{array}$$

22.
$$\begin{array}{r} 111 \ \text{R } 1 \\ 9\overline{)\,1000} \\ \underline{-\ 9} \\ 10 \\ \underline{-\ 9} \\ 10 \\ \underline{-\ 9} \\ 1 \end{array}$$

23.
$$\begin{array}{r} 663 \ \text{R } 6 \\ 32\overline{)\,21222} \\ \underline{-192} \\ 202 \\ \underline{-192} \\ 102 \\ \underline{-96} \\ 6 \end{array}$$

24.
$$\begin{array}{r} 1076 \ \text{R } 60 \\ 65\overline{)\,70000} \\ \underline{-65} \\ 50 \\ \underline{-0} \\ 500 \\ \underline{-455} \\ 450 \\ \underline{-390} \\ 60 \end{array}$$

25.
$$\begin{array}{r} 4000 \\ -2976 \\ \hline 1024 \end{array}$$

26.
$$\begin{array}{r} 10,000 \\ -101 \\ \hline 9,899 \end{array}$$

27.
$$\begin{array}{r} 303 \\ \times\ 101 \\ \hline 303 \\ 00 \\ 30,300 \\ \hline 30,603 \end{array}$$

28.
$$\begin{array}{r} 475 \\ \times\ 100 \\ \hline 47,500 \end{array}$$

29.
$$\begin{array}{r} 0 \\ 7\overline{)\ 0} \\ \underline{-0} \\ 0 \end{array}$$

30. $14 \div 0$ is undefined because 0 times any number is 0, and not 14.

31.
$$\begin{array}{r} 0 \\ 6\overline{)\ 0} \\ \underline{-0} \\ 0 \end{array}$$

32.
$$\begin{array}{r} 0 \\ 105\overline{)\ 0} \\ \underline{-0} \\ 0 \end{array}$$

33.
$$\begin{array}{r} 100 \\ -14 \\ \hline 86 \end{array}$$

34.
$$\begin{array}{r} 43 \\ -21 \\ \hline 22 \end{array}$$

		Tens	Hundreds	Thousands
35.	8625	8630	8600	9000
36.	1553	1550	1600	2000
37.	10,901	10,900	10,900	11,000
38.	432,198	432,200	432,200	432,000

39. A square has all equal sides. Therefore, if one side is 5 feet, each side is 5 feet.

40. Opposite sides of a rectangle have the same length. To find the perimeter add the length of all the sides. $14 + 14 + 7 + 7 = 42$ inches. To find the area, multiply length times width. $14 \times 7 = 98$ square inches.

41. Add up the length of all the sides. $11 + 7 + 8 = 26$ miles.

42. Find the length of the missing sides by looking at the sides directly across from the sides that have no stated value. The bottom side of the figure is 6 meters $(3 + 3)$. The right side of the figure is 7 meters $(3 + 4)$. Add up all the sides. $3 + 7 + 6 + 3 + 3 + 4 = 26$ meters.

43.
$$\begin{array}{r} 1933 \\ +2054 \\ \hline 3987 \end{array}$$

The northern boundary of the United States is 3987 miles.

44.
$$\begin{array}{r} 14 \\ +29 \\ \hline 43 \end{array}$$

It takes 43 muscles to frown.

45.
$$\begin{array}{r} 206\ \text{R } 12 \\ 48\overline{)\ 9900} \\ \underline{-96} \\ 30 \\ \underline{-0} \\ 300 \\ \underline{-288} \\ 12 \end{array}$$

206 cases can be filled with 12 cans left over. Yes, there are enough cases to fill a 200 case order.

46.
$$
\begin{array}{r}
540 \\
\times\ \ 33 \\
\hline
1620 \\
16200 \\
\hline
17{,}820
\end{array}
$$

The video players cost a total of $17,820.

Section 1.8

Practice Problems

1. $2 \cdot 2 \cdot 2 = 2^3$

2. $3 \cdot 3 = 3^2$

3. $10 \cdot 10 \cdot 10 \cdot 10 \cdot 10 \cdot 10 = 10^6$

4. $5 \cdot 5 \cdot 4 \cdot 4 \cdot 4 = (5 \cdot 5)(4 \cdot 4 \cdot 4) = 5^2 \cdot 4^3$

5. $2^3 = 2 \cdot 2 \cdot 2 = 8$

6. $5^2 = 5 \cdot 5 = 25$

7. $10^1 = 10$

8. $4 \cdot 5^2 = 4(5 \cdot 5) = 4 \cdot 25 = 100$

9. $16 \div 4 - 2 = 4 - 2$
   $\qquad\qquad = 2$

10. $18 \div 3^2 \cdot 2^2 = 18 \div 9 \cdot 4$
    $\qquad\qquad\quad = 2 \cdot 4$
    $\qquad\qquad\quad = 8$

11. $(9-8)^3 + 3 \cdot 2^4 = 1^3 + 3 \cdot 2^4$
    $\qquad\qquad\qquad = 1 + 3 \cdot 16$
    $\qquad\qquad\qquad = 1 + 48$
    $\qquad\qquad\qquad = 49$

12. $24 \div [20 - (3 \cdot 4)] + 2^3 - 5$
    $= 24 \div [20 - 12] + 2^3 - 5$
    $= 24 \div 8 + 8 - 5$
    $= 3 + 8 - 5$
    $= 6$

13. $\dfrac{60 - 5^2 + 1}{3(1+1)} = \dfrac{60 - 25 + 1}{3(2)}$
    $\qquad\qquad\quad = \dfrac{36}{6}$
    $\qquad\qquad\quad = 6$

14. Area of a square $= (\text{side})^2$
    $\qquad\qquad\qquad = (11 \text{ centimeters})^2$
    $\qquad\qquad\qquad = 121 \text{ square centimeters}$

Calculator Explorations

1. Press the keys $3\ \boxed{y^x}\ 6\ \boxed{= \text{or ENTER}}$. The display will read 729.

2. Press the keys $5\ \boxed{y^x}\ 6\ \boxed{= \text{or ENTER}}$. The display will read 15,625.

3. Press the keys $4\ \boxed{y^x}\ 5\ \boxed{= \text{or ENTER}}$. The display will read 1024.

4. Press the keys $7\ \boxed{y^x}\ 6\ \boxed{= \text{or ENTER}}$. The display will read 117,649.

5. Press the keys $2\ \boxed{y^x}\ 11\ \boxed{= \text{or ENTER}}$. The display will read 2048.

6. Press the keys $6\ \boxed{y^x}\ 8\ \boxed{= \text{or ENTER}}$. The display will read 1,679,616.

7. Press the keys $7\ \boxed{y^x}\ 4\ \boxed{+}\ 5\ \boxed{y^x}\ 3\ \boxed{= \text{or ENTER}}$. The display will read 2526.

8. Press the keys 12 $\boxed{y^x}$ 4 $\boxed{-}$ 8 $\boxed{y^x}$ 4 $\boxed{= \text{or ENTER}}$. The display will read 16,640.

9. Press the keys 63 $\boxed{\times}$ 75 $\boxed{-}$ 43 $\boxed{\times}$ 10 $\boxed{= \text{or ENTER}}$. The display will read 4295.

10. Press the keys 8 $\boxed{\times}$ 22 $\boxed{+}$ 7 $\boxed{\times}$ 16 $\boxed{= \text{or ENTER}}$. The display will read 288.

11. Press the keys 4 $\boxed{\times}$ $\boxed{(}$ 15 $\boxed{\div}$ 3 $\boxed{+}$ 2 $\boxed{)}$ $\boxed{-}$ 10 $\boxed{\times}$ 2 $\boxed{= \text{or ENTER}}$. The display will read 8.

12. Press the keys 155 $\boxed{-}$ 2 $\boxed{\times}$ $\boxed{(}$ 17 $\boxed{+}$ 3 $\boxed{)}$ $\boxed{+}$ 185 $\boxed{= \text{or ENTER}}$. The display will read 300.

Exercise Set 1.8

1. $3 \cdot 3 \cdot 3 \cdot 3 = 3^4$

3. $7 \cdot 7 \cdot 7 \cdot 7 \cdot 7 \cdot 7 \cdot 7 \cdot 7 = 7^8$

5. $12 \cdot 12 \cdot 12 = 12^3$

7. $6 \cdot 6 \cdot 5 \cdot 5 \cdot 5 = (6 \cdot 6)(5 \cdot 5 \cdot 5) = 6^2 \cdot 5^3$

9. $9 \cdot 9 \cdot 9 \cdot 8 = (9 \cdot 9 \cdot 9)8 = 9^3 \cdot 8$

11. $3 \cdot 2 \cdot 2 \cdot 2 \cdot 2 \cdot 2 = 3(2 \cdot 2 \cdot 2 \cdot 2 \cdot 2) = 3 \cdot 2^5$

13. $3 \cdot 2 \cdot 2 \cdot 5 \cdot 5 \cdot 5 = 3(2 \cdot 2)(5 \cdot 5 \cdot 5) = 3 \cdot 2^2 \cdot 5^3$

15. $5^2 = 5 \cdot 5 = 25$

17. $5^3 = 5 \cdot 5 \cdot 5 = 125$

19. $2^6 = 2 \cdot 2 \cdot 2 \cdot 2 \cdot 2 \cdot 2 = 64$

21. $2^{10} = 2 \cdot 2 \cdot 2 \cdot 2 \cdot 2 \cdot 2 \cdot 2 \cdot 2 \cdot 2 \cdot 2 = 1024$

23. $7^1 = 7$

25. $3^5 = 3 \cdot 3 \cdot 3 \cdot 3 \cdot 3 = 243$

27. $2^8 = 2 \cdot 2 \cdot 2 \cdot 2 \cdot 2 \cdot 2 \cdot 2 \cdot 2 = 256$

29. $4^3 = 4 \cdot 4 \cdot 4 = 64$

31. $9^2 = 9 \cdot 9 = 81$

33. $9^3 = 9 \cdot 9 \cdot 9 = 729$

35. $10^2 = 10 \cdot 10 = 100$

37. $10^4 = 10 \cdot 10 \cdot 10 \cdot 10 = 10,000$

39. $10^1 = 10$

41. $1920^1 = 1920$

43. $3^6 = 3 \cdot 3 \cdot 3 \cdot 3 \cdot 3 \cdot 3 = 729$

45. $15 + 3 \cdot 2 = 15 + 6$
$$= 21$$

47. $20 - 4 \cdot 3 = 20 - 12$
$$= 8$$

49. $5 \cdot 9 - 16 = 45 - 16$
$$= 29$$

51. $28 \div 4 - 3 = 7 - 3$
$$= 4$$

53. $14 + \dfrac{24}{8} = 14 + 3$
$$= 17$$

55. $6 \cdot 5 + 8 \cdot 2 = 30 + 8 \cdot 2$
$$= 30 + 16$$
$$= 46$$

57. $0 \div 6 + 4 \cdot 7 = 0 + 4 \cdot 7$
$$= 0 + 28$$
$$= 28$$

59. $6 + 8 \div 2 = 6 + 4$
$$= 10$$

61. $(6+8) \div 2 = 14 \div 2$
$$= 7$$

63. $\left(6^2 - 4\right) \div 8 = (36 - 4) \div 8$
$$= 32 \div 8$$
$$= 4$$

65. $\left(3 + 5^2\right) \div 2 = (3 + 25) \div 2$
$$= 28 \div 2$$
$$= 14$$

67. $6^2 \cdot (10 - 8) = 36 \cdot (10 - 8)$
$$= 36 \cdot 2$$
$$= 72$$

69. $\dfrac{18 + 6}{2^4 - 4} = \dfrac{24}{16 - 4}$
$$= \dfrac{24}{12}$$
$$= 2$$

71. $(2 + 5) \cdot (8 - 3) = 7 \cdot (8 - 3)$
$$= 7 \cdot 5$$
$$= 35$$

73. $\dfrac{7(9 - 6) + 3}{3^2 - 3} = \dfrac{7 \cdot 3 + 3}{9 - 3}$
$$= \dfrac{21 + 3}{6}$$
$$= \dfrac{24}{6}$$
$$= 4$$

75. $5 \div 0 + 24$ is undefined because $5 \div 0$ is undefined.

77. $3^4 - [35 - (12 - 6)] = 3^4 - [35 - 6]$
$$= 81 - 29$$
$$= 52$$

79. $(7 \cdot 5) + [9 \div (3 \div 3)] = (7 \cdot 5) + [9 \div 1]$
$$= 35 + 9$$
$$= 44$$

81. $8 \cdot [4 + (6 - 1) \cdot 2] - 50 \cdot 2$
$$= 8 \cdot [4 + 5 \cdot 2] - 50 \cdot 2$$
$$= 8 \cdot [4 + 10] - 100$$
$$= 8 \cdot 14 - 100$$
$$= 112 - 100$$
$$= 12$$

83. $7^2 - \left\{18 - [40 \div (4 \cdot 2) + 2] + 5^2\right\}$
$$= 7^2 - \left\{18 - [40 \div 8 + 2] + 5^2\right\}$$
$$= 49 - \{18 - [5 + 2] + 25\}$$
$$= 49 - \{18 - 7 + 25\}$$
$$= 49 - 36$$
$$= 13$$

85. Area of a square $= (\text{side})^2$
$$= (20 \text{ miles})^2$$
$$= 400 \text{ square miles}$$

87. Area of a square $= (\text{side})^2$
$$= (8 \text{ centimeters})^2$$
$$= 64 \text{ square centimeters}$$

89. Area of base $= (\text{side})^2$
$$= (100 \text{ meters})^2$$
$$= 10,000 \text{ square meters}$$

91. $(2 + 3) \cdot 6 - 2 = 5 \cdot 6 - 2$
$$= 30 - 2$$
$$= 28$$

93. $24 \div (3 \cdot 2) + 2 \cdot 5 = 24 \div 6 + 2 \cdot 5$
$$= 4 + 10$$
$$= 14$$

95. Missing side lengths are $60 - 40 = 20$ feet and $30 - 12 = 18$ feet.
Perimeter of one home $= 12 + 60 + 30 + 40 + 18 + 20 = 180$ feet.
Total perimeter $= 7 \times 180 = 1260$ feet.

97. $\left(7 + 2^4\right)^5 - \left(3^5 - 2^4\right)^2$
$$= (7 + 16)^5 - \left(3^5 - 2^4\right)^2$$
$$= 23^5 - (243 - 16)^2$$
$$= 6,436,343 - 227^2$$
$$= 6,436,343 - 51,529$$
$$= 6,384,814$$

Section 1.9

Practice Problems

1. Replace x with 5 in the expression $x - 2$.
$$x - 2 = 5 - 2 = 3$$

2. $y(x-3) = 7(3-3)$
$= 7(0)$
$= 0$

3. $\dfrac{y+6}{x} = \dfrac{8+6}{2}$
$= \dfrac{14}{2}$
$= 7$

4. $25 - z^3 + 1 = 25 - (2)^3 + 1$
$= 25 - 8 + 1$
$= 18$

5. $\dfrac{5(F-32)}{9} = \dfrac{5(41-32)}{9}$
$= \dfrac{5(9)}{9}$
$= 5$

6. a. In words: twice a number
Translate: $2 \cdot x$ or $2x$

b. In words: 8 increased by a number
Translate: $x + 8$

c. In words: 10 minus a number
Translate: $10 - x$

d. In words: 10 subtracted from a number
Translate: $x - 10$

e. In words: the quotient of 6 and a number
Translate: $6 \div x$ or $\dfrac{6}{x}$

Exercise Set 1.9

1. $3 + 2z = 3 + 2(3)$
$= 3 + 6$
$= 9$

3. $6xz - 5x = 6(2)(3) - 5(2)$
$= 36 - 10$
$= 26$

5. $z - x + y = 3 - 2 + 5$
$= 6$

7. $3x - z = 3 \cdot 2 - 3$
$= 6 - 3$
$= 3$

9. $y^3 - 4x = 5^3 - 4(2)$
$= 125 - 4(2)$
$= 125 - 8$
$= 117$

11. $2xy^2 - 6 = 2(2)(5)^2 - 6$
$= 2(2)(25) - 6$
$= 100 - 6$
$= 94$

13. $8 - (y - x) = 8 - (5 - 2)$
$= 8 - 3$
$= 5$

15. $y^4 + (z - x) = 5^4 + (3 - 2)$
$= 5^4 + 1$
$= 625 + 1$
$= 626$

17. $\dfrac{6xy}{z} = \dfrac{6 \cdot 2 \cdot 5}{3}$
$= \dfrac{60}{3}$
$= 20$

19. $\dfrac{2y-2}{x} = \dfrac{2 \cdot 5 - 2}{2}$
$= \dfrac{10-2}{2}$
$= \dfrac{8}{2}$
$= 4$

21. $\dfrac{x+2y}{z} = \dfrac{2 + 2 \cdot 5}{3}$
$= \dfrac{2+10}{3}$
$= \dfrac{12}{3}$
$= 4$

23. $\dfrac{5x}{y} - \dfrac{10}{y} = \dfrac{5 \cdot 2}{5} - \dfrac{10}{5}$
$= \dfrac{10}{5} - \dfrac{10}{5}$
$= 0$

25. $2y^2 - 4y + 3 = 2 \cdot 5^2 - 4 \cdot 5 + 3$
$= 2 \cdot 25 - 4 \cdot 5 + 3$
$= 50 - 20 + 3$
$= 33$

27. $(3y - 2x)^2 = (3 \cdot 5 - 2 \cdot 2)^2$
$= (15 - 4)^2$
$= (11)^2$
$= 121$

29. $(xy+1)^2 = (2 \cdot 5 + 1)^2$
$$= (10+1)^2$$
$$= (11)^2$$
$$= 121$$

31. $2y(4z - x) = 2 \cdot 5(4 \cdot 3 - 2)$
$$= 2 \cdot 5(12 - 2)$$
$$= 2 \cdot 5(10)$$
$$= 10(10)$$
$$= 100$$

33. $xy(5 + z - x) = 2 \cdot 5(5 + 3 - 2)$
$$= 2 \cdot 5(8 - 2)$$
$$= 2 \cdot 5(6)$$
$$= 10(6)$$
$$= 60$$

35. $\dfrac{7x + 2y}{3x} = \dfrac{7 \cdot 2 + 2 \cdot 5}{3 \cdot 2}$
$$= \dfrac{14 + 10}{6}$$
$$= \dfrac{24}{6}$$
$$= 4$$

37.

t	1	2	3	4
$16t^2$	$16(1)^2$	$16(2)^2$	$16(3)^2$	$16(4)^2$
	$16 \cdot 1$	$16 \cdot 4$	$16 \cdot 9$	$16 \cdot 16$
	16	64	144	256

39. $x + 5$

41. $x + 8$

43. $20 - x$

45. $512x$

47. $x \div 2$ or $\dfrac{x}{2}$

49. $5x + (17 + x)$

51. $5x$

53. $11 - x$

55. $x - 5$

57. $6 \div x$ or $\dfrac{6}{x}$

59. $50 - 8x$

61. $x^4 - y^2 = (23)^4 - (72)^2$ Substitute
$$= 279,841 - 5184 \text{ Exponentiate}$$
$$= 274,657 \qquad \text{Subtract}$$

63. $x^2 + 5y - 112$
$$= (23)^2 + 5(72) - 112 \text{ Substitute}$$
$$= 529 + 360 - 112 \qquad \text{Exponentiate}$$
$$= 777 \qquad\qquad \text{Add and subtract}$$

65. Compare expressions:
$$\frac{x}{3} = \left(\frac{1}{3}\right)x$$
$$\left(\frac{1}{3}\right)x < 2x < 5x$$
$5x$ is the largest.

67.

t	1	2	3	4
$16t^2$	16	64	144	256

As t gets larger, $16t^2$ gets larger.

Chapter 1 Review

1. 5<u>4</u>80
   ↓
   hundreds

2. <u>4</u>6,200,120
   ↓
   ten millions

3. 5480 = five thousand, four hundred eighty

4. 46,200,120 = forty-six million, two hundred thousand, one hundred twenty

5. 6279 = 6000 + 200 + 70 + 9

6. 403,225,000 = 400,000,000 + 3,000,000 + 200,000 + 20,000 + 5000

7. Fifty-nine thousand, eight hundred = 59,800

8. Six billion, three hundred four million = 6,304,000,000

9. In 1990, Houston had a population of 1,630,553 people.

10. In 1980, Los Angeles had a population of 2,968,528 people.

11. $\begin{array}{r} 1,321,045 \\ -789,704 \\ \hline 531,341 \end{array}$

The population of Phoenix increased by 531,341 people from 1980 to 2000.

12. $\begin{array}{r} 1,027,974 \\ -951,270 \\ \hline 76,704 \end{array}$

The population of Detroit decreased by 76,704 people from 1990 to 2000.

13. $7 + 6 = 13$

14. $8 + 9 = 17$

15. $3 + 0 = 3$

16. $0 + 10 = 10$

17. $\begin{array}{r} 1 \\ 25 \\ 8 \\ +\ 5 \\ \hline 38 \end{array}$

18. $\begin{array}{r} 27 \\ +41 \\ \hline 68 \end{array}$

19. $\begin{array}{r} 32 \\ +24 \\ \hline 56 \end{array}$

20. $\begin{array}{r} 1 \\ 19 \\ +21 \\ \hline 40 \end{array}$

21. $\begin{array}{r} 11 \\ 47 \\ +63 \\ \hline 110 \end{array}$

22. $\begin{array}{r} 11 \\ 77 \\ +43 \\ \hline 120 \end{array}$

23. $\begin{array}{r} 11 \\ 567 \\ +383 \\ \hline 950 \end{array}$

24. $\begin{array}{r} 111 \\ 463 \\ +787 \\ \hline 1250 \end{array}$

25. $\begin{array}{r} 121 \\ 591 \\ 623 \\ +497 \\ \hline 1711 \end{array}$

26. $\begin{array}{r} 111 \\ 5982 \\ 1647 \\ +2238 \\ \hline 9867 \end{array}$

27. $\begin{array}{r} 11 \\ 714 \\ +7318 \\ \hline 8032 \end{array}$

The total distance from Chicago to New Delhi via New York City is 8032 miles.

28. $\begin{array}{r} 1111 \\ 62,589 \\ 65,340 \\ +69,770 \\ \hline 197,699 \end{array}$

Sean Cruise's total earnings during the three years is $197,699.

29. $\begin{array}{r} 2 \\ 50 \\ 72 \\ 72 \\ +82 \\ \hline 276 \end{array}$

The perimeter is 276 feet.

30. $\begin{array}{r} 11 \\ 20 \\ +35 \\ \hline 66 \end{array}$

The perimeter is 66 kilometers.

31. $\begin{array}{r} 42 \\ -9 \\ \hline 33 \end{array}$

Check: $\begin{array}{r} 1 \\ 33 \\ +9 \\ \hline 42 \end{array}$

32. $\begin{array}{r} 67 \\ -24 \\ \hline 43 \end{array}$

Check: $\begin{array}{r} 43 \\ +24 \\ \hline 67 \end{array}$

33.   93
        − 79
        ‾‾14‾‾

Check:
     1
     14
   + 79
   ‾‾93‾‾

34.   60
        − 27
        ‾‾33‾‾

Check:
     1
     33
   + 27
   ‾‾60‾‾

35.   599
       − 237
       ‾‾362‾‾

Check:
    362
  + 237
  ‾‾599‾‾

36.   462
       − 397
       ‾‾‾65‾‾

Check:
    11
    6 5
  + 397
  ‾‾462‾‾

37.   583
       − 279
       ‾‾304‾‾

Check:
     1
    304
  + 279
  ‾‾583‾‾

38.   600
       − 124
       ‾‾476‾‾

Check:
    11
    476
  + 124
  ‾‾600‾‾

39.   4000
       − 1886
       ‾‾2114‾‾

Check:
    111
    2114
  + 1886
  ‾‾4000‾‾

40.   4268
       − 3947
       ‾‾‾321‾‾

Check:
     1
     321
   + 3947
   ‾‾4268‾‾

41.   712
       − 315
       ‾‾397‾‾

Check:
    11
    397
  + 315
  ‾‾712‾‾

Bob Roma has 397 pages left.

42.   18,425   16,826
       − 1 599   − 1 200
       ‾‾16,826‾‾   ‾‾15,626‾‾

Check:
    1 11
    15,626
    1 200
  + 1 599
  ‾‾18,425‾‾

Shelly Winters paid $15,626 for the car.

43. During May, when it was $100.

44. During August, when it was $490.

45. During April and May.

46. During July, August, and September.

47. To round 93 to the nearest ten, observe that the digit in the ones place is 3. Since this digit is less than 5, we do not add 1 to the digit in the tens place. The number 93 rounded to the nearest ten is 90.

48. To round 45 to the nearest ten, observe that the digit in the ones place is 5. Since this digit is at least 5, we need to add 1 to the digit in the tens place. The number 45 rounded to the nearest ten is 50.

49. To round 467 to the nearest ten, observe that the digit in the ones place is 7. Since this digit is at least 5, we need to add 1 to the digit in the tens place. The number 467 rounded to the nearest ten is 470.

50. To round 493 to the nearest hundred, observe that the digit in the tens place is 9. Since this digit is at least 5, we need to add 1 to the digit in the hundreds place. The number 493 rounded to the nearest hundred it 500.

51. To round 4832 to the nearest hundred, observe that the digit in the tens place is 3. Since this digit is less than 5, we do not add 1 to the digit in the hundreds place. The number 4832 rounded to the nearest hundred is 4800.

52. To round 57,534 to the nearest thousand, observe that the digit in the hundreds place is 5. Since this digit is at least 5, we need to add 1 to the digit in the thousands place. The number 57,534 rounded to the nearest thousand is 58,000.

53. To round 49,683,712 to the nearest million, observe that the digit in the hundred-thousands place is 6. Since this digit is at least 5, we need to add 1 to the digit in the millions place. The number 49,683,712 rounded to the nearest million is 50,000,000.

54. To round 768,542 to the nearest hundred-thousand, observe that the digit in the ten-thousands place is 6. Since this digit is at least 5, we need to add 1 to the digit in the hundred-thousands place. The number 768,542 rounded to the nearest hundred-thousand is 800,000.

55.
$$\begin{array}{rll} 4892 & \text{rounds to} & 4900 \\ 647 & \text{rounds to} & 600 \\ +\,1867 & \text{rounds to} & +\,1900 \\ \hline & & 7400 \end{array}$$
$4892 + 647 + 1867$ is approximately 7400.

56.
$$\begin{array}{rll} 5925 & \text{rounds to} & 5900 \\ -\,1787 & \text{rounds to} & -\,1800 \\ \hline & & 4100 \end{array}$$
$5925 - 1787$ is approximately 4100.

57. When rounding to the nearest million, 68,490,000 rounds to 68,000,000.

58. When rounding to the nearest thousand, 679,967 rounds to 680,000.

59. $6 \cdot 7 = 42$

60. $8 \cdot 3 = 24$

61. $5(0) = 0$

62. $0(9) = 0$

63.
$$\begin{array}{r} 47 \\ \times\ 30 \\ \hline 0 \\ 1410 \\ \hline 1410 \end{array}$$

64.
$$\begin{array}{r} 69 \\ \times\ 42 \\ \hline 138 \\ 2760 \\ \hline 2898 \end{array}$$

65. $20(8)(5) = 20 \cdot 40$
$$= 800$$

66. $25(9 \times 4) = 25 \cdot 36$
$$= 900$$

67.
$$\begin{array}{r} 48 \\ \times\ 77 \\ \hline 336 \\ 3360 \\ \hline 3696 \end{array}$$

68.
$$\begin{array}{r} 77 \\ \times\ 22 \\ \hline 154 \\ 1540 \\ \hline 1694 \end{array}$$

69. $49 \cdot 49 \cdot 0 = 0$, because anything times zero is zero.

70. $62 \cdot 88 \cdot 0 = 0$, because anything times zero is zero.

71.
$$\begin{array}{r} 586 \\ \times\ 29 \\ \hline 5\,274 \\ 11,720 \\ \hline 16,994 \end{array}$$

72.
$$\begin{array}{r} 242 \\ \times\ 37 \\ \hline 1694 \\ 7260 \\ \hline 8954 \end{array}$$

73.
$$\begin{array}{r} 642 \\ \times\,177 \\ \hline 4\,494 \\ 44,940 \\ 64,200 \\ \hline 113,634 \end{array}$$

74.
$$\begin{array}{r} 347 \\ \times\,129 \\ \hline 3\,123 \\ 6\,940 \\ 34,700 \\ \hline 44,763 \end{array}$$

75.
$$\begin{array}{r} 1026 \\ \times\,\ 401 \\ \hline 1\,026 \\ 00 \\ 410,400 \\ \hline 411,426 \end{array}$$

76.
$$\begin{array}{r} 2107 \\ \times\,302 \\ \hline 4\,214 \\ 00 \\ 632,100 \\ \hline 636,314 \end{array}$$

77.   49   rounds to   50
       × 32   rounds to   × 30
$$\overline{1500}$$

49 · 32 is approximately 1500.

78.   586   rounds to   600
       × 357   rounds to   × 400
$$\overline{240,000}$$

586 · 357 is approximately 240,000.

79.   5231   rounds to   5200
       × 243   rounds to   × 200
$$\overline{1,040,000}$$

5231 · 243 is approximately 1,040,000.

80.   7836   rounds to   7800
       × 912   rounds to   × 900
$$\overline{7,020,000}$$

7836 · 912 is approximately 7,020,000.

81. $8 \times 3 = 24$

There are 24 grams of fat in 3 ounces of Swiss cheese.

82.
$$\begin{array}{r} 5283 \\ \times\,927 \\ \hline 36,981 \\ 105,660 \\ 4,754,700 \\ \hline 4,897,341 \end{array}$$

The tuition collected totaled $4,897,341.

83.
$$\begin{array}{r} 12 \\ \times\,5 \\ \hline 60 \end{array}$$

The area is 60 square miles.

84.
$$\begin{array}{r} 20 \\ \times\,25 \\ \hline 100 \\ 400 \\ \hline 500 \end{array}$$

The area is 500 square centimeters.

85.
$$6\overline{)\,18} \quad \begin{array}{r} 3 \\ \hline \end{array}$$
$$\begin{array}{r} -18 \\ \hline 0 \end{array}$$

Check: $3 \cdot 6 = 18$

86.
$$9\overline{)\,36} \quad \begin{array}{r} 4 \\ \hline \end{array}$$
$$\begin{array}{r} -36 \\ \hline 0 \end{array}$$

Check: $4 \cdot 9 = 36$

87.
$$7\overline{)\,42} \quad \begin{array}{r} 6 \\ \hline \end{array}$$
$$\begin{array}{r} -42 \\ \hline 0 \end{array}$$

Check: $6 \cdot 7 = 42$

88.
$$5\overline{)\,25} \quad \begin{array}{r} 5 \\ \hline \end{array}$$
$$\begin{array}{r} -25 \\ \hline 0 \end{array}$$

Check: $5 \cdot 5 = 25$

89.
$$5\overline{)\,27} \quad \begin{array}{r} 5 \text{ R } 2 \\ \hline \end{array}$$
$$\begin{array}{r} -25 \\ \hline 2 \end{array}$$

Check: $5 \cdot 5 + 2 = 27$

90.
$$4\overline{)\,18} \quad \begin{array}{r} 4 \text{ R } 2 \\ \hline \end{array}$$
$$\begin{array}{r} -16 \\ \hline 2 \end{array}$$

Check: $4 \cdot 4 + 2 = 18$

91. $16 \div 0$ is undefined

92. $0 \div 8 = 0$
Check: $0 \cdot 8 = 0$

93. $9 \div 9 = 1$
Check: $9 \cdot 1 = 9$

94. $10 \div 1 = 10$
Check: $10 \cdot 1 = 10$

95. $918 \div 0$ is undefined

96. $0 \div 668 = 0$
Check: $668 \cdot 0 = 0$

97.
$$\begin{array}{r} 15 \\ 5\overline{)75} \\ \underline{-5} \\ 25 \\ \underline{-25} \\ 0 \end{array}$$

Check: $15 \cdot 5 = 75$

98.
$$\begin{array}{r} 19\text{ R }7 \\ 8\overline{)159} \\ \underline{-8} \\ 79 \\ \underline{-72} \\ 7 \end{array}$$

Check: $19 \cdot 8 + 7 = 159$

99.
$$\begin{array}{r} 24\text{ R }2 \\ 26\overline{)626} \\ \underline{-52} \\ 106 \\ \underline{-104} \\ 2 \end{array}$$

Check: $24 \cdot 26 + 2 = 626$

100.
$$\begin{array}{r} 56 \\ 6\overline{)336} \\ \underline{-30} \\ 36 \\ \underline{-36} \\ 0 \end{array}$$

Check: $56 \cdot 6 = 336$

101.
$$\begin{array}{r} 1\text{ R }17 \\ 32\overline{)49} \\ \underline{-32} \\ 17 \end{array}$$

Check: $1 \cdot 32 + 17 = 49$

102.
$$\begin{array}{r} 35\text{ R }15 \\ 19\overline{)680} \\ \underline{-57} \\ 110 \\ \underline{-95} \\ 15 \end{array}$$

Check: $35 \cdot 19 + 15 = 680$

103.
$$\begin{array}{r} 500 \\ 20\overline{)10000} \\ \underline{-100} \\ 00 \\ \underline{-0} \\ 00 \\ \underline{-0} \\ 0 \end{array}$$

Check: $500 \cdot 20 = 10,000$

104.
$$\begin{array}{r} 21\text{ R }6 \\ 43\overline{)909} \\ \underline{-86} \\ 49 \\ \underline{-43} \\ 6 \end{array}$$

Check: $21 \cdot 43 + 6 = 909$

105.
$$\begin{array}{r} 506 \\ 47\overline{)23782} \\ \underline{-235} \\ 28 \\ \underline{-0} \\ 282 \\ \underline{-282} \\ 0 \end{array}$$

Check: $506 \cdot 47 = 23,782$

106.
$$\begin{array}{r} 16 \\ 30\overline{)480} \\ \underline{-30} \\ 180 \\ \underline{-180} \\ 0 \end{array}$$

Check: $16 \cdot 30 = 480$

107.
$$\begin{array}{r} 199\text{ R }8 \\ 16\overline{)3192} \\ \underline{-16} \\ 159 \\ \underline{-144} \\ 152 \\ \underline{-144} \\ 8 \end{array}$$

Check: $199 \cdot 16 + 8 = 3192$

108.

$$25\overline{)5000}$$
$$\underline{-50}$$
$$00$$
$$\underline{-0}$$
$$00$$
$$\underline{-0}$$
$$0$$

with quotient 200.

Check: $200 \cdot 25 = 5000$

109.

$$12\overline{)5496}$$
$$\underline{-48}$$
$$69$$
$$\underline{-60}$$
$$96$$
$$\underline{-96}$$
$$0$$

with quotient 458.

Check: $458 \cdot 12 = 5496$
There are 458 feet in 5496 inches.

110. Add the numbers, then divide by four.

```
  76              51
  49          4) 204
  32             -20
+ 47              04
 204              -4
                   0
```

The average is $\dfrac{204}{4} = 51$.

111. $7 \cdot 7 \cdot 7 \cdot 7 = 7^4$

112. $3 \cdot 3 \cdot 3 = 3^3$

113. $4 \cdot 2 \cdot 2 \cdot 2 = 4 \cdot 2^3$

114. $5 \cdot 5 \cdot 7 \cdot 7 \cdot 7 = 5^2 \cdot 7^3$

115. $7^2 = 7 \cdot 7 = 49$

116. $2^6 = 2 \cdot 2 \cdot 2 \cdot 2 \cdot 2 \cdot 2 = 64$

117. $5^3 \cdot 3^2 = 5 \cdot 5 \cdot 5 \cdot 3 \cdot 3 = 1125$

118. $4^1 \cdot 10^2 \cdot 7^2 = 4 \cdot 10 \cdot 10 \cdot 7 \cdot 7 = 19{,}600$

119. $18 \div 3 + 7 = 6 + 7$
$$ = 13$$

120. $12 - 8 \div 4 = 12 - 2$
$$ = 10$$

121. $\dfrac{6^2 - 3}{3^2 + 2} = \dfrac{36 - 3}{9 + 2}$
$$= \dfrac{33}{11}$$
$$= 3$$

122. $\dfrac{16 - 8}{2^3} = \dfrac{8}{8}$
$$= 1$$

123. $2 + 3[1 + (20 - 17) \cdot 3] = 2 + 3[1 + 3 \cdot 3]$
$$= 2 + 3[1 + 9]$$
$$= 2 + 3[10]$$
$$= 2 + 30$$
$$= 32$$

124. $21 - \left[2^4 - (7 - 5) - 10\right] + 8 \cdot 2$
$$= 21 - \left[2^4 - 2 - 10\right] + 8 \cdot 2$$
$$= 21 - [16 - 2 - 10] + 16$$
$$= 21 - 4 + 16$$
$$= 33$$

125. Area $= (\text{side})^2$
$$= (7 \text{ meters})^2$$
$$= 49 \text{ square meters}$$

126. Area $= (\text{side})^2$
$$= (3 \text{ inches})^2$$
$$= 9 \text{ square inches}$$

127. $\dfrac{2 \cdot 5}{2} = \dfrac{10}{2} = 5$

128 $4(5) - 3 = 20 - 3 = 17$

129. $\dfrac{5 + 7}{0} = \dfrac{12}{0}$ is undefined

130. $\dfrac{0}{5(5)} = 0$

131. $5^3 - 2 \cdot 2 = 125 - 4 = 121$

132. $\dfrac{7 + 5}{3(2)} = \dfrac{12}{6} = 2$

133. $(0 + 2)^2 = 2^2 = 4$

134. $\dfrac{100}{5}+\dfrac{0}{3}=20+0=20$

135. $x-5$

136. $x+7$

137. $10\div(x+1)$

138. $5(x+3)$

139.

x	0	1	2	3
$8x^2$	$8(0)^2$	$8(1)^2$	$8(2)^2$	$8(3)^2$
	0	8	32	72

Chapter 1 Test

1. $59+82=141$

2. $600-487=113$

3.
$$\begin{array}{r}496\\\times\;\;30\\\hline000\\1488\\\hline14,880\end{array}$$

4.
$$\begin{array}{r}766\ R\ 42\\69\overline{)52896}\\-483\\\hline459\\-414\\\hline456\\-414\\\hline42\end{array}$$

$$\begin{array}{r}7666\\\times\;\;69\\\hline52854\\+\;\;42\\\hline52896\end{array}$$

5. $2^3\cdot5^2=8\cdot25=200$

6. $6^1\cdot2^3=6\cdot2\cdot2\cdot2=48$

7. $98\div1=98$

8. $0\div49=0$

9. $62\div0$ is undefined.

10. $(2^4-5)=(16-5)\cdot3$
$=11\cdot3$
$=33$

11. $16+9\div3\cdot4-7=16+12-7=21$

12. $2[(6-4)^2+(22-19)^2]+10$
$=2[2^2+3^2]+10$
$=2[4+9]+10$
$=2(13)+10$
$=26+10$
$=36$

13. 52,369 rounded to the nearest thousand is 52,000.

14.
$$\begin{array}{rr}6289&6300\\5403&5400\\+\;1957&+\;2000\\\hline&13,700\end{array}$$

15.
$$\begin{array}{rr}4267&4300\\-2738&-\;2700\\\hline&1600\end{array}$$

16.
$$\begin{array}{r}\$17\\29\overline{)493}\\-29\\\hline203\\-203\\\hline0\end{array}$$
$$\begin{array}{r}17\\\times\;29\\\hline\$493\end{array}$$

17.
$$\begin{array}{r}17\\\times\;7\\\hline\$119\end{array}$$

18.
$$\begin{array}{r}725\\-\;599\\\hline\$126\end{array}$$ more expensive

19.
$$\begin{array}{r}11\\-\;4\\\hline7\end{array}$$
7 billion more tablets per year are taken for heart disease.

20.
$$\begin{array}{r} 34,000 \\ \times\ \underline{\quad 5} \\ 170,000 \end{array}$$
During a five-day work week the FBI receives over 170,000 fingerprint cards.

21. $5[(2)^3 - 2] = 5[8 - 2] = 5 \cdot 6 = 30$

22. $\dfrac{3(7) - 5}{2(8)} = \dfrac{21 - 5}{16} = 1$

23. a. $17x$

b. $20 - 2x$

24. Perimeter
= length + width + length + width
= 20 yards + 10 yards + 20 yards + 10 yards
= 60 yards

Area = length · width
= (20 yards)(10 yards)
= 200 square yards

25. Area $= (\text{side})^2 = (5 \text{ cm})^2 = 25$ sq cm
Perimeter $= 4(\text{side}) = 4(5 \text{ cm}) = 20$ cm

26. Cast Away earned $233,630,478 in 2000.

27.
$$\begin{array}{r} 215,397,307 \\ -\ 171,383,253 \\ \hline 44,014,054 \end{array}$$

In 2000, Mission Impossible 2 earned $44,014,054 more than the Matrix did in 1999.

28.
$$\begin{array}{r} 431,065,444 \\ -\ 260,031,035 \\ \hline 171,034,439 \end{array}$$

The top-grossing movie in 1999 earned $171,034,439 more than the top-grossing movie in 2000.

Chapter 2

1. If 0 represents the line of scrimmage, a loss of 22 yards is –22.

2.

3. $-31 > -36$

4. $|{-8}| = 8$, because -8 is 8 units from 0.

5. The opposite of -12 is $-(-12) = 12$.

6. $-19 + 8$
   We are adding two numbers with different signs.
   $|{-19}| = 19, |8| = 8$
   $19 - 8 = 11$
   -19 has the larger absolute value and its sign is $-$.
   $-19 + 8 = -11$

7. $x + y = -6 + (-11)$
   We are adding two numbers with the same sign.
   $|{-6}| = 6, |{-11}| = 11$
   $6 + 11 = 17$
   Their common sign is negative, so the sum is negative.
   $-6 + (-11) = -17$

8. $-9 + 5 + 7 = -4 + 7 = 3$
   The temperature was 3°F at 9 a.m.

9. $-9 - (-14) = -9 + 14 = 5$

10. $4 - 6 - (-2) + 8 = 4 + (-6) + 2 + 8$
    $= -2 + 2 + 8$
    $= 0 + 8$
    $= 8$

11. $m - n = -5 - 10 = -5 + (-10) = -15$

12. $88 + 35 - 72 - 55 = 88 + 35 + (-72) + (-55)$
    $= 123 + (-72) + (-55)$
    $= 51 + (-55)$
    $= -4$

13. $(-8)(13) = -104$

14. $\dfrac{-36}{-4} = 9$

15. $\dfrac{x}{y} = \dfrac{-96}{-2} = 48$

16. $xy = 4 \cdot (-5) = -20$

17. $(-20) \cdot 3 = -60$

18. $-5^2 = -(5)(5) = -25$

19. $\dfrac{9 - 17}{-6 + 2} = \dfrac{9 + (-17)}{-6 + 2} = \dfrac{-8}{-4} = 2$

20. $(-2) \cdot |{-7}| - (-6) = (-2) \cdot 7 + 6$
    $= -14 + 6$
    $= -8$

21. $x - y^2 = 2 - (-6)^2$
    $= 2 - 36$
    $= 2 + (-36)$
    $= -34$

22. Add the integers, then divide by 5 (the number of integers).

$$\frac{-17 + 10 + (-9) + 5 + (-19)}{5} = \frac{-30}{5} = -6$$

Section 2.1

Practice Problems

1. a. If 0 represents the surface of the earth, then 800 feet below the surface can be represented by –800 feet.

   b. If 0 represents a balance of $0, then $2 million loss can be represented by –2 million dollars.

2.

3. a. 0 is to the right of -3, so $0 > -3$.

   b. -5 is to the left of 5, so $-5 < 5$.

   c. -8 is to the right of -12, so $-8 > -12$.

4. a. $|{-4}| = 4$, because -4 is 4 units from 0.

   b. $|2| = 2$, because 2 is 2 units from 0.

   c. $|{-8}| = 8$, because 8 is 8 units from 0.

5. a. The opposite of 7 is -7.

   b. The opposite of -17 is $-(-17)$ or 17.

39

6. a. $-|-2| = -2$

b. $-|5| = -5$

c. $-(-11) = 11$

7.   Substitute x with -9.
$-|-9| = -9$

8.   Venus has the highest temperature. It is $867°$ F.

Exercise Set 2.1

1.   If 0 represents ground level, then 1445 feet underground is -1445.

3.   If 0 represents sea level, then 14,433 feet above sea level is $+14,494$.

5.   Above 0 is $+118$.

7.   If 0 represents sea level, then 11,730 feet below sea level is $-11,730$.

9.   A net loss is -1683 million.

11.   Joe, below sea level, is at -135. Sara, below sea level, is at -157. Sara is deeper in the water.

13.   A loss is -81.

15.

17.

19.

21.

23. $4 > 0$

25. $-7 < -5$

27. $-30 > -35$

29. $-26 < 26$

31. $|5| = 5$, because 5 is 5 units from 0.

33. $|-8| = 8$, because -8 is 8 units from 0.

35. $|0| = 0$, because 0 is 0 units from 0.

37. $|-5| = 5$, because -5 is 5 units from 0.

39.   The opposite of 5 is -5.

41.   The opposite of -4 is $-(-4) = 4$.

43.   The opposite of 23 is -23.

45.   The opposite of -10 is $-(-10) = 10$.

47. $|-7| = 7$, because -7 is 7 units from 0.

49. $-|20| = -20$
The opposite of the absolute value of 20 is the opposite of 20.

51. $-|-3| = -3$
The opposite of the absolute value of -3 is the opposite of 3.

53. $-(-8) = 8$
The opposite of negative 8 is 8.

55. $|-14| = 14$, because -14 is 14 units from 0.

57. $-(-29) = 29$
The opposite of negative 29 is 29.

59. $|-(-8)| = |8| = 8$

61. $-|-3| = -3$

63. $|-23| = 23$

65. $-|4| = -4$

67. $-3 > -5$

69. $|-9| \ ? \ |-14|$
$\quad 9 \ ? \ 14$
$\quad 9 < 14$

71. $|-33| \ ? \ -(-33)$
$\quad 33 \ ? \ 33$
$\quad 33 = 33$

73. $-|-10| \ ? \ -(-10)$
$\quad -10 \ ? \ 10$
$\quad -10 < 10$

75. $0 \ ? \ -9$
$\quad 0 > -9$

77. $|0| \ ? \ |-9|$
$\quad 0 \ ? \ 9$
$\quad 0 < 9$

79. $-|-2|$? $-|-10|$
$-2 > -10$

81. $-(-12)$? $-(-18)$
$12 < 18$

83.　$2^2 = 4$
$-|3| = -3$
$-(-5) = 5$
$-|-8| = -8$
$-8, -3, 4, 5$　or　$-|-8|, -|3|, 2^2, -(-5)$

85.　$|-1| = 1$
$-|-6| = -6$
$-(-6) = 6$
$-|1| = -1$
$-6, -1, 1, 6$　or　$-|-6|, -|1|, |-1|, -(-6)$

87.　$-(-2) = 2$
$5^2 = 25$
$-10 = -10$
$-|-9| = -9$
$|-12| = 12$
$-10, -9, 2, 12, 25$　or　$-10, -|-9|, -(-2), |-12|, 5^2$

89. Maracaibo Lake is at 0, which is sea level.

91. Eyre Lake, at 52 feet below sea level, has the second lowest elevation.

93. Earth, with an average temperature of $56°$ F, is closest to $0°$ F.

95. Saturn, with an average temperature of $-218°$ F, is closest to $-200°$ F.

97. $0 + 13 = 13$

99.　　15
　　$+ \ 20$
　　$\overline{35}$

101.　　47
　　　236
　　$+ \ 77$
　　$\overline{360}$

103. $-12 < -8$
　　D

105. $-(-|-5|) = -(-5) = 5$

107. False; consider $-1 > -2$.

109. True; consider the values on a number line.

111. False; consider $a = -3$, then $-a = -(-3) = 3$.

113. Answers will vary.

Section 2.2

Practice Problems

1. $5 + (-1) = 4$

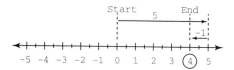

2. $-6 + (-2) = -8$

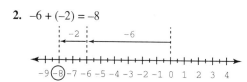

3. $-8 + 3 = -5$

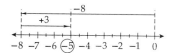

4. $|-3| = 3$, $|-9| = 9$, and $3 + 9 = 12$
Their common sign is negative, so the sum is negative.
$(-3) + (-9) = -12$

5. $-12 + (-3) = -15$

6. $9 + 5 = 14$

7. $|-3| = 3$, $|9| = 9$, and $9 - 3 = 6$
9 has the larger absolute value and its sign is an understood +: $-3 + 9 = 6$.

8. $|2| = 2$, $|-8| = 8$, and $8 - 2 = 6$
-8 has the larger absolute value and its sign is $-$:
$2 + (-8) = -6$

9. $-46 + 20 = -26$

10. $8 + (-6) = 2$

11. $-2 + 0 = -2$

12. $15 + (-15) = 0$

13. $-80 + 80 = 0$

14. $8 + (-3) + (-13) = 5 + (-13)$
$$= -8$$

15. $5 + (-3) + 12 + (-14) = 2 + 12 + (-14)$
$$= 14 + (-14)$$
$$= 0$$

16. $x + y = -4 + 1 = -3$

17. $x + y = -11 + (-6) = 17$

18. $-8 + 4 + 7 = 3$
The temperature at 8 a.m. was 3° Fahrenheit.

Calculator Explorations

The following may vary depending on your calculator.

1. Press the keys 256 $\boxed{+/-}$ $\boxed{+}$ 97 $\boxed{= \text{or ENTER}}$.
The display will read $-$ 159.

2. Press the keys 811 $\boxed{+}$ 1058 $\boxed{+/-}$ $\boxed{= \text{or ENTER}}$.
The display will read $-$ 247.

3. Press the keys 6 $\boxed{\times}$ 15 $\boxed{+}$ 46 $\boxed{+/-}$
$\boxed{= \text{or ENTER}}$. The display will read 44.

4. 129 $\boxed{+/-}$ $\boxed{+}$ 10 $\boxed{\times}$ 48 $\boxed{= \text{or ENTER}}$.
The display will read 351.

5. 108650 $\boxed{+/-}$ $\boxed{+}$ 786205 $\boxed{+/-}$ $\boxed{= \text{or ENTER}}$.
The display will read $-894,855$.

6. 196662 $\boxed{+/-}$ $\boxed{+}$ 129856 $\boxed{+/-}$ $\boxed{= \text{or ENTER}}$.
The display will read $-326,518$.

Mental Math

1. $5 + 0 = 5$

2. $(-2) + 0 = -2$

3. $0 + (-35) = -35$

4. $0 + 3 = 3$

5. $-12 + 12 = 0$

6. $48 + (-48) = 0$

7. $28 + (-28) = 0$

8. $-9 + 9 = 0$

Exercise Set 2.2

1. $-1 + (-6) = -7$

3. $-4 + 7 = 3$

5. $-13 + 7 = -6$

7. $|23| + |12| = 35$
Common sign is positive, so answer is +35.

9. $|-6| + |-2| = 8$
Common sign is negative, so answer is –8.

11. $|-43| - |43| = 0$
Sign does not matter.

13. $|6| - |-2| = 4$
$6 > 2$ so answer is +4.

15. $|8| - |-6| = 2$
$8 > 6$ so answer is +2.

17. $|-5| - |3| = 2$
$5 > 3$ so answer is –2.

19. $|-2| + |-7| = 9$
Common sign is negative, so answer is –9.

21. $|-12| + |-12| = 24$
Common sign is negative, so answer is –24.

23. $|-25| + |-32| = 57$
Common sign is negative, so answer is –57.

25. $|-123| + |-100| = 223$
Common sign is negative, so answer is –223.

27. $|7| - |-7| = 0$
Sign does not matter.

29. $|12| - |-5| = 7$
$12 > 5$, so answer is $+7$.

31. $|-6| - |3| = 3$
$6 > 3$, so answer is -3.

33. $|-12| - |3| = 9$
$12 > 3$, so answer is -9.

35. $|56| - |-26| = 30$
$56 > 26$, so answer is $+30$.

37. $|57| - |-37| = 20$
$57 > 37$, so answer is $+20$.

39. $|93| - |-42| = 51$
$93 > 42$, so answer is $+51$.

41. $|-67| - |34| = 33$
$67 > 34$, so answer is -33.

43. $|-144| - |124| = 20$
$144 > 124$, so answer is -20.

45. $|-82| + |-43| = 125$
Common sign is negative, so -125.

47. $-4 + 2 + (-5)$ add from left to right
$= -2 + (-5)$
$= -7$

49. $-52 + (-77) + (-117)$ add from left to right
$= -129 + (-117)$ add from left to right
$= -246$

51. $12 + (-4) + (-4) + 12$ add from left to right
$= 8 + (-4) + 12$ add from left to right
$= 4 + 12$
$= 16$

53. $(-10) + 14 + 25 + (-16)$ add from left to right
$= 4 + 25 + (-16)$ add from left to right
$= 29 + (-16)$
$= 13$

55. $-8 + (-14) + (-11)$ add from left to right
$= -22 + (-11)$ add from left to right
$= -33$

57. $|-26| - |5| = 21$
$26 > 5$, so answer is -21.

59. $5 + (-1) + 17$ add from left to right
$= 4 + 17$ add from left to right
$= 21$

61. $-14 + (-31) = -45$

63. $13 + 14 + (-18)$ add from left to right
$= 27 + (-18)$ add from left to right
$= 9$

65. $-87 + 87 = 0$

67. $-3 + (-8) + 12 + (-1)$ add from left to right
$= -11 + 12 + (-1)$ add from left to right
$= 1 + (-1)$
$= 0$

69. $0 + (-103) = -103$

71. $x + y$ substitute values
$= (-2) + 3$ add from left to right
$= 1$

73. $x + y$ substitute values
$= (-20) + (-50)$ add from left to right
$= -70$

75. $x + y$ substitute values
$= 3 + (-30)$ add from left to right
$= -27$

77. The net income for Gateway Inc. in 2000 was $236,630,000.

79. $-1,031,062 + (-297,718) = -1,328,780,000$
The total net income for 2001 and 2002 was $-\$1,328,780,000$.

81. $-10 + 12 = 2$
The temperature at 11 p.m. was 2°C.

83. $75,083 + (-10,412) + (-1,786) + 96,398$
$= 64,671 + (-1,786) + 96,398$
$= 62,885 + 96,398$
$= 159,283$
The net income is $159,283.

85. Team 1 Total $= -2 + (-13) + 20 + 2$
$= 7$
Team 2 Total $= 5 + 11 + (-7) + (-3)$
$= 6$
$7 > 6$ so the winning team is Team 1.

87. $-66 + 26 = -40$
Kansas's record low is -40° F.

43

89. $-230 + (-370) + (-346)$
$= -600 + (-346)$
$= -946$
The total U.S. trade balance is $-\$946$ billion.

91. $44 - 0 = 44$

93. $52 - 52 = 0$

95. $87 - 59 = 28$

97. $-8602 + (-1056) = -9658$

99. $-|-56| + |-56| = -56 + 56 = 0$

101. True; add any two negative numbers on a number line to verify.

103. False; consider $5 + (-1) = 4$.

105. Answers will vary.

Section 2.3

Practice Problems

1. $12 - 7 = 12 + (-7) = 5$

2. $-6 - 4 = -6 + (-4) = -10$

3. $11 - (-14) = 11 + 14 = 25$

4. $-9 - (-1) = -9 + 1 = -8$

5. $5 - 9 = 5 + (-9) = -4$

6. $-12 - 4 = -12 + (-4) = -16$

7. $-2 - (-7) = -2 + 7 = 5$

8. $-10 - 5 = -10 + (-5) = -15$

9. $-4 - 3 - 7 - (-5) = -4 + (-3) + (-7) + 5$
$= -7 + (-7) + 5$
$= -14 + 5$
$= -9$

10. $3 + (-5) - 6 - (-4) = 3 + (-5) + (-6) + 4$
$= -2 + (-6) + 4$
$= -8 + 4$
$= -4$

11. $x - y = -2 - 14 = -2 + (-14) = -16$

12. $y - z = -3 - (-4) = -3 + 4 = 1$

13. $29,028 - (-1312)$
$= 29,028 + 1312$
$= 30,340$
Mount Everest is 30,340 feet higher than the Dead Sea.

Exercise Set 2.3

1. $5 - 5 = 5 + (-5) = 0$

3. $8 - 3 = 8 + (-3) = 5$

5. $3 - 8 = 3 + (-8) = -5$

7. $7 - (-7) = 7 + (7) = 14$

9. $-5 - (-8) = -5 + (8) = 3$

11. $-14 - 4 = -14 + (-4) = -18$

13. $2 - 16 = 2 + (-16) = -14$

15. $-10 - (-10) = -10 + 10 = 0$

17. $-15 - (-15) = -15 + 15 = 0$

19. $3 - 7 = 3 + (-7) = -4$

21. $30 - 45 = 30 + (-45) = -15$

23. $-4 - 10 = -4 + (-10) = -14$

25. $-230 - 0 = -230 + 0 = -230$

27. $4 - (-6) = 4 + 6 = 10$

29. $-7 - (-3) = -7 + 3 = -4$

31. $-16 - (-23) = -16 + 23 = 7$

33. $-20 - 18 = -20 + (-18) = -38$

35. $-20 - (-3) = -20 + (3) = -17$

37. $2 - (-11) = 2 + (11) = 13$

39. $7 - 3 - 2 = 7 + (-3) + (-2)$
$= 4 + (-2)$
$= 2$

41. $12 - 5 - 7 = 12 + (-5) + (-7)$
$= 7 + (-7)$
$= 0$

43. $-5 - 8 - (-12) = -5 + (-8) + 12$
$= -13 + 12$
$= -1$

45. $-10 + (-5) - 12 = -10 + (-5) + (-12)$
$$= -15 + (-12)$$
$$= -27$$

47. $12 - (-34) + (-6) = 12 + 34 + (-6)$
$$= 46 + (-6)$$
$$= 40$$

49. $-(-6) - 12 + (-16) = 6 + (-12) + (-16)$
$$= -6 + (-16)$$
$$= -22$$

51. $-9 - (-12) + (-7) - 4 = -9 + 12 + (-7) + (-4)$
$$= 3 + (-7) + (-4)$$
$$= -4 + (-4)$$
$$= -8$$

53. $-3 + 4 - (-23) - 10 = -3 + 4 + 23 + (-10)$
$$= 1 + 23 + (-10)$$
$$= 24 + (-10)$$
$$= 14$$

55. $x - y$
$= (-3) - (5)$ show substitution exactly
$= -3 + (-5)$ change subtraction to addition
$= -8$

57. $x - y$
$= 6 - (-30)$ show substitution exactly
$= 6 + (30)$ change subtraction to addition
$= 36$

59. $x - y$
$= (-4) - (-4)$ show substitution exactly
$= -4 + (4)$ change subtraction to addition
$= 0$

61. $x - y$
$= (1) - (-18)$ show substitution exactly
$= 1 + (18)$ change subtraction to addition
$= 19$

63. $59 - (-369) = 59 + 369 = 428$
The difference in temperature is 428 degrees.

65. $-330 - (-369) = -330 + 369 = 39$
The difference in temperature is 39 degrees.

67. To find how many degrees warmer, subtract the coldest temperature from the warmest temperature.
$136 - (-129) = 136 + 129 = 265$
136°F is 265°F warmer than -129°F.

69. Subtract check amounts from the checking account, and add the deposit.
$125 - 117 + 45 - 69$
$= 125 + (-117) + 45 + (-69)$
$= 8 + 45 + (-69)$
$= 53 + (-69)$
$= -16$
Aaron has overdrawn his checking account by $16.

71. $-6 + (-3) + 4 + (-7)$ add from left to right
$= -9 + 4 + (-7)$ add from left to right
$= -5 + (-7)$
$= -12°C$

73. $-282 - (-436) = -282 + 436 = 154$
The difference in elevation is 154 feet.

75. $-436 - (-505) = -436 + 505 = 69$
The difference in elevation is 69 feet.

77. $600 - (-52) = 600 + 52 = 652$ feet

79. $144 - 0 = 144$ feet

81. $663 - 912 = 663 + (-912) = -249$
The U.S. trade balance in 1998 was
-$249 billion.

83. $436 \cdot 0 = 0$

85. $436 \cdot 1 = 436$

87.
```
    23
 ×  46
  138
 + 92
 1058
```

89. $5^2 - 6 \cdot 2 + 8 = 25 - 6 \cdot 2 + 8$
$$= 25 - 12 + 8$$
$$= 13 + 8$$
$$= 21$$

91. $x - y - z$ show substitution exactly
$= (-4) - (3) - (15)$ change subtraction to addition
$= -4 + (-3) + (-15)$ add left to right
$= -7 + (-15)$
$= -22$

93. $a + b - c$ show substitution exactly
$= (-16) + (14) - (-22)$ change subtraction to addition
$= -16 + 14 + 22$ add from left to right
$= -2 + 22$
$= 20$

95. $|-3|-|-7| = 3-7 = 3+(-7) = -4$

97. $|-6|-|6| = 6-6 = 6+(-6) = 0$

99. $-8067 - 1129 = -8067 + (-1129) = -9196$

101. False. $|-8-3| = |-8+(-3)| = |-11| = 11$

103. Answers may vary.

Integrated Review

1. If 0 represents an elevation of 0 feet, then 29,028 feet above sea level is 29,028.

2. If 0 represents an elevation of 0 feet, then 35,840 feet below sea level is –35,840.

3. If 0 represents sea level, then 7 miles below sea level is – 7.

4.

5. 0 is to the right of –3, so $0 > -3$.

6. –15 is to the left of –5, so $-15 < -5$.

7. –1 is to the left of 1, so $-1 < 1$.

8. –2 is to the right of –7, so $-2 > -7$.

9. $|-1| = 1$, because –1 is 1 unit from 0.

10. $-|-4| = -4$

11. $|-8| = 8$, because –8 is 8 units from 0.

12. $-(-5) = 5$

13. The opposite of 6 is –6.

14. The opposite of –3 is $-(-3) = 3$.

15. The opposite of 89 is –89.

16. The opposite of 0 is 0.

17. $-7 + 12 = 5$

18. $-9 + (-11) = -20$

19. $25 + (-35) = -10$

20. $1 - 3 = 1 + (-3) = -2$

21. $26 - (-26) = 26 + 26 = 52$

22. $-2 - 1 = -2 + (-1) = -3$

23. $-18 - (-102) = -18 + 102 = 84$

24. $-8 + (-6) + 20 = -14 + 20 = 6$

25. $-11 - 7 - (-19) = -11 + (-7) + 19$
$= -18 + 19 = 1$

26. $-4 + (-8) - 16 - (-9) = -4 + (-8) + (-16) + 9$
$= -12 + (-16) + 9$
$= -28 + 9$
$= -19$

27. $26 - 14 = 26 + (-14) = 12$

28. $-12 - (-8) = -12 + 8 = -4$

29. $|18| > 0, |-3| > 0, |-21| > 0$
$18 > 0, 3 > 0, 21 > 0$
b, c, d

30. $|0| > -5, |3| > -5, |-1| > -5, |-1000| > -5$
$0 > -5, 3 - 5, 1 - 5, 1000 - 5$
a, b, c, d

31. $-1 + 11 = 10$

32. $-1 - 11 = -1 + (-11) = -12$

33. $11 - (-1) = 11 + 1 = 12$

34. $11 + (-1) = 10$

Section 2.4

Practice Problems

1. $-2 \cdot 6 = -12$

2. $-4(-3) = 12$

3. $0 \cdot (-10) = 0$

4. $5(-15) = -75$

5. $7(-2)(-4) = -14(-4) = 56$

6. $(-5)(-6)(-1) = 30(-1) = -30$

7. $(-2)(-5)(-6)(-1) = 10(-6)(-1)$
$= -60(-1)$
$= 60$

8. $(-3)^4 = (-3)(-3)(-3)(-3)$
$\qquad = 9(-3)(-3)$
$\qquad = -27(-3)$
$\qquad = 81$

9. $-9^2 = -(9 \cdot 9) = -81$

10. $\dfrac{28}{-7} = -4$

11. $-18 \div (-2) = 9$

12. $\dfrac{-60}{10} = -6$

13. $\dfrac{-1}{0}$ is undefined because there is no number that gives a product of -1 when multiplied by 0.

14. $\dfrac{0}{-2} = 0$ because $0 \cdot (-2) = 0$.

15. $xy = 5(-9) = -45$

16. $\dfrac{x}{y} = \dfrac{-9}{-3} = 3$

17. $4(-12) = -48$
The card player's total score was -48.

Exercise Set 2.4

1. $-2(-3) = 6$

3. $-4(9) = -36$

5. $8(-8) = -64$

7. $0(-14) = 0$

9. $6(-4)(2) = -24(2) = -48$

11. $-1(-2)(-4) = 2(-4) = -8$

13. $-4(4)(-5) = -16(-5) = 80$

15. $10(-5)(0) = -50(0) = 0$

17. $-5(3)(-1)(-1)$
$\qquad = -15(-1)(-1)$
$\qquad = 15(-1)$
$\qquad = -15$

19. $-2^2 = -(2)(2) = -4$

21. $(-3)^3 = (-3)(-3)(-3) = 9(-3) = -27$

23. $-5^2 = -(5)(5) = -25$

25. $(-2)^3 = (-2)(-2)(-2) = 4(-2) = -8$

27. $-24 \div 6 = -4$

29. $\dfrac{-30}{6} = -5$

31. $\dfrac{-88}{-11} = 8$

33. $\dfrac{0}{14} = 0$

35. $\dfrac{2}{0}$ is undefined.

37. $\dfrac{39}{-3} = -13$

39. $-12(0) = 0$

41. $-4(3) = -12$

43. $-9 \cdot 6 = -54$

45. $-7(-6) = 42$

47. $-3(-4)(-2) = 12(-2) = -24$

49. $(-4)^2 = (-4)(-4) = 16$

51. $-\dfrac{10}{5} = -2$

53. $-\dfrac{56}{8} = -7$

55. $-12 \div 3 = -4$

57. $4(-4)(-3) = -16(-3) = 48$

59. $-30(6)(-2)(-3) = -180(-2)(-3)$
$\qquad\qquad\qquad = 360(-3)$
$\qquad\qquad\qquad = -1080$

61. $3 \cdot (-2) \cdot 0 = (-6) \cdot 0 = 0$

63. $\dfrac{100}{-20} = -5$

65. $240 \div (-40) = -6$

67. $\dfrac{-12}{-4} = 3$

69. $-1^4 = -(1)(1)(1)(1) = -1$

71. $(-3)^5 = (-3)(-3)(-3)(-3)(-3)$
$= 9 \cdot (-3)(-3)(-3)$
$= (-27)(-3)(-3)$
$= 81 \cdot (-3)$
$= -243$

73. $-2(3)(5)(-6) = (-6)(5)(-6)$
$= (-30)(-6)$
$= 180$

75. $(-1)^{32} = (-1)(-1)\cdots(-1)$ 32 factors
$= (-1)(-1)(-1)(-1)\cdots(-1)$ 30 factors
$= (1)(-1)(-1)\cdots(-1)$ 30 factors
$= (-1)(-1)\cdots(-1)$ 30 factors
Repeating the pattern 15 more times, we find that
$(-1)^{32} = 1$.

77. $-2(-2)(-5) = 4(-5) = -20$

79.
```
    42
×   23
   126
   840
   966
```
$-42 \cdot 23 = -966$

81.
```
     25
×    82
     50
   2000
   2050
```
$25 \cdot (-82) = -2050$

83. $a \cdot b = (-4) \cdot (7)$ substitute
$= -28$

85. $a \cdot b = (3) \cdot (-2)$ substitute
$= -6$

87. $a \cdot b = (-5) \cdot (-5)$ substitute
$= 25$

89. $\dfrac{x}{y}$

$= \dfrac{5}{-5}$ show substitution exactly

$= -1$

91. $\dfrac{x}{y}$

$= \dfrac{-12}{0}$ show substitution exactly

undefined   division by zero

93. $\dfrac{x}{y}$

$= \dfrac{-36}{-6}$ show substitution exactly

$= 6$

95. $x \cdot y$
$= (-4)(-2)$ show substitution exactly
$= 8$

$\dfrac{x}{y}$

$= \dfrac{-4}{-2}$ show substitution exactly

$= 2$

97. $x \cdot y$
$= (0)(-6)$ show substitution exactly
$= 0$ multiplication property of zero

$\dfrac{x}{y}$

$= \dfrac{0}{-6}$ show substitution exactly

$= 0$ zero division property

99. $3(-70) = -210$
The melting point of nitrogen is $-210°$ C.

101. $-3(63) = -189$
The melting point of argon is $-189°$ C.

103. $(-4)(3) = -12$
A loss of 12 yards

105. $5(-20) = -100$
He is at a depth of 100 feet.

107. $-2420 \cdot 3 = -7260$
Kmart's income would be –$7260 million.

109. a. $192 - 27 = 165$
There was a change of 165 condors.

b. 1987 to 2002 is 15 years.
$\dfrac{165}{15} = 11$
There was a change of 11 condors per year.

111. $\dfrac{-4+(-2)+1+1}{4} = \dfrac{-4}{4} = -1$

His average score per round was –1.

113. $(3 \cdot 5)^2 = (3 \cdot 5)(3 \cdot 5) = (15)(15) = 225$

115. $90 + 12^2 - 5^3 = 90 + 12 \cdot 12 - 5 \cdot 5 \cdot 5$
$$= 90 + 144 - 125$$
$$= 109$$

117. $12 \div 4 - 2 + 7 = 3 - 2 + 7 = 8$

119. true; product of two different signs is negative.

121. true; product of two same signs is positive.

123. positive; product of an even number of negatives is positive.

125. negative; product of an odd number of negatives is negative.

127. $(-5)^{17}, (-2)^{17}, (-2)^{12}, (-5)^{12}$

129. a. $2131 - 2190 = -59$
There was a change of –59 radio stations.

    b. $4(-59) = -236$
The change will be –236 radio stations.

    c. 2006 is 4 years from 2002.
$2131 - 236 = 1895$
There will be 1895 radio stations in 2006.

131. Answers may vary.

133. $87^2 - (-12)^5 = 7569 - (-248,832)$
$$= 7569 + 248,832$$
$$= 256,401$$

Section 2.5

Practice Problems

1. $(-2)^4 = (-2)(-2)(-2)(-2)$
$$= 4(-2)(-2)$$
$$= -8(-2)$$
$$= 16$$

2. $-2^4 = -(2)(2)(2)(2)$
$$= -4(2)(2)$$
$$= -8(2)$$
$$= -16$$

3. $3 \cdot 6^2 = 3 \cdot (6 \cdot 6) = 3 \cdot 36 = 108$

4. $\dfrac{25}{5(-1)} = \dfrac{25}{-5} = -5$

5. $\dfrac{-18+6}{-3-1} = \dfrac{-12}{-4} = 3$

6. $-20 + 2 \cdot 7 + 4 = -20 + 14 + 4$
$$= -6 + 4$$
$$= -2$$

7. $-2^3 + (-4)^2 + 1^5 = -8 + 16 + 1$
$$= 8 + 1$$
$$= 9$$

8. $2(2-8) + (-12) - 3 = 2(-6) + (-12) - 3$
$$= -12 + (-12) - 3$$
$$= -24 - 3$$
$$= -27$$

9. $(-5) \cdot |-4| + (-3) + 2^3 = -5 \cdot 4 + (-3) + 2^3$
$$= -5 \cdot 4 + (-3) + 8$$
$$= -20 + (-3) + 8$$
$$= -23 + 8$$
$$= -15$$

10. $4(-6) \div \left[3(5-7)^2\right] = 4(-6) \div \left[3(-2)^2\right]$
$$= 4(-6) \div [3 \cdot (4)]$$
$$= 4(-6) \div (12)$$
$$= -24 \div 12$$
$$= -2$$

11. $x^2 = (-12)^2 = (-12)(-12) = 144$
$-x^2 = -(-12)^2 = -(-12)(-12) = -144$

12. $5y^2 = 5(3)^2 = 5(9) = 45$
$5y^2 = 5(-3)^2 = 5(9) = 45$

13. $x^2 + y = (-5)^2 + (-2) = 25 + (-2) = 23$

14. $4 - x^2 = 4 - (-9)^2 = 4 - 81 = -77$

15. Add temperature and divide by 7 (the number of months).

$$\dfrac{15 + (-1) + (-11) + (-14) + (-16) + (-14) + (-1)}{7}$$
$$= \dfrac{-42}{7} = -6$$

The average temperature from Oct. through April is $-6°$ F.

Calculator Explorations

The answers may vary depending on what type of calculator you have.

1. Press the keys $\boxed{(}$ 120 $\boxed{+/-}$ $\boxed{-}$ 360 $\boxed{)}$ $\boxed{\div}$

10 $\boxed{+/-}$ $\boxed{=\text{ or ENTER}}$.

The display will read 48.

2. Press the keys 4750 $\boxed{\div}$ $\boxed{(}$ 2 $\boxed{+/-}$ $\boxed{+}$ 17 $\boxed{+/-}$

$\boxed{)}$ $\boxed{=\text{ or ENTER}}$.

The display will read -250.

3. Press the keys $\boxed{(}$ 316 $\boxed{+/-}$ $\boxed{+}$ 458 $\boxed{+/-}$ $\boxed{)}$

$\boxed{\div}$ $\boxed{(}$ 28 $\boxed{+}$ 25 $\boxed{+/-}$ $\boxed{)}$ $\boxed{=\text{ or ENTER}}$.

The display will read -258.

4. Press the keys $\boxed{(}$ 234 $\boxed{+/-}$ $\boxed{+}$ 86 $\boxed{)}$ $\boxed{\div}$

$\boxed{(}$ 18 $\boxed{+/-}$ $\boxed{+}$ 16 $\boxed{)}$ $\boxed{=\text{ or ENTER}}$.

The display will read 74.

Mental Math

1. -3^2 base: 3; exponent: 2

2. $(-3)^2$ base: -3; exponent: 2

3. $4 \cdot 2^3$ base: 2; exponent: 3

4. $9 \cdot 5^6$ base: 5; exponent: 6

5. $(-7)^5$ base: -7; exponent: 5

6. -9^4 base: -9; exponent: 4

7. $5^7 \cdot 10$ base: 5; exponent: 7

8. $2^8 \cdot 11$ base: 2; exponent: 8

Exercise Set 2.5

1. $(-4)^3 = (-4)(-4)(-4) = 16(-4) = -64$

3. $-4^3 = -(4)(4)(4) = -64$

5. $6 \cdot 2^2 = 6 \cdot 4 = 24$

7. $-1(-2) + 1$ multiply before adding
$= 2 + 1$
$= 3$

9. $9 - 12 - 4$ change to addition
$= 9 + (-12) + (-4)$ add from left to right
$= -3 + (-4)$
$= -7$

11. $4 + 3(-6)$ multiply before adding
$= 4 + (-18)$
$= -14$

13. $5(-9) + 2$ multiply before adding
$= -45 + 2$
$= -43$

15. $(-10) + 4 \div 2$ divide before adding
$= (-10) + 2$
$= -8$

17. $6 + 7 \cdot 3 - 40 = 6 + 21 - 40$
$= 27 - 40$
$= -13$

19. $\dfrac{16 - 13}{-3}$ simplify numerator

$= \dfrac{3}{-3}$

$= -1$

21. $\dfrac{24}{10 + (-4)}$ simplify the bottom of the fraction bar first

$= \dfrac{24}{6}$

$= 4$

23. $5(-3) - (-12)$ multiply before adding
$= -15 - (-12)$ change to addition
$= -15 + 12$
$= -3$

25. $(-19) - 12(3)$ multiply before adding
$= (-19) - 36$ change to addition
$= (-19) + (-36)$
$= -55$

27. $-8 + 4^2$ exponents first
$= -8 + 16$
$= 8$

29. $(8 + (-4))^2$ grouping symbols first
$= [4]^2$
$= 16$

31. $8 \cdot 6 - 3 \cdot 5 + (-20) = 48 - 15 + (-20)$
$= 33 + (-20)$
$= 13$

33. $16-(-3)^4$ exponents first
$= 16-(81)$ change to addition
$= 16+(-81)$
$= -65$

35. $|5+3|\cdot 2^3$ grouping symbols first
$= |8|\cdot 2^3$ exponents before multiplication
$= 8\cdot 8$
$= 64$

37. $7\cdot 8^2+4$ exponents first
$= 7\cdot 64+4$ multiply before adding
$= 448+4$
$= 452$

39. $5^3-(4-2^3)$ exponents inside grouping
                    symbols first
$= 5^3-(4-8)$ grouping symbols next
$= 5^3-(-4)$ exponents before subtraction
$= 125-(-4)$ change subtraction to addition
$= 125+4$
$= 129$

41. $|3-12|\div 3$
$= |-9|\div 3$
$= 9\div 3$
$= 3$

43. $-(-2)^2 = -4$

45. $(5-9)^2\div(4-2)^2$ grouping symbols first
$= (-4)^2\div(2)^2$ exponents next
$= 16\div 4$
$= 4$

47. $|8-24|\cdot(-2)\div(-2)$ grouping symbol first
$= |-16|\cdot(-2)\div(-2)$ absolute value
$= 16\cdot(-2)\div(-2)$ multiply and divide
                       from left to right
$= -32\div(-2)$
$= 16$

49. $(-12-20)\div 16-25$ grouping symbols first
$= (-32)\div 16-25$ divide
$= -2-25$
$= -27$

51. $5(5-2)+(-5)^2-6$ grouping symbols first
$= 5(3)+5^2-6$ exponents next
$= 5(3)+25-6$ multiply before adding
$= 15+25-6$
$= 34$

53. $(2-7)\cdot(6-19)$ grouping symbols first
$= (-5)\cdot(-13)$
$= 65$

55. $2-7\cdot 6-19$ multiply
$= 2-42-19$ subtract from left to right
$= -59$

57. $(-36\div 6)-(4\div 4)$ divide
$= -6-1$
$= -7$

59. -5^2-6^2 exponents first (watch the signs)
$= -25-36$
$= -61$

61. $(-5)^2-6^2$ exponents first (watch the signs)
$= 25-36$
$= -11$

63. $(10-4^2)^2 = (10-16)^2$
$= (-6)^2$
$= (-6)(-6)$
$= 36$

65. $2(8-10)^2-5(1-6)^2$
$= 2(-2)^2-5(-5)^2$
$= 2(-2)(-2)-5(-5)(-5)$
$= 2(-2)(-2)+(-5)(-5)(-5)$
$= (-4)(-2)+(25)(-5)$
$= 8+(-125)$
$= -117$

67. $3(-10)\div(5(-3)-7(-2))$
$= 3(-10)\div(5(-3)+(-7)(-2))$
$= 3(-10)\div(-15+14)$
$= 3(-10)\div(-1)$
$= -30\div -1$
$= 30$

69. $\dfrac{(-7)(-3)-(4)(3)}{3[7\div(3-10)]} = \dfrac{(-7)(-3)+(-4)(3)}{3(7\div(3+(-10)))}$

$= \dfrac{21+(-12)}{3(7\div(-7))}$

$= \dfrac{9}{3(-1)}$

$= \dfrac{9}{-3}$

$= -3$

71. $-5\big[4+5(-3+5)\big]+11$

$= -5\big[4+5(2)\big]+11$

$= -5\big[4+10\big]+11$

$= -5\big[14\big]+11$

$= -70+11$

$= -59$

73. $x+y+z$ show substitution exactly

$= (-2)+4+(-1)$ add from left to right

$= 2+(-1)$

$= 1$

75. $2x-3y-4z = 2(-2)-3(4)-4(-1)$

$= -4-12+4$

$= -16+4$

$= -12$

77. x^2-y show substitution exactly

$= (-2)^2-4$ exponents first

$= 4-4$

$= 0$

79. $\dfrac{5y}{z}$ show substitution exactly

$= \dfrac{5\cdot4}{-1}$ simplify numerator

$= \dfrac{20}{-1}$

$= -20$

81. $x^2 = (-3)^2 = 9$

83. $-z^2 = -(-4)^2 = -16$

85. $10-(-3)^2 = 10-9 = 1$

87. $2x^3-z = 2(-3)^2-(-4)$

$= 2(-27)-(-4)$

$= -54+4$

$= -50$

89. $\dfrac{-10+8+(-4)+2+7+(-5)+(-12)}{7}$

$= \dfrac{-14}{7} = -2$

91. $\dfrac{-17+(-26)+(-20)+(-13)}{4}$

$= \dfrac{-76}{4} = -19$

93. $15-(-13) = 15+13 = 28$
The difference between the highest and lowest score is 28 points.

95. $\dfrac{-13+(-2)+0+5+7+15)}{6}$

$= \dfrac{12}{6} = 2$

97. No; answers may vary.

99. $45\cdot90 = 4050$

101. $90-45 = 45$

103. $p = 4(8) = 32$ in.

105. $p = 2(9)+2(6)$

$= 18+12$

$= 30$ feet

107. $2\cdot(7-5)\cdot3 = 2\cdot(2)\cdot3 = 4\cdot3 = 12$

109. $-6\cdot(10-4) = -6\cdot6 = -36$

111. $(-12)^4 = (-12)(-12)(-12)(-12)$

$= 144(-12)(-12)$

$= -1728(-12)$

$= 20,736$

113. x^3-y^2

$= 21^3-(-19)^2$ substitute

$= 21\cdot21\cdot21-(-19)(-19)$

$= 21\cdot21\cdot21+(19)(-19)$

$= 441\cdot21+(-361)$

$= 9261+(-361)$

$= 8900$

115. $(xy+z)^x$

$= [2\cdot(-5)+7]^2$ substitute

$= (-3)^2$

$= (-3)(-3)$

$= 9$

117. Answers may vary.

Chapter 2 Review

1. 1435 feet down in a mine is represented as -1435.

2. 7562 meters above sea level is represented as 7562.

3.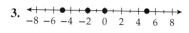

4.

5. $|-12| = 12$

6. $|0| = 0$

7. $-|6| = -6$

8. $-(-9) = 9$

9. $-|-9| = -0$

10. $-(-2) = 2$

11. $-18 > -20$

12. $-5 < 5$

13. $123 > -198$

14. $8 - 12 = -4 > -16$

15. $-(-12) = 12$

16. $-(-(-3)) = -3$

17. False

18. True

19. True

20. True

21. $5 + (-3) = 2$

22. $18 + (-4) = 14$

23. $-12 + 16 = 4$

24. $-23 + 40 = 17$

25. $-8 + (-15) = -23$

26. $-5 + (-17) = -22$

27. $-24 + 3 = -21$

28. $-89 + 19 = -70$

29. $15 + (-15) = 0$

30. $-24 + 24 = 0$

31. $-43 + (-108) = -151$

32. $-100 + (-506) = -606$

33. $-0 + (-5) + (-7) = -14 + (-7) = -21$
Annik Sorenstam's total score was -21.

34. $-1 + 3 + (-5) + 3 = 2 + (-5) + 3 = -3 + 3 = 0$
Joanne Morley's total score was 0.

35. $-15 - 5 = -20$
The temperature was $-20°$C at 6 a.m.

36. $-127 + (-23) = -150$
The divers current depth is -150 feet.

37. $-56 + 155 = 99$
The high temperature for London is $99°$ F.

38. $-13 + 125 = 112$
The high temperature for Los Angeles is $112°$ F.

39. $12 - 4 = 12 + (-4) = 8$

40. $-12 - 4 = -12 + (-4) = -16$

41. $8 - 19 = 8 + (-19) = -11$

42. $-8 - 19 = -8 + (-19) = -27$

43. $7 - (-13) = 7 + 13 = 20$

44. $-6 - (-14) = -6 + 14 = 8$

45. $16 - 16 = 16 + (-16) = 0$

46. $-16 - 16 = -16 + (-16) = -32$

47. $-12 - (-12) = -12 + 12 = 0$

48. $|-5| - |-12| = 5 - 12 = 5 + (-12) = -7$

49. $-(-5) - 12 + (-3) = 5 + (-12) + (-3) = -10$

50. $-8 + |-12| - 10 - |-3| = -8 + 12 + (-10) - 3$
$= -8 + 12 + (-10) + (-3)$
$= 4 + (-10) + (-3)$
$= -6 + (-3)$
$= -9$

51. $142 - 125 + 43 - 85 = 142 + (-125) + 43 + (-85)$
$$= 17 + 43 + (-85)$$
$$= 60 + (-85)$$
$$= -25$$
The balance of his account represented as an integer is –25.

52. $600 - (-92) = 600 + 92 = 692$ feet

53. $32 - 35 = 32 + (-35) = -3$
The low temperature for ReyKjavik is $-3°$ F.

54. $10 - 14 = 10 + (-4) = -4$
The low temperature for Berlin is $-4°$ F.

55. $|-5| - |-6| = 5 - 6$
$5 - 6 = 5 - 6$ True

56. $|-5 - (-6)| = 5 + 6$
$|-5 + 6| = 11$
$|1| = 11$
$1 = 11$ False

57. True

58. True

59. $(-3) \cdot (-7) = 21$

60. $(-6) \cdot (3) = -18$

61. $-4 \cdot 16 = -64$

62. $(-5) \cdot (-12) = 60$

63. $(-5)^2 = (-5)(-5) = 25$

64. $(-1)^5 = (-1)(-1)(-1)(-1)(-1) = -1$

65. $12(-3)(0) = 0$

66. $-1(6)(2)(-2) = -6(2)(-2) = -12(-2) = 24$

67. $-15 \div 3 = -5$

68. $\dfrac{-24}{-8} = 3$

69. $0 \div (-3) = 0$

70. $\dfrac{-46}{0}$ is undefined.

71. $\dfrac{100}{-5} = -20$

72. $\dfrac{-72}{8} = -9$

73. $\dfrac{-38}{-1} = 38$

74. $\dfrac{45}{-9} = -5$

75. $-5(2) = -10$
The team lost 10 yards.

76. $-50(4) = -200$
The bettor lost $200.

77. $3(-9) = -27$
The low temperature for Bucharest is $-27°$ F.

78. $30 \div (-10) = -3$
The low temperature for Geneva is $-3°$ F.

79. $-56 \div (-2) = 28$
The low temperature for Capetown is $28°$ F.

80. $2(-13) = -26$
The low temperature for Stockholm is $-26°$ F.

81. $(-7)^2 = (-7)(-7) = 49$

82. $-7^2 = -(7)(7) = -49$

83. $-2^5 = -(2)(2)(2)(2)(2) = -32$

84. $(-2)^5 = (-2)(-2)(-2)(-2)(-2) = -32$

85. $5 - 8 + 3 = 0$

86. $-3 + 12 + (-7) - 10 = -3 + 12 + (-7) + (-10)$
$$= -8$$

87. $-10 + 3 \cdot (-2) = -10 + (-6) = -16$

88. $5 - 10 \cdot (-3) = 5 - (-30) = 5 + 30 = 35$

89. $16 \cdot (-2) + 4 = -32 + 4 = -28$

90. $3 \cdot (-12) - 8 = -36 + (-8) = -44$

91. $5 + 6 \div (-3) = 5 - 2 = 3$

92. $-6 + (-10) \div (-2) = -6 + 5 = -1$

93. $16 + (-3) \cdot 12 \div 4 = 16 + (-36) \div 4$
$$= 16 + (-9)$$
$$= 7$$

94. $(-12) + 25 \cdot 1 \div (-5) = (-12) + 25 \div (-5)$
$$= (-12) + (-5)$$
$$= -17$$

95. $4^3 - (8-3)^2 = 4^3 - 5^2 = 64 - 25 = 39$

96. $4^3 - 90 = 64 + (-90) = -26$

97. $-(-4) \cdot |-3| - 5 = 4 \cdot 3 - 5$
$$= 12 - 5$$
$$= 12 + (-5)$$
$$= 7$$

98. $|5-1|^2 \cdot (-5) = |4|^2 \cdot (-5)$
$$= 4^2 \cdot (-5)$$
$$= 16 \cdot (-5)$$
$$= -80$$

99. $\dfrac{(-4)(-3) - (-2)(-1)}{-10 + 5} = \dfrac{12 - 2}{-10 + 5}$
$$= \dfrac{12 + (-2)}{-10 + 5}$$
$$= \dfrac{10}{-5}$$
$$= -2$$

100. $\dfrac{4(12 - 18)}{-10 \div (-2 - 3)} = \dfrac{4[12 + (-18)]}{-10 \div [-2 + (-3)]}$
$$= \dfrac{4(-6)}{-10 \div (-5)}$$
$$= \dfrac{-24}{2}$$
$$= -12$$

101. $\dfrac{-18 + 25 + (-30) + 7 + 0 + (-2)}{6} = \dfrac{-18}{6} = -3$

102. $\dfrac{-45 + (-40) + (-30) + (-25)}{4} = \dfrac{-140}{4} = -35$

103. $2(-2) - 1 = -4 - 1 = -5$

104. $1^2 + (-2)^2 = 1 + 4 = 5$

105. $\dfrac{3(-2)}{6} = \dfrac{-6}{6} = -1$

106. $\dfrac{5(1) - (-2)}{-1} = \dfrac{5 + 2}{-1} = \dfrac{7}{-1} = -7$

107. $x^2 = (-2)^2 = 4$

108. $-x^2 = -(-2)^2 = -4$

109. $7 - x^2 = 7 - (-2)^2$
$$= 7 - 4$$
$$= 3$$

110. $100 - x^3 = 100 - (-2)^3$
$$= 100 - (-8)$$
$$= 100 + 8$$
$$= 108$$

Chapter 2 Test

1. $-5 + 8 = 3$

2. $18 - 24 = 18 + (-24) = -6$

3. $5 \cdot (-20) = -100$

4. $(-16) \div (-4) = 4$

5. $(-18) + (-12) = -30$

6. $-7 - (-19) = -7 + 19 = 12$

7. $(-5) \cdot (-13) = 65$

8. $\dfrac{-25}{-5} = 5$

9. $|-25| + (-13) = 25 + (-13) = 12$

10. $14 - |-20| = 14 - 20$
$$= 14 + (-20)$$
$$= -6$$

11. $|5| \cdot |-10| = 5 \cdot 10 = 50$

12. $\dfrac{|-10|}{-|-5|} = \dfrac{10}{-5} = -2$

13. $(-8) + 9 \div (-3) = -8 + (-3) = -11$

14. $-7 + (-32) - 12 + 5 = -7 + (-32) + (-12) + 5$
$$= -51 + 5$$
$$= -46$$

15. $(-5)^3 - 24 \div (-3) = (-125) - 24 \div (-3)$
$$= (-125) - (-8)$$
$$= -125 + 8$$
$$= -117$$

16. $(5-9)^2 \cdot (8-2)^3 = (-4)^2 \cdot (6)^3$
$$= 16 \cdot 216$$
$$= 3456$$

17. $-(-7)^2 \div 7 \cdot (-4) = -49 \div 7 \cdot (-4)$
$$= -7 \cdot (-4)$$
$$= 28$$

18. $3 - (8-2)^3 = 3 - (6)^3 = 3 - 216 = -213$

19. $-6 + (-15) \div (-3) = -6 + 5 = -1$

20. $\dfrac{4}{2} - \dfrac{8^2}{16} = \dfrac{4}{2} - \dfrac{64}{16} = 2 - 4 = -2$

21. $\dfrac{(-3)(-2)+12}{-1(-4-5)} = \dfrac{6+12}{-1(-9)} = \dfrac{18}{9} = 2$

22. $\dfrac{|25-30|^2}{2(-6)+7} = \dfrac{|-5|^2}{2(-6)+7}$
$$= \dfrac{5^2}{-12+7}$$
$$= \dfrac{25}{-5}$$
$$= -5$$

23. $5(-8) - [6 - (2-4)] + (12-16)^2$
$$= 5(-8) - [6 - (-2)] + (-4)^2$$
$$= 5(-8) - [6 + 2] + (-4)^2$$
$$= 5(-8) - 8 + (-4)^2$$
$$= 5(-8) - 8 + 16$$
$$= -40 - 8 + 16$$
$$= -48 + 16$$
$$= -32$$

24. $-2^3 - 2^2 = -8 - 4 = -12$

25. $3(0) + (-3) = 0 + (-3) = -3$

26. $|-3| + |0| + |2| = 3 + 0 + 2 = 5$

27. $\dfrac{3(2)}{2(-3)} = \dfrac{6}{-6} = -1$

26. $5 - (-3) = 5 + 3 = 8$

27. $14,893 - 147 = 14,893 + (-147) = 14,746$
His final elevation is 14,746 feet.

28. $2(-3)^3 = 2(-27) = -54$

29. $10 - (-3)^2 = 10 - 9 = 1$

30. $7(0) + 3(-3) - 4(2) = 0 + (-9) - 8$
$$= -9 - 8$$
$$= -17$$

31. Sea level is 0. Each descent is –22.
$4(-22) = -88$
Her elevation is 88 feet below sea level.

32. $129 - 79 - 40 + 35 = 50 - 40 + 35$
$$= 10 + 35$$
$$= 45$$
His new balance is $45.

33. $6288 - (-25,354) = 6288 + 25,354 = 31,642$
The difference in elevation is 31,642 feet.

34. $1495 + (-5315) = -3820$
The elevation of the lake's deepest point is
–3820 feet or 3820 feet below sea level.

35. $\dfrac{-12 + (-13) + 0 + 9}{4} = \dfrac{-16}{4} = -4$

Chapter 2 Cumulative Review

1. 4 is in the ten-thousands place.

2. 4 is in the hundreds place.

3. 4 is in the tens place.

4. 4 is in the thousands place.

5. 4 is in the millions place.

6. 4 is in the hundreds-thousands place.

7. $5 < 50$
$101 > 0$
$29 > 27$

8. $12 < 4$
$13 > 31$
$82 > 79$

9. $\overset{2}{13}$
2
7
8
$\underline{+9}$
39

10.
$$\begin{array}{r} \overset{|}{1}1 \\ 3 \\ 9 \\ +\,16 \\ \hline 39 \end{array}$$

11.
$$\begin{array}{r} 7826 \\ -\,505 \\ \hline 7321 \end{array}$$
$$\begin{array}{r} 7321 \\ \text{Check:} +\,505 \\ \hline 7826 \end{array}$$

12.
$$\begin{array}{r} 3285 \\ -\,272 \\ \hline 3013 \end{array}$$
$$\begin{array}{r} 3013 \\ \text{Check:} +\,272 \\ \hline 3285 \end{array}$$

13. $6052 - 3612 = 2440$
The radius of Mercury is 2440 km.

14. $762 - 237 = 525$
C.J. will have $525 in her account.

15. To round 568 to the nearest ten, observe that the digit in the ones place is at least 5. Therefore we need to add 1 to the digit in the tens place. 568 rounded to the nearest ten is 570.

16. To round 468 to the nearest hundred, observe that the digit in the tens place is at last 5. Therefore we need to add 1 to the digit in the hundreds place. 568 rounded to the nearest hundred is 600.

17.
$$\begin{array}{r} 4725 \text{ rounds to } 4700 \\ 2879 \text{ rounds to} - 2900 \\ \hline 1800 \end{array}$$

18.
$$\begin{array}{r} 8394 \text{ rounds to } 8000 \\ 2913 \text{ rounds to} - 3000 \\ \hline 5000 \end{array}$$

19. **a.** $3(4 + 5) = 3 \cdot 4 + 3 \cdot 5$

  b. $10(6 + 8) = 10 \cdot 6 + 10 \cdot 8$

  c. $2(7 + 3) = 2 \cdot 7 + 2 \cdot 3$

20. **a.** $5(2 + 12) = 5 \cdot 2 + 5 \cdot 12$

  b. $9(3 + 6) = 9 \cdot 3 + 9 \cdot 6$

  c. $4(8 + 1) = 4 \cdot 8 + 4 \cdot 1$

21.
$$\begin{array}{r} 631 \\ \times\,125 \\ \hline 3155 \\ 12,620 \\ 63,100 \\ \hline 78,875 \end{array}$$

22.
$$\begin{array}{r} 299 \\ \times\,104 \\ \hline 1196 \\ 00 \\ 29,900 \\ \hline 31,096 \end{array}$$

23. $42 \div 7 = 6$
Check: $6 \cdot 7 = 42$

$\dfrac{81}{9} = 9$
Check: $9 \cdot 9 = 81$

$$\begin{array}{r} 6 \\ 4\overline{)\,24} \\ \underline{-24} \\ 0 \end{array}$$
Check: $6 \cdot 4 = 24$

24. $\dfrac{35}{5} = 7$
Check: $7 \cdot 5 = 35$

$64 \div 8 = 8$
Check: $8 \cdot 8 = 64$

$$\begin{array}{r} 12 \\ 4\overline{)\,48} \\ \underline{-4} \\ 08 \\ \underline{-\,8} \\ 0 \end{array}$$
Check: $12 \cdot 4 = 48$

25.
$$\begin{array}{r} 741 \\ 5\overline{)\,3705} \\ \underline{-35} \\ 20 \\ \underline{-\,20} \\ 05 \\ \underline{-\,5} \\ 0 \end{array}$$
Check: $741 \cdot 5 = 3705$

26.
$$\begin{array}{r} 456 \\ 8\overline{)\ 3648} \\ -32 \\ \overline{44} \\ -\ 40 \\ \overline{48} \\ -48 \\ \overline{0} \end{array}$$

Check: $456 \cdot 8 = 3648$

27.
$$\begin{array}{r} 6\ \text{R}\ 2 \\ 9\overline{)\ 56} \\ -54 \\ \overline{2} \end{array}$$

Because there is a remainder of 2, six boxes would not be enough. They would need 7 boxes to send all 56 pairs.

28. $324 \div 36 = 9$
Each ticket cost $9.

29. $8^2 = 8 \cdot 8 = 64$

30. $5^3 = 5 \cdot 5 \cdot 5 = 25 \cdot 5 = 125$

31. $7^1 = 7$

32. $4^1 = 4$

33. $5 \cdot 6^2 = 5 \cdot 36 = 180$

34. $2^3 \cdot 7 = 8 \cdot 7 = 56$

35.
$$\begin{aligned} \frac{7 - 2 \cdot 3 + 3^2}{2^2 + 1} &= \frac{7 - 2 \cdot 3 + 9}{4 + 1} \\ &= \frac{7 - 6 + 9}{4 + 1} \\ &= \frac{1 + 9}{4 + 1} \\ &= \frac{10}{5} \\ &= 2 \end{aligned}$$

36.
$$\begin{aligned} \frac{6^2 + 4 \cdot 4 + 2^3}{37 - 5^2} &= \frac{36 + 4 \cdot 4 + 8}{37 - 25} \\ &= \frac{36 + 16 + 8}{37 - 25} \\ &= \frac{52 + 8}{37 - 25} \\ &= \frac{60}{12} \\ &= 5 \end{aligned}$$

37. $8 + 7 = 15$

38. $5 + 9 = 14$

39.   **a.** $\left|-2\right| = 2$
   b. $\left|5\right| = 5$
   c. $\left|0\right| = 0$

40. $\left|4\right| = 4$
$\left|-7\right| = 7$

41. $-2 + 5 = 3$

42. $8 + (-3) = 5$

43. $8 -(-6) = 8 + 6 = 14$

44. $-2 - (-7) = -2 + 7 = 5$

45. $-7 \cdot 3 = -21$

46. $5(-2) = -10$

47. $0 \cdot (-4) = 0$

48. $-6 \cdot 9 = = 54$

49.
$$\begin{aligned} 3(4 - 7) + (-2) - 5 &= 3(-3) + (-2) - 5 \\ &= -9 + (-2) - 5 \\ &= -11 - 5 \\ &= -16 \end{aligned}$$

50.
$$\begin{aligned} 4 - 8(7 - 3) - (-1) &= 4 - 8(4) - (-1) \\ &= 4 - 32 - (-1) \\ &= -28 - (-1) \\ &= -28 + 1 \\ &= -27 \end{aligned}$$

Chapter 3

Pretest

1. $9x - 4 + 6x + 8 = 9x + 6x - 4 + 8$
$$= (9 + 6)x + 4$$
$$= 15x + 4$$

2. $3(2x - 1) - (x - 8)$
$$= 3(2x - 1) + (-1)(x - 8)$$
$$= 3 \cdot 2x - 3 \cdot 1 + (-1)(x) + (-1)(-8)$$
$$= 6x - 3 - x + 8$$
$$= 6x - x - 3 + 8$$
$$= 5x + 5$$

3. $8(7b) = (8 \cdot 7)b$
$$= 56b$$

4. $-5(2y - 7) = -5 \cdot 2y + (-5)(-7)$
$$= -10y + 35$$

5. perimeter $= 4a + 17 + 9a$
$$= 13a + 17$$
The perimeter is $(13a + 17)$ inches.

6. area $=$ length $\cdot$ width
$$= (4x - 1) \cdot 3$$
$$= 3(4x - 1)$$
$$= 3 \cdot 4x - 3 \cdot 1$$
$$= 12x - 3$$
The area is $(12x - 3)$ square feet.

7. $2y - 3 = -5$
$$2(-4) - 3 = -5$$
$$-8 - 3 = -5$$
$$-11 = -5 \text{ False}$$
No, -4 is not a solution.

8. $-7 = x + 5$
$$-7 - 5 = x + 5 - 5$$
$$-12 = x$$

9. $9n + 3 - 8n = 8 - 14$
$$n + 3 = -6$$
$$n + 3 - 3 = -6 - 3$$
$$n = -9$$

10. $-6x = 42$
$$\frac{-6x}{-6} = \frac{42}{-6}$$
$$x = -7$$

11. $2m - 9m = -77$
$$-7m = -77$$
$$\frac{-7m}{-7} = \frac{-77}{-7}$$
$$m = 11$$

12. $2(x - 12)$

13. $3x$

14. $18 - 3x = -9$
$$18 - 3x - 18 = -9 - 18$$
$$-3x = -27$$
$$\frac{-3x}{-3} = \frac{-27}{-3}$$
$$x = 9$$

15. $8a - 5 = 2a + 7$
$$8a - 5 + 5 = 2a + 7 + 5$$
$$8a = 2a + 12$$
$$8a - 2a = 2a + 12 - 2a$$
$$6a = 12$$
$$\frac{6a}{6} = \frac{12}{6}$$
$$a = 2$$

16. $4(x + 1) = 9x - 1$
$$4x + 4 = 9x - 1$$
$$4x + 4 - 4 = 9x - 1 - 4$$
$$4x = 9x - 5$$
$$4x - 9x = 9x - 5 - 9x$$
$$-5x = -5$$
$$\frac{-5x}{-5} = \frac{-5}{-5}$$
$$x = 1$$

17. $-2(3x + 4) - 10 = 0$
$$-2.3x + (-2)(4) - 10 = 0$$
$$-6x - 8 - 10 = 0$$
$$-6x - 18 = 0$$
$$-6x - 18 + 18 = 0 + 18$$
$$-6x = 18$$
$$\frac{-6x}{-6} = \frac{18}{-6}$$
$$x = -3$$

18. $\frac{54}{-6} = -9$

19. $x - 5 = 12$

20.
$$68 = 9x + 5$$
$$68 - 5 = 9x + 5 - 5$$
$$63 = 9x$$
$$\frac{63}{9} = \frac{9x}{9}$$
$$7 = x$$

Section 3.1

Practice Problems

1. a. $8m - 11m = (8 - 11)m$
$$= -3m$$

   b. $5a + a = 5a + 1a$
$$= (5 + 1)a$$
$$= 6a$$

   c. $-y^2 + 3y^2 + 7 = -1y^2 + 3y^2 + 7$
$$= (-1 + 3)y^2 + 7$$
$$= 2y^2 + 7$$

2. $8m + 5 + m - 4 = 8m + 5 + m + (-4)$
$$= 8m + m + 5 + (-4)$$
$$= (8 + 1)m + 5 + (-4)$$
$$= 9m + 1$$

3. $7y + 11y - 8 = 18y - 8$

4. $2y - 6 + y + 7 = 2y + y - 6 + 7$
$$= 3y + 1$$

5. $-9y + 2 - 4y - 8x + 12 - x$
$$= -9y + 2 + (-4y) + (-8x) + 12 + (-x)$$
$$= -9y + (-4y) + (-8x) + (-x) + 2 + 12$$
$$= -13y - 9x + 14$$

6. $7(8a) = (7 \cdot 8)a$
$$= 56a$$

7. $-5(9x) = (-5 \cdot 9)x$
$$= -45x$$

8. $7(y + 2) = 7 \cdot y + 7 \cdot 2$
$$= 7y + 14$$

9. $4(7a - 5) = 4 \cdot 7a + 4 \cdot (-5)$
$$= 28a - 20$$

10. $6(5 - y) = 6 \cdot 5 - 6 \cdot y = 30 - 6y$

11. $5(y - 3) - 8 + y = 5 \cdot y - 5 \cdot 3 - 8 + y$
$$= 5y - 15 - 8 + y$$
$$= 6y - 23$$

12. $5(2x - 3) + 7(x - 1)$
$$= 5 \cdot 2x - 5 \cdot 3 + 7 \cdot x - 7 \cdot 1$$
$$= 10x - 15 + 7x - 7$$
$$= 10x + (-15) + 7x + (-7)$$
$$= 17x - 22$$

13. $-(y + 1) + 3y - 12 = -1(y + 1) + 3y + (-12)$
$$= -1 \cdot y + (-1)(1) + 3y + (-12)$$
$$= -y + (-1) + 3y + (-12)$$
$$= 2y - 13$$

14. Find the sum of the lengths of the sides. A square has 4 sides of equal length.
$$\text{perimeter} = 2x + 2x + 2x + 2x$$
$$= 8x$$
The perimeter is $8x$ centimeters.

15. $A = \text{length} \cdot \text{width}$
$$= (12y + 9) \cdot 3$$
$$= 3(12y + 9)$$
$$= 3 \cdot 12y + 3 \cdot 9$$
$$= 36y + 27$$
The area is $(36y + 27)$ square yards.

Mental Math

1. The numerical coefficient of $5y$ is 5.

2. The numerical coefficient of $-2z$ is -2.

3. The numerical coefficient of z is 1.

4. The numerical coefficient of $3xy^2$ is 3.

5. The numerical coefficient of $11a$ is 11.

6. The numerical coefficient of $-x$ is -1.

Exercise Set 3.1

1. $3x + 5x = (3 + 5)x = 8x$

3. $5n - 9n = (5 - 9)n = -4n$

5. $4c + c - 7c = (4 + 1 - 7)c = -2c$

7. $5x - 7x + x - 3x = (5 - 7 + 1 - 3)x = -4x$

9. $4a + 3a + 6a - 8 = (4 + 3 + 6)a - 8 = 13a - 8$

11. $6(5x) = (6 \cdot 5)x = 30x$

13. $-2(11y) = (-2 \cdot 11)y = -22y$

15. $12(6a) = (12 \cdot 6)a = 72a$

17. $2(y + 2) = 2 \cdot y + 2 \cdot 2 = 2y + 4$

19. $5(a-8) = 5 \cdot a + 5 \cdot (-8) = 5a - 40$

21. $-4(3x+7) = -4 \cdot 3x + (-4) \cdot 7$
$\qquad = -12x - 28$

23. $2(x+4) + 7 = 2 \cdot x + 2 \cdot 4 + 7$
$\qquad = 2x + 8 + 7$
$\qquad = 2x + 15$

25. $-4(6n-5) + 3n = -4 \cdot 6n + (-4) \cdot (-5) + 3n$
$\qquad = -24n + 20 + 3n$
$\qquad = -21n + 20$

27. $5(3c-1) + 8 = 5 \cdot 3c - 5 \cdot 1 + 8$
$\qquad = 15c - 5 + 8$
$\qquad = 15c + 3$

29. $3 + 6(w+2) + w = 3 + 6 \cdot w + 6 \cdot 2 + w$
$\qquad = 3 + 6w + 12 + w$
$\qquad = 6w + w + 3 + 12$
$\qquad = 7w + 15$

31. $2(3x+1) + 5(x-2)$
$\qquad = 2(3x) + 2(1) + 5(x) - 5(2)$
$\qquad = 6x + 2 + 5x - 10$
$\qquad = 6x + 5x + 2 + (-10)$
$\qquad = 11x - 8$

33. $-(5x-1) - 10 = -1(5x-1) - 10$
$\qquad = -1 \cdot 5x + (-1) \cdot (-1) - 10$
$\qquad = -5x + 1 - 10$
$\qquad = -5x - 9$

35. $18y - 20y = (18-20)y = -2y$

37. $z - 8z = (1-8)z = -7z$

39. $9d - 3c - d = 9d - d - 3c = 8d - 3c$

41. $2y - 6 + 4y - 8 = 2y + 4y - 6 - 8$
$\qquad = 6y - 14$

43. $5q + p - 6q - p = p - p + 5q - 6q$
$\qquad = -q$

45. $2(x+1) + 20 = 2 \cdot x + 2 \cdot 1 + 20$
$\qquad = 2x + 2 + 20$
$\qquad = 2x + 22$

47. $5(x-7) - 8x = 5 \cdot x - 5 \cdot 7 - 8x$
$\qquad = 5x - 35 - 8x$
$\qquad = 5x - 8x - 35$
$\qquad = -3x - 35$

49. $-5(z+3) + 2z = -5 \cdot z + (-5) \cdot 3 + 2z$
$\qquad = -5z - 15 + 2z$
$\qquad = -5z + 2z - 15$
$\qquad = -3z - 15$

51. $8 - x + 4x - 2 - 9x$
$\qquad = -x + 4x - 9x + 8 - 2$
$\qquad = -6x + 6$

53. $-7(x+5) + 5(2x+1)$
$\qquad = -7 \cdot x + (-7) \cdot 5 + 5 \cdot 2x + 5 \cdot 1$
$\qquad = -7x - 35 + 10x + 5$
$\qquad = -7x + 10x - 35 + 5$
$\qquad = 3x - 30$

55. $3r - 5r + 8 + r = 3r - 5r + r + 8$
$\qquad = -r + 8$

57. $-3(n-1) - 4n = -3 \cdot n - (-3) \cdot 1 - 4n$
$\qquad = -3n + 3 - 4n$
$\qquad = -3n - 4n + 3$
$\qquad = -7n + 3$

59. $4(z-3) + 5z - 2 = 4 \cdot z - 4 \cdot 3 + 5z - 2$
$\qquad = 4z - 12 + 5z - 2$
$\qquad = 4z + 5z - 12 - 2$
$\qquad = 9z - 14$

61. $6(2x-1) - 12x = 6 \cdot 2x - 6 \cdot 1 - 12x$
$\qquad = 12x - 6 - 12x$
$\qquad = 12x - 12x - 6$
$\qquad = -6$

63. $-(4x-5) + 5 = -1(4x-5) + 5$
$\qquad = -1 \cdot 4x - (-1) \cdot 5 + 5$
$\qquad = -4x + 5 + 5$
$\qquad = -4x + 10$

65. $-(4xy-10) + 2(3xy+5)$
$\qquad = -1(4xy-10) + 2 \cdot 3xy + 2 \cdot 5$
$\qquad = -1 \cdot 4xy - (-1) \cdot 10 + 6xy + 10$
$\qquad = -4xy + 10 + 6xy + 10$
$\qquad = -4xy + 6xy + 10 + 10$
$\qquad = 2xy + 20$

67. $3a + 4(a+3) = 3a + 4 \cdot a + 4 \cdot 3$
$\qquad = 3a + 4a + 12$
$\qquad = 7a + 12$

69. $5y - 2(y-1) + 3 = 5y - 2y - 2(-1) + 3$
$\qquad = 3y + 2 + 3$
$\qquad = 3y + 5$

71. There are five sides, each of length
$-5x + 11$ inches, so the perimeter is:
$$5(-5x+11) = 5(-5x) + 5(11)$$
$$= -(25x + 55) \text{ inches}$$

73. $5y + 16 + 3y + 4y + 2y + 6$
$$= 5y + 3y + 4y + 2y + 16 + 6$$
$$= (14y + 22) \text{ meters}$$

75. There are three sides of length $2a$ feet, two sides of length 6 feet, and one side of length $5a$ feet, so the perimeter is:
$$3(2a) + 2 \cdot 6 + 5a = 6a + 12 + 5a$$
$$= 6a + 5a + 12$$
$$= (11a + 12) \text{ feet}$$

77. Area $= (\text{side})^2$
$$= (4z)^2$$
$$= (4z)(4z)$$
$$= (4)(4)(z)(z)$$
$$= 16z^2 \text{ square centimeters}$$

79. $A = \text{length} \cdot \text{width}$
$$= 20(5x - 7)$$
$$= 100x - 140$$
$$= (100x - 140) \text{ square inches}$$

81. $-13 + 10 = -3$

83. $-4 - (-12) = -4 + 12 = 8$

85. $-4 + 4 = 0$

87. $9684q - 686 - 4860q + 12,960$
$$= (9684 - 4860)q + (12,960 - 686)$$
$$= 4824q + 12,274$$

89. Answers may vary.

91. Add the areas of the two rectangles.
Area = (length) $\cdot$ (width)
$$\binom{\text{Area of left}}{\text{rectangle}} + \binom{\text{Area of right}}{\text{rectangle}}$$
$$= 7(2x + 1) + 3(2x + 3)$$
$$= 7(2x) + 7(1) + 3(2x) + 3(3)$$
$$= 14x + 7 + 6x + 9$$
$$= (14 + 6)x + 16$$
$$= (20x + 16)$$
The area is $(20x + 16)$ square miles.

93. Answers will vary.

Section 3.2

Practice Problems

1.
$$3(y - 6) = 6$$
$$3(4 - 6) = 6$$
$$3(-2) = 6$$
$$-6 = 6 \quad \text{False}$$
Since $-6 = 6$ is false, 4 is not a solution of the equation.

2.
$$-4x - 3 = 5$$
$$-4(-2) - 3 = 5$$
$$8 - 3 = 5$$
$$5 = 5 \quad \text{True}$$
Since $5 = 5$ is true, -2 is a solution of the equation.

3.
$$y - 5 = -3$$
$$y - 5 + 5 = -3 + 5$$
$$y = 2$$

4.
$$z + 9 = 1$$
$$z + 9 - 9 = 1 - 9$$
$$z = -8$$

5.
$$10x = -2 + 9x$$
$$10x - 9x = -2 + 9x - 9x$$
$$1x = -2 \text{ or } x = -2$$

6.
$$x + 6 = 1 - 3$$
$$x + 6 = -2$$
$$x + 6 - 6 = -2 - 6$$
$$x = -8$$

7. $-6y - 1 + 7y = 17$
$$y - 1 = 17$$
$$y - 1 + 1 = 17 + 1$$
$$y = 18$$

8.
$$13x = 4(3x - 1)$$
$$13x = 4 \cdot 3x - 4 \cdot 1$$
$$13x = 12x - 4$$
$$13x - 12x = 12x - 4 - 12x$$
$$1x = -4 \text{ or } x = -4$$

Exercise Set 3.2

1. $x - 8 = 2$
$$10 - 8 = 2$$
$$2 = 2 \quad \text{True}$$
Yes, 10 is a solution.

3. $z + 8 = 14$
$6 + 8 = 14$
$14 = 14$ True
Yes, 6 is a solution.

5. $x + 12 = 7$
$-5 + 12 = 7$
$7 = 7$ True
Yes, –5 is a solution.

7. $7f = 64 - f$
$7(8) = 64 - 8$
$56 = 64 - 8$
$56 = 56$ True
Yes, 8 is a solution.

9. $h - 8 = -8$
$0 - 8 = -8$
$-8 = -8$ True
Yes, 0 is a solution.

11. $4c + 2 - 3c = -1 + 6$
$4(3) + 2 - 3(3) = 5$
$12 + 2 - 9 = 5$
$14 - 9 = 5$
$5 = 5$ True
Yes, 3 is a solution.

13. $a + 5 = 23$
$a + 5 - 5 = 23 - 5$
$a = 18$
Check: $a + 5 = 23$
$18 + 5 = 23$
$23 = 23$ True
The solution is 18.

15. $d - 9 = 17$
$d - 9 + 9 = 17 + 9$
$d = 26$
Check: $d - 9 = 17$
$26 - 9 = 17$
$17 = 17$ True
The solution is 26.

17. $7 = y - 2$
$7 + 2 = y - 2 + 2$
$9 = y$
Check: $7 = y - 2$
$7 = 9 - 2$
$7 = 7$ True
The solution is 9.

19. $-12 = x + 4$
$-12 - 4 = x + 4 - 4$
$-16 = x$
Check: $-12 = x + 4$
$-12 = -16 + 4$
$-12 = -12$ True
The solution is –16.

21. $3x = 2x + 11$
$3x - 2x = 2x + 11 - 2x$
$x = 11$
Check: $3x = 2x + 11$
$3(11) = 2(11) + 11$
$33 = 22 + 11$
$33 = 33$ True
The solution is 11.

23. $-4 + y = 2y$
$-4 + y - y = 2y - y$
$-4 = y$
Check: $-4 + y = 2y$
$-4 + (-4) = 2(-4)$
$-8 = -8$ True
The solution is –4.

25. $x - 3 = -1 + 4$
$x - 3 = 3$
$x - 3 + 3 = 3 + 3$
$x = 6$
Check: $x - 3 = -1 + 4$
$6 - 3 = -1 + 4$
$3 = 3$ True
The solution is 6.

27. $y + 1 = -3 + 4$
$y + 1 = 1$
$y + 1 - 1 = 1 - 1$
$y = 0$
Check: $y + 1 = -3 + 4$
$0 + 1 = -3 + 4$
$1 = 1$ True
The solution is 0.

29. $-7 + 10 = m - 5$
$3 = m - 5$
$3 + 5 = m - 5 + 5$
$8 = m$
Check: $-7 + 10 = m - 5$
$-7 + 10 = 8 - 5$
$3 = 3$ True
The solution is 8.

31. $-2-3 = -4+x$
$-5 = -4+x$
$-5+4 = -4+x+4$
$-1 = x$
Check: $-2-3 = -4+x$
$-2-3 = -4+(-1)$
$-5 = -5$ True

The solution is -1.

33. $2(5x-3) = 11x$
$2 \cdot 5x - 2 \cdot 3 = 11x$
$10x-6 = 11x$
$10x-6-10x = 11x-10x$
$-6 = x$
Check: $2(5x-3) = 11x$
$2(5 \cdot (-6)-3) = 11 \cdot (-6)$
$2(-30-3) = -66$
$2(-33) = -66$
$-66 = -66$ True

The solution is -6.

35. $3y = 2(y+12)$
$3y = 2 \cdot y + 2 \cdot 12$
$3y = 2y+24$
$3y-2y = 2y+24-2y$
$y = 24$
Check: $3y = 2(y+12)$
$3 \cdot 24 = 2(24+12)$
$72 = 2(36)$
$72 = 72$ True

The solution is 24.

37. $-8x+4+9x = -1+7$
$x+4 = 6$
$x+4-4 = 6-4$
$x = 2$
Check: $-8x+4+9x = -1+7$
$-8(2)+4+9(2) = -1+7$
$-16+4+18 = 6$
$6 = 6$ True

The solution is 2.

39. $2-2 = 5x-4x$
$0 = x$
Check: $2-2 = 5x-4x$
$2-2 = 5(0)-4(0)$
$0 = 0-0$
$0 = 0$ True

The solution is 0.

41. $7x+14-6x = -4-10$
$x+14 = -14$
$x+14-14 = -14-14$
$x = -28$
Check: $7x+14-6x = -4-10$
$7(-28)+14-6(-28) = -4-10$
$-196+14+168 = -14$
$-14 = -14$ True

The solution is -28.

43. $57 = y-16$
$57+16 = y-16+16$
$73 = y$

45. $67 = z+67$
$67+(-67) = z+67+(-67)$
$0 = z$

47. $x+5 = 4-3$
$x+5 = 1$
$x+5+(-5) = 1+(-5)$
$x = -4$

49. $z-23 = -88$
$z-23+23 = -88+23$
$z = -65$

51. $7a+7-6a = 20$
$a+7 = 20$
$a+7+(-7) = 20+(-7)$
$a = 13$

53. $-12+x = -15$
$-12+x+12 = -15+12$
$x = -3$

55. $-8-9 = 3x+5-2x$
$-17 = x+5$
$-17-5 = x+5-5$
$-22 = x$

57. $8(3x-2) = 25x$
$8 \cdot 3x - 8 \cdot 2 = 25x$
$24x-16 = 25x$
$24x-16-24x = 25x-24x$
$-16 = x$

59. $7x+7-6x = 10$
$x+7 = 10$
$x+7+(-7) = 10+(-7)$
$x = 3$

61.
$$50y = 7(7y + 4)$$
$$50y = 7 \cdot 7y + 7 \cdot 4$$
$$50y = 49y + 28$$
$$50y - 49y = 49y + 28 - 49y$$
$$y = 28$$

63. 2400

65. $2400 - 200 = 2200$ more trumpeter swans in 2000 than in 1985.

67. $\dfrac{8}{8} = 1$

69. $\dfrac{-3}{-3} = 1$

71. Answers may vary.

73. No; answers may vary.

75.
$$x - 76,862 = 86,102$$
$$x - 76,862 + 76,862 = 86,102 + 76,862$$
$$x = 162,964$$

77.
$$5^3 = x + 4^4$$
$$125 = x + 16$$
$$125 - 16 = x + 16 - 16$$

79.
$$\left|-13\right| + 3^2 = 100y - \left|-20\right| - 99y$$
$$13 + 3^2 = 100y - 20 - 99y$$
$$13 + 9 = y - 20$$
$$22 = y - 20$$
$$22 + 20 = y - 20 + 22$$
$$42 = y$$

81.
$$T = P + R$$
$$5560 = P + 1933$$
$$5560 - 1933 = P + 1933 - 1933$$
$$3627 = P$$
The total passing yardage was 3627 yards.

83.
$$I = R - E$$
$$6671 = R - 213,141$$
$$6671 + 213,141 = R - 213,141 + 213,141$$
$$219,812 = R$$
The total revenues were \$219,812 million.

Section 3.3

Practice Problems

1.
$$\frac{x}{-4} = 7$$
$$-4 \cdot \frac{x}{-4} = 7 \cdot (-4)$$
$$\frac{-4}{-4} x = 7 \cdot (-4)$$
$$1x = -28 \ \ or \ \ x = -28$$

2.
$$3y = -18$$
$$\frac{3y}{3} = \frac{-18}{3}$$
$$\frac{3}{3} \cdot y = \frac{-18}{3}$$
$$1y = -6 \text{ or } y = -6$$

3.
$$-16 = 8x$$
$$\frac{-16}{8} = \frac{8x}{8}$$
$$\frac{-16}{8} = \frac{8}{8} \cdot x$$
$$-2 = x \text{ or } x = -2$$

4.
$$-3y = -27$$
$$\frac{-3y}{-3} = \frac{-27}{-3}$$
$$\frac{-3}{-3} \cdot y = \frac{-27}{-3}$$
$$y = 9$$

5.
$$10 = 2m - 4m$$
$$10 = -2m$$
$$\frac{10}{-2} = \frac{-2m}{-2}$$
$$-5 = m \text{ or } m = -5$$

6.
$$-8 + 6 = -a$$
$$-2 = -a$$
$$\frac{-2}{-1} = \frac{-1a}{-1}$$
$$2 = a$$

7.
$$-4 - 10 = 4y + 3y$$
$$-14 = 7y$$
$$\frac{-14}{7} = \frac{7y}{7}$$
$$-2 = y$$

8. a. The sum of -3 and a number is $-3 + x$.

b. -5 decreased by a number is $-5 - x.$.

c. Three times a number is $3x$.

   d. A number subtracted from 83 is $83 - x$.

   e. The quotient of a number and 4 is $\dfrac{x}{4}$.

9. a. The product of 5 and a number is $5x$. The product of 5 and a number decreased by 25 is $5x - 25$.

   b. The sum of a number and 3 is $x + 3$. Twice the sum of a number and 3 is $2(x + 3)$.

   c. Twice a number is $2x$. The quotient of 39 and twice a number is $\dfrac{39}{2x}$.

Exercise Set 3.3

1. $5x = 20$
    $$\frac{5x}{5} = \frac{20}{5} \quad \text{divide by 5}$$
    $$x = 4$$

3. $-3z = 12$
    $$\frac{-3z}{-3} = \frac{12}{-3} \quad \text{divide by } -3$$
    $$z = -4$$

5. $\dfrac{x}{7} = 1$
    $$7 \cdot \frac{x}{7} = 1 \cdot 7$$
    $$x = 7$$

7. $\dfrac{z}{-9} = 9$
    $$-9 \cdot \frac{z}{-9} = 9(-9)$$
    $$z = -81$$

9. $4y = 0$
    $$\frac{4y}{4} = \frac{0}{4} \quad \text{divide by 4}$$
    $$y = 0$$

11. $2z = -34$
    $$\frac{2z}{2} = \frac{-34}{2} \quad \text{divide by 2}$$
    $$z = -17$$

13. $\dfrac{x}{-8} = -4$
    $$-8 \cdot \frac{x}{-8} = -4(-8)$$
    $$x = 32$$

15. $\dfrac{y}{-20} = 3$
    $$-20 \cdot \frac{y}{-20} = 3(-20)$$
    $$y = -60$$

17. $-3x = -15$
    $$\frac{-3x}{-3} = \frac{-15}{-3} \quad \text{divide by } -3$$
    $$x = 5$$

19. $\dfrac{x}{-17} = 0$
    $$-17 \cdot \frac{x}{-17} = 0(-17)$$
    $$x = 0$$

21. $2w - 12w = 40 \quad \text{combine like terms}$
    $$-10w = 40$$
    $$\frac{-10w}{-10} = \frac{40}{-10} \quad \text{divide by } -10$$
    $$w = -4$$

23. $16 = 10t - 8t \quad \text{combine like terms}$
    $$16 = 2t$$
    $$\frac{16}{2} = \frac{2t}{2} \quad \text{divide by 2}$$
    $$8 = t$$

25. $2z = 12 - 14 \quad \text{combine like terms}$
    $$2z = -2$$
    $$\frac{2z}{2} = \frac{-2}{2} \quad \text{divide by 2}$$
    $$z = -1$$

27. $4 - 10 = \dfrac{z}{-3}$
    $$-6 = \frac{z}{-3}$$
    $$-3(-6) = \frac{z}{-3}(-3)$$
    $$18 = z$$

29. $-3x - 3x = 50 - 2 \quad \text{combine like terms}$
    $$-6x = 48$$
    $$\frac{6x}{-6} = \frac{48}{-6} \quad \text{divide by } -6$$
    $$x = -8$$

31. $\dfrac{x}{5} = -26 + 16$

$\dfrac{x}{5} = -10$

$5 \cdot \dfrac{x}{5} = -10 \cdot 5$

$x = -50$

33. $-10x = 10$

$\dfrac{-10x}{-10} = \dfrac{10}{-10}$ divide by -10

$x = -1$

35. $5x = -35$

$\dfrac{5x}{5} = \dfrac{-35}{5}$ divide by 5

$x = -7$

37. $0 = 3x$

$\dfrac{0}{3} = \dfrac{3x}{3}$ divide by 3

$0 = x$

39. $24 = t + 3t$ combine like terms

$24 = 4t$

$\dfrac{24}{4} = \dfrac{4t}{4}$ divide by 4

$6 = t$

41. $10z - 3z = -63$ combine like terms

$7z = -63$

$\dfrac{7z}{7} = \dfrac{-63}{7}$ divide by 7

$z = -9$

43. $3z - 10z = -63$ combine like terms

$-7z = -63$

$\dfrac{-7z}{-7} = \dfrac{-63}{-7}$ divide by -7

$z = 9$

45. $12 = 13y - 10y$ combine like terms

$12 = 3y$

$\dfrac{12}{3} = \dfrac{3y}{3}$ divide by 3

$4 = y$

47. $-4x = 20 - (-4)$ combine like terms

$-4x = 20 + 4$

$-4x = 24$

$\dfrac{-4x}{-4} = \dfrac{24}{-4}$ divide by -4

$x = -6$

49. $18 - 11 = \dfrac{x}{-5}$

$7 = \dfrac{x}{-5}$

$-5 \cdot 7 = \dfrac{x}{-5} \cdot -5$

$-35 = x$

51. $-20 - (-50) = \dfrac{x}{9}$

$-20 + 50 = \dfrac{x}{9}$

$30 = \dfrac{x}{9}$

$9 \cdot 30 = \dfrac{x}{9} \cdot 9$

$270 = x$

53. $10p - 11p = 25$ combine like terms

$-1p = 25$

$\dfrac{-1p}{-1} = \dfrac{25}{-1}$ divide by -1

$p = -25$

55. $6x - x = 4 - 14$ combine like terms

$5x = -10$

$\dfrac{5x}{5} = \dfrac{-10}{5}$ divide by 5

$x = -2$

57. $10 = 7t - 12t$ combine like terms

$10 = -5t$

$\dfrac{10}{-5} = \dfrac{-5t}{-5}$ divide by -5

$-2 = t$

59. $5 - 5 = 3x + 2x$ combine like terms

$0 = 5x$

$\dfrac{0}{5} = \dfrac{5x}{5}$ divide by 5

$0 = x$

61. $4r - 9r = -20$ combine like terms

$-5r = -20$

$\dfrac{-5r}{-5} = \dfrac{-20}{-5}$ divide by -5

$r = 4$

63.
$$\frac{x}{-4} = -1 - (-8)$$
$$\frac{x}{-4} = -1 + 8$$
$$\frac{x}{-4} = 7$$
$$-4 \cdot \frac{x}{-4} = 7(-4)$$
$$x = -28$$

65. $3w - 12w = -27$ combine like terms
$$-9w = -27$$
$$\frac{-9w}{-9} = \frac{-27}{-9} \text{ divide by } -9$$
$$w = 3$$

67. $-36 = 9u - 10u$ combine like terms
$$-36 = -1u$$
$$\frac{-36}{-1} = \frac{-1u}{-1} \qquad \text{divide by } -1$$
$$36 = u$$

69. $23x - 25x = 7 - 9$ combine like terms
$$-2x = -2$$
$$\frac{-2x}{-2} = \frac{-2}{-2} \text{ divide by } -2$$
$$x = 1$$

71. Let x represent a number. The sum of -7 and a number is $-7 + x$.

73. Let x represent a number. The product of -11 and a number is $-11x$.

75. Let x represent a number. A number divided by -12 is $\frac{x}{-12}$ or $-\frac{x}{12}$.

77. Let x represent a number. Eleven subtracted from a number is $x - 11$.

79. Let x represent a number. 7 times a number is $7x$. Thus, negative ten decreased by 7 times a number is $-10 - 7x$.

81. Let x represent a number. The product of -13 and a number is $-13x$.

83. Let x represent a number. The quotient of seventeen and a number is $\frac{17}{x}$. Thus, the quotient

of seventeen and a number increased by -15 is
$$\frac{17}{x} + (-15).$$

85. Let x represent a number. The product of 4 and a number is $4x$. Thus, seven added to the product of 4 and a number is $4x + 7$.

87. Let x represent a number. Twice a number is $2x$. Thus, twice a number, decreased by 17 is $2x - 17$.

89. Let x represent a number. The sum of a number and 15 is $x + 15$. Thus, the product of -6 and the sum of a number and 15 is $-6(x + 15)$.

91. Let x represent a number. The product of a number and -5 is $-5x$. Thus, the quotient of 45 and the product of a number and -5 is $\frac{45}{-5x}$.

93. $3x + 10 = 3(-5) + 10 = -15 + 10 = -5$

95. $\frac{x-5}{2} = \frac{-5-5}{2} = \frac{-10}{2} = -5$

97. $\frac{3x+4}{x+4} = \frac{3(-5)+4}{-5+4} = \frac{-15+4}{-1} = \frac{-11}{-1} = 11$

99. Answers may vary.

101.
$$-25x = 900$$
$$\frac{-25x}{-25} = \frac{900}{-25}$$
$$x = -36$$

103.
$$\frac{y}{72} = -86 - (-1029)$$
$$\frac{y}{72} = -86 + 1029$$
$$\frac{y}{72} = 943$$
$$72 \cdot \frac{y}{72} = 943 \cdot 72$$
$$y = 67,896$$

105.
$$\frac{x}{-2} = 5^2 - |-10| - (-9)$$
$$\frac{x}{-2} = 25 - 10 + 9$$
$$\frac{x}{-2} = 24$$
$$-2 \cdot \frac{x}{-2} = 24(-2)$$
$$x = 48$$

107.
$$d = r \cdot t$$
$$780 = 65t$$
$$\frac{780}{65} = \frac{65t}{65}$$
$$12 = t$$
It will take 12 hours.

109.
$$d = r \cdot t$$
$$232 = r \cdot 4$$
$$\frac{232}{4} = \frac{r \cdot 4}{4}$$
$$58 = r$$
The driver should drive at 58 miles per hour

Integrated Review

1. $7x + x = 7x + 1x$
$$= (7 + 1)x$$
$$= 8x$$

2. $6y - 10y = (6 - 10)y$
$$= -4y$$

3. $2a + 5a - 9a - 2 = (2 + 5 - 9)a - 2$
$$= -2a - 2$$

4. $6a - 12 - a - 14 = 6a - a - 12 - 14$
$$= (6 - 1)a - 12 - 14$$
$$= 5a - 26$$

5. $-2(4x + 7) = -2 \cdot 4x + (-2)(7) = -8x - 14$

6. $-3(2x - 10) = -3(2x) + (-3)(-10)$
$$= -6x + 30$$

7. $5(y + 2) - 20 = 5 \cdot y + 5 \cdot 2 - 20$
$$= 5y + 10 - 20$$
$$= 5y - 10$$

8. $12x + 3(x - 6) - 13 = 12x + 3 \cdot x + 3(-6) - 13$
$$= 12x + 3x - 18 - 13$$
$$= 15x - 31$$

9. $A = \text{length} \cdot \text{width}$
$$= (4x - 2) \cdot 3$$
$$= 3(4x - 2)$$
$$= 3 \cdot 4x - 3 \cdot 2$$
$$= 12x - 6$$
The area is $(12x - 6)$ square meters.

10. $P = a + b + c$
$$= x + 7 + (x + 2)$$
$$= x + 7 + 1(x + 2)$$
$$= x + 7 + 1 \cdot x + 1 \cdot 2)$$
$$= x + 7 + x + 2$$
$$= x + x + 7 + 2$$
$$= 2x + 9$$
The perimeter is $(2x + 9)$ feet.

11.
$$x + 7 = 20$$
$$x + 7 - 7 = 20 - 7$$
$$x = 13$$
Check: $x + 7 = 20$
$$13 + 7 = 20$$
$$20 = 20 \ \text{True}$$
The solution is 13.

12.
$$-11 = x - 2$$
$$-11 + 2 = x - 2 + 2$$
$$-9 = x$$
Check: $-11 = x - 2$
$$-11 = -9 - 2$$
$$-11 = -11 \ \text{True}$$
The solution is –9.

13.
$$11x = 55$$
$$\frac{11x}{11} = \frac{55}{11}$$
$$x = 5$$
Check: $11x = 55$
$$11(5) = 55$$
$$55 = 55 \ \text{True}$$
The solution is 5.

14.
$$-7y = 0$$
$$\frac{-7y}{-7} = \frac{0}{-7}$$
$$y = 0$$
Check: $-7y = 0$
$$-7(0) = 0$$
$$0 = 0 \ \text{True}$$
The solution is 0.

15.
$$\frac{x}{-3} = -13$$
$$-3 \cdot \frac{x}{-3} = -13 \cdot (-3)$$
$$x = 39$$

16.
$$\frac{z}{-5} = -11$$
$$-5 \cdot \frac{z}{-5} = -11 \cdot (-5)$$
$$x = 55$$

17.
$$12 = 11x - 14x$$
$$12 = -3x$$
$$\frac{12}{-3} = \frac{-3x}{-3}$$
$$-4 = x$$
Check: $12 = 11x - 14x$
$$12 = 11(-4) - 14(-4)$$
$$12 = -44 - (-56)$$
$$12 = -44 + 56$$
$$12 = 12 \text{ True}$$
The solution is –4.

18.
$$8y + 7y = -45$$
$$15y = -45$$
$$\frac{15y}{15} = \frac{-45}{15}$$
$$y = -3$$
Check: $8y + 7y = -45$
$$8(-3) + 7(-3) = -45$$
$$-24 + (-21) = -45$$
$$-45 = -45 \text{ True}$$
The solution is –3.

19.
$$-3x = -15$$
$$\frac{-3x}{-3} = \frac{-15}{-3}$$
$$x = 5$$
Check: $-3x = -15$
$$-3(5) = -15$$
$$-15 = -15 \text{ True}$$
The solution is 5.

20.
$$-2m = -1.6$$
$$\frac{-2m}{-2} = \frac{-16}{-2}$$
$$m = 8$$
Check: $-2m = -16$
$$-2(8) = -16$$
$$-16 = -16 \text{ True}$$
The solution is 8.

21.
$$x - 12 = -45 + 23$$
$$x - 12 = -22$$
$$x - 12 + 12 = -22 + 12$$
$$x = -1$$
Check: $x - 12 = -45 + 23$
$$-10 - 12 = -45 + 23$$
$$-22 = -22 \text{ True}$$
The solution is –10.

22. $6 - (-5) = x + 5$
$$6 + 5 = x + 5$$
$$11 = x + 5$$
$$11 - 5 = x + 5 - 5$$
$$6 = x$$
Check: $6 - (-5) = x + 5$
$$6 - (-5) = 6 + 5$$
$$6 + 5 = 11$$
$$11 = 11 \text{ True}$$
The solution is 6.

23.
$$6(3x - 4) = 19x$$
$$6 \cdot 3x - 6 \cdot 4 = 19x$$
$$18x - 24 = 19x$$
$$18x - 24 - 18x = 19x - 18x$$
$$-24 = x$$
Check: $6(3x - 4) = 19x$
$$6(3(-24) - 4) = 19(-24)$$
$$6(-72 - 4) = -456$$
$$6(-76) = -456$$
$$-456 = -456 \text{ True}$$
The solution is –24.

24.
$$25x = 6(4x - 9)$$
$$25x = 6 \cdot 4x + 6(-9)$$
$$25x = 24x - 54$$
$$25x - 24x = 24x - 54 - 24x$$
$$x = -54$$
Check: $25x = 6(4x - 9)$
$$25(054) = 6[4(-54) - 9]$$
$$-1350 = 6(-216 - 9)$$
$$-1350 = 6(-225)$$
$$-1350 = -1350 \text{ True}$$
The solution is – 54.

25.
$$-36x - 10 + 37x = -12 - (-14)$$
$$-36x + 37x - 10 = -12 + 14$$
$$x - 10 = 2$$
$$x - 10 + 1- = 2 + 10$$
$$x = 12$$

$\text{Check: } -36x - 10 + 37x = -12 - (-14)$
$-36(12) - 10 + 37(12) = -12 - (-14)$
$-432 - 10 + 444 = -12 + 14$
$-442 + 444 = -12 + 14$
$2 = 2 \text{ True}$
The solution is 12.

26. $-8 + (-14) = -80y + 20 + 81y$
$-8 + (-14) = -80y + 81y + 20$
$-22 = y + 20$
$-22 - 20 = y + 20 - 20$
$-42 = y$

$\text{Check: } -8 + (-14) = -80y + 20 + 81y$
$-8 + (-14) = -80(-42) + 20 + 81(-42)$
$-22 = 3360 + 20 - 3402$
$-22 = 3380 - 3402$
$-22 = -22 \text{ True}$
The solution is -42.

27.
$$\frac{x}{13} = -1 - (-3)$$
$$\frac{x}{13} = -1 + 3$$
$$\frac{x}{13} = 2$$
$$13 \cdot \frac{x}{13} = 2 \cdot 13$$
$$x = 26$$

$\text{Check: } \dfrac{x}{13} = -1 - (-3)$
$$\frac{26}{13} = -1 - (-3)$$
$$2 = -1 + 3$$
$$2 = 2 \text{ True}$$
The solution is 26.

28.
$$\frac{y}{4} = 7 - 10$$
$$\frac{y}{4} = -3$$
$$4 \cdot \frac{y}{4} = -3 \cdot 4$$
$$y = -12$$

$\text{Check: } \dfrac{y}{4} = 7 - 10$
$$\frac{12}{4} = 7 - 10$$
$$-3 = -3 \text{ True}$$
The solution is -12.

29. $-8z - 2z = 26 - (-4)$
$-10z = 26 + 4$
$-10z = 30$
$$\frac{-10z}{-10} = \frac{30}{-10}$$
$$z = -3$$

$\text{Check: } -8z - 2z = 26 - (-4)$
$-8(-3) - 2(-3) = 26 - (-4)$
$24 + 6 = 26 + 4$
$30 = 30 \text{ True}$
The solution is -3.

30. $-12 + (-13) = 5x - 10x$
$-25 = -5x$
$$\frac{-25}{-5} = \frac{-5x}{-5}$$
$$5 = x$$

$\text{Check: } -12 + (-13) = 5x - 10x$
$-12 + (-13) = 5(5) - 10(5)$
$-25 = 25 - 50$
$-25 = -25 \text{ True}$
The solution is 5.

31. The difference of a number and 10 is $x - 10$.

32. The sum of -20 and a number is $-20 + x$.

33. The product of ten and a number is $10x$.

34. The quotient of ten and a number is $\dfrac{10}{x}$ or $10 \div x$.

35. The product of -2 and a number is $-2x$. Five added to the product of -2 and a number is $-2x + 5$.

36. The difference of a number and 1 is $x - 1$. The product of -4 and the difference of a number and 1 is $-4(x - 1)$.

Section 3.4

Practice Problems

1. $5y + 2 = 17$
$5y + 2 - 2 = 17 - 2$
$5y = 15$
$$\frac{5y}{5} = \frac{15}{5}$$
$$y = 3$$

2. $45 = -10 - y$
$45 + 10 = -10 - y + 10$
$55 = -1y$
$$\frac{55}{-1} = \frac{-1y}{-1}$$
$$-55 = y$$

3. $7x + 12 = 3x - 4$
$7x + 12 - 12 = 3x - 4 - 12$
$7x = 3x - 16$
$7x - 3x = 3x - 16 - 3x$
$4x = -16$
$$\frac{4x}{4} = \frac{-16}{4}$$
$$x = -4$$

4.
$$6(a-5) = 4(a+1)$$
$$6a - 30 = 4a + 4$$
$$6a - 30 - 4a = 4a + 4 - 4a$$
$$2a - 30 = 4$$
$$2a - 30 + 30 = 4 + 30$$
$$2a = 34$$
$$\frac{2a}{2} = \frac{34}{2}$$
$$a = 17$$

5.
$$4(x+3) = 12$$
$$4x + 12 = 12$$
$$4x + 12 - 12 = 12 - 12$$
$$4x = 0$$
$$\frac{4x}{4} = \frac{0}{4}$$
$$x = 0$$

6. a. $110 - 80 = 30$

   b. $3(-9 + 11) = 6$

   c. $\dfrac{2(12)}{-6} = -4$

Calculator Explorations

The following answers may vary depending on what type of calculator you have.

1. $76(12 - 25) = -988$
Press the keys 76 $\boxed{\times}$ $\boxed{(}$ 12 − 25 $\boxed{)}$ $\boxed{= \text{or ENTER}}$. The display will read 988.
Yes

2. $-47(35) + 862 = -783$
Press the keys 47 $\boxed{+/-}$ $\boxed{\times}$ 35 $\boxed{+}$ 862 $\boxed{= \text{or ENTER}}$. The display will read −783.
Yes

3. $-170 + 562 = 3(-170) + 900$
Press the keys 170 $\boxed{+/-}$ $\boxed{+}$ 562 $\boxed{= \text{or ENTER}}$. The display will read 391.
Press the keys 3 $\boxed{\times}$ 170 $\boxed{+/-}$ $\boxed{+}$ 900 $\boxed{= \text{or ENTER}}$. The display will read 390.
391 $\neq$ 390.
No

4. $55(-18 + 10) = 75(-18) + 910$
Press the keys 55 $\boxed{(}$ 18 $\boxed{+/-}$ $\boxed{+}$ 10 $\boxed{)}$ $\boxed{= \text{or ENTER}}$. The display will read − 440.
Press the keys 75 $\boxed{\times}$ 18 $\boxed{+/-}$ $\boxed{+}$ 910 $\boxed{= \text{or ENTER}}$. The display will read − 440.
− 440 = − 440.
Yes

5. $29(-21) - 1034 = 619 - 210 - 362$
Press the keys 29 $\boxed{\times}$ 21 $\boxed{+/-}$ $\boxed{-}$ 1034 $\boxed{= \text{or ENTER}}$. The display will read −1643.
Press the keys 61 $\boxed{\times}$ 21 $\boxed{+/-}$ $\boxed{-}$ 362 $\boxed{= \text{or ENTER}}$. The display will read −1643.
−1643 = −1643
Yes

6. $-38(25) + 205 = 25(25) + 120$
Press the keys 38 $\boxed{+/-}$ $\boxed{\times}$ 25 $\boxed{+}$ 205 $\boxed{= \text{or ENTER}}$. The display will read −745.
Press the keys 25 $\boxed{\times}$ 25 $\boxed{+}$ 120 $\boxed{= \text{or ENTER}}$. The display will read 745.
−745 $\neq$ 745
No

Exercise Set 3.4

1.
$$2x - 6 = 0$$
$$2x - 6 + 6 = 0 + 6$$
$$2x = 6$$
$$\frac{2x}{2} = \frac{6}{2}$$
$$x = 3$$

3.
$$\frac{n}{3} + 10 = 0$$
$$\frac{n}{5} + 10 - 10 = 0 - 10$$
$$\frac{n}{5} = -10$$
$$5 \cdot \frac{n}{5} = -10 \cdot 5$$
$$n = -50$$

5.
$$6 - n = 10$$
$$6 - n - 6 = 10 - 6$$
$$-n = 4$$
$$\frac{-n}{-1} = \frac{4}{-1}$$
$$n = -4$$

7.
$$10x + 15 = 6x + 3$$
$$10x + 15 - 15 = 6x + 3 - 15$$
$$10x = 6x - 12$$
$$10x - 6x = 6x - 12 - 6x$$
$$4x = -12$$
$$\frac{4x}{4} = \frac{-12}{4}$$
$$x = -3$$

9.
$$3x - 7 = 4x + 5$$
$$3x - 7 + 7 = 4x + 5 + 7$$
$$3x = 4x + 12$$
$$3x - 4x = 4x + 12 - 4x$$
$$-x = 12$$
$$\frac{-x}{-1} = \frac{12}{-1}$$
$$x = -12$$

11.
$$3(x - 1) = 12$$
$$3x - 3 = 12$$
$$3x - 3 + 3 = 12 + 3$$
$$3x = 15$$
$$\frac{3x}{3} = \frac{15}{3}$$
$$x = 5$$

13.
$$-2(y + 4) = 2$$
$$-2y - 8 = 2$$
$$-2y - 8 + 8 = 2 + 8$$
$$-2y = 10$$
$$\frac{-2y}{-2} = \frac{10}{-2}$$
$$y = -5$$

15.
$$35 = 17 + 3(x - 2)$$
$$35 = 17 + 3x - 6$$
$$35 = 11 + 3x$$
$$35 - 11 = 11 + 3x - 11$$
$$24 = 3x$$
$$\frac{24}{3} = \frac{3x}{3}$$
$$8 = x$$

17.
$$8 - t = 3$$
$$8 - t - 8 = 3 - 8$$
$$-t = -5$$
$$\frac{-t}{-1} = \frac{-5}{-1}$$
$$t = 5$$

19.
$$0 = 4x - 4$$
$$0 + 4 = 4x - 4 + 4$$
$$4 = 4x$$
$$\frac{4}{4} = \frac{4x}{4}$$
$$1 = x$$

21.
$$\frac{x}{-2} - 8 = 0$$
$$\frac{x}{-2} - 8 + 8 = 0 + 8$$
$$\frac{x}{-2} = 8$$
$$-2 \cdot \frac{x}{-2} = 8(-2)$$
$$x = -16$$

23. $7 = 4c - 1$
$$7 + 1 = 4c - 1 + 1$$
$$8 = 4c$$
$$\frac{8}{4} = \frac{4c}{4}$$
$$2 = c$$

25. $3r + 4 = 19$
$$3r + 4 - 4 = 19 - 4$$
$$3r = 15$$
$$\frac{3r}{3} = \frac{15}{3}$$
$$r = 5$$

27. $2x - 1 = -7$
$$2x - 1 + 1 = -7 + 1$$
$$2x = -6$$
$$\frac{2x}{2} = \frac{-6}{2}$$
$$x = -3$$

29. $2 = 3z - 4$
$$2 + 4 = 3z - 4 + 4$$
$$6 = 3z$$
$$\frac{6}{3} = \frac{3z}{3}$$
$$2 = z$$

31. $5x - 2 = -12$
$$5x - 2 + 2 = -12 + 2$$
$$5x = -10$$
$$\frac{5x}{5} = \frac{-10}{5}$$
$$x = -2$$

33. $-7c + 1 = -20$
$$-7c + 1 - 1 = -20 - 1$$
$$-7c = -21$$
$$\frac{-7c}{-7} = \frac{-21}{-7}$$
$$c = 3$$

35. $9 = \frac{x}{2} - 15$
$$9 + 15 = \frac{x}{2} - 15 + 15$$
$$24 = \frac{x}{2}$$
$$2 \cdot 24 = \frac{x}{2} \cdot 2$$
$$48 = x$$

37. $8m + 79 = -1$
$$8m + 79 - 79 = -1 - 79$$
$$8m = -80$$
$$\frac{8m}{8} = \frac{-80}{8}$$
$$m = -10$$

39. $10 + 4v = -6$
$$10 + 4v - 10 = -6 - 10$$
$$4v = -16$$
$$\frac{4v}{4} = \frac{-16}{4}$$
$$v = -4$$

41. $-5 = -13 - 8k$
$$-5 + 13 = -13 - 8k + 13$$
$$8 = -8k$$
$$\frac{8}{-8} = \frac{-8k}{-8}$$
$$-1 = k$$

43. $4x + 3 = 2x + 11$
$$4x + 3 - 3 = 2x + 11 - 3$$
$$4x = 2x + 8$$
$$4x - 2x = 2x + 8 - 2x$$
$$2x = 8$$
$$\frac{2x}{2} = \frac{8}{2}$$
$$x = 4$$

45. $-2y - 10 = 5y + 18$
$$-2y - 10 + 10 = 5y + 18 + 10$$
$$-2y = 5y + 28$$
$$-2y - 5y = 5y + 28 - 5y$$
$$-7y = 28$$
$$\frac{-7y}{-7} = \frac{28}{-7}$$
$$y = -4$$

47. $-8n + 1 = -6n - 5$
$$-8n + 1 - 1 = -6n - 5 - 1$$
$$-8n = -6n - 6$$
$$-8n + 6n = -6n - 6 + 6n$$
$$-2n = -6$$
$$\frac{-2n}{-2} = \frac{-6}{-2}$$
$$n = 3$$

49.
$$9 - 3x = 14 + 2x$$
$$9 - 3x - 9 = 14 + 2x - 9$$
$$-3x = 5 + 2x$$
$$-3x - 2x = 5 + 2x - 2x$$
$$-5x = 5$$
$$\frac{-5x}{-5} = \frac{5}{-5}$$
$$x = -1$$

51.
$$2(y - 3) = y - 6$$
$$2y - 6 = y - 6$$
$$2y - 6 + 6 = y - 6 + 6$$
$$2y = y$$
$$2y - y = y - y$$
$$y = 0$$

53.
$$2t - 1 = 3(t + 7)$$
$$2t - 1 = 3t + 21$$
$$2t - 1 + 1 = 3t + 21 + 1$$
$$2t = 3t + 22$$
$$2t - 3t = 3t + 22 - 3t$$
$$-1t = 22$$
$$\frac{-t}{-1} = \frac{22}{-1}$$
$$t = -22$$

55.
$$3(5c - 1) - 2 = 13c + 3$$
$$15c - 3 - 2 = 13c + 3$$
$$15c - 5 = 13c + 3$$
$$15c - 5 + 5 = 13c + 3 + 5$$
$$15c = 13c + 8$$
$$15c - 13c = 13c + 8 - 13c$$
$$2c = 8$$
$$\frac{2c}{2} = \frac{8}{2}$$
$$c = 4$$

57.
$$10 + 5(z - 2) = 4z + 1$$
$$10 + 5z - 10 = 4z + 1$$
$$5z = 4z + 1$$
$$5z - 4z = 4z + 1 - 4z$$
$$z = 1$$

59.
$$7(6 + w) = 6(2 + w)$$
$$42 + 7w = 12 + 6w$$
$$42 + 7w - 6w = 12 + 6w - 6w$$
$$42 + w = 12$$
$$42 + w - 42 = 12 - 42$$
$$w = -30$$

61. The sum of -42 and 16 is -26 translates to $-42 + 16 = -26$.

63. The product of -5 and -29 gives 145 translates to $-5(-29) = 145$.

65. Three times the difference of -14 and 2 amounts to -48 translates to $3(-14 - 2) = -48$.

67. The quotient of 100 and twice 50 is equal to 1 translates to $\frac{100}{2(50)} = 1$.

69. 2002 shows the greatest increase in the number of electronically filed returns.

71. $73 - 35 = 38$
From 2000 to 2007 the number of electronically filed returns is expected to increase by 38 million.

73. $x^3 - 2xy$ substitute $x = 3$, $y = -1$
$$= 3^3 - 2(3)(-1)$$
$$= 27 - (-6)$$
$$= 27 + 6$$
$$= 33$$

75. $y^5 - 4x^2$ substitute $x = 3$, $y = -1$
$$= (-1)^5 - 4(3)^2$$
$$= (-1)(-1)(-1)(-1)(-1) - 4(3)(3)$$
$$= -1 - 36$$
$$= -37$$

77. $(2x - y)^2$ substitute $x = 3$, $y = -1$
$$= [2(3) - (-1)]^2$$
$$= (6 + 1)^2$$
$$= (7)^2$$
$$= 49$$

79. $4xy + 6y^2$ substitute $x = 3$, $y = -1$
$$= 4(3)(-1) + 6(-1)^2$$
$$= -12 + 6 \cdot 1$$
$$= -12 + 6$$
$$= -6$$

81.
$$(-8)^2 + 3x = 5x + 4^3$$
$$64 + 3x = 5x + 64$$
$$64 + 3x - 5x = 5x + 64 - 5x$$
$$64 - 2x = 64$$
$$64 - 2x - 64 = 64 - 64$$
$$-2x = 0$$
$$\frac{-2x}{-2} = \frac{0}{-2}$$
$$x = 0$$

83.
$$2^3(x+4) = 3^2(x+4)$$
$$8(x+4) = 9(x+4)$$
$$8x+32 = 9x+36$$
$$8x+32-9x = 9x+36-9x$$
$$-x+32 = 36$$
$$-x+32-32 = 36-32$$
$$-x = 4$$
$$-\frac{1x}{-1} = \frac{4}{-1}$$
$$x = -4$$

85. No, answers may vary.

Section 3.5

Practice Problems

1. a. Five times a number is $5x$. Five times a number is 20 is $5x = 20$.

b. The sum of a number and –5 is $x+(-5)$. The sum of a number and –5 yields 14 is $x+(-5) = 14$.

c. Ten subtracted from a number is $x-10$. Ten subtracted from a number amounts to –23 is $x-10 = -23$.

d. Five times a number is $5x$. Five times a number added to 7 is equal to –8 is $7+5x = -8$.

e. The sum of a number and 4 is $x+4$. The quotient of 6 and the sum of a number and 4 gives 1 is $\frac{6}{x+4} = 1$.

2. Let x = the unknown number.
$$x+2 = 3x+6$$
$$x+2-2 = 3x+6-2$$
$$x = 3x+4$$
$$x-3x = 3x+4-3x$$
$$-2x = 4$$
$$\frac{-2x}{-2} = \frac{4}{-2}$$
$$x = -2$$
The unknown number is –2.

3. Let x = the number of delegates the U.S. sent. Then, $x-19$ = the number of delegates Japan sent.

$$x+x-19 = 121$$
$$2x-19 = 121$$
$$2x-19+19 = 121+19$$
$$2x = 140$$
$$\frac{2x}{2} = \frac{140}{2}$$
$$x = 70$$
The United States sent 70 delegates.

4. Let x = the amount son receives. Then $2x$ = the amount husband receives.
$$x+2x = 21,000$$
$$3x = 21,000$$
$$\frac{3x}{3} = \frac{21,000}{3}$$
$$x = 7000$$
$$2x = 2\cdot7000$$
$$2x = 14,000$$
Her son receives $7000 and her husband receives $14,000.

Exercise Set 3.5

1. A number added to –5 is –7 translates to $-5+x = -7$.

3. Three times a number yields 27 translates to $3x = 27$.

5. A number subtracted from –20 amounts to 104 translates to $-20-x = 104$.

7. Twice the sum of a number and –1 is equal to 50 translates to $2[x+(-1)] = 50$.

9. $3x+9 = 33$
$3x = 24$
$x = 8$

11. $9x = 54$
$x = 6$

13. $3+4+x = 16$
$7+x = 16$
$x = 9$

15. $72 = 24+8x$
$48 = 8x$
$6 = x$

17. $x-3 = 45-x$
$2x = 48$
$x = 24$

19. $3(x-5) = 9$
$3x-15 = 9$
$3x = 24$
$x = 8$

21. $8 - x = \dfrac{15}{5}$

$8 - x = 3$

$-x = -5$

$x = 5$

23. $3x + 13 = 3 + 5x$

$10 = 2x$

$5 = x$

25. $5x - 40 = x + 8$

$4x = 48$

$x = 12$

27. $x - 3 = \dfrac{10}{5}$

$x - 3 = 2$

$x = 5$

29. Let x = Gore's votes. Then $x + 5$ = Bush's votes

$x + x + 5 = 527$

$2x + 5 = 527$

$2x + 5 - 5 = 527 - 5$

$2x = 522$

$x = 261$

Gore had 261 electoral votes, and Bush had 261 +5 = 266 electoral votes.

31. Let x = Kelp growth. Then $2x$ = bamboo growth.

$x + 2x = 54$

$3x = 54$

$x = 18$

Kelp can grow 18 inches in one day, and bamboo can grow $2 \cdot 18 = 36$ inches in one day.

33. Let x = the number of U.S. universities. Then $x + 2649$ = the number of universities in India.

$x + x + 2649 = 14{,}165$

$2x + 2649 = 14{,}165$

$2x = 11{,}516$

$x = 5758$

The U.S. has 5758 universities, and India has $5758 + 2649 = 8407$ universities.

35. Let x = the cost of the Game Cube. Then $3x$ = the cost of the games.

$x + 3x = 600$

$4x = 600$

$x = 150$

The Game Cube costs \$150, and the games cost $3(150) = \$450$.

37. Let x = the capacity of Neyland Stadium. Then $x + 4647$ = the capacity of Michigan Stadium.

$x + x + 4647 = 210{,}355$

$2x + 4647 = 210{,}355$

$2x = 205{,}708$

$x = 102{,}854$

Neyland Stadium has a capacity of 102,854 and Michigan Stadium has a capacity of $102{,}854 + 4647 = 107{,}501$.

39. Let x = the native American population of Washington state. Then $3x$ = the native American population of California.

$x + 3x = 412$

$4x = 412$

$x = 103$

The native American population of Washington state is 103 thousand. The native American population of California is $3 \cdot 103 = 309$ thousand.

41. Let x = the points scored by the Sooners. Then $x + 12$ = the points scored by the Huskies.

$x + x + 12 = 152$

$2x + 12 = 152$

$2x = 140$

$x = 70$

The Huskies scored $70 + 12 = 82$ points during the game.

43. Let x = the amount of food a finch eats. Then $x + 5$ = the amount of food a crow eats.

$x + x + 5 = 13$

$2x + 5 = 13$

$2x = 8$

$x = 4$

The finch eats 4 oz of food a day, and the crow eats $4 + 5 = 9$ oz of food a day.

45. To round 586 to the nearest ten, observe that the digit in the ones place is 6. Since this digit is at least 5, we need to add 1 to the digit in the tens place. The number 586 rounded to the nearest ten is 590.

47. To round 1026 to the nearest hundred, observe that the digit in the tens place is 2. Since this digit is less than 5, we do not add 1 to the digit in the hundreds place. The number 1026 rounded to the nearest hundred is 1000.

49. To round 2986 to the nearest thousand observe that the digit in the hundreds place is 9. Since this digit is at least 5, we add 1 to the digit in the thousands place. The number 2986 rounded to the nearest thousand is 3000.

51. Answers may vary.

53. $P = A + C$
$165,000 = 156,750 + C$
$8250 = C$
The agent's commission will be $8250.

55. $P = C + M$
$12 = 7 + M$
$12 - 7 = 7 + M - 7$
$5 = M$
The markup of the cat food is $5.

Chapter 3 Review

1. $3y + 7y - 15 = 10y - 15$

2. $2y - 10 - 8y = -6y - 10$

3. $8a + a - 7 - 15a = -6a - 7$

4. $y + 3 - 9y - 1 = -8y + 2$

5. $2(x + 5) = 2x + 10$

6. $-3(y + 8) = -3y - 24$

7. $7x + 3(x - 4) + x = 7x + 3x - 12 + x$
$= 11x - 12$

8. $-(3m + 2) - m - 10 = -1 \cdot 3m + (-1)(2) - m - 10$
$= -3m - 2 - m - 10$
$= -4m - 12$

9. $3(5a - 2) - 20a + 10 = 15a - 6 - 20a + 10$
$= -5a + 4$

10. $6y + 3 + 2(3y - 6) = 6y + 3 + 6y - 12$
$= 12y - 9$

11. $P = 3 + 2x + 3 + 2x$
$= 4x + 6$
The perimeter is $(4x + 6)$ yards.

12. $P = 5y + 5y + 5y + 5y = 20y$
The perimeter is $20y$ meters.

13. $A = 3(2x - 1) = 6x - 3$
The area is $(6x - 3)$ square yards.

14. $A = 10(x - 2) + 7(5x + 4)$
$= 10x - 20 + 35x + 28$
$= 45x + 8$
The area is $(45x + 8)$ square centimeters.

15. $85(7068x - 108) + 42x$
$= 600,780x - 9180 + 42x$
$= 600,822x - 9180$

16. $-4268y + 120(63y - 32)$
$= -4268y + 7560y - 3840$
$= 3292y - 3840$

17. $5(2 - 4)\ 0\ -10$
$5(-2)\ 0\ -10$
$-10 = -10$ True
Yes, it is a solution.

18. $6(0) + 2\ 0\ 23 + 4(0)$
$0 + 2\ 0\ 23 + 0$
$2 = 23$ False
No, it is not a solution.

19. $z - 5 = -7$
$z - 5 + 5 = -7 + 5$
$z = -2$

20. $3x + 10 = 4x$
$3x + 10 - 3x = 4x - 3x$
$10 = x$

21. $n + 18 = 10 - (-2)$
$n + 18 = 10 + 2$
$n + 18 = 12$
$n + 18 - 18 = 12 - 18$
$n = -6$

22. $c - 5 = -13 + 7$
$c - 5 = -6$
$c - 5 + 5 = -6 + 5$
$c = -1$

23. $7x + 5 - 6x = -20$
$x + 5 = -20$
$x + 5 - 5 = -20 - 5$
$x = -25$

24. $17x = 2(8x - 4)$
$17x = 2 \cdot 8x - 2 \cdot 4$
$17x = 16x - 8$
$17x - 16x = 16x - 8 - 16x$
$x = -8$

25. $-3y = -21$
$\dfrac{-3y}{-3} = \dfrac{-21}{-3}$
$y = 7$

26. $-8x = 72$

$$\frac{-8x}{-8} = \frac{72}{-8}$$

$$x = -9$$

27. $-5n = -5$

$$\frac{-5n}{-5} = \frac{-5}{-5}$$

$$n = 1$$

28. $-3a = 15$

$$\frac{-3a}{-3} = \frac{15}{-3}$$

$$a = -5$$

29. $\dfrac{x}{-6} = 2$

$$-6 \cdot \frac{x}{16} = 2 \cdot (-6)$$

$$x = -12$$

30. $\dfrac{y}{-15} = -3$

$$-15 \cdot \frac{y}{-15} = -3 \cdot (-15)$$

$$y = 45$$

31. $-5t + 32 + 4t = 32$

$$-t + 32 = 32$$

$$-t + 32 - 32 = 32 - 32$$

$$-t = 0$$

$$t = 0$$

32. $3z + 72 - 2z = -56$

$$z + 72 = -56$$

$$z + 72 - 72 = -56 - 72$$

$$z = -128$$

33. $\dfrac{z}{4} = -8 - (-6)$

$$\frac{z}{4} = -8 + 6$$

$$\frac{z}{4} = -2$$

$$4 \cdot \frac{z}{4} = -2 \cdot 4$$

$$z = -8$$

34. $-1 + (-8) = \dfrac{x}{5}$

$$-9 = \frac{x}{5}$$

$$-9 \cdot 5 = \frac{x}{5} \cdot 5$$

$$-45 = x$$

35. $6y - 7y = 100 - 105$

$$-y = -5$$

$$\frac{-1y}{1} = \frac{-5}{-1}$$

$$y = 5$$

36. $19x - 16x = 45 - 60$

$$3x = -15$$

$$\frac{3x}{3} = \frac{-15}{3}$$

$$x = -5$$

37. The product of -5 and a number is $-5x$.

38. Three subtracted from a number is $x - 3$.

39. The sum of -5 and a number is $-5 + x$.

40. The quotient of -2 and a number is $\dfrac{-2}{x}$.

41. Twice a number is $2x$. Eleven added to twice a number is $2x + 11$.

42. The product of -5 and a number is $-5x$. The product of -5 and a number, decreased by 50 is $-5x - 50$.

43. The sum of a number and 6 is $x + 6$. The quotient of 70 and the sum of a number and 6 is $\dfrac{70}{x + 6}$.

44. The difference of a number and 13 is $x - 13$. Twice the difference of a number and 13 is $2(x - 13)$.

45. $3x - 4 = 11$

$$3x - 4 + 4 = 11 + 4$$

$$3x = 15$$

$$\frac{3x}{3} = \frac{15}{3}$$

$$x = 5$$

46. $6y + 1 = 73$

$$6y + 1 - 1 = 73 - 1$$

$$6y = 72$$

$$\frac{6y}{6} = \frac{72}{6}$$

$$y = 12$$

47. $14 - y = -3$

$$14 - y - 14 = -3 - 14$$

$$-y = -17$$

$$\frac{-y}{-1} = \frac{-17}{-1}$$

$$y = 17$$

48.
$$7 - z = 0$$
$$7 - z + z = 0 + z$$
$$7 = z$$

49. $4z - z = -6$
$$3z = -6$$
$$\frac{3z}{3} = \frac{-6}{3}$$
$$z = -2$$

50. $t - 9t = -64$
$$-8t = -64$$
$$\frac{-8t}{-8} = \frac{-64}{-8}$$
$$t = 8$$

51.
$$2x + 5 = 7x - 100$$
$$2x + 5 - 7x = 7x - 100 - 7x$$
$$-5x + 5 = -100$$
$$-5x + 5 - 5 = -100 - 5$$
$$-5x = -105$$
$$\frac{-5x}{-5} = \frac{-105}{5}$$
$$x = 21$$

52.
$$-6x - 4 = x + 66$$
$$-6x - 4 - x = x + 66 - x$$
$$-7x - 4 = 66$$
$$-7x - 4 + 4 = 66 + 4$$
$$-7x = 70$$
$$\frac{-7x}{7} = \frac{70}{-7}$$
$$x = -10$$

53.
$$2x + 7 = 6x - 1$$
$$2x + 7 - 7 = 6x - 1 - 7$$
$$2x = 6x - 8$$
$$2x - 6x = 6x - 8 - 6x$$
$$-4x = -8$$
$$\frac{-4x}{-4} = \frac{-8}{-4}$$
$$x = 2$$

54.
$$5x - 18 = -4x$$
$$5x - 18 + 18 = -4x + 18$$
$$5x = -4x + 18$$
$$5x + 4x = -4x + 18 + 4x$$
$$9x = 18$$
$$\frac{9x}{9} = \frac{18}{9}$$
$$x = 2$$

55.
$$\frac{x}{9} + 3 = 0$$
$$\frac{x}{9} + 3 - 3 = 0 - 3$$
$$\frac{x}{9} = -3$$
$$9 \cdot \frac{x}{9} = -3 \cdot 9$$
$$x = -27$$

56.
$$\frac{z}{-2} - 11 = 0$$
$$\frac{z}{-2} - 11 + 11 = 0 + 11$$
$$\frac{z}{-2} = 11$$
$$-2 \cdot \frac{z}{-2} = 11 \cdot (-2)$$
$$z = -22$$

57.
$$5(n - 3) = 7 + 3n$$
$$5n - 15 = 7 + 3n$$
$$5n - 15 + 15 = 7 + 3n + 15$$
$$5n = 22 + 3n$$
$$5n - 3n = 22 + 3n - 3n$$
$$2n = 22$$
$$\frac{2n}{2} = \frac{22}{2}$$
$$n = 11$$

58.
$$7(2 + x) = 4x - 1$$
$$14 + 7x = 4x - 1$$
$$14 + 7x - 14 = 4x - 1 - 14$$
$$7x = 4x - 15$$
$$7x - 4x = 4x - 15 - 4x$$
$$3x = -15$$
$$\frac{3x}{3} = \frac{-15}{3}$$
$$x = -5$$

59. $20 - (-8) = 28$

60. $5(2 + (-6)) = -20$

61. $\dfrac{-75}{5 + 20} = -3$

62. $-2 - 19 = -21$

63. $2x - 8 = 40$

64. $\dfrac{x}{2} - 12 = 10$

65. $x - 3 = x \div 4$ or $x - 3 = \dfrac{x}{4}$

66. $6x = x + 2$

67.
$$40 - 5x = 3x$$
$$40 - 5x + 5x = 3x + 5x$$
$$40 = 8x$$
$$\frac{40}{8} = \frac{8x}{8}$$
$$5 = x$$

68.
$$3x = 2(x - 8)$$
$$3x = 2x - 16$$
$$3x - 2x = 2x - 16 - 2x$$
$$x = -16$$

69. Let I = votes recieved by the Independent candidate.
$I + 272$ = votes received by the Democratic candidate.
$18,500 - 14,000 = 4500$ votes
$$I + (I + 272) = 4500$$
$$2I + 272 = 4500$$
$$2I + 272 - 272 = 4500 - 272$$
$$2I = 4228$$
$$\frac{2I}{2} = \frac{4228}{2}$$
$$I = 2114$$
$I + 272 = 2114 + 272 = 2386$
The Democratic candidate received 2386 votes.

70. Let x = the number of video tapes. Then $2x$ = the number of DVDs.
$$x + 2x = 126$$
$$3x = 126$$
$$\frac{3x}{3} = \frac{126}{3}$$
$$x = 42$$
The number of DVDs $= 2x = 2(42) = 84$.
Rajiv has 84 DVDs.

Chapter 3 Test

1. $7x - 5 - 12x + 10 = -5x + 5$

2. $-2(3y + 7) = -6y - 14$

3.
$$-(3z + 2) - 5z - 18 = -1 \cdot 3z - 1 \cdot 2 - 5z - 18$$
$$= -3z - 2 - 5z - 18$$
$$= -8z - 20$$

4. $P = a + b + c$
$$= 5x + 5 + 5x + 5 + 5x + 5$$
$$= 15x + 15$$
The perimeter is $(15x + 15)$ inches.

5. $A = LW$
$$= 4(3x - 1)$$
$$= 12x - 4$$
The area is $(12x - 4)$ square meters.

6.
$$9x = -90$$
$$\frac{9x}{9} = \frac{-90}{9}$$
$$x = -10$$

8.
$$12 = y - 3y$$
$$12 = -2y$$
$$\frac{12}{-2} = \frac{-2y}{-2}$$
$$-6 = y$$

9.
$$\frac{x}{2} = -5 - (-2)$$
$$\frac{x}{2} = -5 + 2$$
$$\frac{x}{2} = -3$$
$$2 \cdot \frac{x}{2} = -3 \cdot 2$$
$$x = -6$$

10.
$$5 + 4z = 37$$
$$5 + 4z - 5 = 37 - 5$$
$$4z = 32$$
$$\frac{4z}{4} = \frac{32}{4}$$
$$z = 8$$

11.
$$5x + 12 - 4x - 14 = 22$$
$$x - 2 = 22$$
$$x - 2 + 2 = 22 + 2$$
$$x = 24$$

12.
$$-4x + 7 = 15$$
$$-4x + 7 - 7 = 15 - 7$$
$$-4x = 8$$
$$\frac{-4x}{-4} = \frac{8}{-4}$$
$$x = -2$$

13.
$$2(x - 6) = 0$$
$$2x - 12 = 0$$
$$2x - 12 + 12 = 0 + 12$$
$$2x = 12$$
$$\frac{2x}{2} = \frac{12}{2}$$
$$x = 6$$

14.
$$5x - 2 = x - 10$$
$$5x - 2 + 2 = x - 10 + 2$$
$$5x = x - 8$$
$$5x - x = x - 8 - x$$
$$4x = -8$$
$$\frac{4x}{4} = \frac{-8}{4}$$
$$x = -2$$

15.
$$4(5x + 3) = 2(7x + 6)$$
$$20x + 12 = 14x + 12$$
$$20x + 12 - 12 = 14x + 12 - 12$$
$$20x = 14x$$
$$20x - 14x = 14x - 14x$$
$$6x = 0$$
$$\frac{6x}{6} = \frac{0}{6}$$
$$x = 0$$

16. a. $-23 + x$

    b. $-2 - 3x$

17. a. $2 \cdot 5 + (-15) = -5$

    b. $3x + 6 = -30$

18.
$$3x - 5x = 4$$
$$-2x = 4$$
$$\frac{-2x}{-2} = \frac{4}{-2}$$
$$x = -2$$

19. Let x = the number of free throws Maria made. Then $2x$ = the number of free throws Paula made.
$$2x + x = 12$$
$$3x = 12$$
$$\frac{3x}{3} = \frac{12}{3}$$
$$x = 4$$
Paula's throws $= 2x = 2 \cdot 4 = 8$, so Paula made 8 free throws.

20. Let x = the number of women entered in the race. Then $x + 112$ = the number of men entered in the space.
$$x + (x + 112) = 600$$
$$2x + 112 = 600$$
$$2x + 112 - 112 = 600 - 112$$
$$2x = 488$$
$$x = 244$$
244 women entered the race.

Chapter 3 Cumulative Review

1. One hundred six million, fifty-two thousand, four hundred forty-seven.

2. Two hundred seventy-two thousand, four.

3. $P = 3 + 1 + 3 + 2 + 4 = 13$
Perimeter is 13 inches.

4. $P = 6 + 3 + 6 + 3 = 18$
Perimeter is 18 inches.

5.
$$\begin{array}{r} 900 \\ -174 \\ \hline 726 \end{array}$$
Check: $\begin{array}{r} 726 \\ +174 \\ \hline 900 \end{array}$

6.
$$\begin{array}{r} 17{,}801 \\ -8216 \\ \hline 9{,}585 \end{array}$$
Check: $\begin{array}{r} 9585 \\ +8216 \\ \hline 17{,}801 \end{array}$

7. Since there is an 8 in the tens place, 248,982 rounded to the nearest hundred is 249,000.

8. Since there is a 4 in the hundreds place, 844,497 rounded to the nearest thousand is 844,000.

9.
$$\begin{array}{r} 25 \\ \times 8 \\ \hline 200 \end{array}$$

10.
$$\begin{array}{r} 395 \\ \times 74 \\ \hline 1580 \\ 27{,}650 \\ \hline 29{,}230 \end{array}$$

11.
$$\begin{array}{r} 208 \\ 9\overline{)1872} \\ -18 \\ \hline 07 \\ -\ 0 \\ \hline 72 \\ -72 \\ \hline 0 \end{array}$$
Check: $208 \cdot 9 = 1872$

12.
$$\begin{array}{r} 86 \\ 46\overline{)3956} \\ -368 \\ \hline 276 \\ -276 \\ \hline 0 \end{array}$$
Check: $86 \cdot 46 = 3956$

13. $2 \cdot 4 - 3 \div 3 = 8 - 3 \div 3$
$$= 8 - 1$$
$$= 7$$

14. $8 \cdot 4 + 9 \div 3 = 32 + 9 \div 3$
$$= 32 + 3$$
$$= 35$$

15. $5^2 + 4 - 3 = 25 + 4 - 3$
$$= 29 - 3$$
$$= 26$$

16. $2(2)^2 + 5 - 3 = 2(4) + 5 - 3$
$$= 8 + 5 - 3$$
$$= 13 - 3$$
$$= 10$$

17. a. $-7 < 7$
  b. $0 > -4$
  c. $-9 > -11$

18. a. $-14 < 0$
  b. $8 > -8$

19. $5 + (-2) = 3$

20. $-3 + (-4) = -7$

21. $-5 + (-1) = -6$

22. $3 + (-7) = -4$

23. $2 + 6 = 8$

24. $21 + 15 + (-19) = 36 + (v19) = 17$

25. $-4 - 10 = -4 + (-10) = -14$

26. $-2 - 3 = -2 + (v3) = -5$

27. $6 - (-5) = 6 + 5 = 11$

28. $19 - (-10) = 19 + 10 = 29$

29. $-11 - (-7) = -11 + 7 = -4$

30. $-16 - (-13) = -16 + 13 = -3$

31. $\dfrac{-12}{6} = -2$

32. $\dfrac{-30}{-5} = 6$

33. $-20 \div (-4) = 5$

34. $26 \div (-2) = -13$

35. $\dfrac{48}{-3} = -16$

36. $\dfrac{-120}{12} = -10$

37. $(-3)^2 = (-3)(-3) = 9$

38. $-2^5 = -(2)(2)(2)(2)(2) = -32$

39. $-3^2 = -(3)(3) = -9$

40. $(-5)^2 = (-5)(-5) = 25$

41. $2y - 6 + 4y + 8 = 2y + 4y - 6 + 8$
$$= (2 + 4)y - 6 + 8$$
$$= 6y + 2$$

42. $6x + 2 - 3x + 7 = 6x - 3x + 2 + 7$
$$= (6 - 3)x + 2 + 7$$
$$= 3x + 9$$

43. $3(-1) + 1 = 3$
$$-3 + 1 = 3$$
$$-2 = 3 \text{ False}$$
-1 is not a solution

44. $5(2) - 3 = 7$
$$10 - 3 = 7$$
$$7 = 7 \text{ True}$$
2 is the solution

45. $-12x = -36$
$$\dfrac{-12x}{-12} = \dfrac{-36}{-12} \text{-}$$
$$x = 3$$

46. $7y - 4y = 15$
$$3y = 15$$
$$\dfrac{3y}{3} = \dfrac{15}{3}$$
$$y = 5$$

47. $2x - 6 = 18$
$$2x - 6 + 6 = 18 + 6$$
$$2x = 24$$
$$\dfrac{2x}{2} = \dfrac{24}{2}$$
$$x = 12$$

48.
$$3a + 5 = -1$$
$$3a + 5 - 5 = -1 - 5$$
$$3a = -6$$
$$\frac{3a}{3} = \frac{-6}{3}$$
$$a = -2$$

49. Let x = the cost of the software. Let $4x$ = the cost of the computer system.
$$x + 4x = 2100$$
$$5x = 2100$$
$$\frac{5x}{5} = \frac{2100}{5}$$
$$x = 420$$
The cost of the software is $420. The cost of the computer system is $4x = 4(420) = \$1680$.

50. Let x = a number.
$$2x + 4 = 3x - 7$$
$$2x + 4 - 3x = 3x - 7 - 3x$$
$$-x + 4 = -7$$
$$-x + 4 - 4 = -7 - 4$$
$$-x = -11$$
$$\frac{-1x}{-1} = \frac{-11}{-1}$$
$$x = 11$$
Rose's number is 11.

Chapter 4

Pretest

1. The figure has 8 equal parts. Three parts are shaded. The fraction that is shaded is $\dfrac{3}{8}$.

2. $\dfrac{5}{6} = \dfrac{5}{6} \cdot 1 = \dfrac{5}{6} \cdot \dfrac{3}{3} = \dfrac{5 \cdot 3}{6 \cdot 3} = \dfrac{15}{18}$

3. $\dfrac{0}{-4} = 0 \div -4 = 0$

4. $140 = 2 \cdot 70$
$= 2 \cdot 2 \cdot 35$
$= 2 \cdot 2 \cdot 5 \cdot 7 \text{ or } 2^2 \cdot 5 \cdot 7$

5. $\dfrac{30}{54} = \dfrac{6 \cdot 5}{6 \cdot 9} = \dfrac{5}{9}$

6. Number of milligrams $\rightarrow 450$
Number of milligrams in a gram $\rightarrow \overline{1000}$
$= \dfrac{5 \cdot 9 \cdot 10}{5 \cdot 2 \cdot 10 \cdot 10} = \dfrac{9}{20}$

7. $\dfrac{3}{4} \cdot \dfrac{24}{15} = \dfrac{3 \cdot 24}{4 \cdot 15} = \dfrac{3 \cdot 6 \cdot 4}{4 \cdot 3 \cdot 5} = \dfrac{6}{5}$

8. $\dfrac{5x}{7} \div 10x = \dfrac{5x}{7} \cdot \dfrac{1}{10x}$
$= \dfrac{5x \cdot 1}{7 \cdot 10x}$
$= \dfrac{5x}{7 \cdot 5x \cdot 2x}$
$= \dfrac{1}{14x}$

9. $\dfrac{8}{11} - \dfrac{3}{11} = \dfrac{8-3}{11} = \dfrac{5}{11}$

10. $-\dfrac{3}{10} + \dfrac{2}{10} = \dfrac{-3+2}{10} = \dfrac{-1}{10} = -\dfrac{1}{10}$

11. $\left(-\dfrac{2}{3}\right)^3 = \left(-\dfrac{2}{3}\right)\left(-\dfrac{2}{3}\right)\left(-\dfrac{2}{3}\right)$
$= -\dfrac{2 \cdot 2 \cdot 2}{3 \cdot 3 \cdot 3}$
$= -\dfrac{8}{27}$

12. $x \div y = \dfrac{2}{9} \div -\dfrac{2}{3}$
$= \dfrac{2}{9} \cdot -\dfrac{3}{2}$
$= -\dfrac{2 \cdot 3}{9 \cdot 2}$
$= -\dfrac{2 \cdot 3}{3 \cdot 3 \cdot 2}$
$= -\dfrac{1}{3}$

13. $\dfrac{5}{9} + \dfrac{1}{12} = \dfrac{5}{9} \cdot 1 + \dfrac{1}{12} \cdot 1$
$= \dfrac{5}{9} \cdot \dfrac{4}{4} + \dfrac{1}{12} \cdot \dfrac{3}{3}$
$= \dfrac{5 \cdot 4}{9 \cdot 4} + \dfrac{1 \cdot 3}{12 \cdot 3}$
$= \dfrac{20}{36} + \dfrac{3}{36}$
$= \dfrac{20+3}{36}$
$= \dfrac{23}{36}$

14. $x - y = -\dfrac{3}{14} - \left(-\dfrac{2}{7}\right)$
$= -\dfrac{3}{14} + \dfrac{2}{7}$
$= -\dfrac{3}{14} + \dfrac{2}{7} \cdot 1$
$= -\dfrac{3}{14} + \dfrac{2}{7} \cdot \dfrac{2}{2}$
$= -\dfrac{3}{14} + \dfrac{2 \cdot 2}{7 \cdot 2}$
$= -\dfrac{3}{14} + \dfrac{4}{14}$
$= \dfrac{-3+4}{14}$
$= \dfrac{1}{14}$

15. $\dfrac{\frac{x}{3}}{\frac{7}{9}} = \dfrac{x}{3} \div \dfrac{7}{9}$

$\phantom{\dfrac{\frac{x}{3}}{\frac{7}{9}}} = \dfrac{x}{3} \cdot \dfrac{9}{7}$

$\phantom{\dfrac{\frac{x}{3}}{\frac{7}{9}}} = \dfrac{x \cdot 9}{3 \cdot 7}$

$\phantom{\dfrac{\frac{x}{3}}{\frac{7}{9}}} = \dfrac{x \cdot 3 \cdot 3}{3 \cdot 7}$

$\phantom{\dfrac{\frac{x}{3}}{\frac{7}{9}}} = \dfrac{3x}{7}$

16. $\left(\dfrac{2}{5}\right)^2 - 2 = \left(\dfrac{2}{5}\right)\left(\dfrac{2}{5}\right) - 2$

$\phantom{\left(\dfrac{2}{5}\right)^2 - 2} = \dfrac{2 \cdot 2}{5 \cdot 5} - 2 \cdot 1$

$\phantom{\left(\dfrac{2}{5}\right)^2 - 2} = \dfrac{4}{25} - 2 \cdot \dfrac{25}{25}$

$\phantom{\left(\dfrac{2}{5}\right)^2 - 2} = \dfrac{4}{25} - \dfrac{50}{25}$

$\phantom{\left(\dfrac{2}{5}\right)^2 - 2} = \dfrac{4 - 50}{25}$

$\phantom{\left(\dfrac{2}{5}\right)^2 - 2} = \dfrac{-46}{25}$

$\phantom{\left(\dfrac{2}{5}\right)^2 - 2} = -\dfrac{46}{25}$

17. $\dfrac{x}{4} + 3 = \dfrac{1}{8}$

$8\left(\dfrac{x}{4} + 3\right) = 8 \cdot \dfrac{1}{8}$

$8 \cdot \dfrac{x}{4} + 8 \cdot 3 = 1$

$2x + 24 = 1$

$2x + 24 - 24 = 1 - 24$

$2x = -23$

$\dfrac{2x}{2} = \dfrac{-23}{2}$

$x = -\dfrac{23}{2}$

18. $2\dfrac{3}{5} = \dfrac{5 \cdot 2 + 3}{5} = \dfrac{10 + 3}{5} = \dfrac{13}{5}$

19. $3\dfrac{1}{5} \cdot 2\dfrac{3}{4} = \dfrac{5 \cdot 3 + 1}{5} \cdot \dfrac{4 \cdot 2 + 3}{4}$

$\phantom{3\dfrac{1}{5} \cdot 2\dfrac{3}{4}} = \dfrac{15 + 1}{5} \cdot \dfrac{8 + 3}{4}$

$\phantom{3\dfrac{1}{5} \cdot 2\dfrac{3}{4}} = \dfrac{16}{5} \cdot \dfrac{11}{4}$

$\phantom{3\dfrac{1}{5} \cdot 2\dfrac{3}{4}} = \dfrac{16 \cdot 11}{5 \cdot 4}$

$\phantom{3\dfrac{1}{5} \cdot 2\dfrac{3}{4}} = \dfrac{4 \cdot 4 \cdot 11}{5 \cdot 4}$

$\phantom{3\dfrac{1}{5} \cdot 2\dfrac{3}{4}} = \dfrac{44}{5}$

20.

$\begin{array}{ccccc} & 5\dfrac{2}{3} & = & 5\dfrac{2 \cdot 2}{3 \cdot 2} & = & 5\dfrac{4}{6} \\ + & 4\dfrac{1}{6} & = & + \, 4\dfrac{1}{6} & = & + \, 4\dfrac{1}{6} \\ \hline & & & & & 9\dfrac{5}{6} \end{array}$

Section 4.1

Practice Problems

1. $\dfrac{9}{2}$ $\begin{array}{l} \leftarrow \quad \text{numerator} \\ \leftarrow \quad \text{denominator} \end{array}$

2. $\dfrac{10y}{17}$ $\begin{array}{l} \leftarrow \quad \text{numerator} \\ \leftarrow \quad \text{denominator} \end{array}$

3. 3 out of 8 equal parts are shaded: $\dfrac{3}{8}$.

4. 1 out of 6 equal parts is shaded: $\dfrac{1}{6}$.

5.

6.

7. Each part is $\dfrac{1}{3}$, and there are 8 parts shaded, or

$\dfrac{8}{3}$.

8. Each part is $\dfrac{1}{4}$, and there are 5 parts shaded, or

$\dfrac{5}{4}$.

9. 7 out of 9 planets: $\dfrac{7}{9}$.

10. a.

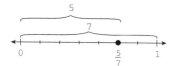

b.

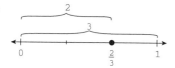

c.

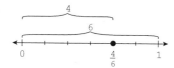

11. a.

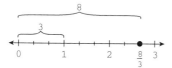

b.

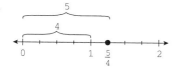

c.

12. $\dfrac{9}{9} = 9 \div 9 = 1$

13. $\dfrac{-6}{-6} = -6 \div -6 = 1$

14. $\dfrac{0}{-1} = 0 \div (-1) = 0$

15. $\dfrac{4}{1} = 4 \div 1 = 4$

16. $\dfrac{-13}{0}$ is undefined

17. $\dfrac{-13}{1} = -13 \div 1 = -13$

18. Since $4 \cdot 5 = 20$, we multiply the numerator and denominator of $\dfrac{1}{4}$ by 5.

$$\frac{1}{4} = \frac{1 \cdot 5}{4 \cdot 5} = \frac{5}{20}$$

Then $\dfrac{1}{4}$ is equivalent to $\dfrac{5}{20}$.

19. Since $7 \cdot 6 = 42$, we multiply the numerator and denominator of $\dfrac{3x}{7}$ by 6.

$$\frac{3x}{7} = \frac{3x \cdot 6}{7 \cdot 6} = \frac{18x}{42}$$

Then $\dfrac{3x}{7}$ is equivalent to $\dfrac{18x}{42}$.

20. Recall that $4 = \dfrac{4}{1}$ and $1 \cdot 6 = 6$.

$$\frac{4}{1} = \frac{4 \cdot 6}{1 \cdot 6} = \frac{24}{6}$$

21. $4x \cdot 5 = 20x$. Multiply the numerator and denominator by 5.

$$\frac{9}{4x} = \frac{9 \cdot 5}{4x \cdot 5} = \frac{45}{20x}$$

Mental Math

1. $\dfrac{1}{2}$ $\begin{array}{l}\leftarrow \text{ numerator}\\ \leftarrow \text{ denominator}\end{array}$

2. $\dfrac{1}{4}$ $\begin{array}{l}\leftarrow \text{ numerator}\\ \leftarrow \text{ denomiantor}\end{array}$

3. $\dfrac{10}{3}$ $\begin{array}{l}\leftarrow \text{ numerator}\\ \leftarrow \text{ denominator}\end{array}$

4. $\dfrac{53}{21}$ $\begin{array}{l}\leftarrow \text{ numerator}\\ \leftarrow \text{ denominator}\end{array}$

5. $\dfrac{3z}{7}$ $\begin{array}{l}\leftarrow \text{ numerator}\\ \leftarrow \text{ denominator}\end{array}$

6. $\dfrac{11x}{15}$ $\begin{array}{l}\leftarrow \text{ numerator}\\ \leftarrow \text{ denominator}\end{array}$

Exercise Set 4.1

1. 1 out of 3 equal parts is shaded: $\frac{1}{3}$.

3. 4 out of 7 equal parts are shaded: $\frac{4}{7}$

5. 7 out of 12 equal parts are shaded: $\frac{7}{12}$.

7. 3 out of 7 equal parts are shaded: $\frac{3}{7}$.

9. 7 out of 8 equal parts are shaded: $\frac{4}{9}$.

11. 5 out of 8 pieces are gone: $\frac{7}{8}$.

13.

15.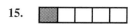

17.

19.

21. $\frac{11}{4}$

23. $\frac{11}{3}$

25. $\frac{3}{2}$

27. $\frac{4}{3}$

29. $\frac{17}{6}$

31. $\frac{14}{9}$

33. Freshmen → $\frac{42}{131}$
Students →

Thus, $\frac{42}{131}$ of the students are freshmen.

35. 131 – 42 = 89 non-freshmen
Non - freshmen → $\frac{89}{131}$
Students →

Thus, $\frac{89}{131}$ of the students are not freshmen.

37. Injury - related visits → $\frac{4}{10}$
Total vists →

Thus, $\frac{4}{10}$ of the visits are injury-related.

39.
Born in Virginia → $\frac{8}{43}$
U.S. Presidents →

Thus, $\frac{8}{43}$ of the presidents were born in Virginia.

41. Gigabytes currently used → $\frac{17}{32}$
Gigabytes on hard drive →

Thus, $\frac{17}{32}$ of the hard drive is being used.

43. Number of days → $\frac{11}{31}$
Days in March →

Thus, 11 days represents $\frac{11}{31}$ of the month.

45. Number of sophomores → $\frac{10}{31}$
Number of students →

Thus, the sophomores are $\frac{10}{31}$ of the class.

47. **a.** Number of legal states → $\frac{40}{50}$
Number of states →
Thus, consumer fireworks are legal in $\frac{40}{50}$ of the states.

b. 50 – 40 = 10
Consumer fireworks are illegal in 10 states.

c. Number of illegal states → $\dfrac{10}{50}$

Number of states →

Thus, consumer fireworks are illegal in

$\dfrac{10}{50}$ of the states.

49. To graph $\dfrac{1}{4}$ on a number line, divide the

distance from 0 to 1 into 4 equal parts. Then start at 0 and count over 1 part.

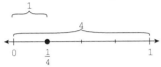

51. To graph $\dfrac{4}{7}$ on a number line, divide the

distance from 0 to 1 into 7 equal parts. Then start at 0 and count over 4 parts.

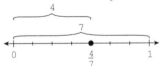

53. To graph $\dfrac{8}{5}$ on a number line, divide the

distance from 0 to 1 into 5 equal parts and divide the distance from 1 to 2 into 5 equal parts. Then start at 0 and count over 8 parts.

55. To graph $\dfrac{7}{3}$ on a number line, divide the

distances from 0 to 1, 1 to 2, and 2 to 3 into 3 equal parts. Then start at 0 and count over 7 parts.

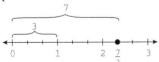

57. To graph $\dfrac{3}{8}$ on a number line, divide the distance

from 0 to 1 into 8 equal parts. Then start at 0 and count over 3 parts.

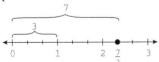

59. $\dfrac{12}{12} = 12 \div 12 = 1$

61. $\dfrac{-5}{1} = -5 \div 1 = -5$

63. $\dfrac{0}{-2} = 0 \div -2 = 0$

65. $\dfrac{-8}{-8} = -8 \div (-8) = 1$

67. $\dfrac{-9}{0}$ is undefined.

69. $\dfrac{3}{1} = 3 \div 1 = 3$

71. $\dfrac{4}{7} = \dfrac{?}{35}$

$\dfrac{4 \cdot 5}{7 \cdot 5} = \dfrac{20}{35}$

73. $\dfrac{2}{3} = \dfrac{?}{21}$

$\dfrac{2 \cdot 7}{3 \cdot 7} = \dfrac{14}{21}$

75. $\dfrac{2y}{5} = \dfrac{?}{25}$

$\dfrac{2y \cdot 5}{5 \cdot 5} = \dfrac{10y}{25}$

77. $\dfrac{1}{2} = \dfrac{?}{30}$

$\dfrac{1 \cdot 15}{2 \cdot 15} = \dfrac{15}{30}$

79. $\dfrac{10}{7x} = \dfrac{?}{21x}$

$\dfrac{10 \cdot 3}{7x \cdot 3} = \dfrac{30}{21x}$

81. $2 = \dfrac{?}{5}$

$\dfrac{2}{1} = \dfrac{?}{5}$

$\dfrac{2 \cdot 5}{1 \cdot 5} = \dfrac{10}{5}$

83. $\dfrac{3}{4} = \dfrac{?}{12}$

$\dfrac{3 \cdot 3}{4 \cdot 3} = \dfrac{9}{12}$

85. $\dfrac{2y}{3} = \dfrac{?}{12}$

$\dfrac{2y \cdot 4}{3 \cdot 4} = \dfrac{8y}{12}$

87. $\dfrac{1}{2} = \dfrac{?}{12}$

$\dfrac{1 \cdot 6}{2 \cdot 6} = \dfrac{6}{12}$

89. $\dfrac{4}{3} = \dfrac{?}{36x}$

$\dfrac{4 \cdot 12x}{3 \cdot 12x} = \dfrac{48x}{36x}$

91. $\dfrac{5}{9} = \dfrac{?}{36x}$

$\dfrac{5 \cdot 4x}{9 \cdot 4x} = \dfrac{20x}{36x}$

93. $1 = \dfrac{?}{36x}$

$\dfrac{1}{1} = \dfrac{?}{36x}$

$\dfrac{1 \cdot 36x}{1 \cdot 36x} = \dfrac{36x}{36x}$

95. Denmark: $\dfrac{13 \cdot 4}{25 \cdot 4} = \dfrac{52}{100}$

Finland: $\dfrac{39 \cdot 2}{50 \cdot 2} = \dfrac{78}{100}$

Israel: $\dfrac{87}{100}$

Italy: $\dfrac{21 \cdot 4}{25 \cdot 4} = \dfrac{84}{100}$

Japan: $\dfrac{59}{100}$

Norway: $\dfrac{83}{100}$

Singapore: $\dfrac{67}{100}$

South Korea: $\dfrac{6 \cdot 10}{10 \cdot 10} = \dfrac{60}{100}$

Sweden: $\dfrac{79}{100}$

United States: $\dfrac{9 \cdot 5}{20 \cdot 5} = \dfrac{45}{100}$

97. The smallest numerator of all the fractions with a denominator of 100 is 45, which is the United States.

99. $3^2 = 3 \cdot 3 = 9$

101. $5^3 = 5 \cdot 5 \cdot 5 = 125$

103. $7^2 = 7 \cdot 7 = 49$

105. $2^3 \cdot 3 = 2 \cdot 2 \cdot 2 \cdot 3 = 24$

107. $9\overline{)2088}$ = 232

$\dfrac{2}{9} = \dfrac{2 \cdot 232}{9 \cdot 232} = \dfrac{464}{2088}$

109. Answers may vary.

111. Total affiliates = 1651 + 634 = 2285

$\dfrac{1651}{2285}$ of Habitat for Humanity's affiliates are in the U.S.

113. Total number of Wendy's Corporation restaurants = 6253 + 2348 + 14 + 26 + 210 = 8851.

$\dfrac{6253}{8851}$ of the restaurants are actually Wendy's.

Section 4.2

Practice Problems

1.

$28 = 2 \cdot 2 \cdot 7 \cdot 5$ or $2^2 \cdot 7$

2.

$$60$$
$$\diagup\ \diagdown$$
$$6 \cdot 10$$
$$\diagup\ \big|\quad \big|\ \diagdown$$
$$2 \cdot 3 \cdot 2 \cdot 5$$

$$60 = 2 \cdot 2 \cdot 3 \cdot 5 \text{ or } 2^2 \cdot 3 \cdot 5$$

3.

$$297$$
$$\diagup\ \diagdown$$
$$9 \cdot 33$$
$$\diagup\ \big|\quad \big|\ \diagdown$$
$$3 \cdot 3 \cdot 3 \cdot 11$$

$$297 = 3 \cdot 3 \cdot 3 \cdot 11 \text{ or } 3^3 \cdot 11$$

4. $\dfrac{30}{45} = \dfrac{2 \cdot 3 \cdot 5}{3 \cdot 3 \cdot 5} = \dfrac{2}{3}$

5. $\dfrac{39}{51} = \dfrac{3 \cdot 13}{3 \cdot 17} = \dfrac{13}{17}$

6. $\dfrac{45}{105y} = \dfrac{3 \cdot 3 \cdot 5}{3 \cdot 5 \cdot 7 \cdot y} = \dfrac{3}{7y}$

7. $\dfrac{9a}{50a} = \dfrac{3 \cdot 3 \cdot a}{2 \cdot 5 \cdot 5 \cdot a} = \dfrac{9}{50}$

8. $\dfrac{38}{4} = \dfrac{2 \cdot 19}{2 \cdot 2} = \dfrac{19}{2}$

9. $\dfrac{7a^3}{56a^2} = \dfrac{7 \cdot a \cdot a \cdot a}{2 \cdot 2 \cdot 2 \cdot 7 \cdot a \cdot a} = \dfrac{a}{8}$

10. $\dfrac{12}{80} = \dfrac{2 \cdot 2 \cdot 3}{2 \cdot 2 \cdot 2 \cdot 2 \cdot 5} = \dfrac{3}{2 \cdot 2 \cdot 5} = \dfrac{3}{20}$

Calculator Explorations

The keys pressed may vary depending on what type of calculator you have.

1. Press the keys 128 $\boxed{a^{b/\!c}}$ 224 $\boxed{\text{= or ENTER}}$.

The display will read $\dfrac{4}{7}$.

2. Press the keys 231 $\boxed{a^{b/\!c}}$ 396 $\boxed{\text{= or ENTER}}$.

The display will read $\dfrac{7}{12}$.

3. Press the keys 340 $\boxed{a^{b/\!c}}$ 459 $\boxed{\text{= or ENTER}}$.

The display will read $\dfrac{20}{27}$.

4. Press the keys 999 $\boxed{a^{b/\!c}}$ 1350 $\boxed{\text{= or ENTER}}$.

The display will read $\dfrac{37}{50}$.

5. Press the keys 810 $\boxed{a^{b/\!c}}$ 432 $\boxed{\text{= or ENTER}}$.

The display will read $\dfrac{15}{8}$.

6. Press the keys 315 $\boxed{a^{b/\!c}}$ 225 $\boxed{\text{= or ENTER}}$.

The display will read $\dfrac{7}{5}$.

7. Press the keys 243 $\boxed{a^{b/\!c}}$ 54 $\boxed{\text{= or ENTER}}$.

The display will read $\dfrac{9}{2}$.

8. Press the keys 689 $\boxed{a^{b/\!c}}$ 455 $\boxed{\text{= or ENTER}}$.

The display will read $\dfrac{53}{35}$.

Mental Math

1. Yes, we know that 2430 is divisible by 2 because its ones digit is 0.
Yes, we know that 2430 is divisible by 3 because the sum of its digits, $2 + 4 + 3 + 0 = 9$, is divisible by 3.
Yes, we know that 2430 is divisible by 5 because its ones digit is 0.

2. $15 = 3 \cdot 5$

3. $10 = 2 \cdot 5$

4. $6 = 2 \cdot 3$

5. $21 = 3 \cdot 7$

6. $4 = 2 \cdot 2 \text{ or } 2^2$

7. $9 = 3 \cdot 3 = 3^2$

8. $14 = 2 \cdot 7$

Exercise Set 4.2

1. $20 = 2 \cdot 10$
$2 \cdot 2 \cdot 5 = 2^2 \cdot 5$

3. $48 = 6 \cdot 8$
$2 \cdot 3 \cdot 2 \cdot 4$
$2 \cdot 3 \cdot 2 \cdot 2 \cdot 2 = 2^4 \cdot 3$

5. $45 = 9 \cdot 5$
$3 \cdot 3 \cdot 5 \text{ or } 3^2 \cdot 5$

7. $240 = 2 \cdot 120$
$2 \cdot 2 \cdot 60$
$2 \cdot 2 \cdot 2 \cdot 30$
$2 \cdot 2 \cdot 2 \cdot 2 \cdot 15$
$2 \cdot 2 \cdot 2 \cdot 2 \cdot 3 \cdot 5 = 2^4 \cdot 3 \cdot 5$

9. $\dfrac{3}{12} = \dfrac{3}{3 \cdot 4} = \dfrac{1}{4}$

11. $\dfrac{7x}{35} = \dfrac{7 \cdot x}{7 \cdot 5} = \dfrac{x}{5}$

13. $\dfrac{14}{16} = \dfrac{2 \cdot 7}{2 \cdot 8} = \dfrac{7}{8}$

15. $\dfrac{24a}{30a} = \dfrac{2 \cdot 2 \cdot 2 \cdot 3 \cdot a}{2 \cdot 3 \cdot 5 \cdot a} = \dfrac{4}{5}$

17. $\dfrac{35}{42} = \dfrac{7 \cdot 5}{7 \cdot 2 \cdot 3} = \dfrac{5}{6}$

19. $\dfrac{30x^2}{36x} = \dfrac{2 \cdot 3 \cdot 5 \cdot x \cdot x}{2 \cdot 2 \cdot 3 \cdot 3 \cdot x} = \dfrac{5x}{6}$

21. $\dfrac{16}{24} = \dfrac{2 \cdot 2 \cdot 2 \cdot 2}{2 \cdot 2 \cdot 2 \cdot 3} = \dfrac{2}{3}$

23. $\dfrac{45xz}{60z} = \dfrac{3 \cdot 3 \cdot 5 \cdot x \cdot z}{2 \cdot 2 \cdot 3 \cdot 5 \cdot z} = \dfrac{3x}{4}$

25. $\dfrac{39ab}{26a^2} = \dfrac{3 \cdot 13 \cdot a \cdot b}{2 \cdot 13 \cdot a \cdot a} = \dfrac{3b}{2a}$

27. $\dfrac{63}{72} = \dfrac{3 \cdot 3 \cdot 7}{2 \cdot 2 \cdot 2 \cdot 3 \cdot 3} = \dfrac{7}{8}$

29. $\dfrac{21}{49} = \dfrac{3 \cdot 7}{7 \cdot 7} = \dfrac{3}{7}$

31. $\dfrac{24y}{40} = \dfrac{2 \cdot 2 \cdot 2 \cdot 3 \cdot y}{2 \cdot 2 \cdot 2 \cdot 5} = \dfrac{3y}{5}$

33. $\dfrac{36z}{63z} = \dfrac{3 \cdot 3 \cdot 2 \cdot 2 \cdot z}{3 \cdot 3 \cdot 7 \cdot z} = \dfrac{4}{7}$

35. $\dfrac{72x^3y^2}{90xy} = \dfrac{2 \cdot 2 \cdot 2 \cdot 3 \cdot 3 \cdot x \cdot x \cdot x \cdot y \cdot y}{2 \cdot 3 \cdot 3 \cdot 5 \cdot x \cdot y}$
$= \dfrac{4x^2y}{5}$

37. $\dfrac{12}{15} = \dfrac{2 \cdot 2 \cdot 3}{3 \cdot 5} = \dfrac{4}{5}$

39. $\dfrac{25x^2}{40x} = \dfrac{5 \cdot 5 \cdot x \cdot x}{2 \cdot 2 \cdot 2 \cdot 5 \cdot x} = \dfrac{5x}{8}$

41. $\dfrac{27xy}{90y} = \dfrac{3 \cdot 3 \cdot 3 \cdot x \cdot y}{2 \cdot 3 \cdot 3 \cdot 5 \cdot y} = \dfrac{3x}{10}$

43. $\dfrac{36a^3bc^2}{24ab^4c^2} = \dfrac{2 \cdot 2 \cdot 3 \cdot 3 \cdot a \cdot a \cdot a \cdot b \cdot c \cdot c}{2 \cdot 2 \cdot 2 \cdot 3 \cdot a \cdot b \cdot b \cdot b \cdot b \cdot c \cdot c}$
$= \dfrac{3a^2}{2b^3}$

45. $\dfrac{40xy}{64xyz} = \dfrac{2 \cdot 2 \cdot 2 \cdot 5 \cdot x \cdot y}{2 \cdot 2 \cdot 2 \cdot 2 \cdot 2 \cdot 2 \cdot x \cdot y \cdot z}$
$= \dfrac{5}{8z}$

47. $\dfrac{6 \text{ hours}}{8 \text{ hours}} = \dfrac{2 \cdot 3}{2 \cdot 2 \cdot 2} = \dfrac{3}{2 \cdot 2} = \dfrac{3}{4}$
6 hours represents $\dfrac{3}{4}$ of a work shift.

49. $\dfrac{2640 \text{ feet}}{5280 \text{ feet}} = \dfrac{2 \cdot 2 \cdot 2 \cdot 2 \cdot 3 \cdot 5 \cdot 11}{2 \cdot 2 \cdot 2 \cdot 2 \cdot 2 \cdot 3 \cdot 5 \cdot 11} = \dfrac{1}{2}$
2640 feet represents $\dfrac{1}{2}$ mile

51. $\dfrac{261}{414} = \dfrac{3 \cdot 3 \cdot 29}{2 \cdot 3 \cdot 3 \cdot 23} = \dfrac{29}{46}$
$\dfrac{29}{46}$ of individuals who have flown in space were Americans.

53. $16,000 - 8800 = 7200$

Number of male students $\rightarrow$ $\dfrac{7200}{16,000}$

Number of students $\rightarrow$

$$\frac{7200}{16,000} = \frac{9 \cdot 800}{20 \cdot 800}$$
$$= \frac{9}{20}$$

$\dfrac{9}{20}$ of the students are male.

55. a. $\dfrac{16}{50} = \dfrac{2 \cdot 2 \cdot 2 \cdot 2}{2 \cdot 5 \cdot 5} = \dfrac{8}{25}$

$\dfrac{8}{25}$ of states have at least one Ritz-Carlton.

b. $50 - 16 = 34$

34 states have no Ritz-Carlton.

c. $\dfrac{34}{50} = \dfrac{2 \cdot 7}{2 \cdot 25} = \dfrac{17}{25}$

$\dfrac{17}{25}$ of states have no Ritz-Carlton.

57. $\dfrac{10}{24} = \dfrac{2 \cdot 5}{2 \cdot 2 \cdot 2 \cdot 3} = \dfrac{5}{12}$

$\dfrac{5}{12}$ of the width is concrete.

59. Education is $\dfrac{1}{10}$.

61. Answers will vary.

63. $\dfrac{x^3}{9} = \dfrac{(-3)^3}{9} = \dfrac{(-3)(-3)(-3)}{9} = \dfrac{-27}{9} = -3$

65. $2y = 2(-7) = -14$

67. $3z - y = 3(2) - 6 = 6 - 6 = 0$

69. $a^2 + 2b + 3 = 4^2 + 2(5) + 3$
$$= 16 + 10 + 3$$
$$= 29$$

71. d

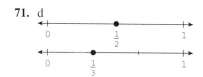

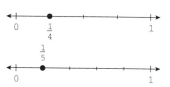

73. False, $\dfrac{14}{42} = \dfrac{2 \cdot 7}{2 \cdot 3 \cdot 7} = \dfrac{1}{3}$

75. True

77. $\dfrac{372}{620} = \dfrac{2 \cdot 2 \cdot 3 \cdot 31}{2 \cdot 2 \cdot 5 \cdot 31} = \dfrac{3}{5}$

79. $\dfrac{36}{100} = \dfrac{2 \cdot 2 \cdot 3 \cdot 3}{2 \cdot 2 \cdot 5 \cdot 5} = \dfrac{3 \cdot 3}{5 \cdot 5} = \dfrac{9}{25}$

$\dfrac{9}{25}$ of the donors have A Rh-positive blood type.

81. $3 + 1 = 4$

$\dfrac{4}{100} = \dfrac{2 \cdot 2}{2 \cdot 2 \cdot 5 \cdot 5} = \dfrac{1}{5 \cdot 5} = \dfrac{1}{25}$

$\dfrac{1}{25}$ of the donors have AB blood type (either Rh-positive or Rh-negative).

83. $7 + 6 + 1 + 1 = 15$

$\dfrac{15}{100} = \dfrac{3 \cdot 5}{2 \cdot 2 \cdot 5 \cdot 5} = \dfrac{3}{20}$

$\dfrac{3}{20}$ of the donors have the negative Rh factor.

85. 105, 900, 2235, and 1470 are divisible by 3 because the sum of their digits are divisible by 3. 105, 900, 235, and 1470 are also divisible by 5 because their last digit is either 0 or 5.

87. 15; answers may vary.

Section 4.3

Practice Problems

1. $\dfrac{3}{8} \cdot \dfrac{5}{7} = \dfrac{3 \cdot 5}{8 \cdot 7} = \dfrac{15}{56}$

2. $\dfrac{1}{3} \cdot \dfrac{1}{6} = \dfrac{1 \cdot 1}{3 \cdot 6} = \dfrac{1}{18}$

3. $\dfrac{6}{11} \cdot \dfrac{5}{8} = \dfrac{6 \cdot 5}{11 \cdot 8} = \dfrac{2 \cdot 3 \cdot 5}{11 \cdot 2 \cdot 4} = \dfrac{3 \cdot 5}{11 \cdot 4} = \dfrac{15}{44}$

4. $\dfrac{4}{15} \cdot \dfrac{3}{8} = \dfrac{4 \cdot 3}{15 \cdot 8} = \dfrac{4 \cdot 3}{3 \cdot 5 \cdot 4 \cdot 2} = \dfrac{1 \cdot 1}{5 \cdot 2} = \dfrac{1}{10}$

5. $\frac{1}{22} \cdot \left(-\frac{11}{28}\right) = -\frac{1 \cdot 11}{22 \cdot 28} = -\frac{1 \cdot 11}{2 \cdot 11 \cdot 28} = -\frac{1}{56}$

6. $\frac{9}{5} \cdot \frac{20}{12} = \frac{3 \cdot 3 \cdot 4 \cdot 5}{5 \cdot 3 \cdot 4} = \frac{3}{1} = 3$

7. $\frac{2}{3} \cdot \frac{3y}{2} = \frac{2 \cdot 3 \cdot y}{3 \cdot 2} = \frac{y}{1} = y$

8. $\frac{a^3}{b^2} \cdot \frac{b}{a^2} = \frac{a^3 \cdot b}{b^2 \cdot a^2} = \frac{a \cdot a \cdot a \cdot b}{b \cdot b \cdot a \cdot a} = \frac{a}{b}$

9. a. $\left(\frac{3}{4}\right)^3 = \frac{3}{4} \cdot \frac{3}{4} \cdot \frac{3}{4} = \frac{3 \cdot 3 \cdot 3}{4 \cdot 4 \cdot 4} = \frac{27}{64}$

   b. $\left(-\frac{4}{5}\right)^2 = \left(-\frac{4}{5}\right)\left(-\frac{4}{5}\right) = \frac{4 \cdot 4}{5 \cdot 5} = \frac{16}{25}$

10. $\frac{3}{2} \div \frac{14}{5} = \frac{3}{2} \cdot \frac{5}{14} = \frac{3 \cdot 5}{2 \cdot 14} = \frac{15}{28}$

11. $\frac{4}{9} \div \frac{1}{2} = \frac{4}{9} \cdot \frac{2}{1} = \frac{4 \cdot 2}{9 \cdot 1} = \frac{8}{9}$

12. $\frac{10}{4} \div \frac{2}{9} = \frac{10}{4} \cdot \frac{9}{2} = \frac{2 \cdot 5 \cdot 9}{4 \cdot 2} = \frac{45}{4}$

13. $\frac{3y}{4} \div 5y^3 = \frac{3y}{4} \cdot \frac{1}{5y^3} = \frac{3 \cdot y \cdot 1}{4 \cdot 5 \cdot y \cdot y \cdot y} = \frac{3}{20y^2}$

14. $\left(-\frac{2}{3} \cdot \frac{9}{14}\right) \div \frac{7}{15} = \left(-\frac{2 \cdot 3 \cdot 3}{3 \cdot 2 \cdot 7}\right) \div \frac{7}{15} = \left(-\frac{3}{7}\right) \div \frac{7}{15}$

    $= -\frac{3}{7} \cdot \frac{15}{7} = -\frac{45}{49}$

15. a. $xy = \left(-\frac{3}{4}\right) \cdot \frac{9}{2} = -\frac{3 \cdot 9}{4 \cdot 2} = -\frac{27}{8}$

    b. $x \div y = -\frac{3}{4} \div \frac{9}{2} = -\frac{3}{4} \cdot \frac{2}{9} = -\frac{3 \cdot 2}{2 \cdot 2 \cdot 3 \cdot 3}$

       $= -\frac{1}{6}$

16. $2x = -\frac{9}{4}$

    $2 \cdot -\frac{9}{8} \stackrel{?}{=} -\frac{9}{4}$

    $-\frac{2 \cdot 9}{2 \cdot 4} \stackrel{?}{=} -\frac{9}{4}$

$-\frac{9}{4} = -\frac{9}{4}$ True.

The statement is true, so $-\frac{9}{8}$ is a solution.

17. $\frac{1}{3} \cdot 20,439 = \frac{1}{3} \cdot \frac{20,439}{1}$

    $= \frac{1 \cdot 20,439}{3 \cdot 1}$

    $= \frac{1 \cdot 3 \cdot 6813}{3 \cdot 1}$

    $= \frac{1 \cdot 6813}{1}$

    $= \frac{6813}{1}$

    $= 6813$

    6813 species are at risk.

Mental Math

1. $\frac{1}{3} \cdot \frac{2}{5} = \frac{2}{15}$

2. $\frac{2}{3} \cdot \frac{4}{7} = \frac{8}{21}$

3. $\frac{6}{5} \cdot \frac{1}{7} = \frac{6}{35}$

4. $\frac{7}{3} \cdot \frac{2}{3} = \frac{14}{9}$

5. $\frac{3}{1} \cdot \frac{3}{8} = \frac{9}{8}$

6. $\frac{2}{1} \cdot \frac{7}{11} = \frac{14}{11}$

Exercise Set 4.3

1. $\frac{7}{8} \cdot \frac{2}{3} = \frac{7 \cdot 2}{8 \cdot 3} = \frac{7 \cdot 2}{2 \cdot 2 \cdot 2 \cdot 3} = \frac{7}{2 \cdot 2 \cdot 3} = \frac{7}{12}$

3. $-\frac{2}{7} \cdot \frac{5}{8} = -\frac{2 \cdot 5}{7 \cdot 8} = -\frac{2 \cdot 5}{7 \cdot 2 \cdot 2 \cdot 2} = -\frac{5}{28}$

5. $-\frac{1}{2} \cdot \frac{2}{15} = -\frac{1 \cdot 2}{2 \cdot 15} = -\frac{1}{15}$

7. $\dfrac{18x}{20} \cdot \dfrac{36}{99} = \dfrac{18 \cdot x \cdot 36}{20 \cdot 99}$

$= \dfrac{9 \cdot 2 \cdot x \cdot 4 \cdot 9}{4 \cdot 5 \cdot 9 \cdot 11}$

$= \dfrac{2 \cdot x \cdot 9}{5 \cdot 11} = \dfrac{18x}{55}$

9. $3a^2 \cdot \dfrac{1}{4} = \dfrac{3 \cdot a^2 \cdot 1}{4} = \dfrac{3a^2}{4}$

11. $\dfrac{x^3}{y^3} \cdot \dfrac{y^2}{x} = \dfrac{x^2 \cdot x \cdot y^2}{y^2 \cdot y \cdot x} = \dfrac{x^2}{y}$

13. $\left(\dfrac{1}{5}\right)^3 = \dfrac{1}{5} \cdot \dfrac{1}{5} \cdot \dfrac{1}{5} = \dfrac{1 \cdot 1 \cdot 1}{5 \cdot 5 \cdot 5} = \dfrac{1}{125}$

15. $\left(-\dfrac{2}{3}\right)^2 = \left(-\dfrac{2}{3}\right) \cdot \left(-\dfrac{2}{3}\right) = \dfrac{2 \cdot 2}{3 \cdot 3} = \dfrac{4}{9}$

17. $\left(-\dfrac{2}{3}\right)^3 \cdot \dfrac{1}{2} = \left(-\dfrac{2}{3}\right) \cdot \left(-\dfrac{2}{3}\right) \cdot \left(-\dfrac{2}{3}\right) \cdot \left(\dfrac{1}{2}\right)$

$= -\dfrac{2 \cdot 2 \cdot 2 \cdot 1}{3 \cdot 3 \cdot 3 \cdot 2}$

$= -\dfrac{4}{27}$

19. $\dfrac{2}{3} \div \dfrac{5}{6} = \dfrac{2}{3} \cdot \dfrac{6}{5} = \dfrac{2 \cdot 2 \cdot 3}{3 \cdot 5} = \dfrac{4}{5}$

21. $-\dfrac{6}{15} \div \dfrac{12}{5} = -\dfrac{6}{15} \cdot \dfrac{5}{12}$

$= -\dfrac{6 \cdot 5}{3 \cdot 5 \cdot 2 \cdot 6}$

$= -\dfrac{1}{6}$

23. $\dfrac{8}{9} \div \dfrac{x}{2} = \dfrac{8}{9} \cdot \dfrac{2}{x} = \dfrac{2 \cdot 2 \cdot 2 \cdot 2}{3 \cdot 3 \cdot x} = \dfrac{16}{9x}$

25. $\dfrac{11y}{20} \div \dfrac{3}{11} = \dfrac{11y}{20} \cdot \dfrac{11}{3} = \dfrac{11 \cdot y \cdot 11}{2 \cdot 2 \cdot 5 \cdot 3} = \dfrac{121y}{60}$

27. $-\dfrac{2}{3} \div 4 = -\dfrac{2}{3} \cdot \dfrac{1}{4} = -\dfrac{2 \cdot 1}{3 \cdot 2 \cdot 2} = -\dfrac{1}{6}$

29. $\dfrac{1}{5x} \div \dfrac{5}{x^2} = \dfrac{1}{5x} \cdot \dfrac{x^2}{5} = \dfrac{x \cdot x}{5 \cdot x \cdot 5} = \dfrac{x}{25}$

31. $\dfrac{2}{3} \cdot \dfrac{5}{9} = \dfrac{2 \cdot 5}{3 \cdot 3 \cdot 3} = \dfrac{10}{27}$

33. $\dfrac{3x}{7} \div \dfrac{5}{6x} = \dfrac{3x}{7} \cdot \dfrac{6x}{5} = \dfrac{3 \cdot x \cdot 2 \cdot 3 \cdot x}{7 \cdot 5} = \dfrac{18x^2}{35}$

35. $-\dfrac{5}{28} \cdot \dfrac{35}{25} = -\dfrac{5 \cdot 5 \cdot 7}{2 \cdot 2 \cdot 7 \cdot 5 \cdot 5} = -\dfrac{1}{4}$

37. $-\dfrac{3}{5} \div -\dfrac{4}{5} = \left(-\dfrac{3}{5}\right) \cdot \left(-\dfrac{5}{4}\right) = \dfrac{3 \cdot 5}{5 \cdot 2 \cdot 2} = \dfrac{3}{4}$

39. $\left(-\dfrac{3}{4}\right)^2 = \left(-\dfrac{3}{4}\right) \cdot \left(-\dfrac{3}{4}\right) = \dfrac{3 \cdot 3}{2 \cdot 2 \cdot 2 \cdot 2} = \dfrac{9}{16}$

41. $\dfrac{x^2}{y} \cdot \dfrac{y^3}{x} = \dfrac{x \cdot x \cdot y \cdot y^2}{y \cdot x} = \dfrac{x \cdot y^2}{1} = xy^2$

43. $7 \div \dfrac{2}{11} = \dfrac{7}{1} \cdot \dfrac{11}{2} = \dfrac{7 \cdot 11}{1 \cdot 2} = \dfrac{77}{2}$

45. $-3x \div \dfrac{x^2}{12} = -\dfrac{3x}{1} \cdot \dfrac{12}{x^2} = -\dfrac{3 \cdot x \cdot 12}{1 \cdot x \cdot x} = -\dfrac{36}{x}$

47. $\left(\dfrac{2}{7} \div \dfrac{7}{2}\right) \cdot \dfrac{3}{4} = \dfrac{2}{7} \cdot \dfrac{2}{7} \cdot \dfrac{3}{4} = \dfrac{2 \cdot 2 \cdot 3}{7 \cdot 7 \cdot 2 \cdot 2} = \dfrac{3}{49}$

49. $-\dfrac{19}{63y} \cdot 9y^2 = -\dfrac{19}{63y} \cdot \dfrac{9y^2}{1}$

$= \dfrac{-19 \cdot 9 \cdot y \cdot y}{7 \cdot 9 \cdot y \cdot 1}$

$= -\dfrac{19y}{7}$

51. $-\dfrac{2}{3} \cdot -\dfrac{6}{11} = \dfrac{2 \cdot 2 \cdot 3}{3 \cdot 11} = \dfrac{4}{11}$

53. $\dfrac{4}{8} \div \dfrac{3}{16} = \dfrac{4}{8} \cdot \dfrac{16}{3} = \dfrac{4 \cdot 8 \cdot 2}{8 \cdot 3} = \dfrac{8}{3}$

55. $\dfrac{21x^2}{10y} \div \dfrac{14x}{25y} = \dfrac{21x^2}{10y} \cdot \dfrac{25y}{14x}$

$= \dfrac{3 \cdot 7 \cdot x \cdot x \cdot 5 \cdot 5 \cdot y}{2 \cdot 5 \cdot y \cdot 2 \cdot 7 \cdot x}$

$= \dfrac{3 \cdot x \cdot 5}{2 \cdot 2}$

$= \dfrac{15x}{4}$

57. $\left(1 \div \dfrac{3}{4}\right) \cdot \dfrac{2}{3} = \dfrac{1}{1} \cdot \dfrac{4}{3} \cdot \dfrac{2}{3} = \dfrac{1 \cdot 2 \cdot 2 \cdot 2}{1 \cdot 3 \cdot 3} = \dfrac{8}{9}$

59. $\dfrac{a^3}{2} \div 30a^3 = \dfrac{a^3}{2} \cdot \dfrac{1}{30a^3}$

$\qquad = \dfrac{a^3}{2 \cdot 30 \cdot a^3}$

$\qquad = \dfrac{1}{60}$

61. $\dfrac{ab^2}{c} \cdot \dfrac{c}{ab} = \dfrac{a \cdot b \cdot b \cdot c}{c \cdot a \cdot b} = \dfrac{b}{1} = b$

63. $\left(\dfrac{1}{2} \cdot \dfrac{2}{3}\right) \div \dfrac{5}{6} = \left(\dfrac{1 \cdot 2}{2 \cdot 3}\right) \cdot \dfrac{6}{5}$

$\qquad = \dfrac{1}{3} \cdot \dfrac{6}{5}$

$\qquad = \dfrac{1 \cdot 2 \cdot 3}{3 \cdot 5}$

$\qquad = \dfrac{2}{5}$

65. $-\dfrac{4}{7} \div \left(\dfrac{4}{5} \cdot \dfrac{3}{7}\right) = -\dfrac{4}{7} \div \left(\dfrac{2 \cdot 2 \cdot 3}{5 \cdot 7}\right)$

$\qquad = -\dfrac{4}{7} \cdot \dfrac{5 \cdot 7}{2 \cdot 2 \cdot 3}$

$\qquad = -\dfrac{4 \cdot 5 \cdot 7}{7 \cdot 4 \cdot 3}$

$\qquad = -\dfrac{5}{3}$

67. a. $xy = \dfrac{2}{5} \cdot \dfrac{5}{6} = \dfrac{2 \cdot 5}{5 \cdot 2 \cdot 3} = \dfrac{1}{3}$

b. $x \div y = \dfrac{2}{5} \div \dfrac{5}{6} = \dfrac{2}{5} \cdot \dfrac{6}{5} = \dfrac{2 \cdot 2 \cdot 3}{5 \cdot 5} = \dfrac{12}{25}$

69. $xy = -\dfrac{4}{5} \cdot \dfrac{9}{11} = -\dfrac{2 \cdot 2 \cdot 3 \cdot 3}{5 \cdot 11} = -\dfrac{36}{55}$

$\qquad x \div y = -\dfrac{4}{5} \div \dfrac{9}{11}$

$\qquad = -\dfrac{4}{5} \cdot \dfrac{11}{9}$

$\qquad = -\dfrac{2 \cdot 2 \cdot 11}{5 \cdot 3 \cdot 3}$

$\qquad = -\dfrac{44}{45}$

71. $\qquad 3x = -\dfrac{5}{6}$

$3\left(-\dfrac{5}{18}\right) = -\dfrac{5}{6}$ $\qquad$ replace x with $-\dfrac{5}{18}$

$-\dfrac{3 \cdot 5}{2 \cdot 3 \cdot 3} = -\dfrac{5}{6}$

$-\dfrac{5}{2 \cdot 3} = -\dfrac{5}{6}$

$-\dfrac{5}{6} = -\dfrac{5}{6}$ $\qquad$ True

Yes, it is a solution.

73. $\qquad -\dfrac{1}{2}z = \dfrac{1}{10}$

$-\dfrac{1}{2} \cdot \dfrac{2}{5} = \dfrac{1}{10}$ $\qquad$ replace z with $\dfrac{2}{5}$

$-\dfrac{1 \cdot 2}{2 \cdot 5} = \dfrac{1}{10}$

$-\dfrac{1}{5} = \dfrac{1}{10}$ $\qquad$ False

No, it is not a solution.

75. $\dfrac{5}{6}(36) = \dfrac{5 \cdot 6 \cdot 6}{6 \cdot 1} = \dfrac{30}{1}$

30 gallons are normally in the vat.

77. $\dfrac{2}{3} \cdot 2757 = \dfrac{2 \cdot 3 \cdot 919}{3} = 1838$

The sale price of the cruise is $1838

79. $\dfrac{1}{2} \cdot \dfrac{3}{8} = \dfrac{3}{16}$

The radius is $\dfrac{3}{16}$ in.

81. $\dfrac{2}{5} \cdot 2170 = \dfrac{2 \cdot 5 \cdot 434}{5} = 868$

He has hiked 868 miles.

83. $\dfrac{7}{10} \cdot 31,050 = \dfrac{7 \cdot 10 \cdot 3,105}{10} = 21,735$

21,735 tornadoes occurred during that time.

85. Let x = size of Jorge's wrist
(wrist size)
= (fraction of waist) · (waist size)

$$x = \frac{1}{4} \cdot \frac{34}{1}$$

$$= \frac{1 \cdot 2 \cdot 17}{2 \cdot 2 \cdot 1}$$

$$= \frac{17}{2}$$

Jorge's wrist is about $\frac{17}{2}$ inches.

87. $9 \cdot \frac{1}{3} = \frac{9}{1} \cdot \frac{1}{3} = \frac{3 \cdot 3}{3} = 3$
3 feet of the 9-foot post should be buried.

89. $2 \div \frac{1}{12} = 2 \cdot 12 = 24$
There are 24 doses available.

91. $\frac{5}{14} \cdot \frac{1}{5} = \frac{5 \cdot 1}{14 \cdot 5} = \frac{1}{14}$
The area is $\frac{1}{14}$ square foot.

93. $90 = 2 \cdot 3 \cdot 3 \cdot 5$ or $2 \cdot 3^2 \cdot 5$

95. $65 = 5 \cdot 13$

97. $126 = 2 \cdot 3 \cdot 3 \cdot 7$ or $2 \cdot 3^2 \cdot 7$

99. $10,300,000 \cdot \frac{7}{10} = 7,210,000$ households

101. Answers may vary.

103. $5144 \div \frac{1}{3} = 5144 \cdot 3 = 15,432$
There are 15,432 flowering plant species that are native to the United States.

105. $\frac{42}{25} \cdot \frac{125}{36} \div \frac{7}{6}$

$$= \frac{6 \cdot 7 \cdot 5 \cdot 5 \cdot 5}{5 \cdot 5 \cdot 6 \cdot 6} \div \frac{7}{6}$$

$$= \frac{35}{6} \cdot \frac{6}{7}$$

$$= \frac{5 \cdot 7 \cdot 6}{6 \cdot 7}$$

$$= 5$$

Section 4.4

Practice Problems

1. $\frac{5}{9} + \frac{2}{9} = \frac{5+2}{9} = \frac{7}{9}$

2. $\frac{5}{8} + \frac{1}{8} = \frac{5+1}{8} = \frac{6}{8} = \frac{3 \cdot 2}{4 \cdot 2} = \frac{3}{4}$

3. $\frac{10}{11} + \frac{1}{11} + \frac{7}{11} = \frac{10+1+7}{11} = \frac{18}{11}$

4. $\frac{7}{12} - \frac{2}{12} = \frac{7-2}{12} = \frac{5}{12}$

5. $\frac{9}{10} - \frac{1}{10} = \frac{9-1}{10} = \frac{8}{10} = \frac{4 \cdot 2}{5 \cdot 2} = \frac{4}{5}$

6. $-\frac{8}{5} + \frac{4}{5} = \frac{-8+4}{5} = \frac{-4}{5}$ or $-\frac{4}{5}$

7. $\frac{2}{5} - \frac{3y}{5} = \frac{2-3y}{5}$

8. $\frac{4}{11} - \frac{6}{11} - \frac{3}{11} = \frac{4-6-3}{11} = \frac{-5}{11}$ or $-\frac{5}{11}$.

9. $x + y = -\frac{10}{12} + \frac{5}{12} = \frac{-10+5}{12} = \frac{-5}{12}$ or $-\frac{5}{12}$

10. Solve: $\frac{7}{10} = x - \frac{1}{10}$

$$\frac{7}{10} + \frac{1}{10} = x - \frac{1}{10} + \frac{1}{10}$$

$$\frac{8}{10} = x$$

$$\frac{4}{5} = x$$

11. $\frac{3}{4} + \frac{1}{4} = \frac{3+1}{4} = \frac{4}{4} = 1$
She practiced 1 hour.

12. 9 laps on Monday =
$$\frac{1}{8} + \frac{1}{8} + \frac{1}{8} + \frac{1}{8} + \frac{1}{8} + \frac{1}{8} + \frac{1}{8} + \frac{1}{8} + \frac{1}{8}$$ miles

3 laps on Wednesday = $\frac{1}{8} + \frac{1}{8} + \frac{1}{8} = \frac{3}{8}$ miles

$$\frac{9}{8} - \frac{3}{8} = \frac{9-3}{8} = \frac{6}{8} = \frac{2 \cdot 3}{2 \cdot 4} = \frac{3}{4}$$ miles

He went $\frac{3}{4}$ mile farther on Monday.

13. Since 15 is not divisible by 12, we check multiples of 15.
$2 \cdot 15 = 30$
30 is not divisible by 12.
$3 \cdot 15 = 45$
45 is not divisible by 12.
$4 \cdot 15 = 60$
60 is divisible by 12.
60 is the LCD.

14. $14 = 2 \cdot 7$
$35 = 5 \cdot 7$
$LCD = 2 \cdot 5 \cdot 7 = 70$

15. $4 = 2 \cdot 2$
$15 = 3 \cdot 5$
$10 = 2 \cdot 5$
$LCD = 2 \cdot 2 \cdot 3 \cdot 5 = 60$

16. $y = y$
$11 = 11$
$LCD = 11 \cdot y = 11y$

Mental Math

1. Since $\frac{7}{8}$ and $\frac{7}{10}$ have different denominators, they are unlike fractions.

2. Since $\frac{2}{3}$ and $\frac{2}{9}$ have different denominators, they are unlike fractions.

3. Since $\frac{9}{10}$ and $\frac{1}{10}$ have the same denominator, they are like fractions.

4. Since $\frac{8}{11}$ and $\frac{2}{11}$ have the same denominator, they are like fractions.

5. Since $\frac{2}{31}, \frac{30}{31}$, and $\frac{19}{31}$ have the same denominator, they are like fractions.

6. Since $\frac{3}{10}, \frac{3}{11}$, and $\frac{3}{13}$ have different denominators, they are unlike fractions.

7. Since $\frac{5}{12}, \frac{7}{12}$, and $\frac{12}{11}$ have different denominators, they are unlike fractions.

8. Since $\frac{1}{5}, \frac{2}{5}$, and $\frac{4}{5}$ have the same denominator, they are like fractions.

9. $\frac{3}{7} + \frac{2}{7} = \frac{3+2}{7} = \frac{5}{7}$

10. $\frac{5}{9} + \frac{2}{9} = \frac{5+2}{9}$
$= \frac{7}{9}$

11. $\frac{10}{11} - \frac{4}{11} = \frac{10-4}{11} = \frac{6}{11}$

12. $\frac{9}{13} - \frac{5}{13} = \frac{9-5}{13} = \frac{4}{13}$

13. $\frac{5}{11} + \frac{2}{11} = \frac{5+2}{11} = \frac{7}{11}$

14. $\frac{4}{7} + \frac{2}{7} = \frac{4+2}{7} = \frac{6}{7}$

15. $\frac{9}{15} - \frac{1}{15} = \frac{9-1}{15} = \frac{8}{15}$

16. $\frac{3}{15} - \frac{1}{15} = \frac{3-1}{15} = \frac{2}{15}$

Exercise Set 4.4

1. $-\frac{1}{2} + \frac{1}{2} = \frac{-1+1}{2} = \frac{0}{2} = 0$

3. $\frac{2}{9x} + \frac{4}{9x} = \frac{2+4}{9x} = \frac{6}{9x} = \frac{2 \cdot 3}{3 \cdot 3 \cdot x} = \frac{2}{3x}$

5. $-\frac{4}{13} + \frac{2}{13} + \frac{1}{13} = \frac{-4+2+1}{13} = \frac{-1}{13} = -\frac{1}{13}$

7. $\frac{7}{18} + \frac{3}{18} + \frac{2}{18} = \frac{7+3+2}{18} = \frac{12}{18} = \frac{2 \cdot 6}{3 \cdot 6} = \frac{2}{3}$

9. $\frac{1}{y} - \frac{4}{y} = \frac{1-4}{y} = \frac{-3}{y} = -\frac{3}{y}$

11. $\frac{7a}{4} - \frac{3}{4} = \frac{7a-3}{4}$

13. $\frac{1}{8} - \frac{7}{8} = \frac{1-7}{8} = \frac{-6}{8} = -\frac{3 \cdot 2}{4 \cdot 2} = -\frac{3}{4}$

15. $\dfrac{20}{21} - \dfrac{10}{21} - \dfrac{17}{21} = \dfrac{20 - 10 - 17}{21}$

$\qquad\qquad = \dfrac{-7}{21}$

$\qquad\qquad = -\dfrac{7}{3 \cdot 7}$

$\qquad\qquad = -\dfrac{1}{3}$

17. $\dfrac{9x}{15} + \dfrac{1x}{15} = \dfrac{9x + 1x}{15} = \dfrac{10x}{15} = \dfrac{5 \cdot 2x}{5 \cdot 3} = \dfrac{2x}{3}$

19. $\dfrac{7x}{16} - \dfrac{15x}{16} = \dfrac{7x - 15x}{16}$

$\qquad\qquad = \dfrac{-8x}{16}$

$\qquad\qquad = -\dfrac{8 \cdot x}{2 \cdot 8}$

$\qquad\qquad = -\dfrac{x}{2}$

21. $\dfrac{15}{16z} - \dfrac{3}{16z} = \dfrac{15 - 3}{16z} = \dfrac{12}{16z} = \dfrac{4 \cdot 3}{4 \cdot 4 \cdot z} = \dfrac{3}{4z}$

23. $\dfrac{3}{10} - \dfrac{6}{10} = \dfrac{3 - 6}{10} = \dfrac{-3}{10} = -\dfrac{3}{10}$

25. $\dfrac{15}{17} + \dfrac{5}{17} + \dfrac{14}{17} = \dfrac{15 + 5 + 14}{17}$

$\qquad\qquad = \dfrac{34}{17}$

$\qquad\qquad = \dfrac{17 \cdot 2}{17}$

$\qquad\qquad = \dfrac{2}{1}$

$\qquad\qquad = 2$

27. $\dfrac{9}{12} - \dfrac{7}{12} - \dfrac{10}{12} = \dfrac{9 - 7 - 10}{12}$

$\qquad\qquad = \dfrac{-8}{12}$

$\qquad\qquad = -\dfrac{2 \cdot 4}{3 \cdot 4}$

$\qquad\qquad = -\dfrac{2}{3}$

29. $\dfrac{x}{4} + \dfrac{3x}{4} - \dfrac{2x}{4} + \dfrac{x}{4} = \dfrac{x + 3x - 2x + x}{4} = \dfrac{3x}{4}$

31. $x + y = \dfrac{3}{4} + \dfrac{2}{4} = \dfrac{5}{4}$

33. $x - y = -\dfrac{1}{5} - \left(-\dfrac{3}{5}\right)$

$\qquad\qquad = -\dfrac{1}{5} + \dfrac{3}{5}$

$\qquad\qquad = \dfrac{-1 + 3}{5}$

$\qquad\qquad = \dfrac{2}{5}$

35. $x - y + z = \dfrac{3}{12} - \dfrac{5}{12} + \left(-\dfrac{7}{12}\right)$

$\qquad\qquad = \dfrac{3 - 5 - 7}{12}$

$\qquad\qquad = \dfrac{-9}{12}$

$\qquad\qquad = -\dfrac{3 \cdot 3}{3 \cdot 4}$

$\qquad\qquad = -\dfrac{3}{4}$

37. $\quad x + \dfrac{1}{3} = -\dfrac{1}{3}$

$\quad x + \dfrac{1}{3} - \dfrac{1}{3} = -\dfrac{1}{3} - \dfrac{1}{3}$

$\qquad\qquad x = \dfrac{-1 - 1}{3} = \dfrac{-2}{3} = -\dfrac{2}{3}$

Check:

$x + \dfrac{1}{3} = -\dfrac{1}{3}$

$-\dfrac{2}{3} + \dfrac{1}{3} = -\dfrac{1}{3}$

$\dfrac{-2 + 1}{3} = -\dfrac{1}{3}$

$\dfrac{-1}{3} = -\dfrac{1}{3}$

$-\dfrac{1}{3} = -\dfrac{1}{3}$ True

39.
$$y - \frac{3}{13} = -\frac{2}{13}$$
$$y - \frac{3}{13} + \frac{3}{13} = -\frac{2}{13} + \frac{3}{13}$$
$$y = \frac{-2+3}{13} = \frac{1}{13}$$

Check:
$$y - \frac{3}{13} = -\frac{2}{13}$$
$$\frac{1}{13} - \frac{3}{13} = -\frac{2}{13}$$
$$\frac{1-3}{13} = -\frac{2}{13}$$
$$\frac{-2}{13} = -\frac{2}{13}$$
$$-\frac{2}{13} = -\frac{2}{13} \quad \text{True}$$

41.
$$3x - \frac{1}{5} - 2x = \frac{1}{5} + \frac{2}{5}$$
$$(3x - 2x) - \frac{1}{5} = \frac{1+2}{5}$$
$$x - \frac{1}{5} = \frac{3}{5}$$
$$x - \frac{1}{5} + \frac{1}{5} = \frac{3}{5} + \frac{1}{5}$$
$$x = \frac{4}{5}$$

Check:
$$3x - \frac{1}{5} - 2x = \frac{1}{5} + \frac{2}{5}$$
$$3 \cdot \frac{4}{5} - \frac{1}{5} - 2 \cdot \frac{4}{5} = \frac{1+2}{5}$$
$$\frac{12}{5} - \frac{1}{5} - \frac{8}{5} = \frac{3}{5}$$
$$\frac{12-1-8}{5} = \frac{3}{5}$$
$$\frac{11-8}{5} = \frac{3}{5}$$
$$\frac{3}{5} = \frac{3}{5} \quad \text{True}$$

43. The perimeter is the distance around. Add the lengths of the sides.
$$\frac{4}{20} + \frac{7}{20} + \frac{9}{20} = \frac{4+7+9}{20} = \frac{20}{20} = 1$$
The perimeter is 1 inch.

45. The perimeter is the distance around. A rectangle has 2 sets of equal sides. Add the lengths of the sides.

$$\frac{5}{12} + \frac{7}{12} + \frac{5}{12} + \frac{7}{12} = \frac{5+7+5+7}{12}$$
$$= \frac{24}{12}$$
$$= \frac{2 \cdot 12}{1 \cdot 12}$$
$$= 2$$
The perimeter is 2 meters.

47. Find the total workout time. Add the times in the morning and in the evening.
$$\frac{7}{8} + \frac{5}{8} = \frac{7+5}{8} = \frac{12}{8} = \frac{3 \cdot 4}{2 \cdot 4} = \frac{3}{2}$$
He worked out $\frac{3}{2}$ hours.

49. The fraction of employees enrolled in each plan in order from smallest to largest are
$$\frac{7}{100}, \frac{14}{100}, \frac{29}{100}, \text{ and } \frac{50}{100}.$$
Thus, the health plans in order from the smallest fraction of employees to the largest fraction of employees are Traditional fee-for-service, Point-of-Service, Health Maintenance Organization, and Preferred Provider Organization.

51.
$$\frac{29}{100} + \frac{14}{100} + \frac{7}{100} = \frac{29+14+7}{100} = \frac{50}{100} = \frac{1}{2}$$
$\frac{1}{2}$ of the employees are not covered by Preferred Provider Organization.

53. Subtract $\frac{18}{50}$ from $\frac{39}{50}$.
$$\frac{39}{50} - \frac{18}{50} = \frac{39-18}{50} = \frac{21}{50}$$
$\frac{21}{50}$ of the states had maximum speed limits that were less than 70 mph.

55. $3 = 3$
$4 = 2 \cdot 2$
$\text{LCD} = 3 \cdot 2 \cdot 2 = 12$

57. $9 = 3 \cdot 3$
$15 = 3 \cdot 5$
$\text{LCD} = 3 \cdot 3 \cdot 5 = 45$

59. $12 = 2 \cdot 2 \cdot 3$
$18 = 2 \cdot 3 \cdot 3$
$\text{LCD} = 2 \cdot 2 \cdot 3 \cdot 3 = 36$

61. $24 = 2 \cdot 2 \cdot 2 \cdot 3$
$x = x$
$LCD = 2 \cdot 2 \cdot 2 \cdot 3 \cdot x = 24x$

63. $25 = 5 \cdot 5$
$15 = 3 \cdot 5$
$6 = 2 \cdot 3$
$LCD = 2 \cdot 3 \cdot 5 \cdot 5 = 150$

65. $18 = 2 \cdot 3 \cdot 3$
$21 = 3 \cdot 7$
$LCD = 2 \cdot 3 \cdot 3 \cdot 7 = 126$

67. $15 = 3 \cdot 5$
$25 = 5 \cdot 5$
$LCD = 3 \cdot 5 \cdot 5 = 75$

69. $8 = 2 \cdot 2 \cdot 2$
$24 = 2 \cdot 2 \cdot 2 \cdot 3$
$LCD = 2 \cdot 2 \cdot 2 \cdot 3 = 24$

71. $25 = 5 \cdot 5$
$10 = 2 \cdot 5$
$LCD = 5 \cdot 5 \cdot 2 = 50$

73. $a = a$
$12 = 2 \cdot 2 \cdot 3$
$LCD = 2 \cdot 2 \cdot 3 \cdot a = 12a$

75. $3 = 3$
$21 = 3 \cdot 7$
$56 = 2 \cdot 2 \cdot 2 \cdot 7$
$LCD = 2 \cdot 2 \cdot 2 \cdot 3 \cdot 7 = 168$

77. $11 = 11$
$33 = 3 \cdot 11$
$121 = 11 \cdot 11$
$LCD = 3 \cdot 11 \cdot 11 = 363$

79. $\dfrac{4}{5} \cdot \dfrac{3}{7} = \dfrac{4 \cdot 3}{5 \cdot 7} = \dfrac{12}{35}$

81. $-2 + 10 = 8$

83. $\dfrac{2}{5} \div \dfrac{1}{2} = \dfrac{2}{5} \cdot \dfrac{2}{1} = \dfrac{2 \cdot 2}{5 \cdot 1} = \dfrac{4}{5}$

85. $-12 - 16 = -12 + (-16) = -28$

87. $\dfrac{4}{11} + \dfrac{5}{11} - \dfrac{3}{11} + \dfrac{2}{11} = \dfrac{4 + 5 - 3 + 2}{11} = \dfrac{8}{11}$

89. Subtract the sum of $\dfrac{38}{50}$ and $\dfrac{7}{50}$ from the total of $\dfrac{50}{50}$.

$\dfrac{50}{50} - \left(\dfrac{38}{50} + \dfrac{7}{50}\right) = \dfrac{50}{50} - \dfrac{45}{50}$
$= \dfrac{50 - 45}{45}$
$= \dfrac{5}{50}$
$= \dfrac{1 \cdot 5}{10 \cdot 5}$
$= \dfrac{1}{10}$

$\dfrac{1}{10}$ of American men over age 65 are either single or divorced.

91. Answers may vary.

Section 4.5

Practice Problems

1. $\dfrac{4}{7} + \dfrac{3}{14}$:
Step 1. The LCD for the denominators 7 and 14 is 14.
Step 2. $\dfrac{4}{7} = \dfrac{4 \cdot 2}{7 \cdot 2} = \dfrac{8}{14}$; $\dfrac{3}{14}$ has a denominator of 14.
Step 3. $\dfrac{4}{7} + \dfrac{3}{14} = \dfrac{8}{14} + \dfrac{3}{14} = \dfrac{11}{14}$
Step 4. $\dfrac{11}{14}$ is in simplest form.

2. $\dfrac{3}{7} - \dfrac{9}{10}$:
Step 1. The LCD for denominators 7 and 10 is 70.
Step 2. $\dfrac{3}{7} = \dfrac{3 \cdot 10}{7 \cdot 10} = \dfrac{30}{70}$ and $\dfrac{9}{10} = \dfrac{9 \cdot 7}{10 \cdot 7} = \dfrac{63}{70}$
Step 3. $\dfrac{3}{7} - \dfrac{9}{10} = \dfrac{30}{70} - \dfrac{63}{70} = \dfrac{30 - 63}{70} = \dfrac{-33}{70}$
or $-\dfrac{33}{70}$
Step 4. $-\dfrac{33}{70}$ is in simplest form.

3. $-\dfrac{1}{5}+\dfrac{3}{20}$:

The LCD denominators 5 and 20 is 20.

$$-\dfrac{1}{5}+\dfrac{3}{20}=\dfrac{-1\cdot4}{5\cdot4}+\dfrac{3}{20}$$
$$=\dfrac{-4}{20}+\dfrac{3}{20}$$
$$=\dfrac{-1}{20}\text{ or }-\dfrac{1}{20}$$

4. $5+\dfrac{3y}{4}$:

Recall that $5=\dfrac{5}{1}$. The LCD for denominators 1 and 4 is 4.

$$\dfrac{5}{1}+\dfrac{3y}{4}=\dfrac{5\cdot4}{1\cdot4}+\dfrac{3y}{4}=\dfrac{20}{4}+\dfrac{3y}{4}=\dfrac{20+3y}{4}$$

5. $\dfrac{5}{8}-\dfrac{1}{3}-\dfrac{1}{12}$:

The LCD of 8, 3 and 12 is 24.

$$\dfrac{5}{8}-\dfrac{1}{3}-\dfrac{1}{12}=\dfrac{5\cdot3}{8\cdot3}-\dfrac{1\cdot8}{3\cdot8}-\dfrac{1\cdot2}{12\cdot2}$$
$$=\dfrac{15}{24}-\dfrac{8}{24}-\dfrac{2}{24}$$
$$=\dfrac{5}{24}$$

6. $\dfrac{3}{8}=\dfrac{3\cdot5}{8\cdot5}=\dfrac{15}{40}$ and $\dfrac{7}{20}=\dfrac{7\cdot2}{20\cdot2}=\dfrac{14}{40}$

Since $15>14$, $\dfrac{15}{40}>\dfrac{14}{40}$. Therefore, $\dfrac{3}{8}>\dfrac{7}{20}$.

7. $-\dfrac{17}{20}$ and $-\dfrac{4}{5}=-\dfrac{4\cdot4}{5\cdot4}=-\dfrac{16}{20}$

Since $-17<-16$, $-\dfrac{17}{20}<-\dfrac{16}{20}$.

Therefore, $-\dfrac{17}{20}<-\dfrac{4}{5}$.

8. $x+y=\dfrac{5}{11}+\dfrac{4}{9}$

The LCD of 11 and 9 is 99.

$$\dfrac{5}{11}+\dfrac{4}{9}=\dfrac{5\cdot9}{11\cdot9}+\dfrac{4\cdot11}{9\cdot11}=\dfrac{45}{99}+\dfrac{44}{99}=\dfrac{89}{99}$$

9. $y-\dfrac{2}{3}=\dfrac{5}{12}$

$$y-\dfrac{2}{3}+\dfrac{2}{3}=\dfrac{5}{12}+\dfrac{2}{3}$$
$$y=\dfrac{5}{12}+\dfrac{2\cdot4}{3\cdot4}$$
$$y=\dfrac{5}{12}+\dfrac{8}{12}$$
$$y=\dfrac{13}{12}$$

10. The phrase "total amount" tells us to add. Add the three amounts: $\dfrac{3}{5}+\dfrac{2}{10}+\dfrac{2}{15}$.

The LCD for the denominators 5, 10, and 15 is 30.

$$\dfrac{3}{5}=\dfrac{3\cdot6}{5\cdot6}=\dfrac{18}{30},\ \dfrac{2}{10}=\dfrac{2\cdot3}{10\cdot3}=\dfrac{6}{30},$$
$$\dfrac{2}{15}=\dfrac{2\cdot2}{15\cdot2}=\dfrac{4}{30}$$
$$\dfrac{3}{5}+\dfrac{2}{10}+\dfrac{2}{15}=\dfrac{18}{30}+\dfrac{6}{30}+\dfrac{4}{30}=\dfrac{28}{30}$$
$$\dfrac{28}{30}=\dfrac{14\cdot2}{15\cdot2}=\dfrac{14}{15}$$

The homeowner needs $\dfrac{14}{15}$ of a cubic yard. Yes, she bought enough because 1 or $\dfrac{15}{15}$ is greater than $\dfrac{14}{15}$.

11. The phrase "find the difference" tells us to subtract. Subtract $\dfrac{2}{3}$ from $\dfrac{4}{5}$: $\dfrac{4}{5}-\dfrac{2}{3}$.

The LCD for the denominators 5 and 3 is 15.

$$\dfrac{4}{5}=\dfrac{4\cdot3}{5\cdot3}=\dfrac{12}{15},\ \dfrac{2\cdot5}{3\cdot5}=\dfrac{10}{15}$$
$$\dfrac{4}{5}-\dfrac{2}{3}=\dfrac{12}{15}-\dfrac{10}{15}=\dfrac{2}{15}$$

$\dfrac{2}{15}$ is in simplest form.

The difference in the lengths is $\dfrac{2}{15}$ of a foot.

Calculator Explorations

Use the calculator keystrokes discussed on page 292 of your textbook.

1. $\dfrac{1}{16}+\dfrac{2}{5}=\dfrac{37}{80}$

2. $\dfrac{3}{20} + \dfrac{2}{25} = \dfrac{23}{100}$

3. $\dfrac{4}{9} + \dfrac{7}{8} = \dfrac{95}{72}$

4. $\dfrac{9}{11} + \dfrac{5}{12} = \dfrac{163}{132}$

5. $\dfrac{10}{17} + \dfrac{12}{19} = \dfrac{394}{323}$

6. $\dfrac{14}{31} + \dfrac{15}{21} = \dfrac{253}{217}$

Mental Math

1. The LCD of 2 and 3 is $2 \cdot 3 = 6$.

2. The LCD of 2 and 4 is 4.

3. The LCD of 6 and 12 is 12.

4. The LCD of 5 and 10 is 10.

5. The LCD of 7 and 8 is $7 \cdot 2^3 = 56$.

6. The LCD of 24 and 3 is 24.

7. The LCD of 12 and 4 is 12.

8. The LCD of 3 and 11 is $3 \cdot 11 = 33$.

Exercise Set 4.5

1. The LCD of 3 and 6 is 6.
$$\frac{2}{3} + \frac{1}{6} = \frac{2 \cdot 2}{3 \cdot 2} + \frac{1}{6} = \frac{4}{6} + \frac{1}{6} = \frac{5}{6}$$

3. The LCD of 2 and 3 is 6.
$$\frac{1}{2} - \frac{1}{3} = \frac{1 \cdot 3}{2 \cdot 3} - \frac{1 \cdot 2}{3 \cdot 2} = \frac{3}{6} - \frac{2}{6} = \frac{1}{6}$$

5. The LCD of 11 and 33 is 33.
$$\begin{aligned} -\frac{2}{11} + \frac{2}{33} &= -\frac{2 \cdot 3}{11 \cdot 3} + \frac{2}{33} \\ &= -\frac{6}{33} + \frac{2}{33} \\ &= -\frac{4}{33} \end{aligned}$$

7. The LCD of 14 and 7 is 14.
$$\frac{3x}{14} - \frac{3}{7} = \frac{3x}{14} - \frac{3 \cdot 2}{7 \cdot 2} = \frac{3x}{14} - \frac{6}{14} = \frac{3x - 6}{14}$$

9. The LCD of 35 and 7 is 35.
$$\begin{aligned} \frac{11}{35} + \frac{2}{7} &= \frac{11}{35} + \frac{2 \cdot 5}{7 \cdot 5} \\ &= \frac{11}{35} + \frac{10}{35} \\ &= \frac{21}{35} \\ &= \frac{3 \cdot 7}{5 \cdot 7} \\ &= \frac{3}{5} \end{aligned}$$

11. The LCD of 1 and 12 is 12.
$$\begin{aligned} \frac{2y}{1} - \frac{5}{12} &= \frac{2y \cdot 12}{1 \cdot 12} - \frac{5}{12} \\ &= \frac{24y}{12} - \frac{5}{12} \\ &= \frac{24y - 5}{12} \end{aligned}$$

13. The LCD of 12 and 9 is 36.
$$\frac{5}{12} - \frac{1}{9} = \frac{5 \cdot 3}{12 \cdot 3} - \frac{1 \cdot 4}{9 \cdot 4} = \frac{15}{36} - \frac{4}{36} = \frac{11}{36}$$

15. The LCD of 7 and 1 is 7.
$$\frac{5}{7} + 1 = \frac{5}{7} + \frac{1}{1} = \frac{5}{7} + \frac{1 \cdot 7}{1 \cdot 7} = \frac{5}{7} + \frac{7}{7} = \frac{12}{7}$$

17. The LCD of 11 and 9 is 99.
$$\begin{aligned} \frac{5a}{11} + \frac{4a}{9} &= \frac{5a \cdot 9}{11 \cdot 9} + \frac{4a \cdot 11}{9 \cdot 11} \\ &= \frac{45a}{99} + \frac{44a}{99} \\ &= \frac{89a}{99} \end{aligned}$$

19. The LCD of 3 and 6 is 6.
$$\frac{2y}{3} - \frac{1}{6} = \frac{2y \cdot 2}{3 \cdot 2} - \frac{1}{6} = \frac{4y}{6} - \frac{1}{6} = \frac{4y - 1}{6}$$

21. The LCD of 2 and x is $2x$.
$$\frac{1}{2} + \frac{3}{x} = \frac{1 \cdot x}{2 \cdot x} + \frac{3 \cdot 2}{x \cdot 2} = \frac{x}{2x} + \frac{6}{2x} = \frac{x + 6}{2x}$$

23. The LCD of 11 and 33 is 33.
$$\begin{aligned} -\frac{2}{11} - \frac{2}{33} &= -\frac{2 \cdot 3}{11 \cdot 3} - \frac{2}{33} \\ &= -\frac{6}{33} - \frac{2}{33} \\ &= -\frac{8}{33} \end{aligned}$$

25. The LCD of 14 and 7 is 14.

$$\frac{9}{14} - \frac{3}{7} = \frac{9}{14} - \frac{3 \cdot 2}{7 \cdot 2} = \frac{9}{14} - \frac{6}{14} = \frac{3}{14}$$

27. The LCD of 35 and 7 is 35.

$$\frac{11y}{35} - \frac{2}{7} = \frac{11y}{35} - \frac{2 \cdot 5}{7 \cdot 5}$$
$$= \frac{11y}{35} - \frac{10}{35}$$
$$= \frac{11y - 10}{35}$$

29. The LCD of 9 and 12 is 36.

$$\frac{1}{9} - \frac{5}{12} = \frac{1 \cdot 4}{9 \cdot 4} - \frac{5 \cdot 3}{12 \cdot 3} = \frac{4}{36} - \frac{15}{36} = -\frac{11}{36}$$

31. The LCD of 15 and 12 is 60.

$$\frac{7}{15} - \frac{5}{12} = \frac{7 \cdot 4}{15 \cdot 4} - \frac{5 \cdot 5}{12 \cdot 5}$$
$$= \frac{28}{60} - \frac{25}{60}$$
$$= \frac{3}{60}$$
$$= \frac{3}{3 \cdot 20}$$
$$= \frac{1}{20}$$

33. The LCD of 7 and 8 is 56.

$$\frac{5}{7} - \frac{1}{8} = \frac{5 \cdot 8}{7 \cdot 8} - \frac{1 \cdot 7}{8 \cdot 7} = \frac{40}{56} - \frac{7}{56} = \frac{33}{56}$$

35. The LCD of 8 and 16 is 16.

$$\frac{7}{8} + \frac{3}{16} = \frac{7 \cdot 2}{8 \cdot 2} + \frac{3}{16} = \frac{14}{16} + \frac{3}{16} = \frac{17}{16}$$

37. $\dfrac{5}{9} + \dfrac{3}{9} = \dfrac{8}{9}$

39. The LCD of 11 and 3 is 33.

$$\frac{5}{11} + \frac{y}{3} = \frac{5 \cdot 3}{11 \cdot 3} + \frac{y \cdot 11}{3 \cdot 11}$$
$$= \frac{15}{33} + \frac{11y}{33}$$
$$= \frac{15 + 11y}{33}$$

41. The LCD of 6 and 7 is 42.

$$-\frac{5}{6} - \frac{3}{7} = -\frac{5 \cdot 7}{6 \cdot 7} - \frac{3 \cdot 6}{7 \cdot 6}$$
$$= -\frac{35}{42} - \frac{18}{42}$$
$$= -\frac{53}{42}$$

43. The LCD of 9 and 6 is 18.

$$\frac{7}{9} - \frac{1}{6} = \frac{7 \cdot 2}{9 \cdot 2} - \frac{1 \cdot 3}{6 \cdot 3} = \frac{14}{18} - \frac{3}{18} = \frac{11}{18}$$

45. The LCD of 3 and 13 is 39.

$$\frac{2a}{3} + \frac{6a}{13} = \frac{2a \cdot 13}{3 \cdot 13} + \frac{6a \cdot 3}{13 \cdot 3}$$
$$= \frac{26a}{39} + \frac{18a}{39}$$
$$= \frac{44a}{39}$$

47. The LCD of 30 and 12 is 60.

$$\frac{7}{30} - \frac{5}{12} = \frac{7 \cdot 2}{30 \cdot 2} - \frac{5 \cdot 5}{12 \cdot 5}$$
$$= \frac{14}{60} - \frac{25}{60}$$
$$= -\frac{11}{60}$$

49. The LCD of 9 and y is $9y$.

$$\frac{5}{9} + \frac{1}{y} = \frac{5 \cdot y}{9 \cdot y} + \frac{1 \cdot 9}{y \cdot 9} = \frac{5y}{9y} + \frac{9}{9y} = \frac{5y + 9}{9y}$$

51. The LCD of 5 and 9 is 45.

$$\frac{4}{5} + \frac{4}{9} = \frac{4 \cdot 9}{5 \cdot 9} + \frac{4 \cdot 5}{9 \cdot 5} = \frac{36}{45} + \frac{20}{45} = \frac{56}{45}$$

53. The LCD of $9x$ and 8 is $72x$.

$$\frac{5}{9x} + \frac{1}{8} = \frac{5 \cdot 8}{9x \cdot 8} + \frac{1 \cdot 9x}{8 \cdot 9x}$$
$$= \frac{40}{72x} + \frac{9x}{72x}$$
$$= \frac{40 + 9x}{72x}$$

55. The LCD of 5, 3, and 10 is 30.

$$-\frac{2}{5} + \frac{1}{3} - \frac{3}{10} = -\frac{2 \cdot 6}{5 \cdot 6} + \frac{1 \cdot 10}{3 \cdot 10} - \frac{3 \cdot 3}{10 \cdot 3}$$
$$= -\frac{12}{30} + \frac{10}{30} - \frac{9}{30}$$
$$= -\frac{11}{30}$$

57. The LCD of 2, 4, and 16 is 16.

$$\frac{x}{2}+\frac{x}{4}+\frac{2x}{16}=\frac{x\cdot 8}{2\cdot 8}+\frac{x\cdot 4}{4\cdot 4}+\frac{2x}{16}$$

$$=\frac{8x}{16}+\frac{4x}{16}+\frac{2x}{16}$$

$$=\frac{14x}{16}$$

$$=\frac{2\cdot 7\cdot x}{2\cdot 4}$$

$$=\frac{7x}{8}$$

59. The LCD of 5, 4, and 2 is 20.

$$\frac{6}{5}-\frac{3}{4}+\frac{1}{2}=\frac{6\cdot 4}{5\cdot 4}-\frac{3\cdot 5}{4\cdot 5}+\frac{1\cdot 10}{2\cdot 10}$$

$$=\frac{24}{20}-\frac{15}{20}+\frac{10}{20}$$

$$=\frac{19}{20}$$

61. The LCD of 12, 24, and 6 is 24.

$$-\frac{9}{12}+\frac{17}{24}-\frac{1}{6}=-\frac{9\cdot 2}{12\cdot 2}+\frac{17}{24}-\frac{1\cdot 4}{6\cdot 4}$$

$$=-\frac{18}{24}+\frac{17}{24}-\frac{4}{24}$$

$$=-\frac{5}{24}$$

63. The LCD of 8, 7, and 14 is 56.

$$\frac{3x}{8}+\frac{2x}{7}-\frac{5}{14}=\frac{3x\cdot 7}{8\cdot 7}+\frac{2x\cdot 8}{7\cdot 8}-\frac{5\cdot 4}{14\cdot 4}$$

$$=\frac{21x}{56}+\frac{16x}{56}-\frac{20}{56}$$

$$=\frac{37x-20}{56}$$

65. $\dfrac{2\cdot 10}{7\cdot 10}=\dfrac{20}{70}<\dfrac{21}{70}=\dfrac{3\cdot 7}{10\cdot 7}$

67. $\dfrac{5}{6}>-\dfrac{13}{15}$

A positive number is always greater than a negative number.

69. $-\dfrac{3\cdot 7}{4\cdot 7}=-\dfrac{21}{28}>\dfrac{-22}{28}=-\dfrac{11\cdot 2}{14\cdot 2}$

71. $x+y=\dfrac{1}{3}+\dfrac{3}{4}$

$$=\frac{1\cdot 4}{3\cdot 4}+\frac{3\cdot 3}{4\cdot 3}$$

$$=\frac{4}{12}+\frac{9}{12}$$

$$=\frac{13}{12}$$

73. $xy=\dfrac{1}{3}\cdot\dfrac{3}{4}=\dfrac{1\cdot 3}{3\cdot 4}=\dfrac{1}{4}$

75. $2y+x=2\cdot\dfrac{3}{4}+\dfrac{1}{3}$

$$=\frac{2}{1}\cdot\frac{3}{4}+\frac{1}{3}$$

$$=\frac{2\cdot 3}{1\cdot 2\cdot 2}+\frac{1}{3}$$

$$=\frac{3}{2}+\frac{1}{3}$$

$$=\frac{3\cdot 3}{2\cdot 3}+\frac{1\cdot 2}{3\cdot 2}$$

$$=\frac{9}{6}+\frac{2}{6}$$

$$=\frac{11}{6}$$

77.

$$x-\frac{1}{12}=\frac{5}{6}$$

$$x-\frac{1}{12}+\frac{1}{12}=\frac{5}{6}+\frac{1}{12}$$

$$x=\frac{5\cdot 2}{6\cdot 2}+\frac{1}{12}$$

$$x=\frac{10}{12}+\frac{1}{12}$$

$$=\frac{11}{12}$$

Check:

$$x-\frac{1}{12}=\frac{5}{6}$$

$$\frac{11}{12}-\frac{1}{12}=\frac{5}{6}$$

$$\frac{10}{12}=\frac{5}{6}$$

$$\frac{5\cdot 2}{6\cdot 2}=\frac{5}{6}$$

$$\frac{5}{6}=\frac{5}{6} \quad \text{True}$$

79.
$$\frac{2}{5} + y = -\frac{3}{10}$$

$$\frac{2}{5} + y - \frac{2}{5} = -\frac{3}{10} - \frac{2}{5}$$

$$y = -\frac{3}{10} - \frac{2 \cdot 2}{5 \cdot 2}$$

$$y = -\frac{3}{10} - \frac{4}{10}$$

$$= -\frac{7}{10}$$

Check:
$$\frac{2}{5} + y = -\frac{3}{10}$$

$$\frac{2}{5} + \left(-\frac{7}{10}\right) = -\frac{3}{10}$$

$$\frac{2 \cdot 2}{5 \cdot 2} - \frac{7}{10} = -\frac{3}{10}$$

$$\frac{4}{10} - \frac{7}{10} = -\frac{3}{10}$$

$$-\frac{3}{10} = -\frac{3}{10} \quad \text{True}$$

81.
$$7z + \frac{1}{16} - 6z = \frac{3}{4}$$

$$(7z - 6z) + \frac{1}{16} = \frac{3}{4}$$

$$z + \frac{1}{16} = \frac{3}{4}$$

$$z + \frac{1}{16} - \frac{1}{16} = \frac{3}{4} - \frac{1}{16}$$

$$z = \frac{3 \cdot 4}{4 \cdot 4} - \frac{1}{16}$$

$$z = \frac{12}{16} - \frac{1}{16}$$

$$= \frac{11}{16}$$

Check:
$$7z + \frac{1}{16} - 6z = \frac{3}{4}$$

$$7 \cdot \frac{11}{16} + \frac{1}{16} - 6 \cdot \frac{11}{16} = \frac{3}{4}$$

$$\frac{77}{16} + \frac{1}{16} - \frac{66}{16} = \frac{3}{4}$$

$$\frac{12}{16} = \frac{3}{4}$$

$$\frac{3 \cdot 4}{4 \cdot 4} = \frac{3}{4}$$

$$\frac{3}{4} = \frac{3}{4} \quad \text{True}$$

83.
$$-\frac{2}{9} = x - \frac{5}{6}$$

$$-\frac{2}{9} + \frac{5}{6} = x - \frac{5}{6} + \frac{5}{6}$$

$$-\frac{2 \cdot 2}{9 \cdot 2} + \frac{5 \cdot 3}{6 \cdot 3} = x$$

$$-\frac{4}{18} + \frac{15}{18} = x$$

$$\frac{11}{18} = x$$

Check:
$$-\frac{2}{9} = x - \frac{5}{6}$$

$$-\frac{2}{9} = \frac{11}{18} - \frac{5}{6}$$

$$-\frac{2}{9} = \frac{11}{18} - \frac{5 \cdot 3}{6 \cdot 3}$$

$$-\frac{2}{9} = \frac{11}{18} - \frac{15}{18}$$

$$-\frac{2}{9} = -\frac{4}{18}$$

$$-\frac{2}{9} = -\frac{2 \cdot 2}{2 \cdot 9}$$

$$-\frac{2}{9} = -\frac{2}{9} \quad \text{True}$$

85. Add the lengths of the 4 sides. A parallelogram has 2 sets of equal sides.
$$\frac{1}{3} + \frac{4}{5} + \frac{1}{3} + \frac{4}{5} = \frac{1 \cdot 5}{3 \cdot 5} + \frac{4 \cdot 3}{5 \cdot 3} + \frac{1 \cdot 5}{3 \cdot 5} + \frac{4 \cdot 3}{5 \cdot 3}$$

$$= \frac{5}{15} + \frac{12}{15} + \frac{5}{15} + \frac{12}{15}$$

$$= \frac{34}{15}$$

The perimeter is $\frac{34}{15}$ centimeters.

87. Add the lengths of the 4 sides.
$$\frac{1}{4} + \frac{1}{5} + \frac{1}{2} + \frac{3}{4} = \frac{1 \cdot 5}{4 \cdot 5} + \frac{1 \cdot 4}{5 \cdot 4} + \frac{1 \cdot 10}{2 \cdot 10} + \frac{3 \cdot 5}{4 \cdot 5}$$

$$= \frac{5}{20} + \frac{4}{20} + \frac{10}{20} + \frac{15}{20}$$

$$= \frac{34}{20}$$

$$= \frac{2 \cdot 17}{2 \cdot 10}$$

$$= \frac{17}{10}$$

The perimeter is $\frac{17}{10}$ meters.

89. Subtract $\dfrac{5}{264}$ from $\dfrac{1}{4}$.

$$\frac{1}{4} - \frac{5}{264} = \frac{1 \cdot 66}{4 \cdot 66} - \frac{5}{264} = \frac{66 - 5}{264} = \frac{61}{264}$$

A killer bee will chase a person $\dfrac{61}{264}$ mile farther.

91. $\dfrac{1}{2} + \dfrac{5}{8} + \dfrac{1}{4} = \dfrac{1 \cdot 4}{2 \cdot 4} + \dfrac{5}{8} + \dfrac{1 \cdot 2}{4 \cdot 2}$

$$= \frac{4}{8} + \frac{5}{8} + \frac{2}{8}$$

$$= \frac{11}{8}$$

The total length is $\dfrac{11}{8}$ in.

93. Subtract $\dfrac{4}{25}$ from $\dfrac{13}{20}$.

$$\frac{13}{20} - \frac{4}{25} = \frac{13 \cdot 5}{20 \cdot 5} - \frac{4 \cdot 4}{25 \cdot 4}$$

$$= \frac{65}{100} - \frac{16}{100}$$

$$= \frac{49}{100}$$

$\dfrac{49}{100}$ of students name math or science as their favorite subject.

95. Add the fractions for 1 or 2 times per week and 3 times per week.

$$\frac{23}{50} + \frac{31}{100} = \frac{23 \cdot 2}{50 \cdot 2} + \frac{31}{100} = \frac{46}{100} + \frac{81}{100} = \frac{77}{100}$$

$\dfrac{77}{100}$ of Americans eat pasta 1, 2, or 3 times per week.

97. Less than 50 miles per week includes 10 to 49 miles and less than 10 miles. Add these amounts.

$$\frac{23}{100} + \frac{3}{50} = \frac{23}{100} + \frac{3 \cdot 2}{50 \cdot 2} = \frac{23}{100} + \frac{6}{100} = \frac{29}{100}$$

$\dfrac{29}{100}$ of adults drive less than 50 miles in an average week.

99. $\left(\dfrac{5}{6}\right)^2 = \dfrac{5}{6} \cdot \dfrac{5}{6} = \dfrac{5 \cdot 5}{6 \cdot 6} = \dfrac{25}{36}$

101. $\left(-\dfrac{5}{6}\right)^2 = -\dfrac{5}{6} \cdot -\dfrac{5}{6} = \dfrac{5 \cdot 5}{6 \cdot 6} = \dfrac{25}{36}$

103. 57,236 rounded to the nearest hundred is 57,200.

105. 327 rounded to the nearest ten is 330.

107. $\dfrac{30}{55} + \dfrac{1000}{1760} = \dfrac{30 \cdot 32}{55 \cdot 32} + \dfrac{1000}{1760}$

$$= \frac{960}{1760} + \frac{1000}{1760}$$

$$= \frac{1960}{1760}$$

$$= \frac{49 \cdot 40}{44 \cdot 40}$$

$$= \frac{49}{44}$$

109. Answers may vary.

111.

$$x = \frac{5}{117} = \frac{71}{27}$$

$$x - \frac{5}{117} + \frac{5}{117} = \frac{71}{27} + \frac{5}{117}$$

$$x = \frac{71 \cdot 13}{27 \cdot 13} + \frac{5 \cdot 3}{117 \cdot 3}$$

$$x = \frac{923}{351} + \frac{15}{351}$$

$$x = \frac{938}{351}$$

113. $\dfrac{94}{579} + \dfrac{23}{193} = \dfrac{94}{579} + \dfrac{23 \cdot 3}{193 \cdot 3}$

$$= \frac{94}{579} + \frac{69}{579} = \frac{163}{579}$$

$\dfrac{163}{579}$ of the worlds land area is accounted for by North and South America.

115. $\dfrac{163}{579} \cdot 57,900,000 = \dfrac{163 \cdot 579 \cdot 100,000}{579}$

$$= 16,300,000$$

The combined land area of North and South America is 16,300,000 square miles.

117. Subtract $\dfrac{18}{193}$ from 1, which represents all of the land area added together.

$$1 - \frac{18}{193} = \frac{1 \cdot 193}{1 \cdot 193} - \frac{18}{193} = \frac{193}{193} - \frac{18}{193} = \frac{175}{193}$$

$\dfrac{175}{193}$ of the world's land area is inhabited.

119.

$$\text{military parks} = \frac{3 \cdot 3}{128 \cdot 3} = \frac{9}{384}$$

$$\text{national preserves} = \frac{1 \cdot 16}{24 \cdot 16} = \frac{16}{384}$$

Since $\dfrac{9}{384} < \dfrac{16}{384}$, the national preserves is the larger category.

121.

$$1 - 2 \text{ videos} = \frac{127 \cdot 2}{500 \cdot 2} = \frac{254}{1000}$$

$$3 - 4 \text{ videos} = \frac{31 \cdot 5}{200 \cdot 5} = \frac{155}{1000}$$

Since $\dfrac{254}{1000} > \dfrac{155}{1000}$, the 1 - 2 video rental category is larger.

Integrated Review

1. The figure has 4 equal parts. One part is shaded. The fraction shaded is $\dfrac{1}{4}$.

2. The figure has 6 equal parts. Three parts are shaded. The fraction shaded is $\dfrac{3}{6}$ or $\dfrac{1}{2}$.

3. Each figure has 4 equal parts. Seven parts are shaded. The fraction shaded is $\dfrac{7}{4}$.

4. Number of people getting less than 8 hours of sleep $\rightarrow \dfrac{73}{85}$
   Total number of people surveyed $\qquad\qquad\rightarrow$

5. $6 = 2 \cdot 3$

6. $70 = 2 \cdot 35 = 2 \cdot 5 \cdot 7$

7. $252 = 2 \cdot 126$
   $\quad = 2 \cdot 2 \cdot 63$
   $\quad = 2 \cdot 2 \cdot 7 \cdot 9$
   $\quad = 2 \cdot 2 \cdot 7 \cdot 3 \cdot 3$
   $\quad = 2^2 \cdot 3^2 \cdot 7$

8. $\dfrac{2}{14} = \dfrac{2}{2 \cdot 7} = \dfrac{1}{7}$

9. $\dfrac{20}{24} = \dfrac{4 \cdot 5}{4 \cdot 6} = \dfrac{5}{6}$

10. $\dfrac{18}{38} = \dfrac{2 \cdot 9}{2 \cdot 19} = \dfrac{9}{19}$

11. $\dfrac{42}{110} = \dfrac{2 \cdot 21}{2 \cdot 55} = \dfrac{21}{55}$

12. $\dfrac{32}{64} = \dfrac{32}{2 \cdot 32} = \dfrac{1}{2}$

13. $\dfrac{72}{80} = \dfrac{8 \cdot 9}{8 \cdot 10} = \dfrac{9}{10}$

14. Number of states that are not adjacent to any other state $\rightarrow \dfrac{2}{}$
Number of states $ \rightarrow \dfrac{}{50}$

$\dfrac{2}{50} = \dfrac{2}{2 \cdot 25} = \dfrac{1}{25}$

15. $\dfrac{1}{5} + \dfrac{3}{5} = \dfrac{1+3}{5} = \dfrac{4}{5}$

16. $\dfrac{1}{5} - \dfrac{3}{5} = \dfrac{1-3}{5} = \dfrac{-2}{5} = -\dfrac{2}{5}$

17. $\dfrac{1}{5} \cdot \dfrac{3}{5} = \dfrac{1 \cdot 3}{5 \cdot 5} = \dfrac{3}{25}$

18. $\dfrac{1}{5} \div \dfrac{3}{5} = \dfrac{1}{5} \cdot \dfrac{5}{3} = \dfrac{1 \cdot 5}{5 \cdot 3} = \dfrac{1}{3}$

19. $\dfrac{2}{3} \div \dfrac{5}{6} = \dfrac{2}{3} \cdot \dfrac{6}{5} = \dfrac{2 \cdot 6}{3 \cdot 5} = \dfrac{2 \cdot 2 \cdot 3}{3 \cdot 5} = \dfrac{4}{5}$

20. $\dfrac{2}{3} \cdot \dfrac{5}{6} = \dfrac{2 \cdot 5}{3 \cdot 6} = \dfrac{2 \cdot 5}{3 \cdot 2 \cdot 3} = \dfrac{5}{9}$

21. $\dfrac{2}{3} - \dfrac{5}{6} = \dfrac{2 \cdot 2}{3 \cdot 2} - \dfrac{5}{6} = \dfrac{4}{6} - \dfrac{5}{6} = \dfrac{4-5}{6} = \dfrac{-1}{6} = -\dfrac{1}{6}$

22. $\dfrac{2}{3} + \dfrac{5}{6} = \dfrac{2 \cdot 2}{3 \cdot 2} + \dfrac{5}{6}$
$\phantom{\dfrac{2}{3} + \dfrac{5}{6}} = \dfrac{4}{6} + \dfrac{5}{6}$
$\phantom{\dfrac{2}{3} + \dfrac{5}{6}} = \dfrac{4+5}{6}$
$\phantom{\dfrac{2}{3} + \dfrac{5}{6}} = \dfrac{9}{6}$
$\phantom{\dfrac{2}{3} + \dfrac{5}{6}} = \dfrac{3 \cdot 3}{3 \cdot 2}$
$\phantom{\dfrac{2}{3} + \dfrac{5}{6}} = \dfrac{3}{2}$

23. $-\dfrac{1}{7} \cdot -\dfrac{7}{18} = \dfrac{1 \cdot 7}{7 \cdot 18} = \dfrac{1}{18}$

24. $-\dfrac{4}{9} \cdot -\dfrac{3}{7} = \dfrac{4 \cdot 3}{9 \cdot 7} = \dfrac{4 \cdot 3}{3 \cdot 3 \cdot 7} = \dfrac{4}{21}$

25. $-\dfrac{7}{8} \div 6 = -\dfrac{7}{8} \div \dfrac{6}{1} = -\dfrac{7}{8} \cdot \dfrac{1}{6} = -\dfrac{7 \cdot 1}{8 \cdot 6} = -\dfrac{7}{48}$

26. $-\dfrac{9}{10} \div 5 = -\dfrac{9}{10} \div \dfrac{5}{1} = -\dfrac{9}{10} \cdot \dfrac{1}{5} = -\dfrac{9 \cdot 1}{10 \cdot 5} = -\dfrac{9}{50}$

27. $\dfrac{7}{8} + \dfrac{1}{20} = \dfrac{7 \cdot 5}{8 \cdot 5} + \dfrac{1 \cdot 2}{20 \cdot 2} = \dfrac{35}{40} + \dfrac{2}{40} = \dfrac{37}{40}$

28. $\dfrac{5}{12} - \dfrac{1}{9} = \dfrac{5 \cdot 3}{12 \cdot 3} - \dfrac{1 \cdot 4}{9 \cdot 4} = \dfrac{15}{36} - \dfrac{4}{36} = \dfrac{11}{36}$

29. $\dfrac{9}{11} - \dfrac{2}{3} = \dfrac{9 \cdot 3}{11 \cdot 3} - \dfrac{2 \cdot 11}{3 \cdot 11} = \dfrac{27}{33} - \dfrac{22}{33} = \dfrac{5}{33}$

30. $\dfrac{2}{9} + \dfrac{1}{18} = \dfrac{2 \cdot 2}{9 \cdot 2} + \dfrac{1}{18} = \dfrac{4}{18} + \dfrac{1}{18} = \dfrac{5}{18}$

31. $\dfrac{2}{9} + \dfrac{1}{18} + \dfrac{1}{3} = \dfrac{2 \cdot 2}{9 \cdot 2} + \dfrac{1}{18} + \dfrac{1 \cdot 6}{3 \cdot 6}$
$\phantom{\dfrac{2}{9} + \dfrac{1}{18} + \dfrac{1}{3}} = \dfrac{4}{18} + \dfrac{1}{18} + \dfrac{6}{18}$
$\phantom{\dfrac{2}{9} + \dfrac{1}{18} + \dfrac{1}{3}} = \dfrac{11}{18}$

32. $\dfrac{3}{10} + \dfrac{1}{5} + \dfrac{6}{25} = \dfrac{3 \cdot 5}{10 \cdot 5} + \dfrac{1 \cdot 10}{5 \cdot 10} + \dfrac{6 \cdot 2}{25 \cdot 2}$
$\phantom{\dfrac{3}{10} + \dfrac{1}{5} + \dfrac{6}{25}} = \dfrac{15}{50} + \dfrac{10}{50} + \dfrac{12}{50}$
$\phantom{\dfrac{3}{10} + \dfrac{1}{5} + \dfrac{6}{25}} = \dfrac{37}{50}$

34. $\dfrac{7}{8} - \left(\dfrac{1}{16} + \dfrac{1}{16}\right) = \dfrac{7}{8} - \dfrac{2}{16}$

$\phantom{\dfrac{7}{8} - \left(\dfrac{1}{16} + \dfrac{1}{16}\right)} = \dfrac{7}{8} - \dfrac{1}{8}$

$\phantom{\dfrac{7}{8} - \left(\dfrac{1}{16} + \dfrac{1}{16}\right)} = \dfrac{6}{8}$

$\phantom{\dfrac{7}{8} - \left(\dfrac{1}{16} + \dfrac{1}{16}\right)} = \dfrac{3}{4}$

The inner diameter is $\dfrac{3}{4}$ ft.

Section 4.6

Practice Problems

1. $\dfrac{\frac{7y}{10}}{\frac{1}{5}} = \dfrac{7y}{10} \div \dfrac{1}{5} = \dfrac{7y}{10} \cdot \dfrac{5}{1} = \dfrac{7 \cdot y \cdot 5}{2 \cdot 5} = \dfrac{7y}{2}$

2. $\dfrac{\frac{1}{2} + \frac{1}{6}}{\frac{3}{4} - \frac{2}{3}} = \dfrac{\frac{1 \cdot 3}{2 \cdot 3} + \frac{1}{6}}{\frac{3 \cdot 3}{4 \cdot 3} - \frac{2 \cdot 4}{3 \cdot 4}}$

$\phantom{\dfrac{\frac{1}{2} + \frac{1}{6}}{\frac{3}{4} - \frac{2}{3}}} = \dfrac{\frac{3}{6} + \frac{1}{6}}{\frac{9}{12} + \frac{8}{12}}$

$\phantom{\dfrac{\frac{1}{2} + \frac{1}{6}}{\frac{3}{4} - \frac{2}{3}}} = \dfrac{\frac{4}{6}}{\frac{1}{12}}$

$\phantom{\dfrac{\frac{1}{2} + \frac{1}{6}}{\frac{3}{4} - \frac{2}{3}}} = \dfrac{4}{6} \div \dfrac{1}{12}$

$\phantom{\dfrac{\frac{1}{2} + \frac{1}{6}}{\frac{3}{4} - \frac{2}{3}}} = \dfrac{4}{6} \cdot \dfrac{12}{1}$

$\phantom{\dfrac{\frac{1}{2} + \frac{1}{6}}{\frac{3}{4} - \frac{2}{3}}} = \dfrac{4 \cdot 6 \cdot 2}{6 \cdot 1}$

$\phantom{\dfrac{\frac{1}{2} + \frac{1}{6}}{\frac{3}{4} - \frac{2}{3}}} = \dfrac{8}{1}$ or 8

3. $\dfrac{\frac{1}{2} + \frac{1}{6}}{\frac{3}{4} - \frac{2}{3}} = \dfrac{12\left(\frac{1}{2} + \frac{1}{6}\right)}{12\left(\frac{3}{4} - \frac{2}{3}\right)}$

$\phantom{\dfrac{\frac{1}{2} + \frac{1}{6}}{\frac{3}{4} - \frac{2}{3}}} = \dfrac{\left(12 \cdot \frac{1}{2}\right) + \left(12 \cdot \frac{1}{6}\right)}{\left(12 \cdot \frac{3}{4}\right) - \left(12 \cdot \frac{2}{3}\right)}$

$\phantom{\dfrac{\frac{1}{2} + \frac{1}{6}}{\frac{3}{4} - \frac{2}{3}}} = \dfrac{6 + 2}{9 - 8}$

$\phantom{\dfrac{\frac{1}{2} + \frac{1}{6}}{\frac{3}{4} - \frac{2}{3}}} = \dfrac{8}{1}$ or 8

4. $\dfrac{\frac{3}{4}}{\frac{x}{5} - 1} = \dfrac{20\left(\frac{3}{4}\right)}{20\left(\frac{x}{5} - 1\right)}$

$\phantom{\dfrac{\frac{3}{4}}{\frac{x}{5} - 1}} = \dfrac{20 \cdot \frac{3}{4}}{\left(20 \cdot \frac{x}{5}\right) - (20 \cdot 1)}$

$\phantom{\dfrac{\frac{3}{4}}{\frac{x}{5} - 1}} = \dfrac{15}{4x - 20}$

5. $\left(2 - \dfrac{2}{3}\right)^3$:

First evaluate $2 - \dfrac{2}{3}$.

$2 - \dfrac{2}{3} = \dfrac{2}{1} - \dfrac{2}{3} = \dfrac{2 \cdot 3}{1 \cdot 3} - \dfrac{2}{3} = \dfrac{6}{3} - \dfrac{2}{3} = \dfrac{4}{3}$

Next, evaluate $\left(\dfrac{4}{3}\right)^3$.

$\left(\dfrac{4}{3}\right)^3 = \dfrac{4}{3} \cdot \dfrac{4}{3} \cdot \dfrac{4}{3} = \dfrac{4 \cdot 4 \cdot 4}{3 \cdot 3 \cdot 3} = \dfrac{64}{27}$

6. $\left(-\dfrac{1}{2} + \dfrac{1}{5}\right)\left(\dfrac{7}{8} + \dfrac{1}{8}\right) = \left(\dfrac{-1 \cdot 5}{2 \cdot 5} + \dfrac{1 \cdot 2}{5 \cdot 2}\right)\left(\dfrac{8}{8}\right)$

$\phantom{\left(-\dfrac{1}{2} + \dfrac{1}{5}\right)\left(\dfrac{7}{8} + \dfrac{1}{8}\right)} = \left(\dfrac{-5}{10} + \dfrac{2}{10}\right)(1)$

$\phantom{\left(-\dfrac{1}{2} + \dfrac{1}{5}\right)\left(\dfrac{7}{8} + \dfrac{1}{8}\right)} = \left(-\dfrac{3}{10}\right)(1)$

$\phantom{\left(-\dfrac{1}{2} + \dfrac{1}{5}\right)\left(\dfrac{7}{8} + \dfrac{1}{8}\right)} = -\dfrac{3}{10}$

7. $-\dfrac{3}{5} - xy = -\dfrac{3}{5} - \left(\dfrac{3}{10} \cdot \dfrac{2}{3}\right)$

$\phantom{-\dfrac{3}{5} - xy} = -\dfrac{3}{5} - \left(\dfrac{3 \cdot 2}{2 \cdot 5 \cdot 3}\right)$

$\phantom{-\dfrac{3}{5} - xy} = -\dfrac{3}{5} - \dfrac{1}{5}$

$\phantom{-\dfrac{3}{5} - xy} = \dfrac{-3 - 1}{5}$

$\phantom{-\dfrac{3}{5} - xy} = \dfrac{-4}{5}$

$\phantom{-\dfrac{3}{5} - xy} = -\dfrac{4}{5}$

Exercise Set 4.6

1. $\dfrac{\frac{1}{8}}{\frac{3}{4}} = \dfrac{1}{8} \div \dfrac{3}{4} = \dfrac{1}{8} \cdot \dfrac{4}{3} = \dfrac{1 \cdot 4}{2 \cdot 4 \cdot 3} = \dfrac{1}{6}$

3. $\dfrac{\frac{9}{10}}{\frac{21}{10}} = \dfrac{9}{10} \div \dfrac{21}{10} = \dfrac{9}{10} \cdot \dfrac{10}{21} = \dfrac{3 \cdot 3 \cdot 10}{10 \cdot 3 \cdot 7} = \dfrac{3}{7}$

5. $\dfrac{\frac{2x}{27}}{\frac{4}{9}} = \dfrac{2x}{27} \div \dfrac{4}{9} = \dfrac{2x}{27} \cdot \dfrac{9}{4} = \dfrac{2 \cdot x \cdot 3 \cdot 3}{3 \cdot 3 \cdot 3 \cdot 2 \cdot 2} = \dfrac{x}{6}$

7. $\dfrac{\frac{3}{4}+\frac{2}{5}}{\frac{1}{2}+\frac{3}{5}} = \dfrac{20\left(\frac{3}{4}+\frac{2}{5}\right)}{20\left(\frac{1}{2}+\frac{3}{5}\right)} = \dfrac{15+8}{10+12} = \dfrac{23}{22}$

9. $\dfrac{\frac{3x}{4}}{5-\frac{1}{8}} = \dfrac{8 \cdot \left(\frac{3x}{4}\right)}{8 \cdot \left(\frac{5}{1}-\frac{1}{8}\right)}$

$\quad = \dfrac{6x}{8 \cdot \left(\frac{5}{1}\right) - 8\left(\frac{1}{8}\right)}$

$\quad = \dfrac{6x}{40-1}$

$\quad = \dfrac{6x}{39}$

$\quad = \dfrac{3 \cdot 2 \cdot x}{3 \cdot 13}$

$\quad = \dfrac{2x}{13}$

11. $\dfrac{1}{5} + \dfrac{1}{3} \cdot \dfrac{1}{4} = \dfrac{1}{5} + \dfrac{1}{12}$

$\quad = \dfrac{1 \cdot 12}{5 \cdot 12} + \dfrac{1 \cdot 5}{12 \cdot 5}$

$\quad = \dfrac{12}{60} + \dfrac{5}{60}$

$\quad = \dfrac{17}{60}$

13. $\dfrac{5}{6} \div \dfrac{1}{3} \cdot \dfrac{1}{4} = \dfrac{5}{6} \cdot \dfrac{3}{1} \cdot \dfrac{1}{4}$

$\quad = \dfrac{5 \cdot 3}{2 \cdot 3} \cdot \dfrac{1}{4}$

$\quad = \dfrac{5}{2} \cdot \dfrac{1}{4} = \dfrac{5}{8}$

15. $2^2 - \left(\dfrac{1}{3}\right)^2 = 4 - \dfrac{1}{9}$

$\quad = \dfrac{4 \cdot 9}{1 \cdot 9} - \dfrac{1}{9}$

$\quad = \dfrac{36}{9} - \dfrac{1}{9}$

$\quad = \dfrac{35}{9}$

17. $\left(\dfrac{2}{9}+\dfrac{4}{9}\right)\left(\dfrac{1}{3}-\dfrac{9}{10}\right) = \left(\dfrac{6}{9}\right)\left(\dfrac{1 \cdot 10}{3 \cdot 10} - \dfrac{9 \cdot 3}{10 \cdot 3}\right)$

$\quad = \left(\dfrac{6}{9}\right)\left(\dfrac{10}{30} - \dfrac{27}{30}\right)$

$\quad = \dfrac{6}{9} \cdot -\dfrac{17}{30}$

$\quad = -\dfrac{6 \cdot 17}{9 \cdot 5 \cdot 6}$

$\quad = -\dfrac{17}{45}$

19. $\left(\dfrac{7}{8}-\dfrac{1}{2}\right) \div \dfrac{3}{11} = \left(\dfrac{7}{8} - \dfrac{1 \cdot 4}{2 \cdot 4}\right) \div \dfrac{3}{11}$

$\quad = \left(\dfrac{7}{8} - \dfrac{4}{8}\right) \cdot \dfrac{11}{3}$

$\quad = \dfrac{3}{8} \cdot \dfrac{11}{3}$

$\quad = \dfrac{3 \cdot 11}{8 \cdot 3}$

$\quad = \dfrac{11}{8}$

21. $2 \cdot \left(\dfrac{1}{4}+\dfrac{1}{5}\right) + 2 = 2 \cdot \left(\dfrac{1 \cdot 5}{4 \cdot 5} + \dfrac{1 \cdot 4}{5 \cdot 4}\right) + 2$

$\quad = 2 \cdot \left(\dfrac{5}{20} + \dfrac{4}{20}\right) + 2$

$\quad = 2\left(\dfrac{9}{20}\right) + 2$

$\quad = \dfrac{2 \cdot 9}{2 \cdot 10} + 2$

$\quad = \dfrac{9}{10} + \dfrac{2 \cdot 10}{1 \cdot 10}$

$\quad = \dfrac{9}{10} + \dfrac{20}{10}$

$\quad = \dfrac{29}{10}$

23.
$$\left(\frac{3}{4}\right)^2 \div \left(\frac{3}{4}-\frac{1}{12}\right) = \left(\frac{3}{4}\right)^2 \div \left(\frac{3\cdot 3}{4\cdot 3}-\frac{1}{12}\right)$$
$$= \left(\frac{3}{4}\right)^2 \div \left(\frac{9}{12}-\frac{1}{12}\right)$$
$$= \left(\frac{3}{4}\right)^2 \div \frac{8}{12}$$
$$= \frac{9}{16}\cdot\frac{12}{8}$$
$$= \frac{9\cdot 3\cdot 4}{4\cdot 4\cdot 8}$$
$$= \frac{27}{32}$$

25.
$$\left(\frac{2}{3}-\frac{5}{9}\right)^2 = \left(\frac{2\cdot 3}{3\cdot 3}-\frac{5}{9}\right)^2$$
$$= \left(\frac{6}{9}-\frac{5}{9}\right)^2$$
$$= \left(\frac{1}{9}\right)^2$$
$$= \frac{1}{81}$$

27.
$$\left(\frac{3}{4}+\frac{1}{8}\right)^2 - \left(\frac{1}{2}+\frac{1}{8}\right)$$
$$= \left(\frac{3\cdot 2}{4\cdot 2}+\frac{1}{8}\right)^2 - \left(\frac{1\cdot 4}{2\cdot 4}+\frac{1}{8}\right)$$
$$= \left(\frac{6}{8}+\frac{1}{8}\right)^2 - \left(\frac{4}{8}+\frac{1}{8}\right)$$
$$= \left(\frac{7}{8}\right)^2 - \frac{5}{8}$$
$$= \frac{49}{64}-\frac{5\cdot 8}{8\cdot 8}$$
$$= \frac{49}{64}-\frac{40}{64}$$
$$= \frac{9}{64}$$

29.
$$5y-z = 5\left(\frac{2}{5}\right)-\left(\frac{5}{6}\right)$$
$$= 2-\frac{5}{6}$$
$$= \frac{2\cdot 6}{6}-\frac{5}{6}$$
$$= \frac{12}{6}-\frac{5}{6}$$
$$= \frac{7}{6}$$

31.
$$\frac{x}{z} = \frac{-\frac{1}{3}}{\frac{5}{6}}$$
$$= -\frac{1}{3}\div\frac{5}{6}$$
$$= -\frac{1}{3}\cdot\frac{6}{5}$$
$$= -\frac{1\cdot 2\cdot 3}{3\cdot 5}$$
$$= -\frac{2}{5}$$

33.
$$x^2-yz = \left(-\frac{1}{3}\right)^2 - \left(\frac{2}{5}\right)\left(\frac{5}{6}\right)$$
$$= \frac{1}{9} - \left(\frac{2}{5}\right)\left(\frac{5}{6}\right)$$
$$= \frac{1}{9} - \frac{2\cdot 5}{5\cdot 2\cdot 3}$$
$$= \frac{1}{9} - \frac{1}{3}$$
$$= \frac{1}{9} - \frac{3}{9}$$
$$= -\frac{2}{9}$$

35.
$$\frac{\frac{5}{24}}{\frac{1}{12}} = \frac{5}{24}\div\frac{1}{12} = \frac{5}{24}\cdot\frac{12}{1} = \frac{5\cdot 12}{2\cdot 12} = \frac{5}{2}$$

37.
$$\left(\frac{3}{2}\right)^3 + \left(\frac{1}{2}\right)^3 = \frac{27}{8}+\frac{1}{8} = \frac{28}{8} = \frac{7\cdot 4}{2\cdot 4} = \frac{7}{2}$$

39.
$$\left(-\frac{1}{3}\right)^2 + \frac{1}{3} = \frac{1}{9}+\frac{1}{3} = \frac{1}{9}+\frac{3}{9} = \frac{4}{9}$$

41.
$$\frac{2+\frac{1}{6}}{1-\frac{4}{3}} = \frac{6\left(2+\frac{1}{6}\right)}{6\left(1-\frac{4}{3}\right)} = \frac{12+1}{6-8} = \frac{13}{-2} = -\frac{13}{2}$$

43.
$$\left(1-\frac{2}{5}\right)^2 = \left(\frac{5}{5}-\frac{2}{5}\right)^2 = \left(\frac{3}{5}\right)^2 = \frac{9}{25}$$

45.
$$\left(\frac{3}{4}-1\right)\left(\frac{1}{8}+\frac{1}{2}\right)=\left(\frac{3}{4}-\frac{4}{4}\right)\left(\frac{1}{8}+\frac{4}{8}\right)$$
$$=\left(-\frac{1}{4}\right)\left(\frac{5}{8}\right)$$
$$=-\frac{1\cdot 5}{4\cdot 8}$$
$$=-\frac{5}{32}$$

47. $\left(-\frac{2}{9}-\frac{7}{9}\right)^4=\left(-\frac{9}{9}\right)^4=(-1)^4=1$

49.
$$\frac{\left(\frac{1}{2}-\frac{3}{8}\right)}{\left(\frac{3}{4}+\frac{1}{2}\right)}=\frac{8\left(\frac{1}{2}-\frac{3}{8}\right)}{8\left(\frac{3}{4}+\frac{1}{2}\right)}$$
$$=\frac{8\cdot\frac{1}{2}-8\cdot\frac{3}{8}}{8\cdot\frac{3}{4}+8\cdot\frac{1}{2}}$$
$$=\frac{4-3}{6+4}$$
$$=\frac{1}{10}$$

51.
$$\left(\frac{3}{4}\div\frac{6}{5}\right)-\left(\frac{3}{4}\cdot\frac{6}{5}\right)=\left(\frac{3}{4}\cdot\frac{5}{6}\right)-\left(\frac{3}{2\cdot 2}\cdot\frac{2\cdot 3}{5}\right)$$
$$=\frac{3\cdot 5}{4\cdot 3\cdot 2}-\frac{3\cdot 2\cdot 3}{2\cdot 2\cdot 5}$$
$$=\frac{5}{8}-\frac{9}{10}$$
$$=\frac{5\cdot 5}{8\cdot 5}-\frac{9\cdot 4}{10\cdot 4}$$
$$=\frac{25}{40}-\frac{36}{40}$$
$$=-\frac{11}{40}$$

53.
$$\frac{\frac{x}{3}+2}{5+\frac{1}{3}}=\frac{3\left(\frac{x}{3}+2\right)}{3\left(5+\frac{1}{3}\right)}$$
$$=\frac{3\cdot\frac{x}{3}+3\cdot 2}{3\cdot 5+3\cdot\frac{1}{3}}$$
$$=\frac{x+6}{15+1}$$
$$=\frac{x+6}{16}$$

55. $2^3=2\cdot 2\cdot 2=8$

57. $5^2=5\cdot 5=25$

59. $\frac{1}{3}(3x)=\frac{1}{3}\cdot\frac{3x}{1}=\frac{1\cdot 3\cdot x}{3\cdot 1}=x$

61. $\frac{2}{3}\left(\frac{3}{2}a\right)=\frac{2}{3}\cdot\frac{3}{2}\cdot\frac{a}{1}=\frac{2\cdot 3\cdot a}{3\cdot 2\cdot 1}=\frac{a}{1}=a$

63. No; answers may vary.

65.
$$\frac{2+x}{y}=\frac{2+\frac{3}{4}}{-\frac{4}{7}}$$
$$=\frac{28\left(2+\frac{3}{4}\right)}{28\left(-\frac{4}{7}\right)}$$
$$=\frac{28\cdot 2+28\cdot\frac{3}{4}}{-16}$$
$$=\frac{56+21}{-16}$$
$$=-\frac{77}{16}$$

67.
$$x^2+7y=\left(\frac{3}{4}\right)^2+7\left(-\frac{4}{7}\right)$$
$$=\frac{9}{16}+\frac{7}{1}\cdot-\frac{4}{7}$$
$$=\frac{9}{16}+\left(-\frac{7\cdot 4}{1\cdot 7}\right)$$
$$=\frac{9}{16}-\frac{4}{1}$$
$$=\frac{9}{16}-\frac{4\cdot 16}{1\cdot 16}$$
$$=\frac{9}{16}-\frac{64}{16}$$
$$=-\frac{55}{16}$$

69. $\frac{\frac{1}{2}+\frac{3}{4}}{2}=\frac{4\left(\frac{1}{2}+\frac{3}{4}\right)}{4\cdot 2}=\frac{4\cdot\frac{1}{2}+4\cdot\frac{3}{4}}{8}=\frac{2+3}{8}=\frac{5}{8}$

71.
$$\frac{\frac{1}{4}+\frac{2}{14}}{2}=\frac{28\left(\frac{1}{4}+\frac{2}{14}\right)}{28\cdot 2}$$
$$=\frac{28\cdot\left(\frac{1}{4}\right)+28\cdot\left(\frac{2}{14}\right)}{56}$$
$$=\frac{7+4}{56}$$
$$=\frac{11}{56}$$

73. The average is halfway between a and b.

75. False, the average of two numbers is between the two numbers.

77. False, consider $-\dfrac{2}{3}+\dfrac{1}{3}=-\dfrac{1}{3}$.

79. True, consider $\dfrac{9}{4}-\dfrac{5}{4}=\dfrac{4}{4}=1$.

81. no; answer may vary.

Section 4.7

Practice Problems

1. $\dfrac{1}{5}y=2$

$5\cdot\dfrac{1}{2}y=5\cdot2$

$1\cdot y=10$ or $y=10$

2. $\dfrac{5}{7}b=25$

$\dfrac{7}{5}\cdot\dfrac{5}{7}b=\dfrac{7}{5}\cdot25$

$1b=\dfrac{7\cdot25}{5}$

$b=35$

3. $-\dfrac{7}{10}x=\dfrac{2}{5}$

$-\dfrac{10}{7}\cdot-\dfrac{7}{10}x=-\dfrac{10}{7}\cdot\dfrac{2}{5}$

$1x=-\dfrac{10\cdot2}{7\cdot5}$

$x=-\dfrac{4}{7}$

4. $5x=-\dfrac{3}{4}$

$\dfrac{1}{5}\cdot5x=\dfrac{1}{5}\cdot-\dfrac{3}{4}$

$1x=-\dfrac{1\cdot3}{5\cdot4}$

$x=-\dfrac{3}{20}$

5. $\dfrac{y}{8}+\dfrac{3}{4}=2$

$8\left(\dfrac{y}{8}+\dfrac{3}{4}\right)=8(2)$

$8\left(\dfrac{y}{8}\right)+8\left(\dfrac{3}{4}\right)=8(2)$

$y+6=16$

$y+6+(-6)=16+(-6)$

$y=10$

6. $\dfrac{x}{5}-x=\dfrac{1}{5}$

$5\left(\dfrac{x}{5}-x\right)=5\cdot\dfrac{1}{5}$

$5\left(\dfrac{x}{5}\right)-5(x)=5\cdot\dfrac{1}{5}$

$x-5x=1$

$-4x=1$

$\dfrac{-4x}{-4}=\dfrac{1}{-4}$

$x=-\dfrac{1}{4}$

7. $\dfrac{y}{2}=\dfrac{y}{5}+\dfrac{3}{2}$

$10\left(\dfrac{y}{2}\right)=10\left(\dfrac{y}{5}+\dfrac{3}{2}\right)$

$10\left(\dfrac{y}{2}\right)=10\left(\dfrac{y}{5}\right)+10\left(\dfrac{3}{2}\right)$

$5y=2y+15$

$5y-2y=2y+15-2y$

$3y=15$

$\dfrac{3y}{3}=\dfrac{15}{3}$

$y=5$

8. $\dfrac{9}{10}-\dfrac{y}{3}=\dfrac{9\cdot3}{10\cdot3}-\dfrac{y\cdot10}{3\cdot10}=\dfrac{27}{30}-\dfrac{10y}{30}=\dfrac{27-10y}{30}$

Exercise Set 4.7

1. $7x=2$

$\dfrac{7x}{7}=\dfrac{2}{7}$

$x=\dfrac{2}{7}$

3. $\dfrac{1}{4}x=3$

$4\dfrac{1}{4}x=4\cdot3$

$x=12$

5. $\dfrac{2}{9}y=-6$

$\dfrac{9}{2}\cdot\dfrac{2}{9}y=\dfrac{9}{2}\cdot-6$

$y=-27$

7.
$$-\frac{4}{9}z = -\frac{3}{2}$$
$$-\frac{9}{4}\cdot-\frac{4}{9}z = -\frac{9}{4}\cdot-\frac{3}{2}$$
$$z = \frac{27}{8}$$

9.
$$7a = \frac{1}{3}$$
$$\frac{1}{7}\cdot 7a = \frac{1}{7}\cdot\frac{1}{3}$$
$$a = \frac{1}{21}$$

11.
$$-3x = -\frac{6}{11}$$
$$-\frac{1}{3}\cdot-3x = -\frac{1}{3}\cdot-\frac{6}{11}$$
$$x = \frac{1\cdot 6}{3\cdot 11}$$
$$x = \frac{2\cdot 3}{3\cdot 11}$$
$$x = \frac{2}{11}$$

13. Multiply both sides of the equation by 3.
$$\frac{x}{3}+2 = \frac{7}{3}$$
$$3\left(\frac{x}{3}+2\right) = 3\cdot\frac{7}{3}$$
$$x+6 = 7$$
$$x+6-6 = 7-6$$
$$x = 1$$

15. Multiply both sides of the equation by the LCD of 5 and 10, 10.
$$\frac{x}{5}-\frac{5}{10} = 1$$
$$10\left(\frac{x}{5}-\frac{5}{10}\right) = 10\cdot 1$$
$$2x-5 = 10$$
$$2x-5+5 = 10+5$$
$$2x = 15$$
$$\frac{2x}{2} = \frac{15}{2}$$
$$x = \frac{15}{2}$$

17. Multiply both sides of the equation by the LCD of 2, 5, and 10: 10.
$$\frac{1}{2}-\frac{3}{5} = \frac{x}{10}$$
$$10\left(\frac{1}{2}-\frac{3}{5}\right) = 10\left(\frac{x}{10}\right)$$
$$5-6 = x$$
$$-1 = x$$

19. Multiply both sides of the equation by the LCD of 3 and 5, 15.
$$\frac{x}{3} = \frac{x}{5}-2$$
$$15\left(\frac{x}{3}\right) = 15\left(\frac{x}{5}-2\right)$$
$$5x = 3x-30$$
$$5x-3x = 3x-30-3x$$
$$2x = -30$$
$$\frac{2x}{2} = -\frac{30}{2}$$
$$x = -15$$

21. $\dfrac{x}{7}-\dfrac{4}{3} = \dfrac{x\cdot 3}{7\cdot 3}-\dfrac{4\cdot 7}{3\cdot 7} = \dfrac{3x}{21}-\dfrac{28}{21}$
$$= \frac{3x-28}{21}$$

23. $\dfrac{y}{2}+5 = \dfrac{y}{2}+\dfrac{5\cdot 2}{1\cdot 2} = \dfrac{y}{2}+\dfrac{10}{2} = \dfrac{y+10}{2}$

25. $\dfrac{3x}{10}+\dfrac{x}{6} = \dfrac{3x\cdot 3}{10\cdot 3}+\dfrac{x\cdot 5}{6\cdot 5}$
$$= \frac{9x}{30}+\frac{5x}{30}$$
$$= \frac{14x}{30}$$
$$= \frac{2\cdot 7x}{2\cdot 15x}$$
$$= \frac{7x}{15}$$

27.
$$\frac{3}{8}x = \frac{1}{2}$$
$$\frac{8}{3}\cdot\frac{3}{8}x = \frac{8}{3}\cdot\frac{1}{2}$$
$$x = \frac{2\cdot 4}{3\cdot 2}$$
$$x = \frac{4}{3}$$

29. $\dfrac{2}{3} - \dfrac{x}{5} = \dfrac{4}{15}$

$$15\left(\dfrac{2}{3} - \dfrac{x}{5}\right) = 15\left(\dfrac{4}{15}\right)$$
$$10 - 3x = 4$$
$$10 - 10 - 3x = 4 - 10$$
$$-3x = -6$$
$$\dfrac{-3x}{-3} = \dfrac{-6}{-3}$$
$$x = 2$$

31. $\dfrac{9}{14} z = \dfrac{27}{20}$

$$\left(\dfrac{14}{9}\right)\left(\dfrac{9}{14}\right)z = \left(\dfrac{14}{9}\right)\left(\dfrac{27}{20}\right)$$
$$z = \dfrac{2 \cdot 7 \cdot 9 \cdot 3}{9 \cdot 2 \cdot 10}$$
$$= \dfrac{7 \cdot 3}{10}$$
$$= \dfrac{21}{10}$$

33. $-3m - 5m = \dfrac{4}{7}$

$$-8m = \dfrac{4}{7}$$
$$\left(-\dfrac{1}{8}\right)(-8m) = \left(-\dfrac{1}{8}\right)\left(\dfrac{4}{7}\right)$$
$$m = -\dfrac{1 \cdot 4}{2 \cdot 4 \cdot 7}$$
$$m = -\dfrac{1}{14}$$

35. $\dfrac{x}{4} + 1 = \dfrac{1}{4}$

$$4\left(\dfrac{x}{4} + 1\right) = 4 \cdot \dfrac{1}{4}$$
$$x + 4 = 1$$
$$x + 4 - 4 = 1 - 4$$
$$x = -3$$

37. $\dfrac{1}{5} y = 10$

$$5\left(\dfrac{1}{5} y\right) = 5 \cdot 10$$
$$y = 50$$

39. $\dfrac{5}{9} - \dfrac{2}{3} = \dfrac{5}{9} - \dfrac{2 \cdot 3}{3 \cdot 3} = \dfrac{5}{9} - \dfrac{6}{9} = -\dfrac{1}{9}$

41. $-\dfrac{3}{4} x = \dfrac{9}{2}$

$$-\dfrac{4}{3} \cdot -\dfrac{3}{4} x = -\dfrac{4}{3} \cdot \dfrac{9}{2}$$
$$x = -\dfrac{2 \cdot 2 \cdot 3 \cdot 3}{3 \cdot 2}$$
$$x = -6$$

43. $\dfrac{x}{2} - x = -2$

$$2\left(\dfrac{x}{2} - x\right) = 2(-2)$$
$$x - 2x = -4$$
$$-x = -4$$
$$\dfrac{-x}{-1} = \dfrac{-4}{-1}$$
$$x = 4$$

45. $-\dfrac{5}{8} y = \dfrac{3}{16} - \dfrac{9}{16}$

$$-\dfrac{5}{8} y = -\dfrac{6}{16}$$
$$-\dfrac{5}{8} y = -\dfrac{2 \cdot 3}{2 \cdot 8}$$
$$-\dfrac{5}{8} y = -\dfrac{3}{8}$$
$$\left(-\dfrac{8}{5}\right)\left(-\dfrac{5}{8} y\right) = \left(-\dfrac{8}{5}\right)\left(-\dfrac{3}{8}\right)$$
$$y = \dfrac{8 \cdot 3}{5 \cdot 8}$$
$$y = \dfrac{3}{5}$$

47. $17x - 25x = \dfrac{1}{3}$

$$-8x = \dfrac{1}{3}$$
$$\left(-\dfrac{1}{8}\right)(-8x) = \left(-\dfrac{1}{8}\right)\left(\dfrac{1}{3}\right)$$
$$x = -\dfrac{1}{24}$$

49. $\dfrac{7}{6} x = \dfrac{1}{4} - \dfrac{2}{3}$

$$12\left(\dfrac{7}{6} x\right) = 12\left(\dfrac{1}{4} - \dfrac{2}{3}\right)$$
$$14x = 3 - 8$$
$$14x = -5$$
$$\dfrac{14x}{14} = \dfrac{-5}{14}$$
$$x = -\dfrac{5}{14}$$

51.
$$\frac{b}{4} = \frac{b}{12} + \frac{2}{3}$$
$$12\left(\frac{b}{4}\right) = 12\left(\frac{b}{12} + \frac{2}{3}\right)$$
$$3b = b + 8$$
$$3b - b = b + 8 - b$$
$$2b = 8$$
$$\frac{2b}{2} = \frac{8}{2}$$
$$b = 4$$

53.
$$\frac{x}{3} + 2 = \frac{x}{2} + 8$$
$$6\left(\frac{x}{3} + 2\right) = 6\left(\frac{x}{2} + 8\right)$$
$$2x + 12 = 3x + 48$$
$$2x + 12 - 2x = 3x + 48 - 2x$$
$$12 = x + 48$$
$$12 - 48 = x + 48 - 48$$
$$-36 = x$$

55.
$$3 + \frac{1}{2} = \frac{3}{1} + \frac{1}{2}$$
$$= \frac{3 \cdot 2}{1 \cdot 2} + \frac{1}{2}$$
$$= \frac{6}{2} + \frac{1}{2}$$
$$= \frac{6+1}{2}$$
$$= \frac{7}{2}$$

57.
$$5 + \frac{9}{10} = \frac{5}{1} + \frac{9}{10}$$
$$= \frac{5 \cdot 10}{1 \cdot 10} + \frac{9}{10}$$
$$= \frac{50}{10} + \frac{9}{10}$$
$$= \frac{50+9}{10}$$
$$= \frac{59}{10}$$

59.
$$9 - \frac{5}{6} = \frac{9}{1} - \frac{5}{6}$$
$$= \frac{9 \cdot 6}{1 \cdot 6} - \frac{5}{6}$$
$$= \frac{54}{6} - \frac{5}{6}$$
$$= \frac{54-5}{6}$$
$$= \frac{49}{6}$$

61. Answers will vary.

63.
$$\frac{19}{53} = \frac{353x}{1431} + \frac{23}{27}$$
$$1431\left(\frac{19}{53}\right) = 1431\left(\frac{353x}{1431} + \frac{23}{27}\right)$$
$$513 = 353x + 1219$$
$$513 - 1219 = 353x + 1219 - 1219$$
$$-706 = 353x$$
$$\frac{-706}{353} = \frac{353x}{353}$$
$$-2 = x$$

Section 4.8

Practice Problems

1. Each part is $\frac{1}{3}$, and there are 8 parts shaded, or 2 wholes and 2 more parts: $\frac{8}{3}$ or $2\frac{2}{3}$.

2. Each part is $\frac{1}{4}$, and there are 5 parts shaded, or 1 whole and 1 more part: $\frac{5}{4}$ or $1\frac{1}{4}$.

3. a. $2\frac{5}{7} = \frac{7 \cdot 2 + 5}{7} = \frac{19}{7}$

   b. $5\frac{1}{3} = \frac{3 \cdot 5 + 1}{3} = \frac{16}{3}$

   c. $9\frac{3}{10} = \frac{10 \cdot 9 + 3}{10} = \frac{93}{10}$

   d. $1\frac{1}{5} = \frac{5 \cdot 1 + 1}{5} = \frac{6}{5}$

4. a.

$$5\overline{)\,8} \\ \,\underline{-5} \\ \,3$$

$$\frac{8}{5} = 1\frac{3}{5}$$

b.

$$6\overline{)\,17} \\ \,\underline{-12} \\ \,5$$

$$\frac{17}{6} = 2\frac{5}{6}$$

c.

$$4\overline{)\,48} \\ \,\underline{-4} \\ \,08 \\ \,\underline{-8} \\ \,0$$

$$\frac{48}{4} = 12$$

d.

$$4\overline{)\,35} \\ \,\underline{-32} \\ \,3$$

$$\frac{35}{4} = 8\frac{3}{4}$$

e.

$$7\overline{)\,51} \\ \,\underline{-49} \\ \,2$$

$$\frac{51}{7} = 7\frac{2}{7}$$

f.

$$20\overline{)\,21} \\ \,\underline{-20} \\ \,1$$

$$\frac{21}{20} = 1\frac{1}{20}$$

5.

$$2\frac{1}{2} \cdot \frac{8}{15} = \frac{5}{2} \cdot \frac{8}{15}$$
$$= \frac{5 \cdot 8}{2 \cdot 15}$$
$$= \frac{5 \cdot 2 \cdot 4}{2 \cdot 5 \cdot 3}$$
$$= \frac{4}{3} \text{ or } 1\frac{1}{3}$$

6.

$$3\frac{1}{5} \cdot 2\frac{3}{4} = \frac{16}{5} \cdot \frac{11}{4}$$
$$= \frac{16 \cdot 11}{5 \cdot 4}$$
$$= \frac{4 \cdot 4 \cdot 11}{5 \cdot 4}$$
$$= \frac{4 \cdot 11}{5}$$
$$= \frac{44}{5} \text{ or } 8\frac{4}{5}$$

7.

$$\frac{2}{3} \cdot 18 = \frac{2}{3} \cdot \frac{18}{1}$$
$$= \frac{2 \cdot 18}{3 \cdot 1}$$
$$= \frac{2 \cdot 3 \cdot 6}{3 \cdot 1}$$
$$= \frac{2 \cdot 6}{1 \cdot 1}$$
$$= \frac{12}{1} \text{ or } 12$$

8.

$$\frac{4}{9} \div 5 = \frac{4}{9} \div \frac{5}{1} = \frac{4}{9} \cdot \frac{1}{5} = \frac{4 \cdot 1}{9 \cdot 5} = \frac{4}{45}$$

9.

$$\frac{8}{15} \div 3\frac{4}{5} = \frac{8}{15} \div \frac{19}{5}$$
$$= \frac{8}{15} \cdot \frac{5}{19}$$
$$= \frac{8 \cdot 5}{15 \cdot 19}$$
$$= \frac{8 \cdot 5}{5 \cdot 3 \cdot 19}$$
$$= \frac{8}{3 \cdot 19}$$
$$= \frac{8}{57}$$

10. $3\dfrac{2}{5} \div 2\dfrac{2}{15} = \dfrac{17}{5} \div \dfrac{32}{15}$

$\qquad\qquad = \dfrac{17}{5} \cdot \dfrac{15}{32}$

$\qquad\qquad = \dfrac{17 \cdot 15}{5 \cdot 32}$

$\qquad\qquad = \dfrac{17 \cdot 5 \cdot 3}{5 \cdot 32}$

$\qquad\qquad = \dfrac{17 \cdot 3}{32}$

$\qquad\qquad = \dfrac{51}{32}$ or $1\dfrac{19}{32}$

11.
$$
\begin{array}{rcl}
4\dfrac{2}{5} & = & 4\dfrac{4}{10} \\[2mm]
+\ 5\dfrac{3}{10} & = & +\ 5\dfrac{3}{10} \\[1mm]
\hline
& & 9\dfrac{7}{10}
\end{array}
$$

12.
$$
\begin{array}{rcl}
2\dfrac{5}{14} & = & 2\dfrac{5}{14} \\[2mm]
+\ 5\dfrac{6}{7} & = & +\ 5\dfrac{12}{14} \\[1mm]
\hline
& & 7\dfrac{17}{14} = 7 + 1\dfrac{3}{14} = 8\dfrac{3}{14}
\end{array}
$$

13.
$$
\begin{array}{rcl}
10 & = & 10 \\[2mm]
2\dfrac{1}{7} & = & 2\dfrac{5}{35} \\[2mm]
+\ 3\dfrac{1}{5} & = & +\ 3\dfrac{7}{35} \\[1mm]
\hline
& & 15\dfrac{12}{35}
\end{array}
$$

14.
$$
\begin{array}{rcl}
29\dfrac{7}{8} & = & 29\dfrac{14}{16} \\[2mm]
-\ 13\dfrac{3}{16} & = & -\ 13\dfrac{3}{16} \\[1mm]
\hline
& & 16\dfrac{11}{16}
\end{array}
$$

15.
$$
\begin{array}{rclcl}
9\dfrac{7}{15} & = & 9\dfrac{7}{15} & = & 8\dfrac{22}{15} \\[2mm]
-\ 5\dfrac{4}{5} & = & -\ 5\dfrac{12}{15} & = & -\ 5\dfrac{12}{15} \\[1mm]
\hline
& & & & 3\dfrac{10}{15} = 3\dfrac{2}{3}
\end{array}
$$

16.
$$
\begin{array}{rcl}
25 & = & 24\dfrac{9}{9} \\[2mm]
-10\dfrac{2}{9} & = & -10\dfrac{2}{9} \\[1mm]
\hline
& & 14\dfrac{7}{9}
\end{array}
$$

17. The phrase "how much larger" tells us to subtract. Subtract $19\dfrac{5}{12}$ feet from $23\dfrac{1}{4}$ feet.

$$
\begin{array}{rclcl}
23\dfrac{1}{4} & = & 23\dfrac{3}{12} & = & 22\dfrac{15}{12} \\[2mm]
-19\dfrac{5}{12} & = & -19\dfrac{5}{12} & = & -19\dfrac{5}{12} \\[1mm]
\hline
& & & & 3\dfrac{10}{12} = 3\dfrac{5}{6}
\end{array}
$$

The girth of the largest known American Beech tree is $3\dfrac{5}{6}$ feet larger than the girth of the largest known Sugar Maple tree.

18. $30 \div 2\dfrac{1}{7} = \dfrac{30}{1} \div \dfrac{15}{7}$

$\qquad\qquad = \dfrac{30}{1} \cdot \dfrac{7}{15}$

$\qquad\qquad = \dfrac{30 \cdot 7}{1 \cdot 15}$

$\qquad\qquad = \dfrac{15 \cdot 2 \cdot 7}{1 \cdot 15}$

$\qquad\qquad = \dfrac{2 \cdot 7}{1}$

$\qquad\qquad = \dfrac{14}{1}$

$\qquad\qquad = 14$

14 dresses can be made.

19. $-7\dfrac{3}{7} = -\dfrac{7 \cdot 7 + 3}{3} = -\dfrac{52}{7}$

20. $-4\dfrac{10}{11} = -\dfrac{11 \cdot 4 + 10}{11} = -\dfrac{54}{11}$

21. $-\dfrac{29}{8} = -3\dfrac{5}{8}$

$$
\begin{array}{r}
3 \\
8\overline{)\ 29} \\
-24 \\
\hline
5
\end{array}
$$

22. $-\dfrac{31}{5} = -6\dfrac{1}{5}$

$$\begin{array}{r} 6 \\ 5\overline{)31} \\ -30 \\ \hline 1 \end{array}$$

23. $3\dfrac{3}{4}\cdot\left(-2\dfrac{3}{5}\right)=\dfrac{15}{4}\cdot\left(-\dfrac{13}{5}\right)$

$\quad=-\dfrac{3\cdot5\cdot13}{4\cdot5}$

$\quad=-\dfrac{39}{4}$ or $-9\dfrac{3}{4}$

24. $-1\dfrac{2}{7}\div4\dfrac{1}{4}=-\dfrac{9}{7}\div\dfrac{17}{4}$

$\quad=-\dfrac{9}{7}\cdot\dfrac{4}{17}$

$\quad=-\dfrac{36}{119}$

25. $7\dfrac{2}{3}+\left(-11\dfrac{3}{4}\right)$

Subtract the absolute values.

$$\begin{array}{rcl} 11\dfrac{3\cdot3}{4\cdot3} & = & 11\dfrac{9}{12} \\ -7\dfrac{2\cdot4}{3\cdot4} & = & -7\dfrac{8}{12} \\ \hline & & 4\dfrac{1}{12} \end{array}$$

Since $-11\dfrac{3}{4}$ has the larger absolute value, the

answer is $-4\dfrac{1}{12}$.

26. $-9\dfrac{2}{7}-15\dfrac{11}{14}$

Add the absolute values.

$$\begin{array}{rcl} 9\dfrac{2\cdot2}{7\cdot2} & = & 9\dfrac{4}{14} \\ +15\dfrac{11}{14} & = & +15\dfrac{11}{14} \\ \hline & & 24\dfrac{15}{14} \end{array}$$

Since $\dfrac{15}{14}=1\dfrac{1}{14}$, $24+1\dfrac{1}{14}=25\dfrac{1}{14}$.

Keep the common sign: $-25\dfrac{1}{14}$

Calculator Explorations

Press the keys as instructed on p.328 of your textbook.

1. $25\dfrac{5}{11}=\dfrac{280}{11}$

2. $67\dfrac{14}{15}=\dfrac{1019}{15}$

3. $107\dfrac{31}{35}=\dfrac{3776}{35}$

4. $186\dfrac{17}{21}=\dfrac{3923}{21}$

5. $\dfrac{365}{14}=26\dfrac{1}{14}$

6. $\dfrac{290}{13}=22\dfrac{4}{13}$

7. $\dfrac{2769}{30}=92\dfrac{3}{10}$

8. $\dfrac{3941}{17}=231\dfrac{14}{17}$

Exercise Set 4.8

1. Each part is $\dfrac{1}{4}$, and there are 11 parts shaded, or 2 wholes and 3 more parts.

  a. $\dfrac{11}{4}$

  b. $2\dfrac{3}{4}$

3. Each part is $\dfrac{1}{3}$, and there are 11 parts shaded, or 3 wholes and 2 more parts.

  a. $\dfrac{11}{3}$

  b. $3\dfrac{2}{3}$

5. Each part is $\dfrac{1}{2}$, and there are 3 parts shaded or 1 whole part and 1 more part.

a. $\dfrac{3}{2}$

b. $1\dfrac{1}{2}$

7. Each part is $\dfrac{1}{3}$, and there are 4 parts shaded, or 1 whole and 1 more part.

a. $\dfrac{4}{3}$

b. $1\dfrac{1}{3}$

9. $2\dfrac{1}{3} = \dfrac{2\cdot 3 + 1}{3} = \dfrac{7}{3}$

11. $3\dfrac{3}{8} = \dfrac{3\cdot 8 + 3}{8} = \dfrac{27}{8}$

13. $11\dfrac{6}{7} = \dfrac{11\cdot 7 + 6}{7} = \dfrac{83}{7}$

15. $\begin{array}{r} 1 \\ 7\overline{)13} \\ \underline{-7} \\ 6 \end{array}$

$\dfrac{13}{7} = 1\dfrac{6}{7}$

17. $\begin{array}{r} 3 \\ 15\overline{)\,47} \\ \underline{-45} \\ 2 \end{array}$

$\dfrac{47}{15} = 3\dfrac{2}{15}$

19. $\begin{array}{r} 4 \\ 8\overline{)\,37} \\ \underline{-32} \\ 5 \end{array}$

$\dfrac{37}{8} = 4\dfrac{5}{8}$

21. $2\dfrac{2}{3}\cdot\dfrac{1}{7} = \dfrac{8}{3}\cdot\dfrac{1}{7} = \dfrac{8\cdot 1}{3\cdot 7} = \dfrac{8}{21}$

23. $8 \div 1\dfrac{5}{7} = 8 \div \dfrac{12}{7}$

$\qquad = \dfrac{8}{1}\cdot\dfrac{7}{12}$

$\qquad = \dfrac{2\cdot 4\cdot 7}{4\cdot 3}$

$\qquad = \dfrac{14}{3}$

$\qquad = 4\dfrac{2}{3}$

25. $3\dfrac{2}{3}\cdot 1\dfrac{1}{2} = \dfrac{11}{3}\cdot\dfrac{3}{2} = \dfrac{11\cdot 3}{3\cdot 2} = \dfrac{11}{2} = 5\dfrac{1}{2}$

27. $2\dfrac{2}{3} \div \dfrac{1}{7} = \dfrac{8}{3} \div \dfrac{1}{7} = \dfrac{8}{3}\cdot\dfrac{7}{1} = \dfrac{8\cdot 7}{3\cdot 1} = \dfrac{56}{3} = 18\dfrac{2}{3}$

29. $4\dfrac{7}{10} + 2\dfrac{1}{10} = 6\dfrac{8}{10} = 6\dfrac{4}{5}$

31. $\begin{array}{rcl} 15\dfrac{4}{7} & = & 15\dfrac{8}{14} \\ + \; 9\dfrac{11}{14} & = & 9\dfrac{11}{14} \\ \hline & & 24\dfrac{19}{14} = 25\dfrac{5}{14} \end{array}$

33. $\begin{array}{rcl} 3\dfrac{5}{8} & = & 3\dfrac{15}{24} \\ 2\dfrac{1}{6} & = & 2\dfrac{4}{24} \\ + \; 7\dfrac{3}{4} & = & 7\dfrac{18}{24} \\ \hline & & 12\dfrac{37}{24} = 13\dfrac{13}{24} \end{array}$

35. $\begin{array}{r} 4\dfrac{7}{10} \\ - \; 2\dfrac{1}{10} \\ \hline 2\dfrac{6}{10} = 2\dfrac{3}{5} \end{array}$

37. $\begin{array}{rcl} 10\dfrac{13}{14} & = & 10\dfrac{13}{14} \\ - \; 3\dfrac{4}{7} & = & - \; 3\dfrac{8}{14} \\ \hline & & 7\dfrac{5}{14} \end{array}$

39.
$$9\frac{1}{5} = 9\frac{5}{25} = 8\frac{30}{25}$$
$$-8\frac{6}{25} = -8\frac{6}{25} = -8\frac{6}{25}$$
$$\frac{24}{25}$$

41.
$$2\frac{3}{4}$$
$$+1\frac{1}{4}$$
$$3\frac{4}{4} = 3+1 = 4$$

43.
$$15\frac{4}{7} = 15\frac{8}{14} = 14\frac{22}{14}$$
$$-9\frac{11}{14} = -9\frac{11}{14} = -9\frac{11}{14}$$
$$5\frac{11}{14}$$

45. $3\frac{1}{9}\cdot 2 = \frac{28}{9}\cdot\frac{2}{1} = \frac{56}{9} = 6\frac{2}{9}$

47. $1\frac{2}{3}\div 2\frac{1}{5} = \frac{5}{3}\div\frac{11}{5} = \frac{5}{3}\cdot\frac{5}{11} = \frac{25}{33}$

49. $22\frac{4}{9}+13\frac{5}{18} = 22\frac{8}{18}+13\frac{5}{18} = 35\frac{13}{18}$

51.
$$5\frac{2}{3} = 5\frac{4}{6}$$
$$-3\frac{1}{6} = -3\frac{1}{6}$$
$$2\frac{3}{6} = 2\frac{1}{2}$$

53.
$$15\frac{1}{5} = 15\frac{6}{30}$$
$$20\frac{3}{10} = 20\frac{9}{30}$$
$$+37\frac{2}{15} = +37\frac{4}{30}$$
$$72\frac{19}{30}$$

55.
$$6\frac{4}{7} = 6\frac{8}{14} = 6\frac{22}{14}$$
$$-5\frac{11}{14} = -5\frac{11}{14} = -5\frac{11}{14}$$
$$\frac{11}{14}$$

57. $4\frac{2}{7}\cdot 1\frac{3}{10} = \frac{30}{7}\cdot\frac{13}{10} = \frac{3\cdot10\cdot13}{7\cdot10} = \frac{39}{7} = 5\frac{4}{7}$

59.
$$6\frac{2}{11} = 6\frac{6}{33}$$
$$3 = 3$$
$$+4\frac{10}{33} = 4\frac{10}{33}$$
$$13\frac{16}{33}$$

61. The phrase "total duration" tells us to add. Find the sum of the three durations.
$$4\frac{14}{15} = 4\frac{56}{60}$$
$$4\frac{7}{60} = 4\frac{7}{60}$$
$$+1\frac{2}{3} = +1\frac{40}{60}$$
$$9\frac{103}{60} = 10\frac{43}{60}$$

The total duration is $10\frac{43}{60}$ minutes.

63. The phrase "how much longer" tells us to subtract. Subtract $4\frac{7}{60}$ minutes from $4\frac{14}{15}$ minutes.
$$4\frac{14}{15} = 4\frac{56}{60}$$
$$-4\frac{7}{60} = -4\frac{7}{60}$$
$$\frac{49}{60}$$

The June 21, 2001 eclipse will be $\frac{49}{60}$ minutes longer than the March 29, 2006 eclipse.

65. $6\cdot 3\frac{1}{4} = \frac{6}{1}\cdot\frac{13}{4}$
$$= \frac{2\cdot3\cdot13}{1\cdot2\cdot2}$$
$$= \frac{39}{2}$$
$$= 19\frac{1}{2}$$

The sidewalk is $19\frac{1}{2}$ inches wide.

67. $423 \div 28\frac{1}{5} = \frac{423}{1} \div \frac{141}{5}$

$\qquad = \frac{3 \cdot 141}{1} \cdot \frac{5}{141}$

$\qquad = 15$

He purchased 15 shares.

69. Subtract $1\frac{1}{2}$ inches from $1\frac{9}{16}$ inches.

$$\begin{array}{rcl} 1\frac{9}{16} & = & 1\frac{9}{16} \\ -\ 1\frac{1}{2} & = & -\ 1\frac{8}{16} \\ \hline & & \frac{1}{16} \end{array}$$

The entrance holes for Mountain Bluebirds should be $\frac{1}{16}$ inch wider than the entrance for Eastern Bluebirds.

71. The phrase "cuts off" tells us to subtract.

First subtract $2\frac{1}{2}$ feet from $15\frac{2}{3}$ feet. Then subtract $3\frac{1}{4}$ feet from that result.

$$\begin{array}{rcl} 15\frac{2}{3} & = & 15\frac{4}{6} \\ -2\frac{1}{2} & = & -2\frac{3}{6} \\ \hline & & 13\frac{1}{6} \end{array}$$

$$\begin{array}{rclcl} 13\frac{1}{6} & = & 13\frac{2}{12} & = & 12\frac{14}{12} \\ -3\frac{1}{4} & = & -3\frac{3}{12} & = & -3\frac{3}{12} \\ \hline & & & & 9\frac{11}{12} \end{array}$$

No, the pipe will be $\frac{1}{12}$ of a foot short.

73. $58\frac{3}{4} \div 7\frac{1}{2} = \frac{235}{4} \div \frac{15}{2}$

$\qquad = \frac{235}{4} \cdot \frac{2}{15}$

$\qquad = \frac{5 \cdot 47 \cdot 2}{2 \cdot 2 \cdot 3 \cdot 5}$

$\qquad = \frac{47}{6}$ or $7\frac{5}{6}$

$7\frac{5}{6}$ gallons were used each hour.

75.
$$\begin{array}{rcl} 65\frac{9}{10} & = & 65\frac{9}{10} \\ -56\frac{1}{2} & = & -56\frac{5}{10} \\ \hline & & 9\frac{4}{10} = 9\frac{2}{5} \end{array}$$

Spain's standard guage is $9\frac{2}{5}$ wider than the U.S. standard guage.

77. The phrase "how much more" tells us to subtract.

Subtract $3\frac{3}{5}$ inches from $11\frac{1}{4}$ inches.

$$\begin{array}{rclcl} 11\frac{1}{4} & = & 11\frac{5}{20} & = & 10\frac{25}{20} \\ -3\frac{3}{5} & = & -3\frac{12}{20} & = & -3\frac{12}{20} \\ \hline & & & & 7\frac{13}{20} \end{array}$$

Tucson gets $7\frac{13}{20}$ inches more, on average, than Yuma.

79. $2 \cdot 1\frac{3}{4} = \frac{2}{1} \cdot \frac{7}{4}$

$\qquad = \frac{2 \cdot 7}{1 \cdot 4}$

$\qquad = \frac{2 \cdot 7}{1 \cdot 2 \cdot 2}$

$\qquad = \frac{7}{1 \cdot 2}$

$\qquad = \frac{7}{2}$ or $3\frac{1}{2}$

The area is $\frac{7}{2}$ or $3\frac{1}{2}$ square yards.

81. $A = lw$

$A = \frac{3}{4} \cdot 1\frac{1}{4} = \frac{3}{4} \cdot \frac{5}{4} = \frac{5}{16}$

The area of the computer chip is $\frac{15}{16}$ sq. in.

83. Find the distance around. Add the lengths of the three sides.

$$2\frac{1}{3}$$
$$2\frac{1}{3}$$
$$+\ 2\frac{1}{3}$$
$$\overline{\hspace{1cm}}$$
$$6\frac{3}{3}=7$$

The perimeter is 7 miles.

85. Find the distance around. Add the lengths of the four sides.

$$3\ \ =3$$
$$5\frac{1}{3}=5\frac{8}{24}$$
$$5\ \ =5$$
$$+\ 7\frac{7}{8}=7\frac{21}{24}$$
$$\overline{\hspace{2cm}}$$
$$20\frac{29}{24}=21\frac{5}{24}$$

The perimeter is $21\frac{5}{24}$ meters.

87. $\dfrac{1}{20}\cdot 30=\dfrac{1\cdot 3\cdot 10}{2\cdot 10}=\dfrac{3}{2}$ or $1\dfrac{1}{2}$

The life expectancy of circulating paper money is $1\frac{1}{2}$ years.

89. The phrase "overall height' tells us to add. Add the two heights.

$$152\frac{1}{6}\ =152\frac{1}{6}$$
$$+\ 154\frac{1}{2}\ =154\frac{3}{6}$$
$$\overline{\hspace{3cm}}$$
$$306\frac{4}{6}=306\frac{2}{3}$$

The overall height is $306\frac{2}{3}$ feet.

91.
$$15\frac{1}{5}\div 24=\frac{76}{5}\div\frac{24}{1}$$
$$=\frac{76}{5}\cdot\frac{1}{24}$$
$$=\frac{76\cdot 1}{5\cdot 24}$$
$$=\frac{4\cdot 19\cdot 1}{5\cdot 4\cdot 6}$$
$$=\frac{19\cdot 1}{5\cdot 6}$$
$$=\frac{19}{30}$$

On average $\dfrac{19}{30}$ inch fell each hour.

93.
$$-4\frac{2}{5}\cdot 2\frac{3}{10}=-\frac{22}{5}\cdot\frac{23}{10}$$
$$=-\frac{2\cdot 11\cdot 23}{5\cdot 2\cdot 5}$$
$$=-\frac{253}{25}$$
$$=-10\frac{3}{25}$$

95.
$$-\ 5\frac{1}{8}\ =\ -5\frac{1}{8}$$
$$-19\frac{3}{4}\ =\ -19\frac{6}{8}$$
$$\overline{\hspace{2.5cm}}$$
$$-24\frac{7}{8}$$

97.
$$-31\frac{2}{15}=-31\frac{8}{60}=-30\frac{68}{60}$$
$$+17\frac{3}{20}=+17\frac{9}{60}=\ +17\frac{9}{60}$$
$$\overline{\hspace{4cm}}$$
$$-13\frac{59}{60}$$

99.
$$1\frac{3}{4}\div\left(-3\frac{1}{2}\right)=\frac{7}{4}\div\left(-\frac{7}{2}\right)$$
$$=\frac{7}{4}\cdot\left(-\frac{2}{7}\right)$$
$$=-\frac{7\cdot 2}{2\cdot 2\cdot 7}$$
$$=-\frac{1}{2}$$

101.

$$-13\frac{5}{6} = -13\frac{20}{24} = -12\frac{44}{24}$$
$$+11\frac{7}{8} = +11\frac{21}{24} = +11\frac{21}{24}$$
$$\overline{\hspace{3cm}} \quad -1\frac{23}{24}$$

103.

$$-7\frac{3}{10} \div (-100) = -\frac{73}{10} \div \left(-\frac{100}{1}\right)$$
$$= -\frac{73}{10} \cdot \left(-\frac{1}{100}\right)$$
$$= \frac{73}{1000}$$

105.

$$-3\frac{1}{6} \cdot \left(-2\frac{3}{4}\right) = -\frac{19}{6} \cdot \left(-\frac{11}{4}\right)$$
$$= \frac{209}{24}$$
$$= 8\frac{17}{24}$$

107.

$$-21\frac{5}{12} = -21\frac{5}{12}$$
$$-10\frac{3}{4} = -10\frac{9}{12}$$
$$\overline{\hspace{3cm}} \quad -31\frac{14}{12} = -32\frac{2}{12} = -32\frac{1}{6}$$

109. $2x - 5 + 7x - 8 = 2x + 7x - 5 - 8$
$\qquad\qquad\qquad\quad = 9x - 13$

111. $3(y - 2) - 6y = 3y - 6 - 6y$
$\qquad\qquad\qquad = 3y - 6y - 6$
$\qquad\qquad\qquad = -3y - 6$

113. $2^3 + 3^2 = 2 \cdot 2 \cdot 2 + 3 \cdot 3 = 8 + 9 = 17$

115. $\dfrac{7 - 3}{2^2} = \dfrac{4}{4} = 1$

117. Weight of Supreme box:

$$2\frac{1}{4} \text{ lb} = 2\frac{1}{4} \text{ lb}$$
$$+3\frac{1}{2} \text{ lb} = +3\frac{2}{4} \text{ lb}$$
$$\overline{\hspace{3cm}} \quad 5\frac{3}{4} \text{ lb} = 5\frac{6}{8} \text{ lb}$$

Weight of Deluxe box:

$$1\frac{3}{8} \text{ lb} = 1\frac{3}{8} \text{ lb}$$
$$+4\frac{1}{4} \text{ lb} = +4\frac{2}{8} \text{ lb}$$
$$\overline{\hspace{3cm}} \quad 5\frac{5}{8} \text{ lb}$$

The Supreme box is heavier.

$$5\frac{6}{8} \text{ lb}$$
$$-5\frac{5}{8} \text{ lb}$$
$$\overline{\hspace{2cm}} \quad \frac{1}{8} \text{ lb}$$

It is $\dfrac{1}{8}$ pound heavier.

119. Answers may vary.

121. Answers may vary.

Chapter 4 Review

1. $\dfrac{3}{4}$ ← Three parts shaded
$\qquad$ ← Four equal parts

So the answer expressed as a fraction is $\dfrac{3}{4}$.

2. $\dfrac{2}{5}$ ← Two parts shaded
$\qquad$ ← Five equal parts

So the answer expressed as a fraction is $\dfrac{2}{5}$.

3. To graph $\dfrac{7}{9}$ on a number line, divide the distance from 0 to 1 into 9 equal parts. Then start at 0 and count over 7 parts.

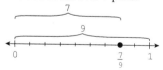

4. To graph $\dfrac{4}{7}$ on a number line, divide the distance from 0 to 1 into 7 equal parts. Then start at 0 and count over 4 parts.

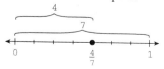

5. To graph $\dfrac{5}{4}$ on a number line, divide the distances from 0 to 1 and 1 to 2 into 4 equal parts. Then start at 0 and count over 5 parts.

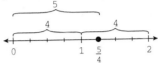

6. To graph $\dfrac{7}{5}$ on a number line, divide the distances from 0 to 1 and from 1 to 2 into 5 equal parts. Then start at 0 and count over 7 parts.

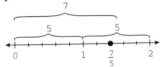

7. $\dfrac{\text{Number closed}}{\text{Total number}} = \dfrac{35}{242}$

    $\dfrac{35}{242}$ of job specialties are closed to women.

8. $\dfrac{43}{50}$ of the U.S. Armed Forces are men.

9. $\dfrac{2}{3} = \dfrac{2 \cdot 10}{3 \cdot 10} = \dfrac{20}{30}$

10. $\dfrac{5}{8} = \dfrac{5 \cdot 7}{8 \cdot 7} = \dfrac{35}{56}$

11. $\dfrac{7a}{6} = \dfrac{7a \cdot 7}{6 \cdot 7} = \dfrac{49a}{42}$

12. $\dfrac{9b}{4} = \dfrac{9b \cdot 5}{4 \cdot 5} = \dfrac{45b}{20}$

13. $\dfrac{4}{5x} = \dfrac{4 \cdot 10}{5x \cdot 10} = \dfrac{40}{50x}$

14. $\dfrac{5}{9y} = \dfrac{5 \cdot 2}{9y \cdot 2} = \dfrac{10}{18y}$

15. $\dfrac{12}{28} = \dfrac{2 \cdot 2 \cdot 3}{2 \cdot 2 \cdot 7} = \dfrac{3}{7}$

16. $\dfrac{15}{27} = \dfrac{3 \cdot 5}{3 \cdot 9} = \dfrac{5}{9}$

17. $\dfrac{25x}{75x^2} = \dfrac{5 \cdot 5 \cdot x}{3 \cdot 5 \cdot 5 \cdot x \cdot x} = \dfrac{1}{3x}$

18. $\dfrac{36y^3}{72y} = \dfrac{36y \cdot y^2}{2 \cdot 36y} = \dfrac{y^2}{2}$

19. $\dfrac{29ab}{32abc} = \dfrac{29 \cdot a \cdot b}{32 \cdot a \cdot b \cdot c} = \dfrac{29}{32c}$

20. $\dfrac{18xyz}{23xy} = \dfrac{18z}{23}$

21. $\dfrac{45x^2 y}{27xy^3} = \dfrac{3 \cdot 3 \cdot 5 \cdot x \cdot x \cdot y}{3 \cdot 3 \cdot 3 \cdot x \cdot y \cdot y^2} = \dfrac{5x}{3y^2}$

22. $\dfrac{42ab^2 c}{30abc^3} = \dfrac{2 \cdot 3 \cdot 7a \cdot b \cdot b \cdot c}{2 \cdot 3 \cdot 5a \cdot b \cdot c \cdot c^2} = \dfrac{7b}{5c^2}$

23. $\dfrac{\text{inches in the part}}{\text{inches in a foot}} = \dfrac{8}{12} = \dfrac{4 \cdot 2}{4 \cdot 3} = \dfrac{2}{3}$

    8 inches is $\dfrac{2}{3}$ of a foot.

24. $1 - \dfrac{6}{15} = \dfrac{15 - 6}{15} = \dfrac{9}{15} = \dfrac{3 \cdot 3}{3 \cdot 5} = \dfrac{3}{5}$

    $\dfrac{3}{5}$ of the cars are not white.

25. $\dfrac{3}{5} \cdot \dfrac{1}{2} = \dfrac{3 \cdot 1}{5 \cdot 2} = \dfrac{3}{10}$

26. $-\dfrac{6}{7} \cdot \dfrac{5}{12} = -\dfrac{6 \cdot 5}{7 \cdot 2 \cdot 6} = -\dfrac{5}{14}$

27. $\dfrac{7}{8x} \cdot -\dfrac{2}{3} = -\dfrac{7 \cdot 2}{4 \cdot 2 \cdot x \cdot 3} = -\dfrac{7}{12x}$

28. $\dfrac{6}{15} \cdot \dfrac{5y}{8} = \dfrac{2 \cdot 3 \cdot 5y}{3 \cdot 5 \cdot 2 \cdot 4} = \dfrac{y}{4}$

29. $-\dfrac{24x}{5} \cdot -\dfrac{15}{8x^3} = \dfrac{3 \cdot 8 \cdot x \cdot 3 \cdot 5}{5 \cdot 8 \cdot x \cdot x \cdot x} = \dfrac{9}{x^2}$

30. $\dfrac{27y^3}{21} \cdot \dfrac{7}{18y^2} = \dfrac{3 \cdot 9 \cdot y \cdot y^2 \cdot 7}{3 \cdot 7 \cdot 2 \cdot 9 \cdot y^2} = \dfrac{y}{2}$

31. $\left(-\dfrac{1}{3}\right)^3 = -\dfrac{1}{3} \cdot \dfrac{1}{3} \cdot \dfrac{1}{3} = -\dfrac{1 \cdot 1 \cdot 1}{3 \cdot 3 \cdot 3} = -\dfrac{1}{27}$

32. $\left(-\dfrac{5}{12}\right)^2 = -\dfrac{5}{12} \cdot -\dfrac{5}{12} = \dfrac{5 \cdot 5}{12 \cdot 12} = \dfrac{25}{144}$

33. $\dfrac{x^3}{y} \cdot \dfrac{y^3}{x} = \dfrac{x \cdot x^2 \cdot y \cdot y^2}{y \cdot x} = x^2 y^2$

34. $\dfrac{ac}{b} \cdot \dfrac{b^2}{a^3 c} = \dfrac{a \cdot c \cdot b \cdot b}{b \cdot a \cdot a^2 \cdot c} = \dfrac{b}{a^2}$

35. $xy = \dfrac{2}{3} \cdot \dfrac{1}{5} = \dfrac{2 \cdot 1}{3 \cdot 5} = \dfrac{2}{15}$

36. $ab = -7 \cdot \dfrac{9}{10} = -\dfrac{7}{1} \cdot \dfrac{9}{10} = -\dfrac{7 \cdot 9}{1 \cdot 10} = -\dfrac{63}{10}$

37. $-\dfrac{3}{4} \div \dfrac{3}{8} = -\dfrac{3}{4} \cdot \dfrac{8}{3} = -\dfrac{3 \cdot 2 \cdot 4}{4 \cdot 3} = -2$

38. $\dfrac{21a}{4} \div \dfrac{7a}{5} = \dfrac{21a}{4} \cdot \dfrac{5}{7a} = \dfrac{3 \cdot 7 \cdot a \cdot 5}{4 \cdot 7 \cdot a} = \dfrac{15}{4}$

39. $\dfrac{18x}{5} \div \dfrac{2}{5x} = \dfrac{18x}{5} \cdot \dfrac{5x}{2}$
$= \dfrac{2 \cdot 9 \cdot x \cdot 5 \cdot x}{5 \cdot 2}$
$= 9x^2$

40. $-\dfrac{9}{2} \div -\dfrac{1}{3} = \dfrac{9}{2} \cdot \dfrac{3}{1} = \dfrac{9 \cdot 3}{2 \cdot 1} = \dfrac{27}{2}$

41. $-\dfrac{5}{3} \div 2y = -\dfrac{5}{3} \cdot \dfrac{1}{2y} = -\dfrac{5 \cdot 1}{3 \cdot 2y} = -\dfrac{5}{6y}$

42. $\dfrac{5x^2}{y} \div \dfrac{10x^3}{y^3} = \dfrac{5x^2}{y} \cdot \dfrac{y^3}{10x^3} = \dfrac{5x^2 y \cdot y^2}{y \cdot 2 \cdot 5 \cdot x \cdot x^2} = \dfrac{y^2}{2x}$

43. $x \div y = \dfrac{9}{7} \div \dfrac{3}{4} = \dfrac{9}{7} \cdot \dfrac{4}{3} = \dfrac{3 \cdot 3 \cdot 4}{7 \cdot 3} = \dfrac{12}{7}$

44. $a \div b = -5 \div \dfrac{2}{3} = -\dfrac{5}{1} \cdot \dfrac{3}{2} = -\dfrac{5 \cdot 3}{1 \cdot 2} = -\dfrac{15}{2}$

45. $A = \dfrac{11}{6} \cdot \dfrac{7}{8} = \dfrac{77}{48}$ or $1\dfrac{29}{48}$ sq. ft.

46. $A = \left(\dfrac{2}{3}\right)^2 = \dfrac{2}{3} \cdot \dfrac{2}{3} = \dfrac{4}{9}$ sq. m

47. $\dfrac{7}{11} + \dfrac{3}{11} = \dfrac{7+3}{11} = \dfrac{10}{11}$

48. $\dfrac{4}{9} + \dfrac{2}{9} = \dfrac{6}{9} = \dfrac{2}{3}$

49. $\dfrac{1}{12} - \dfrac{5}{12} = \dfrac{1-5}{12} = \dfrac{-4}{12} = -\dfrac{4}{12} = -\dfrac{4}{4 \cdot 3} = -\dfrac{1}{3}$

50. $\dfrac{3}{y} - \dfrac{1}{y} = \dfrac{2}{y}$

51. $\dfrac{11x}{15} + \dfrac{x}{15} = \dfrac{11x + x}{15}$
$= \dfrac{12x}{15}$
$= \dfrac{3 \cdot 4 \cdot x}{3 \cdot 5}$
$= \dfrac{4x}{5}$

52. $\dfrac{4y}{21} - \dfrac{3}{21} = \dfrac{4y-3}{21}$

53. $\dfrac{4}{15} + \dfrac{3}{15} - \dfrac{2}{15} = \dfrac{4+3-2}{15} = \dfrac{5}{15} = \dfrac{5}{3 \cdot 5} = \dfrac{1}{3}$

54. $\dfrac{4}{15} - \dfrac{3}{15} - \dfrac{2}{15} = \dfrac{4-3-2}{15} = \dfrac{-1}{15} = -\dfrac{1}{15}$

55. $3 = 3$
$x = x$
$\text{LCD} = 3x$

56. $4 = 2 \cdot 2$
$8 = 2 \cdot 2 \cdot 2$
$12 = 2 \cdot 2 \cdot 3$
$\text{LCD} = 2 \cdot 2 \cdot 2 \cdot 3 = 24$

57. $z + \dfrac{1}{5} = 1$
$\dfrac{4}{5} + \dfrac{1}{5} = 1$
$\dfrac{5}{5} = 1$
$1 = 1$
Yes, it is a solution.

58. $x - \dfrac{2}{4} = \dfrac{1}{4}$
$\dfrac{3}{4} - \dfrac{2}{4} = \dfrac{1}{4}$
$\dfrac{1}{4} = \dfrac{1}{4}$
Yes, it is a solution.

59. $\dfrac{3}{8} + \dfrac{1}{8} = \dfrac{4}{8} = \dfrac{4 \cdot 1}{4 \cdot 2} = \dfrac{1}{2}$

She studied $\dfrac{1}{2}$ hour.

60. $\dfrac{5}{8} + \dfrac{1}{8} - \dfrac{3}{8} = \dfrac{3}{8}$

$\dfrac{3}{8}$ gallon is left.

61. $\dfrac{3}{8} + \dfrac{2}{8} + \dfrac{1}{8} = \dfrac{6}{8} = \dfrac{2 \cdot 3}{2 \cdot 4} = \dfrac{3}{4}$

He did $\dfrac{3}{4}$ of his homework.

62. Recall that perimeter means distance around. Find the sum of the lengths of the four sides.

$\dfrac{3}{16} + \dfrac{9}{16} + \dfrac{3}{16} + \dfrac{9}{16} = \dfrac{3+9+3+9}{16}$

$= \dfrac{24}{16}$

$= \dfrac{3 \cdot 8}{2 \cdot 8}$

$= \dfrac{3}{2}$ or $1\dfrac{1}{2}$

The perimeter is $\dfrac{3}{2}$ or $1\dfrac{1}{2}$ miles.

63. $\dfrac{7}{18} + \dfrac{2}{9} = \dfrac{7}{18} + \dfrac{4}{18} = \dfrac{11}{18}$

64. $\dfrac{4}{13} - \dfrac{1}{26} = \dfrac{4 \cdot 2}{13 \cdot 2} - \dfrac{1}{26} = \dfrac{8}{26} - \dfrac{1}{26} = \dfrac{7}{26}$

65. $-\dfrac{1}{3} + \dfrac{1}{4} = -\dfrac{4}{12} + \dfrac{3}{12} = -\dfrac{1}{12}$

66. $-\dfrac{2}{3} + \dfrac{1}{4} = \dfrac{-2 \cdot 4}{3 \cdot 4} + \dfrac{1 \cdot 3}{4 \cdot 3} = \dfrac{-8}{12} + \dfrac{3}{12} = \dfrac{-5}{12} = -\dfrac{5}{12}$

67. $\dfrac{5x}{11} + \dfrac{2}{55} = \dfrac{25x}{55} + \dfrac{2}{55} = \dfrac{25x + 2}{55}$

68. $\dfrac{4}{15} + \dfrac{b}{5} = \dfrac{4}{15} + \dfrac{b \cdot 3}{5 \cdot 3} = \dfrac{4 + 3b}{15}$

69. $\dfrac{5y}{12} - \dfrac{2y}{9} = \dfrac{5y \cdot 3}{12 \cdot 3} - \dfrac{2y \cdot 4}{9 \cdot 4} = \dfrac{15y}{36} - \dfrac{8y}{36} = \dfrac{7y}{36}$

70. $\dfrac{7x}{18} + \dfrac{2x}{9} = \dfrac{7x}{18} + \dfrac{2x \cdot 2}{9 \cdot 2} = \dfrac{7x + 4x}{18} = \dfrac{11x}{18}$

71. $\dfrac{4}{9} + \dfrac{5}{y} = \dfrac{4y}{9y} + \dfrac{45}{9y} = \dfrac{4y + 45}{9y}$

72. $-\dfrac{9}{14} - \dfrac{3}{7} = -\dfrac{9}{14} - \dfrac{3 \cdot 2}{7 \cdot 2} = -\dfrac{9}{14} - \dfrac{6}{14} = -\dfrac{15}{14}$

73. $\dfrac{4}{25} + \dfrac{23}{75} + \dfrac{7}{50} = \dfrac{24}{150} + \dfrac{46}{150} + \dfrac{21}{150} = \dfrac{91}{150}$

74. $\dfrac{2}{3} - \dfrac{2}{9} - \dfrac{1}{6} = \dfrac{2 \cdot 6}{3 \cdot 6} - \dfrac{2 \cdot 2}{9 \cdot 2} - \dfrac{1 \cdot 3}{6 \cdot 3}$

$= \dfrac{12}{18} - \dfrac{4}{18} - \dfrac{3}{18}$

$= \dfrac{5}{18}$

75. $a - \dfrac{2}{3} = \dfrac{1}{6}$

$a - \dfrac{2}{3} + \dfrac{2}{3} = \dfrac{1}{6} + \dfrac{2}{3}$

$a = \dfrac{1}{6} + \dfrac{4}{6}$

$a = \dfrac{5}{6}$

76. $9x + \dfrac{1}{5} - 8x = -\dfrac{7}{10}$

$(9x - 8x) + \dfrac{1}{5} = -\dfrac{7}{10}$

$x + \dfrac{1}{5} - \dfrac{1}{5} = -\dfrac{7}{10} - \dfrac{1}{5}$

$x = -\dfrac{7}{10} - \dfrac{1 \cdot 2}{5 \cdot 2}$

$x = \dfrac{-7 - 2}{10}$

$= -\dfrac{9}{10}$

77. Find the sum of the lengths of the four sides.

$\dfrac{2}{9} + \dfrac{5}{6} + \dfrac{2}{9} + \dfrac{5}{6} = \dfrac{4}{9} + \dfrac{10}{6}$

$= \dfrac{4 \cdot 2}{9 \cdot 2} + \dfrac{10 \cdot 3}{6 \cdot 3}$

$= \dfrac{8}{18} + \dfrac{30}{18}$

$= \dfrac{38}{18}$

$= \dfrac{19}{9}$

The perimeter is $\dfrac{19}{9}$ meters.

78. Find the sum of the three sides.

$$\frac{1}{5}+\frac{3}{5}+\frac{7}{10}=\frac{2\cdot 1}{2\cdot 5}+\frac{2\cdot 3}{2\cdot 5}+\frac{7}{10}$$
$$=\frac{2+6+7}{10}$$
$$=\frac{15}{10}$$
$$=\frac{3\cdot 5}{2\cdot 5}$$
$$=\frac{3}{2}$$

The perimeter is $\frac{3}{2}$ feet.

79.
$$x+\frac{1}{3}=\frac{35}{11}$$
$$\frac{8}{11}+\frac{1}{3}=\frac{35}{11}$$
$$\frac{24}{33}+\frac{11}{33}=\frac{105}{33}$$
$$\frac{35}{33}\neq\frac{105}{33}$$

No, it is not a solution.

80.
$$\frac{1}{9}y-\frac{1}{4}=\frac{1}{4}$$
$$\frac{1}{9}\left(\frac{9}{2}\right)-\frac{1}{4}=\frac{1}{4}$$
$$\frac{1}{2}-\frac{1}{4}=\frac{1}{4}$$
$$\frac{2}{4}-\frac{1}{4}=\frac{1}{4}$$
$$\frac{1}{4}=\frac{1}{4}$$

Yes, it is a solution.

81. $\frac{9}{25}+\frac{3}{50}=\frac{9\cdot 2}{25\cdot 2}+\frac{3}{50}=\frac{18+3}{50}=\frac{21}{50}$

$\frac{21}{50}$ have type A blood.

82. $\frac{2}{3}-\frac{5}{12}=\frac{8}{12}-\frac{5}{12}=\frac{3}{12}=\frac{1}{4}$

The difference is $\frac{1}{4}$ yard.

83. $\dfrac{\frac{2x}{5}}{\frac{7}{10}}=\frac{2x}{5}\div\frac{7}{10}=\frac{2x}{5}\cdot\frac{10}{7}=\frac{4x}{7}$

84. $\dfrac{\frac{3y}{7}}{\frac{11}{7}}=\frac{7\cdot\frac{3y}{7}}{7\cdot\frac{11}{7}}=\frac{3y}{11}$

85. The LCD of 4 and 8 is 8.

$$\frac{2+\frac{3}{4}}{1-\frac{1}{8}}=\frac{8\left(2+\frac{3}{4}\right)}{8\left(1-\frac{1}{8}\right)}$$
$$=\frac{8\cdot 2+8\cdot\frac{3}{4}}{8\cdot 1-8\cdot\frac{1}{8}}$$
$$=\frac{16+6}{8-1}$$
$$=\frac{22}{7}$$

86. The LCD of 3 and 6 is 6.

$$\frac{\frac{5}{6}+2}{\frac{11}{3}-1}=\frac{6\left(\frac{5}{6}+2\right)}{6\left(\frac{11}{3}-1\right)}=\frac{6\cdot\frac{5}{6}+6\cdot 2}{6\cdot\frac{11}{3}-6\cdot 1}=\frac{5+12}{22-6}=\frac{17}{16}$$

87. The LCD of 5, 2, 4, and 10 is 20.

$$\frac{\frac{2}{5}-\frac{1}{2}}{\frac{3}{4}-\frac{7}{10}}=\frac{20\left(\frac{2}{5}-\frac{1}{2}\right)}{20\left(\frac{3}{4}-\frac{7}{10}\right)}$$
$$=\frac{20\cdot\frac{2}{5}-20\cdot\frac{1}{2}}{20\cdot\frac{3}{4}-20\cdot\frac{7}{10}}$$
$$=\frac{8-10}{15-14}$$
$$=\frac{-2}{1}$$
$$=-2$$

88. The LCD of 6, 4, and $12y$ is $12y$.

$$\frac{\frac{5}{6}-\frac{1}{4}}{\frac{-1}{12y}}=\frac{12y\left(\frac{5}{6}-\frac{1}{4}\right)}{12y\left(\frac{-1}{12y}\right)}$$
$$=\frac{12y\left(\frac{5}{6}\right)-12y\left(\frac{1}{4}\right)}{12y\left(\frac{-1}{12y}\right)}$$
$$=\frac{10y-3y}{-1}$$
$$=\frac{7y}{-1}$$
$$=-7y$$

89. $2x+y=2\cdot\frac{1}{2}+\left(-\frac{2}{3}\right)=1-\frac{2}{3}=\frac{3}{3}-\frac{2}{3}=\frac{1}{3}$

90. $\dfrac{x}{y+z} = \dfrac{\frac{1}{2}}{-\frac{2}{3}+\frac{4}{5}}$

$\qquad = \dfrac{30\left(\frac{1}{2}\right)}{30\left(-\frac{2}{3}+\frac{4}{5}\right)}$

$\qquad = \dfrac{15}{30\left(-\frac{2}{3}\right)+30\left(\frac{4}{5}\right)}$

$\qquad = \dfrac{15}{-20+24}$

$\qquad = \dfrac{15}{4}$

91. $\dfrac{x+y}{z} = \dfrac{\frac{1}{2}+\left(-\frac{2}{3}\right)}{\frac{4}{5}}$

$\dfrac{\frac{1}{2}-\frac{2}{3}}{\frac{4}{5}} = \dfrac{30\left(\frac{1}{2}-\frac{2}{3}\right)}{30\left(\frac{4}{5}\right)}$

$\qquad = \dfrac{30\cdot\frac{1}{2}-30\cdot\frac{2}{3}}{24}$

$\qquad = \dfrac{15-20}{24}$

$\qquad = -\dfrac{5}{24}$

92. $x+y+z = \dfrac{1}{2}+\left(-\dfrac{2}{3}\right)+\dfrac{4}{5}$

$\qquad = \dfrac{15}{30}+\dfrac{-20}{30}+\dfrac{24}{30}$

$\qquad = \dfrac{19}{30}$

93. $y^2 = \left(-\dfrac{2}{3}\right)^2 = -\dfrac{2}{3}\cdot-\dfrac{2}{3} = \dfrac{2\cdot2}{3\cdot3} = \dfrac{4}{9}$

94. $x-z = \dfrac{1}{2}-\dfrac{4}{5} = \dfrac{5}{10}-\dfrac{8}{10} = -\dfrac{3}{10}$

95. $\qquad -\dfrac{3}{5}x = 6$

$-\dfrac{5}{3}\cdot-\dfrac{3}{5}x = -\dfrac{5}{3}\cdot6$

$\qquad x = -10$

96. $\qquad \dfrac{2}{9}y = -\dfrac{4}{3}$

$\dfrac{9}{2}\cdot\dfrac{2}{9}y = \dfrac{9}{2}\cdot\left(-\dfrac{4}{3}\right)$

$\qquad y = -\dfrac{9\cdot4}{2\cdot3}$

$\qquad = -\dfrac{3\cdot3\cdot2\cdot2}{2\cdot3}$

$\qquad = -\dfrac{3\cdot2}{1}$

$\qquad = -6$

97. $\qquad \dfrac{x}{7}-3 = -\dfrac{6}{7}$

$\qquad 7\left(\dfrac{x}{7}-3\right) = 7\cdot-\dfrac{6}{7}$

$\qquad 7\cdot\dfrac{x}{7}-7\cdot3 = -6$

$\qquad x-21 = -6$

$\qquad x-21+21 = -6+21$

$\qquad x = 15$

98. $\qquad \dfrac{y}{5}+2 = \dfrac{11}{5}$

$\qquad 5\left(\dfrac{y}{5}+2\right) = 5\cdot\dfrac{11}{5}$

$\qquad 5\cdot\dfrac{y}{5}+5\cdot2 = 11$

$\qquad y+10 = 11$

$\qquad y+10-10 = 11-10$

$\qquad y = 1$

99. $\qquad \dfrac{1}{6}+\dfrac{x}{4} = \dfrac{17}{12}$

$\qquad 12\left(\dfrac{1}{6}+\dfrac{x}{4}\right) = 12\cdot\dfrac{17}{12}$

$\qquad 12\cdot\dfrac{1}{6}+12\cdot\dfrac{x}{4} = 17$

$\qquad 2+3x = 17$

$\qquad 2+3x-2 = 17-2$

$\qquad 3x = 5$

$\qquad \dfrac{3x}{3} = \dfrac{15}{3}$

$\qquad x = 5$

100.

$$\frac{x}{5} - \frac{5}{4} = \frac{x}{2} - \frac{1}{20}$$

$$20\left(\frac{x}{5} - \frac{5}{4}\right) = 20\left(\frac{x}{2} - \frac{1}{20}\right)$$

$$20 \cdot \frac{x}{5} - 20 \cdot \frac{5}{4} = 20 \cdot \frac{x}{2} - 20 \cdot \frac{1}{20}$$

$$4x - 25 = 10x - 1$$

$$4x - 25 + 25 = 10x - 1 + 25$$

$$4x = 10x + 24$$

$$4x - 10x = 10x + 24 - 10x$$

$$-6x = 24$$

$$\frac{-6x}{-6} = \frac{24}{-6}$$

$$x = -4$$

101.

$$4\overline{)15} \quad \begin{array}{r} 3 \\ \underline{-12} \\ 3 \end{array}$$

$$\frac{15}{4} = 3\frac{3}{4}$$

102. $\dfrac{39}{13} = \dfrac{3 \cdot 13}{13} = 3$

103. $\dfrac{7}{7} = 1$

104.

$$4\overline{)125} \quad \begin{array}{r} 31 \\ \underline{-12} \\ 5 \\ \underline{-4} \\ 1 \end{array}$$

$$\frac{125}{4} = 31\frac{1}{4}$$

105. $2\dfrac{1}{5} = \dfrac{2 \cdot 5 + 1}{5} = \dfrac{11}{5}$

106. $5 = \dfrac{5}{1}$

107. $3\dfrac{8}{9} = \dfrac{3 \cdot 9 + 8}{9} = \dfrac{35}{9}$

108. $3 = \dfrac{3}{1}$

109.

$$\begin{array}{r} 31\dfrac{2}{7} = 31\dfrac{6}{21} \\ + \ 14\dfrac{10}{21} = 14\dfrac{10}{21} \\ \hline 45\dfrac{16}{21} \end{array}$$

110.

$$\begin{array}{r} 24\dfrac{4}{5} \\ + \ 35\dfrac{1}{5} \\ \hline 59\dfrac{5}{5} = 59 + 1 = 60 \end{array}$$

111.

$$\begin{array}{r} 69\dfrac{5}{22} = \quad 69\dfrac{5}{22} = \quad 68\dfrac{27}{22} \\ - \ 36\dfrac{7}{11} = - \ 36\dfrac{14}{22} = - \ 36\dfrac{14}{22} \\ \hline 32\dfrac{13}{22} \end{array}$$

112.

$$\begin{array}{r} 36\dfrac{3}{20} = \quad 36\dfrac{9}{60} = \quad 35\dfrac{69}{60} \\ - \ 32\dfrac{5}{6} = - \ 32\dfrac{50}{60} = - \ 32\dfrac{50}{60} \\ \hline 3\dfrac{19}{60} \end{array}$$

113.

$$\begin{array}{r} 29\dfrac{2}{9} = 29\dfrac{4}{18} \\ 27\dfrac{7}{18} = 27\dfrac{7}{18} \\ + \ 54\dfrac{2}{3} = 54\dfrac{12}{18} \\ \hline 110\dfrac{23}{18} = 110 + 1\dfrac{5}{8} = 111\dfrac{5}{18} \end{array}$$

114.

$$\begin{array}{r} 7\dfrac{3}{8} = 7\dfrac{9}{24} \\ 9\dfrac{5}{6} = 9\dfrac{20}{24} \\ + \ 3\dfrac{1}{12} = 3\dfrac{2}{24} \\ \hline 19\dfrac{31}{24} = 19 + 1\dfrac{7}{24} = 20\dfrac{7}{24} \end{array}$$

115. $1\dfrac{5}{8} \cdot \dfrac{2}{3} = \dfrac{13}{8} \cdot \dfrac{2}{3} = \dfrac{13 \cdot 2}{4 \cdot 2 \cdot 3} = \dfrac{13}{12} = 1\dfrac{1}{12}$

116. $3\dfrac{6}{11} \cdot \dfrac{5}{13} = \dfrac{39}{11} \cdot \dfrac{5}{13} = \dfrac{3 \cdot 13 \cdot 5}{11 \cdot 13} = \dfrac{15}{11} = 1\dfrac{4}{11}$

117. $4\frac{1}{6}\cdot 2\frac{2}{5}=\frac{25}{6}\cdot\frac{12}{5}=\frac{5\cdot5\cdot6\cdot2}{6\cdot5}=\frac{10}{1}=10$

118. $5\frac{2}{3}\cdot 2\frac{1}{4}=\frac{17}{3}\cdot\frac{9}{4}=\frac{17\cdot3\cdot3}{3\cdot4}=\frac{51}{4}=12\frac{3}{4}$

119. $6\frac{3}{4}\div 1\frac{2}{7}=\frac{27}{4}\div\frac{9}{7}=\frac{27}{4}\cdot\frac{7}{9}=\frac{3\cdot9\cdot7}{4\cdot9}=\frac{21}{4}=5\frac{1}{4}$

120. $5\frac{1}{2}\div 2\frac{1}{11}=\frac{11}{2}\div\frac{23}{11}$
$=\frac{11}{2}\cdot\frac{11}{23}$
$=\frac{11\cdot11}{2\cdot23}$
$=\frac{121}{46}$
$=2\frac{29}{46}$

121. $\frac{7}{2}\div 1\frac{1}{2}=\frac{7}{2}\div\frac{3}{2}=\frac{7}{2}\cdot\frac{2}{3}=\frac{7\cdot2}{2\cdot3}=\frac{7}{3}$ or $2\frac{1}{3}$

122. $1\frac{3}{5}\div\frac{1}{4}=\frac{8}{5}\cdot\frac{4}{1}=\frac{8\cdot4}{5\cdot1}=\frac{32}{5}=6\frac{2}{5}$

123. $\begin{array}{rcl}3\frac{3}{4}&=&3\frac{15}{20}\\ +\ 2\frac{3}{5}&=&2\frac{12}{20}\\ \hline &&5\frac{27}{20}=5+1\frac{7}{20}=6\frac{7}{20}\end{array}$

Their combined weight is $6\frac{7}{20}$ pounds.

124. $\begin{array}{rcl}50&=&49\frac{2}{2}\\ -\ 5\frac{1}{2}&=&-\ 5\frac{1}{2}\\ \hline &&44\frac{1}{2}\end{array}$

The amount remaining on the reel is $44\frac{1}{2}$ yards.

125. $\begin{array}{rclclcl}62\frac{3}{10}&=&62\frac{3}{10}&=&61\frac{13}{10}\\ -\ 54\frac{1}{2}&=&-\ 54\frac{5}{10}&=&-\ 54\frac{5}{10}\\ \hline &&&&7\frac{8}{10}=7\frac{4}{5}\end{array}$

The annual snowfall was $7\frac{4}{5}$ inches below normal.

126. $2\frac{1}{4}\cdot 3\frac{1}{3}=\frac{9}{4}\cdot\frac{10}{3}$
$=\frac{9\cdot10}{4\cdot3}$
$=\frac{90}{12}$
$=\frac{2\cdot3\cdot3\cdot5}{2\cdot2\cdot3}$
$=\frac{15}{2}$
$=7\frac{1}{2}$

The area is $7\frac{1}{2}$ square feet.

127. Find the sum of 4 sides.
$1\frac{1}{4}+1\frac{1}{4}+1\frac{1}{4}+1\frac{1}{4}=\frac{5}{4}+\frac{5}{4}+\frac{5}{4}+\frac{5}{4}$
$=\frac{20}{4}$
$=5$

The perimeter is 5 feet.

128. $\frac{7}{10}\cdot 2\frac{1}{8}=\frac{7}{10}\cdot\frac{17}{8}$
$=\frac{7\cdot17}{10\cdot8}$
$=\frac{119}{80}$ or $1\frac{39}{80}$

The area is $\frac{119}{80}$ or $1\frac{39}{80}$ square inches.

129. Find the sum of the eight sides of his flower beds.
$\frac{2}{3}+\frac{2}{3}+\frac{2}{3}+\frac{2}{3}+\frac{7}{8}+\frac{1}{3}+\frac{7}{8}+\frac{1}{3}$
$=\frac{2+2+2+2+1+1}{3}+\frac{7+7}{8}$
$=\frac{10}{3}+\frac{14}{8}$
$=\frac{10\cdot8}{3\cdot8}+\frac{14\cdot3}{8\cdot3}$
$=\frac{80}{24}+\frac{42}{24}$
$=\frac{122}{24}$
$=\frac{2\cdot61}{2\cdot12}$
$=\frac{61}{12}$ or $5\frac{1}{12}$

The total perimeter of his flower beds is $5\frac{1}{12}$ meters.

130. $58 \cdot 3\frac{1}{2} = \frac{58}{1} \cdot \frac{7}{2} = 203$ calories

131. $3\frac{1}{3} \cdot 4 = \frac{10}{3} \cdot \frac{4}{1} = \frac{40}{3}$ grams or $13\frac{1}{3}$ grams

132. $5\frac{1}{4} \div 5 = \frac{21}{4} \cdot \frac{1}{5} = \frac{21 \cdot 1}{4 \cdot 5} = \frac{21}{20}$ or $1\frac{1}{20}$

He walks $\frac{21}{20}$ or $1\frac{1}{20}$ mile each day.

133.
$$12\frac{1}{7} = 12\frac{2}{14}$$
$$+\ 15\frac{4}{14} = +15\frac{3}{14}$$
$$\overline{\hspace{2cm}}$$
$$27\frac{5}{14}$$

Answer: $27\frac{5}{14}$

134. $-3\frac{1}{5} \div \left(-2\frac{7}{10}\right) = -\frac{16}{5} \div \left(-\frac{27}{10}\right)$

$$= -\frac{16}{5} \cdot \left(-\frac{10}{27}\right)$$

$$= \frac{16 \cdot 2 \cdot 5}{5 \cdot 27}$$

$$= \frac{32}{27} \text{ or } 1\frac{5}{27}$$

135. $-2\frac{1}{4} \cdot 1\frac{3}{4} = -\frac{9}{4} \cdot \frac{7}{4}$

$$= -\frac{63}{16} \text{ or } -3\frac{15}{16}$$

136.
$$24\frac{7}{10} = 24\frac{28}{40} = 23\frac{68}{40}$$
$$-\ 23\frac{7}{8} = -\ 23\frac{35}{40} = 23\frac{35}{40}$$
$$\overline{\hspace{3cm}}$$
$$\frac{33}{40}$$

Answer: $-\frac{33}{40}$

Chapter 4 Test

1. $7\frac{2}{3} = \frac{3 \cdot 7 + 2}{3} = \frac{23}{3}$

2. $3\frac{6}{11} = \frac{11 \cdot 3 + 6}{11} = \frac{39}{11}$

3.
$$\begin{array}{r} 4 \\ 5\overline{)\ 23} \\ \underline{-20} \\ 3 \end{array}$$
$$\frac{23}{5} = 4\frac{3}{5}$$

4.
$$\begin{array}{r} 18 \\ 4\overline{)\ 75} \\ \underline{-4} \\ 35 \\ \underline{-32} \\ 3 \end{array}$$
$$\frac{75}{4} = 18\frac{3}{4}$$

5. $\frac{54}{210} = \frac{9 \cdot 6}{35 \cdot 6} = \frac{9}{35}$

6. $-\frac{42}{70} = -\frac{3 \cdot 14}{5 \cdot 14} = -\frac{3}{5}$

7. $\frac{4}{4} \div \frac{3}{4} = \frac{4}{4} \cdot \frac{4}{3} = \frac{4}{3}$

8. $-\frac{4}{3} \cdot \frac{4}{4} = -\frac{4}{3}$

9. $\frac{7x}{9} + \frac{x}{9} = \frac{7x + x}{9} = \frac{8x}{9}$

10. $\frac{1}{7} - \frac{3}{x} = \frac{1 \cdot x}{7 \cdot x} - \frac{3 \cdot 7}{x \cdot 7}$

$$= \frac{x}{7x} - \frac{21}{7x}$$

$$= \frac{x - 21}{7x}$$

11. $\frac{xy^3}{z} \cdot \frac{z}{xy} = \frac{x \cdot y \cdot y^2 \cdot z}{z \cdot x \cdot y} = \frac{y^2}{1} = y^2$

12. $-\frac{2}{3} \cdot -\frac{8}{15} = \frac{2 \cdot 8}{3 \cdot 15} = \frac{16}{45}$

13. $\frac{9a}{10} + \frac{2}{5} = \frac{9a}{10} + \frac{2 \cdot 2}{5 \cdot 2} = \frac{9a + 4}{10}$

14. $-\frac{8}{15y} - \frac{2}{15y} = \frac{-8 - 2}{15y} = \frac{-10}{15y} = -\frac{2}{3y}$

15. $8y^3 \div \dfrac{y}{3} = \dfrac{8y^3}{1} \div \dfrac{y}{3}$

$\quad = \dfrac{8y^3}{1} \cdot \dfrac{3}{y}$

$\quad = \dfrac{8 \cdot 3 \cdot y \cdot y^2}{y}$

$\quad = \dfrac{24y^2}{1}$

$\quad = 24y^2$

16. $5\dfrac{1}{4} \div \dfrac{7}{12} = \dfrac{21}{4} \cdot \dfrac{12}{7} = \dfrac{3 \cdot 7 \cdot 3 \cdot 4}{4 \cdot 7} = 9$

17. $3\dfrac{7}{8} = 3\dfrac{7 \cdot 5}{8 \cdot 5} = 3\dfrac{35}{40}$

$7\dfrac{2}{5} = 7\dfrac{2 \cdot 8}{5 \cdot 8} = 7\dfrac{16}{40}$

$\underline{2\dfrac{3}{4} = 2\dfrac{3 \cdot 10}{4 \cdot 10} = 2\dfrac{30}{40}}$

$\qquad\qquad 12\dfrac{81}{40} = 12 + 2\dfrac{1}{40} = 14\dfrac{1}{40}$

18. $\dfrac{3a}{8} \cdot \dfrac{16}{6a^3} = \dfrac{3a \cdot 2 \cdot 8}{8 \cdot 3 \cdot 2a \cdot a^2} = \dfrac{2 \cdot 3 \cdot 8 \cdot a}{2 \cdot 3 \cdot 8 \cdot a \cdot a^2} = \dfrac{1}{a^2}$

19. $-\dfrac{16}{3} \div -\dfrac{3}{12} = \dfrac{16}{3} \cdot \dfrac{12}{3} = \dfrac{16 \cdot 3 \cdot 4}{3 \cdot 3} = \dfrac{64}{3}$

20. $3\dfrac{1}{3} \cdot 6\dfrac{3}{4} = \dfrac{10}{3} \cdot \dfrac{27}{4} = \dfrac{5 \cdot 9}{2} = \dfrac{45}{2}$ or $22\dfrac{1}{2}$

21. $12 \div 3\dfrac{1}{3} = 12 \div \dfrac{10}{3}$

$\quad = 12 \cdot \dfrac{3}{10}$

$\quad = \dfrac{2 \cdot 6 \cdot 3}{2 \cdot 5}$

$\quad = \dfrac{18}{5}$

$\quad = 3\dfrac{3}{5}$

22. $\left(\dfrac{14}{5} \cdot \dfrac{25}{21} \right) \div 10 = \dfrac{14}{5} \cdot \dfrac{25}{21} \cdot \dfrac{1}{10} = \dfrac{2 \cdot 7 \cdot 5 \cdot 5}{5 \cdot 3 \cdot 7 \cdot 2 \cdot 5} = \dfrac{1}{3}$

23. $\dfrac{11}{12} - \dfrac{3}{8} + \dfrac{5}{24} = \dfrac{11 \cdot 2}{12 \cdot 2} - \dfrac{3 \cdot 3}{8 \cdot 3} + \dfrac{5}{24}$

$\quad = \dfrac{22}{24} - \dfrac{9}{24} + \dfrac{5}{24}$

$\quad = \dfrac{22 - 9 + 5}{24}$

$\quad = \dfrac{18}{24}$

$\quad = \dfrac{3 \cdot 6}{4 \cdot 6}$

$\quad = \dfrac{3}{4}$

24. $\dfrac{\frac{5x}{7}}{\frac{20x^2}{21}} = \dfrac{21 \cdot \frac{5x}{7}}{21 \cdot \frac{20x^2}{21}} = \dfrac{15x}{20x^2} = \dfrac{3 \cdot 5x}{4 \cdot 5 \cdot x \cdot x} = \dfrac{3}{4x}$

25. $\dfrac{5 + \frac{3}{7}}{2 - \frac{1}{2}} = \dfrac{14\left(5 + \frac{3}{7}\right)}{14\left(2 - \frac{1}{2}\right)} = \dfrac{14 \cdot 5 + 14 \cdot \frac{3}{7}}{14 \cdot 2 - 14 \cdot \frac{1}{2}} = \dfrac{70 + 6}{28 - 7} = \dfrac{76}{21}$

26. $\qquad -\dfrac{3}{8}x = \dfrac{3}{4}$

$\quad -\dfrac{8}{3} \cdot -\dfrac{3}{8}x = -\dfrac{8}{3} \cdot \dfrac{3}{4}$

$\qquad\qquad x = -\dfrac{8 \cdot 3}{3 \cdot 4}$

$\qquad\qquad x = -2$

27. $\qquad \dfrac{x}{5} + x = -\dfrac{24}{5}$

$\quad 5 \cdot \left(\dfrac{x}{5} + x \right) = 5 \cdot -\dfrac{24}{5}$

$\quad 5 \cdot \dfrac{x}{5} + 5x = -24$

$\qquad\quad x + 5x = -24$

$\qquad\qquad 6x = -24$

$\qquad\qquad \dfrac{6x}{6} = -\dfrac{24}{6}$

$\qquad\qquad x = -4$

28.
$$\frac{2}{3}+\frac{x}{4}=\frac{5}{12}+\frac{x}{2}$$
$$12\left(\frac{2}{3}+\frac{x}{4}\right)=12\left(\frac{5}{12}+\frac{x}{2}\right)$$
$$12\left(\frac{2}{3}\right)+12\left(\frac{x}{4}\right)=12\left(\frac{5}{12}\right)+12\left(\frac{x}{2}\right)$$
$$8+3x=5+6x$$
$$8+3x-6x=5+6x-6x$$
$$8-3x=5$$
$$8-3x-8=5-8$$
$$-3x=-3$$
$$\frac{-3x}{-3}=\frac{-3}{-3}$$
$$x=1$$

29. $-5x=-5\left(-\dfrac{1}{2}\right)=\dfrac{5}{2}$

30. $x \div y = \dfrac{1}{2} \div 3\dfrac{7}{8} = \dfrac{1}{2} \div \dfrac{31}{8} = \dfrac{1}{2} \cdot \dfrac{8}{31} = \dfrac{1 \cdot 2 \cdot 4}{2 \cdot 31} = \dfrac{4}{31}$

31. $\dfrac{280 \text{ calories}}{560 \text{ calories}} = \dfrac{28 \cdot 10}{28 \cdot 2 \cdot 10} = \dfrac{1}{2}$

$\dfrac{1}{2}$ of the calories are from fat.

32. The phrase "How long is the remaining" tells us to subtract. Subtract $2\dfrac{3}{4}$ feet from $6\dfrac{1}{2}$ feet.

$$
\begin{array}{ccccc}
6\dfrac{1}{2} & = & 6\dfrac{2}{4} & = & 5\dfrac{6}{4} \\
-\ 2\dfrac{3}{4} & = & -\ 2\dfrac{3}{4} & = & -\ 2\dfrac{3}{4} \\
\hline
& & & & 3\dfrac{3}{4}
\end{array}
$$

The remaining piece is $3\dfrac{3}{4}$ feet.

33. Find the sum of the fractions representing Back Woods and Westward.
$$\frac{3}{16}+\frac{1}{8}=\frac{3}{16}+\frac{1\cdot 2}{8\cdot 2}$$
$$=\frac{3}{16}+\frac{2}{16}$$
$$=\frac{5}{16}$$

$\dfrac{5}{16}$ of backpack sales go to Back Woods and Westward.

34. Multiply the fraction representing Wilderness, Inc. $\left(\dfrac{1}{4}\right)$ by 500,000.
$$\frac{1}{4}\cdot 500,000 = \frac{1}{4}\cdot\frac{500,000}{1}$$
$$=\frac{1\cdot 500,000}{4\cdot 1}$$
$$=\frac{1\cdot 4\cdot 125,000}{4\cdot 1}$$
$$=\frac{1\cdot 125,000}{1}$$
$$=\frac{125,000}{1}$$
$$=125,000$$

Wilderness, Inc. sells 125,000 backpacks each year.

35. Area = length $\cdot$ width
$$=(100+10+10)\cdot\left(53\frac{1}{3}+10+10\right)$$
$$=120\cdot 73\frac{1}{3}$$
$$=\frac{120}{1}\cdot\frac{220}{3}$$
$$=\frac{120\cdot 220}{1\cdot 3}$$
$$=\frac{40\cdot 220}{1}$$
$$=\frac{8800}{1}$$
$$=8800$$

8800 square yards of turf are needed.

36. $1\dfrac{8}{9}\cdot\dfrac{2}{3}=\dfrac{17}{9}\cdot\dfrac{2}{3}=\dfrac{17\cdot 2}{9\cdot 3}=\dfrac{34}{27}$ or $1\dfrac{7}{27}$

The area of the figure is $\dfrac{34}{27}$ or $1\dfrac{7}{27}$ square miles.

37.
$$258 \div 10\frac{3}{4} = \frac{258}{1} \div \frac{43}{4}$$
$$=\frac{258}{1}\cdot\frac{4}{43}$$
$$=\frac{258\cdot 4}{1\cdot 43}$$
$$=\frac{43\cdot 6\cdot 4}{1\cdot 43}$$
$$=\frac{24}{1}$$
$$=24$$

We can expect the car to travel 24 miles.

38. $120 \cdot \dfrac{3}{4} = \dfrac{120}{1} \cdot \dfrac{3}{4}$

$\qquad = \dfrac{120 \cdot 3}{1 \cdot 4}$

$\qquad = \dfrac{4 \cdot 30 \cdot 3}{4}$

$\qquad = \dfrac{30 \cdot 3}{1}$

$\qquad = 90$

The stock sold for $90 after the spill.

Chapter 4 Cumulative Review

1. 126 in words is one hundred twenty-six.

2. 115 in words is one hundred fifteen.

3. 3005 in words is three thousand, five.

4. 6573 in words is six thousand, five hundred seventy-three.

5. $\quad\begin{array}{r} 23 \\ +136 \\ \hline 159 \end{array}$

6. $\quad\begin{array}{r} 587 \\ +44 \\ \hline 631 \end{array}$

7. $\quad\begin{array}{r} 43 \\ -29 \\ \hline 14 \end{array}$

   Check: $\begin{array}{r} 14 \\ +29 \\ \hline 43 \end{array}$

8. $\quad\begin{array}{r} 995 \\ -62 \\ \hline 933 \end{array}$

   Check: $\begin{array}{r} 933 \\ +62 \\ \hline 995 \end{array}$

9. Since there is a 3 in the hundreds place, 278,362 rounded to the nearest thousand is 278,000.

10. Since there is a 6 in the ones place, 1436 rounded to the nearest ten is 1440.

11. $1510 \times 42 = 63,420$
    42 disks can hold 63,420 thousand bytes

12. $435 \times 3 = 1305$
    He travels a total of 1305.

13. $\begin{array}{r} 7089 \text{ R } 5 \\ 8\overline{)56717} \\ \underline{-56} \\ 07 \\ \underline{-0} \\ 71 \\ \underline{-64} \\ 77 \\ \underline{-72} \\ 5 \end{array}$

    Check: $7089 \times 8 + 5 = 56,712 + 5 = 56717$

14. $\begin{array}{r} 379 \text{ R } 10 \\ 12\overline{)4558} \\ \underline{-36} \\ 95 \\ \underline{-84} \\ 118 \\ \underline{-108} \\ 10 \end{array}$

    Check: $379 \times f12 + 10 - 4548 + 10 = 4558$

15. $4 \cdot 4 \cdot 4 = 4^3$

16. $7 \cdot 7 = 7^2$

17. $6 \cdot 6 \cdot 6 \cdot 8 \cdot 8 \cdot 8 \cdot 8 \cdot 8 = 6^3 \cdot 8^5$

18. $9 \cdot 9 \cdot 9 \cdot 9 \cdot 5 \cdot 5 = 9^4 \cdot 5^2$

19. $2(x - y) = 2(8 - 4)$
    $\qquad = 2(4)$
    $\qquad = 8$

20. $8a + 3(b - 5) = 8 \cdot 5 + 3(9 - 5)$
    $\qquad = 8 \cdot 5 + 3(4)$
    $\qquad = 40 + 12$
    $\qquad = 52$

21. 150 ft. below the surface is represented by -150.

22. $21°$ F below zero is represented by -21.

23.

24.

25. $7-8-(-5)-1=7-8+5-1=3$

26. $6+(-8)--(-9)+3=6+(-8)+9+3=10$

27. $(-5)^2=(-5)(-5)=25$

28. $-2^4=-(2)(2)(2)(2)=-16$

29. $\dfrac{12-16}{-1+3}=\dfrac{-4}{2}=-2$

30. $\begin{aligned}\left(20-5^2\right)^2&=(20-25)^2\\&=(-5)^2\\&=25\end{aligned}$

31. $5(3y)=(5\cdot3)y=15y$

32. $12(3c)=(12\cdot3)c=36c$

33. $-2(4x)=(-2\cdot4)x=-8x$

34. $-7(14a)=(-7\cdot14)a=-98a$

35. $\begin{aligned}-8&=x+1\\-8-1&=x+1-1\\-9&=x\end{aligned}$

36. $\begin{aligned}x-3&=5\\x-3+3&=5+3\\x&=8\end{aligned}$

37. $\begin{aligned}8x-9x&=12-17\\-x&=-5\\\dfrac{-1x}{-1}&=\dfrac{-5}{-1}\\x&=5\end{aligned}$

38. $\begin{aligned}2x+5x&=0-7\\7x&=-7\\\dfrac{7x}{7}&=\dfrac{-7}{7}\\x&=-1\end{aligned}$

39. a. The product 7 and 6 is 42 translates to: $7\cdot6=42$.

    b. Twice the sum of 3 and 5 is equal to 16 translates to: 2(3+5)=16.

    c. The quotient of –45 and 5 yields –9 translates to $\dfrac{-45}{5}=-9$.

40. a. The sum of 4 and 3 is 7 translates to: 4+3=7.

    b. Four times the difference of 5 and 2 equals 12 translates to: 4(5–2)=12.

    c. The product –4 and –6 yields 24 translates to (–4)(–6)=24.

41. $\begin{aligned}3+2x&=x-6\\3+2x-x&=x-6-x\\3+x&=-6\\3+x-3&=-6-3\\x&=-9\end{aligned}$

42. $\begin{aligned}4+3x&=x-6\\4+3x-x&=x-6-x\\4+2x&=-6\\4+2x-4&=-6-4\\2x&=-10\\\dfrac{2x}{2}&=\dfrac{-10}{2}\\x&=-5\end{aligned}$

43. $\dfrac{9x}{11}=\dfrac{9x\cdot4}{11\cdot4}=\dfrac{36x}{44}$

44. $\dfrac{2a}{3}=\dfrac{2a\cdot5}{3\cdot5}=\dfrac{10a}{15}$

45. $\begin{aligned}45&=5\cdot9\\&=5\cdot3\cdot3\\&=3\cdot3\cdot5\ \text{or}\ 3^2\cdot5\end{aligned}$

46. $\begin{aligned}92&=2\cdot46\\&=2\cdot2\cdot23\ \text{or}\ 2^2\cdot23\end{aligned}$

47. $\dfrac{2}{3}\cdot\dfrac{5}{11}=\dfrac{10}{33}$

48. $\dfrac{1}{7}\cdot\dfrac{2}{5}=\dfrac{2}{35}$

49. $\dfrac{1}{4}\cdot\dfrac{1}{2}=\dfrac{1}{8}$

50. $\dfrac{3}{5}\cdot\dfrac{1}{5}=\dfrac{3}{25}$

Chapter 5

1. $0.27 = \dfrac{27}{100}$

2. Since $0 < 1$, $0.205 < 0.213$.

3. 54.651 rounded to the nearest tenth is 54.7. We round up because the digit in the hundredths place is greater than or equal to 5.

4.
$$
\begin{array}{r}
\overset{2\ 1}{38.410} \\
14.032 \\
+\ 7.600 \\
\hline
60.042
\end{array}
$$

5.
$$
\begin{array}{r}
3.4 \quad \text{1 decimal} \\
\times\ 2.1 \quad \text{1 decimal} \\
\hline
34 \\
680 \\
\hline
7.14 \quad \text{2 decimal places}
\end{array}
$$

6. $(2.016)(100) = 201.6$

7. $0.4\overline{)16.24}$

Move decimal points 1 place.
$$
\begin{array}{r}
40.6 \\
4.\overline{)\ 162.4} \\
-16 \\
\hline
02 \\
-0 \\
\hline
24 \\
-24 \\
\hline
0
\end{array}
$$
$16.24 \div 0.4 = 40.6$

8. $\dfrac{891}{10,000} = 0.0891$

9. $x - y = 12.3 - 0.61 = 11.69$
$$
\begin{array}{r}
12.30 \\
-\ 0.61 \\
\hline
11.69
\end{array}
$$

10. $-9.8 - 6.2x - 7.9 + 1.4x$
$= -9.8 - 7.9 - 6.2x + 1.4x$
$= -17.7 - 4.8x$

11. $xy = (4.2)(0.03) = 0.126$
$$
\begin{array}{r}
4.2 \quad \text{1 decimal place} \\
\times\ 0.03 \quad \text{2 decimal places} \\
\hline
0.126 \quad \text{3 decimal places}
\end{array}
$$

12. Circumference $= 2\pi r$
$= 2\pi \cdot 6$
$= 12\pi$
$\approx 12(3.14)$
$= 37.68$

The circumference is 12π inches which is approximately 37.68 inches.

13. $\dfrac{\$576}{20} = \$28.80$
$$
\begin{array}{r}
28.8 \\
20\overline{)\ 576.0} \\
-40 \\
\hline
176 \\
-160 \\
\hline
160 \\
-160 \\
\hline
0
\end{array}
$$

14. $0.2(6.9 - 3.01) = 0.2(3.89) = 0.778$

15. $\dfrac{3}{8} = 0.375$
$$
\begin{array}{r}
0.375 \\
8\overline{)\ 3.000} \\
-2\,4 \\
\hline
60 \\
-56 \\
\hline
40 \\
-40 \\
\hline
0
\end{array}
$$

16. $\dfrac{9}{11} \approx 0.81818 < 0.8182$

$\dfrac{9}{11} < 0.8182$

17.
$$4(x + 0.22) = 2x - 3.4$$
$$4x + 0.88 = 2x - 3.4$$
$$4x + 0.88 - 0.88 = 2x - 3.4 - 0.88$$
$$4x = 2x - 4.28$$
$$4x - 2x = 2x - 4.28 - 2x$$
$$2x = -4.28$$
$$\frac{2x}{2} = -\frac{4.28}{2}$$
$$x = -2.14$$

18. $\sqrt{\dfrac{36}{49}} = \dfrac{6}{7}$ since $\dfrac{6}{7} \cdot \dfrac{6}{7} = \dfrac{36}{49}$.

19. $\sqrt{46} \approx 6.78$

20.
$$a^2 + b^2 = c^2$$
$$9^2 + 12^2 = c^2$$
$$81 + 144 = c^2$$
$$225 = c^2$$
$$\sqrt{225} = c$$
$$15 = c$$
The length of the hypotenuse is 15 inches.

Section 5.1

Practice Problems

1. a. 0.08 is eight hundredths

   b. −500.025 is negative five hundred and twenty-five thousandths.

   c. 0.0329 is three hundred twenty-nine ten-thousandths.

2. Ninety-seven and twenty-eight hundredths

3. Seventy-two and one thousand eighty-five ten-thousandths.

4. *Two hundred seven and* _____ $^{40}/_{100}$

5. 300.96

6. 39.042

5. $0.037 = \dfrac{37}{1000}$

6. $14.97 = 14\dfrac{97}{100}$

9. $0.12 = \dfrac{12}{100} = \dfrac{3}{25}$

10. $57.8 = 57\dfrac{8}{10} = 57\dfrac{4}{5}$

11. $-209.986 = -209\dfrac{986}{1000} = -209\dfrac{493}{500}$

12. The tens, ones, and tenths places are all the same. The hundredths places are different. Since $0 < 8$, then $13.208 < 13.28$.

13. In the tenths place, 1 is greater than 0 so $0.12 > 0.086$.

14. The tenths and the hundredths places are the same. The thousandths places are different. Since $-9 < 0$, $-0.029 < -0.0209$.

15. To round 123.7817 to the nearest thousandth, observe that the digit in the ten-thousandths place is 7. Since this digit is at least 5, we need to add 1 to the digit in the thousandths place. The number 123.7817 rounded to the nearest thousandth is 123.782.

16. To round −0.072 to the nearest hundredth, observe that the digit in the thousandths place is 2. Since this is less than 5, we do not add 1 to the digit in the hundredths place. The number −0.072 rounded to the nearest hundredth is −0.07.

17. To round 1.2789 to the nearest hundredth, observe that the digit in the thousandths place is 8. Since this digit is at least 5, we need to add 1 to the digit in the hundredths place. The number 1.0789 rounded to the nearest hundredth is 1.28. The price is $1.28.

18. To round 24.43 to the nearest tenth, observe that the digit in the hundredths place is 3. Since this digit is less than 5, we do not add 1 to the digit in the tenths place. The number 24.43 rounded to the nearest tenth is 24.4. The bill is $24.40.

Mental Math

1. 70
    ↑ tens

2. 700
    ↑ hundreds

3. 0.7
    ↑ tenths

4. 0.07
    ↑ hundredths

Exercise Set 5.1

1. 6.52 is six and fifty-two hundredths.

3. 16.23 is sixteen and twenty-three hundredths.

5. −3.205 is negative three and two hundred five thousandths.

7. 167.009 is one hundred sixth-seven and nine thousanths.

9. *Three hundred twenty-one and* ___ $^{42}/_{100}$

11. *Fifty-nine and* ___ $^{68}/_{100}$

13. Six and five-tenths is 6.5.

15. Nine and eight-hundredths is 9.08.

17. Negative five and six hundred twenty-five thousandths is −5.625.

19. Sixty-four ten-thousandths is 0.0064.

21. Sixty-four and sixteen hundredths is 64.16.

23. Five and four tenths is 5.4.

25. $0.3 = \dfrac{3}{10}$

27. $0.27 = \dfrac{27}{100}$

29. $-5.47 = -5\dfrac{47}{100}$

31. $0.048 = \dfrac{48}{1000} = \dfrac{6}{125}$

33. $7.07 = 7\dfrac{7}{100}$

35. $15.802 = 15\dfrac{802}{1000} = 15\dfrac{401}{500}$

37. $0.3005 = \dfrac{3005}{10,000} = \dfrac{601}{2000}$

39. $487.32 = 487\dfrac{32}{100} = 487\dfrac{8}{25}$

41. 0.15 0.16
    ↑   ↑
    5 < 6 so
    0.15 < 0.16

43. −0.57 < −0.54

45. 0.098 0.1
    ↑   ↑
    0 < 1 so
    0.098 < 0.1

47. 0.54900 0.549
    ↑   ↑
    0 =   0 so
    0.54900 = 0.549

49. 167.908 167.980
    ↑   ↑
    0 <   8 so
    167.908 < 167.980

51. 420,000   0.000042
    ↑   ↑
    4   >   0 so
    420,000 > 0.000042

53. −1.0621 < −1.07

55. −7.052 < −7.0052

57. −0.023 > −0.024

59. To round 0.57 to the nearest tenth, observe that the digit in the hundredths place is 7. Since this digit is at least 5, we need to add 1 to the digit in the tenths place. The number 0.57 rounded to the nearest tenth is 0.6.

61. To round 0.234 to the nearest hundredth, observe that the digit in the thousandths place is 4. Since this digit is less than 5, we do not add 1 to the digit in the hundredths place. The number 0.234 rounded to the nearest hundredth is 0.23.

63. To round 0.5942 to the nearest thousandth, observe that the digit in the ten-thousandths place is 2. Since this digit is less than 5, we do not add 1 to the digit in the thousandths place. The number 0.5942 rounded to the nearest thousandth is 0.594.

65. To round 98,207.23 to the nearest ten, observe that the digit in the ones place is 7. Since this digit is at least 5, we need to add 1 to the digit in the tens place. The number 98,207.32 rounded to the nearest ten is 98,210.

67. To round 12,999 to the nearest tenth, observe that the digit in the hundredths place is 9. Since this digit is at least 5, we need to add 1 to the digit in the tenths place. The number 12.999 rounded to the nearest tenth is 13.0.

69. To round –17.667 to the nearest hundredth, observe that the digit in the thousandths place is 7. Since this digit is less than 5, we do not need to add 1 to the digit in the tenths place. The number –17.667 rounded to the nearest hundredth is –17.67.

71. To round –0.501 to the nearest tenth, observe that the digit in the hundredths place is 0. Since the digit is less than 5, we do not add 1 to the digit in the tenths place. The number –0.501 rounded to the nearest tenth is –0.5.

73. To round 0.067 to the nearest hundredth, observe that the digit in the thousandths place is 7. Since this digit is at least 5, we need to add 1 to the digit in the hundredths place. The number 0.067 rounded to the nearest hundredth is 0.07. The amount is $0.07.

75. To round 26.95 to the nearest one, observe that the digit in the tenths place is 9. Since this digit is at least 5, we need to add 1 to the digit in the ones place. The number 26.95 rounded to the nearest one is 27. The amount is $27.

77. To round 0.1992 to the nearest hundredth, observe that the digit in the thousandths place is 9. Since the digit is at least 5, we need to add 1 the digit in the hundredths place. The number 0.1992 rounded to the nearest hundredth is 0.2. The amount is $0.20.

79. 0.26559 rounds to 0.27
0.26499 rounds to 0.26
0.25786 rounds to 0.26
0.25186 rounds to 0.25
Therefore, 0.26499 and 0.25786 round to 0.26.

81. Since there is a 9 in the tenths place, 15.99 rounded to the nearest dollar is $16.

83. Since there is a 5 in the thousandths place, 2.34528 rounded to the nearest hundredth is 2.35.

85. To round 24.6229 to the nearest thousandth, observe that the digit in the ten-thousandths place is 9. Since this digit is at least 5, we need to add 1 to the digit in the thousandths place. The number 24.6229 rounded to the nearest thousandth is 24.623. The length is 24.623 hours.

87. To round 135.74 to the nearest one, observe that the digit in the tenths place is 7. Since this digit is at least 5, we need to add 1 to the digit in the ones place. The number 135.74 rounded to the nearest one is 136. The record is 136 mph

89. Since there is a 3 in the tenths place, 31.3833 rounded to the nearest whole point is 31.

91. Compare each place value.
0.10299, 0.1037, 0.1038, 0.9

93. 3452
$\underline{+2314}$
5766

95. 94
$\underline{-23}$
71

97. 482
$\underline{-239}$
243

99. Compare each place value. 228.040 is the highest average score bowled by Parker Bohn.

101. Compare each place value and list from greatest to least.
226.130, 225.490, 225.370, 222.980, 222.830, 222.008, 219.702, 218.158, 215.432.

103. Answers may vary.

105. 0.0000203 in words is two hundred three ten-millionths.

Section 5.2

Practice Problems

1. a. 15.520
$\underline{+2.371}$
17.891

b. 20.060
$\underline{+17.612}$
37.672

c. 0.125
$\underline{+122.800}$
122.925

2. a. $1\ 1\ 1$
34.5670
129.4300
$\underline{+2.8903}$
166.8873

b. 1
11.210
46.013
$\underline{+362.526}$
419.749

3. 27.00000
$\underline{+0.00043}$
27.00043

4. Subtract the absolute values.
99.2
$\underline{-8.1}$
91.1
Thus, $8.1 + (-99.2) = -91.1$.

5. 5.80
$\underline{-3.92}$
1.88
Check:
$1\ 1$
1.88
$\underline{+3.92}$
5.80 or 5.8

6. 53.00
$\underline{-29.31}$
23.69
Check:
$1\ 1\ 1$
23.69
$\underline{+29.31}$
53.00 or 53

7. $1\ 16$
26.99
$\underline{-18.00}$
8.99
Check:
8.99
$\underline{+18.00}$
26.99

8. To subtract 9.6, add the opposite of 9.6, or −9.6.
$-3.4 - 9.6 = -3.4 + (-9.6)$
To add two numbers with the same sign, add their absolute values.

$$\begin{array}{r} 3.4 \\ + \ 9.6 \\ \hline 13.0 \end{array}$$

The sign in the answer is the common sign.
Thus, $(-3.4) + (-9.6) = -13$.

9. $-1.05 - (-7.23) = -1.05 + 7.23$

$$\begin{array}{r} 7.23 \\ -1.05 \\ \hline 6.18 \end{array}$$

10. $y - z = 11.6 - 10.8$
$\qquad = 0.8$

$$\begin{array}{r} 11.6 \\ -10.8 \\ \hline 0.8 \end{array}$$

11. $\qquad y - 4.3 = 7.8$
$12.1 - 4.3 \ \overset{?}{=} \ 7.8$
$\qquad\qquad 7.8 = 7.8 \ \text{ True}$
Yes, 12.1 is a solution.

12. $-4.3y + 7.8 - 20.1y + 14.6$
$= (-4.3y) + (-20.1y) + 7.8 + 14.6$
$= (-24.4y) + 22.4$
$= -24.4y + 22.4$

13. The phrase "total monthly cost" tells us to add.
Find the sum of the three expenses.

$$\begin{array}{r} {\scriptstyle 111} \\ 52.70 \\ 536.50 \\ + \ 87.50 \\ \hline 676.70 \end{array}$$

The total monthly cost is \$676.70.

14. The phrase "how much taller" tells us to subtract.
Subtract 70.8 from 72.6.

$$\begin{array}{r} 72.6 \\ -70.8 \\ \hline 1.8 \end{array}$$

Check:

$$\begin{array}{r} 1.8 \\ + \ 70.8 \\ \hline 72.6 \end{array}$$

The difference in average height is 1.8 inches.

Calculator Explorations

1. Press the keys 315.782 $\boxed{+}$ 12.96 $\boxed{= \text{ or ENTER}}$.
The display will read 328.742.

2. Press the keys 29.68 $\boxed{+}$ 85.902 $\boxed{= \text{ or ENTER}}$.
The display will read 115.582.

3. Press the keys 6.249 $\boxed{-}$ 1.0076 $\boxed{= \text{ or ENTER}}$.
The display will read 5.2414.

4. Press the keys 5.238 $\boxed{-}$ 0.682 $\boxed{= \text{ or ENTER}}$.
The display will read 4.556.

5. Press the keys 12.555 $\boxed{+}$ 224.987 $\boxed{+}$ 5.2 $\boxed{+}$
622.65 $\boxed{= \text{ or ENTER}}$.
The display will read 865.392.

6. Press the keys 47.006 $\boxed{+}$ 0.17 $\boxed{+}$ 313.259 $\boxed{+}$
139.088 $\boxed{= \text{ or ENTER}}$.
The display will read 499.523.

Mental Math

1. $$\begin{array}{r} 0.3 \\ + \ 0.2 \\ \hline 0.5 \end{array}$$

2. $$\begin{array}{r} 0.4 \\ + 0.5 \\ \hline 0.9 \end{array}$$

3. $$\begin{array}{r} 1.00 \\ + 0.26 \\ \hline 1.26 \end{array}$$

4. $$\begin{array}{r} 3.00 \\ + 0.19 \\ \hline 3.19 \end{array}$$

5. $$\begin{array}{r} 7.6 \\ + \ 1.3 \\ \hline 8.9 \end{array}$$

6. 4.5
$$\begin{array}{r} 4.5 \\ +3.2 \\ \hline 7.7 \end{array}$$

7. 0.9
$$\begin{array}{r} 0.9 \\ -0.3 \\ \hline 0.6 \end{array}$$

8. 0.6
$$\begin{array}{r} 0.6 \\ -0.2 \\ \hline 0.4 \end{array}$$

Exercise Set 5.2

1. 1.3
$$\begin{array}{r} 1.3 \\ +2.2 \\ \hline 3.5 \end{array}$$

3. $5.7 = 5.70$
$$\begin{array}{r} 5.70 \\ +1.13 \\ \hline 6.83 \end{array}$$

5. 24.6000
$$\begin{array}{r} 24.6000 \\ 2.3900 \\ +0.0678 \\ \hline 27.0578 \end{array}$$

7. 45.023
$$\begin{array}{r} 45.023 \\ 3.006 \\ +8.403 \\ \hline 56.432 \end{array}$$

9. $-2.6 + (-5.97)$
Add the absolute values.
$$\begin{array}{r} 2.60 \\ +5.97 \\ \hline 8.57 \end{array}$$
Attach the common sign.
-8.57

11. $15.78 + (-4.62)$
Subtract the absolute values.
$$\begin{array}{r} 15.78 \\ -4.62 \\ \hline 11.16 \end{array}$$
Attach the sign of the number with the larger

absolute value.
11.16

13. 8.8
$$\begin{array}{r} 8.8 \\ -2.3 \\ \hline 6.5 \end{array}$$

15. 18.0
$$\begin{array}{r} 18.0 \\ -2.7 \\ \hline 15.3 \end{array}$$

17. 654.90
$$\begin{array}{r} 654.90 \\ -56.67 \\ \hline 598.23 \end{array}$$

19. 23.0
$$\begin{array}{r} 23.0 \\ -6.7 \\ \hline 16.3 \end{array}$$

21. $-1.12 - 5.2 = -1.12 + (-5.2)$
Add the absolute values.
$$\begin{array}{r} 1.2 \\ +5.20 \\ \hline 6.32 \end{array}$$
Attach the common sign.
-6.32

23. $7.7 - 14.1 = 7.7 + (-14.1)$
Subtract the absolute values.
$$\begin{array}{r} 14.1 \\ -7.7 \\ \hline 6.4 \end{array}$$
Attach the sign of the number with the larger
absolute value.
-6.4

25. $-2.6 - (-5.7) = -2.6 + 5.7$
$$\begin{array}{r} 5.7 \\ -2.6 \\ \hline 3.1 \end{array}$$

27. 0.9
$$\begin{array}{r} 0.9 \\ +2.2 \\ \hline 3.1 \end{array}$$

29. $-5.9 - 4 = -5.9 + (-4)$
Add the absolute values.
$$\begin{array}{r} 5.9 \\ +4.0 \\ \hline 9.9 \end{array}$$

Attach the common sign.
–9.9

31.   45.67
   $\underline{-20.00}$
    25.67

33.   –6.06 + 0.44
Subtract the absolute values.
    6.06
  $\underline{-\ 0.44}$
    5.62
Attach the sign of the number with the largest absolute value.
–5.62

35.   900.34
  $\underline{-123.45}$
   776.89

37.   3490.23
  $\underline{+8493.09}$
  11,983.32

39.   234.89
  $\underline{+230.67}$
   465.56

41.   50.2 – 600 = 50.2 + (–600)
Subtract the absolute values.
  600.0
$\underline{-\ 50.2}$
  549.8
Attach the sign of the number with the larger absolute value.
–549.8

43.   923.5
  $\underline{-\ 61.9}$
   861.6

45.   100.009
    6.080
  $\underline{+9.034}$
  115.123

47.   1000.0
  $\underline{-123.4}$
   876.6

49.   –0.003 + 0.091
Subtract the absolute values.
    0.091
  $\underline{-\ 0.003}$
    0.088
Attach the sign of the number with the larger absolute value.
0.088

51.   500.000
  $\underline{-\ 34.098}$
   465.902

53.   –102.40
  $\underline{-78.04}$
  –180.44

55. $-2.9 - (-1.8) = -2.9 + 1.8$
    –2.9
  $\underline{+1.8}$
    –1.1

57. $x + z = 3.6 + 0.21 = 3.81$

59. $x - z = 3.6 - 0.21 = 3.39$

61. $y - x + z = 5 - 3.6 + 0.217$
             $= 5.00 - 3.60$
             $= 1.40 + 0.21$
             $= 1.61$

63. $x + 2.7 = 9.3$
    $7 + 2.7 = 9.3$
       $9.7 = 9.3$ False
No, it is not a solution.

65. $27.4 - y = 16$
   $27.4 - 11.4 = 16$
          $16 = 16$
Yes, it is a solution.

67. $2.3 + x = 5.3 - x$
   $2.3 + 1 = 5.3 - 1$
       $3.3 \neq 4.3$ False
No, it is not a solution.

69. $30.7x + 17.6 - 23.8x - 10.7$
    $= 30.7x + (-23.8x) + 17.6 + (-10.7)$
    $= 6.9x + 6.9$

71. $-8.61 + 4.23y - 2.36 - 0.76y$
    $= -8.61 + (-2.36) + 4.23y + (-0.76y)$
    $= -10.97 + 3.47y$

73. The phrase "total monthly cost" tells us to add.
Find the sum of the four expenses.

2 1 1 1

275.36

83.00

81.60

+ 14.75

454.71

The total monthly cost is $454.71.

75. The phrase "By how much did the price change"
tells us to subtract. Subtract 0.979 from 1.039.

1.039

− 0.979

0.060

Check:

1 1

0.060

+ 0.979

1.039

The price changed by $0.06.

77. Subtract the cost of the book from what she paid
($20 + $20 = $40).

40.00

− 32.48

7.52

Check:

11 1

7.52

+ 32.48

40.00 or 40

Her change was $7.52.

79. "How much more" tells us to subtract 136.8 from
150.1.

150.1

−136.8

13.3

The average American consumed 13.3 more
pounds of sugar in 2000 than 1990.

81. "How much faster" tells us to subtract 35.2 from
321.0

321.0

−35.2

285.8

The highest speed is 285.8 mph faster than the
average wind speed.

83. To find Green's speed, we must add the old
record and the increase.

1 1 11

633.468

+ 129.567

763.035

The new record by Green is 763.035 mph.

85. The phrase "total amount" tells us to add. Find
the sum of the 3 concert's earnings.

121.2

103.5

+109.7

334.4

The total amount of money these three concert's
have earned is $334.4 million.

87. To find the total amount of snow Blue Canyon
receives we must add Marquette's snow fall to
that of the stated increase.

1

129.2

+ 111.6

240.8

Blue Canyon receives an average of 240.8 inches
of snow annually.

89. Find the sum of the lengths of the three sides.

12.40

29.34

+ 25.70

67.44

The architect needs 67.44 feet of border material.

91.   160.875

−148.466

12.409

The average Daytona 500 winning speed was
12.409 mph slower in 1989 than in 1969.

93. 2059.817

− 15.467

2044.350

The last Mercury mission was 2044.35 minutes
longer than the first Mercury mission.

95. Compare the five numbers, finding the largest.
Switzerland has the largest number of 22 pounds.
Switzerland has the greatest chocolate
consumption per person.

97. Subtract 13.9 from 22.

$$\begin{array}{r} 22.0 \\ -\ 13.9 \\ \hline 8.1 \end{array}$$

Check:

$$\begin{array}{r} 1\ 1 \\ 8.1 \\ +\ 13.9 \\ \hline 22.0 \text{ or } 22 \end{array}$$

The difference in consumption is 8.1 pounds per person.

99.

Country	Pounds of Chocolate per person
Switzerland	22.0
Norway	16.0
Germany	15.8
United Kingdom	14.5
Belgium	13.9

101. $\left(\dfrac{1}{5}\right)^3 = \dfrac{1}{5} \cdot \dfrac{1}{5} \cdot \dfrac{1}{5} = \dfrac{1}{125}$

103. $\dfrac{25}{36} \cdot \dfrac{24}{40} = \dfrac{25}{36} \cdot \dfrac{3 \cdot 8}{5 \cdot 8}$

$= \dfrac{25 \cdot 3}{36 \cdot 5}$

$= \dfrac{5 \cdot 5 \cdot 3}{3 \cdot 12 \cdot 5}$

$= \dfrac{5 \cdot 1}{12 \cdot 1}$

$= \dfrac{5}{12}$

105.
$$\begin{array}{lll} 2 \text{ quarters} & = & 0.50 \\ 3 \text{ dimes} & = & 0.30 \\ 4 \text{ nickels} & = & 0.20 \\ 2 \text{ pennies} & = & +0.02 \\ \hline & & \$1.02 \end{array}$$

107. 5 nickels, 2 dimes, and 1 nickel; 1 dime and 3 nickels; 1 quarter

109. Answers may vary.

111. $14.271 - 8.968x + 1.333 - 201.815x + 101.239x = -109.544x + 15.604$Section 5.3

113. $10.68 - (2.3 + 2.3) = 10.68 - 46$

$$\begin{array}{r} 10.68 \\ -4.60 \\ \hline 6.08 \text{ inches} \end{array}$$

Section 5.3

Practice Problems

1.
$$\begin{array}{r} 45.9 \\ \times\ 0.42 \\ \hline 918 \\ 18360 \\ 000 \\ \hline 19.278 \end{array}$$

2.
$$\begin{array}{r} 0.112 \\ \times\ 0.6 \\ \hline 672 \\ 00 \\ \hline 0.0672 \end{array}$$

3.
$$\begin{array}{r} 0.0721 \\ \times\ 48 \\ \hline 5768 \\ 28840 \\ \hline 3.4608 \end{array}$$

4. The product of a positive number and a negative number is a negative number.
$(5.4)(-1.3) = -7.02$

5. To find 23.7×10, note that 10 has 1 zero. Therefore, we move the decimal point of 23.7 to the right 1 place. The product is 237.

6. To find 203.004×100, note that 100 has 2 zeros. Therefore, we move the decimal point of 203.004 to the right 2 places. The product is 20,300.4.

7. To find 1.15×1000, note that 1000 has 3 zeros. Therefore, we move the decimal point of 1.15 to the right 3 places. The product is 1150.

8. To find 7.62×0.1, note that 0.1 has 1 decimal place. Therefore, we move the decimal point of 7.62 to the left 1 place. The product is 0.762.

9. To find 1.9×0.01, note that 0.01 has 2 decimal places. Therefore, we move the decimal point of 1.9 to the left 2 places. The product is 0.019.

10. To find 7682×0.001, note that 0.001 has 3 decimal places. Therefore, we move the decimal

point of 7682 to the left 3 places. The product is
7.682.

11. 2158 thousand = 2158 × 1000
                   = 2,158,000
     There are 2,158,000 farms in the U.S.

12. Recall that $7y$ means $7 \cdot y$.
     $7y = (7)(-0.028)$ -0.028
                        $\times \quad 7$
     $= -0.196 \leftarrow$ -0.196

13. $-4x = 22$
     $-4(-5.5) = 22$
          $22 = 22$ True
     Since 22 = 22 is a true statement, −5.5 is a
     solution.

14. Circumference = $2 \cdot \pi \cdot$ radius
                   $= 2 \cdot \pi \cdot 11$
                   $= 22\pi$
                   $= 22(3.14)$
                   $= 69.08$
     The circumference is $22\pi \approx 69.08$ meters.

15. Multiply 60.5 by 5.6.
          60.5
     $\times \quad 5.6$
          3630
          3025
          338.80 or 338.8
     She needs 338.8 ounces of fertilizer.

Exercise Set 5.3

1.   0.2 1 decimal place
     $\times$ 0.6 1 decimal place
        0.12 2 decimal places

3.   1.2 1 decimal place
     $\times$ 0.5 2 decimal places
        0.60 2 decimal places
     0.6   The trailing 0 can be dropped.

5. $(-2.3)(7.65)$
        7.65 2 decimal places
     $\times$ − 2.3 1 decimal place
        2295
        15300
        −17.595   3 decimal places

7. $(-6.89)(-5.7)$
        6.89   2 decimal places
     $\times$ 5.7   1 decimal place
        4823
        34450
        39.273   3 decimal places

9. 6.5 3 10 = 65

11. 6.5 3 0.1 = 0.65

13. $(-7.093)(1000) = -7093$

15. $(-9.83)(-0.01) = (9.83)(0.01) = 0.0983$

17.   5.62 2 decimal places
     $\times$ 7.7 1 decimal place
        3934
        39340
        43.274   3 decimal places

19.   1.0047 4 decimal places
     $\times$ 8.2   1 decimal place
        20094
        80376
        8.23854   5 decimal places

21. $(147.9)(100) = 14,790$

23. $(937.62)(-0.01) = -9.3762$

25.   49.02 3 decimals
     $\times$ 0.023 3 decimal places
        14706
        98080
        1.12746   5 decimal places

27.   −0.023   3 decimal places
     $\times$ 6.28   2 decimal places
        184
        0460
        13800
        −0.14444 5 decimal places

29. 5.5 billion = $5.5 \times 1,000,000,000$
               $= 5,500,000,000$

31. 36.4 million = $36.4 \times 1,000,000$
                 $= 36,400,000$

33. 1.6 million = $1.6 \times 1,000,000$
                = 1,600,000

35. Recall that xy means $x \cdot y$.
$xy = (3)(-0.2)$

$\begin{array}{r} 3.0 \\ \times \,-0.2 \\ \hline -0.60 \end{array}$

$= -0.6 \quad \leftarrow$

37. $xz - y = 3(5.7) - (-0.2)$
$= 17.1 + 0.2$
$= 17.3$

39. $SA = 2LW + 2WH + 2HL$
$= 2(10)(2.1) + 2(2.1)(0.6) + 2(0.6)(10)$
$= 42 + 2.52 + 12$
$= 44.52 + 12$
$= 56.52$

41. $0.6x = 4.92$ Show substitution exactly.
$0.6(14.2) = 4.92$
$8.52 = 4.92$ False
No, it is not a solution.

43. $-3x = -2.4$
$-3(0.08) = -2.4$
$-0.24 = -2.4$ False
No, it is not a solution.

45. $3.5y = -14$
$3.5(-4) = -14$
$-14.0 = -14$
$-14 = -14$ True
Yes, it is a solution.

47. Circumference $= 2 \cdot \pi \cdot$ radius
$C = 2 \cdot \pi \cdot 4 = 8\pi$
$C \approx 8(3.14) = 25.12$
The circumference is 8π meters, which is approximately 25.12 meters.

49. Circumference $= \pi \cdot$ diameter
$C = \pi \cdot 10 = 10\pi$
$C \approx 10(3.14) = 31.4$
The circumference is 10π centimeters, which is approximately 31.4 centimeters.

51. Circumference $= 2 \cdot \pi \cdot$ radius
$C = 2 \cdot \pi \cdot 9.1 = 18.2\pi$
$C \approx 57.148$
The circumference is 18.2π yards, which is approximately 57.148 yards.

53. Circumference $= \pi \cdot$ diameter
$C = \pi \cdot 250 = 250\pi$
$C \approx 250(3.14) = 785$
The circumference of the ferris wheel is 250π feet which is approximately 785 feet.

55. One revolution is equal to the circumference.
$C = \pi d$
$C = \pi(135)$
$C = 135\pi$ meters
$C \approx 135(3.14) = 423.9$ meters
One revolution is 135π meters which is approximately 423.9 meters.

57. a. $C = 2 \cdot \pi \cdot 10 = 20\pi \approx 20(3.14) = 62.8$ m
$C = 2 \cdot \pi \cdot 20$
$= 40\pi$
$\approx 40(3.14)$
$= 125.6$ m

b. yes

59. Multiply the number of ounces by the number of grams of fat in 1 ounce to get the total amount of fat.

$\begin{array}{r} 6.2 \\ \times \, 4 \\ \hline 24.8 \end{array}$

There are 24.8 grams of fat in a 4-ounce serving of cream cheese.

61. To find 2.8×1000, note that 1000 has 3 zeros. Therefore, we move the decimal point of 2.8 to the right 3 places. The product is 2800. The farmer received $2800.

63. Multiply 39.37 by 1.65.

$\begin{array}{r} 39.37 \\ \times \, 1.65 \\ \hline 19685 \\ 236220 \\ 393700 \\ \hline 64.9605 \end{array}$

She is about 64.9605 inches tall.

65. Multiply the number of hours by the hourly wage.

$\begin{array}{r} 13.88 \\ \times \, 40 \\ \hline 0 \\ 55520 \\ \hline 555.20 \end{array}$

His pay was $555.20

67. $675 \times 118.07 = 79,697.25$ yen

69. $350 \times 1.4695 \approx 514$ Canadian dollars

71.
$$
\begin{array}{r}
26 \\
5\overline{)130} \\
\underline{-10} \\
30 \\
\underline{-30} \\
0
\end{array}
$$

73.
$$
\begin{array}{r}
36 \\
56\overline{)2016} \\
\underline{-168} \\
336 \\
\underline{-336} \\
0
\end{array}
$$

75.
$$
\begin{array}{r}
8 \\
365\overline{)2920} \\
\underline{-2920} \\
0
\end{array}
$$

77. $-\dfrac{24}{7} \div \dfrac{8}{21} = -\dfrac{24}{7} \cdot \dfrac{21}{8}$

$= -\dfrac{24 \cdot 21}{7 \cdot 8}$

$= -\dfrac{8 \cdot 3 \cdot 7 \cdot 3}{7 \cdot 8}$

$= -\dfrac{3 \cdot 3}{1 \cdot 1}$

$= -\dfrac{9}{1}$

$= -9$

79. $(20.6)(1.86)(100,000) = 3,831,600$ miles

81. Answers may vary.

83. $4\pi r^2 = 4(3.14)(7.68)^2$
$= 4(3.14)(58.9824)$
$= 12.56(58.9824)$
≈ 740.82

Section 5.4

Practice Problems

1.
$$
\begin{array}{r}
0.71 \\
48\overline{)34.08} \\
\underline{-336} \\
48 \\
\underline{-48} \\
0
\end{array}
$$

2. $5.6\overline{)166.88}$ becomes
$$
\begin{array}{r}
29.8 \\
56\overline{)1668.8} \\
\underline{-112} \\
548 \\
\underline{-504} \\
448 \\
\underline{-448} \\
0
\end{array}
$$

3. Recall that a negative number divided by a negative number gives a positive quotient.
$$
\begin{array}{r}
0.027 \\
104\overline{)2.808} \\
\underline{-2\,08} \\
728 \\
\underline{-728} \\
0
\end{array}
$$
Thus $-2.808 \,(-104) = 0.027$.

4. $0.57\overline{)23.4}$ becomes
$$
\begin{array}{r}
41.052 \approx 41.05 \\
57.\overline{)2340.000} \\
\underline{-228} \\
60 \\
\underline{-57} \\
30 \\
\underline{-0} \\
300 \\
\underline{-285} \\
150 \\
\underline{-114} \\
36
\end{array}
$$

5. To find 28×1000, note that 1000 has 3 zeros. Therefore, we move the decimal point of 28 to the left 3 places. The quotient is 0.028.

6. To find 8.56×100, note that 100 has 2 zeros. Therefore, we move the decimal point of 8.56 to the left 2 places. The quotient is 0.0856.

7. $x \div y = 0.035 \div 0.02$

$0.02\overline{)0.035}$ becomes $\quad 2\overline{)3.50}^{\,1.75}$

$= 1.75$

8. $\dfrac{x}{100} = 3.9$

$\dfrac{39}{100} = 3.9$

$0.39 = 3.9$ False

Since $0.39 = 3.9$ is a false statement, 39 is not a solution.

9.
```
          11.84
1250) 14,800.00
     −1250
      2300
     − 1250
      10500
     −10000
       5000
      − 5000
         0
```
He needs 12 bags.

Exercise Set 5.4

1.
```
   0.094
5) 0.470
  − 45
    20
   −20
     0
```
$0.47 \div 5 = 0.094$

3. $0.06)\overline{18.00}$

Move the decimal points 2 places.
```
    300
6.) 1800.
   −18
    00
   −0
    00
   −0
     0
```
$−18 \div 0.06 = −300$

5. $0.82)\overline{4.756}$

Move the decimal points 2 places.
```
     5.8
82.) 475.6
    −410
     656
    −656
       0
```
$4.756 \div 0.82 = 5.8$

7. $5.5)\overline{36.3}$

Move the decimal points 1 place.
```
      6.6
55.) 363.0
    −330
     330
    −330
       0
```
The answer is negative.
$−36.3 \div 5.5 = −6.6$

9. $2.4)\overline{429.34}$

Move the decimal points one place.
```
     178....
24.) 4293.4
    −24
     189
    −168
     213
    −192
      21
```
178 rounded to the nearest hundred is 200.

11. $0.023)\overline{0.549}$

Move the decimal points 3 places.
```
     23.869
23.) 549.00
    −46
     89
    −69
     200
    −184
     160
    −138
     220
    −207
      13
```
23.869 rounded to the nearest hundredth is 23.87.

13. $0.4\overline{)45.23}$

Move the decimal points one place.

$$\begin{array}{r} 113.0 \\ 4.\overline{)\,452.300} \\ \underline{-4} \\ 05 \\ \underline{-4} \\ 12 \\ \underline{-12} \\ 03 \\ \underline{-0} \\ 3 \end{array}$$

-113.0 rounded to the nearest ten is -110.

15. 54.982×100 Move decimal point 2 places to the left.

$= 0.54982$

17. $12.9(-1000)$ Move the decimal point 3 places to the left and attach the negative sign.

$= -0.0129$

19. 87×10 Move the decimal point 1 place to the left.

$= 8.7$

21.
$$\begin{array}{r} 0.413 \\ 3\overline{)\,1.239} \\ \underline{-1\,2} \\ 03 \\ \underline{-3} \\ 09 \\ \underline{-9} \\ 0 \end{array}$$

$1.239 \times 3 = 0.413$

23. $0.6\overline{)4.2}$

Move the decimal points 1 place.

$$\begin{array}{r} 7. \\ 6.\overline{)\,42.} \\ \underline{-42} \\ 0 \end{array}$$

The answer is negative.
$-4.2 \times 0.6 = -7$

25. $0.27\overline{)1.296}$

Move the decimal points 2 places.

$$\begin{array}{r} 4.8 \\ 27.\overline{)\,129.6} \\ \underline{-108} \\ 21\,6 \\ \underline{-21\,6} \\ 0 \end{array}$$

$1.296 \div 0.27 = 4.8$

27. $0.02\overline{)42.}$

Move the decimal points 2 places.

$$\begin{array}{r} 2100. \\ 2.\overline{)\,4200.} \\ \underline{-4200} \\ 0 \end{array}$$

29. $-18 \times -0.6 = 180 \div -6 = 30$

31. $35 \div 0.005 = 35{,}000 \div 5 = 7000$

33. $1.6\overline{)1.104}$

Move the decimal points 1 place.

$$\begin{array}{r} 0.69 \\ 16.\overline{)\,11.04} \\ \underline{-96} \\ 1\,44 \\ \underline{-1\,44} \\ 0 \end{array}$$

The answer is negative.
$-1.104 \div 1.6 = -0.69$

35. -2.4×-100 Move the decimal point 2 places to the left.

$= 0.024$ The answer is positive.

37. $\dfrac{4.615}{0.071} = \dfrac{4615}{71} = 65$

39. $8.9\overline{)0.00263}$

Move the decimal points 1 place.

$$\begin{array}{r} 0.00029\ldots \\ 89.\overline{)\,0.02630} \end{array}$$

0.00029 rounded to the nearest ten-thousandth is 0.0003.

41. $0.0043\overline{)500}$

Move the decimal points 4 places.

$$
\begin{array}{r}
116279. \\
43.\overline{)\,5000000.} \\
\underline{-43} \\
70 \\
\underline{-43} \\
270 \\
\underline{-258} \\
120 \\
\underline{-86} \\
340 \\
\underline{-301} \\
390 \\
\underline{-387} \\
3
\end{array}
$$

116,279 rounded to the nearest ten-thousand is 120,000.

43. $z \div y = 4.52 \ 4 \ 0.8$

$0.8\overline{)4.52}$

Move the decimal points one place.

$$
\begin{array}{r}
5.65 \\
8.\overline{)\,45.20} \\
\underline{-40} \\
52 \\
\underline{-48} \\
40 \\
\underline{-40} \\
0
\end{array}
$$

45. $x \div y = 5.65 \div -0.8 = -7.0625$

$0.8\overline{)5.65}$

Move the decimal point 1 place.

$$
\begin{array}{r}
7.0625 \\
8.\overline{)\,56.5000} \\
\underline{-56} \\
0\,5 \\
\underline{-\,0} \\
50 \\
\underline{-48} \\
20 \\
\underline{-16} \\
40 \\
\underline{-40} \\
0
\end{array}
$$

47. $x \div 5 = 5.65 \div 5 = 1.13$

$$
\begin{array}{r}
1.13 \\
5\overline{)\,5.65} \\
\underline{-5} \\
06 \\
\underline{-5} \\
15 \\
\underline{-15} \\
0
\end{array}
$$

49. $\dfrac{x}{4} = 3.04$

$\dfrac{12.16}{4} = 3.04$

$3.04 = 3.04$ True

Yes, it is a solution.

51. $\dfrac{x}{4.3} = 2$

$\dfrac{0.86}{4.3} = 2$

$0.2 = 2$ False

Not, it is not a solution.

53. $\dfrac{z}{10} = 0.8$

$\dfrac{8}{10} = 0.8$

$08. = 0.8$ True

Yes, it is a solution.

55. Divide the total amount by the amount per month to get the number of months.

$73.86\overline{)1772.64}$

Move the decimal points 2 places.

$$
\begin{array}{r}
24 \\
7386.\overline{)\,177,264.} \\
\underline{-147\,72} \\
29\,544 \\
\underline{-\,29\,544} \\
0
\end{array}
$$

It will be paid off in 24 months.

57. There are 52 weeks per year and 40 hours per week. Therefore, there are $52 \times 40 = 2080$ hours per year.

$$\begin{array}{r} 2\,734.508 \\ 2080\overline{)5,687,777.000} \\ \underline{-4160} \\ 15277 \\ \underline{-14560} \\ 7177 \\ \underline{-6240} \\ 9377 \\ \underline{-8320} \\ 10570 \\ \underline{-10400} \\ 1700 \\ \underline{-0} \\ 17000 \\ \underline{-16640} \\ 360 \end{array}$$

His hourly wage would be \$2734.51.

59.
$$\begin{array}{r} 202.14 \approx 202.1 \\ 39.\overline{)7883.50} \\ \underline{-78} \\ 08 \\ \underline{-0} \\ 83 \\ \underline{-78} \\ 55 \\ \underline{-39} \\ 160 \\ \underline{-156} \\ 4 \end{array}$$

She needs to buy 202.1 pounds.

61. $39.37\overline{)200}$

Move the decimal points 2 places.
$$\begin{array}{r} 5.08 \approx 5.1 \\ 3937.\overline{)20,000.00} \\ \underline{-19\,685} \\ 3150 \\ \underline{-0} \\ 31500 \\ \underline{-31496} \\ 4 \end{array}$$

There are 5.1 meters in 200 inches.

63.
$$\begin{array}{r} 11.40 \approx 11.41 \text{ boxes} \\ 64\overline{)730.00} \\ \underline{-66} \\ 90 \\ \underline{-64} \\ 260 \\ \underline{-256} \\ 40 \\ \underline{-0} \\ 40 \end{array}$$

65.
$$\begin{array}{r} 132.5 \\ 24\overline{)3180.0} \\ \underline{-24} \\ 78 \\ \underline{-72} \\ 60 \\ \underline{-48} \\ 120 \\ \underline{-120} \\ 0 \end{array}$$

Their average speed was 132.5 mph.

67. $6 \times 4 = 24$ teaspoons

69. $24 \div 4 = 6$ doses per day
$48 \div 6 = 8$ days

71. To round 345.219 to the nearest hundredth, observe that the digit in the thousandths place is 9. Since this digit is at least 5, we need to add 1 to the digit in the hundredths place. The number 345.219 rounded to the nearest hundredth is 345.22.

73. To round −1000.994 to the nearest tenth, observe that the digit in the hundredths place is 9. Since this digit is at least 5, we need to add 1 to the digit in the tenths place. The number −1000.994 rounded to the nearest tenth is −1001.0.

75. $2 + 3 \cdot 6 = 2 + 18 = 20$

77. $20 - 10 \div (-5) = 20 + 2 = 22$

79. $(86 + 78 + 91 + 85) \div 4 = 340 \div 4$

$$
\begin{array}{r}
85 \\
4\overline{)\,340} \\
\underline{-32} \\
20 \\
\underline{-20} \\
0
\end{array}
$$

The average is 85.

81. $(9.6 + 8.5 + 4.1 + 4.1 + 9.8) \div 5$
$= 36.1 \div 5$

$$
\begin{array}{r}
8.6 \\
5\overline{)\,36.10} \\
\underline{-35} \\
11 \\
\underline{-10} \\
10 \\
\underline{-10} \\
0
\end{array}
$$

83.

$$
\begin{aligned}
A &= lw \\
38.7 &= l(4.5) \\
\frac{38.7}{4.5} &= l \\
8.6 &= l
\end{aligned}
$$

         The length is 8.6 feet.

85. Answers may vary.

87. 75 mph $\div$ 1.15

$1.15\overline{)75}$

Move the decimal points 2 places.

$$
\begin{array}{r}
65.21 \approx 65.2 \\
115.\overline{)\,7500.00} \\
\underline{-690} \\
600 \\
\underline{-575} \\
250 \\
\underline{-230} \\
200 \\
\underline{-115} \\
85
\end{array}
$$

95 mph $\div$ 1.15

$1.15\overline{)95}$

Move the decimal points 2 places.

$$
\begin{array}{r}
82.60 \approx 82.6 \\
115.\overline{)\,9500.00} \\
\underline{-920} \\
300 \\
\underline{-230} \\
70\ 0 \\
\underline{-69\ 0} \\
1\ 00 \\
\underline{-\ 0} \\
1\ 00
\end{array}
$$

The wind speed range for a Category 1 hurricane is from 65.2 knots to 82.6 knots.

Integrated Review

1.
$$
\begin{array}{r}
1.60 \\
+0.97 \\
\hline
2.57
\end{array}
$$

2.
$$
\begin{array}{r}
3.20 \\
+0.85 \\
\hline
4.05
\end{array}
$$

3.
$$
\begin{array}{r}
9.8 \\
-0.9 \\
\hline
8.9
\end{array}
$$

4.
$$
\begin{array}{r}
10.2 \\
-6.7 \\
\hline
3.5
\end{array}
$$

5.
$$
\begin{array}{r}
0.8 \\
\times\ 0.2 \\
\hline
0.16
\end{array}
$$

6.
$$
\begin{array}{r}
0.6 \\
\times 0.4 \\
\hline
0.24
\end{array}
$$

7.
$$
\begin{array}{r}
0.27 \\
8\overline{)\,2.16} \\
\underline{-1\ 6} \\
56 \\
\underline{-56} \\
0
\end{array}
$$

8.

$$
\begin{array}{r}
0.52 \\
6\overline{)\,3.12} \\
\underline{-30} \\
12 \\
\underline{-12} \\
0
\end{array}
$$

9.

$$
\begin{array}{r}
9.6 \\
\times 0.5 \\
\hline
4.80
\end{array}
\quad \text{or } (9.6)(-0.5) = -4.8
$$

10.

$$
\begin{array}{r}
8.7 \\
\times\, 0.7 \\
\hline
6.09
\end{array}
\quad (-8.7)(-0.7) = 6.09
$$

11.

$$
\begin{array}{r}
123.60 \\
-48.04 \\
\hline
75.56
\end{array}
$$

12.

$$
\begin{array}{r}
325.20 \\
-\,36.08 \\
\hline
289.12
\end{array}
$$

13. $-25 + 0.026 = -24.974$

14.

$$
\begin{array}{r}
44.000 \\
-0.125 \\
\hline
43.875
\end{array}
\quad 0.125 + (-44) = -43.875
$$

15.

$3.4\overline{)29.24}$ becomes

$$
\begin{array}{r}
8.6 \\
34\overline{)\,292.4} \\
\underline{-272} \\
204 \\
\underline{-204} \\
0
\end{array}
$$

-8.6
The answer is negative.

16.

$1.9\overline{)10.26}$ becomes

$$
\begin{array}{r}
5.4 \\
19\overline{)102.6} \\
\underline{95} \\
76 \\
\underline{76} \\
0
\end{array}
\quad -10.26 \div (-1.9) = 5.4
$$

17. $-2.8 \times 100 = -280$

18. $1.6 \times 1000 = 1600$

19.

$$
\begin{array}{r}
96210 \\
7.028 \\
+121.700 \\
\hline
224.938
\end{array}
$$

20.

$$
\begin{array}{r}
0.268 \\
1.940 \\
+142.881 \\
\hline
145.079
\end{array}
$$

21.

$$
\begin{array}{r}
0.56 \\
46\overline{)\,25.76} \\
\underline{-230} \\
276 \\
\underline{-276} \\
0
\end{array}
$$

22.

$$
\begin{array}{r}
-0.63 \\
43\overline{)\,27.09} \\
\underline{-258} \\
129 \\
\underline{-129} \\
0
\end{array}
$$

23.

$$
\begin{array}{r}
12.004 \\
\times\, 2.3 \\
\hline
36012 \\
240080 \\
\hline
26.6092
\end{array}
$$

24.

$$
\begin{array}{r}
28.006 \\
\times\, 5.2 \\
\hline
56012 \\
1400300 \\
\hline
145.6312
\end{array}
$$

25.

$$
\begin{array}{r}
10.0 \\
-\,4.6 \\
\hline
5.4
\end{array}
$$

26.

$$
\begin{array}{r}
18.00 \\
-\,0.26 \\
\hline
17.74
\end{array}
$$

$0.26 - 18 = -17.74$

27.

$$
\begin{array}{r}
268.19 \\
+\,146.25 \\
\hline
414.44
\end{array}
$$

$-268.19 - 414.44 = -414.44$

28.   860.18
        + 434.85
        ‾‾‾‾‾‾‾‾
         1295.03
        −860.18 − 434.85 = −1295.03

29.   0.087)$\overline{2.958}$ becomes

             34
        87.)$\overline{\ 2958}$
         −261
        ‾‾‾‾‾
          348
         −348
         ‾‾‾‾
            0
        −34
        The answer is negative.

30.   0.061)$\overline{1.708}$ becomes

             28
        61.)$\overline{\ 1708}$
         −122
        ‾‾‾‾‾
          488
         −488
         ‾‾‾‾
            0
        −28
        The answer is negative.

31.   160.00
         −43.19
        ‾‾‾‾‾‾‾
         116.81

32.   120.00
         − 101.21
        ‾‾‾‾‾‾‾‾
           18.79

33.   15.62
          × 10
        ‾‾‾‾‾‾
         156.20
        Answer: 156.2

34.
              1.562
        10)$\overline{\ 15.620}$
         −10
        ‾‾‾‾
          56
         − 50
         ‾‾‾‾
           62
          −60
          ‾‾‾
           20
          −20
          ‾‾‾
            0

35.   15.62
         +10.00
        ‾‾‾‾‾‾
         25.62

36.   15.62
         −10.00
        ‾‾‾‾‾‾
          5.62

37. The tenths place in 0.38 is less than the tenths place in 0.5. Thus, the cookie can be labeled "Fat Free."

            32.09 ≈ 32.1
38.   75.)$\overline{\ 2407.00}$
         −225
        ‾‾‾‾‾
          157
         − 150
         ‾‾‾‾‾
           70
           −0
          ‾‾‾
          700
         −675
         ‾‾‾‾
           25

His average number of points per game is 32.1.

Section 5.5

Practice Problems

1.   65.34 Estimate   65
         −14.68   −15
        ‾‾‾‾‾‾   ‾‾‾‾
         50.66   50
        The estimated difference is $50, so $50.66 is reasonable.

2.   30.26 Estimate   30
          × 2.98   × 3
         ‾‾‾‾‾‾   ‾‾‾‾
          24208   90
        272340
        605200
        ‾‾‾‾‾‾‾
        90.1748
        The answer 90.1748 is reasonable.

3. 91.5)$\overline{713.7}$ Estimate $90\overline{)720}^{\,8}$

        becomes
                  7.8
        915.)$\overline{\ 7137.0}$
         −6405
        ‾‾‾‾‾‾
          732 0
         −732 0
         ‾‾‾‾‾‾
              0
        The estimate is 8, so 7.8 is reasonable.

4.   79.2 Estimate   79
         −53.7   − 54
        ‾‾‾‾‾   ‾‾‾‾‾
                            25
        The estimate is 25 miles.

5. Round each number to the nearest ten. Since $50 \div 10 = 5$, the calculator display 19.612 is not reasonable.

6. $-8.6(3.2 - 1.8) = -8.6(1.4)$
$$= -12.04$$

7. $(0.7)^2 = (0.7)(0.7)$
$$= 0.49$$

8. $\dfrac{8.78 - 2.8}{20} = \dfrac{5.98}{20} = 0.299$

9. $1.7y - 2 = 1.7(2.3) - 2$
$$= 3.91 - 2$$
$$= 1.91$$

10. $3x + 7.5 = 1.2$
$3(-2.1) + 7.50 \; 1.2$
$-6.3 + 7.50 \; 1.2$
$1.2 = 1.2$ True
Since $1.2 = 1.2$ is a true statement, -2.1 is a solution.

Exercise Set 5.5

1. $4.9 - 2.1 = 2.8$
$5 - 2 = 3$
3 is close to 2.8, so the answer is reasonable.

3.
$$\begin{array}{r} 6 \\ \times\,483.11 \\ \hline 2898.66 \end{array} \quad \text{Estimate:} \begin{array}{r} 6 \\ \times\,500 \\ \hline 3000 \end{array}$$
3000 is close to 2898.66, so the answer is reasonable.

5. $62.16 \times 14.8 = 4.2$
$60 \times 15 = 4$
4 is close to 4.2 so the answer is reasonable.

7.
$$\begin{array}{r} 69.2 \\ 32.1 \\ +\,48.5 \\ \hline 149.7 \end{array} \quad \begin{array}{r} 70 \\ 30 \\ +\,50 \\ \hline 150 \end{array}$$
149.8 is close to 150, so the answer is reasonable.

9.
$$\begin{array}{r} 34.92 \\ -12.03 \\ \hline 22.89 \end{array} \quad \begin{array}{r} 35 \\ -12 \\ \hline 23 \end{array}$$
23 is close to 22.89 so the answer is reasonable.

11. $2(12.2) + 2(5.9) \approx 2(12) + 2(6)$
$$= 24 + 12$$
$$= 36 \text{ inches}$$

13. $11.8 + 12.9 + 14.2 \approx 12 + 13 + 14 = 39$ ft

15. $3.14(7)(2) = 43.96$ meters

17.
$$\begin{array}{r} 51.6 \\ 30\overline{)\,1550.0} \\ -150 \\ \hline 50 \\ -30 \\ \hline 200 \\ -180 \\ \hline 20 \end{array}$$
Their car will use about 52 gallons.

19. 398.79 is approximately 400
5 years is $5 \times 12 = 60$ months.
$60 \times 400 = 124000$
They will pay about $24,000.

21. $19.9 + 15.1 + 10.9 + 6.7 = ?$
Estimate:
$20 + 15 + 11 + 7 = 53$ miles
The distance is about 53 miles.

23. $600.8 million $\rightarrow$ $600 million
$461.0 million $\rightarrow$ $500 million
$435.0 million $\rightarrow$ $400 million
$431.1 million $\rightarrow$ $400 million
$403.7 million $\rightarrow$ $400 million
$357.1 million $\rightarrow$ $400 million
The estimate is $2700 million

25. 501 rounded to the nearest 10 is 500.
271 rounded to the nearest 10 is 270.
$$\begin{array}{r} 00 \\ \times\,270 \\ \hline 0 \\ 35000 \\ 100000 \\ \hline 135,000 \end{array}$$
The population is about 135,000 people.

27. $9 \times 40 = 360$
c.

29. $78.6 \div 100 = 0.786$
b.

31. $100 \times 40 = 4000$
Not reasonable

33. $1000 - 100 = 900$
Reasonable

35. $(0.4)^2 = (0.4)(0.4) = 0.16$

37. $\dfrac{1+0.8}{-0.6} = \dfrac{1.8}{-0.6} = \dfrac{18}{-6} = -3$

39. $1.4(2 - 1.8) = 1.4(0.2) = 0.28$

41. $4.83 \div 2.1 = 2.3$

43. $(-2.3)^2(0.3 + 0.7) = (-2.3)^2(1)$
$$= 5.29(1)$$
$$= 5.29$$

45. $(3.1 + 0.7)(2.9 - 0.9) = (3.8)(2.0) = 7.6$

47. $\dfrac{(4.5)^2}{100} = \dfrac{20.25}{100} = 0.2025$

49. $\dfrac{7+0.74}{-6} = \dfrac{7.74}{-6} = -1.29$

51. $z^2 = (-2.4)^2 = 5.76$

53. $x - y = 6 - (0.3) = 5.7$

55. $4y - z = 4(0.3) - (-2.4) = 1.2 + 2.4 = 3.6$

57. $7x + 2.1 = -7$
$$7(-1.3) + 2.1 = -7$$
$$-9.1 + 2.1 = -7$$
$$-7 = -7 \quad \text{True}$$
Yes, -1.3 is a solution.

59. $x - 6.5 = 2x + 1.8$
$$-4.7 - 6.5 = 2(-4.7) + 1.8$$
$$-11.2 = -9.4 + 1.8$$
$$-11.2 = -7.6 \qquad \text{False}$$
No, -4.7 is not a solution.

61. $\dfrac{3}{4} \cdot \dfrac{5}{12} = \dfrac{3 \cdot 5}{4 \cdot 3 \cdot 4} = \dfrac{5}{16}$

63.
$$-\dfrac{36}{56} \div \dfrac{30}{35} = -\dfrac{36}{56} \cdot \dfrac{35}{30}$$
$$= -\dfrac{2 \cdot 2 \cdot 3 \cdot 3 \cdot 5 \cdot 7}{2 \cdot 2 \cdot 2 \cdot 7 \cdot 2 \cdot 3 \cdot 5}$$
$$= -\dfrac{3}{4}$$

65. $\dfrac{5}{12} - \dfrac{1}{3} = \dfrac{5}{12} - \dfrac{4}{12} = \dfrac{1}{12}$

67. $1.96(7.852 - 3.147)^2 = 1.96(4.705)^2$
$$= 1.96(22.137025)$$
$$= 43.388569$$
Estimate: $2(8 - 3)^2 = 2(5)^2 = 2(25) = 50$
The result is reasonable.

69. Answers may vary.

71. Square first; answers may vary.

Section 5.6

Practice Problems

1. a. $\dfrac{2}{5} = 2 \div 5$

$$\begin{array}{r} 0.4 \\ 5{\overline{\smash{\big)}\,2.0}} \\ \underline{-2\,0} \\ 0 \end{array}$$

$$\dfrac{2}{5} = 0.4$$

b. $\dfrac{9}{40} = 9 \div 40$

$$\begin{array}{r} 0.225 \\ 40{\overline{\smash{\big)}\,9.000}} \\ \underline{-8\,0} \\ 100 \\ \underline{-80} \\ 200 \\ \underline{-200} \\ 0 \end{array}$$

$$\dfrac{9}{40} = 0.225$$

2.
$$\begin{array}{r} 0.375 \\ 8{\overline{\smash{\big)}\,3.000}} \\ \underline{-24} \\ 60 \\ \underline{-56} \\ 40 \\ \underline{-40} \\ 0 \end{array}$$

$$-\dfrac{3}{8} = -0.375$$

3. a.

$$\begin{array}{r} 0.833\ldots \\ 6\overline{)\,5.000} \\ \underline{-4\,8} \\ 20 \\ \underline{-18} \\ 20 \\ \underline{-18} \\ 2 \end{array}$$

$$\frac{5}{6} = 0.8\overline{3} \approx 0.83$$

b.

$$\begin{array}{r} 0.22\ldots \\ 9\overline{)\,2.00} \\ \underline{-1\,8} \\ 20 \\ \underline{-18} \\ 2 \end{array}$$

$$\frac{2}{9} = 0.\overline{2} \approx 0.2$$

4.

$$\begin{array}{r} 0.3636 \\ 11\overline{)\,4.0000} \\ \underline{-33} \\ 70 \\ \underline{-66} \\ 40 \\ \underline{-33} \\ 70 \\ \underline{-66} \\ 4 \end{array}$$

$$\frac{4}{11} = -0.\overline{36} \approx 0.364$$

5.

$$\begin{array}{r} 0.1111\ldots \\ 9\overline{)\,1.0000} \\ \underline{-9} \\ 10 \\ \underline{-9} \\ 10 \end{array}$$

$$\frac{1}{9} = 0.\overline{1} \approx 0.111$$

6.

$$\frac{1}{5} = 1 \div 5$$

$$\begin{array}{r} 0.2 \\ 5\overline{)\,1.0} \\ \underline{-1\,0} \\ 0 \end{array}$$

$$\frac{1}{5} = 0.20$$

Since $0.20 < 0.25$, $\dfrac{1}{5} < 0.25$.

7. a.

$$\begin{array}{r} 0.5 \\ 2\overline{)\,1.0} \\ \underline{-1\,0} \\ 0 \end{array}$$

$$\frac{1}{2} = 0.50$$

Since $0.50 < 0.54$, $\dfrac{1}{2} < 0.54$.

b. Since $\dfrac{2}{9} = 0.\overline{2}$, $0.\overline{2} = \dfrac{2}{9}$.

c.

$$\begin{array}{r} 0.714 \\ 7\overline{)\,5.000} \\ \underline{-4\,9} \\ 10 \\ \underline{-7} \\ 30 \\ \underline{-28} \\ 2 \end{array}$$

Since $\dfrac{5}{7} \approx 0.714$ and $0.714 < 0.72$,

$$\frac{5}{7} < 0.72.$$

8. a.

Original number	$\frac{1}{3}$	0.302	$\frac{3}{8}$
Decimals	0.333…	0.302	0.375
Compare in order	2nd	1st	3rd

Then, written in order: 0.302, $\dfrac{1}{3}$, $\dfrac{3}{8}$

b.

Original number	1.26	$1\frac{1}{4}$	$1\frac{2}{5}$
Decimals	1.26	1.25	1.40
Compare in order	2nd	1st	3rd

Then, written in order: $1\frac{1}{4}$, 1.26, $1\frac{2}{5}$

c.

Original number	0.4	0.41	$\frac{5}{7}$
Decimals	0.40	0.41	≈ 0.714
Compare in order	1st	2nd	3rd

Then, written in order: 0.4, 0.41, $\frac{5}{7}$

9. area $= \frac{1}{2} \cdot$ base $\cdot$ height

$\qquad = \frac{1}{2} \cdot 7 \cdot 2.1$

$\qquad = 0.5 \cdot 7 \cdot 2.1$

$\qquad = 7.35$

The area is 7.35 square meters.

Exercise Set 5.6

1. $\frac{1}{5} = 0.2$

$$\begin{array}{r} 0.2 \\ 5\overline{)\,1.0} \\ \underline{-1\,0} \\ 0 \end{array}$$

3. $\frac{4}{8} = 0.5$

$$\begin{array}{r} 0.5 \\ 8\overline{)\,4.0} \\ \underline{-4\,0} \\ 0 \end{array}$$

5. $\frac{3}{4} = 0.75$

$$\begin{array}{r} 0.75 \\ 4\overline{)\,3.00} \\ \underline{-2\,8} \\ 20 \\ \underline{-20} \\ 0 \end{array}$$

7. $-\frac{2}{25} = -0.08$

$$\begin{array}{r} 0.08 \\ 25\overline{)\,2.00} \\ \underline{-2\,00} \\ 0 \end{array}$$

9. $\frac{3}{8} = 0.375$

$$\begin{array}{r} 0.375 \\ 8\overline{)\,3.000} \\ \underline{-2\,4} \\ 60 \\ \underline{-56} \\ 40 \\ \underline{-40} \\ 0 \end{array}$$

11. $\frac{11}{12} = 0.91\overline{6}$

$$\begin{array}{r} 0.9166\ldots \\ 12\overline{)\,11.0000} \\ \underline{-10\,8} \\ 20 \\ \underline{-12} \\ 80 \\ \underline{-72} \\ 80 \\ \underline{-72} \\ 8 \end{array}$$

13. $\dfrac{17}{40} = 0.425$

$$\begin{array}{r} 0.425 \\ 40\overline{)\ 17.000} \\ -16\ 0 \\ \hline 1\ 00 \\ -\ 80 \\ \hline 200 \\ -200 \\ \hline 0 \end{array}$$

15. $\dfrac{9}{20} = 0.45$

$$\begin{array}{r} 0.45 \\ 20\overline{)\ 9.00} \\ -8\ 0 \\ \hline 1\ 00 \\ -1\ 00 \\ \hline 0 \end{array}$$

17. $-\dfrac{1}{3} = -0.\overline{3}$

$$\begin{array}{r} 0.33\ldots \\ 3\overline{)1.00} \\ -9 \\ \hline 10 \\ -9 \\ \hline 1 \end{array}$$

19. $\dfrac{7}{16} = 0.4375$

$$\begin{array}{r} 0.4375 \\ 16\overline{)\ 7.0000} \\ -6\ 4 \\ \hline 60 \\ -48 \\ \hline 120 \\ -112 \\ \hline 80 \\ -80 \\ \hline 0 \end{array}$$

21. $\dfrac{2}{9} = 0.\overline{2}$

$$\begin{array}{r} 0.22\ldots \\ 9\overline{)\ 2.00} \\ -18 \\ \hline 20 \\ -18 \\ \hline 2 \end{array}$$

23. $\dfrac{5}{3} = 1.\overline{6}$

$$\begin{array}{r} 1.66\ldots \\ 3\overline{)\ 5.00} \\ -3 \\ \hline 2\ 0 \\ -1\ 8 \\ \hline 20 \\ -18 \\ \hline 2 \end{array}$$

25. $0.\overline{3} \approx 0.333\ldots \approx 0.33$

27. $0.4375 \approx 0.44$

29. $0.\overline{2} = 0.222\ldots \approx 0.2$

31. $1.\overline{6} = 1.666\ldots \approx 1.7$

33.
$$\begin{array}{r} 0.668 \\ 1048\overline{)\ 701.000} \\ -6288 \\ \hline 7220 \\ -6288 \\ \hline 9320 \\ -8384 \\ \hline 936 \end{array}$$

$\dfrac{701}{1048} \approx 0.67$

35.
$$\begin{array}{r} 0.44 \\ 25\overline{)\ 11.00} \\ -10\ 0 \\ \hline 1\ 00 \\ -1\ 00 \\ \hline 0 \end{array}$$

$\dfrac{11}{25} = 0.44$

37.

$$\begin{array}{r} 0.615 \\ 91\overline{)56.000} \\ -546 \\ \hline 140 \\ -91 \\ \hline 490 \\ -455 \\ \hline 35 \end{array}$$

$$\frac{56}{91} \approx 0.62$$

39. $2 < 9$, so $0.562 < 0.569$

41. $2 > 1$, so $0.823 > 0.813$

43. $-0.0923 > -0.0932$

45. $\frac{2}{3} = \frac{4}{6}$ and $\frac{4}{6} < \frac{5}{6}$, so $\frac{2}{3} < \frac{5}{6}$

47. $\frac{5}{9} = 0.\overline{5} = 0.555\cdots$

$\frac{51}{91} \approx 0.5604$

$0.5\overline{5} < 0.5604$, so $\frac{5}{9} < \frac{51}{91}$.

49. $\frac{4}{7} \approx 0.5714$ and $0.5714 > 0.14$,

so $\frac{4}{7} > 0.14$.

51. $\frac{18}{13} \approx 1.3846$

$1.38 < 1.3846$, so $1.38 < \frac{18}{13}$.

53. $\frac{456}{64} = 7.125$

$7.123 < 7.125$, so $7.123 < \frac{456}{64}$

55. $0.32,\ 0.34,\ 0.35$

57. $0.49 = 0.490$

$0.49,\ 0.491,\ 0.498$

59. $\frac{3}{4} = 0.75$

$0.73,\ \frac{3}{4},\ 0.78$

61. $\frac{4}{7} \approx 0.571$

$0.412,\ 0.453,\ \frac{4}{7}$

63. $\frac{42}{8} = 5.25$

$5.23,\ \frac{42}{8},\ 5.34$

65. $\frac{12}{5} = 2.4,\ \frac{17}{8} = 2.125$

$\frac{17}{8},\ 2.37,\ \frac{12}{5}$

67. Area $= \frac{1}{2} \cdot \text{base} \cdot \text{height}$

$= \frac{1}{2} \times 5.7 \times 9$

$= 0.5 \times 5.7 \times 9$

$= 25.65$

The area is 25.65 square inches.

69. Area $= \frac{1}{2} \cdot \text{base} \cdot \text{height}$

$= \frac{1}{2} \cdot 5.2 \cdot 3.6$

$= 0.5 \cdot 5.2 \cdot 3.6$

$= 9.36$

The area is 9.36 square centimeters.

71. Area $= \text{base} \cdot \text{height}$

$= 0.62 \cdot \frac{2}{5}$

$= 0.62 \cdot 0.4$

$= 0.248$

The area is 0.248 square yards.

73. $2^3 = 2 \cdot 2 \cdot 2 = 8$

75. $6^2 \cdot 2 = 6 \cdot 6 \cdot 2 = 72$

77. $\left(\frac{1}{3}\right)^4 = \frac{1}{3} \cdot \frac{1}{3} \cdot \frac{1}{3} \cdot \frac{1}{3} = \frac{1}{81}$

79. $\left(\frac{3}{5}\right)^2 = \frac{3}{5} \cdot \frac{3}{5} = \frac{9}{25}$

81. $\left(\frac{2}{5}\right)\left(\frac{5}{2}\right)^2 = \frac{2}{5} \cdot \frac{5}{2} \cdot \frac{5}{2} = \frac{5}{2}$

83. $\dfrac{2321}{10,569} \approx 0.202$

85.

	Estimate
2131	2100
1179	1800
813	800
713	700
603	600
+ 547	+ 500
	5900
	stations

87.

$$8\overline{)5.000} = 0.625$$

$-4\,8$

$\quad 20$

$\quad -16$

$\quad\quad 40$

$\quad\quad -40$

$\quad\quad\quad 0$

You should enter 0.625 as the margin width.

89. Answers may vary.

91. $\dfrac{3}{4} - (9.6)(5) = 0.75 - 48$
$= -47.25$

93. $\left(\dfrac{1}{10}\right)^2 + (1.6)(2.1) = \dfrac{1}{100} + (1.6)(2.1)$
$= 0.01 + 3.36$
$= 3.37$

95. $\dfrac{3}{8}(4.7 - 5.9) = 0.375(4.7 - 5.9)$
$= 0.375 \cdot -12$
$= -0.45$

Section 5.7

Practice Problems

1. $z + 0.9 = 1.3$
$z + 0.9 - 0.9 = 1.3 - 0.9$
$z = 0.4$

2. $0.17x = -0.34$
$\dfrac{0.17x}{0.17} = \dfrac{-0.34}{0.17}$
$x = -2$

3. $2.9 = 1.7 + 0.3x$
$2.9 - 1.7 = 1.7 + 0.3x - 1.7$
$1.2 = 0.3x$
$\dfrac{1.2}{0.3} = \dfrac{0.3x}{0.3}$
$4 = x$ or $x = 4$

4. $8x + 4.2 = 10x + 11.6$
$8x + 4.2 - 10x = 10x + 11.6 - 10x$
$-2x + 4.2 = 11.6$
$-2x + 4.2 - 4.2 = 11.6 - 4.2$
$-2x = 7.4$
$\dfrac{-2x}{-2} = \dfrac{7.4}{-2}$
$x = -3.7$

5. $6.3 - 5x = 3(x + 2.9)$
$6.3 - 5x = 3x + 8.7$
$6.3 - 5x - 6.3 = 3x + 8.7 - 6.3$
$-5x = 3x + 2.4$
$-5x - 3x = 3x + 2.4 - 3x$
$-8x = 2.4$
$\dfrac{-8x}{-8} = \dfrac{2.4}{-8}$
$x = -0.3$

6. $0.2y + 2.6 = 4$
$10(0.2y + 2.6) = 10(4)$
$2y + 26 = 40$
$2y + 26 - 26 = 40 - 26$
$2y = 14$
$\dfrac{2y}{2} = \dfrac{14}{2}$
$y = 7$

Exercise Set 5.7

1. $x + 1.2 = 7.1$
$x + 1.2 - 1.2 = 7.1 - 1.2$
$x = 5.9$

3. $-5y = 2.15$
$\dfrac{-5y}{-5} = \dfrac{2.15}{-5}$
$y = -0.43$

5. $6.2 = y - 4$
$6.2 + 4 = y - 4 + 4$
$10.2 = y$

7. $3.1x = -13.95$
$$\frac{3.1x}{3.1} = \frac{-13.95}{3.1}$$
$$x = -4.5$$

9. $2(x-1.3) = 5.8$
$$2x - 2.6 = 5.8$$
$$-3.5x + 2.8 = -11.2$$
$$-3.5x + 2.8 - 2.8 = -11.2 - 2.8$$
$$-3.5x = -14$$
$$\frac{-3.5x}{-3.5} = \frac{-14}{-3.5}$$
$$x = 4$$

11. $6x + 8.65 = 3x + 10$
$$6x + 8.65 - 8.65 = 3x + 10 - 8.65$$
$$6x = 3x + 1.35$$
$$6x - 3x = 3x - 3x + 1.35$$
$$3x = 1.35$$
$$\frac{3x}{3} = \frac{1.35}{3}$$
$$x = 0.45$$

13. $2(x-1.3) = 5.8$
$$2x - 2.6 = 5.8$$
$$2x - 2.6 + 2.6 = 5.8 + 2.6$$
$$2x = 8.4$$
$$\frac{2x}{2} = \frac{8.4}{2}$$
$$x = 4.2$$

15. $0.4x + 0.7 = -0.9$
$$4x + 7 = -9$$
$$4x + 7 - 7 = -9 - 7$$
$$4x = -16$$
$$\frac{4x}{4} = \frac{-16}{4}$$
$$x = -4$$

17. $7x - 10.8 = x$
$$70x - 108 = 10x$$
$$70x - 108 + 108 = 10x + 108$$
$$70x = 10x + 108$$
$$70x - 10x = 10x - 10x + 108$$
$$60x = 108$$
$$\frac{60x}{60} = \frac{108}{60}$$
$$x = 1.8$$

19. $2.1x + 5 - 1.6x = 10$
$$21x + 50 - 16x = 100$$
$$5x + 50 = 100$$
$$5x + 50 - 50 = 100 - 50$$
$$5x = 50$$
$$\frac{5x}{5} = \frac{50}{5}$$
$$x = 10$$

21. $y - 3.6 = 4$
$$y - 3.6 + 3.6 = 4 + 3.6$$
$$y = 7.6$$

23. $-0.02x = -1.2$
$$-2x = -120$$
$$\frac{-2x}{-2} = \frac{-120}{-2}$$
$$x = 60$$

25. $6.5 = 10x + 7.2$
$$65 = 100x + 72$$
$$65 - 72 = 100x + 72 - 72$$
$$-7 = 100x$$
$$-0.07 = x$$

27. $2.7x - 25 = 1.2x + 5$
$$2.7x - 25 - 1.2x = 1.2x + 5 - 1.2x$$
$$1.5x - 25 = 5$$
$$1.5x - 25 + 25 = 5 + 25$$
$$1.5x = 30$$
$$\frac{1.5x}{1.5} = \frac{30}{1.5}$$
$$x = 20$$

29. $200x - 0.67 = 100x + 0.81$
$$200x - 0.67 + 0.67 = 100x + 0.81 + 0.67$$
$$200x = 100x + 1.48$$
$$200x - 100x = 100x - 100x + 1.48$$
$$100x = 1.48$$
$$x = 0.0148$$

31. $3(x + 2.71) = 2x$
$$3x + 8.13 = 2x$$
$$3x - 2x = -8.13$$
$$x = -8.13$$

33. $8x - 5 = 10x - 8$
$$8x - 5 - 10x = 10x - 8 - 10x$$
$$-2x - 5 = -8$$
$$-2x - 5 + 5 = -8 + 5$$
$$-2x = -3$$
$$\frac{-2x}{-2} = \frac{-3}{-2}$$
$$x = 1.5$$

35.
$$1.2 + 0.3x = 0.9$$
$$12 + 3x = 9$$
$$12 - 12 + 3x = 9 - 12$$
$$3x = -3$$
$$\frac{3x}{3} = \frac{-3}{3}$$
$$x = -1$$

37.
$$0.9x + 2.65 = 0.5x + 5.45$$
$$90x + 265 = 50x + 545$$
$$90x + 265 - 265 = 50x + 545 - 265$$
$$90x - 50x = 50x - 50x + 280$$
$$40x = 280$$
$$x = 7$$

39.
$$4x + 7.6 = 2(3x - 3.2)$$
$$4x + 7.6 = 6x - 6.4$$
$$4x - 6x + 7.6 - 7.6 = 6x - 6x - 6.4 - 7.6$$
$$-2x = -14$$
$$x = 7$$

41.
$$0.7x + 13.8 = x - 2.16$$
$$0.7x + 13.8 - x = x - 2.16 - x$$
$$-0.3x + 13.8 = x - 2.16 - x$$
$$-0.3x + 13.8 - 13.8 = -2.16 - 13.8$$
$$-0.3x = -15.96$$
$$\frac{-0.3x}{-0.3} = \frac{-15.96}{-0.3}$$
$$x = 53.2$$

43. $2x - 6 + 4x - 10 = (2x + 4x) + (-6 - 10) = 6x - 16$

45. $3(x - 5) + 10 = 3x - 15 + 10 = 3x - 5$

47. $5y - 1.2 - 7y + 8 = (5y - 7y) + (8 - 1.2)$
$$= -2y + 6.8$$

49. Answers may vary.

51.
$$-5.25x = -40.33575$$
$$\frac{-5.25x}{-5.25} = \frac{-40.33575}{-5.25}$$
$$x = 7.683$$

53.
$$1.95y + 6.834 = 7.65y - 19.8591$$
$$19.8591 + 6.834 = 7.65y - 1.95y$$
$$26.6931 = 5.7y$$
$$\frac{26.6931}{5.7} = \frac{5.7y}{5.7}$$
$$4.683 = y$$

Section 5.8

Practice Problems

1. $\sqrt{100} = 10$ because $10^2 = 100$ and 10 is positive.

2. $\sqrt{64} = 8$ because $8^2 = 64$ and 8 is positive.

3. $\sqrt{121} = 11$ because $11^2 = 121$ and 11 is positive.

4. $\sqrt{0} = 0$ because $0^2 = 0$.

5. $\sqrt{\frac{1}{4}} = \frac{1}{2}$ because $\frac{1}{2} \cdot \frac{1}{2} = \frac{1}{4}$.

6. $\sqrt{\frac{9}{16}} = \frac{3}{4}$

7. $\sqrt{11} \approx 3.317$

8. $\sqrt{29} \approx 5.385$

9.
$$a^2 + b^2 = c^2$$
$$12^2 + 16^2 = c^2$$
$$144 + 256 = c^2$$
$$400 = c^2$$
$$c = \sqrt{400}$$
$$c = 20$$

The hypotenuse is 20 feet.

10.
$$a^2 + b^2 = c^2$$
$$9^2 + 7^2 = c^2$$
$$81 + 49 = c^2$$
$$130 = c^2$$
$$c = \sqrt{130}$$
$$c \approx 11$$

The length of the hypotenuse is exactly $\sqrt{130}$ kilometers, which is approximately 11 kilometers.

11.
$$a^2 + b^2 = c^2$$
$$a^2 + 7^2 = 11^2$$
$$a^2 + 49 = 121$$
$$a^2 = 72$$
$$a = \sqrt{72}$$
$$a \approx 8.49$$

The length of the leg is exactly $\sqrt{72}$ feet, which is approximately 8.49 feet.

12.

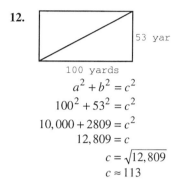

53 yar

100 yards

$$a^2 + b^2 = c^2$$
$$100^2 + 53^2 = c^2$$
$$10,000 + 2809 = c^2$$
$$12,809 = c$$
$$c = \sqrt{12,809}$$
$$c \approx 113$$

The diagonal of the football field is exactly $\sqrt{12,809}$ yards, which is approximately 113 yards.

Calculator Explorations

Depending on what type of calculator you have, you will either press the $\boxed{\sqrt{}}$ key before or after the number of which you wish to take the square root. Then press $\boxed{= \text{or ENTER}}$.

1. $\sqrt{1024} = 32$

2. $\sqrt{676} = 26$

3. $\sqrt{15} \approx 3.872983346 \approx 3.873$

4. $\sqrt{19} \approx 4.358898944 \approx 4.359$

5. $\sqrt{97} \approx 9.848857802 \approx 9.849$

6. $\sqrt{56} \approx 7.483314774 \approx 7.483$

Exercise Set 5.8

1. $\sqrt{4} = 2$ because $2^2 = 4$.

3. $\sqrt{625} = 25$ because $25^2 = 625$.

5. $\sqrt{\dfrac{1}{81}} = \dfrac{1}{9}$ because $\dfrac{1}{9} \cdot \dfrac{1}{9} = \dfrac{1}{81}$.

7. $\sqrt{\dfrac{144}{64}} = \dfrac{12}{8} = \dfrac{3}{2}$ because $\dfrac{12}{8} \cdot \dfrac{12}{8} = \dfrac{144}{64}$.

9. $\sqrt{256} = 16$ because $16^2 = 256$.

11. $\sqrt{\dfrac{9}{4}} = \dfrac{3}{2}$ because $\dfrac{3}{2} \cdot \dfrac{3}{2} = \dfrac{9}{4}$.

13. $\sqrt{3} \approx 1.732$

15. $\sqrt{15} \approx 3.873$

17. $\sqrt{14} \approx 3.742$

19. $\sqrt{47} \approx 6.856$

21. $\sqrt{8} \approx 2.828$

23. $\sqrt{26} \approx 5.099$

25. $\sqrt{71} \approx 8.426$

27. $\sqrt{7} \approx 2.646$

29.
$$a^2 + b^2 = c^2$$
$$5^2 + 12^2 = c^2$$
$$25 + 144 = c^2$$
$$169 = c^2$$
$$c = \sqrt{169}$$
$$c = 13$$

The length of the hypotenuse is 13 inches.

31.
$$a^2 + b^2 = c^2$$
$$10^2 + b^2 = 12^2$$
$$100 + b^2 = 144$$
$$b^2 = 44$$
$$b = \sqrt{44}$$
$$b \approx 6.633$$

The length of the leg is approximately 6.633 centimeters.

33.

c

4

3

$$a^2 + b^2 = c^2$$
$$3^2 + 4^2 = c^2$$
$$9 + 16 = c^2$$
$$25 = c^2$$
$$c = \sqrt{25}$$
$$c = 5$$

35.

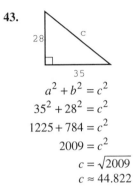

$$a^2 + b^2 = c^2$$
$$a^2 + 6^2 = 10^2$$
$$a^2 + 36 = 100$$
$$a^2 = 64$$
$$a = \sqrt{64}$$
$$a = 8$$

37.

$$a^2 + b^2 = c^2$$
$$10^2 + 14^2 = c^2$$
$$100 + 196 = c^2$$
$$296 = c^2$$
$$c = \sqrt{296}$$
$$c \approx 17.205$$

39.

$$a^2 + b^2 = c^2$$
$$2^2 + 16^2 = c^2$$
$$4 + 256 = c^2$$
$$260 = c^2$$
$$c = \sqrt{260}$$
$$c \approx 16.125$$

41.

$$a^2 + b^2 = c^2$$
$$5^2 + b^2 = 13^2$$
$$25 + b^2 = 169$$
$$b^2 = 144$$
$$b = 12$$

43.

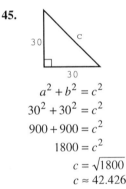

$$a^2 + b^2 = c^2$$
$$35^2 + 28^2 = c^2$$
$$1225 + 784 = c^2$$
$$2009 = c^2$$
$$c = \sqrt{2009}$$
$$c \approx 44.822$$

45.

$$a^2 + b^2 = c^2$$
$$30^2 + 30^2 = c^2$$
$$900 + 900 = c^2$$
$$1800 = c^2$$
$$c = \sqrt{1800}$$
$$c \approx 42.426$$

47.

$$a^2 + b^2 = c^2$$
$$a^2 + 1^2 = 2^2$$
$$a^2 + 1 = 4$$
$$a^2 = 3$$
$$a = \sqrt{3}$$
$$a \approx 1.732$$

49.

$$a^2 + b^2 = c^2$$
$$100^2 + 100^2 = c^2$$
$$10,000 + 10,000 = c^2$$
$$20,000 = c^2$$
$$c = \sqrt{20,000}$$
$$c \approx 141.42$$

The length is approximately 141.42 yards.

51.
$$a^2 + b^2 = c^2$$
$$20^2 + b^2 = 32^2$$
$$400 + b^2 = 1024$$
$$b^2 = 624$$
$$b = \sqrt{624}$$
$$b \approx 25.0$$

The height is approximately 25.0 feet.

53.
$$a^2 + b^2 = c^2$$
$$300^2 + 160^2 = c^2$$
$$90,000 + 25,600 = c^2$$
$$115,600 = c^2$$
$$c = \sqrt{115,600}$$
$$c = 340$$

The length is 340 feet.

55. $\dfrac{10}{12} = \dfrac{2 \cdot 5}{2 \cdot 6} = \dfrac{5}{6}$

57. $\dfrac{24}{60} = \dfrac{2 \cdot 2 \cdot 2 \cdot 3}{2 \cdot 3 \cdot 2 \cdot 5} = \dfrac{2}{5}$

59. $\dfrac{30}{72} = \dfrac{2 \cdot 3 \cdot 5}{2 \cdot 36} = \dfrac{2 \cdot 3 \cdot 5}{2 \cdot 6 \cdot 6} = \dfrac{2 \cdot 3 \cdot 5}{2 \cdot 2 \cdot 3 \cdot 2 \cdot 3} = \dfrac{5}{12}$

61. $\sqrt{38}$ is between 6 and 7.
$\sqrt{38} \approx 6.164$

63. $\sqrt{101}$ is between 10 and 11.
$\sqrt{101} \approx 10.050$

65. Answers may vary.

Chapter 5 Review

1. 23.45
↑
tenths

2. 0.000345
↑
hundred thousandths

3. -23.45 is negative twenty-three and forty-five hundredths.

4. 0.00345 is three hundred forty-five hundred thousandths.

5. 109.23 is one hundred nine and twenty-three hundredths.

6. 200.000032 is two hundred and thirty-two millionths

7. 2.15

8. −503.102

9. 16,025.0014

10. $0.16 = \dfrac{16}{100} = \dfrac{4}{25}$

11. $-12.023 = -12\dfrac{23}{1000}$

12. $1.0045 = 1\dfrac{45}{10,000} = 1\dfrac{9}{2000}$

13. $0.00231 = \dfrac{231}{100,000}$

14. $25.25 = 25\dfrac{25}{100} = 25\dfrac{1}{4}$

15. 0.49   0.43
↑   ↑
9 > 3
0.49 > 0.43

16. $0.973 = 0.9730$

17. $-402.00032 < -402.000032$

18. $-0.230505 > -0.23505$

19. 0.623 to the nearest tenth is 0.6.

20. 0.9384 to the nearest hundredth is 0.94.

21. 42.895 to the nearest hundredth is 42.90.

22. 16.34925 to the nearest thousandth is 16.349.

23. 13,490.5 people rounded to the nearest hundred is 13,500 people.

24. $10.75 = 10\dfrac{75}{100} = 10\dfrac{3}{4}$ teaspoons

25.   2.4
\+ 7.1
―――
9.5

26.   3.9
\+ 1.2
―――
5.1

27. $-6.4 + (-0.88)$
Add the absolute values.
6.40
\+ 0.88
――――
7.28
Attach the common sign.
-7.28

28. Subtract the absolute values.
19.02
-6.98
――――
12.04
Since $19.02 > 6.98$, the answer is negative. The answer is -12.04.

29.   200.490
16.820
\+ 103.002
―――――
320.312

30.   100.45000
48.29000
\+ 0.00236
――――――
148.74236

31.   4.9
-3.2
―――
1.7

32.   5.23
-2.74
―――
2.49

33. Add the absolute values.
892.1
$+432.4$
――――
1324.5
Attach the common sign.
-1324.5

34. Subtract the absolute values.
10.200
-0.064
―――――
10.136
Since $10.2 > 0.064$, the answer is negative. The answer is -10.136.

35.   100.00
-34.98
―――
65.02

36.   200.00000
-0.00198
―――――――
199.99802

37.   8920.70
\+ 684.81
――――――
9605.51
The DJIA opened at 9605.51.

38. $x - y = 1.2 - 6.9 = -5.7$

39. $2.3x + 6.5 + 1.9x + 6.3 = 2.3x + 1.9x + 6.5 + 6.3$
$= 4.2x + 12.8$

40. $8.6y - 7.61 + 1.29y + 3.44$
$= 8.6y + 1.29y - 7.61 + 3.44$
$= 9.89y - 4.17$

41. $7.2 \times 10 = 72$

42. $9.345 \times 1000 = 9345$

43.   34.02 2 decimal places
$\times\ 2.3$ 1 decimal place
――――
10206
68040
――――
78.246 3 decimal places
The answer is negative.
$-34.02 \times 2.3 = -78.246$

44. -839.02 2 decimal places
$\times (-87.3)$ 1 decimal place
――――――
251706
5873140
\+67121600
――――――
73246446 3 decimal places

45. $C = 2 \cdot \pi \cdot r = 2 \cdot \pi \cdot 7 = 14\pi$ meters
$C \approx 14(3.14) = 43.96$ meters

46.   0.625
$\times\ 102$
―――
1250
\+ 62 500
――――
63.750 rounded to the nearest tenth is 63.8 miles.

47. $21 \div 0.3$
$\dfrac{21}{0.3} = \dfrac{210}{3} = 70$

48. $0.03\overline{)0.0063}$

Move decimal points 2 places.

$$
\begin{array}{r}
0.21 \\
3.\overline{)0.63} \\
\underline{-6} \\
03 \\
\underline{-\ 3} \\
0
\end{array}
$$

The answer is negative.
$-0.0063 \div 0.03 = -0.21$

49. $0.005\overline{)24.5}$

Move decimal point 3 places.

$$
\begin{array}{r}
4900 \\
5.\overline{)\ 24500.} \\
\underline{-20} \\
45 \\
\underline{-45} \\
00 \\
\underline{-0} \\
00 \\
\underline{-0} \\
0
\end{array}
$$

The answer is negative.
$24.5 \div (-0.005) = -4900$

50. $2.3\overline{)54.98}$

Move decimal points 1 place.

$$
\begin{array}{r}
23.9043 \approx 23.904 \\
23.\overline{)\ 549.8000} \\
\underline{-46} \\
89 \\
\underline{-69} \\
20\,8 \\
\underline{-20\,7} \\
10 \\
\underline{-0} \\
100 \\
\underline{-92} \\
80 \\
\underline{-69} \\
11
\end{array}
$$

$54.98 \div 2.3 \approx 23.904$

51.

$$
\begin{array}{r}
8.0588 \approx 8.059 \\
34\overline{)\ 274.0000} \\
\underline{-272} \\
2\,0 \\
\underline{-0} \\
2\,00 \\
\underline{-1\,70} \\
300 \\
\underline{-272} \\
280 \\
\underline{-272} \\
8
\end{array}
$$

52.

$$
\begin{array}{r}
158.25 \\
20\overline{)\ 3165.00} \\
\underline{-20} \\
116 \\
\underline{-100} \\
165 \\
\underline{-160} \\
50 \\
\underline{-40} \\
100 \\
\underline{-100} \\
0
\end{array}
$$

$-3165 \div (-20) = 158.25$

53. $3.28\overline{)24.00}$

Move decimal points 2 places.

$$
\begin{array}{r}
7.31 \approx 7.3 \\
328.\overline{)\ 2400.00} \\
\underline{-2296} \\
1040 \\
\underline{-984} \\
560 \\
\underline{-328} \\
232
\end{array}
$$

There are about 7.3 meters in 24 feet.

54. $69.71\overline{)3136.95}$

Move decimal points 2 places.

$$
\begin{array}{r}
45 \\
6971\overline{)\ 313695} \\
\underline{-27884} \\
34855 \\
\underline{-34855} \\
0
\end{array}
$$

The loan will be paid off in 45 months.

55.　2.4　　　　2
　　　6.7　　　　7
　　 $+9.1$　　 $+9$
　　 18.2　　　 18

56.　15.9　　　16
　　 $+34.1$　　 $+34$
　　 50.0　　　50

57.　340.03　　340
　　-240.98　-241
　　 99.05　　 99

58.　100.0　　100
　 $-\ 45.9$　 -46
　　 54.1　　 54

59.　　6.02　　6
　　$\times\ 5.91$　$\times\ 6$
　　　602　　 36
　　5 4180
　　30 1000
　　35.5782

60.　 0.205　　0.2
　　$\times\ 1.72$　$\times\ 1.7$
　　　410　　 0.34
　　14350
　　20500
　　0.35260

61.　$1.9\overline{)62.13}$

becomes

$$\begin{array}{r}32.7\\19.\overline{)\ 621.3}\\-57\\\hline 51\\-38\\\hline 13\ 3\\-13\ 3\\\hline 0\end{array}\qquad\begin{array}{r}31\\2\overline{)\ 62}\\-6\\\hline 02\\-2\\\hline 0\end{array}$$

62.　$19.8\overline{)601.92}$

becomes

$$\begin{array}{r}30.4\\198.\overline{)\ 6019.2}\\-594\\\hline 79\\-0\\\hline 79\ 2\\-79\ 2\\\hline 0\end{array}\qquad\begin{array}{r}30.1\\20\overline{)\ 602.0}\\-60\\\hline 02\\-0\\\hline 2\ 0\\-2\ 0\\\hline 0\end{array}$$

63.　　99
　　　37
　　　28
　　　22
　　$+14$
　　 200

The total average consumption is 200 quadrillion BTU.

64.　$77.3\times115.9\approx77\times116=8932$
The area is about 8932 square feet.

65.　1.07　　Estimate　　　1
　　1.89　　　　　　　　2
　 $+\ 0.99$　　　　　　 $+\ 1$
　　　　　　　　　　　　 4

Yes, $5 is enough.

66.　$(-7.6)(1.9)+2.5=-14.44+2.5=-11.94$

67.　$2.3^2-1.4=5.29-1.4=3.89$

68.　$\dfrac{(-3.2)^2}{100}=\dfrac{10.24}{100}=0.1024$

69.　$(2.6+1.4)(4.5-3.6)=4(0.9)=3.6$

70.

$$\begin{array}{r}0.8\\5\overline{)\ 4.0}\\-40\\\hline 0\end{array}$$

$$\frac{4}{5}=0.8$$

71.

$$\begin{array}{r}0.9230\approx0.923\\13\overline{)\ 12.0000}\\-117\\\hline 30\\-26\\\hline 40\\-39\\\hline 10\\-0\\\hline 10\end{array}$$

$$-\frac{12}{13}\approx-0.923$$

72.

$$0.4285 \approx 0.429$$

$$
\begin{array}{r}
7\overline{)\,3.0000} \\
-2\,8 \\
\hline
20 \\
-14 \\
\hline
60 \\
-56 \\
\hline
40 \\
-35 \\
\hline
5
\end{array}
$$

$$-\frac{3}{7} \approx -0.429$$

73.

$$0.2166\ldots = 0.21\overline{6}$$

$$
\begin{array}{r}
60\overline{)\,13.0000} \\
-12\,0 \\
\hline
1\,00 \\
-60 \\
\hline
400 \\
-360 \\
\hline
400 \\
-360 \\
\hline
40
\end{array}
$$

$$\frac{13}{60} = 0.21\overline{6} \approx 0.217$$

74.

$$0.1125 \approx 0.113$$

$$
\begin{array}{r}
80\overline{)\,9.0000} \\
-8\,0 \\
\hline
1\,00 \\
-80 \\
\hline
200 \\
-160 \\
\hline
400 \\
-400 \\
\hline
0
\end{array}
$$

$$\frac{9}{80} = 0.1125 \approx 0.113$$

75.

$$51.0571 \approx 51.057$$

$$
\begin{array}{r}
175\overline{)\,8935.0000} \\
-875 \\
\hline
185 \\
-175 \\
\hline
100 \\
-0 \\
\hline
1000 \\
-875 \\
\hline
1250 \\
-1225 \\
\hline
250 \\
-175 \\
\hline
75
\end{array}
$$

$$\frac{8935}{175} \approx 51.057$$

76. $0.3920 = 0.392$

77. $\dfrac{4}{7} \approx 0.5714$

$$\frac{5}{8} = 0.625$$

$$\frac{4}{7} < \frac{5}{8}$$

78. $\dfrac{5}{17} \approx 0.294$

$$0.293 < \frac{5}{17}$$

79. $\dfrac{6}{11} \approx 0.545$

$$\frac{6}{11} < 0.55$$

80. $0.832, 0.837, 0.839$

81. $\dfrac{3}{7} \approx 0.4286$

$$0.42, \ \frac{3}{7}, \ 0.43$$

82. $\dfrac{18}{11} \approx 1.636, \ \dfrac{19}{12} \approx 1.583$

$$\frac{19}{12}, \ 1.63, \ \frac{18}{11}$$

83. $\dfrac{6}{7} \approx 0.8571, \ \dfrac{8}{9} = 0.\overline{8} \approx 0.8889, \ \dfrac{3}{4} = 0.75$

$$\frac{3}{4}, \ \frac{6}{7}, \ \frac{8}{9}$$

84. $\text{Area} = \dfrac{1}{2} \cdot \text{base} \cdot \text{height}$

$\quad\quad\quad = 0.5 \cdot 4.6 \cdot 3$

$\quad\quad\quad = 6.9$

The area is 6.9 square feet.

85. $\text{Area} = \dfrac{1}{2} \cdot \text{base} \cdot \text{height}$

$\quad\quad\quad = 0.5 \cdot 5.2 \cdot 2.1$

$\quad\quad\quad = 5.46$

The area is 5.46 square inches.

86. $\quad\quad x + 3.9 = 4.2$

$\quad x + 3.9 - 3.9 = 4.2 - 3.9$

$\quad\quad\quad\quad\quad x = 0.3$

87. $\quad\quad\quad 70 = y + 22.81$

$\quad 70 - 22.81 = y + 22.81 - 22.81$

$\quad\quad\quad 47.19 = y$

88. $\quad 2x = 17.2$

$\quad \dfrac{2x}{2} = \dfrac{17.2}{2}$

$\quad\quad x = 8.6$

89. $\quad\quad 1.1y = 88$

$\quad 10(1.1y) = 10(88)$

$\quad\quad\quad 11y = 880$

$\quad\quad\quad \dfrac{11y}{11} = \dfrac{880}{11}$

$\quad\quad\quad\quad y = 80$

90. $\quad \dfrac{x}{4} = 0.12$

$\quad 4\left(\dfrac{x}{4}\right) = 4(0.12)$

$\quad\quad\quad x = 0.48$

91. $\quad 6.8 = \dfrac{y}{5}$

$\quad (6.8)5 = \dfrac{y}{5} \cdot 5$

$\quad 34.0 = y$

92. $\quad\quad x + 0.78 = 1.2$

$\quad x + 0.78 - 0.78 = 1.2 - 0.78$

$\quad\quad\quad\quad\quad x = 0.42$

93. $\quad 0.56 = 2x$

$\quad \dfrac{0.56}{2} = \dfrac{2x}{2}$

$\quad 0.28 = x$

94. $\quad\quad\quad 1.3x - 9.4 = 0.4x + 8.6$

$\quad 1.3x - 0.4x - 9.4 = 0.4x - 0.4x + 8.6$

$\quad\quad\quad 0.9x - 9.4 + 9.4 = 8.6 + 9.4$

$\quad\quad\quad\quad\quad 0.9x = 18$

$\quad\quad\quad\quad\quad \dfrac{0.9x}{0.9} = \dfrac{18}{0.9}$

$\quad\quad\quad\quad\quad x = 20$

95. $\quad\quad 3(x - 1.1) = 5x - 5.3$

$\quad\quad\quad 3x - 3.3 = 5x - 5.3$

$\quad 3x - 3.3 + 3.3 = 5x - 5.3 + 3.3$

$\quad\quad\quad\quad 3x = 5x - 2$

$\quad\quad 3x - 5x = 5x - 5x - 2$

$\quad\quad\quad\quad -2x = -2$

$\quad\quad\quad\quad\quad x = 1$

96. $\sqrt{64} = 8$ since $8^2 = 64$.

97. $\sqrt{144} = 12$ since $12^2 = 144$.

98. $\sqrt{36} = 6$ since $6^2 = 36$.

99. $\sqrt{1} = 1$ since $1^2 = 1$.

100. $\sqrt{\dfrac{4}{25}} = \dfrac{2}{5}$ since $\left(\dfrac{2}{5}\right)^2 = \dfrac{4}{25}$.

101. $\sqrt{\dfrac{1}{100}} = \dfrac{1}{10}$ since $\left(\dfrac{1}{10}\right)^2 = \dfrac{1}{100}$.

102. $\quad a^2 + b^2 = c^2$

$\quad 12^2 + 5^2 = c^2$

$\quad 144 + 25 = c^2$

$\quad\quad\quad 169 = c^2$

$\quad\quad \sqrt{169} = c$

$\quad\quad\quad 13 = c$

103. $\quad a^2 + b^2 = c^2$

$\quad 20^2 + 21^2 = c^2$

$\quad 400 + 441 = c^2$

$\quad\quad\quad 841 = c^2$

$\quad\quad \sqrt{841} = c$

$\quad\quad\quad 29 = c$

104. $a^2 + b^2 = c^2$
$9^2 + b^2 = 14^2$
$81 + b^2 = 196$
$b^2 = 115$
$b = \sqrt{115}$
$b \approx 10.7$

105. $a^2 + b^2 = c^2$
$124^2 + b^2 = 155^2$
$15,376 + b^2 = 24,025$
$b^2 = 8649$
$b = \sqrt{8649}$
$b = 93$

106. $a^2 + b^2 = c^2$
$66^2 + 56^2 = c^2$
$4356 + 3136 = c^2$
$7492 = c^2$
$\sqrt{7492} = c$
$86.6 \approx c$

107. $a^2 + b^2 = c^2$
$20^2 + 20^2 = c^2$
$400 + 400 = c^2$
$800 = c^2$
$\sqrt{800} = c$
$28.28 \approx c$
The diagonal is approximately 28.28 centimeters.

108. $a^2 + b^2 = c^2$
$90^2 + b^2 = 126^2$
$8100 + b^2 = 15,876$
$b^2 = 7776$
$b = \sqrt{7776}$
$b \approx 88.2$
The height of the building is approximately 88.2 feet.

Chapter 5 Test

1. 45.092 is forty-five and ninety-two thousandths.

2. Three thousand and fifty-nine thousandths is 3000.059.

3.   2.893
        4.210
     + 10.492
     ⎯⎯⎯⎯⎯
       17.595

4.   −47.92
        − 3.28
       ⎯⎯⎯⎯
        −51.20

5. $9.83 - 30.25 = 9.83 + (-30.25)$
Subtract the absolute values.
     30.25
    −9.83
    ⎯⎯⎯
    20.42
Since $30.25 > 9.83$, the answer is negative.
−20.42

6.   10.2
     × 4.01
    ⎯⎯⎯⎯
       102
         0
    40 800
    ⎯⎯⎯⎯
    40.902

7. $0.23 \overline{)0.00843}$
becomes
          $0.0366\ldots \approx 0.037$
    $23 \overline{)0.8430}$
       $\underline{-69}$
        153
       $\underline{-138}$
        150
       $\underline{-138}$
         15
$(-0.00843) \div (-0.23) \approx 0.037$

8. 34.8923 rounded to the nearest tenth is 34.9.

9. 0.8623 rounded to the nearest thousandth is 0.862.

10. $25.0909 < 25.9090$

11. $\dfrac{4}{9} = 0.444\ldots$

$\dfrac{4}{9} < 0.445$

12. $0.345 = \dfrac{345}{1000} = \dfrac{69}{200}$

13. $-24.73 = -24\dfrac{73}{100}$

14. $-\dfrac{13}{26} = -\dfrac{1}{2} = -0.5$

15. $\dfrac{16}{17} \approx 0.941$

$$
\begin{array}{r}
0.9411 \\
17\overline{)16.0000} \\
-153 \\
\hline
70 \\
-68 \\
\hline
20 \\
-17 \\
\hline
30 \\
-17 \\
\hline
13
\end{array}
$$

16. $(-0.6)^2 + 1.57 = 0.36 + 1.57 = 1.93$

17. $\dfrac{0.23 + 1.63}{-0.3} = \dfrac{1.86}{-0.3}$

$$= -\dfrac{186}{30}$$

$$= -\dfrac{62 \cdot 3}{10 \cdot 3}$$

$$= -\dfrac{62}{10}$$

$$= -6.2$$

18. $2.4x - 3.6 - 1.9x - 9.8$
$= (2.4 - 1.9)x - 3.6 - 9.8$
$= 0.5x - 13.4$

19. $\sqrt{49} = 7$

20. $\sqrt{157} = 12.530$

21. $\sqrt{\dfrac{64}{100}} = \dfrac{8}{10} = \dfrac{4}{5}$

22. $0.2x + 1.3 = 0.7$
$10(0.2x + 1.3) = 10(0.7)$
$2x + 13 = 7$
$2x + 13 - 13 = 7 - 13$
$2x = -6$
$x = -3$

23. $2(x + 5.7) = 6x - 3.4$
$2x + 11.4 = 6x - 3.4$
$2x - 2x + 11.4 = 6x - 2x - 3.4$
$11.4 = 4x - 3.4$
$11.4 + 3.4 = 4x - 3.4 + 3.4$
$14.8 = 4x$
$3.7 = x$

24. $a^2 + b^2 = c^2$
$4^2 + 4^2 = c^2$
$16 + 16 = c^2$
$32 = c^2$
$\sqrt{32} = c$
$5.66 \approx c$
The length of the hypotenuse is approximately 5.66 centimeters.

25. Area $= \dfrac{1}{2} \cdot$ base $\cdot$ height
$= 0.5 \cdot 4.2 \cdot 1.1$
$= 2.31$
The area is 2.31 square miles.

26. $A = 123.8(80) = 9904$
9904 square feet of lawn
$9904 \times 0.02 = 198.08$
She needs 198.08 ounces of insecticide.

27. Circumference $= 2 \cdot \pi \cdot$ radius
$= 2 \cdot \pi \cdot 9$
$= 18\pi$
$\approx 18(3.14)$
$= 56.52$
The circumference is 18π miles ≈ 56.52 miles.

28.

$$
\begin{array}{r}
12.4 \approx 12 \\
700\overline{)8740.0} \\
-700 \\
\hline
1740 \\
-1400 \\
\hline
3400 \\
-2800 \\
\hline
600
\end{array}
$$

It takes 12 CDs to hold as much data as a DVD.

29.

	14.2	Estimate	14
	16.1		16
+	23.7		+ 24
			54

The total distance is about 54 miles.

Cumulative Review

1.
$$\begin{array}{r} 34,285 \\ +149,761 \\ \hline 184,046 \end{array}$$

2.
$$\begin{array}{r} 5,785 \\ +210,199 \\ \hline 215,984 \end{array}$$

3.
$$\begin{array}{r} 300 \\ 600 \\ 1100 \\ +300 \\ \hline 2300 \end{array}$$

4.
$$\begin{array}{r} 200 \\ 400 \\ 900 \\ +1400 \\ \hline 2900 \end{array}$$

5.
$$\begin{array}{r} 401 \;\; \text{R 2} \\ 17\overline{)\,6819} \\ -68 \\ \hline 01 \\ 0 \\ \hline 19 \\ -17 \\ \hline 2 \end{array}$$

6.
$$\begin{array}{r} 146 \;\; \text{R 3} \\ 14\overline{)\,2047} \\ -14 \\ \hline 64 \\ 56 \\ \hline 87 \\ -84 \\ \hline 3 \end{array}$$

7. $\dfrac{21 - 5(3)}{3} = \dfrac{21 - 15}{3} = \dfrac{6}{3} = 2$

8. $\dfrac{2(7) + 4}{3} = \dfrac{14 + 4}{3} = \dfrac{18}{3} = 6$

9. a. -11
    b. 2
    c. 0

10. a. 7
    b. -4
    c. 1

11. $-2 + (-21) = -23$

12. $-7 + (-15) = -22$

13. $2 \cdot 5^2 = 2.25 = 50$

14. $4 \cdot 2^3 = 4 \cdot 8 = 32$

15. $-3^2 = -(3)(3) = -9$

16. $(-2)^5 = (-2)(-2)(-2)(-2)(-2) = -32$

17. $(-3)^2 = (-3)(-3) = 9$

18. $-7^2 = -(7)(7) = -49$

19. a. $3x + 2x = 5x$
    b. $y - 7y = -6y$
    c. $3x^2 + 5x^2 - 2 = 8x^2 - 2$

20. a. $2a - 5a = -3a$
    b. $-3z^2 - z^2 = -4z^2$
    c. $4k + 2 + 7k = 4k + 7k + 2 = 11k + 2$

21.
$$\begin{aligned} 5x + 2 - 4x &= 7 - 9 \\ x + 2 &= -2 \\ x + 2 - 2 &= -2 - 2 \\ x &= -4 \end{aligned}$$

22.
$$\begin{aligned} 7x - 3 &= 6x + 2 \\ 7x - 3 - 6x &= 6x + 2 - 6x \\ x - 3 &= 2 \\ x - 3 + 3 &= 2 + 3 \\ x &= 5 \end{aligned}$$

23.
$$\begin{aligned} -5x &= 15 \\ \frac{-5x}{-5} &= \frac{15}{-5} \\ x &= -3 \end{aligned}$$

24. $-21 = -7x$
$$\frac{-21}{-7} = \frac{-7x}{-7}$$
$$3 = x$$

25.
$$7(x-2) = 9x - 6$$
$$7x - 14 = 9x - 6$$
$$7x - 14 - 9x = 9x - 6 - 9x$$
$$-2x - 14 = -6$$
$$-2x - 14 + 14 = -6 + 14$$
$$-2x = 8$$
$$\frac{-2x}{-2} = \frac{8}{-2}$$
$$x = -4$$

26.
$$2(x+4) = -x - 1$$
$$2x + 8 = -x - 1$$
$$2x + 8 + x = -x - 1 + x$$
$$3x + 8 = -1$$
$$3x + 8 - 8 = -1 - 8$$
$$3x = -9$$
$$\frac{3x}{3} = \frac{-9}{3}$$
$$x = -3$$

27. Let x = votes received by Thomas' challenger. Then $x + 110{,}280$ = Thomas' votes.
$$x + x + 110{,}280 = 204{,}358$$
$$2x + 110{,}280 = 204{,}358$$
$$2x + 110{,}280 - 110{,}280 = 204{,}358 - 110{,}280$$
$$2x = 94{,}078$$
$$\frac{2x}{x} = \frac{94{,}078}{2}$$
$$x = 47{,}039$$
Thomas' votes = $47{,}039 + 110{,}280 = 157{,}319$.

28.
$$84 + 3x = 153$$
$$84 + 3x - 84 = 153 - 84$$
$$3x = 79$$
$$x = 23$$

29. numerator = 3
denominator = 7

30. numerator = 2
denominator = $5a$

31. numerator = $13x$
denominator = 5

32. numerator = $7y$
denominator = $3x$

33. $\dfrac{12}{20} = \dfrac{2 \cdot 6}{5 \cdot 6} = \dfrac{2}{5}$

34. $\dfrac{64}{112} = \dfrac{4 \cdot 16}{7 \cdot 16} = \dfrac{4}{7}$

35. $-\dfrac{1}{4} \cdot \dfrac{1}{2} = -\dfrac{1}{8}$

36. $\left(-\dfrac{1}{3}\right)\left(-\dfrac{1}{4}\right) = \dfrac{1}{12}$

37. $\dfrac{2}{7} + \dfrac{3}{7} = \dfrac{5}{7}$

38. $\dfrac{2}{5} + \dfrac{3}{5} = \dfrac{5}{5} = 1$

39. $\dfrac{7}{8} + \dfrac{6}{8} + \dfrac{3}{8} = \dfrac{16}{8} = 2$

40. $\dfrac{2}{3} + \dfrac{1}{3} + \dfrac{2}{3} = \dfrac{5}{3}$ or $1\dfrac{2}{3}$

41. $\dfrac{2}{5} + \dfrac{4}{15} = \dfrac{2 \cdot 3}{5 \cdot 3} + \dfrac{4}{15}$
$$= \dfrac{6}{15} + \dfrac{4}{15}$$
$$= \dfrac{10}{15}$$
$$= \dfrac{2}{3}$$

42. $\dfrac{3}{4} + \dfrac{5}{12} = \dfrac{3 \cdot 3}{4 \cdot 3} + \dfrac{5}{12}$
$$= \dfrac{9}{12} + \dfrac{5}{12}$$
$$= \dfrac{14}{12}$$
$$= \dfrac{7}{6} \text{ or } 1\dfrac{1}{6}$$

43. $\dfrac{\frac{x}{4}}{\frac{3}{2}} = \dfrac{x}{4} \div \dfrac{3}{2} = \dfrac{x}{4} \cdot \dfrac{2}{3} = \dfrac{x \cdot 2}{2 \cdot 2 \cdot 3} = \dfrac{x}{6}$

44.

$$\frac{\frac{2}{3}}{\frac{4x}{9}} = \frac{2}{3} \div \frac{4x}{9} = \frac{2}{3} \cdot \frac{9}{4x} = \frac{2 \cdot 3 \cdot 3}{3 \cdot 2 \cdot 2x} = \frac{3}{2x}$$

45.

$$\frac{3}{5}a = 9$$
$$\frac{5}{3} \cdot \frac{3}{5}a = 9 \cdot \frac{5}{3}$$
$$a = \frac{3 \cdot 3 \cdot 5}{3}$$
$$a = 15$$

46.

$$\frac{2}{3}y = 12$$
$$\frac{3}{2} \cdot \frac{2}{3}y = 12 \cdot \frac{3}{2}$$
$$y = \frac{2 \cdot 6 \cdot 3}{2}$$
$$y = 18$$

47.
```
  763.7651
   22.0010
 +43.8900
  829.6561
```

48.
```
   89.2700
   14.3610
 +127.2318
  230.8628
```

49.
```
    23.6
   ×0.78
    1888
   16520
  18.408
```

50.
```
     43.8
   ×0.645
     2190
    17520
   262800
   27.2510
```
        Answer: 27.251

Chapter 6

1. $\dfrac{5.1}{7.9} = \dfrac{51}{79}$

2. $\dfrac{30}{20} = \dfrac{3}{2}$

3. $\dfrac{22}{x} = \dfrac{66}{12}$

$12(22) = 66(x)$

$\dfrac{264}{66} = \dfrac{66x}{66}$

$4 = x$

4. $\dfrac{x}{8} = \dfrac{0.6}{2.4}$

$2.4(x) = 8(0.6)$

$\dfrac{2.4x}{2.4} = \dfrac{4.8}{2.4}$

$x = 2$

5. $\dfrac{1 \text{ in}}{20 \text{ mi}} = \dfrac{5\frac{3}{8} \text{ in}}{x \text{ mi}}$

$1(x) = 20\left(5\frac{3}{8}\right)$

$x = \dfrac{20}{1} \cdot \dfrac{43}{8}$

$x = \dfrac{215}{2}$ or $107\frac{1}{2}$

$5\frac{3}{8}$ inches represents $107\frac{1}{2}$ miles

6. $\dfrac{12}{100} = 12\%$

7. $57\% = 57.\% = 0.57$

8. $2.75 = 275\%$

9. $7.5\% = \dfrac{7.5}{100} = \dfrac{75}{1000} = \dfrac{3}{40}$

10. $\dfrac{3}{20} = \dfrac{3 \cdot 5}{20 \cdot 5} = \dfrac{15}{100} = 15\%$

11. $18\% \cdot 50 = x$

12. $4\% \cdot x = 89$

13. $\dfrac{82}{b} = \dfrac{90}{100}$

14. $\dfrac{48}{112} = \dfrac{p}{100}$

15. $x \cdot 80 = 16$

$\dfrac{x \cdot 80}{80} = \dfrac{16}{80}$

$x = 0.2$

$x = 20\%$

16 is 20% of 80.

16. $x = 1.5\% \cdot 220$

$x = 0.015 \cdot 220$

$x = 3.3$

3.3 is 1.5% of 220.

17. $32 = 16\% \cdot x$

$32 = 0.16 \cdot x$

$\dfrac{32}{0.16} = \dfrac{0.16 \cdot x}{0.16}$

$200 = x$

32 is 16% of 200.

18. What number is 1.2% of 250?

$x = 1.2\% \cdot 250$

$x = 0.012 \cdot 250$

$x = 3$

3 lightbulbs were defective.

19. What number is 2% of 4200?

$x = 2\% \cdot 4200$

$x = 0.02 \cdot 4200$

$x = 84$

The enrollment decreased by 84 students. The current enrollment is 4200 − 84 = 4316 students.

20. $\$34.93 = r \cdot \$499$

$\dfrac{\$34.93}{\$499} = \dfrac{r \cdot \$499}{\$499}$

$0.07 = r$

$7\% = r$

The sales tax rate is 7%.

21. $\$448 = 2\% \cdot x$

$\$448 = 0.02 \cdot x$

$\dfrac{\$448}{0.02} = \dfrac{0.02 \cdot x}{0.02}$

$\$22,400 = x$

His sales were $22,400.

22. discount = $12\% \cdot \$650$
$= 0.12 \cdot \$650$
$= \$78$
sales price = $\$650 - 78 = \$572$

23. simple interest = principal $\cdot$ rate $\cdot$ time
$= \$600 \cdot 8\% \cdot 3$
$= \$600 \cdot (0.08) \cdot 3$
$= \$144$

24. The compound interest factor for 6 years at 6% compounded quarterly is 1.42950.
total amount = $\$5000 \cdot 1.42950 = \$7147.50$

25. monthly payment $= \dfrac{\text{principal interest}}{\text{number of payments}}$
$= \dfrac{\$700 + \$196}{2 \cdot 12}$
$= \dfrac{\$896}{24}$
$\approx \$37.33$

Section 6.1

Practice Problems

1. a. $\dfrac{3}{7}$ **b.** $\dfrac{40 \text{ min}}{3 \text{ hours}} = \dfrac{40 \text{ min}}{180 \text{ min}} = \dfrac{2}{9}$

2. $\dfrac{1.68}{4.8} = \dfrac{1.68 \cdot 100}{4.8 \cdot 100} = \dfrac{168}{48} = \dfrac{7 \cdot 24}{8 \cdot 57} = \dfrac{7}{2}$

3. a. $\dfrac{\text{shortest side}}{\text{longest side}} = \dfrac{6 \text{ m}}{10 \text{ m}} = \dfrac{3 \cdot 2}{5 \cdot 2} = \dfrac{3}{5}$

b. $\dfrac{\text{longest side}}{\text{perimeter}} = \dfrac{10 \text{ m}}{6 \text{ m} + 8 \text{ m} + 10 \text{ m}}$
$= \dfrac{10 \text{m}}{24 \text{ m}}$
$= \dfrac{5 \cdot 2}{12 \cdot 2}$
$= \dfrac{5}{12}$

4. $\dfrac{3}{8} = \dfrac{63}{x}$
$3(x) = 8(63)$
$\dfrac{3x}{3} = \dfrac{504}{3}$
$x = 168$

5. $\dfrac{2x+1}{7} = \dfrac{x-3}{5}$
$7(x-3) = 5(2x+1)$
$7x - 21 = 10x + 5$
$7x - 10x = 5 + 21$
$\dfrac{-3x}{-3} = \dfrac{26}{-3}$
$x = -\dfrac{26}{3}$

6. $\dfrac{12 \text{ feet}}{1 \text{ inch}} = \dfrac{n \text{ feet}}{3\frac{1}{2} \text{ inches}}$
$\dfrac{12}{1} = \dfrac{n}{3\frac{1}{2}}$
$1 \cdot n = 12 \cdot 3\frac{1}{2}$
$n = \dfrac{12}{1} \cdot \dfrac{7}{2}$
$n = 42$
$3\dfrac{1}{2}$ inches corresponds to 42 feet.

7. $\dfrac{14 \text{ gallons}}{3 \text{ ounces}} = \dfrac{n \text{ gallons}}{16 \text{ ounces}}$
$\dfrac{14}{3} = \dfrac{n}{16}$
$3 \cdot n = 14 \cdot 16$
$3n = 224$
$\dfrac{3n}{3} = \dfrac{224}{3}$
$n = 74\dfrac{2}{3}$
$74\dfrac{2}{3}$ gallons of gas can be treated with a 16-ounce bottle of alcohol.

Exercise Set 6.1

1. $\dfrac{2}{15}$

3. $\dfrac{10}{12} = \dfrac{5}{6}$

5. $\dfrac{5 \text{ quarts}}{3 \text{ gallons}} = \dfrac{5 \text{ quarts}}{12 \text{ quarts}} = \dfrac{5}{12}$

7. $\dfrac{4 \text{ nickels}}{2 \text{ dollars}} = \dfrac{4 \text{ nickels}}{40 \text{ nickels}} = \dfrac{1}{10}$

9. $\dfrac{175 \text{ cm}}{5 \text{ m}} = \dfrac{175 \text{ cm}}{500 \text{ cm}} = \dfrac{7}{20}$

11. $\dfrac{190 \text{ min}}{3 \text{ hours}} = \dfrac{190 \text{ min}}{180 \text{ min}} = \dfrac{19}{18}$

13. $\dfrac{\text{length}}{\text{width}} = \dfrac{94 \text{ feet}}{50 \text{ feet}} = \dfrac{47 \cdot 2}{25 \cdot 2} = \dfrac{47}{25}$

15. perimeter = 8 + 15 + 17 = 40 feet
$\dfrac{\text{longest side}}{\text{perimeter}} = \dfrac{17 \text{ feet}}{40 \text{ feet}} = \dfrac{17}{40}$

17. $\dfrac{\text{calories from fat}}{\text{total calories}} = \dfrac{200}{450} = \dfrac{4 \cdot 50}{9 \cdot 50} = \dfrac{4}{9}$

19. $\dfrac{\text{red blood cells}}{\text{platelet cells}} = \dfrac{600}{40} = \dfrac{40 \cdot 15}{40 \cdot 1} = \dfrac{15}{1}$

21. Answers may vary

23. $\dfrac{2}{3} = \dfrac{x}{6}$
$3(x) = 2(6)$
$\dfrac{3x}{3} = \dfrac{12}{3}$
$x = 4$

25. $\dfrac{x}{10} = \dfrac{5}{9}$
$9(x) = 5(10)$
$\dfrac{9x}{9} = \dfrac{50}{9}$
$x = \dfrac{50}{9}$

27. $\dfrac{4x}{6} = \dfrac{7}{2}$
$2(4x) = 7(6)$
$\dfrac{8x}{8} = \dfrac{42}{8}$
$x = \dfrac{21}{4}$

29. $\dfrac{x-3}{x} = \dfrac{4}{7}$
$4(x) = 7(x-3)$
$4x = 7x - 21$
$4x - 7x = -21$
$\dfrac{-3x}{-3} = \dfrac{-21}{-3}$
$x = 7$

31. $\dfrac{x+1}{2x+3} = \dfrac{2}{3}$
$2(2x+3) = 3(x+1)$
$4x + 6 = 3x + 3$
$4x - 3x = 3 - 6$
$x = -3$

33. $\dfrac{9}{5} = \dfrac{12}{3x+2}$
$9(3x+2) = 5(12)$
$27x + 18 = 60$
$27x = 60 - 18$
$\dfrac{27x}{27} = \dfrac{42}{27}$
$x = \dfrac{14}{9}$

35. $\dfrac{3}{x+1} = \dfrac{5}{2x}$
$3(2x) = 5(x+1)$
$6x = 5x + 5$
$6x - 5x = 5$
$x = 5$

37. $\dfrac{15}{3x-4} = \dfrac{5}{x}$
$15(x) = 5(3x-4)$
$15x = 15x - 20$
$15x - 15x = -20$
$0 = -20$
No Solution

39. $\dfrac{100 \text{ Earth}}{3 \text{ Mars}} = \dfrac{4100 \text{ Earth}}{x \text{ Mars}}$
$100(x) = 3(4100)$
$100x = 12,300$
$x = 123$
The elephant would weigh 123 pounds.

41. $\dfrac{110 \text{ calories}}{28.4 \text{ grams}} = \dfrac{x \text{ calories}}{42.6 \text{ grams}}$

$28.4(x) = 42.6(110)$

$\dfrac{28.4x}{28.4} = \dfrac{4686}{28.4}$

$x = 165$

42.6 grams of this cereal contain 165 calories.

43. Let n = the number of people.

$\dfrac{1 \text{ person}}{625 \text{ square feet of lawn}} = \dfrac{n \text{ people}}{3750 \text{ square feet of lawn}}$

$625n = 3750$

$\dfrac{625n}{625} = \dfrac{3750}{625}$

$n = 6$

The lawn supplies enough oxygen for 6 people.

45. Let n = the estimated height of Statue of Liberty.

$\dfrac{42 \text{ feet}}{2 \text{ feet}} = \dfrac{n \text{ feet}}{5\frac{1}{3} \text{ feet}}$

$2n = 42 \cdot 5\frac{1}{3}$

$2n = \dfrac{42}{1} \cdot \dfrac{16}{3}$

$2n = 224$

$\dfrac{2n}{2} = \dfrac{224}{2}$

$n = 112$

The estimate height is 112 feet. The actual height is 111 feet 1 inch. The difference in the estimated height and the actual height is

$112 - 111\frac{1}{2} = \dfrac{11}{12}$ of a foot or 11 inches.

47. Let n = the number of pounds of sugar.

$\dfrac{1 \text{ pound of sugar}}{2\frac{1}{4} \text{ cups packed sugar}} = \dfrac{n \text{ pounds sugar}}{6 \text{ cups packed sugar}}$

$2\frac{1}{4} \cdot n = 1 \cdot 6$

$\dfrac{9}{4} \cdot n = 6$

$\dfrac{4}{9} \cdot \dfrac{9}{4} \cdot n = \dfrac{4}{9} \cdot \dfrac{6}{1}$

$n = \dfrac{8}{3}$

$n = 2\frac{2}{3}$

$2\frac{2}{3}$ pounds of sugar will be required.

49. Let xn= men who blame fast food.

$\dfrac{2}{5} = \dfrac{n}{40}$

$5n = 40 \cdot 2$

$5n = 80$

$\dfrac{5n}{5} = \dfrac{80}{5}$

$n = 16$

16 men blame fast food.

51. Let n = the number of visits including a prescription.

$\dfrac{7 \text{ prescriptions}}{10 \text{ visits}} = \dfrac{n \text{ prescriptions}}{620 \text{ visits}}$

$10n = 7 \cdot 620$

$10n = 4340$

$\dfrac{10n}{10} = \dfrac{4340}{10}$

$n = 434$

434 emergency room visits included a prescription.

53. Let n = the number of cups of rock salt.

$\dfrac{5}{1} = \dfrac{12}{n}$

$1 \cdot 12 = 5n$

$12 = 5n$

$\dfrac{12}{5} = \dfrac{5n}{5}$

$2.4 = n$

Mix 2.4 cups of rock salt with the ice.

55. a. $\dfrac{50}{1} = \dfrac{5}{x}$

$50x = 5$

$\dfrac{50x}{50} = \dfrac{5}{50}$

$x = \dfrac{1}{10}$ or   0.1 gallon

b. $\dfrac{1 \text{ gal}}{128 \text{ fl. oz.}} = \dfrac{0.1 \text{ gal}}{x}$

$x = 12.8$

When rounded to the nearest whole ounces, the answer is 13 fluid oz.

57. a. $\dfrac{150 \text{ mg}}{20 \text{ lb}} = \dfrac{x}{275 \text{ lb}}$

$20x = 150 \cdot 275$

$20x = 41{,}250$

$\dfrac{20x}{20} = \dfrac{41{,}250}{20}$

$x = 2062.5 \text{ mg}$

b. 24 hours $\div$ 8 = 3 doses a day

3 doses $\times$ 500 mg = 1500 mg

He is not receiving the proper dosage.

59. $15 = 3 \cdot 5$

61. $20 = 4 \cdot 5$

$= 2 \cdot 2 \cdot 5$

$= 2^2 \cdot 5$

63. $200 = 2 \cdot 100$

$= 2 \cdot 4 \cdot 25$

$= 2 \cdot 2 \cdot 2 \cdot 5 \cdot 5$

$= 2^3 \cdot 5^2$

65. $32 = 4 \cdot 8$

$= 2 \cdot 2 \cdot 2 \cdot 4$

$= 2 \cdot 2 \cdot 2 \cdot 2 \cdot 2$

$= 2^5$

67. $\dfrac{15 \text{ mg}}{1 \text{ mL}} = \dfrac{12 \text{ mg}}{x}$

$15x = 12$

$\dfrac{15x}{15} = \dfrac{12}{15}$

$x = 0.8 \text{ mL}$

69. $\dfrac{8 \text{ mg}}{1 \text{ mL}} = \dfrac{10 \text{ mg}}{x}$

$8x = 10$

$\dfrac{8x}{8} = \dfrac{10}{8}$

$x = 1.25 \text{ mL}$

Section 6.2

Practice Problems

1. $\dfrac{23}{100} = 23\%$

2. $\dfrac{29}{100} = 29\%$

3. $89\% = 89.\% = 0.89$

4. $2.7\% = 0.027$

5. $150\% = 150.\% = 1.5$

6. $0.69\% = 0.0069$

7. $500\% = 500.\% = 5$

8. $0.19 = 19.\% = 19\%$

9. $1.75 = 175.\% = 175\%$

10. $0.044 = 004.4\% = 4.4\%$

11. $0.7 = 070.\% = 70\%$

12. $25\% = \dfrac{25}{100} = \dfrac{1 \cdot 25}{4 \cdot 25} = \dfrac{1}{4}$

13. $2.3\% = \dfrac{2.3}{100} = \dfrac{2.3 \cdot 10}{100 \cdot 10} = \dfrac{23}{1000}$

14. $150\% = \dfrac{150}{100} = \dfrac{3 \cdot 50}{2 \cdot 50} = \dfrac{3}{2}$

15. $66\dfrac{2}{3}\% = \dfrac{66\frac{2}{3}}{100}$

$= \dfrac{\frac{200}{3}}{100}$

$= \dfrac{200}{3} \div 100$

$= \dfrac{200}{3} \cdot \dfrac{1}{100}$

$= \dfrac{2}{3}$

16. $8\% = \frac{8}{100} = \frac{2 \cdot 4}{25 \cdot 4} = \frac{2}{25}$

17. $\frac{1}{2} = \frac{1}{2} \cdot 100\% = \frac{100}{2}\% = 50\%$

18. $\frac{7}{40} = \frac{7}{40} \cdot 100\% = \frac{700}{40}\% = \frac{35}{2}\% = 17\frac{1}{2}\%$

19. $2\frac{1}{4} = \frac{9}{4} \cdot 100\% = \frac{900}{4}\% = 225\%$

20. $\frac{3}{17} = \frac{3}{17} \cdot 100\% = \frac{300}{17}\% \approx 17.65\%$

$$
\begin{array}{r}
17.647 \approx 17.65 \\
17\overline{)300.000} \\
\underline{-17} \\
130 \\
\underline{-119} \\
11\,0 \\
\underline{-10\,2} \\
80 \\
\underline{-\,68} \\
120 \\
\underline{-119} \\
1
\end{array}
$$

21. $25\% = 25.\% = 0.25$

22. $1\frac{1}{4} = \frac{5}{4} \cdot 100\% = \frac{500}{4}\% = 125\%$

Mental Math

1. $\frac{13}{100} = 13\%$

2. $\frac{92}{100} = 92\%$

3. $\frac{87}{100} = 87\%$

4. $\frac{71}{100} = 71\%$

5. $\frac{1}{100} = 1\%$

6. $\frac{2}{100} = 2\%$

Exercise Set 6.2

1. $\frac{81}{100} = 81\%$

3. $\frac{9}{100} = 9\%$

5. The largest section of the circle graph is chocolate chip. Therefore, chocolate chip was the most preferred cookie.
$\frac{52}{100} = 52\%$

7. $\frac{12}{100} = 12\%$

9. $48\% = 48.\% = 0.48$

11. $6\% = 6.\% = 0.06$

13. $100\% = 100.\% = 1.00 = 1$

15. $61.3\% = 0.613$

17. $2.8\% = 0.028$

19. $64\frac{1}{4}\% = 6.25\% = 0.625$

21. $300\% = 300.\% = 3.00 = 3$

23. $32.58\% = 0.3258$

25. $73.7\% = 0.737$

27. $25\% = 25.\% = 0.25$

29. $11.1\% = 0.111$

31. $46.2\% = 0.462$

33. $3.1 = 3.10 = 310.\% = 310\%$

35. $29 = 29.00 = 2900.\% = 2900\%$

37. $0.003 = 000.3\% = 0.3\%$

39. $0.22 = 022.\% = 22\%$

41. $0.056 = = 005.6\% = 5.6\%$

43. $0.3328 = 033.28\% = 33.28\%$

45. $3.00 = 300.\% = 300\%$

47. $0.7 = 0.70 = 070.\% = 70\%$

49. $0.10 = 010.\% = 10\%$

51. $0.324 = 32.4\%$

53. $0.38 = 038.\% = 38\%$

55. $4\% = \dfrac{4}{100} = \dfrac{4 \cdot 1}{4 \cdot 25} = \dfrac{1}{25}$

57. $4.5\% = \dfrac{4.5}{100} = \dfrac{45}{1000} = \dfrac{5 \cdot 9}{5 \cdot 200} = \dfrac{9}{200}$

59. $175\% = \dfrac{175}{100} = \dfrac{25 \cdot 7}{25 \cdot 4} = \dfrac{7}{4} = 1\dfrac{3}{4}$

61. $73\% = \dfrac{73}{100}$

63. $12.5\% = \dfrac{12.5}{100} = \dfrac{125}{1000} = \dfrac{125 \cdot 1}{125 \cdot 8} = \dfrac{1}{8}$

65. $6.25\% = \dfrac{6.25}{100} = \dfrac{625}{10,000} = \dfrac{625}{625 \cdot 16} = \dfrac{1}{16}$

67. $10\dfrac{1}{3}\% = \dfrac{10\frac{1}{3}}{100}$

$= \dfrac{\frac{31}{3}}{100}$

$= \dfrac{31}{3} \div 100$

$= \dfrac{31}{3} \cdot \dfrac{1}{100}$

$= \dfrac{31}{300}$

69. $22\dfrac{3}{8}\% = \dfrac{22\frac{3}{8}}{100}$

$= \dfrac{\frac{179}{8}}{100}$

$= \dfrac{179}{8} \div 100$

$= \dfrac{179}{8} \cdot \dfrac{1}{100}$

$= \dfrac{179}{800}$

71. $\dfrac{3}{4} = \dfrac{3}{4} \cdot 100\% = \dfrac{300}{4}\% = 75\%$

73. $\dfrac{7}{10} = \dfrac{7}{10} \cdot 100\% = \dfrac{700}{10}\% = 70\%$

75. $\dfrac{2}{5} = \dfrac{2}{5} \cdot 100\% = \dfrac{200}{5}\% = 40\%$

77. $\dfrac{59}{100} = \dfrac{59}{100} \cdot 100\% = \dfrac{59 \cdot 100}{100}\% = 59\%$

79. $\dfrac{17}{50} = \dfrac{17}{50} \cdot 100\% = \dfrac{1700}{50}\% = 34\%$

81. $\dfrac{3}{8} = \dfrac{3}{8} \cdot 100\%$

$= \dfrac{300}{8}\%$

$= \dfrac{4 \cdot 75}{4 \cdot 2}\%$

$= \dfrac{75}{2}\%$

$= 37\dfrac{1}{2}\%$

83. $\dfrac{5}{16} = \dfrac{5}{16} \cdot 100\% = \dfrac{500}{16}\% = 31\dfrac{1}{4}\%$

85. $\dfrac{2}{3} = \dfrac{2}{3} \cdot 100\% = \dfrac{200}{3}\% = 66\dfrac{2}{3}\%$

87. $2\dfrac{1}{2} = \dfrac{5}{2} \cdot 100\% = \dfrac{500}{2}\% = 250\%$

89. $1\dfrac{9}{10} = \dfrac{19}{10} \cdot 100\% = \dfrac{1900}{10}\% = 190\%$

91. $\dfrac{7}{11} = \dfrac{7}{11} \cdot 100\% = \dfrac{700}{11}\% \approx 63.64\%$

$$\begin{array}{r} 63.636 \approx 63.64 \\ 11\overline{)\,700.000} \\ \underline{-66} \\ 40 \\ \underline{-33} \\ 70 \\ \underline{-66} \\ 40 \\ \underline{-33} \\ 70 \\ \underline{-66} \\ 4 \end{array}$$

93. $\frac{4}{15} = \frac{4}{15} \cdot 100\% = \frac{400}{15}\% \approx 26.67\%$

$$\begin{array}{r} 26.666 \approx 26.67 \\ 15\overline{)400.00} \\ \underline{-30} \\ 100 \\ \underline{-90} \\ 100 \\ \underline{-90} \\ 100 \\ \underline{-90} \\ 10 \end{array}$$

95. $\frac{1}{7} = \frac{1}{7} \cdot 100\% = \frac{100}{7}\% \approx 14.29\%$

$$\begin{array}{r} 14.285 \approx 14.29 \\ 7\overline{)100.000} \\ \underline{-7} \\ 30 \\ \underline{-28} \\ 2\,0 \\ \underline{-1\,4} \\ 60 \\ \underline{-56} \\ 40 \\ \underline{-35} \\ 5 \end{array}$$

97. $\frac{11}{12} = \frac{11}{12} \cdot 100\% = \frac{1100}{12}\% \approx 91.67\%$

$$\begin{array}{r} 91.666 \approx 91.67 \\ 12\overline{)1100.000} \\ \underline{-108} \\ 20 \\ \underline{-12} \\ 8\,0 \\ \underline{-7\,2} \\ 80 \\ \underline{-72} \\ 80 \\ \underline{-72} \\ 8 \end{array}$$

99.

Percent	Decimal	Fraction
35%	0.35	$\frac{7}{20}$
20%	0.2	$\frac{1}{5}$
50%	0.5	$\frac{1}{2}$
70%	0.7	$\frac{7}{10}$
37.5%	0.375	$\frac{3}{8}$

101.

Percent	Decimal	Fraction
40%	0.4	$\frac{2}{5}$
23.5%	0.235	$\frac{47}{200}$
80%	0.8	$\frac{4}{5}$
$33\frac{1}{3}\%$	$0.33\overline{3}$	$\frac{1}{3}$
87.5%	0.875	$\frac{7}{8}$
7.5%	0.075	$\frac{3}{40}$

103. $24.9\% = 0.249 = \frac{249}{1000}$

105. $\frac{17}{200} = \frac{17}{200} \cdot 100\% = \frac{1700}{200}\% = \frac{17}{2}\% = 8.5\%$

$$\begin{array}{r} 8.5 \\ 2\overline{)17.0} \\ \underline{-16} \\ 10 \\ \underline{-10} \\ 0 \end{array}$$

107. $20.7\% = 0.207 = \frac{207}{1000}$

109. $\frac{1}{4} = \frac{1}{4} \cdot 100\% = \frac{100}{4}\% = 25\%$

111. $0.4\% = 0.004 = \frac{4}{1000} = \frac{1}{250}$

113. $12\% = \frac{12}{100} = \frac{3}{25}$

115. $7.1\% = 0.071 = \frac{71}{1000}$

117. $3n = 45$
$$\frac{3n}{3} = \frac{45}{3}$$
$$n = 15$$

119. $-8n = 80$
$$\frac{-8n}{-8} = \frac{80}{-8}$$
$$n = -10$$

121.
$$-6n = -72$$
$$\frac{-6n}{-6} = \frac{-72}{-6}$$
$$n = 12$$

123. $\dfrac{3}{4} = \dfrac{75}{100} = 75\%$

125. $\dfrac{4}{5} = \dfrac{80}{100} = 80\%$

127. $\dfrac{850}{736} \approx 1.155 = 115.5\%$

129. A fraction written as a percent is greater than 100% when the numerator is <u>greater</u> than the denominator.

131. Answers may vary.

133. Computer software engineers applications is predicted to be the fastest growing occupation.

135. $62\% = 62.\% = 0.62$

Section 6.3

Practice Problems

1. $6 = x \cdot 24$

2. $1.8 = 20\% \cdot x$

3. $x = 40\% \cdot 3.6$

4. $42\% \cdot 50 = x$

5. $15\% \cdot x = 9$

6. $x \cdot 150 = 90$

7.
$$x = 20\% \cdot 85$$
$$x = 0.2 \cdot 85$$
$$x = 17$$
The number is 17.

8.
$$90\% \cdot 150 = x$$
$$0.9 \cdot 150 = x$$
$$135 = x$$
The number is 135.

9.
$$15\% \cdot x = 1.2$$
$$0.15 \cdot x = 1.2$$
$$\frac{0.15 \cdot x}{0.15} = \frac{1.2}{0.15}$$
$$x = 8$$
The number is 8.

10.
$$27 = 4\frac{1}{2}\% \cdot x$$
$$27 = 0.045 \cdot x$$
$$\frac{27}{0.045} = \frac{0.045 \cdot x}{0.045}$$
$$600 = x$$
The number is 600.

11.
$$x \cdot 80 = 8$$
$$\frac{x \cdot 80}{80} = \frac{8}{80}$$
$$x = 0.10$$
$$x = 10\%$$
The percent is 10%.

12.
$$35 = x \cdot 25$$
$$\frac{35}{25} = \frac{x \cdot 25}{25}$$
$$1.4 = x$$
$$140\% = x$$
The percent is 140%.

Mental Math

1. percent: 42
base: 50
amount: 21

2. percent: 30
base: 65
amount: 19.5

3. percent: 125
base: 86
amount: 107.5

4. percent: 110
base: 90
amount: 99

Exercise Set 6.3

1. $15\% \cdot 72 = x$

3. $30\% \cdot x = 80$

5. $x \cdot 90 = 20$

7. $1.9 = 40\% \cdot x$

9. $x = 9\% \cdot 43$

11.
$$10\% \cdot 35 = x$$
$$0.10 \cdot 35 = x$$
$$3.5 = x$$

13. $x = 14\% \cdot 52$
$x = 0.14 \cdot 52$
$x = 7.28$

15. $3000 = 5\% \cdot x$
$30 = 0.05x$
$\dfrac{30}{0.05} = \dfrac{0.05x}{0.05}$
$600 = x$

17. $1.2 = 12\% \cdot x$
$1.2 = 0.12x$
$\dfrac{1.2}{0.12} = \dfrac{0.12x}{0.12}$
$10 = x$

19. $66 = x \cdot 60$
$\dfrac{66}{60} = \dfrac{x \cdot 60}{60}$
$1.1 = x$
$110\% = x$

21. $16 = x \cdot 50$
$\dfrac{16}{50} = \dfrac{x \cdot 50}{50}$
$0.32 = x$
$32\% = x$

23. $0.1 = 10\% \cdot x$
$0.1 = 0.10x$
$\dfrac{0.1}{0.10} = \dfrac{0.10x}{0.10}$
$1 = x$

25. $125\% \cdot 36 = x$
$1.25 \cdot 36 = x$
$45 = x$

27. $82.5 = 16\dfrac{1}{2}\% \cdot x$
$82.5 = 0.165 \cdot x$
$\dfrac{82.5}{0.165} = \dfrac{0.165 \cdot x}{0.165}$
$500 = x$

29. $2.58 = x \cdot 50$
$\dfrac{2.58}{50} = \dfrac{x \cdot 50}{50}$
$0.0516 = x$
$5.16\% = x$

31. $x = 42\% \cdot 60$
$x = 0.42 \cdot 60$
$x = 25.2$

33. $x \cdot 150 = 67.5$
$\dfrac{x \cdot 150}{150} = \dfrac{67.5}{150}$
$x = 0.45$
$x = 45\%$

35. $120\% \cdot x = 42$
$1.2 \cdot x = 42$
$\dfrac{1.2 \cdot x}{1.2} = \dfrac{42}{1.2}$
$x = 35$

37. $\dfrac{27}{n} = \dfrac{9}{10}$
$9 \cdot n = 27 \cdot 10$
$\dfrac{9 \cdot n}{9} = \dfrac{270}{9}$
$n = 30$

39. $\dfrac{n}{5} = \dfrac{8}{11}$
$5 \cdot 8 = 11 \cdot n$
$\dfrac{40}{11} = \dfrac{11 \cdot n}{11}$
$3\dfrac{7}{11} = n$

41. $\dfrac{17}{12} = \dfrac{n}{20}$

43. $\dfrac{8}{9} = \dfrac{14}{n}$

45. $1.5\% \cdot 45,775 = x$
$0.015 \cdot 45,775 = x$
$686.625 = x$

47. $22,113 = 180\% \cdot x$
$22,113 = 1.8 \cdot x$
$\dfrac{22,113}{1.8} = \dfrac{1.8 \cdot x}{1.8}$
$12,285 = x$

Section 6.4

Practice Problems

1. $\dfrac{55}{b} = \dfrac{15}{100}$

2. $\dfrac{35}{70} = \dfrac{p}{100}$

3. $\dfrac{a}{68} = \dfrac{25}{100}$

4. $\dfrac{520}{b} = \dfrac{65}{100}$

5. $\dfrac{65}{50} = \dfrac{p}{100}$

6. $\dfrac{a}{80} = \dfrac{36}{100}$

7.
$$\dfrac{a}{120} = \dfrac{8}{100}$$
$$a \cdot 100 = 120 \cdot 8$$
$$a \cdot 100 = 960$$
$$\dfrac{a \cdot 100}{100} = \dfrac{960}{100}$$
$$a = 9.6$$
Therefore, 9.6 is 8% of 120.

8.
$$\dfrac{60}{b} = \dfrac{75}{100}$$
$$b \cdot 75 = 6000$$
$$\dfrac{b \cdot 75}{75} = \dfrac{6000}{75}$$
$$b = 80$$
Therefore, 75% of 80 is 60.

9.
$$\dfrac{15}{b} = \dfrac{5}{100}$$
$$5 \cdot b = 1500$$
$$\dfrac{5 \cdot b}{5} = \dfrac{1500}{5}$$
$$b = 300$$
Therefore, 15 is 5% of 300.

10.
$$\dfrac{5}{40} = \dfrac{p}{100}$$
$$40 \cdot p = 500$$
$$\dfrac{40 \cdot p}{40} = \dfrac{500}{40}$$
$$p = 12.5$$
Therefore, 12.5% of 40 is 5.

11.
$$\dfrac{336}{160} = \dfrac{p}{100}$$
$$160 \cdot p = 33,600$$
$$\dfrac{160 \cdot p}{160} = \dfrac{33,600}{160}$$
$$p = 210$$
Therefore, 210% of 160 is 336.

Mental Math

1. amount: 12.6
   base: 42
   percent: 30

2. amount: 201
   base: 300
   percent: 67

3. amount: 102
   base: 510
   percent: 20

4. amount: 248
   base: 620
   percent: 40

Exercise Set 6.4

1. $\dfrac{a}{65} = \dfrac{32}{100}$

3. $\dfrac{75}{b} = \dfrac{40}{100}$

5. $\dfrac{70}{200} = \dfrac{p}{100}$

7. $\dfrac{2.3}{b} = \dfrac{58}{100}$

9. $\dfrac{a}{130} = \dfrac{19}{100}$

11.
$$\dfrac{a}{55} = \dfrac{10}{100}$$
$$\dfrac{a}{55} = \dfrac{1}{10}$$
$$a \cdot 10 = 55 \cdot 1$$
$$a \cdot 10 = 55$$
$$\dfrac{a \cdot 10}{10} = \dfrac{55}{10}$$
$$a = 5.5$$
Therefore, 10% of 55 is 5.5.

13.
$$\dfrac{a}{105} = \dfrac{18}{100}$$
$$\dfrac{a}{105} = \dfrac{9}{50}$$
$$a \cdot 50 = 105 \cdot 9$$
$$\dfrac{a \cdot 50}{50} = \dfrac{945}{50}$$
$$a = 18.9$$
Therefore, 18% of 105 is 18.9.

15.
$$\dfrac{60}{b} = \dfrac{15}{100}$$
$$\dfrac{60}{b} = \dfrac{3}{20}$$
$$60 \cdot 20 = b \cdot 3$$
$$1200 = b \cdot 3$$
$$\dfrac{1200}{3} = \dfrac{b \cdot 3}{3}$$
$$400 = b$$
Therefore, 15% of 400 is 60.

17.
$$\frac{7.8}{b} = \frac{78}{100}$$
$$\frac{7.8}{b} = \frac{39}{50}$$
$$7.8 \cdot 50 = b \cdot 39$$
$$390 = b \cdot 39$$
$$\frac{390}{39} = \frac{b \cdot 39}{39}$$
$$10 = b$$
Therefore, 78% of 10 is 7.8.

19.
$$\frac{105}{84} = \frac{p}{100}$$
$$\frac{5}{4} = \frac{p}{100}$$
$$5 \cdot 100 = 4 \cdot p$$
$$500 = 4 \cdot p$$
$$\frac{500}{4} = \frac{4 \cdot p}{4}$$
$$125 = p$$
Therefore, 125% of 84 is 105.

21.
$$\frac{14}{50} = \frac{p}{100}$$
$$\frac{7}{25} = \frac{p}{100}$$
$$7 \cdot 100 = 25 \cdot p$$
$$700 = 25 \cdot p$$
$$\frac{700}{25} = \frac{25 \cdot p}{25}$$
$$28 = p$$
Therefore, 28% of 50 is 14.

23.
$$\frac{2.9}{b} = \frac{10}{100}$$
$$\frac{2.9}{b} = \frac{1}{10}$$
$$2.9 \cdot 10 = b \cdot 1$$
$$29 = b$$
Therefore, 10% of 29 is 2.9.

25.
$$\frac{a}{80} = \frac{2.4}{100}$$
$$a \cdot 100 = 80 \cdot 2.4$$
$$a \cdot 100 = 192$$
$$\frac{a \cdot 100}{100} = \frac{192}{100}$$
$$a = 1.92$$
Therefore, 2.4% of 80 is 1.92.

27.
$$\frac{160}{b} = \frac{16}{100}$$
$$\frac{160}{b} = \frac{4}{25}$$
$$160 \cdot 25 = b \cdot 4$$
$$4000 = b \cdot 4$$
$$\frac{4000}{4} = \frac{b \cdot 4}{4}$$
$$1000 = b$$
Therefore, 16% of 1000 is 160.

29.
$$\frac{348.6}{166} = \frac{p}{100}$$
$$348.6 \cdot 100 = 166 \cdot p$$
$$34{,}860 = 166 \cdot p$$
$$\frac{34{,}860}{166} = \frac{166 \cdot p}{166}$$
$$210 = p$$
Therefore, 210% of 166 is 348.6.

31.
$$\frac{a}{62} = \frac{89}{100}$$
$$a \cdot 100 = 62 \cdot 89$$
$$a \cdot 100 = 5518$$
$$\frac{a \cdot 100}{100} = \frac{5518}{100}$$
$$a = 55.18$$
Therefore, 89% of 62 is 55.18.

33.
$$\frac{3.6}{8} = \frac{p}{100}$$
$$3.6 \cdot 100 = 8 \cdot p$$
$$360 = 8 \cdot p$$
$$\frac{360}{8} = \frac{8 \cdot p}{8}$$
$$45 = p$$
Therefore, 45% of 8 is 3.6.

35.
$$\frac{119}{b} = \frac{140}{100}$$
$$\frac{119}{b} = \frac{7}{5}$$
$$119 \cdot 5 = b \cdot 7$$
$$595 = b \cdot 7$$
$$\frac{595}{7} = \frac{b \cdot 7}{7}$$
$$85 = b$$
Therefore, 140% of 85 is 119.

37. $\dfrac{11}{16} + \dfrac{3}{16} = \dfrac{11+3}{16} = \dfrac{14}{16} = \dfrac{7 \cdot 2}{8 \cdot 2} = \dfrac{7}{8}$

39.
$$3\frac{1}{2} = 3\frac{15}{30}$$
$$\underline{-\frac{11}{30}} = \underline{-\frac{11}{30}}$$
$$3\frac{4}{30} = 3\frac{2}{15}$$

41.
$$\overset{1}{}0.41$$
$$\underline{+\ 0.29}$$
$$0.70 \text{ or } 0.7$$

43.
$$2.38$$
$$\underline{-\ 0.19}$$
$$2.19$$

Check:
$$\overset{1}{}2.19$$
$$\underline{+\ 0.19}$$
$$2.38$$

45.
$$\frac{a}{53,862} = \frac{22.3}{100}$$
$$a \cdot 100 = 53,862 \cdot 22.3$$
$$a \cdot 100 = 1,201,122.6$$
$$\frac{a \cdot 100}{100} = \frac{1,201,122.6}{100}$$
$$a = 12,011.226$$

Therefore, 22.3% of 53,862 rounded to the nearest tenth is 12,011.2.

47.
$$\frac{8652}{b} = \frac{119}{100}$$
$$8652 \cdot 100 = b \cdot 119$$
$$865,200 = b \cdot 119$$
$$\frac{865,200}{119} = \frac{b \cdot 119}{119}$$
$$7270.6 \approx b$$

Therefore, to the nearest tenth 8625 is 119% of 7270.6.

Integrated Review

1. $0.12 = 12\%$

2. $0.68 = 68\%$

3. $\frac{1}{4} = 0.25 = 25\%$

4. $\frac{1}{2} = 0.50 = 50\%$

5. $\frac{12 \text{ inches}}{18 \text{ inches}} = \frac{12}{18} = \frac{2 \cdot 6}{3 \cdot 6} = \frac{2}{3}$

6. $\frac{\$26 \text{ hundred million}}{\$8 \text{ hundred million}} = \frac{26}{8} = \frac{13 \cdot 2}{4 \cdot 2} = \frac{13}{4}$

7.
$$\frac{3.5}{12.5} = \frac{7}{z}$$
$$3.5(z) = 7(12.5)$$
$$\frac{3.5z}{3.5} = \frac{87.5}{3.5}$$
$$z = 25$$

8.
$$\frac{x+7}{3} = \frac{2x}{5}$$
$$3(2x) = 5(x+7)$$
$$6x = 5x + 35$$
$$6x - 5x = 35$$
$$x = 35$$

9.
$$\frac{5 \text{ boxes}}{3 \text{ weeks}} = \frac{144 \text{ boxes}}{x \text{ weeks}}$$
$$5(x) = 3(144)$$
$$\frac{5x}{5} = \frac{532}{5}$$
$$x \approx 86$$

10. 1 month $\approx$ 4 weeks
$$\frac{5 \text{ boxes}}{3 \text{ weeks}} = \frac{x \text{ boxes}}{4 \text{ weeks}}$$
$$3(x) = 5(4)$$
$$\frac{3x}{3} = \frac{20}{3}$$
$$x \approx 7$$
7 boxes should be purchased.

11. $0.12 = 12\%$

12. $0.68 = 68\%$

13. $\frac{1}{4} = 0.25 = 25\%$

14. $\frac{1}{2} = 0.50 = 50\%$

15. $5.2 = 520\%$

16. $7.8 = 780\%$

17. $\frac{3}{50} = \frac{3}{50} \cdot \frac{2}{2} = \frac{6}{100} = 6\%$

18. $\frac{11}{25} = \frac{11}{25} \cdot \frac{4}{4} = \frac{44}{100} = 44\%$

19. $2\frac{1}{2} = \frac{5}{2} = \frac{5}{2} \cdot \frac{50}{50} = \frac{250}{100} = 250\%$

20. $3\dfrac{1}{4} = \dfrac{13}{4} = \dfrac{3}{14} \cdot \dfrac{25}{25} = \dfrac{325}{100} = 325\%$

21. $0.03 = 3\%$

22. $0.05 = 5\%$

23. $65\% = 65.\% = 0.65$

24. $31\% = 31.\% = 0.31$

25. $8\% = 8.\% = 0.08$

26. $7\% = 7.\% = 0.07$

27. $142\% = 142.\% = 1.42$

28. $538\% = 538.\% = 5.38$

29. $2.9\% = 0.029$

30. $6.6\% = 0.066$

31. $3\% = \dfrac{3}{100}$

32. $8\% = \dfrac{8}{100} = \dfrac{2}{25}$

33. $5.25\% = \dfrac{5.25}{100} = \dfrac{525}{10,000} = \dfrac{21}{400}$

34. $12.75\% = \dfrac{12.75}{100} = \dfrac{1275}{10,000} = \dfrac{51}{400}$

35. $38\% = \dfrac{38}{100} = \dfrac{19}{50}$

36. $45\% = \dfrac{45}{100} = \dfrac{9}{20}$

37. $12\dfrac{1}{3}\% = \dfrac{37}{3}\% = \dfrac{37}{3} \div 100 = \dfrac{37}{3} \cdot \dfrac{1}{100} = \dfrac{37}{300}$

38. $16\dfrac{2}{3} = \dfrac{50}{3}\%$

$= \dfrac{50}{3} \div 100$

$= \dfrac{50}{3} \cdot \dfrac{1}{100}$

$= \dfrac{50}{300}$

$= \dfrac{1}{6}$

39. $\dfrac{a}{70} = \dfrac{12}{100}$

$\dfrac{a}{70} = \dfrac{3}{25}$

$a \cdot 25 = 70 \cdot 3$

$a \cdot 25 = 210$

$\dfrac{a \cdot 25}{25} = \dfrac{210}{25}$

$a = 8.4$

12% of 70 is 8.4.

40. $\dfrac{36}{b} = \dfrac{36}{100}$

$\dfrac{36}{b} = \dfrac{9}{25}$

$36 \cdot 25 = b \cdot 9$

$900 = b \cdot 9$

$\dfrac{900}{9} = \dfrac{b \cdot 9}{9}$

$100 = b$

36 is 36% of 100.

41. $\dfrac{212.5}{b} = \dfrac{85}{100}$

$\dfrac{212.5}{b} = \dfrac{17}{20}$

$212.5 \cdot 20 = b \cdot 17$

$4250 = b \cdot 17$

$\dfrac{4250}{17} = \dfrac{b \cdot 17}{17}$

$250 = b$

212.5 is 85% of 250.

42. $\dfrac{66}{55} = \dfrac{p}{100}$

$66 \cdot 100 = 55 \cdot p$

$6600 = 55 \cdot p$

$\dfrac{6600}{55} = \dfrac{55 \cdot p}{55}$

$120 = p$

66 is 120% of 55.

43. $\dfrac{23.8}{85} = \dfrac{p}{100}$

$23.8 \cdot 100 = 85 \cdot p$

$2380 = 85 \cdot p$

$\dfrac{2380}{85} = \dfrac{85 \cdot p}{85}$

$28 = p$

23.8 is 28% of 85.

44. $\dfrac{a}{200} = \dfrac{38}{100}$

$\dfrac{a}{200} = \dfrac{19}{50}$

$a \cdot 50 = 200 \cdot 19$

$a \cdot 50 = 3800$

$\dfrac{a \cdot 50}{50} = \dfrac{3800}{50}$

$a = 76$

38% of 200 is 76.

45. $\dfrac{a}{44} = \dfrac{25}{100}$

$\dfrac{a}{44} = \dfrac{1}{4}$

$a \cdot 4 = 44 \cdot 1$

$a \cdot 4 = 44$

$\dfrac{a \cdot 4}{4} = \dfrac{44}{4}$

$a = 11$

11 is 25% of 44.

46. $\dfrac{128.7}{99} = \dfrac{p}{100}$

$128.7 \cdot 100 = 99 \cdot p$

$12{,}870 = 99 \cdot p$

$\dfrac{12{,}870}{99} = \dfrac{99 \cdot p}{99}$

$130 = p$

130% of 99 is 128.7.

47. $\dfrac{215}{250} = \dfrac{p}{100}$

$\dfrac{43}{50} = \dfrac{p}{100}$

$43 \cdot 100 = 50 \cdot p$

$4300 = 50 \cdot p$

$\dfrac{4300}{50} = \dfrac{50 \cdot p}{50}$

$86 = p$

86% of 250 is 215.

48. $\dfrac{a}{84} = \dfrac{45}{100}$

$\dfrac{a}{84} = \dfrac{9}{20}$

$a \cdot 20 = 84 \cdot 9$

$a \cdot 20 = 756$

$\dfrac{a \cdot 20}{20} = \dfrac{756}{2}$

$a = 37.8$

37.8 is 45% of 84.

49. $\dfrac{63}{b} = \dfrac{42}{100}$

$\dfrac{63}{b} = \dfrac{21}{50}$

$63 \cdot 50 = b \cdot 21$

$3150 = b \cdot 21$

$\dfrac{3150}{21} = \dfrac{b \cdot 21}{21}$

$150 = b$

63 is 42% of 150.

50. $\dfrac{58.9}{b} = \dfrac{95}{100}$

$\dfrac{58.9}{b} = \dfrac{19}{20}$

$58.9 \cdot 20 = b \cdot 19$

$1178 = b \cdot 19$

$\dfrac{1178}{19} = \dfrac{b \cdot 19}{19}$

$62 = b$

58.9 is 95% of 62.

Section 6.5

Practice Problems

1. 61 is what percent of 106%?

$61 = x \cdot 106$

$\dfrac{61}{106} = \dfrac{x \cdot 106}{106}$

$0.575 \approx x$

About 58% of Ohio nursing schools have RN degrees.

2. 775 is 31% of what number?

$775 = 31\% \cdot x$

$775 = 0.31 \cdot x$

$\dfrac{775}{0.31} = \dfrac{0.31 \cdot x}{0.31}$

$2500 = x$

There are 2500 students that go to Euclid University.

3. 130 is what percent of 190?

$130 = x \cdot 190$

$\dfrac{130}{190} = \dfrac{x \cdot 190}{190}$

$0.684 \approx x$

$68.4\% \approx x$

About 68.4% of the calories are from fat.

4. What number is 10% of 122 million?

$x = 10\% \cdot 122$

$x = 0.10 \cdot 122$

$x = 12.2$

The increase in vehicles is 12.2 million. The number of vehicles in 2000 is 122 million + 12.2 million = 134.2 million.

5. percent increase $= \dfrac{\text{amount of increase}}{\text{original amount}}$

$= \dfrac{333 - 285}{285}$

$= \dfrac{48}{285}$

≈ 0.168

$= 16.8\%$

The attendance increased by about 16.8%.

6. percent decrease $= \dfrac{\text{amount of decrease}}{\text{original amount}}$

$= \dfrac{20,145 - 18,430}{20,145}$

$= \dfrac{1715}{20,145}$

≈ 0.085

$= 8.5\%$

The population decreased by about about 8.5%.

Exercise Set 6.5

1. Let n = the number of bolts inspected.

$1.5\% \cdot n = 24$

$0.015 \cdot n = 24$

$\dfrac{0.015 \cdot n}{0.015} = \dfrac{24}{0.015}$

$n = 1600$

1600 bolts were inspected.

3. Let x = the hours billed per 40 hour week.

$x = 75\% \cdot 40$

$x = (0.75)(40)$

$x = 30$

The owner can bill 30 hours.

5. Let x = the percent of income spent on food.

$\$300 = x \cdot \$2000$

$\dfrac{300}{2000} = \dfrac{x \cdot 2000}{2000}$

$0.15 = x$

$0.15 \cdot 100\% = x$

$15\% = x$

She spends 15% of her monthly income on food.

7. Let x = the number of defective components.

$x = 1.04\% \cdot 28,350$

$x = 0.0104 \cdot 28,350$

$x = 294.84$

$x \approx 295$

295 defective components are expected.

9. Let x = the percent of the members of the 108th Congress that attended a community college.

$73 = x \cdot 535$

$\dfrac{73}{535} = \dfrac{x \cdot 535}{535}$

$0.136 \approx x$

$0.136 \cdot 100\% = x$

$13.6\% = x$

13.6% of the members of the 108th Congress have attended a community school.

11. Let n = the number of registered dental hygienists in the U.S.

$98.3\% \cdot n = 98,400$

$0.983 \cdot n = 98,400$

$\dfrac{0.983n}{0.983} = \dfrac{98,400}{0.983}$

$n \approx 100,102$

There are 100,102 dental hygienists in the U.S.

13. Let x = the percent of calories from fat.

$35 = x \cdot 120$

$\dfrac{35}{120} = \dfrac{x \cdot 120}{120}$

$0.292 = x$

$0.292 \cdot 100\% = x$

$29.2\% = x$

29.2% of the food's total calories is from fat.

15. $x = 8\% \cdot 6200$

$x = 0.08 \cdot 6200$

$x = 496$

Ace Furniture Company increased production by 496 chairs.

$6200 + 496 = 6696$

The new number of chairs produced each month is 6696.

17. 20% of $170 is what number?

$20\% \cdot \$170 = n$

$0.2 \cdot \$170 = n$

$\$34.00 = n$

Their new bill is $170 − $34 = $136.

19. 4.5% of \$19,286 is what number?
$$4.5\% \cdot \$19,286 = n$$
$$0.045 \cdot \$19,286 = n$$
$$\$867.87 = n$$
The increase is \$867.87. The new price is
\$19,286 + \$867.87 = \$20,153.87.

21. 33% of 26.8 million is what number?
$$33\% \cdot 26.8 \text{ million} = n$$
$$0.33 \cdot 26,800,000 = n$$
$$8,844,000 = n$$
projected population:
26.8 million + 8.844 million
= 35.644 million
The increase is 8.844 million. The projected
population is 35.644 million.

	Original Amount	New Amount	Amount of Increase	Percent Increase
23.	40	50	$50 - 40 = 10$	$\frac{10}{40} = 0.25 = 25\%$
25.	85	187	$187 - 85 = 102$	$\frac{102}{85} = 1.2 = 120\%$

	Original Amount	New Amount	Amount of Decrease	Percent Decrease
27.	8	6	$8 - 6 = 2$	$\frac{2}{8} = 0.25 = 25\%$
29.	160	40	$160 - 40 = 120$	$\frac{120}{160} = 0.75 = 75\%$

31. percent decrease $= \frac{150-84}{150}$
$$= \frac{66}{150}$$
$$= 0.44$$
$$= 44\%$$

33. percent increase $= \frac{23.7-19.5}{19.5}$
$$= \frac{4.2}{19.5}$$
$$\approx 0.215$$
$$= 21.5\%$$

35. percent decrease $= \frac{10,845-10,700}{10,845}$
$$= \frac{145}{10,845}$$
$$\approx 0.013$$
$$= 1.3\%$$

37. percent decrease $= \frac{52.1-6.7}{52.1}$
$$= \frac{45.4}{52.1}$$
$$\approx 0.871$$
$$= 87.1\%$$

39. percent increase $= \frac{300,000-75,000}{75,000}$
$$= \frac{225,000}{75,000}$$
$$= 3$$
$$= 300\%$$

41. percent increase $= \frac{29,000-16,000}{16,000}$
$$= \frac{13,000}{16,000}$$
$$= 0.8125$$
$$= 81.25\% \text{ or } 81.3\% \text{ when}$$
rounded to the
nearest tenth

43. percent decrease $= \frac{272.6-76}{272.6}$
$$= \frac{196.6}{272.6}$$
$$\approx 0.721$$
$$= 72.1\%$$

45. percent increase $= \dfrac{110,000,000 - 16,000,000}{16,000,000}$

$= \dfrac{94,000,000}{16,000,000}$

$= 5.875$

$= 587.5\%$

47. percent increase $= \dfrac{28,700 - 26,518}{26,518}$

$= \dfrac{2182}{26,518}$

≈ 0.082

$= 8.2\%$

49.
$$\begin{array}{r} 0.12 \\ \times\ 38 \\ \hline 96 \\ 360 \\ \hline 4.56 \end{array}$$

51.
$$\begin{array}{r} 9.20 \\ +\ 1.98 \\ \hline 11.18 \end{array}$$

53.
$$\begin{array}{r} 78.00 \\ -\ 19.46 \\ \hline 58.54 \end{array}$$

55. The increased number is double the original number. Answers may vary.

Section 6.6

Practice Problems

1. tax $= 6\% \cdot \$29.90$

$= 0.06 \cdot \$29.9$

$= \$1.79$

total $= \$29.90 + \$1.79$

$= \$31.69$

The tax is \$1.79 and the total is \$31.69.

2. $\$1080 = r \cdot \$13,500$

$\dfrac{\$1080}{\$13,500} = \dfrac{r \cdot 13,500}{13,500}$

$0.08 = r$

$8\% = r$

The sales tax rate is 8%.

3. commission $= 6.6\% \cdot \$37,632$

$= 0.066 \cdot \$37,632$

$= \$2483.712$

His commission is \$2483.71.

4. $\$1290 = r \cdot \$8600$

$\dfrac{\$1290}{\$8600} = \dfrac{r \cdot 8600}{8600}$

$0.15 = r$

$15\% = r$

The commission rate is 15%.

5. discount $= 15\% \cdot \$700$

$= 0.15 \cdot \$700$

$= \$105$

sale price $= \$700 - \$105$

$= \$595$

The discount is \$105 and the sale price is \$595.

Exercise Set 6.6

1. tax $= 5\% \cdot \$150.00$

$= 0.05 \cdot \$150.00$

$= \$7.50$

The sales tax is \$7.50.

3. tax $= 7.5\% \cdot \$799$

$= 0.075 \cdot \$799$

$= \$59.925$

total $= \$799 + \$59.925$

$= \$858.925$

The total price is \$858.93.

5. $\$54 = r \cdot \$600$

$\dfrac{\$54}{\$600} = r$

$0.09 = r$

$9\% = r$

The sales tax rate is 9%.

7. tax $= 8.5\% \cdot \$220$

$= 0.085 \cdot \$220$

$= \$18.70$

total $= \$220 + \$18.70$

$= \$238.70$

The total price is \$238.70.

9. tax $= 6.5\% \cdot \$1800$

$= 0.065 \cdot \$1800$

$= \$117$

total $= \$1800 + \$117 = \$1917$

The total price is \$1917.

11. $\$920 = 8\% \cdot n$

$\$920 = 0.08 \cdot n$

$\dfrac{\$920}{0.08} = n$

$\$11,500 = n$

The purchase price is \$11,500.

13. total purchase $= \$90 + \$15 = \$105$

tax $= 7\% \cdot \$105$

$= 0.07 \cdot \$105$

$= \$7.35$

total $= \$105 + \$7.35 = \$112.35$

The total price is $112.35.

15. $\$98.70 = r \cdot \$1645$

$\dfrac{\$98.70}{\$1645} = r$

$0.06 = r$

$6\% = r$

The sales tax rate is 6%.

17. commission $= 4\% \cdot \$1,236,856$

$= 0.04 \cdot \$1,236,856$

$= \$49,474.24$

Her commission was $49,474.24.

19. $\$1380.40 = r \cdot \$9860.00$

$\dfrac{\$1380.40}{\$9860.00} = r$

$0.14 = r$

$14\% = r$

The commission rate is 14%.

21. commission $= 1.5\% \cdot \$125,900$

$= 0.015 \cdot \$125,900$

$= \$1888.50$

His commission is $1888.50.

23. $2565 = 3\% \cdot x$

$2565 = 0.03 \cdot x$

$\dfrac{2565}{0.03} = x$

$85,500 = x$

$85,500 is the selling price of the house.

	Original Price	Discount Rate	Amount of Discount	Sale Price
25.	$68.00	10%	$68.00 · 10% = $68.00 · 0.10 = $6.80	$68.00 − $6.80 = $61.20
27.	$96.50	50%	$96.50 · 50% = $9650 · 0.5 = $48.25	$96.50 − $48.25 = $48.25
29.	$215.00	35%	$215.00 · 35% = $215.00 · 0.35 = $75.25	$215.00 − $75.25 = $139.75
31.	$21,700.00	15%	$21,700.00 · 15% = $21,700· 0.15 =$3255.00	$21,700.00 − $3255.00 = $18,445.00

33. discount $= 15\% \cdot \$300$

$= 0.15 \cdot \$300$

$= \$45$

sale price $= \$300 - \$45$

$= \$255$

	Original Price	Discount Rate	Amount of Discount	Sale Price
35.	$75.00	20%	$75 \cdot 0.2 = \$15$	$75.00 − 15.00 = $60.00
37.	$120.00	$\dfrac{39.60}{120} = 33\%$	$39.60	$120.00 − 39.60 = $80.40
39.	$\dfrac{370}{0.40} = \$925$	40%	$370.00	$925 − $370 = $555.00

41. $2000 \cdot 0.3 \cdot 2 = 600 \cdot 2 = 1200$

43. $400 \cdot 0.03 \cdot 11 = 12 \cdot 11 = 132$

45. $600 \cdot 0.04 \cdot \dfrac{2}{3} = 24 \cdot \dfrac{2}{3}$

$\qquad\qquad = \dfrac{24}{1} \cdot \dfrac{2}{3}$

$\qquad\qquad = \dfrac{24 \cdot 2}{3}$

$\qquad\qquad = \dfrac{48}{3}$

$\qquad\qquad = 16$

47. discount $= \$24{,}966 \cdot 15\%$

$\qquad\qquad = 24{,}966 \cdot 0.15$

$\qquad\qquad = \$3744.90$

discount price $= \$24{,}966 - \$3744.90$

$\qquad\qquad\qquad = \$21{,}221.10$

tax $= \$21{,}221.10 \cdot 7.5\%$

$\qquad = 21{,}221.10 \cdot 0.075$

$\qquad = \$1591.58$

total price $= \$21{,}221.10 + \$1591.58 = \$22{,}812.68$

49. 60% discount:

$\$50 \cdot 60\% = \$50 \cdot 0.6 = \$30$

discount price $= \$50 - \$30 = \$20$

30% discount followed by a 35% discount

$\$50 \cdot 30\% = \$50 \cdot 0.3 = \$15$

$\$50 - \$15 = \$35$

$\$35 \cdot 35\% = \$35 \cdot 0.35 = \$12.25$

discount price $= \$35 - \$12.25 = \$22.75$

A discount of 60% is better.

	Bill Amount	10%	15%	20%
51.	$15.89	$1.60	$2.40	$3.20
53.	$9.33	$0.90	$1.35	$1.80

Section 6.7

Practice Problems

1. $I = P \cdot R \cdot T$

$\quad = \$750 \cdot 8\% \cdot 3$

$\quad = \$750 \cdot 0.08 \cdot 3$

$\quad = \$180$

2. time $= 9$ months $= \dfrac{9}{12}$ year $= \dfrac{3}{4}$ year

$I = P \cdot R \cdot T$

$\quad = \$800 \cdot 20\% \cdot \dfrac{3}{4}$

$\quad = \$800 \cdot 0.2 \cdot \dfrac{3}{4}$

$\quad = \$120$

She paid $120 in interest.

3. time $= 6$ months $= \dfrac{6}{12}$ year $= \dfrac{1}{2}$ year

$I = P \cdot R \cdot T$

$\quad = \$500 \cdot 12\% \cdot \dfrac{1}{2}$

$\quad = \$500 \cdot 0.12 \cdot \dfrac{1}{2}$

$\quad = \$30$

total amount $= \$500 + \$30$

$\qquad\qquad\quad = \$530$

4. total amount

$= $ original principal $\cdot$ compound interest factor

$= \$5500 \cdot 1.41902$

$= \$7804.61$

5. interest earned

$= $ total amount $-$ original principal

$= \$9933.14 - \$5500$

$= \$4433.14$

6. monthly payment

$= \dfrac{\text{principal} + \text{interest}}{\text{total number of payments}}$

$= \dfrac{\$3000 + \$1123.58}{3 \cdot 12}$

$\approx \$114.54$

The monthly payment is $114.54

Calculator Explorations

1. $\left(1 + \dfrac{0.09}{4}\right)^{(4 \cdot 5)} \approx 1.56051$

2. $\left(1 + \dfrac{0.14}{365}\right)^{(365 \cdot 15)} \approx 8.16288$

3. $\left(1 + \dfrac{0.11}{1}\right)^{(1 \cdot 20)} \approx 8.06231$

4. $\left(1 + \dfrac{0.07}{2}\right)^{(2 \cdot 1)} \approx 1.07123$

5. Compound interest factor $= \left(1 + \dfrac{0.06}{4}\right)^{(4 \cdot 4)}$

≈ 1.26899

$\$500 \cdot 1.26899 \approx \$634.50$

6. Compound interest factor $= \left(1 + \dfrac{0.05}{365}\right)^{(365 \cdot 19)}$

≈ 2.58554

$\$2500 \cdot 2.58554 = \$6463.85$

Exercise Set 6.7

1. simple interest $=$ principal $\cdot$ rate $\cdot$ time
$= \$200 \cdot 8\% \cdot 2$
$= \$200 \cdot (0.08) \cdot 2$
$= \$32$

3. simple interest $=$ principal $\cdot$ rate $\cdot$ time
$= \$160 \cdot 11.5\% \cdot 4$
$= \$160 \cdot (0.115) \cdot 4$
$= \$73.60$

5. simple interest $=$ principal $\cdot$ rate $\cdot$ time
$= \$5000 \cdot 10\% \cdot 1\frac{1}{2}$
$= \$5000 \cdot (0.10) \cdot 1.5$
$= \$750$

7. simple interest $=$ principle $\cdot$ rate $\cdot$ time
$= \$375 \cdot 18\% \cdot \dfrac{6}{12}$
$= \$375 \cdot (0.18) \cdot (0.5)$
$= \$33.75$

9. simple interest $=$ principal $\cdot$ rate $\cdot$ time
$= \$2500 \cdot 16\% \cdot \dfrac{21}{12}$
$= \$2500 \cdot (0.16) \cdot 1.75$
$= \$700$

11. simple interest $=$ principal $\cdot$ rate $\cdot$ time
$= \$62,500 \cdot 12.5\% \cdot 2$
$= \$62,500 \cdot (0.125) \cdot 2$
$= \$15,625$
total $= \$62,500 + \$15,625 = \$78,125.$
The total amount paid is $78,125.

13. simple interest $=$ principal $\cdot$ rate $\cdot$ time
$= \$5000 \cdot 9\% \cdot \dfrac{15}{12}$
$= \$5000 \cdot (0.09) \cdot 1.25$
$= \$562.50$
total $= \$5000 + \$562.50 = \$5562.50$
The total amount received is $5562.50

15. simple interest $=$ principal $\cdot$ rate $\cdot$ time
$= \$8500 \cdot 12\% \cdot 4$
$= \$8500 \cdot (0.12) \cdot 4$
$= \$4080$
total $= \$8500 + \$4080 = \$12,580$
She pays back a total of $12,580.

17. total $=$ principal $\cdot$ compound interest factor
$= \$6150(7.61226)$
$= \$46,815.399$
The total amount is $46,815.40.

19. total $=$ principal $\cdot$ compound interest factor
$= \$1560(1.49176)$
$= \$2327.1456$
The total amount is $2327.15.

21. total $=$ principal $\cdot$ compound interest factor
$= \$10,000(5.81636)$
$= \$58,163.60$
The total amount is $58,163.60.

23. total $=$ principal $\cdot$ compound interest factor
$= \$2675(1.09000)$
$= \$2915.75$
compound interest
$=$ total amount $-$ original principal
$= \$2915.75 - \$2675$
$= \$240.75$
The interest earned is $240.75.

25. total $=$ original principal $\cdot$ compound interest factor
$= \$2000(1.46933)$
$= \$2938.66$
compound interest $=$ total amount $-$ original principal
$= \$2938.66 - \$2000$
$= \$938.66$
The interest earned is $938.66.

27. total = original principal $\cdot$ compound interest factor
$$= \$2000(1.48595)$$
$$= \$2971.90$$

compound interest = total amount $-$ original principal
$$= \$2971.90 - \$2000$$
$$= \$971.90$$
The interest earned is \$971.90.

29. monthly payment $= \dfrac{\text{principal} + \text{interest}}{\text{number of payments}}$
$$= \dfrac{\$1500 + \$61.88}{6}$$
$$= \dfrac{\$1561.88}{6}$$
$$\approx \$260.31$$
The monthly payment is \$260.31.

31. monthly payment $= \dfrac{\text{principal} + \text{interest}}{\text{number of payments}}$
$$= \dfrac{\$20,000 + \$10,588.70}{48}$$
$$= \dfrac{\$30,588.70}{48}$$
$$\approx \$637.26$$
The monthly payment is \$637.26.

33. $-5 + (-24) = -29$

35. $(-5)(-10) = 50$

37. $\dfrac{7-10}{3} = \dfrac{-3}{3} = -1$

39. Answers may vary.

41. Answers may vary.

Chapter 6 Review

1. $\dfrac{20 \text{ cents}}{1 \text{ dollar}} = \dfrac{20 \text{ cents}}{100 \text{ cents}} = \dfrac{1}{5}$

2. $\dfrac{4}{6} = \dfrac{2}{3}$

3. $\dfrac{x}{2} = \dfrac{12}{4}$
$$4(x) = 2(12)$$
$$\dfrac{4x}{4} = \dfrac{24}{4}$$
$$x = 6$$

4. $\dfrac{20}{1} = \dfrac{x}{25}$
$$1(x) = 20(25)$$
$$x = 500$$

5. $\dfrac{32}{100} = \dfrac{100}{x}$
$$32(x) = 100(100)$$
$$\dfrac{32x}{32} = \dfrac{10,000}{32}$$
$$x = 312.5$$

6. $\dfrac{20}{2} = \dfrac{c}{5}$
$$2(c) = 20(5)$$
$$\dfrac{2c}{2} = \dfrac{100}{2}$$
$$c = 50$$

7. $\dfrac{2}{x-1} = \dfrac{3}{x+3}$
$$3(x-1) = 2(x+3)$$
$$3x - 3 = 2x + 6$$
$$3x - 2x = 6 + 3$$
$$x = 9$$

8. $\dfrac{4}{y-3} = \dfrac{2}{y-3}$
$$4(y-3) = 2(y-3)$$
$$4y - 12 = 2y - 6$$
$$4y - 2y = -6 + 12$$
$$\dfrac{2y}{2} = \dfrac{6}{2}$$
$$y = 3$$
Since the denominator $3 - 3 = 0$, the expression is undefined. Therefore, the answer is "No Solution".

9. $\dfrac{y+2}{y} = \dfrac{5}{3}$
$$5(y) = 3(y+2)$$
$$5y = 3y + 6$$
$$5y - 3y = 6$$
$$\dfrac{2y}{2} = \dfrac{6}{2}$$
$$y = 3$$

10. $\dfrac{x-3}{3x+2} = \dfrac{2}{6}$
$6(x-3) = 2(3x+2)$
$6x - 18 = 6x + 4$
$6x - 6x = 4 + 18$
$0 = 22$
No Solution

11. $\dfrac{300 \text{ parts}}{20 \text{ min.}} = \dfrac{x \text{ parts}}{45 \text{ min.}}$
$20(x) = 45(300)$
$\dfrac{20x}{20} = \dfrac{13,500}{20}$
$x = 675$
675 parts can be processed.

12. $\dfrac{\$90.00}{8 \text{ hours}} = \dfrac{\$x}{3 \text{ hours}}$
$8(x) = 3(90.00)$
$\dfrac{8x}{8} = \dfrac{270.00}{8}$
$x = 33.75$
He would charge $33.75.

13. $\dfrac{37}{100} = 37\%$

14. $\dfrac{77}{100} = 77\%$

15. $83\% = 0.83$

16. $75\% = 0.75$

17. $73.5\% = 0.735$

18. $1.5\% = 0.015$

19. $125\% = 1.25$

20. $145\% = 1.45$

21. $0.5\% = 0.005$

22. $0.7\% = 0.007$

23. $200\% = 2.00$ or 2

24. $400\% = 4.00$ or 4

25. $26.25\% = 0.2625$

26. $85.34\% = 0.8534$

27. $2.6 = 260\%$

28. $0.055 = 5.5\%$

29. $0.35 = 35\%$

30. $1.02 = 102\%$

31. $0.725 = 72.5\%$

32. $0.25 = 25\%$

33. $0.076 = 7.6\%$

34. $0.085 = 8.5\%$

35. $0.75 = 75\%$

36. $0.65 = 65\%$

37. $4.00 = 400\%$

38. $9.00 = 900\%$

39. $1\% = \dfrac{1}{100}$

40. $10\% = \dfrac{10}{100} = \dfrac{1}{10}$

41. $25\% = \dfrac{25}{100} = \dfrac{1}{4}$

42. $8.5\% = \dfrac{8.5}{100} = \dfrac{85}{1000} = \dfrac{17}{200}$

43. $10.2\% = \dfrac{10.2}{100} = \dfrac{102}{1000} = \dfrac{51}{500}$

44. $16\dfrac{2}{3}\% = \dfrac{16\frac{2}{3}}{100}$
$= 16\dfrac{2}{3} \div 100$
$= \dfrac{50}{3} \cdot \dfrac{1}{100}$
$= \dfrac{50}{300}$
$= \dfrac{1}{6}$

45. $33\dfrac{1}{3}\% = \dfrac{33\frac{1}{3}}{100} = 33\dfrac{1}{3} \div 100 = \dfrac{100}{3} \cdot \dfrac{1}{100} = \dfrac{1}{3}$

46. $110\% = \dfrac{110}{100} = \dfrac{11}{10}$ or $1\dfrac{1}{10}$

47. $\dfrac{1}{5} = \dfrac{1}{5} \cdot 100\% = \dfrac{100\%}{5} = 20\%$

48. $\dfrac{7}{10} = \dfrac{7}{10} \cdot 100\% = 70\%$

49. $\dfrac{5}{6} \cdot 100\% = \dfrac{500\%}{6} = \dfrac{250\%}{3} = 83\dfrac{1}{3}\%$

50. $\dfrac{5}{8} = \dfrac{5}{8} \cdot 100\%$

$= \dfrac{500\%}{8}$

$= \dfrac{125}{2}\%$

$= 62\dfrac{1}{2}\%$ or 62.5%

51. $1\dfrac{2}{3} = \dfrac{5}{3} = \dfrac{5}{3} \cdot 100\% = \dfrac{500\%}{3} = 166\dfrac{2}{3}\%$

52. $1\dfrac{1}{4} = \dfrac{5}{4} = \dfrac{5}{4} \cdot 100\% = 125\%$

53. $\dfrac{3}{5} = \dfrac{3}{5} \cdot 100\% = \dfrac{300\%}{5} = 60\%$

54. $\dfrac{1}{16} = \dfrac{1}{16} \cdot 100\%$

$= \dfrac{100\%}{16}$

$= \dfrac{25}{4}\%$

$= 6\dfrac{1}{4}\%$ or 6.25%

55. $90\% = \dfrac{90}{100} = \dfrac{9}{10}$; $10\% = \dfrac{10}{100} = \dfrac{1}{10}$

56. $96\% = \dfrac{96}{100} = \dfrac{24}{25}$

57. $\dfrac{7}{10} = \dfrac{7}{10} \cdot 100\% = 70\%$

58. $150\% = 1.50$ or 1.5

59. $1250 = 1.25\% \cdot n$
$1250 = 0.0125n$
$\dfrac{1250}{0.0125} = n$
$100{,}000 = n$

60. $n = 33\dfrac{1}{3}\% \cdot 24{,}000$

$n = \dfrac{33\frac{1}{3}}{100} \cdot 24{,}000$

$n = 33\dfrac{1}{3} \cdot 240$

$n = \dfrac{100}{3} \cdot 240$

$n = 8000$

61. $124.2 = n \cdot 540$
$\dfrac{124.2}{540} = n$
$0.23 = n$
$23\% = n$

62. $22.9 = 20\% \cdot n$
$22.9 = 0.2n$
$\dfrac{22.9}{0.2} = n$
$114.5 = n$

63. $n = 40\% \cdot 7500$
$n = (0.40)(7500)$
$n = 3000$

64. $693 = n \cdot 462$
$\dfrac{693}{462} = n$
$1.5 = n$
$150\% = n$

65. $\dfrac{104.5}{b} = \dfrac{25}{100}$
$b \cdot 25 = 104.5 \cdot 100$
$b \cdot 25 = 10{,}450$
$b = \dfrac{10{,}450}{25}$
$b = 418$
Therefore, 25% of 418 is 104.5.

66. $\dfrac{16.5}{b} = \dfrac{5.5}{100}$
$b \cdot 5.5 = 16.5 \cdot 100$
$b \cdot 5.5 = 1650$
$b = \dfrac{1650}{5.5}$
$b = 300$
Therefore, 5.5% of 300 is 16.5.

67. $\dfrac{a}{180} = \dfrac{36}{100}$

$a \cdot 100 = 36 \cdot 180$

$a \cdot 100 = 6480$

$a = \dfrac{6480}{100}$

$a = 64.8$

Therefore, 36% of 180 is 64.8.

68. $\dfrac{63}{35} = \dfrac{p}{100}$

$63 \cdot 100 = 35 \cdot p$

$6300 = 35 \cdot p$

$\dfrac{6300}{35} = p$

$180 = p$

Therefore, 180% of 35 is 63.

69. $\dfrac{93.5}{85} = \dfrac{p}{100}$

$93.5 \cdot 100 = 85 \cdot p$

$9350 = 85 \cdot p$

$\dfrac{9350}{85} = p$

$110 = p$

Therefore, 110% of 85 is 93.5.

70. $\dfrac{a}{500} = \dfrac{33}{100}$

$a \cdot 100 = 500 \cdot 33$

$a \cdot 100 = 16,500$

$a = \dfrac{16,500}{100}$

$a = 165$

Therefore, 33% of 500 is 165.

71. What percent of 2000 is 1320?

$n \cdot 2000 = 1320$

$n = \dfrac{1320}{2000}$

$n = 0.66$

$n = 66\%$

72. What percent of 12,360 is 2000?

$n \cdot 12,360 = 2000$

$n = \dfrac{2000}{12,360} \approx 0.16$

About 16% of entering freshmen are enrolled in Basic College Mathematics.

73. percent increase $= \dfrac{\text{amount of increase}}{\text{original amount}}$

$= \dfrac{33 - 16}{16}$

$= \dfrac{17}{16}$

$= 1.0625$

$= 106.25\%$

74. percent decrease $= \dfrac{\text{amount of decrease}}{\text{original amount}}$

$= \dfrac{675 - 534}{675}$

$= \dfrac{141}{675}$

$= 0.208\overline{8}$

$\approx 20.9\%$

75. decrease $= 4\% \cdot \$215,000$

$= 0.04 \cdot 215,000 = \$8600$

Next year $=$ this year $-$ decrease

$= \$215,000 - \$8600 = \$206,400$

76. 15% of \$11.50 is what number?

$(0.15)(\$11.50) = n$

$\$1.725 = n$

New hourly rate is

$\$11.50 + \$1.725 = \$13.225 \approx \$13.23$

77. Sales tax is

$(5.5\%)(\$250) = (0.055)(\$250) = \$13.75.$

Total price of the coat is

$\$250 + \$13.75 = \$263.75.$

78. Sales tax is

$(4.5\%)(\$25.50) = (0.045)(\$25.50)$

$= \$1.1475$

$\approx \$1.15$

79. Commission $= 5\% \cdot \$100,000$

$= 0.05 \cdot \$100,000$

$= \$5000$

80. Commission $= (7.5\%)(\$4005)$

$= (0.075)(\$4005)$

$= \$300.375$

$\approx \$300.38$

81. discount $= 30\% \cdot \$3000$

$= 0.3 \cdot \$3000$

$= \$900$

sale price $= \$3000 - \$900$

$= \$2100$

The discount is \$900 and the sale price is \$2100.

82. discount $= 10\% \cdot \$90$
$= 0.1 \cdot \$90$
$= \$9$
sale price $= \$90 - \$9$
$= \$81$
The discount is $9 and the sale price is $81.

83. simple interest $=$ principal $\cdot$ rate $\cdot$ time
$= \$4000 \cdot 12\% \cdot \dfrac{3}{12}$
$= \$4000 \cdot 0.12 \cdot 0.25$
$= \$120$

84. simple interest $=$ principle $\cdot$ rate $\cdot$ time
$= \$1200 \cdot 15\% \cdot \dfrac{8}{12}$
$= \$1200 \cdot 0.15 \cdot \dfrac{2}{3}$
$= \$120$
total due $= \$1200 + \$120 = \$1320$

85. The compound interest factor for 15 years at 12% compounded annually is 5.47357.
total amount $= \$5500 \cdot 5.47357$
$= \$30,104.635$
The total is $30,104.64.

86. The compound interest factor for 10 years at 11% compounded semiannually is 2.91776.
total amount $= \$6000 \cdot 2.91776$
$= \$17,506.56$
The total is $17,506.56.

87. The compound interest factor for 5 years at 12% compounded quarterly is 1.80611.
total amount $= \$100 \cdot 1.80611 \approx \$180.61$
Interest earned
$=$ total amount $-$ original principal
$= \$180.61 - \$100 = \$80.61$

88. The compound interest factor for 20 years at 18% compounded quarterly is 33.83010.
Total amount $= \$1000 \cdot 33.83010$
$= \$33,830.10$
Interest earned $= \$33,830.10 - \$1000$
$= \$32,830.10$

Chapter 6 Test

1. $85\% = 85.\% = 0.85$

2. $500\% = 500.\% = 5$

3. $0.6\% = 0.006$

4. $0.056 = 5.6\%$

5. $6.1 = 6.10 = 610.\% = 610\%$

6. $0.35 = 35\%$

7. $120\% = \dfrac{120}{100} = \dfrac{6}{5}$

8. $38.5\% = \dfrac{38.5}{100} = \dfrac{385}{1000} = \dfrac{77}{200}$

9. $0.2\% = \dfrac{0.2}{100} = \dfrac{2}{1000} = \dfrac{1}{500}$

10. $\dfrac{11}{20} = \dfrac{11}{20} \cdot \dfrac{5}{5} = \dfrac{55}{100} = 55\%$

11. $\dfrac{3}{8} = 0.375 = 37.5\%$

12. $1\dfrac{3}{4} = \dfrac{7}{4} = \dfrac{7}{4} \cdot \dfrac{25}{25} = \dfrac{175}{100} = 175\%$

13. $\dfrac{1}{5} = \dfrac{1}{5} \cdot 100\% = \dfrac{100}{5}\% = 20\%$

14. $64\% = \dfrac{64}{100} = \dfrac{16}{25}$

15. $n = 42\% \cdot 80$
$n = (0.42)(80)$
$n = 33.6$
Therefore, 42% of 80 is 33.6.

16. $0.6\% \cdot n = 7.5$
$0.006 \cdot n = 7.5$
$n = \dfrac{7.5}{0.006}$
$n = 1250$
Therefore, 0.6% of 1250 is 7.5.

17. $567 = x \cdot 756$
$\dfrac{567}{756} = \dfrac{x \cdot 756}{x}$
$0.75 = x$
$75\% = x$
Therefore, 75% of 756 is 567.

18. 12% of 320 is the amount of copper.
$12\% \cdot 320 = n$
$0.12 \cdot 320 = n$
$38.4 = n$
The alloy contains 38.4 pounds of copper.

19. 20% of what is $11,350?
$$0.20n = \$11,350$$
$$n = \frac{\$11,350}{0.20}$$
$$n = \$56,750$$
The value is $56,750.

20. tax $= 1.25\% \cdot \$354$
$$= (0.0125)(\$354)$$
$$= \$4.425$$
$$\approx \$4.43$$
Total price is $354 + $4.43 = $358.43.

21. percent increase $= \dfrac{26,460 - 25,200}{25,200}$
$$= \frac{1260}{25,200}$$
$$= 0.05$$
$$= 5\%$$
The population increased 5%.

22. discount $= 15\% \cdot \$120$
$$= 0.15 \cdot \$120$$
$$= \$18$$
sale price $= \$120 - \$18$
$$= \$102$$

23. commission $= 4\% \cdot \$9875$
$$= 0.04 \cdot \$9875$$
$$= \$395$$
His commission is $395.

24. $\$1.53 = r \cdot \$152.99$
$$\frac{\$1.53}{\$152.99} = r$$
$$0.01 \approx r$$
$$1\% = r$$

25. simple interest $=$ principal $\cdot$ rate $\cdot$ time
$$= \$2000 \cdot 9.25\% \cdot 3\frac{1}{2}$$
$$= \$2000 \cdot (0.0925) \cdot 3.5$$
$$= \$647.50$$

26. The compound interest factor for 5 years at 8% compounded annually is 1.46933.
total amount $= \$1365 \cdot 1.46933$
$$= \$2005.63545$$
The total amount is $2005.64.

27. interest $=$ principal $\cdot$ rate $\cdot$ time
$$\text{interest} = \$400 \cdot 13.5\% \cdot \frac{6}{12}$$
$$= \$400 \cdot (0.135) \cdot 0.5$$
$$= \$27.00$$
Total amount due the bank $= \$400 + \$27$
$$= \$427$$

28. percent decrease $= \dfrac{125,587 - 118,346}{125,587}$
$$= \frac{7241}{125,587}$$
$$\approx 0.058$$
$$= 5.8\%$$
The percent decrease is about 5.8%.

29. $\dfrac{5}{y+1} = \dfrac{4}{y+2}$
$$5(y+2) = 4(y+1)$$
$$5y + 10 = 4y + 4$$
$$5y - 4y = 4 - 10$$
$$y = -6$$

30. $\dfrac{85 \text{ bulbs}}{3 \text{ defective}} = \dfrac{510 \text{ bulbs}}{x \text{ defective}}$
$$85(x) = 3(510)$$
$$\frac{85x}{85} = \frac{1530}{85}$$
$$x = 18$$
18 defective bulbs should be found.

Cumulative Review

1.   236
            $\times 86$
            1416
           18880
          20,296

2.   409
            $\times 76$
            2454
          $+28630$
          31,084

3. $-3 - 7 = -10$

4. $8 - (-2) = 10$

5.
$$x - 2 = 1$$
$$x - 2 + 2 = 1 + 2$$
$$x = 3$$

6.
$$x + 4 = 3$$
$$x + 4 - 4 = 3 - 4$$
$$x = -1$$

7.
$$3(2x - 6) + 6 = 0$$
$$6x - 18 + 6 = 0$$
$$6x - 12 = 0$$
$$6x - 12 + 12 = 0 + 12$$
$$6x = 12$$
$$\frac{6x}{6} = \frac{12}{6}$$
$$x = 2$$

8.
$$5(x - 2) = 3x$$
$$5x - 10 = 3x$$
$$5x - 10 - 5x = 3x - 5x$$
$$-10 = -2x$$
$$\frac{-10}{-2} = \frac{-2x}{-2}$$
$$5 = x$$

9.
$$3 = \frac{3 \cdot 7}{1 \cdot 7} = \frac{21}{7}$$

10.
$$8 = \frac{8 \cdot 5}{1 \cdot 5} = \frac{40}{5}$$

11.
$$\frac{84x}{90} = \frac{14 \cdot 6x}{15 \cdot 6} = \frac{14x}{15}$$

12.
$$\frac{10y}{32} = \frac{5 \cdot 2y}{16 \cdot 2} = \frac{5y}{16}$$

13.
$$-\frac{5}{16} \div \left(-\frac{3}{4}\right) = -\frac{5}{16} \cdot \left(-\frac{4}{3}\right) = \frac{5 \cdot 4}{4 \cdot 4 \cdot 3} = \frac{5}{12}$$

14.
$$-\frac{2}{5} \div \frac{7}{10} = -\frac{2}{5} \cdot \frac{10}{7} = -\frac{2 \cdot 2 \cdot 5}{5 \cdot 7} = -\frac{4}{7}$$

15.
$$-\frac{8}{10} - \left(-\frac{3}{10}\right) = \frac{-8 + 3}{10} = -\frac{5}{10} = -\frac{1}{2}$$

16.
$$2\left(\frac{2}{5}\right) + 3\left(-\frac{1}{5}\right) = \frac{2 \cdot 2}{1 \cdot 5} - \frac{3 \cdot 1}{1 \cdot 5}$$
$$= \frac{4}{5} - \frac{3}{5}$$
$$= \frac{1}{5}$$

17.
$$-\frac{3}{4} - \frac{1}{14} + \frac{6}{7} = -\frac{3 \cdot 7}{4 \cdot 7} - \frac{1 \cdot 2}{14 \cdot 2} + \frac{6 \cdot 4}{7 \cdot 4}$$
$$= \frac{-21 - 2 + 24}{28}$$
$$= \frac{1}{28}$$

18.
$$\frac{2}{9} + \frac{7}{15} - \frac{1}{3} = \frac{2 \cdot 5}{9 \cdot 5} + \frac{7 \cdot 3}{15 \cdot 3} - \frac{1 \cdot 15}{3 \cdot 15}$$
$$= \frac{10 + 21 - 15}{45}$$
$$= \frac{16}{45}$$

19.
$$\frac{\frac{1}{2} + \frac{3}{8}}{\frac{3}{4} - \frac{1}{6}} = \frac{24\left(\frac{1}{2} + \frac{3}{8}\right)}{24\left(\frac{3}{4} - \frac{1}{6}\right)} = \frac{12 + 9}{18 - 4} = \frac{21}{14} = \frac{3}{2}$$

20.
$$\frac{\frac{2}{3} + \frac{1}{6}}{\frac{3}{4} - \frac{3}{5}} = \frac{60\left(\frac{2}{3} + \frac{1}{6}\right)}{60\left(\frac{3}{4} - \frac{3}{5}\right)} = \frac{40 + 10}{45 - 36} = \frac{50}{9}$$

21.
$$\frac{x}{2} = \frac{x}{3} + \frac{1}{2}$$
$$\left(\frac{x}{2}\right) = 6\left(\frac{x}{3} + \frac{1}{2}\right)$$
$$3x = 2x + 3$$
$$3x - 2x = 2x + 3 - 2x$$
$$y = 3$$

22.
$$\frac{x}{2}+\frac{1}{5}=3-\frac{x}{5}$$
$$10\left(\frac{x}{2}+\frac{1}{5}\right)=10\left(3-\frac{x}{5}\right)$$
$$5x+2=30-2x$$
$$5x+2+2x=30-2x+2x$$
$$7x+2=30$$
$$7x+2-2=30-2$$
$$7x=28$$
$$\frac{7x}{7}=\frac{28}{7}$$
$$x=4$$

23.
a. $4\frac{2}{9}=\frac{9\cdot4+2}{9}=\frac{38}{9}$

b. $1\frac{8}{11}=\frac{11\cdot1+8}{11}=\frac{19}{11}$

24.
a. $3\frac{2}{5}=\frac{5\cdot3+2}{5}=\frac{17}{5}$

b. $6\frac{2}{7}=\frac{7\cdot6+2}{7}=\frac{44}{7}$

25.
$$0.125=\frac{125}{1000}=\frac{1}{8}$$

26.
$$0.85=\frac{85}{100}=\frac{17}{20}$$

27.
$$-105.083=-105\frac{83}{1000}$$

28.
$$17.015=17\frac{15}{1000}=17\frac{3}{200}$$

29.
$$\begin{array}{r}85.00\\-17.31\\\hline67.69\end{array}$$

30.
$$\begin{array}{r}38.00\\-10.06\\\hline27.94\end{array}$$

31. $7.68\times10=76.8$

32. $12.483\times100=1248.3$

33. $(-76.3)(1000)=-76,300$

34. $-853.75\times10=-8537.5$

35.
$$\frac{720}{100}=7.2$$
$$7.2=7.2\ \text{True}$$
720 is a solution

36.
$$\frac{470}{100}=4.75$$
$$4.70=4.75\ \text{False}$$
470 is not a solution

37.
$$\sqrt{\frac{4}{25}}=\frac{2}{5}$$

38.
$$\sqrt{\frac{9}{16}}=\frac{3}{4}$$

39.
$$\frac{2.5}{3.15}=\frac{250}{315}=\frac{50}{63}$$

40.
$$\frac{5.8}{7.6}=\frac{58}{76}=\frac{29}{38}$$

41.
$$\frac{5}{2}=\frac{x}{7}$$
$$2x=35$$
$$x=17.5$$
17.5 miles

42.
$$\frac{7}{6}=\frac{x}{30}$$
$$6x=210$$
$$x=35$$
35 problems

43.
$$1.9\%=\frac{1.9}{100}=\frac{19}{1000}$$

44.
$$2.3\%=\frac{2.3}{100}=\frac{23}{1000}$$

45.
$$33\frac{1}{3}\%=33\frac{1}{3}\%\div100=\frac{100}{3}\div\frac{100}{1}$$
$$=\frac{100}{3}\cdot\frac{1}{100}=\frac{1}{3}$$

46.
$$108\%=\frac{108}{100}=1\frac{8}{100}=1\frac{2}{25}$$

Chapter 7

Pretest

1. The lowest point occurs at April. The least number of burglaries occurred in April.

2. July had 400 burglaries.

3. September had 700 burglaries.

4.   Dawn Miller's Day

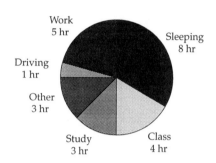

	Class Intervals (Scores)	Tally	Class Frequency (# of Exams)
5.	60 – 69	I I	2
6.	70 – 79	I I I I	4
7.	80 – 89	I I I I	4
8.	90 – 99	ⅢⅡ I	6

9.

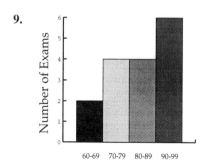

10. mean = $\dfrac{28+36+81+73+28+74+31+74+64+25+74}{11}$

$= \dfrac{588}{11}$

≈ 53.5

median: write the numbers in order to identify the middle number.

25, 28, 28, 31, 36, 64, 73, 74, 74, 74, 81

median = 64

mode: 74 is the mode because it is the number that occurs most often.

11. possible outcomes: 1, 2, 3, 4, 5, 6

probability of a 4 = $\dfrac{1}{6}$

12. possible outcomes: 1, 2, 3, 4, 5, 6

probability of a number greater than 3 = $\dfrac{3}{6} = \dfrac{1}{2}$

13. possible outcomes: 1, 2, 3, 4, 5, 6

probability of a 3 or a 5 = $\dfrac{2}{6} = \dfrac{1}{3}$

Section 7.1

Practice Problems

1. a. Each symbol indicates 50 billion kilowatt hours. Sweden shows 1.5 pictures which would indicate 1.5 × 50 = 75 billion kilowatt hours.

   b. Sweden has 1.5 symbols and Russia has 2.5 symbols which make 4 symbols altogether, 40 × 5 = 200 billion kilowatt hours.

2. a. The bar for insects is between 30 and 40. Therefore there are approximately 35 endangered insects.

   b. The shortest bars belong to amphibians and arachnids.

3.
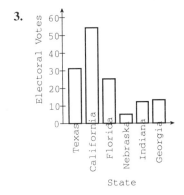

4. Look on the left to locate 70 – 79 under the Student Scores headline. Look to the right and you'll see a frequency of 10.

5. To find the amount of students who socred less than 60, add together the frequencies from the Student Scores 40 – 49 and 50 – 59. 1 + 3 = 4.

6.

Class Intervals (Credit Card Balances)	Tally	Class Frequency (Number of Months)
$0 – $49	III	3
$50 – $99	IIII	4
$100 – $149	II	2
$150 – $199	I	1
$200 – $249	I	1
$250 – $299	I	1

7.

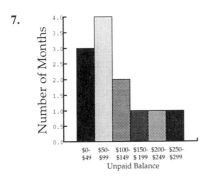

8. a. The month with the lowest temperature corresponds to the lowest point. Follow the lowest point down to the horizontal month scale, which reads January.

    b. Locate 25°F on the vertical scale and move across horizontally until you reach a darkened point. The month for that point is December.

    c. The points above the temperature of 70°F represent the months June, July, and August.

Exercise Set 7.1

1. The year 2002 has the most cars, so the greatest number of automobiles was manufactured in 2002.

3. There are eight cars for 2000, and each car represents 500 automobiles. Approximately 8 · 500 = 4000 automobiles were manufactured in 2000.

5. Compare each year with the previous year to see that the production of automobiles decreased from the previous year in 1998, 1999, and 2003.

7. The pictograph must show 8 cars for 4000 manufactured automobiles $\left(\frac{4000}{500} = 8 \right)$. The years 1997 and 2000 both show 8 cars.

9. The year 1997 has 7.5 chickens and each chicken represents 3 ounces of chicken, so approximately 7.5 · 3 = 22.5 ounces of chicken were consumed per person per week in 1997.

11. To be greater than 21 ounces, the pictograph must show more than seven chickens $\left(\frac{21}{3} = 7 \right)$. The years 1997, 1999, and 2001 have more than seven chickens.

13. There is one more chicken for 2001 than for 1995, so there was an increase of approximately 1 · 3 = 3 ounces per person per week.

15. The pictograph shows more chickens each year. This indicates a trend of increasing consumption of chicken per person per week in the United States.

17. The tallest bar corresponds to the month of April, so April has the most tornado-related deaths.

19. Draw a horizontal line from the top of the bar above May to the scale on the left. The approximate number of tornado-related deaths is 19.

21. Look for bars that extend above the horizontal line at 5. The months of February, March, April,

May, and June have over 5 tornado-related deaths.

23. The longest bar corresponds to Tokyo with an estimated population of 34.5 million or 34,500,000 people.

25. New York City is the largest, with an estimated population of 21.4 million or 21,400,000 people.

27. Tokyo   =   34.5 million
     Sao Paulo   =   −18.5 million
                       16.0 million

Tokyo is larger than Sao Paulo by 16 million or 16,000,000 people.

29.

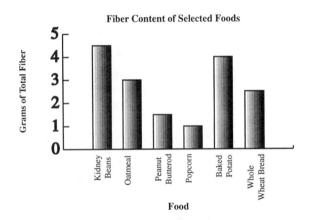

31.

33. The bar goes up to 15. 15 adults drive between 100-149 miles per week.

35. $0 - 49 = 28$ adults
$50 - 99 = 17$ adults
$100 - 149 = 15$ adults
$29 + 17 + 15 = 61$ adults drive fewer than 150 miles per week.

37. $100 - 149 = 15$ adults
$149 - 199 = 9$ adults
$15 + 9 = 24$ adults drive between $100 - 199$ miles per week.

39. $250 - 299 = 21$ adults
$200 - 249 = 9$ adults
$21 - 9 = 12$ adults more drive $250 - 299$ miles per week than they drive $200 - 249$ miles per week.

41. $\text{ratio} = \dfrac{\text{adults who drive } 150 \ - \ 199 \text{ miles}}{\text{total adults surveyed}} = \dfrac{9}{100}$

43. The highest bar is in the $45 - 54$ age range.

45. The $55 - 64$ age range bar goes up to 17 million householders.

47. Under $25 = 5$ million
$25 - 34 = 17$ million
$35 - 44 = 23$ million
$5 + 17 + 23 = 45$ million householders.

49. Answer may vary.

Class Intervals (Scores)	Tally	Class Frequency (Number of Games)
51. 70 – 79	I	1
53. 90 – 99	卌 III	8

Class Intervals (Acct. Balances)	Tally	Class Frequency (Number of People)
55. $0 – $99	卌 I	6
57. $200 – $299	卌 I	6
59. $400 – $499	II	2

61.

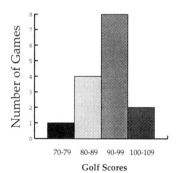

63. In 1994, there was an average of approximately 2.7 field goals per game.

65. 1982 had the highest average number of field goals per game.

67. The average number of field goals per game decreased between 1998 and 2000.

69. $30\% \cdot 12 = 0.3 \cdot 12 = 3.6$

71. $10\% \cdot 62 = 0.1 \cdot 62 = 6.2$

73. $\dfrac{1}{4} = 0.25 = 25\%$

75. $\dfrac{17}{50} = 0.34 = 34\%$

77. 83°F was the high temperature reading on Thursday.

79. The lowest temperature occurred on Sunday wit 68°F.

81. The greatest difference between high and low temperatures occurred on Tuesday with a difference of $86 - 73 = 13°F$.

83. Answers may vary.

Section 7.2

Practice Problems

1. $\dfrac{10 \text{ people preferring oatmeal raisin cookies}}{100 \text{ people}} = \dfrac{10}{100} = \dfrac{1}{10}$

2. Two + Three + Four or More $= 15\% + 6\% + 3\% = 24\%$

3. Four or more $= 3\%$
$= 3\% \cdot 288,400,000$
$= 0.03 \cdot 288,400,000$
$= 8,652,000$ Americans

4. Freshman $30\% \cdot 360° = 108°$
Sophomores $27\% \cdot 360° = 97.2° \approx 97°$
Juniors $25\% \cdot 360° = 90°$
Seniors $18\% \cdot 360° = 64.8° \approx 65°$

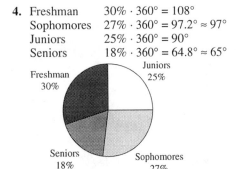

Exercise Set 7.2

1. The largest sector, or 320 students, corresponds to where most college students live. Most college students live at parent or guardian's home.

3. $\dfrac{\text{Students living in campus housing}}{\text{total students}}$

   $= \dfrac{180}{700} = \dfrac{9}{35}$

5. $\dfrac{\text{Students living in campus housing}}{\text{students living at home}}$

   $= \dfrac{180}{320} = \dfrac{9}{16}$

7. The largest sector is 30% which corresponds to Asia which is the largest continent.

9. Asia + Europe = 30% + 7% = 37%
   37% of the land on Earth is accounted for by Asia and Europe.

11. Asia $= 30\% \cdot 57,000,000$
    $= 0.30 \cdot 57,000,000$
    $= 17,100,000$ square miles

11. Austrailia $= 5\% \cdot 57,000,000$
    $= 0.05 \cdot 57,000,000$
    $= 2,850,000$ square miles

15. The sectors which represent fiction are "Adult Fiction" and Children's Fiction."
    percent = 33% + 22% = 55%

17. The second-largest sector is 25% which corresponds to "Nonfiction." Nonfiction is the second-largest category of books.

19. amount $= 25\% \cdot 125,600$
    $= 0.25 \cdot 125,600$
    $= 31,400$ books
    This library has 31,400 nonfiction books.

21. amount $= 22\% \cdot 125,600$
    $= 0.25 \cdot 125,600$
    $= 31,400$ books
    This library has 27,632 books in children's fiction.

23. amount $= (17\% + 3\%) \cdot 125,600$
    $= 20\% \cdot 125,600$
    $= 0.2 \cdot 125,600$
    $= 25,120$
    This library has 25,120 books in reference or other category.

25. United States $75\% \cdot 360° = 270°$
    Japan $11\% \cdot 360° = 40°$
    Germany $6\% \cdot 360° = 20°$
    Other Countries $8\% \cdot 360° = 30°$

27. Under 3 days $7\% \cdot 360° = 25°$
    3 – 10 days $18\% \cdot 360° = 65°$
    11 – 20 days $14\% \cdot 360° = 50°$
    21 or more days $61\% \cdot 360° = 220°$

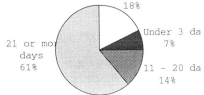

29. $20 = 4 \cdot 5 = 2 \cdot 2 \cdot 5 = 2^2 \cdot 5$

31. $40 = 8 \cdot 5 = 2 \cdot 2 \cdot 2 \cdot 5 = 2^3 \cdot 5$

33. $85 = 5 \cdot 17$

35. Pacific; answers may vary.

37. Pacific Ocean:
    $49\% \cdot 264,489,800 = 0.49 \cdot 264,489,800$
    $= 129,600,002$
    The Pacific Ocean is 129,600,002 square kilometers.

39. Indian Ocean:
    $21\% \cdot 264,489,800 = 0.21 \cdot 264,489,800$
    $= 55,542,858$
    The Indian Ocean is 55,542,858 square kilometers.

41. $21.5\% \cdot 2800 = 0.215 \cdot 2800 = 602$ respondents spend $0–$15 online each month.

43. at least $15 + over $175 = $175
$= 59.8\% + 18.7\% = 78.5\%$
$0.785 \cdot 2800 = 2198$ respondents.

Integrated Review

1. In 1995 the graph has 6.9 pictures. Each picture represents 10 pounds. The approximate number of pounds of beef and veal consumed per person is $10 \cdot 6.9 = 69$ pounds.

2. For the year 1980, the graph has 7.8 pictures. Each picture represents 10 pounds. The approximate number of pounds of beef and veal consumed per person is $10 \cdot 7.8 = 78$ pounds.

3. The number of pounds of beef and veal consumed was the greatest in 1985.

4. The number of pounds of beef and veal consumed was the least in 1995 and 2000.

5. The dam with the greatest height is represented by the tallest bar. The height of this bar is approximately 755 feet. Therefore, the Oroville Dam has the greatest height of approximately 755 feet.

6. The bar with a height between 625 feet and 650 feet is the one representing New Bullards Bar Dam. The New Bullards Bar Dam has a height of approximately 635 feet.

7. Find the difference in the heights of the bars representing these dams.
$725 - 710 = 15$
The Hoover Dam is approximately 15 feet taller than the Glen Canyon Dam.

8. There are 4 bars that have heights over 700 feet. Therefore, there are 4 United States dams that are over 700 feet.

9. Locate the highest points. Thursday and Saturday with temperatures of 100°F are the days with the highest temperature.

10. Locate the lowest point. Monday with a temperature of 82°F is the day with the lowest temperature.

11. There are three points below 90°F. The days corresponding to these points are Sunday, Monday, and Tuesday.

45. $\text{ratio} = \dfrac{\$0 - \$15}{\$15 - \$75} = \dfrac{602}{1674} = \dfrac{301}{837}$

47. No; answers may vary.

12. There are four points above 90°F. The days corresponding to these points are Wednesday, Thursday, Friday, and Saturday.

13. Whole milk: $35\% \cdot 200 = 70$ quart containers

14. Skim milk: $26\% \cdot 200 = 52$ quart containers

15. Buttermilk: $1\% \cdot 200 = 2$ quart containers

16. Flavored reduced fat and skim milk:
$3\% \cdot 200 = 6$ quart containers

	Class Intervals (Scores)	Tally	Class Frequency (# of Quizzes)
17.	50 – 59	I I	2
18.	60 – 69	I	1
19.	70 – 79	III	3
20.	80 – 89	TH II I	6
21.	90 – 99	TH II	5

22.

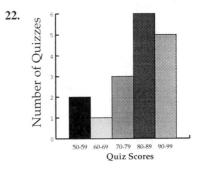

Section 7.3

Practice Problems

1. $\text{mean} = \dfrac{77 + 85 + 86 + 91 + 88}{5}$
$= \dfrac{427}{5}$
$= 85.4$

2. grade point average

$$= \frac{4 \cdot 2 + 2 \cdot 4 + 3 \cdot 5 + 1 \cdot 2 + 4 \cdot 2}{2 + 4 + 5 + 2 + 2}$$

$$= \frac{41}{15}$$

$$\approx 2.73$$

3. Because the list is in numerical order, the median is the middle number, 24.

4. First list the scores in numerical order. Then find the middle number, which will be the mean of the two middle numbers since there is an even number of scores.

43, 65, 71, 78, 88, 89, 95, 95

median $= \frac{78 + 88}{2} = \frac{166}{2} = 83$

5. The number 15 occurs most often. Therefore, 15 is the mode.

6. First write the numbers in numerical order.

15, 15, 15, 16, 18, 26, 26, 30, 31, 35

Since there is an even number of items, the median is the mean of the two middle numbers.

median $= \frac{18 + 26}{2} = \frac{44}{2} = 22$

The mode is 15, since 15 occurs most often.

Mental Math

1. $\frac{3 + 5}{2} = \frac{8}{2} = 4$

2. $\frac{10 + 20}{2} = \frac{30}{2} = 15$

3. $\frac{1 + 3 + 5}{3} = \frac{9}{3} = 3$

4. $\frac{7 + 7 + 7}{3} = \frac{21}{3} = 7$

Exercise Set 7.3

1. Mean: $\frac{21 + 28 + 16 + 42 + 38}{5} = \frac{145}{5} = 29$

Median: Write the numbers in order.

16, 21, 28, 38, 42

The middle number is 28.

Mode: There is no mode, since there is no number that occurs more often than the others.

3. Mean: $\frac{7.6 + 8.2 + 8.2 + 9.6 + 5.7 + 9.1}{6} = \frac{48.4}{6}$

≈ 8.1

Median: Write the numbers in order.

5.7, 7.6, 8.2, 8.2, 9.1, 9.6

Since there is an even number of items, find the average of the two middle numbers.

$\frac{8.2 + 8.2}{2} = \frac{16.4}{2} = 8.2$

Mode: 8.2 occurs most often.

5. Mean: $\frac{0.2 + 0.3 + 0.5 + 0.6 + 0.6 + 0.9 + 0.2 + 0.7 + 1.1}{9} = \frac{5.1}{9}$

≈ 0.6

Median: Write the numbers in order.

0.2, 0.2, 0.3, 0.5, 0.6, 0.6, 0.7, 0.9, 1.1

The middle number is 0.6.

Mode: Since 0.2 and 0.6 occur most often, there are two modes, 0.2 and 0.6.

7. Mean: $\frac{231 + 543 + 601 + 293 + 588 + 109 + 334 + 268}{8} = \frac{2967}{8}$

≈ 370.9

Median: Write the numbers in order.

109, 231, 268, 293, 334, 543, 588, 601

Since there is an even number of items, find the average of the two middle numbers.

$\frac{293 + 334}{2} = \frac{627}{2} = 313.5$

Mode: There is no mode since there is no number that occurs more often than the others.

9. Mean: $\dfrac{1483+1483+1450+1381+1283}{5} = \dfrac{7080}{5} = 1416$ feet

11. Median: Arrange from smallest to largest. Then, since there is an even number of items, find the average of the two middle numbers: 1227, 1250, 1260, <u>1283</u>, <u>1381</u>, 1450, 1483, 1483

    median $= \dfrac{1283+1381}{2} = \dfrac{2664}{2} = 1332$ feet

13. Answers may vary.

15.

Grade	Point Value	Credit Hours	$\left(\dfrac{\text{Point}}{\text{Value}}\right) \cdot \left(\dfrac{\text{Credit}}{\text{Hours}}\right)$
B	3	3	9
C	2	3	6
A	4	4	16
C	2	4	8
Totals		14	39

Grade Point Average $= \dfrac{39}{14} \approx 2.79$

17.

Grade	Point Value	Credit Hours	$\left(\dfrac{\text{Point}}{\text{Value}}\right) \cdot \left(\dfrac{\text{Credit}}{\text{Hours}}\right)$
A	4	3	12
A	4	3	12
B	3	4	12
B	3	1	3
B	3	2	6
Totals		13	45

Grade Point Average $= \dfrac{45}{13} \approx 3.46$

19. Mean:
    $\dfrac{7.8+6.9+7.5+4.7+6.9+7.0}{6} = \dfrac{40.8}{6}$
    $= 6.8$

    The mean time is 6.8 seconds.

21. The most common time is 6.9 seconds.

23. Write the numbers in order.
    74, 77, 85, 86, 91, 95
    Since there is an even number of scores, find the average of the middle two numbers.
    median $= \dfrac{85+86}{2} = \dfrac{171}{2} = 85.5$

25. mean $= \dfrac{78+80+66+68+71+64+82+71+70+65+70+75+77+86+72}{15} = \dfrac{1095}{15} = 73$

27. Since 70 and 71 occur more often than the other numbers, the modes are 70 and 71.

29. Nine: the rates of 66, 68, 71, 64, 71, 70, 65, 70, and 72 are below the mean of 73.

31. $\frac{6}{18} = \frac{2 \cdot 3}{2 \cdot 3 \cdot 3} = \frac{1}{3}$

33. $\frac{18}{30} = \frac{2 \cdot 3 \cdot 3}{2 \cdot 3 \cdot 5} = \frac{3}{5}$

35. $\frac{55}{75} = \frac{5 \cdot 11}{5 \cdot 15} = \frac{11}{15}$

37. There are 5 numbers, so the median is the middle number, 37. The mode is 35 so it must occur two times since the others occur only once. Now we have 35, 35, 37, 40, ___.
Let x = the unknown number.
Since the mean is 38,
$$38 = \frac{35 + 35 + 37 + 40 + x}{5}$$
$$5 \cdot 38 = 147 + x$$
$$190 = 147 + x$$
$$190 - 147 = 147 + x - 147$$
$$43 = x$$

The list is 35, 35, 37, 40, 43.

39. Yes; answers may vary.

Section 7.4

Practice Problems

1.

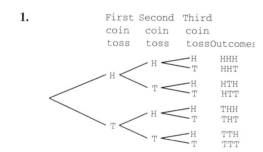

There are 8 outcomes.

2.

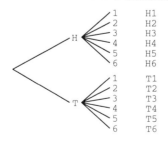

There are 12 outcomes.

3. Possible outcomes: HHH, HHT, HTH, HTT, THH, THT, TTH, TTT

$$\text{probability} = \frac{\text{number of ways the event can occur}}{\text{number of possible outcomes}}$$

$$= \frac{1}{8}$$

4. Possible outcomes: 1, 2, 3, 4, 5, 6

probability

$$= \frac{\text{number of ways the event can occur}}{\text{number of possible outcomes}}$$

$$= \frac{2}{6}$$

$$= \frac{1}{3}$$

5. probability

$$= \frac{\text{number of ways the event can occur}}{\text{number of possible outcomes}}$$

$$= \frac{2}{4}$$

$$= \frac{1}{2}$$

Mental Math

1. $\frac{1}{2}$

2. $\frac{1}{2}$

3. $\frac{1}{2}$

4. $\frac{1}{2}$

Exercise Set 7.4

1.

```
                              Outcomes
                    1         a1
              a     2         a2
                    3         a3
                    1         e1
              e     2         e2
                    3         e3
                    1         i1
              i     2         i2
                    3         i3
                    1         o1
              o     2         o2
                    3         o3
                    1         u1
              u     2         u2
                    3         u3
```

There are 15 outcomes.

3.

```
                    Outcomes
        Red         Red
        Blue        Blue
        Yellow      Yellov
```

There are 3 outcomes.

5.   Outcomes

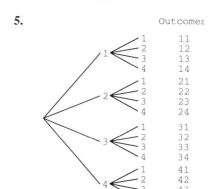

There are 16 outcomes.

7.   Outcomes

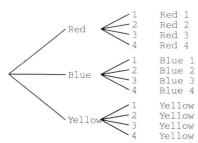

There are 12 outcomes.

9.   Outcomes

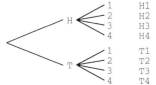

There are 8 outcomes.

11. possible outcomes: 1, 2, 3, 4, 5, 6
probability of a 5 $= \frac{1}{6}$

13. possible outcomes: 1, 2, 3, 4, 5, 6
probability of a 1 or a 4 $= \frac{2}{6} = \frac{1}{3}$

15. possible outcomes: 1, 2, 3, 4, 5, 6
probability of an even number $= \frac{3}{6} = \frac{1}{2}$

17. possible outcomes: 1, 2, 3
probability of a 2 $= \frac{1}{3}$

19. possible outcomes: 1, 2, 3
    probability of an odd number $= \frac{2}{3}$

21. possible outcomes: red, blue, yellow, yellow, green, green, green
    probability of a red $= \frac{1}{7}$

23. possible outcomes: red, blue, yellow, yellow, green, green, green
    probability of yellow $= \frac{2}{7}$

25. probability $= \dfrac{\text{blood pressure higher}}{\text{total participants}} = \dfrac{38}{200} = \dfrac{19}{100}$

27. probability $= \dfrac{\text{blood pressure unchanged}}{\text{total participants}} = \dfrac{10}{200} = \dfrac{1}{20}$

29. $\dfrac{1}{2} + \dfrac{1}{3} = \dfrac{1}{2} \cdot \dfrac{3}{3} + \dfrac{1}{3} \cdot \dfrac{2}{2}$
    $= \dfrac{1 \cdot 3}{2 \cdot 3} + \dfrac{1 \cdot 2}{3 \cdot 2}$
    $= \dfrac{3}{6} + \dfrac{2}{6}$
    $= \dfrac{5}{6}$

31. $\dfrac{1}{2} \cdot \dfrac{1}{3} = \dfrac{1 \cdot 1}{2 \cdot 3} = \dfrac{1}{6}$

33. $5 \div \dfrac{3}{4} = \dfrac{5}{1} \cdot \dfrac{4}{3} = \dfrac{5 \cdot 4}{1 \cdot 3} = \dfrac{20}{3}$ or $6\dfrac{2}{3}$

35. There are 52 possible outcomes.
    There is one King of hearts.
    probability of King of Hearts $= \dfrac{1}{52}$

37. There are 52 possible outcomes.
    There are four kings.
    probability of a King $= \dfrac{4}{52} = \dfrac{1}{13}$

39. There are 52 possible outcomes.
    There are 13 hearts.
    probability of a heart $= \dfrac{13}{52} = \dfrac{1}{4}$

41.

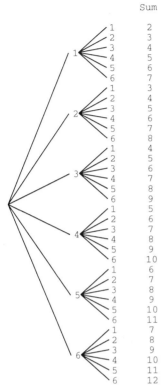

There are 36 possible outcomes. Three outcomes result in a sum of 4.

probability of a sum of 4 $= \frac{3}{36} = \frac{1}{12}$

43. There are 36 possible outcomes. None of the outcomes results is a sum of 0 (see diagram in solution for **37.**)

probability of a sum of 0 $= \frac{0}{36} = 0$

45. Answers may vary.

Chapter 7 Review

1. Each symbol represents 500,000 homes. There are 8 symbols for the Midwest.
   $8 \cdot 500,000 = 4,000,000$

2. Each symbol represents 500,000 homes. There are 3.5 symbols for the Northeast.
   $3.5 \cdot 500,000 = 1,750,000$

3. The South contains the most symbols.

4. The Northeast contains the least symbols.

5. 4,000,000 or more housing would be at least 8 symbols. The Midwest, South, and West each have more than 8 symbols.

6. The Northeast has less than 8 symbols.

7. The bar above 1960 is approximately 7.5 high, so approximately 7.5% of persons age 25 or more completed 4 or more years of college in 1960.

8. The tallest bar is for the year 2000, so 2000 had the greatest percentage of persons age 25 or more completing 4 or more years of college.

9. The years 1980, 1990, and 2000 all have bars of height 15 or more, so those years had 15% or more persons age 25 or more completing 4 or more years of college.

10. Answers may vary.

11. The line above 2003 is approximately at $2,100,000.

12. The line above 1997 is at $1,200,000.

13. The line remains the same between 1991 and 1992. The line decreases between 2000 and 2001 and between 2001 and 2002.

14. The steepest increase is between 1999 and 2000.

15. The line is below $1,000,000 in 1990, 1991, 1992, 1993, and 1994.

16. At 21 – 25, the bar goes up to 4. 4 employees.

17. At 41 – 45, the bar goes up to 1. 1 employee.

18. At 36 – 40, the bar goes up to 8. At 41 – 45 the bar goes up to 1. 8 + 1 = 9 employees.

19. At 16 – 20 the bar goes up to 6. At 21 – 25 the bar goes up to 4. At 26 – 30 the bar goes up to 8. 6 + 4 + 8 = 18 employees.

	Class Intervals (Temperatures)	Tally	Class Frequency (# of Months)
20.	80° –89°	₪	5
21.	90° – 99°	|||	3
22.	100° – 109°	||||	4

23.

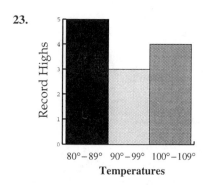

24. The largest sector of the circle graph represents the largest budget item, which is House Mortgage.

25. The smallest sector of the circle graph represents the smallest budget item, which is Utilities.

26. Add the two amounts of the two sectors:
$975 + $250 = $1225

27. Add the two amounts of the two sectors:
$400 + $300 = $700

28. ratio $= \dfrac{\text{house mortgage}}{\text{monthly budget}} = \dfrac{\$975}{\$4000} = \dfrac{39}{160}$

29. ratio $= \dfrac{\text{food}}{\text{monthly budget}} = \dfrac{\$700}{\$4000} = \dfrac{7}{40}$

30. ratio $= \dfrac{\text{car expenses}}{\text{food}} = \dfrac{500}{700} = \dfrac{5}{7}$

31. amount $= 40\% \cdot 50 = 20$ states

32. amount $= 22\% \cdot 50 = 11$ states

33. amount $= 2\% \cdot 50 = 1$ state

34. amount $= (22\% + 36\%) \cdot 50$
$= 58\% \cdot 50$
$= 29$ states

35. Mean $= \dfrac{13 + 23 + 33 + 14 + 6}{5}$
$= \dfrac{89}{5}$
$= 17.8$
Median: Write the numbers in order to find the middle number. Write the numbers in order.
6, 13, 14, 23, 33
The median is the middle number: Median = 14.
Mode: Since each number occurs only once, there is no mode.

36. Mean $= \dfrac{45 + 21 + 60 + 86 + 64}{5}$
$= \dfrac{276}{5}$
$= 55.2$
Median: Write the numbers in order to find the middle number. Write the numbers in order.
21, 45, 60, 64, 86
The median is the middle number: Median = 60.
Mode: Since each number occurs only once, there is no mode.

37. Mean $= \dfrac{\$14,000 + \$20,000 + \$12,000 + \$20,000 + \$36,000 + \$45,000}{6} = \dfrac{\$147,000}{6} = \$24,500$
Median: Write the numbers in order to find the middle number. Write the dollar amounts in order.
$12,000; $14,000; $20,000; $20,000; $36,000; $45,000
The median is the average of the two middle dollar amounts.
median $= \dfrac{\$20,000 + \$20,000}{2} = \$20,000$
Mode: $20,000 occurs more often than the other numbers, so $20,000 is the mode.

38. Average $= \dfrac{560 + 620 + 123 + 400 + 410 + 300 + 400 + 780 + 430 + 450}{10} = \dfrac{4473}{10} = 447.3$

Median: Write the numbers in order to find the middle number. Write the numbers in order.
123, 300, 400, 400, 410, 430, 450, 560, 620, 780
The median is the average of the two middle numbers.

median $= \dfrac{410 + 430}{2} = 420$

Mode: The number 400 occurs more often than the other numbers, so 400 is the mode

39.

Grade	Point Value	Credit Hours	$\left(\dfrac{\text{Point}}{\text{Value}}\right) \cdot \left(\dfrac{\text{Credit}}{\text{Hours}}\right)$
A	4	3	12
A	4	3	12
C	2	2	4
B	3	3	9
C	2	1	2
Totals		12	39

Grade Point Average $= \dfrac{39}{12} = 3.25$

40.

Grade	Point Value	Credit Hours	$\left(\dfrac{\text{Point}}{\text{Value}}\right) \cdot \left(\dfrac{\text{Credit}}{\text{Hours}}\right)$
B	3	3	9
B	3	4	12
C	2	2	4
D	1	2	2
B	3	3	9
Totals		14	36

Grade Point Average $= \dfrac{36}{14} \approx 2.57$

41.

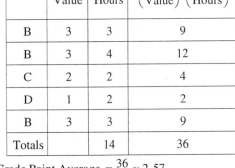

There are 10 outcomes.

42.

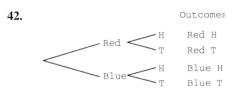

There are 4 outcomes.

43.

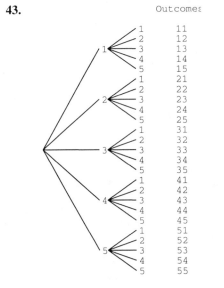

There are 25 outcomes.

44.

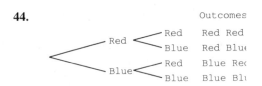

There are 4 outcomes.

45.

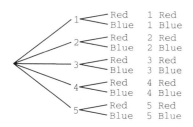

There are 10 outcomes.

46. possible outcomes: 1, 2, 3, 4, 5, 6

probability of a $4 = \dfrac{1}{6}$

47. possible outcomes: 1, 2, 3, 4, 5, 6

probability of a $3 = \dfrac{1}{6}$

48. possible outcomes: 1, 2, 3, 4, 5

probability of a $4 = \dfrac{1}{5}$

49. possible outcomes: 1, 2, 3, 4, 5

probability of a $3 = \dfrac{1}{5}$

50. possible outcomes: 1, 2, 3, 4, 5

probability of a 1, 3, or $5 = \dfrac{3}{5}$

51. possible outcomes: 1, 2, 3, 4, 5

probability of a 2 or a $4 = \dfrac{2}{5}$

Chapter 7 Test

1. The second week has $4\dfrac{1}{2}$ bills and each bill represents \$50. $4.5 \cdot \$50 = \$225$ was collected during the second week.

2. The most bills are for week 3 with 7 bills. Week 3 took in the most money:
$7 \cdot \$50 = \$350$

3.

Week	Number of Bills	$\left(\begin{array}{c}\text{Number} \\ \text{of Bills}\end{array}\right) \cdot \$50$
1	3	\$150
2	4.5	\$225
3	7	\$350
4	5.5	\$275
5	2	\$100
Total		\$1100

4. The bars for the months of June, August, and September have heights above 9. June, August, and September normally have more than 9 centimeters of monthly precipitation in Chicago.

5. The shortest bar is above the month of February. February has the least amount of normal monthly precipitation with 3 centimeters.

6. The months of March and November show a normal monthly precipitation of 7 centimeters.

7.

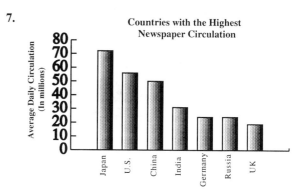

8. $\dfrac{\text{number who prefer rock}}{\text{number surveyed}} = \dfrac{85}{200} = \dfrac{17}{40}$

9. $\dfrac{\text{number who prefer country music}}{\text{number who prefer jazz}} = \dfrac{62}{44} = \dfrac{31}{22}$

10. amount $= 31\% \cdot 132,000,000$
$= 40,920,000$ people

11. amount $= 16\% \cdot 132,000,000$
$= 21,120,000$ people

12. The bar goes up to 9. 9 students.

13. $5 + 6 = 11$

14.

Class Intervals (Scores)	Tally	Class Frequency (# of Students)
40 – 49	I	1
50 – 59	III	3
60 – 69	IIII	4
70 – 79	ⅢⅡ	5
80 – 89	ⅢⅡ III	8
90 – 99	IIII	4

15.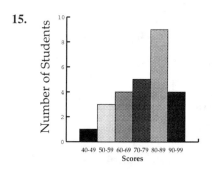

16. Mean $= \dfrac{26 + 32 + 42 + 43 + 49}{5}$
$= \dfrac{192}{5}$
$= 38.4$
Median: Write the numbers in order.
26, 32, 42, 43, 49
The median is the middle number, so
median $= 42$.
Mode: Since each number occurs only once, there is no mode.

17. Mean
$= \dfrac{8 + 10 + 16 + 16 + 14 + 12 + 12 + 13}{8}$
$= \dfrac{101}{8}$
$= 12.625$
Median: Write the numbers in order.
8, 10, 12, 12, 13, 14, 16, 16
The median is the average of the two middle numbers.
Median $= \dfrac{12 + 13}{2} = 12.5$
Mode: Since 12 and 16 occur more often than the other numbers, there are two modes: 12 and 16.

18.

Grade	Point Value	Credit Hours	$\left(\dfrac{Point}{Value}\right) \cdot \left(\dfrac{Credit}{Hours}\right)$
A	4	3	12
B	3	3	9
C	2	3	6
B	3	4	12
A	4	1	4
Totals		14	43

Grade Point Average $= \dfrac{43}{14} \approx 3.07$

19.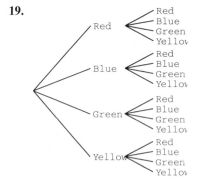

20.

```
        H < H
          < T
        T < H
          < T
```

21. possible outcomes: 1, 2, 3, 4, 5, 6, 7, 8, 9, 10
probability of a 6 $= \dfrac{1}{10}$

22. possible outcomes: 1, 2, 3, 4, 5, 6, 7, 8, 9, 10
probability of a 3 or a 4 $= \dfrac{2}{10} = \dfrac{1}{5}$

Cumulative Review

1.
$$4^3 + [3^2 - (10 \div 2) - 7 \cdot 3 = 4^3[3^2 - 5] - 7 \cdot 3$$
$$= 4^3 + [9 - 5] - 7 \cdot 3$$
$$= 4^3 + 4 - 7 \cdot 3$$
$$= 64 + 4 - 7 \cdot 3$$
$$= 64 + 4 - 21$$
$$= 68 - 21$$
$$= 47$$

2.
$$7^2 - \left[5^3 = (6 \div 3)\right] + 4 \cdot 2 = 7^2 - \left[5^3 + 2\right] + 4 \cdot 2$$
$$= 7^2 - [125 + 2] + 4 \cdot 2$$
$$= 7^2 - 127 + 4 \cdot 2$$
$$= 49 - 127 + 4 \cdot 2$$
$$= 49 - 127 + 8$$
$$= -78 + 8$$
$$= -70$$

3. $-3 - 9 = -12$

4. $7 - (-2) = 7 + 2 = 9$

5.
$$3y - 7y = 12$$
$$-4y = 12$$
$$\frac{-4y}{-4} = \frac{12}{-4}$$
$$y = -3$$

6.
$$2x - 6x = 24$$
$$-4x = 24$$
$$\frac{-4x}{-4} = \frac{24}{-4}$$
$$x = -6$$

7.
$$\frac{x}{4} + 1 = \frac{4}{3}$$
$$6\left(\frac{x}{6} + 1\right) = 6\left(\frac{4}{3}\right)$$
$$x + 6 = 8$$
$$x + 6 - 6 = 8 - 6$$
$$x = 2$$

8.
$$\frac{7}{2} + \frac{a}{4} = 1$$
$$4\left(\frac{7}{2} + \frac{a}{4}\right) = 4(1)$$
$$14 + a = 4$$
$$14 + a - 14 = 4 - 14$$
$$a = -10$$

9.
$$2\frac{1}{3} = 2\frac{8}{24}$$
$$+5\frac{3}{8} = +5\frac{9}{24}$$
$$\overline{7\frac{17}{24}}$$

10.
$$3\frac{2}{5} = 3\frac{8}{20}$$
$$+4\frac{3}{4} = +4\frac{15}{20}$$
$$\overline{7\frac{23}{20}}$$

$$\frac{23}{20} = 1\frac{3}{20}$$
$$7 + 1\frac{3}{20} = 8\frac{3}{20}$$

11.
$$5\frac{6}{10} = 5\frac{3}{5}$$

12.
$$2\frac{8}{10} = 2\frac{4}{5}$$

13.
$$\begin{array}{r} 3.500 \\ -0.068 \\ \hline 3.432 \end{array}$$

14.
$$\begin{array}{r} 7.400 \\ -0.073 \\ \hline 7.327 \end{array}$$

15.
$$\begin{array}{r} 0.283 \\ \times\, 0.3 \\ \hline 0.0849 \end{array}$$

16.
$$\begin{array}{r} 0.147 \\ \times\, 0.2 \\ \hline 0.0294 \end{array}$$

17.
$$\begin{array}{r} 0.052 \\ 115{\overline{\smash{\big)}\,5.980}} \\ \underline{-575} \\ 230 \\ \underline{-230} \\ 0 \end{array}$$

18.

$$
\begin{array}{r}
0.136 \\
205\overline{)27.880} \\
\underline{-205} \\
738 \\
\underline{-615} \\
1230 \\
\underline{-1230} \\
0
\end{array}
$$

19. $(-1.3)^2 + 2.4 = 1.69 + 2.4 = 4.09$

20. $(-2.7)^2 = 7.29$

21.

$$
\begin{array}{r}
0.25 \\
4\overline{)1.00} \\
\underline{-8} \\
20 \\
\underline{-20} \\
0
\end{array}
$$

22.

$$
\begin{array}{r}
0.375 \\
8\overline{)3.000} \\
\underline{-24} \\
60 \\
\underline{-56} \\
40 \\
\underline{-40} \\
0
\end{array}
$$

23.
$$
\begin{aligned}
5(x - 0.36) &= -x + 2.4 \\
5x - 1.8 &= -x + 2.4 \\
5x - 1.8 + x &= -x + 2.4 + x \\
6x - 1.8 &= 2.4 \\
6x - 1.8 + 1.8 &= 2.4 + 1.8 \\
6x &= 4.2 \\
\frac{6x}{6} &= \frac{4.2}{6} \\
x &= 0.7
\end{aligned}
$$

24.
$$
\begin{aligned}
4(0.35 - x) &= x - 7 \\
1.4 - 4x &= x - 7 \\
1.4 - 4x - x &= x - 7 - x \\
1.4 - 5x &= -7 \\
1.4 - 5x - 1.4 &= -7 - 1.4 \\
-5x &= -8.4 \\
\frac{-5x}{-5} &= \frac{-8.4}{-5} \\
x &= 1.68
\end{aligned}
$$

25. $\sqrt{32} \approx 5.657$

26. $\sqrt{60} \approx 7.746$

27. $4.6\% = 0.046$

28. $32\% = 32.\% = 0.32$

29. $0.74\% = 0.0074$

30. $2.7\% = 0.027$

31. $x = 0.35 \cdot 60$
$x = 21$

32. $x = .40 \cdot 36$
$x = 14.4$

33. $20.8 = 0.40 \cdot x$
$\dfrac{20.8}{0.40} = x$
$52 = x$

34. $9.5 = 0.25 \cdot x$
$\dfrac{9.5}{0.25} = x$
$38 = x$

35. cost $\cdot$ rate = sales tax
$300 \cdot x = 22.50$
$x = \dfrac{22.50}{300}$
$x = 0.075$
The sales taxs rate is 7.5%

36. $3.00 \cdot x = 0.13$
$x = \dfrac{0.13}{2.00}$
$x = 0.065$
The sales taxs rate is 6.5%

37. (loan + interest) ÷ how many payments.
$(2000 + 435.88) \div 24 = 2435.88 \div 24 \approx 101.50$.
The monthly payments are \$101.50.

38. $(1600 + 128.60) \div 12 = 1728.60 \div 12 = 144.05$.
The monthly payments are \$144.05.

39. median: middle number or average of the two
middle numbers when arranged from lowest to highes
55, 67, 75, 86, 91, 91
median = $\dfrac{75 + 86}{2} = \dfrac{161}{2} = 80.5$

40.   43, 46, 47, 50, 52, 83

$$\text{median} = \frac{47 + 50}{2} = \frac{97}{2} = 48.5$$

41.   possible outcomes: 1, 2, 3, 4, 5, 6

probability of a 3 or 4 $= \dfrac{2}{6} = \dfrac{1}{3}$

42.   possible outcomes: 1, 2, 3, 4, 5, 6

probability of an even number (2, 4, or 6) $= \dfrac{3}{6} = \dfrac{1}{2}$

Chapter 8

Pretest

1. Since the angle is between 0° and 90°, it is an acute angle.

2. Since the angle is 180°, it is a straight angle.

3. The supplement of an angle that measures 92° is an angle that measures 180° − 92° = 88°.

4. Since $\angle x$ and the 55° angle are vertical angles, $\angle x = 55°$. Since $\angle y$ and the 55° angle are supplementary angles, $\angle y = 180° − 55° = 125°$. Since $\angle y$ and $\angle z$ are vertical angles, $\angle z = 125°$.

5. Since the sum of the measures of the angles of a triangle is 180°, $\angle x = 180° − 40° − 30° = 110°$.

6. $11 \text{ feet} \cdot \dfrac{1 \text{ yard}}{3 \text{ feet}} = \dfrac{11 \text{ yards}}{3} = 3\dfrac{2}{3} \text{ yards}$

7. To convert centimeters to kilometers, move the decimal point 5 places to the left.
   6,250,000 cm = 62.5 km

8. $P = 2l + 2w$
   $= 2 \cdot 24 \text{ inches} + 2 \cdot 6 \text{ inches}$
   $= 48 \text{ inches} + 12 \text{ inches}$
   $= 60 \text{ inches}$

9. $C = 2\pi r$
   $= 2\pi \cdot 9 \text{ yards}$
   $= 18\pi \text{ yards}$
   $\approx 18 \cdot 3.14 \text{ yards}$
   $= 56.52 \text{ yards}$

10. $A = \dfrac{1}{2}bh$
    $= \dfrac{1}{2} \cdot 4 \text{ cm} \cdot 3 \text{ cm}$
    $= 6 \text{ square centimeters}$

11.
```
        7 lb   12 oz
   2) 15 lb    8 oz
      −14
       1 lb = 16 oz
             24 oz
            −24 oz
              0
```

12.
```
   9 gal 1 qt  =    8 gal 5 qt
  −     2qt    −        2 qt
                   8 gal 3 qt
```

13. To convert liters to milliliters, move the decimal point 3 places to the right.
    25 L = 25,000 ml

14. $C = \dfrac{5}{9}(F - 32)$
    $= \dfrac{5}{9}(118 - 32)$
    $= \dfrac{5}{9}(86)$
    ≈ 47.8
    $118°F \approx 47.8°C$

15. Since the triangles are similar, we can compare any of the corresponding sides to find the ratio.
    $\dfrac{5}{10} = \dfrac{1}{2}$

16. $\dfrac{6}{18} = \dfrac{2}{n}$
    $18 \cdot 2 = 6n$
    $36 = 6n$
    $\dfrac{36}{6} = \dfrac{6n}{6}$
    $6 = n$

17. $\dfrac{\text{tree height}}{\text{shadow length}} = \dfrac{\text{tree height}}{\text{shadow length}}$
    $\dfrac{40 \text{ feet}}{22 \text{ feet}} = \dfrac{36 \text{ feet}}{x \text{ feet}}$
    $\dfrac{40}{22} = \dfrac{36}{x}$
    $22 \cdot 36 = 40x$
    $792 = 40x$
    $\dfrac{792}{40} = \dfrac{40x}{40}$
    $19.8 = x$
    A 36-foot tree casts a 19.8-foot shadow.

Section 8.1

Practice Problems

1. a. The figure has two endpoints. It is line segment RS, or $\overline{RS}$.

b. The figure is part of a line with one endpoint. It is ray AB, or $\overrightarrow{AB}$.

c. The figure extends indefinitely in two directions. It is line EF, or $\overleftrightarrow{EF}$.

d. The figure is two rays with a common endpoint. It is $\angle HVT$, $\angle TVH$, or $\angle V$.

2. Two other ways to name $\angle z$ are $\angle RTS$ or $\angle STR$.

3. a. $\angle M$ is an acute angle. It measures between $0°$ and $90°$.

6. $\angle y = 136° - 97° = 39°$

7. Since $\angle ABY$ and $\angle ZBC$ are vertical angles, $\angle ABY = 46°$. Since $\angle ABZ$ and $\angle YBC$ are vertical angles, $\angle ABZ = 134°$.

8. Since $\angle a$ and the $112°$ angle are vertical angles, the measure of $\angle a$ is $112°$. $\angle a$ and $\angle b$ are supplementary angles, so $\angle b$ measures $180° - 112° = 68°$. $\angle b$ and $\angle c$ are vertical angles, so $\angle c$ measures $68°$.

9. Since $\angle w$ and $\angle x$ are vertical angles and $\angle w = 40°$, $\angle x = 40°$. $\angle y$ and $\angle w$ are corresponding angles, so $\angle y = 40°$. $\angle y$ and $\angle z$ are supplementary angles, so $\angle z = 180° - 40° = 140°$.

Exercise Set 8.1

1. The figure extends indefinitely in two directions. It is line yz, or $\overleftrightarrow{yz}$.

3. The figure has two endpoints. It is line segment LM, or $\overline{LM}$.

5. The figure has two endpoints. It is line segment PQ, or $\overline{PQ}$.

7. The figure is part of a line with one endpoint. It is ray UW, or $\overrightarrow{UW}$.

9. $\angle ABC = 15°$

11. $\angle CBD = 50°$

b. $\angle N$ is a straight angle.

c. $\angle O$ is an obtuse angle. It measures between $90°$ and $180°$.

d. $\angle P$ is a right angle.

4. The complement of an angle that measures $36°$ is an angle that measures $90° - 36° = 54°$.

5. The supplement of an angle that measures $88°$ is an angle that measures $180° - 88° = 92°$.

13. $\angle DBA = 50° + 15° = 65°$

15. $\angle CBE = 50° + 45° = 95°$

17. $90°$

19. $0°$; $90°$

21. $\angle S$ is a straight angle.

23. $\angle R$ is a right angle.

25. Since $\angle Q$ measures between $90°$ and $180°$, it is an obtuse angle.

27. $\angle N$ is a right angle.

29. The complement of an angle that measures $17°$ is an angle that measures $90° - 17° = 73°$.

31. The supplement of an angle that measures $17°$ is an angle that measures $180° - 17° = 163°$.

33. The complement of a $48°$ angle is an angle that measures $90° - 48° = 42°$.

35. The supplement of a $125°$ angle is an angle that measures $180° - 125° = 55°$.

37. $\angle MNP$ and $\angle RNO$ are complementary angles since $60° + 30° = 90°$. $\angle PNQ$ and $\angle QNR$ are complementary angles since $52° + 38° = 90°$.

39. $\angle SPT$ and $\angle TPQ$ are supplementary angles since $45° + 135° = 180°$. $\angle SPR$ and $\angle RPQ$ are supplementary angles

since $135° + 45° = 180°$.
$\angle SPT$ and $\angle SPR$ are supplementary angles since $45° + 135° = 180°$.
$\angle TPQ$ and $\angle QPR$ are supplementary angles since $135° + 45° = 180°$.

41. The supplement of a $125.2°$ angle is $180° - 125.2° = 54.8°$.

43. $\angle x = 120° - 88° = 32°$

45. $\angle x = 90° - 15° = 75°$

47. Since $\angle x$ and the $35°$ angle are vertical angles, $\angle x = 35°$. $\angle x$ and $\angle y$ are supplementary angles, so $\angle y = 180° - 35° = 145°$. $\angle y$ and $\angle z$ are vertical angles, so $\angle z = 145°$.

49. Since $\angle x$ and the $103°$ angle are supplementary angles, $\angle x = 180° - 103° = 77°$. $\angle y$ and the $103°$ angle are vertical angles, so $\angle y = 103°$. $\angle x$ and $\angle z$ are vertical angles, so $\angle z = 77°$.

51. $\angle x$ and the $80°$ angle are adjacent angles, so $\angle x = 180° - 80° = 100°$. $\angle y$ and the $80°$ angle are alternate interior angles, so $\angle y = 80°$. $\angle x$ and $\angle z$ are corresponding angles, so $\angle z = 100°$.

53. $\angle x$ and the $46°$ angle are supplementary angles, so $\angle x = 180° - 46° = 134°$. $\angle y$ and the $46°$ angle are corresponding angles, so $\angle y = 46°$. $\angle x$ and $\angle z$ are corresponding angles, so $\angle z = 134°$.

55. $\dfrac{7}{8} + \dfrac{1}{4} = \dfrac{7}{8} + \dfrac{2}{8} = \dfrac{9}{8}$ or $1\dfrac{1}{8}$

57. $\dfrac{7}{8} \cdot \dfrac{1}{4} = \dfrac{7 \cdot 1}{8 \cdot 4} = \dfrac{7}{32}$

59. $3\dfrac{1}{3} - 2\dfrac{1}{2} = \dfrac{10}{3} - \dfrac{5}{2} = \dfrac{20}{6} - \dfrac{15}{6} = \dfrac{5}{6}$

61. $3\dfrac{1}{3} \div 2\dfrac{1}{2} = \dfrac{10}{3} \div \dfrac{5}{2}$
$= \dfrac{10}{3} \cdot \dfrac{2}{5}$
$= \dfrac{10 \cdot 2}{3 \cdot 5}$
$= \dfrac{20}{15}$
$= \dfrac{4}{3}$ or $1\dfrac{1}{3}$

63. $\angle a$ and the $60°$ angle are alternate interior angles, so $\angle a = 60°$.
$\angle a$, $\angle b$, and the $70°$ angle form a straight angle, so
$\angle b = 180° - 70° - \angle a$
$= 180° - 70° - 60°$
$= 50°$.
$\angle c$ and the angle that is $\angle a$ and $\angle b$ together are alternate interior angles, so
$\angle c = 60° + 50° = 110°$.
$\angle c$ and $\angle d$ are adjacent angles, so
$\angle d = 180° - 110° = 70°$.
$\angle e$ and the $60°$ angle are adjacent angles, so
$\angle e = 180° - 60° = 120°$.

65. $x + x = 90°$
$2x = 90°$
$x = 45°$

67. No; answers may vary.

Section 8.2

Practice Problems

1. $5 \text{ ft} = \dfrac{5 \text{ ft}}{1} \cdot \dfrac{12 \text{ in.}}{1 \text{ ft}}$
$= 5 \cdot 12 \text{ in.}$
$= 60 \text{ in.}$

2. $7 \text{ yd} = \dfrac{7 \text{ yd}}{1} \cdot \dfrac{3 \text{ ft}}{1 \text{ yd}}$
$= 7 \cdot 3 \text{ ft}$
$= 21 \text{ ft}$

3. $\begin{array}{r} 5 \\ 12\overline{)\,68} \\ -60 \\ \hline 8 \end{array}$

$68 \text{ in.} = 5 \text{ ft } 8 \text{ in.}$

4.
$$5 \text{ yd} = \frac{5 \text{ yd}}{1} \cdot \frac{3 \text{ ft}}{1 \text{ yd}} = 15 \text{ ft}$$
$$5 \text{ yd } 2 \text{ ft} = 15 \text{ ft} + 2 \text{ ft} = 17 \text{ ft}$$

5.
$$\begin{array}{r} 4 \text{ ft } 8 \text{ in.} \\ + 8 \text{ ft } 11 \text{ in.} \\ \hline 12 \text{ ft } 19 \text{ in.} = 12 \text{ ft} + 1 \text{ ft } 7 \text{ in.} \\ = 13 \text{ ft } 7 \text{ in.} \end{array}$$

6.
$$\begin{array}{r} 4 \text{ ft } 7 \text{ in.} \\ \times \quad 4 \\ \hline 16 \text{ ft } 28 \text{ in.} = 16 \text{ ft} + 2 \text{ ft } 4 \text{ in.} \\ = 18 \text{ ft } 4 \text{ in.} \end{array}$$

7.
$$\begin{array}{r} 9 \text{ ft } 3 \text{ in.} \\ 2{\overline{\smash{)}\,18 \text{ ft } 6 \text{ in.}}} \\ \underline{-18 \text{ ft}} \\ 0 \quad 6 \text{ in.} \\ \underline{-6 \text{ in.}} \\ 0 \end{array}$$

8.
$$\begin{array}{r} 5 \text{ ft } 8 \text{ in.} = \quad 4 \text{ ft } 20 \text{ in.} \\ -1 \text{ ft } 9 \text{ in.} = -1 \text{ ft } \quad 9 \text{ in.} \\ \hline 3 \text{ ft } 11 \text{ in.} \end{array}$$

9. $3.5 \text{ m} = \dfrac{3.5 \text{ m}}{1} \cdot \dfrac{0.001 \text{ km}}{1 \text{ m}}$
$$= 0.0035 \text{ km}$$

10. To convert meters to millimeters, move decimal point 3 places to the right.
2.5 m = 2500 mm

11. 640 m = 0.64 km   or   2.1 km = 2100 m
$$\begin{array}{cc} 2.1 \text{ km} & 2100 \text{ m} \\ -0.64 \text{ km} & -640 \text{ m} \\ \hline 1.46 \text{ km} \text{ or} & 1460 \text{ m} \end{array}$$

12.
$$\begin{array}{r} 18.3 \text{ hm} \\ \times \quad 5 \\ \hline 91.5 \text{ hm} \end{array}$$

13. 0.8 m = 80 cm or 45 cm = 0.45 m
$$\begin{array}{cc} 80 \text{ cm} & 0.80 \text{ m} \\ +45 \text{ cm} & 0.45 \text{ m} \\ \hline 125 \text{ cm} \text{ or} & 1.25 \text{ m} \end{array}$$
The scarf will be 125 cm or 1.25 m long.

Mental Math

1. 12 in. = 1 ft

2. 6 ft. = 2 yd

3. 24 in. = 2 ft

4. 36 in. = 3 ft

5. 36 in. = 1 yd

6. 2 yd = 6 ft = 72 in.

7. No; 30 meters is too long.

8. Yes

9. Yes

10. No; 4 kilometers is much too long.

11. No; 50 kilometers is too long.

12. Yes

Exercise Set 8.2

1. $60 \text{ in.} = 60 \text{ in.} \cdot \dfrac{1 \text{ ft}}{12 \text{ in.}} = \dfrac{60 \text{ ft}}{12} = 5 \text{ ft}$
60 inches is 5 feet.

3. $12 \text{ yd} = 12 \text{ yd} \cdot \dfrac{3 \text{ ft}}{1 \text{ yd}} = 12 \cdot 3 \text{ ft} = 36 \text{ ft}$

5. $42,240 \text{ ft} = 42,240 \text{ ft} \cdot \dfrac{1 \text{ mi}}{5280 \text{ ft}}$
$$= \frac{42,240 \text{ mi}}{5280}$$
$$= 8 \text{ mi}$$
42,240 feet is 8 miles.

7. $102 \text{ in.} = 102 \text{ in.} \cdot \dfrac{1 \text{ ft}}{12 \text{ in.}} = \dfrac{102 \text{ ft}}{12} = 8\dfrac{1}{2} \text{ ft}$

9. $10 \text{ ft} = 10 \text{ ft} \cdot \dfrac{1 \text{ yd}}{3 \text{ ft}} = \dfrac{10 \text{ yd}}{3} = 3\dfrac{1}{3} \text{ yd}$
10 feet is $3\dfrac{1}{3}$ yards.

11. $6.4 \text{ mi} = 6.4 \text{ mi} \cdot \dfrac{5280 \text{ ft}}{1 \text{ mi}}$
$$= 6.4 \cdot 5280 \text{ ft}$$
$$= 33,792 \text{ ft}$$

13. 40 ft ÷ 3 = 13 with remainder 1
40 ft = 13 yd 1 ft

15. 41 in. ÷ 12 = 3 with remainder 5
41 in. = 3 ft 5 in.

17. 10,000 ft ÷ 5280 = 1 with remainder 4720
10,000 ft = 1 mi 4720 ft

19. $5 \text{ ft} = 5 \text{ ft} \cdot \frac{12 \text{ in.}}{1 \text{ ft}} = 60 \text{ in.}$
5 ft 2 in. = 60 in. + 2 in. = 62 in.

21. $5 \text{ yd} = 5 \text{ yd} \cdot \frac{3 \text{ ft}}{1 \text{ yd}} = 15 \text{ ft}$
5 yd 2 ft = 15 ft + 2 ft = 17 ft

23. $2 \text{ yd} = 2 \text{ yd} \cdot \frac{36 \text{ in.}}{1 \text{ yd}} = 72 \text{ in.}$
$1 \text{ ft} = 1 \text{ ft} \cdot \frac{12 \text{ in.}}{1 \text{ ft}} = 12 \text{ in.}$
2 yd 1 ft = 72 in. + 12 in. = 84 in.

25.   5 ft 8 in.
       + 6 ft 7 in.
       ‾‾‾‾‾‾‾‾‾‾‾‾‾
       11 ft 15 in. = 11 ft + 1 ft 3 in. = 12 ft 3 in.

27.   12 yd 2 ft
       + 9 yd 2 ft
       ‾‾‾‾‾‾‾‾‾‾‾
       21 yd 4 ft = 21 yd + 1 yd 1 ft = 22 yd 1 ft

29.   24 ft 8 in.
       − 16 ft 3 in.
       ‾‾‾‾‾‾‾‾‾‾‾
        8 ft 5 in.

31.   16 ft 3 in. =   15 ft 15 in.
       − 10 ft 9 in. = − 10 ft 9 in.
       ‾‾‾‾‾‾‾‾‾‾‾‾   ‾‾‾‾‾‾‾‾‾‾‾‾
                          5 ft 6 in.

33. $\begin{array}{r} 3 \text{ ft } 4 \text{ in.} \\ 2\overline{)\,6 \text{ ft } 8 \text{ in.}} \\ \underline{-6 \text{ ft}} \\ 0 \quad 8 \text{ in.} \\ \underline{-8 \text{ in.}} \\ 0 \end{array}$

35.   12 yd 2 ft
       ×   4
       ‾‾‾‾‾‾‾‾‾‾‾‾
       48 yd 8 ft = 48 yd + 2 yd 2 ft
                  = 50 yd 2 ft

37.   6 ft 10 in.
       + 3 ft 8 in.
       ‾‾‾‾‾‾‾‾‾‾‾‾
        9 ft 18 in. = 9 ft + 1 ft 6 in.
                    = 10 ft 6 in.
The bamboo is 10 ft 6 in. tall.

39.   16 ft 5 in =   15 ft 17 in
       − 2 ft 6 in = − 2 ft 6 in
       ‾‾‾‾‾‾‾‾‾‾‾   ‾‾‾‾‾‾‾‾‾‾‾
                          13 ft 11 in
The hand is 13 ft 11 in longer than the eye is wide.

41.   1 ft 9 in.
       ×   9
       ‾‾‾‾‾‾‾‾‾‾‾
        9 ft 81 in. = 9 ft + 6 ft 9 in.
                    = 15 ft 9 in.
9 stacks would extend 15 ft 9 in. from the wall.

43. $\begin{array}{r} 3 \text{ ft } 1 \text{ in.} \\ 3\overline{)\,9 \text{ ft } 3 \text{ in.}} \\ \underline{-9 \text{ ft}} \\ 0 \quad 3 \text{ in.} \\ \underline{-3 \text{ in.}} \\ 0 \end{array}$

Each cut piece will be 3 ft 1 in. long.

45. Perimeter = 24 ft 9 in. + 18 ft 6 in. + 24 ft 9 in. + 18 ft 6 in.
            = 84 ft 30 in.
            = 84 ft + 2 ft 6 in.
            = 86 ft 6 in.
She must purchase 86 ft 6 in. of fencing material.

47. $79 \text{ ft} = 79 \text{ ft} \cdot \frac{1 \text{ yd}}{3 \text{ ft}} = \frac{79}{3} \text{ yd}$
$\frac{79}{3} \cdot 4 = \frac{316}{3} = 105\frac{1}{3}$
4 trucks are $105\frac{1}{3}$ yd long.

49. To convert meters to centimeters, move the decimal 2 places to the right.
40 m = 4000 cm

51. To convert millimeters to centimeters, move the decimal 1 place to the right.
40 mm = 4.0 cm = 4 cm

53. To convert meters to kilometers, move the decimal 3 places to the left.
300 m = 0.300 km = 0.3 km

55. To convert millimeters to meters, move the decimal 3 places to the left.
1400 mm = 1.4 m

57. To convert centimeters to meters, move the decimal 2 places to the left.
1500 cm = 15 m

59. To convert centimeters to millimeters, move the decimal 1 place to the right.
8.3 cm = 83 mm

61. To convert millimeters to decimeters, move the decimal 2 places to the left.
20.1 mm = 0.201 dm

63. To convert meters to millimeters, move the decimal 3 places to the right.
0.04 m = 0040. mm = 40 mm

65.
$$\begin{array}{r} 8.60 \text{ m} \\ + 0.34 \text{ m} \\ \hline 8.94 \text{ m} \end{array}$$

67.
$$\begin{array}{rcl} 2.9 \text{ m} &=& 2.90 \text{ m} \\ + 40.0 \text{ mm} &=& 0.04 \text{ m} \\ \hline && 2.94 \text{ m or } 2940 \text{ mm} \end{array}$$

69.
$$\begin{array}{rcl} 24.8 \text{ mm} &=& 2.48 \text{ cm} \\ - 1.19 \text{ cm} &=& - 1.19 \text{ cm} \\ \hline && 1.29 \text{ cm or } 12.9 \text{ mm} \end{array}$$

71.
$$\begin{array}{rcl} 15 \text{ km} &=& 15.000 \text{ km} \\ - 2360 \text{ m} &=& - 2.360 \text{ km} \\ \hline && 12.640 \text{ km or } 12,640 \text{ m} \end{array}$$

73.
$$\begin{array}{r} 18.3 \text{ m} \\ \times \quad 3 \\ \hline 5.49 \text{ m} \end{array}$$

75.
$$\begin{array}{r} 1.55 \\ 4)\overline{6.2} \\ \underline{-4} \\ 2.2 \\ \underline{-2\,0} \\ 20 \\ \underline{-20} \\ 0 \end{array}$$
6.2 km ÷ 4 = 1.55 km

77. 3.4 m + 5.8 m − 8 cm
= 3.4 m + 5.8 m − 0.08 m
= 9.12 m
The tied ropes are 9.12 m long.

79. 80 mm − 5.33 cm
= 80 mm − 53.3 mm
= 26.7 mm
The ice must be 26.7 mm thicker.

81. 25(1 m + 65 cm) = 25(100 cm + 65 cm)
= 25(165 cm)
= 4125 cm or 41.25 m
4125 cm or 41.25 m of wood must be ordered.

83.
$$\begin{array}{r} 3.35 \\ 20)\overline{67.00} \\ \underline{-60} \\ 70 \\ \underline{-60} \\ 100 \\ \underline{-100} \\ 0 \end{array}$$
67 m ÷ 20 = 3.35 m
Each piece will be 3.35 m long.

85. 5.988 km + 21 m = 5988 m + 21 m
= 6009 m or 6.009 km
The elevation is 6009 m or 6.009 km.

87. 3.429 m ÷ 22.86 cm = 3.429 m ÷ 0.2286 m
$0.2286)\overline{3.429}$
Move the decimal points 4 places.

$$\begin{array}{r} 15 \\ 2286.\overline{)\ 34290.} \\ -2286 \\ \hline 11430 \\ -11430 \\ \hline 0 \end{array}$$

15 tiles are needed.

89. $0.86 = 86\%$

91. $\dfrac{13}{100} = 13\%$

93. $\dfrac{1}{4} = \dfrac{25}{100} = 25\%$

95. Answers may vary.

97. A square has 4 equal sides.

$$\begin{array}{r} 6.575 \\ 4\overline{)\ 26.300} \\ -24 \\ \hline 2\,3 \\ -2\,0 \\ \hline 30 \\ -28 \\ \hline 20 \\ -20 \\ \hline 0 \end{array}$$

Each side will be 6.575 m long.

Section 8.3

Practice Problems

1. Perimeter
   $= 60 \text{ feet} + 60 \text{ feet} + 80 \text{ feet} + 80 \text{ feet}$
   $= 280 \text{ feet}$

2. $P = 2l + 2w$
   $= 2 \cdot 22 \text{ centimeters} + 2 \cdot 10 \text{ centimeters}$
   $= 44 \text{ centimeters} + 20 \text{ centimeters}$
   $= 64 \text{ centimeters}$

3. $P = 4s = 4 \cdot 50 \text{ yards} = 200 \text{ yards}$

4. $P = a + b + c = 5 \text{ cm} + 9 \text{ cm} + 7 \text{ cm} = 21 \text{ cm}$

5. Perimeter $= 3 \text{ km} + 7 \text{ km} + 3 \text{ km} + 4 \text{ km}$
   $= 17 \text{ km}$

6. There are two sides of the room that are unknown. One side is 20 m – 15 m = 5 m, and the other side is 26 m – 7 m = 19 m. The perimeter of the room is
   5 m + 19 m + 15 m + 26 m + 20 m + 7 m = 92 m.

7. First find the perimeter of the room.
   $P = 2l + 2w$
   $= 2 \cdot 60 \text{ feet} + 2 \cdot 120 \text{ feet}$
   $= 120 \text{ feet} + 240 \text{ feet}$
   $= 360 \text{ feet}$
   The cost for the fencing is
   cost $= 1.90 \cdot 360 = 684$
   The cost of the fencing is $684.

8. $C = \pi d = \pi \cdot 20 \text{ yards} = 20\pi \text{ yards}$
   If we use 3.14 as an approximation of π, then the circumference is approximately
   20 yards $\cdot$ 3.14 = 62.8 yards.

Exercise Set 8.3

1. $P = 2l + 2w$
   $= 2 \cdot 17 \text{ feet} + 2 \cdot 15 \text{ feet}$
   $= 34 \text{ feet} + 30 \text{ feet}$
   $= 64 \text{ feet}$

3. $P = 4s = 4(9 \text{ centimeters}) = 36 \text{ centimeters}$

5. $P = a + b + c$
   $= 5 \text{ inches} + 7 \text{ inches} + 9 \text{ inches}$
   $= 21 \text{ inches}$

7. $P = 2l + 2w$
$= 2(35 \text{ centimeters}) + 2(25 \text{ centimeters})$
$= 70 \text{ centimeters} + 50 \text{ centimeters}$
$= 120 \text{ centimeters}$

9. $P = 10 \text{ feet} + 8 \text{ feet} + 8 \text{ feet} + 15 \text{ feet} + 7 \text{ feet}$
$= 48 \text{ feet}$

11. $P = 12 \text{ inches} + 3 \text{ inches} + 15 \text{ inches} + 24 \text{ inches} + 12 \text{ inches}$
$= 66 \text{ inches}$

13. $P = 5 \text{ feet} + 3 \text{ feet} + 2 \text{ feet} + 7 \text{ feet} + 4 \text{ feet}$
$= 21 \text{ feet}$

15. $P = 4s = 4(15 \text{ feet}) = 60 \text{ feet}$

17. $P = 2l + 2w$
$= 2(120 \text{ yards}) + 2(53 \text{ yards})$
$= 240 \text{ yards} + 106 \text{ yards}$
$= 346 \text{ yards}$

19. $P = 2l + 2w$
$= 2(8 \text{ feet}) + 2(3 \text{ feet})$
$= 16 \text{ feet} + 6 \text{ feet}$
$= 22 \text{ feet}$

21. Since 22 feet of stripping is needed,
cost $= \$3(22) = \$66$.

23. $P = 6(6 \text{ inches}) = 36 \text{ inches}$

25. $P = 4s = 4(7 \text{ inches}) = 28 \text{ inches}$

27. First find the perimeter of the room.
$P = 2l + 2w$
$= 2(6 \text{ feet}) + 2(8 \text{ feet})$
$= 12 \text{ feet} + 16 \text{ feet}$
$= 28 \text{ feet}$
The cost of the wallpaper is
$c = 0.86(28) = \$24.08$.

29. The missing lengths are:
$28 \text{ meters} - 20 \text{ meters} = 8 \text{ meters}$
$20 \text{ meters} - 17 \text{ meters} = 3 \text{ meters}$
$P = 8 \text{ meters} + 3 \text{ meters} + 20 \text{ meters} + 20 \text{ meters} + 28 \text{ meters} + 17 \text{ meters}$
$= 96 \text{ meters}$

31. The missing length is: $3 \text{ feet} + 6 \text{ feet} + 4 \text{ feet} = 13 \text{ feet}$
$P = 13 \text{ feet} + 15 \text{ feet} + 3 \text{ feet} + 5 \text{ feet} + 6 \text{ feet} + 5 \text{ feet} + 4 \text{ feet} + 15 \text{ feet}$
$= 66 \text{ feet}$

33. The missing lengths are:
12 miles + 10 miles = 22 miles
8 miles + 34 miles = 42 miles
$P = 12$ miles $+ 34$ miles $+ 10$ miles $+ 8$ miles $+ 22$ miles $+ 42$ miles
$= 128$ miles

35. $C = \pi d$
$= \pi 17$ centimeters
$\approx 3.14 \cdot 17$ centimeters
$= 53.38$ centimeters

37. $C = 2\pi r$
$= 2\pi \cdot 8$ miles
$= 16\pi$ miles
$\approx 16 \cdot 3.14$ miles
$= 50.24$ miles

39. $C = \pi d$
$= \pi \cdot 26$ meters
$= 26\pi$ meters
$\approx 26 \cdot 3.14$ meters
$= 81.64$ meters

41. $C = 2\pi r$
$= 2\pi \cdot 5$ feet
$= 10\pi$ feet
$\approx 10 \cdot \dfrac{22}{7}$ feet
$= \dfrac{220}{7}$ feet
$= 31\dfrac{3}{7}$ feet

43. $C = \pi d$
$= \pi \cdot 4000$ feet
$= 4000\pi$ feet
$\approx 4000 \cdot 3.14$ feet
$= 12,560$ feet

45. $5 + 6 \cdot 3 = 5 + 18 = 23$

47. $(20 - 16) \div 4 = 4 \div 4 = 1$

49. $(18 + 8) - (12 + 4) = 26 - 16 = 10$

51. $(72 \div 2) \cdot 6 = 36 \cdot 6 = 216$

57. $P = 2L + 2W$
$30 = 2 \cdot 9 + 2W$
$30 = 18 + 2W$
$12 = 2W$
$6 = W$
The width of the rectangle is 6 feet.

59. Perimeter = add the 3 sides of the square to half of the circumference of the circular part.
$P = 6 + 6 + 6 + \dfrac{1}{2}(2 \cdot 3.14 \cdot 3)$
$= 18 + \dfrac{1}{2}(18.84)$
$= 18 + 9.42$
≈ 27.4 meters

53. a. Circumference of the smaller circle:
$C = 2\pi r$
$= 2\pi \cdot 10$ meters
$= 20\pi$ meters
$\approx 20 \cdot 3.14$ meters
$= 62.8$ meters
Circumference of the larger circle:
$C = 2\pi r$
$= 2\pi \cdot 20$ meters
$= 40\pi$ meters
$\approx 40 \cdot 3.14$ meters
$= 125.6$ meters

b. Yes, the circumference is doubled.

55. The perimeter of the skating rink is equal to the circumference of a circle with radius 5 m plus two sides of a rectangle, each of length 22 m.
Perimeter $= 2\pi \cdot 5$ m $+ 2 \cdot 22$ m
$= 10\pi$ m $+ 44$ m
$\approx 10 \cdot 3.14$ m $+ 44$ m
$= 75.4$ m

Section 8.4

Practice Problems

1. $A = \dfrac{1}{2}bh$
$= \dfrac{1}{2} \cdot 8$ in. $\cdot 6\dfrac{1}{4}$ in.
$= \dfrac{1}{2} \cdot \dfrac{8}{1} \cdot \dfrac{25}{4}$ square inches
$= 25$ square inches

2. $A = \dfrac{1}{2}(b + B)h$

$= \dfrac{1}{2} \cdot (4 \text{ yd} + 10 \text{ yd}) \cdot 4.1 \text{ yd}$

$= \dfrac{1}{2} \cdot 14 \text{ yd} \cdot 4.1 \text{ yd}$

$= 28.7 \text{ square yards}$

3. Split the figure into two rectangles, and find the sum of the areas of the rectangles.

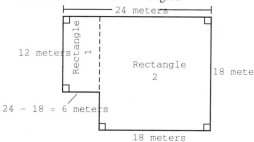

The area of rectangle 1
$= (6 \text{ meters})(12 \text{ meters})$
$= 72 \text{ square meters}$

The area of rectangle 2
$= (18 \text{ meters})(18 \text{ meters})$
$= 324 \text{ square meters}$

The area of the figure
$= 324 \text{ square meters} + 72 \text{ square meters}$
$= 396 \text{ square meters}$

4. $A = \pi r^2$

$= \pi \cdot (7 \text{ centimeters})^2$
$= 49\pi \text{ square centimeters}$
$\approx 49 \cdot 3.14 \text{ square centimeters}$
$= 153.86 \text{ square centimeters}$

5.

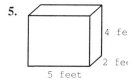

4 fe

2 fee

5 feet

$V = lwh$
$= 5 \text{ feet} \cdot 2 \text{ feet} \cdot 4 \text{ feet}$
$= 40 \text{ cubic feet}$

6. $\frac{1}{2}$ centimeter

$V = \dfrac{4}{3}\pi r^3$

$= \dfrac{4}{3}\pi \cdot \left(\dfrac{1}{2} \text{ centimeter}\right)^3$

$= \dfrac{1}{8} \cdot \dfrac{4}{3}\pi \text{ cubic centimeters}$

$= \dfrac{1}{6}\pi \text{ cubic centimeters}$

$\approx \dfrac{1}{6} \cdot \dfrac{22}{7} \text{ cubic centimeters}$

$= \dfrac{11}{21} \text{ cubic centimeters}$

7. $V = \pi r^2 h$

$= \pi \cdot (5 \text{ inches})^2 \cdot 7 \text{ inches}$
$= 25 \cdot 7 \cdot \pi \text{ cubic inches}$
$= 175\pi \text{ cubic inches}$
$\approx 175 \cdot 3.14 \text{ cubic inches}$
$= 549.5 \text{ cubic inches}$

8. $V = \dfrac{1}{3}s^2 h$

$= \dfrac{1}{3} \cdot (3 \text{ meters})^2 \cdot 5.1 \text{ meters}$

$= \dfrac{1}{3} \cdot 9 \cdot 5.1 \text{ cubic meters}$

$= 15.3 \text{ cubic meters}$

Exercise Set 8.4

1. $A = lw$

$= 3.5 \text{ meters} \cdot 2 \text{ meters}$
$= 7 \text{ square meters}$

3. $A = \dfrac{1}{2}bh$

$= \dfrac{1}{2} \cdot 6\dfrac{1}{2} \text{ yards} \cdot 3 \text{ yards}$

$= \dfrac{1}{2} \cdot \dfrac{13}{2} \cdot \dfrac{3}{1} \text{ square yards}$

$= \dfrac{39}{4} \text{ or } 9\dfrac{3}{4} \text{ square yards}$

5. $A = \dfrac{1}{2}bh$

$\quad = \dfrac{1}{2} \cdot 6 \text{ yards} \cdot 5 \text{ yards}$

$\quad = \dfrac{1}{2} \cdot 6 \cdot 5 \text{ square yards}$

$\quad = 15 \text{ square yards}$

7. $r = \dfrac{d}{2}$

$\quad = \dfrac{3 \text{ inches}}{2}$

$\quad = 1.5 \text{ inches}$

$A = \pi r^2$

$\quad = \pi(1.5 \text{ inches})^2$

$\quad = 2.25\pi \text{ square inches}$

$\quad \approx 2.25(3.14) \text{ square inches}$

$\quad = 7.065 \text{ square inches}$

9. $A = bh$

$\quad = 7 \text{ feet} \cdot 5.25 \text{ feet}$

$\quad = 36.75 \text{ square feet}$

11. $A = \dfrac{1}{2}(b + B)h$

$\quad = \dfrac{1}{2} \cdot (5 \text{ meters} + 9 \text{ meters}) \cdot 4 \text{ meters}$

$\quad = \dfrac{1}{2} \cdot 14 \cdot 4 \text{ square meters}$

$\quad = 28 \text{ square meters}$

13. $A = \dfrac{1}{2}(b + B)h$

$\quad = \dfrac{1}{2} \cdot (4 \text{ yards} + 7 \text{ yards}) \cdot 4 \text{ yards}$

$\quad = \dfrac{1}{2} \cdot 11 \text{ yards} \cdot 4 \text{ yards}$

$\quad = \dfrac{1}{2} \cdot 11 \cdot 4 \text{ square yards}$

$\quad = 22 \text{ square yards}$

15. $A = bh$

$\quad = 7 \text{ feet} \cdot 5\dfrac{1}{4} \text{ feet}$

$\quad = 7 \cdot \dfrac{21}{4} \text{ square feet}$

$\quad = \dfrac{147}{4} \text{ or } 36\dfrac{3}{4} \text{ square feet}$

17. $A = bh$

$\quad = 5 \text{ inches} \cdot 4\dfrac{1}{2} \text{ inches}$

$\quad = 5 \cdot \dfrac{9}{2} \text{ square inches}$

$\quad = \dfrac{45}{2} \text{ or } 22\dfrac{1}{2} \text{ square inches}$

19. Area of rectangle $= bh$

$\qquad\qquad\qquad = 7 \text{ centimeters} \cdot 3 \text{ centimeters}$

$\qquad\qquad\qquad = 21 \text{ square centimeters}$

Area of triangle $= \dfrac{1}{2}bh$

$\qquad\qquad = \dfrac{1}{2} \cdot \left(7 - 1\dfrac{1}{2} - 1\dfrac{1}{2}\right) \text{ centimeters} \cdot 2 \text{ centimeters}$

$\qquad\qquad = \dfrac{1}{2} \cdot \left(\dfrac{14}{2} - \dfrac{3}{2} - \dfrac{3}{2}\right) \cdot 2 \text{ square centimeters}$

$\qquad\qquad = \dfrac{1}{2} \cdot \dfrac{8}{2} \cdot 2 \text{ square centimeters}$

$\qquad\qquad = 4 \text{ square centimeters}$

Total area $= 21 \text{ square centimeters} + 4 \text{ square centimeters}$

$\qquad\qquad = 25 \text{ square centimeters}$

21.

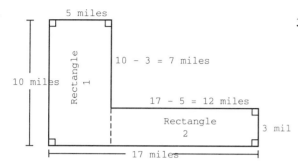

Area of rectangle 1 = bh
$$= 5 \text{ miles} \cdot 10 \text{ miles}$$
$$= 50 \text{ square miles}$$
Area of rectangle 2 = bh
$$= 12 \text{ miles} \cdot 3 \text{ miles}$$
$$= 36 \text{ square miles}$$
Total area = 50 square miles + 36 square miles
$$= 86 \text{ square miles}$$

23. Area of square = s^2
$$= (3 \text{ centimeters})^2$$
$$= 9 \text{ square centimeters}$$
Area of parallelogram = $b \cdot h$
$$= (3 \text{ centimeters})(5 \text{ centimeters})$$
$$= 15 \text{ square centimeters}$$

Total area = 9 square centimeters + 15 square centimeters = 24 square centimeters

25. $A = \pi r^2$
$$= \pi (6 \text{ inches})^2$$
$$= 36\pi \text{ square inches}$$
$$\approx 36 \cdot \frac{22}{7} \text{ square inches}$$
$$\approx 113.1 \text{ square inches}$$

27. $V = lwh$
$$= 6 \text{ inches} \cdot 4 \text{ inches} \cdot 3 \text{ inches}$$
$$= 72 \text{ cubic inches}$$

29. $V = s^3$
$$= (8 \text{ centimeters})^3$$
$$= 512 \text{ cubic centimeters}$$

31. $V = \frac{1}{3}\pi r^2 h$
$$= \frac{1}{3} \cdot \pi \cdot (2 \text{ yards})^2 \cdot (3 \text{ yards})$$
$$= 4\pi \text{ cubic yards}$$
$$\approx 4 \cdot \frac{22}{7} \text{ cubic yards}$$
$$= \frac{88}{7} \text{ or } 12\frac{4}{7} \text{ cubic yards}$$

33. $V = \frac{4}{3}\pi r^3$
$$= \frac{4}{3} \cdot \pi \cdot \left(\frac{10 \text{ inches}}{2}\right)^3$$
$$= \frac{4}{3} \cdot 125 \cdot \pi \text{ cubic inches}$$
$$= \frac{500}{3}\pi \text{ cubic inches}$$
$$\approx \frac{500}{3} \cdot \frac{22}{7} \text{ cubic inches}$$
$$= \frac{11,000}{21} \text{ cubic inches}$$
$$= 523\frac{17}{21} \text{ cubic inches}$$

35. $V = \frac{1}{3}s^2 h$
$$= \frac{1}{3} \cdot (5 \text{ centimeters})^2 \cdot 9 \text{ centimeters}$$
$$= 75 \text{ cubic centimeters}$$

37. $V = s^3$
$$= \left(1\frac{1}{3} \text{ inches}\right)^3$$
$$= \left(\frac{4}{3}\right)^3 \text{ cubic inches}$$
$$= \frac{64}{27} \text{ cubic inches}$$
$$= 2\frac{10}{27} \text{ cubic inches}$$

39. $V = lwh$
$$= 2 \text{ feet} \cdot 1.4 \text{ feet} \cdot 3 \text{ feet}$$
$$= 8.4 \text{ cubic feet}$$

41. $A = lw$
$$= 500 \text{ feet} \cdot 225 \text{ feet}$$
$$= 113,625 \text{ square feet}$$

43. Area of one panel = lw
$$= 6 \text{ feet} \cdot 7 \text{ feet}$$
$$= 42 \text{ square feet}$$
Area of four panels $= 4 \cdot 42$ square feet
$$= 168 \text{ square feet}$$

45. $V = \dfrac{1}{3} s^2 h$
$$= \dfrac{1}{3} \cdot (12 \text{ centimeters})^2 \cdot 20 \text{ centimeters}$$
$$= \dfrac{2880}{3} \text{ cubic centimeters}$$
$$= 960 \text{ cubic centimeters}$$

47. $A = \dfrac{1}{2}(b + B)h$
$$= \dfrac{1}{2} \cdot (90 \text{ feet} + 140 \text{ feet}) \cdot 80 \text{ feet}$$
$$= \dfrac{1}{2} \cdot 230 \cdot 80 \text{ square feet}$$
$$= 9200 \text{ square feet}$$

49. Area of shaded part
$$= \dfrac{1}{2}(b + B)h$$
$$= \dfrac{1}{2} \cdot (25 \text{ feet} + 36 \text{ feet}) \cdot 12 \dfrac{1}{2} \text{ feet}$$
$$= \dfrac{1}{2} \cdot 61 \text{ feet} \cdot \dfrac{25}{2} \text{ feet}$$
$$= \dfrac{1}{2} \cdot \dfrac{61}{1} \cdot \dfrac{25}{2} \text{ square feet}$$
$$= \dfrac{1525}{4} \text{ square feet}$$
$$= 381 \dfrac{1}{4} \text{ square feet}$$
The area of the shaded part to the nearest foot, is 381 square feet.

51. $V = \dfrac{4}{3} \pi r^3$
$$= \dfrac{4}{3} \pi (7 \text{ inches})^3$$
$$= \dfrac{1372}{3} \pi \text{ cubic inches or } 457 \dfrac{1}{3} \pi \text{ cubic inches}$$

53. $V = lwh$
$$= 2 \text{ feet} \cdot 2 \dfrac{1}{2} \text{ feet} \cdot 1 \dfrac{1}{2} \text{ feet}$$
$$= 7 \dfrac{1}{2} \text{ cubic feet}$$

55. $V = \dfrac{1}{3} \pi r^2 h; \ r = \dfrac{1}{2} d$
$$= \dfrac{1}{3} \cdot \dfrac{22}{7} \cdot (2 \text{ feet})^2 \cdot 3 \text{ feet}$$
$$= \dfrac{264}{21} \text{ cubic feet}$$
$$= 12 \dfrac{4}{7} \text{ cubic feet}$$

57. $V = \dfrac{4}{3} \pi r^3$
$$= \dfrac{4}{3} \pi (3 \text{ inches})^3$$
$$= 36\pi \text{ cubic inches}$$
$$= 36(3.14) \text{ cubic inches}$$
$$\approx 113.04 \text{ cubic inches}$$

59. $V = \dfrac{1}{3} s^2 h$
$$= \dfrac{1}{3}(5 \text{ inches})^2 \cdot 1.3 \text{ inches}$$
$$= 10 \dfrac{5}{6} \text{ cubic inches}$$

61. $5^2 = 25$

63. $3^2 = 9$

65. $1^2 + 2^2 = 1 + 4 = 5$

67. $4^2 + 2^2 = 16 + 4 = 20$

69. perimeter.

71. area

73. area

75. perimeter

77. Area of a 12-inch pizza
$$= \pi r^2$$
$$= \pi \left(\frac{12}{2} \text{ inches} \right)^2$$
$$= \pi (6 \text{ inches})^2$$
$$= 36\pi \text{ square inches}$$

Area of two 8-inch pizzas
$$= 2(\pi r^2)$$
$$= 2 \cdot \pi \left(\frac{8}{2} \text{ inches} \right)^2$$
$$= 2\pi (4 \text{ inches})^2$$
$$= 2\pi \cdot 16 \text{ square inches}$$
$$= 32\pi \text{ square inches}$$
The 12-inch pizza is
$$\frac{\$10}{36\pi \text{ square inches}} \approx \$0.08 \text{ per square inch.}$$
The two 8-inch pizzas are $\dfrac{\$9}{32\pi \text{ square inches}} \approx \$0.09$ per square inch.
The 12-inch pizza is the better buy.

79. 8 inches $= \dfrac{8}{12}$ feet $= \dfrac{2}{3}$ feet
$$A = lw$$
$$= 2 \text{ feet} \cdot \frac{2}{3} \text{ feet}$$
$$= \frac{4}{3} \text{ or } 1\frac{1}{3} \text{ square feet}$$
2 feet = 24 inches
$$A = lw$$
$$= 24 \text{ inches} \cdot 8 \text{ inches}$$
$$= 192 \text{ square inches}$$

81. Area of skating rink = area of rectangle + area of circle
$$A = lw + \pi r^2$$
$$= 22 \text{ meters} \cdot 10 \text{ meters} + 3.14 \, (5 \text{ meters})^2$$
$$= 220 \text{ square meters} + 78.5 \text{ square meters}$$
$$= 298.5 \text{ square meters}$$

83. $V = \dfrac{1}{3}s^2 h$
$$= \frac{1}{3} \cdot (230 \text{ meters})^2 \cdot 146.5 \text{ meters}$$
$$\approx 2,583,283 \text{ cubic meters}$$

85. $V = \dfrac{1}{3}s^2 h$
$$= \frac{1}{3} \cdot (344 \text{ meters})^2 \cdot 65.5 \text{ meters}$$
$$\approx 2,583,669 \text{ cubic meters}$$

87. $V = \pi r^2 h$

$\qquad = (3.14)(16.3 \text{ feet})^2 (32 \text{ feet})$

$\qquad \approx 26,695.5 \text{ cubic feetw}$

89. No; answers may vary.

Integrated Review

1. The supplement of a 27° angle is 180° − 27° = 153°. The complement of a 27° angle is 90° − 27° = 63°.   **2.** Since ∠x and the 105° angle are supplementary angles, ∠x = 180° − 105° = 75°. ∠y and the 105° angle are vertical angles, so ∠y = 105°. ∠x and ∠z are vertical angles, so ∠z = 75°.

3. Since ∠x and the 52° angle are supplementary angles, ∠x = 180° − 52° = 128°. ∠y and the 52° angle are corresponding angles, so ∠y = 52°. ∠y and ∠z are supplementary angles, so ∠z = 180° − 52° = 128°.

4. ∠x = 180° − 90° − 38° = 52°

5. $36 \text{ in.} = \dfrac{36 \text{ in.}}{1} \cdot \dfrac{1 \text{ ft}}{12 \text{ in.}} = 3 \text{ ft}$

6. $10,560 \text{ ft} = \dfrac{10,560 \text{ ft}}{1} \cdot \dfrac{1 \text{ mi}}{5280 \text{ ft}} = 2 \text{ mi}$

7. $20 \text{ ft} = \dfrac{20 \text{ ft}}{1} \cdot \dfrac{1 \text{ yd}}{3 \text{ ft}} = \dfrac{20}{3} \text{ yd} = 6\dfrac{2}{3} \text{ yd}$

8. $6 \text{ yd} = \dfrac{6 \text{ yd}}{1} \cdot \dfrac{3 \text{ ft}}{1 \text{ yd}} = 18 \text{ ft}$

9. $2.1 \text{ mi} = \dfrac{2.1 \text{ mi}}{1} \cdot \dfrac{5280 \text{ ft}}{1 \text{ mi}} = 11,088 \text{ ft}$

10. $3.2 \text{ ft} = \dfrac{3.2 \text{ ft}}{1} \cdot \dfrac{12 \text{ in.}}{1 \text{ ft}} = 38.4 \text{ in.}$

11. 30 m = 3000 cm

12. 24 mm = 2.4 cm

13. 2000 mm = 2 m

14. 18 m = 1800 cm

15. 7.2 cm = 72 mm

16. 600 m = 0.6 km

17. $P = 4s = 4 \cdot (5 \text{ meters}) = 20 \text{ meters}$

$A = s^2 = (5 \text{ meters})^2 = 25 \text{ square meters}$

18. $P = a + b + c$

$\qquad = 3 \text{ feet} + 4 \text{ feet} + 5 \text{ feet}$

$\qquad = 12 \text{ feet}$

$A = \dfrac{1}{2} bh$

$\quad = \dfrac{1}{2} \cdot 4 \text{ feet} \cdot 3 \text{ feet}$

$\quad = 6 \text{ square feet}$

19. $C = 2\pi r$

$\qquad = 2 \cdot \pi \cdot (3 \text{ centimeters})$

$\qquad = 6\pi \text{ centimeters}$

$\qquad \approx 6 \cdot 3.14 \text{ centimeters}$

$\qquad = 18.84 \text{ centimeters}$

$A = \pi r^2$

$\qquad = \pi \cdot (3 \text{ centimeters})^2$

$\qquad = 9\pi \text{ square centimeters}$

$\qquad \approx 9 \cdot 3.14 \text{ square centimeters}$

$\qquad = 28.26 \text{ square centimeters}$

20. Perimeter

$\qquad = 11 \text{ miles} + 5 \text{ miles} + 11 \text{ miles} + 5 \text{ miles}$

$\qquad = 32 \text{ miles}$

$A = bh$

$\qquad = 11 \text{ miles} \cdot 4 \text{ miles}$

$\qquad = 44 \text{ square miles}$

21. $P = 2l + 2w$

$\qquad = 2 \cdot 14 \text{ feet} + 2 \cdot 17 \text{ feet}$

$\qquad = 28 \text{ feet} + 34 \text{ feet}$

$\qquad = 62 \text{ feet}$

$A = lw$

$\qquad = 14 \text{ feet} \cdot 17 \text{ feet}$

$\qquad = 238 \text{ square feet}$

22. $V = s^3$

$\qquad = (4 \text{ inches})^3$

$\qquad = 64 \text{ cubic inches}$

23. $V = lwh$

$\quad = 2 \text{ feet} \cdot 3 \text{ feet} \cdot 5.1 \text{ feet}$

$\quad = 30.6 \text{ cubic feet}$

24. $V = \dfrac{1}{3} s^2 h$

$\quad = \dfrac{1}{3} \cdot (10 \text{ centimeters})^2 \cdot 12 \text{ centimeters}$

$\quad = 400 \text{ cubic centimeters}$

25. $V = \dfrac{4}{3} \pi r^3$

$\quad = \dfrac{4}{3} \cdot \pi \cdot \left(\dfrac{16 \text{ miles}}{2} \right)^3$

$\quad = \dfrac{4}{3} \cdot 512 \cdot \pi \text{ cubic miles}$

$\quad = \dfrac{2048}{3} \pi \text{ cubic miles}$

$\quad \approx \dfrac{2048}{3} \cdot \dfrac{22}{7} \text{ cubic miles}$

$\quad = \dfrac{45{,}056}{21} \text{ or } 2145\dfrac{11}{21} \text{ cubic miles}$

Section 8.5

Practice Problems

1. $4500 \text{ lb} = \dfrac{4500 \text{ lb}}{1} \cdot \dfrac{1 \text{ ton}}{2000 \text{ lb}}$

$\quad = \dfrac{4500 \text{ tons}}{2000}$

$\quad = \dfrac{9}{4} \text{ tons}$

$\quad = 2\dfrac{1}{4} \text{ tons}$

2. $56 \text{ oz} = \dfrac{56 \text{ oz}}{1} \cdot \dfrac{1 \text{ lb}}{16 \text{ oz}}$

$\quad = \dfrac{56 \text{ lb}}{16}$

$\quad = \dfrac{7}{2} \text{ lb}$

$\quad = 3\dfrac{1}{2} \text{ lb}$

3.
$$
\begin{array}{r}
8 \text{ tons} \quad 100 \text{ lb} = \quad 7 \text{ tons } 2100 \text{ lb} \\
- 5 \text{ tons } 1200 \text{ lb} = -5 \text{ tons } 1200 \text{ lb} \\
\hline
2 \text{ tons} \quad 900 \text{ lb}
\end{array}
$$

4.
$$
\begin{array}{r}
4 \text{ lb } 11 \text{ oz} \\
\times \qquad 8 \\
\hline
32 \text{ lb } 88 \text{ oz} = 32 \text{ lb} + 5 \text{ lb } 8 \text{ oz} \\
= 37 \text{ lb } 8 \text{ oz}
\end{array}
$$

$$
\begin{array}{r}
5 \\
16{\overline{\smash{\big)}\,88}} \\
\underline{-80} \\
8
\end{array}
$$

5.
$$
\begin{array}{r}
1 \text{ lb } 6 \text{ oz} \\
4{\overline{\smash{\big)}\,5 \text{ lb } 8 \text{ oz}}} \\
\underline{-4} \\
1 = \underline{16 \text{ oz}} \\
24 \text{ oz} \\
\underline{-24} \\
0
\end{array}
$$

6.
$$
\begin{array}{r}
5 \text{ lb } 14 \text{ oz} \\
+ \qquad 6 \text{ oz} \\
\hline
5 \text{ lb } 20 \text{ oz} = 5 \text{ lb} + 1 \text{ lb } 4 \text{ oz} \\
= 6 \text{ lb } 4 \text{ oz}
\end{array}
$$

7. $3.41 \text{ g} = \dfrac{3.41 \text{ g}}{1} \cdot \dfrac{1000 \text{ mg}}{1 \text{ g}}$

$\quad = 3140 \text{ mg}$

8. To convert centigrams to grams, move the decimal point 2 places to the left.

$\quad 56.2 \text{ cg} = \dfrac{56.2 \text{ cg}}{1} \cdot \dfrac{1 \text{ g}}{100 \text{ cg}}$

$\quad\quad = 0.562 \text{ g}$

9. $3.1 \text{ dg} = 0.31 \text{ g}$ or $2.5 \text{ g} = 25 \text{ dg}$

$$
\begin{array}{cc}
\begin{array}{r}
2.50 \text{ g} \\
- 0.31 \text{ g} \\
\hline
2.19 \text{ g}
\end{array}
&
\begin{array}{r}
25.0 \text{ dg} \\
- 3.1 \text{ dg} \\
\hline
21.9 \text{ dg}
\end{array}
\end{array}
$$

$\quad\quad\quad\quad\quad\quad \text{or}$

10.
$$
\begin{array}{r}
12.6 \text{ kg} \\
\times \ 4 \\
\hline
50.4 \text{ kg}
\end{array}
$$

11.
$$
\begin{array}{r}
22.9 \approx 23 \\
24{\overline{\smash{\big)}\,550.0}} \\
\underline{-48} \\
70 \\
\underline{-48} \\
22\,0 \\
\underline{-216} \\
4
\end{array}
$$

Each bag weighs approximately 23 kg.

Mental Math

1. 16 ounces = 1 lb

2. 32 ounces = 2 lb

3. 1 ton = 2000 lb

4. 2 tons = 4000 lb

5. 1 pound = 16 oz

6. 6 pounds = 96 oz

7. 2000 pounds = 1 ton

8. 4000 pounds = 2 tons

9. No

10. No

11. Yes

12. Yes

13. No

14. No

Exercise Set 8.5

1. $2\text{ lb} = 2\text{ lb}\cdot\dfrac{16\text{ oz}}{1\text{ lb}} = 2\cdot16\text{ oz} = 32\text{ oz}$

3. $5\text{ tons} = 5\text{ tons}\cdot\dfrac{2000\text{ lb}}{1\text{ ton}}$
$= 5\cdot2000\text{ lb}$
$= 10,000\text{ lb}$

5. $12,000\text{ lb} = 12,000\text{ lb}\cdot\dfrac{1\text{ ton}}{2000\text{ lb}}$
$= \dfrac{12,000\text{ tons}}{2000}$
$= 6\text{ tons}$

7. $60\text{ oz} = 60\text{ oz}\cdot\dfrac{1\text{ lb}}{16\text{ oz}}$
$= \dfrac{60\text{ lb}}{16}$
$= \dfrac{15}{4}\text{ lb}$
$= 3\dfrac{3}{4}\text{ lb}$

9. $3500\text{ lb} = 3500\text{ lb}\cdot\dfrac{1\text{ ton}}{2000\text{ lb}}$
$= \dfrac{3500\text{ tons}}{2000}$
$= \dfrac{7}{4}\text{ tons}$
$= 1\dfrac{3}{4}\text{ tons}$

11. $16.25\text{ lb} = 16.25\text{ lb}\cdot\dfrac{16\text{ oz}}{1\text{ lb}}$
$= 16.25\cdot16\text{ oz}$
$= 260\text{ oz}$

13. $4.9\text{ tons} = 4.9\text{ tons}\cdot\dfrac{2000\text{ lb}}{1\text{ ton}}$
$= 4.9\cdot2000\text{ lb}$
$= 9800\text{ lb}$

15. $4\dfrac{3}{4}\text{ lb} = 4\dfrac{3}{4}\text{ lb}\cdot\dfrac{16\text{ oz}}{1\text{ lb}}$
$= \dfrac{19}{4}\cdot16\text{ oz}$
$= 19\cdot4\text{ oz}$
$= 76\text{ oz}$

17. $2950\text{ lb} = 2950\text{ lb}\cdot\dfrac{1\text{ ton}}{2000\text{ lb}}$
$= \dfrac{2950\text{ tons}}{2000}$
$= 1.475\text{ tons}$
$\approx 1.5\text{ tons}$

19.   34 lb 12 oz
  + 18 lb 14 oz
  52 lb 26 oz = 52 lb + 1 lb 10 oz
       = 53 lb 10 oz

21.   6 tons 1540 lb
  + 2 tons 850 lb
  8 tons 2390 lb = 8 tons + 1 ton 390 lb
       = 9 tons 390 lb

23.   5 tons 1050 lb
  − 2 tons 875 lb
  3 tons 175 lb

25.   12 lb 4 oz = 11 lb 20 oz
  − 3 lb 9 oz = − 3 lb 9 oz
       8 lb 11 oz

27.
$$\begin{array}{r} 5 \text{ lb } 3 \text{ oz} \\ \times \quad\quad 6 \\ \hline 30 \text{ lb } 18 \text{ oz} = 30 \text{ lb} + 1 \text{ lb } 2 \text{ oz} = 31 \text{ lb } 2 \text{ oz} \end{array}$$

29.
$$\begin{array}{r} 1 \text{ ton} \quad 700 \text{ lb} \\ 5 \overline{) \ 6 \text{ tons } 1500 \text{ lb}} \\ \underline{-5 \text{ tons}} \\ 1 \text{ ton} = 2000 \text{ lb} \\ 3500 \text{ lb} \\ \underline{- \ 3500 \text{ lb}} \\ 0 \end{array}$$

31.
$$\begin{array}{r} 1 \text{ lb } 10 \text{ oz} \\ + \ 3 \text{ lb } 14 \text{ oz} \\ \hline 4 \text{ lb } 24 \text{ oz} = 4 \text{ lb} + 1 \text{ lb } 8 \text{ oz} = 5 \text{ lb } 8 \text{ oz} \end{array}$$
She has 5 lb 8 oz of rice.

33.
$$\begin{array}{rcr} 64 \text{ lb } \ 8 \text{ oz} = & & 63 \text{ lb } 24 \text{ oz} \\ - \ 28 \text{ lb } 10 \text{ oz} = & & - \ 28 \text{ lb } 10 \text{ oz} \\ \hline & & 35 \text{ lb } 14 \text{ oz} \end{array}$$
His zucchini was 35 lb 14 oz below the record.

35. 4 boxes · 10 packages = 40 total packages
$$\begin{array}{r} 3 \text{ lb } \quad 4 \text{ oz} \\ \times \quad\quad 40 \\ \hline 120 \text{ lb } 160 \text{ oz} = 120 \text{ lb} + 10 \text{ lb} = 130 \text{ lb} \end{array}$$
4 boxes weigh 130 lb.

37.
$$\begin{array}{rcr} 55 \text{ lb } 4 \text{ oz} = & & 54 \text{ lb } 20 \text{ oz} \\ - \ 2 \text{ lb } 8 \text{ oz} = & & - \ 2 \text{ lb } \ 8 \text{ oz} \\ \hline & & 52 \text{ lb } 12 \text{ oz} \end{array}$$

$$\begin{array}{r} 52 \text{ lb } 12 \text{ oz} \\ \times \quad\quad 4 \\ \hline 208 \text{ lb } 48 \text{ oz} = 208 \text{ lb} + 3 \text{ lb} = 211 \text{ lb} \end{array}$$
There are 211 lb of pineapple in 4 boxes.

39. $6\frac{3}{4} \text{ oz} \cdot 12 = \frac{27}{4} \text{ oz} \cdot 12 = 81 \text{ oz}$

$81 \text{ oz} \cdot \frac{1 \text{ lb}}{16 \text{ oz}} = 5 \text{ lb } 1 \text{ oz}$

A dozen bags will weigh 5 lb 1 oz.

41. To convert grams to kilograms, move the decimal 3 places to the left.
500 g = 0.5 kg

43. To convert grams to milligrams, move the decimal 3 places to the right.
4 g = 4000 mg

45. To convert kilograms to grams, move the decimal 3 places to the right.
25 kg = 25,000 g

47. To convert milligrams to grams, move the decimal 3 places to the left.
48 mg = 0.048 g

49. To convert grams to kilograms, move the decimal 3 places to the left.
6.3 g = 0.0063 kg

51. To convert grams to milligrams, move the decimal 3 places to the right.
15.14 g = 15,140 mg

53. To convert kilograms to grams, move the decimal 3 places to the right.
4.01 kg = 4010 g

55.
$$\begin{array}{r} 3.8 \text{ mg} \\ + \ 9.7 \text{ mg} \\ \hline 13.5 \text{ mg} \end{array}$$

57. 205 mg = 0.205 g or 5.61 g = 5610 mg
$$\begin{array}{rclcr} 0.205 \text{ g} & = & & & 205 \text{ mg} \\ + \ 5.610 \text{ g} & = & & + & 5610 \text{ mg} \\ \hline 5.815 \text{ g} & \text{or} & & & 5815 \text{ mg} \end{array}$$

59. 9 g = 9000 mg or 7150 mg = 7.15 g
$$\begin{array}{rclcr} 9000 \text{ mg} & = & & & 9.00 \text{ g} \\ -7150 \text{ mg} & = & & - & 7.15 \text{ g} \\ \hline 1850 \text{ mg} & \text{or} & & & 1.85 \text{ g} \end{array}$$

61. 1.61 kg = 1610 g or 250 g = 0.25 kg
$$\begin{array}{rcr} 1610 \text{ g} & & 1.61 \text{ kg} \\ -250 \text{ g} & & -0.25 \text{ kg} \\ \hline 1360 \text{ g} & & 1.36 \text{ kg} \end{array}$$

63.
$$\begin{array}{r} 5.2 \text{ kg} \\ \times \ 2.6 \\ \hline 312 \\ 1040 \\ \hline 13.52 \text{ kg} \end{array}$$

65.
$$\begin{array}{r} 2.125 \text{ kg} \\ 8 \overline{) \ 17.000 \text{ kg}} \\ \underline{-16} \\ 1 \ 0 \\ \underline{- \ 8} \\ 20 \\ \underline{-16} \\ 40 \\ \underline{-40} \\ 0 \end{array}$$

67.   336 g
          × 24
          ──────
          1344
          6720
          ──────
          8064 g = 8.064 kg
24 cans weigh 8.064 kg.

69. 0.09 g − 60 mg = 90 mg − 60 mg
                      = 30 mg
The extra-strength tablet contains 30 mg more medication.

71. 0.6 g − 350 mg = 600 mg − 350 mg
                      = 250 mg
He can have 250 mg more sodium.

73. 3 · 16 · 3 mg = 144 mg
3 cartons contain 144 mg of perservatives.

75. 6.432 kg − 12 · 26 g = 6.432 kg − 312 g
                           = 6.432 kg − 0.312 kg
                           = 6.12 kg

There is 6.12 kg of oatmeal in the carton.

77. 0.3 kg + 0.15 kg + 400 g
     = 0.3 kg + 0.15 kg + 0.4 kg
     = 0.85 kg or 850 g
The package weighs 0.85 kg or 850 g.

79.   198 g
           12
          ──────
          396
          1980
          ──────
          2376 g = 2.376 kg
A dozen bags weigh about 2.38 kg.

81. $\dfrac{1}{4} = \dfrac{1 \cdot 25}{4 \cdot 25} = \dfrac{25}{100} = 0.25$

83. $\dfrac{4}{25} = \dfrac{4 \cdot 4}{25 \cdot 4} = \dfrac{16}{100} = 0.16$

85. $\dfrac{7}{8} = \dfrac{7 \cdot 125}{8 \cdot 125} = \dfrac{875}{1000} = 0.875$

87. Answers may vary.

Section 8.6

Practice Problems

1. 43 pints $= \dfrac{43 \text{ pints}}{1} \cdot \dfrac{1 \text{ qt}}{2 \text{ pints}}$
            $= \dfrac{43}{2}$ qt
            $= 21\dfrac{1}{2}$ qt

2. 26qt $= \dfrac{26 \text{ qt}}{1} \cdot \dfrac{4 \text{ c}}{1 \text{ qt}}$
         $= 104$ c

3.   1 gal 1 qt   0 gal 5 qt
        −   2 qt   −   2 qt
        ──────────   ──────────
                                   3 qt

4.   2 gal 3 qt
        ×   2
        ──────────────
        4 gal 6 qt = 4 gal + 1 gal 2 qt
                   = 5 gal 2 qt

5.   3 gal   1 pt
        2) 6 gal 1 qt
           −6
           ──────
            0   1 qt = 2 pt
                        − 2 pt
                        ──────
                             0

6.   15 gal 3 qt
        + 4 gal 3 qt
        ────────────────
        19 gal 6 qt = 19 gal + 1 gal 2 qt
                    = 20 gal 2 qt

7. 2100 ml $= \dfrac{2100 \text{ ml}}{1} \cdot \dfrac{1 \text{ L}}{1000 \text{ ml}}$
         $= \dfrac{2100}{1000}$ L
         $= 2.1$ L

8. To convert decaliters to liters, move the decimal one place to the right.
2.13 dal = 21.3 L

9. 1250 ml = 1.25 L or 2.9 L = 2900 ml

        1250 ml   1.25 L
     + 2900 ml   + 2.90 L
     ──────────   ──────────
        4150 ml   4.15 L

10.
$$\begin{array}{r} 11.3 \text{ L} \\ 13\overline{)146.9 \text{ L}} \\ \underline{-13} \\ 16 \\ \underline{-13} \\ 39 \\ \underline{-39} \\ 0 \end{array}$$

11.
$$\begin{array}{r} 28.6 \\ \times\ \ 85 \\ \hline 1430 \\ 22880 \\ \hline 24310 \end{array}$$
2431 L can be pumped in 85 minutes.

Mental Math

1. $2 \text{ c} = 1 \text{ pt}$

2. $4 \text{ c} = 2 \text{ pt}$

3. $4 \text{ qt} = 1 \text{ gal}$

4. $8 \text{ qt} = 2 \text{ gal}$

5. $2 \text{ pt} = 1 \text{ qt}$

6. $6 \text{ pt} = 3 \text{ qt}$

7. $8 \text{ fl oz} = 1 \text{ c}$

8. $24 \text{ fl oz} = 3 \text{ c}$

9. $1 \text{ pt} = 2 \text{ c}$

10. $3 \text{ pt} = 6 \text{ c}$

11. $1 \text{ gal} = 4 \text{ qt}$

12. $2 \text{ gal} = 8 \text{ qt}$

13. No

14. Yes

15. No

16. Yes

Exercise Set 8.6

1. $32 \text{ fl oz} = 32 \text{ fl oz} \cdot \dfrac{1 \text{ c}}{8 \text{ fl oz}} = \dfrac{32 \text{ c}}{8} = 4 \text{ c}$

3. $8 \text{ qt} = 8 \text{ qt} \cdot \dfrac{2 \text{ pt}}{1 \text{ qt}} = 8 \cdot 2 \text{ pt} = 16 \text{ pt}$

5. $10 \text{ qt} = 10 \text{ qt} \cdot \dfrac{1 \text{ gal}}{4 \text{ qt}} = \dfrac{10 \text{ gal}}{4} = 2\dfrac{1}{2} \text{ gal}$

7. $80 \text{ fl oz} = 80 \text{ fl oz} \cdot \dfrac{1 \text{ pt}}{16 \text{ fl oz}} = \dfrac{80 \text{ pt}}{16} = 5 \text{ pt}$

9. $2 \text{ qt} = 2 \text{ qt} \cdot \dfrac{4 \text{ c}}{1 \text{ qt}} = 2 \cdot 4 \text{ c} = 8 \text{ c}$

11. $120 \text{ fl oz} = 120 \text{ fl oz} \cdot \dfrac{1 \text{ c}}{8 \text{ fl oz}} \cdot \dfrac{1 \text{ pt}}{2 \text{ c}} \cdot \dfrac{1 \text{ qt}}{2 \text{ pt}}$
$$= \dfrac{120 \text{ qt}}{8 \cdot 2 \cdot 2}$$
$$= \dfrac{120 \text{ qt}}{32}$$
$$= \dfrac{15 \text{ qt}}{4}$$
$$= 3\dfrac{3}{4} \text{ qt}$$

13.
$$6 \text{ gal} = 6 \text{ gal} \cdot \dfrac{4 \text{ qt}}{1 \text{ gal}} \cdot \dfrac{2 \text{ pt}}{1 \text{ qt}} \cdot \dfrac{2 \text{ c}}{1 \text{ pt}} \cdot \dfrac{8 \text{ fl oz}}{1 \text{ c}}$$
$$= 6 \cdot 4 \cdot 2 \cdot 2 \cdot 8 \text{ fl oz}$$
$$= 768 \text{ fl oz}$$

15. $4\dfrac{1}{2} \text{ pt} = \dfrac{9}{2} \text{ pt} \cdot \dfrac{2 \text{ c}}{1 \text{ pt}} = 9 \text{ c}$

17. $2\dfrac{3}{4} \text{ gal} = \dfrac{11}{4} \text{ gal} \cdot \dfrac{4 \text{ qt}}{1 \text{ gal}} \cdot \dfrac{2 \text{ pt}}{1 \text{ qt}}$
$$= \dfrac{11 \cdot 4 \cdot 2 \text{ pt}}{4}$$
$$= 22 \text{ pt}$$

19.
$$\begin{array}{r} 4 \text{ gal } 3 \text{ qt} \\ + 5 \text{ gal } 2 \text{ qt} \\ \hline 9 \text{ gal } 5 \text{ qt} \end{array} = 9 \text{ gal} + 1 \text{ gal } 1 \text{ qt} = 10 \text{ gal } 1 \text{ qt}$$

21.
$$\begin{array}{r} 1 \text{ c } \ 5 \text{ fl oz} \\ + 2 \text{ c } \ 7 \text{ fl oz} \\ \hline 3 \text{ c } 12 \text{ fl oz} \end{array} = 3 \text{ c} + 1 \text{ c } 4 \text{ fl oz} = 4 \text{ c } 4 \text{ fl oz}$$

23.
$$\begin{array}{rcl} 3 \text{ gal} & = & 2 \text{ gal } 4 \text{ qt} \\ - 1 \text{ gal } 3 \text{ qt} & = & - 1 \text{ gal } 3 \text{ qt} \\ \hline & & 1 \text{ gal } 1 \text{ qt} \end{array}$$

25.
$$\begin{array}{rcl} 3 \text{ gal } 1 \text{ qt} & = & 2 \text{ gal } 4 \text{ qt } 2 \text{ pt} \\ - \qquad 1 \text{ qt } 1 \text{ pt} & = & - \qquad 1 \text{ qt } 1 \text{ pt} \\ \hline & & 2 \text{ gal } 3 \text{ qt } 1 \text{ pt} \end{array}$$

27.
$$\begin{array}{r} 1 \text{ pt } 1 \text{ c} \\ \times \quad\quad 3 \\ \hline \end{array}$$
$$3 \text{ pt } 3 \text{ c} = 3 \text{ pt} + 1 \text{ pt } 1 \text{ c}$$
$$= 4 \text{ pt } 1 \text{ c} = 2 \text{ qt } 1 \text{ c}$$

29.
$$\begin{array}{r} 8 \text{ gal } 2 \text{ qt} \\ \times \quad\quad 2 \\ \hline \end{array}$$
$$16 \text{ gal } 4 \text{ qt} = 16 \text{ gal} + 1 \text{ gal} = 17 \text{ gal}$$

31.
$$\begin{array}{r} 4 \text{ gal} \quad 3 \text{ qt} \\ 2\overline{)\ 9 \text{ gal} \quad 2 \text{ qt}} \\ \underline{-8 \text{ gal}} \\ 1 \text{ gal} = \underline{4 \text{ qt}} \\ 6 \text{ qt} \\ \underline{-6 \text{ qt}} \\ 0 \end{array}$$

33. $1\dfrac{1}{2} \text{ qt} = \dfrac{3}{2}\text{qt} \cdot \dfrac{2 \text{ pt}}{1 \text{ qt}} \cdot \dfrac{2 \text{ c}}{1 \text{ qt}} \cdot \dfrac{8 \text{ fl oz}}{1 \text{ c}}$

$\qquad = \dfrac{3 \cdot 2 \cdot 2 \cdot 8 \text{ fl oz}}{2}$

$\qquad = 48 \text{ fl oz}$

One can holds 48 fl oz.

35. $64 \text{ fl oz} = 64 \text{ fl oz} \cdot \dfrac{1 \text{ c}}{8 \text{ fl oz}} \cdot \dfrac{1 \text{ pt}}{2 \text{ c}} \cdot \dfrac{1 \text{ qt}}{2 \text{ pt}}$

$\qquad = \dfrac{64 \text{ qt}}{8 \cdot 2 \cdot 2}$

$\qquad = 2 \text{ qt}$

Individuals should drink 2 qt of water daily.

37.
$$\begin{array}{r} 5 \text{ pt } 1 \text{ c} \\ + 2 \text{ pt } 1 \text{ c} \\ \hline 7 \text{ pt } 2 \text{ c} \end{array} = 7 \text{ pt} + 1 \text{ pt} = 8 \text{ pt} = 4 \text{ qt} = 1 \text{ gal}$$
Yes, the fruit punch can be poured into the container.

39. $\dfrac{1}{30} \text{ gal} \cdot \dfrac{4 \text{ qt}}{1 \text{ gal}} \cdot \dfrac{2 \text{ pt}}{1 \text{ qt}} \cdot \dfrac{2 \text{ c}}{1 \text{ pt}} \cdot \dfrac{8 \text{ oz}}{1 \text{ c}} \approx 4.3 \text{ oz}$

41. $12 \text{ fl oz} \cdot 24 = 288 \text{ fl oz}$

$\qquad 288 \text{ fl oz} = 288 \text{ fl oz} \cdot \dfrac{1 \text{ c}}{8 \text{ fl oz}} \cdot \dfrac{1 \text{ pt}}{2 \text{ c}} \cdot \dfrac{1 \text{ qt}}{2 \text{ pt}}$

$\qquad\qquad = \dfrac{288 \text{ qt}}{8 \cdot 2 \cdot 2}$

$\qquad\qquad = 9 \text{ qt}$

There are 9 quarts in a case of Pepsi.

43. To convert liters to milliliters move the decimal 3 places to the right.
$5 \text{ L} = 5000 \text{ ml}$

45. To convert milliliters to liters, move the decimal 3 places to the left.
$4500 \text{ ml} = 4.5 \text{ L}$

47. To convert liters to kiloliters move the decimal 3 places to the left.
$410 \text{ L} = 0.41 \text{ kl}$

49. To convert milliliters to liters move the decimal 3 places to the left.
$64 \text{ ml} = 0.064 \text{ L}$

51. To convert kiloliters to liters, move the decimal 3 places to the right.
$0.16 \text{ kl} = 160 \text{ L}$

53. To convert liters to milliliters move the decimal 3 places to the right.
$3.6 \text{ L} = 3600 \text{ ml}$

55. To convert liters to kiloliters, move the decimal 3 places to the left.
$0.16 \text{ L} = 0.00016 \text{ kl}$

57.
$$\begin{array}{r} 2.9 \text{ L} \\ + 19.6 \text{ L} \\ \hline 22.5 \text{ L} \end{array}$$

59. $2700 \text{ ml} = 2.7 \text{ L}$ or $1.8 \text{ L} = 1800 \text{ ml}$
$$\begin{array}{r} 2.7 \text{ L} = \quad 2700 \text{ ml} \\ + \ 1.8 \text{ L} = + 1800 \text{ ml} \\ \hline 4.5 \text{ L or} \quad 4500 \text{ ml} \end{array}$$

61. $8.6 \text{ L} = 8600 \text{ ml}$ or $190 \text{ ml} = 0.19 \text{ L}$
$$\begin{array}{r} 8600 \text{ ml} = \quad 8.60 \text{ L} \\ -190 \text{ ml} = -0.19 \text{ L} \\ \hline 8410 \text{ ml or} \quad 8.41 \text{ L} \end{array}$$

63. $11,400 \text{ ml} = 11.4 \text{ L}$ or $0.8 \text{ L} = 800 \text{ ml}$
$$\begin{array}{r} 11.4 \text{ L} = \quad 11,400 \text{ ml} \\ -0.8 \text{ L} = - \quad 800 \text{ ml} \\ \hline 10.6 \text{ L or} \quad 10,600 \text{ ml} \end{array}$$

65.
$$\begin{array}{r} 480 \text{ ml} \\ \times \quad\quad 8 \\ \hline 3840 \text{ ml} \end{array}$$

67. $0.5\overline{)81.2}$
Move decimal points 1 place.

$$5.) \overline{) \begin{array}{r} 162.4 \\ 812.0 \end{array}}$$

$$\begin{array}{r} \underline{-5} \\ 31 \\ \underline{-30} \\ 12 \\ \underline{-10} \\ 20 \\ \underline{-20} \\ 0 \end{array}$$

$81.2 \text{ L} \div 0.5 = 162.4 \text{ L}$

69.
$$\begin{array}{rl} 2 \text{ L} = & 2.00 \text{ L} \\ \underline{-410 \text{ ml}} = & \underline{-0.41 \text{ L}} \\ & 1.59 \text{ L} \end{array}$$

1.59 liters remain in the bottle.

71. 354 ml = 0.354 L

$$\begin{array}{rl} \text{gasoline} & 18.600 \text{ L} \\ \underline{+ \text{ dry gas}} & \underline{+ \ 0.354 \text{ L}} \\ & 18.954 \text{ L} \end{array}$$

There are 18.954 L of gasoline in the tank.

73. $44.3 \overline{) \$14.00} \rightarrow 443 \overline{) \begin{array}{r} 0.3160 \\ 140.0000 \end{array}}$

$$\begin{array}{r} \underline{-132 \ 9} \\ 7 \ 10 \\ \underline{-4 \ 43} \\ 2 \ 670 \\ \underline{-2 \ 658} \\ 120 \end{array}$$

The cost is about $0.316 per liter.

75.
$$\begin{array}{rl} 1.89 \text{ L} = & 1890 \text{ mL} \\ \underline{-946 \text{ mL}} = & \underline{-946 \text{ mL}} \\ & 944 \text{ mL} \end{array}$$

The larger bottle contains 944 ml more.

77. $0.7 = \dfrac{7}{10}$

79. $0.03 = \dfrac{3}{100}$

81. $0.006 = \dfrac{6}{1000} = \dfrac{3}{500}$

83. Answers may vary.

85. Each line represents 0.1 cc. B=1.5 cc

87. Each line represents 0.1 cc. D=2.7 cc

89. Each line represents 2u or 0.02 cc. B=54u or 0.54 cc.

91. Each line represents 2u or 0.02 cc. D=86u or 0.86 cc.

Section 8.7

Practice Problems

1. $1.5 \text{ cm} \cdot \dfrac{1 \text{ in}}{2.54 \text{ cm}} \approx 0.59 \text{ in}$

2. $8 \text{ oz} \cdot \dfrac{28.35 \text{ g}}{1 \text{ oz}} = 226.8 \text{ g}$

3. $237 \text{ ml} \cdot \dfrac{1 \text{ fl oz}}{29.57 \text{ ml}} \approx 8 \text{ fl oz}$

4.
$$\begin{aligned} F &= \frac{9}{5}C + 32 \\ &= \frac{9}{5} \cdot 50 + 32 \\ &= 90 + 32 \\ &= 122 \end{aligned}$$
50°C is 122°F

5.
$$\begin{aligned} F &= 1.8C + 32 \\ &= 1.8 \cdot 18 + 32 \\ &= 32.4 + 32 \\ &= 64.4 \end{aligned}$$
18°C is 64.4°F

6.
$$\begin{aligned} C &= \frac{5}{9}(F - 32) \\ &= \frac{5}{9} \cdot (113 - 32) \\ &= \frac{5}{9} \cdot 81 \\ &= 45 \end{aligned}$$
113°F is 45°C

7.
$$\begin{aligned} C &= \frac{5}{9}(F - 32) \\ &= \frac{5}{9} \cdot (102.8 - 32) \\ &= \frac{5}{9} \cdot 70.8 \\ &= 39.\overline{3} \end{aligned}$$
102.8°C is approximately 39.3°F

Mental Math

1. Yes
2. No
3. No
4. Yes
5. No
6. No
7. Yes
8. No

Exercise Set 8.7

1. $578 \text{ ml} \cdot \dfrac{1 \text{ fl oz}}{29.57 \text{ ml}} \approx 19.55 \text{ fl oz}$

3. $86 \text{ in} \cdot \dfrac{2.54 \text{ cm}}{1 \text{ in}} \approx 218.44 \text{ cm}$

5. $1000 \text{ g} \cdot \dfrac{0.04 \text{ oz}}{1 \text{ g}} = 40 \text{ oz}$

7. $93 \text{ km} \cdot \dfrac{0.62 \text{ mi}}{1 \text{ km}} = 57.66 \text{ mi}$

9. $14.5 \text{ L} \cdot \dfrac{0.26 \text{ gal}}{1 \text{ L}} = 3.77 \text{ gal}$

11. $30 \text{ lb} \cdot \dfrac{1 \text{ kg}}{2.20 \text{ lb}} \approx 13.64 \text{ km}$

13. $10 \text{ cm} \cdot \dfrac{1 \text{ in}}{2.54 \text{ cm}} \approx 3.94 \text{ in}$

15. $70 \text{ mi} \cdot \dfrac{1.61 \text{ km}}{1 \text{ mi}} = 112.7 \text{ km per hr}$

17. $200 \text{ mg} = 0.2\text{g} \cdot \dfrac{0.04 \text{ oz}}{1 \text{ g}} = 0.008 \text{ oz}$

19. $15 \text{ stone} \cdot \dfrac{14 \text{ lb}}{1 \text{ stone}} = 210 \text{ lb} + 10 \text{ lb} = 220 \text{ lb}$

    $220 \text{ lb} \cdot \dfrac{1 \text{ kg}}{2.20 \text{ lb}} = 100 \text{ kg}$

    Yes, 100 kg is approximately equal to 15 stone 10 pounds.

21. $12 \text{ fl oz} \cdot \dfrac{29.57 \text{ ml}}{1 \text{ fl oz}} \approx 355 \text{ ml}$

    Since 335 ml < 380 ml, 380 ml is larger.

23. $3\dfrac{1}{2} \text{ in} = 3.5 \text{ in} \cdot \dfrac{2.54 \text{ cm}}{1 \text{ in}} = 8.89 \text{ cm} \approx 90 \text{ mm}$

25. $1.5 \text{ lb} - 1.25 \text{ lb} = 0.25 \text{ lb} \cdot \dfrac{16 \text{ oz}}{1 \text{ lb}} = 4 \text{ oz}$

    $4 \text{ oz} \cdot \dfrac{28.35 \text{ g}}{1 \text{ oz}} = 113.4 \text{ g}$

27. $167 \text{ km} \cdot \dfrac{1 \text{ mi}}{1.61 \text{ km}} \approx 104 \text{ mph}$

29. $8 \text{ m} \cdot \dfrac{3.28 \text{ ft}}{1 \text{ m}} = 26.24 \text{ ft}$

31. $4.5 \text{ km} \cdot \dfrac{0.62 \text{ mi}}{1 \text{ km}} \approx 3 \text{ mi}$

33. $24 \text{ hr} \div 4 = 6$ doses for 1 day
    $6 \text{ doses} \cdot 7 \text{ days} = 42$ doses for 1 week
    $42 \text{ doses} \cdot 5 \text{ ml} = 210 \text{ ml}$ of medicine is needed
    $210 \text{ ml} \cdot \dfrac{1 \text{ fl oz}}{29.57 \text{ ml}} \approx 7.1$ fl oz which is 8 fl oz
    when rounded up to the next whole flu oz.

35. A
37. B
39. C
41. D
43. D

45. $C = \dfrac{5}{9}(F - 32)$

    $C = \dfrac{5}{9} \cdot (41 - 32)$

    $= \dfrac{5}{9} \cdot (9)$

    $= 5$

    $41° \text{ F} = 5° \text{ C}$

47. $C = \dfrac{5}{9}(F - 32)$

$\quad C = \dfrac{5}{9} \cdot (104 - 32)$

$\quad\quad = \dfrac{5}{9} \cdot (72)$

$\quad\quad = 5(8)$

$\quad\quad = 40$

$\quad 104°F = 40°C$

49. $F = \dfrac{9}{5}C + 32$

$\quad F = \dfrac{9}{5} \cdot (115) + 32$

$\quad\quad = 108 + 32$

$\quad\quad = 140$

$\quad 60°C = 140°F$

51. $F = \dfrac{9}{5}C + 32$

$\quad F = \dfrac{9}{5} \cdot (115) + 32$

$\quad\quad = 9(23) + 32$

$\quad\quad = 207 + 32$

$\quad\quad = 239$

$\quad 115°C = 239°F$

53. $C = \dfrac{5}{9}(F - 32)$

$\quad C = \dfrac{5}{9} \cdot (62 - 32)$

$\quad\quad = \dfrac{5}{9} \cdot (30)$

$\quad\quad = \dfrac{150}{9}$

$\quad\quad \approx 16.7$

$\quad 62°F \approx 16.7°C$

55. $C = \dfrac{5}{9}(F - 32)$

$\quad C = \dfrac{5}{9} \cdot (142.1 - 32)$

$\quad\quad = \dfrac{5}{9} \cdot (110.1)$

$\quad\quad = \dfrac{550.5}{9}$

$\quad\quad \approx 61.2$

$\quad 142.1°F \approx 61.2°C$

57. $F = 1.8C + 32$

$\quad F = 1.8(92) + 32$

$\quad\quad = 165.6 + 32$

$\quad\quad = 197.6$

$\quad 92°C = 197.6°F$

59. $F = 1.8C + 32$

$\quad F = 1.8(16.3) + 32$

$\quad\quad = 29.34 + 32$

$\quad\quad = 61.34$

$\quad 16.3°C \approx 61.3°F$

61. $C = \dfrac{5}{9}(F - 32)$

$\quad\quad = \dfrac{5}{9}(122 - 32)$

$\quad\quad = \dfrac{5}{9}(90)$

$\quad\quad = \dfrac{450}{9}$

$\quad\quad = 50° \text{ C}$

$\quad 122° \text{ F} = 50° \text{ C}$

63. $F = 1.8C + 32$

$\quad F = 1.8(27) + 32$

$\quad\quad = 48.6 + 32$

$\quad\quad = 80.6$

$\quad 27°C = 80.6°F$

65. $C = \dfrac{5}{9}(F - 32)$

$\quad C = \dfrac{5}{9} \cdot (70 - 32)$

$\quad\quad = \dfrac{5}{9} \cdot (38)$

$\quad\quad = \dfrac{190}{9}$

$\quad\quad \approx 21.1$

$\quad 70°F \approx 21.1°C$

67. $C = \dfrac{5}{9}(F - 32)$

$\quad C = \dfrac{5}{9} \cdot (100.2 - 32)$

$\quad\quad = \dfrac{5}{9} \cdot (68.2)$

$\quad\quad = \dfrac{341}{9}$

$\quad\quad \approx 37.9$

$\quad 100.2°F \approx 37.9°C$

69. $F = 1.8C + 32$

$\quad F = 1.8 \cdot 118 + 32$

$\quad\quad = 212.4 + 32$

$\quad\quad = 244.4$

$\quad 118°C = 244.4°F$

71. $C = \frac{5}{9}(F - 32)$

$C = \frac{5}{9} \cdot (500 - 32)$

$= \frac{5}{9} \cdot (468)$

$= 5(52)$

$= 260$

$500°F = 260°C$

73. $C = \frac{5}{9}(F - 32)$

$C = \frac{5}{9} \cdot (864 - 32)$

$= \frac{5}{9} \cdot (832)$

$= \frac{4160}{9}$

≈ 462.2

$864°F \approx 462.2°C$

75. $-6 \cdot 4 + 5 \div (-1) = -24 + (-5) = -29$

77. $\frac{-10 + 8}{-10 - 8} = \frac{-2}{-18} = \frac{1}{9}$

79. $3 + 5(17 - 19) - 8 = 3 + 5(-2) - 8$

$= 3 + (-10) - 8$

$= -7 - 8$

$= -15$

81. $3\big[(-1 + 5) \cdot (6 - 8)\big] = 3\big[4(-2)\big]$

$= 3\big[-8\big]$

$= -24$

83. $\text{BSA} = \sqrt{\frac{90 \times 182}{3600}} \approx 2.13 \text{ sq m}$

85. $40 \text{ in} \cdot \frac{2.54 \text{ cm}}{1 \text{ in}} = 101.6 \text{ cm}$

$\text{BSA} = \sqrt{\frac{50 \times 101.6}{3600}} \approx 1.19 \text{ sq m}$

87. $60 \text{ in} \cdot \frac{254 \text{ cm}}{1 \text{ in}} \approx 152 \text{ cm}$

$150 \text{ lb} \cdot \frac{0.45 \text{ kg}}{1 \text{ lb}} \approx 68 \text{ kg}$

$\text{BSA} = \sqrt{\frac{68 \times 152}{3600}} \approx 1.70 \text{ sq m}$

89. $10 \cdot 2.13 = 21.3 \text{ mg}$

$12 \cdot 2.13 = 25.56 \text{ mg}$

The dosage range would be 21.3 mg - 25.56 mg.

91. $A = lw \text{ (in meters)}$

$= 20 \text{ meters} \cdot 40 \text{ meters}$

$= 800 \text{ square meters}$

Convert to feet:

$20 \text{ m} \cdot \frac{3.28 \text{ ft}}{1 \text{ m}} = 65.6 \text{ ft}$

$40 \text{ m} \cdot \frac{3.28 \text{ ft}}{1 \text{ m}} = 131.2 \text{ ft}$

$A = 65.6 \text{ feet} \cdot 131.2 \text{ feet}$

$= 8606.72 \text{ square feet}$

93. $C = \frac{5}{9} \cdot (918,000,000 - 32)$

$= \frac{4,589,999,840}{9}$

$= 509,999,982$

$\approx 510,000,000$

$918,000,000°F \approx 510,000,000°C$

Section 8.8

Practice Problems

1. MNO is congruent to RQS because of Side-Angle-Side (SAS).

2. We are given the lengths of two corresponding sides. Their ratio is $\frac{9 \text{ meters}}{13 \text{ meters}} = \frac{9}{13}$.

3. Since the triangles are similar, corresponding sides are in proportion.

$\frac{10}{5} = \frac{n}{4}$

$5n = 40$

$\frac{5n}{5} = \frac{40}{5}$

$n = 8$

The missing length is 8 units.

4. The triangles formed are similar triangles, so

$$\frac{5}{n} = \frac{8}{200}$$

$$8n = 1000$$

$$n = \frac{1000}{8}$$

$$n = 125 \text{ feet}$$

The height of the building is 125 feet.

Exercise Set 8.8

1. congruent; Side-Side-Side (SSS)

3. congruent; Angle-Side-Angle (ASA)

5. Since the triangles are similar, we can compare any of the corresponding sides to find the ratio.

$$\frac{22}{11} = \frac{2}{1}$$

7. Since the triangles are similar, we can compare any of the corresponding sides to find the ratio.

$$\frac{12}{8} = \frac{3}{2}$$

9.
$$\frac{3}{n} = \frac{6}{9}$$

$$6n = 27$$

$$\frac{6n}{6} = \frac{27}{6}$$

$$n = 4.5$$

11.
$$\frac{12}{4} = \frac{18}{n}$$

$$72 = 12n$$

$$\frac{72}{12} = \frac{12n}{12}$$

$$6 = n$$

13.
$$\frac{n}{3.75} = \frac{12}{9}$$

$$45 = 9n$$

$$\frac{45}{9} = \frac{9n}{9}$$

$$5 = n$$

15.
$$\frac{18}{n} = \frac{40}{30}$$

$$40n = 540$$

$$\frac{40n}{40} = \frac{540}{40}$$

$$n = 13.5$$

17.
$$\frac{n}{3.25} = \frac{17.5}{3.25}$$

$$56.875 = 3.25n$$

$$\frac{56.875}{3.25} = \frac{3.25n}{3.25}$$

$$17.5 = n$$

19.
$$\frac{n}{2} = \frac{8\frac{1}{2}}{2\frac{1}{8}}$$

$$\left(2\frac{1}{8}\right)n = (2)8\frac{1}{2}$$

$$\frac{17}{8}n = 2 \cdot \frac{17}{2}$$

$$\frac{8}{17} \cdot \frac{17}{8}n = \frac{8}{17} \cdot \frac{17}{1}$$

$$n = 8$$

21.
$$\frac{34}{n} = \frac{16}{10}$$

$$16n = 340$$

$$\frac{16n}{16} = \frac{340}{16}$$

$$n = 21.25$$

23. $\dfrac{\text{height of building}}{\text{height of flagpole}} = \dfrac{\text{shadow of building}}{\text{shadow of flagpole}}$

$$\frac{n}{40} = \frac{25}{2}$$

$$2n = 40 \cdot 25$$

$$2n = 1000$$

$$\frac{2n}{2} = \frac{1000}{2}$$

$$n = 500$$

The height of the building is 500 feet.

25.
$$\frac{5}{4} = \frac{x}{48}$$

$$4x = 5 \cdot 48$$

$$4x = 240$$

$$x = 60$$

The height of the tree is 60 feet.

27. $\dfrac{30}{24} = \dfrac{18}{x}$

$30x = 432$

$x = 14.4$

The shadow is 14.4 feet long.

29. $\dfrac{14 + 17 + 21 + 18}{4} = \dfrac{70}{4} = 17.5$

31. $\dfrac{76 + 79 + 88}{3} = \dfrac{243}{3} = 81$

33. $\dfrac{5.2}{n} = \dfrac{7.8}{12.6}$

$7.8n = 65.52$

$n = 8.4$

35. Answers may vary.

37. $\dfrac{3 \text{ in}}{x} = \dfrac{\frac{1}{4} \text{ in}}{1 \text{ ft}}$; $\dfrac{4\frac{1}{2} \text{ in}}{x} = \dfrac{\frac{1}{4} \text{ in}}{1 \text{ ft}}$

$\dfrac{1}{4}x = 3$ $\dfrac{1}{4}x = 4\dfrac{1}{2}$

$4 \cdot \dfrac{1}{4}x = 3 \cdot 4$ $4 \cdot \dfrac{1}{4}x = \dfrac{9}{2} \cdot \dfrac{4}{1}$

$x = 12$ $x = 18$

$3 \text{ in} = 12 \text{ ft}$

$4\dfrac{1}{2} \text{ in} = 18 \text{ ft}$

The dimensions of the deck are 12 ft by 18 ft.

Chapter 8 Review

1. $\angle A$ is a right angle.

2. $\angle B$ is a straight angle.

3. $\angle C$ is an acute angle.

4. $\angle D$ is an obtuse angle.

5. The complement of a 25° angle is $90° - 25° = 65°$.

6. The supplement of a 105° angle is $180° - 105° = 75°$.

7. The supplement of a 72° angle is $180° - 72° = 108°$.

8. The complement of a 1° angle is $90° - 1° = 89°$.

9. $\angle x = 90° - 32° = 58°$

10. $\angle x = 180° - 82° = 98°$

11. $\angle x = 105° - 15° = 90°$

12. $\angle x = 45° - 20° = 25°$

13. 47° and 133° are supplementary angles.

14. 47° and 43° are complementary angles.
58° and 32° are complementary angles.

15. $\angle x$ and the 80° angle are vertical angles, so $\angle x = 80°$. $\angle x$ and $\angle y$ are supplementary angles, so $\angle y = 180° - 80° = 100°$. $\angle y$ and $\angle z$ are vertical angles, so $\angle z = 100°$.

16. $\angle x$ and the 25° angle are supplementary angles, so $\angle x = 180° - 25° = 155°$. $\angle x$ and $\angle y$ are vertical angles, so $\angle y = 155°$. $\angle z$ and the 25° angle are vertical angles, so $\angle z = 25°$.

17. $\angle x$ and the 53° angle are vertical angles, so $\angle x = 53°$. $\angle y$ and the 53° angle are corresponding angles, so $\angle y = 53°$. $\angle y$ and $\angle z$ are supplementary angles, so $\angle z = 180° - 53° = 127°$.

18. $\angle x$ and the 42° angle are vertical angles, so $\angle x = 42°$. $\angle y$ and the 42° angle are corresponding angles, so $\angle y = 42°$. $\angle y$ and $\angle z$ are supplementary angles, so $\angle z = 180° - 42° = 138°$.

19. $108 \text{ in.} = 108 \text{ in.} \cdot \dfrac{1 \text{ ft}}{12 \text{ in.}} = 9 \text{ ft}$

20. $72 \text{ ft} = 72 \text{ ft} \cdot \dfrac{1 \text{ yd}}{3 \text{ ft}}$
$= 24 \text{ yd}$

21. $2.5 \text{ mi} = 2.5 \text{ mi} \cdot \dfrac{5280 \text{ ft}}{1 \text{ mi}} = 13{,}200 \text{ ft}$

22. $6.25 \text{ ft} = 6.25 \text{ ft} \cdot \dfrac{12 \text{ in.}}{1 \text{ ft}}$
$= 75 \text{ in.}$

23.

$$\begin{array}{r} 17 \\ 3\overline{\smash{)}52} \\ -3 \\ \hline 22 \\ -21 \\ \hline 1 \end{array}$$

52 ft = 17 yd 1 ft

24.

$$\begin{array}{r} 3 \\ 12\overline{\smash{)}46} \\ -36 \\ \hline 10 \end{array}$$

46 in. = 3 ft 10 in.

25. 42 m = 4200 cm

26. 82 cm = 820 mm

27. 12.18 mm = 0.01218 m

28. 2.31 m = 0.00231 km

29.

$$\begin{array}{r} 4 \text{ yd } 2 \text{ ft} \\ + 16 \text{ yd } 2 \text{ ft} \\ \hline 20 \text{ yd } 4 \text{ ft} \end{array} = 20 \text{ yd} + 1 \text{ yd } 1 \text{ ft}$$
$$= 21 \text{ yd } 1 \text{ ft}$$

30.

$$\begin{array}{rclr} 12 \text{ ft } 1 \text{ in.} & = & 11 \text{ ft } 13 \text{ in.} \\ - 4 \text{ ft } 8 \text{ in.} & = & - 4 \text{ ft } 8 \text{ in.} \\ \hline & & 7 \text{ ft } 5 \text{ in.} \end{array}$$

31.

$$\begin{array}{r} 8 \text{ ft } 3 \text{ in.} \\ \times 5 \\ \hline 40 \text{ ft } 15 \text{ in.} \end{array} = 40 \text{ ft} + 1 \text{ ft } 3 \text{ in.}$$
$$= 41 \text{ ft } 3 \text{ in.}$$

32.

$$\begin{array}{r} 3 \text{ ft} 8 \text{ in.} \\ 2\overline{\smash{)}7 \text{ ft} 4 \text{ in.}} \\ \underline{-6 \text{ ft}} \\ 1 \text{ ft} = \underline{12 \text{ in.}} \\ 16 \text{ in.} \\ \underline{-16 \text{ in.}} \\ 0 \end{array}$$

33. 8 cm = 80 mm or 15 mm = 1.5 cm

$$\begin{array}{r} 80 \text{ mm} \\ +15 \text{ mm} \\ \hline 95 \text{ mm} \end{array} \qquad \begin{array}{r} 8.0 \text{ cm} \\ + 1.5 \text{ cm} \\ \hline 9.5 \text{ cm} \end{array}$$

34. 4 m = 400 cm or 126 cm = 1.26 m

$$\begin{array}{r} 400 \text{ cm} \\ +126 \text{ cm} \\ \hline 526 \text{ cm} \end{array} \qquad \begin{array}{r} 4.00 \text{ m} \\ + 1.26 \text{ m} \\ \hline 5.26 \text{ m} \end{array}$$

35. 9.3 km = 9300 m or 183 m = 0.183 km

$$\begin{array}{r} 9300 \text{ m} \\ -183 \text{ m} \\ \hline 9117 \text{ m} \end{array} \qquad \begin{array}{r} 9.300 \text{ km} \\ - 0.183 \text{ km} \\ \hline 9.117 \text{ km} \end{array}$$

36. 4100 mm = 4.1 m or 3 m = 3000 mm

$$\begin{array}{r} 4.1 \text{ m} \\ -3.0 \text{ m} \\ \hline 1.1 \text{ m} \end{array} \qquad \begin{array}{r} 4100 \text{ mm} \\ -3000 \text{ mm} \\ \hline 1100 \text{ mm} \end{array}$$

37.

$$\begin{array}{r} 333 \text{ yd } 1 \text{ ft} \\ - 163 \text{ yd } 2 \text{ ft} \end{array} \qquad \begin{array}{r} 332 \text{ yd } 4 \text{ ft} \\ - 163 \text{ yd } 2 \text{ ft} \\ \hline 169 \text{ yd } 2 \text{ ft} \end{array}$$

169 yards 2 feet of cloth remain.

38.

$$\begin{array}{r} 6 \text{ ft } 4 \text{ in.} \\ \times 20 \\ \hline 120 \text{ ft } 80 \text{ in.} \end{array} = 120 \text{ ft} + 6 \text{ ft } 8 \text{ in.}$$
$$= 126 \text{ ft } 8 \text{ in.}$$

126 feet 8 inches of framing material is needed.

39. The round-trip distance is
2(217 km) = 434 km.
$$\frac{434}{4} = 108.5$$
Each must drive 108.5 kilometers.

40. 30 cm = 0.3 m

$$\begin{array}{r} 0.8 \text{ m} \\ \times 0.3 \text{ m} \\ \hline 0.24 \end{array} \text{ square meters}$$

41. Perimeter
= 27 meters + 17 meters + 27 meters + 17 meters
= 88 meters

42. $P = a + b + c$
= 11 centimeters + 7 centimeters + 12 centimeters
= 30 centimeters

43. The missing lengths are:
10 meters − 7 meters = 3 meters
8 meters − 5 meters = 3 meters
Perimeter = 8 meters + 7 meters + 3 meters + 3 meters + 5 meters + 10 meters
= 36 meters

44. The missing length is: 5 feet + 4 feet + 11 feet = 20 feet
Perimeter = 22 feet + 20 feet + 22 feet + 11 feet + 3 feet + 4 feet + 3 feet + 5 feet
= 90 feet

45. $P = 2l + 2w$
$= 2 \cdot 6 \text{ feet} + 2 \cdot 10 \text{ feet}$
$= 12 \text{ feet} + 20 \text{ feet}$
$= 32 \text{ feet}$

46. $P = 4s = 4 \cdot 110 \text{ feet} = 440 \text{ feet}$

47. $C = \pi d$
$= \pi \cdot 1.7 \text{ inches}$
$= 1.7\pi \text{ inches}$
$\approx 1.7 \cdot 3.14 \text{ inches}$
$= 5.338 \text{ inches}$

48. $C = 2\pi r$
$= 2 \cdot \pi \cdot 5 \text{ yards}$
$= 10\pi \text{ yards}$
$\approx 10 \cdot 3.14 \text{ yards}$
$= 31.4 \text{ yards}$

49. $A = \dfrac{1}{2}(b + B)h$
$= \dfrac{1}{2} \cdot (12 \text{ feet} + 36 \text{ feet}) \cdot 10 \text{ feet}$
$= 240 \text{ square feet}$

50. $A = \dfrac{1}{2}bh$
$= \dfrac{1}{2} \cdot 20 \text{ meters} \cdot 14 \text{ meters}$
$= 140 \text{ square meters}$

51. $A = lw$
$= 40 \text{ centimeters} \cdot 15 \text{ centimeters}$
$= 600 \text{ square centimters}$

52. $A = bh$
$= 21 \text{ yards} \cdot 9 \text{ yards}$
$= 189 \text{ square yards}$

53. $A = \pi r^2$
$= \pi \cdot (7 \text{ feet})^2$
$= 49\pi \text{ square feet}$
$\approx 49 \cdot 3.14 \text{ square feet}$
$= 153.86 \text{ square feet}$

54. $A = \pi r^2$
$= \pi \cdot (2 \text{ inches})^2$
$= 4\pi \text{ square inches}$
$\approx 4 \cdot 3.14 \text{ square inches}$
$= 12.56 \text{ square inches}$

55. $A = \dfrac{1}{2}bh$
$= \dfrac{1}{2} \cdot 34 \text{ inches} \cdot 7 \text{ inches}$
$= 119 \text{ square inches}$

56.

$A = \dfrac{1}{2}(b + B)h$
$= \dfrac{1}{2} \cdot (32 \text{ centimeters} + 64 \text{ centimeters}) \cdot 26 \text{ centime}$
$= \dfrac{1}{2} \cdot 96 \cdot 26 \text{ square centimeters}$
$= 1248 \text{ square centimeters}$

57.

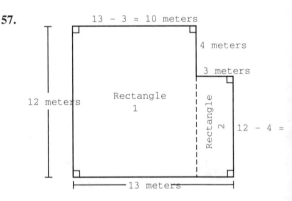

Area of rectangle 1 = 12 meters · 10 meters
= 120 square meters

Area of rectangle 2 = 8 meters · 3 meters
= 24 square meters

Total area = 120 square meters + 24 square meters
= 144 square meters

58. $A = lw$
$= 36 \text{ feet} \cdot 12 \text{ feet}$
$= 432 \text{ square feet}$

59. $A = lw$
$$= 13 \text{ feet} \cdot 10 \text{ feet}$$
$$= 130 \text{ square feet}$$

60. $V = s^3$
$$= \left(2\frac{1}{2} \text{ inches}\right)^3$$
$$= \left(\frac{5}{2} \text{ inches}\right)^3$$
$$= \frac{125}{8} \text{ or } 15\frac{5}{8} \text{ cubic inches}$$

61. $V = lwh$
$$= 7 \text{ feet} \cdot 2 \text{ feet} \cdot 6 \text{ feet}$$
$$= 84 \text{ cubic feet}$$

62. $V = \pi r^2 h$
$$= \pi \cdot (20 \text{ centimeters})^2 \cdot 50 \text{ centimeters}$$
$$= 20{,}000\pi \text{ cubic centimeters}$$
$$\approx 20{,}000 \cdot \frac{22}{7} \text{ cubic centimeters}$$
$$= 62{,}857\frac{1}{7} \text{ cubic centimeters}$$

63. $V = \frac{1}{3}\pi r^2 h$
$$= \frac{1}{3} \cdot \pi \cdot \left(5\frac{1}{4} \text{ inches}\right)^2 \cdot 12 \text{ inches}$$
$$= \frac{1}{3} \cdot \left(\frac{21}{4}\right)^2 \cdot 12 \cdot \pi \text{ cubic inches}$$
$$= \frac{441}{4}\pi \text{ cubic inches}$$
$$\approx \frac{441}{4} \cdot \frac{22}{7} \text{ cubic inches}$$
$$= \frac{693}{2} \text{ or } 346\frac{1}{2} \text{ cubic inches}$$

64. $V = \frac{1}{3}s^2 h$
$$= \frac{1}{3} \cdot (2 \text{ feet})^2 \cdot 2 \text{ feet}$$
$$= \frac{1}{3} \cdot 4 \cdot 2 \text{ cubic feet}$$
$$= \frac{8}{3} \text{ or } 2\frac{2}{3} \text{ cubic feet}$$

65. $V = \pi r^2 h$
$$= \pi \cdot (3.5 \text{ inches})^2 \cdot 8 \text{ inches}$$
$$= 98\pi \text{ cubic inches}$$
$$\approx 98 \cdot 3.14 \text{ cubic inches}$$
$$= 307.72 \text{ cubic inches}$$

66. Volume $= 3lwh$
$$= 3 \cdot 2\frac{1}{2} \text{ feet} \cdot 1\frac{1}{2} \text{ feet} \cdot \frac{2}{3} \text{ feet}$$
$$= 3 \cdot \frac{5}{2} \cdot \frac{3}{2} \cdot \frac{2}{3} \text{ cubic feet}$$
$$= \frac{15}{2} \text{ or } 7\frac{1}{2} \text{ cubic feet}$$

67. $V = \pi r^2 h$
$$= \pi \cdot \left(\frac{1 \text{ foot}}{2}\right)^2 \cdot 2 \text{ feet}$$
$$= \frac{1}{4} \cdot 2 \cdot \pi \text{ cubic feet}$$
$$= \frac{1}{2}\pi \text{ or } 0.5\pi \text{ cubic feet}$$

68. $V = lwh$
$$= 15 \text{ feet} \cdot 12 \text{ feet} \cdot 7 \text{ feet}$$
$$= 1260 \text{ cubic feet}$$

69. Volume of first box $= (3 \text{ feet})^3$
$$= 27 \text{ cubic feet}$$
Volume of second box $= (1.2 \text{ feet})^3$
$$= 1.728 \text{ cubic feet}$$
Total volume
$$= 27 \text{ cubic feet} + 1.728 \text{ cubic feet}$$
$$= 28.728 \text{ cubic feet}$$

70. $66 \text{ oz} = 66 \text{ oz} \cdot \dfrac{1 \text{ lb}}{16 \text{ oz}} = 4.125 \text{ lb}$

71. $2.3 \text{ tons} = 2.3 \text{ tons} \cdot \dfrac{2000 \text{ lb}}{1 \text{ ton}}$
$$= 4600 \text{ lb}$$

72.
$$\begin{array}{r} 3 \\ 16\overline{\smash{)}52} \\ -48 \\ \hline 4 \end{array}$$
$52 \text{ oz} = 3 \text{ lb } 4 \text{ oz}$

73.
$$\begin{array}{r} 4 \\ 2000\overline{\smash{)}8200} \\ -8000 \\ \hline 200 \end{array}$$
$8200 \text{ lb} = 4 \text{ tons } 200 \text{ lb}$

74. $1400 \text{ mg} = 1.4 \text{ g}$

75. 40 kg = 40,000 g

76. 2.1 hg = 21 dag

77. 0.03 mg = 0.0003 dg

78.
$$\begin{array}{r} 6 \text{ lb } 5 \text{ oz} \\ - 2 \text{ lb } 12 \text{ oz} \\ \hline \end{array} \qquad \begin{array}{r} 5 \text{ lb } 21 \text{ oz} \\ - 2 \text{ lb } 12 \text{ oz} \\ \hline 3 \text{ lb } 9 \text{ oz} \end{array}$$

79.
$$\begin{array}{r} 5 \text{ tons } 1600 \text{ lb} \\ + 4 \text{ tons } 1200 \text{ lb} \\ \hline 9 \text{ tons } 2800 \text{ lb} = 9 \text{ tons} + 1 \text{ ton } 800 \text{ lb} \\ = 10 \text{ tons } 800 \text{ lb} \end{array}$$

80.
$$\begin{array}{r} 2 \text{ tons } 750 \text{ lb} \\ 3{\overline{\smash{\big)}\, 6 \text{ tons } 2250 \text{ lb}}} \\ \underline{-6 \text{ tons}} \\ 0 2250 \text{ lb} \\ \underline{-2250 \text{ lb}} \\ 0 \end{array}$$

81.
$$\begin{array}{r} 8 \text{ lb } 6 \text{ oz} \\ \times \phantom{8 \text{ lb} } 4 \\ \hline 32 \text{ lb } 24 \text{ oz} = 32 \text{ lb} + 1 \text{ lb } 8 \text{ oz} \\ = 33 \text{ lb } 8 \text{ oz} \end{array}$$

82. 1300 mg = 1.3 g or 3.6 g = 3600 mg
$$\begin{array}{r} 1.3 \text{ g} \\ + 3.6 \text{ g} \\ \hline 4.9 \text{ g} \end{array} \qquad \begin{array}{r} 1300 \text{ mg} \\ + 3600 \text{ mg} \\ \hline 4900 \text{ mg} \end{array}$$

83. 4.8 kg = 4800 g or 4200 g = 4.2 kg
$$\begin{array}{r} 4800 \text{ g} \\ + 4200 \text{ g} \\ \hline 9000 \text{ g} \end{array} \qquad \begin{array}{r} 4.8 \text{ kg} \\ + 4.2 \text{ kg} \\ \hline 9.0 \text{ kg} = 9 \text{ kg} \end{array}$$

84. 9.3 g = 9300 mg or 1200 mg = 1.2 g
$$\begin{array}{r} 9300 \text{ mg} \\ - 1200 \text{ mg} \\ \hline 8100 \text{ mg} \end{array} \qquad \begin{array}{r} 9.3 \text{ g} \\ - 1.2 \text{ g} \\ \hline 8.1 \text{ g} \end{array}$$

85.
$$\begin{array}{r} 6.3 \text{ kg} \\ \times \phantom{6.3 \text{ k}} 8 \\ \hline 50.4 \text{ kg} \end{array}$$

86.
$$\begin{array}{r} 1 \text{ lb } 12 \text{ oz} \\ + 2 \text{ lb } 8 \text{ oz} \\ \hline 3 \text{ lb } 20 \text{ oz} = 3 \text{ lb} + 1 \text{ lb } 4 \text{ oz} \\ = 4 \text{ lb } 4 \text{ oz} \end{array}$$
He ordered 4 pounds 4 ounces of candy.

87.
$$\begin{array}{r} 9 \text{ tons } 1075 \text{ lb} \\ 4{\overline{\smash{\big)}\, 38 \text{ tons } 300 \text{ lb}}} \\ \underline{-36 \text{ tons}} \\ 2 \text{ tons} = 4000 \text{ lb} \\ \hline 4300 \text{ lb} \\ \underline{- 4300 \text{ lb}} \\ 0 \end{array}$$
Each township receives 9 tons 1075 pounds of cinders.

88. 450 g = 0.45 kg
$$\begin{array}{r} 8.30 \text{ kg} \\ - 0.45 \text{ kg} \\ \hline 7.85 \text{ kg} \end{array}$$
She received 7.85 kilograms of flour.

89.
$$\begin{array}{r} 1.1625 \text{ kg} \\ 8{\overline{\smash{\big)}\, 9.3000 \text{ kg}}} \\ \underline{-8} \\ 13 \\ \underline{- 8} \\ 50 \\ \underline{-48} \\ 20 \\ \underline{-16} \\ 40 \\ \underline{-40} \\ 0 \end{array}$$
Each receives 1.1625 kilograms of syrup.

90. $16 \text{ pt} = 16 \text{ pt} \cdot \dfrac{1 \text{ qt}}{2 \text{ pt}} = 8 \text{ qt}$

91. $40 \text{ fl oz} = 40 \text{ fl oz} \cdot \dfrac{1 \text{ c}}{8 \text{ fl oz}} = 5 \text{ c}$

92. $6.75 \text{ gal} = 6.75 \text{ gal} \cdot \dfrac{4 \text{ qt}}{1 \text{ gal}} = 27 \text{ qt}$

93. $8.5 \text{ pt} = 8.5 \text{ pt} \cdot \dfrac{2 \text{ c}}{1 \text{ pt}} = 17 \text{ c}$

94.
$$\begin{array}{r} 4 \\ 2{\overline{\smash{\big)}\, 9}} \\ \underline{-8} \\ 1 \end{array}$$
9 pt = 4 qt 1 pt

95.
$$\begin{array}{r} 3 \\ 4{\overline{\smash{\big)}\, 15}} \\ \underline{-12} \\ 3 \end{array}$$
15 qt = 3 gal 3 qt

96. 3.8 L = 3800 ml

97. 4.2 ml = 0.042 dl

98. 14 hl = 1.4 kl

99. 30.6 L = 3060 cl

100.
$$\begin{array}{r} 1 \text{ qt } 1 \text{ pt} \\ + \ 3 \text{ qt } 1 \text{ pt} \\ \hline 4 \text{ qt } 2 \text{ pt} = 4 \text{ qt} + 1 \text{ qt} \\ = 5 \text{ qt} \\ = 1 \text{ gal } 1 \text{ qt} \end{array}$$

101.
$$\begin{array}{r} 3 \text{ gal } 2 \text{ qt } 1 \text{ pt} \\ \times \qquad\qquad 2 \\ \hline 6 \text{ gal } 4 \text{ qt } 2 \text{ pt} = 6 \text{ gal} + 1 \text{ gal} + 1\text{qt} \\ = 7 \text{ gal } 1 \text{ qt} \end{array}$$

102. 0.946 L = 946 ml or 210 ml = 0.210 L
$$\begin{array}{rr} 946 \text{ ml} & 0.946 \text{ L} \\ -210 \text{ ml} & -\ 0.210 \text{ L} \\ \hline 736 \text{ ml} & 0.736 \text{ L} \end{array}$$

103. 6.1 L = 6100 ml or 9400 ml = 9.4 L
$$\begin{array}{rr} 6100 \text{ ml} & 6.1 \text{ L} \\ +9400 \text{ ml} & +9.4 \text{ L} \\ \hline 15,500 \text{ ml} & 15.5 \text{ L} \end{array}$$

104.
$$\begin{array}{rcl} 4 \text{ gal } 2 \text{ qt} & = & 3 \text{ gal } 6 \text{ qt} \\ -\ 1 \text{ gal } 3 \text{ qt} & = & -\ 1 \text{ gal } 3 \text{ qt} \\ \hline & & 2 \text{ gal } 3 \text{ qt} \end{array}$$
2 gal 3 qt of tea remains.

105. 1 c 4 fl oz = 8 fl oz + 4 fl oz
$$= 12 \text{ fl oz}$$
12 fl oz ÷ 2 = 6 fl oz
6 fluid ounces of beef broth should be used.

106. 85 ml · 8 · 16 = 10,880 ml = 10.88 L
8 boxes contain 10.88 liters of polish.

107. 6 L + 1300 ml + 2.6 L
= 6 L + 1.3 L + 2.6 L
= 9.9 L
Yes, since 9.9 L < 10 L, it will fit.

108. $7 \text{ m} \cdot \dfrac{3.28 \text{ ft}}{1 \text{ m}} = 22.96 \text{ ft}$

109. $11.5 \text{ yd} \cdot \dfrac{1\text{m}}{1.09 \text{ yd}} \approx 10.55 \text{ m}$

110. $17.5 \text{ L} \cdot \dfrac{1 \text{ gal}}{3.79 \text{ L}} \approx 4.62 \text{ gal}$

111. $7.8 \text{ L} \cdot \dfrac{1.06 \text{ qt}}{1 \text{ L}} \approx 8.27 \text{ qt}$

112. $15 \text{ oz} \cdot \dfrac{28.35 \text{ g}}{1 \text{ oz}} = 425.25 \text{ g}$

113. $23 \text{ lb} \cdot \dfrac{1 \text{ kg}}{2.20 \text{ lb}} \approx 10.45 \text{ kg}$

114. $100 \text{ m} \cdot \dfrac{1.09 \text{ yd}}{1\text{m}} = 109 \text{ yd}$

115. $82 \text{ kg} \cdot \dfrac{2.20 \text{ lb}}{1 \text{ kg}} = 180.4 \text{ lb}$

116. $3 \text{ L} \cdot \dfrac{1.06 \text{ qt}}{1 \text{ L}} = 318 \text{ qt}$

117. $1.2 \text{ mm} = 0.12 \text{ cm} \cdot \dfrac{1 \text{ in}}{2.54 \text{ cm}} \cdot 50 \approx 2.36 \text{ in}$

118. $F = \dfrac{9}{5} \cdot 245 + 32 = 441 + 32 = 473$
245°C = 473°F

119. $F = \dfrac{9}{5} \cdot 160 + 32$
$= 288 + 32$
$= 320$
160°C = 320°F

120. F = 1.8(42) + 32
$= 75.6 + 32$
$= 107.6$
42°C = 107.6°F

121. F = 1.8 · 86 + 32
$= 154.8 + 32$
$= 186.8° \text{F}$
86°C = 186.8°F

122. $C = \dfrac{5}{9} \cdot (93.2 - 32)$
$= \dfrac{5}{9} \cdot 61.2$
$= \dfrac{306.0}{9}$
$= 34$
93.2°F = 34°C

123. $C = \frac{5}{9} \cdot (51.8 - 32)$

$= \frac{5}{9} \cdot 19.8$

$= \frac{99}{9}$

$= 11$

$51.8°F = 11°C$

124. $C = \frac{5}{9} \cdot (41.3 - 32)$

$= \frac{5}{9} \cdot 9.3$

$= \frac{46.5}{9}$

$= 5.1\overline{6}$

≈ 5.2

$41.3°F \approx 5.2°C$

125. $C = \frac{5}{9} \cdot (80 - 32)$

$= \frac{5}{9} \cdot 48$

$= \frac{240}{9}$

$= 26.\overline{6}$

≈ 26.7

$80°F \approx 26.7°C$

126. $C = \frac{5}{9} \cdot (35 - 32)$

$= \frac{5}{9} \cdot 3$

$= \frac{15}{9}$

$= 1.\overline{6}$

≈ 1.7

$35°F \approx 1.7°C$

127. $F = \frac{9}{5} \cdot 165 + 32$

$= 297 + 32$

$= 329$

$165°C = 329°F$

128. $\frac{20}{8} = \frac{x}{15}$

$20 \cdot 15 = 8x$

$300 = 8x$

$\frac{300}{8} = \frac{8x}{4}$

$\frac{75}{2} = x$

$37.5 = x$

129. $\frac{x}{20} = \frac{16}{24}$

$20 \cdot 16 = 24x$

$320 = 24x$

$\frac{320}{24} = \frac{24x}{24}$

$\frac{40}{3} = x$

$13\frac{1}{3} = x$

130. $\frac{x}{5.8} = \frac{24}{8}$

$8x = (5.8)(24)$

$8x = 139.2$

$\frac{8x}{8} = \frac{139.2}{8}$

$x = 17.4$

131. $\frac{8\frac{2}{3}}{n} = \frac{12\frac{1}{2}}{9\frac{3}{8}}$

$\frac{\frac{26}{3}}{n} = \frac{\frac{25}{2}}{\frac{75}{8}}$

$\left(\frac{26}{3}\right)\left(\frac{75}{8}\right) = \left(\frac{25}{2}\right)n$

$\frac{325}{4} = \frac{25}{2}x$

$\frac{2}{25} \cdot \frac{325}{4} = \frac{2}{25} \cdot \frac{25}{2}x$

$\frac{13}{2} = x$

$6\frac{1}{2} = x$

132. Let x = building height.

$$\frac{\text{man shadow}}{\text{building shadow}} = \frac{\text{man height}}{\text{building height}}$$

$$\frac{7\text{ feet}}{42\text{ feet}} = \frac{5\frac{1}{2}\text{ feet}}{x\text{ feet}}$$

$$\frac{7}{42} = \frac{5\frac{1}{2}}{x}$$

$$7x = \left(5\frac{1}{2}\right)(42)$$

$$7x = \frac{11}{2} \cdot 42$$

$$7x = 231$$

$$\frac{7x}{7} = \frac{231}{7}$$

$$x = 33$$

The building is 33 feet tall.

133. $$\frac{2\text{ inches}}{24\text{ feet}} = \frac{x\text{ inches}}{10\text{ feet}} = \frac{y\text{ inches}}{26\text{ feet}}$$

$$\frac{2}{24} = \frac{x}{10}$$

$$2 \cdot 10 = 24x$$

$$20 = 24x$$

$$\frac{20}{24} = \frac{24x}{24}$$

$$\frac{5}{6} = x$$

$$\frac{2}{24} = \frac{y}{26}$$

$$2 \cdot 26 = 24y$$

$$52 = 24y$$

$$\frac{52}{24} = \frac{24y}{24}$$

$$\frac{13}{6} = y$$

$$2\frac{1}{6} = y$$

x is $\frac{5}{6}$ inches and y is $2\frac{1}{6}$ inches.

134. They are congruent because of Angle-Side-Angle (ASA).

135. They are not congruent.

Chapter 8 Test

1. The complement of a 78° angle is $90° - 78° = 12°$.

2. The supplement of a 124° angle is $180° - 124° = 56°$.

3. $\angle x = 90° - 40° = 50°$

4. Since $\angle x$ and the 62° angle are supplementary angles, $\angle x = 180° - 62° = 118°$. $\angle y$ and the 62° angle are vertical angles, so $\angle y = 62°$. $\angle x$ and $\angle z$ are vertical angles, so $\angle z = 118°$.

5. $\angle x$ and the 73° angle are vertical angles, so $\angle x = 73°$. $\angle y$ and the 73° angle are corresponding angles, so $\angle y = 73°$. $\angle z$ and $\angle y$ are vertical angles, so $\angle z = 73°$.

6. $d = 2r$
$d = 2(3.1\text{ m})$
$d = 6.2\text{ m}$

7. $r = \frac{1}{2}d$
$r = \frac{1}{2}(20\text{ in})$
$r = 10\text{ in}$

8. $C = 2\pi r$
$= 2 \cdot \pi \cdot 9\text{ inches}$
$= 18\pi\text{ inches}$
$\approx 18 \cdot 3.14\text{ inches}$
$= 56.52\text{ inches}$

$A = \pi r^2$
$= \pi \cdot (9\text{ inches})^2$
$= 81\pi\text{ square inches}$
$\approx 81 \cdot 3.14\text{ square inches}$
$= 254.34\text{ square inches}$

9. $P = 2l + 2w$
$= 2 \cdot 7\text{ yards} + 2 \cdot 5.3\text{ yards}$
$= 14\text{ yards} + 10.6\text{ yards}$
$= 24.6\text{ yards}$

$A = lw$
$= 7\text{ yards} \cdot 5.3\text{ yards}$
$= 37.1\text{ square yards}$

10.

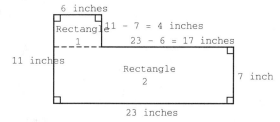

Perimeter = 6 inches + 4 inches + 17 inches + 7 inches + 23 inches + 11 inches
= 68 inches
Area of rectangle 1 = 6 inches · 4 inches
= 24 square inches
Area of rectangle 2 = 7 inches · 23 inches
= 161 square inches
Total area = 161 square inches + 24 square inches
= 185 square inches

11. $V = \pi r^2 h$
$= \pi \cdot (2 \text{ inches})^2 \cdot 5 \text{ inches}$
$= 20\pi \text{ cubic inches}$
$\approx 20 \cdot \dfrac{22}{7} \text{ cubic inches}$
$= \dfrac{440}{7} \text{ or } 62\dfrac{6}{7} \text{ cubic inches}$

12. $V = lwh$
$= 3 \text{ feet} \cdot 5 \text{ feet} \cdot 2 \text{ feet}$
$= 30 \text{ cubic feet}$

13. $P = 4s = 4 \cdot 4 \text{ inches} = 16 \text{ inches}$

14. $V = lwh$
$= 3 \text{ feet} \cdot 3 \text{ feet} \cdot 2 \text{ feet}$
$= 18 \text{ cubic feet}$

15. $A = lw$
$= 123.8 \text{ feet} \cdot 80 \text{ feet}$
$= 9904 \text{ square feet}$

16.
$$12\overline{)280}$$
23
-24
40
-36
4
280 in. = 23 ft 4 in.

17. $2\dfrac{1}{2} \text{ gal} = \dfrac{5}{2}\text{gal} \cdot \dfrac{4 \text{ qt}}{1 \text{ gal}} = 10 \text{ qt}$

18. $30 \text{ oz} = 30 \text{ oz} \cdot \dfrac{1 \text{ lb}}{16 \text{ oz}} = 1.875 \text{ lb}$

19. $2.8 \text{ tons} = 2.8 \text{ tons} \cdot \dfrac{2000 \text{ lb}}{1 \text{ ton}} = 5600 \text{ lb}$

20. $2.4 \text{ km} = 2400 \text{ m}$

21. $3.6 \text{ cm} = 36 \text{ mm}$

22. $4.3 \text{ dg} = 0.43 \text{ g}$

23. $0.83 \text{ L} = 830 \text{ ml}$

24. $7 \text{ kg} \cdot \dfrac{2.20 \text{ lb}}{1 \text{ kg}} = 15.4 \text{ lb}$

25. $8.5 \text{ in} \cdot \dfrac{2.54 \text{ cm}}{1 \text{ in}} = 21.59 \text{ cm}$

26. $C = \dfrac{5}{9} \cdot (84 - 32)$
$= \dfrac{5}{9} \cdot 52$
$= \dfrac{260}{9}$
$= 28.\overline{8}$
≈ 28.9
$84°F \approx 28.9°C$

27. $F = 1.8 \cdot 12.6 + 32$
$ = 22.68 + 32$
$ = 54.68$
$12.6°C = 54.7°F$

28. $8.4 \text{ m} \cdot \dfrac{1}{3} = 2.8 \text{ m}$
$8.4 \text{ m} - 2.8 \text{ m} = 5.6 \text{ m}$
The maples will be 5.6 meters tall after the cutting.

29. $20 \text{ gal} = 19 \text{ gal } 4 \text{ qt}$

$19 \text{ gal } 4 \text{ qt}$
$\underline{-\ 15 \text{ gal } 1 \text{ qt}}$
$4 \text{ gal } 3 \text{ qt}$

4 gal 3 qt of oil remains.

30. $340 \text{ cm} = 3.4 \text{ m}$

88.0 m
$\underline{+\ 3.4 \text{ m}}$
91.4 m

The span is 91.4 m long.

31. $2 \text{ ft } 9 \text{ in.}$
$\underline{\times \phantom{2 \text{ ft } 9 \text{ i}} 6}$
$12 \text{ ft } 54 \text{ in.} = 12 \text{ ft} + 4 \text{ ft } 6 \text{ in.}$
$\phantom{12 \text{ ft } 54 \text{ in.}} = 16 \text{ ft } 6 \text{ in. or } 16\dfrac{1}{2} \text{ ft}$

16 ft 6 inches or $16\dfrac{1}{2}$ feet of material is needed for 6 scarves.

32. $4667 \text{ gal} = \dfrac{4667}{1} \text{ gal} \cdot \dfrac{4 \text{ qt}}{1 \text{ gal}} \cdot \dfrac{2 \text{ pt}}{1 \text{ qt}}$
$\phantom{4667 \text{ gal}} = 4667 \cdot 4 \cdot 2 \text{ pt}$
$\phantom{4667 \text{ gal}} = 37{,}336 \text{ pt}$
Thus, 37,336 pints of ice cream were used.

33. $5 \text{ g} \cdot \dfrac{0.04 \text{ oz}}{1 \text{ g}} = 0.2 \text{ oz}$

34. $5 \text{ gal} \cdot \dfrac{3.79 \text{ L}}{1 \text{ gal}} = 18.95 \text{ L}$

35. $5 \text{ km} \cdot \dfrac{1 \text{ mi}}{1.61 \text{ km}} \approx 3.1 \text{ mi}$

36. $\dfrac{5}{8} = \dfrac{n}{12}$
$8n = 5 \cdot 12$
$8n = 60$
$\dfrac{8n}{8} = \dfrac{60}{8}$
$n = 7.5$

37. $\dfrac{\text{tower's shadow}}{\text{Tamara's shadow}} = \dfrac{\text{tower's height}}{\text{Tamara's height}}$

$\dfrac{48 \text{ feet}}{4 \text{ feet}} = \dfrac{x \text{ feet}}{5\frac{3}{4} \text{ feet}}$

$4x = 48 \cdot 5\dfrac{3}{4}$

$4x = 48 \cdot \dfrac{23}{4}$

$4x = 276$

$\dfrac{4x}{4} = \dfrac{276}{4}$

$x = 69$

The tower is 69 feet tall.

Cumulative Review

1. $3a - 6 = a + 4$
$3a - 6 - a = a + 4 - a$
$2a - 6 = 4$
$2a - 6 + 6 = 4 + 6$
$2a = 10$
$\dfrac{2a}{2} = \dfrac{10}{2}$
$a = 5$

2. $2x + 1 = 3x - 5$
$2x + 1 - 3x = 3x - 5 - 3x$
$-x + 1 = -5$
$-x + 1 - 1 = -5 - 1$
$-x = -6$
$\dfrac{-x}{-1} = \dfrac{-6}{-1}$
$x = 6$

3.
   a. $\left(\dfrac{2}{5}\right)^4 = \left(\dfrac{2}{5}\right)\left(\dfrac{2}{5}\right)\left(\dfrac{2}{5}\right)\left(\dfrac{2}{5}\right) = \dfrac{16}{625}$

   b. $\left(-\dfrac{1}{4}\right)^2 = \left(-\dfrac{1}{4}\right)\left(-\dfrac{1}{4}\right) = \dfrac{1}{16}$

4.

a. $\left(-\dfrac{1}{3}\right)^3 = \left(-\dfrac{1}{3}\right)\left(-\dfrac{1}{3}\right)\left(-\dfrac{1}{3}\right) = -\dfrac{1}{27}$

b. $\left(\dfrac{3}{7}\right)^2 = \left(\dfrac{3}{7}\right)\left(\dfrac{3}{7}\right) = \dfrac{9}{49}$

5.

$$
\begin{aligned}
1\tfrac{4}{5} &= \ 1\tfrac{8}{10}\\
4 &= \ 4\\
+\,2\tfrac{1}{2} &= +\,2\tfrac{5}{10}\\
\hline
&\ \ 7\tfrac{13}{10} = 7+1\tfrac{3}{10} = 8\tfrac{3}{10}
\end{aligned}
$$

6.

$$
\begin{aligned}
2\tfrac{1}{3} &= \ 2\tfrac{5}{15}\\
4\tfrac{2}{5} &= \ 4\tfrac{6}{15}\\
+\,3 &= +\,3\\
\hline
&\ \ 9\tfrac{11}{15}
\end{aligned}
$$

7.
$$
\begin{aligned}
&11.1x - 6.3 + 8.9x - 4.6\\
&= 11.1x + 8.9x - 6.3 - 4.6\\
&= 20x - 10.9
\end{aligned}
$$

8.
$$
\begin{aligned}
&2.5y + 3.7 - 1.3y - 1.9\\
&= 2.5y - 1.3y + 3.7 - 1.9\\
&= 1.2y + 1.8
\end{aligned}
$$

9.
$$\dfrac{0.7 + 1.84}{0.4} = \dfrac{2.54}{0.4} = 6.35$$

10.
$$\dfrac{0.12 + 0.96}{0.5} = \dfrac{1.08}{0.5} = 2.16$$

11.
$$0.\overline{7} = 0.\overline{7} = \dfrac{7}{9}$$

12.
$$0.43 > 0.40 = \dfrac{2}{5}$$

13.
$$
\begin{aligned}
0.5y + 2.3 &= 1.65\\
0.5y + 2.3 - 2.3 &= 1.65 - 2.3\\
0.5y &= -0.65\\
\dfrac{0.5y}{0.5} &= \dfrac{-0.65}{0.5}\\
y &= -1.3
\end{aligned}
$$

14.
$$
\begin{aligned}
0.4x - 9.3 &= 2.7\\
0.4x - 9.3 + 9.3 &= 2.7 + 9.3\\
0.4x &= 12\\
\dfrac{0.4x}{0.4} &= \dfrac{12}{0.4}\\
x &= 30
\end{aligned}
$$

15. Two sides of the square with the diagonal will form a right triangle, therefore we use the Pythagorean Theorem. The diagonal is C.
$$
\begin{aligned}
a^2 + b^2 &= c^2\\
300^2 + 300^2 &= c^2\\
90,000 + 90,000 &= c^2\\
180,000 &= c^2\\
\sqrt{180,000} &= c\\
424 &\approx c
\end{aligned}
$$
The diagonal is 424 feet.

16. The length, width, and diagonal of the rectangle will form a right triangle, so we will use the Pythagorean Theorem. The diagonal is C.
$$
\begin{aligned}
a^2 + b^2 &= c^2\\
200^2 + 125^2 &= c^2\\
40,000 + 15,625 &= c^2\\
55,625 &= c^2\\
\sqrt{55,625} &= c\\
236 &\approx c
\end{aligned}
$$
The diagonal is 236 feet.

17.

a. $\dfrac{\text{width}}{\text{length}} = \dfrac{5}{7}$

b. $\dfrac{\text{length}}{\text{perimeter}} = \dfrac{7}{5+7+5+7} = \dfrac{7}{24}$

18.

a. $\dfrac{\text{side}}{\text{perimeter}} = \dfrac{9}{9+9+9+9} = \dfrac{9}{36} = \dfrac{1}{4}$

b. $\dfrac{\text{perimeter}}{\text{area}} = \dfrac{36}{9^2} = \dfrac{36}{81} = \dfrac{4}{9}$

19.
$$
\begin{aligned}
\dfrac{4}{25} &= \dfrac{x}{140}\\
25x &= 560\\
x &= 22.4
\end{aligned}
$$
The standard dose is 22.4 cc

20.

$$\frac{2}{3} = \frac{5}{x}$$
$$2x = 15$$
$$x = 7.5$$

7.5 cups of flour is needed

21.

$$\frac{17}{100} = 17\%$$

22.

$$\frac{17}{100} = 17\%$$

23.

$$13 = 0.065 \cdot x$$
$$\frac{13}{0.065} = x$$
$$200 = x$$

24.

$$54 = 0.045 \cdot x$$
$$\frac{54}{0.045} = x$$
$$1200 = x$$

25.

$$x = .30 \cdot 9$$
$$x = 2.7$$

26.

$$x = .42 \cdot 30$$
$$x = 12.6$$

27.

$$\text{percent increase} = \frac{45 - 34}{34} = \frac{11}{34} \approx 32\%$$

28.

$$\text{percent increase} = \frac{19 - 15}{15} = \frac{4}{15} \approx 27\%$$

29.

sales tax $= \$85.50 \cdot 0.075 = \$6.41$
total price $= \$85.50 + \$6.41 = \$91.91$

30.

sales tax $= \$375 \cdot 0.08 = \$30$
total price $= \$375 + \$30 = \$405$

31. Arrange numbers from smallest to largest
25, 54, 56, 57, 60, 71, 98
Median: the middle number which is 57.

32. Arrange numbers from smallest to largest
60, 72, 83, 89, 85
Median: the middle number which is 83.

33.

$$\frac{\text{number of ways the event can occur}}{\text{number of possible outcomes}} = \frac{1}{4}$$

34.

$$\frac{\text{number of ways the event can occur}}{\text{number of possible outcomes}} = \frac{2}{7}$$

35. $90° - 48° = 42°$

36. $180° - 137° = 43°$

37.

$$8 \text{ ft} \cdot \frac{12 \text{ in}}{1 \text{ ft}} = 96 \text{ inches}$$

38.

$$7 \text{ yd} \cdot \frac{3 \text{ ft}}{1 \text{ yd}} = 21 \text{ feet}$$

39.

$$\begin{array}{r} 8 \text{ tons } 1000 \text{ lb} = 7 \text{ tons } 3000 \text{ lb} \\ -3 \text{ tons } 1350 \text{ lb} = -3 \text{ tons } 1350 \text{ lb} \\ \hline 4 \text{ tons } 1650 \text{ lb} \end{array}$$

40.

$$\begin{array}{r} 9 \text{ lb } 3 \text{ oz} \\ +8 \text{ lb } 15 \text{ oz} \\ \hline 17 \text{ lb } 18 \text{ oz} = 181 \text{ lb } 2 \text{ oz} \end{array}$$

41.

$$C = \frac{5}{9}(F - 32)$$
$$C = \frac{5}{9}(59 - 32)$$
$$C = \frac{135}{9}$$
$$C = 15$$

59° F is equal to 15° C

42.

$$C = \frac{5}{9}(86 - 32)$$
$$C = \frac{270}{9}$$
$$C = 30$$

86° F is equal to 30° C

Chapter 9

Chapter 9 Pretest

1. $5(2x+9)-3 = 10x+45-3$
$$= 10x+42$$

2. $-5(2y-3)+1 = -10y+15+1$
$$= -10y+16$$

3. $\quad 3-x = -12$
$$3-x-3 = -12-3$$
$$-x = -15$$
$$\frac{-x}{-1} = \frac{-15}{-1}$$
$$x = 15$$

4. $12-(5-4b) = 9+3b$
$$12-5+4b = 9+3b$$
$$7+4b = 9+3b$$
$$7+4b-3b = 9+3b-3b$$
$$7+b = 9$$
$$7+b-7 = 9-7$$
$$b = 2$$

5. $\quad \dfrac{2}{3}m = -8$
$$\frac{3}{2}\left(\frac{2}{3}m\right) = \frac{3}{2}(-8)$$
$$m = -12$$

6. $\quad -7-3y = 17+5y$
$$-7-3y-5y = 17+5y-5y$$
$$-7-8y = 17$$
$$-7-8y+7 = 17+7$$
$$-8y = 24$$
$$\frac{-8y}{-8} = \frac{24}{-8}$$
$$y = -3$$

7. $3(1-4x)+2(5x) = 9$
$$3-12x+10x = 9$$
$$3-2x = 9$$
$$3-2x-3 = 9-3$$
$$-2x = 6$$
$$\frac{-2x}{-2} = \frac{6}{-2}$$
$$x = -3$$

8. $\quad 0.20x+0.15(60) = 0.75(18)$
$$100\left[0.20x+0.15(60)\right] = 100\left[0.75(18)\right]$$
$$20x+15(60) = 75(18)$$
$$20x+900 = 1350$$
$$20x+900-900 = 1350-900$$
$$20x = 450$$
$$\frac{20x}{20} = \frac{450}{20}$$
$$x = 22.5$$

9.
$$2(x-1) = 2x+5$$
$$2x-2 = 2x+5$$
$$2x-2-2x = 2x+5-2x$$
$$-2 = 5, \text{ false}$$

There is no solution

10. Let $x =$ the unknown number

$$3\left[x+(-2)\right] = x+2$$
$$3x-6 = x+2$$
$$3x-x-6 = x+2-x$$
$$2x-6 = 2$$
$$2x-6+6 = 2+6$$
$$2x = 8$$
$$\frac{2x}{2} = \frac{8}{2}$$
$$x = 4$$

The number is 4

11. Let $x =$ the smaller integer and
$x+2 =$ the next even integer

$$3x = 2(x+2)+16$$
$$3x = 2x+4+16$$
$$3x = 2x+20$$
$$3x-2x = 2x-2x+20$$
$$x = 20$$
$$x+2 = 20+2 = 22$$

The integers are 20 and 22

12. $V = \dfrac{1}{3}Ah;\ V = 60,\ h = 4$

$$60 = \frac{1}{3}A(4)$$
$$\frac{3}{4}(60) = \frac{3}{4}\left(\frac{1}{3}\right)A(4)$$
$$45 = A$$

13. $A = \dfrac{1}{2}bh;\ A = 18,\ h = 4$

$$18 = \frac{1}{2}b(4)$$
$$18 = 2b$$
$$\frac{18}{2} = \frac{2b}{2}$$
$$9 = b$$

The base is 9 feet.

14.
$$2x+y = 8$$
$$2x+y-2x = 8-2x$$
$$y = 8-2x$$

15. Commutative Property of Multiplication

16. Associative Property of Addition

17. Identity Property of Addition

18.
$$-4+x \le 2$$
$$-4+4+x \le 2+4$$
$$x \le 6$$

19.
$$-\frac{3}{2}y > 6$$
$$-\frac{2}{3}\left(-\frac{3}{2}y\right) < -\frac{2}{3}(6)$$
$$y < -4$$

271

20.
$$-5x+3 \le 4(x-6)$$
$$-5x+3 \le 4x-24$$
$$-5x-4x+3 \le 4x-4x-24$$
$$-9x+3 \le -24$$
$$-9x+3-3 \le -24-3$$
$$-9x \le -27$$
$$\frac{-9x}{-9} \ge \frac{-27}{-9}$$
$$x \ge 3$$

Practice Problems 9.1

1. False, since 8 is to the right of 6 on the number line.

2. True, since 100 is to the right of 10 on the number line.

3. True, since 21=21.

4. True, since 21=21.

5. True, since 0 is to the left of 5 on the number line.

6. True, since 25 is to the right of 22 on the number line.

7. **a.** $14 \ge 14$
   b. $0 < 5$
   c. $9 \ne 10$

8. -282 represents 282 feet below sea level.

9.

10. **a.** The natural numbers are 6 and 913.
    b. The whole numbers are 0, 6 and 913.
    c. The integers are -100, 0, 6 and 913.
    d. The rational numbers are -100, $-2/5$, 0, 6 and 913.
    e. The irrational number is π.
    f. The real numbers are all numbers in the given set.

Exercise Set 9.1

1. $4 < 10$

3. $7 > 3$

5. $6.26 = 6.26$

7. $0 < 7$

9. $32 < 212$

11. True, since 11=11.

13. False, since 10 is to the left of 11 on the number line.

15. False, since 11 is to the left of 24 on the number line.

17. True, since 7 is to the right of 0 on the number line.

19. $30 \le 45$

21. $20 \le 25$

23. $6 > 0$

25. $-12 < -10$

27. $7 < 11$

29. $5 \ge 4$

31. $15 \ne -2$

33. $14,494$ represents an altitude of 14,494 feet.
-282 represents 282 feet below sea level.

35. $-34,841$ represents a population decrease of 34,841.

37. 475 represents a deposit of $475.
-195 represents a withdrawal of $195.

39.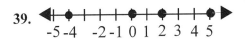

41.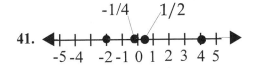

43.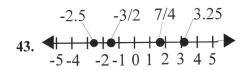

45. The number 0 belongs to the sets of: whole numbers, integers, rational numbers, and real numbers.

47. The number -2 belongs to the sets of: integers, rational numbers, and real numbers.

49. The number 2650 belongs to the sets of: natural numbers, whole numbers, integers, rational numbers, and real numbers.

51. The number 2/3 belongs to the sets of: rational numbers and real numbers.

53. False. Rational numbers may be non-integers.

55. True

57. False. Negative numbers may be irrational.

59. False. Irrational numbers are real.

61. $\left|-5\right| > -4$ since $5 > -4$

63. $\left|-1\right| = \left|1\right|$ since $1 = 1$

65. $\left|-2\right| < \left|-3\right|$ since $2 < 3$

67. $\left|0\right| < \left|-8\right|$ since $8 < 8$

69. False, since $\dfrac{1}{2}$ is to the right of $\dfrac{1}{3}$ on the number line.

71. True, since $5.3 = 5.3$

73. False, since -9.6 is to the left of -9.1 on the number line.

75. True, since $-\dfrac{2}{3}$ is to the left of $-\dfrac{1}{5}$ on the number line.

77. Blue Ridge Parkway has the most visitors.

79. Blue Ridge Parkway had more visitors than Golden Gate National Recreation Area: $19.0 \geq 14.5$

81. $-0.04 > -26.7$

83. The sun is brighter since $-26.7 < -0.04$.

85. The sun is brighter since -26.7 is to the left of all other numbers listed.

87. Answers may vary.

Practice Problems 9.2

1. a. $7 \cdot y = y \cdot 7$
   b. $4 + x = x + 4$

2. a. $5 \cdot (-3 \cdot 6) = (5 \cdot -3) \cdot 6$
   b. $(-2 + 7) + 3 = -2 + (7 + 3)$

3. Commutative property

4. Associative property

5. $(-3 + x) + 17 = [x + (-3)] + 17$
   $= x + (-3 + 17) = x + 14$

6. $4(5x) = (4 \cdot 5)x = 20x$

7. $5(x + y) = 5x + 5y$

8. $-3(2 + 7x) = -3(2) + (-3)(7x) = -6 - 21x$

9. $4(x + 6y - 2z) = 4(x) + 4(6y) - 4(2z)$
   $= 4x + 24y - 8z$

10. $-1(3 - a) = -1(3) - (-1)(a) = -3 + a$

11. $-(8 + a - b) = -1(8 + a - b)$
   $= -1(8) + (-1)(a) - (-1)(b) = -8 - a + b$

12. $9(2x + 4) + 9 = 9(2x) + 9(4) + 9$
   $= 18x + 36 + 9 = 18x + 45$

13. $9 \cdot 3 + 9 \cdot y = 9(3 + y)$

14. $4x + 4y = 4(x + y)$

15. Additive inverse property

16. Commutative property of addition

17. Associative property of addition

18. Commutative property of addition

19. Multiplicative inverse property

20. Identity element for addition

21. Commutative and associative properties of multiplication

Exercise Set 9.2

1. $x + 16 = 16 + x$

3. $-4 \cdot y = y \cdot (-4)$

5. $xy = yx$

7. $2x + 13 = 13 + 2x$

9. $(xy) \cdot z = x \cdot (yz)$

11. $2 + (a + b) = (2 + a) + b$

13. $4 \cdot (ab) = 4a \cdot (b)$

15. $(a + b) + c = a + (b + c)$

17. $8 + (9 + b) = (8 + 9) + b = 17 + b$

19. $4(6y) = (4 \cdot 6)y = 24y$

21. $\dfrac{1}{5}(5y) = \left(\dfrac{1}{5} \cdot 5\right)y = 1 \cdot y = y$

23. $(13 + a) + 13 = (a + 13) + 13 = a + (13 + 13)$
$$= a + 26$$

25. $-9(8x) = (-9 \cdot 8)x = -72x$

27. $\dfrac{3}{4}\left(\dfrac{4}{3}s\right) = \left(\dfrac{3}{4} \cdot \dfrac{4}{3}\right)s = 1s = s$

29. Answers may vary

31. $4(x + y) = 4x + 4y$

33. $9(x - 6) = 9x - 9 \cdot 6 = 9x - 54$

35. $2(3x + 5) = 2(3x) + 2(5) = 6x + 10$

37. $7(4x - 3) = 7(4x) - 7(3) = 28x - 21$

39. $3(6 + x) = 3(6) + 3x = 18 + 3x$

41. $-2(y - z) = -2y - (-2)z = -2y + 2z$

43. $-7(3y + 5) = -7(3y) + (-7)(5) = -21y - 35$

45. $5(x + 4m + 2) = 5x + 5(4m) + 5(2)$
$$= 5x + 20m + 10$$

47. $-4(1 - 2m + n) = -4(1) - (-4)(2m) + (-4)n$
$$= -4 + 8m - 4n$$

49. $-(5x + 2) = -1(5x + 2) = -1(5x) + (-1)(2)$
$$= -5x - 2$$

51. $-(r - 3 - 7p) = -1(r - 3 - 7p)$
$$= -1r - (-1)(3) - (-1)(7p)$$
$$= -r + 3 + 7p$$

53. $\dfrac{1}{2}(6x + 8) = \dfrac{1}{2}(6x) + \dfrac{1}{2}(8)$
$$= \left(\dfrac{1}{2} \cdot 6\right)x + \left(\dfrac{1}{2} \cdot 8\right) = 3x + 4$$

55. $-\dfrac{1}{3}(3x - 9y) = -\dfrac{1}{3}(3x) - \left(-\dfrac{1}{3}\right)(9y)$
$$= \left(-\dfrac{1}{3} \cdot 3\right)x - \left(-\dfrac{1}{3} \cdot 9\right)y = -1 \cdot x + 3 \cdot y$$
$$= -x + 3y$$

57. $3(2r+5)-7 = 3(2r)+3(5)-7$
$$= 6r+15+(-7) = 6r+8$$

59. $-9(4x+8)+2 = -9(4x)+(-9)(8)+2$
$$= -36x-72+2 = -36x-70$$

61. $-4(4x+5)-5 = -4(4x)+(-4)(5)-5$
$$= -16x+(-20)+(-5) = -16x-25$$

63. $4\cdot1+4\cdot y = 4(1+y)$

65. $11x+11y = 11(x+y)$

67. $(-1)\cdot5+(-1)\cdot x = -1(5+x) = -(5+x)$

69. $30a+30b = 30(a+b)$

71. The additive inverse of 16 is -16 since
$16+(-16) = 0$

73. The additive inverse of -8 is 8 since
$-8+8 = 0$

75. The additive inverse of $-(-1.2)$ is -1.2
since $-(-1.2)+(-1.2) = 1.2+(-1.2) = 0$

77. The additive inverse of $-|-2|$ is 2 since
$-|-2|+2 = -2+2 = 0$

79. The multiplicative inverse of $\frac{2}{3}$ is $\frac{3}{2}$
since $\frac{2}{3}\cdot\frac{3}{2} = 1$

81. The multiplicative inverse of $-\frac{5}{6}$ is $-\frac{6}{5}$
since $-\frac{5}{6}\cdot-\frac{6}{5} = 1$

83. The multiplicative inverse of $3\frac{5}{6}$ is $\frac{6}{23}$
since $3\frac{5}{6}\cdot\frac{6}{23} = \frac{23}{6}\cdot\frac{6}{23} = 1$

85. The multiplicative inverse of -2 is $-\frac{1}{2}$
since $-2\cdot-\frac{1}{2} = 1$

87. Commutative property of multiplication

89. Associative property of addition

91. Distributive property

93. Associative property of multiplication

95. Identity property of addition

97. Distributive property

99. Associative and commutative properties
of multiplication

101. $y-x^2 = 3-(-1)^2 = 3-1 = 2$

103. $a-b^2 = 2-(-5)^2 = 2-25 = -23$

105. $yz-y^2-x = (-5)(0)-(-5)^2$
$$= (-5)(0)-25$$
$$= 0-25$$
$$= -25$$

107.

Expression	Opposite	Reciprocal
8	−8	$\dfrac{1}{8}$

109.

Expression	Opposite	Reciprocal
x	$-x$	$\dfrac{1}{x}$

111.

Expression	Opposite	Reciprocal
$2x$	$-2x$	$\dfrac{1}{2x}$

113. **a**. Commutative property of addition

b. Commutative property of addition

c. Associative property of addition

115. Answers may vary

117. No

119. Yes

Practice Problems 9.3

1. $5(3x-1)+2=12x+6$

$$15x-5+2=12x+6$$
$$15x-3=12x+6$$

$$15x-12x-3=12x-12x+6$$
$$3x-3=6$$
$$3x-3+3=6+3$$
$$3x=9$$
$$\frac{3x}{3}=\frac{9}{3}$$
$$x=3$$

2. $9(5-x)=-3x$

$$45-9x=-3x$$
$$45-9x+9x=-3x+9x$$
$$45=6x$$
$$\frac{45}{6}=\frac{6x}{6}$$
$$\frac{15}{2}=x$$

3. $\dfrac{5}{2}x-1=\dfrac{3}{2}x-4$

$$2\left(\frac{5}{2}x-1\right)=2\left(\frac{3}{2}x-4\right)$$
$$5x-2=3x-8$$
$$5x-3x-2=3x-3x-8$$
$$2x-2=-8$$
$$2x-2+2=-8+2$$
$$2x=-6$$
$$\frac{2x}{2}=\frac{-6}{2}$$
$$x=-3$$

277

4. $\dfrac{3(x-2)}{5} = 3x+6$

$5\left(\dfrac{3(x-2)}{5}\right) = 5(3x+6)$

$3(x-2) = 15x+30$

$3x-6 = 15x+30$

$3x-15x-6 = 15x-15x+30$

$-12x-6 = 30$

$-12x-6+6 = 30+6$

$-12x = 36$

$\dfrac{-12x}{-12} = \dfrac{36}{-12}$

$x = -3$

5. $0.06x-0.10(x-2) = -0.02(8)$

$100\big[0.06x-0.10(x-2)\big] = 100\big[-0.02(8)\big]$

$6x-10(x-2) = -2(8)$

$6x-10x+20 = -16$

$-4x+20 = -16$

$-4x+20-20 = -16-20$

$-4x = -36$

$\dfrac{-4x}{-4} = \dfrac{-36}{-4}$

$x = 9$

6. $5(2-x)+8x = 3(x-6)$

$10-5x+8x = 3x-18$

$10+3x = 3x-18$

$10+3x-3x = 3x-3x-18$

$10 = -18$

There is no solution

7. $-6(2x+1)-14 = -10(x+2)-2x$

$-12x-6-14 = -10x-20-2x$

$-12x-20 = -12x-20$

$-12x+12x-20 = -12x+12x-20$

$-20 = -20$

Every real number is a solution

Graphing Calculator Explorations 9.3

1. Solution

2. Solution

3. Not a solution

4. Not a solution

5. Solution

6. Solution

Exercise Set 9.3

1. $-4y+10 = -2(3y+1)$

$-4y+10 = -6y-2$

$-4y+6y+10 = -6y+6y-2$

$2y+10 = -2$

$2y+10-10 = -2-10$

$2y = -12$

$\dfrac{2y}{2} = \dfrac{-12}{2}$

$y = -6$

3.
$$9x - 8 = 10 + 15x$$
$$9x - 15x - 8 = 10 + 15x - 15x$$
$$-6x - 8 = 10$$
$$-6x - 8 + 8 = 10 + 8$$
$$-6x = 18$$
$$\frac{-6x}{-6} = \frac{18}{-6}$$
$$x = -3$$

5.
$$-2(3x - 4) = 2x$$
$$-6x + 8 = 2x$$
$$-6x + 6x + 8 = 2x + 6x$$
$$8 = 8x$$
$$\frac{8}{8} = \frac{8x}{8}$$
$$1 = x$$

7.
$$4(2n - 1) = (6n + 4) + 1$$
$$8n - 4 = 6n + 4 + 1$$
$$8n - 4 = 6n + 5$$
$$8n - 6n - 4 = 6n - 6n + 5$$
$$2n - 4 = 5$$
$$2n - 4 + 4 = 5 + 4$$
$$2n = 9$$
$$\frac{2n}{2} = \frac{9}{2}$$
$$n = \frac{9}{2}$$

9. $5(2x - 1) - 2(3x) = 1$
$$10x - 5 - 6x = 1$$
$$4x - 5 = 1$$
$$4x - 5 + 5 = 1 + 5$$
$$4x = 6$$
$$\frac{4x}{4} = \frac{6}{4}$$
$$x = \frac{3}{2}$$

11. $6(x - 3) + 10 = -8$
$$6x - 18 + 10 = -8$$
$$6x - 8 = -8$$
$$6x - 8 + 8 = -8 + 8$$
$$6x = 0$$
$$\frac{6x}{6} = \frac{0}{6}$$
$$x = 0$$

13. $8 - 2(a - 1) = 7 + a$
$$8 - 2a + 2 = 7 + a$$
$$-2a + 10 = 7 + a$$
$$-2a + 2a + 10 = 7 + a + 2a$$
$$10 = 7 + 3a$$
$$10 - 7 = 7 - 7 + 3a$$
$$3 = 3a$$
$$\frac{3}{3} = \frac{3a}{3}$$
$$1 = a$$

15.
$$4x + 3 = 2x + 11$$
$$4x - 2x + 3 = 2x - 2x + 11$$
$$2x + 3 = 11$$
$$2x + 3 - 3 = 11 - 3$$
$$2x = 8$$
$$\frac{2x}{2} = \frac{8}{2}$$
$$x = 4$$

17.
$$-2y - 10 = 5y + 18$$
$$-2y - 5y - 10 = 5y - 5y + 18$$
$$-7y - 10 = 18$$
$$-7y - 10 + 10 = 18 + 10$$
$$-7y = 28$$
$$\frac{-7y}{-7} = \frac{28}{-7}$$
$$y = -4$$

19.
$$-3(t - 5) + 2t = 5t - 4$$
$$-3t + 15 + 2t = 5t - 4$$
$$-t + 15 = 5t - 4$$
$$-t - 5t + 15 = 5t - 5t - 4$$
$$-6t + 15 = -4$$
$$-6t + 15 - 15 = -4 - 15$$
$$-6t = -19$$
$$\frac{-6t}{-6} = \frac{-19}{-6}$$
$$t = \frac{19}{6}$$

21.
$$5y + 2(y - 6) = 4(y + 1) - 2$$
$$5y + 2y - 12 = 4y + 4 - 2$$
$$7y - 12 = 4y + 2$$
$$7y - 4y - 12 = 4y - 4y + 2$$
$$3y - 12 = 2$$

$$3y - 12 + 12 = 2 + 12$$
$$3y = 14$$
$$\frac{3y}{3} = \frac{14}{3}$$
$$y = \frac{14}{3}$$

23.
$$\frac{3}{4}x - \frac{1}{2} = 1$$
$$4\left(\frac{3}{4}x - \frac{1}{2}\right) = 4(1)$$
$$3x - 2 = 4$$
$$3x - 2 + 2 = 4 + 2$$
$$3x = 6$$
$$\frac{3x}{3} = \frac{6}{3}$$
$$x = 2$$

25.
$$x + \frac{5}{4} = \frac{3}{4}x$$
$$4\left(x + \frac{5}{4}\right) = 4\left(\frac{3}{4}x\right)$$
$$4x + 5 = 3x$$
$$4x - 3x + 5 = 3x - 3x$$
$$x + 5 = 0$$
$$x + 5 - 5 = 0 - 5$$
$$x = -5$$

27.
$$\frac{x}{2} - 1 = \frac{x}{5} + 2$$
$$10\left(\frac{x}{2} - 1\right) = 10\left(\frac{x}{5} + 2\right)$$
$$5x - 10 = 2x + 20$$
$$5x - 2x - 10 = 2x - 2x + 20$$
$$3x - 10 = 20$$
$$3x - 10 + 10 = 20 + 10$$

$$3x = 30$$

$$\frac{3x}{3} = \frac{30}{3}$$

$$x = 10$$

29. $\dfrac{6(3-z)}{5} = -z$

$$5\left[\frac{6(3-z)}{5}\right] = 5(-z)$$

$$6(3-z) = -5z$$

$$18 - 6z = -5z$$

$$18 - 6z + 6z = -5z + 6z$$

$$18 = z$$

31. $0.06 - 0.01(x+1) = -0.02(2-x)$

$$100\left[0.06 - 0.01(x+1)\right] = 100\left[-0.02(2-x)\right]$$

$$6 - (x+1) = -2(2-x)$$

$$6 - x - 1 = -4 + 2x$$

$$5 - x = -4 + 2x$$

$$5 - x - 2x = -4 + 2x - 2x$$

$$5 - 3x = -4$$

$$5 - 5 - 3x = -4 - 5$$

$$-3x = -9$$

$$\frac{-3x}{-3} = \frac{-9}{-3}$$

$$x = 3$$

33. $\dfrac{3(x-5)}{2} = \dfrac{2(x+5)}{3}$

$$6\left[\frac{3(x-5)}{2}\right] = 6\left[\frac{2(x+5)}{3}\right]$$

$$9(x-5) = 4(x+5)$$

$$9x - 45 = 4x + 20$$

$$9x - 4x - 45 = 4x - 4x + 20$$

$$5x - 45 = 20$$

$$5x - 45 + 45 = 20 + 45$$

$$5x = 65$$

$$\frac{5x}{5} = \frac{65}{5}$$

$$x = 13$$

35. $0.50x + 0.15(70) = 0.25(142)$

$$100\left[0.50x + 0.15(70)\right] = 100\left[0.25(142)\right]$$

$$50x + 15(70) = 25(142)$$

$$50x + 1050 = 3550$$

$$50x + 1050 - 1050 = 3550 - 1050$$

$$50x = 2500$$

$$\frac{50x}{50} = \frac{2500}{50}$$

$$x = 50$$

37. $0.12(y-6) + 0.06y = 0.08y - 0.07(10)$

$$100\left[0.12(y-6) + 0.06y\right] = 100\left[0.08y - 0.07(10)\right]$$

$$12(y-6) + 6y = 8y - 7(10)$$

$$12y - 72 + 6y = 8y - 70$$

$$18y - 72 = 8y - 70$$

$$18y - 8y - 72 = 8y - 8y - 70$$

$$10y - 72 = -70$$

$$10y - 72 + 72 = -70 + 72$$

$$10y = 2$$

$$\frac{10y}{10} = \frac{2}{10}$$

$$y = \frac{1}{5} = 0.2$$

39. $\dfrac{2(x+1)}{4} = 3x - 2$

$4\left[\dfrac{2(x+1)}{4}\right] = 4(3x-2)$

$2(x+1) = 12x - 8$

$2x + 2 = 12x - 8$

$2x - 12x + 2 = 12x - 12x - 8$

$-10x + 2 = -8$

$-10x + 2 - 2 = -8 - 2$

$-10x = -10$

$\dfrac{-10x}{-10} = \dfrac{-10}{-10}$

$x = 1$

41. $x + \dfrac{7}{6} = 2x - \dfrac{7}{6}$

$6\left(x + \dfrac{7}{6}\right) = 6\left(2x - \dfrac{7}{6}\right)$

$6x + 7 = 12x - 7$

$6x - 12x + 7 = 12x - 12x - 7$

$-6x + 7 = -7$

$-6x + 7 - 7 = -7 - 7$

$-6x = -14$

$\dfrac{-6x}{-6} = \dfrac{-14}{-6}$

$x = \dfrac{14}{6}$

$x = \dfrac{7}{3}$

43. $\dfrac{9}{2} + \dfrac{5}{2}y = 2y - 4$

$2\left(\dfrac{9}{2} + \dfrac{5}{2}y\right) = 2(2y - 4)$

$9 + 5y = 4y - 8$

$9 + 5y - 4y = 4y - 4y - 8$

$9 + y = -8$

$9 - 9 + y = -8 - 9$

$y = -17$

45. Answers may vary

47. $5x - 5 = 2(x+1) + 3x - 7$

$5x - 5 = 2x + 2 + 3x - 7$

$5x - 5 = 5x - 5$

$5x - 5x - 5 = 5x - 5x - 5$

$-5 = -5$

Every real number is a solution.

49. $\dfrac{x}{4} + 1 = \dfrac{x}{4}$

$4\left(\dfrac{x}{4} + 1\right) = 4\left(\dfrac{x}{4}\right)$

$x + 4 = x$

$x - x + 4 = x - x$

$4 = 0$

There is no solution.

51. $3x - 7 = 3(x+1)$

$3x - 7 = 3x + 3$

$3x - 3x - 7 = 3x - 3x + 3$

$-7 = 3$

There is no solution.

53. $2(x+3)-5=5x-3(1+x)$

$2x+6-5=5x-3-3x$

$2x+1=2x-3$

$2x-2x+1=2x-2x-3$

$1=-3$

There is no solution.

55. Answers may vary

57. $x+(2x-3)+(3x-5)=x+2x-3+3x-5$

$=6x-8$

The perimeter is $(6x-8)$ meters

59. $-8-x$

61. $-3+2x$

63. $9(x+20)$

65. $1000(7x-10)=50(412+100x)$

$7000x-10,000=20,600+5000x$

$7000x-5000x-10,000$

$\qquad =20,600+5000x-5000x$

$2000x-10,000=20,600$

$2000x-10,000+10,000$

$\qquad =20,600+10,000$

$2000x=30,600$

$\dfrac{2000x}{2000}=\dfrac{30,600}{2000}$

$x=15.3$

67. $0.035x+5.112=0.010x+5.107$

$1000(0.035x+5.112)=1000(0.010x+5.107)$

$35x+5112=10x+5107$

$35x-10x+5112=10x-10x+5107$

$25x+5112=5107$

$25x+5112-5112=5107-5112$

$25x=-5$

$\dfrac{25x}{25}=\dfrac{-5}{25}$

$x=-\dfrac{1}{5}=-0.2$

69. Since the perimeter is the sum of the lengths of the sides,

$x+x+x+2x+2x=28$

$7x=28$

$\dfrac{7x}{7}=\dfrac{28}{7}$

$x=4$

$2x=2(4)=8$

The lengths are 4 cm and 8 cm.

Integrated Review-Real Numbers and Solving Linear Equations

1. Whole numbers, integers, rational numbers, real numbers

2. Natural numbers, whole numbers, integers, rational numbers, real numbers

3. Rational numbers, whole numbers, rational numbers, real numbers

4. Natural numbers, whole numbers, rational numbers, real numbers

5. Integers, rational numbers, real numbers

6. Rational numbers, real numbers

7. Rational numbers, real numbers

8. Irrational numbers, real numbers

9. $7(d-3)+10 = 7d-21+10$
$$= 7d-11$$

10. $9(z+7)-15 = 9z+63-15$
$$= 9z+48$$

11. $-4(3y-4)+12y = -12y+16+12y$
$$= 16$$

12. $-3(2x+5)-6x = -6x-15-6x$
$$= -12x-15$$

13. $\quad 2x-7 = 6x-27$
$2x-6x-7 = 6x-6x-27$
$-4x-7 = -27$
$-4x-7+7 = -27+7$
$-4x = -20$
$\dfrac{-4x}{-4} = \dfrac{-20}{-4}$
$x = 5$

14. $\quad 3+8y = 3y-2$
$3+8y-3y = 3y-3y-2$
$3+5y = -2$
$3-3+5y = -2-3$
$5y = -5$
$\dfrac{5y}{5} = \dfrac{-5}{5}$
$y = -1$

15. $-3a+6+5a = 7a-8a$
$2a+6 = -a$
$2a-2a+6 = -a-2a$
$6 = -3a$
$\dfrac{6}{-3} = \dfrac{-3a}{-3}$
$-2 = a$

16. $\quad 4b-8-b = 10b-3b$
$3b-8 = 7b$
$3b-3b-8 = 7b-3b$
$-8 = 4b$
$\dfrac{-8}{4} = \dfrac{4b}{4}$
$-2 = b$

17. $\quad -\dfrac{2}{3}x = \dfrac{5}{9}$
$-\dfrac{3}{2}\left(-\dfrac{2}{3}x\right) = -\dfrac{3}{2}\left(\dfrac{5}{9}\right)$
$x = -\dfrac{5}{6}$

18. $\quad -\dfrac{3}{8}y = -\dfrac{1}{16}$
$-\dfrac{8}{3}\left(-\dfrac{3}{8}y\right) = -\dfrac{8}{3}\left(-\dfrac{1}{16}\right)$
$y = \dfrac{1}{6}$

19. $\quad 10 = -6n+16$
$10-16 = -6n+16-16$
$-6 = -6n$
$\dfrac{-6}{-6} = \dfrac{-6n}{-6}$
$1 = n$

284

20.
$$-5 = -2m + 7$$
$$-5 - 7 = -2m + 7 - 7$$
$$-12 = -2m$$
$$\frac{-12}{-2} = \frac{-2m}{-2}$$
$$6 = m$$

21. $3(5c - 1) - 2 = 13c + 3$
$$15c - 3 - 2 = 13c + 3$$
$$15c - 5 = 13c + 3$$
$$15c - 13c - 5 = 13c - 13c + 3$$
$$2c - 5 = 3$$
$$2c - 5 + 5 = 3 + 5$$
$$2c = 8$$
$$\frac{2c}{2} = \frac{8}{2}$$
$$c = 4$$

22. $4(3t + 4) - 20 = 3 + 5t$
$$12t + 16 - 20 = 3 + 5t$$
$$12t - 4 = 3 + 5t$$
$$12t - 5t - 4 = 3 + 5t - 5t$$
$$7t - 4 = 3$$
$$7t - 4 + 4 = 3 + 4$$
$$7t = 7$$
$$\frac{7t}{7} = \frac{7}{7}$$
$$t = 1$$

23.
$$\frac{2(z + 3)}{3} = 5 - z$$
$$3\left[\frac{2(z + 3)}{3}\right] = 3(5 - z)$$
$$2z + 6 = 15 - 3z$$

$$2z + 3z + 6 = 15 - 3z + 3z$$
$$5z + 6 = 15$$
$$5z + 6 - 6 = 15 - 6$$
$$5z = 9$$
$$\frac{5z}{5} = \frac{9}{5}$$
$$z = \frac{9}{5}$$

24.
$$\frac{3(w + 2)}{4} = 2w + 3$$
$$4\left[\frac{3(w + 2)}{4}\right] = 4(2w + 3)$$
$$3w + 6 = 8w + 12$$
$$3w - 8w + 6 = 8w - 8w + 12$$
$$-5w + 6 = 12$$
$$-5w + 6 - 6 = 12 - 6$$
$$-5w = 6$$
$$\frac{-5w}{-5} = \frac{6}{-5}$$
$$w = -\frac{6}{5}$$

25.
$$-2(2x - 5) = -3x + 7 - x + 3$$
$$-4x + 10 = -4x + 10$$
$$-4x + 4x + 10 = -4x + 4x + 10$$
$$10 = 10$$
Every real number is a solution

26.
$$-4(5x - 2) = -12x + 4 - 8x + 4$$
$$-20x + 8 = -20x + 8$$
$$-20x + 20x + 8 = -20x + 20x + 8$$
$$8 = 8$$
Every real number is a solution

27.
$$0.02(6t-3)=0.04(t-2)+0.02$$
$$100\left[0.02(6t-3)\right]=100\left[0.04(t-2)+0.02\right]$$
$$2(6t-3)=4(t-2)+2$$
$$12t-6=4t-8+2$$
$$12t-6=4t-6$$
$$12t-4t-6=4t-4t-6$$

$$8t-6=-6$$
$$8t-6+6=-6+6$$
$$8t=0$$
$$\frac{8t}{8}=\frac{0}{8}$$
$$t=0$$

28.
$$0.03(m+7)=0.02(5-m)+0.03$$
$$100\left[0.03(m+7)\right]=100\left[0.02(5-m)+0.03\right]$$
$$3(m+7)=2(5-m)+3$$
$$3m+21=10-2m+3$$
$$3m+21=13-2m$$
$$3m+2m+21=13-2m+2m$$
$$5m+21=13$$
$$5m+21-21=13-21$$
$$5m=-8$$
$$\frac{5m}{5}=\frac{-8}{5}$$
$$m=-\frac{8}{5}=-1.6$$

29.
$$-3y=\frac{4(y-1)}{5}$$
$$5(-3y)=5\left[\frac{4(y-1)}{5}\right]$$
$$-15y=4y-4$$

$$-15y-4y=4y-4y-4$$
$$-19y=-4$$
$$\frac{-19y}{-19}=\frac{-4}{-19}$$
$$y=\frac{4}{19}$$

30.
$$-4x=\frac{5(1-x)}{6}$$
$$6(-4x)=6\left[\frac{5(1-x)}{6}\right]$$
$$-24x=5-5x$$
$$-24x+5x=5-5x+5x$$
$$-19x=5$$
$$\frac{-19x}{-19}=\frac{5}{-19}$$
$$x=-\frac{5}{19}$$

31.
$$\frac{5}{3}x-\frac{7}{3}=x$$
$$3\left(\frac{5}{3}x-\frac{7}{3}\right)=3(x)$$
$$5x-7=3x$$
$$5x-5x-7=3x-5x$$
$$-7=-2x$$
$$\frac{-7}{-2}=\frac{-2x}{-2}$$
$$\frac{7}{2}=x$$

32. $\dfrac{7}{5}n + \dfrac{3}{5} = -n$

$$5\left(\dfrac{7}{5}n + \dfrac{3}{5}\right) = 5(-n)$$

$$7n + 3 = -5n$$

$$7n - 7n + 3 = -5n - 7n$$

$$3 = -12n$$

$$\dfrac{3}{-12} = \dfrac{-12n}{-12}$$

$$-\dfrac{1}{4} = n$$

Practice Problems 9.4

1.   Let $x =$ the number.

$$3(x - 5) = 2x - 3$$

$$3x - 15 = 2x - 3$$

$$3x - 2x - 15 = 2x - 2x - 3$$

$$x - 15 = -3$$

$$x - 15 + 15 = -3 + 15$$

$$x = 12$$

The number $= 12$

2. Let $x =$ length of the shorter piece and $5x =$ length of the longer piece.

$$x + 5x = 18$$

$$6x = 18$$

$$\dfrac{6x}{6} = \dfrac{18}{6}$$

$$x = 3$$

$$5x = 5(3) = 15$$

The shorter piece $= 3$ ft. and the longer piece $= 15$ ft

3. Let $x =$ the number of electoral votes for Texas and $x + 22 =$ the number for California.

$$x + x + 22 = 86$$

$$2x + 22 = 86$$

$$2x + 22 - 22 = 86 - 22$$

$$2x = 64$$

$$\dfrac{2x}{2} = \dfrac{64}{2}$$

$$x = 32$$

$$x + 22 = 32 + 22 = 54$$

Texas had 32 electoral votes
California had 54 electoral votes.

4. Let $x =$ the number of miles driven and $0.20 =$ the charge per mile.

$$34 + 0.20x = 104$$

$$34 - 34 + 0.20x = 104 - 34$$

$$0.20x = 70$$

$$\dfrac{0.20x}{0.20} = \dfrac{70}{0.20}$$

$$x = 350$$

350 miles were driven

5. Let $x =$ the measure of the smallest angle, $2x =$ the measure of the second angle, and $3x =$ the measure of the third.

$$x + 2x + 3x = 180$$

$$6x = 180$$

$$\dfrac{6x}{6} = \dfrac{180}{6}$$

$$x = 30$$

$$2x = 2(30) = 60$$
$$3x = 3(30) = 90$$

The 3 angles are $30°$, $60°$, $90°$

6. Let x = first integer

Then $x + 1$ = second integer

$$x + (x + 1) = x + x + 1 = 2x + 1$$

Exercise Set 9.4

1.   Let x = the number.

$$5\left(2x + \frac{1}{5}\right) = 5\left(3x - \frac{4}{5}\right)$$
$$10x + 1 = 15x - 4$$
$$10x - 15x + 1 = 15x - 15x - 4$$
$$-5x + 1 = -4$$
$$-5x + 1 - 1 = -4 - 1$$
$$-5x = -5$$
$$\frac{-5x}{-5} = \frac{-5}{-5}$$
$$x = 1$$

The number = 1

3.   Let x = the number.

$$2(x - 8) = 3(x + 3)$$
$$2x - 16 = 3x + 9$$
$$2x - 2x - 16 = 3x - 2x + 9$$
$$-16 = x + 9$$
$$-16 - 9 = x + 9 - 9$$
$$-25 = x$$

The number = -25

5.   Let x = the number.

$$2x(3) = 5x - \frac{3}{4}$$
$$6x = 5x - \frac{3}{4}$$
$$6x - 5x = 5x - 5x - \frac{3}{4}$$
$$x = -\frac{3}{4}$$

The number = $-\frac{3}{4}$

7.   Let x = the number.

$$3(x + 5) = 2x - 1$$
$$3x + 15 = 2x - 1$$
$$3x - 2x + 15 = 2x - 2x - 1$$
$$x + 15 = -1$$
$$x + 15 - 15 = -1 - 15$$
$$x = -16$$

The number = -16

9. Let x = the salary of the govenor of Oregon and $x + 83,400$ = the salary of the govenor of Michigan.

$$x + x + 83,400 = 270,600$$
$$2x + 83,400 = 270,600$$
$$2x + 83,400 - 83,400 = 270,600 - 83,400$$
$$2x = 187,200$$
$$\frac{2x}{2} = \frac{187,200}{2}$$
$$x = 93,600$$
$$x + 83,400 = 93,600 + 83,400 = 177,000$$

The govenor of Oregon makes $93,600 and the govenor of Michigan makes $177,000.

11. Let x = length of the first piece,
$2x$ = length of the second piece,
and $5x$ = length of the third piece.

$$x + 2x + 5x = 40$$
$$8x = 40$$
$$\frac{8x}{8} = \frac{40}{8}$$
$$x = 5$$

$$2x = 2(5) = 10$$
$$5x = 5(5) = 25$$

The lengths are 5, 10, and 25 inches

13. Let x = the number of miles driven,
0.29 = the charge per mile, and
24.95 = the charge per day.

$$2(24.95) + 0.29x = 100$$
$$49.90 + 0.29x = 100$$
$$49.90 - 49.90 + 0.29x = 100 - 49.90$$
$$0.29x = 50.10$$
$$\frac{0.29x}{0.29} = \frac{50.10}{0.29}$$
$$x = 172$$

172 miles were driven

15. Let x = the measure of each of the two
equal angle, and $2x + 30$ = the measure
of the third.

$$x + x + 2x + 30 = 180$$
$$4x + 30 = 180$$
$$4x + 30 - 30 = 180 - 30$$
$$4x = 150$$

$$\frac{4x}{4} = \frac{150}{4}$$
$$x = 37.5$$
$$2x + 30 = 2(37.5) + 30 = 105$$

The 3 angles are $37.5°, 37.5°, 105°$

17. Let x = the number of votes for
cerulean and $x + 3366$ = the number
for blue.

$$x + x + 3366 = 19,278$$
$$2x + 3366 = 19,278$$
$$2x + 3366 - 3366 = 19,278 - 3366$$
$$2x = 15,912$$
$$\frac{2x}{2} = \frac{15,912}{2}$$
$$x = 7956$$
$$x + 3366 = 7956 + 3366 = 11,322$$

Cerulean had 7956 votes.
Blue had 11,322 votes.

19. Let x = the measure of the smaller
angle and $3x$ = the measure of the other.

$$x + 3x = 180$$
$$4x = 180$$
$$\frac{4x}{4} = \frac{180}{4}$$
$$x = 45$$
$$3x = 3(45) = 135$$

The 2 angles are $45°, 135°$.

21. Let x = length of the shorter piece
and $2x + 2$ = length of the longer piece.

$$x + 2x + 2 = 17$$
$$3x + 2 = 17$$

$$3x + 2 - 2 = 17 - 2$$
$$3x = 15$$
$$\frac{3x}{3} = \frac{15}{3}$$
$$x = 5$$

$$2x + 2 = 2(5) + 2 = 12$$

The shorter piece = 5 ft. and the longer piece = 12 ft

23. Let $x =$ diameter and $5x + 8 =$ height.
$$x + 5x + 8 = 14$$
$$6x + 8 = 14$$
$$6x + 8 - 8 = 14 - 8$$
$$6x = 6$$
$$\frac{6x}{6} = \frac{6}{6}$$
$$x = 1$$
$$5x + 8 = 5(1) + 8 = 13$$
The diameter = 1 meter. and the height = 13 meters.

25. Let $x =$ the area of the Gobi Desert and $7x =$ the area of the Sahara Desert.
$$x + 7x = 4,000,000$$
$$8x = 4,000,000$$
$$\frac{8x}{8} = \frac{4,000,000}{8}$$
$$x = 500,000$$
$$7x = 7(500,000) = 3,500,000$$
Gobi Desert: 500,000 sq mi.
Sahara Desert: 3,500,000 sq mi.

27. Answers may vary

29. Texas and Florida

31. Let $x =$ the amount spent by Pennsylvania and $2x - 8.1 =$ the amount spent by Hawaii.
$$x + 2x - 8.1 = 60.9$$
$$3x - 8.1 = 60.9$$
$$3x - 8.1 + 8.1 = 60.9 + 8.1$$
$$3x = 69$$
$$\frac{3x}{3} = \frac{69}{3}$$
$$x = 23$$
$$2x - 8.1 = 2(23) - 8.1 = 37.9$$
Pennsylvania spent $23 million.
Hawaii spends $37.9 million.

33. Let $x =$ the floor area of the Empire State Building.
$$3x = 6.5$$
$$\frac{3x}{3} = \frac{6.5}{3}$$
$$x = \frac{6.5}{3} \approx 2.2$$
The floor area of the Empire State Building is about 2.2 million sq ft.

35. Let $x =$ Purdue's score and $x + 2 =$ NotreDame's score.
$$x + x + 2 = 134$$
$$2x + 2 = 134$$
$$2x + 2 - 2 = 134 - 2$$
$$2x = 132$$
$$\frac{2x}{2} = \frac{132}{2}$$
$$x = 66$$

$x + 2 = 66 + 2 = 68$

Purdue's score was 66 and
NotreDame's score was 68.

37. Let x = number of medals won by
Germany, $x + 1$ = number of medals
won by Australia, and $x + 2$ = number
of medals won by China.

$$x + x + 1 + x + 2 = 174$$
$$3x + 3 = 174$$
$$3x + 3 - 3 = 174 - 3$$
$$3x = 171$$
$$\frac{3x}{3} = \frac{171}{3}$$
$$x = 57$$

$x + 1 = 57 + 1 = 58$, $x + 2 = 57 + 2 = 59$

Germany won 57 medals.

Australia won 58 medals.

China won 59 medals.

39. Let x = the measure of the smallest
angle, $x + 2$ = the measure of the second,
and $x + 4$ = the measure of the third.

$$x + x + 2 + x + 4 = 180$$
$$3x + 6 = 180$$
$$3x + 6 - 6 = 180 - 6$$
$$3x = 174$$
$$\frac{3x}{3} = \frac{174}{3}$$
$$x = 58$$

$x + 2 = 58 + 2 = 60$

$x + 4 = 58 + 4 = 62$

The 3 angles are $58°$, $60°$, $62°$

41. $\dfrac{1}{2}(x - 1) = 37$

43. $\dfrac{3(x + 2)}{5} = 0$

45. Let $W = 7$ and $L = 10$

$2W + 2L = 2(7) + 2(10) = 14 + 20 = 34$

47. Let $r = 15$

$\pi r^2 = \pi (15)^2 = 225\pi$

49. Answers may vary

51. Let $L = 1.6W$

$$P = 2W + 2L$$
$$78 = 2W + 2(1.6W)$$
$$78 = 2W + 3.2W$$
$$78 = 5.2W$$
$$\frac{78}{5.2} = \frac{5.2W}{5.2}$$
$$15 = W$$

$1.6W = 1.6(15) = 24$

Width = 15 ft, Length = 24 ft

53. Answers may vary

Practice Problems 9.5

1. Let $d = 1180$ and $r = 50$

$$d = rt$$
$$1180 = 50t$$
$$\frac{1180}{50} = \frac{50t}{50}$$
$$23.6 = t$$

They will drive 23.6 hours

2. Let $A = 450$ and $w = 18$

$$A = lw$$
$$450 = l(18)$$
$$\frac{450}{18} = \frac{18l}{18}$$
$$l = 25$$

The length of the deck is 25 ft

3. $C = 2\pi r$

$$\frac{C}{2\pi} = \frac{2\pi r}{2\pi}$$
$$\frac{C}{2\pi} = r$$

4. $P = 2l + 2w$

$$P - 2l = 2l - 2l + 2w$$
$$P - 2l = 2w$$
$$\frac{P - 2l}{2} = \frac{2w}{2}$$
$$\frac{P - 2l}{2} = w$$

5. $A = \dfrac{a+b}{2}$

$$2A = 2\left(\frac{a+b}{2}\right)$$
$$2A = a + b$$
$$2A - a = a - a + b$$
$$2A - a = b$$

Exercise Set 9.5

1. Let $A = 45$ and $b = 15$

$$A = bh$$
$$45 = 15h$$
$$\frac{45}{15} = \frac{15h}{15}$$
$$3 = h$$

3.   Let $S = 102$, $l = 7$, and $w = 3$

$$S = 4lw + 2wh$$
$$102 = 4(7)(3) + 2(3)h$$
$$102 = 84 + 6h$$
$$102 - 84 = 84 - 84 + 6h$$
$$18 = 6h$$
$$\frac{18}{6} = \frac{6h}{6}$$
$$3 = h$$

5. Let $A = 180$, $B = 11$, and $b = 7$

$$A = \frac{1}{2}(B + b)h$$
$$180 = \frac{1}{2}(11 + 7)h$$
$$2(180) = 2\left[\frac{1}{2}(18)h\right]$$

$$360 = 18h$$

$$\frac{360}{18} = \frac{18h}{18}$$

$$20 = h$$

7. Let $P = 30$, $a = 8$, and $b = 10$

$$P = a + b + c$$

$$30 = 8 + 10 + c$$

$$30 = 18 + c$$

$$30 - 18 = 18 - 18 + c$$

$$12 = c$$

9. Let $C = 15.7$, and $\pi = 3.14$

$$C = 2\pi r$$

$$15.7 = 2(3.14) r$$

$$15.7 = 6.28r$$

$$\frac{15.7}{6.28} = \frac{6.28r}{6.28}$$

$$2.5 = r$$

11. Let $I = 3750$, $P = 25,000$, and $R = 0.05$

$$I = PRT$$

$$3750 = 25,000(0.05)T$$

$$3750 = 1250T$$

$$\frac{3750}{1250} = \frac{1250T}{1250}$$

$$3 = T$$

13. Let $V = 565.2$, $r = 6$, and $\pi = 3.14$

$$V = \frac{1}{3}\pi r^2 h$$

$$565.2 = \frac{1}{3}(3.14)(6)^2 h$$

$$565.2 = 37.68h$$

$$\frac{565.2}{37.68} = \frac{37.68h}{37.68}$$

$$15 = h$$

15. Let $A = 52,400$ and $l = 400$

$$A = lw$$

$$52,400 = 400w$$

$$\frac{52,400}{400} = \frac{400w}{400}$$

$$131 = w$$

The width is 131 ft

17. Let $t = 2.5$ and $r = 55$

$$d = rt$$

$$d = 55(2.5)$$

$$d = 137.5$$

They are 137.5 miles apart.

19. Let $F = 122$

$$C = \frac{5}{9}(F - 32)$$

$$C = \frac{5}{9}(122 - 32)$$

$$C = \frac{5}{9}(90)$$

$$C = 50°\,C$$

21. Let $l = 8$, $w = 3$, and $h = 6$

$$V = lwh$$

$$V = 8(3)(6) = 144$$

Let x = number of fish and volume

per fish $= 1.5$

$$144 = 1.5x$$

$$\frac{144}{1.5} = \frac{1.5x}{1.5}$$

$$96 = x$$

96 piranhas can be placed in the tank.

23. Let $A = 1,813,500$ and $w = 150$

$$A = lw$$

$$1,813,500 = l(150)$$

$$\frac{1,813,500}{150} = \frac{150l}{150}$$

$$12,090 = l$$

The length is 12,090 ft

25. Let $d = 25,000$ and $r = 4000$

$$d = rt$$

$$25,000 = 4000t$$

$$\frac{25,000}{4000} = \frac{4000t}{4000}$$

$$6.25 = t$$

It will take 6.25 hours

27. Let $h = 60$, $B = 130$, and $b = 70$

$$A = \frac{1}{2}(B + b)h$$

$$A = \frac{1}{2}(130 + 70)60 = \frac{1}{2}(200)(60) = 6000$$

Let x = number of bags of fertilizer

and the area per bag $= 4000$.

$$4000x = 6000$$

$$\frac{4000x}{4000} = \frac{6000}{4000}$$

$$x = 1.5$$

Two bags must be purchased.

29. Let $l = 199$, $w = 78.5$, and $h = 33$

$$V = lwh$$

$$V = 199(78.5)(33) = 515,509.5$$

The volume must be 515,509.5 cu in.

31. Let $d = 16$, so $r = 8$

$$A = \pi r^2 = \pi(8)^2 = 64\pi$$

Let $d = 10$, so $r = 5$

$$A = 2\pi r^2 = 2\pi(5)^2 = 50\pi$$

One 16 inch pizza has more area and

therefore gives more pizza for the price.

33. Let $C = -78.5$

$$F = \frac{9}{5}C + 32 = \frac{9}{5}(-78.5) + 32$$

$$= -141.3 + 32 = -109.3$$

The equivalent temperature is $-109°$ F.

35. Let $d = 93,000,000$ and $r = 186,000$

$$d = rt$$

$$93,000,000 = 186,000t$$

$$\frac{93,000,000}{186,000} = \frac{186,000t}{186,000}$$

$$500 = t$$

It will take 500 seconds or $8\frac{1}{3}$ minutes.

37. Let $\pi = 3.14$ and $d = 9.5$ so $r = 4.75$

$$V = \frac{4}{3}\pi r^3 = \frac{4}{3}(3.14)(4.75)^3 = 449$$

The volume is 449 cu in.

39. Let $C = 167$

$$F = \frac{9}{5}C + 32 = \frac{9}{5}(167) + 32$$

$$= 300.6 + 32 = 332.6$$

The equivalent temperature is $332.6°$F.

41. Let $t = 1$ and $r = 270,000$

$$d = rt = 270,000(1) = 270,000 \text{ miles}$$

Let $x =$ number of times around when it is 25,120 miles per time.

$$25,120x = 270,000$$

$$\frac{25,120x}{25,120} = \frac{270,000}{25,120}$$

$$x = 10.7$$

It can circle the world about 10.7 times.

43. $20\dfrac{\text{miles}}{\text{hour}}$

$$= 20\frac{\text{miles}}{\text{hour}}\left(\frac{5280 \text{ feet}}{1 \text{ mile}}\right)\left(\frac{1 \text{ hour}}{3600 \text{ seconds}}\right)$$

$$= \frac{88}{3} \text{ feet/second}$$

Let $d = 1300$ and $r = \dfrac{88}{3}$

$$d = rt$$

$$1300 = \frac{88}{3}t$$

$$\frac{3}{88}(1300) = \frac{3}{88}\left(\frac{88}{3}t\right)$$

$$44.3 = t$$

It will take about 44.3 seconds.

45. Let $d = 42.8$ and $r = 552$

$$d = rt$$

$$42.8 = 552t$$

$$\frac{42.8}{552} = \frac{552t}{552}$$

$$\frac{42.8}{552} = t$$

$$\frac{42.8 \text{ hour}}{552}\left(\frac{60 \text{ min}}{1 \text{ hour}}\right) = 4.65 \text{ min}$$

It will last about 4.65 minutes.

47. $f = 5gh$

$$\frac{f}{5g} = \frac{5gh}{5g}$$

$$\frac{f}{5g} = h$$

49. $V = LWH$

$$\frac{V}{LH} = \frac{LWH}{LH}$$

$$\frac{V}{LH} = W$$

51. $3x + y = 7$

$$3x - 3x + y = 7 - 3x$$

$$y = 7 - 3x$$

53. $A = P + PRT$

$$A - P = P - P + PRT$$

$$A - P = PRT$$

$$\frac{A - P}{PT} = \frac{PRT}{PT}$$

$$\frac{A - P}{PT} = R$$

55. $V = \dfrac{1}{3} Ah$

$$3V = 3\left(\frac{1}{3} Ah\right)$$

$$3V = Ah$$

$$\frac{3V}{h} = \frac{Ah}{h}$$

$$\frac{3V}{h} = A$$

57. $P = a + b + c$

$$P - b - c = a + b - b + c - c$$

$$P - b - c = a$$

59. $S = 2\pi rh + 2\pi r^2$

$$S - 2\pi r^2 = 2\pi rh + 2\pi r^2 - 2\pi r^2$$

$$S - 2\pi r^2 = 2\pi rh$$

$$\frac{S - 2\pi r^2}{2\pi r} = \frac{2\pi rh}{2\pi r}$$

$$\frac{S - 2\pi r^2}{2\pi r} = h$$

61. $32\% = 32(0.01) = 0.32$

63. $200\% = 200(0.01) = 2$

65. $0.17 = 0.17(100\%) = 17\%$

67. $7.2 = 7.2(100\%) = 720\%$

69. $N = R + \dfrac{V}{G}$

$$N - R = R - R + \frac{V}{G}$$

$$N - R = \frac{V}{G}$$

$$G(N - R) = G\frac{V}{G}$$

$$G(N - R) = V$$

71. The original box has a volume

$V = LWH$

The altered box, has a length $2L$, a width $2W$, a height $2H$ and a new volume

$V = 2L(2W)(2H) = 8LWH$.

The volume is multiplied by 8.

73. Let $C = F$

$$F = \frac{9}{5}C + 32$$

$$F = \frac{9}{5}F + 32$$

$$F - \frac{9}{5}F = \frac{9}{5}F - \frac{9}{5}F + 32$$

$$-\frac{4}{5}F = 32$$

$$-\frac{5}{4}\left(-\frac{4}{5}F\right) = -\frac{5}{4}(32)$$

$$F = -40$$

The measurements are the same
number at $-40°$.

Practice Problems 9.6

1. $x \geq -2$

2. $5 > x$

3. $x - 6 \geq -11$

$$x \geq -5$$

4. $-3x \leq 12$

$$\frac{-3x}{-3} \geq \frac{12}{-3}$$

$$x \geq -4$$

5. $5x > -20$

$$x > -4$$

6. $-3x + 11 \leq -13$

$$-3x \leq -24$$

$$\frac{-3x}{-3} \geq \frac{-24}{-3}$$

$$x \geq 8$$

$$\{x \mid x \geq 8\}$$

7. $-6x - 3 > -4(x + 1)$

$$-6x - 3 > -4x - 4$$

$$-2x - 3 > -4$$

$$-2x > -1$$

$$\frac{-2x}{-2} < \frac{-1}{-2}$$

$$x < \frac{1}{2}$$

$$\left\{x \mid x < \frac{1}{2}\right\}$$

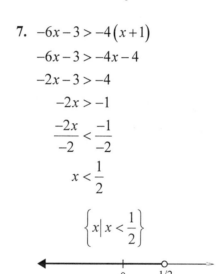

297

8. $3(x+5)-1 \geq 5(x-1)+7$

$3x+15-1 \geq 5x-5+7$

$3x+14 \geq 5x+2$

$-2x+14 \geq 2$

$-2 \geq -12$

$\dfrac{-2x}{-2} \leq \dfrac{-12}{-2}$

$x \leq 6$

$\{x | x \leq 6\}$

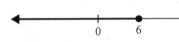

9. Let x = the amount of sales and

$0.04x$ = the amount earned from sales.

$600 + 0.04x \geq 3000$

$0.04x \geq 2400$

$x \geq 60,000$

He must sell at least $60,000.

Mental Math 9.6

1. $5x > 10$

$x > 2$

2. $4x < 20$

$x < 5$

3. $2x \geq 6$

$x \geq 8$

4. $9x \leq 63$

$x \leq 7$

5. -5 is not a solution to $x \geq -3$.

6. $|-6|$ is not a solution to $x < 6$.

7. 4.1 is not a solution to $x < 4.01$.

8. -4 is not a solution to $x \geq -3$.

Exercise Set 9.6

1. $x \leq -1$

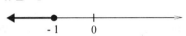

3. $x > \dfrac{1}{2}$

5. $y < 4$

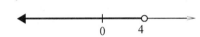

7. $-2 \leq m$

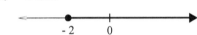

9. $x - 2 \geq -7$

$x \geq -5$

$\{x | x \geq -5\}$

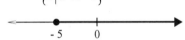

11. $-9 + y < 0$

$y < 9$

$\{y | y < 9\}$

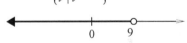

13. $3x - 5 > 2x - 8$

$x - 5 > -8$

$x > -3$

$\{x \mid x > -3\}$

15. $4x - 1 \le 5x - 2x$

$4x - 1 \le 3x$

$x - 1 \le 0$

$x \le 1$

$\{x \mid x \le 1\}$

17. $2x < -6$

$x < -3$

$\{x \mid x < -3\}$

19. $-8x \le 16$

$\dfrac{-8x}{-8} \ge \dfrac{16}{-8}$

$x \ge -2$

$\{x \mid x \ge -2\}$

21. $-x > 0$

$\dfrac{-x}{-1} < \dfrac{0}{-1}$

$x < 0$

$\{x \mid x < 0\}$

23. $\dfrac{3}{4}y \ge -2$

$y \ge -\dfrac{8}{3}$

$\left\{y \mid y \ge -\dfrac{8}{3}\right\}$

25. $-0.6y < -1.8$

$\dfrac{-0.6y}{-0.6} > \dfrac{-1.8}{-0.6}$

$y > 3$

$\{y \mid y > 3\}$

27. When multiplying or dividing by a negative number, the direction of the inequality sign must be reversed.

29. $3x - 7 < 6x + 2$

$-3x - 7 < 2$

$-3x < 9$

$\dfrac{-3x}{-3} > \dfrac{9}{-3}$

$x > -3$

$\{x \mid x > -3\}$

31. $5x - 7x \le x + 2$

$-2x \le x + 2$

$-3x \le 2$

$\dfrac{-3x}{-3} \le \dfrac{2}{-3}$

$x \le -\dfrac{2}{3}$

$\left\{ x \middle| x \le -\dfrac{2}{3} \right\}$

33. $-6x + 2 \ge 2(5 - x)$

$-6x + 2 \ge 10 - 2x$

$-4x + 2 \ge 10$

$-4x \ge 8$

$\dfrac{-4x}{-4} \le \dfrac{8}{-4}$

$x \le -2$

$\left\{ x \middle| x \le -2 \right\}$

35. $4(3x - 1) \le 5(2x - 4)$

$12x - 4 \le 10x - 20$

$2x - 4 \le -20$

$2x \le -16$

$x \le -8$

$\left\{ x \middle| x \le -8 \right\}$

37. $3(x + 2) - 6 > -2(x - 3) + 14$

$3x + 6 - 6 > -2x + 6 + 14$

$3x > -2x + 20$

$5x > 20$

$x > 4$

$\left\{ x \middle| x > 4 \right\}$

39. $-2(x - 4) - 3x < -(4x + 1) + 2x$

$-2x + 8 - 3x < -4x - 1 + 2x$

$-5x + 8 < -2x - 1$

$-3x + 8 < -1$

$-3x < -9$

$\dfrac{-3x}{-3} > \dfrac{-9}{-3}$

$x > 3$

$\left\{ x \middle| x > 3 \right\}$

41. $\dfrac{1}{2}(x - 5) < \dfrac{1}{3}(2x - 1)$

$6 \left[\dfrac{1}{2}(x - 5) \right] < 6 \left[\dfrac{1}{3}(2x - 1) \right]$

$3x - 15 < 4x - 2$

$-x - 15 < -2$

$-x < 13$

$\dfrac{-x}{-1} > \dfrac{13}{-1}$

$x > -13$

$\left\{ x \middle| x > -13 \right\}$

43. $-5x + 4 \le -4(x - 1)$

$-5x + 4 \le -4x + 4$

$-x + 4 \le 4$

$-x \le 0$

$\dfrac{-x}{-1} \ge \dfrac{0}{-1}$

$x \ge 0$

$\left\{ x \middle| x \ge 0 \right\}$

45. Let x = the unknown number.
$$2x + 6 > -14$$
$$2x > -20$$
$$x > -10$$
All numbers greater than -10.

47. Let x = the length and 15 = the width.
$$P = 2l + 2w$$
$$2x + 2(15) \le 100$$
$$2x + 30 \le 100$$
$$2x \le 70$$
$$x \le 35$$
The maximum length is 35 cm.

49. Let x = his score on the third game.
$$\frac{146 + 201 + x}{3} \ge 180$$
$$3\left(\frac{146 + 201 + x}{3}\right) \ge 3(180)$$
$$347 + x \ge 540$$
$$x \ge 193$$
He must score at least 193.

51. $3^4 = (3)(3)(3)(3) = 81$

53. $1^8 = (1)(1)(1)(1)(1)(1)(1)(1) = 1$

55. $\left(\frac{7}{8}\right)^2 = \left(\frac{7}{8}\right)\left(\frac{7}{8}\right) = \frac{49}{64}$

57. Approximately 1000

59. The greatest increase is between 2000 and 2001, where the graph is the steepest.

61. 2001

63. Let x = his score on the final exam.
$$\frac{75 + 83 + 85 + 2x}{5} \ge 80$$
$$5\left(\frac{243 + 2x}{5}\right) \ge 5(80)$$
$$243 + 2x \ge 400$$
$$2x \ge 157$$
$$x \ge 78.5$$
He must score at least 78.5.

Chapter 9 Review

1. $8 < 10$

2. $7 > 2$

3. $-4 > -5$

4. $\frac{12}{2} > -8$

5. $|-7| < |-8|$

6. $|-9| > -9$

7. $-|-1| = -1$

8. $|-14| = -(-14)$

9. $1.2 > 1.02$

10. $-\frac{3}{2} < -\frac{3}{4}$

11. $4 \ge -3$

12. $6 \neq 5$

13. $0.03 < 0.3$

14. $400 > 155$

15. a. The natural numbers are 1 and 3.
   b. The whole numbers are 0, 1, and 3.
   c. The integers are -6, 0, 1, and 3.
   d. The rational numbers are $-6, 0, 1,$ $1\frac{1}{2}$, 3, and 9.62.
   e. The irrational number is π.
   f. The real numbers are all numbers in the given set.

16. a. The natural numbers are 2 and 5.
   b. The whole numbers are 2 and 5.
   c. The integers are -3, 2, and 5.
   d. The rational numbers are $-3, -1.6,$ $2, 5, \frac{11}{2}$, and 15.1.
   e. The irrational numbers are $\sqrt{5}$ and 2π.
   f. The real numbers are all numbers in the given set.

17. Friday

18. Wednesday

19. Commutative property of addition

20. Multiplicative identity property

21. Distributive property

22. Additive inverse property

23. Associative property of addition

24. Commutative property of multiplication

25. Distributive property

26. Associative property of multiplication

27. Multiplicative inverse property

28. Additive identity property

29.
$$5x + 25 = 20$$
$$5x + 25 - 25 = 20 - 25$$
$$\frac{5x}{5} = -\frac{5}{5}$$
$$x = -1$$

30. $5x - 6 + x = 4x$
$$6x - 6 = 4x$$
$$-6 = -2x$$
$$3 = x$$

31. $-y + 4y = -y$
$$3y = -y$$
$$4y = 0$$
$$y = 0$$

32. $-5x + \dfrac{3}{7} = \dfrac{10}{7}$
$$-5x = \frac{7}{7}$$
$$-5x = 1$$
$$x = -\frac{1}{5}$$

33. $\dfrac{5}{3}x + 4 = \dfrac{2}{3}x$

$$\dfrac{3}{3}x + 4 = 0$$

$$x = -4$$

34. $-(5x+1) = -7x+3$

$$-5x - 1 = -7x + 3$$

$$2x - 1 = 3$$

$$2x = 4$$

$$x = 2$$

35. $-4(2x+1) = -5x+5$

$$-8x - 4 = -5x + 5$$

$$-3x - 4 = 5$$

$$-3x = 9$$

$$x = -3$$

36. $-6(2x-5) = -3(9+4x)$

$$-12x + 30 = -27 - 12x$$

$$30 = -27$$

There is no solution.

37. $3(8y-1) = 6(5+4y)$

$$24y - 3 = 30 + 24y$$

$$-3 = 30$$

There is no solution.

38. $\dfrac{3(2-z)}{5} = z$

$$3(2-z) = 5z$$

$$6 - 3z = 5z$$

$$6 = 8z$$

$$\dfrac{6}{8} = z$$

$$\dfrac{3}{4} = z$$

39. $\dfrac{4(n+2)}{5} = -n$

$$4(n+2) = -5n$$

$$4n + 8 = -5n$$

$$8 = -9n$$

$$-\dfrac{8}{9} = n$$

40. $0.5(2n-3) - 0.1 = 0.4(6+2n)$

$$10\left[0.5(2n-3) - 0.1\right] = 10\left[0.4(6+2n)\right]$$

$$5(2n-3) - 1 = 4(6+2n)$$

$$10n - 15 - 1 = 24 + 8n$$

$$10n - 16 = 24 + 8n$$

$$2n - 16 = 24$$

$$2n = 40$$

$$n = 20$$

41. $-9 - 5a = 3(6a-1)$

$$-9 - 5a = 18a - 3$$

$$-9 = 23a - 3$$

$$-6 = 23a$$

$$-\dfrac{6}{23} = a$$

42. $\dfrac{5(c+1)}{6} = 2c-3$

$$5(c+1) = 6(2c-3)$$
$$5c+5 = 12c-18$$
$$-7c+5 = -18$$
$$-7c = -23$$
$$c = \dfrac{23}{7}$$

43. $\dfrac{2(8-a)}{3} = 4-4a$

$$2(8-a) = 3(4-4a)$$
$$16-2a = 12-12a$$
$$10a+16 = 12$$
$$10a = -4$$
$$a = \dfrac{-4}{10}$$
$$a = -\dfrac{2}{5}$$

44. $200(70x-3560) = -179(150x-19,300)$

$$14,000x-712,000 = -26,850x+3,454,700$$
$$40,850x-712,000 = 3,454,700$$
$$40,850x = 4,166,700$$
$$x = 102$$

45. $1.72y-0.04y = 0.42$

$$1.68y = 0.42$$
$$\dfrac{1.68y}{1.68} = \dfrac{0.42}{1.68}$$
$$y = 0.25$$

46. Let x = the first even integer.

$$\text{Sum } = x+(x+2)+(x+4) = 3x+6$$

47. Let x = the length and
$10x+50.5$ = the height.

$$x+10x+50.5 = 7327$$
$$11x+50.5 = 7327$$
$$11x = 7276.5$$
$$x = 661.5$$
$$10x+50.5 = 10(661.5)+50.5 = 6665.5$$

The height is 6665.5 inches.

48. Let x = the length of the shorter piece
and $2x$ = the length of the other.

$$x+2x = 12$$
$$3x = 12$$
$$x = 4$$
$$2x = 8$$

The lengths are 4 feet and 8 feet.

49. Let x = the number of Keebler plants
and $2x-1$ = the number of Kellogg plants.

$$x+2x-1 = 53$$
$$3x-1 = 53$$
$$3x = 54$$
$$x = 18$$
$$2x-1 = 2(18)-1 = 35$$

There were 18 Keebler plants
and 35 Kellogg plants.

50. Let $x =$ the first integer, $x + 1 =$ the second integer, and $x + 2 =$ the third.

$$x + x + 1 + x + 2 = -114$$
$$3x + 3 = -114$$
$$3x = -117$$
$$x = -39$$

$x + 1 = -38$, and $x + 2 = -37$

The integers are $-39, -38, -37$.

51. Let $x =$ the unknown number.

$$\frac{x}{3} = x - 2$$
$$x = 3(x - 2)$$
$$x = 3x - 6$$
$$-2x = -6$$
$$x = 3$$

The number is 3.

52. Let $x =$ the unknown number.

$$2(x + 6) = -x$$
$$2x + 12 = -x$$
$$12 = -3x$$
$$-4 = x$$

The number is -4.

53. Let $P = 46$ and $l = 14$.

$$P = 2l + 2w$$
$$46 = 2(14) + 2w$$
$$46 = 28 + 2w$$
$$18 = 2w$$
$$9 = w$$

54. Let $V = 192$, $l = 8$, and $w = 6$.

$$V = lwh$$
$$192 = 8(6)h$$
$$192 = 48h$$
$$4 = h$$

55.
$$y = mx + b$$
$$y - b = mx$$
$$\frac{y - b}{x} = m$$

56.
$$r = vst - 5$$
$$r + 5 = vst$$
$$\frac{r + 5}{vt} = s$$

57. $2y - 5x = 7$
$$-5x = -2y + 7$$
$$x = \frac{-2y + 7}{-5} = \frac{2y - 7}{5}$$

58. $3x - 6y = -2$
$$-6y = -3x - 2$$
$$y = \frac{-3x - 2}{-6} = \frac{3x + 2}{6}$$

59. $C = \pi D$
$$\frac{C}{D} = \pi$$

60. $C = 2\pi r$
$$\frac{C}{2r} = \pi$$

61. Let $V = 900$, $l = 20$, and $h = 3$.

$$V = lwh$$
$$900 = 20w(3)$$
$$900 = 60w$$
$$15 = w$$

Width $= 15$ meters

62. Let $F = 104$

$$C = \frac{5}{9}(F - 32) = \frac{5}{9}(104 - 32) = \frac{5}{9}(72)$$
$$= 40$$

The temperature was $40°$ C.

63. $x \leq -2$

64. $x > 0$

65. $x - 5 \leq -4$
$$x \leq 1$$
$$\{x \mid x \leq 1\}$$

66. $x + 7 > 2$
$$x > -5$$
$$\{x \mid x > -5\}$$

67. $-2x \geq -20$
$$\frac{-2x}{-2} \leq \frac{-20}{-2}$$
$$x \leq 10$$
$$\{x \mid x \leq 10\}$$

68. $-3x > 12$
$$\frac{-3x}{-3} < \frac{12}{-3}$$
$$x < -4$$
$$\{x \mid x < -4\}$$

69. $5x - 7 > 8x + 5$
$$-3x - 7 > 5$$
$$-3x > 12$$
$$\frac{-3x}{-3} < \frac{12}{-3}$$
$$x < -4$$
$$\{x \mid x < -4\}$$

70. $x + 4 \geq 6x - 16$
$$-5x + 4 \geq -16$$
$$-5x \geq -20$$
$$\frac{-5x}{-5} \leq \frac{-20}{-5}$$
$$x \leq 4$$
$$\{x \mid x \leq 4\}$$

71. $\frac{2}{3}y > 6$
$$y > 9$$
$$\{y \mid y > 9\}$$

72. $-0.5y \leq 7.5$
$$\frac{-0.5y}{-0.5} \geq \frac{7.5}{-0.5}$$
$$y \geq -15$$
$$\{y \mid y \geq -15\}$$

73. $-2(x-5) > 2(3x-2)$

$$-2x+10 > 6x-4$$
$$-8x+10 > -4$$
$$-8x > -14$$
$$\frac{-8x}{-8} < \frac{-14}{-8}$$
$$x < \frac{7}{4}$$
$$\left\{ x \middle| x < \frac{7}{4} \right\}$$

74. $4(2x-5) \le 5x-1$

$$8x-20 \le 5x-1$$
$$3x-20 \le -1$$
$$3x \le 19$$

$$x \le \frac{19}{3}$$
$$\left\{ x \middle| x \le \frac{19}{3} \right\}$$

75. Let x = the amount of sales then
$0.05x$ = her commission.

$$175 + 0.05x \ge 300$$
$$0.05x \ge 125$$
$$x \ge 2500$$

Sales must be at least $2500.

76. Let x = his score on the fourth round.

$$\frac{76+82+79+x}{4} < 80$$
$$237 + x < 320$$
$$x < 83$$

His score must be less than 83.

Chapter 9 Test

1. $|-7| > 5$

2. $(9+5) \ge 4$

3. a. The natural numbers are 1 and 7.

   b. The whole numbers are 0, 1 and 7.

   c. The integers are -5, -1, $0, 1$, and 7.

   d. The rational numbers are

$$-5, \ -1, \ \frac{1}{4}, \ 0, 1, \ 7, \text{ and } 11.6.$$

   e. The irrational numbers are $\sqrt{7}$ and 3π.

   f. The real numbers are all numbers
     in the given set.

4. Associative property of addition

5. Commutative property of multiplication

6. Distributive property

7. Multiplicative inverse property

8. The opposite of -9 is 9.

9. The reciprocal of $-\dfrac{1}{3}$ is -3.

10. $7 + 2(5y-3) = 7 + 10y - 6$
$$= 10y + 1$$

11. $4(x-2) - 3(2x-6) = 4x - 8 - 6x + 18$
$$= -2x + 10$$

12. $4(n-5) = -(4-2n)$

$4n - 20 = -4 + 2n$

$2n - 20 = -4$

$2n = 16$

$n = 8$

13. $-2(x-3) = x + 5 - 3x$

$-2x + 6 = -2x + 5$

$6 = 5$

No solution.

14. $4z + 1 - z = 1 + z$

$3z + 1 = 1 + z$

$2z + 1 = 1$

$2z = 0$

$z = 0$

15. $\dfrac{2(x+6)}{3} = x - 5$

$2(x+6) = 3(x-5)$

$2x + 12 = 3x - 15$

$12 = x - 15$

$27 = x$

16. $\dfrac{1}{2} - x + \dfrac{3}{2} = x - 4$

$2\left(\dfrac{1}{2} - x + \dfrac{3}{2}\right) = 2(x-4)$

$1 - 2x + 3 = 2x - 8$

$-2x + 4 = 2x - 8$

$-4x + 4 = -8$

$-4x = -12$

$x = 3$

17. $-0.3(x-4) + x = 0.5(3-x)$

$10\left[-0.3(x-4) + x\right] = 10\left[0.5(3-x)\right]$

$-3(x-4) + 10x = 5(3-x)$

$-3x + 12 + 10x = 15 - 5x$

$7x + 12 = 15 - 5x$

$12x + 12 = 15$

$12x = 3$

$x = \dfrac{3}{12} = \dfrac{1}{4} = 0.25$

18. $-4(a+1) - 3a = -7(2a-3)$

$-4a - 4 - 3a = -14a + 21$

$-7a - 4 = -14a + 21$

$7a - 4 = 21$

$7a = 25$

$a = \dfrac{25}{7}$

19. Let x = the number.

$x + \dfrac{2}{3}x = 35$

$3x + 2x = 105$

$5x = 105$

$x = 21$

The number is 21.

20. Let $l = 35,$ and $w = 20.$

$2A = 2lw = 2(35)(20) = 1400$

Let x = the number of gallons needed
at 200 square feet per gallon.

$1400 = 200x$

$7 = x$

7 gallons are needed.

21. Let $y = -14$, $m = -2$, and $b = -2$.

$$y = mx + b$$
$$-14 = -2x - 2$$
$$-12 = -2x$$
$$6 = x$$

22.

$$V = \pi r^2 h$$
$$\frac{V}{\pi r^2} = \frac{\pi r^2 h}{\pi r^2}$$
$$\frac{V}{\pi r^2} = h$$

23. $3x - 4y = 10$

$$-4y = -3x + 10$$
$$y = \frac{-3x + 10}{-4}$$
$$= \frac{3x - 10}{4}$$

24.

$$3x - 5 > 7x + 3$$
$$-4x - 5 > 3$$
$$-4x > 8$$
$$\frac{-4x}{-4} < \frac{8}{-4}$$
$$x < -2$$
$$\{x \mid x < -2\}$$

25. $-0.3x \geq 2.4$

$$\frac{-0.3x}{-0.3} \leq \frac{2.4}{-0.3}$$
$$x \leq -8$$
$$\{x \mid x \leq -8\}$$

26. $-5(x - 1) + 6 \leq -3(x + 4) + 1$

$$-5x + 5 + 6 \leq -3x - 12 + 1$$
$$-5x + 11 \leq -3x - 11$$
$$-2x + 11 \leq -11$$
$$-2x \leq -22$$
$$\frac{-2x}{-2} \geq \frac{-22}{-2}$$
$$x \geq 11$$
$$\{x \mid x \geq 11\}$$

27. $\dfrac{2(5x + 1)}{3} > 2$

$$2(5x + 1) > 6$$
$$10x + 2 > 6$$
$$10x > 4$$
$$x > \frac{4}{10} = \frac{2}{5}$$
$$\left\{ x \mid x > \frac{2}{5} \right\}$$

28. Let $x =$ the number of public libraries in Indiana and $x + 650 =$ the number in New York.

$$x + x + 650 = 1504$$
$$2x + 650 = 1504$$
$$2x = 854$$
$$x = 427$$
$$x + 650 = 427 + 650 = 1077$$

There are 427 public libraries in Indiana and 1077 in New York.

Chapter 9 Cumulative Review

1. a) $-(-4) = 4$ b) $-|-5| = -5$ c) $-|-6| = -6$

2. a) $|0| \; ? \; 2$ b) $|-5| \; ? \; |5|$ c) $|-3| \; ? \; |-2|$
    $0 < 2$ $5 = 5$ $3 > 2$

    d) $|5| \; ? \; |6|$ e) $|-7| \; ? \; |6|$
    $5 < 6$ $7 > 6$

3. $-2\left[-3 + 2(-1+6)\right] - 5 = -2\left[-3 + 2(5)\right] - 5$
    $= -2\left[-3 + 10\right] - 5$
    $= -2[7] - 5$
    $= -14 - 5$
    $= -19$

4. $\dfrac{3 + |4-3| + 2^2}{6-3} = \dfrac{3 + |1| + 2^2}{6-3}$
    $= \dfrac{3 + 1 + 4}{6-3}$
    $= \dfrac{8}{3}$

5. $-18 + 10 = -8$

6. $(-8) + (-11) = -19$

7. $12 + (-8) = 4$

8. $(-2) + 10 = 8$

9. $-3 + 4 + (-11) = 1 + (-11) = -10$

10. $0.2 + (-0.5) = -0.3$

11. $\dfrac{2}{3} - \dfrac{10}{11} = \dfrac{2 \cdot 11}{3 \cdot 11} - \dfrac{10 \cdot 3}{11 \cdot 3} = \dfrac{22}{33} - \dfrac{30}{33} = -\dfrac{8}{33}$

12. $\dfrac{2}{5} - \dfrac{39}{40} = \dfrac{2 \cdot 8}{5 \cdot 8} - \dfrac{39}{40} = \dfrac{16}{40} - \dfrac{39}{40} = -\dfrac{23}{40}$

13. $2 - \dfrac{x}{3} = \dfrac{2 \cdot 3}{1 \cdot 3} - \dfrac{x}{3} = \dfrac{6}{3} - \dfrac{x}{3} = \dfrac{6-x}{3}$

14. $5 + \dfrac{x}{2} = \dfrac{5 \cdot 2}{1 \cdot 2} + \dfrac{x}{2} = \dfrac{10}{2} + \dfrac{x}{2} = \dfrac{10+x}{2}$

15. $2x + y^2 = 2\left(-\dfrac{1}{2}\right) + \left(\dfrac{1}{3}\right)$
    $= 2\left(-\dfrac{1}{2}\right) + \dfrac{1}{9}$

16. $2y + x^2 = 2\left(\dfrac{1}{3}\right) + \left(-\dfrac{1}{2}\right)^2$
    $= 2\left(\dfrac{1}{3}\right) + \dfrac{1}{4}$
    $= \dfrac{2}{3} + \dfrac{1}{4}$
    $= \dfrac{2 \cdot 4}{3 \cdot 4} + \dfrac{1 \cdot 3}{4 \cdot 3}$
    $= \dfrac{8}{12} + \dfrac{3}{12}$
    $= \dfrac{11}{12}$

17. $-4\dfrac{2}{5} \cdot 1\dfrac{3}{11}$

$= \dfrac{-22}{5} \cdot \dfrac{14}{11}$

$= -\dfrac{2 \cdot 11 \cdot 14}{5 \cdot 11}$

$= -\dfrac{2 \cdot 14}{5}$

$= -\dfrac{28}{5}$ or $-5\dfrac{3}{5}$

18. $-2\dfrac{1}{2} \cdot \left(-2\dfrac{1}{2}\right)$

$= -\dfrac{5}{2} \cdot \left(-\dfrac{5}{2}\right)$

$= \dfrac{5 \cdot 5}{2 \cdot 2}$

$= \dfrac{25}{4}$ or $6\dfrac{1}{4}$

19. $-2\dfrac{1}{3} \div \left(-2\dfrac{1}{2}\right)$

$= -\dfrac{7}{3} \div \left(-\dfrac{5}{2}\right)$

$= -\dfrac{7}{3} \cdot \left(-\dfrac{2}{5}\right)$

$= \dfrac{14}{15}$

20. $3\dfrac{3}{5} \div \left(-3\dfrac{1}{3}\right)$

$= \dfrac{18}{5} \div \left(-\dfrac{10}{3}\right)$

$= \dfrac{18}{5} \cdot \left(-\dfrac{3}{10}\right)$

$= -\dfrac{2 \cdot 9 \cdot 3}{5 \cdot 2 \cdot 5}$

$= \dfrac{9 \cdot 3}{5 \cdot 5}$

$= -\dfrac{27}{25}$ or $-1\dfrac{2}{25}$

21. $(-1.3)^2 + 2.4 = 1.69 + 2.4 = 4.09$

22. $1.2(7.3 - 9.3) = 1.2(-2) = -2.4$

23. $\sqrt{49} = 7$

24. $\sqrt{64} = 8$

25. $\sqrt{\dfrac{4}{25}} = \dfrac{2}{5}$

26. $\sqrt{\dfrac{9}{100}} = \dfrac{3}{10}$

27. $1.2x + 5.8 = 8.2$

$\qquad 1.2x = 8.2 - 5.8$

$\qquad \dfrac{1.2x}{1.2} = \dfrac{2.4}{1.2}$

$\qquad\qquad x = 2$

28. $1.3x - 2.6 = -9.1$

$$1.3x = -9.1 + 2.6$$

$$\frac{1.3x}{1.3} = \frac{-6.5}{1.3}$$

$$x = -5$$

29. $8 \geq 8$

True

30. $-4 \leq -4$

True

31. $8 \leq 8$

True

32. $-4 \geq -4$

True

33. $23 \leq 0$

False

34. $-8 \leq 0$

True

35. $0 \leq 23$

True

36. $0 \leq -8$

False

37. $-5(-3 + 2z) = -5(-3) + (-5)(2z)$

$$= 15 - 10z$$

38. $-4(2x - 1) = -4(2x) + (-4)(-1)$

$$= -8x + 4$$

39. $4(3x + 7) + 10 = 4(3x) + 4(7) + 10$

$$= 12x + 28 + 10$$

$$= 12x + 38$$

40. $9 + 2(5x + 6) = 9 + 2(5x) + 2(6)$

$$= 9 + 10x + 12$$

$$= 10x + 21$$

41.

$$\frac{2(a + 3)}{3} = 6a + 2$$

$$3\left(\frac{2(a + 3)}{3}\right) = 3(6a + 2)$$

$$2(a + 3) = 3(6a + 2)$$

$$2a + 6 = 18a + 6$$

$$2a - 18a = 6 - 6$$

$$\frac{-16a}{-16} = \frac{0}{-16}$$

$$a = 0$$

42.

$$\frac{x}{2} + \frac{x}{5} = 3$$

$$10\left(\frac{x}{2} + \frac{x}{5}\right) = 10(3)$$

$$10\left(\frac{x}{2}\right) + 10\left(\frac{x}{5}\right) = 10(3)$$

$$5x + 2x = 30$$

$$\frac{7x}{7} = \frac{30}{7}$$

$$x = \frac{30}{7}$$

43. Let x = the number of Democrats.

Then $x + 10$ = the number of Republicans.

$$x + x + 10 = 430$$
$$2x + 10 = 430$$
$$2x = 430 - 10$$
$$\frac{2x}{2} = \frac{420}{2}$$
$$x = 210$$

There were 210 Democrats and $210 + 10 = 220$ Republicans in the 107th Congress.

44. The sum of a number and 2 is $x + 2$.

Three times the sum of a number and 2 is $3(x+2)$. 9 times the number is $9x$.

Full translation: $\quad 3(x+2) = 9x$

Solve: $\qquad\qquad 3x + 6 = 9x$
$$3x - 9x = -6$$
$$\frac{-6x}{-6} = \frac{-6}{-6}$$
$$x = 1$$

45. $d = rt$

$$\frac{31,680}{400} = \frac{400t}{400}$$
$$79.2 = t$$

It would take 79.2 years.

46. $V = lwh$

$$\frac{V}{lh} = \frac{lwh}{lh}$$
$$\frac{V}{lh} = w$$

47. $-1 > x$ or $x < -1$

48. $-3x < -30$

$$\frac{-3x}{-3} < \frac{-30}{-3}$$
$$x > 10$$
$$\{x \mid x > 10\}$$

49. $2(x-3) - 5 \le 3(x+2) - 18$
$$2x - 6 - 5 \le 3x + 6 - 18$$
$$2x - 11 \le 3x - 12$$
$$2x - 3x \le -12 + 11$$
$$\frac{-1x}{-1} \le \frac{-1}{-1}$$
$$x \ge 1$$
$$\{x \mid x \ge 1\}$$

50. $10 + x < 6x - 10$
$$x - 6x < -10 - 10$$
$$\frac{-5x}{-5} < \frac{-20}{-5}$$
$$x > 4$$
$$\{x \mid x > 4\}$$

Chapter 10 Pretest

1. $\left(-\dfrac{3}{4}\right)^2 = \left(-\dfrac{3}{4}\right)\left(-\dfrac{3}{4}\right) = \dfrac{9}{16}$

2. $\left(4y^6\right)\left(2y^7\right) = 4 \cdot 2 \cdot y^6 \cdot y^7 = 8y^{13}$

3. $\dfrac{a^9 b^{16}}{a^{12} b^5} = \left(a^{9-12}\right)\left(b^{16-5}\right) = a^{-3}b^{11} = \dfrac{b^{11}}{a^3}$

4. $4^0 + 2x^0 = 1 + 2 \cdot 1 = 1 + 2 = 3$

5. $\left(-\dfrac{1}{6}\right)^{-3} = \left(-\dfrac{1}{6}\right)^{-3} = \dfrac{(-1)^{-3}}{6^{-3}} = \dfrac{6^3}{(-1)^3}$

$= \dfrac{216}{-1} = -216$

6. $\left(\dfrac{m^{-2}n}{m^6 n^{-8}}\right)^{-2} = \dfrac{m^4 n^{-2}}{m^{-12} n^{16}} = \left(m^{4-(-12)}\right)\left(n^{-2-16}\right)$

$= m^{16} n^{-18} = \dfrac{m^{16}}{n^{18}}$

7. $12x^2 + 3x - 5 - 8x^2 + 7x$

$= 12x^2 - 8x^2 + 3x + 7x - 5$

$= 4x^2 + 10x - 5$

8. $0.000000814 = 8.14 \times 10^{-7}$

9. The degree of $8x - 4x^5 + 6x^3 + 10$ is 5.

10. $-3x^3 + 2x^2 - 4 = -3(-1)^3 + 2(-1)^2 - 4$

$= -3(-1) + 2(1) - 4 = 3 + 2 - 4 = 1$

11. $\left(4x^2 - 3x + 9\right) + \left(6x^2 + 3x - 8\right)$

$= 4x^2 - 3x + 9 + 6x^2 + 3x - 8$

$= 4x^2 + 6x^2 - 3x + 3x + 9 - 8$

$= 10x^2 + 1$

12. $\left(6y^2 - 4\right) - \left(-3y^2 + 5y - 1\right)$

$= 6y^2 - 4 + 3y^2 - 5y + 1$

$= 6y^2 + 3y^2 - 5y - 4 + 1$

$= 9y^2 - 5y - 4 + 1$

$= 9y^2 - 5y - 3$

13. $\left(2a^2 + 3ab - 7b^2\right) - \left(-3a^2 + 3ab + 9b^2\right)$

$= 2a^2 + 3ab - 7b^2 - 3a^2 - 3ab - 9b^2$

$= 2a^2 - 3a^2 + 3ab - 3ab - 7b^2 - 9b^2$

$= -a^2 - 16b^2$

14. $\left(-\dfrac{2}{7}n^6\right)\left(\dfrac{21}{16}n^3\right) = -\dfrac{2}{7} \cdot \dfrac{21}{16} \cdot n^6 \cdot n^3$

$= -\dfrac{42}{112}n^9 = -\dfrac{3}{8}n^9$

15. $-2t^2\left(3t^5 + 4t^3 - 8\right)$

$= -2t^2\left(3t^5\right) + \left(-2t^2\right)\left(4t^3\right) - \left(-2t^2\right)(8)$

$= -6t^7 - 8t^5 + 16t^2$

16. $\left(2y - 1\right)\left(5y + 6\right)$

$= 2y(5y) + 5y(-1) + 2y(6) + (-1)(6)$

$= 10y^2 - 5y + 12y - 6$

$= 10y^2 + 7y - 6$

17. $(7a-5)^2 = (7a-5)(7a-5)$

$\quad = (7a)(7a) + (7a)(-5) + (-5)(7a) + (-5)(-5)$

$\quad = 49a^2 - 35a - 35a + 25$

$\quad = 49a^2 - 70a + 25$

18. $(4b+9)(4b-9)$

$\quad = (4b)(4b) + (4b)(-9) + (9)(4b) + (9)(-9)$

$\quad = 16b^2 - 36b + 36b - 81 = 16b^2 - 81$

19. $\dfrac{16p^4 - 8p^3 + 20p^2}{4p} = \dfrac{16p^4}{4p} - \dfrac{8p3}{4p} + \dfrac{20p^2}{4p}$

$\qquad\qquad\qquad = 4p - 2p^2 + 5p$

20. $\begin{array}{r} 5x+2 \\ x-6\overline{)5x^2 - 28x - 12} \\ \underline{5x^2 - 30x} \\ 2x - 12 \\ \underline{2x - 12} \\ 0 \end{array}$

Thus, $\dfrac{5x^2 - 28x - 12}{x-6} = 5x + 2.$

Practice Problems 10.1

1. $3^4 = 3 \cdot 3 \cdot 3 \cdot 3 = 81$

2. $7^1 = 7$

3. $(-2)^3 = (-2)(-2)(-2) = -8$

4. $-2^3 = -(2 \cdot 2 \cdot 2) = -8$

5. $\left(\dfrac{2}{3}\right)^2 = \left(\dfrac{2}{3}\right)\left(\dfrac{2}{3}\right) = \dfrac{4}{9}$

6. $5 \cdot 6^2 = 5 \cdot 6 \cdot 6 = 180$

7. a. $3x^2 = 3(4)^2 = 3 \cdot 4 \cdot 4 = 48$

    b. $\dfrac{x^4}{-8} = \dfrac{(-2)^4}{-8} = \dfrac{(-2)(-2)(-2)(-2)}{-8}$

$\qquad = \dfrac{16}{-8} = -2$

8. $7^3 \cdot 7^2 = 7^{3+2} = 7^5$

9. $x^4 \cdot x^9 = x^{4+9} = x^{13}$

10. $r^5 \cdot r = r^5 \cdot r^1 = r^{5+1} = r^6$

11. $s^6 \cdot s^2 \cdot s^3 = s^{6+2+3} = s^{11}$

12. $(-3)^9(-3) - (-3)^9(-3)^1 = (-3)^{9+1} = (-3)^{10}$

13. $(6x^3)(-2x^9) = 6 \cdot (-2) \cdot x^3 \cdot x^9 = -12x^{12}$

14. $(9^4)^{10} = 9^{4 \cdot 10} = 9^{40}$

15. $(z^6)^3 = z^{6 \cdot 3} = z^{18}$

16. $(xy)^7 = x^7 y^7$

17. $(3y)^4 = 3^4 y^4 = 81y^4$

18. $(-2p^4 q^2 r)^3 = (-2)^3 (p^4)^3 (q^2)^3 r^3$

$\qquad\qquad\qquad = -8p^{12} q^6 r^3$

19. $\left(\dfrac{r}{s}\right)^6 = \dfrac{r^6}{s^6}, \; s \neq 0$

20. $\left(\dfrac{5x^6}{9y^3}\right)^2 = \dfrac{5^2 (x^6)^2}{9^2 (y^3)^2} = \dfrac{25x^{12}}{81y^6}, \; y \neq 0$

21. $\dfrac{y^7}{y^3} = y^{7-3} = y^4$

22. $\dfrac{5^9}{5^6} = 5^{9-6} = 5^3 = 125$

23. $\dfrac{(-2)^{14}}{(-2)^{10}} = (-2)^{14-10} = (-2)^4 = 16$

24. $\dfrac{7a^4b^{11}}{ab} = 7 \cdot \dfrac{a^4}{a^1} \cdot \dfrac{b^{11}}{b^1} = 7a^{4-1}b^{11-1} = 7a^3b^{10}$

25. $8^0 = 1$

26. $(2r^2s)^0 = 1$

27. $(-5)^0 = 1$

28. $-5^0 = -1 \cdot 5^0 = -1 \cdot 1 = -1$

29. a. $\dfrac{x^7}{x^4} = x^{7-4} = x^3$

    b. $\left(3y^4\right)^4 = 3^4 \left(y^4\right)^4 = 81y^{16}$

    c. $\left(\dfrac{x}{4}\right)^3 = \dfrac{x^3}{4^3} = \dfrac{x^3}{64}$

Mental Math 10.1

1. 3^2

    base: 3

    exponent: 2

2. 5^4

    base: 5

    exponent: 4

3. $(-3)^6$

    base: -3

    exponent: 6

4. -3^7

    base: 3

    exponent: 7

5. -4^2

    base: 4

    exponent: 2

6. $(-4)^3$

    base: -4

    exponent: 3

7. $5 \cdot 3^4$

    base: 5; exponent: 1

    base: 3; exponent: 4

8. $9 \cdot 7^6$

    base: 9; exponent: 1

    base: 7; exponent: 6

9. $5x^2$

    base: 5; exponent: 1

    base: x; exponent: 2

10. $(5x)^2$

    base: $5x$

    exponent: 2

Exercise Set 10.1

1. $7^2 = 7 \cdot 7 = 49$

3. $(-5)^1 = -5$

5. $-2^4 = -2 \cdot 2 \cdot 2 \cdot 2 = -16$

7. $(-2)^4 = (-2)(-2)(-2)(-2) = 16$

9. $\left(\dfrac{1}{3}\right)^3 = \left(\dfrac{1}{3}\right)\left(\dfrac{1}{3}\right)\left(\dfrac{1}{3}\right) = \dfrac{1}{27}$

11. $7 \cdot 2^4 = 7 \cdot 2 \cdot 2 \cdot 2 \cdot 2 = 112$

13. Answers may vary.

15. $x^2 = (-2)^2 = (-2)(-2) = 4$

17. $5x^3 = 5(3)^3 = 5 \cdot 3 \cdot 3 \cdot 3 = 135$

19. $2xy^2 = 2(3)(5)^2 = 2(3)(5)(5) = 150$

21. $\dfrac{2z^4}{5} = \dfrac{2(-2)^4}{5} = \dfrac{2(-2)(-2)(-2)(-2)}{5} = \dfrac{32}{5}$

23. $x^2 \cdot x^5 = x^{2+5} = x^7$

25. $(-3)^3 \cdot (-3)^9 = (-3)^{3+9} = (-3)^{12}$

27. $(5y^4)(3y) = 5(3)y^{4+1} = 15y^5$

29. $(4z^{10})(-6z^7)(z^3) = 4(-6)z^{10+7+3} = -24z^{20}$

31. $(4x^2)(5x^3) = 4(5)x^{2+3} = 20x^5$ sq ft

33. $(x^9)^4 = x^{9 \cdot 4} = x^{36}$

35. $(pq)^7 = p^7 q^7$

37. $(2a^5)^3 = 2^3 a^{5 \cdot 3} = 8a^{15}$

39. $\left(\dfrac{m}{n}\right)^9 = \dfrac{m^9}{n^9}$

41. $(x^2 y^3)^5 = x^{2 \cdot 5} y^{3 \cdot 5} = x^{10} y^{15}$

43. $\left(\dfrac{-2xz}{y^5}\right)^2 = \dfrac{(-2)^2 x^2 z^2}{y^{5 \cdot 2}} = \dfrac{4x^2 z^2}{y^{10}}$

45. $\left(8z^5\right)^2 = 8^2 z^{5 \cdot 2} = 64z^{10}$

The area is $64z^{10}$ sq. decimeters.

47. $\left(3y^4\right)^3 = 3^3 y^{4 \cdot 3} = 27y^{11}$

The volume is $27y^{12}$ cubic feet.

49. $\dfrac{x^3}{x} = \dfrac{x^3}{x^1} = x^{3-1} = x^2$

51. $\dfrac{(-2)^5}{(-2)^3} = (-2)^{5-3} = (-2)^2 = 4$

53. $\dfrac{p^7 q^{20}}{pq^{15}} = p^{7-1} q^{20-15} = p^6 q^5$

55. $\dfrac{7x^2 y^6}{14x^2 y^3} = \dfrac{7}{14} x^{2-2} y^{6-3} = \dfrac{1}{2} x^0 y^3 = \dfrac{y^3}{2}$

57. $(2x)^0 = 1$

59. $-2x^0 = -2(1) = -2$

61. $5^0 + y^0 = 1 + 1 = 2$

63. Answers may vary.

65. $-5^2 = -5 \cdot 5 = -25$

67. $\left(\dfrac{1}{4}\right)^3 = \dfrac{1^3}{4^3} = \dfrac{1}{64}$

69. $\dfrac{z^{12}}{z^4} = z^{12-4} = z^8$

71. $(9xy)^2 = 9^2 x^2 y^2 = 81x^2 y^2$

73. $(6b)^0 = 1$

75. $2^3 + 2^5 = 8 + 32 = 40$

77. $b^4 b^2 = b^{4+2} = b^6$

79. $a^2 a^3 a^4 = a^{2+3+4} = a^9$

81. $(2x^3)(-8x^4) = 2(-8)x^{3+4} = -16x^7$

83. $(4a)^3 = 4^3 a^3 = 64a^3$

85. $(-6xyz^3)^2 = (-6)^2 x^2 y^2 z^{3 \cdot 2} = 36x^2 y^2 z^6$

87. $\left(\dfrac{3y^5}{6x^4}\right)^3 = \dfrac{3^3 y^{5 \cdot 3}}{6^3 x^{4 \cdot 3}} = \dfrac{27y^{15}}{216x^{12}} = \dfrac{y^{15}}{8x^{12}}$

89. $\dfrac{3x^5}{x^4} = 3x^{5-4} = 3x$

91. $\dfrac{2x^3 y^2 z}{xyz} = 2x^{3-1} y^{2-1} z^{1-1} = 2x^2 y$

93. $5 - 7 = 5 + (-7) = -2$

95. $3 - (-2) = 3 + 2 = 5$

97. $-11 - (-4) = -11 + 4 = -7$

99. $V = x^3 = 7^3 = 7 \cdot 7 \cdot 7 = 343$
The volume is 343 cubic meters.

101. We use the volume formula.

103. $x^{5a} x^{4a} = x^{5a+4a} = x^{9a}$

105. $(a^b)^5 = a^{b \cdot 5} = a^{5b}$

107. $\dfrac{x^{9a}}{x^{4a}} = x^{9a-4a} = x^{5a}$

109. $A = P\left(1 + \dfrac{r}{12}\right)^6$
$A = 1000\left(1 + \dfrac{0.09}{12}\right)^6$
$A = 1000(1.0075)^6$
$A = 1045.85$
You need $1045.85 to pay off the loan.

Practice Problems 10.2

1. $5^{-3} = \dfrac{1}{5^3} = \dfrac{1}{125}$

2. $7x^{-4} = 7 \cdot \dfrac{1}{x^4} = \dfrac{7}{x^4}$

3. $5^{-1} + 3^{-1} = \dfrac{1}{5^1} + \dfrac{1}{3^1} = \dfrac{3}{15} + \dfrac{5}{15} = \dfrac{8}{15}$

4. $(-3)^{-4} = \dfrac{1}{(-3)^4} = \dfrac{1}{81}$

5. $\left(\dfrac{6}{7}\right)^{-2} = \dfrac{6^{-2}}{7^{-2}} = \dfrac{7^2}{6^2} = \dfrac{49}{36}$

6. $\dfrac{x}{x^{-4}} = \dfrac{x^1}{x^{-4}} = x^{1-(-4)} = x^5$

7. $\dfrac{y^{-9}}{z^{-5}} = \dfrac{z^5}{y^9}$

8. $\dfrac{y^{-4}}{y^6} = y^{-4-6} = y^{-10} = \dfrac{1}{y^{10}}$

9. $\dfrac{\left(x^5\right)^3 x}{x^4} = \dfrac{x^{15}x^1}{x^4} = x^{15+1-4} = x^{12}$

10. $\left(\dfrac{9x^3}{y}\right)^{-2} = \dfrac{9^{-2}x^{-6}}{y^{-2}} = \dfrac{y^2}{9^2 x^6} = \dfrac{y^2}{81x^6}$

11. $\left(a^{-4}b^7\right)^{-5} = a^{20}b^{-35} = \dfrac{a^{20}}{b^{35}}$

12. $\dfrac{(2x)^4}{x^8} = \dfrac{2^4 x^4}{x^8} = 2^4 x^{4-8} = 16x^{-4} = \dfrac{16}{x^4}$

13. $\dfrac{y^{-10}}{\left(y^5\right)^4} = \dfrac{y^{-10}}{y^{20}} = y^{-10-20} = y^{-30} = \dfrac{1}{y^{30}}$

14. $\left(4a^2\right)^{-3} = 4^{-3}a^{-6} = \dfrac{1}{4^3 a^6} = \dfrac{1}{64a^6}$

15. $\dfrac{\left(3x^{-2}y\right)^{-2}}{4x^7 y} = \dfrac{3^{-2}x^4 y^{-2}}{4x^7 y} = \dfrac{x^{4-7}y^{-2-1}}{3^2 (4)}$

$= \dfrac{x^{-3}y^{-3}}{36} = \dfrac{1}{36x^3 y^3}$

16.   a. $420,000 = 4.2 \times 10^5$

       b. $0.00017 = 1.7 \times 10^{-4}$

       c. $9,060,000,000 = 9.06 \times 10^9$

       d. $0.000007 = 7 \times 10^{-6}$

17.   a. $3.062 \times 10^{-4} = 40.0003062$

       b. $5.21 \times 10^4 = 52,100$

       c. $9.6 \times 10^{-5} = 0.000096$

       d. $6.002 \times 10^6 = 6,002,000$

18.   a. $\left(9 \times 10^7\right)\left(4 \times 10^{-9}\right) = 9 \cdot 4 \cdot 10^7 \cdot 10^{-9}$

           $= 36 \times 10^{-2} = 0.36$

       b. $\dfrac{8 \times 10^4}{2 \times 10^{-3}} = \dfrac{8}{2} \times 10^{4-(-3)} = 4 \times 10^7$

           $= 40,000,000$

Mental Math 10.2

1. $5x^{-2} = \dfrac{5}{x^2}$

2. $3x^{-3} = \dfrac{3}{x^3}$

3. $\dfrac{1}{y^{-6}} = y^6$

4. $\dfrac{1}{x^{-3}} = x^3$

5. $\dfrac{4}{y^{-3}} = 4y^3$

6. $\dfrac{16}{y^{-7}} = 16y^7$

Exercise Set 10.2

1. $4^{-3} = \dfrac{1}{4^3} = \dfrac{1}{64}$

3. $7x^{-3} = 7 \cdot \dfrac{1}{x^3} = \dfrac{7}{x^3}$

5. $\left(-\dfrac{1}{4}\right)^{-3} = \dfrac{(-1)^{-3}}{(4)^{-3}} = \dfrac{4^3}{(-1)^3} = \dfrac{64}{-1} = -64$

7. $3^{-1} + 2^{-1} = \dfrac{1}{3} + \dfrac{1}{2} = \dfrac{2}{6} + \dfrac{3}{6} = \dfrac{5}{6}$

9. $\dfrac{1}{p^{-3}} = p^3$

11. $\dfrac{p^{-5}}{q^{-4}} = \dfrac{q^4}{p^5}$

13. $\dfrac{x^{-2}}{x} = x^{-2-1} = x^{-3} = \dfrac{1}{x^3}$

15. $\dfrac{z^{-4}}{a^{-7}} = z^{-4-(-7)} = z^3$

17. $2^0 + 3^{-1} = 1 + \dfrac{1}{3} = \dfrac{3}{3} + \dfrac{1}{3} = \dfrac{4}{3}$

19. $(-3)^{-2} = \dfrac{1}{(-3)^2} = \dfrac{1}{9}$

21. $\dfrac{-1}{p^{-4}} = 1\left(p^4\right) = -p^4$

23. $-2^0 - 3^0 = -1(1) - 1 = -2$

25. $\dfrac{x^2 x^5}{x^3} = x^{2+5-3} = x^4$

27. $\dfrac{p^2 p}{p^{-1}} = p^{2+1-(-1)} = p^{2+1+1} = p^4$

29. $\dfrac{\left(m^5\right)^4 m}{m^{10}} = m^{5(4)+1-10} = m^{20+1-10} = m^{11}$

31. $\dfrac{r}{r^{-3} r^{-2}} = r^{1-(-3)-(-2)} = r^{1+3+2} = r^6$

33. $\left(x^5 y^3\right)^{-3} = x^{5(-3)} y^{3(-3)} = x^{-15} y^{-9} = \dfrac{1}{x^{15} y^9}$

35. $\dfrac{\left(x^2\right)^3}{x^{10}} = \dfrac{x^6}{x^{10}} = x^{6-10} = x^{-4} = \dfrac{1}{x^4}$

37. $\dfrac{\left(a^5\right)^2}{\left(a^3\right)^4} = \dfrac{a^{10}}{a^{12}} = a^{10-12} = a^{-2} = \dfrac{1}{a^2}$

39. $\dfrac{8k^4}{2k} = \dfrac{8}{2} \cdot k^{4-1} = 4k^3$

41. $\dfrac{-6m^4}{-2m^3} = \dfrac{-6}{-2} \cdot m^{4-3} = 3m$

43. $\dfrac{-24a^6 b}{6ab^2} = \dfrac{-24}{6} \cdot a^{6-1} b^{1-2} = -4a^5 b^{-1}$

$= -\dfrac{4a^5}{b}$

45. $\dfrac{6x^2 y^3}{-7xy^5} = -\dfrac{6}{7} x^{2-1} y^{3-5} = -\dfrac{6}{7} x^1 y^{-2}$

$= -\dfrac{6x}{7y^2}$

47. $\left(a^{-5}b^2\right)^{-6} = a^{-5(-6)}b^{2(-6)} = a^{30}b^{-12} = \dfrac{a^{30}}{b^{12}}$

49. $\left(\dfrac{x^{-2}y^4}{x^3y^7}\right)^2 = \dfrac{x^{-2(2)}y^{4(2)}}{x^{3(2)}y^{7(2)}} = \dfrac{x^{-4}y^8}{x^6y^{14}}$

$\qquad = x^{-4-6}y^{8-14} = x^{-10}y^{-6} = \dfrac{1}{x^{10}y^6}$

51. $\dfrac{4^2z^{-3}}{4^3z^{-5}} = 4^{2-3}z^{-3-(-5)} = 4^{-1}z^2 = \dfrac{z^2}{4}$

53. $\dfrac{2^{-3}x^{-4}}{2^2x} = 2^{-3-2}x^{-4-1} = 2^{-5}x^{-5} = \dfrac{1}{2^5x^5} = \dfrac{1}{32x^5}$

55. $\dfrac{7ab^{-4}}{7^{-1}a^{-3}b^2} = 7^{1-(-1)}a^{1-(-3)}b^{-4-2}$

$\qquad = 7^2a^4b^{-6}$

$\qquad = \dfrac{49a^4}{b^6}$

57. $\left(\dfrac{a^{-5}b}{ab^3}\right)^{-4} = \dfrac{a^{-5(-4)}b^{-4}}{a^{-4}b^{3(-4)}} = \dfrac{a^{20}b^{-4}}{a^{-4}b^{-12}}$

$\qquad = a^{20-(-4)}b^{-4-(-12)}$

$\qquad = a^{24}b^8$

59. $\dfrac{\left(xy^3\right)^5}{(xy)^{-4}} = \dfrac{x^5y^{3(5)}}{x^{-4}y^{-4}} = \dfrac{x^5y^{15}}{x^{-4}y^{-4}}$

$\qquad = x^{5-(-4)}y^{15-(-4)}$

$\qquad = x^9y^{19}$

61. $\dfrac{\left(-2xy^{-3}\right)^{-3}}{\left(xy^{-1}\right)^{-1}} = \dfrac{(-2)^{-3}x^{-3}y^9}{x^{-1}y^1}$

$\qquad = (-2)^{-3}x^{-3-(-1)}y^{9-1}$

$\qquad = -\dfrac{y^8}{8x^2}$

63. $\dfrac{\left(a^4b^{-7}\right)^{-5}}{\left(5a^2b^{-1}\right)^{-2}} = \dfrac{a^{-20}b^{35}}{5^{-2}a^{-4}b^2}$

$\qquad = 5^2a^{-20-(-4)}b^{35-2}$

$\qquad = 25a^{-16}b^{33}$

$\qquad = \dfrac{25b^{33}}{a^{16}}$

65. $\left(\dfrac{3x^{-2}}{z}\right)^3 = \dfrac{3^3x^{-6}}{z^3} = \dfrac{27}{x^6z^3}$

The volume is $\dfrac{27}{x^6z^3}$ cubic inches.

67. $78,000 = 7.8 \times 10^4$

69. $0.00000167 = 1.67 \times 10^{-6}$

71. $0.00635 = 6.35 \times 10^{-3}$

73. $1,160,000 = 1.16 \times 10^6$

75. $15,600,000 = 1.56 \times 10^7$

77. $13,600 = 1.36 \times 10^4$

79. $284,000,000 = 2.84 \times 10^8$

81. $8.673 \times 10^{-10} = 0.0000000008673$

83. $3.3 \times 10^{-2} = 0.033$

85. $2.032 \times 10^4 = 20,320$

87. $3.97 \times 10^{-24} = 0.00000000000000000000000397$

89. $7.0 \times 10^8 = 700,000,000$

91. $\left(1.2 \times 10^{-3}\right)\left(3 \times 10^{-2}\right) = 1.2 \cdot 3 \cdot 10^{-3} \cdot 10^{-2}$

$$= 3.6 \times 10^{-5}$$
$$= 0.000036$$

93. $\left(4 \times 10^{-10}\right)\left(7 \times 10^{-9}\right) = 4 \cdot 7 \cdot 10^{-10} \cdot 10^{-9}$

$$= 28 \times 10^{-19}$$
$$= 0.0000000000000000028$$

95. $\dfrac{8 \times 10^{-1}}{16 \times 10^{5}} = \dfrac{8}{16} \times 10^{-1-5}$

$$= 0.5 \times 10^{-6}$$
$$= 0.0000005$$

97. $\dfrac{1.4 \times 10^{-2}}{7 \times 10^{-8}} = \dfrac{1.4}{7} \times 10^{-2-(-8)}$

$$= 0.2 \times 10^{6}$$
$$= 200,000$$

99. $7.5 \times 10^{5} \dfrac{\text{gallons}}{\text{second}} \left(\dfrac{3600 \text{ seconds}}{1 \text{ hour}}\right) = 27,000 \times 10^{5}$

$$= 2.7 \times 10^{4} \times 10^{5} = 2.7 \times 10^{9}$$

2.7×10^{9} gallons flows over Niagra Falls
in one hour.

101. $3x - 5x + 7 = (3 - 5)x + 7 = -2x + 7$

103. $y - 10 + y = (1 + 1)y - 10 = 2y - 10$

105. $7x + 2 - 8x - 6 = (7 - 8)x + (2 - 6) = -x - 4$

107. $\left(2.63 \times 10^{12}\right)\left(-1.5 \times 10^{-10}\right)$

$$= 2.63 \cdot (-1.5) \cdot 10^{12} \cdot 10^{-10}$$
$$= -3.945 \times 10^{2} = -394.5$$

109. $d = r \cdot t$

$$238,857 = \left(1.86 \times 10^{5}\right)t$$
$$t = \dfrac{238,857}{1.86 \times 10^{5}}$$
$$t = \dfrac{2.38857}{1.86} \times 10^{5-5}$$
$$t = 1.3 \text{ seconds}$$

111. $a^{-4m} \cdot a^{5m} = a^{-4m+5m} = a^{m}$

113. $(3y^{2z})^{3} = 3^{3}y^{2z \cdot 3} = 27y^{6z}$

115. Answers may vary.

Practice Problems 10.3

1. $-6x^{6} + 4x^{5} + 7x3 - 9x^{2} - 1$

Term	Coefficient
$7x^{3}$	7
$-9x^{2}$	-9
$-6x^{6}$	-6
$4x^{5}$	4
-1	-1

2. $-15x^{3} + 2x^{2} - 5$

The term $-15x^{3}$ has degree 3.

The term $2x^{2}$ has degree 2.

The term -5 has degree 0 because
-5 is $-5x^{0}$.

3. a. The degree of the binomial $-6x+14$ is
1 because $-6x$ is $-6x^1$.

b. The degree of the polynomial $9x-3x^6+2$
is 6, the greatest degree of any of its terms.
It is not a monomial, binomial, or trinomial.

c. The degree of the trinomial $10x^2-6x-6$ is
2, the greatest degree of any of its terms.

4. a. $-2x+10 = -2(-1)+10 = 2+10 = 12$

b. $6x^2+11x-20 = 6(-1)^2+11(-1)-20$
$= 6-11-20 = -25$

5. $-16t^2+1821 = -16(3)^2+1821$
$= -16(9)+1821 = -144+1821 = 1677$
The height of the object at 3 seconds is
16,777 feet.
$-16t^2+1821 = -16(7)^2+1821$
$= -16(49)+1821$
$= 1037$
The height of the object at 7 seconds is
1037 feet.

6. $-6y+8y = (-6+8)y = 2y$

7. $14y^2+3-10y^2-9 = 14y^2-10y^2+3-9 = 4y^2-6$

8. $7x^3+x^3 = 7x^3+1x^3 = 8x^3$

9. $23x^2-6x-x-15 = 23x^2-7x-15$

10. $\frac{2}{7}x^3 - \frac{1}{4}x + 2 - \frac{1}{2}x^3 + \frac{3}{8}x$

$= \left(\frac{2}{7}-\frac{1}{2}\right)x^3 + \left(-\frac{1}{4}+\frac{3}{8}\right)x + 2$

$= \left(\frac{4}{14}-\frac{7}{14}\right)x^3 + \left(-\frac{2}{8}+\frac{3}{8}\right)x + 2$

$= -\frac{3}{14}x^3 + \frac{1}{8}x + 2$

11. Area $= 5 \cdot x + x \cdot x + 4 \cdot 5 + x \cdot x + 8 \cdot x$
$= 5x + x^2 + 20 + x^2 + 8x$
$= 2x^2 + 13x + 20$

12. $-2x^3y^2+4-8xy+3x^3y+5xy^2$

Terms	Degree	Degree of Polynomial
$-2x^3y^2$	3+2 or 5	5(highest degree)
4	0	
$-8xy$	1+1 = 2	
$3x^3y$	3+1 or 4	
$5xy^2$	1+2 or 3	

13. $11ab-6a^2-ba+8b^2$
$= (11-1)ab-6a^2+8b^2$
$= 10ab-6a^2+8b^2$

14. $7x^2y^2+2y^2-4y^2x^2+x^2-y^2+5x^2$
$= (7-4)x^2y^2+(2-1)y^2+(1+5)x^2$
$= 3x^2y^2+y^2+6x^2$

Exercise Set 10.3

1. $x^2 - 3x + 5$

Term	Coefficient
x^2	1
$-3x$	-3
5	5

3. $-5x^4 + 3.2x^2 + x - 5$

Term	Coefficient
$-5x^4$	-5
$3.2x^2$	3.2
x	1
-5	-5

5. $x + 2$

The degree is 1 since x is x^1. It is a binomial because it has two terms.

7. $9m^3 - 5m^2 + 4m - 8$

The degree is 3, the greatest degree of any of its terms. It is none of these because it has more than three terms.

9. $12x^4 - x^2 - 12x^2 = 12x^4 - 13x^2$

The degree is 4, the greatest degree of any of its terms. It is a binomial because the simplified form has two terms.

11. $3z - 5$

The degree is 1 because $3z$ is $3z^1$. It is a binomial because it has two terms.

13. Answers may vary.

15. Answers may vary.

17. a. $x + 6 = 0 + 6 = 6$

b. $x + 6 = -1 + 6 = 5$

19. a. $x^2 - 5x - 2 = 0^2 - 5(0) - 2 = -2$

b. $x^2 - 5x - 2 = (-1)^2 - 5(-1) - 2$
$= 1 + 5 - 2 = 4$

21. a. $x^3 - 15 = 0^3 - 15 = -15$

b. $x^3 - 15 = (-1)^3 - 15 = -1 - 15 = -16$

23. $-16t^2 + 200t = -16(1)^2 + 200(1)$
$= -16 + 200 = 184$ feet

25. $-16t^2 + 200t = -16(7.6)^2 + 200(7.6)$
$= -924.16 + 1520 = 595.84$ feet

27. Let $x = 15$
$0.97x^2 - 0.91x + 7.46$
$= 0.97(15)^2 - 0.91(15) + 7.46$
$= 218.25 - 13.65 + 7.46$
$= 212.06$
Expect 212.06 wireless telephone subscribers in 2005.

29. $14x^2 + 9x^2 = (14 + 9)x^2 = 23x^2$

31. $15x^2 - 3x^2 - y$
$(15 - 3)x^2 - y = 12x^2 - y$

33. $8s - 5s + 4s = (8 - 5 + 4)s = 7s$

35. $0.1y^2 - 1.2y^2 + 6.7 - 1.9$
$= (0.1 - 1.2)y^2 + (6.7 - 1.9)$
$= -1.1y^2 + 4.8$

37. $5x + 3 + 4x + 3 + 2x + 6 + 3x + 7x$
$= (5x + 4x + 2x + 3x + 7x) + (3 + 3 + 6)$
$= 21x + 12$

39. $(2x)^2 + 7x + x^2 + 5x = 4x^2 + x^2 + 7x + 5x$
$= 5x^2 + 12x$

41. $9ab - 6a + 5b - 3$

Terms	Degree	Degree of Polynomial
$9ab$	$1+1$ or 2	2(highest degree)
$-6a$	1	
$5b$	1	
-3	0	

43. $x^3y - 6 + 2x^2y^2 + 5y^3$

Terms	Degree	Degree of Polynomial
x^3y	$3+1$ or 4	4
-6	0	
$2x^2y^2$	$2+2$ or 4	
$5y^3$	3	

45. $3ab - 4a + 6ab - 7a = (3+6)ab + (-4-7)a$
$= 9ab - 11a$

47. $4x^2 - 6xy + 3y^2 - xy$
$= 4x^2 + (-6-1)xy + 3y^2$
$= 4x^2 - 7xy + 3y^2$

49. $5x^2y + 6xy^2 - 5yx^2 + 4 - 9y^2x$
$= (5-5)x^2y + (6-9)xy^2 + 4$
$= -3xy^2 + 4$

51. $14y^3 - 9 + 3a^2b^2 - 10 - 19b^2a^2$
$= 14y^3 + (-9-10) + (3-19)a^2b^2$
$= 14y^3 - 19 - 16a^2b^2$

53. $4 + 5(2x + 3) = 4 + 10x + 15 = 10x + 19$

55. $2(x - 5) + 3(5 - x) = 2x - 10 + 15 - 3x = -x + 5$

57. Answers may vary.

59. $1.85x^2 - 3.76x + 9.25x^2 + 10.76 - 4.21x$
$= (1.85 + 9.25)x^2 (-3.76 - 4.21)x + 10.76$
$= 11.1x^2 - 7.97x + 10.76$

Practice Problems 10.4

1. $(3x^5 - 7x^3 + 2x - 1) + (3x^3 - 2x)$
$= 3x^5 - 7x^3 + 2x - 1 + 3x^3 - 2x$
$= 3x^5 + (-7x^3 + 3x^3) + (2x - 2x) - 1$
$= 3x^5 - 4x^3 - 1$

2. $(5x^2 - 2x + 1) + (-6x^2 + x - 1)$
$= 5x^2 - 2x + 1 - 6x^2 + x - 1$
$= (5x^2 - 6x^2) + (-2x + x) + (1 - 1)$
$= -x^2 - x$

3. $9y^2 - 6y + 55$
$\underline{\hspace{1.2cm} 4y + 3}$
$9y^2 - 2y + 8$

4. $(9x+5)-(4x-3)=(9x+5)+\left[-(4x-3)\right]$
$=(9x+5)+(-4x+3)=5x+8$

5. $\left(4x^3-10x^2+1\right)-\left(-4x^3+x^2-11\right)$
$=\left(4x^3-10x^2+1\right)+\left(4x^3-x^2+11\right)$
$=4x^3+4x^3-10x^2-x^2+1+11$
$=8x^3-11x^2+12$

6. $\quad 2y^2-2y+7$
$\quad -\left(6y^2-3y+2\right)$
$\overline{}$

$\quad 2y^2-2y+7$
$\quad -6y^2+3y-2$
$\overline{\quad -4y^2+y+5}$

7. $\left[(4x-3)+(12x-5)\right]-(3x+1)$
$=4x-3+12x-5-3x-1$
$=4x+12x-3x-3-5-1$
$=13x-9$

8. $\left(2a^2-ab+6b^2\right)-\left(-3a^2+ab-7b^2\right)$
$=2a^2-ab+6b^2+3a^2-ab+7b^2$
$=5a^2-2ab+13b^2$

9. $\left(5x^2y^2+3-9x^2y+y^2\right)$
$\qquad -\left(-x^2y^2+7-8xy^2+2y^2\right)$
$=5x^2y^2+3-9x^2y+y^2$
$\qquad +x^2y^2-7+8xy^2-2y^2$
$=6x^2y^2-4-9x^2y-y^2+8xy^2$

Exercise Set 10.4

1. $(3x+7)+(9x+5)=3x+7+9x+5$
$=(3x+9x)+(7+5)=12x+12$

3. $(-7x+5)+\left(-3x^2+7x+5\right)$
$=-7x+5+\left(-3x^2\right)+7x+5$
$=-3x^2+(-7x+7x)+(5+5)$
$=-3x^2+10$

5. $\left(-5x^2+3\right)+\left(2x^2+1\right)$
$=-5x^2+3+2x^2+1$
$=\left(-5x^2+2x^2\right)+(3+1)$
$=-3x^2+4$

7. $\left(-3y^2-4y\right)+\left(2y^2+y-1\right)$
$=-3y^2-4y+2y^2+y-1$
$=\left(-3y^2+2y^2\right)+(-4y+y)-1$
$=-y^2-3y-1$

9. $\quad 3t^2+4$
$\quad +5t^2-8$
$\overline{\quad 8t^2-4}$

11. $\quad 10a^3-8a^2+9$
$\quad +5a^3+9a^2+7$
$\overline{\quad 15a^3+a^2+16}$

13. $(2x+5)-(3x-9)=(2x+5)+(-3x+9)$
$=2x+5+(-3x)+9=(2x-3x)+(5+9)$
$=-x+14$

15. $3x - (5x - 9) = 3x + (-5x + 9)$

$= 3x + (-5x) + 9 = -2x + 9$

17. $(2x^2 + 3x - 9) - (-4x + 7)$

$= (2x^2 + 3x - 9) + (4x - 7)$

$= 2x^2 + 3x - 9 + 4x - 7$

$= 2x^2 + (3x + 4x) + (-9 - 7)$

$= 2x^2 + 7x - 16$

19. $(-7y^2 + 5) - (-8y^2 + 12)$

$= (-7y^2 + 5) + (8y^2 - 12)$

$= -7y^2 + 5 + 8y^2 - 12$

$= (-7y^2 + 8y^2) + (5 - 12)$

$= y^2 - 7$

21. $(5x + 8) - (-2x^2 - 6x + 8)$

$= (5x + 8) + (2x^2 + 6x - 8)$

$= 5x + 8 + 2x^2 + 6x - 8$

$= 2x^2 + (5x + 6x) + (8 - 8)$

$= 2x^2 + 11x$

23. $4z^2 - 8z + 3$

$\underline{-(6z^2 + 8z - 3)}$

$4z^2 - 8z + 3$

$\underline{+(-6z^2 - 8z + 3)}$

$-2z^2 - 16z + 6$

25. $5u^5 - 4u^2 + 3u - 7$

$\underline{-(3u^5 + 6u^2 - 8u + 2)}$

$5u^5 - 4u^2 + 3u - 7$

$\underline{+(-3u^5 - 6u^2 + 8u - 2)}$

$2u^5 - 10u^2 + 11u - 9$

27. $(3x + 5) + (2x - 14) 3x + 5 + 2x - 14$

$= 5x - 9$

29. $(7y + 7) - (y - 6) = 7y + 7 - y + 6$

$= 6y + 13$

31. $(x^2 + 2x + 1) - (3x^2 - 6x + 2)$

$= x^2 + 2x + 1 - 3x^2 + 6x - 2$

$= -2x^2 + 8x - 1$

33. $(3x^2 + 5x - 8) + (5x^2 + 9x + 12) - (x^2 - 14)$

$= 3x^2 + 5x - 8 + 5x^2 + 9x + 12 - x^2 + 14$

$= 7x^2 + 14x + 18$

35. $(7x - 3) - 4x = 7x - 3 - 4x = 3x - 3$

37. $(4x^2 - 6x + 1) + (3x^2 + 2x + 1)$

$= 4x^2 - 6x + 1 + 3x^2 + 2x + 1$

$= 7x^2 - 4x + 2$

39. $(7x^2 + 3x + 9) - (5x + 7)$

$= 7x^2 + 3x + 9 - 5x - 7$

$= 7x^2 - 2x + 2$

41. $\left[(8y^2 + 7) + (6y + 9)\right] - (4y^2 - 6y - 3)$

$= 8y^2 + 7 + 6y + 9 - 4y^2 + 6y + 3$

$= 4y^2 + 12y + 19$

43. $\left(x^2 - 9x + 2\right) + \left(2x^2 - 6x + 1\right) - \left(3x^2 - 4\right)$

$= x^2 - 9x + 2 + 2x^2 - 6x + 1 - 3x^2 + 4$

$= -15x + 7$

45. $\left(9a + 6b - 5\right) + \left(-11a - 7b + 6\right)$

$= 9a + 6b - 5 - 11a - 7b + 6$

$= -2a - b + 1$

47. $\left(4x^2 + y^2 + 3\right) - \left(x^2 + y^2 - 2\right)$

$= 4x^2 + y^2 + 3 - x^2 - y^2 + 2$

$= 3x^2 + 5$

49. $\left(x^2 + 2xy - y^2\right) + \left(5x^2 - 4xy + 20y^2\right)$

$= x^2 + 2xy - y^2 + 5x^2 - 4xy + 20y^2$

$= 6x^2 - 2xy + 19y^2$

51. $\left(11r^2s + 16rs - 3 - 2r^2s^2\right) - \left(3sr^2 + 5 - 9r^2s^2\right)$

$= 11r^2s + 16rs - 3 - 2r^2s^2 - 3sr^2 - 5 + 9r^2s^2$

$= 8r^2s + 16rs + 7r^2s^2 - 8$

53. $3x(2x) = 3 \cdot 2 \cdot x \cdot x = 6x^2$

55. $\left(12x^3\right)\left(-x^5\right) = \left(12x^3\right)\left(-1x^5\right)$

$= (12)(-1)\left(x^3\right)\left(x^5\right) = -12x^8$

57. $10x^2(20xy^2) = 10 \cdot 20x^2 \cdot x \cdot y^2 = 200x^3y^2$

59. $\left(-x^2 + 3x\right) + \left(2x^2 + 5\right) + \left(4x - 1\right)$

$= -x^2 + 3x + 2x^2 + 5 + 4x - 1$

$= \left(x^2 + 7x + 4\right)$ feet

61. $\left(4y^2 + 4y + 1\right) - \left(y^2 - 10\right)$

$= 4y^2 + 4y + 1 - y^2 + 10$

$= \left(3y^2 + 4y + 11\right)$ meters

63. $\left[\left(1.2x^2 - 3x + 9.1\right) - \left(7.8x^2 - 3.1 + 8\right)\right]$

$+ \left(1.2x - 6\right)$

$= 1.2x^2 - 3x + 9.1 - 7.8x^2 + 3.1 - 8 + 1.2x - 6$

$= -6.6x^2 - 1.8x - 4.9$

65. $\left(-0.26x^2 + 4.58x + 14\right)$

$+ \left(-0.30x^2 + 5.74x + 21.72\right)$

$= -0.26x^2 - 0.30x^2 + 4.58x + 5.74x + 14 + 21.72$

$= -0.56x^2 + 10.32x + 35.72$

67. a. $2x$

b. x^2

c. $-2x$

d. x^2; answers may vary

Practice Problems 10.5

1. $10x \cdot 9x = (10 \cdot 9)(x \cdot x) = 90x^2$

2. $8x^3(-11x^7) = 8 \cdot (-11)(x^3 \cdot x^7) = -88x^{10}$

3. $\left(-5x^4\right)\left(-x\right) = \left(-5x^4\right)\left(-1x\right)$

$= (-5)(-1)\left(x^4 \cdot x\right) = 5x^5$

4. $4x\left(x^2 + 4x + 3\right) = 4x\left(x^2\right) + 4x\left(4x\right) + 4x\left(3\right)$

$= 4x^3 + 16x^2 + 12x$

5. $8x\left(7x^4 + 1\right) = 8x\left(7x^4\right) + 8x\left(1\right)$

$= 56x^5 + 8x$

6. $-2x^3\left(3x^2 - x + 2\right)$

$= -2x^3\left(3x^2\right) - 2x^3\left(-x\right) - 2x^3\left(2\right)$

$= -6x^5 + 2x^4 - 4x^3$

7. $(4x+5)(3x-4)$

$= 4x(3x) + 4x(-4) + 5(3x) + 5(-4)$

$= 12x^2 - 16x + 15x - 20$

$= 12x^2 - x - 20$

8. $(3x-2y)^2 = (3x-2y)(3x-2y)$

$= 3x(3x) + 3x(-2y) - 2y(3x) - 2y(-2y)$

$= 9x^2 - 6xy - 6xy + 4y^2$

$= 9x^2 - 12xy + 4y^2$

9. $(x+3)(2x^2 - 5x + 4)$

$= x(2x^2) + x(-5x) + x(4) + 3(2x^2) + 3(-5x) + 3(4)$

$= 2x^3 - 5x^2 + 4x + 6x^2 - 15x + 12$

$= 2x^3 + x^2 - 11x + 12$

10.

$$
\begin{array}{r}
y^2 - 4y + 5 \\
3y^2 \qquad\quad +1 \\
\hline
y^2 - 4y + 5 \\
3y^4 - 12y^3 + 15y^2 \\
\hline
3y^4 - 12y^3 + 16y^2 - 4y + 5
\end{array}
$$

11.

$$
\begin{array}{r}
4x^2 \quad - x - 1 \\
3x^2 + 6x - 2 \\
\hline
-8x^2 + 2x + 2 \\
24x^3 - 6x^2 - 6x \\
12x^4 - \quad 3x^3 - 3x^2 \\
\hline
12x^4 + \quad 21x^3 - 17x^2 - 4x + 2
\end{array}
$$

Mental Math 10.5

1. $x^3 \cdot x^5 = x^8$

2. $x^2 \cdot x^6 = x^8$

3. $y^4 y = y^{10}$

4. $y^9 \cdot y = y^{10}$

5. $x^7 \cdot x^7 = x^{14}$

6. $x^{11} \cdot x^{11} = x^{22}$

Exercise Set 10.5

1. $8x^2 \cdot 3x = (8 \cdot 3)(x^2 \cdot x) = 24x^3$

3. $(-3.1x^3)(4x^9) = (-3.1 \cdot 4)(x^3 \cdot x^9)$

$= -12.4x^{12}$

5. $(-x^3)(x) = (-1)(-1)(x^3 \cdot x) = x^4$

7. $\left(-\dfrac{1}{3}y^2\right)\left(\dfrac{2}{5}y\right) = \left(-\dfrac{1}{3} \cdot \dfrac{2}{5}\right)(y^2 \cdot y) = -\dfrac{2}{15}y^3$

9. $(2x)(-3x^2)(4x^5) = (2)(-3)(4)(x \cdot x^2 \cdot x^5) = -24x^8$

11. $3x(2x+5) = 3x(2x) + 3x(5) = 6x^2 + 15x$

13. $7x(x^2 + 2x - 1)$

$= 7x(x^2) + 7x(2x) + 7x(-1)$

$= 7x^3 + 14x^2 - 7x$

15. $-2a(a+4) = -2a(a) + (-2a)(4) = -2a^2 - 8a$

17. $3x(2x^2 - 3x + 4)$

$= 3x(2x^2) + 3x(-3x) + 3x(4)$

$= 6x^3 - 9x^2 + 12x$

19. $3a(a^2 + 2) = 3a(a^2) + 3a(2) = 3a^3 + 6a$

21. $-2a^2(3a^2 - 2a + 3)$

$= -2a^2(3a^2) - 2a^2(-2a) - 2a^2(3)$

$= -6a^4 + 4a^3 - 6a^2$

23. $3x^2 y(2x^3 - x^2 y^2 + 8y^3)$

$= 3x^2 y(2x^3) + 3x^2 y(-x^2 y^2) + 3x^2 y(8y^3)$

$= 6x^5 y - 3x^4 y^3 + 24x^2 y^4$

25. $x^2 + 3x = x(x + 3)$

27. $(x + 4)(x + 3) = x(x) + x(3) + 4(x) + 4(3)$

$= x^2 + 3x + 4x + 12 = x^2 + 7x + 12$

29. $(a + 7)(a - 2) = a(a)a(-2) + 7(a) + 7(-2)$

$= a^2 - 2a + 7a - 14$

$= a^2 + 5a - 14$

31. $\left(x + \dfrac{2}{3}\right)\left(x - \dfrac{1}{3}\right)$

$= x(x) + x\left(-\dfrac{1}{3}\right) + \dfrac{2}{3}(x) + \dfrac{2}{3}\left(-\dfrac{1}{3}\right)$

$= x^2 - \dfrac{1}{3}x + \dfrac{2}{3}x - \dfrac{2}{9}$

$= x^2 + \dfrac{1}{3}x - \dfrac{2}{9}$

33. $(3x^2 + 1)(4x^2 + 7)$

$= 3x^2(4x^2) + 3x^2(7) + 1(4x^2) + 1(7)$

$= 12x^4 + 21x^2 + 4x^2 + 7$

$= 12x^4 + 25x^2 + 7$

35. $(4x - 3)(3x - 5)$

$= 4x(3x) + 4x(-5) - 3(3x) - 3(-5)$

$= 12x^2 - 20x - 9x + 15$

$= 12x^2 - 29x + 15$

37. $(1 - 3a)(1 - 4a)$

$= 1(1) + 1(-4a) - 3a(1) - 3a(-4a)$

$= 1 - 4a - 3a + 12a^2$

$= 1 - 7a + 12a^2$

39. $(2y - 4)^2 = (2y - 4)(2y - 4)$

$= 2y(2y) + 2y(-4) - 4(2y) - 4(-4)$

$= 4y^2 - 8y - 8y + 16$

$= 4y^2 - 16y + 16$

41. $(x - 2)(x^2 - 3x + 7)$

$= x(x^2) + x(-3x) + x(7)$

$\qquad - 2(x^2) - 2(-3x) - 2(7)$

$= x^3 - 3x^2 + 7x - 2x^2 + 6x - 14$

$= x^3 - 5x^2 + 13x - 14$

43. $(x + 5)(x^3 - 3x + 4) = x(x^3) + x(-3x)$

$\qquad + x(4) + 5(x^3) + 5(-3x) + 5(4)$

$= x^4 - 3x^2 + 4x + 5x^3 - 15x + 20$

$= x^4 + 5x^3 - 3x^2 - 11x + 20$

45. $(2a-3)(5a^2-6a+4) = 2a(5a^2) + 2a(-6a)$
$\qquad + 2a(4) - 3(5a^2) - 3(-6a) - 3(4)$
$\qquad = 10a^3 - 12a^2 + 8a - 15a^2 + 18a - 12$
$\qquad = 10a^3 - 27a^2 + 26a - 12$

47. $(7xy - y)^2 = (7xy - y)(7xy - y)$
$\qquad = 7xy(7xy) + 7xy(-y) - y(7xy) - y(-y)$
$\qquad = 49x^2y^2 - 7xy^2 - 7xy^2 + y^2$
$\qquad = 49x^2y^2 - 14xy^2 + y^2$

49. $x^2 + 2x + 3x + 2(3) = x^2 + 5x + 6$

51.
$$
\begin{array}{r}
2x - 11 \\
6x + \ 1 \\
\hline
2x - 11 \\
12x^2 - 66x \\
\hline
12x^2 - 64x - 11
\end{array}
$$

53.
$$
\begin{array}{r}
2x^2 + \ 4x - 1 \\
x + 3 \\
\hline
6x^2 + 12x - 3 \\
2x^3 + \ 4x^2 - \ \ x \\
\hline
2x^3 + 10x^2 + 11x - 3
\end{array}
$$

55.
$$
\begin{array}{r}
x^2 + 5x - \ 7 \\
x^2 - 7x - \ 9 \\
\hline
9x^2 - 45x + 63 \\
-7x^3 - 35x^2 + 49x \\
x^4 + 5x^3 - \ 7x^2 \\
\hline
x^4 - 2x^3 - 51x^2 + 4x + 63
\end{array}
$$

57. $(5x)^2 = 5^2 x^2 = 25x^2$

59. $(-3y^3)^2 = (-3)^2 y^{3\cdot 2} = 9y^6$

61. At $t = 0$, value = $7000

63. At $t = 0$, value $= \$7000$
At $t = 1$, value $= \$6500$
$\$7000 - \$6500 = \$500$

65. Answers may vary.

67. $(2x - 5)(2x + 5)$
$\qquad = 2x(2x) + 2x(5) - 5(2x) - 5(5)$
$\qquad = 4x^2 + 10x - 10x - 25 = 4x^2 - 25$
$\qquad (4x^2 - 25)$ square yards

69. $\dfrac{1}{2}(3x - 2)(4x) = 2x(3x - 2)$
$\qquad = 2x(3x) + 2x(-2) = 6x^2 - 4x$
$\qquad (6x^2 - 4x)$ square inches

71. a. $(3x + 5) + (3x + 7) = 3x + 5 + 3x + 7$
$\qquad = 6x + 12$
Answers may vary.
 b. $(3x + 5)(3x + 7)$
$\qquad = 3x(3x) + 3x(7) + 5(3x) + 5(7)$
$\qquad = 9x^2 + 21x + 15x + 35$
$\qquad = 9x^2 + 36x + 35$
Answers may vary.

73. a. $(a+b)(a-b) = a^2 - ab + ab - b^2$

$= a^2 - b^2$

b. $(2x+3y)(2x-3y)$

$= (2x)^2 - 6xy + 6xy - (3y)^2$

$= 4x^2 - 9y^2$

c. $(4x+7)(4x-7)$

$= (4x)^2 - 28x + 28x - 7^2$

$= 16x^2 - 49$

d. Answers may vary.

Practice Problems 10.6

1. $(x+7)(x-5)$

$= (x)(x) + (x)(-5) + (7)(x) + (7)(-5)$

$= x^2 - 5x + 7x - 35 = x^2 + 2x - 35$

2. $(6x-1)(x-4)$

$= 6x(x) + 6x(-4) + (-1)(x) + (-1)(-4)$

$= 6x^2 - 24x - x + 4$

$= 6x^2 - 25x + 4$

3. $(2y^2 + 3)(y-4)$

$= (2y^2)(y) + (2y^2)(-4) + (3)(y) + (3)(-4)$

$= 2y^3 - 8y^2 + 3y - 12$

4. $(2x+9)^2 = (2x+9)(2x+9)$

$= 2x(2x) + 2x(9) + 9(2x) + 9(9)$

$= 4x^2 + 18x + 18x + 81$

$= 4x^2 + 36x + 81$

5. $(y+3)^2 = y^2 + 2(3) + 3^2$

$= y^2 + 6y + 9$

6. $(r-s)^2 = r^2 - 2rs + s^2$

7. $(6x+5)^2 = (6x)^2 + 2(6x)(5) + 5^2$

$= 36x^2 + 60x + 25$

8. $(x^2 - 3y)^2 = (x^2)^2 - 2(x^2)(3y) + (3y)^2$

$= x^4 - 6x^2 y + 9y^2$

9. $(x+7)(x-7) = x^2 - 7^2 = x^2 - 49$

10. $(4y+5)(4y-5) = (4y)^2 - 5^2$

$= 16y^2 - 25$

11. $\left(x - \dfrac{1}{3}\right)\left(x + \dfrac{1}{3}\right) = x^2 - \left(\dfrac{1}{3}\right)^2 = x^2 - \dfrac{1}{9}$

12. $(3a-b)(3a+b) - (3a)^2 - b^2 = 9a^2 - b^2$

13. $(2x^2 - 6y)(2x^2 + 6y) = (2x^2)^2 - (6y)^2$

$= 4x^4 - 36y^2$

14. $(7x-1)^2 = (7x)^2 - 2(7x)(1) + 1^2$

$= 49x^2 - 14x + 1$

15. $(5y+3)(2y-5)$

$= 5y(2y) + 5y(-5) + 3(2y) + 3(-5)$

$= 10y^2 - 25y + 6y - 15$

$= 10y^2 - 19y - 15$

16. $(2a-1)(2a+1) = (2a)^2 - 1^2 = 4a^2 - 1$

Exercise Set 10.6

1. $(x+3)(x+4) = x^2 + 4x + 3x + 12$
$$= x^2 + 7x + 12$$

3. $(x-5)(x+10) = x^2 + 10x - 5x - 50$
$$= x^2 + 5x - 50$$

5. $(5x-6)(x+2) = 5x^2 + 10x - 6x - 12$
$$= 5x^2 + 4x - 12$$

7. $(y-6)(4y-1) = 4y^2 - 1y - 24y + 6$
$$= 4y^2 - 25y + 6$$

9. $(2x+5)(3x-1) = 6x^2 - 2x + 15x - 5$
$$= 6x^2 + 13x - 5$$

11. $(y^2 + 7)(6y + 4) = 6y^3 + 4y^2 + 42y + 28$

13. $\left(x - \frac{1}{3}\right)\left(x + \frac{2}{3}\right) = x^2 + \frac{2}{3}x - \frac{1}{3}x - \frac{2}{9}$
$$= x^2 + \frac{1}{3}x - \frac{2}{9}$$

15. $(4-3a)(2-5a) = 8 - 20a - 6a + 15a^2$
$$= 8 - 26a + 15a^2$$

17. $(x+5y)(2x-y) = 2x^2 - xy + 10xy - 5y^2$
$$= 2x^2 + 9xy - 5y^2$$

19. $(x+2)^2 = x^2 + 2(x)(2) + 2^2$
$$= x^2 + 4x + 4$$

21. $(2x-1)^2 = (2x)^2 - 2(2x)(1) + (1)^2$
$$= 4x^2 - 4x + 1$$

23. $(3a-5)^2 = (3a)^2 - 2(3a)(5) + 5^2$
$$= 9a^2 - 30a + 25$$

25. $(x^2 + 5)^2 = (x^2)^2 + 2(x^2)(5) + 5^2$
$$= x^4 + 10x^2 + 25$$

27. $\left(y - \frac{2}{7}\right)^2 = y^2 - 2(y)\left(\frac{2}{7}\right) + \left(\frac{2}{7}\right)^2$
$$= y^2 - \frac{4}{7}y + \frac{4}{49}$$

29. $(2a-3)^2 = (2a)^2 - 2(2a)(3) + 3^2$
$$= 4a^2 - 12a + 9$$

31. $(5x+9)^2 = (5x)^2 + 2(5x)(9) + 9^2$
$$= 25x^2 + 90x + 81$$

33. $(3x-7y)^2 = (3x)^2 - 2(3x)(7y) + (7y)^2$
$$= 9x^2 - 42xy + 49y^2$$

35. $(4m+5n)^2 = (4m)^2 + 2(4m)(5n) + (5n)^2$
$$= 16m^2 + 40mn + 25n^2$$

37. Answers may vary.

39. $(a-7)(a+7) = a^2 - 7^2 = a^2 - 49$

41. $(x+6)(x-6) = x^2 - 6^2 = x^2 - 36$

43. $(3x-1)(3x+1) = (3x)^2 - 1^2 = 9x^2 - 1$

45. $(x^2 + 5)(x^2 - 5) = (x^2)^2 - 5^2 = x^4 - 25$

47. $(2y^2 - 1)(2y^2 + 1) = (2y^2)^2 - 1^2 = 4y^4 - 1$

49. $(4-7x)(4+7x) = 4^2 - (7x)^2 = 16 - 49x^2$

51. $\left(3x-\dfrac{1}{2}\right)\left(3x+\dfrac{1}{2}\right)=\left(3x\right)^2-\left(\dfrac{1}{2}\right)^2$

$$=9x^2-\dfrac{1}{4}$$

53. $\left(9x+y\right)\left(9x-y\right)=\left(9x\right)^2-y^2=81x^2-y^2$

55. $\left(2m+5n\right)\left(2m-5n\right)=\left(2m\right)^2-\left(5n\right)^2$

$$=4m^2-25n^2$$

57. $\left(a+5\right)\left(a+4\right)=a^2+4a+5a+20$

$$=a^2+9a+20$$

59. $\left(a-7\right)^2=a^2-2\left(a\right)\left(7\right)+7^2$

$$=a^2-14a+49$$

61. $\left(4a+1\right)\left(3a-1\right)=12a^2-4a+3a-1$

$$=12a^2-a-1$$

63. $(x+2)(x-2)=x^2-2^2=x^2-4$

65. $\left(3a+1\right)^2=\left(3a\right)^2+2\left(3a\right)\left(1\right)+1^2$

$$=9a^2+6a+1$$

67. $\left(x+y\right)\left(4x-y\right)=4x^2-xy+4xy-y^2$

$$=4x^2+3xy-y^2$$

69. $\left(a-\dfrac{1}{2}y\right)\left(a+\dfrac{1}{2}y\right)=a^2-\left(\dfrac{1}{2}y\right)^2$

$$=a^2-\dfrac{1}{4}y^2$$

71. $\left(3b+7\right)\left(2b-5\right)=6b^2-15b+14b-35$

$$=6b^2-b-35$$

73. $\left(x^2+10\right)\left(x^2-10\right)=\left(x^2\right)^2-\left(10\right)^2$

$$=x^4-100$$

75. $\left(4x+5\right)\left(4x-5\right)=\left(4x\right)^2-5^2$

$$=16x^2-25$$

77. $\left(5x-6y\right)^2=\left(5x\right)^2-2\left(5x\right)\left(6y\right)+\left(6y\right)^2$

$$=25x^2-60xy+36y^2$$

79. $\left(2r-3s\right)\left(2r+3s\right)=\left(2r\right)^2-\left(3s\right)^2$

$$=4r^2-9s^2$$

81. $\dfrac{50b^{10}}{70b^5}=\dfrac{10\cdot5\cdot b^5\cdot b^5}{10\cdot7\cdot b^5}=\dfrac{5b^5}{7}$

83. $\dfrac{8a^{17}b^5}{-4a^7b^{10}}=\dfrac{4\cdot2\cdot a^7\cdot a^{10}\cdot b^5}{4\cdot(-1)\cdot a^7\cdot b^5\cdot b^5}=-\dfrac{2a^{10}}{b^5}$

85. $\dfrac{2x^4y^{12}}{3x^4y^4}=\dfrac{2\cdot x^4\cdot y^4\cdot y^8}{3\cdot x^4\cdot y^4}=\dfrac{2y^8}{3}$

87. $\left(2x+1\right)^2=\left(2x\right)^2+2\left(2x\right)\left(1\right)+1^2$

$$=4x^2+4x+1$$

$\left(4x^2+4x+1\right)$ square feet

89. $\left(5x-3\right)^2-\left(x+1\right)^2$

$$=\left[\left(5x\right)^2-2\left(5x\right)\left(3\right)+3^2\right]-\left[x^2+2\left(x\right)\left(1\right)+1^2\right]$$

$$=\left(25x^2-30x+9\right)-\left(x^2+2x+1\right)$$

$$=25x^2-30x+9-x^2-2x-1$$

$$=\left(24x^2-32x+8\right)\text{ square meters}$$

Integrated Review 10.6

1. $\left(5x^2\right)\left(7x^3\right) = \left(5 \cdot 7\right)\left(x^2 \cdot x^3\right)$
$= 35x^5$

2. $\left(4y^2\right)\left(8y^7\right) = \left(4 \cdot 8\right)\left(y^2 \cdot y^7\right)$
$= 32y^9$

3. $-4^2 = -(4 \cdot 4) = -16$

4. $(-4)^2 = (-4)(-4) = 16$

5. $(x-5)+(2x+1) = x-5+2x+1$
$= 3x-4$

6. $(3x-2)+(x+5) = 3x-2+x+5$
$= 4x+3$

7. $(4y-3)(4y+3) = (4y)^2 - 3^2$
$= 16y^2 - 9$

8. $(7x-1)(7x+1) = (7x)^2 - 1^2$
$= 49x^2 - 1$

9. $\dfrac{7x^9 y^{12}}{x^3 y^{10}} = 7x^{9-3} y^{12-10}$
$= 7x^6 y^2$

10. $\dfrac{20a^2 b^8}{14a^2 b^2} = \dfrac{10a^{2-2} b^{8-2}}{7}$
$= \dfrac{10b^6}{7}$

11. $\left(12m^7 n^6\right)^2 = 12^2 m^{7 \cdot 2} n^{6 \cdot 2}$
$= 144m^{14} n^{12}$

12. $\left(4y^9 z^{10}\right)^3 = 4^3 y^{9 \cdot 3} z^{10 \cdot 3}$
$= 64y^{27} z^{30}$

13. $(4y-3)(4y+3) = (4y)^2 - 3^2$
$= 16y^2 - 9$

14. $(7x-1)(7x+1) = (7x)^2 - 1^2$
$= 49x^2 - 1$

15. $\left(x^{-7} y^5\right)^9 = x^{-63} y^{45}$
$= \dfrac{y^{45}}{x^{63}}$

16. $\left(3^{-1} x^9\right)^3 = 3^{-3} x^{27}$
$= \dfrac{x^{27}}{3^3}$
$= \dfrac{x^{27}}{27}$

17. $\left(7x^2 - 2x + 3\right) - \left(5x^2 + 9\right)$
$= 7x^2 - 2x + 3 - 5x^2 - 9$
$= 2x^2 - 2x - 6$

18. $\left(10x^2 + 7x - 9\right) - \left(4x^2 - 6x + 2\right)$
$= 10x^2 + 7x - 9 - 4x^2 + 6x - 2$
$= 6x^2 + 13x - 11$

19. $0.7y^2 - 1.2 + 1.8y^2 - 6y + 1$
$= 2.5y^2 - 6y - 0.2$

20. $7.8x^2 - 6.8x - 3.3 + 0.6x^2 - 9$
$= 8.4x^2 - 6.8x - 12.3$

21. $(x+4)^2 = (x+4)(x+4)$

$\qquad = x^2 + 2(x)(4) + 4^2$

$\qquad = x^2 + 8x + 16$

22. $(y-9)^2 = (y-9)(y-9)$

$\qquad = y^2 - 2(y)(9) + 9^2$

$\qquad = y^2 - 18y + 81$

23. $(x+4)(x+4) = x+4+x+4$

$\qquad = 2x+8$

24. $(y-9)(y-9) = y-9+y-9$

$\qquad = 2y-18$

25. $7x^2 - 6xy + 4(y^2 - xy)$

$\qquad = 7x^2 - 6xy + 4y^2 - 4xy$

$\qquad = 7x^2 - 10xy + 4y^2$

26. $5a^2 - 3ab + 6(6^2 - a^2)$

$\qquad = 5a^2 - 3ab + 6b^2 - 6a^2$

$\qquad = -a^2 - 3ab + 6b^2$

27. $(x-3)(x^2 + 5x - 1)$

$\qquad = x(x^2) + x(5x) + x(-1) - 3(x^2)$

$\qquad\quad -3(5x) - 3(-1)$

$\qquad = x^3 + 5x^2 - x - 3x^2 - 15x + 3$

$\qquad = x^3 + 2x^2 - 16x + 3$

28. $(x+1)(x^2 - 3x - 2)$

$\qquad = x(x^2) + x(-3x) + x(-2) + 1(x^2)$

$\qquad\quad +1(-3x) + 1(-2)$

$\qquad = x^3 - 3x^2 - 2x + x^2 - 3x - 2$

$\qquad = x^3 - 2x^2 - 5x - 2$

29. $(2x-7)(3x+10)$

$\qquad = 2x(3x) + 2x(10) - 7(3x) - 7(10)$

$\qquad = 6x^2 + 20x - 21x - 70$

$\qquad = 6x^2 - x - 70$

30. $(5x-1)(4x+5)$

$\qquad = 5x(4x) + 5x(5) - 1(4x) - 1(5)$

$\qquad = 20x^2 + 25x - 4x - 5$

$\qquad = 20x^2 + 21x - 5$

31. $(2x-7)(x^2 - 6x + 1)$

$\qquad = 2x(x^2) - 2x(6x) + 2x(1) - 7(x^2)$

$\qquad\quad -7(-6x) - 7(1)$

$\qquad = 2x^3 - 12x^2 + 2x - 7x^2 + 42x - 7$

$\qquad = 2x^3 - 19x^2 + 44x - 7$

32. $(5x-1)(x^2 + 2x - 3)$

$\qquad = 5x(x^2) + 5x(2x) + 5x(-3) - 1(x^2)$

$\qquad\quad -1(2x) - 1(-3)$

$\qquad = 5x^3 + 10x^2 - 15x - x^2 - 2x + 3$

$\qquad = 5x^3 + 9x^2 - 17x + 3$

Practice Problems 10.7

1. $\dfrac{25x^3 + 5x^2}{5x^2} = \dfrac{25x^3}{5x^2} + \dfrac{5x^2}{5x^2} = 5x + 1$

2. $\dfrac{30x^7 + 10x^2 - 5x}{5x^2} = \dfrac{30x^7}{5x^2} + \dfrac{10x^2}{5x^2} - \dfrac{5x}{5x^2}$

$\qquad = 6x^5 + 2 - \dfrac{1}{x}$

3. $\dfrac{12x^3y^3 - 18xy + 6y}{3xy} = \dfrac{12x^3y^3}{3xy} - \dfrac{18xy}{3xy} + \dfrac{6y}{3xy}$

$$= 4x^2y^2 - 6 + \dfrac{2}{x}$$

4.
$$
\begin{array}{r}
x + 7 \\
x+5{\overline{\smash{\big)}\,x^2 + 12x + 35}} \\
\underline{x^2 + 5x} \\
7x + 35 \\
\underline{7x + 35} \\
0
\end{array}
$$

The quotient is $x + 7$.

5.
$$
\begin{array}{r}
3x + 5 \\
2x-1{\overline{\smash{\big)}\,6x^2 + 7x - 5}} \\
\underline{6x^2 - 3x} \\
10x - 5 \\
\underline{10x - 5} \\
0
\end{array}
$$

The quotient is $3x + 5$.

6.
$$
\begin{array}{r}
3x^2 - 2x + 1 \\
3x+2{\overline{\smash{\big)}\,9x^3 + 0x^2 - x + 5}} \\
\underline{9x^3 + 6x^2} \\
-6x^2 - x \\
\underline{-6x^2 - 4x} \\
3x + 5 \\
\underline{3x + 2} \\
3
\end{array}
$$

$$\dfrac{5 - x + 9x^3}{3x + 2} = 3x^2 - 2x + 1 + \dfrac{3}{3x + 2}$$

7.
$$
\begin{array}{r}
x^2 + x + 1 \\
x-1{\overline{\smash{\big)}\,x^3 + 0x^2 + 0x - 1}} \\
\underline{x^3 - x^2} \\
x^2 + 0x \\
\underline{x^2 - x} \\
x - 1 \\
\underline{x - 1} \\
0
\end{array}
$$

$$\dfrac{x^3 - 1}{x - 1} = x^2 + x + 1$$

Mental Math 10.7

1. $\dfrac{a^6}{a^4} = a^2$

2. $\dfrac{y^2}{y} = y$

3. $\dfrac{a^3}{a} = a^2$

4. $\dfrac{p^8}{p^3} = p^5$

5. $\dfrac{k^5}{k^2} = k^3$

6. $\dfrac{k^7}{k^5} = k^2$

Exercise Set 10.7

1. $\dfrac{20x^2 + 5x + 9}{5} = \dfrac{20x^2}{5} + \dfrac{5x}{5} + \dfrac{9}{5}$

$= 4x^2 + x + \dfrac{9}{5}$

3. $\dfrac{12x^4 + 3x^2}{x} = \dfrac{12x^4}{x} + \dfrac{3x^2}{x} = 12x^3 + 3x$

5. $\dfrac{15p^3 + 18p^2}{3p} = \dfrac{15p^3}{3p} + \dfrac{18p^2}{3p} = 5p^2 + 6p$

7. $\dfrac{-9x^4 + 18x^5}{6x^5} = \dfrac{-9x^4}{6x^5} + \dfrac{18x^5}{6x^5} = -\dfrac{3}{2x} + 3$

9. $\dfrac{-9x^5 + 3x^4 - 12}{3x^3} = \dfrac{-9x^5}{3x^3} + \dfrac{3x^4}{3x^3} - \dfrac{12}{3x^3}$

$= -3x^2 + x - \dfrac{4}{x^3}$

11. $\dfrac{4x^4 - 6x^3 + 7}{-4x^4} = \dfrac{4x^4}{-4x^4} - \dfrac{6x^3}{-4x^4} + \dfrac{7}{-4x^4}$

$= -1 + \dfrac{3}{2x} - \dfrac{7}{4x^4}$

13. $\dfrac{a^2b^2 - ab^3}{ab} = \dfrac{a^2b^2}{ab} - \dfrac{ab^3}{ab} = ab - b^2$

15. $\dfrac{2x^2y + 8x^2y^2 - xy^2}{2xy} = \dfrac{2x^2y}{2xy} + \dfrac{8x^2y^2}{2xy} - \dfrac{xy^2}{2xy}$

$= x + 4xy - \dfrac{y}{2}$

17. $\begin{array}{r} x+1 \\ x+3\overline{\smash{\big)}\,x^2 + 4x + 3} \\ \underline{x^2 + 3x} \\ x+3 \\ \underline{x+3} \\ 0 \end{array}$

$\dfrac{x^2 + 4x + 3}{x + 3} = x + 1$

19. $\begin{array}{r} 2x+3 \\ x+5\overline{\smash{\big)}\,2x^2 + 13x + 15} \\ \underline{2x^2 + 10x} \\ 3x+15 \\ \underline{3x+15} \\ 0 \end{array}$

$\dfrac{2x^2 + 13x + 15}{x + 5} = 2x + 3$

21. $\begin{array}{r} 2x+1 \\ x-4\overline{\smash{\big)}\,2x^2 - 7x + 3} \\ \underline{2x^2 - 8x} \\ x+3 \\ \underline{x-4} \\ 7 \end{array}$

$\dfrac{2x^2 - 7x + 3}{x - 4} = 2x + 1 + \dfrac{7}{x - 4}$

23. $\begin{array}{r} 4x+9 \\ 2x-3\overline{\smash{\big)}\,8x^2 + 6x - 27} \\ \underline{8x^2 - 12x} \\ 18x-27 \\ \underline{18x-27} \\ 0 \end{array}$

$\dfrac{8x^2 + 6x - 27}{2x - 3} = 4x + 9$

25.
$$3a+2\overline{\smash{\big)}9a^3-3a^2-3a+4} \quad\quad \overset{3a^2-3a+1}{}$$

$$\underline{9a^3+6a^2}$$
$$-9a^2-3a$$
$$\underline{-9a^2-6a}$$
$$3a+4$$
$$\underline{3a+2}$$
$$2$$

$$\frac{9a^3-3a^2-3a+4}{3a+2}=3a^2-3a+1+\frac{2}{3a+2}$$

27.
$$b+4\overline{\smash{\big)}2b^3+9b^2+6b-4} \quad\quad \overset{2b^2+b+2}{}$$

$$\underline{2b^3+8b^2}$$
$$b^2+6b$$
$$\underline{b^2+4b}$$
$$2b-4$$
$$\underline{2b+8}$$
$$-12$$

$$\frac{2b^3+9b^2+6b-4}{b+4}=2b^2+b+2-\frac{12}{b+4}$$

29.
$$2x+1\overline{\smash{\big)}8x^2+10x+1} \quad\quad \overset{4x+3}{}$$

$$\underline{8x^2+\ 4x}$$
$$6x+1$$
$$\underline{6x+3}$$
$$-2$$

$$\frac{8x^2+10x+1}{2x+1}=4x+3-\frac{2}{2x+1}$$

31.
$$x-2\overline{\smash{\big)}2x^3+2x^2-17x+8} \quad\quad \overset{2x^2+6x-5}{}$$

$$\underline{2x^3-4x^2}$$
$$6x^2-17x$$
$$\underline{6x^2-12x}$$
$$-5x+\ 8$$
$$\underline{-5x+10}$$
$$-2$$

$$\frac{2x^3+2x^2-17x+8}{x-2}=2x^2+6x-5-\frac{2}{x-2}$$

33.
$$x-3\overline{\smash{\big)}x^3+0x^2+0x-27} \quad\quad \overset{x^2+3x+9}{}$$

$$\underline{x^3-3x^2}$$
$$3x^2+0x$$
$$\underline{3x^2-9x}$$
$$9x-27$$
$$\underline{9x-27}$$
$$0$$

$$\frac{x^3-27}{x-3}=x^2+3x+9$$

35.
$$x+2\overline{\smash{\big)}-3x^2+0x+1} \quad\quad \overset{-3x+6}{}$$

$$\underline{-3x^2-6x}$$
$$6x+\ 1$$
$$\underline{6x+12}$$
$$-11$$

$$\frac{1-3x^2}{x+2}=-3x+6-\frac{11}{x+2}$$

37.

$$\begin{array}{r} 2b-1 \\ 2b-1\overline{\smash{\big)}\,4b^2-4b-5} \\ \underline{4b^2-2b} \\ -2b-5 \\ \underline{-2b+1} \\ -6 \end{array}$$

$$\frac{-4b+4b^2-5}{2b-1} = 2b-1-\frac{6}{2b-1}$$

39. $12 = 4 \cdot 3$

41. $20 = -5 \cdot (-4)$

43. $9x^2 = 3x \cdot 3x$

45. $36x^2 = 4x \cdot 9x$

47.

$$\begin{array}{r} x^3-x^2+x \\ x^2+x\overline{\smash{\big)}\,x^5+0x^4+0x^3+x^2} \\ \underline{x^5+x^4} \\ -x^4+0x^3 \\ \underline{-x^4-x^3} \\ x^3+x^2 \\ \underline{x^3+x^2} \\ 0 \end{array}$$

$$\frac{x^5+x^2}{x^2+x} = x^3-x^2+x$$

49. $\dfrac{12x^3+4x-16}{4} = \dfrac{12x^3}{4} + \dfrac{4x}{x} - \dfrac{16}{4}$

$= 3x^3 + x - 4$

Each side is $\left(3x^2 + x - 4\right)$ feet.

51.

$$\begin{array}{r} 2x+5 \\ 5x+3\overline{\smash{\big)}\,10x^2+31x+15} \\ \underline{10x^2+6x} \\ 25+15 \\ \underline{25+15} \\ 0 \end{array}$$

The height is $\left(2x+5\right)$ meters.

53. Answers may vary.

Chapter 10 Review

1. 3^2

base: 3

exponent: 2

2. $(-5)^4$

base: -5

exponent: 4

3. -5^4

base: 5

exponent: 4

4. x^2

base: x

exponent: 6

5. $8^3 = 8 \cdot 8 \cdot 8 = 512$

6. $(-6)^2 = (-6)(-6) = 36$

7. $-6^2 = -6 \cdot 6 = -36$

8. $-4^3 - 4^0 = -4 \cdot 4 \cdot 4 - 1 = -65$

9. $(3b)^0 = 1$

10. $\dfrac{8b}{8b} = 1$

11. $y^2 \cdot y^2 = y^{2+7} = y^9$

12. $x^9 \cdot x^5 = x^{9+5} = x^{14}$

13. $(2x^5)(-3x^6) = 2(-3) \cdot (x^5 \cdot x^6) = -6x^{11}$

14. $(-5y^3)(4y^4) = (-5 \cdot 4)(y^3 \cdot y^4) = -20y^7$

15. $(x^4)^2 = x^{4 \cdot 2} = x^8$

16. $(y^3)^5 = y^{3 \cdot 5} = y^{15}$

17. $(3y^6)^4 = 3^4 y^{6 \cdot 4} = 81y^{24}$

18. $(2x^3)^3 = 2^3 x^{3 \cdot 3} = 8x^9$

19. $\dfrac{x^9}{x^4} = x^{9-4} = x^5$

20. $\dfrac{z^{12}}{z^5} = z^{12-5} = z^7$

21. $\dfrac{a^5 b^4}{ab} = a^{5-1} b^{4-1} = a^4 b^3$

22. $\dfrac{x^4 y^6}{xy} = x^{4-1} y^{6-1} = x^3 y^5$

23. $\dfrac{12xy^6}{3x^4 y^{10}} = \dfrac{12}{3} \cdot x^{1-4} \cdot y^{6-10}$
$= 4x^{-3} y^{-4}$
$= \dfrac{4}{x^3 y^4}$

24. $\dfrac{2x^7 y^8}{8xy^2} = \dfrac{2}{8} \cdot x^{7-1} y^{8-2}$
$= \dfrac{x^6 y^6}{4}$

25. $5a^7 (2a^4)^3$
$= 5a^7 (2^3 a^{4 \cdot 3})$
$= 5a^7 (8a^{12})$
$= 5 \cdot 8 a^{7+12}$
$= 40a^{19}$

26. $(2x)^2 (9x)$
$= (2^2 \cdot x^2)(9x)$
$= 4x^2 \cdot 9x$
$= 4 \cdot 9 \cdot x^{2+1}$
$= 36x^3$

27. $(-5a)^0 + 7^0 + 8^0$
$= 1 + 1 + 1$
$= 3$

28. $8x^0 + 9x^0$
$= 8 \cdot 1 + 1$
$= 9$

29. $\left(\dfrac{3x^4}{4y}\right)^3$
$= \dfrac{3^3 x^{4 \cdot 3}}{4^3 y^3}$
$= \dfrac{27x^{12}}{64y^3}$
Answer: b

30. $\left(\dfrac{5a^6}{b^3}\right)^{} = \dfrac{5^2 a^{6\cdot2}}{b^{3\cdot2}} = \dfrac{25a^{12}}{b^6}$

Answer: c

31. $7^{-2} = \dfrac{1}{7^2} = \dfrac{1}{49}$

32. $-7^{-2} = -\dfrac{1}{7^2} = -\dfrac{1}{49}$

33. $2x^{-4} = \dfrac{2}{x^4}$

34. $(2x)^{-4} = \dfrac{1}{(2x)^4} = \dfrac{1}{16x^4}$

35. $\left(\dfrac{1}{5}\right)^{-3} = \dfrac{1^{-3}}{5^{-3}} = \dfrac{5^3}{1^3} = 125$

36. $\left(\dfrac{-2}{3}\right)^{-2} = \dfrac{(-2)^{-2}}{3^{-2}} = \dfrac{3}{(-2)^2} = \dfrac{9}{4}$

37. $2^0 + 2^{-4} = 1 + \dfrac{1}{2^4} = \dfrac{16}{16} + \dfrac{1}{16} = \dfrac{17}{16}$

38. $6^{-1} - 7^{-1} = \dfrac{1}{6} - \dfrac{1}{7} = \dfrac{7}{42} - \dfrac{6}{42} = \dfrac{1}{42}$

39. $\dfrac{x^5}{x^{-3}} = x^{5-(-3)} = x^8$

40. $\dfrac{z^4}{z^{-4}} = z^{4-(-4)} = z^8$

41. $\dfrac{r^{-3}}{r^{-4}} = r^{-3-(-4)} = r^1 = r$

42. $\dfrac{y^{-2}}{y^{-5}} = y^{-2-(-5)} = y^3$

43. $\left(\dfrac{bc^{-2}}{bc^{-3}}\right)^4 = \dfrac{b^4 c^{-8}}{b^4 c^{-12}} = b^{4-4} c^{-8-(-12)} = c^4$

44. $\left(\dfrac{x^{-3} y^{-4}}{x^{-2} y^{-5}}\right)^{-3} = \dfrac{x^9 y^{12}}{x^6 y^{15}} = x^{9-6} y^{12-15} = \dfrac{x^3}{y^3}$

45. $\dfrac{x^{-4} y^{-6}}{x^2 y^7} = x^{-4-2} y^{-6-7} = x^{-6} y^{-13} = \dfrac{1}{x^6 y^{13}}$

46. $\dfrac{a^5 b^{-5}}{a^{-5} b^5} = a^{5-(-5)} b^{-5-5}$

$= a^{10} b^{-10}$

$= \dfrac{a^{10}}{b^{10}}$

47. $0.00027 = 2.7 \times 10^{-4}$

48. $0.8868 = 8.868 \times 10^{-1}$

49. $80,800,000 = 8.08 \times 10^7$

50. $-868,000 = -8.68 \times 10^5$

51. $1,302,079,000 = 1.302079 \times 10^9$

52. $150,000 = 1.5 \times 10^5$ light years

53. $8.67 \times 10^5 = 867,000$

54. $3.86 \times 10^{-3} = 0.00386$

55. $8.6 \times 10^{-4} = 0.00086$

56. $8.936 \times 10^5 = 893,600$

57. $1.43128 \times 10^{15} = 1,431,280,000,000,000$ cu. km

58. $1 \times 10^{-10} = 0.0000000001$ m

59. $\left(8 \times 10^4\right)\left(2 \times 10^{-7}\right)$

$= \left(8 \times 2\right) \times \left(10^4 \times 10^{-7}\right)$

$= 16 \times 10^{-3}$

$= 0.016$

60. $\dfrac{8 \times 10^4}{2 \times 10^{-7}}$

$= \dfrac{8}{2} \times \left(10^{4-(-7)}\right)$

$= 4 \times 10^{11}$

$= 400,000,000,000$

61. The degree is 5 because y^5 is the term with the highest degree.

62. The degree is 2 because $9y^2$ is the term with the highest degree.

63. The degree is 5 because $-28x^2 y^3$ is the term with the highest degree.

64. The degree is 5 because $6x^2 y^2 z^2$ is the term with the highest degree.

65. $2(1)^2 + 20(1) = 22$

$2(3)^2 + 20(3) = 78$

$2(5.1)^2 + 20(5.1) = 154.02$

$2(10)^2 + 20(10) = 400$

x	1	3	5.1	10
$2x^2 + 20x$	22	78	154.02	400

66. $7a^2 - 4a^2 - a^2 = (7-4-1)a^2$

$= 2a^2$

67. $9y + y - 14y = (9+1-14)y$

$= -4y$

68. $6a^2 - 4a + 9a^2 = (6+9)a^2 + 4a$

$= 15a^2 + 4a$

69. $21x^2 + 3x + x^2 + 6$

$= (21+1)x^2 + 3x + 6$

$= 22x^2 + 3x + 6$

70. $4a^2 b - 3b^2 - 8q^2 - 10a^2 b + 7q^2$

$= \left(4a^2 b - 10a^2 b\right) - 3b^2 + \left(-8q^2 + 7q^2\right)$

$= -6a^2 b - 3b^2 - q^2$

71. $2s^{14} + 3s^{13} + 12s^{12} - s^{10}$

Cannot be combined.

72. $\left(3x^2 + 2x + 6\right) + \left(5x^2 + x\right)$

$= 3x^2 + 2x + 6 + 5x^2 + x$

$= 8x^2 + 3x + 6$

73. $\left(2x^5 + 3x^4 + 4x^3 + 5x^2\right) + \left(4x^2 + 7x + 6\right)$

$= 2x^5 + 3x^4 + 4x^3 + 5x^2 + 4x^2 + 7x + 6$

$= 2x^5 + 3x^4 + 4x^3 + 9x^2 + 7x + 6$

74. $\left(-5y^2 + 3\right) - \left(2y^2 + 4\right)$

$= -5y^2 + 3 - 2y^2 - 4$

$= -7y^2 - 1$

75. $\left(2m^7 + 3x^4 + 7m^6\right) - \left(8m^7 + 4m^2 + 6x^4\right)$

$= 2m^7 + 3x^4 + 7m^6 - 8m^7 - 4m^2 - 6x^4$

$= -6m^7 - 3x^4 + 7m^6 - 4m^2$

76. $\left(3x^2 - 7xy + 7y^2\right) - \left(4x^2 - xy + 9y^2\right)$

$= 3x^2 - 7xy + 7y^2 - 4x^2 + xy - 9y^2$

$= -x^2 - 6xy - 2y^2$

77. $\left(-9x^2 + 6x + 2\right) + \left(4x^2 - x - 1\right)$

$= -9x^2 + 6x + 2 + 4x^2 - x - 1$

$= -5x^2 + 5x + 1$

78. $\left[\left(x^2 + 7x + 9\right) + \left(x^2 + 4\right)\right] - \left(4x^2 + 8x - 7\right)$

$= x^2 + 7x + 9 + x^2 + 4 - 4x^2 - 8x + 7$

$= -2x^2 - x + 20$

79. $6(x + 5) = 6x + 6(5)$

$= 6x + 30$

80. $9(x - 7) = 9x - 9(7)$

$= 9x - 63$

81. $4(2a + 7) = 4(2a) + 4(7)$

$= 8a + 28$

82. $9(6a - 3) = 9(6a) - 9(3)$

$= 54a - 27$

83. $-7x\left(x^2 + 5\right) = -7\left(x^2\right) - 7x(5)$

$= -7x^3 - 35x$

84. $-8y\left(4y^2 - 6\right) = -8y\left(4y^2\right) - 8y(-6)$

$= -32y^3 + 48y$

85. $-2\left(x^3 - 9x^2 + x\right) = -2\left(x^3\right) - 2\left(-9x^2\right) - 2(x)$

$= -2x^3 + 18x^2 - 2x$

86. $-3a\left(a^2b + ab + b^2\right)$

$= -3a\left(a^2b\right) - 3a(ab) - 3a\left(b^2\right)$

$= -3a^3b - 3a^2b - 3ab^2$

87. $\left(3a^3 - 4a + 1\right)(-2a)$

$= 3a^3(-2a) - 4a(-2a) + 1(-2a)$

$= -6a^4 + 8a^2 - 2a$

88. $\left(6b^3 - 4b + 2\right)(7b)$

$= 6b^3(7b) - 4b(7b) + 2(7b)$

$= 42b^4 - 28b^2 + 14b$

89. $(2x + 2)(x - 7)$

$= 2x(x) + 2x(-7) + 2(x) + 2(-7)$

$= 2x^2 - 12x - 14$

90. $(2x - 5)(3x + 2)$

$= 2x(3x) + 2x(2) - 5(3x) - 5(2)$

$= 6x^2 + 4x - 15x - 10$

$= 6x^2 - 11x - 10$

91. $(4a - 1)(a + 7) = 4a^2 + 28a - a - 7$

$= 4a^2 + 27a - 7$

92. $(6a - 1)(7a + 3) = 42a^2 + 18a - 7a - 3$

$= 42a^2 + 11a - 3$

93. $(x + 7)\left(x^3 + 4x - 5\right)$

$= x^4 + 4x^2 - 5x + 7x^3 + 28x - 35$

$= x^4 + 7x^3 + 4x^2 + 23x - 35$

94. $(x+2)(x^5+x+1)$

$= x^6 + x^2 + x + 2x^5 + 2x + 2$

$= x^6 + 2x^5 + x^2 + 3x + 2$

95. $(x^2+2x+4)(x^2+2x-4)$

$= x^4 + 2x^3 - 4x^2 + 2x^3 + 4x^2 - 8x$

$\qquad + 4x^2 + 8x - 16$

$= x^4 + 4x^3 + 4x^2 - 16$

96. $(x^3+4x+4)(x^3+4x-4)$

$= x^6 + 4x^4 - 4x^3 + 4x^4 + 16x^2 - 16x$

$\qquad + 4x^3 + 16x - 16$

$= x^6 + 8x^4 + 16x^2 - 16$

97. $(x+7)^3$

$= (x+7)(x+7)(x+7)$

$= \left(x^2 + 7x + 7x + 49\right)(x+7)$

$= \left(x^2 + 14x + 49\right)(x+7)$

$= x^3 + 7x^2 + 14x^2 + 98x + 49x + 343$

$= x^3 + 21x^2 + 147x + 343$

98. $(2x-5)^3$

$= (2x-5)(2x-5)(2x-5)$

$= \left(4x^2 - 10x - 10x + 25\right)(2x-5)$

$= \left(4x^2 - 20x + 25\right)(2x-5)$

$= 8x^3 - 20x^2 - 40x^2 + 100x + 50x - 125$

$= 8x^3 - 60x^2 + 150x - 125$

99. $(x+7)^2 = x^2 + 2(x)(7) + 7^2$

$\qquad\qquad = x^2 + 14x + 49$

100. $(x-5)^2 = x^2 - 2(x)(5) + 5^2$

$\qquad\qquad = x^2 - 10x + 25$

101. $(3x-7)^2 = (3x)^2 - 2(3x)(7) + 7^2$

$\qquad\qquad = 9x^2 - 42x + 49$

102. $(4x+2)^2 = (4x)^2 + 2(4x)(2) + 2^2$

$\qquad\qquad = 16x^2 + 16x + 4$

103. $(5x-9)^2 = (5x)^2 - 2(5x)(9) + 9^2$

$\qquad\qquad = 25x^2 - 90x + 81$

104. $(5x+1)(5x-1) = (5x)^2 - 1^2$

$\qquad\qquad\qquad = 25x^2 - 1$

105. $(7x+4)(7x-4) = (7x)^2 - 4^2$

$\qquad\qquad\qquad = 49x^2 - 16$

106. $(a+2b)(a-2b) = a^2 - (2b)^2$

$\qquad\qquad\qquad = a^2 - 4b^2$

107. $(2x-6)(2x+6) = (2x)^2 - 6^2$

$\qquad\qquad\qquad = 4x^2 - 36$

108. $\left(4a^2-2b\right)\left(4a^2+2b\right) = \left(4a^2\right)^2 - (2b)^2$

$\qquad\qquad\qquad\qquad = 16a^4 - 4b^2$

109. $(3x-1)(3x-1) = 9x^2 - 2(3x) + 1$

$\qquad\qquad\qquad = \left(9x^2 - 6x + 1\right)$ sq m

110. $(5x+2)(x-1) = 5x^2 - 5x + 2x - 2$

$\qquad\qquad\qquad = \left(5x^2 - 3x - 2\right)$ sq mi

111.
$$\frac{x^2+21x+49}{7x^2}=\frac{x^2}{7x^2}+\frac{21x}{7x^2}+\frac{49}{7x^2}$$
$$=\frac{1}{7}+\frac{3}{x}+\frac{7}{x^2}$$

112.
$$\frac{5a^3-15ab^2+20ab}{-5ab}$$
$$=\frac{5a^3b}{-5ab}-\frac{15ab^2}{-5ab}+\frac{20ab}{-5ab}$$
$$=-a^2+3b-4$$

113.
$$\begin{array}{r} a+1 \\ a-2\overline{)a^2-a+4} \\ \underline{a^2-2a} \\ a+4 \\ \underline{a-2} \\ 6 \end{array}$$
$$\left(a^2-a+4\right)\div\left(a-2\right)=a+1+\frac{6}{a-2}$$

114.
$$\begin{array}{r} 4x \\ x+5\overline{)4x^2+20x+7} \\ \underline{4x^2+20x} \\ 7 \end{array}$$
$$\left(4x^2+20x+7\right)\div\left(x+5\right)=4x+\frac{7}{x+5}$$

115.
$$\begin{array}{r} a^2+3a+8 \\ a-2\overline{)a^3+\ a^2+2a+6} \\ \underline{a^3-2a^2} \\ 3a^2+2a \\ \underline{3a^2-6a} \\ 8a+\ 6 \\ \underline{8a-16} \\ 22 \end{array}$$
$$\frac{a^3+a^2+2a+6}{a-2}=a^2+3a+8+\frac{22}{a-2}$$

116.
$$\begin{array}{r} 3b^2-4b \\ 3b-2\overline{)9b^3-18b^2+8b-1} \\ \underline{9b^3-6b^2} \\ -12b^2+8b \\ \underline{-12b^2+8b} \\ -1 \end{array}$$
$$\frac{9b^3-18b^2+8b-1}{3b-2}=3b^2-4b-\frac{1}{3b-2}$$

117.
$$\begin{array}{r} 2x^3-x^2+2 \\ 2x-1\overline{)4x^4-4x^3+x^2+4x-3} \\ \underline{4x^4-2x^3} \\ -2x^3+x^2 \\ \underline{-2x^2+x^2} \\ 4x-3 \\ \underline{4x-2} \\ -1 \end{array}$$
$$\frac{4x^4-4x^3+x^2+4x-3}{2x-1}$$
$$=2x^3-x^2+2-\frac{1}{2x-1}$$

118.
$$\begin{array}{r} -x^2-16x-117 \\ x-6\overline{)-4x^3-10x^2-21x+18} \\ \underline{-x^3+10x^2} \\ -16x^2-21x \\ \underline{-16x^2+96x} \\ -117x+18 \\ \underline{-117x+702} \\ -684 \end{array}$$
$$\frac{-10x^2-x^3-21x+18}{x-6}$$
$$=-x^2-16x-117-\frac{684}{x-6}$$

119. Width $= \dfrac{15x^3 - 3x^2 + 60}{3x^2}$

$\qquad = \left(5x - 1 + \dfrac{20}{x^2}\right)$ ft

120. Length $= \dfrac{21a^3b^6 + 3a - 3}{3}$

$\qquad = \left(7a^3b^6 + a - 1\right)$ units

Chapter 10 Test

1. $2^5 = 2 \cdot 2 \cdot 2 \cdot 2 \cdot 2 = 32$

2. $(-3)^4 = (-3)(-3)(-3)(-3) = 81$

3. $-3^4 = -3 \cdot 3 \cdot 3 \cdot 3 = -81$

4. $4^{-3} = \dfrac{1}{4^3} = \dfrac{1}{64}$

5. $\left(3x^2\right)\left(-5x^9\right) = (3)(-5)\left(x^2 \cdot x^9\right)$

$\qquad = -15x^{11}$

6. $\dfrac{y^7}{y^2} = y^{7-2} = y^5$

7. $\dfrac{r^{-8}}{r^{-3}} = r^{-8-(-3)} = r^{-5} = \dfrac{1}{r^5}$

8. $\left(\dfrac{x^2 y^3}{x^3 y^{-4}}\right)^2 = \dfrac{x^4 y^6}{x^6 y^{-8}}$

$\qquad = x^{4-6} y^{6-(-8)}$

$\qquad = x^{-2} y^{14}$

$\qquad = \dfrac{y^{14}}{x^2}$

9. $\left(\dfrac{6^2 x^{-4} y^{-1}}{6^3 x^{-3} y^7}\right) = 6^{2-3} x^{-4-(-3)} y^{-1-7}$

$\qquad = 6^{2-3} x^{-4-(-3)} y^{-1-7}$

$\qquad = 6^{-1} x^{-1} y^{-8}$

$\qquad = \dfrac{1}{6xy^8}$

10. $563,000 = 5.63 \times 10^5$

11. $0.0000863 = 8.63 \times 10^{-5}$

12. $1.5 \times 10^{-3} = 0.0015$

13. $6.23 \times 10^4 = 62,300$

14. $\left(1.2 \times 10^5\right)\left(3 \times 10^{-7}\right)$

$\qquad = (1.2)(3) \times 10^{5-7}$

$\qquad = 3.6 \times 10^{-2}$

$\qquad = 0.036$

15. The degree is 5 because $9x^3 yz$ or $9x^3 y^1 z^1$ is the term with the highest degree.

16. $5x^2 + 4x - 7x^2 + 11 + 8x$

$\qquad = \left(5x^2 - 7x^2\right) + (4x + 8x) + 11$

$\qquad = -2x^2 + 12x + 11$

17. $\left(8x^3 + 7x^2 + 4x - 7\right) + \left(8x^3 - 7x - 6\right)$

$\qquad = 8x^3 + 7x^2 + 4x - 7 + 8x^3 - 7x - 6$

$\qquad = 16x^3 + 7x^2 - 3x - 13$

18. $\quad 5x^3 + x^2 + 5x - 2$

$\quad\quad \underline{-\left(8x^3 - 4x^2 + x - 7\right)}$

$\quad\quad\quad 5x^3 + x^2 + 5x - 2$

$\quad\quad\quad \underline{-\ 8x^3 + 4x^2 - x + 7}$

$\quad\quad -3x^3 + 5x^2 + 4x + 5$

19. $\left[\left(8x^2 + 7x + 5\right) + \left(x^3 - 8\right)\right] - \left(4x + 2\right)$

$\quad = 8x^2 + 7x + 5 + x^3 - 8 - 4x - 2$

$\quad = x^3 + 8x^2 + 3x - 5$

20. $\left(3x + 7\right)\left(x^2 + 5x + 2\right)$

$\quad = 3x^3 + 15x^2 + 6x + 7x^2 + 35x + 14$

$\quad = 3x^3 + 22x^2 + 41x + 14$

21. $3x^2\left(2x^2 - 3x + 7\right)$

$\quad = 3x^2\left(2x^2\right) + 3x^2\left(-3x\right) + 3x\left(7\right)$

$\quad = 6x^4 - 9x^3 + 21x$

22. $\left(x + 7\right)\left(3x - 5\right) = 3x^2 - 5x + 21x - 35$

$\quad\quad\quad\quad\quad\quad\quad = 3x^2 + 16x - 35$

23. $\left(4x - 2\right)^2 = \left(4x\right)^2 - 2\left(4x\right)\left(2\right) + 2^2$

$\quad\quad\quad\quad\quad = 16x^2 - 16x + 4$

24. $\left(x^2 - 9b\right)\left(x^2 + 9b\right) = \left(x^2\right)^2 - \left(9b\right)^2$

$\quad\quad\quad\quad\quad\quad\quad\quad = x^4 - 81b^2$

25. $-16t^2 + 1516$

$\quad t = 0: \ 16\left(0\right)^2 + 1516 = 1516 \text{ ft}$

$\quad t = 3: \ -16\left(3\right)^2 + 1516 = 1372 \text{ ft}$

$\quad t = 6: \ -16\left(6\right)^2 + 1516 = 940 \text{ ft}$

$\quad t = 9: \ -16\left(9\right)^2 + 1516 = 220 \text{ ft}$

26. $A = lw$

$\quad = \left(2x + 3\right)\left(2x - 3\right)$

$\quad = \left(4x^2 - 9\right) \text{ sq in.}$

27. $\dfrac{4x^2 + 2xy - 7x}{8xy} = \dfrac{4x^2}{8xy} + \dfrac{2xy}{8xy} - \dfrac{7x}{8xy}$

$\quad\quad\quad\quad\quad\quad = \dfrac{x}{2y} + \dfrac{1}{4} - \dfrac{7}{8y}$

28. $\begin{array}{r} x + 2 \\ x+5\overline{)x^2 + 7x + 10} \end{array}$

$\quad\quad\quad \underline{x^2 + 5x}$

$\quad\quad\quad\quad\quad 2x + 10$

$\quad\quad\quad\quad\quad \underline{2x + 10}$

$\quad\quad\quad\quad\quad\quad\quad 0$

$\quad \dfrac{x^2 + 7x + 10}{x + 5} = x + 2$

29. $\begin{array}{r} 9x^2 - 6x + 4 \\ 3x+2\overline{)27x^3 + 0x^2 + 0x - 8} \end{array}$

$\quad\quad\quad \underline{27x^3 + 18x^2}$

$\quad\quad\quad\quad\quad -18x^2 + \ 0x$

$\quad\quad\quad\quad\quad \underline{-18x^2 - 12x}$

$\quad\quad\quad\quad\quad\quad\quad\quad 12x - 8$

$\quad\quad\quad\quad\quad\quad\quad\quad \underline{12x + 8}$

$\quad\quad\quad\quad\quad\quad\quad\quad\quad -16$

$\quad \dfrac{27x^3 - 8}{3x + 2} = 9x^2 - 6x + 4 - \dfrac{16}{3x + 2}$

Cumulative Review Chapter 10

1. $8^2 = 8 \cdot 8 = 64$

2. $5^3 = 5 \cdot 5 \cdot 5 = 25 \cdot 5 = 125$

3. $2^5 = 2 \cdot 2 \cdot 2 \cdot 2 \cdot 2 = 4 \cdot 2 \cdot 2 \cdot 2 = 8 \cdot 2 \cdot 2$
$\quad = 16 \cdot 2 = 32$

4. $3^3 = 3 \cdot 3 \cdot 3 = 9 \cdot 3 = 27$

5. a) $7 + x$

  b) $15 - x$

  c) $2x$

  d) $\dfrac{x}{5}$

  e) $x - 2$

6. a) $x + 3$

  b) $3x$

  c) $2x$

  d) $10 - x$

  e) $5x + 7$

7. $2(3 + x) - 15 = 2(3) + 2(x) - 15$
$\quad\quad\quad\quad\quad\quad = 6 + 2x - 15$
$\quad\quad\quad\quad\quad\quad = 2x - 9$

8. $5x + 10$; cannot simplify further

9. $-2(x - 5) + 4(2x + 2)$
$\quad = -2(x) + (-2)(-5) + 4(2x) + 4(2)$
$\quad = -2x + 10 + 8x + 8$
$\quad = 6x + 18$

10. $-2(y + 0.3z - 1)$
$\quad = -2(y) + (-2)(0.3z) + (-2)(-1)$
$\quad = -2y - 0.6z + 2$

11. $y - 5 = -2 - 6$
$\quad\quad y - 5 = -8$
$\quad\quad\quad y = -8 + 5$
$\quad\quad\quad y = -3$

12. $\quad \dfrac{y}{7} = 20$

$\quad 7\left(\dfrac{y}{7}\right) = 7(20)$

$\quad\quad y = 140$

13. $7(x - 2) = 9x - 6$
$\quad\quad 7x - 14 = 9x - 6$
$\quad\quad 7x - 9x = -6 + 14$
$\quad\quad \dfrac{-2x}{-2} = \dfrac{8}{-2}$
$\quad\quad\quad x = -4$

14. $6(2a - 1) - (11a + 6) = 7$
$\quad\quad 12a - 6 - 11a - 6 = 7$
$\quad\quad\quad\quad\quad\quad\quad a = 19$

15. $\quad \dfrac{3}{5}a = 9$

$\quad \dfrac{5}{3}\left(\dfrac{3}{5}a\right) = \dfrac{5}{3}(9)$

$\quad\quad\quad a = \dfrac{5 \cdot 9}{3}$

$\quad\quad\quad a = 15$

16. $\dfrac{2}{3}y = 16$

$$\dfrac{3}{2}\left(\dfrac{2}{3}y\right) = \dfrac{3}{2}(16)$$

$$y = \dfrac{3 \cdot 16}{2}$$

$$y = 24$$

17. $3y = -\dfrac{2}{11}$

$$11(3y) = 11\left(-\dfrac{2}{11}\right)$$

$$\dfrac{33y}{33} = \dfrac{-2}{33}$$

$$y = -\dfrac{2}{33}$$

18. $5y = -\dfrac{1}{5}$

$$5(5y) = 5\left(-\dfrac{1}{5}\right)$$

$$\dfrac{25y}{25} = \dfrac{-1}{25}$$

$$y = -\dfrac{1}{25}$$

19. $0.125 = \dfrac{125}{1000} = \dfrac{1}{8}$

20. $0.250 = \dfrac{250}{1000} = \dfrac{1}{4}$

21. $23.5 = 23\dfrac{5}{10} = 23\dfrac{1}{2}$

22. $10.75 = 10\dfrac{75}{100} = 10\dfrac{3}{4}$

23. $-105.083 = -105\dfrac{83}{1000}$

24. $-31.07 = -31\dfrac{7}{100}$

25. $x - y = 2.8 - 0.92 = 1.88$

26. $x - y = -1.2 - 7.6 = -8.8$

27. $xy = (2.3)(0.44) = 1.012$

28. $xy = (-6.1)(0.5) = -3.05$

29. a) 11, 112
   b) 0, 11, 112
   c) $-3, -2, 0, 11, 112$
   d) $-3, -2, 0, \frac{1}{4}, 11, 112$
   e) $\sqrt{2}$
   f) $-3, -2, 0, \frac{1}{4}, \sqrt{2}, 11, 112$

30. $-2\dfrac{1}{2}$ belongs to the following sets:

rational numbers and real numbers

31.
$$0.25x + 0.10(x - 3) = 0.05(22)$$
$$100\left[0.25x + 0.10(x - 3)\right] = 100\left[0.05(22)\right]$$
$$25x + 10(x - 3) = 5(22)$$
$$25x + 10x - 30 = 110$$
$$35x - 30 = 110$$
$$35x = 110 + 30$$
$$\dfrac{35x}{35} = \dfrac{140}{35}$$
$$x = 4$$

350

32.
$$0.6x - 10 = 1.4x - 14$$
$$10(0.6x - 10) = 10(1.4x - 14)$$
$$6x - 100 = 14x - 140$$
$$6x - 14x = -140 + 100$$
$$\frac{-8x}{-8} = \frac{-40}{-8}$$
$$x = 5$$

33. $2(x + 4) = 4x - 12$
$$2x + 8 = 4x - 12$$
$$2x - 4x = -12 - 8$$
$$\frac{-2x}{-2} = \frac{-20}{-2}$$
$$x = 10$$

34. $3(x - 2) = 5x - 10$
$$3x - 6 = 5x - 10$$
$$3x - 5x = -10 + 6$$
$$\frac{-2x}{-2} = \frac{-4}{-2}$$
$$x = 2$$

35.
$$\text{Let } x = \text{length}$$
$$2L + 2W = P$$
$$2(x) + 2(30) = 140$$
$$2x + 60 = 140$$
$$2x = 140 - 60$$
$$\frac{2x}{2} = \frac{80}{2}$$
$$x = 40$$

The length of the garden is 40 feet.

36. Let x = width
$$LW = A$$
$$\frac{63x}{63} = \frac{2016}{63}$$
$$x = 32$$

The width of the house is 32 feet.

37. $-4x + 7 \geq -9$
$$-4x \geq -9 - 7$$
$$\frac{-4x}{-4} \geq \frac{-16}{-4}$$
$$\{x \mid x \leq 4\}$$

38. $3x + 4 \geq 2x - 6$
$$3x - 2x \geq -6 - 4$$
$$x \geq -10$$
$$\{x \mid x \geq -10\}$$

39. a) $x^7 \cdot x^4 = x^{7+4} = x^{11}$

     b) $\left(\dfrac{1}{2}\right)^4 = \dfrac{1}{2^4} = \dfrac{1}{16}$

     c) $\left(9y^5\right)^2 = 9^2\left(y^5\right)^2 = 81y^{5\cdot2} = 81y^{10}$

40. a) $y \cdot y^5 = y^1 \cdot y^5 = y^6$

     b) $\left(\dfrac{2}{3}\right)^3 = \dfrac{2^3}{3^3} = \dfrac{8}{27}$

     c) $\left(8x^3\right)^2 = 8^2\left(x^3\right)^2 = 64x^6$

41. $\left(\dfrac{3a^2}{b}\right)^{-3} = \left(\dfrac{b}{3a^2}\right)^3 = \dfrac{b^3}{3^3 a^6} = \dfrac{b^3}{27a^6}$

42. $\left(\dfrac{2x^3}{y}\right)^{-2} = \left(\dfrac{y}{2x^3}\right)^2 = \dfrac{y^2}{2^2 x^6} = \dfrac{y^2}{4x^6}$

43. $\left(5y^3\right)^{-2} = \dfrac{1}{\left(5y^3\right)^2} = \dfrac{1}{5^2 y^6} = \dfrac{1}{25y^6}$

44. $\left(3x^7\right)^{-3} = \dfrac{1}{\left(3x^7\right)^3} = \dfrac{1}{3^3 x^{21}} = \dfrac{1}{27x^{21}}$

45. $9x^3 + x^3 = 9x^3 + 1x^3 = 10x^3$

46. $9x^3 - x^3 = 8x^3$

47. $5x^2 + 6x - 9x - 3 = 5x^2 - 3x - 3$

48. $2x - x^2 + 5x - 4x^2$
$= -x^2 - 4x^2 + 2x + 5x$
$= -5x^2 + 7x$

49. $7x\left(x^2 + 2x + 5\right)$
$= 7x\left(x^2\right) + 7x\left(2x\right) + 7x\left(5\right)$
$= 7x^3 + 14x^2 + 35x$

50. $-2x\left(x^2 - x + 1\right)$
$= -2x\left(x^2\right) + \left(-2x\right)\left(-x\right) + \left(-2x\right)\left(1\right)$
$= -2x^3 + 2x^2 - 2x$

51. $\dfrac{9x^5 - 12x^2 + 3x}{3x^2} = \dfrac{9x^5}{3x^2} - \dfrac{12x^2}{3x^2} + \dfrac{3x}{3x^2}$
$= 3x^3 - 4 + \dfrac{1}{x}$

52. $\dfrac{4x^7 - 12x^2 + 2x}{2x} = \dfrac{4x^7}{2x} - \dfrac{12x^2}{2x} + \dfrac{2x}{2x}$
$= 2x^6 - 6x + 1$

Chapter 11

Chapter 11 Pretest

1. $2x^3y - 6x^2y^2 = 2x^2y(x - 3y)$

2. $xy + 6x - 4y - 24 = (xy + 6x) + (-4y - 24)$
   $= x(y + 6) - 4(y + 6) = (y + 6)(x - 4)$

3. $a^2 + 8a + 12 = (a + 6)(a + 2)$

4. $m^2 + 4m - 3$ is a prime polynomial.

5. $3x^3 - 18x^2 + 15x = 3x(x^2 - 6x + 5)$
   $= 3x(x - 5)(x - 1)$

6. $2x^2 + 5x - 12 = (2x - 3)(x + 4)$

7. $14x^2 + 63x + 70 = 7(2x^2 + 9x + 10)$
   $= 7(2x + 5)(x + 2)$

8. $24b^2 - 25b + 6 = 24b^2 - 16b - 9b + 6$
   $= 8b(3b - 2) - 3(3b - 2) = (3b - 2)(8b - 3)$

9. $15y^2 + 38y + 7 = 15y^2 + 35y + 3y + 7$
   $= 5y(3y + 7) + 1(3y + 7) = (3y + 7)(5y + 1)$

10. $x^2 + 24x + 144 = (x^2) + 2(x)(12) + (12)^2$
    $= (x + 12)(x + 12) = (x + 12)^2$

11. $4x^2 - 12xy + 9y^2$
    $= (2x)^2 - 2(2x)(3y) + (3y)^2$
    $= (2x - 3y)(2x - 3y) = (2x - 3y)^2$

12. $a^2 - 49b^2 = a^2 - (7b)^2 = (a + 7b)(a - 7b)$

13. $1 - 64t^2 = 1^2 - (8t)^2 = (1 + 8t)(1 - 8t)$

14. $25b^2 + 4$ is a prime polynomial.

15. $x^2 + 18x + 81$ is a perfect square trinomial.

16. $(x - 12)(x + 5) = 0$
    $x - 12 = 0$ or $x + 5 = 0$
    $x = 12$ $x = -5$
    The solutions are 12 and -5.

17. $y^2 - 13y = 0$
    $y(y - 13) = 0$
    $y = 0$ or $y - 13 = 0$
                         $y = 13$
    The solutions are 0 and 13.

18. $2m^3 - 2m^2 - 24m = 0$
    $2m(m^2 - m - 12) = 0$
    $2m(m - 4)(m + 3) = 0$

    $2m = 0$ or $m - 4 = 0$ or $m + 3 = 0$
    $m = 0$ $m = 4$ $m = -3$
    The solutions are 0, 4, and -3.

19. Let x = the width. Then $x + 7$ = the length.

$A = lw$

$120 = (x+7)(x)$

$120 = x^2 + 7x$

$0 = x^2 + 7x - 120$

$0 = (x+15)(x-8)$

$x + 15 = 0 \quad$ or $\quad x - 8 = 0$

$\qquad x = -15 \qquad\qquad x = 8$

Since the width cannot be negative, we discard the result -15. The width is 8 inches and the length is $8 + 7 = 15$ inches.

20. Let x = the number

$x + x^2 = 240$

$x^2 + x - 240 = 0$

$(x+16)(x-15) = 0$

$x + 16 = 0 \quad$ or $\quad x - 15 = 0$

$\qquad x = -16 \qquad\qquad x = 15$

The number is -16 or 15.

Practice Problems 11.1

1. a. $6x^2 = 2 \cdot 3 \cdot x^2$

$\quad 9x^4 = 3 \cdot 3 \cdot x^4$

$\quad -12x^5 = -2 \cdot 2 \cdot 3 \cdot x^5$

$\quad \text{GCF} = 3 \cdot x^2 = 3x^2$

b. $-16y = -2 \cdot 2 \cdot 2 \cdot 2 \cdot y$

$\quad -20y^6 = -2 \cdot 2 \cdot 5 \cdot y^6$

$\quad 40y^4 = 2 \cdot 2 \cdot 2 \cdot 5 \cdot y^4$

$\quad \text{GCF} = 2 \cdot 2 \cdot y = 4y$

c. The GCF of a^5, a and a^3 is a.

The GCF of b^4, b^3 and b^2 is b^2.

The GCF of $a^5 b^4$, ab^3, and $a^3 b^2$ is ab^2.

2. a. $10y + 25 = 5(2y + 5)$

b. $x^4 - x^9 = x^4(1 - x^5)$

3. $-10x^3 + 8x^2 - 2x = -2x(5x^2 - 4x + 1)$

4. $4x^3 + 12x = 4x(x^2 + 3)$

5. $\dfrac{2}{5}a^5 - \dfrac{4}{5}a^3 + \dfrac{1}{5}a^2 = \dfrac{1}{5}a^2(2a^3 - 4a + 1)$

6. $6a^3b + 3a^3b^2 + 9a^2b^4$

$= 3a^2b(2a + ab + 3b^3)$

7. $7(p+2) + q(p+2) = (p+2)(7+q)$

8. $ab + 7a + 2b + 14 = a(b+7) + 2(b+7)$

$= (b+7)(a+2)$

9. $28x^3 - 7x^2 + 12x - 3$

$= 7x^2(4x-1) + 3(4x-1)$

$= (4x-1)(7x^2+3)$

10. $2xy + 5y^2 - 4x - 10y$

$= y(2x+5y) - 2(2x+5y)$

$= (2x+5y)(y-2)$

11. $4x^3 + x - 20x^2 - 5$

$= x(4x^2+1) - 5(4x^2+1)$

$= (4x^2+1)(x-5)$

12. $2x - 2 + x^3 - 3x^2 = 2(x-1) + x^2(x-3)$

The polynomial is not factorable by grouping.

13. $3xy - 4 + x - 12y = 3xy + x - 4 - 12y$
$= x(3y + 1) - 4(1 + 3y)$
$= (3y + 1)(x - 4)$

Mental Math 11.1

1. $2 = 2$
$16 = 2 \cdot 2 \cdot 2 \cdot 2$
$GCF = 2$

2. $3 = 3$
$18 = 2 \cdot 3 \cdot 3$
$GCF = 3$

3. $6 = 2 \cdot 3$
$15 = 3 \cdot 5$
$GCF = 3$

4. $20 = 2 \cdot 2 \cdot 5$
$15 = 3 \cdot 5$
$GCF = 5$

5. $14 = 2 \cdot 7$
$35 = 5 \cdot 7$
$GCF = 7$

6. $27 = 3 \cdot 3 \cdot 3$
$36 = 2 \cdot 2 \cdot 3 \cdot 3$
$GCF = 3 \cdot 3 = 9$

Exercise Set 11.1

1. y^2

3. xy^2

5. $8x = 2 \cdot 2 \cdot 2 \cdot x$
$4 = 2 \cdot 2$
$GCF = 2 \cdot 2 = 4$

7. $12y^4 = 2 \cdot 2 \cdot 3 \cdot y^4$
$20y^3 = 2 \cdot 2 \cdot 5 \cdot y^3$
$GCF = 2 \cdot 2 \cdot y^3 = 4y^3$

9. $-10x^2 = -2 \cdot 5 \cdot x^2$
$15x^3 = 3 \cdot 5 \cdot x^3$
$GCF = 5 \cdot x^2 = 5x^2$

11. $12x^3 = 2 \cdot 2 \cdot 3 \cdot x^3$
$-6x^4 = -2 \cdot 3 \cdot x^4$
$3x^5 = 3 \cdot x^5$
$GCF = 3 \cdot x^3 = 3x^3$

13. $-18x^2 y = -2 \cdot 3 \cdot 3 \cdot x^2 \cdot y$
$9x^3 y^3 = 3 \cdot 3 \cdot x^3 \cdot y^3$
$36x^3 y = 2 \cdot 2 \cdot 3 \cdot 3 \cdot x^3 \cdot y$
$GCF = 3 \cdot 3 \cdot x^2 \cdot y = 9x^2 y$

15. $3a + 6 = 3(a + 2)$

17. $30x - 15 = 15(2x - 1)$

19. $x^3 + 5x^2 = x^2(x + 5)$

21. $6y^4 - 2y = 2y(3y^3 - 1)$

23. $32xy - 18x^2 = 2x(16y - 9x)$

25. $4x - 8y + 4 = 4(x - 2y + 1)$

27. $6x^3 - 9x^2 + 12x = 3x(2x^2 - 3x + 4)$

29. $a^7b^6 - a^3b^2 + a^2b^5 - a^2b^2$
$$= a^2b^2(a^5b^4 - a + b^3 - 1)$$

31. $5x^3y - 15x^2y + 10xy = 5xy(x^2 - 3x + 2)$

33. $8x^5 + 16x^4 - 20x^3 + 12$
$$= 4(2x^5 + 4x^4 - 5x^3 + 3)$$

35. $\dfrac{1}{3}x^4 + \dfrac{2}{3}x^3 - \dfrac{4}{3}x^5 + \dfrac{1}{3}x$
$$= \dfrac{1}{3}x(x^3 + 2x^2 - 4x^4 + 1)$$

37. $y(x + 2) + 3(x + 2) = (x + 2)(y + 3)$

39. $8(x + 2) - y(x + 2) = (x + 2)(8 - y)$

41. Answers may vary.

43. $x^3 + 2x^2 + 5x + 10 = x^2(x + 2) + 5(x + 2)$
$$= (x^2 + 5)(x + 2)$$

45. $5x + 15 + xy + 3y = 5(x + 3) + y(x + 3)$
$$= (x + 3)(5 + y)$$

47. $6x^3 - 4x^2 + 15x - 10$
$$= 2x^2(3x - 2) + 5(3x - 2)$$
$$= (2x^2 + 5)(3x - 2)$$

49. $2y - 8 + xy - 4x = 2(y - 4) + x(y - 4)$
$$= (y - 4)(2 + x)$$

51. $2x^3 + x^2 + 8x + 4 = x^2(2x + 1) + 4(2x + 1)$
$$= (2x + 1)(x^2 + 4)$$

53. $4x^2 - 8xy - 3x + 6y$
$$= 4x(x - 2y) - 3(x - 2y)$$
$$= (x - 2y)(4x - 3)$$

55. Answers may vary

57. $(x + 2)(x + 5) = x^2 + 2x + 5x + 10$
$$= x^2 + 7x + 10$$

59. $(b + 1)(b - 4) = b^2 + b - 4b - 4$
$$= b^2 - 3b - 4$$

61. The two numbers are 2 and 6.
$2 \cdot 6 = 12; \ 2 + 6 = 8$

63. The two numbers are -1 and -8.
$-1 \cdot (-8) = 8; \ -1 + (-8) = -9$

65. The two numbers are -2 and 5.
$-2 \cdot 5 = -10; \ -2 + 5 = 3$

67. The two numbers are -8 and 3.
$-8 \cdot 3 = -24; \ -8 + 3 = -5$

69. $12x^2y - 42x^2 - 4y + 14$
$$= 2(6x^2y - 21x^2 - 2y + 7)$$
$$= 2(3x^2(2y - 7) - 1(2y - 7))$$
$$= 2(3x^2 - 1)(2y - 7)$$

71. Subtract the area of the innter rectangle from the area of the outer rectangle.

Outer rectangle: $A = l \cdot w$

$$A = 12x \cdot x^2 = 12x^3$$

Inner rectangle: $A = l \cdot w$

$$A = 2 \cdot x = 2x$$

The area of the shaded region is given by the expression $12x^3 - 2x = 2x\left(6x^2 - 1\right)$.

73. Let l = length of the rectangle.

$$A = l \cdot w$$

$$4n^4 - 24n = 4n \cdot l$$

$$4n\left(n^3 - 6\right) = 4n \cdot l$$

$$\frac{4n\left(n^3 - 6\right)}{4n} = \frac{4n \cdot l}{4n}$$

$$n^3 - 6 = l$$

The length is $\left(n^3 - 6\right)$ units.

75. a. When $x = 0$

$$-8x^2 + 60x + 2000$$

$$= 8(0)^2 + 60(0) + 2000$$

$$= 2000 \text{ billion kilowatt hours}$$

b. When $x = 2$

$$-8x^2 + 60x + 2000$$

$$= -8(2)^2 + 60(2) + 2000$$

$$= 2088 \text{ billion kilowatt hours}$$

c. $-8x^2 + 60x + 2000$

$$= -4\left(2x^2 - 15x - 500\right)$$

Practice Problems 11.2

1. $x^2 + 9x + 20 = (x + 4)(x + 5)$

2. a. $x^2 - 13x + 22 = (x - 11)(x - 2)$

    b. $x^2 - 27x + 50 = (x - 25)(x - 2)$

3. $x^2 + 5x - 36 = (x + 9)(x - 4)$

4. a. $q^2 - 3q - 40 = (q - 8)(q + 5)$

    b. $y^2 + 2y - 48 = (y + 8)(y - 6)$

5. $x^2 + 6x + 15$ is a prime polynomial.

6. a. $x^2 + 6xy + 8y^2 = (x + 4y)(x + 2y)$

    b. $a^2 - 13ab + 30b^2 = (a - 10b)(a - 3b)$

7. $x^4 + 9x^2 + 12 = \left(x^2 + 6\right)\left(x^2 + 2\right)$

8. a. $x^3 + 3x^2 - 4x = x\left(x^2 + 3x - 4\right)$

$$= x(x + 4)(x - 1)$$

    b. $4x^2 - 24x + 36 = 4\left(x^2 - 6x + 9\right)$

$$= 4(x - 3)(x - 3)$$

9. $5x^5 - 25x^4 - 30x^3 = 5x^3\left(x^2 - 5x - 6\right)$

$$= 5x^3(x - 6)(x + 1)$$

Mental Math 11.2

1. $x^2 + 9x + 20 = (x + 4)(x + 5)$

2. $x^2 + 12x + 35 = (x + 5)(x + 7)$

3. $x^2 - 7x + 12 = (x - 4)(x - 3)$

4. $x^2 - 13x + 22 = (x-2)(x-11)$

5. $x^2 + 4x + 4 = (x+2)(x+2)$

6. $x^2 + 10x + 24 = (x+6)(x+4)$

Exercise Set 11.2

1. $x^2 + 7x + 6 = (x+6)(x+1)$

3. $x^2 - 10x + 9 = (x-9)(x-1)$

5. $x^2 - 3x - 18 = (x-6)(x+3)$

7. $x^2 + 3x - 70 = (x+10)(x-7)$

9. $x^2 + 5x + 2$ is a prime polynomial.

11. $x^2 + 8xy + 15y^2 = (x+5y)(x+3y)$

13. $a^4 - 2a^2 - 15 = (a^2 - 5)(a^2 + 3)$

15. $(x-3)(x+8) = x^2 - 3x + 8x - 24$
$$= x^2 + 5x - 24$$

17. Answers may vary.

19. $2z^2 + 20z + 32 = (z^2 + 10z + 16)$
$$= 2(z+8)(z+2)$$

21. $2x^3 - 18x^2 + 40x = 2x(x^2 - 9x + 20)$
$$= 2x(x-5)(x-4)$$

23. $x^2 - 3xy - 4y^2 = (x-4y)(x+y)$

25. $x^2 + 15x + 36 = (x+12)(x+3)$

27. $x^2 - x - 2 = (x-2)(x+1)$

29. $r^2 - 16r + 48 = (r-12)(r-4)$

31. $x^2 + xy - 2y^2 = (x+2y)(x-y)$

33. $3x^2 + 9x - 30 = 3(x^2 + 3x - 10)$
$$= 3(x+5)(x-2)$$

35. $3x^2 - 60x + 108 = 3(x^2 - 20x + 36)$
$$= 3(x-18)(x-2)$$

37. $x^2 - 18x - 144 = (x-24)(x+6)$

39. $r^2 - 3r + 6$ is a prime polynomial.

41. $x^2 - 8x + 15 = (x-5)(x-3)$

43. $6x^3 + 54x^2 + 120x = 6x(x^2 + 9x + 20)$
$$= 6x(x+4)(x+5)$$

45. $4x^2y + 4xy - 12y = 4y(x^2 + x - 3)$

47. $x^2 - 4x - 21 = (x-7)(x+3)$

49. $x^2 + 7xy + 10y^2 = (x+5y)(x+2y)$

51. $64 + 24t + 2t^2 = 2t^2 + 24t + 64$
$$= 2(t^2 + 12t + 32)$$
$$= 2(t+8)(t+4)$$

53. $x^3 - 2x^2 - 24x = x(x^2 - 2x - 24)$
$$= x(x - 6)(x + 4)$$

55. $2t^5 - 14t^4 + 24t^3 = 2t^3(t^2 - 7t + 12)$
$$= 2t^3(t - 4)(t - 3)$$

57. $5x^3y - 25x^2y^2 - 120xy^3$
$$= 5xy(x^2 - 5xy - 24y^2)$$
$$= 5xy(x - 8y)(x + 3y)$$

59. $(2x + 1)(x + 5) = 2x^2 + x + 10x + 5$
$$= 2x^2 + 11x + 5$$

61. $(5y - 4)(3y - 1) = 15y^2 - 12y - 5y + 4$
$$= 15y^2 - 17y + 4$$

63. $(a + 3)(9a - 4) = 9a^2 + 27a - 4a - 12$
$$= 9a^2 + 23a - 12$$

65. $P = 2l + 2w$
$l = x^2 + 10x$ and $w = 4x + 33$, so
$P = 2(x^2 + 10x) + 2(4x + 33)$
$$= 2x^2 + 20x + 8x + 66$$
$$= 2x^2 + 28x + 66 = (x^2 + 14x + 33)$$
$$= 2(x + 11)(x + 3)$$
The perimeter of the rectangle is given by the polynomial $2x^2 + 28x + 66$ which factors as $2(x + 11)(x + 3)$.

67. $y^2(x + 1) - 2y(x + 1) - 15(x + 1)$
$$= (x + 1)(y^2 - 2y - 15)$$
$$= (x + 1)(y - 5)(y + 3)$$

69. $y^2 - 4y + c$ if factorable when c is 3 or 4.

71. $x^2 + bx + 15$ is factorable when b is 8 or 16.

73. $x^{2n} + 5x^n + 6 = (x^n + 2)(x^n + 3)$

Practice Problems 11.3

1. a. $4x^2 + 12x + 5 = (2x + 5)(2x + 1)$
    b. $5x^2 + 27x + 10 = (5x + 2)(x + 5)$

2. a. $6x^2 - 5x + 1 = (3x - 1)(2x - 1)$
    b. $2x^2 - 11x + 12 = (2x - 3)(x - 4)$

3. a. $35x^2 + 4x - 4 = (5x + 2)(7x - 2)$
    b. $4x^2 + 3x - 7 = (4x + 7)(x - 1)$

4. a. $14x^2 - 3xy - 2y^2 = (7x + 2y)(2x - y)$
    b. $12a^2 - 16ab - 3b^2 = (6a + b)(2a - 3b)$

5. a. $3x^3 + 17x^2 + 10x = (3x^2 + 17x + 10)$
$$= x(3x + 2)(x + 5)$$
    b. $6xy^2 + 33xy - 18x = 3x(2y^2 + 11y - 6)$
$$= 3x(2y - 1)(y + 6)$$

6. $-5x^2 - 19x + 4 = -1(5x^2 + 19x - 4)$
$$= -1(5x - 1)(x + 4)$$

Exercise Set 11.3

1. $5x^2 + 22x + 8 = (5x + 2)(x + 4)$

3. $50x^2 + 15x - 2 = (5x + 2)(10x - 1)$

5. $20x^2 - 7x - 6 = (5x + 2)(4x - 3)$

7. $2x^2 + 13x + 15 = (2x + 3)(x + 5)$

9. $8y^2 - 17y + 9 = (y - 1)(8y - 9)$

11. $2x^2 - 9x - 5 = (2x + 1)(x - 5)$

13. $20r^2 + 27r - 8 = (4r - 1)(5r + 8)$

15. $10x^2 + 17x + 3 = (5x + 1)(2x + 3)$

17. $3x^2 + x - 2 = (3x - 2)(x + 1)$

19. $6x^2 - 13xy + 5y^2 = (3x - 5y)(2x - y)$

21. $15x^2 - 16x - 15 = (3x - 5)(5x + 3)$

23. $x^2 - 9x + 20 = (x - 4)(x - 5)$

25. $2x^2 - 7x - 99 = (2x + 11)(x - 9)$

27. $-27t + 7t^2 - 4 = 7t^2 - 27t - 4$
$$= (7t + 1)(t - 4)$$

29. $3a^2 + 10ab + 3b^2 = (3a + b)(a + 3b)$

31. $49x^2 - 7x - 2 = (7x + 1)(7x - 2)$

33. $18x^2 - 9x - 14 = (6x - 7)(3x + 2)$

35. $12x^3 + 11x^2 + 2x = x(12x^2 + 11x + 2)$
$$= x(3x + 2)(4x + 1)$$

37. $21x^2 - 48x - 45 = 3(7x^2 - 16x - 15)$
$$= 3(7x + 5)(x - 3)$$

39. $12x^2 + 7x - 12 = (3x + 4)(4x - 3)$

41. $6x^2y^2 - 2xy^2 - 60y^2 = 2y^2(3x^2 - x - 30)$
$$= 2y^2(3x - 10)(x + 3)$$

43. $4x^2 - 8x - 21 = (2x - 7)(2x + 3)$

45. $3x^2 - 42x + 63 = 3(x^2 - 14x + 21)$

47. $8x^2 + 6x - 27 = (4x + 9)(2x - 3)$

49. $-x^2 + 2x + 24 = -1(x^2 - 2x - 24)$
$$= -1(x + 4)(x - 6)$$

51. $4x^3 - 9x^2 - 9x = x(4x^2 - 9x - 9)$
$$= x(4x + 3)(x - 3)$$

53. $24x^2 - 58x + 9 = (4x - 9)(6x - 1)$

55. $40a^2b + 9ab - 9b = b(40a^2 + 9a - 9)$
$$= b(8a - 3)(5a + 3)$$

57. $15x^4 + 19x^2 + 6 = (3x^2 + 2)(5x^2 + 3)$

59.
$$6y^3 - 8y^2 - 30y = 2y\left(3y^2 - 4y - 15\right)$$
$$= 2y(3y + 5)(y - 3)$$

61.
$$10x^3 + 25x^2y - 15xy^2 = 5x\left(2x^2 + 5xy - 3y^2\right)$$
$$= 5x(2x - y)(x + 3y)$$

63.
$$-14x^2 + 39x - 10 = -1\left(14x^2 - 39x + 10\right)$$
$$= -1(2x - 5)(7x - 2)$$

65. During April and May the unemployment rate was 5.8%.

67. February rate - July rate
$$= 6.4\% - 6.3\% = 0.1\%$$
The employment rate decreased by 0.1% from February to July.

69.
$$4x^2\left(y - 1\right)^2 + 10x(y - 1)^2 + 25(y - 1)^2$$
$$= (y - 1)^2\left(4x^2 + 10x + 25\right)$$

71.
$$-12x^3y^2 + 3x^2y^2 + 15xy^2$$
$$= -3xy^2\left(4x^2 - x - 5\right)$$
$$= -3xy^2(4x - 5)(x + 1)$$

73. $2z^2 + bz - 7$ is factorable when b is 5 or 13.

75. $3x^2 - 8x + c$ is factorable when c is 4 or 5.

Practice Problems 11.4

1. a.
$$3x^2 + 14x + 8 = 3x^2 + 12x + 2x + 8$$
$$= 3x(x + 4) + 2(x + 4)$$
$$= (x + 4)(3x + 2)$$

    b.
$$12x^2 + 19x + 5 = 12x^2 + 15x + 4x + 5$$
$$= 3x(4x + 5) + 1(4x + 5)$$
$$= (4x + 5)(3x + 1)$$

2. a.
$$6x^2y - 7xy - 5y = y\left(x^2 - 7x - 5\right)$$
$$= y\left(6x^2 - 10x + 3x - 5\right)$$
$$= y\left[2x(3x - 5) + 1(3x - 5)\right]$$
$$= y(3x - 5)(2x + 1)$$

    b.
$$30x^2 - 26x + 4 = 2\left(15x^2 - 13x + 2\right)$$
$$= 2\left(15x^2 - 10x - 3x + 2\right)$$
$$= 2\left[5x(3x - 2) - 1(3x - 2)\right]$$
$$= 2(3x - 2)(5x - 1)$$

Exercise Set 11.4

1.
$$x^2 + 3x + 2x + 6 = x(x + 3) + 2(x + 3)$$
$$= (x + 3)(x + 2)$$

3.
$$x^2 - 4x + 7x - 28 = x(x - 4) + 7(x - 4)$$
$$= (x - 4)(x + 7)$$

5.
$$y^2 + 8y - 2y - 16 = y(y + 8) - 2(y + 8)$$
$$= (y + 8)(y - 2)$$

7.
$$3x^2 + 4x + 12x + 16 = x(3x + 4) + 4(3x + 4)$$
$$= (3x + 4)(x + 4)$$

9. $8x^2 - 5x - 24x + 15 = x(8x - 5) - 3(8x - 5)$
$$= (8x - 5)(x - 3)$$

11. $5x^4 - 3x^2 + 25x^2 - 15$
$$= x^2(5x^2 - 3) + 5(5x^2 - 3)$$
$$= (5x^2 - 3)(x^2 + 5)$$

13. a. The numbers are 9 and 2.
$$9 \cdot 2 = 18$$
$$9 + 2 = 11$$
   b. $9x + 2x = 11x$
   c. $6x^2 + 11x + 3 = 6x^2 + 9x + 2x + 3$
$$= 3x(2x + 3) + 1(2x + 3)$$
$$= (2x + 3)(3x + 1)$$

15. a. The numbers are -20 and -3.
$$-20 \cdot (-3) = 60$$
$$-20 + (-3) = -23$$
   b. $-20x - 3x = -23x$
   c. $15x^2 - 23x + 4 = 15x^2 - 20x - 3x + 4$
$$= 5x(3x - 4) - (3x - 4)$$
$$= (3x - 4)(5x - 1)$$

17. $21y^2 + 17y + 2 = 21y^2 + 3y + 14y + 2$
$$= 3y(7y + 1) + 2(7y + 1)$$
$$= (3y + 2)(7y + 1)$$

19. $7x^2 - 4x - 11 = 7x^2 - 11x + 7x - 11$
$$= x(7x - 11) + 1(7x - 11)$$
$$= (7x - 11)(x + 1)$$

21. $10x^2 - 9x + 2 = 10x^2 - 5x - 4x + 2$
$$= 5x(2x - 1) - 2(2x - 1)$$
$$= (2x - 1)(5x - 2)$$

23. $2x^2 - 7x + 5 = 2x^2 - 5x - 2x + 5$
$$= x(2x - 5) - 1(2x - 5) = (2x - 5)(x - 1)$$

25. $4x^2 + 12x + 9 = 4x^2 + 6x + 6x + 9$
$$= 2x(2x + 3) + 3(2x + 3)$$
$$= (2x + 3)(2x + 3)$$
$$= (2x + 3)^2$$

27. $4x^2 - 8x - 21 = 4x^2 - 14x + 6x - 21$
$$= 2x(2x - 7) + 3(2x - 7)$$
$$= (2x - 7)(2x + 3)$$

29. $10x^2 - 23x + 12 = 10x^2 - 15x - 8x + 12$
$$= 5x(2x - 3) - 4(2x - 3)$$
$$= (2x - 3)(5x - 4)$$

31. $2x^3 + 13x^2 + 15x = x(2x^2 + 13x + 15)$
$$= x(2x^2 + 10x + 3x + 15)$$
$$= x[2x(x + 5) + 3(x + 5)] = x(x + 5)(2x + 3)$$

33. $16y^2 - 34y + 18 = 2(8y^2 - 17y + 9)$
$$= 2(8y^2 - 8y - 9y + 9)$$
$$= 2[8y(y - 1) - 9(y - 1)] = 2(y - 1)(8y - 9)$$

35. $6x^2 - 13x + 6 = 6x^2 - 9x - 4x + 6$
$$= 3x(2x - 3) - 2(2x - 3)$$
$$= (2x - 3)(3x - 2)$$

37. $54a^2 - 9a - 30 = 3(18a^2 - 3a - 10)$
$$= 3(18a^2 - 15a + 12a - 10)$$
$$= 3[3a(6a - 5) + 2(6a - 5)]$$
$$= 3(6a - 5)(3a + 2)$$

39. $20a^3 + 37a^2 + 8a$

$= a(20a^2 + 37a + 8)$

$= a(20a^2 + 5a + 32a + 8)$

$= a[5a(4a+1) + 8(4a+1)]$

$= a(4a+1)(5a+8)$

41. $12x^3 - 27x^2 - 27x$

$= 3x(4x^2 - 9x - 9)$

$= 3x(4x^2 - 12x + 3x - 9)$

$= 3x[4x(x-3) + 3(x-3)]$

$= 3x(x-3)(4x+3)$

43. $(x-2)(x+2) = x^2 - 2x + 2x - 4$

$= x^2 - 4$

45. $(y+4)(y+4) = y^2 + 4y + 4y + 16$

$= y^2 + 8y + 16$

47. $(9z+5)(9z-5) = 81z^2 + 45z - 45a - 25$

$= 81z^2 - 25$

49. $(4x-3)^2 = 16x^2 + 2(4x)(-3) + 9$

$= 16x^2 - 24x + 9$

51. $x^{2n} + 2x^n + 3x^n + 6$

$= x^n(x^n + 2) + 3(x^n + 2)$

$= (x^n + 2)(x^n + 3)$

53. $3x^{2n} + 16x^n - 35$

$= 3x^n - 5x^n + 21x^n - 35$

$= x^n(3x^n - 5) + 7(3x^n - 5)$

$= (3x^n - 5)(x^n + 7)$

55. Answers may vary.

Practice Problems 11.5

1. a. Yes; two terms, x^2 and 36, are squares
$(36 = 6^2)$ and the third term of the trinomial,
$12x$, is twice the product of x and $6(2 \cdot x \cdot 6 = 12)$.

 b. Yes; two terms, x^2 and 100, are squares $(100 = 10^2)$,
and the third term of the trinomial, $20x$, is twice the
product of x and $10(2 \cdot x \cdot 10 = 20x)$.

2. a. No; the two terms, $9x^2$ and 25,
$(9x^2 = (3x)^2$ and $25 = 5^2)$ are squares, but the
third term, $20x$, is not twice the product of $3x$
and 5, or its opposite.

 b. No; only one of the terms, $4x^2$, is a square.

3. a. Yes; two terms, $25x^2$ and 1, are squares
$(25x^2 = (5x)^2$ and $1 = 1^2)$, and the third term of
the trinomial, $-10x$, is the opposite of twice the
product of $5x$ and $1(-2 \cdot 5x \cdot 1 = -10x)$.

 b. Yes; two terms, $9x^2$ and 49, are squares
$(9x^2 = (3x)^2$, and $49 = 7^2)$, and the third
term of the trinomial, $-42x$, is the opposite
of twice the product of $3x$ and
$7(-2 \cdot 3x \cdot 7 = -42x)$.

4. $x^2 + 16x + 64 = x^2 + 2 \cdot x \cdot 8 + 8^2$

$= (x+8)^2$

5. $9r^2 + 24rs + 16s^2 = (3r)^2 + 2 \cdot 3r \cdot 4s + (4s)^2$

$= (3r + 4s)^2$

6. $9n^2 - 6n + 1 = (3n)^2 - 2 \cdot 3n \cdot 1 + 1^2$

$= (3n - 1)^2$

7. $9x^2 + 15x + 4 = 9x^2 + 12x + 3x + 4$
$$= 3x(3x+4) + 1(3x+4)$$
$$= (3x+4)(3x+1)$$

8. $12x^3 - 84x^2 + 147x = 3x(4x^2 - 28x + 49)$
$$= 3x(3x+4) + 1(3x+4)$$
$$= (3x+4)(3x+1)$$

9. $x^2 - 9 = x^2 - 3^2 = (x+3)(x-3)$

10. $a^2 - 16 = a^2 - 4^2 = (a+4)(a-4)$

11. $c^2 - \dfrac{9}{25} = c^2 - \left(\dfrac{3}{5}\right)^2 = \left(c+\dfrac{3}{5}\right)\left(c-\dfrac{3}{5}\right)$

12. $s^2 + 9 = s^2 + 3^2$
This is not a difference of squares, it is a prime polynomial.

13. $9s^2 - 1 = (3s)^2 - 1^2 = (3s+1)(3s-1)$

14. $16x^2 - 49y^2 = (4x)^2 - (7y)^2$
$$= (4x+7y)(4x-7y)$$

15. $p^4 - 81 = (p^2)^2 - 9^2 = (p^2+9)(p^2-9)$
$$= (p^2+9)(p^2-3^2)$$
$$= (p^2+9)(p+3)(p-3)$$

16. $9x^3 - 25x = x(9x^2 - 25)$
$$= x\left[(3x)^2 - 5^2\right] = x(3x+5)(3x-5)$$

17. $48x^4 - 3 = 3(16x^4 - 1) = 3\left[(4x^2)^2 - 1^2\right]$
$$= 3(4x^2+1)(4x^2-1)$$
$$= 3(4x^2+1)\left[(2x)^2 - 1^2\right]$$
$$= 3(4x^2+1)(2x+1)(2x-1)$$

18. $-9x^2 + 100 = -1(9x^2 - 100)$
$$= -1\left[(3x)^2 - 10^2\right]$$
$$= -1(3x+10)(3x-10)$$

Mental Math 11.5

1. $1 = 1^2$

2. $25 = 5^2$

3. $81 = 9^2$

4. $64 = 8^2$

5. $9 = 3^2$

6. $100 = 10^2$

7. $9x^2 = (3x)^2$

8. $16y^2 = (4y)^2$

9. $25a^2 = (5a)^2$

10. $81b^2 = (9b)^2$

11. $36p^4 = (6p^2)^2$

12. $4q^4 = (2q^2)^2$

Exercise Set 11.5

1. Yes; two terms, x^2 and 64, are squares $(64 = 8^2)$, and the third term of the trinomial, $16x$, is twice the product of x and $8 (2 \cdot x \cdot 8 = 16x)$.

3. No; the two terms, y^2 and 25, are squares $(25 = 5^2)$, but the third term of the trinomial, $5y$, is not twice the product of y and 5, or its opposite.

5. Yes; two terms, m^2 and 1, are squares $(1 = 1^2)$, and the third term of the trinomial, $-2m$, is the opposite of twice the product of m and $1 (-(2 \cdot m \cdot 1) = -2m)$.

7. No; the two terms, a^2 and 49, are squares $(49 = 7^2)$, but the third term of the trinomial, $-16a$, is not twice the product of a and 7, or its opposite.

9. No; if we first factor out the GCF, 4, we find that only one of the terms, x^2, is a square.

11. Yes; two terms, $25a^2$ and $16b^2$, are squares $(25a^2 = (5a)^2$ and $16b^2 = (4b)^2)$, and the third term of the trinomial, $-40ab$, is the opposite of twice the product of $5a$ and $4b (-(2 \cdot 5a \cdot 4b = -40ab)$.

13. $x^2 + 8x + 16$ is a perfect square trinomial because, x^2 and 16 are squares $(16 = 4^2)$, and $8x$ is twice the product of x and 4 $(2 \cdot x \cdot 4 = 8x)$.

15. $x^2 + 22x + 121 = x^2 + 2 \cdot x \cdot 11 + 11^2$
$$= (x + 11)^2$$

17. $x^2 - 16x + 64 = x^2 - 2 \cdot x \cdot 8 + 8^2$
$$= (x - 8)^2$$

19. $16a^2 - 24a + 9 = (4a)^2 - 2 \cdot 4a \cdot 3 + 3^2$
$$= (4a - 3)^2$$

21. $x^4 + 4x^2 + 4 = (x^2)^2 + 2 \cdot x^2 \cdot 2 + 2^2$
$$= (x^2 + 2)^2$$

23. $2n^2 - 28n + 98 = 2(n^2 - 14x + 49)$
$$= 2(n^2 - 2 \cdot n \cdot 7 + 7^2) = 2(n - 7)^2$$

25. $16y^2 + 40y + 25 = (4y)^2 + 2 \cdot 4y \cdot 5 + 5^2$
$$= (4y + 5)^2$$

27. $x^2y^2 - 10xy + 25 = (xy)^2 - 2 \cdot xy \cdot 5 + 5^2$
$$= (xy - 5)^2$$

29. $m^3 + 18m^2 + 81m = m(m^2 + 18m + 81)$
$$= m(m^2 + 2 \cdot m \cdot 9 + 9^2)$$
$$= m(m + 9)^2$$

31. The trinomial $1 + 6x^2 + x^4 = x^4 + 6x^2 + 1$ is not factorable with integers, and is, therefore, a prime polynomial.

33. $9x^2 - 24xy + 16y^2 = (3x)^2 - 2 \cdot 3x \cdot 4y + (4y)^2$
$$= (3x - 4y)^2$$

35. $x^2 + 14xy + 49y^2 = x^2 + 2\cdot x\cdot 7y + (7y)^2$
$$= (x+7y)^2$$

37. Answers may vary.

39. $x^2 - 4 = x^2 - 2^2 = (x+2)(x-2)$

41. $81 - p^2 = 9^2 - p^2 = (9+p)(9-p)$

43. $-4r^2 + 1 = -1(4r^2 - 1) = -1(2r+1)(2r-1)$

45. $9x^2 - 16 = (3x)^2 - 4^2 = (3x+4)(3x-4)$

47. $16r^2 + 1$ is the sum of two squares, $(4r)^2 + 1^2$, not the difference of two squares. $16r^2 + 1$ is a prime polynomial.

49. $-36 + x^2 = -(6)^2 + x^2 = (-6+x)(6+x)$

51. $m^4 - 1 = (m^2)^2 - 1^1$
$$= (m^2+1)(m^2-1)$$
$$= (m^2+1)(m^2-1^2)$$
$$= (m^2+1)(m+1)(m-1)$$

53. $x^2 - 169y^2 = x^2 - (13y)^2$
$$= (x+13y)(x-13y)$$

55. $18r^2 - 8 = 2(9r^2 - 4)$
$$= 2((3r)^2 - 2^2)$$
$$= 2(3r+2)(3r-2)$$

57. $9xy^2 - 4x = x(9y^2 - 4)$
$$= x((3y)^2 - 2^2)$$
$$= x(3y+2)(3y-2)$$

59. $25y^4 - 100y^2 = 25y^2(y^2 - 4)$
$$= 25y^2(y^2 - 2^2)$$
$$= 25y^2(y+2)(y-2)$$

61. $x^3y - 4xy^3 = xy(x^2 - 4y^2)$
$$= xy(x^2 - (2y)^2)$$
$$= xy(x+2y)(x-2y)$$

63. $225a^2 - 81b^2 = 9(25a^2 - 9b^2)$
$$= 9((5a)^2 - (3b)^2)$$
$$= 9(5a+3b)(5a-3b)$$

65. $12x^2 - 27 = 3(4x^2 - 9) = 3((2x)^2 - 3^2)$
$$= 3(2x+3)(2x-3)$$

67. $49a^2 - 16 = (7a)^2 - 4^2$
$$= (7a+4)(7a-4)$$

69. $169a^2 - 49b^2 = (13a)^2 - (7b)^2$
$$= (13a+7b)(13a-7b)$$

71. $16 - a^2b^2 = 4^2 - (ab)^2$
$$= (4+ab)(4-ab)$$

73. $y^2 - \dfrac{1}{16} = y^2 - \left(\dfrac{1}{4}\right)^2$

$$= \left(y + \dfrac{1}{4}\right)\left(y - \dfrac{1}{4}\right)$$

75. $100 - \dfrac{4}{81}n^2 = 10^2 - \left(\dfrac{2}{9}n\right)^2$

$$= \left(10 + \dfrac{2}{9}n\right)\left(10 - \dfrac{2}{9}n\right)$$

77. $5 - y$, since

$$(5 - y)(5 + y) = 25 - 5y + 5y - y^2$$
$$= 25 - y^2 = 5^2 - y^2$$

79. $y + 5 = 0$

$y + 5 - 5 = 0 - 5$

$y = -5$

81. $3x - 9 = 0$

$3x - 9 + 9 = 0 + 9$

$3x = 9$

$\dfrac{3x}{3} = \dfrac{9}{3}$

$x = 3$

83. $4a + 2 = 0$

$4a + 2 - 2 = 0 - 2$

$4a = -2$

$\dfrac{4a}{4} = \dfrac{-2}{4}$

$a = -\dfrac{1}{2}$

85. The sail is shaped like a triangle. The area of a triangle is given by $A = \dfrac{1}{2}bh$. Use $b = 10$ feet and $h = x$ feet. Then,

$$A = \dfrac{1}{2}bh$$
$$25 = \dfrac{1}{2} \cdot 10 \cdot x$$
$$25 = 5x$$
$$\dfrac{25}{5} = \dfrac{5x}{5}$$
$$5 = x$$

The height, x, is 5 feet.

87. $(y - 6)^2 - z^2 = (y - 6 + z)(y - 6 - z)$

89. $m^2(n + 8) - 9(n + 8) = (n + 8)(m^2 - 9)$

$$= (n + 8)(m^2 - 3^2) = (n + 8)(m + 3)(m - 3)$$

91. $(x^2 + 2x + 1) - 36y^2$

$$= \left[(x + 1)(x + 1)\right] - 36y^2$$
$$= (x + 1)^2 - (6y)^2$$
$$= (x + 1 + 6y)(x + 1 - 6y)$$

93. $x^{2n} - 81 = \left(x^n\right)^2 - 9^2 = \left(x^n + 9\right)\left(x^n - 9\right)$

95. The formula for factoring a perfect square trinomial.

367

97. a. Let $t = 1$.

$$529 - 16t^2 = 529 - 16(1)^2$$
$$= 529 - 16(1) = 529 - 16 = 513$$

After 1 second the height of
the bolt is 513 feet.

b. Let $t = 4$.

$$529 - 16t^2 = 529 - 16(4)^2$$
$$= 529 - 16(16)$$
$$529 - 256 = 273$$

After 4 seconds the height of
the bolt is 273 feet.

c. When the object hits the ground, its
height is zero feet. Thus, to find the
time, t, when the object's height is
zero feet above the ground, we set the
expression $529 - 16t^2$ equal to 0 and
solve for t.

$$529 - 16t^2 = 0$$
$$529 - 16t^2 + 16t^2 = 0 + 16t^2$$
$$529 = 16t^2$$
$$\frac{529}{16} = \frac{16t^2}{16}$$
$$33.0625 = t^2$$
$$\sqrt{33.0625} = \sqrt{t^2}$$
$$5.75 = t$$

Thus, the object will hit the ground
after approximately 6 seconds.

d. $529 - 16t^2 = 23^2 - (4t)^2$
$$= (23 + 4t)(23 - 4t)$$

99. a. Let $t = 2$

$$784 - 16t^2 = 784 - 16(2)^2 = 720$$

After 2 seconds the height is 720 feet.

b. Let $t = 5$

$$784 - 16t^2 = 784 - 16(5)^2$$
$$= 384$$

After 5 seconds the height is 384 feet.

c. When he reaches ground level,
the height is 0.

$$0 = 784 - 16t^2$$
$$16t^2 = 784$$
$$t^2 = 49$$
$$t = \sqrt{49}$$
$$t = 7$$

He reaches ground level
after 7 seconds.

d. $784 - 16t^2 = 16(49 - t^2)$
$$= 16(7^2 - t^2)$$
$$= 16(7 + t)(7 - t)$$

Integrated Review 11.5

1. $x^2 + x - 12 = (x + 4)(x - 3)$

2. $x^2 - 10x + 16 = (x - 2)(x - 8)$

3. $x^2 - x - 6 = (x + 2)(x - 3)$

4. $x^2 + 2x + 1 = (x + 1)(x + 1) = (x + 1)^2$

5. $x^2 - 6x + 9 = (x - 3)(x - 3) = (x - 3)^2$

6. $x^2 + x - 2 = (x+2)(x-1)$

7. $x^2 + x - 6 = (x+3)(x-2)$

8. $x^2 + 7x + 12 = (x+4)(x+3)$

9. $x^2 - 7x + 10 = (x-5)(x-2)$

10. $x^2 - x - 30 = (x-6)(x+5)$

11. $2x^2 - 98 = (x^2 - 49)$
$\qquad = 2(x^2 - 7^2)$
$\qquad = 2(x+7)(x-7)$

12. $3x^2 - 75 = 3(x^2 - 25)$
$\qquad = 3(x^2 - 5^2)$
$\qquad = 3(x+5)(x-5)$

13. $x^2 + 3x + 5x + 15 = x(x+3) + 5(x+3)$
$\qquad = (x+3)(x+5)$

14. $3y - 21 + xy - 7x = 3(y-7) + x(y-7)$
$\qquad = (y-7)(3+x)$

15. $x^2 + 6x - 16 = (x+8)(x-2)$

16. $x^2 - 3x - 28 = (x-7)(x+4)$

17. $4x^3 + 20x^2 - 56x = 4x(x^2 + 5x - 14)$
$\qquad = 4x(x+7)(x-2)$

18. $6x^3 - 6x^2 - 120x = 6x(x^2 - x - 20)$
$\qquad = 6x(x-5)(x+4)$

19. $12x^2 + 34x + 24 = 2(6x^2 + 17x + 12)$
$\qquad = 2(6x^2 + 9x + 8x + 12)$
$\qquad = 2[3x(2x+3) + 4(2x+3)]$
$\qquad = 2(2x+3)(3x+4)$

20. $8a^2 + 6ab - 5b^2 = 8a^2 + 10ab - 4ab - 5b^2$
$\qquad = 2a(4a+5b) - b(4a+5b)$
$\qquad = (4a+5b)(2a-b)$

21. $4a^2 - b^2 = (2a)^2 - b^2 = (2a+b)(2a-b)$

22. $x^2 - 25y^2 = x^2 - (5y)^2 = (x+5y)(x-5y)$

23. $28 - 13x - 6x^2 = 28 - 21x + 8x - 6x^2$
$\qquad = 7(4-3x) + 2x(4-3x) = (4-3x)(7+2x)$

24. $20 - 3x - 2x^2 = 20 - 8x + 5x - 2x^2$
$\qquad = 4(5-2x) + x(5-2x)$
$\qquad = (5-2x)(4+x)$

25. $x^2 - 2x + 4$ is a prime polynomial.

26. $a^2 + a - 3$ is a prime polynomial.

27. $6y^2 + y - 15 = 6y^2 + 10y - 9y - 15$
$\qquad = 2y(3y+5) - 3(3y+5)$
$\qquad = (3y+5)(2y-3)$

28. $4x^2 - x - 5 = 4x^2 - 5x + 4x - 5$
$\qquad = x(4x-5) + 1(4x-5)$
$\qquad = (4x-5)(x+1)$

29. $18x^3 - 63x^2 + 9x = 9x(2x^2 - 7x + 1)$

30. $12a^3 - 24a^2 + 4a = 4a(3a^2 - 6a + 1)$

31. $16a^2 - 56a + 49 = (4a)^2 - 2 \cdot 4a \cdot 7 + 7^2$
$$= (4a - 7)^2$$

32. $25p^2 - 70p + 49 = (5p)^2 - 2 \cdot 5p \cdot 7 + 7^2$
$$= (4a - 7)^2$$

33. $14 + 5x - x^2 = (7 - x)(2 + x)$

34. $3 - 2x - x^2 = (3 + x)(1 - x)$

35. $3x^4y + 6x^3y - 72x^2y = 3x^2y(x^2 + 2x - 24)$
$$= 3x^2y(x + 6)(x - 4)$$

36. $2x^3y + 8x^2y^2 - 10xy^3 = 2xy(x^2 + 4xy - 5y^2)$
$$= 2xy(x + 5y)(x - y)$$

37. $12x^3y + 243xy = 3xy(4x^2 + 81)$

38. $6x^3y^2 + 8xy^2 = 2xy^2(3x^2 + 4)$

39. $2xy - 72x^3 = 2xy(1 - 36x^2)$
$$= 2xy(1^2 - (6x)^2) - 2xy(1 + 6x)(1 - 6x)$$

40. $2x^3 - 18x = 2x(x^2 - 9)$
$$= 2x(x^2 - 3^2)$$
$$= 2x(x + 3)(x - 3)$$

41. $x^3 + 6x^2 - 4x - 24 = x^2(x + 6) - 4(x + 6)$
$$= (x + 6)(x^2 - 4) = (x + 6)(x^2 - 2^2)$$
$$= (x + 6)(x + 2)(x - 2)$$

42. $x^3 - 2x^2 - 36x + 72$
$$= x^2(x - 2) - 36(x - 2)$$
$$= (x - 2)(x^2 - 36) = (x - 2)(x^2 - 6^2)$$
$$= (x - 2)(x + 6)(x - 6)$$

43. $6a^3 + 10a^2 = 2a^2(3a + 5)$

44. $4n^2 - 6n = 2n(2n - 3)$

45. $3x^3 - x^2 + 12x - 4 = x^2(3x - 1) + 4(3x - 1)$
$$= (3x - 1)(x^2 + 4)$$

46. $x^3 - 2x^2 + 3x - 6 = x^2(x - 2) + 3(x - 2)$
$$= (x - 2)(x^2 + 3)$$

47. $6x^2 + 18xy + 12y^2 = 6(x^2 + 3xy + 2y^2)$
$$= 6(x + 2)(x + y)$$

48. $12x^2 + 46xy - 8y^2 = 2(6x^2 + 23xy - 4y^2)$
$$= 2(6x^2 + 24xy - xy - 4y^2)$$
$$= 2[6x(x + 4y) - y(x + 4y)]$$
$$= 2(x + 4y)(6x - y)$$

49. $5(x + y) + x(x + y) = (x + y)(5 + x)$

50. $7(x - y) + y(x - y) = (x - y)(7 + y)$

51. $14t^2 - 9t + 1 = 14t^2 - 7t - 2t + 1$
$$= 7t(2t - 1) - 1(2t - 1)$$
$$= (2t - 1)(t - 1)$$

52. $3t^2 - 5t + 1$ is a prime polynomial.

53. $3x^2 + 2x - 5 = 3x^2 + 5x - 3x - 5$
$$= x(3x + 5) - 1(3x + 5)$$
$$= (3x + 5)(x - 1)$$

54. $7x^2 + 19x - 6 = 7x^2 + 21x - 2x - 6$
$$= 7x(x + 3) - 2(x + 3)$$
$$= (x + 3)(7x - 2)$$

55. $1 - 8a - 20a^2 = 1 - 10a + 2a - 20a^2$
$$= 1(1 - 10a) + 2a(1 - 10a)$$
$$= (1 - 10a)(1 + 2a)$$

56. $1 - 7a - 60a^2 = 1 - 12a + 5a - 60a^2$
$$= 1(1 - 12a) + 5a(1 - 12a)$$
$$= (1 - 12a)(1 + 5a)$$

57. $x^4 - 10x^2 + 9 = (x^2 - 9)(x^2 - 1)$
$$= (x^2 - 3^2)(x^2 - 1^2)$$
$$= (x + 3)(x - 3)(x + 1)(x - 1)$$

58. $x^4 - 13x^2 + 36 = (x^2 - 9)(x^2 - 4)$
$$= (x^2 - 3^2)(x^2 - 2^2)$$
$$= (x + 3)(x - 3)(x + 2)(x - 2)$$

59. $x^2 - 23x + 120 = (x - 15)(x - 8)$

60. $y^2 + 22y + 96 = (y + 16)(y + 6)$

61. $x^2 - 14x - 48$ is prime.

62. $16a^2 - 56ab + 49b^2$
$$= (4a)^2 - 2(4a)(7b) + (7b)^2$$
$$= (4a - 7b)^2$$

63. $25p^2 - 70pq + 49q^2$
$$= (5p)^2 - 2(5p)(7q) + (7q)^2$$
$$= (5p - 7q)^2$$

64. $7x^2 + 24xy + 9y = 7x^2 + 3xy + 21xy + 9y^2$
$$= x(7x + 3y) + 3y(7x + 3y)$$
$$= (7x + 3y)(x + 3y)$$

65. $-x^2 - x + 30 = -1(x^2 + x - 30)$
$$= -1(x + 6)(x + 5)$$

66. $-x^2 + 6x - 8 = -1(x^2 - 6x + 8)$
$$= -1(x - 2)(x + -4)$$

67. $3rs - s + 12r - 4 = s(3r - 1) + 4(3r - 1)$
$$= (3r - 1)(s + 4)$$

68. $x^3 - 2x^2 + 3x - 6 = x^2(x - 2) + 3(x - 2)$
$$= (x - 2)(x^2 + 3)$$

69. $4x^2 - 8xy - 3x + 6y$
$$= 4x(x - 2y) - 3(x - 2y)$$
$$= (x - 2y)(4x - 3)$$

70. $4x^2 - 2xy - 7yz + 14xz$
$$= 2x(2x - y) + 7z(-y + 2x)$$
$$= (2x - y)(2x + 7z)$$

71. $x^2 + 9xy - 36y^2 = (x + 12y)(x - 3y)$

72. $3x^2 + 10xy - 8y^2 = 3x^2 - 2xy + 12xy - 8y^2$
$$= x(3x - 2y) + 4y(3x - 2y)$$

73. $x^4 - 14x^2 - 32 = (x^2 + 2)(x^2 - 16)$
$$= (x^2 + 2)(x + 4)(x - 4)$$

74. $x^4 - 22x^2 - 75 = (x^2 + 3)(x^2 - 25)$
$$= (x^2 + 3)(x + 5)(x - 5)$$

75. Answers may vary.

76. Yes. $9(x^2 + 9y^2)$

Practice Problems 11.6

1. $(x - 7)(x + 2) = 0$
$x - 7 = 0$ or $x + 2 = 0$
$x = 7$ $x = -2$
The solutions are 7 and -2.

2. $(x - 10)(3x + 1) = 0$
$x - 10 = 0$ or $3x + 1 = 0$
$x = 10$ $3x = -1$
$$x = -\frac{1}{3}$$
The solutions are 10 and $-\frac{1}{3}$.

3. a. $y(y + 3) = 0$
$y = 0$ or $y + 3 = 0$
$y = -3$
The solutions are 0 and -3.

b. $x(4x - 3) = 0$
$x = 0$ or $4x - 3 = 0$
$4x = 3$
$$x = \frac{3}{4}$$
The solutions are 0 and $\frac{3}{4}$.

4. $x^2 - 3x - 18 = 0$
$(x - 6)(x + 3) = 0$
$x - 6 = 0$ or $x + 3 = 0$
$x = 6$ $x = -3$
The solutions are 6 and -3.

5. $x^2 - 14x = -24$
$x^2 - 14x + 24 = 0$
$(x - 12)(x - 2) = 0$
$x - 12 = 0$ or $x - 2 = 0$
$x = 12$ $x = 2$
The solutions are 12 and 2.

6. a. $x(x - 4) = 5$
$x^2 - 4x = 5$
$x^2 - 4x - 5 = 0$
$(x - 5)(x + 1) = 0$
$x - 5 = 0$ or $x + 1 = 0$
$x = 5$ $x = -1$
The solutions are 5 and -1.

b. $x(3x + 7) = 6$
$3x^2 + 7x = 6$
$3x^2 + 7x - 6 = 0$
$(3x - 2)(x + 3) = 0$
$3x - 2 = 0$ or $x + 3 = 0$
$3x = 2$ $x = -3$
$$x = \frac{2}{3}$$
The solutions are $\frac{2}{3}$ and -3.

7. $2x^3 - 18x = 0$

$\quad 2x(x^2 - 9) = 0$

$\quad 2x(x + 3)(x - 3) = 0$

$\quad 2x = 0 \quad$ or $\quad x + 3 = 0 \quad$ or $\quad x - 3 = 0$

$\quad\quad x = 0 \quad\quad\quad\quad x = -3 \quad\quad\quad\quad x = 3$

The solutions are 0, -3, and 3.

8. $(x + 3)(3x^2 - 20x - 7) = 0$

$\quad (x + 3)(3x + 1)(x - 7) = 0$

$\quad x + 3 = 0 \quad$ or $\quad 3x + 1 = 0 \quad$ or $\quad x - 7 = 0$

$\quad\quad x = -3 \quad\quad\quad\quad x = -1 \quad\quad\quad\quad x = 7$

$\quad\quad\quad\quad\quad\quad\quad\quad x = -\dfrac{1}{3}$

The solutions are -3, $-\dfrac{1}{3}$, and 7.

Mental Math 11.6

1. $(a - 3)(a - 7) = 0$

$\quad a - 3 = 0 \quad$ or $\quad a - 7 = 0$

$\quad\quad a = 3 \quad\quad\quad\quad a = 7$

The solutions are 3 and 7.

2. $(a - 5)(a - 2) = 0$

$\quad a - 5 = 0 \quad$ or $\quad a - 2 = 0$

$\quad\quad a = 5 \quad\quad\quad\quad a = 2$

The solutions are 5 and 2.

3. $(x + 8)(x + 6) = 0$

$\quad x + 8 = 0 \quad$ or $\quad x + 6 = 0$

$\quad\quad x = -8 \quad\quad\quad\quad x = -6$

The solutions are -8 and -6.

4. $(x + 2)(x + 3) = 0$

$\quad x + 2 = 0 \quad$ or $\quad x + 3 = 0$

$\quad\quad x = -2 \quad\quad\quad\quad x = -3$

The solutions are -2 and -3.

5. $(x + 1)(x - 3) = 0$

$\quad x + 1 = 0 \quad$ or $\quad x - 3 = 0$

$\quad\quad x = -1 \quad\quad\quad\quad x = 3$

The solutions are -1 and 3.

6. $(x - 1)(x + 2) = 0$

$\quad x - 1 = 0 \quad$ or $\quad x + 2 = 0$

$\quad\quad x = 1 \quad\quad\quad\quad x = -2$

The solutions are 1 and -2.

Exercise Set 11.6

1. $(x - 2)(x + 1) = 0$

$\quad x - 2 = 0 \quad$ or $\quad x + 1 = 0$

$\quad\quad x = 2 \quad\quad\quad\quad x = -1$

The solutions are 2 and -1.

3. $(x - 6)(x - 7) = 0$

$\quad x - 6 = 0 \quad$ or $\quad x - 7 = 0$

$\quad\quad x = 6 \quad\quad\quad\quad x = 7$

The solutions are 6 and 7.

5. $(x + 9)(x + 17) = 0$

$\quad x + 9 = 0 \quad$ or $\quad x + 17 = 0$

$\quad\quad x = -9 \quad\quad\quad\quad x = -17$

The solutions are -9 and -17.

7. $x(x + 6) = 0$

$\quad x = 0 \quad$ or $\quad x + 6 = 0$

$\quad\quad\quad\quad\quad\quad\quad\quad x = -6$

The solutions are 0 and -6.

9. $3x(x-8) = 0$

$3x = 0$ or $x - 8 = 0$

$x = 0$ $x = 8$

The solutions are 0 and 8.

11. $(2x+3)(4x-5) = 0$

$2x + 3 = 0$ or $4x - 5 = 0$

$2x = -3$ $4x = 5$

$x = -\dfrac{3}{2}$ $x = \dfrac{5}{4}$

The solutions are $-\dfrac{3}{2}$ and $\dfrac{5}{4}$.

13. $(2x-7)(7x+2) = 0$

$2x - 7 = 0$ or $7x + 2 = 0$

$2x = 7$ $7x = -2$

$x = \dfrac{7}{2}$ $x = -\dfrac{2}{7}$

The solutions are $\dfrac{7}{2}$ and $-\dfrac{2}{7}$.

15. $\left(x - \dfrac{1}{2}\right)\left(x + \dfrac{1}{3}\right) = 0$

$x - \dfrac{1}{2} = 0$ or $x + \dfrac{1}{3} = 0$

$x = \dfrac{1}{2}$ $x = -\dfrac{1}{3}$

The solutions are $\dfrac{1}{2}$ and $-\dfrac{1}{3}$.

17. $(x+0.2)(x+1.5) = 0$

$x + 0.2 = 0$ or $x + 1.5 = 0$

$x = -0.2$ $x = -1.5$

The solutions are -0.2 and -1.5.

19. If $x = 6$ and $x = -1$ are the solutions, then

$x = 6$ or $x = -1$

$x - 6 = 0$ $x + 1 = 0$

$(x-6)(x+1) = 0$

21. $x^2 - 13x + 36 = 0$

$(x-9)(x-4) = 0$

$x - 9 = 0$ or $x - 4 = 0$

$x = 9$ $x = 4$

The solutions are 9 and 4.

23. $x^2 + 2x - 8 = 0$

$(x+4)(x-2) = 0$

$x + 4 = 0$ or $x - 2 = 0$

$x = -4$ $x = 2$

The solutions are -4 and 2.

25. $x^2 - 7x = 0$

$x(x-7) = 0$

$x = 0$ or $x - 7 = 0$

$x = 7$

The solutions are 0 and 7.

27. $x^2 + 20x = 0$

$x(x+20) = 0$

$x = 0$ or $x + 20 = 0$

$x = -20$

The solutions are 0 and -20.

29. $x^2 = 16$

$x^2 - 16 = 0$

$x^2 - 4^2 = 0$

$(x + 4)(x - 4) = 0$

$x + 4 = 0$ or $x - 4 = 0$

     $x = -4$ $x = 4$

The solutions are -4 and 4.

31. $x^2 - 4x = 32$

$x^2 - 4x - 32 = 0$

$(x - 8)(x + 4) = 0$

$x - 8 = 0$ or $x + 4 = 0$

     $x = 8$ $x = -4$

The solutions are 8 and -4.

33. $x(3x - 1) = 14$

$3x^2 - x = 14$

$3x^2 - x - 14 = 0$

$(3x - 7)(x + 2) = 0$

$3x - 7 = 0$ or $x + 2 = 0$

     $3x = 7$ $x = -2$

     $x = \dfrac{7}{3}$

The solutions are $\dfrac{7}{3}$ and -2.

35. $3x^2 + 19x - 72 = 0$

$(3x - 8)(x + 9) = 0$

$3x - 8 = 0$ or $x + 9 = 0$

     $3x = 9$ $x = -9$

     $x = \dfrac{8}{3}$

The solutions are $\dfrac{8}{3}$ and -9.

37. $4x^3 - x = 0$

$x(4x^2 - 1) = 0$

$x(2x + 1)(2x - 1) = 0$

$x = 0$ or $2x + 1 = 0$ or $2x - 1 = 0$

                     $x = -\dfrac{1}{2}$ $x = \dfrac{1}{2}$

The solutions are 0, $-\dfrac{1}{2}$, and $\dfrac{1}{2}$.

39. $4(x - 7) = 6$

$4x - 28 = 6$

$4x = 34$

$x = \dfrac{34}{4}$

$x = \dfrac{17}{2}$

The solution is $\dfrac{17}{2}$.

41. $(4x - 3)(16x^2 - 24x + 9) = 0$

$(4x - 3)(4x - 3)^2 = 0$

$(4x - 3)^3 = 0$

$4x - 3 = 0$

$4x = 3$

$x = \dfrac{3}{4}$

The solution is $\dfrac{3}{4}$.

43. $4y^2 - 1 = 0$

$(2y+1)(2y-1) = 0$

$2y+1 = 0$ or $2y-1 = 0$

$2y = -1$ $2y = 1$

$y = -\dfrac{1}{2}$ $y = \dfrac{1}{2}$

The solutions are $-\dfrac{1}{2}$ and $\dfrac{1}{2}$.

45. $(2x+3)(2x^2 - 5x - 3) = 0$

$(2x+3)(2x+1)(x-3) = 0$

$2x+3 = 0$ or $2x+1 = 0$ or $x-3 = 0$

$2x = -3$ $2x = -1$ $x = 3$

$x = -\dfrac{3}{2}$ $x = -\dfrac{1}{2}$

The solutions are $-\dfrac{3}{2}$, $-\dfrac{1}{2}$, and 3.

47. $x^2 - 15 = -2x$

$x^2 + 2x - 15 = 0$

$(x+5)(x-3) = 0$

$x+5 = 0$ or $x-3 = 0$

$x = -5$ $x = 3$

The solutions are -5 and 3.

49. $5x^2 - 6x - 8 = 0$

$(5x+4)(x-2) = 0$

$5x+4 = 0$ or $x-2 = 0$

$5x = -4$ $x = 2$

$x = -\dfrac{4}{5}$

The solutions are $-\dfrac{4}{5}$ and 2.

51. $30x^2 - 11x = 30$

$30x^2 - 11x - 30 = 0$

$(5x-6)(6x+5) = 0$

$5x-6 = 0$ or $6x+5 = 0$

$5x = 6$ $6x = -5$

$x = \dfrac{6}{5}$ $x = -\dfrac{5}{6}$

The solutions are $\dfrac{6}{5}$ and $-\dfrac{5}{6}$.

53. $6y^2 - 22y - 40 = 0$

$2(3y^2 - 11y - 20) = 0$

$2(3y+4)(y-5) = 0$

$3y+4 = 0$ or $y-5 = 0$

$3y = -4$ $y = 5$

$y = -\dfrac{4}{3}$

The solutions are $-\dfrac{4}{3}$ and 5.

55. $(y-2)(y+3) = 6$

$y^2 - 2y + 3y - 6 = 6$

$y^2 + y - 12 = 0$

$(y+4)(y-3) = 0$

$y+4 = 0$ or $y-1 = 0$

$y = -4$ $y = 3$

The solutions are -4 and 3.

57. $x^3 - 12x^2 + 32x = 0$

$x(x^2 - 12x + 32) = 0$

$x(x-8)(x-4) = 0$

$x = 0$ or $x - 8 = 0$ or $x - 4 = 0$

                      $x = 8$ $x = 4$

The solutions are 0, 8, and 4.

59. If the solutions are $x = 5$ and $x = 7$,

then, by the zero factor property,

       $x = 5$ or $x = 7$

$x - 5 = 0$ $x - 7 = 0$

$(x-5)(x-7) = 0$

$x^2 - 5x - 7x + 35 = 0$

$x^2 - 12x + 35 = 0$

61. $\dfrac{3}{5} + \dfrac{4}{9} = \dfrac{3 \cdot 9}{5 \cdot 9} + \dfrac{4 \cdot 5}{9 \cdot 5}$

$= \dfrac{27}{45} + \dfrac{20}{45}$

$= \dfrac{27 + 20}{45} = \dfrac{47}{45}$

63. $\dfrac{7}{10} - \dfrac{5}{12} = \dfrac{7 \cdot 6}{10 \cdot 6} - \dfrac{5 \cdot 5}{12 \cdot 5}$

$= \dfrac{42}{60} - \dfrac{25}{60}$

$= \dfrac{42 - 25}{60}$

$= \dfrac{17}{60}$

65. $\dfrac{4}{5} \cdot \dfrac{7}{8} = \dfrac{4 \cdot 7}{5 \cdot 8}$

$= \dfrac{4 \cdot 7}{5 \cdot 2 \cdot 4}$

$= \dfrac{7}{10}$

67. The equation is not written in standard form.

69. a. When $x = 0$;

$y = -16x^2 + 20x + 300$

$y = -16(0^2) + 20(0) + 300$

$= -16(0) + 20(0) + 300$

$= 0 + 0 + 300 = 300$

When $x = 1$:

$y = -16x^2 + 20x + 300$

$y = -16(1)^2 + 20(1) + 300$

$= -16(1) + 20(1) + 300$

$= -16 + 20 + 300 + 304$

When $x = 2$:

$y = -16x^2 + 20x + 300$

$y = -16(2)^2 + 20(2) + 300$

$= -16(4) + 20(2) + 300$

$= -64 + 40 + 300$

$= 276$

When $x = 3$:

$y = -16x^2 + 20x + 300$

$y = -16(3^2) + 20(3) + 300$

$= -16(9) + 20(3) + 300$

$= -144 + 60 + 300$

$= 216$

When $x = 4$:

$y = -16x^2 + 20x + 300$

$y = -16(4^2) + 20(4) + 300$

$\quad = -16(16) + 20(4) + 300$

$\quad = -256 + 80 + 300$

$\quad = 124$

When $x = 5$:

$y = -16x^2 + 20x + 300$

$y = -16(5^2) + 20(5) + 300$

$\quad = -16(25) + 20(5) + 300$

$\quad = -400 + 100 + 300$

$\quad = 0$

When $x = 6$:

$y = -16x^2 + 20x + 300$

$y = -16(6^2) + 20(6) + 300$

$\quad = -16(36) + 20(6) + 300$

$\quad = -576 + 120 + 300$

$\quad = -156$

b. The compass strikes the ground after 5 seconds, when the height, y, is zero feet.

c. The maximum height was approximately 304 feet.

71. $(x-3)(3x+4) = (x+2)(x-6)$

$3x^2 - 9x + 4x - 12 = x^2 + 2x - 6x - 12$

$3x^2 - 5x - 12 = x^2 - 4x - 12$

$2x^2 - x = 0$

$x(2x-1) = 0$

$x = 0 \quad$ or $\quad 2x - 1 = 0$

$\qquad\qquad\qquad\qquad 2x = 1$

$\qquad\qquad\qquad\qquad x = \dfrac{1}{2}$

The solutions are 0 and $\dfrac{1}{2}$.

73. $(2x-3)(x+8) = (x-6)(x+4)$

$2x^2 - 3x + 16x - 24 = x^2 - 6x + 4x - 24$

$2x^2 + 13x - 24 = x^2 - 2x - 24$

$x^2 + 15x = 0$

$x(x+15) = 0$

$x = 0 \quad$ or $\quad x + 15 = 0$

$\qquad\qquad\qquad\qquad x = -15$

The solutions are 0 and -15.

Practice Problems 11.7

1. Find t when $h = 0$.

$h = -16t^2 + 144$

$0 = -16t^2 + 144$

$0 = -16(t^2 - 9)$

$0 = -16(t+3)(t-3)$

$t + 3 = 0 \quad$ or $\quad t - 3 = 0$

$\quad t = -3 \qquad\qquad t = 3$

Since the time cannot be negative, the solution is 3 seconds.

2. Let x = the unknown number.

$x^2 - 2x = 63$

$x^2 - 2x - 63 = 0$

$(x-9)(x+7) = 0$

$x - 9 = 0$ or $x + 7 = 0$

$x = 9$ $x = -7$

The two numbers are 9 and -7.

3. Let x = the width of the rectangle. Then $x + 5$ = the length of the rectangle.

$A = lw$

$176 = (x+5)(x)$

$176 = x^2 + 5x$

$0 = x^2 + 5x - 176$

$0 = (x+16)(x-11)$

$x + 16 = 0$ or $x - 11 = 0$

$x = -16$ $x = 11$

Since the dimensions cannot be negative, we discard $x = -16$. The width is 11 feet and the length is $11 + 5 = 16$ feet.

4. a. Let x = the first integer. Then $x + 2$ = the next consecutive odd integer.

$x(x+2) - 23 = x + (x+2)$

$x^2 + 2x - 23 = 2x + 2$

$x^2 - 25 = 0$

$(x+5)(x-5) = 0$

$x + 5 = 0$ or $x - 5 = 0$

$x = -5$ $x = 5$

The integers are -5 and -3 or 5 and 7.

b. Let x = length of the shorter leg. Then $x + 7$ = length of the longer leg. By the Pythagorean theorem

$x^2 + (x+7)^2 = 13^2$

$x^2 + x^2 + 14x + 49 = 169$

$2x^2 + 14x + 49 = 169$

$2x^2 + 14x - 120 = 0$

$2(x^2 + 7x - 60) = 0$

$2(x+12)(x-5) = 0$

$x + 12 = 0$ or $x - 5 = 0$

$x = -12$ $x = 5$

Since the length cannot be negative, we discard $x = -12$. The legs are 5 meters and $5 + 7 = 12$ meters.

Exercise Set 11.7

1. Let x = the width, then $x + 4$ = the length.

3. Let x = the first odd integer, then $x + 2$ = the next consecutive odd integer.

5. Let x = the base, then $4x + 1$ = the height.

7. Let x = the length of one side.

$A = x^2$

$121 = x^2$

$0 = x^2 - 121$

$0 = x^2 - 11^2$

$0 = (x+11)(x-11)$

$x + 11 = 0$ or $x - 11 = 0$

     $x = -11$ $x = 11$

Since the length cannot be negative, the sides are 11 units long.

9. The perimeter is the sum of the lengths of the sides.

$120 = (x+5) + (x^2 - 3x) + (3x-8)(x+3)$

$120 = x + 5 + x^2 - 3x + 3x - 8 + x + 3$

$120 = x^2 + 2x$

$0 = x^2 + 2x - 120$

$x^2 + 2x - 120 = 0$

$(x+12)(x-10) = 0$

$x + 12 = 0$ or $x - 10 = 0$

     $x = -12$ $x = 10$

Since the dimensions cannot be negative, the lengths of the sides are:

$10 + 5 = 15$ cm, $10^2 - 3(10) = 70$ cm,

$3(10) - 8 = 22$ cm, and $10 + 3 = 13$ cm.

11. $x + 5$ = the base and $x - 5$ = the height.

$A = bh$

$96 = (x+5)(x-5)$

$96 = x^2 + 5x - 5x - 25$

$96 = x^2 - 25$

$0 = x^2 - 121$

$x^2 - 121 = 0$

$(x+11)(x-11) = 0$

$x + 11 = 0$ or $x - 11 = 0$

     $x = -11$ $x = 11$

Since the dimensions cannot be negative, $x = 11$. The base is $11 + 5 = 16$ miles, and the height is $11 - 5 = 6$ miles.

13. Find t when $h = 0$.

$h = -16t^2 + 64t + 80$

$0 = -16t^2 + 64t + 80$

$0 = -16(t^2 - 4t - 5)$

$0 = -16(t-5)(t+1)$

$t - 5 = 0$ or $t + 1 = 0$

    $t = 5$ $t = -1$

Since the time t cannot be negative, the object hits the ground after 5 seconds.

15. Let x = the width then $2x - 7$ = the length.

$A = lw$

$30 = (2x - 7)(x)$

$30 = 2x^2 - 7x$

$0 = 2x^2 - 7x - 30$

$0 = (2x + 5)(x - 6)$

$2x + 5 = 0$ or $x - 6 = 0$

$\quad x = -\dfrac{5}{2} \qquad\qquad x = 6$

Since the dimensions cannot be negative, the width is 6 cm and the length is $2(6) - 7 = 5$ cm.

17. Let n = 12.

$D = \dfrac{1}{2}n(n - 3)$

$D = \dfrac{1}{2} \cdot 12(12 - 3) = 6(9) = 54$

A polygon with 12 sides has 54 diagonals.

19. Let D = 35 and solve for n.

$D = \dfrac{1}{2}n(n - 3)$

$35 = \dfrac{1}{2}n(n - 3)$

$35 = \dfrac{1}{2}n^2 - \dfrac{3}{2}n$

$0 = \dfrac{1}{2}n^2 - \dfrac{3}{2}n - 35$

$0 = \dfrac{1}{2}(n^2 - 3n - 70)$

$0 = \dfrac{1}{2}(n - 10)(n + 7)$

$n - 10 = 0$ or $n + 7 = 0$

$\quad n = 10 \qquad\qquad n = -7$

The polygon has 10 sides.

21. Let x = the unknown number.

$x + x^2 = 132$

$x^2 + x - 132 = 0$

$(x + 12)(x - 11) = 0$

$x + 12 = 0$ or $x - 11 = 0$

$\quad x = -12 \qquad\qquad x = 11$

The two numbers are -12 and 11.

23. Let x = the rate (in mph) of the slower boat, then $x + 7$ = the rate (in mph) of the faster boat. After one hour, the slower boat has traveled x miles and the faster boat has traveled $x + 7$ miles. By the Pythagorean theorem,

$x^2 + (x + 7)^2 = 17^2$

$x^2 + x^2 + 14x + 49 = 289$

$2x^2 + 14x + 49 = 289$

$2x^2 + 14x - 240 = 0$

$2(x^2 + 7x - 120) = 0$

$2(x + 15)(x - 8) = 0$

$x + 15 = 0$ or $x - 8 = 0$

     $x = -15$ $x = 8$

Since the rate cannot be negative, the slower boat travels at 8 mph. The faster boat travels at $8 + 7 = 15$ mph.

25. Let x = the first number, then $20 - x$ = the other number.

$x^2 + (20 - x)^2 = 218$

$x^2 + 400 - 40x + x^2 = 218$

$2x^2 - 40x + 400 = 218$

$2x^2 - 40x + 182 = 0$

$2(x^2 - 20x + 91) = 0$

$2(x - 13)(x - 7) = 0$

$x - 13 = 0$ or $x - 7 = 0$

     $x = 13$ $x = 7$

The numbers are 13 and 7.

27. Let x = the length of a side of the original square. Then $x + 3$ = the length of a side of the larger square.

$64 = (x + 3)^2$

$64 = x^2 + 6x + 9$

$0 = x^2 + 6x - 55$

$0 = (x + 11)(x - 5)$

$x + 11 = 0$ or $x - 5 = 0$

     $x = -11$ $x = -5$

Since the length cannot be negative, the sides of the original square are 5 inches long.

29. Let x = the length of the shorter leg. Then $x + 4$ = the length of the longer leg and $x + 8$ = the length of the hypotenuse. By the Pythagorean theorem,

$x^2 + (x + 4)^2 = (x + 8)^2$

$x^2 + x^2 + 8x + 16 = x^2 + 16x + 64$

$x^2 - 8x - 48 = 0$

$(x - 12)(x + 4) = 0$

$x - 12 = 0$ or $x + 4 = 0$

     $x = 12$ $x = -4$

Since the length cannot be negative, the sides of the triangle are 12 mm, $12 + 4 = 16$ mm, and $12 + 8 = 20$ mm.

31. Let x = the height of the triangle, then $2x$ = the base.

$A = \dfrac{1}{2}bh$

$100 = \dfrac{1}{2}(2x)(x)$

$100 = x^2$

$0 = x^2 - 100$

$0 = (x + 10)(x - 10)$

$x + 10 = 0$ or $x - 10 = 0$

     $x = -10$ $x = 10$

Since the altitude cannot be negative, the height of the triangle is 10 km.

33. Let x = the length of the shorter leg,
then $x + 12$ = the length of the longer leg
and $2x - 12$ = the length of the hypotenuse.
By the Pythagorean theorem,

$$x^2 + (x+12)^2 = (2x-12)^2$$
$$x^2 + x^2 + 24x + 144 = 4x^2 - 48x + 144$$
$$0 = 2x^2 - 72x$$
$$0 = 2x(x-36)$$
$$2x = 0 \quad \text{or} \quad x - 36 = 0$$
$$x = 0 \qquad\qquad x = 36$$

Since the length cannot be zero feet,
the shorter leg is 36 feet long.

35. Find t when $h = 0$.

$$h = -16t^2 + 1444$$
$$0 = -16t^2 + 1444$$
$$0 = -4(4t^2 - 361)$$
$$0 = -4(2t+19)(2t-19)$$
$$2t + 19 = 0 \quad \text{or} \quad 2t - 19 = 0$$
$$2t = -19 \qquad\qquad 2t = 19$$
$$t = -9.5 \qquad\qquad t = 9.5$$

Since the time cannot be negative, the
solution is 9.5 seconds.

37. Let $P = 100$ and $A = 144$

$$A = P(1+r)^2$$
$$144 = 100(1+r)^2$$
$$1.2 = 1 + r$$
$$0.2 = r$$

The interest rate is 20%.

39. Let x = the length and $x - 7$ = the width.

$$A = lw$$
$$120 = (x-7)(x)$$
$$120 = x^2 - 7x$$
$$0 = x^2 - 7x - 120$$
$$0 = (x+8)(x-15)$$
$$x + 8 = 0 \quad \text{or} \quad x - 15 = 0$$
$$x = -8 \qquad\qquad x = 15$$

Since the length cannot be negative,
the length is 15 miles. The width is
$15 - 7 = 8$ miles.

41. Let $C = 9500$

$$C = x^2 - 15x + 50$$
$$9500 = x^2 - 15x + 50$$
$$0 = x^2 - 15x - 9450$$
$$0 = (x+90)(x-105)$$
$$x + 90 = 0 \quad \text{or} \quad x - 105 = 0$$
$$x = -90 \qquad\qquad x = 105$$

Since the number of units cannot
be negative the solution is 105 units.

43. 9600 thousand acres

45. 9500 thousand acres

47. end of 1998

49. Answers may vary

51. Pool: x = length and $x + 6$ = width.
Total: $x + 8$ = length and $x + 14$ = width.

$$A_{\text{Total}} = l_{\text{Total}} w_{\text{Total}} - l_{\text{Pool}} w_{\text{Pool}}$$

$576 = (x+14)(x+8) - (x+6)(x)$

$576 = x^2 + 22x + 112 - x^2 - 6x$

$576 = 16x + 112$

$464 = 16x$

$29 = x$

$x + 6 = 29 + 6 = 35$

The length is 35 meters. The width is 29 meters.

Chapter 11 Review

1. $6x^2 - 15x = 3x(2x - 5)$

2. $4x^5 + 2x - 10x^4 = 2x(2x^4 + 1 - 5x^3)$

3. $5m + 30 = 5(m + 6)$

4. $20x^3 + 12x^2 + 24x = 4x(5x^2 + 3x + 6)$

5. $3x(2x+3) - 5(2x+3) = (2x+3)(3x-5)$

6. $5x(x+1) - (x+1) = (x+1)(5x-1)$

7. $3x^2 - 3x + 2x - 2 = 3x(x-1) + 2(x-1)$
$= (x-1)(3x+2)$

8. $6x^2 + 10x - 3x - 5 = 2x(3x+5) - 1(3x+5)$
$= (3x+5)(2x-1)$

9. $3a^2 + 9ab + 3b^2 + ab$
$= 3a(a+3b) + b(3b+a)$
$= 3a(a+3b) + b(a+3b)$
$= (a+3b)(3a+b)$

10. $x^2 + 6x + 8 = (x+4)(x+2)$

11. $x^2 - 11x + 24 = (x-8)(x-3)$

12. $x^2 + x + 2$ is a prime polynomial.

13. $x^2 - 5x - 6 = (x-6)(x+1)$

14. $x^2 + 2x - 8 = (x+4)(x-2)$

15. $x^2 + 4xy - 12xy^2 = (x+6y)(x-2y)$

16. $x^2 + 8xy + 15y^2 = (x+5y)(x+3y)$

17. $72 - 18x - 2x^2 = 2(36 - 9x - x^2)$
$= 2(3-x)(12+x)$

18. $32 + 12x - 4x^2 = 4(8 + 3x - x^2)$

19. $5y^3 - 50y^2 + 120y = 5y(y^2 - 10y + 24)$
$= 5y(y-6)(y-4)$

20. To factor $x^2 + 2x - 48$, think of two numbers whose product is -48 and whose sum is 2.

21. Factor out the GCF, which is 3.

22. $2x^2 + 13x + 6 = 2x^2 + 12x + x + 6$
$= 2x(x+6) + 1(x+6)$
$= (x+6)(2x+1)$

23. $4x^2 + 4x - 3 = 4x^2 + 6x - 2x - 3$
$$= 2x(2x+3) - 1(2x+3)$$
$$= (2x+3)(2x-1)$$

24. $6x^2 + 5xy - 4y^2 = 6x^2 + 8xy - 3xy - 4y^2$
$$= 2x(3x+4y) - y(3x+4y)$$
$$= (3x+4y)(2x-y)$$

25. $x^2 - x + 2$ is a prime polynomial.

26. $2x^2 - 23x - 39 = 2x^2 - 26x + 3x - 39$
$$= 2x(x-13)(x-13)$$
$$= (x-13)(2x+3)$$

27. $18x^2 - 9xy - 20y^2$
$$= 18x^2 - 24xy + 15xy - 20y^2$$
$$= 6x(3x-4y) + 5y(3x-4y)$$
$$= (3x-4y)(6x+5y)$$

28. $10y^3 + 25y^2 - 60y$
$$= 5y(2y^2 + 5y - 12)$$
$$= 5y(2y^2 + 8y - 3y - 12)$$
$$= 5y[2y(y+4) - 3(y+4)]$$
$$= 5y(y+4)(2y-3)$$

29. The perimeter is the sum of the lengths of the sides.
$$P = (x^2 - 2) + (x^2 - 4x) + (3x^2 - 5x)$$
$$= x^2 - 2 + x^2 - 4x + 3x^2 - 5x$$
$$= 5x^2 - 9x - 2$$
$$= (5x+1)(x-2)$$

30. $l = 6x^2 - 14x$ and $w = 2x^2 + 3$.
$$P = 2l + 2w$$
$$P = 2(6x^2 - 14x) + 2(2x^2 + 3)$$
$$= 12x^2 - 28x + 4x^2 + 6$$
$$= 16x^2 - 28x + 6$$
$$= 2(8x^2 - 14x + 3)$$
$$= 2(4x-1)(2x-3)$$

31. Yes; two terms, x^2 and 9, are squares $(9 = 3^2)$, and the third term of the trinomial, $6x$, is twice the product of x and $3 \, (2 \cdot x \cdot 3 = 6x)$.

32. No; the two terms, x^2 and 64, are squares $(64 = 8^2)$, but the third term of the trinomial, $8x$, is not twice the product of x and 8, or its opposite.

33. No; the two terms, $9m^2$ and 16, are squares $(9m^2 = (3m)^2$ and $16 = 4^2)$, but the third term of the trinomial, $-12m$, is not twice the product of $3m$ and 4, or its opposite.

34. Yes; two terms, $4y^2$ and 49, are squares $(4y^2 = (2y)^2$ and $49 = 7^2)$, and the third term of the trinomial, $-28y$, is the opposite of twice the product of $2y$ and 7.

35. Yes; $x^2 - 9 = x^2 - 3^2$ is the difference of squares.

36. No; $x^2 + 16$ is the sum of two squares, $x^2 + 16 = x^2 + 4^2$.

37. Yes; $4x^2 - 25y^2 = (2x)^2 - (5y)^2$ is the difference of two squares.

38. No; only one of the terms, 1, is a square.

39. $x^2 - 81 = x^2 - 9^2 = (x+9)(x-9)$

40. $x^2 + 12x + 36 = (x+6)(x+6) = (x+6)^2$

41. $4x^2 - 9 = (2x)^2 - 3^2 = (2x+3)(2x-3)$

42. $9t^2 - 25s^2 = (3t)^2 - (5s)^2 = (3t+5s)(3t-5s)$

43. $16x^2 + y^2$ is a prime polynomial.

44. $n^2 - 18n + 81 = (n-9)(n-9) = (n-9)^2$

45. $3r^2 + 36r + 108 = 3(r^2 + 12r + 36)$
$= 3(r+6)(r+6) = 3(r+6)^2$

46. $9y^2 - 42y + 49 = (3y-7)(3y-7)$
$= (3y-7)^2$

47. $5m^8 - 5m^6 = 5m^6(m^2 - 1) = 5m^6(m^2 - 1^2)$
$= 5m^6(m+1)(m-1)$

48. $4x^2 - 28xy + 49y^2 = (2x-7y)(2x-7y)$
$= (2x-7y)^2$

49. $3x^2 y + 6xy^2 + 3y^3 = 3y(x^2 + 2xy + y^2)$
$= 3y(x+y)(x+y)$
$= 3y(x+y)^2$

50. $16x^4 - 1 = (4x^2)^2 - 1^2$
$= (4x^2 + 1)(4x^2 - 1)$
$= (4x^2 + 1)((2x)^2 - 1^2)$
$= (4x^2 + 1)(2x+1)(2x-1)$

51. $(x+6)(x-2) = 0$
$x+6 = 0$ or $x-2 = 0$
$x = -6$ $x = 2$
The solutions are -6 and 2.

52. $3x(x+1)(7x-2) = 0$
$3x = 0$ or $x+1 = 0$ or $7x-2 = 0$
$x = 0$ $x = -1$ $7x = 2$
$x = \frac{2}{7}$
The solutions are 0, -1, and $\frac{2}{7}$.

53. $4(5x+1)(x+3) = 0$
$5x+1 = 0$ or $x+3 = 0$
$5x = -1$ $x = -3$
$x = -\frac{1}{5}$
The solutions are $-\frac{1}{5}$ and -3.

54. $x^2 + 8x + 7 = 0$

$(x + 7)(x + 1) = 0$

$x + 7 = 0$ or $x + 1 = 0$

$x = -7$ $x = -1$

The solutions are -7 and -1.

55. $x^2 - 2x - 24 = 0$

$(x - 6)(x + 4) = 0$

$x - 6 = 0$ or $x + 4 = 0$

$x = 6$ $x = -4$

The solutions are 6 and -4.

56. $x^2 + 10x = -25$

$x^2 + 10x + 25 = 0$

$(x + 5)(x + 5) = 0$

$x + 5 = 0$ or $x + 5 = 0$

$x = -5$ $x = -5$

The solution is -5.

57. $x(x - 10) = -16$

$x^2 - 10x = -16$

$x^2 - 10x + 16 = 0$

$(x - 8)(x - 2) = 0$

$x - 8 = 0$ or $x - 2 = 0$

$x = 8$ $x = 2$

The solutions are 8 and 2.

58. $(3x - 1)(9x^2 + 3x + 1) = 0$

$3x - 1 = 0$ or $9x^2 + 3x + 1 = 0$

$9x^2 + 3x + 1$ is a prime polynomial.

$3x - 1 = 0$

$3x = 1$

$x = \dfrac{1}{3}$

59. $56x^2 - 5x - 6 = 0$

$56x^2 + 16x - 21x - 6 = 0$

$8x(7x + 2)(8x - 3) = 0$

$(7x + 2)(8x - 3) = 0$

$7x + 2 = 0$ or $8x - 3 = 0$

$7x = -2$ $8x = 3$

$x = -\dfrac{2}{7}$ $x = \dfrac{3}{8}$

The solutions are $-\dfrac{2}{7}$ and $\dfrac{3}{8}$.

60. $m^2 = 6m$

$m^2 - 6m = 0$

$m(m - 6) = 0$

$m = 0$ or $m - 6 = 0$

$m = 6$

The solutions are 0 and 6.

61. $r^2 = 25$

$r^2 - 25 = 0$

$r^2 - 5^2 = 0$

$(r + 5)(r - 5) = 0$

$x + 5 = 0$ or $x - 5 = 0$

$x = -5$ $x = 5$

The solutions are -5 and 5.

62. If $x = 4$ and $x = 5$ are the solutions, then by the zero factor property

$x = 4$ or $x = 5$

$x - 4 = 0$ $x - 5 = 0$

$(x - 4)(x - 5) = 0$

$x^2 - 4x - 5x + 20 = 0$

$x^2 - 9x + 20 = 0$

63. Let x = the width, then $2x$ = the length.
$P = 2l + 2w$
$24 = 2(2x) + 2x$
$24 = 4x + 2x$
$24 = 6x$
$4 = x$
The width is 4 inches and the length is
$2 \cdot 4 = 8$ inches. Thus, (c) is the correct
answer.

64. Let x = the width, then $3x + 1$ = the length.
$A = lw$
$80 = (3x + 1)(x)$
$80 = 3x^2 + x$
$0 = 3x^2 + x - 80$
$0 = (3x + 16)(x - 5)$
$3x + 16 = 0$ or $x - 5 = 0$
$3x = -16$ $x = 5$
$x = -\dfrac{16}{3}$
Since the width cannot be negative,
the width is 5 meters and the length is
$3(5) + 1 = 16$ meters. Thus (d) is the
correct answer.

65. $x^2 = 81$
$x^2 - 81 = 0$
$(x + 9)(x - 9) = 0$
$x + 9 = 0$ or $x - 9 = 0$
$x = -9$ $x = 9$
Since the length cannot be negative, the
sides are 9 units long.

66. The perimeter is the sum of the lengths
of the sides.
$47 = (2x + 3) + (3x + 1) + (x^2 - 3x) + (x + 3)$
$47 = 2x + 3 + 3x + 1 + x^2 - 3x + x + 3$
$47 = x^2 + 3x + 7$
$0 = x^2 + 3x - 40$
$0 = (x + 8)(x - 5)$
$x + 8 = 0$ or $x - 5 = 0$
$x = -8$ $x = 5$

Since the lengths cannot be negative,
$x = 5$. The lengths of the sides are
$2(5) + 3 = 13$ units,
$3(5) + 1 = 16$ units, $5^2 - 3(5) = 10$
units, and $5 + 3 = 8$ units.

67. Let x = the width of the flag. Then
$2x - 15$ = the length of the flag.
$A = lw$
$500 = (2x - 15)(x)$
$500 = 2x^2 - 15x$
$0 = 2x^2 - 15x - 500$
$0 = (2x + 25)(x - 20)$

68. Let x = the height of the sail, then
$4x$ = the base of the sail.

$$A = \frac{1}{2}bh$$

$$162 = \frac{1}{2}(4x)(x)$$

$$162 = 2x^2$$

$$0 = 2x^2 - 162$$

$$0 = 2(x^2 - 81)$$

$$0 = 2(x+9)(x-9)$$

$$x + 9 = 0 \quad \text{or} \quad x - 9 = 0$$

$$x = -9 \qquad\qquad x = 9$$

Since the dimensions cannot be negative, the height is 9 yards and the base is $4 \cdot 9 = 36$ yards.

69. Let x = the first integer. Then
$x + 1$ = the next consecutive integer.

$$x(x+1)380$$

$$x^2 + x = 380$$

$$x^2 + x - 380 = 0$$

$$(x+20)(x-19) = 0$$

$$x + 20 = 0 \quad \text{or} \quad x - 19 = 0$$

$$x = -21 \qquad\qquad x = 19$$

The integers are 19 and 20.

70. a. Let h = 2800 and solve for t.

$$h = -16t^2 + 440t$$

$$2800 = -16t^2 + 440t$$

$$0 = -16t^2 + 440t - 2800$$

$$0 = -8(2t^2 - 55t + 350)$$

$$0 = -8(2t - 35)(t - 10)$$

$$2t - 35 = 0 \quad \text{or} \quad t - 10 = 0$$

$$2t = 35 \qquad\qquad t = 10$$

$$t = \frac{35}{2}$$

$$t = 17.5$$

The solutions are 17.5 and 10 sec

Answers may vary.

b. Find t when $h = 0$.

$$h = -16t^2 + 440t$$

$$0 = 16t^2 + 440t$$

$$0 = -8t(2t - 55)$$

$$-8t = 0 \quad \text{or} \quad 2t - 55 = 0$$

$$t = 0 \qquad\qquad 2t = 55$$

$$t = \frac{55}{2}$$

$$t = 27.5$$

27.5 seconds after being fired, the rocket will reach the ground again.

71. Let x = the length of the longer leg,
then $x - 8$ = the length of the shorter leg
and $x + 8$ = the length of the hypotenuse.
By the Pythagorean theorem,

$$x^2 + (x-8)^2 = (x+8)^2$$
$$x^2 + x^2 - 16x + 64 = x^2 + 16x + 64$$

$$x^2 - 32x = 0$$
$$x(x - 32) = 0$$
$$x = 0 \quad \text{or} \quad x = 32$$

Since the length cannot be zero cm,
the length of the longer leg is 32 cm.

Chapter 11 Test

1. $9x^2 - 3x = 3x(3x - 1)$

2. $x^2 + 11x + 28 = (x + 7)(x + 4)$

3. $y^2 + 22y + 121 = (y + 11)(y + 11)$
$$= (y + 11)^2$$

4. $4(a + 3) - y(a + 3) = (a + 3)(4 - y)$

5. $y^2 - 8y - 48 = (y - 12)(y + 4)$

6. $3a^2 + 3ab - 7a - 7b = 3a(a + b) - 7(a + b)$
$$= (a + b)(3a - 7)$$

7. $3x^2 - 5x + 2 = (3x - 2)(x - 1)$

8. $180 - 5x^2 = 5(36 - x^2)$
$$= 5(6^2 - x^2)$$
$$= 5(6 + x)(6 - x)$$

9. $3x^3 - 21x^2 + 30x = 3x(x^2 - 7x + 10)$
$$= 3x(x - 5)(x - 2)$$

10. $6t^2 - t - 5 = (6t + 5)(t - 1)$

11. $xy^2 - 7y^2 - 4x + 28$
$$= y^2(x - 7) - 4(x - 7)$$
$$= (x - 7)(y^2 - 4)$$
$$= (x - 7)(y^2 - 2^2)$$
$$= (x - 7)(y + 2)(y - 2)$$

12. $x - x^5 = x(1 - x^4)$
$$= x\left(1 - (x^2)^2\right)$$
$$= x(1 + x^2)(1 - x^2)$$
$$= x(1 + x^2)(1 + x)(1 - x)$$

13. $x^2 + 14xy + 24y^2 = (x + 12y)(x + 2y)$

14. $\qquad x^2 + 5x = 14$
$$x^2 + 5x - 14 = 0$$
$$(x + 7)(x - 2) = 0$$
$$x + 7 = 0 \quad \text{or} \quad x - 2 = 0$$
$$x = -7 \qquad\qquad x = 2$$
The solutions are -7 and 2.

15.
$$x(x+6) = 7$$
$$x^2 + 6x = 7$$
$$x^2 + 6x - 7 = 0$$
$$(x+7)(x-1) = 0$$
$$x + 7 = 0 \quad \text{or} \quad x - 1 = 0$$
$$x = -7 \qquad\qquad x = 1$$
The solutions are -7 and 1.

16. $3x(2x-3)(3x+4) = 0$
$$3x = 0 \quad \text{or} \quad 2x - 3 = 0 \quad \text{or} \quad 3x + 4 = 0$$
$$x = 0 \qquad\qquad 2x = 3 \qquad\qquad 3x = -4$$
$$x = \frac{3}{2} \qquad\qquad x = -\frac{4}{3}$$
The solutions are 0, $\frac{3}{2}$, and $-\frac{4}{3}$.

17.
$$5t^3 - 45t = 0$$
$$5t(t^2 - 0) = 0$$
$$5t(t+3)(t-3) = 0$$
$$5t = 0 \quad \text{or} \quad t + 3 = 0 \quad \text{or} \quad t - 3 = 0$$
$$t = 0 \qquad\qquad t = -3 \qquad\qquad t = 3$$
The solutions are 0, -3, and 3.

18.
$$t^2 - 2t - 15 = 0$$
$$(t-5)(t+3) = 0$$
$$x - 5 = 0 \quad \text{or} \quad t + 3 = 0$$
$$t = 5 \qquad\qquad t = -3$$
The solutions are 5 and -3.

19. $(x-1)(3x^2 - x - 2) = 0$
$$(x-1)(3x+2)(x-1) = 0$$
$$(x-1)^2(3x+2) = 0$$
$$x - 1 = 0 \quad \text{or} \quad 3x + 2 = 0$$
$$x = 1 \qquad\qquad 3x = -2$$
$$x = -\frac{2}{3}$$
The solutions are 1 and $-\frac{2}{3}$.

20. Let x = the height of the triangle, then $x + 9$ = the base.
$$A = \frac{1}{2}bh$$
$$68 = \frac{1}{2}(x+9)(x)$$
$$68 = \frac{1}{2}x^2 + \frac{9}{2}x$$
$$0 = \frac{1}{2}x^2 + \frac{9}{2}x - 68$$
$$0 = \frac{1}{2}(x^2 + 9x - 136)$$
$$0 = \frac{1}{2}(x+17)(x-8)$$
$$x + 17 = 0 \quad \text{or} \quad x - 8 = 0$$
$$x = -17 \qquad\qquad x = 8$$
Since the length of the base cannot be negative, the base is $8 + 9 = 17$ feet.

21. Let x = the first number, then
$17 - x$ = the other number.

$$x^2 + (17 - x)^2 = 145$$
$$x^2 + 289 - 34x + x^2 = 145$$
$$2x^2 - 34x + 144 = 0$$
$$2(x^2 - 17x + 72) = 0$$
$$2(x - 9)(x - 8) = 0$$

$x - 9 = 0$ or $x - 8 = 0$
$x = 9$ $\qquad\qquad x = 8$

The numbers are 8 and 9.

22. Find t when $h = 0$.

$$h = -16t^2 + 1089$$
$$0 = -16t^2 + 1089$$
$$16t^2 = 1089$$
$$t^2 = 68.0625$$
$$t = 8.25$$

It reaches the ground after 8.25 seconds.

23. Let x = the length of the shorter leg, then $x + 5$ = the length of the longer leg and $x + 10$ = the length of the hypotenuse. By the Pythagorean theorem,

$$x^2 + (x + 5)^2 = (x + 10)^2$$
$$x^2 + x^2 + 10x + 25 = x^2 + 20x + 100$$
$$x^2 - 10x - 75 = 0$$
$$(x - 15)(x + 5) = 0$$

$x - 15 = 0$ or $x + 5 = 0$
$x = 15$ $\qquad\qquad x = -5$

Since the lengths cannot be negative, the length of the shorter leg is 15 cm, the longer leg is $15 + 5 = 20$ cm, and the hypotenuse is $15 + 10 = 25$ cm.

Cumulative Review Chapter 11

1. $x + 2y - z = 3 + 2(-5) - (-4)$
$= 3 - 10 + 4$
$= -7 + 4$
$= -3$

2. $5x - y = 5(-2) - 4 = -10 - 4 = -14$

3. $7 - x^2 = 7 - (-4)^2 = 7 - 16 = -9$

4. $x^3 - y^3 = (-2)^3 - (4)^3 = -8 - 64 = -72$

5. $2y - 6 + 4y + 8 = 6y + 2$

6. $-5a - 3 + a + 2 = -4a - 1$

7. $4x + 2 - 5x + 3 = -x + 5$

8. $2.3x + 5x - 6 = 2.3x + 5.0x - 6$
$$= 7.3x - 6$$

9. $4(6 - 3) = 12$
$$4(3) = 12$$
$$12 = 12 \quad \text{True}$$
6 is a solution.

10. $3(2) + 10 = 8(2)$
$$6 + 10 = 16$$
$$16 = 16 \quad \text{True}$$
2 is a solution.

11. $3(3x - 5) = 10x$
$$9x - 15 = 10x$$
$$9x - 10x = 15$$
$$\frac{-1x}{-1} = \frac{15}{-1}$$
$$x = -15$$

12. $2(7x - 1) = 15x$
$$14x - 2 = 15x$$
$$14x - 15x = 2$$
$$\frac{-1x}{-1} = \frac{2}{-1}$$
$$x = -2$$

13. $\dfrac{-12x}{-12} = \dfrac{-36}{-12}$
$$x = 3$$

14. $\dfrac{-7x}{-7} = \dfrac{42}{-7}$
$$x = -6$$

15. $\dfrac{x - 5}{3} = \dfrac{x + 2}{5}$
$$5(x - 5) = 3(x + 2)$$
$$5x - 25 = 3x + 6$$
$$5x - 3x = 6 + 25$$
$$\frac{2x}{2} = \frac{31}{2}$$
$$x = \frac{31}{2}$$

16. $\dfrac{x + 1}{2} = \dfrac{x - 7}{3}$
$$3(x + 1) = 2(x - 7)$$
$$3x + 3 = 2x - 14$$
$$3x - 2x = -14 - 3$$
$$x = -17$$

17. a) $9 \leq 11$
     b) $8 > 1$
     c) $3 \neq 4$

18. a) $5 \geq 1$
     b) $2 \neq -4$

19. $3(x - 4) = 3x - 12$
$$3x - 12 = 3x - 12$$
$$3x - 3x = -12 + 12$$
$$0 = 0$$
All real numbers

20. $2(x + 5) = 2x + 9$
$$2x + 10 = 2x + 9$$
$$2x - 2x = 9 - 10$$
$$0 = -1$$
No solution

21. $V = lwh$

$$\frac{V}{wh} = \frac{lwh}{wh}$$

$$\frac{V}{wh} = l$$

22. $3x - 2y = 5$

$$\frac{3x}{3} = \frac{2y+5}{3}$$

$$x = \frac{2y+5}{3}$$

23. $\left(5^3\right)^6 = 5^{3\cdot6} = 5^{18}$

24. $\left(7^9\right)^2 = 7^{9\cdot2} = 7^{18}$

25. $\left(y^8\right)^2 = y^{8\cdot2} = y^{16}$

26. $\left(x^{11}\right)^3 = x^{11\cdot3} = x^{33}$

27. $\dfrac{\left(x^3\right)^4 x}{x^7} = \dfrac{x^{12}x^1}{x^7} = \dfrac{x^{13}}{x^7} = x^6$

28. $\dfrac{\left(y^3\right)^9 \cdot y}{y^6} = \dfrac{y^{27}\cdot y^1}{y^6} = \dfrac{y^{28}}{y^6} = y^{22}$

29. $\left(y^{-3}z^6\right)^{-6} = \left(y^{-3}\right)^{-6}\left(z^6\right)^{-6}$

$$= y^{18}z^{-36}$$

$$= y^{18} \cdot \frac{1}{z^{36}}$$

$$= \frac{y^{18}}{z^{36}}$$

30. $\left(xy^{-4}\right)^{-2} = \left(x\right)^{-2}\left(y^{-4}\right)^{-2}$

$$= x^{-2}y^8$$

$$= \frac{1}{x^2} \cdot y^8$$

$$= \frac{y^8}{x^2}$$

31. $\dfrac{x^{-7}}{\left(x^4\right)^3} = \dfrac{x^{-7}}{x^{12}} = x^{-7-12} = x^{-19} = \dfrac{1}{x^{19}}$

32. $\dfrac{\left(y^2\right)^5}{y^{-3}} = \dfrac{y^{10}}{y^{-3}} = y^{10-(-3)} = y^{13}$

33. $-3x + 7x = 4x$

34. $y + y = 1y + 1y = 2y$

35. $11x^2 + 5 + 2x^2 - 7 = 13x^2 - 2$

36. $8y - y^2 + 4y - y^2 = 12y - 2y^2$

37. $(2x - y)^2 = (2x - y)(2x - y)$

$$= 2x(2x - y) - y(2x - y)$$

$$= 4x^2 - 2xy - 2xy + y^2$$

$$= 4x^2 - 4xy + y^2$$

38. $(3x + 1)^2 = (3x + 1)(3x + 1)$

$$= 3x(3x + 1) + 1(3x + 1)$$

$$= 9x^2 + 3x + 3x + 1$$

$$= 9x^2 + 6x + 1$$

39. $(t + 2)^2 = (t)^2 + 2(t)(2) + (2)^2$

$$= t^2 + 4t + 4$$

40. $(x-4)^2 = (x)^2 - 2(x)(4) + (4)^2$
$$= x^2 - 8x + 16$$

41. $(x^2 - 7y)^2 = (x^2)^2 - 2(x^2)(7y) + (7y)^2$
$$= x^4 - 14x^2 y + 49 y^2$$

42. $(x^2 + 7y)^2 = (x^2)^2 + 2(x^2)(7y) + (7y)^2$
$$= x^4 + 14x^2 y + 49 y^2$$

43. $\dfrac{8x^2 y^2 - 16xy + 2x}{4xy} = \dfrac{8x^2 y^2}{4xy} - \dfrac{16xy}{4xy} + \dfrac{2x}{4xy}$
$$= 2xy - 4 + \dfrac{1}{2y}$$

44. $\dfrac{20a^2 b^3 - 5ab + 10b}{5ab} = \dfrac{20a^2 b^3}{5ab} - \dfrac{5ab}{5ab} + \dfrac{10b}{5ab}$
$$= 4ab^2 - 1 + \dfrac{2}{a}$$

45. $5(x+3) + y(x+3) = (x+3)(5+y)$

46. $9(y-2) + x(y-2) = (y-2)(9+x)$

47. $x^4 + 5x^2 + 6 = (x^2 + 2)(x^2 + 3)$

48. $x^4 - 4x^2 - 5 = (x^2 + 1)(x^2 - 5)$

49. $6x^2 - 2x - 20 = 2(3x^2 - x - 10)$
$$= 2(x-2)(3x+5)$$

50. $10x^2 + 25x + 10 = 5(2x^2 + 5x + 2)$
$$= 5(x+2)(2x+1)$$

51. $h = -16t^2 + 256$

Since the ground has a height of zero,
Let $h = 0$.
$$0 = -16t^2 + 256$$
$$16t^2 - 256 = 0$$
$$\dfrac{16}{16}(t^2 - 16) = \dfrac{0}{16}$$
$$t^2 - 16 = 0$$
$$(t+4)(t-4) = 0$$
$$t + 4 = 0 \quad \text{or} \quad t - 4 = 0$$
$$t = -4 \qquad\qquad t = 4$$

Since time cannot be negative, we only use $t = 4$. The lugage will hit the ground in 4 seconds.

52. Let $x = $ a number.
$$x^2 + 2x = 120$$
$$x^2 + 2x - 120 = 0$$
$$(x-10)(x+12) = 0$$
$$x - 10 = 0 \quad \text{or} \quad x + 12 = 0$$
$$x = 10 \quad \text{or} \qquad x = -12$$
$$x = 10, -12$$

Chapter   12

Chapter 12 Pretest

1. Find the values for x that make the denominator 0.
$$x^2 - 9x - 10 = 0$$
$$(x-10)(x+1) = 0$$
$$x - 10 = 0 \quad \text{or} \quad x + 1 = 0$$
$$x = 10 \qquad\qquad x = -1$$

The rational expression $\dfrac{x+2}{x^2-9x-10}$ is undefined when $x = 10$ or when $x = -1$.

2. $\dfrac{4x+32}{x^2+10x+16} = \dfrac{4(x+8)}{(x+8)(x+2)} = \dfrac{4}{x+2}$

3. Factor each denominator.
$$5x + 10 = 5(x+2)$$
$$2x^2 + 10x + 12 = 2(x^2 + 5x + 6)$$
$$= 2(x+3)(x+2)$$
$$\text{LCD} = 2 \cdot 5(x+2)(x+3)$$
$$= 10(x+2)(x+3)$$

4. $\dfrac{y^2-8y+7}{2y-14} \cdot \dfrac{6y+18}{y^2+2y-3}$
$$= \dfrac{(y-7)(y-1)}{2(y-7)} \cdot \dfrac{2\cdot3(y+3)}{(y+3)(y-1)}$$
$$= \dfrac{(y-7)(y-1)\cdot 2\cdot3(x+3)}{2(y-7)\cdot(y+3)(y-1)}$$

5. $\dfrac{5x^3}{x^2-25} \div \dfrac{x^6}{(x+5)^2} = \dfrac{5x^3}{x^2-25} \cdot \dfrac{(x+5)^2}{x^6}$
$$= \dfrac{5x^3}{(x+5)(x-5)} \cdot \dfrac{(x+5)^2}{x^3\cdot x^3}$$
$$= \dfrac{5x^3\cdot(x+5)^2}{(x+5)(x-5)\cdot x^3\cdot x^3} = \dfrac{5(x+5)}{x^3(x-5)}$$

6. $\dfrac{b}{b^2-9b-22} + \dfrac{2}{b^2-9b-22}$
$$= \dfrac{b+2}{b^2-9b-22} = \dfrac{b+2}{(b-11)(b+2)}$$
$$= \dfrac{1}{b-11}$$

7. $\dfrac{3}{x-1} - 4 = \dfrac{3}{x-1} - \dfrac{4(x-1)}{1(x-1)} = \dfrac{3-4(x-1)}{x-1}$
$$= \dfrac{3-4x+4}{x-1} = \dfrac{7-4x}{x-1}$$

8. $\dfrac{2}{x-5} - \dfrac{7}{5-x} = \dfrac{2}{x-5} - \dfrac{7}{-(x-5)}$
$$= \dfrac{2}{x-5} - \dfrac{-7}{x-5} = \dfrac{2-(-7)}{x-5} = \dfrac{9}{x-5}$$

9.
$$\frac{x}{x^2-16}+\frac{3}{x^2-7x+12}$$
$$=\frac{x}{(x+4)(x-4)}+\frac{3}{(x-4)(x-3)}$$
$$=\frac{x(x-3)}{(x+4)(x-4)(x-3)}$$
$$+\frac{3(x+4)}{(x+4)(x-4)(x-3)}$$
$$=\frac{x(x-3)+3(x+4)}{(x+4)(x-4)(x-3)}$$
$$=\frac{x^2-3x+3x+12}{(x+4)(x-4)(x-3)}$$
$$=\frac{x^2+12}{(x+4)(x-4)(x-3)}$$

10.
$$\frac{5}{b}+\frac{3}{5}=\frac{4}{5b}$$
$$5b\left(\frac{5}{b}+\frac{3}{5}\right)=5b\left(\frac{4}{5b}\right)$$
$$5b\left(\frac{5}{b}\right)+5b\left(\frac{3}{5}\right)=4$$
$$25+3b=4$$
$$3b=-21$$
$$b=-7$$

11. $9+\frac{7}{d-7}=\frac{d}{d-7}$
$$(d-7)\left(9+\frac{7}{d-7}\right)=(d-7)\left(\frac{d}{d-7}\right)$$
$$(d-7)(9)+(d-7)\left(\frac{7}{d-7}\right)=d$$
$$9d-63+7=d$$
$$-56=-8d.$$

$d=7$
However, $d=7$ makes the denominators 0 in the original equation. The equation has no solution.

12. $\frac{4y+5}{y^2+5y+6}+\frac{3}{y+3}=\frac{2}{y+2}$
$$y^2+5y+6=(y+3)(y+2)$$
$$(y+3)(y+2)\left(\frac{4y+5}{(y+3)(y+2)}+\frac{3}{y+3}\right)$$
$$=(y+3)(y+2)\left(\frac{2}{y+2}\right)$$
$$(y+3)(y+2)\left(\frac{4y+5}{(y+3)(y+2)}\right)$$
$$+(y+3)(y+2)\left(\frac{3}{y+3}\right)=2(y+3)$$
$$4y+5+3(y+2)=2(y+3)$$
$$4y+5+3y+6=2y+6$$
$$5y=-5$$
$$y=-1$$

13. $\frac{2A}{b}=h$
$$b\left(\frac{2A}{b}\right)=b(h)$$
$$2A=bh$$
$$\frac{2A}{h}=\frac{bh}{h}$$
$$\frac{2A}{h}=b$$

14. $\dfrac{\frac{12m^3}{5n^2}}{\frac{4m^6}{25n^8}} = \dfrac{12m^3}{5n^2} \cdot \dfrac{25n^8}{4m^6}$

$= \dfrac{12m^3 \cdot 25n^8}{5n^2 \cdot 4m^6}$

$= \dfrac{3 \cdot 4 \cdot 5 \cdot 5m^3 \cdot n^6 \cdot n^2}{5 \cdot 4m^3 \cdot m^3 \cdot n^2}$

$= \dfrac{3 \cdot 5n^6}{m^3}$

$= \dfrac{15n^6}{m^3}$

15. $\dfrac{16 - \frac{1}{a^2}}{\frac{4}{a} + \frac{1}{a^2}} = \dfrac{a^2\left(16 - \frac{1}{a^2}\right)}{a^2\left(\frac{4}{a} + \frac{1}{a^2}\right)} = \dfrac{16a^2 - 1}{4a + 1}$

$= \dfrac{(4a+1)(4a-1)}{(4a+1)} = 4a - 1$

16. $\dfrac{3}{x} = \dfrac{9}{15}$

$45 = 9x$

$5 = x$

17. Let $x =$ the unknown number.

$\left(10 \cdot \dfrac{1}{x}\right) + x = 7$

$\dfrac{10}{x} + x = 7$

$x\left(\dfrac{10}{x} + x\right) = x(7)$

$10 + x^2 = 7x$

$x^2 - 7x + 10 = 0$

$(x-5)(x-2) = 0$

$x - 5 = 0 \quad \text{or} \quad x - 2 = 0$

$x = 5 \qquad\qquad x = 2$

The number is 2 or 5.

18. Let $x =$ the time in hours it takes if they work together. Then $\dfrac{1}{x} =$ the part of the job they complete is 1 hour. Since Sonya completes $\dfrac{1}{5}$ of the job in 1 hour, and her daughter completes $\dfrac{1}{8}$ of the job in one hour,

$\dfrac{1}{5} + \dfrac{1}{8} = \dfrac{1}{x}$

$40x\left(\dfrac{1}{5}\right) + 40x\left(\dfrac{1}{8}\right) = 40x\left(\dfrac{1}{x}\right)$

$8x + 5x = 40$

$13x = 40$

$x = \dfrac{40}{13}$

$x = 3\dfrac{1}{13}$

It will take $3\dfrac{1}{13}$ hrs if they work together.

19. Let $r =$ the rate of the plane in still air. Then $r + 25 =$ the rate with a tail wind and $r - 25 =$ the rate against the wind. Since

$d = rt, \ t = \dfrac{d}{r}.$

With a tail wind:

$\dfrac{495}{r + 25} = t$

Against the wind:

$\dfrac{405}{r - 25} = t$

$$\frac{495}{r+25} = \frac{405}{r-25}$$

$$(r+25)(r-25)\left(\frac{495}{r+25}\right)$$

$$= (r+25)(r-25)\left(\frac{405}{r-25}\right)$$

$$495(r-25) = 405(r+25)$$

$$495r - 12,375 = 405r + 10,125$$

$$90r = 22,500$$

$$r = 250$$

The rate of the plane in still air is 250 mph.

Practice Problems 12.1

1. a. $\dfrac{x-3}{5x+1} = \dfrac{4-3}{5(4)+1} = \dfrac{1}{20+1} = \dfrac{1}{21}$

    b. $\dfrac{x-3}{5x+1} = \dfrac{-3-3}{5(-3)+1} = \dfrac{-6}{-15+1} = \dfrac{-6}{-14}$

       $= \dfrac{-2\cdot 3}{-2\cdot 7} = \dfrac{3}{7}$

2. a. $x+2 = 0$

       $x = -2$

    The expression is undefined when $x = -2$.

    b. $x^2 + 5x + 4 = 0$

       $(x+4)(x+1) = 0$

       $x+4 = 0$ or $x+1 = 0$

          $x = -4$ $x = -1$

    The expression is undefined when $x = -4$ or $x = -1$.

c. The denominator of $\dfrac{x^2 - 3x + 2}{5}$ is never zero, so there are no values of x for which the expression is undefined.

3. $\dfrac{x^4 + x^3}{5x+5} = \dfrac{x^3(x+1)}{5(x+1)} = \dfrac{x^3}{5}$

4. $\dfrac{x^2 + 11x + 18}{x^2 + x - 2} = \dfrac{(x+2)(x+9)}{(x+2)(x-1)} = \dfrac{x+9}{x-1}$

5. $\dfrac{x^2 + 10x + 25}{x^2 + 5x} = \dfrac{(x+5)(x+5)}{x(x+5)} = \dfrac{x+5}{x}$

6. $\dfrac{x+5}{x^2 - 25} = \dfrac{x+5}{(x-5)(x+5)} = \dfrac{1}{x-5}$

7. a. $\dfrac{x+4}{4+x} = \dfrac{x+4}{x+4} = 1$

    b. $\dfrac{x-4}{4-x} = \dfrac{x-4}{(-1)(x-4)} = \dfrac{1}{-1} = -1$

Mental Math 12.1

1. $x = 0$

2. $x = 3$

3. $x = 0,\ x = 1$

4. $x = 5,\ x = 6$

Exercise Set 12.1

1. $\dfrac{x+5}{x+2} = \dfrac{2+5}{2+2} = \dfrac{7}{4}$

3. $\dfrac{y^3}{y^2-1} = \dfrac{(-2)^3}{(-2)^2-1} = \dfrac{-8}{4-1} = \dfrac{-8}{3} = -\dfrac{8}{3}$

5. $\dfrac{x^2+8x+2}{x^2-x-6} = \dfrac{2^2+8(2)+2}{2^2-2-6}$

$= \dfrac{4+16+2}{4-8}$

$= \dfrac{22}{-4}$

$= \dfrac{11\cdot 2}{-2\cdot 2}$

$= -\dfrac{11}{2}$

7. a. $\dfrac{150x^2}{x^2+3} = \dfrac{150(1)^2}{1^2+3} = \dfrac{150}{4} = 37.5$

The revenue is approximately \$37.5 million at the end of the first year.

b. $\dfrac{150x^2}{x^2+3} = \dfrac{150(2)^2}{2^2+3} = \dfrac{150(4)}{4+3} = \dfrac{600}{7}$

$= 85.7$

The revenue is approximately \$85.7 million at the end of the second year.

c. $\$85.7 - \$37.5 = \$48.2$ million

9. $2x = 0$

$x = 0$

The expression is undefined when $x = 0$.

11. $x + 2 = 0$

$x = -2$

The expression is undefined when $x = -2$.

13. $2x - 8 = 0$

$2x = 8$

$x = 4$

The expression is undefined when $x = 4$.

15. $15x + 30 = 0$

$15x = -30$

$x = -2$

The expression is undefined when $x = -2$.

17. The denominator is never zero so there are no values for which

$\dfrac{x^2-5x-2}{4}$ is undefined.

19. Answers may vary.

21. $\dfrac{2}{8x+16} = \dfrac{2}{8(x+2)} = \dfrac{2}{2\cdot 4(x+2)} = \dfrac{1}{4(x+2)}$

23. $\dfrac{x-2}{x^2-4} = \dfrac{x-2}{(x+2)(x-2)} = \dfrac{1}{x+2}$

25. $\dfrac{2x-10}{3x-30} = \dfrac{2(x-5)}{3(x-10)}$; does not simplify

27. $\dfrac{x+7}{7+x} = \dfrac{x+7}{x+7} = 1$

29. $\dfrac{x-7}{7-x} = \dfrac{x-7}{-1(x-7)} = \dfrac{1}{-1} = -1$

31. $\dfrac{-5a-5b}{a+b} = \dfrac{-5(a+b)}{a+b} = -5$

33. $\dfrac{x+5}{x^2-4x-45} = \dfrac{x+5}{(x-9)(x+5)} = \dfrac{1}{x-9}$

35. $\dfrac{5x^2+11x+2}{x+2} = \dfrac{(5x+1)(x+2)}{x+2} = 5x+1$

37. $\dfrac{x+7}{x^2+5x-14} = \dfrac{x+7}{(x-2)(x+7)} = \dfrac{1}{x-2}$

39. $\dfrac{2x^2+3x-2}{2x-1} = \dfrac{(2x-1)(x+2)}{2x-1} = x+2$

41. $\dfrac{x^2+7x+10}{x^2-3x-10} = \dfrac{(x+5)(x+2)}{(x-5)(x+2)} = \dfrac{x+5}{x-5}$

43. $\dfrac{3x^2+7x+2}{3x^2+13x+4} = \dfrac{(x+2)(3x+1)}{(x+4)(3x+1)} = \dfrac{x+2}{x+4}$

45. $\dfrac{2x^2-8}{4x-8} = \dfrac{2(x^2-4)}{4(x-2)}$

$= \dfrac{2(x+2)(x-2)}{2\cdot 2(x-2)}$

$= \dfrac{x+2}{2}$

47. $\dfrac{11x^2-22x^3}{6x-12x^2} = \dfrac{11x^2(1-2x)}{6x(1-2x)}$

$= \dfrac{11x\cdot x(1-2x)}{6\cdot x(1-2x)}$

$= \dfrac{11x}{6}$

49. $\dfrac{2-x}{x-2} = \dfrac{-1(x-2)}{x-2} = -1$

51. $\dfrac{x^2-1}{x^2-2x+1} = \dfrac{(x-1)(x+1)}{(x-1)(x-1)}$

$= \dfrac{x+1}{x-1}$

53. $\dfrac{m^2-6m+9}{m^2-9} = \dfrac{(m-3)(m-3)}{(m+3)(m-3)}$

$= \dfrac{m-3}{m+3}$

55. $\dfrac{1}{3}\cdot\dfrac{9}{11} = \dfrac{1\cdot 9}{3\cdot 11} = \dfrac{3\cdot 3}{3\cdot 11} = \dfrac{3}{11}$

57. $\dfrac{5}{6}\cdot\dfrac{10}{11}\cdot\dfrac{2}{3} = \dfrac{5\cdot 10\cdot 2}{6\cdot 11\cdot 3}$

$= \dfrac{5\cdot 2\cdot 5\cdot 2}{3\cdot 2\cdot 11\cdot 3}$

$= \dfrac{5\cdot 5\cdot 2}{3\cdot 11\cdot 3} = \dfrac{50}{99}$

59. $\dfrac{1}{3}\div\dfrac{1}{4} = \dfrac{1}{3}\cdot\dfrac{4}{1} = \dfrac{4}{3}$

61. $\dfrac{13}{20}\div\dfrac{2}{9} = \dfrac{13}{20}\cdot\dfrac{9}{2} = \dfrac{13\cdot 9}{20\cdot 2} = \dfrac{117}{40}$

63. $\dfrac{x^2 + xy + 2x + 2y}{x+2} = \dfrac{x(x+y) + 2(x+y)}{x+2}$

$$= \dfrac{(x+y)(x+2)}{x+2}$$

$$= x + y$$

65. $\dfrac{5x + 15 - xy - 3y}{2x+6} = \dfrac{5(x+3) - y(x+3)}{2(x+3)}$

$$= \dfrac{(x+3)(5-y)}{2(x+3)}$$

$$= \dfrac{5-y}{2}$$

67. Answers may vary.

69. $P = \dfrac{R-C}{R}$

$P = \dfrac{20.9 - 15.7}{20.9} = \dfrac{5.2}{20.9} \approx 0.249$

The company's gross profit margin was 24.9% in thye year 2003.

71. Let $h = 150$, $d = 30$, $t = 1$, $r = 31$, $b = 472$

$S = \dfrac{h + d + 2t + 3r}{b}$

$S = \dfrac{150 + 30 + 2(1) + 3(31)}{472}$

$= \dfrac{275}{472}$

$= 0.583$

The slugging percentage is 58.3%.

Practice Problems 12.2

1. a. $\dfrac{16y}{3} \cdot \dfrac{1}{x^2} = \dfrac{16y \cdot 1}{3 \cdot x^2} = \dfrac{16y}{3x^2}$

b. $\dfrac{-5a^3}{3b^3} \cdot \dfrac{2b^2}{15a} = \dfrac{-5a^3 \cdot 2b^2}{3b^3 \cdot 15a}$

$$= \dfrac{-1 \cdot 5 \cdot 2 \cdot a \cdot a^2 \cdot b^2}{3 \cdot 3 \cdot 5 \cdot a \cdot b \cdot b^2} = -\dfrac{2a^2}{9b}$$

2. $\dfrac{6x+6}{7} \cdot \dfrac{14}{x^2 - 1} = \dfrac{6(x+1)}{7} \cdot \dfrac{2 \cdot 7}{(x-1)(x+1)}$

$$= \dfrac{6(x+1) \cdot 2 \cdot 7}{7 \cdot (x-1)(x+1)} = \dfrac{12}{x-1}$$

3. $\dfrac{4x+8}{7x^2 - 14x} \cdot \dfrac{3x^2 - 5x - 2}{9x^2 - 1}$

$$= \dfrac{4(x+2)}{7x(x-2)} \cdot \dfrac{(3x+1)(x-2)}{(3x+1)(3x-1)}$$

$$= \dfrac{4(x+2)(3x+1)(x-2)}{7x(x-2)(3x+1)(3x-1)}$$

$$= \dfrac{4(x+2)}{7x(3x-1)}$$

4. $\dfrac{7x^2}{6} \div \dfrac{x}{2y} = \dfrac{7x^2}{6} \cdot \dfrac{2y}{x} = \dfrac{7x \cdot x \cdot 2y}{2 \cdot 3 \cdot x} = \dfrac{7xy}{3}$

5. $\dfrac{(2x+3)(x-4)}{6} \div \dfrac{3x - 12}{2}$

$$= \dfrac{(2x+3)(x-4)}{6} \cdot \dfrac{2}{3x - 12}$$

$$= \dfrac{(2x+3)(x-4)}{2 \cdot 3 \cdot 3(x-4)} = \dfrac{2x+3}{9}$$

6. $\dfrac{10x+4}{x^2-4} \div \dfrac{5x^3+2x^2}{x+2} = \dfrac{10x+4}{x^2-4} \cdot \dfrac{x+2}{5x^3+2x^2}$

$= \dfrac{2(5x+2)\cdot(x+2)}{(x-2)(x+2)\cdot x^2(5x+2)} = \dfrac{2}{x^2(x-2)}$

7. $\dfrac{3x^2-10x+8}{7x-14} \div \dfrac{9x-12}{21}$

$= \dfrac{3x^2-10x+8}{7x-14} \cdot \dfrac{21}{9x-12}$

$= \dfrac{(3x-4)(x-2)\cdot 3\cdot 7}{7(x-2)\cdot 3(3x-4)} = \dfrac{1}{1} = 1$

8. a. $\dfrac{x+3}{x} \cdot \dfrac{7}{x+3} = \dfrac{(x+3)\cdot 7}{x\cdot(x+3)} = \dfrac{7}{x}$

b. $\dfrac{x+3}{x} \div \dfrac{7}{x+3} = \dfrac{x+3}{x} \cdot \dfrac{x+3}{7}$

$= \dfrac{(x+3)\cdot(x+3)}{x\cdot 7} = \dfrac{(x+3)^2}{7x}$

c. $\dfrac{3-x}{x^2+6x+5} \cdot \dfrac{2x+10}{x^2-7x+12}$

$= \dfrac{-1(x-3)(2)(x+5)}{(x+1)(x+5)(x-3)(x-4)}$

$= -\dfrac{2}{(x+1)(x-4)}$

9. $21,444$ sq yd $= 21,444$ sq yd $\cdot \dfrac{9 \text{ sq ft}}{1 \text{ sq yd}}$

$= 192,996$ sq ft

10. 40.9 ft/sec

$= \dfrac{40.9 \text{ feet}}{1 \text{ second}} \cdot \dfrac{3600 \text{ seconds}}{1 \text{ hour}} \cdot \dfrac{1 \text{ mile}}{5280 \text{ feet}}$

≈ 27.9 miles/hour

Mental Math 12.2

1. $\dfrac{2}{y} \cdot \dfrac{x}{3} = \dfrac{2x}{3y}$

2. $\dfrac{3x}{4} \cdot \dfrac{1}{y} = \dfrac{3x}{4y}$

3. $\dfrac{5}{7} \cdot \dfrac{y^2}{x^2} = \dfrac{5y^2}{7x^2}$

4. $\dfrac{x^5}{11} \cdot \dfrac{4}{z^3} = \dfrac{4x^5}{11z^3}$

5. $\dfrac{9}{x} \cdot \dfrac{x}{5} = \dfrac{9x}{5x} = \dfrac{9}{5}$

6. $\dfrac{y}{7} \cdot \dfrac{3}{y} = \dfrac{3y}{7y} = \dfrac{3}{7}$

Exercise Set 12.2

1. $\dfrac{3x}{y^2} \cdot \dfrac{7y}{4x} = \dfrac{3x\cdot 7y}{y^2\cdot 4x} = \dfrac{3\cdot 7\cdot x\cdot y}{4\cdot x\cdot y\cdot y} = \dfrac{3\cdot 7}{4\cdot y} = \dfrac{21}{4y}$

3. $\dfrac{8x}{2} \cdot \dfrac{x^5}{4x^2} = \dfrac{8x\cdot x^5}{2\cdot 4x^2} = \dfrac{2\cdot 4\cdot x\cdot x\cdot x^4}{2\cdot 4\cdot x\cdot x} = x^4$

5. $-\dfrac{5a^2b}{30a^2b^2} \cdot b^3 = -\dfrac{5a^2b\cdot b^3}{30a^2b^2}$

$= -\dfrac{5\cdot a^2\cdot b\cdot b\cdot b^2}{5\cdot 6\cdot a^2\cdot b^2} = -\dfrac{b\cdot b}{6} = -\dfrac{b^2}{6}$

7. $\dfrac{x}{2x-14} \cdot \dfrac{x^2-7x}{5} = \dfrac{x\cdot(x^2-7x)}{(2x-14)\cdot 5}$

$= \dfrac{x\cdot x(x-7)}{2(x-7)\cdot 5} = \dfrac{x\cdot x}{2\cdot 5} = \dfrac{x^2}{10}$

9. $\dfrac{6x+6}{5}\cdot\dfrac{10}{36x+36}=\dfrac{(6x+6)\cdot10}{5\cdot(36x+36)}$

$=\dfrac{6(x+1)\cdot2\cdot5}{5\cdot36(x+1)}=\dfrac{6\cdot5\cdot2\cdot(x+1)}{6\cdot5\cdot2\cdot3\cdot(x+1)}$

$=\dfrac{1}{3}$

11. $\dfrac{m^2-n^2}{m+n}\cdot\dfrac{m}{m^2-mn}=\dfrac{(m^2-n^2)\cdot m}{(m+n)\cdot(m^2-mn)}$

$=\dfrac{(m-n)(m+n)\cdot m}{(m+n)\cdot m\cdot(m-n)}=1$

13. $\dfrac{x^2-25}{x^2-3x-10}\cdot\dfrac{x+2}{x}=\dfrac{(x^2-25)\cdot(x+2)}{(x^2-3x-10)\cdot x}$

$=\dfrac{(x-5)(x+5)\cdot(x+2)}{(x-5)(x+2)\cdot x}=\dfrac{x+5}{x}$

15. $A=\dfrac{2x}{x^2-25}\cdot\dfrac{x+5}{9x}=\dfrac{2x\cdot(x+5)}{(x^2-25)\cdot9x}$

$=\dfrac{2\cdot x\cdot(x+5)}{9\cdot x\cdot(x+5)(x-5)}=\dfrac{2}{9(x-5)}$

17. $\dfrac{5x^7}{2x^5}\div\dfrac{10x}{4x^3}=\dfrac{5x^7}{2x^5}\cdot\dfrac{4x^3}{10x}$

$=\dfrac{5\cdot x^2\cdot x^5\cdot2\cdot2x\cdot x^2}{2x^5\cdot2\cdot5\cdot x}$

$=x^4$

19. $\dfrac{8x^2}{y^3}\div\dfrac{4x^2y^3}{6}=\dfrac{8x^2}{y^3}\cdot\dfrac{6}{4x^2y^3}$

$=\dfrac{2\cdot4\cdot x^2\cdot6}{y^3\cdot4x^2y^3}$

$=\dfrac{12}{y^6}$

21. $\dfrac{(x-6)(x+4)}{4x}\div\dfrac{2x-12}{8x^2}$

$=\dfrac{(x-6)(x+4)}{4x}\cdot\dfrac{8x^2}{2x-12}$

$=\dfrac{(x-6)(x+4)\cdot2\cdot4\cdot x\cdot x}{4x\cdot2(x-6)}$

$=x(x+4)$

23. $\dfrac{3x^2}{x^2-1}\div\dfrac{x^5}{(x+1)^2}=\dfrac{3x^2}{x^2-1}\cdot\dfrac{(x+1)^2}{x^5}$

$=\dfrac{3x^2\cdot(x+1)(x+1)}{(x-1)(x+1)\cdot x^2\cdot x^3}$

$=\dfrac{3(x+1)}{x^3(x-1)}$

25. $\dfrac{m^2-n^2}{m+n}\div\dfrac{m}{m^2+nm}$

$=\dfrac{m^2-n^2}{m+n}\cdot\dfrac{m^2+nm}{m}$

$=\dfrac{(m-n)(m+n)\cdot m(m+n)}{(m+n)\cdot m}$

$=(m-n)(m+n)=m^2-n^2$

27. $\dfrac{x+2}{7-x} \div \dfrac{x^2-5x+6}{x^2-9x+14} = \dfrac{x+2}{7-x} \cdot \dfrac{x^2-9x+14}{x^2-5x+6}$

$= \dfrac{(x+2)\cdot(x-7)(x-2)}{-1(x-7)\cdot(x-3)(x-2)}$

$= -\dfrac{x+2}{x-3}$

29. $\dfrac{\dfrac{x^2+7x+10}{x-1}}{\div} \dfrac{x^2+2x-15}{x-1}$

$= \dfrac{x^2+7x+10}{x-1} \cdot \dfrac{x-1}{x^2+2x-15}$

$= \dfrac{(x+5)(x+2)\cdot(x-1)}{(x-1)\cdot(x+5)(x-3)} = \dfrac{x+2}{x-3}$

31. $\dfrac{5x-10}{12} \div \dfrac{4x-8}{8} = \dfrac{5x-10}{12} \cdot \dfrac{8}{4x-8}$

$= \dfrac{5(x-2)\cdot 2\cdot 4}{6\cdot 2\cdot 4(x-2)} = \dfrac{5}{6}$

33. $\dfrac{x^2+5x}{8} \cdot \dfrac{9}{3x+15} = \dfrac{x(x+5)\cdot 3\cdot 3}{8\cdot 3(x+5)} = \dfrac{3x}{8}$

35. $\dfrac{7}{6p^2+q} \div \dfrac{14}{18p^2+3q}$

$= \dfrac{7}{6p^2+q} \cdot \dfrac{18p^2+3q}{14}$

$= \dfrac{7\cdot 3\left(6p^2+q\right)}{\left(6p^2+q\right)\cdot 7\cdot 2} = \dfrac{3}{2}$

37. $\dfrac{3x+4y}{x^2+4xy+4y^2} \cdot \dfrac{x+2y}{2}$

$= \dfrac{(3x+4y)\cdot(x+2y)}{(x+2y)(x+2y)\cdot 2}$

$= \dfrac{3x+4y}{2(x+2y)}$

39. $\dfrac{(x+2)^2}{x-2} \div \dfrac{x^2-4}{2x-4} = \dfrac{(x+2)^2}{x-2} \cdot \dfrac{2x-4}{x^2-4}$

$= \dfrac{(x+2)(x+2)\cdot 2(x-2)}{(x-2)\cdot(x+2)(x-2)} = \dfrac{2(x+2)}{x-2}$

41. $\dfrac{3y}{3-x} \div \dfrac{12xy}{x^2-9} = \dfrac{3y}{3-x} \cdot \dfrac{x^2-9}{12xy}$

$= \dfrac{3y(x+3)(x-3)}{-(x-3)(12xy)}$

$= -\dfrac{x+3}{4x}$

43. $\dfrac{a^2+7a+12}{a^2+5a+6} \cdot \dfrac{a^2+8a+15}{a^2+5a+4}$

$= \dfrac{(a+3)(a+4)\cdot(a+5)(a+3)}{(a+3)(a+2)\cdot(a+4)(a+1)}$

$= \dfrac{(a+5)(a+3)}{(a+2)(a+1)}$

45. 1 square foot is 12 inches by 12 inches or 144 square inches.

$10 \text{ sq ft} \cdot \dfrac{144 \text{ sq in}}{1 \text{ sq ft}} = 1440 \text{ sq in.}$

47. $90,000 \text{ cu in} = 90,000 \text{ cu in}$

$\left(\dfrac{1 \text{ cu ft}}{1728 \text{ cu in}}\right)\left(\dfrac{1 \text{ cu yd}}{27 \text{ cu ft}}\right) = 1.93 \text{ cu yd}$

49. $\dfrac{50 \text{ miles}}{1 \text{ hour}} \cdot \dfrac{1 \text{ hour}}{3600 \text{ seconds}} = \dfrac{5280 \text{ feet}}{1 \text{ mile}}$

$= \dfrac{50 \cdot 5280}{3600} \text{ feet/sec} \approx 73 \text{ feet/sec}$

51. $3,705,793$ sq ft

$= 3,705,793 \text{ sq ft} \left(\dfrac{1 \text{ sq yd}}{9 \text{ sq ft}} \right)$

$\approx 411,755$ sq yd

53. $763\dfrac{\text{mi}}{\text{hr}} = 763\dfrac{\text{mi}}{\text{hr}} \left(\dfrac{1 \text{ hr}}{3600 \text{ sec}} \right) \left(\dfrac{5280 \text{ ft}}{\text{mi}} \right)$

$\approx 1119 \dfrac{\text{ft}}{\text{sec}}$

55. $\dfrac{1}{5} + \dfrac{4}{5} = \dfrac{5}{5} = 1$

57. $\dfrac{9}{9} - \dfrac{19}{9} = -\dfrac{10}{9}$

59. $\dfrac{6}{5} + \left(\dfrac{1}{5} - \dfrac{8}{5} \right) = \dfrac{6}{5} + \left(-\dfrac{7}{5} \right) = -\dfrac{1}{5}$

61. $\left(\dfrac{x^2 - y^2}{x^2 + y^2} \div \dfrac{x^2 - y^2}{3x} \right) \cdot \dfrac{x^2 + y^2}{6}$

$= \dfrac{x^2 - y^2}{x^2 + y^2} \cdot \dfrac{3x}{x^2 - y^2} \cdot \dfrac{x^2 + y^2}{6}$

$= \dfrac{(x^2 - y^2) \cdot 3x \cdot (x^2 + y^2)}{(x^2 + y^2) \cdot (x^2 - y^2) \cdot 2 \cdot 3} = \dfrac{x}{2}$

63. $\left(\dfrac{2a+b}{b^2} \cdot \dfrac{3a^2 - 2ab}{ab + 2b^2} \right) \div \dfrac{a^2 - 3ab + 2b^2}{5ab - 10b^2}$

$= \dfrac{2a+b}{b^2} \cdot \dfrac{3a^2 - 2ab}{ab + 2b^2} \cdot \dfrac{5ab - 10b^2}{a^2 - 3ab + 2b^2}$

$= \dfrac{(2a+b) \cdot (3a^2 - 2ab) \cdot (5ab - 10b^2)}{b^2 \cdot (ab + 2b^2) \cdot (a^2 - 3ab + 2b^2)}$

$= \dfrac{(2a+b) \cdot a(3a - 2b) \cdot 5b(a - 2b)}{b^2 \cdot b(a + 2b) \cdot (a - 2b)(a - b)}$

$= \dfrac{5a(2a+b)(3a - 2b)}{b^2 (a + 2b)(a - b)}$

65. Answers may vary.

67. $\$2000 = \dfrac{\$2000}{1} \cdot \dfrac{1 \text{ euro}}{\$1.09} = \dfrac{2000}{1.09}$ euros

$= 1834.86$ euros

Practice Problems 12.3

1. $\dfrac{8x}{3y} + \dfrac{x}{3y} = \dfrac{8x + x}{3y} = \dfrac{9x}{3y} = \dfrac{3x}{y}$

2. $\dfrac{3x}{3x - 7} - \dfrac{7}{3x - 7} = \dfrac{3x - 7}{3x - 7} = \dfrac{1}{1} = 1$

3. $\dfrac{2x^2 + 5x}{x + 2} - \dfrac{4x + 6}{x + 2} = \dfrac{2x^2 + 5x - (4x + 6)}{x + 2}$

$= \dfrac{2x^2 + 5x - 4x - 6}{x + 2} = \dfrac{2x^2 + x - 6}{x + 2}$

$= \dfrac{(2x - 3)(x + 2)}{x + 2} = 2x - 3$

4. a. $9 = 3 \cdot 3 = 3^2$ and $15 = 3 \cdot 5$

     LCD $= 3^2 \cdot 5 = 9 \cdot 5 = 45$

   b. $6x^3 = 2 \cdot 3 \cdot x^3$ and $8x^5 = 2^3 \cdot x^5$

     LCD $= 2^3 \cdot 3 \cdot x^5 = 8 \cdot 3 \cdot x^5 = 24x^5$

5. Since $a + 5$ and $a - 5$ are completely factored and each factor appears once, the LCD $= (a + 5)(a - 5)$.

6. $(x - 4)^2 = (x - 4)^2$

     $3x - 12 = 3(x - 4)$

       LCD $= 3(x - 4)^2$

7. $y^2 + 2y - 3 = (y + 3)(y - 1)$

     $y^2 - 3y + 2 = (y - 2)(y - 1)$

       LCD $= (y + 3)(y - 1)(y - 2)$

8. Since $x - 4$ and $4 - x$ are opposites, LCD $= x - 4$ or LCD $= 4 - x$.

9. $\dfrac{2x}{5y} = \dfrac{2x(4x^2 y)}{5y(4x^2 y)} = \dfrac{8x^3 y}{20x^2 y^2}$

10. $\dfrac{3}{x^2 - 25} = \dfrac{3}{(x + 5)(x - 5)}$

     $= \dfrac{3(x - 3)}{(x + 5)(x - 5)(x - 3)}$

     $= \dfrac{3x - 9}{(x + 5)(x - 5)(x - 3)}$

Mental Math 12.3

1. $\dfrac{2}{3} + \dfrac{1}{3} = \dfrac{3}{3} = 1$

2. $\dfrac{5}{11} + \dfrac{1}{11} = \dfrac{6}{11}$

3. $\dfrac{3x}{9} + \dfrac{4x}{9} = \dfrac{7x}{9}$

4. $\dfrac{3y}{8} + \dfrac{2y}{8} = \dfrac{5y}{8}$

5. $\dfrac{8}{9} - \dfrac{7}{9} = \dfrac{1}{9}$

6. $\dfrac{14}{12} - \dfrac{3}{12} = \dfrac{11}{12}$

7. $\dfrac{7y}{5} + \dfrac{10y}{5} = \dfrac{17y}{5}$

8. $\dfrac{12x}{7} - \dfrac{4x}{7} = \dfrac{8x}{7}$

Exercise Set 12.3

1. $\dfrac{a}{13} + \dfrac{9}{13} = \dfrac{a + 9}{13}$

3. $\dfrac{4m}{3n} + \dfrac{5m}{3n} = \dfrac{4m + 5m}{3n} = \dfrac{9m}{3n} = \dfrac{3m}{n}$

5. $\dfrac{4m}{m - 6} - \dfrac{24}{m - 6} = \dfrac{4m - 24}{m - 6} = \dfrac{4(m - 6)}{m - 6} = 4$

7. $\dfrac{9}{3 + y} + \dfrac{y + 1}{3 + y} = \dfrac{9 + y + 1}{3 + y} = \dfrac{y + 10}{3 + y}$

9. $\dfrac{5x+4}{x-1}-\dfrac{2x+7}{x-1}=\dfrac{5x+4-(2x+7)}{x-1}$

$=\dfrac{5x+4-2x-7}{x-1}=\dfrac{3x-3}{x-1}=\dfrac{3(x-1)}{x-1}=3$

11. $\dfrac{a}{a^2+2a-15}-\dfrac{3}{a^2+2x-15}=\dfrac{a-3}{a^2+2a-15}$

$=\dfrac{a-3}{(a+5)(a-3)}=\dfrac{1}{a+5}$

13. $\dfrac{2x+3}{x^2-x-30}-\dfrac{x-2}{x^2-x-30}$

$=\dfrac{2x+3-(x-2)}{x^2-x-30}$

$=\dfrac{2x+3-x+2}{x^2-x-30}=\dfrac{x+5}{x^2-x-30}$

$=\dfrac{x+5}{(x-6)(x+5)}=\dfrac{1}{x-6}$

15. $P=\dfrac{5}{x-2}+\dfrac{5}{x-2}+\dfrac{5}{x-2}+\dfrac{5}{x-2}$

$=\dfrac{5+5+5+5}{x-2}=\dfrac{20}{x-2}$

The perimeter is $\dfrac{20}{x-2}$ meters.

17. Answers may vary.

19. $2x=2\cdot x$

$4x^3=2^2\cdot x^3$

$LCD=2^2\cdot x^3=4x^3$

21. $8x=2\ \cdot x$

$2x+4=2(x+2)$

$LCD=2^3\cdot x\cdot(x+2)=8x(x+2)$

23. $x+3=x+3$

$x-2=x-2$

$LCD=(x+3)(x-2)$

25. $x+6=x+6$

$3x+18=3\cdot(x+6)$

$LCD=3(x+6)$

27. $3x+3=3\cdot(x+1)$

$2x^2+4x+2=2(x^2+2x+1)=2\cdot(x+1)^2$

$LCD=2\cdot3(x+1)^2$

$=6(x+1)^2$

29. $x-8=x-8$

$8-x=-(x-8)$

$LCD=x-8$ or $8-x$

31. $x^2+3x-4=(x+4)(x-1)$

$x^2+2x-3=(x+3)(x-1)$

$LCD=(x+4)(x+3)(x-1)$

33. Answers may vary

35. $\dfrac{3}{2x}=\dfrac{3(2x)}{2x(2x)}=\dfrac{6x}{4x^2}$

37. $\dfrac{6}{3a}=\dfrac{6(4b^2)}{3a(4b^2)}=\dfrac{24b^2}{12ab^2}$

39. $\dfrac{9}{x+3}=\dfrac{9(2)}{(x+3)(2)}=\dfrac{18}{2(x+3)}$

408

41. $\dfrac{9a+2}{5a+10} = \dfrac{9a+2}{5(a+2)}$

$\qquad = \dfrac{(9a+2)(b)}{5(a+2)(b)}$

$\qquad = \dfrac{9ab+2b}{5b(a+2)}$

43. $\dfrac{x}{x^3+6x^2+8x} = \dfrac{x}{x(x^2+6x+8)}$

$\qquad\qquad = \dfrac{x}{x(x+4)(x+2)(x+1)}$

$\qquad\qquad = \dfrac{x(x+1)}{x(x+4)(x+2)(x+1)}$

$\qquad\qquad = \dfrac{x^2+x}{x(x+4)(x+2)(x+1)}$

45. $\dfrac{9y-1}{15x^2-30} = \dfrac{(9y-1)(2)}{(15x^2-30)2} = \dfrac{18y-2}{30x^2-60}$

47. LCD = 21

$\dfrac{2}{3}+\dfrac{5}{7} = \dfrac{2(7)}{3(7)}+\dfrac{5(3)}{7(3)} = \dfrac{14}{21}+\dfrac{15}{21} = \dfrac{29}{21}$

49. Since $6=2\cdot 3$ and $4=2^2$,

LCD $= 2^2 \cdot 3 = 12$.

$\dfrac{2}{6}-\dfrac{3}{4} = \dfrac{2(2)}{6(2)}-\dfrac{3(3)}{4(3)} = \dfrac{4}{12}-\dfrac{9}{12} = \dfrac{4-9}{12}$

$\qquad = -\dfrac{5}{12}$

51. Since $12 = 2^2 \cdot 3$ and $20 = 2^2 \cdot 5$,

LCD $= 2^2 \cdot 3 \cdot 5 = 60$.

$\dfrac{1}{12}+\dfrac{3}{20} = \dfrac{1(5)}{12(5)}+\dfrac{3(3)}{20(3)} = \dfrac{5}{60}+\dfrac{9}{60} = \dfrac{14}{60}$

$\qquad = \dfrac{7(2)}{30(2)} = \dfrac{7}{30}$

53. Since $8=2^3$ and $12=2^2 \cdot 3$, the least common multiple of 8 and 12 is $2^2 \cdot 3 = 24$. Since $8 \cdot 3 = 24$ and $12 \cdot 2 = 24$, buy three packages of hot dogs and two packages of buns.

55. Answers may vary.

Practice Problems 12.4

1. a. LCD $= 5 \cdot 3 = 15$

$\dfrac{y}{5}-\dfrac{3y}{15} = \dfrac{y(3)}{5(3)}-\dfrac{3y}{15} = \dfrac{3y}{15}-\dfrac{3y}{15}$

$\qquad = \dfrac{3y-3y}{15} = \dfrac{0}{15} = 0$

b. $8x = 2^3 \cdot x$

$10x^2 = 2 \cdot 5 \cdot x^2$

LCD $= 2^3 \cdot \cdot x^2 = 8 \cdot 5 \cdot x^2 = 40x^2$

$\dfrac{5}{8x}+\dfrac{11}{10x^2} = \dfrac{5(5x)}{8x(5x)}+\dfrac{11(4)}{10x^2(4)}$

$\qquad = \dfrac{25x}{40x^2}+\dfrac{44}{40x^2} = \dfrac{25x+44}{40x^2}$

2. Since $x^2 - 9 = (x+3)(x-3)$, the

LCD $= (x+3)(x-3)$.

$\dfrac{10x}{x^2-9} - \dfrac{5}{x+3}$

$= \dfrac{10x}{(x+3)(x-3)} - \dfrac{5(x-3)}{(x+3)(x-3)}$

$= \dfrac{10x - 5(x-3)}{(x+3)(x-3)} = \dfrac{10x - 5x + 15}{(x+3)(x-3)}$

$= \dfrac{5x + 15}{(x+3)(x-3)} = \dfrac{5(x+3)}{(x+3)(x-3)}$

$= \dfrac{5}{x-3}$

3. $\dfrac{5}{7x} + \dfrac{2}{x+1} = \dfrac{5(x+1)}{7x(x+1)} + \dfrac{2(7x)}{7x(x+1)}$

$= \dfrac{5(x+1) + 2(7x)}{7x(x+1)} = \dfrac{5x + 5 + 14x}{7x(x+1)}$

$= \dfrac{19x + 5}{7x(x+1)}$

4. $\dfrac{10}{x-6} - \dfrac{15}{6-x} = \dfrac{10}{x-6} - \dfrac{15}{-(x-6)}$

$= \dfrac{10}{x-6} - \dfrac{-15}{x-6} = \dfrac{10 - (-15)}{x-6} = \dfrac{25}{x-6}$

5. $2 + \dfrac{x}{x+5} = \dfrac{2}{1} + \dfrac{x}{x+5} = \dfrac{2(x+5)}{1(x+5)} + \dfrac{x}{x+5}$

$= \dfrac{2x + 10 + x}{x+5} = \dfrac{3x + 10}{x+5}$

6. $\dfrac{4}{3x^2+2x} - \dfrac{3x}{12x+8} = \dfrac{4}{x(3x+2)} - \dfrac{3x}{4(3x+2)}$

$= \dfrac{4(4)}{x(3x+2)(4)} - \dfrac{3x(x)}{4(3x+2)(x)} = \dfrac{16 - 3x^2}{4x(3x+2)}$

7. $\dfrac{6x}{x^2+4x+4} + \dfrac{x}{x^2-4}$

$= \dfrac{6x}{(x+2)^2} + \dfrac{x}{(x+2)(x-2)}$

$= \dfrac{6x(x-2)}{(x+2)^2(x-2)} + \dfrac{x(x+2)}{(x+2)(x-2)(x+2)}$

$= \dfrac{6x^2 - 12x + x^2 + 2x}{(x+2)^2(x-2)}$

$= \dfrac{7x^2 - 10x}{(x+2)^2(x-2)} = \dfrac{x(7x-10)}{(x+2)^2(x-2)}$

Exercise Set 12.4

1. LCD $= 2\cdot3\cdot x = 6x$

$\dfrac{4}{2x} + \dfrac{9}{3x} = \dfrac{4(3)}{2x(3)} + \dfrac{9(2)}{3x(2)} = \dfrac{12}{6x} + \dfrac{18}{6x}$

$= \dfrac{30}{6x} = \dfrac{5(6)}{6x} = \dfrac{5}{x}$

3. LCD $= 5b$

$\dfrac{15a}{b} + \dfrac{6b}{5} = \dfrac{15a(5)}{b(5)} + \dfrac{6b(b)}{5(b)} = \dfrac{75a}{5b} + \dfrac{6b^2}{5b}$

$= \dfrac{75a + 6b^2}{5b}$

5. LCD $= 2x^2$

$\dfrac{3}{x} + \dfrac{5}{2x^2} = \dfrac{3(2x)}{x(2x)} + \dfrac{5}{2x^2} = \dfrac{6x}{2x^2} + \dfrac{5}{2x^2}$

$= \dfrac{6x + 5}{2x^2}$

7. $2x+2=2(x+1)$

$\text{LCD} = 2(x+1)$

$$\frac{6}{x+1}+\frac{10}{2x+2}=\frac{6}{x+1}+\frac{10}{2(x+1)}$$

$$=\frac{6(2)}{(x+1)2}+\frac{10}{2(x+1)}=\frac{12}{2(x+1)}+\frac{10}{2(x+1)}$$

$$=\frac{12+10}{2(x+1)}=\frac{22}{2(x+1)}=\frac{2\cdot 11}{2(x+1)}=\frac{11}{x+1}$$

9. $x+2=x+2$

$x^2-4=(x-2)(x+2)$

$\text{LCD}=(x-2)(x+2)$

$$\frac{3}{x+2}-\frac{1}{x^2-4}=\frac{3}{x+2}-\frac{1}{(x-2)(x+2)}$$

$$=\frac{3(x-2)}{(x+2)(x-2)}-\frac{1}{(x-2)(x+2)}$$

$$=\frac{3x-6}{(x-2)(x+2)}-\frac{1}{(x-2)(x+2)}$$

$$=\frac{3x-6-1}{(x-2)(x+2)}=\frac{3x-7}{(x-2)(x+2)}$$

11. $\text{LCD}=4x(x-2)$

$$\frac{3}{4x}+\frac{8}{x-2}=\frac{3(x-2)}{4x(x-2)}+\frac{8(4x)}{(x-2)(4x)}$$

$$=\frac{3x-6}{4x(x-2)}+\frac{32x}{4x(x-2)}=\frac{3x-6+32x}{4x(x-2)}$$

$$=\frac{35x-6}{4x(x-2)}$$

13. $$\frac{6}{x-3}+\frac{8}{3-x}=\frac{6}{x-3}+\frac{8}{-(x-3)}$$

$$=\frac{6}{x-3}+\frac{-8}{x-3}=\frac{6+(-8)}{x-3}=-\frac{2}{x-3}$$

15. $$\frac{-8}{x^2-1}-\frac{7}{1-x^2}=\frac{8}{-(x^2-1)}-\frac{7}{1-x^2}$$

$$=\frac{8}{1-x^2}-\frac{7}{1-x^2}=\frac{8-7}{1-x^2}$$

$$=\frac{1}{1-x^2}\quad\text{or}\quad -\frac{1}{x^2-1}$$

17. $$\frac{5}{x}+2=\frac{5}{x}+\frac{2}{1}=\frac{5}{x}+\frac{2(x)}{1(x)}=\frac{5+2x}{x}$$

19. $$\frac{5}{x-2}+6=\frac{5}{x-2}+\frac{6}{1}=\frac{5}{x-2}+\frac{6(x-2)}{1(x-2)}$$

$$=\frac{5}{x-2}+\frac{6x-12}{x-2}=\frac{5+6x-12}{x-2}=\frac{6x-7}{x-2}$$

21. $$\frac{y+2}{y+3}-2=\frac{y+2}{y+3}-\frac{2}{1}=\frac{y+2}{y+3}-\frac{2(y+3)}{y+3}$$

$$=\frac{y+2}{y+3}-\frac{2y+6}{y+3}=\frac{y+2-(2y+6)}{y+3}$$

$$=\frac{y+2-2y-6}{y+3}=\frac{-y-4}{y+3}=\frac{-(y+4)}{y+3}$$

$$=-\frac{y+4}{y+3}$$

23. $$\frac{-x+2}{x}-\frac{x-6}{4x}=\frac{(-x+2)}{x(4)}-\frac{(x-6)}{4x}$$

$$=\frac{-4x+8-(x-6)}{4x}$$

$$=\frac{-4x+8-x+6}{4x}$$

$$=\frac{-5x+14}{4x}$$

25. $\dfrac{5x}{x+2} - \dfrac{3x-4}{x+2} = \dfrac{5x-(3x-4)}{x+2}$

$= \dfrac{5x-3x+4}{x+2} = \dfrac{2x+4}{x+2} = \dfrac{2(x+2)}{x+2} = 2$

27. $\dfrac{3x^4}{x} - \dfrac{4x^2}{x^2} = \dfrac{3x^4(x)}{x(x)} - \dfrac{4x^2}{x^2} = \dfrac{3x^5}{x^2} - \dfrac{4x^2}{x^2}$

$= \dfrac{3x^5 - 4x^2}{x^2} = \dfrac{x^2(3x^3 - 4)}{x^2} = 3x^3 - 4$

29. $\dfrac{1}{x+3} - \dfrac{1}{(x+3)^2} = \dfrac{1(x+3)}{(x+3)(x+3)} - \dfrac{1}{(x+3)^2}$

$= \dfrac{x+3}{(x+3)^2} - \dfrac{1}{(x+3)^2} = \dfrac{x+3-1}{(x+3)^2} = \dfrac{x+2}{(x+3)^2}$

31. $\dfrac{4}{5b} + \dfrac{1}{b-1} = \dfrac{4(b-1)}{5b(b\text{-}1)} + \dfrac{1(5b)}{(b-1)(5b)}$

$= \dfrac{4b-4}{5b(b\text{-}1)} + \dfrac{5b}{5b(b\text{-}1)} = \dfrac{4b-4+5b}{5b(b\text{-}1)}$

$= \dfrac{9b-4}{5b(b\text{-}1)}$

33. $\dfrac{2}{m} + 1 = \dfrac{2}{m} + \dfrac{1}{1} = \dfrac{2}{m} + \dfrac{1(m)}{1(m)} = \dfrac{2+m}{m}$

35. $\dfrac{6}{1-2x} - \dfrac{4}{2x-1} = \dfrac{6}{1-2x} - \dfrac{4}{-(1-2x)}$

$= \dfrac{6}{1-2x} - \dfrac{-4}{1-2x} = \dfrac{6-(-4)}{1-2x} = \dfrac{10}{1-2x}$

37. $\dfrac{7}{(x+1)(x-1)} + \dfrac{8}{(x+1)^2}$

$= \dfrac{7(x+1)}{(x+1)(x-1)(x+1)} + \dfrac{8(x-1)}{(x+1)^2(x-1)}$

$= \dfrac{7x+7}{(x+1)^2(x-1)} + \dfrac{8x-8}{(x+1)^2(x-1)}$

$= \dfrac{7x+7+8x-8}{(x+1)^2(x-1)} = \dfrac{15x-1}{(x+1)^2(x-1)}$

39. $\dfrac{x}{x^2-1} - \dfrac{2}{x^2-2x+1}$

$= \dfrac{x}{(x-1)(x+1)} - \dfrac{2}{(x-1)^2}$

$= \dfrac{x(x-1)}{(x-1)(x+1)(x-1)} - \dfrac{2(x+1)}{(x-1)^2(x+1)}$

$= \dfrac{x^2-x}{(x-1)^2(x+1)} - \dfrac{2x+2}{(x-1)^2(x+1)}$

$= \dfrac{x^2-x-(2x+2)}{(x-1)^2(x+1)} = \dfrac{x^2-x-2x-2}{(x-1)^2(x+1)}$

$= \dfrac{x^2-3x-2}{(x-1)^2(x+1)}$

41. $\dfrac{3a}{2a+6} - \dfrac{a-1}{a+3} = \dfrac{3a}{2(a+3)} - \dfrac{a-1}{a+3}$

$= \dfrac{3a}{2(a+3)} - \dfrac{(a-1)(2)}{(a+3)(2)}$

$= \dfrac{3a}{2(a+3)} - \dfrac{2a-2}{2(a+3)}$

$= \dfrac{3a-(2a-2)}{2(a+3)} = \dfrac{3a-2a+2}{2(a+3)} = \dfrac{a+2}{2(a+3)}$

43.
$$\frac{y-1}{2y+3}+\frac{3}{(2y+3)^2}$$
$$=\frac{(y-1)(2y+3)}{(2y+3)(2y+3)}+\frac{3}{(2y+3)^2}$$
$$=\frac{2y^2+y-3+3}{(2y+3)^2}$$
$$=\frac{2y^2+y}{(2y+3)^2}$$
$$=\frac{y(2y+1)}{(2y+3)^2}$$

45.
$$\frac{5}{2-x}+\frac{x}{2x-4}=\frac{5}{-(x-2)}+\frac{x}{2(x-2)}$$
$$=\frac{-5}{x-2}+\frac{x}{2(x-2)}$$
$$=\frac{-5(2)}{(x-2)(2)}+\frac{x}{2(x-2)}$$
$$=\frac{-10}{2(x-2)}+\frac{x}{2(x-2)}=\frac{x-10}{2(x-2)}$$

47.
$$\frac{-7}{y^2-3y+2}-\frac{2}{y-1}=\frac{-7}{(y-1)(y-2)}-\frac{2}{y-1}$$
$$=\frac{-7}{(y-1)(y-2)}-\frac{2(y-2)}{(y-1)(y-2)}$$
$$=\frac{-7-(2y-4)}{(y-1)(y-2)}=\frac{-7-2y+4}{(y-1)(y-2)}$$
$$=\frac{-3-2y}{(y-2)(y-1)}$$

49.
$$\frac{13}{x^2-5x+6}-\frac{5}{x-3}=\frac{13}{(x-3)(x-2)}-\frac{5}{x-3}$$
$$=\frac{13}{(x-3)(x-2)}-\frac{5(x-2)}{(x-3)(x-2)}$$
$$=\frac{13-(5x-10)}{(x-3)(x-2)}=\frac{213-5x+10}{(x-3)(x-2)}$$
$$=\frac{-5x+23}{(x-3)(x-2)}$$

51.
$$\frac{x+8}{x^2-5x-6}+\frac{x+1}{x^2-4x-5}$$
$$=\frac{x+8}{(x-6)(x+1)}+\frac{x+1}{(x-5)(x+1)}$$
$$=\frac{(x+8)(x-5)}{(x-6)(x+1)(x-5)}$$
$$\quad+\frac{(x+1)(x-6)}{(x-5)(x+1)(x-6)}$$
$$=\frac{x^2+3x-40+x^2-5x-6}{(x-6)(x+1)(x-5)}$$
$$=\frac{2x^2-2x-46}{(x-6)(x+1)(x-5)}$$

53. Answers may vary.

55.
$$3x+5=7$$
$$3x+5-5=7-5$$
$$3x=2$$
$$\frac{3x}{3}=\frac{2}{3}$$
$$x=\frac{2}{3}$$

57. $2x^2-x-1=0$
$$(2x+1)(x-1)=0$$
$$2x+1=0 \quad \text{or} \quad x-1=0$$

$$2x = -1 \qquad\qquad x = 1$$

$$x = -\frac{1}{2}$$

The solutions are $x = -\dfrac{1}{2}$ and $x = 1$.

59. $4(x+6)+3 = -3$

$$4x + 24 + 3 = -3$$

$$4x + 27 = -3$$

$$4x + 27 - 27 = -3 - 27$$

$$4x = -30$$

$$\frac{4x}{4} = -\frac{30}{4}$$

$$x = -\frac{30}{4} = \frac{-15 \cdot 2}{2 \cdot 2}$$

$$= -\frac{15}{2}$$

61. $\dfrac{3}{x} - \dfrac{2x(x)}{(x^2-1)(x)} + \dfrac{5}{x+1}$

$$= \frac{3(x^2-1)}{x(x^2-1)} - \frac{2x^2}{x(x^2-1)} + \frac{5(x-1)x}{(x+1)(x-1)x}$$

$$= \frac{3x^2 - 3 - 2x^2 + 5x^2 - 5x}{x(x+1)(x-1)}$$

$$= \frac{6x^2 - 5x - 3}{x(x+1)(x-1)}$$

63. $\dfrac{5}{x^2-4} + \dfrac{2}{x^2-4x+4} - \dfrac{3}{x^2-x-6}$

$$= \frac{5}{(x-2)(x+2)} + \frac{2}{(x-2)^2}$$

$$- \frac{3}{(x-3)(x+2)}$$

$$= \frac{5(x-2)(x-3)}{(x-2)(x+2)(x-2)(x-3)}$$

$$+ \frac{2(x+2)(x-3)}{(x-2)^2(x+2)(x-3)}$$

$$- \frac{3(x-2)^2}{(x-3)(x+2)(x-2)^2}$$

$$= \frac{5(x^2-5x+6)}{(x-2)^2(x+2)(x-3)}$$

$$+ \frac{2(x^2-x-6)}{(x-2)^2(x+2)(x-3)}$$

$$- \frac{3(x^2-4x+4)}{(x-2)^2(x+2)(x-3)}$$

$$= \frac{5x^2 - 25x + 30}{(x-2)^2(x+2)(x-3)}$$

$$+ \frac{2x^2 - 2x - 12}{(x-2)^2(x+2)(x-3)}$$

$$- \frac{3x^2 - 12x + 12}{(x-2)^2(x+2)(x-3)}$$

$$= \frac{4x^2 - 15x + 6}{(x-2)^2(x+2)(x-3)}$$

65. $\dfrac{9}{x^2+9x+14}-\dfrac{3x}{x^2+10x+21}+\dfrac{x+4}{x^2+5x+6}$

$=\dfrac{9}{(x+7)(x+2)}-\dfrac{3x}{(x+7)(x+3)}$

$\qquad +\dfrac{x+4}{(x+2)(x+3)}$

$=\dfrac{9(x+3)-3x(x+2)+(x+4)(x+7)}{(x+7)(x+2)(x+3)}$

$=\dfrac{9x+27-3x^2-6x+x^2+11x+28}{(x+7)(x+2)(x+3)}$

$=\dfrac{-2x^2+14x+55}{(x+7)(x+2)(x+3)}$

67. $\dfrac{3}{x+4}-\dfrac{1}{x-4}$

$=\dfrac{3(x-4)}{(x+4)(x-4)}-\dfrac{1(x+4)}{(x+4)(x-4)}$

$=\dfrac{3x-12}{(x+4)(x-4)}-\dfrac{x+4}{(x+4)(x-4)}$

$=\dfrac{3x-12-(x+4)}{(x+4)(x-4)}=\dfrac{3x-12-x-4}{(x+4)(x-4)}$

$=\dfrac{2x-16}{(x+4)(x-4)}$

The length of the other board is

$\dfrac{2x-16}{(x+4)(x-4)}$ inches.

69. $1-\dfrac{G}{P}=\dfrac{1(P)}{P}-\dfrac{G}{P}=\dfrac{P-G}{P}$

71. Answers may vary.

Practice Problems 12.5

1. $\dfrac{x}{4}+\dfrac{4}{5}=\dfrac{1}{20}$

$20\left(\dfrac{x}{4}+\dfrac{4}{5}\right)=20\left(\dfrac{1}{20}\right)$

$20\left(\dfrac{x}{4}\right)+20\left(\dfrac{4}{5}\right)=20\left(\dfrac{1}{20}\right)$

$5x+16=1$

$5x=-15$

$x=-3$

Check:

$\dfrac{x}{4}+\dfrac{4}{5}=\dfrac{1}{20}$

$\dfrac{-3}{4}+\dfrac{4}{5}\overset{?}{=}\dfrac{1}{20}$

$\dfrac{-15}{20}+\dfrac{16}{20}\overset{?}{=}\dfrac{1}{20}$

$\dfrac{1}{20}=\dfrac{1}{20}$ True

The solution is -3.

2. $\dfrac{x+2}{3}-\dfrac{x-1}{5}=\dfrac{1}{15}$

$15\left(\dfrac{x+2}{3}-\dfrac{x-1}{5}\right)=15\left(\dfrac{1}{15}\right)$

$15\left(\dfrac{x+2}{3}\right)-15\left(\dfrac{x-1}{5}\right)=15\left(\dfrac{1}{15}\right)$

$5(x+2)-3(x-1)=1$

$5x+10-3x+3=1$

$2x+13=1$

$2x=-12$

$x=-6$

Check:

$$\frac{x+2}{3} - \frac{x-1}{5} = \frac{1}{15}$$

$$\frac{-3+2}{3} - \frac{-6-1}{5} \overset{?}{=} \frac{1}{15}$$

$$\frac{-4}{3} - \frac{-7}{5} \overset{?}{=} \frac{1}{15}$$

$$\frac{-20}{15} - \frac{-21}{15} \overset{?}{=} \frac{1}{15}$$

$$\frac{-20+21}{15} \overset{?}{=} \frac{1}{15}$$

$$\frac{1}{15} = \frac{1}{15} \quad \text{True}$$

The solution is -6.

3. $2 + \dfrac{6}{x} = x + 7$

$$x\left(2 + \frac{6}{x}\right) = x(x+7)$$

$$x(2) + x\left(\frac{6}{x}\right) = x^2 + 7x$$

$$2x + 6 = x^2 + 7x$$

$$0 = x^2 + 5x - 6$$

$$0 = (x+6)(x-1)$$

$$x + 6 = 0 \quad \text{or} \quad x - 1 = 0$$

$$x = -6 \qquad\qquad x = 1$$

Check:

$$x = -6 \qquad\text{or}\qquad x = 1$$

$$2 + \frac{6}{x} = x + 7 \qquad 2 + \frac{6}{x} = x + 7$$

$$2 + \frac{6}{-6} \overset{?}{=} -6 + 7 \qquad 2 + \frac{6}{1} \overset{?}{=} 1 + 7$$

$$1 + (-1) \overset{?}{=} 1 \qquad\qquad 2 + 6 \overset{?}{=} 8$$

$$1 = 1 \qquad\qquad\qquad 8 = 8 \quad \text{True}$$

Both -6 and 1 are solutions.

4. $\dfrac{2}{x+3} + \dfrac{3}{x-3} = \dfrac{-2}{x^2 - 9}$

$$(x+3)(x-3)\left(\frac{2}{x+3} + \frac{3}{x-3}\right)$$

$$= (x+3)(x-3)\left(\frac{-2}{x^2 - 9}\right)$$

$$(x+3)(x-3)\left(\frac{2}{x+3}\right)$$

$$\qquad + (x+3)(x-3)\left(\frac{3}{x-3}\right)$$

$$= (x+3)(x-3)\left(\frac{-2}{x^2 - 9}\right)$$

$$2(x-3) + 3(x+3) = -2$$

$$2x - 6 + 3x + 9 = -2$$

$$5x + 3 = -2$$

$$5x = -5$$

$$x = -1$$

Check:

$$\frac{2}{x+3} + \frac{3}{x-3} = \frac{-2}{x^2 - 9}$$

$$\frac{2}{-1+3} + \frac{3}{-1-3} \overset{?}{=} \frac{-2}{(-1)^2 - 9}$$

$$\frac{2}{2} + \frac{3}{-4} \overset{?}{=} \frac{-2}{1-9}$$

$$1 - \frac{3}{4} \overset{?}{=} \frac{-2}{-8}$$

$$\frac{1}{4} = \frac{1}{4} \quad \text{True}$$

The solution is -1.

5. $\dfrac{5x}{x-1} = \dfrac{5}{x-1} + 3$

$(x-1)\left(\dfrac{5x}{x-1}\right) = (x-1)\left(\dfrac{5}{x-1} + 3\right)$

$(x-1)\left(\dfrac{5x}{x-1}\right) = (x-1)\left(\dfrac{5}{x-1} + \right)$

$\phantom{(x-1)\left(\dfrac{5x}{x-1}\right) =} + (x-1)(3)$

$5x = 5 + 3x - 3$

$5x = 3x + 2$

$2x = 2$

$x = 1$

Notice that 1 makes the denominator 0 in the original equation. This equation has no solution.

6. $x - \dfrac{6}{x+3} = \dfrac{2x}{x+3} + 2$

$(x+3)\left(x - \dfrac{6}{x+3}\right) = (x+3)\left(\dfrac{2x}{x+3} + 2\right)$

$(x+3)(x) - (x+3)\left(\dfrac{6}{x+3}\right)$

$= (x+3)\left(\dfrac{2x}{x+3}\right) + (x+3)(2)$

$x^2 + 3x - 6 = 2x + 2x + 6$

$x^2 + 3x - 6 = 4x + 6$

$x^2 - x - 12 = 0$

$(x-4)(x+3) = 0$

$x - 4 = 0 \quad \text{or} \quad x + 3 = 0$

$ x = 4 \qquad\qquad x = -3$

Since -3 would make a denominator $0, -3$ cannot be a solution. The only solution is 4.

7. $\dfrac{1}{a} + \dfrac{1}{b} = \dfrac{1}{x}$

$abx\left(\dfrac{1}{a} + \dfrac{1}{b}\right) = abx\left(\dfrac{1}{x}\right)$

$abx\left(\dfrac{1}{a}\right) + abx\left(\dfrac{1}{b}\right) = abx\left(\dfrac{1}{x}\right)$

$bx + ax = ab$

$bx = ab - ax$

$bx = a(b - x)$

$\dfrac{bx}{b - x} = a$

Mental Math 12.5

1. $\dfrac{x}{5} = 2$

$x = 10$

2. $\dfrac{x}{8} = 4$

$x = 32$

3. $\dfrac{z}{6} = 6$

$z = 36$

4. $\dfrac{y}{7} = 8$

$y = 56$

Exercise Set 12.5

1. $\dfrac{x}{5} + 3 = 9$

$5\left(\dfrac{x}{5} + 3\right) = 5(9)$

$5\left(\dfrac{x}{5}\right) + 5(3) = 5(9)$

$x + 15 = 45$

$x = 30$

Check:

$\dfrac{x}{5} + 3 = 9$

$\dfrac{30}{5} + 3 \overset{?}{=} 9$

$6 + 3 \overset{?}{=} 9$

$9 = 9$ True

The solution is 30.

3. $\dfrac{x}{2} + \dfrac{5x}{4} = \dfrac{x}{12}$

$12\left(\dfrac{x}{2} + \dfrac{5x}{4}\right) = 12\left(\dfrac{x}{12}\right)$

$12\left(\dfrac{x}{2}\right) + 12\left(\dfrac{5x}{4}\right) = 12\left(\dfrac{x}{12}\right)$

$6x + 15x = x$

$21x = x$

$20x = 0$

$x = 0$

Check:

$\dfrac{x}{2} + \dfrac{5x}{4} = \dfrac{x}{12}$

$\dfrac{0}{2} + \dfrac{5 \cdot 0}{4} \overset{?}{=} \dfrac{0}{12}$

$0 + \dfrac{0}{4} \overset{?}{=} 0$

$0 = 0$ True

The solution is 0.

5. $2 - \dfrac{8}{x} = 6$

$x\left(2 - \dfrac{8}{x}\right) = x(6)$

$x(2) - x\left(\dfrac{8}{x}\right) = x(6)$

$2x - 8 = 6x$

$-8 = 4x$

$-2 = x$

Check:

$2 - \dfrac{8}{x} = 6$

$2 - \dfrac{8}{-2} \overset{?}{=} 6$

$2 - (-4) \overset{?}{=} 6$

$2 + 4 \overset{?}{=} 6$

$6 = 6$ True

The solution is -2.

7. $2 + \dfrac{10}{x} = x + 5$

$x\left(2 + \dfrac{10}{x}\right) = x(x + 5)$

$x(2) + x\left(\dfrac{10}{x}\right) = x(x + 5)$

$$2x+10=x^2+5x$$
$$0=x^2+3x-10$$
$$0=(x+5)(x-2)$$
$$x+5=0 \quad \text{or} \quad x-2=0$$
$$x=-5 \qquad\qquad x=2$$

Check:

$x=-5:$
$$2+\frac{10}{x}=x+5$$
$$2+\frac{10}{-5}\overset{?}{=}-5+5$$
$$2+(-2)\overset{?}{=}-5+5$$
$$0=0 \quad \text{True}$$

$x=2:$
$$2+\frac{10}{x}=x+5$$
$$2+\frac{10}{2}\overset{?}{=}2+5$$
$$2+5\overset{?}{=}2+5$$
$$7=7 \quad \text{True}$$

Both -5 and 2 are solutions.

9. $\dfrac{a}{5}=\dfrac{a-3}{2}$
$$10\left(\frac{a}{5}\right)=10\left(\frac{a-3}{2}\right)$$
$$2a=5(a-3)$$
$$2a=5a-15$$
$$-3a=-15$$
$$a=5$$

Check:
$$\frac{a}{5}=\frac{a-3}{2}$$
$$\frac{5}{5}\overset{?}{=}\frac{5-3}{2}$$
$$\frac{5}{5}\overset{?}{=}\frac{2}{2}$$
$$1=1 \quad \text{True}$$
The solution is 5.

11. $\dfrac{x-3}{5}+\dfrac{x-2}{2}=\dfrac{1}{2}$
$$10\left(\frac{x-3}{5}+\frac{x-2}{2}\right)=10\left(\frac{1}{2}\right)$$
$$10\left(\frac{x-3}{5}\right)+10\left(\frac{x-2}{2}\right)=10\left(\frac{1}{2}\right)$$
$$2(x-3)+5(x-2)=5$$
$$2x-6+5x-10=5$$
$$7x-16=5$$
$$7x=21$$
$$x=3$$

Check:
$$\frac{x-3}{5}+\frac{x-2}{2}=\frac{1}{2}$$
$$\frac{3-3}{5}+\frac{3-2}{2}\overset{?}{=}\frac{1}{2}$$
$$\frac{0}{5}+\frac{1}{2}\overset{?}{=}\frac{1}{2}$$
$$0+\frac{1}{2}\overset{?}{=}\frac{1}{2}$$
$$\frac{1}{2}=\frac{1}{2} \quad \text{True}$$
The solution is 3.

13. $\dfrac{2}{y} + \dfrac{1}{2} = \dfrac{5}{2y}$

$$2y\left(\dfrac{2}{y} + \dfrac{1}{2}\right) = 2y\left(\dfrac{5}{2y}\right)$$

$$2y\left(\dfrac{2}{y}\right) + 2y\left(\dfrac{1}{2}\right) = 2y\left(\dfrac{5}{2y}\right)$$

$$4 + y = 5$$

$$y = 1$$

Check:

$$\dfrac{2}{y} + \dfrac{1}{2} = \dfrac{5}{2y}$$

$$\dfrac{2}{1} + \dfrac{1}{2} \overset{?}{=} \dfrac{5}{2(1)}$$

$$\dfrac{4}{2} + \dfrac{1}{2} \overset{?}{=} \dfrac{5}{2}$$

$$\dfrac{5}{2} = \dfrac{5}{2} \quad \text{True}$$

The solution is 1.

15. $\dfrac{11}{2x} + \dfrac{2}{3} = \dfrac{7}{2x}$

$$6x\left(\dfrac{11}{2x} + \dfrac{2}{3}\right) = 6x\left(\dfrac{7}{2x}\right)$$

$$6x\left(\dfrac{11}{2x}\right) + 6x\left(\dfrac{2}{3}\right) = 6x\left(\dfrac{7}{2x}\right)$$

$$33 + 4x = 21$$

$$4x = -12$$

$$x = -3$$

Check:

$$\dfrac{11}{2x} + \dfrac{2}{3} = \dfrac{7}{2x}$$

$$\dfrac{11}{2(-3)} + \dfrac{2}{3} \overset{?}{=} \dfrac{7}{2(-3)}$$

$$\dfrac{11}{-6} + \dfrac{2}{3} \overset{?}{=} \dfrac{7}{-6}$$

$$\dfrac{-11}{6} + \dfrac{4}{6} \overset{?}{=} -\dfrac{7}{6}$$

$$\dfrac{-11+4}{6} \overset{?}{=} -\dfrac{7}{6}$$

$$-\dfrac{7}{6} = -\dfrac{7}{6} \quad \text{True}$$

The solution is -3.

17. $2 + \dfrac{3}{a-3} = \dfrac{a}{a-3}$

$$(a-3)\left(2 + \dfrac{3}{a-3}\right) = (a-3)\left(\dfrac{a}{a-3}\right)$$

$$(a-3)(2) + (a-3)\left(\dfrac{3}{a-3}\right)$$

$$= (a-3)\left(\dfrac{a}{a-3}\right)$$

$$2a - 6 + 3 = a$$

$$2a - 3 = a$$

$$-3 = -a$$

$$3 = a$$

In the original equation, 3 makes a denominator 0. This equation has no solution.

19. $\dfrac{3}{2a-5} = -1$

$(2a-5)\left(\dfrac{3}{2a-5}\right) = (2a-5)(-1)$

$3 = -2a + 5$

$-2 = -2a$

$1 = a$

Check:

$\dfrac{3}{2a-5} = -1$

$\dfrac{3}{2(1)-5} \overset{?}{=} -1$

$\dfrac{3}{2-5} \overset{?}{=} -1$

$\dfrac{3}{-3} \overset{?}{=} -1$

$-1 = -1$ True

The solution is 1.

21. $\dfrac{y}{y+4} + \dfrac{4}{y+4} = 3$

$(y+4)\left(\dfrac{y}{y+4} + \dfrac{4}{y+4}\right) = (y+4)(3)$

$(y+4)\left(\dfrac{y}{y+4}\right) + (y+4)\left(\dfrac{4}{y+4}\right)$

$\qquad\qquad\qquad = (y+4)(3)$

$y + 4 = 3y + 12$

$4 = 2y + 12$

$-8 = 2y$

$-\dfrac{8}{2} = y$

$-4 = y$

In the original equation, -4 makes a denominator 0. This equation has no solution.

23. $\dfrac{a}{a-6} = \dfrac{-2}{a-1}$

$(a-6)(a-1)\left(\dfrac{a}{a-6}\right)$

$\qquad\qquad = (a-6)(a-1)\left(\dfrac{-2}{a-1}\right)$

$a(a-1) = -2(a-6)$

$a^2 - a = -2a + 12$

$a^2 + a - 12 = 0$

$(a+4)(a-3) = 0$

$a + 4 = 0 \quad$ or $\quad a - 3 = 0$

$\qquad a = -4 \qquad\qquad a = 3$

Check:

$a = -4:$ $a = 3:$

$\dfrac{a}{a-6} = \dfrac{-2}{a-1}$ $\dfrac{a}{a-6} = \dfrac{-2}{a-1}$

$\dfrac{-4}{-4-6} \overset{?}{=} \dfrac{-2}{-4-1}$ $\dfrac{3}{3-6} \overset{?}{=} \dfrac{-2}{a-1}$

$\dfrac{-4}{-10} \overset{?}{=} \dfrac{-2}{-5}$ $\dfrac{3}{3-6} \overset{?}{=} \dfrac{-2}{3-1}$

$\dfrac{2}{5} = \dfrac{2}{5}$ True $\dfrac{3}{-3} \overset{?}{=} \dfrac{-2}{2}$

$\qquad\qquad\qquad\qquad -1 = -1$ True

The solutions are -4 and 3

25. $\dfrac{2x}{x+2} - 2 = \dfrac{x-8}{x-2}$

$(x+2)(x-2)\left(\dfrac{2x}{x+2}\right)$

$\qquad\qquad = (x+2)(x-2)\left(\dfrac{x-8}{x-2}\right)$

$(x+2)(x-2)\left(\dfrac{2x}{x+2}\right) - (x+2)(x-2)(2)$

$\qquad\qquad = (x+2)(x-2)\left(\dfrac{x-8}{x-2}\right)$

$2x(x-2)-2(x^2-4)=(x+2)(x-8)$

$2x^2-4x-2x^2+8=x^2-6x-16$

$-4x+8=x^2-6x-16$

$0=x^2-2x-24$

$0=(x-6)(x+4)$

$x-6=0 \quad$ or $\quad x+4=0$

$\qquad x=6 \qquad\qquad x=-4$

Check:

$x=6:$

$\dfrac{2x}{x+2}-2=\dfrac{x-8}{x-2}$

$\dfrac{2(6)}{6+2}-2\stackrel{?}{=}\dfrac{6-8}{6-2}$

$\dfrac{12}{8}-2\stackrel{?}{=}-\dfrac{2}{4}$

$\dfrac{3}{2}-\dfrac{4}{2}\stackrel{?}{=}-\dfrac{1}{2}$

$\dfrac{3-4}{2}\stackrel{?}{=}-\dfrac{1}{2}$

$-\dfrac{1}{2}=-\dfrac{1}{2} \quad$ True

$x=-4:$

$\dfrac{2x}{x+2}-2=\dfrac{x-8}{x-2}$

$\dfrac{2(-4)}{-4+2}-2\stackrel{?}{=}\dfrac{-4-8}{-4-2}$

$\dfrac{-8}{-2}-2\stackrel{?}{=}\dfrac{-12}{-6}$

$4-2\stackrel{?}{=}2$

$2=2 \quad$ True

The solutions are 6 and -4.

27. $\dfrac{4y}{y-4}+5=\dfrac{5y}{y-4}$

$(y-4)\left(\dfrac{4y}{y-4}+5\right)=(y-4)\left(\dfrac{5y}{y-4}\right)$

$(y-4)\left(\dfrac{4y}{y-4}\right)+(y-4)(5)=(y-4)\left(\dfrac{5y}{y-4}\right)$

$4y+5y-20=5y$

$9y-20=5y$

$4y-20=0$

$4y=20$

$y=5$

Check:

$\dfrac{4y}{y-4}+5=\dfrac{5y}{y-4}$

$\dfrac{4(5)}{5-4}+5\stackrel{?}{=}\dfrac{5(5)}{5-4}$

$\dfrac{20}{1}+5\stackrel{?}{=}\dfrac{25}{1}$

$25=25 \quad$ True

The solution is 5.

29. $\dfrac{2}{x-2}+1=\dfrac{x}{x+2}$

$(x-2)(x+2)\left(\dfrac{2}{x-2}+1\right)$

$=(x-2)(x+2)\left(\dfrac{x}{x+2}\right)$

$(x-2)(x+2)\left(\dfrac{2}{x-2}\right)+(x-2)(x+2)$

$=(x-2)(x+2)\left(\dfrac{x}{x+2}\right)$

$2(x+2)+(x-2)(x+2)=x(x-2)$

$2x+4+x^2-4=x^2-2x$

$2x+x^2=x^2-2x$

$2x=-2x$

$4x=0$

$x=0$

Check:

$$\frac{2}{x-2}+1=\frac{x}{x+2}$$

$$\frac{2}{0-2}+1\overset{?}{=}\frac{0}{0+2}$$

$$\frac{2}{-2}+1\overset{?}{=}0$$

$$-1+1\overset{?}{=}0$$

$$0=0 \quad \text{True} \qquad \text{The solution is 0.}$$

31. $\dfrac{t}{t-4}=\dfrac{t+4}{6}$

$$6(t-4)\left(\frac{t}{t-4}\right)=6(t-4)\left(\frac{t+4}{6}\right)$$

$$6t=t^2-6t-16$$

$$0=t^2-6t-16$$

$$0=(t-8)(t+2)$$

$$t-8=0 \quad \text{or} \quad t+2=0$$

$$t=8 \qquad\qquad t=-2$$

Check:

$t=8:$	$t=-2:$

$$\frac{t}{t-4}=\frac{t+4}{6} \qquad \frac{t}{t-4}=\frac{t+4}{6}$$

$$\frac{8}{8-4}\overset{?}{=}\frac{8+4}{6} \qquad \frac{-2}{-2-4}\overset{?}{=}\frac{-2+4}{6}$$

$$\frac{8}{4}\overset{?}{=}\frac{12}{6} \qquad\qquad \frac{-2}{-6}\overset{?}{=}\frac{2}{6}$$

$$2=2 \quad \text{True} \qquad \frac{1}{3}=\frac{1}{3} \quad \text{True}$$

The solutions are 8 and -2.

33. $\dfrac{x+1}{3}-\dfrac{x-1}{6}=\dfrac{1}{6}$

$$6\left(\frac{x+1}{3}-\frac{x-1}{6}\right)=6\left(\frac{1}{6}\right)$$

$$6\left(\frac{x+1}{3}\right)-6\left(\frac{x-1}{6}\right)=6\left(\frac{1}{6}\right)$$

$$2(x+1)-(x-1)=1$$

$$2x+2-x+1=1$$

$$x+3=1$$

$$x=-2$$

Check:

$$\frac{x+1}{3}-\frac{x-1}{6}=\frac{1}{6}$$

$$\frac{-2+1}{3}-\frac{-2-1}{6}\overset{?}{=}\frac{1}{6}$$

$$\frac{1}{3}-\frac{-3}{6}\overset{?}{=}\frac{1}{6}$$

$$\frac{2}{6}-\frac{-3}{6}\overset{?}{=}\frac{1}{6}$$

$$\frac{-2-(-3)}{6}\overset{?}{=}\frac{1}{6}$$

$$\frac{-2-(-3)}{6}\overset{?}{=}\frac{1}{6}$$

$$\frac{1}{6}=\frac{1}{6} \quad \text{True}$$

The solution is -2.

35. $\dfrac{y}{2y+2}+\dfrac{2y-16}{4y+4}=\dfrac{2y-3}{y+1}$

$$\frac{y}{2(y+1)}+\frac{2y-16}{4(y+1)}=\frac{2y-3}{y+1}$$

$$4(y+1)\left(\frac{y}{2(y+1)}+\frac{2y-16}{4(y+1)}\right)$$

$$=4(y+1)\left(\frac{2y-3}{y+1}\right)$$

$$4(y+1)\left(\frac{y}{2(y+1)}\right)+4(y+1)\left(\frac{2y-16}{4(y+1)}\right)$$

$$=4(y+1)\left(\frac{2y-3}{y+1}\right)$$

$$2y+2y-16=4(2y-3)$$

$$4y-16=8y-12$$

$$-4y=4$$

$$y=-1$$

In the original equation, -1 makes a

denominator 0.

This equation has no solution.

37. $\dfrac{4r-4}{r^2+5r-14}+\dfrac{2}{r+7}=\dfrac{1}{r-2}$

$$\frac{4r-4}{(r+7)(r-2)}+\frac{2}{r+7}=\frac{1}{r-2}$$

$$(r+7)(r-2)\left(\frac{4r-4}{(r+7)(r-2)}+\frac{2}{r+7}\right)$$

$$=(r+7)(r-2)\left(\frac{1}{r-2}\right)$$

$$(r+7)(r-2)\left(\frac{4r-4}{(r+7)(r-2)}\right)$$

$$+(r+7)(r-2)\left(\frac{2}{r+7}\right)$$

$$=(r+7)(r-2)\left(\frac{1}{r-2}\right)$$

$$4r-4+2(r-2)=(r+7)(1)$$

$$4r-4+2r-4=r+7$$

$$6r-8=r+7$$

$$5r=15$$

$$r=3$$

Check:

$$\frac{4r-4}{r^2+5r-14}+\frac{2}{r+7}=\frac{1}{r-2}$$

$$\frac{4(3)-4}{3^2+5(3)-14}+\frac{2}{3+7}\overset{?}{=}\frac{1}{3-2}$$

$$\frac{12-4}{9+15-14}+\frac{2}{10}\overset{?}{=}\frac{1}{1}$$

$$\frac{8}{10}+\frac{2}{10}\overset{?}{=}1$$

$$\frac{8+2}{10}\overset{?}{=}1$$

$$\frac{10}{10}\overset{?}{=}1$$

$$1=1 \quad \text{True}$$

The solution is 3.

39. $\dfrac{x+1}{x+3}=\dfrac{x^2-11x}{x^2+x-6}-\dfrac{x-3}{x-2}$

$$\frac{x+1}{x+3}=\frac{x^2-11x}{(x+3)(x-2)}-\frac{x-3}{x-2}$$

$$(x+3)(x-2)\left(\frac{x+1}{x+3}\right)$$

$$=(x+3)(x-2)\left(\frac{x^2-11x}{(x+3)(x-2)}-\frac{x-3}{x-2}\right)$$

$$(x+3)(x-2)\left(\frac{x+1}{x+3}\right)$$

$$=(x+3)(x-2)\left(\frac{x^2-11x}{(x+3)(x-2)}\right)$$

$$-(x+3)(x-2)\left(\frac{x-3}{x-2}\right)$$

$$(x-2)(x+1)=x^2-11x-(x+3)(x-3)$$

$$x^2-x-2=x^2-11x-(x^2-9)$$

$x^2 - x - 2 = x^2 - 11x - x^2 + 9$

$x^2 - x - 2 = -11x + 9$

$x^2 + 10x - 11 = 0$

$(x+11)(x-1) = 0$

$x + 11 = 0 \quad \text{or} \quad x - 1 = 0$

$ x = -11 \qquad\quad x = 1$

Check:

$x = -11:$

$\dfrac{x+1}{x+3} = \dfrac{x^2-11x}{x^2+x-6} - \dfrac{x-3}{x-2}$

$\dfrac{-11+1}{-11+3} \overset{?}{=} \dfrac{(-11)^2-11(11)}{(-11)^2+(-11)-6} - \dfrac{-11-3}{-11-2}$

$\dfrac{-10}{-8} \overset{?}{=} \dfrac{121+121}{121-17} - \dfrac{-14}{-13}$

$\dfrac{5}{4} \overset{?}{=} \dfrac{242}{104} - \dfrac{14}{13}$

$\dfrac{5}{4} \overset{?}{=} \dfrac{121}{52} - \dfrac{14}{13}$

$\dfrac{65}{52} \overset{?}{=} \dfrac{121}{52} - \dfrac{56}{52}$

$\dfrac{65}{52} \overset{?}{=} \dfrac{121-56}{52}$

$\dfrac{65}{52} = \dfrac{65}{52} \quad \text{True}$

$x = 1:$

$\dfrac{x+1}{x+3} = \dfrac{x^2-11x}{x^2+x-6} - \dfrac{x-3}{x-2}$

$\dfrac{1+1}{1+3} \overset{?}{=} \dfrac{(1)^2-11(1)}{(1)^2+1-6} - \dfrac{1-3}{1-2}$

$\dfrac{2}{4} \overset{?}{=} \dfrac{1-11}{1+1-6} - \dfrac{-2}{-1}$

$\dfrac{1}{2} \overset{?}{=} \dfrac{-10}{-4} - 2$

$\dfrac{1}{2} \overset{?}{=} \dfrac{5}{2} - \dfrac{4}{2}$

$\dfrac{1}{2} = \dfrac{1}{2} \quad \text{True}$

The solutions are -11 and 1.

41. $R = \dfrac{E}{I}$

$IR = I\left(\dfrac{E}{I}\right)$

$IR = E$

$\dfrac{IR}{R} = \dfrac{E}{R}$

$I = \dfrac{E}{R}$

43. $T = \dfrac{V}{Q}$

$Q(T) = Q\left(\dfrac{V}{Q}\right)$

$QT = V$

$\dfrac{QT}{T} = \dfrac{V}{T}$

$Q = \dfrac{V}{T}$

45. $i = \dfrac{A}{t+B}$

$(t+B)(i) = (t+B)\left(\dfrac{A}{t+B}\right)$

$ti + Bi = A$

$ti = A - Bi$

$\dfrac{ti}{i} = \dfrac{A-Bi}{i}$

$t = \dfrac{A-Bi}{i}$

47.

$$N = R + \frac{V}{G}$$

$$N - R = \frac{V}{G}$$

$$G(N-R) = G\left(\frac{V}{G}\right)$$

$$G(N-R) = V$$

$$\frac{G(N-R)}{N-R} = \frac{V}{N-R}$$

$$G = \frac{V}{N-R}$$

49.

$$\frac{C}{\pi r} = 2$$

$$\pi r\left(\frac{C}{\pi r}\right) = \pi r(2)$$

$$C = 2\pi r$$

$$\frac{C}{2\pi} = \frac{2\pi r}{2\pi}$$

$$\frac{C}{2\pi} = r$$

51.

$$\frac{1}{y} + \frac{1}{3} = \frac{1}{x}$$

$$3xy\left(\frac{1}{y}\right) + 3xy\left(\frac{1}{3}\right) = 3xy\left(\frac{1}{x}\right)$$

$$3x + xy = 3y$$

$$x(3+y) = 3y$$

$$\frac{x(3+y)}{3+y} = \frac{3y}{3+y}$$

$$x = \frac{3y}{y+3}$$

53. The reciprocal of x is $\dfrac{1}{x}$.

55. The reciprocal of x added to the reciprocal of 2 is $\dfrac{1}{x} + \dfrac{1}{2}$.

57. If a tank is filled in 3 hours, the part of the tank filled in 1 hour is $\dfrac{1}{3}$.

59.

$$\frac{20x}{3} + \frac{32x}{6} = 180$$

$$6\left(\frac{180}{3} + \frac{32x}{6}\right) = 6(180)$$

$$6\left(\frac{20x}{3}\right) + 6\left(\frac{32x}{6}\right) = 6(180)$$

$$40x + 32x = 1080$$

$$72x = 1080$$

$$\frac{72x}{72} = \frac{1080}{72}$$

$$x = 15$$

$$\frac{20x}{3} = \frac{20(15)}{3} = 100$$

$$\frac{32x}{6} = \frac{32(15)}{6} = 80$$

The angles are $100°$ and $80°$.

61.

$$\frac{150}{x} + \frac{450}{x} = 90$$

$$x\left(\frac{150}{x} + \frac{450}{x}\right) = x(90)$$

$$x\left(\frac{150}{x}\right) + x\left(\frac{450}{x}\right) = x(90)$$

$$150 + 450 = 90x$$

$$600 = 90x$$

$$\frac{600}{90} = x$$

$$\frac{20}{3} = x$$

$$\frac{150}{x} = \frac{150}{\frac{20}{3}} = 150\left(\frac{3}{20}\right) = \frac{45}{2} = 22.5$$

$$\frac{450}{x} = \frac{450}{\frac{20}{3}} = 450\left(\frac{3}{20}\right) = \frac{135}{2} = 67.5$$

The angles are 22.5° and 67.5°.

63. $\dfrac{4}{a^2 + 4a + 3} + \dfrac{2}{a^2 + a - 6} - \dfrac{3}{a^2 - a - 2} = 0$

$$\frac{4}{(a+3)(a+1)} + \frac{2}{(a+3)(a-2)}$$

$$- \frac{3}{(a-2)(a+1)} = 0$$

$$(a+3)(a+1)(a-2)\left(\begin{array}{c} \dfrac{4}{(a+3)(a+1)} \\[2mm] + \dfrac{2}{(a+3)(a-2)} \\[2mm] - \dfrac{3}{(a-2)(a+1)} \end{array}\right)$$

$$= (a+3)(a+1)(a-2)(0)$$

$$(a+3)(a+1)(a-2)\left(\frac{4}{(a+3)(a+1)}\right)$$

$$+ (a+3)(a+1)(a-2)\left(\frac{2}{(a+3)(a-2)}\right)$$

$$- (a+3)(a+1)(a-2)\left(\frac{3}{(a-2)(a+1)}\right)$$

$$= 0$$

$$4(a-2) + 2(a+1) - 3(a+3) = 0$$
$$4a - 8 + 2a + 2 - 3a - 9 = 0$$
$$3a - 15 = 0$$
$$3a = 15$$
$$a = 5$$

65. No, multiplying both terms in the expression by 4 changes the value of the original expression.

Integrated Review 12.5

1. expression

$$\frac{1}{x} + \frac{2}{3} = \frac{1(3)}{x(3)} + \frac{2(x)}{3(x)} = \frac{3}{3x} + \frac{2x}{3x} = \frac{3 + 2x}{3x}$$

2. expression

$$\frac{3}{a} + \frac{5}{6} = \frac{3(6)}{a(6)} + \frac{5(a)}{6(a)} = \frac{18}{6a} + \frac{5a}{6a} = \frac{18 + 5a}{6a}$$

3. equation

$$\frac{1}{x} + \frac{2}{3} = \frac{3}{x}$$

$$3x\left(\frac{1}{x} + \frac{2}{3}\right) = 3x\left(\frac{3}{x}\right)$$

$$3x\left(\frac{1}{x}\right) + 3x\left(\frac{2}{3}\right) = 3x\left(\frac{3}{x}\right)$$

$$3 + 2x = 9$$
$$2x = 6$$
$$x = 3$$

The solution is 3.

4. equation

$$\frac{3}{a} + \frac{5}{6} = 1$$

$$6a\left(\frac{3}{a} + \frac{5}{6}\right) = 6a(1)$$

$$6a\left(\frac{3}{a}\right) + 6a\left(\frac{5}{6}\right) = 6a$$

$$18 + 5a = 6a$$
$$18 = a$$

The solution is 18.

5. expression

$$\frac{2}{x+1} - \frac{1}{x} = \frac{2(x)}{(x+1)(x)} - \frac{1(x+1)}{x(x+1)}$$

$$= \frac{2x - (x+1)}{x(x+1)} = \frac{x-1}{x(x+1)}$$

6. expression

$$\frac{4}{x-3} - \frac{1}{x} = \frac{4(x)}{(x-3)(x)} - \frac{1(x-3)}{x(x-3)}$$

$$= \frac{4x - (x-3)}{x(x-3)} = \frac{4x - x + 3}{x(x-3)} = \frac{3x+3}{x(x-3)}$$

$$= \frac{3(x+1)}{x(x-3)}$$

7. equation

$$\frac{2}{x+1} - \frac{1}{x} = 1$$

$$x(x+1)\left(\frac{2}{x+1} - \frac{1}{x}\right) = x(x+1)(1)$$

$$x(x+1)\left(\frac{2}{x+1}\right) - x(x+1)\left(\frac{1}{x}\right) = x(x+1)$$

$$2x - (x+1) = x(x+1)$$

$$2x - x - 1 = x^2 + x$$

$$x - 1 = x^2 + x$$

$$-1 = x^2$$

There is no real number solution.

8. equation

$$\frac{4}{x-3} - \frac{1}{x} = \frac{6}{x(x-3)}$$

$$x(x-3)\left(\frac{4}{x-3} - \frac{1}{x}\right) = x(x-3)\left(\frac{6}{x(x-3)}\right)$$

$$x(x-3)\left(\frac{4}{x-3}\right) - x(x-3)\left(\frac{1}{x}\right) = 6$$

$$4x - (x-3) = 6$$

$$4x - x + 3 = 6$$

$$3x + 3 = 6$$

$$3x = 3$$

$$x = 1$$

The solution is 1.

9. expression

$$\frac{15x}{x+8} \cdot \frac{2x+16}{3x} = \frac{15x \cdot (2x+16)}{(x+8) \cdot 3x}$$

$$= \frac{3 \cdot 5 \cdot x \cdot 2 \cdot (x+8)}{(x+8) \cdot 3 \cdot x} = 5 \cdot 2 = 10$$

10. expression

$$\frac{9z+5}{15} \cdot \frac{5z}{81z^2 - 25} = \frac{(9z+5) \cdot 5z}{15 \cdot (81z^2 - 25)}$$

$$= \frac{(9z+5) \cdot 5 \cdot z}{5 \cdot 3 \cdot (9z+5)(9z-5)} = \frac{z}{3(9z-5)}$$

11. expression

$$\frac{2x+1}{x-3} + \frac{3x+6}{x-3} = \frac{2x+1+3x+6}{x-3}$$

$$= \frac{5x+7}{x-3}$$

12. expression

$$\frac{4p-3}{2p+7}+\frac{3p+8}{2p+7}=\frac{4p-3+3p+8}{2p+7}$$

$$=\frac{7p+5}{2p+7}$$

13. equation

$$\frac{x+5}{7}=\frac{8}{2}$$

$$14\left(\frac{x+5}{7}\right)=14\left(\frac{8}{2}\right)$$

$$2(x+5)=56$$

$$2x+10=56$$

$$2x=46$$

$$x=23$$

The solution is 23.

14. equation

$$\frac{1}{2}=\frac{x+1}{8}$$

$$8\left(\frac{1}{2}\right)=8\left(\frac{x+1}{8}\right)$$

$$4=x+1$$

$$3=x$$

The solution is 3.

15. expression

$$\frac{5a+10}{18}\div\frac{a^2-4}{10a}=\frac{5a+10}{18}\cdot\frac{10a}{a^2-4}$$

$$=\frac{5(a+2)\cdot2\cdot5\cdot a}{2\cdot9(a+2)(a-2)}$$

$$=\frac{5\cdot5\cdot a}{9(a-2)}=\frac{25a}{9(a-2)}$$

16. expression

$$\frac{9}{x^2-1}\div\frac{12}{3x+3}=\frac{9}{x^2-1}\cdot\frac{3x+3}{12}$$

$$=\frac{3\cdot3\cdot3(x+1)}{(x-1)(x+1)\cdot3\cdot4}=\frac{3\cdot3}{(x-1)\cdot4}=\frac{9}{4(x-1)}$$

17. expression

$$\frac{x+2}{3x-1}+\frac{5}{(3x-1)^2}$$

$$=\frac{(x+2)(3x-1)}{(3x-1)(3x-1)}+\frac{5}{(3x-1)^2}$$

$$=\frac{3x^2+5x-2+5}{(3x-1)^2}$$

$$=\frac{3x^2+5x+3}{(3x-1)^2}$$

18. expression

$$\frac{4}{(2x-5)^2}+\frac{x+1}{2x-5}$$

$$=\frac{4}{(2x-5)^2}+\frac{(x+1)(2x-5)}{(2x-5)(2x-5)}$$

$$=\frac{4+2x^2-3x-5}{(2x-5)^2}$$

$$=\frac{2x^2-3x-1}{(2x-5)^2}$$

19. expression

$$\frac{x-7}{x}-\frac{x+2}{5x}=\frac{(x-7)(5)}{x(5)}-\frac{x+2}{5x}$$

$$=\frac{5x-25-x-2}{5x}$$

$$=\frac{4x-37}{5x}$$

20. equation

$$\frac{9}{x^2-4}+\frac{2}{x+2}=\frac{-1}{x-2}$$

$$\left(x^2-4\right)\left(\frac{9}{x^2-4}\right)+\left(x^2-4\right)\left(\frac{2}{x+2}\right)$$

$$=\left(x^2-4\right)\left(\frac{-1}{x-2}\right)$$

$$9+(x-2)(2)=(x+2)(-1)$$
$$9+2x-4=-x-2$$
$$2x+5=-x-2$$
$$3x+5=-2$$
$$3x=-7$$
$$x=-\frac{7}{3}$$

The solution is $-\dfrac{7}{3}$.

21. equation

$$\frac{3}{x+3}=\frac{5}{x^2-9}-\frac{2}{x-3}$$

$$\left(x^2-9\right)\left(\frac{3}{x+3}\right)$$

$$=\left(x^2-9\right)\left(\frac{5}{x^2-9}\right)-\left(x^2-9\right)\left(\frac{2}{x-3}\right)$$

$$(x-3)(3)=5-(x+3)(2)$$
$$3x-9=5-2x-6$$
$$3x-9=-2x-1$$
$$5x-9=-1$$
$$5x=8$$
$$x=\frac{8}{5}$$

The solution is $\dfrac{8}{5}$.

22. expression

$$\frac{10x-9}{x}-\frac{x-4}{3x}=\frac{(10x-9)(3)}{x(3)}-\frac{x-4}{3x}$$

$$=\frac{30x-27-x+4}{3x}$$

$$=\frac{29x-23}{3x}$$

23. Answers may vary.

24. Answers may vary.

Practice Problems 12.6

1. Let x = the unknown number.

$$\frac{x}{2}-\frac{1}{3}=\frac{x}{6}$$

$$6\left(\frac{x}{2}-\frac{1}{3}\right)=6\left(\frac{x}{6}\right)$$

$$6\left(\frac{x}{2}\right)-6\left(\frac{1}{3}\right)=6\left(\frac{x}{6}\right)$$

$$3x-2=x$$
$$-2=-2x$$
$$x=1$$

The unknown number is 1.

2.

	Hours to Complete Total Job	Part of Job Completed in 1 Hour
Andrew	2	1/2
Timothy	3	1/3
Together	x	1/x

$$\frac{1}{2} + \frac{1}{3} = \frac{1}{x}$$

$$6x\left(\frac{1}{2}\right) + 6x\left(\frac{1}{3}\right) = 6x\left(\frac{1}{x}\right)$$

$$3x + 2x = 6$$

$$5x = 6$$

$$x = \frac{6}{5} \text{ or } 1\frac{1}{5}$$

Andrew and Timothy can recycle a

batch in $1\frac{1}{5}$ hour.

3. Let r = the motorcycle's speed

	Distance =	rate	time
car	280	$r + 10$	$280/r + 10$
motorcycle	240	r	$240/r$

$$\frac{280}{r + 10} = \frac{240}{r}$$

$$280r = 240(r + 10)$$

$$280r = 240r + 2400$$

$$40r = 2400$$

$$r = 60$$

$$r + 10 = 70$$

The speed of the car is 70 miles per hour
and the speed of the motorcycle is 60
miles per hour.

4. Since the triangles are similar, their
corresponding sides are in proportion.

$$\frac{x}{12} = \frac{15}{9}$$

$$9x = 180$$

$$x = 20$$

The side has length of 20 units.

Mental Math 12.6

1. c

2. a

Exercise Set 12.6

1. $3 \cdot \frac{1}{x} = 9 \cdot \frac{1}{6}$

$$\frac{3}{x} = \frac{9}{6}$$

$$6x\left(\frac{3}{x}\right) = 6x\left(\frac{9}{6}\right)$$

$$18 = 9x$$

$$x = 2$$

The unknown number is 2.

3. $\frac{3 + 2x}{x + 1} = \frac{3}{2}$

$$2(x + 1)\left(\frac{3 + 2x}{x + 1}\right) = 2(x + 1)\left(\frac{3}{2}\right)$$

$$2(3 + 2x) = 3(x + 1)$$

$$6 + 4x = 3x + 3$$

$$x = -3$$

The unknown number is -3.

5. $\frac{2}{x - 3} - \frac{4}{x + 3} = 8 \cdot \frac{1}{x^2 - 9}$

$$(x - 3)(x + 3)\left(\frac{2}{x - 3} - \frac{4}{x + 3}\right)$$

$$= (x - 3)(x + 3)\left(\frac{8}{x^2 - 9}\right)$$

$$(x - 3)(x + 3)\left(\frac{2}{x - 3}\right)$$

$$- (x - 3)(x + 3)\left(\frac{4}{x + 3}\right) = 8$$

$$2(x+3)-4(x-3)=8$$
$$2x+6-4x+12=8$$
$$-2x=-10$$
$$x=5$$

The unknown number is 5.

7. $\dfrac{1}{4}=\dfrac{x}{8}$

$$8\left(\dfrac{1}{4}\right)=8\left(\dfrac{x}{8}\right)$$
$$2=x$$

The unknown number is 2.

9.

	Hours to Complete Total Job	Part of Job Completed in 1 Hour
Experienced	4	1/4
Apprentice	5	1/5
Together	x	1/x

$$\dfrac{1}{4}+\dfrac{1}{5}=\dfrac{1}{x}$$
$$20x\left(\dfrac{1}{4}\right)+20x\left(\dfrac{1}{5}\right)=20x\left(\dfrac{1}{x}\right)$$
$$5x+4x=20$$
$$9x=20$$
$$x=\dfrac{20}{9}\text{ or }2\dfrac{2}{9}$$

The experienced surveyor and apprentice surveyor, working together, can survey the road in $2\dfrac{2}{9}$ hours.

11.

	Minutes to Complete Total Job	Part of Job Completed in 1 Minute
Larger belt	2	1/2
Smaller belt	6	1/6
Both belts	x	1/x

$$\dfrac{1}{2}+\dfrac{1}{6}=\dfrac{1}{x}$$
$$6x\left(\dfrac{1}{2}\right)+6x\left(\dfrac{1}{6}\right)=6x\left(\dfrac{1}{x}\right)$$
$$3x+x=6$$
$$4x=6$$
$$x=\dfrac{6}{4}=\dfrac{3}{2}=1\dfrac{1}{2}$$

Both belts together can move the cans to the storage area in $1\dfrac{1}{2}$ minute.

13.

	Hours to Complete Total Job	Part of Job Completed in 1 Hour
Marcus	6	1/6
Tony	4	1/4
Together	x	1/x

$$\dfrac{1}{6}+\dfrac{1}{4}=\dfrac{1}{x}$$
$$12x\left(\dfrac{1}{6}\right)+12x\left(\dfrac{1}{4}\right)=12x\left(\dfrac{1}{x}\right)$$
$$2x+3x=12$$
$$5x=12$$
$$x=\dfrac{12}{5}=2\dfrac{2}{5}$$
$$45\left(\dfrac{12}{5}\right)=108$$

Together Marcus and Tony work for $2\dfrac{2}{5}$ hours at \$45 per hour. The labor estimate should be \$108.00.

15.

	Hours to Complete Total Job	Part of Job Completed in 1 Hour
Custodian	3	$1/3$
2nd Worker	x	$1/x$
Together	$1\frac{1}{2}$ or $\frac{3}{2}$	$2/3$

$$\frac{1}{3} + \frac{1}{x} = \frac{2}{3}$$

$$3x\left(\frac{1}{3}\right) + 3x\left(\frac{1}{x}\right) = 3x\left(\frac{2}{3}\right)$$

$$x + 3 = 2x$$

$$3 = x$$

It takes the second worker 3 hours to do the job alone.

17.

	Hours to Complete Total Job	Part of Job Completed in 1 Hour
1st Pipe	20	$1/20$
2nd Pipe	15	$1/15$
3rd Pipe	x	$1/x$
3 Pipes Together	6	$1/6$

$$\frac{1}{20} + \frac{1}{15} + \frac{1}{x} = \frac{1}{6}$$

$$60x\left(\frac{1}{20}\right) + 60x\left(\frac{1}{15}\right) + 60x\left(\frac{1}{x}\right)$$
$$= 60x\left(\frac{1}{6}\right)$$

$$3x + 4x + 60 = 10x$$

$$7x + 60 = 10x$$

$$60 = 3x$$

$$20 = x$$

It takes the third pipe 20 hours to fill the pond.

19.

	Distance =	rate ·	time
Trip to Park	3	$3/x$	x
Return Trip	9	$9/x+1$	$x+1$

$$\frac{3}{x} = \frac{9}{x+1}$$

$$3(x+1) = 9x$$

$$3x + 3 = 9x$$

$$3 = 6x$$

$$\frac{1}{2} = x$$

The jogger spends $\frac{1}{2}$ hour on her trip to the park, so her rate is $\dfrac{3}{\frac{1}{2}} = \dfrac{3}{1} \cdot \dfrac{2}{1} = 6$ miles per hour.

21.

	Distance =	rate ·	time
1st portion	20	r	$20/r$
Cooldown portion	16	$r-2$	$16/r-2$

$$\frac{20}{r} = \frac{16}{r-2}$$

$$20(r-2) = 16r$$

$$20r - 40 = 16r$$

$$-40 = -4r$$

$$r = 10 \text{ and } r - 2 = 10 - 2 = 8$$

His speed was 10 miles per hour during the first portion and 8 miles per hour during the cooldown portion.

23.

	Distance =	rate ·	time
Upstream	9	$r-3$	$9/r-3$
Downstream	11	$r+3$	$11/r+3$

$$\frac{9}{r-3} = \frac{11}{r+3}$$

$$9(r+3) = 11(r-3)$$

$$9r + 27 = 11r - 33$$

$$60 = 2r$$

$$r = 30$$

The speed of the boat in still water is

30 miles per hour.

25. Let w = the rate of the wind.

	Distance =	rate ·	time
With the wind	48	$16+w$	$48/16+w$
Into the wind	16	$16-w$	$16/16-w$

$$\frac{48}{16+w} = \frac{16}{16-w}$$

$$48(16-w) = 16(16+w)$$

$$768 - 48w = 256 + 16w$$

$$512 = 64w$$

$$w = 8$$

The rate of the wind is 8 miles per hour.

27. Let r = the speed of the car in still air.

	Distance =	rate ·	time
Into the wind	10	$r-3$	$10/r-3$
With the wind	11	$r+3$	$11/r+3$

$$\frac{10}{r-3} = \frac{11}{r+3}$$

$$10(r+3) = 11(r-3)$$

$$10r + 30 = 11r - 33$$

$$63 = r$$

The speed of the car in still air is 63 miles per hour.

29. $\dfrac{12}{4} = \dfrac{18}{x}$

$$12x = 72$$

$$x = 6$$

31. $\dfrac{x}{3.75} = \dfrac{12}{9}$

$$9x = 45$$

$$x = 5$$

33. $\dfrac{16}{10} = \dfrac{34}{y}$

$$16y = 340$$

$$y = 21.25$$

35. $\dfrac{y}{30} = \dfrac{3}{5}$

$$y = \frac{90}{5}$$

$$y = 18 \text{ feet}$$

37. $\dfrac{x}{8} = \dfrac{20}{6}$

$$x = \frac{160}{6}$$

$$x = \frac{80}{3} = 26\frac{2}{3}$$

The side is $26\dfrac{2}{3}$ feet long.

39. $\dfrac{\frac{3}{4} + \frac{1}{4}}{\frac{3}{8} + \frac{13}{8}} = \dfrac{\frac{3+1}{4}}{\frac{3+13}{8}} = \dfrac{\frac{4}{4}}{\frac{16}{8}} = \dfrac{1}{2}$

41. $\dfrac{\frac{2}{5} + \frac{1}{5}}{\frac{7}{10} + \frac{7}{10}} = \dfrac{\frac{2+1}{5}}{\frac{7+7}{10}} = \dfrac{\frac{3}{5}}{\frac{14}{10}} = \dfrac{3}{5} \div \dfrac{14}{10} = \dfrac{3}{5} \cdot \dfrac{10}{14}$

$$= \frac{3 \cdot 2 \cdot 5}{5 \cdot 2 \cdot 7} = \frac{3}{7}$$

43.

	Distance =	rate ·	time
J	2.459	x	$2.459/x$
C	2.5	$x+3.6$	$2.5/x+3.6$

$$\frac{2.5}{x+3.6} = \frac{2.459}{x}$$

$$2.5x = 2.459x + 8.8524$$

$$0.041x = 8.8524$$

$$x \approx 215.9$$

$$x + 3.6 \approx 219.5$$

Junqueira's speed was 215.9 miles per hour. Castroneves' speed was 219.5 miles per hour.

45. It would take them less than 3 hours but more than $1\frac{1}{2}$ hours.

Practice Problems 12.7

1. $\dfrac{\frac{3}{7}}{\frac{5}{9}} = \dfrac{3}{7} \cdot \dfrac{9}{5} = \dfrac{27}{35}$

2. $\dfrac{\frac{3}{4} - \frac{2}{3}}{\frac{1}{2} + \frac{3}{8}} = \dfrac{\frac{3(3)}{4(3)} - \frac{2(4)}{3(4)}}{\frac{1(4)}{2(4)} + \frac{3}{8}} = \dfrac{\frac{9}{12} - \frac{8}{12}}{\frac{4}{8} + \frac{3}{8}} = \dfrac{\frac{1}{12}}{\frac{7}{8}}$

$= \dfrac{1}{12} \cdot \dfrac{8}{7} = \dfrac{1 \cdot 4 \cdot 2}{3 \cdot 4 \cdot 7} = \dfrac{2}{21}$

3. $\dfrac{\frac{2}{5} - \frac{1}{x}}{\frac{x}{10} - \frac{1}{3}} = \dfrac{\frac{2x}{5x} - \frac{5}{5x}}{\frac{3x}{30} - \frac{10}{30}} = \dfrac{\frac{2x-5}{5x}}{\frac{3x-10}{30}}$

$= \dfrac{2x-5}{5x} \cdot \dfrac{30}{3x-10} = \dfrac{5 \cdot 6(2x-5)}{5 \cdot x(3x-10)}$

$= \dfrac{6(2x-5)}{x(3x-10)}$

4. $\dfrac{\frac{3}{4} - \frac{2}{3}}{\frac{1}{2} + \frac{3}{8}} = \dfrac{24\left(\frac{3}{4} - \frac{2}{3}\right)}{24\left(\frac{1}{2} + \frac{3}{8}\right)} = \dfrac{24\left(\frac{3}{4}\right) - 24\left(\frac{2}{3}\right)}{24\left(\frac{1}{2}\right) + 24\left(\frac{3}{8}\right)}$

$= \dfrac{18-16}{12+9} = \dfrac{2}{21}$

5. $\dfrac{1 + \frac{x}{y}}{\frac{2x+1}{y}} = \dfrac{y\left(1 + \frac{x}{y}\right)}{y\left(\frac{2x+1}{y}\right)} = \dfrac{y(1) + y\left(\frac{x}{y}\right)}{y\left(\frac{2x+1}{y}\right)} = \dfrac{y+x}{2x+1}$

6. $\dfrac{\frac{5}{6y} + \frac{y}{x}}{\frac{y}{3} - x} = \dfrac{6xy\left(\frac{5}{6y} + \frac{y}{x}\right)}{6xy\left(\frac{y}{3} - x\right)} = \dfrac{6xy\left(\frac{5}{6y}\right) + 6xy\left(\frac{y}{x}\right)}{6xy\left(\frac{y}{3}\right) - 6xy(x)}$

$= \dfrac{5x + 6y^2}{2xy^2 - 6x^2 y} = \dfrac{5x + 6y^2}{2xy(y - 3x)}$

Exercise Set 12.7

1. $\dfrac{\frac{1}{2}}{\frac{3}{4}} = \dfrac{1}{2} \cdot \dfrac{4}{3} = \dfrac{1 \cdot 2 \cdot 2}{2 \cdot 3} = \dfrac{2}{3}$

3. $\dfrac{-\frac{4x}{9}}{-\frac{2x}{3}} = -\dfrac{4x}{9} \cdot -\dfrac{3}{2x} = \dfrac{2 \cdot 2 \cdot 3 \cdot x}{3 \cdot 3 \cdot 2 \cdot x} = \dfrac{2}{3}$

5. $\dfrac{\frac{-5}{12x^2}}{\frac{25}{16x^3}} = -\dfrac{5}{12x^2} \cdot \dfrac{16x^3}{25} = -\dfrac{5 \cdot 4 \cdot 4 \cdot x^2 \cdot x}{4 \cdot 3 \cdot x^2 \cdot 5 \cdot 5}$

$= -\dfrac{4x}{15}$

7. $\dfrac{\frac{1}{3}}{\frac{1}{2} - \frac{1}{4}} = \dfrac{12\left(\frac{1}{3}\right)}{12\left(\frac{1}{2} - \frac{1}{4}\right)} = \dfrac{12\left(\frac{1}{3}\right)}{12\left(\frac{1}{2}\right) - 12\left(\frac{1}{4}\right)}$

$= \dfrac{4}{6-3} = \dfrac{4}{3}$

9. $\dfrac{2+\frac{7}{10}}{1+\frac{3}{5}} = \dfrac{10\left(2+\frac{7}{10}\right)}{10\left(1+\frac{3}{5}\right)}$

$= \dfrac{10(2)+10\left(\frac{7}{10}\right)}{10(1)+10\left(\frac{3}{5}\right)} = \dfrac{20+7}{10+6} = \dfrac{27}{16}$

11. $\dfrac{\frac{m}{n}-1}{\frac{m}{n}+1} = \dfrac{n\left(\frac{m}{n}-1\right)}{n\left(\frac{m}{n}+1\right)} = \dfrac{n\left(\frac{m}{n}\right)-n(1)}{n\left(\frac{m}{n}\right)+n(1)} = \dfrac{m-n}{m+n}$

13. $\dfrac{\frac{1}{5}-\frac{1}{x}}{\frac{7}{10}+\frac{1}{x^2}} = \dfrac{10x^2\left(\frac{1}{5}-\frac{1}{x}\right)}{10x^2\left(\frac{7}{10}+\frac{1}{x^2}\right)}$

$= \dfrac{10x^2\left(\frac{1}{5}\right)-10x^2\left(\frac{1}{x}\right)}{10x^2\left(\frac{7}{10}\right)+10x^2\left(\frac{1}{x^2}\right)} = \dfrac{2x^2-10x}{7x^2+10}$

$= \dfrac{2x(x-5)}{7x^2+10}$

15. $\dfrac{1+\frac{1}{y-2}}{y+\frac{1}{y-2}} = \dfrac{(y-2)\left(1+\frac{1}{y-2}\right)}{(y-2)\left(y+\frac{1}{y-2}\right)}$

$= \dfrac{(y-2)(1)+(y-2)\left(\frac{1}{y-2}\right)}{(y-2)(y)+(y-2)\left(\frac{1}{y-2}\right)}$

$= \dfrac{y-2+1}{y^2-2y+1} = \dfrac{y-1}{(y-1)^2} = \dfrac{1}{y-1}$

17. $\dfrac{\frac{4y-8}{16}}{\frac{6y-12}{4}} = \dfrac{4y-8}{16}\cdot\dfrac{4}{6y-12} = \dfrac{4(y-2)\cdot4}{4\cdot4\cdot6(y-2)}$

$= \dfrac{1}{6}$

19. $\dfrac{\frac{x}{y}+1}{\frac{x}{y}-1} = \dfrac{y\left(\frac{x}{y}+1\right)}{n\left(\frac{x}{y}-1\right)} = \dfrac{y\left(\frac{x}{y}\right)+y(1)}{y\left(\frac{x}{y}\right)-y(1)} = \dfrac{x+y}{x-y}$

21. $\dfrac{1}{2+\frac{1}{3}} = \dfrac{3(1)}{3\left(2+\frac{1}{3}\right)} = \dfrac{3(1)}{3(2)+3\left(\frac{1}{3}\right)}$

$= \dfrac{3}{6+1} = \dfrac{3}{7}$

23. $\dfrac{\frac{ax+ab}{x^2-b^2}}{\frac{x+b}{x-b}} = \dfrac{ax+ab}{x^2-b^2}\cdot\dfrac{x-b}{x+b}$

$= \dfrac{a(x+b)\cdot(x-b)}{(x+b)(x-b)\cdot(x+b)} = \dfrac{a}{x+b}$

25. $\dfrac{\frac{8}{x+4}+2}{\frac{12}{x+4}-2} = \dfrac{(x+4)\left(\frac{8}{x+4}+2\right)}{(x+4)\left(\frac{12}{x+4}-2\right)}$

$= \dfrac{(x+4)\left(\frac{8}{x+4}\right)+(x+4)(2)}{(x+4)\left(\frac{12}{x+4}\right)-(x+4)(2)}$

$= \dfrac{8+2x+8}{12-2x-8} = \dfrac{16+2x}{4-2x} = \dfrac{2(8+x)}{2(2-x)}$

$= \dfrac{8+x}{2-x}$

27. $\dfrac{\frac{s}{r}+\frac{r}{s}}{\frac{s}{r}-\frac{r}{s}} = \dfrac{rs\left(\frac{s}{r}+\frac{r}{s}\right)}{rs\left(\frac{s}{r}-\frac{r}{s}\right)} = \dfrac{rs\left(\frac{s}{r}\right)+rs\left(\frac{r}{s}\right)}{rs\left(\frac{s}{r}\right)-rs\left(\frac{r}{s}\right)}$

$= \dfrac{s^2+r^2}{s^2-r^2}$

29. Answers may vary.

31. Steffi Graf

33. Monica Seles, Martina Hingis, Arantxa Sanchez-Vicario

35. $\dfrac{\frac{1}{3}+\frac{3}{4}}{2} = \dfrac{12\left(\frac{1}{3}+\frac{3}{4}\right)}{12(2)} = \dfrac{12\left(\frac{1}{3}\right)+12\left(\frac{3}{4}\right)}{12(2)}$

$= \dfrac{4+9}{24} = \dfrac{13}{24}$

37. $\dfrac{1}{\frac{1}{R_1} + \frac{1}{R_2}} = \dfrac{R_1 R_2 (1)}{R_1 R_2 \left(\frac{1}{R_1} + \frac{1}{R_2}\right)}$

$= \dfrac{R_1 R_2}{R_1 R_2 \left(\frac{1}{R_1}\right) + R_1 R_2 \left(\frac{1}{R_2}\right)} = \dfrac{R_1 R_2}{R_2 + R_1}$

39. $\dfrac{x^{-1} + 2^{-1}}{x^{-2} - 4^{-1}} = \dfrac{\frac{1}{x} + \frac{1}{2}}{\frac{1}{x^2} - \frac{1}{4}} = \dfrac{4x^2 \left(\frac{1}{x} + \frac{1}{2}\right)}{4x^2 \left(\frac{1}{x^2} - \frac{1}{4}\right)}$

$= \dfrac{4x^2 \left(\frac{1}{x}\right) + 4x^2 \left(\frac{1}{2}\right)}{4x^2 \left(\frac{1}{x^2}\right) - 4x^2 \left(\frac{1}{4}\right)} = \dfrac{4x + 2x^2}{4 - x^2}$

$= \dfrac{2x(2 + x)}{(2 - x)(2 + x)} = \dfrac{2x}{2 - x}$

41. $\dfrac{y^{-2}}{1 - y^{-2}} = \dfrac{\frac{1}{y^2}}{1 - \frac{1}{y^2}} = \dfrac{y^2 \left(\frac{1}{y^2}\right)}{y^2 \left(1 - \frac{1}{y^2}\right)}$

$= \dfrac{y^2 \left(\frac{1}{y^2}\right)}{y^2 (1) - y^2 \left(\frac{1}{y^2}\right)} = \dfrac{1}{y^2 - 1}$

Chapter 12 Review

1. The rational expression is undefined when

$x^2 - 4 = 0$

$(x - 2)(x + 2) = 0$

$x - 2 = 0$ or $x + 2 = 0$

$x = 2$ $x = -2$

2. The rational expression is undefined when

$4x^2 - 4x - 15 = 0$

$(2x + 3)(2x - 5) = 0$

$2x + 3 = 0$ or $2x - 5 = 0$

$2x = -3$ $2x = 5$

$x = -\dfrac{3}{2}$ $x = \dfrac{5}{2}$

3. $\dfrac{2 - z}{z + 5} = \dfrac{2 - (-2)}{-2 + 5} = \dfrac{2 + 2}{3} = \dfrac{4}{3}$

4. $\dfrac{x^2 + xy - y^2}{x + y} = \dfrac{5^2 + 5 \cdot 7 - 7^2}{5 + 7}$

$= \dfrac{25 + 35 - 49}{12} = \dfrac{11}{12}$

5. $\dfrac{2x + 6}{x^2 + 3x} = \dfrac{2(x + 3)}{x(x + 3)} = \dfrac{2}{x}$

6. $\dfrac{3x - 12}{x^2 - 4x} = \dfrac{3(x - 4)}{x(x - 4)} = \dfrac{3}{x}$

7. $\dfrac{x + 2}{x^2 - 3x - 10} = \dfrac{x + 2}{(x - 5)(x + 2)} = \dfrac{1}{x - 5}$

8. $\dfrac{x + 4}{x^2 + 5x + 4} = \dfrac{x + 4}{(x + 1)(x + 4)} = \dfrac{1}{x + 1}$

9. $\dfrac{x^3 - 4x}{x^2 + 3x + 2} = \dfrac{x(x^2 - 4)}{(x + 2)(x + 1)}$

$= \dfrac{x(x - 2)(x + 2)}{(x + 2)(x + 1)} = \dfrac{x(x - 2)}{x + 1}$

10. $\dfrac{5x^2 - 125}{x^2 + 2x - 15} = \dfrac{5(x^2 - 25)}{(x-3)(x+5)}$

$= \dfrac{5(x-5)(x+5)}{(x-3)(x+5)} = \dfrac{5(x-5)}{x-3}$

11. $\dfrac{x^2 - x - 6}{x^2 - 3x - 10} = \dfrac{(x-3)(x+2)}{(x-5)(x+2)} = \dfrac{x-3}{x-5}$

12. $\dfrac{x^2 - 2x}{x^2 + 2x - 8} = \dfrac{x(x-2)}{(x+4)(x-2)} = \dfrac{x}{x+4}$

13. $\dfrac{x^2 + xa + xb + ab}{x^2 - xc + bx - bc} = \dfrac{x(x+a) + b(x+a)}{x(x-c) + b(x-c)}$

$= \dfrac{(x+a)(x+b)}{(x-c)(x+b)} = \dfrac{x+a}{x-c}$

14. $\dfrac{x^2 + 5x - 2x - 10}{x^2 - 3x - 2x + 6} = \dfrac{x(x+5) - 2(x+5)}{x(x-3) - 2(x-3)}$

$= \dfrac{(x+5)(x-2)}{(x-3)(x-2)} = \dfrac{x+5}{x-3}$

15. $\dfrac{15x^3 y^2}{z} \cdot \dfrac{z}{5xy^3} = \dfrac{15x^3 y^2 \cdot z}{z \cdot 5xy^3}$

$= \dfrac{3 \cdot 5 \cdot x^2 \cdot x \cdot y^2 \cdot z}{z \cdot 5 \cdot x \cdot y^2 \cdot y} = \dfrac{3x^2}{y}$

16. $\dfrac{-y^3}{8} \cdot \dfrac{9x^2}{y^3} = \dfrac{y^3 \cdot 9x^2}{8 \cdot y^3} = -\dfrac{9x^2}{8}$

17. $\dfrac{x^2 - 9}{x^2 - 4} \cdot \dfrac{x-2}{x+3} = \dfrac{(x^2 - 9) \cdot (x-2)}{(x^2 - 4) \cdot (x+3)}$

$= \dfrac{(x-3)(x+3)(x-2)}{(x+2)(x-2)(x+3)} = \dfrac{x-3}{x+2}$

18. $\dfrac{2x+5}{x-6} \cdot \dfrac{2x}{-x+6} = \dfrac{2x+5}{x-6} \cdot \dfrac{2x}{-(x-6)}$

$= \dfrac{2x+5}{x-6} \cdot \dfrac{-2x}{x-6} = \dfrac{(2x+5) \cdot (-2x)}{(x-6) \cdot (x-6)}$

$= \dfrac{-2x(2x+5)}{(x-6)^2}$

19. $\dfrac{x^2 - 5x - 24}{x^2 - x - 12} \div \dfrac{x^2 - 10x + 16}{x^2 + x - 6}$

$= \dfrac{x^2 - 5x - 24}{x^2 - x - 12} \cdot \dfrac{x^2 + x - 6}{x^2 - 10x + 16}$

$= \dfrac{(x-8)(x+3) \cdot (x+3)(x-2)}{(x-4)(x+3) \cdot (x-8)(x-2)}$

$= \dfrac{x+3}{x-4}$

20. $\dfrac{4x + 4y}{xy^2} \div \dfrac{3x + 3y}{x^2 y} = \dfrac{4x + 4y}{xy^2} \cdot \dfrac{x^2 y}{3x + 3y}$

$= \dfrac{4(x+y) \cdot x \cdot x \cdot y}{x \cdot y \cdot y \cdot 3(x+y)} = \dfrac{4x}{3y}$

21. $\dfrac{x^2 + x - 42}{x-3} \cdot \dfrac{(x-3)^2}{x+7}$

$= \dfrac{(x+7)(x-6) \cdot (x-3)(x-3)}{(x-3) \cdot (x+7)}$

$= (x-6)(x-3)$

22. $\dfrac{2a + 2b}{3} \cdot \dfrac{a-b}{a^2 - b^2} = \dfrac{2(a+b) \cdot (a-b)}{3 \cdot (a+b)(a-b)} = \dfrac{2}{3}$

23. $\dfrac{x^2 - 9x + 14}{x^2 - 5x + 6} \cdot \dfrac{x+2}{x^2 - 5x - 14}$

$= \dfrac{(x-7)(x-2) \cdot (x+2)}{(x-3)(x-2) \cdot (x-7)(x+2)} = \dfrac{1}{x-3}$

24. $(x-3) \cdot \dfrac{x}{x^2 + 3x - 18}$

$= \dfrac{(x-3) \cdot x}{(x-3)(x+6)} = \dfrac{x}{x+6}$

25. $\dfrac{2x^2 - 9x + 9}{8x - 12} \div \dfrac{x^2 - 3x}{2x}$

$= \dfrac{2x^2 - 9x + 9}{9x - 12} \cdot \dfrac{2x}{x^2 - 3x}$

$= \dfrac{(2x-3)(x-3) \cdot 2x}{4(2x-3) \cdot x(x-3)}$

$= \dfrac{2}{4} = \dfrac{1}{2}$

26. $\dfrac{x^2 - y^2}{x^2 + xy} \div \dfrac{3x^2 - 2xy - y^2}{3x^2 + 6x}$

$= \dfrac{x^2 - y^2}{x^2 + xy} \cdot \dfrac{3x^2 + 6x}{3x^2 - 2xy - y^2}$

$= \dfrac{(x-y)(x+y) \cdot 3x(x+2)}{x(x+y) \cdot (3x+y)(x-y)}$

$= \dfrac{3(x+2)}{3x+y}$

27. $\dfrac{x}{x^2 + 9x + 14} + \dfrac{7}{x^2 + 9x + 14}$

$= \dfrac{x+7}{x^2 + 9x + 14} = \dfrac{x+7}{(x+2)(x+7)} = \dfrac{1}{x+2}$

28. $\dfrac{x}{x^2 + 2x - 15} + \dfrac{5}{x^2 + 2x - 15} = \dfrac{x+5}{x^2 + 2x - 15}$

$= \dfrac{x+5}{(x-3)(x+5)} = \dfrac{1}{x-3}$

29. $\dfrac{4x-5}{3x^2} - \dfrac{2x+5}{3x^2} = \dfrac{4x-5-(2x+5)}{3x^2}$

$= \dfrac{4x - 5 - 2x - 5}{3x^2} = \dfrac{2x - 10}{3x^2}$

30. $\dfrac{9x+7}{6x^2} - \dfrac{3x+4}{6x^2} = \dfrac{9x+7-(3x+4)}{6x^2}$

$= \dfrac{9x+7-3x-4}{6x^2} = \dfrac{6x+3}{6x^2} = \dfrac{3(2x+1)}{3 \cdot 2x^2}$

$= \dfrac{2x+1}{2x^2}$

31. $2x = 2 \cdot x$

$7x = 7 \cdot x$

$LCD = 2 \cdot 7 \cdot x = 14x$

32. $x^2 - 5x - 24 = (x-8)(x+3)$

$x^2 + 11x + 24 = (x+8)(x+3)$

$LCD = (x-8)(x+3)(x+8)$

33. $\dfrac{5}{7x} = \dfrac{5(2x^2 y)}{7x(2x^2 y)} = \dfrac{10x^2 y}{14x^3 y}$

34. $\dfrac{9}{4y} = \dfrac{9(4y^2 x)}{4y(4y^2 x)} = \dfrac{36y^2 x}{16y^3 x}$

35. $\dfrac{x+2}{x^2 + 11x + 18} = \dfrac{x+2}{(x+9)(x+2)}$

$= \dfrac{(x+2)(x-5)}{(x+9)(x+2)(x-5)}$

$= \dfrac{x^2 - 3x - 10}{(x+2)(x-5)(x+9)}$

36. $\dfrac{3x-5}{x^2+4x+4}=\dfrac{3x-5}{(x+2)^2}$

$=\dfrac{(3x-5)(x+3)}{(x+2)^2(x+3)}=\dfrac{3x^2+4x-15}{(x+2)^2(x+3)}$

37. $\dfrac{4}{5x^2}-\dfrac{6}{y}=\dfrac{4(y)}{5x^2(y)}-\dfrac{6(5x^2)}{y(5x^2)}=\dfrac{4y-30x^2}{5x^2y}$

38. $\dfrac{2}{x-3}-\dfrac{4}{x-1}$

$=\dfrac{2(x-1)}{(x-3)(x-1)}-\dfrac{4(x-3)}{(x-1)(x-3)}$

$=\dfrac{2(x-1)-4(x-3)}{(x-3)(x-1)}=\dfrac{2x-2-4x+12}{(x-3)(x-1)}$

$=\dfrac{-2x+10}{(x-3)(x-1)}$

39. $\dfrac{x+7}{x+3}-\dfrac{x-3}{x+7}$

$=\dfrac{(x+7)(x+7)}{(x+3)(x+7)}-\dfrac{(x-3)(x+3)}{(x+7)(x+3)}$

$=\dfrac{x^2+14x+49-(x^2-9)}{(x+3)(x+7)}$

$=\dfrac{x^2+14x+49-x^2+9}{(x+3)(x+7)}=\dfrac{14x+58}{(x+3)(x+7)}$

40. $\dfrac{4}{x+3}-2=\dfrac{4}{x+3}-\dfrac{2(x+3)}{x+3}$

$=\dfrac{4-2(x+3)}{x+3}=\dfrac{4-2x-6}{x+3}=\dfrac{-2x-2}{x+3}$

41. $\dfrac{3}{x^2+2x-8}+\dfrac{2}{x^2-3x+2}$

$=\dfrac{3}{(x+4)(x-2)}+\dfrac{2}{(x-1)(x-2)}$

$=\dfrac{3(x-1)}{(x+4)(x-2)(x-1)}$

$+\dfrac{2(x+4)}{(x-1)(x-2)(x+4)}$

$=\dfrac{3(x-1)+2(x+4)}{(x+4)(x-2)(x-1)}$

$=\dfrac{3x-3+2x+8}{(x+4)(x-2)(x-1)}$

$=\dfrac{5x+5}{(x+4)(x-2)(x-1)}$

42. $\dfrac{2x-5}{6x+9}-\dfrac{4}{2x^2+3x}$

$=\dfrac{2x-5}{3(2x+3)}-\dfrac{4}{x(2x+3)}$

$=\dfrac{(2x-5)(x)}{3(2x+3)(x)}-\dfrac{4(3)}{x(2x+3)(3)}$

$=\dfrac{2x^2-5x-12}{3x(2x+3)}=\dfrac{(2x+3)(x-4)}{3x(2x+3)}$

$=\dfrac{x-4}{3x}$

43. $\dfrac{x-1}{x^2-2x+1}-\dfrac{x+1}{x-1}=\dfrac{x-1}{(x-1)^2}-\dfrac{x+1}{x-1}$

$=\dfrac{1}{x-1}=\dfrac{x+1}{x-1}=\dfrac{1-(x+1)}{x-1}$

$=\dfrac{1-x-1}{x-1}=\dfrac{-x}{x-1}=-\dfrac{x}{x-1}$

44. $\dfrac{x-1}{x^2+4x+4}+\dfrac{x-1}{x+2}$

$=\dfrac{x-1}{(x+2)^2}+\dfrac{(x-1)(x+2)}{(x+2)(x+2)}$

$=\dfrac{x-1+(x-1)(x+2)}{(x+2)^2}$

$=\dfrac{x-1+x^2+x-2}{(x+2)^2}$

$=\dfrac{x^2+2x-3}{(x+2)^2}$

45. $P=2l+2w$

$P=2\left(\dfrac{2}{8}\right)+2\left(\dfrac{x+2}{4x}\right)$

$=\dfrac{x}{4}+\dfrac{2(x+2)}{4x}$

$=\dfrac{x\cdot x}{4\cdot x}+\dfrac{2x+4}{4x}$

$=\dfrac{x^2+2x+4}{4x}$

$A=l\cdot w$

$A=\dfrac{x}{8}\cdot\dfrac{x+2}{4x}=\dfrac{x\cdot(x+2)}{8\cdot4x}=\dfrac{x+2}{32}$

The perimeter is $\dfrac{x^2+2x+4}{4x}$ units

and the area is $\dfrac{x+2}{32}$ square units.

46. $P=\dfrac{3x}{4x-4}+\dfrac{2x}{3x-3}+\dfrac{x}{x-1}$

$=\dfrac{3x}{4(x-1)}+\dfrac{2x}{3(x-1)}+\dfrac{x}{x-1}$

$=\dfrac{3x(3)}{4(x-1)(3)}+\dfrac{2x(4)}{3(x-1)(4)}+\dfrac{x(12)}{(x-1)(12)}$

$=\dfrac{9x+8x+12x}{12(x-1)}=\dfrac{29x}{12(x-1)}$

$A=\dfrac{1}{2}\cdot b\cdot h$

$A=\dfrac{1}{2}\cdot\dfrac{x}{x-1}\cdot\dfrac{6y}{5}$

$=\dfrac{1\cdot x\cdot2\cdot3y}{2\cdot(x-1)\cdot5}$

$=\dfrac{3xy}{5(x-1)}$

The perimeter is $\dfrac{29x}{12(x-1)}$ units and the

area is $\dfrac{3xy}{5(x-1)}$ square units.

47. $\dfrac{x+4}{9}=\dfrac{5}{9}$

$9\left(\dfrac{x+4}{9}\right)=9\left(\dfrac{5}{9}\right)$

$x+4=5$

$x=1$

48.
$$\frac{n}{10} = 9 - \frac{n}{5}$$

$$10\left(\frac{n}{10}\right) = 10\left(9 - \frac{n}{5}\right)$$

$$10\left(\frac{n}{10}\right) = 10(9) - 10\left(\frac{n}{5}\right)$$

$$n = 90 - 2n$$

$$3n = 90$$

$$n = 30$$

49.
$$\frac{5y-3}{7} = \frac{15y-2}{28}$$

$$28\left(\frac{5y-3}{7}\right) = 28\left(\frac{15y-2}{28}\right)$$

$$4(5y-3) = 15y-2$$

$$20y - 12 = 15y - 2$$

$$5y = 10$$

$$y = 2$$

50.
$$\frac{2}{x+1} - \frac{1}{x-2} = -\frac{1}{2}$$

$$2(x+1)(x-2)\left(\frac{2}{x+1} - \frac{1}{x-2}\right)$$

$$= 2(x+1)(x-2)\left(-\frac{1}{2}\right)$$

$$2(x+1)(x-2)\left(\frac{2}{x+1}\right)$$

$$-2(x+1)(x-2)\left(\frac{1}{x-2}\right)$$

$$= 2(x+1)(x-2)\left(-\frac{1}{2}\right)$$

$$4(x-2) - 2(x+1) = -(x+1)(x-2)$$

$$4x - 8 - 2x - 2 = -\left(x^2 - x - 2\right)$$

$$2x - 10 = -x^2 + x + 2$$

$$x^2 + x - 12 = 0$$

$$(x+4)(x-3) = 0$$

$$x+4 = 0 \quad \text{or} \quad x-3 = 0$$

$$x = -4 \qquad\qquad x = 3$$

51. $\dfrac{1}{a+3}+\dfrac{1}{a-3}=-\dfrac{5}{a^2-9}$

$(a-3)(a+3)\left(\dfrac{1}{a+3}+\dfrac{1}{a-3}\right)$

$\qquad =(a-3)(a+3)\left(-\dfrac{5}{(a-3)(a+3)}\right)$

$(a-3)(a+3)\left(\dfrac{1}{a+3}\right)$

$\qquad +(a-3)(a+3)\left(\dfrac{1}{a-3}\right)=-5$

$a-3+a+3=-5$

$2a=-5$

$a=-\dfrac{5}{2}$

52. $\dfrac{y}{2y+2}+\dfrac{2y-16}{4y+4}=\dfrac{y-3}{y+1}$

$\dfrac{y}{2(y+1)}+\dfrac{2y-16}{4(y+1)}=\dfrac{y-3}{y+1}$

$4(y+1)\left(\dfrac{y}{2(y+1)}+\dfrac{2y-16}{4(y+1)}\right)$

$\qquad =4(y+1)\left(\dfrac{y-3}{y+1}\right)$

$4(y+1)\left(\dfrac{y}{2(y+1)}\right)+4(y+1)\left(\dfrac{2y-16}{4(y+1)}\right)$

$\qquad =4(y+1)\left(\dfrac{y-3}{y+1}\right)$

$2y+2y-16=4(y-3)$

$4y-16=4y-12$

$-16=-12$ False

This equation has no solution.

53. $\dfrac{4}{x+3}+\dfrac{8}{x^2-9}=0$

$(x-3)(x+3)\left(\dfrac{4}{x+3}+\dfrac{8}{(x-3)(x+3)}\right)$

$\qquad =(x-3)(x+3)(0)$

$(x-3)(x+3)\left(\dfrac{4}{x+3}\right)$

$\qquad +(x-3)(x+3)\left(\dfrac{8}{(x-3)(x+3)}\right)=0$

$4(x-3)+8=0$

$4x-12+8=0$

$4x-4=0$

$4x=4$

$x=1$

54. $\dfrac{2}{x-3}-\dfrac{4}{x+3}=\dfrac{8}{x^2-9}$

$(x-3)(x+3)\left(\dfrac{2}{x-3}-\dfrac{4}{x+3}\right)$

$\qquad =(x-3)(x+3)\left(\dfrac{8}{(x-3)(x+3)}\right)$

$(x-3)(x+3)\left(\dfrac{2}{x-3}\right)$

$\qquad -(x-3)(x+3)\left(\dfrac{4}{x+3}\right)=8$

$2(x+3)-4(x-3)=8$

$2x+6-4x+12=8$

$-2x+18=8$

$-2x=-10$

$x=5$

55. $\dfrac{x-3}{x+1} - \dfrac{x-6}{x+5} = 0$

$(x+1)(x+5)\left(\dfrac{x-3}{x+1} - \dfrac{x-6}{x+5}\right)$

$\qquad = (x+1)(x+5)(0)$

$(x+1)(x+5)\left(\dfrac{x-3}{x+1}\right)$

$\qquad -(x+1)(x+5)\left(\dfrac{x-6}{x+5}\right) = 0$

$(x+5)(x-3) - (x+1)(x-6) = 0$

$x^2 + 2x - 15 - \left(x^2 - 5x - 6\right) = 0$

$x^2 + 2x - 15 - x^2 + 5x + 6 = 0$

$7x - 9 = 0$

$7x = 9$

$x = \dfrac{9}{7}$

56. $x + 5 = \dfrac{6}{x}$

$x(x+5) = x\left(\dfrac{6}{x}\right)$

$x^2 + 5x = 6$

$x^2 + 5x - 6 = 0$

$(x+6)(x-1) = 0$

$x + 6 = 0 \quad$ or $\quad x - 1 = 0$

$\qquad x = -6 \qquad\qquad x = 1$

57. $\dfrac{4A}{5b} = x^2$

$4A = 5bx^2$

$\dfrac{4A}{5x^2} = \dfrac{5bx^2}{5x^2}$

$\dfrac{4A}{5x^2} = b$

58. $\dfrac{x}{7} + \dfrac{y}{8} = 10$

$56\left(\dfrac{x}{7}\right) + 56\left(\dfrac{y}{8}\right) = 56(10)$

$8x + 7y = 560$

$7y = 560 - 8x$

$y = \dfrac{560 - 8x}{7}$

59. $5 \cdot \dfrac{1}{x} = \dfrac{3}{2} \cdot \dfrac{1}{x} + \dfrac{7}{6}$

$\dfrac{5}{x} = \dfrac{3}{2x} + \dfrac{7}{6}$

$6x\left(\dfrac{5}{x}\right) = 6x\left(\dfrac{3}{2x}\right) + 6x\left(\dfrac{7}{6}\right)$

$30 = 9 + 7x$

$21 = 7x$

$x = 3$

The unknown number is 3.

60. $\dfrac{1}{x} = \dfrac{1}{4-x}$

$4 - x = x$

$4 = 2x$

$2 = x$

The unknown number is 2.

61.

	Distance	=	rate	·	time
1st car	90		r		$90/r$
2nd car	60		$r-10$		$60/r-10$

$\dfrac{90}{r} = \dfrac{60}{r-10}$

$90(r-10) = 60r$

$90r - 900 = 60r$

$-900 = -30r$

$30 = r$

$r - 10 = 30 - 10 = 20$

The rate of the first car is 30 miles per hour and the rate of the second car is 20 miles per hour.

62.

	Distance $=$	rate $\cdot$	time
Upstream	48	$r - 4$	$48/r - 4$
Downstream	72	$r + 4$	$72/r + 4$

$\dfrac{48}{r - 4} = \dfrac{72}{r + 4}$

$48(r + 4) = 72(r - 4)$

$48r + 192 = 72r - 288$

$480 = 24r$

$r = 20$

The speed of the boat in still water is 20 miles per hour.

63.

	Hours to Complete Total Job	Part of Job Completed in 1 Hour
Mark	7	$1/7$
Maria	x	$1/x$
Together	5	$1/5$

$\dfrac{1}{7} + \dfrac{1}{x} = \dfrac{1}{5}$

$35x\left(\dfrac{1}{7}\right) + 35x\left(\dfrac{1}{x}\right) = 35x\left(\dfrac{1}{5}\right)$

$5x + 35 = 7x$

$35 = 2x$

$x = \dfrac{35}{2}$ or $17\dfrac{1}{2}$

It takes Maria $17\dfrac{1}{2}$ hours to complete the job alone.

64.

	Days to Complete Total Job	Part of Job Completed in 1 Day
Pipe A	20	$1/20$
Pipe B	15	$1/15$
Together	x	$1/x$

$\dfrac{1}{20} + \dfrac{1}{25} = \dfrac{1}{x}$

$60x\left(\dfrac{1}{20}\right) + 60x\left(\dfrac{1}{15}\right) = 60x\left(\dfrac{1}{x}\right)$

$3x + 4x = 60$

$7x = 60$

$x = \dfrac{60}{7} = 8\dfrac{4}{7}$

Both pipes fill the pond in $8\dfrac{4}{7}$ days.

65. $\dfrac{2}{3} = \dfrac{10}{x}$

$2x = 30$

$x = 15$

The missing length is 15.

66. $\dfrac{12}{4} = \dfrac{18}{x}$

$12x = 72$

$x = 6$

The missing length is 6.

67. $\dfrac{9}{7\frac{1}{5}} = \dfrac{x}{12}$

$108 = 7\frac{1}{5}x$

$108 = \dfrac{36}{5}x$

$540 = 36x$

$15 = x$

The missing length is 15.

68. $\dfrac{x}{5} = \dfrac{30}{2.5}$

$2.5x = 150$

$x = 60$

The missing length is 60.

69. $\dfrac{\frac{5x}{27}}{-\frac{10xy}{21}} = \dfrac{5x}{27} \cdot -\dfrac{21}{10xy} = -\dfrac{5x \cdot 3 \cdot 7}{3 \cdot 9 \cdot 5 \cdot 2 \cdot x \cdot y}$

$= -\dfrac{7}{18y}$

70. $\dfrac{\frac{8x}{x^2-9}}{\frac{4}{x+3}} = \dfrac{8x}{x^2-9} \cdot \dfrac{x+3}{4}$

$= \dfrac{2 \cdot 4 \cdot x(x+3)}{(x-3)(x+3) \cdot 4} = \dfrac{2x}{x-3}$

71. $\dfrac{\frac{3}{5}+\frac{2}{7}}{\frac{1}{5}+\frac{5}{6}} = \dfrac{\frac{21}{35}+\frac{10}{35}}{\frac{6}{30}+\frac{25}{30}} = \dfrac{\frac{31}{35}}{\frac{31}{30}} = \dfrac{31}{35} \cdot \dfrac{30}{31}$

$= \dfrac{31 \cdot 5 \cdot 6}{5 \cdot 7 \cdot 31} = \dfrac{6}{7}$

72. $\dfrac{2+\frac{1}{x^2}}{\frac{1}{x}+\frac{2}{x^2}} = \dfrac{x^2\left(2+\frac{1}{x^2}\right)}{x^2\left(\frac{1}{x}+\frac{2}{x^2}\right)} = \dfrac{x^2(2)+x^2\left(\frac{1}{x^2}\right)}{x^2\left(\frac{1}{x}\right)+x^2\left(\frac{2}{x^2}\right)}$

$= \dfrac{2x^2+1}{x+2}$

73. $\dfrac{3-\frac{1}{y}}{2-\frac{1}{y}} = \dfrac{y\left(3-\frac{1}{y}\right)}{y\left(2-\frac{1}{y}\right)} = \dfrac{y(3)-y\left(\frac{1}{y}\right)}{y(2)-y\left(\frac{1}{y}\right)}$

$= \dfrac{3y-1}{2y-1}$

74. $\dfrac{\frac{6}{x+2}+4}{\frac{8}{x+2}-4} = \dfrac{(x+2)\left(\frac{6}{x+2}+4\right)}{(x+2)\left(\frac{8}{x+2}-4\right)}$

$= \dfrac{(x+2)\left(\frac{6}{x+2}\right)+(x+2)(4)}{(x+2)\left(\frac{8}{x+2}\right)-(x+2)(4)}$

$= \dfrac{6+4x+8}{8-4x-8} = \dfrac{4x+14}{-4x} = -\dfrac{2(2x+7)}{2 \cdot 2x}$

$= -\dfrac{2x+7}{2x}$

Chapter 12 Test

1. The rational expression is undefined when

$x^2+4x+3 = 0$

$(x+3)(x+1) = 0$

$x+3 = 0 \quad$ or $\quad x+1 = 0$

$\qquad x = -3 \qquad\qquad x = -1$

2. a. $C = \dfrac{100x+3000}{x}$

$= \dfrac{100(200)+3000}{200}$

$= \dfrac{20,000+3000}{200}$

$$= \frac{23,000}{200} = 115$$

The average cost/desk is \$115.

b. $C = \dfrac{100x + 3000}{x}$

$$= \frac{100(1000) + 3000}{1000}$$

$$= \frac{100,000 + 3000}{1000}$$

$$= \frac{103,000}{1000} = 103$$

The average cost/desk is \$103.

3. $\dfrac{3x - 6}{5x - 10} = \dfrac{3(x - 2)}{5(x - 2)} = \dfrac{3}{5}$

4. $\dfrac{x + 10}{x^2 - 100} = \dfrac{x + 10}{(x - 10)(x + 10)} = \dfrac{1}{x - 10}$

5. $\dfrac{x + 6}{x^2 + 12x + 36} = \dfrac{x + 6}{(x + 6)^2} = \dfrac{1}{x + 6}$

6. $\dfrac{7 - x}{x - 7} = \dfrac{-(x - 7)}{x - 7} = -1$

7. $\dfrac{2m^3 - 2m^2 - 12m}{m^2 - 5m + 6} = \dfrac{2m(m^2 - m - 6)}{(m - 3)(m - 2)}$

$$= \frac{2m(m - 3)(m + 2)}{(m - 3)(m - 2)} = \frac{2m(m + 2)}{m - 2}$$

8. $\dfrac{y - x}{x^2 - y^2} = \dfrac{-(x - y)}{(x - y)(x + y)} = -\dfrac{1}{x + y}$

9. $\dfrac{3}{x - 1} \cdot (5x - 5) = \dfrac{3}{x - 1} \cdot 5(x - 1)$

$$= \frac{3 \cdot 5(x - 1)}{x - 1} = 15$$

10. $\dfrac{y^2 - 5y + 6}{2y + 4} \cdot \dfrac{y + 2}{2y - 6}$

$$= \frac{(y - 3)(y - 2) \cdot (y + 2)}{2(y + 2) \cdot 2(y - 3)} = \frac{y - 2}{4}$$

11. $\dfrac{6}{2x + 5} - \dfrac{5 + x}{2x + 5} = \dfrac{6 - (5 + x)}{2x + 5}$

$$= \frac{6 - 5 - x}{2x + 5}$$

$$= \frac{1 - x}{2x + 5}$$

12. $\dfrac{5a}{a^2 - a - 6} - \dfrac{2}{a - 3}$

$$= \frac{5a}{(a - 3)(a + 2)} - \frac{2(a + 2)}{(a - 3)(a + 2)}$$

$$= \frac{5a - 2(a + 2)}{(a - 3)(a + 2)} = \frac{5a - 2a - 4}{(a - 3)(a + 2)}$$

$$= \frac{3a - 4}{(a - 3)(a + 2)}$$

13. $\dfrac{6}{x^2 - 1} + \dfrac{3}{x + 1}$

$$= \frac{6}{(x + 1)(x - 1)} + \frac{3(x - 1)}{(x + 1)(x - 1)}$$

$$= \frac{6 + 3x - 3}{(x + 1)(x - 1)} = \frac{3x + 3}{(x + 1)(x - 1)}$$

$$= \frac{3(x + 1)}{(x + 1)(x - 1)} = \frac{3}{x - 1}$$

14. $\dfrac{x^2-9}{x^2-3x} \div \dfrac{xy+5x+3y+15}{2x+10}$

$\dfrac{x^2-9}{x^2-3x} \cdot \dfrac{2x+10}{xy+5x+3y+15}$

$= \dfrac{(x+3)(x-3)(2)(x+5)}{x(x-3)\left[x(y+5)+3(y+5)\right]}$

$= \dfrac{(x+3)(x-3)(2)(x+5)}{x(x-3)(x+3)(y+5)}$

$= \dfrac{2(x+5)}{x(y+5)}$

15. $\dfrac{x+2}{x^2+11x+18} + \dfrac{5}{x^2-3x-10}$

$= \dfrac{x+2}{(x+9)(x+2)} + \dfrac{5}{(x-5)(x+2)}$

$= \dfrac{(x+2)(x-5)}{(x+9)(x+2)(x-5)}$

$\quad + \dfrac{5(x+9)}{(x-5)(x+2)(x+9)}$

$= \dfrac{(x+2)(x-5)+5(x+9)}{(x+9)(x+2)(x-5)}$

$= \dfrac{x^2-3x-10+5x+45}{(x+9)(x+2)(x-5)}$

$= \dfrac{x^2+2x+35}{(x+9)(x+2)(x-5)}$

16. $\dfrac{4}{y} - \dfrac{5}{3} = \dfrac{-1}{5}$

$15y\left(\dfrac{4}{y} - \dfrac{5}{3}\right) = 15y\left(-\dfrac{1}{5}\right)$

$15y\left(\dfrac{4}{y}\right) - 15y\left(\dfrac{5}{3}\right) = 15y\left(-\dfrac{1}{5}\right)$

$60 - 25y = -3y$

$60 = 22y$

$\dfrac{60}{22} = y$

$y = \dfrac{30}{11}$

17. $\dfrac{5}{y+1} = \dfrac{4}{y+2}$

$5(y+2) = 4(y+1)$

$5y+10 = 4y+4$

$y = -6$

18. $\dfrac{a}{a-3} = \dfrac{3}{a-3} - \dfrac{3}{2}$

$2(a-3)\left(\dfrac{a}{a-3}\right) = 2(a-3)\left(\dfrac{3}{a-3} - \dfrac{3}{2}\right)$

$2a = 2(a-3)\left(\dfrac{3}{a-3}\right) - 2(a-3)\left(\dfrac{3}{2}\right)$

$2a = 6 - 3(a-3)$

$2a = 6 - 3a + 9$

$2a = 15 - 3a$

$5a = 15$

$a = 3$

In the original equation, 3 makes a denominator 0. This equation has no solution.

19.
$$x - \frac{14}{x-1} = 4 - \frac{2x}{x-1}$$

$$x(x-1) - (x-1)\left(\frac{14}{x-1}\right) = 4(x-1) - (x-1)\left(\frac{2x}{x-1}\right)$$

$$x^2 - x - 14 = 4x - 4 - 2x$$

$$x^2 - x - 14 = 2x - 4$$

$$x^2 - 3x - 10 = 0$$

$$(x-5)(x+2) = 0$$

$$x - 5 = 0 \qquad x + 2 = 0$$

$$x = 5 \qquad\qquad x = -2$$

20.
$$\frac{\frac{5x^2}{yz^2}}{\frac{10x}{z^3}} = \frac{5x^2}{yz^2} \cdot \frac{z^3}{10x} = \frac{5 \cdot x \cdot x \cdot z \cdot z^2}{y \cdot z^2 \cdot 2 \cdot 5 \cdot x}$$

$$= \frac{xz}{2y}$$

21.
$$\frac{5 - \frac{1}{y^2}}{\frac{1}{y} + \frac{2}{y^2}} = \frac{y^2\left(5 - \frac{1}{y^2}\right)}{y^2\left(\frac{1}{y} + \frac{2}{y^2}\right)} = \frac{y^2(5) - y^2\left(\frac{1}{y^2}\right)}{y^2\left(\frac{1}{y}\right) + y^2\left(\frac{2}{y^2}\right)}$$

$$= \frac{5y^2 - 1}{y + 2}$$

22.
$$\frac{8}{x} = \frac{10}{15}$$

$$8(15) = 10x$$

$$120 = 10x$$

$$12 = x$$

23. $x + 5 \cdot \dfrac{1}{x} = 6$

$$x + \frac{5}{x} = 6$$

$$x\left(x + \frac{5}{x}\right) = x(6)$$

$$x(x) + x\left(\frac{5}{x}\right) = x(6)$$

$$x^2 + 5 = 6x$$

$$x^2 - 6x + 5 = 0$$

$$(x-5)(x-1) = 0$$

$$x - 5 = 0 \quad \text{or} \quad x - 1 = 0$$

$$x = 5 \qquad\qquad x = 1$$

The unknown number is 5 or 1.

24.

	Distance =	rate ·	time
Upstream	14	$r - 2$	$14/r - 2$
Downstream	16	$r + 2$	$16/r + 2$

$$\frac{14}{r-2} = \frac{16}{r+2}$$

$$14(r+2) = 16(r-2)$$

$$14r + 28 = 16r - 32$$

$$60 = 2r$$

$$r = 30$$

The speed of the boat in still water is 30 miles per hour.

25.

	Hours to Complete Total Job	Part of Job Completed in 1 Hour
1st pipe	12	1/12
2nd pipe	15	1/15
Together	x	$1/x$

$$\frac{1}{12}+\frac{1}{15}=\frac{1}{x}$$

$$60x\left(\frac{1}{12}\right)+60x\left(\frac{1}{15}\right)=60x\left(\frac{1}{x}\right)$$

$$5x+4x=60$$

$$9x=60$$

$$x=\frac{60}{9}=\frac{20}{3}=6\frac{2}{3}$$

Together, the pipes can fill the tank in

$6\frac{2}{3}$ hours.

Chapter 12 Cumulative Review

1. $\frac{9}{20}\cdot100\%=\frac{9\cdot5\cdot20}{20}\%=45\%$

2. $\frac{4}{5}\cdot100\%=\frac{4\cdot5\cdot20}{5}\%=80\%$

3. $\frac{2}{3}\cdot100\%=\frac{200}{3}\%=66\frac{2}{3}\%$

4. $\frac{1}{9}\cdot100\%=\frac{100}{9}\%=11\frac{1}{9}\%$

5. $1\frac{1}{2}=1.5=150\%$

6. $3\frac{3}{4}=3.75=375\%$

7. Commutative Property of Multiplication

8. Commutative Property of Addition

9. Associative Property of Addition

10. Associative Property of Multiplication

11. Let x = the length of the shorter piece.
Then $4x$ = the length of the longer piece.
$$x+4x=10$$
$$\frac{5}{5}x=\frac{10}{5}$$
$$x=2$$
The shorter piece is 2 feet longer, and the longer piece is $4(2)=8$ feet long.

12. Let x = one piece. Since there are two sides of equal length, let x = a second piece. Then the third piece $=x-3$.
$$x+x+x-3=45$$
$$3x-3=45$$
$$3x=45+3$$
$$\frac{3x}{3}=\frac{48}{3}$$
$$x=16$$
The two pieces of equal length are each 16 meters long. The third piece is $16-3=13$ meters.

13. $$y=mx+b$$
$$\frac{y-b}{m}=\frac{mx}{m}$$
$$\frac{y-b}{m}=x$$

14. $$y=mx+b$$
$$y-mx=b$$

15. $x + 4 \le -6$

$\qquad x \le -6 - 4$

$\qquad x \le -10$

16. $x - 1 > -10$

$\qquad x > -10 + 1$

$\qquad x > -9$

$\qquad \{x \mid x > -9\}$

17. $\dfrac{x^5}{x^2} = x^{5-2} = x^3$

18. $\dfrac{x^9}{x} = x^{9-1} = x^8$

19. $\dfrac{4^7}{4^3} = 4^{7-3} = 4^4 = 256$

20. $\dfrac{7^{12}}{7^4} = 7^{12-4} = 7^8$

21. $\dfrac{(-3)^{-5}}{(-3)^2} = (-3)^{5-2} = (-3)^3 = -27$

22. $\dfrac{(-4)^9}{(-4)^7} = (-4)^{9-7} = (-4)^2 = 16$

23. $\dfrac{2x^5 y^2}{xy} = 2x^{5-1} y^{2-1} = 2x^4 y$

24. $\dfrac{13a^5 b}{a^4} = 13a^{5-4} b = 13ab$

25. $2x^{-3} = 2 \cdot \dfrac{1}{x^3} = \dfrac{2}{x^3}$

26. $9x^{-2} = 9 \cdot \dfrac{1}{x^2} = \dfrac{9}{x^2}$

27. $(-2)^{-4} = \dfrac{1}{(-2)^4} = \dfrac{1}{16}$

28. $(-3)^{-3} = \dfrac{1}{(-3)^3} = \dfrac{1}{-27} = -\dfrac{1}{27}$

29. $5x(2x^3 + 6) = 5x(2x^3) + 5x(6)$

$\qquad\qquad\qquad = 10x^4 + 30x$

30. $3y(4y^2 - 2) = 3y(4y^2) + 3y(-2)$

$\qquad\qquad\qquad = 12y^3 - 6y$

31. $-3x^2(5x^2 + 6x - 1) = -15x^4 - 18x^3 + 3x^2$

32. $-5y(7y^2 - 3y + 1) = -35y^3 + 15y^2 - 5y$

33. $\dfrac{4x^2 + 7 + 8x^3}{2x + 3} = \dfrac{8x^3 + 4x^2 + 0x + 7}{2x + 3}$

$$
\begin{array}{r}
4x^2 - 4x + 6 + \frac{-11}{2x+3} \\
2x+3 \overline{\smash{\big)}\ 8x^3 + 4x^2 + 0x + 7} \\
\underline{-8x^3 - 12x^2} \\
-8x^2 + 0x \\
\underline{+8x^2 + 12x} \\
12x + 7 \\
\underline{-12x - 18} \\
-11
\end{array}
$$

34. $\dfrac{6x^2 - 7x + 4}{2x + 1}$

$$2x+1\overline{\smash{\big)}\,6x^2 - 7x + 4} \quad \left(3x - 5 + \tfrac{9}{2x+1}\right)$$

$$\begin{array}{r}
3x - 5 + \frac{9}{2x+1} \\
2x+1{\overline{\smash{\big)}\,6x^2 - 7x + 4}} \\
\underline{-6x^2 - 3x} \\
-10x + 4 \\
\underline{+10x + 5} \\
9
\end{array}$$

35. $x^2 + 7x + 12 = (x+3)(x+4)$

36. $x^2 + 17x + 70 = (x+7)(x+10)$

37. $25x^2 + 20xy + 4y^2 = (5x+2y)(5x+2y)$
$$= (5x+2y)^2$$

38. $36a^2 - 48ab + 16b^2 = 4\left(9a^2 - 12ab + 4b^2\right)$
$$= 4(3a-2b)(3a-2b)$$
$$= 4(3a-2b)^2$$

39. $\quad x^2 - 9x - 22 = 0$
$$(x+2)(x-11) = 0$$
$$x + 2 = 0, \quad x - 11 = 0$$
$$x = -2, 11$$

40. $\quad x^2 + 2x - 15 = 0$
$$(x-3)(x+5) = 0$$
$$x - 3 = 0 \quad x + 5 = 0$$
$$x = 3 \qquad x = -5$$
$$x = -5, 3$$

41. $\dfrac{x^2 + x}{3x} \cdot \dfrac{6}{5x + 5} = \dfrac{x(x+1)}{3x} \cdot \dfrac{6}{5(x+1)}$
$$= \dfrac{6x(x+1)}{15x(x+1)}$$
$$= \dfrac{2}{5}$$

42. $\dfrac{3x - 12}{2} \div \dfrac{5x - 20}{4x} = \dfrac{3x - 12}{2} \cdot \dfrac{4x}{5x - 20}$
$$= \dfrac{3(x-4)}{2} \cdot \dfrac{4x}{5(x-4)}$$
$$= \dfrac{12x(x-4)}{10(x-4)}$$
$$= \dfrac{6x}{5}$$

43. $\dfrac{3x^2 + 2x}{x - 1} - \dfrac{10x - 5}{x - 1}$
$$= \dfrac{3x^2 + 2x - (10x - 5)}{x - 1}$$
$$= \dfrac{3x^2 + 2x - 10x + 5}{x - 1}$$
$$= \dfrac{3x^2 - 8x + 5}{x - 1}$$
$$= \dfrac{(x-1)(3x-5)}{(x-1)}$$
$$= 3x - 5$$

44. $\dfrac{4x}{x + 2} + \dfrac{8}{x + 2}$
$$= \dfrac{4x + 8}{x + 2}$$
$$= \dfrac{4(x+2)}{(x+2)}$$
$$= 4$$

45. $\dfrac{6x}{x^2-4}-\dfrac{3}{x+2}$

$=\dfrac{6x}{(x+2)(x-2)}-\dfrac{3}{(x+2)}$

LCD: $(x+2)(x-2)$

$=\dfrac{6x}{(x+2)(x-2)}-\dfrac{3(x-2)}{(x+2)(x-2)}$

$=\dfrac{6x}{(x+2)(x-2)}-\dfrac{3x-6}{(x+2)(x-2)}$

$=\dfrac{6x-(3x-6)}{(x+2)(x-2)}$

$=\dfrac{6x-3x+6}{(x+2)(x-2)}$

$=\dfrac{3x+6}{(x+2)(x-2)}$

$=\dfrac{3(x+2)}{(x+2)(x-2)}$

$=\dfrac{3}{x-2}$

46. $\dfrac{2}{x-3}+\dfrac{5x}{x^2-9}$

$=\dfrac{2}{(x-3)}+\dfrac{5}{(x+3)(x-3)}$

LCD: $(x-3)(x+3)$

$=\dfrac{2(x+3)}{(x-3)(x+3)}+\dfrac{5x}{(x+3)(x-3)}$

$=\dfrac{2x+6}{(x-3)(x+3)}+\dfrac{5x}{(x-3)(x+3)}$

$=\dfrac{2x+6+5x}{(x-3)(x+3)}$

$=\dfrac{7x+6}{(x-3)(x+3)}$ or $\dfrac{7x+6}{x^2-9}$

47. $\dfrac{t-4}{2}-\dfrac{t-3}{9}=\dfrac{5}{18}$

$18\left(\dfrac{t-4}{2}-\dfrac{t-3}{9}\right)=18\left(\dfrac{5}{18}\right)$

$18\left(\dfrac{t-4}{2}\right)-18\left(\dfrac{t-3}{9}\right)=18\left(\dfrac{5}{18}\right)$

$9(t-4)-2(t-3)=1(5)$

$9t-36-2t+6=5$

$7t-30=5$

$7t=5+30$

$\dfrac{7t}{7}=\dfrac{35}{7}$

$t=5$

48. $\dfrac{y}{2}-\dfrac{y}{4}=\dfrac{1}{6}$

$12\left(\dfrac{y}{2}-\dfrac{y}{4}\right)=12\left(\dfrac{1}{6}\right)$

$12\left(\dfrac{y}{2}\right)-12\left(\dfrac{y}{4}\right)=12\left(\dfrac{1}{6}\right)$

$6(y)-3(y)=2(1)$

$6y-3y=2$

$\dfrac{3y}{3}=\dfrac{2}{3}$

$y=\dfrac{2}{3}$

49. Let x = the time it takes to complete the tour working together.

$$\frac{1}{3}x + \frac{1}{7}x = 1$$

$$21\left(\frac{1}{3}x + \frac{1}{7}x\right) = 21(1)$$

$$7x + 3x = 21$$

$$\frac{10x}{10} = \frac{21}{10}$$

$$x = 2\frac{1}{10}$$

It would take Sam and Frank $2\frac{1}{10}$ hr to complete a quality control tour together.

50. Let x = both machines working together

$$\frac{1}{18}x + \frac{1}{12}x = 1$$

$$36\left(\frac{1}{18}x + \frac{1}{12}x\right) = 36(1)$$

$$2x + 3x = 36$$

$$\frac{5x}{5} = \frac{36}{5}$$

$$x = 7\frac{1}{5}$$

It would take both machines $7\frac{1}{5}$ hr to complete the task working together.

51.
$$\frac{\frac{1}{z} - \frac{1}{2}}{\frac{1}{3} - \frac{z}{6}} = \frac{6z\left(\frac{1}{z} - \frac{1}{2}\right)}{6z\left(\frac{1}{3} - \frac{z}{6}\right)}$$

$$= \frac{6z\left(\frac{1}{z}\right) - 6z\left(\frac{1}{2}\right)}{6z\left(\frac{1}{3}\right) - 6z\left(\frac{z}{6}\right)}$$

$$= \frac{6(1) - 3z(1)}{2z(1) - z(z)}$$

$$= \frac{6 - 3z}{2z - z^2}$$

$$= \frac{3(2 - z)}{z(2 - z)}$$

$$= \frac{3}{z}$$

52.
$$\frac{\frac{x}{9} - \frac{1}{x}}{1 + \frac{3}{x}} = \frac{9x\left(\frac{x}{9} - \frac{1}{x}\right)}{9x\left(1 + \frac{3}{x}\right)}$$

$$= \frac{9x\left(\frac{x}{9}\right) - 9x\left(\frac{1}{x}\right)}{9x(1) + 9x\left(\frac{3}{x}\right)}$$

$$= \frac{x^2 - 9}{9x + 27}$$

$$= \frac{(x + 3)(x - 3)}{9(x + 3)}$$

$$= \frac{x - 3}{9}$$

Chapter 13

Chapter 13 Pretest

1. $(-4,3), (0,-2), (5,0)$

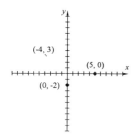

2. $8x - 3y = 2$

If $x = -2$

$8(-2) - 3y = 2$

$-16 - 3x = 2$

$-3x = 18$

$x = -6$

$(-2, -6)$

3. $3x - y = 6$

x	y
0	-6
2	0

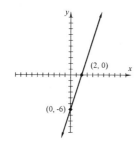

4.

x	y
0	4
-1	0

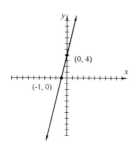

5. $3x + 2y \le 6$

x	y
0	3
2	0

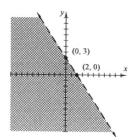

6. $(-7, 8)$ and $(3, 5)$

$$m = \frac{y_2 - y_1}{x_2 - x_1} = \frac{5 - 8}{3 - (-7)} = \frac{-3}{10}$$

7. $4x - 5y = 20$

$-5y = -4x + 20$

$y = \frac{4}{5}x - 4$

$m = \frac{4}{5}$

8. $x = 10$ is a vertical line therefore the slope is undefined.

9. $m = -\frac{1}{3}; (3, -6)$

$y - y_1 = m(x - x_1)$

$y - (-6) = -\frac{1}{3}(x - 3)$

$3(y + 6) = -(x - 3)$

$3y + 18 = -x + 3$

$x + 3y + 18 = 3$

$x + 3y = -15$

455

10. $(0,0)$ and $(-8,1)$

$$m = \frac{y_2 - y_1}{x_2 - x_1} = \frac{1-0}{-8-0} = -\frac{1}{8}$$

Use $m = -\dfrac{1}{8}$; $(0,0)$

$$y - y_1 = m(x - x_1)$$

$$y - 0 = -\frac{1}{8}(x - 0)$$

$$8y = -x$$

$$x + 8y = 0$$

11. $m = \dfrac{2}{7}$; $b = 14$

$$y = mx + b$$

$$y = \frac{2}{7}x + 98$$

$$7y = 2x + 98$$

$$2x - 7y = -98$$

12. $\{(-3,8),(7,-1),(0,6),(2,-1)\}$

domain: $\{-3,0,2,7\}$

range: $\{-1,6,8\}$

13. $\{(1,7),(-8,7),(6,3),(9,2)\}$

It is a function.

14. $\{(0,4),(1,3),(2,-5),(1,10),(-2,-8)\}$

It is not a function because two pair have the same x value.

15. $f(x) = -3x + 8$

  a. $f(-1) = -3(-1) + 8 = 3 + 8 = 11$

  b. $f(0) = -3(0) + 8 = 0 + 8 = 8$

  c. $f(10) = -3(10) + 8 = -30 + 8 = -22$

16. $y = kx$

$$\frac{16}{24} = \frac{k(24)}{24}$$

$$\frac{2}{3} = k$$

$$y = \frac{2}{3}(20)$$

$$y = \frac{40}{3}$$

Practice Problems 13.1

1.

Point $(4,2)$ lies in quadrant I.

Point $(-5,1)$ lies in quadrant II.

Point $(-1,-3)$ lies in quadrant III.

Point $(2,-2)$ lies in quadrant IV.

Points $(0,3),\left(-2\tfrac{1}{2},0\right),(3,0)$, and $(0,-4)$ lies on axes, so they are not in any quadrant.

2. a. (1997, 1148), (1998, 1424), (1999, 1343), (2000, 997), (2001, 1216), (2002, 941)

b.

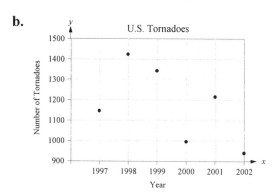

c. The number of tornadoes varies greatly from year to year.

3. $x + 2y = 8$

    a. $x = 0, \; 0 + 2y = 8$

$$y = 4; \; (0,4)$$

    b. $y = 3, \; x + 2(3) = 8$

$$x + 6 = 8$$

$$x = 2; \; (2,3)$$

    c. $x = -4, \; -4 + 2y = 8$

$$2y = 12$$

$$y = 6; \; (-4,6)$$

4. $y = -2x$

    a. $x = -3, \; y = -2(-3) = 6; \; (-3,6)$

    b. $y = 0, \; 0 = -2x, \; x = 0; \; (0,0)$

    c. $y = 10, \; 10 = -2x, \; x = -5; \; (-5,10)$

x	y
-3	6
0	0
-5	10

5. $x = 5$

x	y
5	-2
5	0
5	4

6. $y = -50x + 400$

x	1	2	3	4	5	6	7
y	350	300	250	200	150	100	50

Mental Math 13.1

1. $x + y = 10$

    Answers may vary; Ex. $(5,5),(7,3)$

2. $x + y = 6$

    Answers may vary; Ex. $(0,6),(6,0)$

Exercise Set 13.1

1.

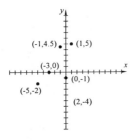

Point $(1, 5)$ lies in quadrant I.

Point $\left(-1, 4\frac{1}{2}\right)$ lies in quadrant II.

Point $(-5, -2)$ lies in quadrant III.

Point $(2, -4)$ lies in quadrant IV.

Point $(-3, 0)$ lies on the *x*-axis.

Point $(0, -1)$ lies on the *y*-axis.

3. When $a = b$.

5. $A : (0, 0)$

7. $C : (3, 2)$

9. $E : (-2, -2)$

11. $G : (2, -1)$

13. $B : (0, -3)$

15. $D : (1, 3)$

17. $F : (-3, -1)$

19.a. $(1995, 438), (1996, 438), (1997, 436),$
$(1998, 435), (1999, 432), (2000, 434)$
$(2001, 436)$

b.

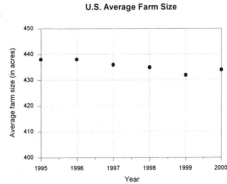

c. The number of tornadoes varies greatly from year to year.

21.a. $(2313, 2), (2085, 1), (2711, 21), (2869, 39),$
$(2920, 42), (4038, 99), (1783, 0), (2493, 9)$

b.

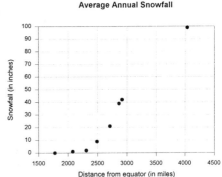

c. The farther from the equator, the more snowfall.

23.a. $(0.50, 10), (0.75, 12), (1.00, 15), (1.25, 16),$
$(1.50, 18), (1.50, 19), (1.75, 19), (2.00, 20)$

b.

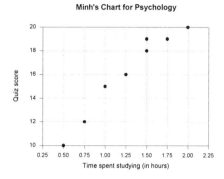

Minh's Chart for Psychology

c. Answers may vary.

25. $x - 4y = 4$

$y = -2, \ x - 4(-2) = 4$

$\qquad x + 8 = 4$

$\qquad\qquad x = -4; \ (-4, -2)$

$x = 4, \ 4 - 4y = 4$

$\qquad -4y = 0$

$\qquad\qquad y = 0; \ (4, 0)$

27. $3x + y = 9$

$x = 0, \ 3(0) + y = 9$

$\qquad 0 + y = 9$

$\qquad\qquad y = 9; \ (0, 9)$

$y = 0, \ 3x + 0 = 9$

$\qquad 3x = 9$

$\qquad\qquad x = 3; \ (3, 0)$

29. $y = -7$

$x = 11, \ y = -7; \ (11, -7)$

$y = -7, \ x = $ any value

31. $x + 3y = 6$

$x = 0, \ 0 + 3y = 6, \ y = 2; \ (0, 2)$

$y = 0, \ x + 3(0) = 6, \ x = 6; \ (6, 0)$

$y = 1, \ x + 3(1) = 6, \ x = 3; \ (3, 1)$

x	y
0	2
6	0
3	1

33. $2x - y = 12$

$x = 0, \ 2(0) - y = 12, \ y = -12; \ (0, -12)$

$y = -2, \ 2x - (-2) = 12$

$\qquad\qquad 2x + 2 = 12$

$\qquad\qquad\quad 2x = 10$

$\qquad\qquad\qquad x = 5; \ (5, -2)$

$x = 3, \ 2(3) - y = 12,$

$\qquad\quad 6 - y = 12$

$\qquad\quad -y = 6$

$\qquad\qquad y = -6; \ (3, -6)$

x	y
0	-12
5	-2
3	-6

35. $2x + 7y = 5$

$x = 0, \ 2(0) + 7y = 5,$

$\qquad\qquad 7y = 5$

$\qquad\qquad y = \dfrac{5}{7}; \ \left(0, \dfrac{5}{7}\right)$

$y = 0, \ 2x + 7(0) = 5$

$$2x = 5$$

$$x = \frac{5}{2}; \ \left(\frac{5}{2}, 0\right)$$

$y = 1, \ 2x + 7(1) = 5,$

$$2x + 7 = 5$$

$$2x = -2$$

$$x = -1; \ (-1, 1)$$

x	y
0	$\frac{5}{7}$
$\frac{5}{2}$	0
-1	1

37. $x = 3$

x	y
3	0
3	-0.5
3	$\frac{1}{4}$

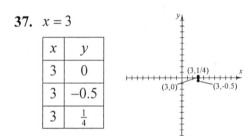

39. $x = -5y$

$y = 0, \ x = -5(0) = 0$

$y = 1, \ x = -5(1) = -5$

$x = 10, \ 10 = -5y, \ y = -2$

x	y
0	0
-5	1
10	-2

41.a. $y = 80x + 5000$

$x = 100, \ y = 80(100) + 5000 = 13,000$

$x = 200, \ y = 80(200) + 5000 = 21,000$

$x = 300, \ y = 80(300) + 5000 = 29,000$

x	100	200	300
y	$13,000$	$21,000$	$29,000$

b.   Let $y = 8600$

$$8600 = 80x + 5000$$

$$3600 = 80x$$

$$45 = x$$

45 desks can be produced

43. $x + y = 5$

$$y = 5 - x$$

45. $2x + 4y = 5$

$$4y = 5 - 2x$$

$$y = \frac{5 - 2x}{4}$$

47. $10x = -5y$

$$-2x = y$$

49.

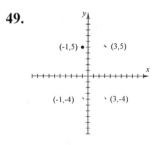

Rectangle is 9 units by 4 units.

Perimeter is $9 + 4 + 9 + 4 = 26$ units.

51. Years 0 to 1: $21 million
Years 1 to 2: $23 million
Years 2 to 3: $24 million
Years 3 to 4: $25 million

53. Answers may vary.

55.a. $y = -4.22x + 985.02$
$x = 4,\ y = -4.22(4) + 985.02 = 968.14$
$x = 7,\ y = -4.22(7) + 985.02 = 955.48$
$x = 10,\ y = -4.22(10) + 985.02 = 942.82$

x	4	7	10
y	968.14	955.48	942.82

b. Let $y = 947$
$947 = -4.22x + 985.02$
$-38.02 = -4.22x$
$9 \approx x$
The year 1999

Practice Problems 13.2

1. $x + 3y = 6$
$x = 0,\ 0 + 3y = 6,\ y = 2;\ (0,2)$
$x = 3,\ 3 + 3y = 6,$
$\quad 3y = 3$
$\quad\quad y = 1;\ (3,1)$
$x = 6,\ 6 + 3y = 6,$
$\quad 3y = 0$
$\quad\quad y = 0;\ (6,0)$

x	y
0	2
3	1
6	0

2. $-2x + 4y = 8$
$x = -2,\ -2(-2) + 4y = 8$
$\quad\quad 4 + 4y = 8$
$\quad\quad\quad 4y = 4$
$\quad\quad\quad\quad y = 1$
$x = 0,\ -2(0) + 4y = 8$
$\quad\quad 4y = 8$
$\quad\quad\ y = 2$
$x = 2,\ -2(2) + 4y = 8$
$\quad\quad -4 + 4y = 8$
$\quad\quad\quad 4y = 12$
$\quad\quad\quad\ y = 3$

x	y
-2	1
0	2
2	3

3. $y = 2x$
$x = -2,\ y = 2(-2) = -4$
$x = 0,\ y = 2(0) = 0$
$x = 2,\ y = 2(2) = 4$

461

x	y
−2	−4
0	0
2	4

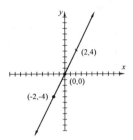

6. $x = 3$

x	y
3	4
3	0
3	−4

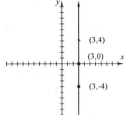

4. $y = -\dfrac{1}{2}x$

$x = -4, \ y = -\dfrac{1}{2}(-4) = 2$

$x = 0, \ y = -\dfrac{1}{2}(0) = 0$

$x = 4, \ y = -\dfrac{1}{2}(4) = -2$

x	y
−4	2
0	0
4	−2

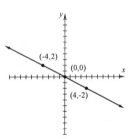

Graphing Calculator Explorations

1. $y = -3x + 7$

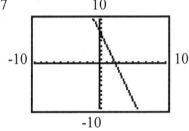

2. $y = -x + 5$

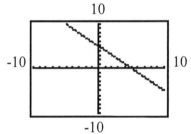

5. $y = 2x + 3$

$x = -2, \ y = 2(-2) + 3 = -4 + 3 = -1$

$x = 0, \ y = 2(0) + 3 = 0 + 3 = 3$

$x = 2, \ y = 2(2) + 3 = 4 + 3 = 7$

x	y
−2	−1
0	3
2	7

3. $y = 2.5x - 7.9$

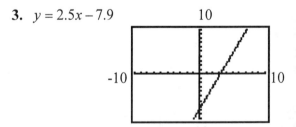

462

4. $y = -1.3x + 5.2$

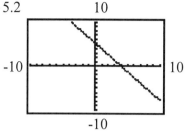

5. $y = -\dfrac{3}{10}x + \dfrac{32}{5}$

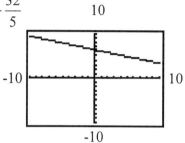

6. $y = \dfrac{2}{9}x - \dfrac{22}{3}$

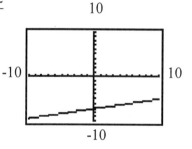

Exercise Set 13.2

1. $x - y = 6$

$$y = 0, \ x - 0 = 6$$
$$x = 6$$
$$x = 4, \ 4 - y = 6$$
$$-y = 2$$
$$y = -2$$
$$y = -1, \ x - (-1) = 6$$
$$x + 1 = 6$$
$$x = 5$$

x	y
6	0
4	−2
5	−1

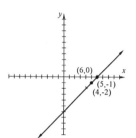

3. $y = -4x$

$$x = 1, \ y = -4(1) = -4$$
$$x = 0, \ y = -4(0) = 0$$
$$x = -1, \ y = -4(-1) = 4$$

x	y
1	−4
0	0
−1	4

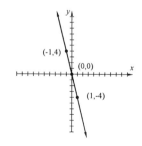

5. $y = \dfrac{1}{3}x$

$x = 0, \ y = \dfrac{1}{3}(0) = 0$

$x = 6, \ y = \dfrac{1}{3}(6) = 2$

$x = -3, \ y = \dfrac{1}{3}(-3) = -1$

x	y
0	0
6	2
-3	-1

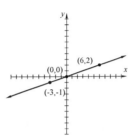

7. $y = -4x + 3$

$x = 0, \ y = -4(0) + 3 = 0 + 3 = 3$

$x = 1, \ y = -4(1) + 3 = -4 + 3 = -1$

$x = 2, \ y = -4(2) + 3 = -8 + 3 = -5$

x	y
0	3
1	-1
2	-5

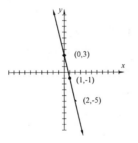

9. $x + y = 1$

x	y
-2	3
0	1
2	-1

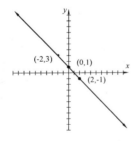

11. $-x + y = 6$

x	y
-6	0
-2	4
0	6

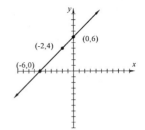

13. $x - 2y = 6$

x	y
-4	-5
0	-3
4	-1

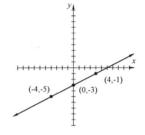

15. $y = 6x + 3$

x	y
-1	-3
0	3
1	9

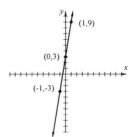

17. $x = -4$

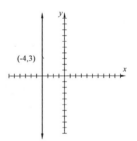

464

19. $y = 3$

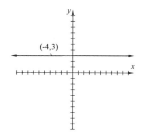

21. $y = x$

x	y
-4	-4
0	0
4	4

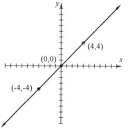

23. $y = 5x$

x	y
-1	-5
0	0
1	5

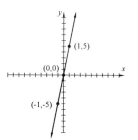

25. $x + 3y = 9$

x	y
-3	4
0	3
3	2

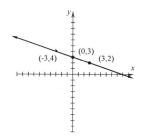

27. $y = \dfrac{1}{2}x - 1$

x	y
-4	-3
0	-1
4	1

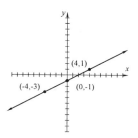

29. $3x - 2y = 12$

x	y
4	0
2	-3
0	-6

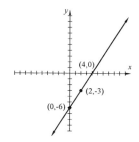

31. $y = 5x$ $y = 5x + 4$

x	y
-1	-5
0	0
1	5

x	y
-1	-1
0	4
1	9

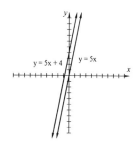

33. $y = -2x$ $y = -2x - 3$

x	y
-2	4
0	0
2	-4

x	y
-2	1
0	-3
2	-7

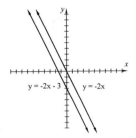

35.

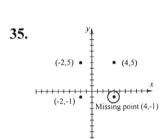

37. $x - y = -3$

$y = 0,\ x - 0 = -3,\ x = -3$

$x = 0,\ 0 - y = -3,\ y = 3$

x	y
0	3
−3	0

39. $y = 2x$

$y = 0,\ 0 = 2x,\ 0 = x$

$x = 0,\ y = 2(0) = 0$

x	y
0	0
0	0

41. $y = x^2$

x	y
0	0
1	1
−1	1
2	4
−2	4

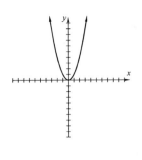

43. $x + y + 5 + 5 = 22$

$x + y + 10 = 22$

$x + y = 12$

Let $x = 3$

$3 + y = 12$

$y = 9$ centimeters

45. $y = 45x + 2214$

a.

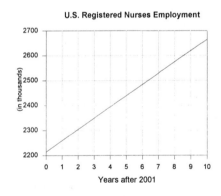

b. Yes. Answers may vary.

466

47. $y = 1.43x + 95$

a.

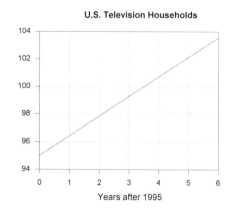

U.S. Television Households

Years after 1995

b. $y = 1.43x + 95$

Let $x = 5$

$y = 1.43(5) + 95 = 7.15 + 95 = 102.15$

$(5, 102.15)$

c. In 2000, there were 102.15 million households in the United States with at least one television.

Practice Problems 13.3

1. x-intercept: $(2, 0)$; y-intercept: $(0, -4)$

2. x-intercepts: $(-4, 0)$, $(2, 0)$
y-intercept: $(0, 2)$

3. x-intercept: none; y-intercept: $(0, 3)$

4. $2x - y = 4$
$y = 0$, $2x - 0 = 4$, $x = 2$
$x = 0$, $2(0) - y = 4$, $y = -4$
x-intercept: $(2, 0)$; y-intercept: $(0, -4)$

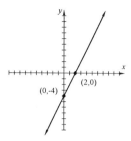

x	y
2	0
0	-4

$(0, -4)$ $(2, 0)$

5. $y = 3x$
$y = 0$, $0 = 3x$, $x = 0$
$x = 0$, $y = 3(0) = 0$
x-intercept: $(0, 0)$; y-intercept: $(0, 0)$
$x = 2$, $y = 3(2) = 6$

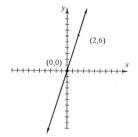

x	y
2	6
0	0

$(0,0)$ $(2,6)$

6. $x = -3$
$y = 0$, $x = -3$
x-intercept: $(-3, 0)$

$(-3, 0)$

7. $y = 4$
$x = 0$, $y = 4$
y-intercept: $(0, 4)$

$(0, 4)$

Graphing Calculator Explorations 13.3

1. $x = 3.78y$

$$y = \frac{x}{3.78}$$

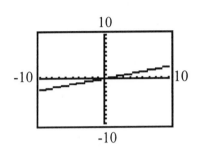

2. $-2.61y = x$

$$y = \frac{x}{-2.61}$$

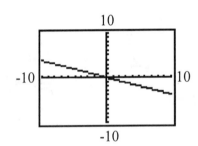

3. $-2.2x + 6.8y = 15.5$

$6.8y = 2.2x + 15.5$

$$y = \frac{2.2}{6.8}x + \frac{15.5}{6.8}$$

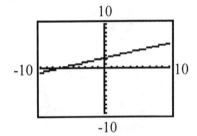

4. $5.9x - 0.8y = -10.4$

$-0.8y = -5.9x - 10.4$

$$y = \frac{5.9}{0.8}x + \frac{10.4}{0.8}$$

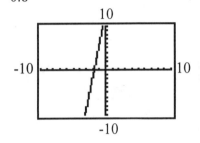

Mental Math 13.3

1. False

2. False

3. True

4. True

Exercise Set 13.3

1. x-intercept: $(-1, 0)$; y-intercept: $(0, 1)$

3. x-intercepts: $(-2, 0), (1, 0), (3, 0)$

y-intercept: $(0, 3)$

5. Infinite

7. 0

9. $x - y = 3$

$y = 0, \ x - 0 = 3, \ x = 3$

$x = 0, \ 0 - y = 3, \ y = -3$

x-intercept: $(3, 0)$; y-intercept: $(0, -3)$

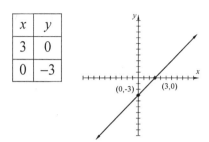

x	y
3	0
0	−3

x	y
−6	0
0	3

15. $2x - 4y = 8$

$y = 0, \ 2x - 4(0) = 8, \ x = 4$

$x = 0, \ 2(0) - 4y = 8, \ y = -2$

x-intercept: $(4, 0)$; y-intercept: $(0, -2)$

x	y
4	0
0	−2

11. $x = 5y$

$y = 0, \ x = 5(0) = 0$

$x = 0, \ 0 = 5y, \ y = 0$

x-intercept: $(0, 0)$; y-intercept: $(0, 0)$

$y = 1, \ x = 5(1) = 5$

x	y
0	0
5	1

17. $x = 2y$

$y = 0, \ x = 2(0) = 0$

$x = 0, \ 0 = 2y, \ y = 0$

x-intercept: $(0, 0)$; y-intercept: $(0, 0)$

$y = 4, \ x = 2(4) = 8$

x	y
4	8
0	0

13. $-x + 2y = 6$

$y = 0, \ -x + 2(0) = 6, \ x = -6$

$x = 0, \ -0 + 2y = 6, \ y = 3$

x-intercept: $(-6, 0)$; y-intercept: $(0, 3)$

19. $y = 3x + 6$

$y = 0$, $0 = 3x + 6$, $x = -2$

$x = 0$, $y = 3(0) + 6 = 6$

x-intercept: $(-2, 0)$; y-intercept: $(0, 6)$

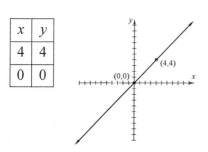

x	y
-2	0
0	6

21. $x = y$

$y = 0$, $x = 0$

$x = 0$, $0 = y$

x-intercept: $(0, 0)$; y-intercept: $(0, 0)$

$y = 4$, $x = 4$

x	y
4	4
0	0

23. $x + 8y = 8$

$y = 0$, $x + 8(0) = 8$, $x = 8$

$x = 0$, $0 + 8y = 8$, $y = 1$

x-intercept: $(8, 0)$; y-intercept: $(0, 1)$

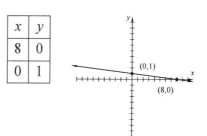

x	y
8	0
0	1

25. $5 = 6x - y$

$y = 0$, $5 = 6x - 0$, $x = \dfrac{5}{6}$

$x = 0$, $5 = 6(0) - y$, $y = -5$

x-intercept: $\left(\dfrac{5}{6}, 0\right)$; y-intercept: $(0, -5)$

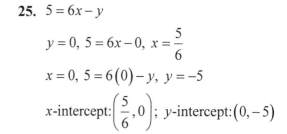

x	y
$\dfrac{5}{6}$	0
0	-5

27. $-x + 10y = 11$

$y = 0$, $-x + 10(0) = 11$, $x = -11$

$x = 0$, $-0 + 10y = 11$, $y = \dfrac{11}{10}$

x-intercept: $(-11, 0)$; y-intercept: $\left(0, \dfrac{11}{10}\right)$

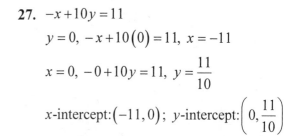

x	y
-11	0
0	$\dfrac{11}{10}$

470

29. $x = -1$

for all values of y.

31. $y = 0$

for all values of x.

33. $y + 7 = 0$

$y = -7$

for all values of x.

35. $x + 3 = 0$

$x = -3$

for all values of y.

37. $\dfrac{-6 - 3}{2 - 8} = \dfrac{-9}{-6} = \dfrac{3}{2}$

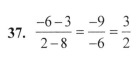

39. $\dfrac{-8 - (-2)}{-3 - (-2)} = \dfrac{-6}{-1} = 6$

41. $\dfrac{0 - 6}{5 - 0} = \dfrac{-6}{5} = -\dfrac{6}{5}$

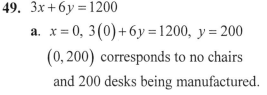

43. $y = 3$

C

45. $x = 3$

A

47. Answers may vary.

49. $3x + 6y = 1200$

    a. $x = 0$, $3(0) + 6y = 1200$, $y = 200$

        $(0, 200)$ corresponds to no chairs

        and 200 desks being manufactured.

    b. $y = 0$, $3x + 6(0) = 1200$, $x = 400$

        $(400, 0)$ corresponds to 400 chairs

        and no desks being manufactured.

    c. $y = 50$, $3x + 6(50) = 1200$

$$3x + 300 = 1200$$

$$3x = 900$$

$$x = 300$$

        300 chairs can be made.

51. Parallel to $y = -1$ is horizontal.

y-intercept is $(0, -4)$, so $y = -4$

for all values of x. $y = -4$

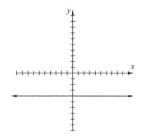

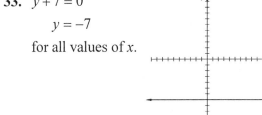

53. $y = 51.6x + 560.2$

    a. $x = 0$, $y = 51.6(0) + 560.2 = 560.2$

    $(0, 560.2)$.

    b. In 1996, the number of Disney
       Stores was about 560.2

Practice Problems 13.4

1. $(-2, 3)$ and $(4, -1)$

$$m = \frac{y_2 - y_1}{x_2 - x_1} = \frac{-1 - 3}{4 - (-2)} = \frac{-4}{6} = -\frac{2}{3}$$

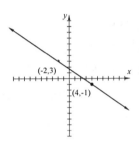

2. $(-2, 1)$ and $(3, 5)$

$$m = \frac{y_2 - y_1}{x_2 - x_1} = \frac{5 - 1}{3 - (-2)} = \frac{4}{5}$$

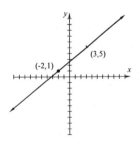

3. $5x + 4y = 10$

$$4y = -5x + 10$$

$$y = -\frac{5}{4}x + \frac{5}{2}$$

$$m = -\frac{5}{4}$$

4. $y = 3$

$$y = 0x + 3$$

$$m = 0$$

5. $x = -2$ for all values of y. Pick two
   points; $(-2, 0)$ and $(-2, 4)$

$$m = \frac{y_2 - y_1}{x_2 - x_1} = \frac{4 - 0}{-2 - (-2)} = \frac{4}{0} \text{ is undefined}$$

6. **a.** $x + y = 5$

        $y = -x + 5$, $m_1 = -1$

      $2x + y = 5$

        $y = -2x + 5$, $m_2 = -2$

    $m_1 \neq m_2$ and $m_1 m_2 \neq -1$, neither

b. $5y = 2x - 3$

$$y = \frac{2}{5}x - \frac{3}{5}, \; m_1 = \frac{2}{5}$$

$$5x + 2y = 1$$

$$2y = -5x + 1$$

$$y = -\frac{5}{2}x + \frac{1}{2}, \; m_2 = -\frac{5}{2}$$

$$m_1 m_2 = \left(\frac{2}{5}\right)\left(-\frac{5}{2}\right) = -1, \text{ perpendicular}$$

c. $y = 2x + 1, \; m_1 = 2$

$$4x - 2y = 8$$

$$-2y = -4x + 8,$$

$$y = 2x - 4, \; m_2 = 2$$

$$m_1 = m_2, \text{ parallel}$$

7. $\text{grade} = \dfrac{\text{rise}}{\text{run}} = \dfrac{3}{20} = 0.15 = 15\%$

8. $(1980, 120)$ and $(1990, 240)$

$$m = \frac{y_2 - y_1}{x_2 - x_1} = \frac{240 - 120}{1990 - 1980} = \frac{120}{10} = 12$$

Each year the sales of food and drink from restaurants increases by $12 billion.

Graphing Calculator Explorations 13.4

1. $y_1 = 3.8x$

$y_2 = 3.8x - 3$

$y_3 = 3.8x + 9$

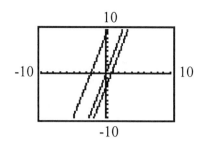

2. $y_1 = -4.9x$

$y_2 = -4.9x + 1$

$y_3 = -4.9x + 8$

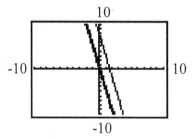

3. $y_1 = \dfrac{1}{4}x$

$y_2 = \dfrac{1}{4}x + 5$

$y_3 = \dfrac{1}{4}x - 8$

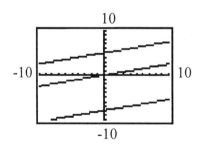

4. $y_1 = -\dfrac{3}{4}x$

$y_2 = -\dfrac{3}{4}x - 5$

$y_3 = -\dfrac{3}{4}x + 6$

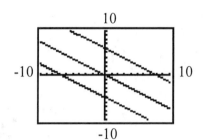

Mental Math 13.4

1. Upward

2. Downward

3. Horizontal

4. Vertical

Exercise Set 13.4

1. $(-1, 2)$ and $(2, -2)$

$m = \dfrac{y_2 - y_1}{x_2 - x_1} = \dfrac{-2 - 2}{2 - (-1)} = -\dfrac{4}{3}$

3. $(1, -2)$ and $(3, 3)$

$m = \dfrac{y_2 - y_1}{x_2 - x_1} = \dfrac{3 - (-2)}{3 - 1} = \dfrac{5}{2}$

5. $(0, 0)$ and $(7, 8)$

$m = \dfrac{y_2 - y_1}{x_2 - x_1} = \dfrac{8 - 0}{7 - 0} = \dfrac{8}{7}$

7. $(-1, 5)$ and $(6, -2)$

$m = \dfrac{y_2 - y_1}{x_2 - x_1} = \dfrac{-2 - 5}{6 - (-1)} = -\dfrac{7}{7} = -1$

9. $(1, 4)$ and $(5, 3)$

$m = \dfrac{y_2 - y_1}{x_2 - x_1} = \dfrac{3 - 4}{5 - 1} = -\dfrac{1}{4}$

11. $(-2, 8)$ and $(1, 6)$

$m = \dfrac{y_2 - y_1}{x_2 - x_1} = \dfrac{6 - 8}{1 - (-2)} = -\dfrac{2}{3}$

13. $(5, 1)$ and $(-2, 1)$

$m = \dfrac{y_2 - y_1}{x_2 - x_1} = \dfrac{1 - 1}{-2 - 5} = \dfrac{0}{-7} = 0$

15. Line 1

17. Line 2

19. $y = 5x - 2,\ m = 5$

21. $2x + y = 7$

$y = -2x + 7,\ m = -2$

23. $2x - 3y = 10$

$-3y = -2x + 10$

$y = \dfrac{2}{3}x - \dfrac{10}{3},\ m = \dfrac{2}{3}$

25. $x = 2y$

$2y = x$

$y = \dfrac{1}{2}x,\ m = \dfrac{1}{2}$

27. $(2,-1)$ and $(2,3)$

$$m = \frac{y_2 - y_1}{x_2 - x_1} = \frac{3-(-1)}{2-2} = \frac{4}{0} \text{ is undefined}$$

29. $x = 1$ is a vertical line, so it has an undefined slope.

31. $y = -3$ is a horizontal line, so it has a slope $m = 0$.

33. $x - 3y = -6$, $-3y = -x - 6$,

$y = \frac{1}{3}x + 2$, $m_1 = \frac{1}{3}$

$3x - y = 0$, $-y = -3x$, $y = 3x$, $m_2 = 3$

$m_1 \neq m_2$ and $m_1 m_2 \neq -1$, neither

35. $10 + 3x = 5y$, $2 + \frac{3}{5}x = y$, $m_1 = \frac{3}{5}$

$5x + 3y = 1$, $3y = -5x + 1$, $y = -\frac{5}{3}x + \frac{1}{3}$

$m_2 = -\frac{5}{3}$

$m_1 m_2 = \left(\frac{3}{5}\right)\left(-\frac{5}{3}\right) = -1$, perpendicular

37. $6x = 5y + 1$, $6x - 1 = 5y$, $\frac{6}{5}x - \frac{1}{5} = y$,

$m_1 = \frac{6}{5}$

$-12x + 10y = 1$, $10y = 12x + 1$,

$y = \frac{12}{10}x + \frac{1}{10}$, $y = \frac{6}{5}x + \frac{1}{10}$, $m_2 = \frac{6}{5}$

$m_1 = m_2$, parallel

39. $(-3,-3)$ and $(0,0)$

$$m = \frac{y_2 - y_1}{x_2 - x_1} = \frac{0-(-3)}{0-(-3)} = \frac{3}{3} = 1$$

a. $m = 1$

b. $m = -1$

41. $(-8,-4)$ and $(3,5)$

$$m = \frac{y_2 - y_1}{x_2 - x_1} = \frac{5-(-4)}{3-(-8)} = \frac{9}{11}$$

a. $m = \frac{9}{11}$

b. $m = -\frac{11}{9}$

43. pitch $= \frac{6}{10} = \frac{3}{5}$

45. grade $= \frac{\text{rise}}{\text{run}} = \frac{2}{16} = 0.125 = 12.5\%$

47. grade $= \frac{\text{rise}}{\text{run}} = \frac{2580}{6450} = 0.40 = 40\%$

49. slope $= \frac{\text{rise}}{\text{run}} = \frac{0.25}{12} = 0.02$

51. $(1999, 99)$ and $(2002, 144)$

$$m = \frac{y_2 - y_1}{x_2 - x_1} = \frac{144 - 99}{2002 - 1999} = \frac{45}{3}$$

$= 15$ million users per year.
Every year there will be 15 million more Internet users.

53. $(5000, 1800)$ and $(20,000, 7200)$

$$m = \frac{y_2 - y_1}{x_2 - x_1} = \frac{7200 - 1800}{20,000 - 5000} = \frac{5400}{15,000}$$
$$= 0.36 \text{ dollars per mile}$$

It costs $0.36 per mile to own and operate a compact car.

55. $y - (-6) = 2(x - 4)$
$$y + 6 = 2x - 8$$
$$y = 2x - 14$$

57. $y - 1 = -6(x - (-2))$
$$y - 1 = -6(x + 2)$$
$$y - 1 = -6x - 12$$
$$y = -6x - 11$$

59. $(0, 0)$ and $(1, 1)$
$$m = \frac{y_2 - y_1}{x_2 - x_1} = \frac{1 - 0}{1 - 0} = 1$$

D

61. A vertical line has undefined slope.

B

63. $(2, 0)$ and $(4, -1)$
$$m = \frac{y_2 - y_1}{x_2 - x_1} = \frac{-1 - 0}{4 - 2} = -\frac{1}{2}$$

E

65. 28.3 miles per gallon

67. 1992 the average was 27.6 miles per gallon.

69. The greatest slope was from 1992 to 1993.

71. $\text{pitch} = \dfrac{\text{rise}}{\text{run}}$
$$\frac{1}{3} = \frac{x}{18}$$
$$3x = 18$$
$$x = 6$$

73. a. $(1994, 782)$ and $(2001, 1132)$

    b. $m = \dfrac{y_2 - y_1}{x_2 - x_1} = \dfrac{1132 - 782}{2001 - 1994} = \dfrac{350}{7} = 50$

    c. For the years 1994 through 2001, the price per acre of U.S. farmland rose $50 every year.

75. $y = -30x + 1485$

    a. $(0, 1485)$

    b. In 1998, there were 1485 million admissions to movie theatres in the U.S. and Canada

    c. $m = -30$

    d. For the years 1998 through 2000, the number of movie theater admissions has decreased at a rate of 30 million per year.

77. $(1, 1)$, $(-4, 4)$ and $(-3, 0)$
$$m_1 = \frac{0 - 1}{-3 - 1} = \frac{1}{4}, \; m_2 = \frac{0 - 4}{-3 - (-4)} = -4$$
$m_1 m_2 = -1$, so the sides are perpendicular.

79. $(2.1, 6.7)$ and $(-8.3, 9.3)$
$$m = \frac{y_2 - y_1}{x_2 - x_1} = \frac{9.3 - 6.7}{-8.3 - 2.1} = \frac{2.6}{-10.4} = -0.25$$

81. $(2.3, 0.2)$ and $(7.9, 5.1)$

$$m = \frac{y_2 - y_1}{x_2 - x_1} = \frac{5.1 - 0.2}{7.9 - 2.3} = \frac{4.9}{5.6} = 0.875$$

83. $y = -\frac{1}{3}x + 2$

$y = -2x + 2$

$y = -4x + 2$

The line becomes steeper.

Practice Problems 13.5

1. $m = \frac{3}{5}, b = -2$

$y = mx + b$

$y = \frac{3}{5}x - 2$

2. $y = \frac{2}{3}x - 4$

$m = \frac{2}{3}, b = -4$

3. $3x + y = 2$

$y = -3x + 2$

$m = \frac{-3}{1}, b = 2$

4. $m = -3; (2, -4)$

$$y - y_1 = m(x - x_1)$$

$$y - (-4) = -3(x - 2)$$

$$y + 4 = -3x + 6$$

$$3x + y + 4 = 6$$

$$3x + y = 2$$

5. $(1, 3)$ and $(5, -2)$

$$m = \frac{y_2 - y_1}{x_2 - x_1} = \frac{-2 - 3}{5 - 1} = -\frac{5}{4}$$

$$m = -\frac{5}{4}; (1, 3)$$

$$y - y_1 = m(x - x_1)$$

$$y - 3 = -\frac{5}{4}(x - 1)$$

$$4(y - 3) = -5(x - 1)$$

$$4y - 12 = -5x + 5$$

$$5x + 4y = 17$$

6. a. $(10, 200)$ and $(9, 250)$

$$m = \frac{y_2 - y_1}{x_2 - x_1} = \frac{250 - 200}{9 - 10} = -50$$

$$m = -50; (10, 200)$$

$$y - y_1 = m(x - x_1)$$

$$y - 200 = -50(x - 10)$$

$$y - 200 = -50x + 500$$

$$y = -50x + 700$$

b. Let $x = 7.50$

$$y = -50(7.50) + 700$$

$$= -375 + 700$$

$$= 325$$

Expect to sell 325 toys

477

Graphing Calculator Explorations 13.5

1. $y_1 = x, \quad y_2 = 6x, \quad y_3 = -6x$

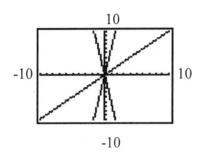

2. $y_1 = -x, \quad y_2 = -5x, \quad y_3 = -10x$

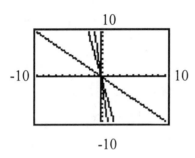

3. $y_1 = \frac{1}{2}x + 2, \quad y_2 = \frac{3}{4}x + 2, \quad y_3 = x + 2$

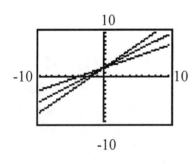

4. $y_1 = x + 1, \quad y_2 = \frac{5}{4}x + 1, \quad y_3 = \frac{5}{2}x + 1$

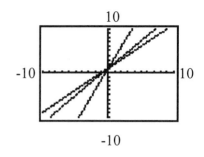

Mental Math 13.5

1. $y = 2x - 1$

$m = 2, \ (0, -1)$

2. $y = -7x + 3$

$m = -7, \ (0, 3)$

3. $y = x + \frac{1}{3}$

$m = 1, \ \left(0, \frac{1}{3}\right)$

4. $y = -x - \frac{2}{9}$

$m = -1, \ \left(0, -\frac{2}{9}\right)$

5. $y = \frac{5}{7}x - 4$

$m = \frac{5}{7}, \ (0, -4)$

6. $y = -\dfrac{1}{4}x + \dfrac{3}{5}$

$m = -\dfrac{1}{4}, \ \left(0, \dfrac{3}{5}\right)$

7. $y - 8 = 3(x - 4)$

$m = 3$

Answers may vary. Example: $(4, 8)$

8. $y - 1 = 5(x - 2)$

$m = 5$

Answers may vary. Example: $(2, 1)$

9. $y + 3 = -2(x - 10)$

$m = -2$

Answers may vary. Example: $(10, -3)$

10. $y + 6 = -7(x - 2)$

$m = -7$

Answers may vary. Example: $(2, -6)$

11. $y = \dfrac{2}{5}(x + 1)$

$m = \dfrac{2}{5}$

Answers may vary. Example: $(-1, 0)$

12. $y = \dfrac{3}{7}(x + 4)$

$m = \dfrac{3}{7}$

Answers may vary. Example: $(-4, 0)$

Exercise Set 13.5

1. $m = 5, \ b = 3$

$y = mx + b$

$y = 5x + 3$

3. $m = \dfrac{2}{3}, \ b = 0$

$y = mx + b$

$y = \dfrac{2}{3}x$

5. $m = -\dfrac{1}{5}, \ b = \dfrac{1}{9}$

$y = mx + b$

$y = -\dfrac{1}{5}x + \dfrac{1}{9}$

7. $y = 2x + 1$

9. $y = \dfrac{2}{3}x + 5$

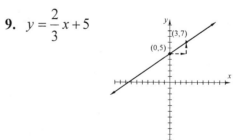

11. $y = -5x$

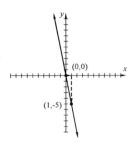

13. $4x + y = 6$

$\quad y = -4x + 6$

15. $4x - 7y = -14$

$\quad -7y = -4x - 14$

$\quad y = \dfrac{4}{7}x + 2$

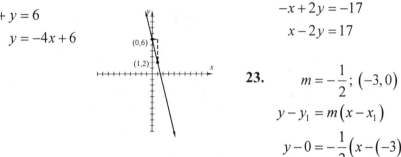

17. $m = 6; \ (2,2)$

$y - y_1 = m(x - x_1)$

$y - 2 = 6(x - 2)$

$y - 2 = 6x - 12$

$-6x + y = 10$

19. $m = -8; \ (-1, -5)$

$y - y_1 = m(x - x_1)$

$y - (-5) = -8(x - (-1))$

$y + 5 = -8x - 8$

$8x + y = -13$

21. $m = \dfrac{1}{2}; \ (5, -6)$

$y - y_1 = m(x - x_1)$

$y - (-6) = \dfrac{1}{2}(x - 5)$

$2(y + 6) = x - 5$

$2y + 12 = x - 5$

$-x + 2y = -17$

$x - 2y = 17$

23. $m = -\dfrac{1}{2}; \ (-3, 0)$

$y - y_1 = m(x - x_1)$

$y - 0 = -\dfrac{1}{2}(x - (-3))$

$2y = -x - 3$

$x + 2y = -3$

25. $(3, 2)$ and $(5, 6)$

$m = \dfrac{y_2 - y_1}{x_2 - x_1} = \dfrac{6 - 2}{5 - 3} = \dfrac{4}{2} = 2$

$m = 2; \ (3, 2)$

$y - y_1 = m(x - x_1)$

$y - 2 = 2(x - 3)$

$y - 2 = 2x - 6$

$-2x + y = -4$

$2x - y = 4$

27. $(-1, 3)$ and $(-2, -5)$

$$m = \frac{y_2 - y_1}{x_2 - x_1} = \frac{-5 - 3}{-2 - (-1)} = \frac{-8}{-1} = 8$$

$m = 8;\ (-1, 3)$

$$y - y_1 = m(x - x_1)$$
$$y - 3 = 8(x - (-1))$$
$$y - 3 = 8x + 8$$
$$-8x + y = 11$$
$$8x - y = -11$$

29. $(2, 3)$ and $(-1, -1)$

$$m = \frac{y_2 - y_1}{x_2 - x_1} = \frac{-1 - 3}{-1 - 2} = \frac{-4}{-3} = \frac{4}{3}$$

$m = \dfrac{4}{3};\ (2, 3)$

$$y - y_1 = m(x - x_1)$$
$$y - 3 = \frac{4}{3}(x - 2)$$
$$3(y - 3) = 4(x - 2)$$
$$3y - 9 = 4x - 8$$
$$-4x + 3y = 1$$
$$4x - 3y = -1$$

31. $(10, 7)$ and $(7, 10)$

$$m = \frac{y_2 - y_1}{x_2 - x_1} = \frac{10 - 7}{7 - 10} = \frac{3}{-3} = -1$$

$m = -1;\ (10, 7)$

$$y - y_1 = m(x - x_1)$$
$$y - 7 = -1(x - 10)$$
$$y - 7 = -x + 10$$
$$x + y = 17$$

33. $(10, 7)$ and $(7, 10)$

$$m = \frac{y_2 - y_1}{x_2 - x_1} = \frac{10 - 7}{7 - 10} = \frac{3}{-3} = -1$$

$m = -1;\ (10, 7)$

$$y - y_1 = m(x - x_1)$$
$$y - 7 = -1(x - 10)$$
$$y - 7 = -x + 10$$
$$x + y = 17$$

35. $(-8, 1)$ and $(0, 0)$

$$m = \frac{y_2 - y_1}{x_2 - x_1} = \frac{0 - 1}{0 - (-8)} = -\frac{1}{8}$$

$m = -\dfrac{1}{8};\ (0, 0)$

$$y - y_1 = m(x - x_1)$$
$$y - 0 = -\frac{1}{8}(x - 0)$$
$$8y = -x$$
$$x + 8y = 0$$

37. a. $(1, 32)$ and $(3, 96)$

$$m = \frac{y_2 - y_1}{x_2 - x_1} = \frac{96 - 32}{3 - 1} = \frac{64}{2} = 32$$

$m = 32;\ (1, 32)$

$$s - s_1 = m(t - t_1)$$
$$s - 32 = 32(t - 1)$$
$$s - 32 = 32t - 32$$
$$s = 32t$$

b. If $t = 4$, then $s = 32(4) = 128$ ft/sec.

39. a. Same

b. 2009 is 11 years past 1998, so $x = 11$.

$y = 1174(11) + 5242$

$= 12,914 + 5242$

$= 18,156$ vehicles

41. a. $(0, 70.3)$ and $(10, 79.6)$

$m = \dfrac{y_2 - y_1}{x_2 - x_1} = \dfrac{79.6 - 70.3}{10 - 0} = \dfrac{9.3}{10} = 0.93$

$m = 0.93; \ (0, 70.3)$

$y - y_1 = m(x - x_1)$

$y - 70.3 = 0.93(x - 0)$

$y - 70.3 = 0.93x$

$y = 0.93x + 70.3.$

b. If $x = 17$,

then $y = 0.93(17) + 70.3 = 86.11$

Expect 86.11 persons per square mile.

43. a. $(0, 191)$ and $(5, 260)$

b. $m = \dfrac{y_2 - y_1}{x_2 - x_1} = \dfrac{260 - 191}{5 - 0} = \dfrac{69}{5} = 13.8$

$m = 13.8; \ (0, 191)$

$y - y_1 = m(x - x_1)$

$y - 191 = 13.8(x - 0)$

$y - 191 = 13.8x$

$y = 13.8x + 191$

c. If $x = 4$,

then $y = 13.8(4) + 191 = 246.2$

Expect \$246.2 million in sales.

45. a. $(3, 10,000)$ and $(5, 8000)$

$m = \dfrac{y_2 - y_1}{x_2 - x_1} = \dfrac{8000 - 10,000}{5 - 3}$

$= \dfrac{-2000}{2} = -1000$

$m = -1000; \ (5, 8000)$

$s - s_1 = m(p - p_1)$

$s - 8000 = -1000(p - 5)$

$s - 8000 = -1000p + 5000$

$s = -1000p + 13,000$

b. If $p = 3.50$,

then $s = -1000(3.5) + 13,000 = 9500$

Expect \$9500 in daily sales.

47. If $x = 2$, then

$x^2 - 3x + 1 = (2)^2 - 3(2) + 1 = 4 - 6 + 1 = -1$

49. If $x = -1$, then

$x^2 - 3x + 1 = (-1)^2 - 3(-1) + 1 = 1 + 3 + 1 = 5$

51. No

53. Yes

55. $y = 2x + 1$

$m = 2, b = 1$

B

57. $y = -3x - 2$

$m = -3, b = -2$

D

59. $y = 3x - 1$, $m_1 = 3$

Same slope: $m_2 = m_1 = 3$; $(-1, 2)$

$$y - y_1 = m_2 (x - x_1)$$
$$y - 2 = 3(x - (-1))$$
$$y - 2 = 3x + 3$$
$$-3x + y = 5$$
$$3x - y = -5$$

61. $y = 3x - 1$, $m_1 = 3$

a. Parallel: $m_2 = m_1 = 3$; $(-1, 2)$

$$y - y_1 = m_2 (x - x_1)$$
$$y - 2 = 3(x - (-1))$$
$$y - 2 = 3x + 3$$
$$-3x + y = 5$$
$$3x - y = -5$$

b. Perpendicular: $m_2 = -\dfrac{1}{m_1} = -\dfrac{1}{3}$;

$(-1, 2)$

$$y - y_1 = m_2 (x - x_1)$$
$$y - 2 = -\dfrac{1}{3}(x - (-1))$$
$$3(y - 2) = -1(x + 1)$$
$$3y - 6 = -x - 1$$
$$x + 3y = 5$$

Integrated Review 13.5

1. $(0, 0)$ and $(2, 4)$

$$m = \dfrac{y_2 - y_1}{x_2 - x_1} = \dfrac{4 - 0}{2 - 0} = \dfrac{4}{2} = 2$$

2. Horizontal line, $m = 0$

3. $(0, 1)$ and $(3, -1)$

$$m = \dfrac{y_2 - y_1}{x_2 - x_1} = \dfrac{-1 - 1}{3 - 0} = -\dfrac{2}{3}$$

4. Vertical line, slope is undefined.

5. $y = -2x$

$m = 2, b = 0$

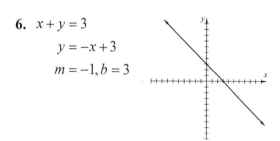

6. $x + y = 3$

$y = -x + 3$

$m = -1, b = 3$

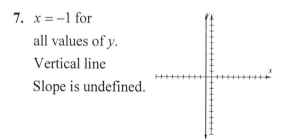

7. $x = -1$ for
all values of y.
Vertical line
Slope is undefined.

483

8. $y = 4$ for all values of x
   Horizontal line
   $m = 0$

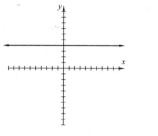

13. $7x + 2y = 11$
    $2y = -7x + 11$
    $y = -\dfrac{7}{2}x + \dfrac{11}{2}$
    $y = mx + b$
    $m = -\dfrac{7}{2}$

9. $x - 2y = 6$
   $-2y = -x + 6$
   $y = \dfrac{1}{2}x - 3$
   $m = \dfrac{1}{2}, b = -3$

14. $2x - y = 0$
    $-y = -2x$
    $y = 2x$
    $y = mx + b$
    $m = 2$

15. $x = 2$, vertical line, slope is undefined.

16. $y = -4$, horizontal line, $m = 0$

10. $y = 3x + 2$
    $m = 3, b = 2$

17. $m = 2, b = -\dfrac{1}{3}$
    $y = mx + b$
    $y = 2x - \dfrac{1}{3}$

18. $m = -4;\ (-1, 3)$
    $y - y_1 = m(x - x_1)$
    $y - 3 = -4(x - (-1))$
    $y - 3 = -4x - 4$
    $4x + y = -1$

11. $y = 3x - 1$
    $y = mx + b$
    $m = 3$

12. $y = -6x + 2$
    $y = mx + b$
    $m = -6$

19. $(2, 0)$ and $(-1, -3)$
    $m = \dfrac{y_2 - y_1}{x_2 - x_1} = \dfrac{-3 - 0}{-1 - 2} = \dfrac{-3}{-3} = 1$
    $m = 1;\ (2, 0)$

$$y - y_1 = m(x - x_1)$$
$$y - 0 = 1(x - 2)$$
$$y = x - 2$$
$$-x + y = -2$$

20. $6x - y = 7,\ -y = -6x + 7,$
$$y = 6x + 7,\ m_1 = 6$$
$$2x + 3y = 4,\ 3y = -2x + 4,$$
$$y = -\frac{2}{3}x + \frac{4}{3},\ m_2 = -\frac{2}{3}$$
$$m_1 \neq m_2 \text{ and } m_1 m_2 \neq -1,\ \text{neither}$$

21. $3x - 6y = 4,\ -6y = -3x + 4,$
$$y = \frac{1}{2}x - \frac{2}{3},\ m_1 = \frac{1}{2}$$
$$y = -2x,\ m_2 = -2$$
$$m_1 m_2 = \left(\frac{1}{2}\right)(-2) = -1,\ \text{perpendicular}$$

22. a. $(1997, 11.6)$ and $(2001, 15.4)$

   b. $m = \dfrac{y_2 - y_1}{x_2 - x_1} = \dfrac{15.4 - 11.6}{2001 - 1997} = \dfrac{3.8}{4} = 0.95$

   c. For the years 1997 through 2001, the number of grill units shipped increased at a rate of 0.95 million per year.

Practice Problems 13.6

1. $\{(-3, 5), (-3, 1), (4, 6), (7, 0)\}$
Domain: $\{-3, 4, 7\}$
Range: $\{0, 1, 5, 6\}$

2. a. Every point has a unique x-value: it is a function.

   b. Two points have the same x-value: it is not a function.

3. a. This is the graph of the relation
$$\{(-3, -2), (-1, -1), (0, 0), (1, 1)\}$$
Every point has a unique x-value: it is a function.

   b. This is the graph of the relation
$$\{(-1, -1), (-1, 2), (1, 0), (3, 1)\}$$
Two points have the same x-value: it is not a function.

4. (a) and (b) pass the vertical line test– they are functions. (c) and (d) do not pass the vertical line test– they are not functions.

5. a. 6:30 A.M.

   b. middle of March and middle of September

6. $f(x) = x^2 + 1$

   a. $f(1) = (1)^2 + 1 = 2;\ (1, 2)$

   b. $f(-3) = (-3)^2 + 1 = 9 + 1 = 10;\ (-3, 10)$

   c. $f(0) = (0)^2 + 1 = 1;\ (0, 1)$

Exercise Set 13.6

1. $\{(2,4),(0,0),(-7,10),(10,-7)\}$
   Domain: $\{-7,0,2,10\}$
   Range: $\{-7,0,4,10\}$

3. $\{(0,-2),(1,-2),(5,-2),\}$
   Domain: $\{0,1,5\}$
   Range: $\{-2\}$

5. Every point has a unique x-value: it is a function.

7. Two points have the same x-value: it is not a function.

9. No

11. Yes

13. Yes

15. No

17. 5:30 A.M.

19. Answers may vary

21. 9:30 A.M.

23. January 1 and December 1

25. Yes: it passes the vertical line test.

27. $4.75 per hour

29. The first year there is a dot above $4.00 is 1992.

31. Yes; answers may vary

33. $f(x) = 2x - 5$
    $f(-2) = 2(-2) - 5 = -4 - 5 = -9$
    $f(0) = 2(0) - 5 = -5$
    $f(3) = 2(3) - 5 = 6 - 5 = 1$

35. $f(x) = x^2 + 2$
    $f(-2) = (-2)^2 + 2 = 4 + 2 = 6$
    $f(0) = (0)^2 + 2 = 2$
    $f(3) = (3)^2 + 2 = 9 + 2 = 11$

37. $f(x) = 3x$
    $f(-2) = 3(-2) = -6$
    $f(0) = 3(0) = 0$
    $f(3) = 3(3) = 9$

39. $f(x) = |x|$
    $f(-2) = |-2| = 2$
    $f(0) = |0| = 0$
    $f(3) = |3| = 3$

41. $h(x) = -5x$
    $h(-1) = -5(-1) = 5$
    $h(0) = -5(0) = 0$
    $h(4) = -5(4) = -20$

43. $h(x) = 2x^2 + 3$
    $h(-1) = 2(-1)^2 + 3 = 2 + 3 = 5$
    $h(0) = 2(0)^2 + 3 = 3$
    $h(4) = 2(4)^2 + 3 = 2 \cdot 16 + 3 = 32 + 3 = 35$

45. $2x + 5 < 7$

$2x < 2$

$x < 1$

47. $-x + 6 \leq 9$

$-x \leq 3$

$\dfrac{-x}{-1} \geq \dfrac{3}{-1}$

$x \geq -3$

49. $P = \dfrac{3}{x} + \dfrac{3}{2x} + \dfrac{5}{x} = \dfrac{6}{2x} + \dfrac{3}{2x} + \dfrac{10}{2x} = \dfrac{19}{2x}$ m

51. $f(x) = 2.59x + 47.24$

    a. $f(46) = 2.59(46) + 47.24 = 166.38$ cm

    b. $f(39) = 2.59(39) + 47.24 = 148.25$ cm

53. Answers may vary

55. $y = x + 7$

    $f(x) = x + 7$

Practice Problems 13.7

1. $x - 4y > 8$

    a. $(-3, 2)$, $-3 - 4(2) \overset{?}{>} 8$

                $-3 - 8 \overset{?}{>} 8$

                $-11 \overset{?}{>} 8$, False

    $(-3, 2)$ is not a solution

    b. $(9, 0)$, $9 - 4(0) \overset{?}{>} 8$

                $9 - 0 \overset{?}{>} 8$

                $9 \overset{?}{>} 8$, True

    $(9, 0)$ is a solution

2. $x - y > 3$

    Test $(0, 0)$

    $0 - 0 \overset{?}{>} 3$, False

    Shade below.

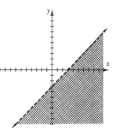

3. $x - 4y \leq 4$

    Test $(0, 0)$

    $0 - 4(0) \overset{?}{\leq} 4$, True

    Shade above.

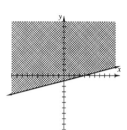

4. $y < 3x$

    Test $(0, 1)$

    $1 \overset{?}{<} 3(0)$, False

    Shade below.

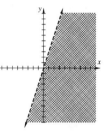

5. $3x + 2y \geq 12$

    Test $(0, 0)$

    $3(0) + 2(0) \overset{?}{\geq} 12$,

    False

    Shade above.

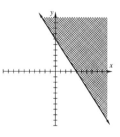

6. $x < 2$

Test $(0,0)$

$0 \overset{?}{<} 2$, True

Shade to the left.

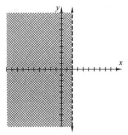

7. $y \geq \frac{1}{4}x + 3$

Test $(0,0)$

$0 \overset{?}{\geq} \frac{1}{4}(0) + 3,$

False

Shade above.

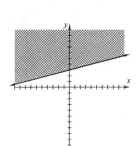

Mental Math 13.7

1. Yes

2. No

3. Yes

4. No

5. $x + y > -5$, $(0,0)$

$0 + 0 \overset{?}{>} -5$

$0 \overset{?}{>} -5$

Yes

6. $2x + 3y < 10$, $(0,0)$

$2(0) + 3(0) \overset{?}{<} 10$

$0 \overset{?}{<} 10$

Yes

7. $x - y \leq -1$, $(0,0)$

$0 - 0 \overset{?}{\leq} -1$

$0 \overset{?}{\leq} -1$

No

8. $\frac{2}{3}x + \frac{5}{6}y > 4$, $(0,0)$

$\frac{2}{3}(0) + \frac{5}{6}(0) \overset{?}{>} 4$

$0 \overset{?}{>} 4$

No

Exercise Set 13.7

1. $x - y > 3$

$(0,3)$, $0 - 3 \overset{?}{>} 3$

$-3 \overset{?}{>} 3$, False

$(0,3)$ is not a solution

$(2,-1)$, $2 - (-1) \overset{?}{>} 3$

$2 + 1 \overset{?}{>} 3$

$3 \overset{?}{>} 3$, False

$(2,-1)$ is not a solution

3. $3x - 5y \leq -4$

$(2,3)$, $3(2) - 5(3) \overset{?}{\leq} -4$

$6 - 15 \overset{?}{\leq} -4$

$-9 \overset{?}{\leq} -4$, True

$(2,3)$ is a solution

$(-1,-1)$, $3(-1) - 5(-1) \overset{?}{\leq} -4$

488

$$-3+5\overset{?}{\le}-4$$
$$2\overset{?}{\le}-4,\ \text{False}$$
$(-1,-1)$ is not a solution

5. $x<-y$

$(0,2),\ 0\overset{?}{<}-2,\ \text{False}$
$(0,2)$ is not a solution
$(-5,1),\ -5\overset{?}{<}-1,\ \text{True}$
$(-5,1)$ is a solution

7. $x+y\le1$
Test $(0,0)$
$0+0\overset{?}{\le}1,\ \text{True}$
Shade below.

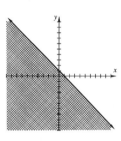

9. $2x-y>-4$
Test $(0,0)$
$2(0)-0\overset{?}{>}-4$
True
Shade below.

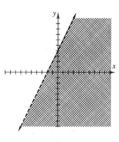

11. $y>2x$
Test $(0,1)$
$1\overset{?}{>}2(0)$
True
Shade above.

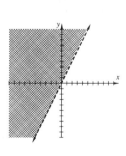

13. $x\le-3y$
Test $(0,1)$
$0\overset{?}{\le}-3(1)$
False
Shade below.

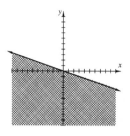

15. $y\ge x+5$
Test $(0,0)$
$0\overset{?}{\ge}0+5$
False
Shade above.

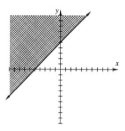

17. $y<4$
Test $(0,0)$
$0\overset{?}{<}4$
True
Shade below.

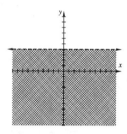

19. $x\ge-3$
Test $(0,0)$
$0\overset{?}{\ge}-3$
True
Shade right.

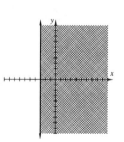

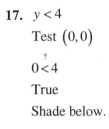

21. $5x + 2y \leq 10$

Test $(0,0)$

$5(0) + 2(0) \overset{?}{\leq} 10$

True

Shade below.

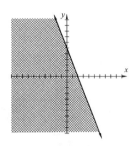

23. $x > y$

Test $(0,1)$

$0 \overset{?}{>} 1$

False

Shade below.

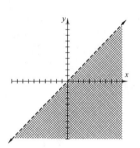

25. $x - y \leq 6$

Test $(0,0)$

$0 - 0 \overset{?}{\leq} 6$

True

Shade above.

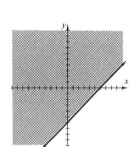

27. $x \geq 0$

Test $(1,0)$

$1 \overset{?}{\geq} 0$

True

Shade right.

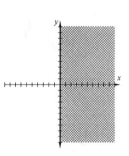

29. $2x + 7y > 5$

Test $(0,0)$

$2(0) + 7(0) \overset{?}{>} 5$

False

Shade above.

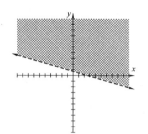

31. $y \geq \dfrac{1}{2}x - 4$

Test $(0,0)$

$0 \overset{?}{\geq} \dfrac{1}{2}(0) - 4$

True

Shade above.

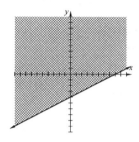

33. $(-2, 1)$

35. $(-3, -1)$

37. $x > 2$

a

39. $y \leq 2x$

b

41. Answers may vary

43. a. $30x + 0.15y \leq 500$

b.

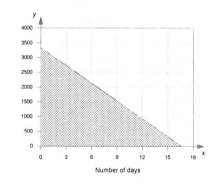

c. Answers may vary

Practice Problems 13.8

1. $y = kx$

$8 = k(4)$

$2 = k$

$y = 2x$

2. $y = kx$

$15 = k(45)$

$\dfrac{15}{45} = k$

$\dfrac{1}{3} = k$

Direct variation equation: $y = \dfrac{1}{3}x$

When $x = 3$:

$y = \dfrac{1}{3}(3)$

$y = 1$

3. $k = \text{slope} = \dfrac{0-(-2)}{0-(-1)} = \dfrac{2}{1} = 2$

$y = 2x$

4. $y = kx$

$5 = \dfrac{k}{4}$

$20 = k$

$y = \dfrac{20}{x}$

5. $y = \dfrac{k}{x}$

$4 = \dfrac{k}{0.8}$

$3.2 = k$

Equation: $y = \dfrac{3.2}{x}$

When $x = 20$

$y = \dfrac{3.2}{20}$

$y = 0.16$

6. $A = kr^2$

$49\pi = k(7)^2$

$49\pi = 49k$

$\pi = k$

$A = \pi(4)^2$

$A = 16\pi$ square feet

7. $d = kt^2$

$144 = k(3)^2$

$144 = 9k$

$16 = k$

$d = 16t^2$

$d = 16(5)^2$

$d = 400$ feet

Mental Math 13.8

1. Direct

2. Inverse

3. Inverse

4. Direct

5. Inverse

6. Direct

7. Direct

8. Inverse

Exercise Set 13.8

1. $y = kx$

$3 = k(6)$

$\dfrac{3}{6} = k$

$\dfrac{1}{2} = k$

$y = \dfrac{1}{2}x$

3. $y = kx$

$-12 = k(-2)$

$6 = k$

$y = 6x$

5. $k = \text{slope} = \dfrac{3-0}{1-0} = \dfrac{3}{1} = 3$

$y = 3x$

7. $k = \text{slope} = \dfrac{2-0}{3-0} = \dfrac{2}{3}$

$y = \dfrac{2}{3}x$

9. $y = \dfrac{k}{x}$

$7 = \dfrac{k}{1}$

$7 = k$

$y = \dfrac{7}{x}$

11. $y = \dfrac{k}{x}$

$0.05 = \dfrac{k}{10}$

$0.5 = k$

$y = \dfrac{0.5}{x}$

13. $y = kx$

15. $h = \dfrac{k}{t}$

17. $z = kx^2$

19. $y = \dfrac{k}{z^3}$

21. $x = \dfrac{k}{\sqrt{y}}$

23. $y = kx$

$20 = k(5)$

$4 = k$

$$y = 4x$$
$$y = 4(10)$$
$$y = 40$$

25. $y = \dfrac{k}{x}$

$$5 = \dfrac{k}{60}$$
$$300 = k$$
$$y = \dfrac{300}{x}$$
$$y = \dfrac{300}{100}$$
$$y = 3$$

27. $z = kx^2$

$$96 = k(4)^2$$
$$96 = 16k$$
$$6 = k$$

$$z = 6x^2$$
$$z = 6(3)^2$$
$$z = 6(9)$$
$$z = 54$$

29. $a = \dfrac{k}{b^3}$

$$\dfrac{3}{2} = \dfrac{k}{2^3}$$
$$\dfrac{3}{2} = \dfrac{k}{8}$$
$$2k = 24$$
$$k = 12$$

$$a = \dfrac{12}{b^3}$$
$$a = \dfrac{12}{3^3}$$
$$a = \dfrac{12}{27}$$
$$a = \dfrac{4}{9}$$

31. $p = kh$

$$112.50 = k(18)$$
$$6.25 = k$$

$$p = 6.25h$$
$$p = 6.25(10)$$
$$p = 62.5$$

$62.50 for 10 hours

33. $c = \dfrac{k}{n}$

$9.00 = \dfrac{k}{5000}$

$45,000 = k$

$c = \dfrac{45,000}{n}$

$c = \dfrac{45,000}{7500}$

$c = 6$

$6.00 to manufacture 7500 headphones

35. $d = kw$

$4 = k(60)$

$\dfrac{4}{60} = k$

$\dfrac{1}{15} = k$

$d = \dfrac{1}{15}w$

$d = \dfrac{1}{15}(80)$

$d = \dfrac{80}{15}$

$d = 5\dfrac{1}{3}$

$5\dfrac{1}{3}$ inches with a 80 lb weight.

37. $w = \dfrac{k}{d^2}$

$180 = \dfrac{k}{4000^2}$

$180 = \dfrac{k}{16,000,000}$

$2,880,000,000 = k$

$w = \dfrac{2,880,000,000}{d^2}$

$w = \dfrac{2,880,000,000}{4010^2}$

$w = \dfrac{2,880,000,000}{16,080,100}$

$w \approx 179$

179 pounds, 10 miles above the Earth's surface.

39. $d = kt^2$

$64 = k(2)^2$

$64 = 4k$

$16 = k$

$d = 16t^2$

$d = 16(10)^2$

$d = 16(100)$

$d = 1600$

1600 ft in 10 seconds

41. $-3x+4y=7$

$\underline{3x-2y=9}$

$2y=16$

43. $5x-0.4y=0.7$

$\underline{-9x+0.4y=-0.2}$

$-4x=0.5$

45. $y=kx$

If x is tripled, y is also tripled. Answers may vary.

47. $p=k\sqrt{l}$

If l is quadrupled (multiplied by 4), since l is square rooted, $\sqrt{4}=2$. Therefore, p is doubled (multiplied by 2). Answers may vary.

Chapter 13 Review

1.-6.

7. $-2+y=6x,\ \ x=7$

$-2+y=6(7)$

$-2+y=42$

$y=44$

$(7,44)$

8. $y=3x+5,\ \ y=-8$

$-8=3x+5$

$-13=3x$

$-\dfrac{13}{3}=x$

$\left(-\dfrac{13}{3},-8\right)$

9. $9=-3x+4y$

$y=0,\ 9=-3x+4(0),\ 9=-3x,\ -3=x$

$y=3,\ 9=-3x+4(3),\ 9=-3x+12$

$-3=-3x,\ 1=x$

$x=9,\ 9=-3(9)+4y,\ 9=-27+4y$

$36=4y,\ 9=y$

x	y
-3	0
1	3
9	9

10. $y=5$ for all values of x.

x	y
7	5
-7	5
0	5

11. $x = 2y$

$y = 0,\ x = 2(0) = 0$

$y = 5,\ x = 2(5) = 10$

$y = -5,\ x = 2(-5) = -10$

x	y
0	0
10	5
−10	−5

12.a. $y = 5x + 2000$

$x = 1,\ y = 5(1) + 2000 = 2005$

$x = 100,\ y = 5(100) + 2000 = 2500$

$x = 1000,\ y = 5(1000) + 2000 = 7000$

x	1	100	1000
y	2005	2500	7000

b. Let $y = 6430$

$6430 = 5x + 2000$

$4430 = 5x$

$886 = x$

886 compact disc holders can be produced.

13. $x - y = 1$

x	y
1	0
0	−1

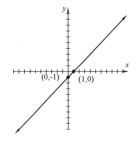

14. $x + y = 6$

x	y
6	0
0	6

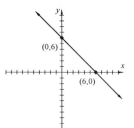

15. $x - 3y = 12$

x	y
12	0
0	−4

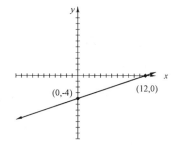

16. $5x - y = -8$

x	y
−2	−2
0	8

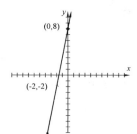

17. $x = 3y$

x	y
0	0
6	2

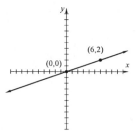

18. $y = -2x$

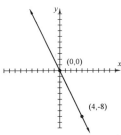

x	y
0	0
4	-8

19. x-intercept: $(4,0)$

y-intercept: $(0,-2)$

20. x-intercepts: $(-2,0),(2,0)$

y-intercepts: $(0,2),(0,-2)$

21. $y = -3$ for all values of x.

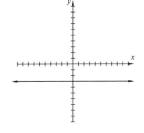

22. $x = 5$ for all values of y.

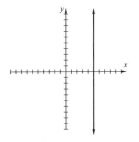

23. $x - 3y = 12$

$y = 0,\ x - 3(0) = 12.\ x = 12$

$x = 0,\ 0 - 3y = 12,\ y = -4$

x-intercept: $(12,0)$

y-intercept: $(0,-4)$

24. $-4x + y = 8$

$y = 0,\ -4x + 0 = 8.\ x = -2$

$x = 0,\ -4(0) + y = 8,\ y = 8$

x-intercept: $(-2,0)$

y-intercept: $(0,8)$

25. $(-1,2)$, and $(3,-1)$

$m = \dfrac{y_2 - y_1}{x_2 - x_1} = \dfrac{-1-2}{3-(-1)} = -\dfrac{3}{4}$

26. $(-2,-2)$, and $(3,-1)$

$m = \dfrac{y_2 - y_1}{x_2 - x_1} = \dfrac{-1-(-2)}{3-(-2)} = \dfrac{1}{5}$

27. $m = 0$

D

28. $m = -1$

B

29. Slope is undefined.

C

30. $m = 4$

A

31. $(2,5)$, and $(6,8)$

$m = \dfrac{y_2 - y_1}{x_2 - x_1} = \dfrac{8-5}{6-2} = \dfrac{3}{4}$

32. $(4,7)$, and $(1,2)$

$m = \dfrac{y_2 - y_1}{x_2 - x_1} = \dfrac{2-7}{1-4} = \dfrac{-5}{-3} = \dfrac{5}{3}$

33. $(1,3)$, and $(-2,-9)$

$$m = \frac{y_2 - y_1}{x_2 - x_1} = \frac{-9-3}{-2-1} = \frac{-12}{-3} = 4$$

34. $(-4,1)$, and $(3,-6)$

$$m = \frac{y_2 - y_1}{x_2 - x_1} = \frac{-6-1}{3-(-4)} = \frac{-7}{7} = -1$$

35. $y = 3x + 7$

$y = mx + b$

$m = 3$

36. $x - 2y = 4$

$-2y = -x + 2$

$y = \frac{1}{2}x - 1$

$y = mx + b$

$m = \frac{1}{2}$

37. $y = -2$

$y = 0x - 2$

$y = mx + b$

$m = 0$

38. $x = 0$

Undefined slope

39. $x - y = -6$, $-y = -x - 6$,

$y = x + 6$, $m_1 = 1$

$x + y = 3$, $y = -x + 3$, $m_2 = -1$

$m_1 m_2 = (1)(-1) = -1$, perpendicular

40. $3x + y = 7$, $y = -3x + 7$, $m_1 = -3$

$-3x - y = 10$, $-y = 3x + 10$,

$y = -3x - 10$, $m_2 = -3$

$m_1 = m_2$, parallel

41. $y = 4x + \frac{1}{2}$, $m_1 = 4$

$4x + 2y = 1$, $2y = -4x + 1$,

$y = -2x + \frac{1}{2}$, $m_2 = -2$

$m_1 \neq m_2$ and $m_1 m_2 \neq -1$, neither

42. $(1995, 39.2)$, and $(2000, 44.0)$

$$m = \frac{y_2 - y_1}{x_2 - x_1} = \frac{44.0 - 39.2}{2000 - 1995} = \frac{4.8}{5} = 0.96$$

Every 1 year, 0.96 million more persons have a bachelor's degree or higher.

43. $(1997, 859)$, and $(2002, 1021)$

$$m = \frac{y_2 - y_1}{x_2 - x_1} = \frac{1021 - 859}{2002 - 1997} = \frac{162}{5} = 32.4$$

Every 1 year, 32.4 million more people go on vacations.

44. $3x + y = 7$

$y = -3x + 7$

$y = mx + b$

$m = -3$, y-intercept $= (0, 7)$

45. $x - 6y = -1$

$\qquad -6y = -x - 1$

$\qquad y = \dfrac{1}{6}x + \dfrac{1}{6}$

$\qquad y = mx + b$

$\qquad m = \dfrac{1}{6}$, y-intercept $= \left(0, \dfrac{1}{6}\right)$

46. $m = -5$, y-intercept $= \left(0, \dfrac{1}{2}\right)$

$\qquad y = mx + b$

$\qquad y = -5x + \dfrac{1}{2}$

47. $m = \dfrac{2}{3}$, y-intercept $= (0, 6)$

$\qquad y = mx + b$

$\qquad y = \dfrac{2}{3}x + 6$

48. $y = 2x + 1$

$\qquad m = 2, b = 1$

$\qquad$ **D**

49. $y = -4x$

$\qquad m = -4, b = 0$

$\qquad$ **C**

50. $y = 2x$

$\qquad m = 2, b = 0$

$\qquad$ **A**

51. $y = 2x - 1$

$\qquad m = 2, b = -1$

$\qquad$ **B**

52. $\qquad m = 4; (2, 0)$

$\qquad y - y_1 = m(x - x_1)$

$\qquad y - 0 = 4(x - 2)$

$\qquad y = 4x - 8$

$\qquad -4x + y = -8$

53. $\qquad m = -3; (0, -5)$

$\qquad y - y_1 = m(x - x_1)$

$\qquad y - (-5) = -3(x - 0)$

$\qquad y + 5 = -3x$

$\qquad 3x + y = -5$

54. $\qquad m = \dfrac{3}{5}; (1, 4)$

$\qquad y - y_1 = m(x - x_1)$

$\qquad y - 4 = \dfrac{3}{5}(x - 1)$

$\qquad 5(y - 4) = 3(x - 1)$

$\qquad 5y - 20 = 3x - 3$

$\qquad -3x + 5y = 17$

55. $\qquad m = -\dfrac{1}{3}; (-3, 3)$

$\qquad y - y_1 = m(x - x_1)$

$\qquad y - 3 = -\dfrac{1}{3}(x - (-3))$

$\qquad 3(y - 3) = -(x + 3)$

$\qquad 3y - 9 = -x - 3$

$\qquad x + 3y = 6$

56. $(1,7)$ and $(2,-7)$

$$m = \frac{y_2 - y_1}{x_2 - x_1} = \frac{-7 - 7}{2 - 1} = \frac{-14}{1} = -14$$

$m = -14; \ (1,7)$

$$y - y_1 = m(x - x_1)$$

$$y - 7 = -14(x - 1)$$

$$y - 7 = -14x + 14$$

$$14x + y = 21$$

57. $(-2,5)$ and $(-4,6)$

$$m = \frac{y_2 - y_1}{x_2 - x_1} = \frac{6 - 5}{-4 - (-2)} = \frac{1}{-2} = -\frac{1}{2}$$

$m = -\frac{1}{2}; \ (-2,5)$

$$y - y_1 = m(x - x_1)$$

$$y - 5 = -\frac{1}{2}(x - (-2))$$

$$2(y - 5) = -(x + 2)$$

$$2y - 10 = -x - 2$$

$$x + 2y = 8$$

58. Two points have the same x-value: it is not a function.

59. Every point has a unique x-value: it is a function.

60. Yes

61. Yes

62. No

63. Yes

64. $f(x) = -2x + 6$

   a. $f(0) = -2(0) + 6 = 6$

   b. $f(-2) = -2(-2) + 6 = 4 + 6 = 10$

   c. $f\left(\frac{1}{2}\right) = -2\left(\frac{1}{2}\right) + 6 = -1 + 6 = 5$

65. $x + 6y < 6$

Test $(0,0)$

$$0 + 6(0) \overset{?}{<} 6$$

True

Shade below.

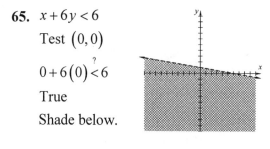

66. $x + y > -2$

Test $(0,0)$

$$0 + 0 \overset{?}{>} -2$$

True

Shade above.

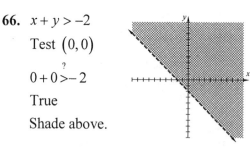

67. $y \geq -7$

Test $(0,0)$

$$0 \overset{?}{\geq} -7$$

True

Shade above.

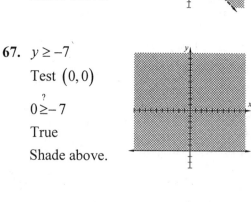

68. $y \leq -4$

Test $(0,0)$

$$0 \overset{?}{\leq} -4$$

False

Shade below.

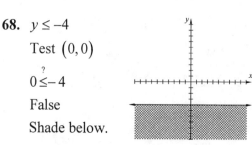

69. $-x \le y$

    Test $(1,0)$

    $-1 \overset{?}{\le} 0$

    True

    Shade above.

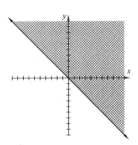

70. $x \ge -y$

    Test $(1,0)$

    $1 \overset{?}{\ge} 0$

    True

    Shade above.

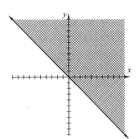

71. $y = kx$

    $40 = k(4)$

    $10 = k$

    $y = 10x$

    $y = 10(11)$

    $y = 110$

72. $y = \dfrac{k}{x}$

    $4 = \dfrac{k}{6}$

    $24 = k$

    $y = \dfrac{24}{x}$

    $y = \dfrac{24}{48}$

    $y = \dfrac{1}{2}$

73. $y = \dfrac{k}{x^3}$

    $12.5 = \dfrac{k}{2^3}$

    $12.5 = \dfrac{k}{8}$

    $100 = k$

    $y = \dfrac{100}{x^3}$

    $y = \dfrac{100}{3^3}$

    $y = \dfrac{100}{27}$

74. $y = kx^2$

    $175 = k(5)^2$

    $175 = 25k$

    $7 = k$

    $y = 7x^2$

    $y = 7(10)^2$

    $y = 7(100)$

    $y = 700$

75.
$$c = \frac{k}{a}$$
$$6600 = \frac{k}{3000}$$
$$19{,}800{,}000 = k$$

$$c = \frac{19{,}800{,}000}{a}$$
$$c = \frac{19{,}800{,}000}{5000}$$
$$c = 3960$$

It cost \$3960 to manufacture 5000 ml of medicine.

76.
$$d = kw$$
$$8 = k(150)$$
$$\frac{8}{150} = k$$
$$\frac{4}{75} = k$$

$$d = \frac{4}{75}w$$
$$d = \frac{4}{75}(90)$$
$$d = \frac{360}{75}$$
$$d = 4\frac{4}{5}$$

A 90 lb weight would stretch the spring $4\frac{4}{5}$ in.

Chapter 13 Test

1. a. $(1980, 38)$, $(1984, 47)$, $(1988, 51)$, $(1992, 54)$, $(1996, 59)$, $(2000, 55)$

b.

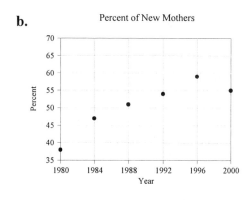

2. $2x + y = 8$

x	y
4	0
0	8

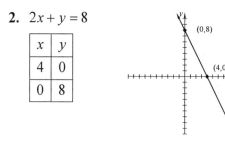

3. $5x - 7y = 10$

x	y
2	0
−5	−5

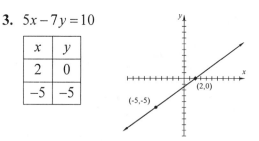

4. $y = -1$
for all values of x

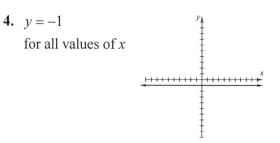

5. $x - 3 = 0$

$x = 3$

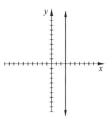

x	y
3	-4
3	0
3	2

6. $y \geq -4x$

Test $(1, 0)$

$0 \overset{?}{\geq} -4(1)$

True

Shade above.

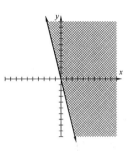

7. $2x - 3y > -6$

Test $(0, 0)$

$2(0) - 3(0) \overset{?}{>} -6$

True

Shade below.

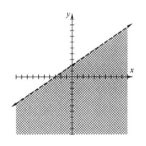

8. $(-1, -1)$, and $(4, 1)$

$m = \dfrac{y_2 - y_1}{x_2 - x_1} = \dfrac{1 - (-1)}{4 - (-1)} = \dfrac{2}{5}$

9. Horizontal line: $m = 0$

10. $(6, -5)$, and $(-1, 2)$

$m = \dfrac{y_2 - y_1}{x_2 - x_1} = \dfrac{2 - (-5)}{-1 - 6} = \dfrac{7}{-7} = -1$

11. $-3x + y = 5$

$y = 3x + 5$

$y = mx + b$

$m = 3$

12. $x = 6$ is a vertical line.

The slope is undefined.

13. $7x - 3y = 2$

$-3y = -7x + 2$

$y = \dfrac{7}{3}x - \dfrac{2}{3}$

slope $(m) = \dfrac{7}{3}$

y-intercept $(b) = -\dfrac{2}{3}$

14. $y = 2x - 6, \ m_1 = 2$

$-4x = 2y, \ -2x = y,$

$y = -2x, \ m_2 = -2$

$m_1 \neq m_2$ and $m_1 m_2 \neq -1$, neither

15. $\quad\quad m = -\dfrac{1}{4}; \ (2, 2)$

$y - y_1 = m(x - x_1)$

$y - 2 = -\dfrac{1}{4}(x - 2)$

$4(y - 2) = -(x - 2)$

$4y - 8 = -x + 2$

$x + 4y = 10$

16. $(0,0)$ and $(6,-7)$

$$m = \frac{y_2 - y_1}{x_2 - x_1} = \frac{-7-0}{6-0} = -\frac{7}{6}$$

$$m = -\frac{7}{6}; \; (0,0)$$

$$y - y_1 = m(x - x_1)$$

$$y - 0 = -\frac{7}{6}(x - 0)$$

$$6y = -7x$$

$$7x + 6y = 0$$

17. $(2,-5)$ and $(1,3)$

$$m = \frac{y_2 - y_1}{x_2 - x_1} = \frac{3-(-5)}{1-2} = \frac{8}{-1} = -8$$

$$m = -8; \; (1,3)$$

$$y - y_1 = m(x - x_1)$$

$$y - 3 = -8(x - 1)$$

$$y - 3 = -8x + 8$$

$$8x + y = 11$$

18. $m = \frac{1}{8}, b = 12$

$$y = mx + b$$

$$y = \frac{1}{8}x + 12$$

$$8y = x + 96$$

$$-x + 8y = 96$$

$$x - 8y = -96$$

19. Yes

20. No

21. Yes

22. Yes

23. $f(x) = 2x - 4$

a. $f(-2) = 2(-2) - 4 = -4 - 4 = -8$

b. $f(0.2) = 2(0.2) - 4 = 0.4 - 4 = -3.6$

c. $f(0) = 2(0) - 4 = -4$

24. $h(x) = x^3 - x$

a. $h(-1) = (-1)^3 - (-1) = -1 + 1 = 0$

b. $h(0) = (0)^3 - (0) = 0$

c. $h(4) = (4)^3 - (4) = 64 - 4 = 60$

25. $2x + 2(2y) = P$

$$2x + 4y = 42$$

$$x + 2y = 21$$

Let $y = 8$

$$x + 2(8) = 21$$

$$x + 16 = 21$$

$$x = 5 \text{ meters}$$

26. slope $= \dfrac{1630 - 1420}{2002 - 2000} = \dfrac{210}{2} = 105$

Every year 105 million more movie tickets are sold.

27. $y = kx$

$$10 = k(15)$$

$$\frac{10}{15} = k$$

$$\frac{2}{3} = k$$

$$y = \frac{2}{3}x$$

$$y = \frac{2}{3}(42)$$

$$y = \frac{84}{3}$$

$$y = 28$$

28. $y = \dfrac{k}{x^2}$

$$8 = \frac{k}{5^2}$$

$$8 = \frac{k}{25}$$

$$200 = k$$

$$y = \frac{200}{x^2}$$

$$y = \frac{200}{15^2}$$

$$y = \frac{200}{225}$$

$$y = \frac{8}{9}$$

Cumulative Review Chapter 13

1. $A = lw$

$$A = (380 \text{ miles})(280 \text{ miles})$$

$$A = 106,400 \text{ sq. mi.}$$

The state of Colorado has an area of 106,400 square miles.

2. $21 \cdot 7 = 147$

There are 147 pecan trees.

3. $1 + (-10) + (-8) + 9 = -9 + (-8) + 9$
$$= -17 + 9 = -8$$

4. $-2 + (-7) + 3 + (-4) = -9 + 3 + (-4)$
$$= -6 + (-4)$$
$$= -10$$

5. $\dfrac{8 \cdot 4}{3x \cdot 4} = \dfrac{32}{12x}$

6. $\dfrac{3 \cdot 4}{2c \cdot 4} = \dfrac{12}{8c}$

7. $\begin{array}{r} 12 = 11\frac{7}{7} \\ -8\frac{3}{7} = -8\frac{3}{7} \\ \hline 3\frac{4}{7} \end{array}$

8. $\begin{array}{r} 15 = 14\frac{5}{5} \\ -4\frac{2}{5} = -4\frac{2}{5} \\ \hline 10\frac{3}{5} \end{array}$

9. $-2x + 5 = -2(3.8) + 5 = -7.6 + 5 = -2.6$

10. $6x - 1 = 6(-2.1) - 1 = -12.6 - 1 = -13.6$

11.
$$\begin{array}{r} 3.142 \\ 7{\overline{\smash{\big)}\,22.000}} \\ \underline{-21} \\ 10 \\ \underline{-7} \\ 30 \\ \underline{-28} \\ 20 \\ \underline{-14} \\ 6 \end{array}$$

$$\frac{22}{7} \approx 3.14$$

12.
$$\begin{array}{r} 1.947 \\ 19{\overline{\smash{\big)}\,37.000}} \\ \underline{-19} \\ 180 \\ \underline{-171} \\ 90 \\ \underline{-76} \\ 140 \\ \underline{-133} \\ 70 \\ \underline{-57} \\ 13 \end{array}$$

$$\frac{37}{19} \approx 1.947$$

13. $2x < -4$

$$\frac{2}{2}x < \frac{-4}{2}$$

$$x < -2$$

$$\{x \mid x < -2\}$$

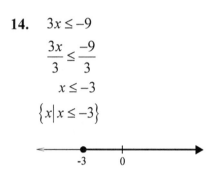

14. $3x \le -9$

$$\frac{3x}{3} \le \frac{-9}{3}$$

$$x \le -3$$

$$\{x \mid x \le -3\}$$

15. a. $-2t^2 + 3t + 6$; degree 2; trinomial

    b. $15x - 10$; degree 1; binomial

    c. $7x + 3x^3 + 2x^2 - 1$; degree 3; none of these

16. a. $-7y + 2$; degree 1; binomial

    b. $8x - x^2 - 1$; degree 2; trinomial

    c. $9y^3 - 6y + 2 + y^2$; degree 3; none of these

17. $\left(-2x^2 + 5x - 1\right) + \left(-2x^2 + x + 3\right)$

$$= -2x^2 - 2x^2 + 5x + x - 1 + 3$$

$$= -4x^2 + 6x + 2$$

18. $\left(9x - 5\right) + \left(x^2 - 6x + 5\right)$

$$= x^2 + 9x - 6x - 5 + 5$$

$$= x^2 + 3x$$

19. $(3y+1)^2 = (3y)^2 + 2(3y)(1) + (1)^2$
$$= 9y^2 + 6y + 1$$

20. $(2x-5)^2 = (2x)^2 + 2(2x)(-5) + (-5)^2$
$$= 4x^2 - 20x + 25$$

21. $-9a^5 + 18a^2 - 3a = 3a(-3a^4 + 6a - 1)$

22. $2x^5 - x^3 = x^3(2x^2 - 1)$

23. $x^2 + 4x - 12 = (x-2)(x+6)$

24. $x^2 + 4x - 21 = (x-3)(x+7)$

25. $8x^2 - 22x + 5 = (2x-5)(4x-1)$

26. $15x^2 + x - 2 = (5x+2)(3x-1)$

27.
$$x^2 - 9x = -20$$
$$x^2 - 9x + 20 = 0$$
$$(x-4)(x-5) = 0$$
$$x - 4 = 0, \quad x - 5 = 0$$
$$x = 4 \qquad x = 5$$
$$x = 4, \ 5$$

28.
$$x^2 - 9x = -14$$
$$x^2 - 9x + 14 = 0$$
$$(x-2)(x-7) = 0$$
$$x - 2 = 0, \quad x - 7 = 0$$
$$x = 2 \qquad x = 7$$
$$x = 2, \ 7$$

29. $\dfrac{2x^2 - 11x + 5}{5x - 25} \div \dfrac{4x - 2}{10} = \dfrac{2x^2 - 11x + 5}{5x - 25} \cdot \dfrac{10}{4x - 2}$
$$= \dfrac{(x-5)(2x-1)}{5(x-5)} \cdot \dfrac{10}{2(2x-1)}$$
$$= \dfrac{10(x-5)(2x-1)}{10(x-5)(2x-1)}$$
$$= 1$$

30. $\dfrac{3x^2 + 17x - 6}{5x + 5} \cdot \dfrac{2x + 2}{4x + 24}$
$$= \dfrac{(x+6)(3x-1)}{5(x+1)} \cdot \dfrac{2(x+1)}{4(x+6)}$$
$$= \dfrac{2(x+6)(3x-1)(x+1)}{20(x+1)(x+6)}$$
$$= \dfrac{3x-1}{10}$$

31. $\dfrac{4b \cdot 3ab}{9a \cdot 3ab} = \dfrac{12ab^2}{27a^2 b}$

32. $\dfrac{7x \cdot 9x^2 y}{11y \cdot 9x^2 y} = \dfrac{63x^3 y}{99x^2 y^2}$

33. $1 + \dfrac{m}{m+1} = \dfrac{m+1}{m+1} + \dfrac{m}{m+1}$
$$= \dfrac{m+1+m}{m+1}$$
$$= \dfrac{2m+1}{m+1}$$

34. $1 - \dfrac{m}{m+1} = \dfrac{m+1}{m+1} - \dfrac{m}{m+1}$
$$= \dfrac{m+1-m}{m+1}$$
$$= \dfrac{1}{m+1}$$

35.
$$3 - \frac{6}{x} = x + 8$$
$$x\left(3 - \frac{6}{x}\right) = x(x+8)$$
$$3x - 6 = x^2 + 8x$$
$$x^2 + 5x + 6 = 0$$
$$(x+2)(x+3) = 0$$

$$x + 2 = 0, \quad x + 3 = 0$$
$$x = -2, \qquad x = -3$$

36.
$$2 + \frac{10}{x} = x + 5$$
$$x\left(2 + \frac{10}{x}\right) = x(x+5)$$
$$2x + 10 = x^2 + 5x$$
$$x^2 + 3x - 10 = 0$$
$$(x-2)(x+5) = 0$$

$$x - 2 = 0, \quad x + 5 = 0$$
$$x = 2, \qquad x = -5$$

37.
$$\frac{\frac{x+1}{y}}{\frac{x}{y}+2} = \frac{y\left(\frac{x+1}{y}\right)}{y\left(\frac{x}{y}+2\right)}$$
$$= \frac{x+1}{x+2y}$$

38.
$$\frac{\frac{x}{2}+2}{\frac{x}{2}-2} = \frac{2\left(\frac{x}{2}+2\right)}{2\left(\frac{x}{2}-2\right)}$$
$$= \frac{x+4}{x-4}$$

39. a. $3(0) + y = 12$
$$y = 12$$
$$(0,\ 12)$$

b. $3x + 6 = 12$
$$3x = 12 - 6$$
$$\frac{3x}{3} = \frac{6}{3}$$
$$x = 2$$
$$(2,\ 6)$$

c. $3(-1) + y = 12$
$$-3 + y = 12$$
$$y = 12 + 3$$
$$y = 15$$
$$(-1,\ 15)$$

40. a. $-0 + 4y = -20$
$$\frac{4y}{4} = \frac{-20}{4}$$
$$y = -5$$
$$(0,\ -5)$$

b. $-x + 4(0) = -20$
$$\frac{-1x}{-1} = \frac{-20}{-1}$$
$$x = 20$$
$$(20,\ 0)$$

c. $-x + 4(-2) = -20$
$$-x - 8 = -20$$
$$-x = -20 + 8$$
$$\frac{-1x}{-1} = \frac{-12}{-1}$$
$$x = 12$$
$$(12,\ -2)$$

41. $2x + y = 5$

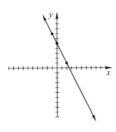

x	y
-1	7
0	5
2	1

42. $y = -2x$

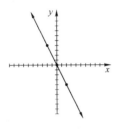

x	y
-2	4
0	0
2	-4

43. Put in $y = mx + b$ form.

$$-2x + 3y = 11$$
$$\frac{3y}{3} = \frac{2x}{3} + \frac{11}{3}$$
$$y = \frac{2}{3}x + \frac{11}{3}$$

Slope $(m) = \dfrac{2}{3}$

44. Put in $y = mx + b$ form.

$$7x + 4y = 10$$
$$\frac{4y}{4} = -\frac{7x}{4} + \frac{10}{4}$$
$$y = -\frac{7}{4}x + \frac{5}{2}$$

Slope $(m) = -\dfrac{7}{4}$

45. $y - y_1 = m(x - x_1)$
$$y - 5 = -2(x + 1)$$
$$y - 5 = -2x - 2$$
$$2x + y = -2 + 5$$
$$2x + y = 3$$

46. $y - y_1 = m(x - x_1)$
$$y + 7 = -5(x - 2)$$
$$y + 7 = -5x + 10$$
$$5x + y = 10 - 7$$
$$5x + y = 3$$

47. a. $g(x) = x^2 - 3$
$$g(2) = (2)^2 - 3$$
$$= 4 - 3$$
$$= 1$$
$$(2, 1)$$

   b. $g(x) = x^2 - 3$
$$g(-2) = (-2)^2 - 3$$
$$= 4 - 3$$
$$= 1$$
$$(-2, 1)$$

   c. $g(x) = x^2 - 3$
$$g(0) = 0^2 - 3$$
$$= 0 - 3$$
$$= -3$$
$$(0, -3)$$

48. a. $f(x) = 3x^2 + 2$

$$f(0) = 3(0)^2 + 2$$
$$= 3(0) + 2$$
$$= 0 + 2$$
$$= 2$$
$$(0,\ 2)$$

b. $f(x) = 3x^2 + 2$

$$f(4) = 3(4)^2 + 2$$
$$= 3(16) + 2$$
$$= 48 + 2$$
$$= 50$$
$$(4,\ 50)$$

c. $f(x) = 3x^2 + 2$

$$f(-1) = 3(-1)^2 + 2$$
$$= 3(1) + 2$$
$$= 3 + 2$$
$$= 5$$
$$(-1,\ 5)$$

Chapter 14

Chapter 14 Pretest

1. $\begin{cases} x+y=5 \\ x-y=7 \end{cases}$

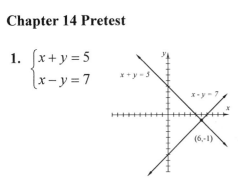

The solution of the system is $(6,-1)$.

2. $\begin{cases} y=4x \\ x=1 \end{cases}$

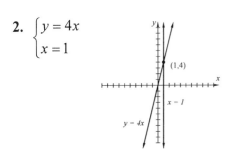

The solution of the system is $(1,4)$.

3. $\begin{cases} x+y=6 \\ x=3y-2 \end{cases}$

Substitute $3y-2$ for x in the first equation.

$3y-2+y=6$

$\quad 4y=8$

$\quad\; y=2$

Let $y=2$ in the second equation.

$x=3(2)-2$

$x=4$

The solution is $(4,2)$.

4. $\begin{cases} 5x+y=13 \\ 4x-5y=22 \end{cases}$

Solve the first equation for y.

$y=13-5x$

Substitute $13-5x$ for y in the second equation.

$4x-5(13-5x)=22$

$\quad 4x-65+25x=22$

$\qquad\qquad 29x=87$

$\qquad\qquad\quad\; x=3$

Let $x=3$ in $y=13-5x$.

$y=13-5(3)$

$y=-2$

The solution is $(3,-2)$.

5. $\begin{cases} 7y=x-6 \\ 2x+3y=-5 \end{cases}$

Solve the first equation for x.

$x=7y+6$

Substitute $7y+6$ for x in the second equation.

$2(7y+6)+3y=-5$

$\quad 14y+12+3y=-5$

$\qquad\qquad\quad 17y=-17$

$\qquad\qquad\qquad y=-1$

Let $y=-1$ in $x=7y+6$.

$x=7(-1)+6$

$x=-1$

The solution is $(-1,-1)$.

6. $\begin{cases} 4x = y + 6 \\ 8x - 2y = 12 \end{cases}$

Solve the first equation for y.

$y = 4x - 6$

Substitute $4x - 6$ for y in the second equation.

$8x - 2(4x - 6) = 12$

$8x - 8x + 12 = 12$

$12 = 12$

The equations in the original system are equivalent and there are an infinite number of solutions.

7. $\begin{cases} x - 5 = 3y \\ 6y - 2x = 10 \end{cases}$

Solve the first equation for x.

$x = 3y + 5$

Substitute $3y + 5$ for x in the second equation.

$6y - 2(3y + 5) = 10$

$6y - 6y - 10 = 10$

$-10 = 10$

The system has no solution.

8. $\begin{cases} 4x + 6y = -14 \\ 6x + y = -1 \end{cases}$

Solve the second equation for y.

$y = -1 - 6x$

Substitute $-1 - 6x$ for y in the first equation.

$4x + 6(-1 - 6x) = -14$

$4x - 6 - 36x = -14$

$-32x = -8$

$x = \dfrac{1}{4}$

Let $x = \dfrac{1}{4}$ in $y = -1 - 6x$.

$y = -1 - 6\left(\dfrac{1}{4}\right)$

$y = -\dfrac{5}{2}$

The solution is $\left(\dfrac{1}{4}, -\dfrac{5}{2}\right)$.

9. $\begin{cases} \dfrac{1}{5}x - y = 3 \\ x - 5y = 15 \end{cases}$

Solve the second equation for x.

$x = 15 + 5y$

Substitute $15 + 5y$ for x in the first equation.

$\dfrac{1}{5}(15 + 5y) - y = 3$

$3 + y - y = 3$

$3 = 3$

The equations in the original system are equivalent and there are an infinite number of solutions.

10. $\begin{cases} y = 3x + 7 \\ y = 10x + 21 \end{cases}$

Substitute $3x + 7$ for y in the second equation.

$3x + 7 = 10x + 21$

$-14 = 7x$

$-2 = x$

Let $x = -2$ in the first equation.

$y = 3(-2) + 7$

$y = 1$

The solution is $(-2, 1)$.

11. $\begin{cases} 2x + y = 11 \\ 3x - y = 29 \end{cases}$

$2x + y = 11$

$\underline{3x - y = 29}$

$5x = 40$

$x = 8$

Substitute 8 for x in the first equation.

$2(8) + y = 11$

$16 + y = 11$

$y = -5$

The solution of the system is $(8, -5)$

12. $\begin{cases} 4x - 3y = 13 \\ 5x - 9y = 53 \end{cases}$

Multiply the first equation by -3.

$-12x + 9y = -39$

$\underline{5x - 9y = 53}$

$-7x = 14$

$x = -2$

Let $x = -2$ in the first equation.

$4(-2) - 3y = 13$

$-8 - 3y = 13$

$-3y = 21$

$y = -7$

The solution of the system is $(-2, -7)$.

13. $\begin{cases} 6x + 8y = 92 \\ 5x - 3y = 9 \end{cases}$

Multiply the first equation by 3 and the second equation by 8.

$18x + 24y = 276$

$\underline{40x - 24y = 72}$

$58x = 348$

$x = 6$

Let $x = 6$ in the first equation.

$6(6) + 8y = 92$

$36 + 8y = 92$

$8y = 56$

$y = 7$

The solution of the system is $(6, 7)$.

14. $\begin{cases} 3x - 4y = 7 \\ -9x + 12y = 21 \end{cases}$

Multiply the first equation by 3.

$9x - 12y = 21$

$\underline{-9x + 12y = 21}$

$0 = 42$

Since this is a false statement, the system has no solution.

15. $\begin{cases} \dfrac{x}{2} + \dfrac{y}{3} = 2 \\ \dfrac{x}{6} - \dfrac{y}{4} = 5 \end{cases}$

Multiply the first equation by 18 and the second equation by 24.

$9x + 6y = 36$

$\underline{4x - 6y = 120}$

$13x = 156$

$x = 12$

Let $x = 12$ in the first equation.

$$\frac{12}{2} + \frac{y}{3} = 2$$

$$6 + \frac{y}{3} = 2$$

$$\frac{y}{3} = -4$$

$$y = -12$$

The solution of the system is $(12, -12)$.

16. $\begin{cases} 6x + 10y = -4 \\ -x + \ \ y = -1 \end{cases}$

Multiply the second equation by 6.

$$6x + 10y = -4$$
$$\underline{-6x + \ 6y = -6}$$
$$16y = -10$$
$$y = -\frac{10}{16}$$
$$y = -\frac{5}{8}$$

Let $y = -\frac{5}{8}$ in the second equation.

$$-x - \frac{5}{8} = -1$$
$$-8x - 5 = -8$$
$$-8x = -3$$
$$x = \frac{3}{8}$$

The solution of the system is $\left(\frac{3}{8}, -\frac{5}{8}\right)$.

17. $\begin{cases} 2x = 8 - 3y \\ 9y = 24 - 6x \end{cases}$

Put in standard form.

$$\begin{cases} 2x + 3y = 8 \\ 6x + 9y = 24 \end{cases}$$

Multiply the first equation by -3.

$$-6x - 9y = -24$$
$$\underline{6x + 9y = 24}$$
$$0 = 0$$

The equations in the original system are equivalent and there are an infinite number of solutions.

18. $\begin{cases} 11x = 5y + 30 \\ 3x + 4y = -24 \end{cases}$

Put in standard form.

$$\begin{cases} 11x - 5y = 30 \\ \ \ 3x + 4y = -24 \end{cases}$$

Multiply the first equation by 4 and the second equation by 5.

$$44x - 20y = 120$$
$$\underline{15x + 20y = -120}$$
$$59x \qquad = 0$$
$$x \qquad = 0$$

Let $x = 0$ in the first equation.

$$11(0) = 5y + 30$$
$$-30 = 5y$$
$$-6 = y$$

The solution of the system is $(0, -6)$.

19. Let x = the first number and y = the second number.

$$\begin{cases} x + y = 97 \\ x - y = 65 \end{cases}$$

$$\begin{array}{r} x + y = 97 \\ x - y = 65 \\ \hline 2x \quad\; = 162 \\ x \quad\; = 81 \end{array}$$

Let $x = 81$ in the first equation.

$$81 + y = 97$$
$$y = 16$$

The numbers are 81 and 16.

20. Let x = the measure of the first angle and y = the measure of the second angle.

$$\begin{cases} x + y = 90 \\ x = 2y - 6 \end{cases}$$

Re write in standard form.

$$\begin{cases} x + y = 90 \\ x - 2y = -6 \end{cases}$$

Multiply the first equation by -1.

$$\begin{array}{r} -x - \; y = -90 \\ x - 2y = -6 \\ \hline -3y = -96 \\ y = 32 \end{array}$$

Let $y = 32$ in the first equation.

$$x + 32 = 90$$
$$x = 58$$

The measures of the angles are $32°$ and $58°$.

Practice Problems 14.1

1. Let $x = 3$ and $y = 9$.

$$5(3) - 2(9) \overset{?}{=} -3 \qquad 9 \overset{?}{=} 3(3)$$
$$15 - 18 \overset{?}{=} -3 \qquad 9 = 9$$
$$-3 = -3 \qquad\qquad \text{True}$$

True

$(3, 9)$ is a solution of the system.

2. Let $x = 3$ and $y = -2$.

$$2(3) - (-2) \overset{?}{=} 8 \qquad 3 + 3(-2) \overset{?}{=} 4$$
$$6 + 2 \overset{?}{=} 8 \qquad\qquad 3 - 6 \overset{?}{=} 4$$
$$8 = 8 \qquad\qquad\qquad -3 = 4$$

True   False

$(3, -2)$ is not a solution of the system.

3. $\begin{cases} -3x + y = -10 \\ x - y = 6 \end{cases}$

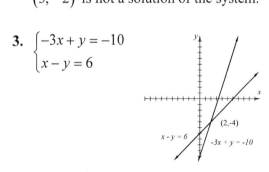

The solution of the system is $(2, -4)$.

4. $\begin{cases} x + 3y = -1 \\ y = 1 \end{cases}$

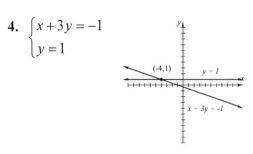

The solution of the system is $(-4, 1)$.

5. $\begin{cases} 3x - y = 6 \\ 6x = 2y \end{cases}$

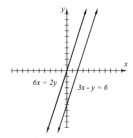

There is no solution.

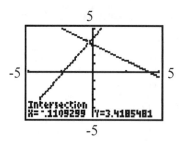

The solution of the system is $(-0.11, 3.42)$.

6. $\begin{cases} 3x + 4y = 12 \\ 9x + 12y = 36 \end{cases}$

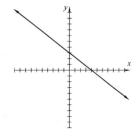

There are an infinite number of solutions.

3. $\begin{cases} 4.3x - 2.9y = 5.6 \\ 8.1x + 7.6y = -14.1 \end{cases}$

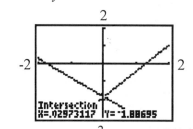

The solution of the system is $(0.03, -1.89)$.

Graphing Calculator Explorations 14.1

1. $\begin{cases} y = -2.68x + 1.21 \\ y = 5.22x - 1.68 \end{cases}$

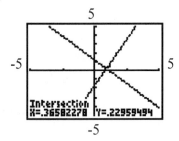

The solution of the system is $(0.37, 0.23)$.

4. $\begin{cases} -3.6x - 8.6y = 10 \\ -4.5x + 9.6y = -7.7 \end{cases}$

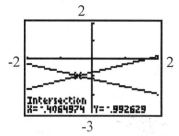

The solution of the system is $(-0.41, -0.99)$.

2. $\begin{cases} y = 4.25x + 3.89 \\ y = -1.88x + 3.21 \end{cases}$

Mental Math 14.1

1. One solution, $(-1, 3)$

2. No solution

3. Infinite number of solutions.

4. One solution, $(3,4)$

5. No solution

6. Infinite number of solutions.

7. One solution, $(3,2)$

8. One solution, $(0,-3)$

Exercise Set 14.1

1. a. Let $x = 2$ and $y = 4$.

$x + y = 8$ $3x + 2y = 21$

$2 + 4 \overset{?}{=} 8$ $3(2) + 2(4) \overset{?}{=} 21$

$6 = 8$ $6 + 8 \overset{?}{=} 21$

False $14 = 21$

             False

$(2,4)$ is not a solution of the system.

b. Let $x = 5$ and $y = 3$.

$x + y = 8$ $3x + 2y = 21$

$5 + 3 \overset{?}{=} 8$ $3(5) + 2(3) \overset{?}{=} 21$

$8 = 8$ $15 + 6 \overset{?}{=} 21$

True $21 = 21$

             True

$(5,3)$ is a solution of the system

3. a. Let $x = 3$ and $y = 4$.

$3x - y = 5$ $x + 2y = 11$

$3(3) - 4 \overset{?}{=} 5$ $3 + 2(4) \overset{?}{=} 11$

$9 - 4 \overset{?}{=} 5$ $3 + 8 = 11$

$5 = 5$ $11 = 11$

True   True

$(3,4)$ is a solution of the system.

b. Let $x = 0$ and $y = -5$.

$3x - y = 5$ $x + 2y = 11$

$3(0) - (-5) \overset{?}{=} 5$ $0 + 2(-5) \overset{?}{=} 11$

$0 + 5 \overset{?}{=} 5$ $0 - 10 \overset{?}{=} 11$

$5 = 5$ $-10 = 11$

True   False

$(0,-5)$ is not a solution of the system

5. a. Let $x = -3$ and $y = -6$.

$2y = 4x$ $2x - y = 0$

$2(-6) \overset{?}{=} 4(-3)$ $2(-3) - (-6) \overset{?}{=} 0$

$-12 = -12$ $-6 + 6 \overset{?}{=} 0$

True $0 = 0$

             True

$(-3,-6)$ is a solution of the system

b. Let $x = 0$ and $y = 0$.

$2y = 4x$ $2x - y = 0$

$2(0) \overset{?}{=} 4(0)$ $2(0) - (0) \overset{?}{=} 0$

$0 = 0$ $0 - 0 \overset{?}{=} 0$

True $0 = 0$

             True

$(0,0)$ is a solution of the system.

7. $\begin{cases} x + y = 4 \\ x - y = 2 \end{cases}$

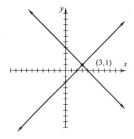

The solution of the system is $(3,1)$.

9. $\begin{cases} x + y = 6 \\ -x + y = -6 \end{cases}$

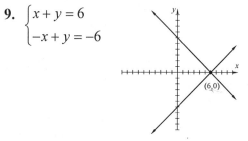

The solution of the system is $(6,0)$.

11. $\begin{cases} y = 2x \\ 3x - y = -2 \end{cases}$

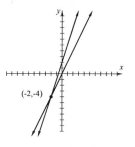

The solution of the system is $(-2,-4)$.

13. $\begin{cases} y = x + 1 \\ y = 2x - 1 \end{cases}$

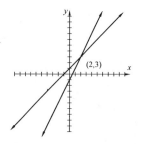

The solution of the system is $(2,3)$.

15. $\begin{cases} 2x + y = 0 \\ 3x + y = 1 \end{cases}$

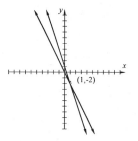

The solution of the system is $(1,-2)$.

17. $\begin{cases} y = -x - 1 \\ y = 2x + 5 \end{cases}$

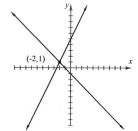

The solution of the system is $(-2,1)$.

19. $\begin{cases} 2x - y = 6 \\ y = 2 \end{cases}$

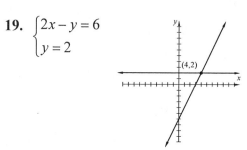

The solution of the system is $(4,2)$.

21. $\begin{cases} x + y = 5 \\ x + y = 6 \end{cases}$

There is no solution.

23. $\begin{cases} 2x + y = 4 \\ x + y = 2 \end{cases}$

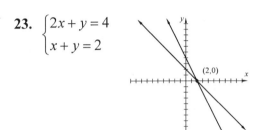

The solution of the system is $(2,0)$.

25. $\begin{cases} x - 2y = 2 \\ 3x + 2y = -2 \end{cases}$

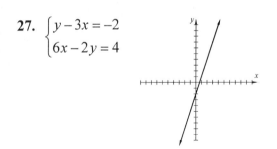

The solution of the system is $(0,-1)$.

27. $\begin{cases} y - 3x = -2 \\ 6x - 2y = 4 \end{cases}$

There are an infinite number of solutions.

29. $\begin{cases} x = 3 \\ y = -1 \end{cases}$

The solution of the system is $(3,-1)$.

31. $\begin{cases} y = x - 2 \\ y = 2x + 3 \end{cases}$

The solution of the system is $(-5,-7)$.

33. $\begin{cases} 2x - 3y = -2 \\ -3x + 5y = 5 \end{cases}$

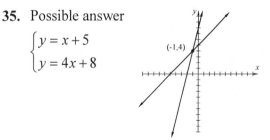

The solution of the system is $(5,4)$.

35. Possible answer

$\begin{cases} y = x + 5 \\ y = 4x + 8 \end{cases}$

37. Possible answer

$\begin{cases} y = -x + 3 \\ y = -x - 2 \end{cases}$

39. 1984, 1988

41. 1996

43.a. Each table includes the point $(4,9)$. Therefore $(4,9)$ is a solution of the system.

b.

c. Yes

45. $-2x + 3(x+6) = 17$

$$-2x + 3x + 18 = 17$$
$$x + 18 = 17$$
$$x = -1$$

The solution is -1.

47. $-y + 12\left(\dfrac{y-1}{4}\right) = 3$

$$-y + 3(y-1) = 3$$
$$-y + 3y - 3 = 3$$
$$2y - 3 = 3$$
$$2y = 6$$
$$y = 3$$

The solution is 3.

49. $3z - (4z - 2) = 9$

$$3z - 4z + 2 = 9$$
$$-z + 2 = 9$$
$$-z = 7$$
$$z = -7$$

The solution is -7.

51. Answers may vary.
Possible answer

$$\begin{cases} 3x - 2y = -2 \\ 6x + 4y = 4 \end{cases}$$

53. Answers may vary.

Practice Problems 14.2

1. $\begin{cases} 2x + 3y = 13 \\ x = y + 4 \end{cases}$

Substitute $y + 4$ for x in the first equation.

$$2(y+4) + 3y = 13$$
$$2y + 8 + 3y = 13$$
$$5y = 5$$
$$y = 1$$

Let $y = 1$ in the second equation.

$$x = 1 + 4$$
$$x = 5$$

The solution is $(5,1)$.

2. $\begin{cases} 4x - y = 2 \\ y = 5x \end{cases}$

Substitute $5x$ for y in the first equation.

$$4x - (5x) = 2$$
$$-x = 2$$
$$x = -2$$

Let $x = -2$ in the second equation.

$$y = 5(-2)$$
$$y = -10$$

The solution is $(-2, -10)$.

3. $\begin{cases} 3x + y = 5 \\ 3x - 2y = -7 \end{cases}$

Solve the first equation for y.

$y = 5 - 3x$

Substitute $5 - 3x$ for y in the second equation.

$3x - 2(5 - 3x) = -7$

$3x - 10 + 6x = -7$

$9x = 3$

$x = \dfrac{1}{3}$

Let $x = \dfrac{1}{3}$ in $y = 5 - 3x$.

$y = 5 - 3\left(\dfrac{1}{3}\right)$

$y = 4$

The solution is $\left(\dfrac{1}{3}, 4\right)$.

4. $\begin{cases} 5x - 2y = 6 \\ -3x + y = -3 \end{cases}$

Solve the second equation for y.

$y = -3 + 3x$

Substitute $-3 + 3x$ for y in the first equation.

$5x - 2(-3 + 3x) = 6$

$5x + 6 - 6x = 6$

$-x = 0$

$x = 0$

Let $x = 0$ in $y = -3 + 3x$.

$y = -3 + 3(0)$

$y = -3$

The solution is $(0, -3)$.

5. $\begin{cases} -x + 3y = 6 \\ y = \dfrac{1}{3}x + 2 \end{cases}$

Substitute $\dfrac{1}{3}x + 2$ for y in the first equation.

$-x + 3\left(\dfrac{1}{3}x + 2\right) = 6$

$-x + x + 6 = 6$

$6 = 6$

The equations in the original system are equivalent and there are an infinite number of solutions.

6. $\begin{cases} 2x - 3y = 6 \\ -4x + 6y = -12 \end{cases}$

Solve the first equation for x.

$2x = 3y + 6$

$x = \dfrac{3}{2}y + 3$

Substitute $\dfrac{3}{2}y + 3$ for x in the second equation.

$-4\left(\dfrac{3}{2}y + 3\right) + 6y = -12$

$-6y - 12 + 6y = -12$

$-12 = -12$

The equations in the original system are equivalent and there are an infinite number of solutions..

Exercise Set 14.2

1. $\begin{cases} x+y=3 \\ x=2y \end{cases}$

   Substitute $2y$ for x in the first equation.

   $2y+y=3$

   $\qquad 3y=3$

   $\qquad\ \ y=1$

   Let $y=1$ in the second equation.

   $x=2(1)$

   $x=2$

   The solution is $(2,1)$.

3. $\begin{cases} x+y=6 \\ y=-3x \end{cases}$

   Substitute $-3x$ for y in the first equation.

   $x+(-3x)=6$

   $\qquad -2x=6$

   $\qquad\quad x=-3$

   Let $x=-3$ in the second equation.

   $y=-3(-3)$

   $y=9$

   The solution is $(-3,9)$.

5. $\begin{cases} 3x+2y=16 \\ x=3y-2 \end{cases}$

   Substitute $3y-2$ for x in the first equation.

   $3(3y-2)+2y=16$

   $\quad 9y-6+2y=16$

   $\qquad\qquad 11y=22$

   $\qquad\qquad\ \ y=2$

Let $y=2$ in the second equation.

$x=3(2)-2$

$x=4$

The solution is $(4,2)$.

7. $\begin{cases} 3x-4y=10 \\ x=2y \end{cases}$

   Substitute $2y$ for x in the first equation.

   $3(2y)-4y=10$

   $\quad 6y-4y=10$

   $\qquad\ \ 2y=10$

   $\qquad\quad y=5$

   Let $y=5$ in the second equation.

   $x=2(5)$

   $x=10$

   The solution is $(10,5)$.

9. $\begin{cases} y=3x+1 \\ 4y-8x=12 \end{cases}$

   Substitute $3x+1$ for y in the second equation.

   $4(3x+1)-8x=12$

   $\quad 12x+4-8x=12$

   $\qquad\qquad 4x=8$

   $\qquad\qquad\ x=2$

   Let $x=2$ in the first equation.

   $y=3(2)+1$

   $y=7$

   The solution is $(2,7)$.

11. $\begin{cases} y = 2x + 9 \\ y = 7x + 10 \end{cases}$

Substitute $2x + 9$ for y in the second equation.

$2x + 9 = 7x + 10$

$-5x = 1$

$x = -\dfrac{1}{5}$

Let $x = -\dfrac{1}{5}$ in the first equation.

$y = 2\left(-\dfrac{1}{5}\right) + 9$

$y = \dfrac{43}{5}$

The solution is $\left(-\dfrac{1}{5}, \dfrac{43}{5}\right)$.

13. $\begin{cases} x + 2y = 6 \\ 2x + 3y = 8 \end{cases}$

Solve the first equation for x.

$x = 6 - 2y$

Substitute $6 - 2y$ for x in the second equation.

$2(6 - 2y) + 3y = 8$

$12 - 4y + 3y = 8$

$-y = -4$

$y = 4$

Let $y = 4$ in $x = 6 - 2y$.

$x = 6 - 2(4)$

$y = -2$

The solution is $(-2, 4)$.

15. $\begin{cases} 2x - 5y = 1 \\ 3x + y = -7 \end{cases}$

Solve the second equation for y.

$y = -7 - 3x$

Substitute $-7 - 3x$ for y in the first equation.

$2x - 5(-7 - 3x) = 1$

$2x + 35 + 15x = 1$

$17x = -34$

$x = -2$

Let $x = -2$ in $y = -7 - 3x$.

$y = -7 - 3(-2)$

$y = -1$

The solution is $(-2, -1)$.

17. $\begin{cases} 2y = x + 2 \\ 6x - 12y = 0 \end{cases}$

Solve the first equation for x.

$x = 2y - 2$

Substitute $2y - 2$ for x in the second equation.

$6(2y - 2) - 12y = 0$

$12y - 12 - 12y = 0$

$-12 = 0$

The system has no solution.

19. $\begin{cases} 4x + y = 11 \\ 2x + 5y = 1 \end{cases}$

Solve the first equation for y.

$y = 11 - 4x$

Substitute $11 - 4x$ for y in the second equation.

$$2x + 5(11 - 4x) = 1$$
$$2x + 55 - 20x = 1$$
$$-18x = -54$$
$$x = 3$$

Let $x = 3$ in $y = 11 - 4x$.

$$y = 11 - 4(3)$$
$$y = -1$$

The solution is $(3, -1)$.

21. $\begin{cases} 2x - 3y = -9 \\ 3x = y + 4 \end{cases}$

Solve the second equation for y.

$$y = 3x - 4$$

Substitute $3x - 4$ for y in the
first equation.

$$2x - 3(3x - 4) = -9$$
$$2x - 9x + 12 = -9$$
$$-7x = -21$$
$$x = 3$$

Let $x = 3$ in $y = 3x - 4$.

$$y = 3(3) - 4$$
$$y = 5$$

The solution is $(3, 5)$.

23. $\begin{cases} 6x - 3y = 5 \\ x + 2y = 0 \end{cases}$

Solve the second equation for x.

$$x = -2y$$

Substitute $-2y$ for x in the
first equation.

$$6(-2y) - 3y = 5$$
$$-12y - 3y = 5$$

$$-15y = 5$$
$$y = -\frac{1}{3}$$

Let $y = -\frac{1}{3}$ in $x = -2y$.

$$x = -2\left(-\frac{1}{3}\right)$$
$$x = \frac{2}{3}$$

The solution is $\left(\frac{2}{3}, -\frac{1}{3}\right)$.

25. $\begin{cases} 3x - y = 1 \\ 2x - 3y = 10 \end{cases}$

Solve the first equation for y.

$$y = 3x - 1$$

Substitute $3x - 1$ for y in the
second equation.

$$2x - 3(3x - 1) = 10$$
$$2x - 9x + 3 = 10$$
$$-7x = 7$$
$$x = -1$$

Let $x = -1$ in $y = 3x - 1$.

$$y = 3(-1) - 1$$
$$y = -4$$

The solution is $(-1, -4)$.

27. $\begin{cases} -x + 2y = 10 \\ -2x + 3y = 18 \end{cases}$

Solve the first equation for x.

$$x = 2y - 10$$

Substitute $2y - 10$ for x in the
second equation.

$$-2(2y-10)+3y=18$$
$$-4y+20+3y=18$$
$$-y=-2$$
$$y=2$$

Let $y=2$ in $x=2y-10$.

$$x=2(2)-10$$
$$x=-6$$

The solution is $(-6,2)$.

29. $\begin{cases} 5x+10y=20 \\ 2x+6y=10 \end{cases}$

Solve the first equation for x.

$$x+2y=4$$
$$x=4-2y$$

Substitute $4-2y$ for x in the second equation.

$$2(4-2y)+6y=10$$
$$8-4y+6y=10$$
$$2y=2$$
$$y=1$$

Let $y=1$ in $x=4-2y$.

$$x=4-2(1)$$
$$x=2$$

The solution is $(2,1)$.

31. $\begin{cases} 3x+6y=9 \\ 4x+8y=16 \end{cases}$

Solve the first equation for x.

$$x+2y=3$$
$$x=3-2y$$

Substitute $3-2y$ for x in the second equation.

$$4(3-2y)+8y=16$$
$$12-8y+8y=16$$
$$12=16$$

The system has no solution.

33. $\begin{cases} \dfrac{1}{3}x-y=2 \\ x-3y=6 \end{cases}$

Solve the second equation for x.

$$x=6+3y$$

Substitute $6+3y$ for x in the first equation.

$$\frac{1}{3}(6+3y)-y=2$$
$$2+y-y=2$$
$$2=2$$

The equations in the original system are equivalent and there are an infinite number of solutions.

35. Answers may vary.

37.
$$3x+2y=6$$
$$-2(3x+2y)=-2(6)$$
$$-6x-4y=-12$$

39.
$$-4x+y=3$$
$$3(-4x+y)=3(3)$$
$$-12x+3y=9$$

41. $3n+6m$
$$\underline{2n-6m}$$
$$5n$$

43.
$$-5a - 7b$$
$$\underline{5a - 8b}$$
$$-15b$$

45.
$$\begin{cases} -5y + 6y = 3x + 2(x - 5) - 3x + 5 \\ \quad\quad y = 3x + 2x - 10 - 3x + 5 \\ \quad\quad y = 2x - 5 \\ \\ 4(x + y) - x + y = -12 \\ 4x + 4y - x + y = -12 \\ \quad\quad 3x + 5y = -12 \end{cases}$$

Substitute $2x - 5$ for y in the second equation.
$$3x + 5(2x - 5) = -12$$
$$3x + 10x - 25 = -12$$
$$13x = 13$$
$$x = 1$$

Let $x = 1$ in $y = 2x - 5$.
$$y = 2(1) - 5$$
$$y = -3$$

The solution is $(1, -3)$.

47. $\begin{cases} y = 5.1x + 14.56 \\ y = -2x - 3.9 \end{cases}$

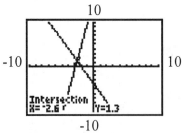

The solution of the system is $(-2.6, 1.3)$.

49. $\begin{cases} 3x + 2y = 14.04 \\ 5x + y = 18.5 \end{cases}$

$$y_1 = -\frac{3}{2}x + 7.02 \quad \text{and} \quad y_2 = -5x + 18.5$$

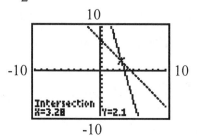

The solution of the system is $(3.28, 2.1)$.

51.a. $\begin{cases} y = -0.49x + 24.75 \\ y = 0.71x + 9.19 \end{cases}$

Use substitution, then solve for x.
$$-0.49x + 24.75 = 0.71x + 9.1$$
$$-0.49x - 0.71x = 9.19 - 24.75$$
$$-1.2x = -15.56$$
$$x \approx 13$$

Substitute 13 for x in the first equation.
$$y = -0.49(13) + 24.75$$
$$y = -6.37$$
$$y \approx 18$$

The solution is $(13, 18)$

b. In $1970 + 13 = 1983$, the percentage of U.S. households used fuel oil equaled the percentage that used electricity. That percentage was 18%.

c.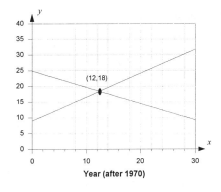

Year (after 1970)

Practice Problems 14.3

1. $\begin{cases} x + y = 13 \\ x - y = 5 \end{cases}$

$\begin{array}{r} x + y = 13 \\ \underline{x - y = 5} \\ 2x = 18 \\ x = 9 \end{array}$

Let $x = 9$ in the first equation.

$9 + y = 13$

$y = 4$

The solution of the system is $(9, 4)$

2. $\begin{cases} 2x - y = -6 \\ -x + 4y = 17 \end{cases}$

Multiply the second equation by 2.

$\begin{array}{r} 2x - y = -6 \\ \underline{-2x + 8y = 34} \\ 7y = 28 \\ y = 4 \end{array}$

Let $y = 4$ in the second equation.

$-x + 4(4) = 17$

$-x + 16 = 17$

$-x = 1$

$x = -1$

The solution of the system is $(-1, 4)$.

3. $\begin{cases} x - 3y = -2 \\ -3x + 9y = 5 \end{cases}$

Multiply the first equation by 3.

$\begin{array}{r} 3x - 9y = -6 \\ \underline{-3x + 9y = 5} \\ 0 = -1 \end{array}$

The system has no solution.

4. $\begin{cases} 2x + 5y = 1 \\ -4x - 10y = -2 \end{cases}$

Multiply the first equation by 2.

$\begin{array}{r} 4x + 10y = 2 \\ \underline{-4x - 10y = -2} \\ 0 = 0 \end{array}$

The equations in the original system are equivalent and there are an infinite number of solutions..

5. $\begin{cases} 4x + 5y = 14 \\ 3x - 2y = -1 \end{cases}$

Multiply the first equation by 2 and the second equation by 5.

$\begin{array}{r} 8x + 10y = 28 \\ \underline{15x - 10y = -5} \\ 23x = 23 \\ x = 1 \end{array}$

Let $x = 1$ in the first equation.

$4(1) + 5y = 14$

$4 + 5y = 14$

$5y = 10$

$y = 2$

The solution of the system is $(1, 2)$.

6. $\begin{cases} -\dfrac{x}{3} + y = \dfrac{4}{3} \\ \dfrac{x}{2} - \dfrac{5}{2}y = -\dfrac{1}{2} \end{cases}$

Multiply the first equation by 3 and the second equation by 2.

$-x + 3y = 4$

$\underline{x - 5y = -1}$

$-2y = 3$

$y = -\dfrac{3}{2}$

Let $y = -\dfrac{3}{2}$ in the first equation.

$-\dfrac{x}{3} + \left(-\dfrac{3}{2}\right) = \dfrac{4}{3}$

$6\left(-\dfrac{x}{3}\right) + 6\left(-\dfrac{3}{2}\right) = 6\left(\dfrac{4}{3}\right)$

$-2x - 9 = 8$

$-2x = 17$

$x = -\dfrac{17}{2}$

The solution of the system is $\left(-\dfrac{17}{2}, -\dfrac{3}{2}\right)$.

Exercise Set 14.3

1. $\begin{cases} 3x + y = 5 \\ 6x - y = 4 \end{cases}$

$3x + y = 5$

$\underline{6x - y = 4}$

$9x \quad = 9$

$x \quad = 1$

Let $x = 1$ in the first equation.

$3(1) + y = 5$

$3 + y = 5$

$y = 2$

The solution of the system is $(1, 2)$

3. $\begin{cases} x - 2y = 8 \\ -x + 5y = -17 \end{cases}$

$x - 2y = \quad 8$

$\underline{-x + 5y = -17}$

$3y = -9$

$y = -3$

Let $y = -3$ in the first equation.

$x - 2(-3) = 8$

$x + 6 = 8$

$x = 2$

The solution of the system is $(2, -3)$.

5. $\begin{cases} 3x + 2y = 11 \\ 5x - 2y = 29 \end{cases}$

$3x + \quad y = 11$

$\underline{5x - 2y = 29}$

$8x \quad = 40$

$x \quad = 5$

Let $x = 5$ in the first equation.

$3(5) + 2y = 11$

$15 + 2y = 11$

$2y = -4$

$y = -2$

The solution of the system is $(5, -2)$

7. $\begin{cases} x + y = 6 \\ x - y = 6 \end{cases}$

$x + y = 6$

$\underline{x - y = 6}$

$2x \quad = 12$

$x \quad = 6$

Let $x = 6$ in the first equation.

$6 + y = 6$

$y = 0$

The solution of the system is $(6, 0)$

9. $\begin{cases} 3x + y = -11 \\ 6x - 2y = -2 \end{cases}$

Multiply the first equation by 2.

$6x + 2y = -22$

$\underline{6x - 2y = -2}$

$12x \quad = -24$

$x \quad = -2$

Let $x = -2$ in the first equation.

$3(-2) + y = -11$

$-6 + y = -11$

$y = -5$

The solution of the system is $(-2, -5)$.

11. $\begin{cases} x + 5y = 18 \\ 3x + 2y = -11 \end{cases}$

Multiply the first equation by -3.

$-3x - 15y = -54$

$\underline{3x + 2y = -11}$

$-13y = -65$

$y = 5$

Let $y = 5$ in the first equation.

$x + 5(5) = 18$

$x + 25 = 18$

$x = -7$

The solution of the system is $(-7, 5)$.

13. $\begin{cases} 2x - 5y = 4 \\ 3x - 2y = 4 \end{cases}$

Multiply the first equation by -3 and the second equation by 2.

$-6x + 15y = -12$

$\underline{6x - 4y = \quad 8}$

$11y = -4$

$y = -\dfrac{4}{11}$

Let $y = -\dfrac{4}{11}$ in the first equation.

$2x - 5\left(-\dfrac{4}{11}\right) = 4$

$2x + \dfrac{20}{11} = 4$

$$11(2x) + 11\left(\frac{20}{11}\right) = 11(4)$$

$$22x + 20 = 44$$

$$22x = 24$$

$$x = \frac{12}{11}$$

The solution of the system is $\left(\dfrac{12}{11}, -\dfrac{4}{11}\right)$.

15. $\begin{cases} 2x + 3y = 0 \\ 4x + 6y = 3 \end{cases}$

Multiply the first equation by -2.

$$-4x - 6y = 0$$

$$\underline{4x + 6y = 3}$$

$$0 = 3$$

The system has no solution.

17. $\begin{cases} 3x + y = 4 \\ 9x + 3y = 6 \end{cases}$

Multiply the first equation by -3.

$$-9x - 3y = -12$$

$$\underline{9x + 3y = 6}$$

$$0 = -6$$

The system has no solution.

19. $\begin{cases} 3x - 2y = 7 \\ 5x + 4y = 8 \end{cases}$

Multiply the first equation by 2.

$$6x - 4y = 14$$

$$\underline{5x + 4y = 8}$$

$$11x = 22$$

$$x = 2$$

Let $x = 2$ in the first equation.

$$3(2) - 2y = 7$$

$$6 - 2y = 7$$

$$-2y = 1$$

$$y = -\frac{1}{2}$$

The solution of the system is $\left(2, -\dfrac{1}{2}\right)$.

21. $\begin{cases} \dfrac{2}{3}x + 4y = -4 \\ 5x + 6y = 18 \end{cases}$

Multiply the first equation by 3 and the second equation by -2.

$$2x + 12y = -12$$

$$\underline{-10x - 12y = 36}$$

$$-8x = -48$$

$$x = 6$$

Let $x = 6$ in the first equation.

$$\frac{2}{3}(6) + 4y = -4$$

$$4 + 4y = -4$$

$$4y = -8$$

$$y = -2$$

The solution of the system is $(6, -2)$.

23. $\begin{cases} 4x - 6y = 8 \\ 6x - 9y = 12 \end{cases}$

Multiply the first equation by 3 and the second equation by -2.

$$12x - 18y = 24$$

$$\underline{-12x + 18y = 24}$$

$$0 = 0$$

The equations in the original system are equivalent and there are an infinite number of solutions..

25.
$$\begin{cases} 8x = -11y - 16 \\ 8x + 11y = -16 \\ \\ 2x + 3y = -4 \end{cases}$$

Multiply the second equation by -4.

$$\begin{array}{r} 8x + 11y = -16 \\ -8x - 12y = 16 \\ \hline -y = 0 \\ y = 0 \end{array}$$

Let $y = 0$ in the second equation.

$$2x + 3(0) = -4$$
$$2x = -4$$
$$x = -2$$

The solution of the system is $(-2, 0)$.

27. Answers may vary.

29.
$$\begin{cases} \dfrac{x}{3} + \dfrac{y}{6} = 1 \\ \dfrac{x}{2} - \dfrac{y}{5} = 0 \end{cases}$$

Multiply the first equation by 6 and the second equation by 4.

$$\begin{cases} 2x + y = 6 \\ 2x - y = 0 \end{cases} \quad \text{Simplified system}$$

$$\begin{array}{r} 4x = 6 \\ x = \dfrac{3}{2} \end{array}$$

Multiply the second equation of the simplified system by -1.

$$\begin{array}{r} 2x + y = 6 \\ -2x + y = 0 \\ \hline 2y = 6 \\ y = 3 \end{array}$$

The solution of the system is $\left(\dfrac{3}{2}, 3 \right)$.

31.
$$\begin{cases} x - \dfrac{y}{3} = -1 \\ -\dfrac{x}{2} + \dfrac{y}{8} = \dfrac{1}{4} \end{cases}$$

Multiply the first equation by 3 and the second equation by 8.

$$\begin{cases} 3x - y = -3 \\ -4x + y = 2 \end{cases} \quad \text{Simplified system}$$

$$\begin{array}{r} -x = -1 \\ x = 1 \end{array}$$

Multiply the first equation of the simplified system by 4 and the second equation by 3.

$$\begin{cases} 12x - 4y = -12 \\ -12x + 3y = 6 \end{cases}$$

$$\begin{array}{r} -y = -6 \\ y = 6 \end{array}$$

The solution of the system is $(1, 6)$.

33. $\begin{cases} \dfrac{x}{3} - y = 2 \\ -\dfrac{x}{2} + \dfrac{3y}{2} = -3 \end{cases}$

Multiply the first equation by 3 and
the second equation by 2.

$\begin{cases} x - 3y = 6 \\ -x + 3y = -6 \end{cases}$ Simplified system

$\overline{ 0 = 0 }$

The equations in the original system
are equivalent and there are an infinite
number of solutions..

35. $\begin{cases} \dfrac{3}{5}x - y = -\dfrac{4}{5} \\ 3x + \dfrac{y}{2} = -\dfrac{9}{5} \end{cases}$

Multiply the first equation by 5 and
the second equation by 10.

$\begin{cases} 3x - 5y = -4 \\ 30x + 5y = -18 \end{cases}$ Simplified system

$\overline{ 33x = -22 }$

$ x = -\dfrac{2}{3}$

Multiply the first equation of the
simplified system by -10.

$\begin{cases} -30x + 50y = 40 \\ 30x + 5y = -18 \end{cases}$

$\overline{ 55y = 22 }$

$ y = \dfrac{2}{5}$

The solution of the system is $\left(-\dfrac{2}{3}, \dfrac{2}{5}\right)$.

37. $\begin{cases} 3.5x + 2.5y = 17 \\ -1.5x - 7.5y = -33 \end{cases}$

Multiply the first equation by 3.

$\begin{cases} 10.5x + 7.5y = 51 \\ -1.5x - 7.5y = -33 \end{cases}$ Simplified system

$\overline{ 9x = 18 }$

$ x = 2$

Multiply the second equation of the
simplified system by 7.

$\begin{cases} 10.5x + 7.5y = 51 \\ -10.5x - 52.5y = -231 \end{cases}$

$\overline{ -45y = -180 }$

$ y = 4$

The solution of the system is $(2, 4)$.

39. $\begin{cases} 0.02x + 0.04y = 0.09 \\ -0.1x + 0.3y = 0.8 \end{cases}$

Multiply the first equation by 100
and the second equation by 20.

$\begin{cases} 2x + 4y = 9 \\ -2x + 6y = 16 \end{cases}$ Simplified system

$\overline{ 10y = 25 }$

$ y = 2.5$

Multiply the first equation of the
simplified system by 3 and the second
equation by -2.

$\begin{cases} 6x + 12y = 27 \\ 4x - 12y = -32 \end{cases}$

$\overline{ 10x = -5 }$

$ x = -0.5$

The solution of the system is $(-0.5, 2.5)$.

41. Let x = a number.

$2x + 6 = x - 3$

43. Let x = a number.

$20 - 3x = 2$

45. Let x = a number.

$4(x + 6) = 2x$

47. $\begin{cases} x + y = 5 \\ 3x + 3y = b \end{cases}$

Multiply the first equation by -3.

$-3x - 3y = -15$

$\underline{3x + 3y = b}$

$0 = b - 15$

a. The system has an infinite number
of solutions if this statement is true.
$b = 15$

b. The system has no solution if this
statement is false. b = any real
number except 15.

49. $\begin{cases} 2x + 3y = 14 \\ 3x - 4y = -69.1 \end{cases}$

Multiply the first equation by 3 and
the second equation by -2.

$6x + 9y = 42$

$\underline{-6x + 8y = 138.2}$

$17y = 180.2$

$y = 10.6$

Let $y = 10.6$ in the first equation.

$$2x + 3(10.6) = 14$$
$$2x + 31.8 = 14$$
$$2x = -17.8$$
$$x = -8.9$$

The solution of the system is $(-8.9, 10.6)$.

51. **b.** $4x - 8y = 6$

Answers may vary.

53.a. $\begin{cases} 3x - y = 514 \\ \underline{-23x + y = 249} \\ -20x = -265 \\ x = 13.25 \end{cases}$

Substitute to complete ordered pair solution.

$$3(13.25) - y = -514$$
$$39.75 - y = -514$$
$$-y = -553.75$$
$$y = 553.75$$

Solution rounded to the nearest whole
number: (13,554)

b. Answers may vary

c. $1994 - 2001$

Integrated Review 14.3

1. $\begin{cases} 2x - 3y = -11 \\ y = 4x - 3 \end{cases}$

   Substitute $4x - 3$ for y in the first equation.

   $2x - 3(4x - 3) = -11$

   $2x - 12x + 9 = -11$

   $-10x = -20$

   $x = 2$

   Let $x = 2$ in the second equation.

   $y = 4(2) - 3$

   $y = 5$

   The solution is $(2, 5)$.

2. $\begin{cases} 4x - 5y = 6 \\ y = 3x - 10 \end{cases}$

   Substitute $3x - 10$ for y in the first equation.

   $4x - 5(3x - 10) = 6$

   $4x - 15x + 50 = 6$

   $-11x = -44$

   $x = 4$

   Let $x = 4$ in the second equation.

   $y = 3(4) - 10$

   $y = 2$

   The solution is $(4, 2)$.

3. $\begin{cases} x + y = 3 \\ x - y = 7 \end{cases}$

   $\begin{aligned} 2x &= 10 \\ x &= 5 \end{aligned}$

   Let $x = 5$ in the first equation.

   $5 + y = 3$

   $y = -2$

   The solution of the system is $(5, -2)$

4. $\begin{cases} x - y = 20 \\ x + y = -8 \end{cases}$

   $\begin{aligned} 2x &= 12 \\ x &= 6 \end{aligned}$

   Let $x = 6$ in the second equation.

   $6 + y = -8$

   $y = -14$

   The solution of the system is $(6, -14)$

5. $\begin{cases} x + 2y = 1 \\ 3x + 4y = -1 \end{cases}$

   Solve the first equation for x.

   $x = 1 - 2y$

   Substitute $1 - 2y$ for x in the second equation.

   $3(1 - 2y) + 4y = -1$

   $3 - 6y + 4y = -1$

   $-2y = -4$

   $y = 2$

   Let $y = 2$ in $x = 1 - 2y$.

   $x = 1 - 2(2)$

   $x = -3$

   The solution is $(-3, 2)$.

6. $\begin{cases} x + 3y = 5 \\ 5x + 6y = -2 \end{cases}$

Solve the first equation for x.

$x = 5 - 3y$

Substitute $5 - 3y$ for x in the second equation.

$5(5 - 3y) + 6y = -2$

$25 - 15y + 6y = -2$

$-9y = -27$

$y = 3$

Let $y = 3$ in $x = 5 - 3y$.

$x = 5 - 3(3)$

$x = -4$

The solution is $(-4, 3)$.

7. $\begin{cases} y = x + 3 \\ 3x - 2y = -6 \end{cases}$

Substitute $x + 3$ for y in the second equation.

$3x - 2(x + 3) = -6$

$3x - 2x - 6 = -6$

$x = 0$

Let $x = 0$ in the first equation.

$y = 0 + 3$

$y = 3$

The solution is $(0, 3)$.

8. $\begin{cases} y = -2x \\ 2x - 3y = -16 \end{cases}$

Substitute $-2x$ for y in the second equation.

$2x - 3(-2x) = -16.$

$2x + 6x = -16$

$8x = -16$

$x = -2$

Let $x = -2$ in the first equation.

$y = -2(-2)$

$y = 4$

The solution is $(-2, 4)$.

9. $\begin{cases} y = 2x - 3 \\ y = 5x - 18 \end{cases}$

Substitute $5x - 18$ for y in the first equation.

$5x - 18 = 2x - 3$

$3x = 15$

$x = 5$

Let $x = 5$ in the second equation.

$y = 5(5) - 18$

$y = 7$

The solution is $(5, 7)$.

10. $\begin{cases} y = 6x - 5 \\ y = 4x - 11 \end{cases}$

Substitute $6x - 5$ for y in the second equation.

$6x - 5 = 4x - 11$

$2x = -6$

$x = -3$

Let $x = -3$ in the first equation.

$y = 6(-3) - 5$

$y = -23$

The solution is $(-3, -23)$.

11. $\begin{cases} x + \dfrac{1}{6}y = \dfrac{1}{2} \\ 3x + 2y = 3 \end{cases}$

Multiply the first equation by 6.

$\begin{cases} 6x + y = 3 \\ 3x + 2y = 3 \end{cases}$ Simplified system

Multiply the first equation of the simplified system by -2.

$\begin{cases} -12x - 2y = -6 \\ \underline{\;\;\;3x + 2y = \;\;3} \\ \;\;\;-9x \qquad = -3 \\ \qquad x \qquad = \dfrac{1}{3} \end{cases}$

Multiply the second equation of the simplified system by -2.

$\begin{cases} 6x + \;\;\;y = \;\;3 \\ \underline{-6x - 4y = -6} \\ \qquad -3y = -3 \\ \qquad\;\; y = 1 \end{cases}$

The solution of the system is $\left(\dfrac{1}{3}, 1 \right)$.

12. $\begin{cases} x + \dfrac{1}{3}y = \dfrac{5}{12} \\ 8x + 3y = 4 \end{cases}$

Multiply the first equation by 12.

$\begin{cases} 12x + 4y = 5 \\ 8x + 3y = 4 \end{cases}$ Simplified system

Multiply the first equation of the simplified system by 2 and the second equation by -3.

$\begin{cases} 24x + 8y = \;\;10 \\ \underline{-24x - 9y = -12} \\ \qquad -y = -2 \\ \qquad\;\; y = 2 \end{cases}$

Multiply the first equation of the simplified system by 3 and the second equation by 4.

$\begin{cases} 36x + 12y = \;\;15 \\ \underline{-32x - 12y = -16} \\ \;\;4x \qquad\quad = -1 \\ \quad x \qquad\qquad = -\dfrac{1}{4} \end{cases}$

The solution of the system is $\left(-\dfrac{1}{4}, 2 \right)$.

13. $\begin{cases} x - 5y = 1 \\ -2x + 10y = 3 \end{cases}$

Multiply the first equation by 2.

$\begin{aligned} 2x - 10y &= 2 \\ \underline{-2x + 10y} &= \underline{3} \\ 0 &= 5 \end{aligned}$

The system has no solution.

14. $\begin{cases} -x + 2y = 3 \\ 3x - 6y = -9 \end{cases}$

Multiply the first equation by 3.

$\begin{aligned} -3x + 6y &= \;\;9 \\ \underline{3x - 6y} &= \underline{-9} \\ 0 &= 0 \end{aligned}$

The equations in the original system are equivalent and there are an infinite number of solutions..

15. $\begin{cases} 0.2x - 0.3y = -0.95 \\ 0.4x + 0.1y = 0.55 \end{cases}$

Multiply both equations by 10.

$\begin{cases} 2x - 3y = -9.5 \\ 4x + y = 5.5 \end{cases}$ Simplified system

Multiply the first equation of the simplified system by -2.

$\begin{cases} -4x + 6y = 19 \\ \underline{4x + y = 5.5} \end{cases}$

$\qquad\qquad 7y = 24.5$

$\qquad\qquad\quad y = 3.5$

Multiply the second equation of the simplified system by 3.

$\begin{cases} 2x - 3y = -9.5 \\ \underline{12x + 3y = 16.5} \end{cases}$

$\quad 14x \quad = 7$

$\qquad x \quad = 0.5$

The solution of the system is $(0.5, 3.5)$.

16. $\begin{cases} 0.08x - 0.04y = -0.11 \\ 0.02x - 0.06y = -0.09 \end{cases}$

Multiply both equations by 100.

$\begin{cases} 8x - 4y = -11 \\ 2x - 6y = -9 \end{cases}$ Simplified system

Multiply the second equation of the simplified system by -4.

$\begin{cases} 8x - 4y = -11 \\ \underline{-8x + 24y = 36} \end{cases}$

$\qquad\quad 20y = 25$

$\qquad\qquad y = 1.25$

Multiply the first equation of the simplified system by -3 and the second equation by 2.

$\begin{cases} -24x + 12y = 33 \\ \underline{\quad 4x - 12y = -18} \end{cases}$

$\;\; -20x \qquad = 15$

$\qquad x \qquad = -0.75$

The solution of the system is $(-0.75, 1.25)$.

17. $\begin{cases} x = 3y - 7 \\ 2x - 6y = -14 \end{cases}$

Substitute $3y - 7$ for x in the second equation.

$2(3y - 7) - 6y = -14$

$\qquad 6y - 14 - 6y = -14$

$\qquad\qquad\qquad 0 = 0$

The equations in the original system are equivalent and there are an infinite number of solutions..

18. $\begin{cases} y = \dfrac{x}{2} - 3 \\ 2x - 4y = 0 \end{cases}$

Substitute $\dfrac{x}{2} - 3$ for y in the second equation.

$2x - 4\left(\dfrac{x}{2} - 3\right) = 0$

$\qquad 2x - 2x + 12 = 0$

$\qquad\qquad\qquad 12 = 0$

There is no solution.

19. Answers may vary.

20. Answers may vary.

Practice Problems 14.4

1. Let x = the first number and

y = the second number.

$$\begin{cases} x + y = 50 \\ \underline{x - y = 22} \end{cases}$$

$$2x \quad = 72$$

$$x \quad = 36$$

Let $x = 36$ in the first equation.

$$36 + y = 50$$

$$y = 14$$

The numbers are 36 and 14.

2. Let C = the number of children and

A = the number of adults.

$$\begin{cases} 5C + 7A = 3379 \\ C + A = 587 \end{cases}$$

Solve the second equation for A.

$$A = 587 - C$$

Substitute $587 - C$ for A in the

first equation.

$$5C + 7(587 - C) = 3379$$

$$5C + 4109 - 7C = 3379$$

$$-2C = -730$$

$$C = 365$$

Let $C = 365$ in $A = 587 - C$.

$$A = 587 - 365$$

$$A = 222$$

There were 365 children and 222 adults.

3. Let x = the speed of the faster car and

y = the speed of the slower car.

	r	$\cdot$ t	$=$ d
Faster car	x	3	$3x$
Slower car	y	3	$3y$

$$\begin{cases} x = y + 10 \\ 3x + 3y = 440 \end{cases}$$

Substitute $y + 10$ for x in the

second equation.

$$3(y + 10) + 3y = 440$$

$$3y + 30 + 3y = 440$$

$$6y = 410$$

$$y = \frac{410}{6} = 68\frac{1}{3}$$

Let $y = 68\frac{1}{3}$ in the first equation.

$$x = 68\frac{1}{3} + 10 = 78\frac{1}{3}$$

The speed of the faster car is $68\frac{1}{3}$ mph.

The speed of the slower car is $78\frac{1}{3}$ mph.

4. Let x = liters of 20% solution and

y = liters of 70% solution.

	Concentration Rate	Liters of Solution	Liters of Pure Alcohol
First solution	20%	x	$0.2x$
Second solution	70%	y	$0.7y$
Mixture	60%	50	$0.6(50)$

$$\begin{cases} x + y = 50 \\ 0.2x + 0.7y = 0.6(50) \end{cases}$$

Multiply the first equation by -2 and the second equation by 10.

$$-2x - 2y = -100$$
$$\underline{2x + 7y = 300}$$
$$5y = 200$$
$$y = 40$$

Let $y = 40$ in the first equation.

$$x + 40 = 50$$
$$x = 10$$

10 liters of 20% alcohol solution and 40 liters of 70% alcohol solution.

Mental Math 14.4

1. c

2. b

3. b

4. c

5. a

6. c

Exercise Set 14.4

1. Let x = the first number and y = the second number.

$$\begin{cases} x + y = 15 \\ x - y = 7 \end{cases}$$

3. Let x = the amount invested in the larger account and y = the amount invested in the smaller account.

$$\begin{cases} x + y = 6500 \\ x = y + 800 \end{cases}$$

5. Let x = the first number and y = the second number.

$$\begin{cases} x + y = 83 \\ \underline{x - y = 17} \end{cases}$$
$$2x = 100$$
$$x = 50$$

Let $x = 50$ in the first equation.

$$50 + y = 83$$
$$y = 33$$

The numbers are 50 and 33.

7. Let x = the first number and y = the second number.

$$\begin{cases} x + 2y = 8 \\ 2x + y = 25 \end{cases}$$

Multiply the first equation by -2.

$$-2x - 4y = -16$$
$$\underline{2x + y = 25}$$
$$-3y = 9$$
$$y = -3$$

Let $y = -3$ in the first equation.

$$x + 2(-3) = 8$$
$$x - 6 = 8$$
$$x = 14$$

The numbers are 14 and -3.

9. Let J = Jackson's points scored

Let H = Holdsclaw's points scored

$$\begin{cases} J = H + 142 \\ J + H = 1174 \end{cases}$$

Using substitution:

$$H + 142 + H = 1174$$
$$2H + 142 = 1174$$
$$2H = 1032$$
$$H = 516$$

Holdsclaw scored 516 points during the 2003 regular season, and Jackson scored $516 + 142 = 658$ points during that season.

11. Let x = the price of an adult's ticket and y = the price of a child's ticket.

$$\begin{cases} 3x + 4y = 159 \\ 2x + 3y = 112 \end{cases}$$

Multiply the first equation by -2 and the second equation by 3.

$$\begin{array}{rcl} -6x - 8y &=& -318 \\ 6x + 9y &=& 336 \\ \hline y &=& 18 \end{array}$$

Let $y = 18$ in the first equation.

$$3x + 4(18) = 159$$
$$3x + 72 = 159$$
$$3x = 87$$
$$x = 29$$

An adult's ticket is \$29 and a child's ticket is \$18.

13. Let x = the number of quarters and y = the number of nickels.

$$\begin{cases} x + y = 80 \\ 0.25x + 0.05y = 14.6 \end{cases}$$

Solve the first equation for y.

$$y = 80 - x$$

Substitute $80 - x$ for y in the second equation.

$$0.25x + 0.05(80 - x) = 14.6$$
$$0.25x + 4 - 0.05x = 14.6$$
$$0.20x = 10.6$$
$$x = 53$$

Let $x = 53$ in $y = 80 - x$.

$$y = 80 - 53$$
$$y = 27$$

There are 53 quarters and 27 nickels.

15. Let x = price of Ohio Art stock and y = price of General Electric stock.

$$\begin{cases} 55x+30y=2348.10 \\ y=x+35.77 \end{cases}$$

Substitute $x+35.77$ for y in the first equation.

$55x+30(x+35.77)=2348.10$

$55x+30x+1073.10=2348.10$

$85x=1275$

$x=15$

Let $x=15$ in the second equation.

$y=15+35.77$

$y=50.77$

Ohio Art Co. was \$15 and General Electric was \$50.77

17. Let x = the cost per hour of labor and y = the cost per ton of material.

$$\begin{cases} 65x+3y=1702.50 \\ 49x+\dfrac{5}{2}y=1349 \end{cases}$$

Multiply the second equation by 2.

$$\begin{cases} 65x+3y=1702.50 \\ 98x+5y=2698 \end{cases} \text{Simplified system}$$

Multiply the first equation of the simplified system by 5 and the second equation by -3.

$$\begin{aligned} 325x+15y &= 8512.5 \\ -294x-15y &= -8094 \\ \hline 31x &= 418.5 \\ x &= 13.5 \end{aligned}$$

Let $x=13.5$ in the first equation.

$65(13.5)+3y=1702.5$

$877.5+3y=1702.5$

$3y=825$

$y=275$

Labor costs \$13.50 per hour and material costs \$275 per ton.

19.

	d	$=$	r	$\cdot$	t
Downstream	18		$x+y$		2
Upstream	18		$x-y$		$4\frac{1}{2}$

$$\begin{cases} 2(x+y)=18 \\ \dfrac{9}{2}(x-y)=18 \end{cases}$$

Multiply the first equation by $\dfrac{1}{2}$ and the second equation by $\dfrac{2}{9}$.

$$\begin{cases} x+y=9 \\ x-y=4 \end{cases} \text{ Simplified system}$$

$$2x \quad = 13$$
$$x \quad = 6.5$$

Multiply the second equation of the simplified system by -1.

$$\begin{cases} x+y=9 \\ -x+y=-4 \end{cases}$$

$$2y=5$$
$$y=2.5$$

Pratap can row 6.5 mph in still water. The rate of the current is 2.5 mph.

21.

d	$=$	r	$\cdot$	t
With the wind	780	$x+y$		$1\frac{1}{2}$
Into the wind	780	$x-y$		2

$$\begin{cases} \frac{3}{2}(x+y)=780 \\ 2(x-y)=780 \end{cases}$$

Multiply the first equation by $\frac{2}{3}$ and

the second equation by $\frac{1}{2}$.

$$\begin{cases} x+y=520 \\ x-y=390 \end{cases} \text{ Simplified system}$$

$$2x \quad = 910$$
$$x \quad = 455$$

Multiply the second equation of the simplified system by -1.

$$\begin{cases} x+y=520 \\ -x+y=-390 \end{cases}$$

$$2y=130$$
$$y=65$$

The plane can fly 455 mph in still air. The speed of the wind is 65 mph.

23. Let x = the time spent walking and y = the time spent on the bicycle.

	r	$\cdot$	t	$=$	d
Walking	4		x		$4x$
Biking	40		y		$40y$

$$\begin{cases} x+y=6 \\ 4x+40y=186 \end{cases}$$

Multiply the first equation by -4.

$$-4x-4y=-24$$
$$4x+40y=186$$
$$36y=162$$
$$y=4.5$$

He spent $4\frac{1}{2}$ hours on the bicycle.

25. Let x = liters of 4% solution and y = liters of 12% solution.

	Concentration Rate	Ounces of Solution	Ounces of Pure Acid
First solution	0.04	x	$0.04x$
Second solution	0.12	y	$0.12y$
Mixture	0.09	12	$0.09(12)$

$$\begin{cases} x + y = 12 \\ 0.04x + 0.12y = 0.09(12) \end{cases}$$

Multiply the first equation by -4
and the second equation by 100.

$$-4x - 4y = -48$$
$$4x + 12y = 108$$
$$\overline{}$$
$$8y = 60$$
$$y = 7.5$$

Let $y = 7.5$ in the first equation.

$$x + 7.5 = 12$$
$$x = 4.5$$

$4\dfrac{1}{2}$ ounces of 4% solution and

$7\dfrac{1}{2}$ ounces of 12% solution.

27. Let $x =$ pounds of \$4.95 per pound
beans and $y =$ pounds of \$2.65 per
pound beans.

	Cost Rate	Pounds of Beans	Dollars Cost
High Quality	4.95	x	$4.95x$
Low Quality	2.65	y	$2.65y$
Mixture	3.95	200	$3.95(200)$

$$\begin{cases} x + y = 200 \\ 4.95x + 2.65y = 3.95(200) \end{cases}$$

Solve the first equation for y.

$$y = 200 - x$$

Substitute $200 - x$ for y in the
second equation.

$$4.95x + 2.65(200 - x) = 3.95(200)$$
$$4.95x + 530 - 2.65x = 790$$
$$2.30x = 260$$
$$x = 113.04$$

Let $x = 113.04$ in the first equation.

$$113.04 + y = 200$$
$$y = 86.96$$

He needs 113 pounds of \$4.95 per
pound beans and 87 pounds of \$2.65
per pound beans.

29. Let $x =$ the first angle and
$y =$ the second angle.

$$\begin{cases} x + y = 90 \\ x = 2y \end{cases}$$

Substitute $2y$ for x in the
first equation.

$$2y + y = 90$$
$$3y = 90$$
$$y = 30$$

Let $y = 30$ in the second equation.

$$x = 2(30)$$
$$x = 60$$

The angles are $60°$ and $30°$.

31. Let $x =$ the first angle and
$y =$ the second angle.

$$\begin{cases} x + y = 90 \\ x = 3y + 10 \end{cases}$$

Substitute $3y + 10$ for x in the
first equation.

$$3y + 10 + y = 90$$
$$4y = 80$$
$$y = 20$$

Let $y = 20$ in the second equation.

$x = 3(20) + 10$

$x = 70$

The angles are 70° and 20°.

33. Let x = the number sold at \$9.50 and y = the number sold at \$7.50.

$$\begin{cases} x + y = 90 \\ 9.5x + 7.5y = 721 \end{cases}$$

Solve the first equation for y.

$y = 90 - x$

Substitute $90 - x$ for y in the second equation.

$9.5x + 7.5(90 - x) = 721$

$9.5x + 675 - 7.5x = 721$

$2x = 46$

$x = 23$

Let $x = 23$ in $y = 90 - x$.

$y = 90 - 23$

$y = 67$

They sold 23 at \$9.50 and 67 at \$7.50.

35. Let x = the rate of the faster group and y = the rate of the slower group.

	r	$\cdot$ t	$=$ d
Slower group	x	240	$240x$
Faster group	y	240	$240y$

$$\begin{cases} x = y - \dfrac{1}{2} \\ 240x + 240y = 1200 \end{cases}$$

Substitute $y - \dfrac{1}{2}$ for x in the second equation.

$240\left(y - \dfrac{1}{2}\right) + 240y = 1200$

$240y - 120 + 240y = 1200$

$480y = 1320$

$y = \dfrac{1320}{480} = 2\dfrac{3}{4}$

Let $y = 2\dfrac{3}{4}$ in the first equation.

$x = 2\dfrac{3}{4} - \dfrac{1}{2} = 2\dfrac{1}{4}$

The rate of the faster group is $2\dfrac{3}{4}$ mph.

The rate of the slower group is $2\dfrac{1}{4}$ mph.

37. Let x = gallons of 30% solution and y = gallons of 60% solution.

	Concentration Rate	Gallons of Solution	Gallons of Pure Fertilizer
First solution	0.30	x	$0.30x$
Second solution	0.60	y	$0.60y$
Mixture	0.50	150	$0.50(150)$

$$\begin{cases} x + y = 150 \\ 0.30x + 0.60y = 0.50(150) \end{cases}$$

Multiply the first equation by -3 and the second equation by 10.

$-3x - 3y = -450$

$\underline{3x + 6y = 750}$

$3y = 300$

$y = 100$

Let $y = 100$ in the first equation.

$x + 100 = 150$

$x = 50$

50 gallons of 30% solution and 100 gallons of 60% solution.

39. Let x = the width and y = the length.

$$\begin{cases} 2x + 2y = 144 \\ y = x + 12 \end{cases}$$

Substitute $x + 12$ for y in the first equation.

$$2x + 2(x + 12) = 144$$
$$2x + 2x + 24 = 144$$
$$4x = 120$$
$$x = 30$$

Let $x = 30$ in the second equation.

$$y = 30 + 12$$
$$y = 42$$

Width = 30 inches, length = 42 inches.

41. $4^2 = 16$

43. $(6x)^2 = 36x^2$

45. $(10y^3)^2 = 100y^6$

47. Let x = the width and y = the length.

$$\begin{cases} 2x + y = 33 \\ y = 2x - 3 \end{cases}$$

Substitute $2x - 3$ for y in the first equation.

$$2x + 2x - 3 = 33$$
$$4x = 36$$
$$x = 9$$

Let $x = 9$ in the second equation.

$$y = 2(9) - 3$$
$$y = 15$$

Width = 9 feet, length = 15 feet.

Chapter 14 Review

1. a. Let $x = 12$ and $y = 4$.

$$2x - 3y = 12 \qquad\qquad 3x + 4y = 1$$
$$2(12) - 3(4) \overset{?}{=} 12 \qquad 3(12) + 4(4) \overset{?}{=} 1$$
$$24 - 12 \overset{?}{=} 12 \qquad\qquad 36 + 16 \overset{?}{=} 1$$
$$12 = 12 \qquad\qquad\qquad 52 = 1$$
$$\text{True} \qquad\qquad\qquad\quad \text{False}$$

$(12, 4)$ is not a solution of the system.

b. Let $x = 3$ and $y = -2$.

$$2x - 3y = 12 \qquad\qquad 3x + 4y = 1$$
$$2(3) - 3(-2) \overset{?}{=} 12 \qquad 3(3) + 4(-2) \overset{?}{=} 1$$
$$6 + 6 \overset{?}{=} 12 \qquad\qquad 9 - 8 \overset{?}{=} 1$$
$$2 = 12 \qquad\qquad\qquad 1 = 1$$
$$\text{True} \qquad\qquad\qquad\quad \text{True}$$

$(3, -2)$ is a solution of the system

2. a. Let $x = \dfrac{3}{4}$ and $y = -3$.

$$4x + y = 0 \qquad\qquad -8x - 5y = 9$$
$$4\left(\frac{3}{4}\right) - 3 \overset{?}{=} 0 \qquad -8\left(\frac{3}{4}\right) - 5(-3) \overset{?}{=} 9$$
$$3 - 3 \overset{?}{=} 0 \qquad\qquad -6 + 15 \overset{?}{=} 9$$
$$0 = 0 \qquad\qquad\qquad 9 = 9$$
$$\text{True} \qquad\qquad\qquad \text{True}$$

$\left(\dfrac{3}{4}, -3\right)$ is a solution of the system.

b. Let $x = -2$ and $y = 8$.

$$4x + y = 0 \qquad -8x - 5y = 9$$

$$4(-2) + 8 \overset{?}{=} 0 \qquad -8(-2) - 5(8) \overset{?}{=} 9$$

$$-8 + 8 \overset{?}{=} 0 \qquad 16 - 40 \overset{?}{=} 9$$

$$0 = 0 \qquad -24 = 9$$

$$\text{True} \qquad\qquad \text{False}$$

$(-2, 8)$ is not a solution of the system

3. a. Let $x = -6$ and $y = -8$.

$$5x - 6y = 18 \qquad 2y - x = -4$$

$$5(-6) - 6(-8) \overset{?}{=} 18 \quad 2(-8) - (-6) \overset{?}{=} -4$$

$$-30 + 48 \overset{?}{=} 18 \qquad -16 + 6 \overset{?}{=} -4$$

$$18 = 18 \qquad -10 = -4$$

$$\text{True} \qquad\qquad \text{False}$$

$(-6, -8)$ is not a solution of the system.

b. Let $x = 3$ and $y = \dfrac{5}{2}$.

$$5x - 6y = 18 \qquad 2y - x = -4$$

$$5(3) - 6\left(\dfrac{5}{2}\right) \overset{?}{=} 18 \quad 2\left(\dfrac{5}{2}\right) - 3 \overset{?}{=} -4$$

$$15 - 15 \overset{?}{=} 18 \qquad 5 - 3 \overset{?}{=} -4$$

$$0 = 18 \qquad 2 = -4$$

$$\text{False} \qquad\qquad \text{False}$$

$\left(3, \dfrac{5}{2}\right)$ is not a solution of the system

4. a. Let $x = 2$ and $y = 2$.

$$2x + 3y = 1 \qquad 3y - x = 4$$

$$2(2) + 3(2) \overset{?}{=} 1 \qquad 3(2) - (2) \overset{?}{=} 4$$

$$4 + 6 \overset{?}{=} 1 \qquad 6 - 2 \overset{?}{=} 4$$

$$10 = 1 \qquad 4 = 4$$

$$\text{False} \qquad\qquad \text{True}$$

$(2, 2)$ is not a solution of the system.

b. Let $x = -1$ and $y = 1$.

$$2x + 3y = 1 \qquad 3y - x = 4$$

$$2(-1) + 3(1) \overset{?}{=} 1 \qquad 3(1) - (-1) \overset{?}{=} 4$$

$$-2 + 3 \overset{?}{=} 1 \qquad 3 + 1 \overset{?}{=} 4$$

$$1 = 1 \qquad 4 = 4$$

$$\text{True} \qquad\qquad \text{True}$$

$(-1, 1)$ is a solution of the system

5. $\begin{cases} x + y = 5 \\ x - y = 1 \end{cases}$

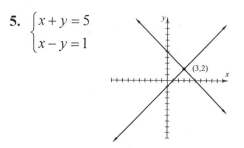

The solution of the system is $(3, 2)$.

6. $\begin{cases} x + y = 3 \\ x - y = -1 \end{cases}$

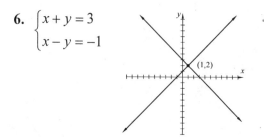

The solution of the system is $(1, 2)$.

7. $\begin{cases} x = 5 \\ y = -1 \end{cases}$

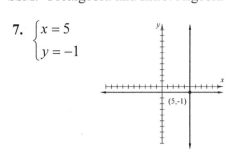

The solution of the system is $(5, -1)$.

8. $\begin{cases} x = -3 \\ y = 2 \end{cases}$

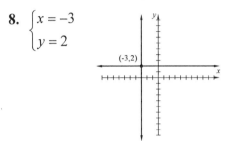

The solution of the system is $(-3, 2)$.

9. $\begin{cases} 2x + y = 5 \\ x = -3y \end{cases}$

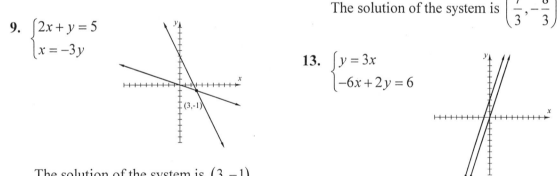

The solution of the system is $(3, -1)$.

10. $\begin{cases} 3x + y = -2 \\ y = -5x \end{cases}$

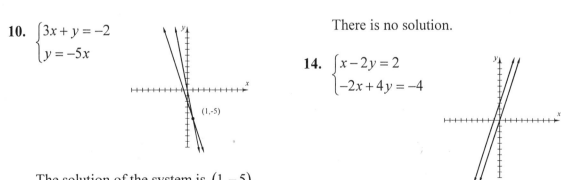

The solution of the system is $(1, -5)$.

11. $\begin{cases} y = 2x + 4 \\ y = -x - 5 \end{cases}$

The solution of the system is $(-3, -2)$.

12. $\begin{cases} y = x - 5 \\ y = -2x + 2 \end{cases}$

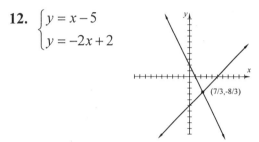

The solution of the system is $\left(\dfrac{7}{3}, -\dfrac{8}{3} \right)$.

13. $\begin{cases} y = 3x \\ -6x + 2y = 6 \end{cases}$

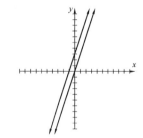

There is no solution.

14. $\begin{cases} x - 2y = 2 \\ -2x + 4y = -4 \end{cases}$

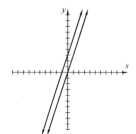

There are an infinite number of solutions.

17. $\begin{cases} y = 2x + 6 \\ 3x - 2y = -11 \end{cases}$

Substitute $2x + 6$ for y in the second equation.

$3x - 2(2x + 6) = -11$

$3x - 4x - 12 = -11$

$-x = 1$

$x = -1$

Let $x = -1$ in the first equation.

$y = 2(-1) + 6$

$y = 4$

The solution is $(-1, 4)$.

15. $\begin{cases} x = 2y \\ 2x - 3y = 2 \end{cases}$

Substitute $2y$ for x in the second equation.

$2(2y) - 3y = 2$

$4y - 3y = 2$

$y = 2$

Let $y = 2$ in the first equation.

$x = 2(2)$

$x = 4$

The solution is $(4, 2)$.

16. $\begin{cases} x = 5y \\ x - 4y = 1 \end{cases}$

Substitute $5y$ for x in the second equation.

$5y - 4y = 1$

$y = 1$

Let $y = 1$ in the first equation.

$x = 5(1)$

$x = 5$

The solution is $(5, 1)$.

18. $\begin{cases} y = 3x - 7 \\ 2x - 3y = 7 \end{cases}$

Substitute $3x - 7$ for y in the second equation.

$2x - 3(3x - 7) = 7$

$2x - 9x + 21 = 7$

$-7x = -14$

$x = 2$

Let $x = 2$ in the first equation.

$y = 3(2) - 7$

$y = -1$

The solution is $(2, -1)$.

19. $\begin{cases} x + 3y = -3 \\ 2x + y = 4 \end{cases}$

Solve the first equation for x.

$x = -3 - 3y$

Substitute $-3 - 3y$ for x in the second equation.

$2(-3 - 3y) + y = 4$

$-6 - 6y + y = 4$

$-5y = 10$

$y = -2$

Let $y = -2$ in $x = -3 - 3y$.

$x = -3 - 3(-2)$

$x = 3$

The solution is $(3, -2)$.

20. $\begin{cases} 3x + y = 11 \\ x + 2y = 12 \end{cases}$

Solve the first equation for y.

$y = 11 - 3x$

Substitute $11 - 3x$ for y in the second equation.

$x + 2(11 - 3x) = 12$

$x + 22 - 6x = 12$

$-5x = -10$

$x = 2$

Let $x = 2$ in $y = 11 - 3x$.

$y = 11 - 3(2)$

$y = 5$

The solution is $(2, 5)$.

21. $\begin{cases} 4y = 2x - 3 \\ x - 2y = 4 \end{cases}$

Solve the second equation for x.

$x = 4 + 2y$

Substitute $4 + 2y$ for x in the first equation.

$4y = 2(4 + 2y) - 3$

$4y = 8 + 4y - 3$

$0 = 5$

The system has no solution.

22. $\begin{cases} 2x = 3y - 18 \\ x + 4y = 2 \end{cases}$

Solve the second equation for x.

$x = 2 - 4y$

Substitute $2 - 4y$ for x in the first equation.

$2(2 - 4y) = 3y - 18$

$4 - 8y = 3y - 18$

$-11y = -22$

$y = 2$

Let $y = 2$ in $x = 2 - 4y$.

$x = 2 - 4(2)$

$x = -6$

The solution is $(-6, 2)$.

23. $\begin{cases} x+y=6 \\ y=-x-4 \end{cases}$

Substitute $-x-4$ for y in the first equation.

$x+(-x-4)=6$

$\quad x-x-4=6$

$\quad\quad -4=6$

There is no solution.

24. $\begin{cases} -3x+y=6 \\ y=3x+2 \end{cases}$

Substitute $3x+2$ for y in the first equation.

$-3x+(3x+2)=6$

$\quad -3x+3x+2=6$

$\quad\quad\quad 2=6$

There is no solution.

25. $\begin{cases} x+y=14 \\ x-y=18 \end{cases}$

$2x\quad=32$

$\;x\quad=16$

Let $x=16$ in the first equation.

$16+y=14$

$\quad y=-2$

The solution of the system is $(16,-2)$

26. $\begin{cases} x+y=9 \\ x-y=13 \end{cases}$

$2x\quad=22$

$\;x\quad=11$

Let $x=11$ in the first equation.

$11+y=9$

$\quad y=-2$

The solution of the system is $(11,-2)$

27. $\begin{cases} 2x+3y=-6 \\ \;\;x-3y=-12 \end{cases}$

$3x\quad=-18$

$\;x\quad=-6$

Let $x=-6$ in the first equation.

$2(-6)+3y=-6$

$\quad -12+3y=-6$

$\quad\quad 3y=6$

$\quad\quad y=2$

The solution of the system is $(-6,2)$

28. $\begin{cases} \;\;4x+\;y=\;15 \\ -4x+3y=-19 \end{cases}$

$4y=-4$

$\;y=-1$

Let $y=-1$ in the first equation.

$4x+(-1)=15$

$\quad 4x-1=15$

$\quad\quad 4x=16$

$\quad\quad x=4$

The solution of the system is $(4,-1)$.

29. $\begin{cases} 2x-3y=-15 \\ x+4y=31 \end{cases}$

Multiply the second equation by -2.

$2x-3y=-15$
$\underline{-2x-8y=-62}$
$-11y=-77$
$y=7$

Let $y=7$ in the second equation.

$x+4(7)=31$
$x+28=31$
$x=3$

The solution of the system is $(3,7)$.

30. $\begin{cases} x-5y=-22 \\ 4x+3y=4 \end{cases}$

Multiply the first equation by -4.

$-4x+20y=88$
$\underline{4x+3y=4}$
$23y=92$
$y=4$

Let $y=4$ in the first equation.

$x-5(4)=-22$
$x-20=-22$
$x=-2$

The solution of the system is $(-2,4)$.

31. $\begin{cases} 2x-6y=-1 \\ -x+3y=\dfrac{1}{2} \end{cases}$

Multiply the second equation by 2.

$2x-6y=-1$
$\underline{-2x+6y=1}$
$0=0$

There are an infinite number of solutions.

32. $\begin{cases} -4x-6y=8 \\ 2x+3y=-3 \end{cases}$

Multiply the second equation by 2.

$-4x-6y=8$
$\underline{4x+6y=-6}$
$0=2$

The system has no solution.

33. $\begin{cases} \dfrac{3}{4}x+\dfrac{2}{3}y=2 \\ x+\dfrac{y}{3}=6 \end{cases}$

Multiply the first equation by 12 and the second equation by -9.

$9x+8y=24$
$\underline{-9x-3y=-54}$
$5y=-30$
$y=-6$

Let $y = -6$ in the second equation.

$$x + \left(\frac{-6}{3}\right) = 6$$

$$x - 2 = 6$$

$$x = 8$$

The solution of the system is $(8, -6)$.

34. $\begin{cases} \dfrac{2}{5}x + \dfrac{3}{4}y = 1 \\ x + 3y = -2 \end{cases}$

Multiply the first equation by 20 and the second equation by -8.

$$8x + 15y = 20$$
$$\underline{-8x - 24y = 16}$$
$$-9y = 36$$
$$y = -4$$

Let $y = -4$ in the second equation.

$$x + 3(-4) = -2$$

$$x - 12 = -2$$

$$x = 10$$

The solution of the system is $(10, -4)$.

35. $\begin{cases} 10x + 2y = 0 \\ 3x + 5y = 33 \end{cases}$

Multiply the first equation by 5 and the second equation by -2.

$$50x + 10y = 0$$
$$\underline{-6x - 10y = -66}$$
$$44x = -66$$
$$x = -\frac{3}{2}$$

Let $x = -\dfrac{3}{2}$ in the first equation.

$$10\left(-\frac{3}{2}\right) + 2y = 0$$

$$-15 + 2y = 0$$

$$2y = 15$$

$$y = \frac{15}{2}$$

The solution of the system is $\left(-\dfrac{3}{2}, \dfrac{15}{2}\right)$.

36. $\begin{cases} 0.6x - 0.3y = -1.5 \\ 0.04x - 0.02y = -0.1 \end{cases}$

Multiply the first equation by 10 and the second equation by 100.

$$\begin{cases} 6x - 3y = -15 \\ 4x - 2y = -10 \end{cases} \quad \text{Simplified system}$$

Multiply the first equation by 2 and the second equation by -3.

$$12x - 6y = -30$$
$$\underline{-12x + 6y = 30}$$
$$0 = 0$$

There are an infinite number of solutions..

37. Let $x =$ the larger number and $y =$ the smaller number.

$$\begin{cases} x + y = 16 \\ 3x - y = 72 \end{cases}$$
$$\overline{4x = 88}$$
$$x = 22$$

Let $x = 22$ in the first equation.

$$22 + y = 16$$

$$y = -6$$

The numbers are -6 and 22.

38. Let x = the number of orchestra seats and y = the number of balcony seats.

$$\begin{cases} x + y = 360 \\ 45x + 35y = 15,150 \end{cases}$$

Solve the first equation for x.

$x = 360 - y$

Substitute $360 - y$ for x in the second equation.

$45(360 - y) + 35y = 15,150$

$16,200 - 45y + 35y = 15,150$

$-10y = -1050$

$y = 105$

Let $y = 105$ in $x = 360 - y$.

$x = 360 - 105$

$x = 255$

There were 255 orchestra seats and 105 balcony seats.

39. Let x = the riverboat's speed in still water and y = the rate of the current.

	d	$=$	r	$\cdot$	t
Downriver	340		$x + y$		14
Upriver	340		$x - y$		19

$$\begin{cases} 14(x + y) = 340 \\ 19(x - y) = 340 \end{cases}$$

Multiply the first equation by $\dfrac{1}{14}$ and the second equation by $\dfrac{1}{19}$.

$$\begin{cases} x + y = \dfrac{340}{14} \approx 24.29 \\ x - y = \dfrac{340}{19} \approx 17.89 \end{cases} \quad \text{Simplified system}$$

$$\begin{array}{ll} 2x & \approx 42.18 \\ x & \approx 21.09 \end{array}$$

Multiply the second equation of the simplified system by -1.

$$\begin{cases} x + y \approx 24.29 \\ -x + y \approx -17.89 \end{cases}$$

$$\begin{array}{l} 2y \approx 6.4 \\ y \approx 3.2 \end{array}$$

The riverboat's speed in still water is 21.1 mph. The rate of the current is 3.2 mph.

40. Let x = amount invested at 6% and y = amount invested at 10%.

$$\begin{cases} x + y = 9000 \\ 0.06x + 0.10y = 652.80 \end{cases}$$

Multiply the first equation by -6 and the second equation by 100.

$$\begin{array}{l} -6x - 6y = -54,000 \\ 6x + 10y = 65,280 \end{array}$$

$$\begin{array}{l} 4y = 11,280 \\ y = 2820 \end{array}$$

Let $y = 2820$ in the first equation.

$x + 2820 = 9000$

$x = 6180$

$6180 invested at 6% and $2820 invested at 10%.

41. Let x = the width and y = the length.
$$\begin{cases} 2x+2y=6 \\ y=1.6x \end{cases}$$
Substitute $1.6x$ for y in the
first equation.
$$2x+2(1.6x)=6$$
$$2x+3.2x=6$$
$$5.2x=6$$
$$x\approx 1.154$$
Let $x=1.154$ in the second equation.
$$y=1.6(1.154)$$
$$y\approx 1.846$$
Width $=1.15$ feet, length $=1.85$ feet.

42. Let x = liters of 6% solution and
y = liters of 14% solution.

	Concentration Rate	Ounces of Solution	Ounces of Pure Acid
First solution	0.06	x	$0.06x$
Second solution	0.14	y	$0.14y$
Mixture	0.12	50	$0.12(50)$

$$\begin{cases} x+y=50 \\ 0.06x+0.14y=0.12(50) \end{cases}$$
Multiply the first equation by -6
and the second equation by 100.
$$-6x-\ 6y=-300$$
$$6x+14y=\ \ 600$$
$$\overline{\ \ \ \ \ \ 8y=\ \ 300}$$
$$y=37.5$$

Let $y=37.5$ in the first equation.
$$x+37.5=50$$
$$x=12.5$$
$12\frac{1}{2}$ cc of 6% solution and
$37\frac{1}{2}$ cc of 14% solution.

43. Let x = the cost of an egg and
y = the cost of a strip of bacon.
$$\begin{cases} 3x+4y=3.80 \\ 2x+3y=2.75 \end{cases}$$
Multiply the first equation by -2 and
the second equation by 3.
$$-6x-8y=-7.60$$
$$6x+9y=\ \ 8.25$$
$$\overline{\ \ \ \ \ \ \ y=\ \ 0.65}$$
Let $y=0.65$ in the first equation.
$$3x+4(0.65)=3.80$$
$$3x+2.60=3.80$$
$$3x=1.20$$
$$x=0.40$$
An egg costs 40¢ and a strip of
bacon costs 65¢.

44. Let x = the time spent walking and
y = the time spent jogging.

	r	$\cdot$ t	$=$ d
Walking	4	x	$4x$
Jogging	7.5	y	$7.5y$

$$\begin{cases} x+y=3 \\ 4x+7.5y=15 \end{cases}$$

Multiply the first equation by -4.

$$-4x - 4y = -12$$
$$\underline{4x + 7.5y = 15}$$
$$3.5y = 3$$
$$y \approx 0.857$$

Let $y = 0.857$ in the first equation.

$$x + 0.857 = 3$$
$$x = 2.143$$

He spent 2.14 hours walking and 0.86 hours jogging.

Chapter 14 Test

1. $\begin{cases} y - x = 6 \\ y + 2x = -6 \end{cases}$

The solution is

$(-4, 2)$

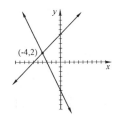

2. $\begin{cases} 4x + 3y = 1 \\ y = -3x + 7 \end{cases}$

$$4x + 3(-3x + 7) = 1$$
$$4x - 9x + 21 = 1$$
$$-5x + 21 = 1$$
$$-5x = -20$$
$$x = 4$$
$$y = -3(4) + 7$$
$$y = -12 + 7$$
$$y = -5$$

Solution: $(4, -5)$

3. $\begin{cases} 3x - 2y = -14 \\ x + 3y = -1 \end{cases}$

Solve 2nd equation for x:

$$x + 3y = -1$$
$$x = -3y - 1$$

Substitute:

$$3(-3y - 1) - 2y = -14$$
$$-9y - 3 - 2y = -14$$
$$-11y - 3 = -14$$
$$-11y = -11$$
$$y = 1$$
$$x + 3(1) = -1$$
$$x + 3 = -1$$
$$x = -4$$

Solution: $(-4, 1)$

4. $\begin{cases} x + y = 28 \\ x - y = 12 \end{cases}$

$$2x = 40$$
$$x = 20$$

Let $x = 20$ in the first equation.

$$20 + y = 28$$
$$y = 8$$

The solution is $(20, 8)$

5. $\begin{cases} 3x+5y=2 \\ 2x-3y=14 \end{cases}$

Multiply the first equation by 3 and the second equation by 5.

$9x+15y=6$

$\underline{10x-15y=70}$

$19x \qquad = 76$

$\qquad x=4$

$2(4)-3y=14$

$\qquad 8-3y=14$

$\qquad\qquad y=-2$

Solution: $(4,-2)$

6. $\begin{cases} x-y=4 \\ x-2y=11 \end{cases}$

Solve the first equation for x.

$x=y+4$

Substitute $y+4$ for x in the second equation.

$y+4-2y=11$

$\qquad -y=7$

$\qquad\quad y=-7$

Let $y=-7$ in $x=y+4$.

$x=-7+4$

$x=-3$

The solution is $(-3,-7)$.

7. $\begin{cases} 8x-4y=12 \\ y=2x-3 \end{cases}$

Substitute $2x-3$ for y in the first equation.

$8x-4(2x-3)=12$

$\qquad 8x-8x+12=12$

$\qquad\qquad 12=12$

There are an infinite number of solutions.

8. $\begin{cases} 3(2x+y)=4x+20 \\ x-2y=3 \end{cases}$

Put the first equation in standard form.

$6x+3y=4x+20$

$2x+3y=20$

$\begin{cases} 2x+3y=20 \\ x-2y=3 \end{cases}$

Multiply the second equation by -2.

$2x+3y=20$

$\underline{-2x+4y=-6}$

$\qquad\quad 7y=14$

$\qquad\quad y=2$

$x-2(2)=3$

$\qquad x-4=3$

$\qquad\quad x=7$

Solution: $(7,2)$

9. $\begin{cases} \dfrac{1}{2}x + 2y = -\dfrac{15}{4} \\ 4x = -y \end{cases}$

Multiply the first equation by 4 and put the second equation in standard form.

$\begin{cases} 2x + 8y = -15 \\ 4x + y = 0 \end{cases}$

Multiply the second simplified equation by -8.

$\begin{array}{r} 2x + 8y = -15 \\ -32x - 8y = 0 \\ \hline -30x \qquad = -15 \end{array}$

$$x = \frac{1}{2}$$

Substitute $\dfrac{1}{2}$ for x in the second equation.

$$4\left(\frac{1}{2}\right) = y$$

$$2 = -y$$

$$-2 = y$$

The solution to the system is $\left(\dfrac{1}{2}, -2\right)$.

10. $\begin{cases} x - \dfrac{2}{3}y = 3 \\ -2x + 3y = 10 \end{cases}$

Multiply the first equation by 3.

$\begin{cases} 3x - 2y = 9 \\ -2x + 3y = 10 \end{cases}$ Simplified system

Multiply the first equation of the simplified system by 2 and the second equation by 3.

$\begin{array}{r} 6x - 4y = 18 \\ -6x + 9y = 30 \\ \hline 5y = 48 \end{array}$

$$y = \frac{48}{5} = 9\frac{3}{5}$$

Multiply the first equation of the simplified system by 3 and the second equation by 2.

$\begin{array}{r} 9x - 6y = 27 \\ -4x + 6y = 20 \\ \hline 5x \qquad = 47 \end{array}$

$$x \qquad = \frac{47}{5} = 9\frac{2}{5}$$

The solution of the system is $\left(9\dfrac{2}{5}, 9\dfrac{3}{5}\right)$.

11. $\begin{cases} 0.01x - 0.06y = -0.23 \\ 0.2x + 0.4y = 0.2 \end{cases}$

Multiply the first equation by 100 and the second equation by 10.

$\begin{cases} x - 6y = -23 \\ 2x + 4y = 2 \end{cases}$ Simplified system

Multiply the first equation of the simplified system by -2.

$$\begin{cases} -2x+12y=46 \\ \underline{2x+4y=2} \end{cases}$$
$$16y=48$$
$$y=3$$

Multiply the first equation of the simplified system by 2 and the second equation by 3.

$$\begin{cases} 2x-12y=-46 \\ \underline{6x+12y=6} \end{cases}$$
$$8x=-40$$
$$x=-5$$

The solution is $(-5,3)$.

12. $\begin{cases} 4x-6y=7 \\ -2x+3y=0 \end{cases}$

To eliminate x:

$$4x-6y=7$$
$$2(-2x+3y)=0$$

$$\begin{array}{r} 4x-6y=7 \\ \underline{-4x+6y=0} \\ 0=7 \end{array}$$

No solution

13. $\begin{cases} \dfrac{x-3}{2}=\dfrac{2-y}{4} \\ \dfrac{7-2x}{3}=\dfrac{y}{2} \end{cases}$

Multiply the first equation by 4 and the second equation by 6.

$$\begin{cases} 2(x-3)=2-y \\ 2x-6=2-y \\ 2x+y=8 \\ \\ 2(7-2x)=3y \\ 14-4x=3x \\ 4x+3y=14 \end{cases}$$

Multiply the first simplified equation by -3.

$$\begin{array}{r} -6x-3y=-24 \\ \underline{4x+3y=14} \\ -2x=-10 \\ x=5 \end{array}$$

Substitute 5 for x in the first simplified equation.

$$2(5)+y=8$$
$$10+y=8$$
$$y=-2$$

The solution to the system is $(5,-2)$.

14. Let x = the first number and y = the second number.

$$\begin{cases} x+y=124 \\ x-y=32 \end{cases}$$

$$\begin{aligned} 2x &= 156 \\ x &= 78 \end{aligned}$$

Let $x = 78$ in the first equation.

$$78+y=124$$
$$y=46$$

The numbers are 78 and 46.

15. Let x = the amount of the 12% solution.
Let y = the amount of the 16% solution.

$$\begin{cases} x+80=y \\ 0.12x+0.22(80)=0.16y \end{cases}$$

Use substitution:

$$0.12x+0.22(80)=0.16(x+80)$$
$$0.12x+17.6=0.16x+12.8$$
$$0.12x-0.16x=12.8-17.6$$
$$-0.04x=-4.8$$
$$x=120$$

120cc of a 12% saline solution should be added.

16. Let x = amount invested at 5%
y = amount invested at 9%

$$\begin{cases} x+y=4000 \\ .05x+.09y=311 \end{cases}$$

$$=\begin{cases} x+y=4000 \\ 5x+9y=31,100 \end{cases}$$

Eliminate x by multiplying -5 times the first equation.

$$-5(x+y=4000)$$
$$-5x-5y=-20,000$$
$$5x+9y=31,100$$

$$\frac{4y}{4}=\frac{11,100}{4}$$
$$y=2775$$

To find x: $\ x+2775-4000$
$$x=4000-2775$$
$$x=1225$$

$1225 invested at 5%
$2775 invested at 9%

17. Let x = the number of farms in Missouri
y = the number of farms in Texas
$$\begin{cases} y = x + 116,000 \\ x + y = 336,000 \end{cases}$$
Use substitution:
$$x + x + 116,000 = 336,000$$
$$2x + 116,000 = 36,000$$
$$2x = 336,000 - 116,000$$
$$\frac{2x}{x} = \frac{220,000}{2}$$
$$x = 110,000$$
Then $y = 110,000 + 116,000 = 226,000$.
Missouri has 110,000 farms, and Texas has 226,000 farms.

Cumulative Review Chapter 14

1. $8 - 15 = 8 + (-15) = -7$

2. $4 - 7 = 4 + (-7) = -3$

3. $-4 - (-5) = -4 + 5 = 1$

4. $3 - (-2) = 3 + 2 = 5$

5. $7x = 6x + 4$
$$7x - 6x = 4$$
$$x = 4$$

6. $4x = -2 + 3x$
$$4x - 3x = -2$$
$$x = -2$$

7. 1.2 is 30% of what number?
$$1.2 = 30\% \cdot x$$

8. 9 is 45% of what number?
$$9 = 45\% \cdot x$$

9. What percent of 50 is 8?
$$x \cdot 50 = 8$$
$$x = \frac{8}{50}$$
$$x = \frac{4}{25} \cdot 100\%$$
$$= \frac{4 \cdot 4 \cdot 25}{25}\%$$
$$= 16\%$$

10. What percent of 16 is 4?
$$x \cdot 16 = 4$$
$$x = \frac{4}{16}$$
$$x = \frac{1}{4} \cdot 100\%$$
$$= \frac{1 \cdot 4 \cdot 25}{4}\%$$
$$= 25\%$$

11. 31 is 4% of the total.
$$31 = 4\% \cdot x$$
$$31 = 0.04 \cdot x$$
$$\frac{31}{0.04} = x$$
$$775 = x$$
There are 775 freshman at Slidell High School.

12. 2% of the total is 29.

$2\% \cdot x = 29$

$0.02 \cdot x = 29$

$x = \dfrac{29}{0.02}$

$x = 1450$

There are 1450 apples in the shipment.

13. $-2(x-5)+10 = -3(x+2)+x$

$-2x+10+10 = -3x-6+x$

$-2x+20 = -2x-6$

$20 = -6$

There is no solution

14. $4(4y+2) = 2(1+6y)+8$

$16y+8 = 2+12y+8$

$16y+8 = 12y+10$

$16y-12y = 10-8$

$\dfrac{4y}{4} = \dfrac{2}{4}$

$y = \dfrac{1}{2}$

15. $-5x+7 < 2(x-3)$

$-5x+7 < 2x-6$

$-7x < -13$

$\dfrac{-7x}{-7} > \dfrac{-13}{-7}$

$x > \dfrac{13}{7}$

$\left\{x \,\middle|\, x > \dfrac{13}{7}\right\}$

16. $-7x+4 \le 3(4-x)$

$-7x+4 \le 12-3x$

$-7x+3x \le 12-4$

$-4x \le 8$

$\dfrac{-4x}{-4} \ge \dfrac{8}{-4}$

$x \ge -2$

$\left\{x \,\middle|\, x \ge -2\right\}$

17. $\left(\dfrac{m}{n}\right)^7 = \dfrac{m^7}{n^7}, \ n \ne 0$

18. $\left(-5x^3\right)\left(-7x^4\right)$

$= (-5)(-7)x^{3+4}$

$= 35x^7$

19. $\left(\dfrac{2x^4}{3y^5}\right)^4 = \dfrac{2^4\left(x^4\right)^4}{3^4\left(y^5\right)^4} = \dfrac{16x^{16}}{81y^{20}}, \ y \ne 0$

20. $\left(\dfrac{5x^2}{4y^3}\right)^2$

$= \dfrac{5^2\left(x^2\right)^2}{4^2\left(y^3\right)^2}$

$= \dfrac{25x^4}{16y^6}$

21. $\left(2x^3+8x^2-6x\right)-\left(2x^3-x^2+1\right)$

$=2x^3+8x^2-6x-2x^3+x^2-1$

$=2x^3-2x^3+8x^2+x^2-6x-1$

$=9x^2-6x-1$

22. $\left(7x+1\right)-\left(-x-3\right)=\left(7x+1\right)-1\left(-x-3\right)$

$=7x+1+x+3$

$=8x+4$

23. $\begin{array}{r}2x+4\\3x-1\overline{)6x^2+10x-5}\end{array}$

$\underline{6x^2-\ 2x}$

$12x-5$

$\underline{12x-4}$

-1

$\dfrac{6x^2+10x-5}{3x-1}=2x+4-\dfrac{1}{3x-1}$

24. $\begin{array}{r}3x+2\\x-1\overline{)\ 3x^2-\ x-4}\end{array}$

$\underline{-3x^2+3x}$

$2x-4$

$\underline{-2x+2}$

-2

$\dfrac{3x^2-x-4}{x-1}=3x+2-\dfrac{2}{x-1}$

25. $\quad x\left(2x-7\right)=4$

$2x^2-7x=4$

$2x^2-7x-4=0$

$\left(2x+1\right)\left(x-4\right)=0$

$2x+1=0\ \ \text{or}\ \ x-4=0$

$x=-\dfrac{1}{2}\qquad x=4$

The solutions are $-\dfrac{1}{2}$ and 4.

26. $\quad x\left(x-5\right)=24$

$x^2-5x=24$

$x^2-5x-24=0$

$\left(x+3\right)\left(x-8\right)=0$

$x+3=0,\ \ x-8=0$

$x=-3,\qquad x=8$

$x=-3,\ 8$

27. Let $x=$ the length of the shorter leg, $x+2=$ the length of the longer leg, and $x+4=$ the length of the hypotenuse.

$\left(x\right)^2+\left(x+2\right)^2=\left(x+4\right)^2$

$x^2+x^2+4x+4=x^2+8x+16$

$2x^2+4x+4=x^2+8x+16$

$x^2-4x-12=0$

$\left(x+2\right)\left(x-6\right)=0$

$x+2=0\ \ \text{or}\ \ x-6=0$

$x=-2\qquad x=6$

Since length cannot be negative, $x=6$ is the only solution.

$x+2=6+2=8$

$x+4=6+4=10$

The lengths are 6, 8 and 10.

28. Let $x =$ a number

$$x + x^2 = 132$$
$$x^2 + x - 132 = 0$$
$$(x-11)(x+12) = 0$$
$$x - 11 = 0, \quad x + 12 = 0$$
$$x = 11, \qquad x = -12$$

Use only the positive solution: $x = 11$.

29. $\dfrac{2y}{2y-7} - \dfrac{7}{2y-7} = \dfrac{2y-7}{2y-7} = 1$

30. $\dfrac{x^2+3}{x+9} + \dfrac{9x-3}{x+9} = \dfrac{x^2+3+9x-3}{x+9}$

$$= \frac{x^2+9x}{x+9}$$
$$= \frac{x(x+9)}{(x+9)}$$
$$= x$$

31. Since $y = -1$ for all x, use $(0,-1)$
and $(2,-1)$.

$$m = \frac{y_2 - y_1}{x_2 - x_1} = \frac{-1-(-1)}{2-0} = \frac{0}{2} = 0$$

32. $x = 2$ is a horizontal line, therefore
its slope (m) is 0.

33. $(2,5)$ and $(-3,4)$

$$m = \frac{y_2 - y_1}{x_2 - x_1} = \frac{4-5}{-3-2} = \frac{-1}{-5} = \frac{1}{5}$$
$$m = \frac{1}{5}; \ (2,5)$$
$$y - y_1 = m(x - x_1)$$
$$y - 5 = \frac{1}{5}(x - 2)$$
$$5(y-5) = 1(x-2)$$
$$5y - 25 = x - 2$$
$$-x + 5y = 23$$
$$x - 5y = -23$$

34. Find the slope: $m = \dfrac{5+6}{-6-5} = \dfrac{11}{-11} = -1$

Use the slope and one point: $m = -1, \ (5, -6)$

$$y + 6 = -1(x - 5)$$
$$y + 6 = -x + 5$$
$$x + y = 5 - 6$$
$$x + y = -1$$

35. Domain is $\{-1, 0, 3\}$

Range is $\{-2, 0, 2, 3\}$

36. Domain: all x values $\{2\}$

Range: all y values $\{3, 0, -2, 4\}$

37. $\begin{cases} x+2y=7 \\ 2x+2y=13 \end{cases}$

Solve the first equation for x.

$x=7-2y$

Substitute $7-2y$ for x in the second equation.

$2(7-2y)+2y=13$

$14-4y+2y=13$

$-2y=-1$

$y=\dfrac{1}{2}$

Let $y=\dfrac{1}{2}$ in $x=7-2y$.

$x=7-2\left(\dfrac{1}{2}\right)$

$x=6$

The solution is $\left(6,\dfrac{1}{2}\right)$.

38. $\begin{cases} 3y=x+6 \\ -x+3=6 \\ \\ 4x+12y=0 \end{cases}$

Multiply the second equation by $\dfrac{1}{4}$

$\begin{array}{r} -x+3y=6 \\ x+3y=0 \\ \hline 6y=6 \\ y=1 \end{array}$

Substitute 1 for y in the first equation.

$3(1)=x+6$

$3=x+6$

$-3=x$

$(-3, 1)$

39. $\begin{cases} -x-\dfrac{y}{2}=\dfrac{5}{2} \\ \dfrac{x}{6}-\dfrac{y}{2}=0 \end{cases}$

Multiply the first equation by -6 and the second equation by 6.

$\begin{cases} 6x+3y=-15 \\ \underline{x-3y=0} \end{cases}$ Simplified system

$\begin{array}{rl} 7x & =-15 \\ \\ x & =-\dfrac{15}{7} \end{array}$

Multiply the second equation of the simplified system by -6.

$$\begin{cases} 6x + 3y = -15 \\ -6x + 18y = 0 \end{cases}$$

$$21y = -15$$

$$y = -\frac{5}{7}$$

The solution of the system is $\left(-\dfrac{15}{7}, -\dfrac{5}{7}\right)$.

40. $\begin{cases} x - \dfrac{3y}{8} = -\dfrac{3}{2} \\ x + \dfrac{y}{9} = \dfrac{13}{3} \end{cases}$

Multiply the first equation by 8 and the second equation by 9

$$\begin{cases} 8x - 3y = -12 \\ 9x + y = 39 \end{cases}$$

Multiply the second simplified equation by 3

$$8x - 3y = -12$$
$$27x + 3y = 117$$

$$35x = 105$$

$$x = 3$$

Substitute 3 for x in the second simplified equation

$$9(3) + y = 39$$

$$27 + y = 39$$

$$y = 12$$

The solution to the system is $(3, 12)$.

41. Let $x =$ the first number and $y =$ the second number.

$$\begin{cases} x + y = 37 \\ x - y = 21 \end{cases}$$

$$2x = 58$$

$$x = 29$$

Let $x = 29$ in the first equation.

$$29 + y = 37$$

$$y = 8$$

The numbers are 29 and 8.

42. Let $x =$ one number

Let $y =$ the other number

$$\begin{cases} x + y = 75 \\ x - y = 9 \end{cases}$$

$$2x = 84$$

$$x = 42$$

Substitute into the first equation.

$$42 + y = 75$$

$$y = 74 - 42$$

$$y = 33$$

42 and 33 are the two numbers.

Chapter   15

Chapter 15 Pretest

1. $-\sqrt{49} = -7$

2. $\sqrt{\dfrac{4}{25}} = \dfrac{2}{5}$

3. $\sqrt[3]{-64} = -4$

4. $\sqrt{120} = \sqrt{4 \cdot 30} = \sqrt{4} \cdot \sqrt{30} = 2\sqrt{30}$

5. $\sqrt{\dfrac{24}{y^6}} = \dfrac{\sqrt{24}}{\sqrt{y^6}} = \dfrac{\sqrt{4} \cdot \sqrt{6}}{\sqrt{\left(y^3\right)^2}} = \dfrac{2\sqrt{6}}{y^3}$

6. $\sqrt[3]{112} = \sqrt[3]{8} \cdot \sqrt[3]{14} = 2\sqrt[3]{14}$

7. $\sqrt{15} + 2\sqrt{15} - 6\sqrt{15} = (1 + 2 - 6)\sqrt{15} = -3\sqrt{15}$

8. $3\sqrt{12} - 2\sqrt{27} = 3\sqrt{4} \cdot \sqrt{3} - 2\sqrt{9} \cdot \sqrt{3}$

$$= 6\sqrt{3} - 6\sqrt{3}$$
$$= 0$$

9. $\sqrt{\dfrac{7}{4}} + \sqrt{\dfrac{7}{25}} = \dfrac{\sqrt{7}}{\sqrt{4}} + \dfrac{\sqrt{7}}{\sqrt{25}} = \dfrac{\sqrt{7}}{2} + \dfrac{\sqrt{7}}{5}$

$$= \dfrac{5\sqrt{7}}{10} + \dfrac{2\sqrt{7}}{10} = \dfrac{(5+2)\sqrt{7}}{10} = \dfrac{7\sqrt{7}}{10}$$

10. $\sqrt{6} \cdot \sqrt{18} = \sqrt{6 \cdot 18} = \sqrt{108} = \sqrt{36 \cdot 3} = 6\sqrt{3}$

11. $\sqrt{2}\left(\sqrt{14} - \sqrt{5}\right) = \sqrt{2} \cdot \sqrt{14} - \sqrt{2} \cdot \sqrt{5}$

$$= \sqrt{28} - \sqrt{10} = \sqrt{4 \cdot 7} - \sqrt{10}$$
$$= 2\sqrt{7} - \sqrt{10}$$

12. $\left(\sqrt{y} - 3\right)^2 = \left(\sqrt{y}\right)^2 - 2(3)\sqrt{y} + (3)^2$

$$= y - 6\sqrt{y} + 9$$

13. $\dfrac{\sqrt{56x^5}}{\sqrt{2x^3}} = \sqrt{\dfrac{56x^5}{2x^3}} = \sqrt{28x^2} = \sqrt{4 \cdot 7x^2}$

$$= 2x\sqrt{7}$$

14. $\sqrt{\dfrac{5}{11}} = \dfrac{\sqrt{5}}{\sqrt{11}} = \dfrac{\sqrt{5}}{\sqrt{11}} \cdot \dfrac{\sqrt{11}}{\sqrt{11}} = \dfrac{\sqrt{55}}{11}$

15. $\dfrac{16}{\sqrt{2a}} = \dfrac{16}{\sqrt{2a}} \cdot \dfrac{\sqrt{2a}}{\sqrt{2a}} = \dfrac{16\sqrt{2a}}{2a} = \dfrac{8\sqrt{2a}}{a}$

16. $\dfrac{3}{2 - \sqrt{x}} = \dfrac{3}{2 - \sqrt{x}} \cdot \dfrac{2 + \sqrt{x}}{2 + \sqrt{x}} = \dfrac{3\left(2 + \sqrt{x}\right)}{4 - x}$

$$= \dfrac{6 + 3\sqrt{x}}{4 - x}$$

17. $\sqrt{x} + 9 = 16$

$$\sqrt{x} = 7$$
$$\left(\sqrt{x}\right)^2 = 7^2$$
$$x = 49$$

18. $\sqrt{x + 4} = \sqrt{x} + 1$

$$\left(\sqrt{x+4}\right)^2 = \left(\sqrt{x} + 1\right)^2$$
$$x + 4 = x + 2\sqrt{x} + 1$$
$$3 = 2\sqrt{x}$$
$$\dfrac{3}{2} = \sqrt{x}$$

$$\left(\frac{3}{2}\right)^2 = \left(\sqrt{x}\right)^2$$

$$\frac{9}{4} = x$$

19. Let b = the length of the unknown leg.

$$a^2 + b^2 = c^2$$
$$6^2 + b^2 = 14^2$$
$$36 + b^2 = 196$$
$$b^2 = 160$$
$$b = \sqrt{160}$$
$$b = 4\sqrt{10}$$

The length of the leg is $4\sqrt{10}$ cm.

20. Let $S = 80$.

$$r = \sqrt{\frac{S}{4\pi}}$$

$$r = \sqrt{\frac{80}{4\pi}} = \sqrt{\frac{20}{\pi}} = \frac{2\sqrt{5}}{\sqrt{\pi}} \approx 2.52$$

The radius is about 2.52 inches.

Practice Problems 15.1

1. $\sqrt{100} = 10$, because $10^2 = 100$ and 10 is positive.

2. $\sqrt{9} = 3$, because $3^2 = 9$ and 3 is positive.

3. $-\sqrt{36} = -6$, because $6^2 = 36$ and the negative sign indicates the negative square root.

4. $\sqrt{\frac{25}{81}} = \frac{5}{9}$, because $\left(\frac{5}{9}\right)^2 = \frac{25}{81}$ and $\frac{5}{9}$ is positive.

5. $\sqrt{1} = 1$, because $1^2 = 1$ and 1 is positive.

6. $\sqrt[3]{27} = 3$, because $3^3 = 27$.

7. $\sqrt[3]{-8} = -2$, because $(-2)^3 = -8$.

8. $\sqrt[3]{\frac{1}{64}} = \frac{1}{4}$, because $\left(\frac{1}{4}\right)^3 = \frac{1}{64}$.

9. $\sqrt[4]{-16}$ is not a real number.

10. $\sqrt[5]{-1} = -1$, because $(-1)^3 = -1$.

11. $\sqrt[4]{81} = 3$, because $3^4 = 81$.

12. $\sqrt[6]{-64}$ is not a real number.

13. $\sqrt{10} \approx 3.162$

14. $\sqrt{x^8} = x^4$, because $\left(x^4\right)^2 = x^8$.

15. $\sqrt{x^{20}} = x^{10}$, because $\left(x^{10}\right)^2 = x^{20}$.

16. $\sqrt{4x^6} = 2x^3$, because $\left(2x^3\right)^2 = 4x^6$.

17. $\sqrt[3]{8y^{12}} = 2y^4$, because $\left(2y^4\right)^3 = 8y^{12}$.

Calculator Explorations 15.1

1. $\sqrt{7} \approx 2.646$

2. $\sqrt{14} \approx 3.742$

3. $\sqrt{11} \approx 3.317$

4. $\sqrt{200} \approx 14.142$

5. $\sqrt{82} \approx 9.055$

6. $\sqrt{46} \approx 6.782$

7. $\sqrt[3]{40} \approx 3.420$

8. $\sqrt[3]{71} \approx 4.141$

9. $\sqrt[4]{20} \approx 2.115$

10. $\sqrt[4]{15} \approx 1.968$

11. $\sqrt[5]{18} \approx 1.783$

12. $\sqrt[6]{2} \approx 1.122$

Exercise Set 15.1

1. $\sqrt{16} = 4$, because $4^2 = 16$ and 4 is positive.

3. $\sqrt{81} = 9$, because $9^2 = 81$ and 9 is positive.

5. $\sqrt{\dfrac{1}{25}} = \dfrac{1}{5}$, because $\left(\dfrac{1}{5}\right)^2 = \dfrac{1}{25}$ and $\dfrac{1}{5}$ is positive.

7. $-\sqrt{100} = -10$, because $10^2 = 100$ and the negative sign indicates the negative square root.

9. $\sqrt{-4}$ is not a real number.

11. $-\sqrt{121} = -11$, because $11^2 = 121$ and the negative sign indicates the negative square root.

13. $\sqrt{\dfrac{9}{25}} = \dfrac{3}{5}$, because $\left(\dfrac{3}{5}\right)^2 = \dfrac{9}{25}$ and $\dfrac{3}{5}$ is positive.

15. $\sqrt{900} = 30$, because $30^2 = 900$ and 30 is positive.

17. $\sqrt{144} = 12$, because $12^2 = 144$ and 12 is positive.

19. $\sqrt{\dfrac{1}{100}} = \dfrac{1}{10}$, because $\left(\dfrac{1}{10}\right)^2 = \dfrac{1}{100}$ and $\dfrac{1}{10}$ is positive.

21. $\sqrt[3]{125} = 5$, because $(5)^3 = 125$.

23. $\sqrt[3]{-64} = -4$, because $(-4)^3 = -64$.

25. $-\sqrt[3]{8} = -2$, because $\sqrt[3]{8} = 2$.

27. $\sqrt[3]{\dfrac{1}{8}} = \dfrac{1}{2}$, because $\left(\dfrac{1}{2}\right)^3 = \dfrac{1}{8}$.

29. $\sqrt[3]{-125} = -5$, because $(-5)^3 = -125$.

31. Answers may vary.

33. $\sqrt[5]{32} = 2$, because $(2)^5 = 32$.

35. $\sqrt[4]{-16}$ is not a real number.

37. $-\sqrt[4]{625} = -5$, because $\sqrt[4]{625} = 5$.

39. $\sqrt[6]{1} = 1$, because $(1)^6 = 1$.

41. $\sqrt{7} \approx 2.646$

43. $\sqrt{12} \approx 3.464$

45. $\sqrt{37} \approx 6.083$

47. $\sqrt{136} \approx 11.662$

49. $\sqrt{2} \approx 1.41$
$90\sqrt{2} \approx 90 \cdot 1.41 = 126.90$ feet

51. $\sqrt{z^2} = z$, because $(z)^2 = z^2$.

53. $\sqrt{x^4} = x^2$, because $\left(x^2\right)^2 = x^4$.

55. $\sqrt{9x^8} = 3x^4$, because $\left(3x^4\right)^2 = 9x^8$.

57. $\sqrt{81x^2} = 9x$, because $(9x)^2 = 81x^2$.

59. $\sqrt{a^2 b^4} = ab^2$, because $\left(ab^2\right)^2 = a^2 b^4$.

61. $\sqrt{16a^6 b^4} = 4a^3 b^2$,
because $\left(4a^3 b^2\right)^2 = 16a^6 b^4$.

63. $50 = 25 \cdot 2$

65. $32 = 16 \cdot 2$ or $32 = 4 \cdot 8$

67. $28 = 4 \cdot 7$

69. $27 = 9 \cdot 3$

71. Let $A = 49$
The length of a side $= \sqrt{A}$
$\sqrt{A} = \sqrt{49} = 7$
The length of a side $= 7$ miles

73. Let $A = 9.61$
The length of a side $= \sqrt{A}$
$\sqrt{A} = \sqrt{9.61} = 3.1$
The length of a side $= 3.1$ inches.

75. $\sqrt{\sqrt{81}} = \sqrt{9} = 3$

77. $y = \sqrt{x}$

x	y
0	0
1	1
3	1.7
4	2
9	3

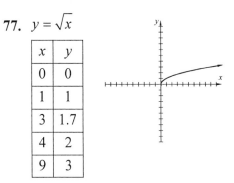

79. $y = \sqrt{x-2}$

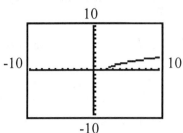

The graph starts at $(2,0)$ because

$x - 2 \geq 0$ for $x \geq 2$

81. $y = \sqrt{x+4}$

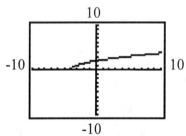

The graph starts at $(-4,0)$ because

$x + 4 \geq 0$ for $x \geq -4$

83. $\sqrt[3]{195,112} = 58$

The length of a side = 58 feet.

Practice Problems 15.2

1. $\sqrt{40} = \sqrt{4 \cdot 10} = \sqrt{4} \cdot \sqrt{10} = 2\sqrt{10}$

2. $\sqrt{18} = \sqrt{9 \cdot 2} = \sqrt{9} \cdot \sqrt{2} = 3\sqrt{2}$

3. $\sqrt{700} = \sqrt{100 \cdot 7} = \sqrt{100} \cdot \sqrt{7} = 10\sqrt{7}$

4. $\sqrt{15}$ can't be simplified.

5. $\sqrt{\dfrac{16}{81}} = \dfrac{\sqrt{16}}{\sqrt{81}} = \dfrac{4}{9}$

6. $\sqrt{\dfrac{2}{25}} = \dfrac{\sqrt{2}}{\sqrt{25}} = \dfrac{\sqrt{2}}{5}$

7. $\sqrt{\dfrac{45}{49}} = \dfrac{\sqrt{45}}{\sqrt{49}} = \dfrac{\sqrt{9} \cdot \sqrt{5}}{7} = \dfrac{3\sqrt{5}}{7}$

8. $\sqrt{x^{11}} = \sqrt{x^{10} \cdot x} = \sqrt{x^{10}} \cdot \sqrt{x} = x^5 \sqrt{x}$

9. $\sqrt{18x^4} = \sqrt{9 \cdot 2x^4} = \sqrt{9x^4} \cdot \sqrt{2} = 3x^2 \sqrt{2}$

10. $\sqrt{\dfrac{27}{x^8}} = \dfrac{\sqrt{27}}{\sqrt{x^8}} = \dfrac{\sqrt{9} \cdot \sqrt{3}}{x^4} = \dfrac{3\sqrt{3}}{x^4}$

11. $\sqrt[3]{40} = \sqrt[3]{8 \cdot 5} = \sqrt[3]{8} \cdot \sqrt[3]{5} = 2\sqrt[3]{5}$

12. $\sqrt[3]{50}$ can't be simplified.

13. $\sqrt[3]{\dfrac{10}{27}} = \dfrac{\sqrt[3]{10}}{\sqrt[3]{27}} = \dfrac{\sqrt[3]{10}}{3}$

14. $\sqrt[3]{\dfrac{81}{8}} = \dfrac{\sqrt[3]{81}}{\sqrt[3]{8}} = \dfrac{\sqrt[3]{27 \cdot 3}}{2} = \dfrac{\sqrt[3]{27} \cdot \sqrt[3]{3}}{2} = \dfrac{3\sqrt[3]{3}}{2}$

Mental Math 15.2

1. $\sqrt{4 \cdot 9} = 6$

2. $\sqrt{9 \cdot 36} = 18$

3. $\sqrt{x^2} = x$

4. $\sqrt{y^4} = y^2$

5. $\sqrt{0} = 0$

6. $\sqrt{1} = 1$

7. $\sqrt{25x^4} = 5x^2$

8. $\sqrt{49x^2} = 7x$

Exercise Set 15.2

1. $\sqrt{20} = \sqrt{4 \cdot 5} = \sqrt{4} \cdot \sqrt{5} = 2\sqrt{5}$

3. $\sqrt{18} = \sqrt{9 \cdot 2} = \sqrt{9} \cdot \sqrt{2} = 3\sqrt{2}$

5. $\sqrt{50} = \sqrt{25 \cdot 2} = \sqrt{25} \cdot \sqrt{2} = 5\sqrt{2}$

7. $\sqrt{33}$ can't be simplified.

9. $\sqrt{60} = \sqrt{4 \cdot 15} = \sqrt{4} \cdot \sqrt{15} = 2\sqrt{15}$

11. $\sqrt{180} = \sqrt{36 \cdot 5} = \sqrt{36} \cdot \sqrt{5} = 6\sqrt{5}$

13. $\sqrt{52} = \sqrt{4 \cdot 13} = \sqrt{4} \cdot \sqrt{13} = 2\sqrt{13}$

15. $\sqrt{\dfrac{8}{25}} = \dfrac{\sqrt{8}}{\sqrt{25}} = \dfrac{\sqrt{4} \cdot \sqrt{2}}{5} = \dfrac{2\sqrt{2}}{5}$

17. $\sqrt{\dfrac{27}{121}} = \dfrac{\sqrt{27}}{\sqrt{121}} = \dfrac{\sqrt{9} \cdot \sqrt{3}}{11} = \dfrac{3\sqrt{3}}{11}$

19. $\sqrt{\dfrac{9}{4}} = \dfrac{\sqrt{9}}{\sqrt{4}} = \dfrac{3}{2}$

21. $\sqrt{\dfrac{125}{9}} = \dfrac{\sqrt{125}}{\sqrt{9}} = \dfrac{\sqrt{25} \cdot \sqrt{5}}{3} = \dfrac{5\sqrt{5}}{3}$

23. $\sqrt{\dfrac{11}{36}} = \dfrac{\sqrt{11}}{\sqrt{36}} = \dfrac{\sqrt{11}}{6}$

25. $-\sqrt{\dfrac{27}{144}} = -\dfrac{\sqrt{27}}{\sqrt{144}} = -\dfrac{\sqrt{9} \cdot \sqrt{3}}{12} = -\dfrac{3\sqrt{3}}{12}$

27. $\sqrt{x^7} = \sqrt{x^6 \cdot x} = \sqrt{x^6} \cdot \sqrt{x} = x^3\sqrt{x}$

29. $\sqrt{x^{13}} = \sqrt{x^{12} \cdot x} = \sqrt{x^{12}} \cdot \sqrt{x} = x^6\sqrt{x}$

31. $\sqrt{75x^2} = \sqrt{25x^2 \cdot 3} = \sqrt{25x^2} \cdot \sqrt{3} = 5x\sqrt{3}$

33. $\sqrt{96x^4} = \sqrt{16x^4 \cdot 6} = \sqrt{16x^4} \cdot \sqrt{6} = 4x^2\sqrt{6}$

35. $\sqrt{\dfrac{12}{y^2}} = \dfrac{\sqrt{12}}{\sqrt{y^2}} = \dfrac{\sqrt{4} \cdot \sqrt{3}}{y} = \dfrac{2\sqrt{3}}{y}$

37. $\sqrt{\dfrac{9x}{y^2}} = \dfrac{\sqrt{9x}}{\sqrt{y^2}} = \dfrac{\sqrt{9} \cdot \sqrt{x}}{y} = \dfrac{3\sqrt{x}}{y}$

39. $\sqrt{\dfrac{88}{x^4}} = \dfrac{\sqrt{88}}{\sqrt{x^4}} = \dfrac{\sqrt{4} \cdot \sqrt{22}}{x^2} = \dfrac{2\sqrt{22}}{x^2}$

41. $\sqrt[3]{24} = \sqrt[3]{8 \cdot 3} = \sqrt[3]{8} \cdot \sqrt[3]{3} = 2\sqrt[3]{3}$

43. $\sqrt[3]{250} = \sqrt[3]{125 \cdot 2} = \sqrt[3]{125} \cdot \sqrt[3]{2} = 5\sqrt[3]{2}$

45. $\sqrt[3]{\dfrac{5}{64}} = \dfrac{\sqrt[3]{5}}{\sqrt[3]{64}} = \dfrac{\sqrt[3]{5}}{4}$

47. $\sqrt[3]{\dfrac{7}{8}} = \dfrac{\sqrt[3]{7}}{\sqrt[3]{8}} = \dfrac{\sqrt[3]{7}}{2}$

49. $\sqrt[3]{\dfrac{15}{64}} = \dfrac{\sqrt[3]{15}}{\sqrt[3]{64}} = \dfrac{\sqrt[3]{15}}{4}$

51. $\sqrt[3]{80} = \sqrt[3]{8\cdot10} = \sqrt[3]{8}\cdot\sqrt[3]{10} = 2\sqrt[3]{10}$

53. $6x + 8x = (6+8)x = 14x$

55. $(2x+3)(x-5) = 2x^2 -10x +3x -15$
$$= 2x^2 -7x -15$$

57. $9y^2 - 9y^2 = 0$

59. $\sqrt{x^6y^3} = \sqrt{x^6y^2y} = \sqrt{x^6y^2}\cdot\sqrt{y} = x^3y\sqrt{y}$

61. $\sqrt{x^2+4x+4} = \sqrt{(x+2)^2} = x+2$

63. $\sqrt[3]{80} = \sqrt[3]{8\cdot10} = \sqrt[3]{8}\cdot\sqrt[3]{10} = 2\sqrt[3]{10}$

The length of each side is $2\sqrt[3]{10}$ inches.

65. Let $A = 120$

The length of a side $= \sqrt{\dfrac{A}{6}}$

$\sqrt{\dfrac{A}{6}} = \sqrt{\dfrac{120}{6}} = \sqrt{20} = \sqrt{4}\cdot\sqrt{5} = 2\sqrt{5}$

The length of a side $= 2\sqrt{5}$ inches

67. Let $A = 150$

The length of a side $= \sqrt{\dfrac{A}{6}}$

$\sqrt{\dfrac{A}{6}} = \sqrt{\dfrac{150}{6}} = \sqrt{25} = 5$

The length of a side $= 5$ inches.

69. Let $n = 1000$
$$C = 100\sqrt[3]{n} + 700$$
$$C = 100\sqrt[3]{1000} + 700$$
$$= 100(10) + 700$$
$$= 1700$$
The cost is $1700

71. Answers may vary.

73. Let $h = 169$ and $w = 64$.
$$B = \sqrt{\dfrac{hw}{3600}}$$
$$B = \sqrt{\dfrac{(169)(64)}{3600}} = \sqrt{\dfrac{10,816}{3600}} = \sqrt{\dfrac{676}{225}}$$
$$= \dfrac{26}{15} \approx 1.7$$
The surface area is about 1.7 sq. m.

Practice Problems 15.3

1. $6\sqrt{11} + 9\sqrt{11} = (6+9)\sqrt{11} = 15\sqrt{11}$

2. $\sqrt{7} - 3\sqrt{7} = (1-3)\sqrt{7} = -2\sqrt{7}$

3. $\sqrt{2} + \sqrt{2} = (1+1)\sqrt{2} = 2\sqrt{2}$

4. $3\sqrt{3} - 3\sqrt{2}$ cannot be simplified.

5. $\sqrt{27} + \sqrt{75} = \sqrt{9}\cdot\sqrt{3} + \sqrt{25}\cdot\sqrt{3}$
$$= 3\sqrt{3} + 5\sqrt{3}$$
$$= 8\sqrt{3}$$

6. $3\sqrt{20} - 7\sqrt{45} = 3\sqrt{4} \cdot \sqrt{5} - 7\sqrt{9} \cdot \sqrt{5}$

$$= 3(2)\sqrt{5} - 7(3)\sqrt{5}$$
$$= 6\sqrt{5} - 21\sqrt{5}$$
$$= -15\sqrt{5}$$

7. $\sqrt{36} - \sqrt{48} - 4\sqrt{3} - \sqrt{9}$

$$= 6 - \sqrt{16} \cdot \sqrt{3} - 4\sqrt{3} - 3$$
$$= 6 - 4\sqrt{3} - 4\sqrt{3} - 3$$
$$= 3 - 8\sqrt{3}$$

8. $\sqrt{9x^4} - \sqrt{36x^3} + \sqrt{x^3}$

$$= 3x^2 - \sqrt{36x^2} \cdot \sqrt{x} + \sqrt{x^2} \cdot \sqrt{x}$$
$$= 3x^2 - 6x\sqrt{x} + x\sqrt{x}$$
$$= 3x^2 - 5x\sqrt{x}$$

Mental Math 15.3

1. $3\sqrt{2} + 5\sqrt{2} = 8\sqrt{2}$

2. $3\sqrt{5} + 7\sqrt{5} = 10\sqrt{5}$

3. $5\sqrt{x} + 2\sqrt{x} = 7\sqrt{x}$

4. $8\sqrt{x} + 3\sqrt{x} = 11\sqrt{x}$

5. $5\sqrt{7} - 2\sqrt{7} = 3\sqrt{7}$

6. $8\sqrt{6} - 5\sqrt{6} = 3\sqrt{6}$

Exercise Set 15.3

1. $4\sqrt{3} - 8\sqrt{3} = (4 - 8)\sqrt{3} = -4\sqrt{3}$

3. $3\sqrt{6} + 8\sqrt{6} - 2\sqrt{6} - 5 = (3 + 8 - 2)\sqrt{6} - 5$

$$= 9\sqrt{6} - 5$$

5. $6\sqrt{5} - 5\sqrt{5} + \sqrt{2} = (6 - 5)\sqrt{5} + \sqrt{2}$

$$= \sqrt{5} + \sqrt{2}$$

7. $2\sqrt{3} + 5\sqrt{3} - \sqrt{3} = (2 + 5 - 1)\sqrt{3} = 6\sqrt{3}$

9. $2\sqrt{2} - 7\sqrt{2} - 6 = (2 - 7)\sqrt{2} - 6$

$$= -5\sqrt{2} - 6$$

11. $12\sqrt{5} - \sqrt{5} - 4\sqrt{5} = (12 - 1 - 4)\sqrt{5} = 7\sqrt{5}$

13. $\sqrt{5} + \sqrt{5} = (1 + 1)\sqrt{5} = 2\sqrt{5}$

15. $6 - 2\sqrt{3} - \sqrt{3} = 6 + (-2 - 1)\sqrt{3} = 6 - 3\sqrt{3}$

17. Answers may vary.

19. $\sqrt{12} + \sqrt{27} = \sqrt{4 \cdot 3} + \sqrt{9 \cdot 3}$

$$= \sqrt{4} \cdot \sqrt{3} + \sqrt{9} \cdot \sqrt{3}$$
$$= 2\sqrt{3} + 3\sqrt{3} = 5\sqrt{3}$$

21. $\sqrt{45} + 3\sqrt{20} = \sqrt{9 \cdot 5} + 3\sqrt{4 \cdot 5}$

$$= \sqrt{9} \cdot \sqrt{5} + 3\sqrt{4} \cdot \sqrt{5}$$
$$= 3\sqrt{5} + 3(2)\sqrt{5}$$
$$= 3\sqrt{5} + 6\sqrt{5}$$
$$= 9\sqrt{5}$$

23. $2\sqrt{54} - \sqrt{20} + \sqrt{45} - \sqrt{24}$

$= 2\sqrt{9 \cdot 6} - \sqrt{4 \cdot 5} + \sqrt{9 \cdot 5} - \sqrt{4 \cdot 6}$

$= 2\sqrt{9} \cdot \sqrt{6} - \sqrt{4} \cdot \sqrt{5} + \sqrt{9} \cdot \sqrt{5} - \sqrt{4} \cdot \sqrt{6}$

$= 2(3)\sqrt{6} - 2\sqrt{5} + 3\sqrt{5} - 2\sqrt{6}$

$= 6\sqrt{6} - 2\sqrt{5} + 3\sqrt{5} - 2\sqrt{6}$

$= 4\sqrt{6} + \sqrt{5}$

25. $4x - 3\sqrt{x^2} + \sqrt{x} = 4x - 3x + \sqrt{x} = x + \sqrt{x}$

27. $\sqrt{25x} + \sqrt{36x} - 11\sqrt{x}$

$= \sqrt{25} \cdot \sqrt{x} + \sqrt{36} \cdot \sqrt{x} - 11\sqrt{x}$

$= 5\sqrt{x} + 6\sqrt{x} - 11\sqrt{x}$

$= 0$

29. $3\sqrt{x^3} - x\sqrt{4x} = 3\sqrt{x^2 \cdot x} - x\sqrt{4x}$

$= 3\sqrt{x^2} \cdot \sqrt{x} - x\sqrt{4} \cdot \sqrt{x}$

$= 3x\sqrt{x} - x(2)\sqrt{x}$

$= x\sqrt{x}$

31. $\sqrt{75} + \sqrt{48} = \sqrt{25} \cdot \sqrt{3} + \sqrt{16} \cdot \sqrt{3}$

$= 5\sqrt{3} + 4\sqrt{3}$

$= 9\sqrt{3}$

33. $\sqrt{8} + \sqrt{9} + \sqrt{18} + \sqrt{81}$

$= \sqrt{4} \cdot \sqrt{2} + 3 + \sqrt{9} \cdot \sqrt{2} + 9$

$= 2\sqrt{2} + 3 + 3\sqrt{2} + 9$

$= 5\sqrt{2} + 12$

35. $\sqrt{\dfrac{5}{9}} + \sqrt{\dfrac{5}{81}} = \dfrac{\sqrt{5}}{\sqrt{9}} + \dfrac{\sqrt{5}}{\sqrt{81}} = \dfrac{\sqrt{5}}{3} + \dfrac{\sqrt{5}}{9}$

$= \dfrac{3\sqrt{5}}{9} + \dfrac{\sqrt{5}}{9} = \dfrac{3\sqrt{5} + \sqrt{5}}{9} = \dfrac{4\sqrt{5}}{9}$

37. $\sqrt{\dfrac{3}{4}} - \sqrt{\dfrac{3}{64}} = \dfrac{\sqrt{3}}{\sqrt{4}} - \dfrac{\sqrt{3}}{\sqrt{64}} = \dfrac{\sqrt{3}}{2} - \dfrac{\sqrt{3}}{8}$

$= \dfrac{4\sqrt{3}}{8} - \dfrac{\sqrt{3}}{8} = \dfrac{4\sqrt{3} - \sqrt{3}}{8} = \dfrac{3\sqrt{3}}{8}$

39. $2\sqrt{45} - 2\sqrt{20} = 2\sqrt{9} \cdot \sqrt{5} - 2\sqrt{4} \cdot \sqrt{5}$

$= 2(3)\sqrt{5} - 2(2)\sqrt{5}$

$= 6\sqrt{5} - 4\sqrt{5}$

$= 2\sqrt{5}$

41. $\sqrt{35} - \sqrt{140} = \sqrt{35} - \sqrt{4} \cdot \sqrt{35}$

$= \sqrt{35} - 2\sqrt{35}$

$= -\sqrt{35}$

43. $3\sqrt{9x} + 2\sqrt{x} = 3\sqrt{9} \cdot \sqrt{x} + 2\sqrt{x}$

$= 3(3)\sqrt{x} + 2\sqrt{x}$

$= 9\sqrt{x} + 2\sqrt{x}$

$= 11\sqrt{x}$

45. $\sqrt{9x^2} + \sqrt{81x^2} - 11\sqrt{x}$

$= \sqrt{9} \cdot \sqrt{x^2} + \sqrt{81} \cdot \sqrt{x^2} - 11\sqrt{x}$

$= 3x + 9x - 11\sqrt{x}$

$= 12x - 11\sqrt{x}$

47. $\sqrt{3x^3} + 3x\sqrt{x} = \sqrt{x^2 \cdot 3x} + 3x\sqrt{x}$

$= \sqrt{x^2} \cdot \sqrt{3x} + 3x\sqrt{x}$

$= x\sqrt{3x} + 3x\sqrt{x}$

49. $\sqrt{32x^2} + \sqrt{32x^2} + \sqrt{4x^2}$

$= \sqrt{16} \cdot \sqrt{x^2} \cdot \sqrt{2} + \sqrt{16} \cdot \sqrt{x^2} \cdot \sqrt{2} + \sqrt{4} \cdot \sqrt{x^2}$

$= 4x\sqrt{2} + 4x\sqrt{2} + 2x$

$= 8x\sqrt{2} + 2x$

51. $\sqrt{40x} + \sqrt{40x^4} - 2\sqrt{10x} - \sqrt{5x^4}$

$= \sqrt{4} \cdot \sqrt{10x} + \sqrt{4x^4} \cdot \sqrt{10} - 2\sqrt{10x} - \sqrt{x^4} \cdot \sqrt{5}$

$= 2\sqrt{10x} + 2x^2\sqrt{10} - 2\sqrt{10x} - x^2\sqrt{5}$

$= 2x^2\sqrt{10} - x^2\sqrt{5}$

53. $(x+6)^2 = x^2 + 2(6)x + 6^2$

$= x^2 + 12x + 36$

55. $(2x-1)^2 = (2x)^2 + 2(-1)(2x) + (-1)^2$

$= 4x^2 - 4x + 1$

57. $\begin{cases} x = 2y \\ x + 5y = 14 \end{cases}$

Substitute $2y$ for x in the second equation.

$2y + 5y = 14$

$7y = 14$

$y = 2$

Let $y = 2$ in the first equation.

$x = 2(2) = 4$

The solution is $(4, 2)$

59. Let $l = 3\sqrt{5}$ and $w = \sqrt{5}$

Perimeter $= 2l + 2w$

$= 2(3\sqrt{5}) + 2(\sqrt{5})$

$= 6\sqrt{5} + 2\sqrt{5}$

$= 8\sqrt{5}$ inches

61. Let $l = 8$ and $w = 3$

Area $=$ area of 2 triangles

$\quad\quad\quad + $ area of 2 rectangles

$= 2\left(\dfrac{3\sqrt{27}}{4}\right) + 2lw$

$= \dfrac{3\sqrt{9} \cdot \sqrt{3}}{2} + 2(8)(3)$

$= \dfrac{9\sqrt{3}}{2} + 48$ square feet

Practice Problems 15.4

1. $\sqrt{5} \cdot \sqrt{2} = \sqrt{5 \cdot 2} = \sqrt{10}$

2. $\sqrt{6} \cdot \sqrt{3} = \sqrt{6 \cdot 3} = \sqrt{18} = \sqrt{9} \cdot \sqrt{2} = 3\sqrt{2}$

3. $\sqrt{10x} \cdot \sqrt{2x} = \sqrt{10x \cdot 2x} = \sqrt{20x^2}$

$= \sqrt{4x^2} \cdot \sqrt{5} = 2x\sqrt{5}$

4. a. $\sqrt{7}\left(\sqrt{7} - \sqrt{3}\right) = \sqrt{7} \cdot \sqrt{7} - \sqrt{7} \cdot \sqrt{3}$

$= \sqrt{49} - \sqrt{21} = 7 - \sqrt{21}$

b. $\left(\sqrt{x} + \sqrt{5}\right)\left(\sqrt{x} - \sqrt{3}\right)$

$= \sqrt{x} \cdot \sqrt{x} - \sqrt{x} \cdot \sqrt{3} + \sqrt{5} \cdot \sqrt{x} - \sqrt{5} \cdot \sqrt{3}$

$= \sqrt{x^2} - \sqrt{3x} + \sqrt{5x} - \sqrt{15}$

$= x - \sqrt{3x} + \sqrt{5x} - \sqrt{15}$

5. a. $\left(\sqrt{3} + 6\right)\left(\sqrt{3} - 6\right) = \left(\sqrt{3}\right)^2 - 6^2$

$= 3 - 36$

$= -33$

b. $\left(\sqrt{5x} + 4\right)^2 = \left(\sqrt{5x}\right)^2 + 2(4)\sqrt{5x} + 4^2$

$= 5x + 8\sqrt{5x} + 16$

6. $\dfrac{\sqrt{15}}{\sqrt{3}} = \sqrt{\dfrac{15}{3}} = \sqrt{5}$

7. $\dfrac{\sqrt{90}}{\sqrt{2}} = \sqrt{\dfrac{90}{2}} = \sqrt{45} = \sqrt{9}\cdot\sqrt{5} = 3\sqrt{5}$

8. $\dfrac{\sqrt{75x^3}}{\sqrt{5x}} = \sqrt{\dfrac{75x^3}{5x}} = \sqrt{15x^2}$
$= \sqrt{x^2}\cdot\sqrt{15} = x\sqrt{15}$

9. $\dfrac{5}{\sqrt{3}} = \dfrac{5}{\sqrt{3}}\cdot\dfrac{\sqrt{3}}{\sqrt{3}} = \dfrac{5\sqrt{3}}{\sqrt{9}} = \dfrac{5\sqrt{3}}{3}$

10. $\dfrac{\sqrt{7}}{\sqrt{20}} = \dfrac{\sqrt{7}}{\sqrt{4}\cdot\sqrt{5}} = \dfrac{\sqrt{7}}{2\sqrt{5}} = \dfrac{\sqrt{7}}{2\sqrt{5}}\cdot\dfrac{\sqrt{5}}{\sqrt{5}}$
$= \dfrac{\sqrt{35}}{2\sqrt{25}} = \dfrac{\sqrt{35}}{10}$

11. $\dfrac{\sqrt{2}}{\sqrt{45x}} = \dfrac{\sqrt{2}}{\sqrt{9}\cdot\sqrt{5x}} = \dfrac{\sqrt{2}}{3\sqrt{5x}} = \dfrac{\sqrt{2}}{3\sqrt{5x}}\cdot\dfrac{\sqrt{5x}}{\sqrt{5x}}$
$= \dfrac{\sqrt{10x}}{3\sqrt{25x^2}} = \dfrac{\sqrt{10x}}{15x}$

12. $\dfrac{3}{1+\sqrt{7}} = \dfrac{3}{1+\sqrt{7}}\cdot\dfrac{1-\sqrt{7}}{1-\sqrt{7}} = \dfrac{3\left(1-\sqrt{7}\right)}{1^2 - \left(\sqrt{7}\right)^2}$
$= \dfrac{3\left(1-\sqrt{7}\right)}{1-7} = \dfrac{3\left(1-\sqrt{7}\right)}{-6} = \dfrac{1-\sqrt{7}}{-2}$
$= \dfrac{-1+\sqrt{7}}{2}$

13. $\dfrac{\sqrt{2}+5}{\sqrt{2}-1} = \dfrac{\sqrt{2}+5}{\sqrt{2}-1}\cdot\dfrac{\sqrt{2}+1}{\sqrt{2}+1}$
$= \dfrac{2+\sqrt{2}+5\sqrt{2}+5}{2-1}$
$= 7+6\sqrt{2}$

14. $\dfrac{7}{2-\sqrt{x}} = \dfrac{7}{2-\sqrt{x}}\cdot\dfrac{2+\sqrt{x}}{2+\sqrt{x}} = \dfrac{7\left(2+\sqrt{x}\right)}{2^2 - \left(\sqrt{x}\right)^2}$
$= \dfrac{7\left(2+\sqrt{x}\right)}{4-x}$

Mental Math 15.4

1. $\sqrt{2}\cdot\sqrt{3} = \sqrt{6}$

2. $\sqrt{5}\cdot\sqrt{7} = \sqrt{35}$

3. $\sqrt{1}\cdot\sqrt{6} = \sqrt{6}$

4. $\sqrt{7}\cdot\sqrt{x} = \sqrt{7x}$

5. $\sqrt{10}\cdot\sqrt{y} = \sqrt{10y}$

6. $\sqrt{x}\cdot\sqrt{y} = \sqrt{xy}$

Exercise Set 15.4

1. $\sqrt{8}\cdot\sqrt{2} = \sqrt{8\cdot 2} = \sqrt{16} = 4$

3. $\sqrt{10}\cdot\sqrt{5} = \sqrt{10\cdot 5} = \sqrt{50} = \sqrt{25}\cdot\sqrt{2} = 5\sqrt{2}$

5. $\sqrt{6}\cdot\sqrt{6} = \sqrt{6\cdot 6} = \sqrt{36} = 6$

7. $\sqrt{2x}\cdot\sqrt{2x} = \sqrt{2x\cdot 2x} = \sqrt{4x^2} = 2x$

9. $\left(2\sqrt{5}\right)^2 = 2^2\left(\sqrt{5}\right)^2 = 4(5) = 20$

11. $\left(6\sqrt{x}\right)^2 = 6^2\left(\sqrt{x}\right)^2 = 36x$

13. $\sqrt{3y}\cdot\sqrt{6x} = \sqrt{3y\cdot 6x} = \sqrt{18xy}$
$= \sqrt{9}\cdot\sqrt{2xy} = 3\sqrt{2xy}$

15. $\sqrt{2xy^2}\cdot\sqrt{8xy} = \sqrt{2xy\cdot 8xy^2} = \sqrt{16x^2y^3}$
$= \sqrt{16x^2y^2}\cdot\sqrt{y} = 4xy\sqrt{y}$

17. $\sqrt{2}\left(\sqrt{5}+1\right) = \sqrt{2}\cdot\sqrt{5} + \sqrt{2}\cdot 1$
$= \sqrt{2\cdot 5} + \sqrt{2\cdot 1} = \sqrt{10} + \sqrt{2}$

19. $\sqrt{10}\left(\sqrt{2}+\sqrt{5}\right) = \sqrt{10}\cdot\sqrt{2} + \sqrt{10}\cdot\sqrt{5}$
$= \sqrt{20} + \sqrt{50} = \sqrt{4}\cdot\sqrt{5} + \sqrt{25}\cdot\sqrt{2}$
$= 2\sqrt{5} + 5\sqrt{2}$

21. $\sqrt{6}\left(\sqrt{5}+\sqrt{7}\right) = \sqrt{6}\cdot\sqrt{5} + \sqrt{6}\cdot\sqrt{7}$
$= \sqrt{30} + \sqrt{42}$

23. $\left(\sqrt{3}+6\right)\left(\sqrt{3}-6\right) = \left(\sqrt{3}\right)^2 - (6)^2$
$= 3 - 36 = -33$

25. $\left(\sqrt{3}+\sqrt{5}\right)\left(\sqrt{2}-\sqrt{5}\right)$
$= \sqrt{3}\cdot\sqrt{2} - \sqrt{3}\cdot\sqrt{5} + \sqrt{5}\cdot\sqrt{2} - \left(\sqrt{5}\right)^2$
$= \sqrt{6} - \sqrt{15} + \sqrt{10} - 5$

27. $\left(2\sqrt{11}+1\right)\left(\sqrt{11}-6\right)$
$= 2\left(\sqrt{11}\right)^2 - 12\sqrt{11} + 1\sqrt{11} - 6$
$= 2(11) - 11\sqrt{11} - 6$
$= 16 - 11\sqrt{11}$

29. $\left(\sqrt{x}+6\right)\left(\sqrt{x}-6\right) = \left(\sqrt{x}\right)^2 - (6)^2 = x - 36$

31. $\left(\sqrt{x}-7\right)^2 = \left(\sqrt{x}\right)^2 - 2(7)\sqrt{x} + (7)^2$
$= x - 14\sqrt{x} + 49$

33. $\left(\sqrt{6y}+1\right)^2 = \left(\sqrt{6y}\right)^2 + 2(1)\sqrt{6y} + (1)^2$
$= 6y + 2\sqrt{6y} + 1$

35. $\dfrac{\sqrt{32}}{\sqrt{2}} = \sqrt{\dfrac{32}{2}} = \sqrt{16} = 4$

37. $\dfrac{\sqrt{21}}{\sqrt{3}} = \sqrt{\dfrac{21}{3}} = \sqrt{7}$

39. $\dfrac{\sqrt{90}}{\sqrt{5}} = \sqrt{\dfrac{90}{5}} = \sqrt{18} = \sqrt{9}\cdot\sqrt{2} = 3\sqrt{2}$

41. $\dfrac{\sqrt{75y^5}}{\sqrt{3y}} = \sqrt{\dfrac{75y^5}{3y}} = \sqrt{25y^4} = 5y^2$

43. $\dfrac{\sqrt{150}}{\sqrt{2}} = \sqrt{\dfrac{150}{2}} = \sqrt{75} = \sqrt{25}\cdot\sqrt{3} = 5\sqrt{3}$

45. $\dfrac{\sqrt{72y^5}}{\sqrt{3y^3}} = \sqrt{\dfrac{72y^5}{3y^3}} = \sqrt{24y^2}$
$= \sqrt{4y^2}\cdot\sqrt{6} = 2y\sqrt{6}$

47. $\dfrac{\sqrt{24x^3y^4}}{\sqrt{2xy}} = \sqrt{\dfrac{24x^3y^4}{2xy}} = \sqrt{12x^2y^3}$

$\qquad = \sqrt{4x^2y^2}\cdot\sqrt{3y} = 2xy\sqrt{3y}$

49. $\dfrac{\sqrt{3}}{\sqrt{5}} = \dfrac{\sqrt{3}}{\sqrt{5}}\cdot\dfrac{\sqrt{5}}{\sqrt{5}} = \dfrac{\sqrt{15}}{\sqrt{25}} = \dfrac{\sqrt{15}}{5}$

51. $\dfrac{7}{\sqrt{2}} = \dfrac{7}{\sqrt{2}}\cdot\dfrac{\sqrt{2}}{\sqrt{2}} = \dfrac{7\sqrt{2}}{\sqrt{4}} = \dfrac{7\sqrt{2}}{2}$

53. $\dfrac{1}{\sqrt{6y}} = \dfrac{1}{\sqrt{6y}}\cdot\dfrac{\sqrt{6y}}{\sqrt{6y}} = \dfrac{\sqrt{6y}}{6y}$

55. $\sqrt{\dfrac{5}{18}} = \dfrac{\sqrt{5}}{\sqrt{18}} = \dfrac{\sqrt{5}}{\sqrt{9}\cdot\sqrt{2}} = \dfrac{\sqrt{5}}{3\sqrt{2}}$

$\qquad = \dfrac{\sqrt{5}}{3\sqrt{2}}\cdot\dfrac{\sqrt{2}}{\sqrt{2}} = \dfrac{\sqrt{10}}{3(2)} = \dfrac{\sqrt{10}}{6}$

57. $\sqrt{\dfrac{3}{x}} = \dfrac{\sqrt{3}}{\sqrt{x}} = \dfrac{\sqrt{3}}{\sqrt{x}}\cdot\dfrac{\sqrt{x}}{\sqrt{x}} = \dfrac{\sqrt{3x}}{x}$

59. $\sqrt{\dfrac{1}{8}} = \dfrac{\sqrt{1}}{\sqrt{8}} = \dfrac{1}{\sqrt{4}\cdot\sqrt{2}} = \dfrac{1}{2\sqrt{2}}$

$\qquad = \dfrac{1}{2\sqrt{2}}\cdot\dfrac{\sqrt{2}}{\sqrt{2}} = \dfrac{\sqrt{2}}{2(2)} = \dfrac{\sqrt{2}}{4}$

61. $\sqrt{\dfrac{2}{15}} = \dfrac{\sqrt{2}}{\sqrt{15}} = \dfrac{\sqrt{2}}{\sqrt{15}}\cdot\dfrac{\sqrt{15}}{\sqrt{15}} = \dfrac{\sqrt{30}}{15}$

63. $\sqrt{\dfrac{3}{20}} = \dfrac{\sqrt{3}}{\sqrt{20}} = \dfrac{\sqrt{3}}{\sqrt{4}\cdot\sqrt{5}} = \dfrac{\sqrt{3}}{2\sqrt{5}}$

$\qquad = \dfrac{\sqrt{3}}{2\sqrt{5}}\cdot\dfrac{\sqrt{5}}{\sqrt{5}} = \dfrac{\sqrt{15}}{2(5)} = \dfrac{\sqrt{15}}{10}$

65. $\dfrac{3x}{\sqrt{2x}} = \dfrac{3x}{\sqrt{2x}}\cdot\dfrac{\sqrt{2x}}{\sqrt{2x}} = \dfrac{3x\sqrt{2x}}{2x} = \dfrac{3\sqrt{2x}}{2}$

67. $\dfrac{8y}{\sqrt{5}} = \dfrac{8y}{\sqrt{5}}\cdot\dfrac{\sqrt{5}}{\sqrt{5}} = \dfrac{8y\sqrt{5}}{5}$

69. $\sqrt{\dfrac{y}{12x}} = \dfrac{\sqrt{y}}{\sqrt{12x}} = \dfrac{\sqrt{y}}{\sqrt{4}\cdot\sqrt{3x}} = \dfrac{\sqrt{y}}{2\sqrt{3x}}$

$\qquad = \dfrac{\sqrt{y}}{2\sqrt{3x}}\cdot\dfrac{\sqrt{3x}}{\sqrt{3x}} = \dfrac{\sqrt{3xy}}{2(3x)} = \dfrac{\sqrt{3xy}}{6x}$

71. $\dfrac{3}{\sqrt{2}+1} = \dfrac{3}{\sqrt{2}+1}\cdot\dfrac{\sqrt{2}-1}{\sqrt{2}-1} = \dfrac{3(\sqrt{2}-1)}{(\sqrt{2})^2-1^2}$

$\qquad = \dfrac{3(\sqrt{2}-1)}{2-1} = \dfrac{3(\sqrt{2}-1)}{1} = 3\sqrt{2}-3$

73. $\dfrac{4}{2-\sqrt{5}} = \dfrac{4}{2-\sqrt{5}}\cdot\dfrac{2+\sqrt{5}}{2+\sqrt{5}} = \dfrac{4(2+\sqrt{5})}{2^2-(\sqrt{5})^2}$

$\qquad = \dfrac{4(2+\sqrt{5})}{4-5} = \dfrac{4(2+\sqrt{5})}{-1} = -8-4\sqrt{5}$

75. $\dfrac{\sqrt{5}+1}{\sqrt{6}-\sqrt{5}} = \dfrac{\sqrt{5}+1}{\sqrt{6}-\sqrt{5}}\cdot\dfrac{\sqrt{6}+\sqrt{5}}{\sqrt{6}+\sqrt{5}}$

$\qquad = \dfrac{\sqrt{30}+5+\sqrt{6}+\sqrt{5}}{(\sqrt{6})^2-(\sqrt{5})^2}$

$\qquad = \dfrac{\sqrt{30}+5+\sqrt{6}+\sqrt{5}}{6-5}$

$\qquad = \sqrt{30}+5+\sqrt{6}+\sqrt{5}$

77. $\dfrac{\sqrt{3}+1}{\sqrt{2}-1} = \dfrac{\sqrt{3}+1}{\sqrt{2}-1} \cdot \dfrac{\sqrt{2}+1}{\sqrt{2}+1}$

$\qquad = \dfrac{\sqrt{6}+\sqrt{3}+\sqrt{2}+1}{2-1}$

$\qquad = \sqrt{6}+\sqrt{3}+\sqrt{2}+1$

79. $\dfrac{5}{2+\sqrt{x}} = \dfrac{5}{2+\sqrt{x}} \cdot \dfrac{2-\sqrt{x}}{2-\sqrt{x}} = \dfrac{5\left(2-\sqrt{x}\right)}{2^2 -\left(\sqrt{x}\right)^2}$

$\qquad = \dfrac{10-5\sqrt{x}}{4-x}$

81. $\dfrac{3}{\sqrt{x}-4} = \dfrac{3}{\sqrt{x}-4} \cdot \dfrac{\sqrt{x}+4}{\sqrt{x}+4} = \dfrac{3\left(\sqrt{x}+4\right)}{\left(\sqrt{x}\right)^2 -4^2}$

$\qquad = \dfrac{3\sqrt{x}+12}{x-16}$

83. $x+5 = 7^2$

$\qquad x+5 = 49$

$\qquad\quad x = 44$

85. $4z^2 +6z-12 = \left(2z\right)^2$

$\qquad 4z^2 +6z-12 = 4z^2$

$\qquad\qquad 6z-12 = 0$

$\qquad\qquad\quad 6z = 12$

$\qquad\qquad\quad z = 2$

87. $9x^2 +5x+4 = \left(3x+1\right)^2$

$\qquad 9x^2 +5x+4 = 9x^2 +6x+1$

$\qquad\qquad\quad -x = -3$

$\qquad\qquad\quad\ \ x = 3$

89. Let $l = 13\sqrt{2}$ and $w = 5\sqrt{6}$.

$\quad A = lw$

$\qquad = 13\sqrt{2}\cdot 5\sqrt{6} = 65\sqrt{12} = 65\sqrt{4}\cdot\sqrt{3}$

$\qquad = 65(2)\sqrt{3} = 130\sqrt{3}$ square meters

91. Answers may vary.

93. $\dfrac{\sqrt{3}+1}{\sqrt{2}-1} = \dfrac{\sqrt{3}+1}{\sqrt{2}-1} \cdot \dfrac{\sqrt{3}-1}{\sqrt{3}-1}$

$\qquad = \dfrac{3-1}{\sqrt{6}-\sqrt{2}-\sqrt{3}+1}$

$\qquad = \dfrac{2}{\sqrt{6}-\sqrt{2}-\sqrt{3}+1}$

Integrated Review 15.4

1. $\sqrt{36} = 6$, because $6^2 = 36$ and 6 is positive.

2. $\sqrt{48} = \sqrt{16}\cdot\sqrt{3} = 4\sqrt{3}$

3. $\sqrt{x^4} = x^2$, because $\left(x^2\right)^2 = x^4$.

4. $\sqrt{y^7} = \sqrt{y^6}\sqrt{y} = y^3\sqrt{y}$

5. $\sqrt{16x^2} = 4x$, because $\left(4x\right)^2 = 16x^2$.

6. $\sqrt{18x^{11}} = \sqrt{9x^{10}}\sqrt{2x} = 3x^5\sqrt{2x}$

7. $\sqrt[3]{8} = 2$, because $\left(2\right)^3 = 8$.

8. $\sqrt[4]{81} = 3$, because $\left(3\right)^4 = 81$.

9. $\sqrt[3]{-27} = -3$, because $\left(-3\right)^3 = -27$.

10. $\sqrt{-4}$ is not a real number.

11. $\sqrt{\dfrac{11}{9}} = \dfrac{\sqrt{11}}{\sqrt{9}} = \dfrac{\sqrt{11}}{3}$

12. $\sqrt[3]{\dfrac{7}{64}} = \dfrac{\sqrt[3]{7}}{\sqrt[3]{64}} = \dfrac{\sqrt[3]{7}}{4}$

13. $-\sqrt{16} = -4$

14. $-\sqrt{25} = -5$

15. $\sqrt{\dfrac{9}{49}} = \dfrac{3}{7}$

16. $\sqrt{\dfrac{1}{64}} = \dfrac{1}{8}$

17. $\sqrt{a^8 b^2} = a^4 b$

18. $\sqrt{x^{10} y^{20}} = x^5 y^{10}$

19. $\sqrt{25 m^6} = 5 m^3$

20. $\sqrt{9 n^{16}} = 3 n^8$

21. $5\sqrt{7} + \sqrt{7} = (5+1)\sqrt{7} = 6\sqrt{7}$

22. $\sqrt{50} - \sqrt{8} = \sqrt{25}\cdot\sqrt{2} - \sqrt{4}\cdot\sqrt{2}$
$= 5\sqrt{2} - 2\sqrt{2} = (5-2)\sqrt{2} = 3\sqrt{2}$

23. $5\sqrt{2} - 5\sqrt{3}$ cannot be simplified.

24. $2\sqrt{x} + \sqrt{25x} - \sqrt{36x} + 3x$
$= 2\sqrt{x} + \sqrt{25}\cdot\sqrt{x} - \sqrt{36}\cdot\sqrt{x} + 3x$
$= 2\sqrt{x} + 5\sqrt{x} - 6\sqrt{x} + 3x$
$= (2+5-6)\sqrt{x} + 3x$
$= \sqrt{x} + 3x$

25. $\sqrt{2}\cdot\sqrt{15} = \sqrt{2\cdot15} = \sqrt{30}$

26. $\sqrt{3}\cdot\sqrt{3} = \sqrt{3\cdot3} = \sqrt{9} = 3$

27. $\left(2\sqrt{7}\right)^2 = 2^2\left(\sqrt{7}\right)^2 = 4(7) = 28$

28. $\left(3\sqrt{5}\right)^2 = 3^2\left(\sqrt{5}\right)^2 = 9(5) = 45$

29. $\sqrt{3}\left(\sqrt{11}+1\right) = \sqrt{3}\cdot\sqrt{11} + \sqrt{3}\cdot1$
$= \sqrt{33} + \sqrt{3}$

30. $\sqrt{6}\left(\sqrt{3}-2\right) = \sqrt{6}\cdot\sqrt{3} - \sqrt{6}\cdot2$
$= \sqrt{18} - 2\sqrt{6} = \sqrt{9}\cdot\sqrt{2} - 2\sqrt{6}$
$= 3\sqrt{2} - 2\sqrt{6}$

31. $\sqrt{8y}\cdot\sqrt{2y} = \sqrt{8y\cdot2y} = \sqrt{16y^2} = 4y$

32. $\sqrt{15x^2}\cdot\sqrt{3x^2} = \sqrt{15x^2\cdot3x^2} = \sqrt{45x^4}$
$= \sqrt{9x^4}\cdot\sqrt{5} = 3x^2\sqrt{5}$

33. $\left(\sqrt{x}-5\right)\left(\sqrt{x}+2\right) = \sqrt{x^2} + 2\sqrt{x} - 5\sqrt{x} - 10$
$= x - 3\sqrt{x} - 10$

34. $\left(3+\sqrt{2}\right)^2 = 3^2 + 2(3)\sqrt{2} + \left(\sqrt{2}\right)^2$

$$= 9 + 6\sqrt{2} + 2$$
$$= 11 + 6\sqrt{2}$$

35. $\dfrac{\sqrt{8}}{\sqrt{2}} = \sqrt{\dfrac{8}{2}} = \sqrt{4} = 2$

36. $\dfrac{\sqrt{45}}{\sqrt{15}} = \sqrt{\dfrac{45}{15}} = \sqrt{3}$

37. $\dfrac{\sqrt{24x^5}}{\sqrt{2x}} = \sqrt{\dfrac{24x^5}{2x}} = \sqrt{12x^4} = \sqrt{4x^4} \cdot \sqrt{3}$

$$= 2x^2\sqrt{3}$$

38. $\dfrac{\sqrt{75a^4b^5}}{\sqrt{5ab}} = \sqrt{\dfrac{75a^4b^5}{5ab}} = \sqrt{15a^3b^4}$

$$= \sqrt{a^2b^4} \cdot \sqrt{15a} = ab^2\sqrt{15a}$$

39. $\sqrt{\dfrac{1}{6}} = \dfrac{\sqrt{1}}{\sqrt{6}} = \dfrac{1}{\sqrt{6}} \cdot \dfrac{\sqrt{6}}{\sqrt{6}} = \dfrac{\sqrt{6}}{6}$

40. $\dfrac{x}{\sqrt{20}} = \dfrac{x}{\sqrt{4} \cdot \sqrt{5}} = \dfrac{x}{2\sqrt{5}} = \dfrac{x}{2\sqrt{5}} \cdot \dfrac{\sqrt{5}}{\sqrt{5}}$

$$= \dfrac{x\sqrt{5}}{2(5)} = \dfrac{x\sqrt{5}}{10}$$

41. $\dfrac{4}{\sqrt{6}+1} = \dfrac{4}{\sqrt{6}+1} \cdot \dfrac{\sqrt{6}-1}{\sqrt{6}-1} = \dfrac{4\left(\sqrt{6}-1\right)}{6-1}$

$$= \dfrac{4\sqrt{6}-4}{5}$$

42. $\dfrac{\sqrt{2}+1}{\sqrt{x}-5} = \dfrac{\sqrt{2}+1}{\sqrt{x}-5} \cdot \dfrac{\sqrt{x}+5}{\sqrt{x}+5}$

$$= \dfrac{\sqrt{2x}+5\sqrt{2}+\sqrt{x}+5}{x-25}$$

Practice Problems 15.5

1. $\sqrt{x-2} = 7$

$$\left(\sqrt{x-2}\right)^2 = 7^2$$
$$x-2 = 49$$
$$x = 51$$

2. $\sqrt{x}+9 = 2$

$$\sqrt{x} = -7$$

The square root cannot be negative, therefore there is no solution.

3. $\sqrt{6x-1} = \sqrt{x}$

$$\left(\sqrt{6x-1}\right)^2 = \left(\sqrt{x}\right)^2$$
$$6x-1 = x$$
$$5x = 1$$
$$x = \dfrac{1}{5}$$

4. $\sqrt{9y^2+2y-10} = 3y$

$$\left(\sqrt{9y^2+2y-10}\right)^2 = (3y)^2$$
$$9y^2+2y-10 = 9y^2$$
$$2y-10 = 0$$
$$2y = 10$$
$$y = 5$$

5. $\sqrt{x+1} - x = -5$

$\sqrt{x+1} = x - 5$

$\left(\sqrt{x+1}\right)^2 = (x-5)^2$

$x + 1 = x^2 - 10x + 25$

$0 = x^2 - 11x + 24$

$0 = (x-3)(x-8)$

$x - 3 = 0 \quad \text{or} \quad x - 8 = 0$

$x = 3 \qquad\qquad x = 8$

Check:

$\sqrt{3+1} - 3 \overset{?}{=} -5 \qquad \sqrt{8+1} - 8 \overset{?}{=} -5$

$\sqrt{4} - 3 \overset{?}{=} -5 \qquad \sqrt{9} - 8 \overset{?}{=} -5$

$2 - 3 \overset{?}{=} -5 \qquad\quad 3 - 8 \overset{?}{=} -5$

$-1 \neq -5 \qquad\qquad -5 = -5$

     False   True

The solution is 8.

6. $\sqrt{x} + 3 = \sqrt{x+15}$

$\left(\sqrt{x}+3\right)^2 = \left(\sqrt{x+15}\right)^2$

$x + 6\sqrt{x} + 9 = x + 15$

$6\sqrt{x} = 6$

$\sqrt{x} = 1$

$\left(\sqrt{x}\right)^2 = (1)^2$

$x = 1$

Exercise Set 15.5

1. $\sqrt{x} = 9$

$\left(\sqrt{x}\right)^2 = 9^2$

$x = 81$

3. $\sqrt{x+5} = 2$

$\left(\sqrt{x+5}\right)^2 = 2^2$

$x + 5 = 4$

$x = -1$

5. $\sqrt{2x+6} = 4$

$\left(\sqrt{2x+6}\right)^2 = 4^2$

$2x + 6 = 16$

$2x = 10$

$x = 5$

7. $\sqrt{x} - 2 = 5$

$\sqrt{x} = 7$

$\left(\sqrt{x}\right)^2 = 7^2$

$x = 49$

9. $3\sqrt{x} + 5 = 2$

$3\sqrt{x} = -3$

The square root cannot be negative, therefore there is no solution.

11. $\sqrt{x+6} + 1 = 3$

$\sqrt{x+6} = 2$

$\left(\sqrt{x+6}\right)^2 = 2^2$

$x + 6 = 4$

$x = -2$

13. $\sqrt{2x+1}+3=5$

$\sqrt{2x+1}=2$

$\left(\sqrt{2x+1}\right)^2=2^2$

$2x+1=4$

$2x=3$

$x=\dfrac{3}{2}$

15. $\sqrt{x}+3=7$

$\sqrt{x}=4$

$\left(\sqrt{x}\right)^2=4^2$

$x=16$

17. $\sqrt{x+6}+5=3$

$\sqrt{x+6}=-2$

The square root cannot be negative, therefore there is no solution.

19. $\sqrt{4x-3}=\sqrt{x+3}$

$\left(\sqrt{4x-3}\right)^2=\left(\sqrt{x+3}\right)^2$

$4x-3=x+3$

$3x=6$

$x=2$

21. $\sqrt{x}=\sqrt{3x-8}$

$\left(\sqrt{x}\right)^2=\left(\sqrt{3x-8}\right)^2$

$x=3x-8$

$-2x=-8$

$x=4$

23. $\sqrt{4x}=\sqrt{2x+6}$

$\left(\sqrt{4x}\right)^2=\left(\sqrt{2x+6}\right)^2$

$4x=2x+6$

$2x=6$

$x=3$

25. $\sqrt{9x^2+2x-4}=3x$

$\left(\sqrt{9x^2+2x-4}\right)^2=\left(3x\right)^2$

$9x^2+2x-4=9x^2$

$2x-4=0$

$2x=4$

$x=2$

27. $\sqrt{16x^2-3x+6}=4x$

$\left(\sqrt{16x^2-3x+6}\right)^2=\left(4x\right)^2$

$16x^2-3x+6=16x^2$

$-3x+6=0$

$-3x=-6$

$x=2$

29. $\sqrt{16x^2+2x+2}=4x$

$\left(\sqrt{16x^2+2x+2}\right)^2=\left(4x\right)^2$

$16x^2+2x+2=16x^2$

$2x+2=0$

$2x=-2$

$x=-1$

A check shows that $x=-1$ is an extraneous solution. Therefore, there is no solution.

31. $\sqrt{2x^2 + 6x + 9} = 3$

$\left(\sqrt{2x^2 + 6x + 9}\right)^2 = (3)^2$

$2x^2 + 6x + 9 = 9$

$2x^2 + 6x = 0$

$2x(x+3) = 0$

$2x = 0 \quad \text{or} \quad x + 3 = 0$

$x = 0 \qquad\qquad x = -3$

33. $\sqrt{x+7} = x + 5$

$\left(\sqrt{x+7}\right)^2 = (x+5)^2$

$x + 7 = x^2 + 10x + 25$

$0 = x^2 + 9x + 18$

$0 = (x+3)(x+6)$

$x + 3 = 0 \quad \text{or} \quad x + 6 = 0$

$x = -3 \qquad x = -6\,(\text{extraneous})$

35. $\sqrt{x} = x - 6$

$\left(\sqrt{x}\right)^2 = (x-6)^2$

$x = x^2 - 12x + 36$

$0 = x^2 - 13x + 36$

$0 = (x-9)(x-4)$

$x - 9 = 0 \quad \text{or} \quad x - 4 = 0$

$x = 9 \qquad x = 4\,(\text{extraneous})$

37. $\sqrt{2x+1} = x - 7$

$\left(\sqrt{2x+1}\right)^2 = (x-7)^2$

$2x + 1 = x^2 - 14x + 49$

$0 = x^2 - 16x + 48$

$0 = (x-12)(x-4)$

$x - 12 = 0 \quad \text{or} \quad x - 4 = 0$

$x = 12 \qquad x = 4\,(\text{extraneous})$

39. $x = \sqrt{2x-2} + 1$

$x - 1 = \sqrt{2x-2}$

$(x-1)^2 = \left(\sqrt{2x-2}\right)^2$

$x^2 - 2x + 1 = 2x - 2$

$x^2 - 4x + 3 = 0$

$(x-1)(x-3) = 0$

$x - 1 = 0 \quad \text{or} \quad x - 3 = 0$

$x = 1 \qquad x = 3$

41. $\sqrt{1-8x} - x = 4$

$\sqrt{1-8x} = x + 4$

$\left(\sqrt{1-8x}\right)^2 = (x+4)^2$

$1 - 8x = x^2 + 8x + 16$

$0 = x^2 + 16x + 15$

$0 = (x+1)(x+15)$

$x + 1 = 0 \quad \text{or} \quad x + 15 = 0$

$x = -1 \qquad x = -15$

(extraneous)

43. $\sqrt{2x+5} - 1 = x$

$\sqrt{2x+5} = x + 1$

$\left(\sqrt{2x+5}\right)^2 = (x+1)^2$

$2x + 5 = x^2 + 2x + 1$

$0 = x^2 - 4$

$0 = (x-2)(x+2)$

$x - 2 = 0 \quad \text{or} \quad x + 2 = 0$

$x = 2 \qquad x = -2$

(extraneous)

45. $\sqrt{x-7} = \sqrt{x} - 1$

$\left(\sqrt{x-7}\right)^2 = \left(\sqrt{x}-1\right)^2$

$x - 7 = x - 2\sqrt{x} + 1$

$2\sqrt{x} = 8$

$\sqrt{x} = 4$

$\left(\sqrt{x}\right)^2 = (4)^2$

$x = 16$

47. $\sqrt{x} + 3 = \sqrt{x+15}$

$\left(\sqrt{x}+3\right)^2 = \left(\sqrt{x+15}\right)^2$

$x + 6\sqrt{x} + 9 = x + 15$

$6\sqrt{x} = 6$

$\sqrt{x} = 1$

$\left(\sqrt{x}\right)^2 = (1)^2$

$x = 1$

49. $\sqrt{x+8} = \sqrt{x} + 2$

$\left(\sqrt{x+8}\right)^2 = \left(\sqrt{x}+2\right)^2$

$x + 8 = x + 4\sqrt{x} + 4$

$4 = 4\sqrt{x}$

$1 = \sqrt{x}$

$1^2 = \left(\sqrt{x}\right)^2$

$1 = x$

51. $3x - 8 = 19$

$3x = 27$

$x = 9$

53. Let x = width and $2x$ = length.

$2(2x + x) = 24$

$2(3x) = 24$

$6x = 24$

$x = 4$

$2x = 2(4) = 8$

The length is 8 inches.

55. $b = \sqrt{\dfrac{V}{2}}$

a. $b = \sqrt{\dfrac{20}{2}} \approx 3.2$

$b = \sqrt{\dfrac{200}{2}} = 10$

$b = \sqrt{\dfrac{2000}{2}} \approx 31.6$

V	20	200	2000
b	3.2	10	31.6

b. No; it increases by a factor of $\sqrt{10}$.

57. Answers may vary.

59. $\sqrt{x+1} = 2x - 3$, $y_1 = \sqrt{x+1}$, $y_2 = 2x - 3$

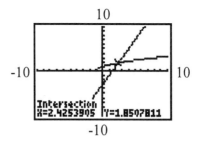

The solution is 2.43.

61. $-\sqrt{x+5} = -7x+1$

$y_1 = -\sqrt{x+5}, \ y_2 = -7x+1$

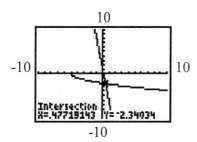

The solution is 0.48.

Practice Problems 15.6

1. $a^2 + b^2 = c^2$

$3^2 + 4^2 = c^2$

$9 + 16 = c^2$

$25 = c^2$

$5 = c$

The length is 5 centimeters

2. $a^2 + b^2 = c^2$

$3^2 + b^2 = 6^2$

$9 + b^2 = 36$

$b^2 = 27$

$b = \sqrt{27}$

$b = 3\sqrt{3}$

The length is $3\sqrt{3}$ miles ≈ 5.20 miles.

3. $\quad a^2 + b^2 = c^2$

$40^2 + b^2 = 65^2$

$1600 + b^2 = 4225$

$b^2 = 2625$

$b = \sqrt{2625}$

$b = 5\sqrt{105}$

The distance is $5\sqrt{105}$ feet ≈ 51.2 feet.

4. $v = \sqrt{2gh}$

$= \sqrt{2(32)(20)}$

$= \sqrt{1280}$

$= 16\sqrt{5}$

The velocity is $16\sqrt{5}$ feet per second ≈ 35.8 feet per second.

Exercise Set 15.6

1. $a^2 + b^2 = c^2$

$2^2 + 3^2 = c^2$

$4 + 9 = c^2$

$13 = c^2$

$\sqrt{13} = c$

The length is $\sqrt{13} \approx 3.61$.

3. $a^2 + b^2 = c^2$

$3^2 + b^2 = 6^2$

$9 + b^2 = 36$

$b^2 = 27$

$b = \sqrt{27}$

$b = 3\sqrt{3}$

The length is $3\sqrt{3} \approx 5.20$.

5.
$$a^2 + b^2 = c^2$$
$$7^2 + 24^2 = c^2$$
$$49 + 576 = c^2$$
$$625 = c^2$$
$$\sqrt{625} = c$$
$$25 = c$$
The length is 25.

7.
$$a^2 + b^2 = c^2$$
$$a^2 + \left(\sqrt{3}\right)^2 = 5^2$$
$$a^2 + 3 = 25$$
$$a^2 = 22$$
$$a = \sqrt{22}$$
The length is $\sqrt{22} \approx 4.69$.

9.
$$a^2 + b^2 = c^2$$
$$4^2 + b^2 = 13^2$$
$$16 + b^2 = 169$$
$$b^2 = 153$$
$$b = \sqrt{153}$$
$$b = 3\sqrt{17}$$
The length is $3\sqrt{17} \approx 12.37$.

11.
$$a^2 + b^2 = c^2$$
$$4^2 + 5^2 = c^2$$
$$16 + 25 = c^2$$
$$41 = c^2$$
$$\sqrt{41} = c$$
The length is $\sqrt{41} \approx 6.40$.

13.
$$a^2 + b^2 = c^2$$
$$a^2 + 2^2 = 6^2$$
$$a^2 + 4 = 36$$
$$a^2 = 32$$
$$a = \sqrt{32}$$
$$a = 4\sqrt{2}$$
The length is $4\sqrt{2} \approx 5.66$.

15.
$$a^2 + b^2 = c^2$$
$$\left(\sqrt{10}\right)^2 + b^2 = 10^2$$
$$10 + b^2 = 100$$
$$b^2 = 90$$
$$b = \sqrt{90}$$
$$b = 3\sqrt{10}$$
The length is $3\sqrt{10} \approx 9.49$.

17.
$$a^2 + b^2 = c^2$$
$$5^2 + 20^2 = c^2$$
$$25 + 400 = c^2$$
$$425 = c^2$$
$$\sqrt{425} = c$$
The length is $\sqrt{425} \approx 20.6$ feet.

19.
$$a^2 + b^2 = c^2$$
$$6^2 + 10^2 = c^2$$
$$36 + 100 = c^2$$
$$136 = c^2$$
$$\sqrt{136} = c$$
The length is $\sqrt{136} \approx 11.7$ feet.

21. $b = \sqrt{\dfrac{3V}{h}}$

$6 = \sqrt{\dfrac{3V}{2}}$

$6^2 = \left(\sqrt{\dfrac{3V}{2}}\right)^2$

$36 = \dfrac{3V}{2}$

$24 = V$

The volume is 24 cubic feet.

23. $s = \sqrt{30\,fd}$

$s = \sqrt{30(0.35)(280)}$

$= \sqrt{2940}$

≈ 54

It was moving at 54 mph.

25. $v = \sqrt{2.5r}$

$v = \sqrt{2.5(300)}$

$= \sqrt{750}$

≈ 27

It can travel at 27 mph.

27. $d = 3.5\sqrt{h}$

$d = 3.5\sqrt{285.4}$

≈ 59.1

You can see 59.1 km.

29. $3^2 = 9,\ (-3)^2 = 9$

The numbers are 3 and -3.

31. $10^2 = 100,\ (-10)^2 = 100$

The numbers are 10 and -10.

33. $8^2 = 64,\ (-8)^2 = 64$

The numbers are 8 and -8.

35. Let y = length of whole base and

z = length of unlabeled section of base.

Find y:

$y^2 + 3^2 = 7^2$

$y^2 + 9 = 49$

$y^2 = 40$

$y = \sqrt{40} = 2\sqrt{10}$

Find z

$z^2 + 3^2 = 5^2$

$z^2 + 9 = 25$

$z^2 = 16$

$z = \sqrt{16} = 4$

Find x:

$x = y - z$

$= 2\sqrt{10} - 4$

37. $a^2 + b^2 = c^2$

$\left[60(3)\right]^2 + \left[30(3)\right]^2 = c^2$

$180^2 + 90^2 = c^2$

$32,400 + 8100 = c^2$

$40,500 = c^2$

$\sqrt{40,500} = c$

$201 \approx c$

They are about 201 miles apart.

39. Answers may vary.

Chapter 15 Review

1. $\sqrt{81} = 9$, because $9^2 = 81$ and 9 is positive.

2. $-\sqrt{49} = -7$, because $\sqrt{49} = 7$.

3. $\sqrt[3]{27} = 3$, because $(3)^3 = 27$.

4. $\sqrt[4]{16} = 2$, because $2^4 = 16$.

5. $-\sqrt{\dfrac{9}{64}} = -\dfrac{3}{8}$, because $\sqrt{\dfrac{9}{64}} = \dfrac{3}{8}$.

6. $\sqrt{\dfrac{36}{81}} = \dfrac{6}{9} = \dfrac{2}{3}$, because $\left(\dfrac{6}{9}\right)^2 = \dfrac{36}{81}$.

7. $\sqrt[4]{16} = 2$, because $2^4 = 16$.

8. $\sqrt[3]{-8} = -2$, because $(-2)^3 = -8$.

9. c

10. a, c

11. $\sqrt{x^{12}} = x^6$, because $\left(x^6\right)^2 = x^{12}$.

12. $\sqrt{x^8} = x^4$, because $\left(x^4\right)^2 = x^8$.

13. $\sqrt{9y^2} = 3y$, because $(3y)^2 = 9y^2$.

14. $\sqrt{25x^4} = 5x^2$, because $\left(5x^2\right)^2 = 25x^4$.

15. $\sqrt{40} = \sqrt{4 \cdot 10} = \sqrt{4} \cdot \sqrt{10} = 2\sqrt{10}$

16. $\sqrt{24} = \sqrt{4 \cdot 6} = \sqrt{4} \cdot \sqrt{6} = 2\sqrt{6}$

17. $\sqrt{54} = \sqrt{9 \cdot 6} = \sqrt{9} \cdot \sqrt{6} = 3\sqrt{6}$

18. $\sqrt{88} = \sqrt{4 \cdot 22} = \sqrt{4} \cdot \sqrt{22} = 2\sqrt{22}$

19. $\sqrt{x^5} = \sqrt{x^4 \cdot x} = \sqrt{x^4} \cdot \sqrt{x} = x^2\sqrt{x}$

20. $\sqrt{y^7} = \sqrt{y^6 \cdot y} = \sqrt{y^6} \cdot \sqrt{y} = y^3\sqrt{y}$

21. $\sqrt{20x^2} = \sqrt{4x^2 \cdot 5} = \sqrt{4x^2} \cdot \sqrt{5} = 2x\sqrt{5}$

22. $\sqrt{50y^4} = \sqrt{25y^4 \cdot 2} = \sqrt{25y^4} \cdot \sqrt{2} = 5y^2\sqrt{2}$

23. $\sqrt[3]{54} = \sqrt[3]{27 \cdot 2} = \sqrt[3]{27} \cdot \sqrt[3]{2} = 3\sqrt[3]{2}$

24. $\sqrt[3]{88} = \sqrt[3]{8 \cdot 11} = \sqrt[3]{8} \cdot \sqrt[3]{11} = 2\sqrt[3]{11}$

25. $\sqrt{\dfrac{18}{25}} = \dfrac{\sqrt{18}}{\sqrt{25}} = \dfrac{\sqrt{9} \cdot \sqrt{2}}{5} = \dfrac{3\sqrt{2}}{5}$

26. $\sqrt{\dfrac{75}{64}} = \dfrac{\sqrt{75}}{\sqrt{64}} = \dfrac{\sqrt{25} \cdot \sqrt{3}}{8} = \dfrac{5\sqrt{3}}{8}$

27. $-\sqrt{\dfrac{50}{9}} = -\dfrac{\sqrt{50}}{\sqrt{9}} = -\dfrac{\sqrt{25} \cdot \sqrt{2}}{3} = -\dfrac{5\sqrt{2}}{9}$

28. $-\sqrt{\dfrac{12}{49}} = -\dfrac{\sqrt{12}}{\sqrt{49}} = -\dfrac{\sqrt{4} \cdot \sqrt{3}}{7} = -\dfrac{2\sqrt{3}}{7}$

29. $\sqrt{\dfrac{11}{x^2}} = \dfrac{\sqrt{11}}{\sqrt{x^2}} = \dfrac{\sqrt{11}}{x}$

30. $\sqrt{\dfrac{7}{y^4}} = \dfrac{\sqrt{7}}{\sqrt{y^4}} = \dfrac{\sqrt{7}}{y^2}$

31. $\sqrt{\dfrac{y^5}{100}} = \dfrac{\sqrt{y^5}}{\sqrt{100}} = \dfrac{\sqrt{y^4} \cdot \sqrt{y}}{10} = \dfrac{y^2\sqrt{y}}{10}$

32. $\sqrt{\dfrac{x^3}{81}} = \dfrac{\sqrt{x^3}}{\sqrt{81}} = \dfrac{\sqrt{x^2} \cdot \sqrt{x}}{9} = \dfrac{x\sqrt{x}}{9}$

33. $5\sqrt{2} - 8\sqrt{2} = (5-8)\sqrt{2} = -3\sqrt{2}$

34. $\sqrt{3} - 6\sqrt{3} = (1-6)\sqrt{3} = -5\sqrt{3}$

35. $6\sqrt{5} + 3\sqrt{6} - 2\sqrt{5} + \sqrt{6}$
$= (6-2)\sqrt{5} + (3+1)\sqrt{6}$
$= 4\sqrt{5} + 4\sqrt{6}$

36. $-\sqrt{7} + 8\sqrt{2} - \sqrt{7} - 6\sqrt{2}$
$= (-1-1)\sqrt{7} + (8-6)\sqrt{2}$
$= -2\sqrt{7} + 2\sqrt{2}$

37. $\sqrt{28} + \sqrt{63} + \sqrt{56}$
$= \sqrt{4} \cdot \sqrt{7} + \sqrt{9} \cdot \sqrt{7} + \sqrt{4} \cdot \sqrt{14}$
$= 2\sqrt{7} + 3\sqrt{7} + 2\sqrt{14}$
$= 5\sqrt{7} + 2\sqrt{14}$

38. $\sqrt{75} + \sqrt{48} - \sqrt{16}$
$= \sqrt{25} \cdot \sqrt{3} + \sqrt{16} \cdot \sqrt{3} - 4$
$= 5\sqrt{3} + 4\sqrt{3} - 4$
$= 9\sqrt{3} - 4$

39. $\sqrt{\dfrac{5}{9}} - \sqrt{\dfrac{5}{36}} = \dfrac{\sqrt{5}}{\sqrt{9}} - \dfrac{\sqrt{5}}{\sqrt{36}} = \dfrac{\sqrt{5}}{3} - \dfrac{\sqrt{5}}{6}$
$= \dfrac{2\sqrt{5}}{6} - \dfrac{\sqrt{5}}{6} = \dfrac{2\sqrt{5} - \sqrt{5}}{6} = \dfrac{\sqrt{5}}{6}$

40. $\sqrt{\dfrac{11}{25}} + \sqrt{\dfrac{11}{16}} = \dfrac{\sqrt{11}}{\sqrt{25}} + \dfrac{\sqrt{11}}{\sqrt{16}} = \dfrac{\sqrt{11}}{5} + \dfrac{\sqrt{11}}{4}$
$= \dfrac{4\sqrt{11}}{20} + \dfrac{5\sqrt{11}}{20} = \dfrac{4\sqrt{11} + 5\sqrt{11}}{20} = \dfrac{9\sqrt{11}}{20}$

41. $\sqrt{45x^2} + 3\sqrt{5x^2} - 7x\sqrt{5} + 10$
$= \sqrt{9x^2} \cdot \sqrt{5} + 3\sqrt{x^2} \cdot \sqrt{5} - 7x\sqrt{5} + 10$
$= 3x\sqrt{5} + 3x\sqrt{5} - 7x\sqrt{5} + 10$
$= -x\sqrt{5} + 10$
$= 10 - x\sqrt{5}$

42. $\sqrt{50x} - 9\sqrt{2x} + \sqrt{72x} - \sqrt{3x}$
$= \sqrt{25} \cdot \sqrt{2x} - 9\sqrt{2x} + \sqrt{36} \cdot \sqrt{2x} - \sqrt{3x}$
$= 5\sqrt{2x} - 9\sqrt{2x} + 6\sqrt{2x} - \sqrt{3x}$
$= 2\sqrt{2x} - \sqrt{3x}$

43. $\sqrt{3} \cdot \sqrt{6} = \sqrt{18} = \sqrt{9} \cdot \sqrt{2} = 3\sqrt{2}$

44. $\sqrt{5} \cdot \sqrt{15} = \sqrt{75} = \sqrt{25} \cdot \sqrt{3} = 5\sqrt{3}$

45. $\sqrt{2}\left(\sqrt{5} - \sqrt{7}\right) = \sqrt{10} - \sqrt{14}$

46. $\sqrt{5}\left(\sqrt{11} + \sqrt{3}\right) = \sqrt{55} + \sqrt{15}$

47. $\left(\sqrt{3} + 2\right)\left(\sqrt{6} - 5\right)$
$= \sqrt{18} - 5\sqrt{3} + 2\sqrt{6} - 10$
$= \sqrt{9} \cdot \sqrt{2} - 5\sqrt{3} + 2\sqrt{6} - 10$
$= 3\sqrt{2} - 5\sqrt{3} + 2\sqrt{6} - 10$

48. $\left(\sqrt{5}+1\right)\left(\sqrt{5}-3\right)=\sqrt{25}-3\sqrt{5}+\sqrt{5}-3$

$$=5-2\sqrt{5}-3$$
$$=2-2\sqrt{5}$$

49. $\left(\sqrt{x}-2\right)^2=\left(\sqrt{x}\right)^2-2\left(2\right)\sqrt{x}+\left(2\right)^2$

$$=x-4\sqrt{x}+4$$

50. $\left(\sqrt{y}+4\right)^2=\left(\sqrt{y}\right)^2+2\left(4\right)\sqrt{y}+\left(4\right)^2$

$$=y+8\sqrt{y}+16$$

51. $\dfrac{\sqrt{27}}{\sqrt{3}}=\sqrt{\dfrac{27}{3}}=\sqrt{9}=3$

52. $\dfrac{\sqrt{20}}{\sqrt{5}}=\sqrt{\dfrac{20}{5}}=\sqrt{4}=2$

53. $\dfrac{\sqrt{160}}{\sqrt{8}}=\sqrt{\dfrac{160}{8}}=\sqrt{20}=\sqrt{4}\cdot\sqrt{5}=2\sqrt{5}$

54. $\dfrac{\sqrt{96}}{\sqrt{3}}=\sqrt{\dfrac{96}{3}}=\sqrt{32}=\sqrt{16}\cdot\sqrt{2}=4\sqrt{2}$

55. $\dfrac{\sqrt{30x^6}}{\sqrt{2x^3}}=\sqrt{\dfrac{30x^6}{2x^3}}=\sqrt{15x^3}=\sqrt{x^2}\cdot\sqrt{15x}$

$$=x\sqrt{15x}$$

56. $\dfrac{\sqrt{54x^5y^2}}{\sqrt{3xy^2}}=\sqrt{\dfrac{54x^5y^2}{3xy^2}}=\sqrt{18x^4}$

$$=\sqrt{9x^4}\cdot\sqrt{2}=3x^2\sqrt{2}$$

57. $\dfrac{\sqrt{2}}{\sqrt{11}}=\dfrac{\sqrt{2}}{\sqrt{11}}\cdot\dfrac{\sqrt{11}}{\sqrt{11}}=\dfrac{\sqrt{22}}{\sqrt{121}}=\dfrac{\sqrt{22}}{11}$

58. $\dfrac{\sqrt{3}}{\sqrt{13}}=\dfrac{\sqrt{3}}{\sqrt{13}}\cdot\dfrac{\sqrt{13}}{\sqrt{13}}=\dfrac{\sqrt{39}}{\sqrt{169}}=\dfrac{\sqrt{39}}{13}$

59. $\sqrt{\dfrac{5}{6}}=\dfrac{\sqrt{5}}{\sqrt{6}}=\dfrac{\sqrt{5}}{\sqrt{6}}\cdot\dfrac{\sqrt{6}}{\sqrt{6}}=\dfrac{\sqrt{30}}{\sqrt{36}}=\dfrac{\sqrt{30}}{6}$

60. $\sqrt{\dfrac{7}{10}}=\dfrac{\sqrt{7}}{\sqrt{10}}=\dfrac{\sqrt{7}}{\sqrt{10}}\cdot\dfrac{\sqrt{10}}{\sqrt{10}}=\dfrac{\sqrt{70}}{\sqrt{100}}=\dfrac{\sqrt{70}}{10}$

61. $\dfrac{1}{\sqrt{5x}}=\dfrac{1}{\sqrt{5x}}\cdot\dfrac{\sqrt{5x}}{\sqrt{5x}}=\dfrac{\sqrt{5x}}{5x}$

62. $\dfrac{5}{\sqrt{3y}}=\dfrac{5}{\sqrt{3y}}\cdot\dfrac{\sqrt{3y}}{\sqrt{3y}}=\dfrac{5\sqrt{3y}}{3y}$

63. $\sqrt{\dfrac{3}{x}}=\dfrac{\sqrt{3}}{\sqrt{x}}=\dfrac{\sqrt{3}}{\sqrt{x}}\cdot\dfrac{\sqrt{x}}{\sqrt{x}}=\dfrac{\sqrt{3x}}{x}$

64. $\sqrt{\dfrac{6}{y}}=\dfrac{\sqrt{6}}{\sqrt{y}}=\dfrac{\sqrt{6}}{\sqrt{y}}\cdot\dfrac{\sqrt{y}}{\sqrt{y}}=\dfrac{\sqrt{6y}}{y}$

65. $\dfrac{3}{\sqrt{5}-2}=\dfrac{3}{\sqrt{5}-2}\cdot\dfrac{\sqrt{5}+2}{\sqrt{5}+2}=\dfrac{3\left(\sqrt{5}+2\right)}{\left(\sqrt{5}\right)^2-2^2}$

$$=\dfrac{3\left(\sqrt{5}+2\right)}{5-4}=\dfrac{3\left(\sqrt{5}+2\right)}{1}=3\sqrt{5}+6$$

66. $\dfrac{8}{\sqrt{10}-3}=\dfrac{8}{\sqrt{10}-3}\cdot\dfrac{\sqrt{10}+3}{\sqrt{10}+3}=\dfrac{8\left(\sqrt{10}+3\right)}{\left(\sqrt{10}\right)^2-3^2}$

$$=\dfrac{8\left(\sqrt{10}+3\right)}{10-9}=\dfrac{8\left(\sqrt{10}+3\right)}{1}=8\sqrt{10}+24$$

67. $\dfrac{\sqrt{2}+1}{\sqrt{3}-1} = \dfrac{\sqrt{2}+1}{\sqrt{3}-1} \cdot \dfrac{\sqrt{3}+1}{\sqrt{3}+1}$

$\qquad = \dfrac{\sqrt{6}+\sqrt{2}+\sqrt{3}+1}{3-1}$

$\qquad = \dfrac{\sqrt{6}+\sqrt{2}+\sqrt{3}+1}{2}$

68. $\dfrac{\sqrt{3}-2}{\sqrt{5}+2} = \dfrac{\sqrt{3}-2}{\sqrt{5}+2} \cdot \dfrac{\sqrt{5}-2}{\sqrt{5}-2}$

$\qquad = \dfrac{\sqrt{15}-2\sqrt{3}-2\sqrt{5}+4}{5-4}$

$\qquad = \sqrt{15}-2\sqrt{3}-2\sqrt{5}+4$

69. $\dfrac{10}{\sqrt{x}+5} = \dfrac{10}{\sqrt{x}+5} \cdot \dfrac{\sqrt{x}-5}{\sqrt{x}-5} = \dfrac{10\left(\sqrt{x}-5\right)}{x-25}$

$\qquad = \dfrac{10\sqrt{x}-50}{x-25}$

70. $\dfrac{8}{\sqrt{x}-1} = \dfrac{8}{\sqrt{x}-1} \cdot \dfrac{\sqrt{x}+1}{\sqrt{x}+1} = \dfrac{8\left(\sqrt{x}+1\right)}{x-1}$

$\qquad = \dfrac{8\sqrt{x}+8}{x-1}$

71. $\quad \sqrt{2x} = 6$

$\qquad \left(\sqrt{2x}\right)^2 = 6^2$

$\qquad\quad 2x = 36$

$\qquad\quad\ x = 18$

72. $\quad \sqrt{x+3} = 4$

$\qquad \left(\sqrt{x+3}\right)^2 = 4^2$

$\qquad\quad x+3 = 16$

$\qquad\qquad x = 13$

73. $\sqrt{x}+3 = 8$

$\qquad \sqrt{x} = 5$

$\qquad \left(\sqrt{x}\right)^2 = 5^2$

$\qquad\quad x = 25$

74. $\sqrt{x}+8 = 3$

$\qquad \sqrt{x} = -5$

The square root cannot be negative, therefore there is no solution.

75. $\quad \sqrt{2x+1} = x-7$

$\qquad \left(\sqrt{2x+1}\right)^2 = (x-7)^2$

$\qquad\quad 2x+1 = x^2-14x+49$

$\qquad\qquad 0 = x^2-16x+48$

$\qquad\qquad 0 = (x-12)(x-4)$

$\qquad x-12 = 0 \quad \text{or} \quad x-4 = 0$

$\qquad\quad x = 12 \qquad\qquad x = 4$

$\qquad\qquad\qquad\qquad\qquad\text{(extraneous)}$

76. $\quad \sqrt{3x+1} = x-1$

$\qquad \left(\sqrt{3x+1}\right)^2 = (x-1)^2$

$\qquad\quad 3x+1 = x^2-2x+1$

$\qquad\qquad 0 = x^2-5x$

$\qquad\qquad 0 = x(x-5)$

$\qquad x = 0 \quad \text{or} \quad x-5 = 0$

$\qquad x = 0 \qquad\qquad x = 5$

$\qquad\text{(extraneous)}$

77.
$$\sqrt{x}+3=\sqrt{x+15}$$
$$\left(\sqrt{x}+3\right)^2=\left(\sqrt{x+15}\right)^2$$
$$x+6\sqrt{x}+9=x+15$$
$$6\sqrt{x}=6$$
$$\sqrt{x}=1$$
$$\left(\sqrt{x}\right)^2=(1)^2$$
$$x=1$$

78.
$$\sqrt{x-5}=\sqrt{x}-1$$
$$\left(\sqrt{x-5}\right)^2=\left(\sqrt{x}-1\right)^2$$
$$x-5=x-2\sqrt{x}+1$$
$$-6=-2\sqrt{x}$$
$$3=\sqrt{x}$$
$$3^2=\left(\sqrt{x}\right)^2$$
$$9=x$$

79.
$$a^2+b^2=c^2$$
$$5^2+b^2=9^2$$
$$25+b^2=81$$
$$b^2=56$$
$$b=\sqrt{56}$$
$$b=2\sqrt{14}$$
The length is $2\sqrt{14}\approx 7.48$.

80.
$$a^2+b^2=c^2$$
$$6^2+9^2=c^2$$
$$36+81=c^2$$
$$117=c^2$$
$$\sqrt{117}=c$$
The length is $\sqrt{117}\approx 10.82$.

81.
$$a^2+b^2=c^2$$
$$20^2+12^2=c^2$$
$$400+144=c^2$$
$$544=c^2$$
$$\sqrt{544}=c$$
$$4\sqrt{34}=c$$
They are $4\sqrt{34}$ feet apart.

82.
$$a^2+b^2=c^2$$
$$a^2+5^2=10^2$$
$$a^2+25=100$$
$$a^2=75$$
$$a=\sqrt{75}$$
$$a=5\sqrt{3}$$
The length is $5\sqrt{3}$ inches.

83.
$$r=\sqrt{\frac{S}{4\pi}}$$
$$r=\sqrt{\frac{72}{4\pi}}\approx 2.4$$
The radius is about 2.4 inches.

84.
$$r=\sqrt{\frac{S}{4\pi}}$$
$$6=\sqrt{\frac{S}{4\pi}}$$
$$6^2=\left(\sqrt{\frac{S}{4\pi}}\right)^2$$
$$36=\frac{S}{4\pi}$$
$$144\pi=S$$
The surface area is 144π square inches.

Chapter 15 Test

1. $\sqrt{16} = 4,$ because $4^2 = 16$ and 4 is positive.

2. $\sqrt[3]{-125} = \sqrt[3]{(-5)(-5)(-5)} = -5$

3. $\sqrt[4]{81} = 3,$ because $3^4 = 81.$

4. $\sqrt{\dfrac{9}{16}} = \dfrac{3}{4},$ because $\left(\dfrac{3}{4}\right)^2 = \dfrac{9}{16}$ and $\dfrac{3}{4}$ is positive.

5. $\sqrt[4]{-81}$ is not a real number.

6. $\sqrt{x^{10}} = x^5,$ because $\left(x^5\right)^2 = x^{10}.$

7. $\sqrt{54} = \sqrt{9}\cdot\sqrt{6} = 3\sqrt{6}$

8. $\sqrt{92} = \sqrt{4}\cdot\sqrt{23} = 2\sqrt{23}$

9. $\sqrt{y^7} = \sqrt{y^6}\cdot\sqrt{y} = y^3\sqrt{y}$

10. $\sqrt{24x^8} = \sqrt{4x^8}\cdot\sqrt{6} = 2x^4\sqrt{6}$

11. $\sqrt[3]{27} = 3$

12. $\sqrt[3]{16} = \sqrt[3]{8}\cdot\sqrt[3]{2} = 2\sqrt[3]{2}$

13. $\sqrt{\dfrac{5}{16}} = \dfrac{\sqrt{5}}{\sqrt{16}} = \dfrac{\sqrt{5}}{4}$

14. $\sqrt{\dfrac{y^3}{25}} = \dfrac{\sqrt{y^3}}{\sqrt{25}} = \dfrac{\sqrt{y^2}\cdot\sqrt{y}}{5} = \dfrac{y\sqrt{y}}{5}$

15. $\sqrt{13} + \sqrt{13} - 4\sqrt{13} = -2\sqrt{13}$

16. $\sqrt{18} - \sqrt{75} + 7\sqrt{3} - \sqrt{8}$
$= \sqrt{9}\cdot\sqrt{2} - \sqrt{25}\cdot\sqrt{3} + 7\sqrt{3} - \sqrt{4}\cdot\sqrt{2}$
$= 3\sqrt{2} - 5\sqrt{3} + 7\sqrt{3} - 2\sqrt{2}$
$= \sqrt{2} + 2\sqrt{3}$

17. $\sqrt{\dfrac{3}{4}} + \sqrt{\dfrac{3}{25}} = \dfrac{\sqrt{3}}{\sqrt{4}} + \dfrac{\sqrt{3}}{\sqrt{25}} = \dfrac{\sqrt{3}}{2} + \dfrac{\sqrt{3}}{5}$
$= \dfrac{5\sqrt{3}}{10} + \dfrac{2\sqrt{3}}{10} = \dfrac{5\sqrt{3}+2\sqrt{3}}{10} = \dfrac{7\sqrt{3}}{10}$

18. $\sqrt{7}\cdot\sqrt{14} = \sqrt{98} = \sqrt{49}\cdot\sqrt{2} = 7\sqrt{2}$

19. $\sqrt{5}\left(\sqrt{5}+2\sqrt{7}\right) = \sqrt{25} + 2\sqrt{35}$
$= 5 + 2\sqrt{35}$

20. $\left(2\sqrt{x}+3\right)\left(2\sqrt{x}-3\right)$
$= 4\sqrt{x^2} - 6\sqrt{x} + 6\sqrt{x} - 9$
$= 4\sqrt{x^2} - 9$
$= 4x - 9$

21. $\dfrac{\sqrt{50}}{\sqrt{10}} = \sqrt{\dfrac{50}{10}} = \sqrt{5}$

22. $\dfrac{\sqrt{40x^4}}{\sqrt{2x}} = \sqrt{\dfrac{40x^4}{2x}} = \sqrt{20x^3} = \sqrt{4x^2}\cdot\sqrt{5x}$
$= 2x\sqrt{5x}$

23. $\sqrt{\dfrac{2}{3}} = \dfrac{\sqrt{2}}{\sqrt{3}} = \dfrac{\sqrt{2}}{\sqrt{3}}\cdot\dfrac{\sqrt{3}}{\sqrt{3}} = \dfrac{\sqrt{6}}{\sqrt{9}} = \dfrac{\sqrt{6}}{3}$

24. $\dfrac{8}{\sqrt{5y}} = \dfrac{8}{\sqrt{5y}} \cdot \dfrac{\sqrt{5y}}{\sqrt{5y}} = \dfrac{8\sqrt{5y}}{5y}$

25. $\dfrac{8}{\sqrt{6}+2} = \dfrac{8}{\sqrt{6}+2} \cdot \dfrac{\sqrt{6}-2}{\sqrt{6}-2} = \dfrac{8\left(\sqrt{6}-2\right)}{\left(\sqrt{6}\right)^2 - 2^2}$

$= \dfrac{8\left(\sqrt{6}-2\right)}{6-4} = \dfrac{8\left(\sqrt{6}-2\right)}{2} = 4\sqrt{6}-8$

26. $\dfrac{1}{3-\sqrt{x}} = \dfrac{1}{3-\sqrt{x}} \cdot \dfrac{3+\sqrt{x}}{3+\sqrt{x}} = \dfrac{3+\sqrt{x}}{9-x}$

27. $\sqrt{x}+8 = 11$

$\sqrt{x} = 3$

$\left(\sqrt{x}\right)^2 = 3^2$

$x = 9$

28. $\sqrt{3x-6} = \sqrt{x+4}$

$\left(\sqrt{3x-6}\right)^2 = \left(\sqrt{x+4}\right)^2$

$3x-6 = x+4$

$2x = 10$

$x = 5$

29. $\sqrt{2x-2} = x-5$

$\left(\sqrt{2x-2}\right)^2 = \left(x-5\right)^2$

$2x-2 = x^2 - 10x + 25$

$0 = x^2 - 12x + 27$

$0 = \left(x-9\right)\left(x-3\right)$

$x-9 = 0 \quad$ or $\quad x-3 = 0$

$x = 9 \qquad\qquad x = 3$

$\qquad\qquad\qquad\qquad$ (extraneous)

30. $a^2 + b^2 = c^2$

$8^2 + b^2 = 12^2$

$64 + b^2 = 144$

$b^2 = 80$

$b = \sqrt{80}$

$b = 4\sqrt{5}$

The length is $4\sqrt{5}$ inches.

31. $r = \sqrt{\dfrac{A}{\pi}}$

$r = \sqrt{\dfrac{15}{\pi}} \approx 2.19$

The radius is about 2.19 meters

Cumulative Review Chapter 15

1. $-5\left(-10\right) = 50$

2. $-\dfrac{2}{3} \cdot \dfrac{4}{7} = -\dfrac{8}{21}$

3. $4\left(2x-3\right)+7 = 3x+5$

$8x - 12 + 7 = 3x + 5$

$8x - 5 = 3x + 5$

$5x = 10$

$x = 2$

4. a. 17%

b. $17\% + 4\% = 21\%$

c. Let x = the unknown number

$x = 0.17\left(253\right) = 43$

43 are traveling soley for business.

5. $3.7(-9) = -3.33$

   $-33.3 = -3.33$ False

   -9 is not a solution.

6. $2.8(6) = 16.8$

   $16.8 = 16.8$ True

   6 is a solution.

7. $\sqrt{\dfrac{1}{36}} = \sqrt{\dfrac{1 \cdot 1}{6 \cdot 6}} = \dfrac{1}{6}$

8. $\sqrt{\dfrac{4}{25}} = \sqrt{\dfrac{2 \cdot 2}{5 \cdot 5}} = \dfrac{2}{5}$

9. $4(2x - 3) + 7 = 3x + 5$

   $8x - 12 + 7 = 3x + 5$

   $8x - 5 = 3x + 5$

   $5x = 10$

   $x = 2$

10. $3(2 - 5x) + 24x = 12$

   $6 - 15x + 24x = 12$

   $6 + 9x = 12$

   $9x = 12 - 6$

   $\dfrac{9x}{9} = \dfrac{6}{9}$

   $x = \dfrac{2}{3}$

11. **a.** $1.02 \times 10^5 = 102,000$

   b. $7.358 \times 10^{-3} = 0.007358$

   c. $8.4 \times 10^7 = 84,000,000$

   d. $3.007 \times 10^{-5} = 0.00003007$

12. **a.** $8.26 \times 10^4 = 82,600$

   b. $9.9 \times 10^{-2} = 0.099$

   c. $1.002 \times 10^5 = 100,200$

   d. $8.039 \times 10^{-3} = 0.008039$

13. $(3x + 2)(2x - 5) = 6x^2 - 15x + 4x - 10$

   $\qquad\qquad\qquad = 6x^2 - 11x - 10$

14. $(5x - 1)(4x + 1) = 5x(4x + 1) - 1(4x + 1)$

   $\qquad\qquad\qquad = 20x^2 + 5x - 4x - 1$

   $\qquad\qquad\qquad = 20x^2 + x - 1$

15. $xy + 2x + 3y + 6 = x(y + 2) + 3(y + 2)$

   $\qquad\qquad\qquad = (y + 2)(x + 3)$

16. $16x^3 - 28x^2 + 12x - 21$

   $= (16x^3 - 28x^2) + (12x - 21)$

   $= 4x^2(4x - 7) + 3(4x - 7)$

   $= (4x - 7)(4x^2 + 3)$

17. $3x^2 + 11x + 6 = (3x + 2)(x + 3)$

18. $9x^2 - 5x - 4 = (x - 1)(9x + 4)$

19. **a.** When $x - 3 = 0$, $x = 0$.

   b. When $x^2 - 3x + 2 = 0$,

   $\qquad (x - 1)(x - 2) = 0$

   $\qquad x = 1$ or $x = 2$.

   c. None, since 3 cannot be zero.

20. a. $\dfrac{x-3}{x};\; x=0$

Undefined at $x=0$.

b. $\dfrac{x+1}{5}$; denominator will never equal zero.

Always defined.

c. $\dfrac{x^2-3}{x^2-4};\; x^2-4=0$

$$(x+2)(x-2)=0$$
$$x+2=0,\; x-2=0$$
$$x=-2 \qquad x=2$$

Undefined at $x=-2,\; x=2$

21. $\dfrac{x^2+4x+4}{x^2+2x}=\dfrac{(x+2)(x+2)}{x(x+2)}=\dfrac{x+2}{x}$

22. $\dfrac{16x^2-4y^2}{4x-2y}=\dfrac{4\left(4x^2-y^2\right)}{2(2x-y)}$

$$=\dfrac{4(2x+y)(2x-y)}{2(2x-y)}$$

$$=2(2x+y)$$

23. a. $\dfrac{a}{4}-\dfrac{2a}{8}$

$$=\dfrac{a\cdot 2}{4\cdot 2}-\dfrac{2a}{8}$$

$$=\dfrac{2a}{8}-\dfrac{2a}{8}$$

$$=\dfrac{2a-2a}{8}$$

$$=\dfrac{0}{8}$$

$$=0$$

b. $\dfrac{3}{10x^2}+\dfrac{7}{25x}$

$\text{LCD}=50x^2$

$$=\dfrac{3\cdot 5}{10x^2\cdot 5}+\dfrac{7\cdot 2x}{25x\cdot 2x}$$

$$=\dfrac{15}{50x^2}+\dfrac{14x}{50x^2}$$

$$=\dfrac{15+14x}{50x^2}$$

24. a. $\dfrac{x}{5}-\dfrac{3x}{10}$

$$=\dfrac{x\cdot 2}{5\cdot 2}-\dfrac{3x}{10}$$

$$=\dfrac{2x}{10}-\dfrac{3x}{10}$$

$$=\dfrac{2x-3x}{10}$$

$$=\dfrac{-x}{10}$$

b. $\dfrac{9}{12a^2}+\dfrac{5}{16a}$

$\text{LCD}=48a^2$

$$=\dfrac{9\cdot 4}{12a^2\cdot 4}+\dfrac{5\cdot 3a}{16a\cdot 3a}$$

$$=\dfrac{36}{48a^2}+\dfrac{15a}{48a^2}$$

$$=\dfrac{36+15a}{48a^2}$$

$$=\dfrac{3(12+5a)}{3\cdot 16a^2}$$

$$=\dfrac{12+5a}{16a^2}$$

25. $\dfrac{4x}{x^2+x-30} + \dfrac{2}{x-5} = \dfrac{1}{x+6}$

$(x-5)(x+6)\left(\dfrac{4x}{x^2+x-30} + \dfrac{2}{x-5}\right)$

$= (x-5)(x+6)\left(\dfrac{1}{x+6}\right)$

$4x + 2(x+6) = 1(x-5)$

$4x + 2x + 12 = x - 5$

$5x = -17$

$x = -\dfrac{17}{5}$

26. $\dfrac{3}{x+3} = \dfrac{12x+19}{x^2+7x+12} - \dfrac{5}{x+4}$

$\dfrac{3}{(x+3)} = \dfrac{12x+19}{(x+3)(x+4)} - \dfrac{5}{(x+4)}$

$LCD = (x+3)(x+4)$

$(x+3)(x+4)\left[\dfrac{3}{(x+3)}\right]$

$= (x+3)(x+4)\left[\dfrac{12x+19}{(x+3)(x+4)} - \dfrac{5}{(x+4)}\right]$

$3(x+4) = 12x+19-5(x+3)$

$3x+12 = 12x+19-5x-15$

$3x+12 = 7x+4$

$3x-7x = 4-12$

$\dfrac{-4x}{-4} = \dfrac{-8}{-4}$

$x = 2$

All expressions are defined. Therefore

2 is the solution.

27. $y = -3$ for all values of x.

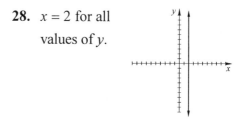

28. $x = 2$ for all values of y.

29. $\sqrt[3]{1} = 1$

30. $\sqrt[3]{8} = \sqrt[3]{2 \cdot 2 \cdot 2} = 2$

31. $\sqrt[3]{-27} = -3$

32. $\sqrt[3]{-8} = \sqrt[3]{(-2)(-2)(-2)} = -2$

33. $\sqrt[3]{\dfrac{1}{125}} = \dfrac{1}{5}$

34. $\sqrt[3]{\dfrac{27}{64}} = \sqrt[3]{\dfrac{3 \cdot 3 \cdot 3}{4 \cdot 4 \cdot 4}} = \dfrac{3}{4}$

35. $\sqrt{54} = \sqrt{9} \cdot \sqrt{6} = 3\sqrt{6}$

36. $\sqrt{40} = \sqrt{4} \cdot \sqrt{10} = 2\sqrt{10}$

37. $\sqrt{200} = \sqrt{100} \cdot \sqrt{2} = 10\sqrt{2}$

38. $\sqrt{125} = \sqrt{25} \cdot \sqrt{5} = 5\sqrt{5}$

39. $7\sqrt{12} - \sqrt{75} = 7\sqrt{4} \cdot \sqrt{3} - \sqrt{25} \cdot \sqrt{3}$
$= 7(2)\sqrt{3} - 5\sqrt{3} = 14\sqrt{3} - 5\sqrt{3} = 9\sqrt{3}$

40. $\sqrt{75} + \sqrt{48} = \sqrt{25} \cdot \sqrt{3} + \sqrt{16} \cdot \sqrt{3}$
$= 5\sqrt{3} + 4\sqrt{3}$
$= 9\sqrt{3}$

41. $2\sqrt{x^2} - \sqrt{25x} + \sqrt{x} = 2x - 5\sqrt{x} + \sqrt{x}$
$= 2x - 4\sqrt{x}$

42. $5\sqrt{x^2} + \sqrt{36x} + \sqrt{49x^2} = 5x + 6\sqrt{x} + 7x$
$= 12x + 6\sqrt{x}$

43. $\dfrac{2}{\sqrt{7}} = \dfrac{2}{\sqrt{7}} \cdot \dfrac{\sqrt{7}}{\sqrt{7}} = \dfrac{2\sqrt{7}}{7}$

44. $\dfrac{4}{\sqrt{5}} = \dfrac{4 \cdot \sqrt{5}}{\sqrt{5} \cdot \sqrt{5}} = \dfrac{4\sqrt{5}}{5}$

45. $\sqrt{x} = \sqrt{5x - 2}$
$\left(\sqrt{x}\right)^2 = \left(\sqrt{5x - 2}\right)^2$
$x = 5x - 2$
$-4x = -2$
$x = \dfrac{1}{2}$

46. $\sqrt{x + 5} = x - 1$
$\left(\sqrt{x + 5}\right)^2 = (x - 1)^2$
$x + 5 = (x)^2 - 2(x)(1) + (1)^2$
$x + 5 = x^2 - 2x + 1$
$0 = x^2 - 2x + 1 - x - 5$
$x^2 - 3x - 4 = 0$
$(x + 1)(x - 4) = 0$

46. $x + 1 = 0, \quad x - 4 = 0$
$\quad x = -1, \qquad x = 4$
Check: $\sqrt{-1 + 5} = -1 - 1$
$\qquad \sqrt{4} = -2$
$\qquad \quad 2 = -2$
-1 is not a solution.
$\sqrt{4 + 5} = 4 - 1$
$\quad \sqrt{9} = 3$
$\qquad 3 = 3$ True
4 is a solution.

Chapter 16

Chapter 16 Pretest

1. $a^2 - 6a = 0$

$a(a - 6) = 0$

$a - 6 = 0$ or $a = 0$

$a = 6$

The solutions are 0 and 6.

2. $2x^2 - 11x = 6$

$2x^2 - 11x - 6 = 0$

$(2x - 1)(x - 6) = 0$

$2x - 1 = 0$ or $x - 6 = 0$

$2x = -1 \qquad x = 6$

$x = -\dfrac{1}{2}$

The solutions are $-\dfrac{1}{2}$ and 6.

3. $b^2 = 144$

$b = \sqrt{144}$ or $b = -\sqrt{144}$

$b = 12 \qquad b = -12$

4. $(2x - 7)^2 = 24$

$2x - 7 = \sqrt{24}$ or $2x - 7 = -\sqrt{24}$

$2x - 7 = 2\sqrt{6} \qquad 2x - 7 = -2\sqrt{6}$

$2x = 7 + 2\sqrt{6} \qquad 2x = 7 - 2\sqrt{6}$

$x = \dfrac{7 + 2\sqrt{6}}{2} \qquad x = \dfrac{7 - 2\sqrt{6}}{2}$

The solutions are $\dfrac{7 + 2\sqrt{6}}{2}$ and $\dfrac{7 - 2\sqrt{6}}{2}$.

5. $x^2 - 14x + 48 = 0$

$x^2 - 14x = -48$

$x^2 - 14x + 49 = -48 + 49$

$(x - 7)^2 = 1$

$x - 7 = \sqrt{1}$ or $x - 7 = -\sqrt{1}$

$x = 7 + 1 \qquad x = 7 - 1$

$x = 8 \qquad x = 6$

The solutions are 6 and 8.

6. $3x^2 - 5x = 2$

$x^2 - \dfrac{5}{3}x = \dfrac{2}{3}$

$x^2 - \dfrac{5}{3}x + \dfrac{25}{36} = \dfrac{2}{3} + \dfrac{25}{36}$

$\left(x - \dfrac{5}{6}\right)^2 = \dfrac{49}{36}$

$x - \dfrac{5}{6} = \sqrt{\dfrac{49}{36}}$ or $x - \dfrac{5}{6} = -\sqrt{\dfrac{49}{36}}$

$x - \dfrac{5}{6} = \dfrac{7}{6} \qquad x - \dfrac{5}{6} = -\dfrac{7}{6}$

$x = \dfrac{12}{6} \qquad x = -\dfrac{2}{6}$

$x = 2 \qquad x = -\dfrac{1}{3}$

The solutions are $-\dfrac{1}{3}$ and 2.

7. $x^2 - 6x - 27 = 0$

$a = 1, b = -6,$ and $c = -27$

$$x = \frac{-b \pm \sqrt{b^2 - 4ac}}{2a}$$

$$x = \frac{-(-6) \pm \sqrt{(-6)^2 - 4(1)(-27)}}{2(1)}$$

$$x = \frac{6 \pm \sqrt{36 + 108}}{2}$$

$$x = \frac{6 \pm \sqrt{144}}{2}$$

$$x = \frac{6 \pm 12}{2}$$

$$x = \frac{6 + 12}{2} = 9 \quad \text{or} \quad x = \frac{6 - 12}{2} = -3$$

The solutions are -3 and 9.

8. $m^2 - \frac{7}{4}m - \frac{3}{2} = 0$

$a = 1, b = -\frac{7}{4},$ and $c = -\frac{3}{2}$

$$m = \frac{-b \pm \sqrt{b^2 - 4ac}}{2a}$$

$$m = \frac{-\left(-\frac{7}{4}\right) \pm \sqrt{\left(-\frac{7}{4}\right)^2 - 4(1)\left(-\frac{3}{2}\right)}}{2(1)}$$

$$= \frac{\frac{7}{4} \pm \sqrt{\frac{49}{16} + \frac{12}{2}}}{2} = \frac{\frac{7}{4} \pm \sqrt{\frac{145}{16}}}{2}$$

$$= \frac{\frac{7}{4} \pm \frac{\sqrt{145}}{4}}{2} = \frac{7 \pm \sqrt{145}}{8}$$

The solutions are $\dfrac{7 + \sqrt{145}}{8}$ and $\dfrac{7 - \sqrt{145}}{8}$.

9. $(2x + 3)(x - 1) = 6$

$2x^2 + x - 3 = 6$

$2x^2 + x - 9 = 0$

$a = 2, b = 1,$ and $c = -9$

$$x = \frac{-b \pm \sqrt{b^2 - 4ac}}{2a}$$

$$x = \frac{-(1) \pm \sqrt{(1)^2 - 4(2)(-9)}}{2(2)}$$

$$= \frac{-1 \pm \sqrt{1 + 72}}{4} = \frac{-1 \pm \sqrt{73}}{4}$$

The solutions are $\dfrac{-1 + \sqrt{73}}{4}$ and $\dfrac{-1 - \sqrt{73}}{4}$.

10. $(5x + 3)^2 = 18$

$5x + 3 = \sqrt{18} \quad \text{or} \quad 5x + 3 = -\sqrt{18}$

$5x + 3 = 3\sqrt{2} \qquad\quad 5x + 3 = -3\sqrt{2}$

$5x = -3 + 3\sqrt{2} \qquad 5x = -3 - 3\sqrt{2}$

$x = \dfrac{-3 + 3\sqrt{2}}{5} \qquad x = \dfrac{-3 - 3\sqrt{2}}{5}$

The solutions are $\dfrac{-3 + 3\sqrt{2}}{5}$ and $\dfrac{-3 - 3\sqrt{2}}{5}$.

11. $8x^2 + 18x + 9 = 0$

$a = 8, b = 18,$ and $c = 9$

$$x = \frac{-b \pm \sqrt{b^2 - 4ac}}{2a}$$

$$x = \frac{-(18) \pm \sqrt{(18)^2 - 4(8)(9)}}{2(8)}$$

$$= \frac{-18 \pm \sqrt{324 - 288}}{16} = \frac{-18 \pm \sqrt{36}}{16}$$

$$= \frac{-18 \pm 6}{16}$$

$$x = \frac{-18+6}{16} = -\frac{3}{4} \quad \text{or} \quad x = \frac{-18-6}{16} = -\frac{3}{2}$$

The solutions are $-\frac{3}{4}$ and $-\frac{3}{2}$.

12.
$$m^2 - 6m = -3$$
$$m^2 - 6m + 9 = -3 + 9$$
$$(m-3)^2 = 6$$
$$m - 3 = \sqrt{6} \quad \text{or} \quad m - 3 = -\sqrt{6}$$
$$m = 3 + \sqrt{6} \qquad m = 3 - \sqrt{6}$$

The solutions are $3 + \sqrt{6}$ and $3 - \sqrt{6}$.

13.
$$\frac{1}{4}x^2 + x - \frac{1}{8} = 0$$
$$x^2 + 4x - \frac{1}{2} = 0$$
$$x^2 + 4x = \frac{1}{2}$$
$$x^2 + 4x + 4 = \frac{1}{2} + 4$$
$$(x+2)^2 = \frac{9}{2} = \frac{18}{4}$$
$$x + 2 = \sqrt{\frac{18}{4}} \quad \text{or} \quad x + 2 = -\sqrt{\frac{18}{4}}$$
$$x = -2 + \frac{3\sqrt{2}}{2} \qquad x = -2 - \frac{3\sqrt{2}}{2}$$

The solutions are $\dfrac{-4+3\sqrt{2}}{4}$ and $\dfrac{-4-3\sqrt{2}}{4}$.

14.
$$(y+7)^2 - 5 = 0$$
$$(y+7)^2 = 5$$
$$y + 7 = \sqrt{5} \quad \text{or} \quad y + 7 = -\sqrt{5}$$
$$y = -7 + \sqrt{5} \qquad y = -7 - \sqrt{5}$$

The solutions are $-7 + \sqrt{5}$ and $-7 - \sqrt{5}$.

15. $y = -3x^2$

x	y
0	0
1	−3
	−12
	−3
	−12

16. $y = x^2 + 3$

x	y
−2	7
−1	4
0	3
1	4
2	7

17. $y = x^2 + 4x$

x	y
−4	0
−3	−3
−2	−4
−1	−3
0	0

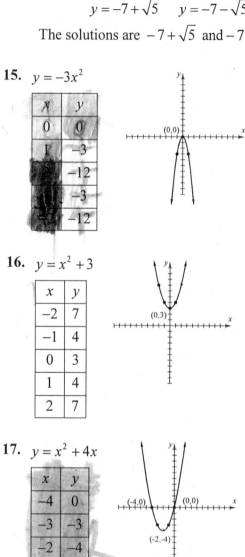

18. $y = x^2 + 2x - 3$

x	y
-3	0
-2	-3
-1	-4
0	-3
1	0

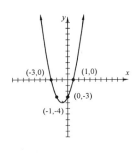

(-3,0)   (1,0)   (0,-3)   (-1,-4)

Practice Problems 16.1

1. $\qquad x^2 - 25 = 0$

$(x+5)(x-5) = 0$

$\qquad x + 5 = 0 \quad \text{or} \quad x - 5 = 0$

$\qquad\qquad x = -5 \qquad\qquad x = 5$

The solutions are -5 and 5

2. $\qquad 2x^2 - 3x = 9$

$\qquad 2x^2 - 3x - 9 = 0$

$(2x+3)(x-3) = 0$

$\qquad\qquad 2x + 3 = 0 \quad \text{or} \quad x - 3 = 0$

$\qquad\qquad\qquad x = -\dfrac{3}{2} \qquad\qquad x = 3$

The solutions are $-\dfrac{3}{2}$ and 3.

3. $x^2 - 16 = 0$

$\qquad x^2 = 16$

$\qquad x = \sqrt{16} = 4 \quad \text{or} \quad x = -\sqrt{16} = -4$

The solutions are -4 and 4.

4. $3x^2 = 11$

$\qquad x^2 = \dfrac{11}{3}$

$\qquad x = \sqrt{\dfrac{11}{3}} \quad \text{or} \quad x = -\sqrt{\dfrac{11}{3}}$

$\qquad x = \sqrt{\dfrac{11}{3}} \cdot \dfrac{\sqrt{3}}{\sqrt{3}} \qquad x = -\sqrt{\dfrac{11}{3}} \cdot \dfrac{\sqrt{3}}{\sqrt{3}}$

$\qquad x = \dfrac{\sqrt{33}}{3} \qquad\qquad x = -\dfrac{\sqrt{33}}{3}$

The solutions are $\dfrac{\sqrt{33}}{3}$ and $-\dfrac{\sqrt{33}}{3}$.

5. $(x-4)^2 = 49$

$\qquad x - 4 = \sqrt{49} \quad \text{or} \quad x - 4 = -\sqrt{49}$

$\qquad x - 4 = 7 \qquad\qquad x - 4 = -7$

$\qquad\qquad x = 4 + 7 = 11 \qquad x = 4 - 7 = -3$

The solutions are -3 and 11.

6. $(x-5)^2 = 18$

$\qquad x - 5 = \sqrt{18} \quad \text{or} \quad x - 5 = -\sqrt{18}$

$\qquad x - 5 = 3\sqrt{2} \qquad\qquad x - 5 = -3\sqrt{2}$

$\qquad\qquad x = 5 + 3\sqrt{2} \qquad x = -5 + 3\sqrt{2}$

The solutions are $-5 \pm 3\sqrt{2}$.

7. $(x+3)^2 = -5$

This equation has no real solution because $\sqrt{-5}$ is not a real number.

8. $(4x+1)^2 = 15$

$\qquad 4x+1 = \sqrt{15} \quad$ or $\quad 4x+1 = -\sqrt{15}$

$\qquad\qquad 4x = -1+\sqrt{15} \qquad 4x = -1-\sqrt{15}$

$\qquad\qquad x = \dfrac{-1+\sqrt{15}}{4} \qquad x = \dfrac{-1-\sqrt{15}}{4}$

The solutions are $\dfrac{-1\pm\sqrt{15}}{4}$.

Exercise Set 16.1

1. $\qquad k^2 - 9 = 0$

$\qquad (k+3)(k-3) = 0$

$\qquad\qquad k+3 = 0 \quad$ or $\quad k-3 = 0$

$\qquad\qquad k = -3 \qquad\qquad k = 3$

The solutions are -3 and 3.

3. $\qquad m^2 + 2m = 15$

$\qquad m^2 + 2m - 15 = 0$

$\qquad (m+5)(m-3) = 0$

$\qquad\qquad m+5 = 0 \quad$ or $\quad m-3 = 0$

$\qquad\qquad m = -5 \qquad\qquad m = 3$

The solutions are -5 and 3.

5. $\qquad 2x^2 - 32 = 0$

$\qquad 2(x^2 - 16) = 0$

$\qquad 2(x+4)(x-4) = 0$

$\qquad\qquad x+4 = 0 \quad$ or $\quad x-4 = 0$

$\qquad\qquad x = -4 \qquad\qquad x = 4$

The solutions are -4 and 4.

7. $\qquad 4a^2 - 36 = 0$

$\qquad 4(a^2 - 9) = 0$

$\qquad 4(a+3)(a-3) = 0$

$\qquad\qquad a+3 = 0 \quad$ or $\quad a-3 = 0$

$\qquad\qquad a = -3 \qquad\qquad a = 3$

The solutions are -3 and 3.

9. $\qquad x^2 + 7x = -10$

$\qquad x^2 + 7x + 10 = 0$

$\qquad (x+5)(x+2) = 0$

$\qquad\qquad x+5 = 0 \quad$ or $\quad x+2 = 0$

$\qquad\qquad x = -5 \qquad\qquad x = -2$

The solutions are -5 and -2.

11. $x^2 = 64$

$\qquad x = \sqrt{64} = 8 \quad$ or $\quad x = -\sqrt{64} = -8$

The solutions are ± 8.

13. $x^2 = 21$

$\qquad x = \sqrt{21} \quad$ or $\quad x = -\sqrt{21}$

The solutions are $\pm\sqrt{21}$.

15. $x^2 = \dfrac{1}{25}$

$\qquad x = \sqrt{\dfrac{1}{25}} = \dfrac{1}{5} \quad$ or $\quad x = -\sqrt{\dfrac{1}{25}} = -\dfrac{1}{5}$

The solutions are $\pm\dfrac{1}{5}$.

17. $x^2 = -4$

This equation has no real solution because $\sqrt{-4}$ is not a real number.

19. $3x^2 = 13$

$$x^2 = \frac{13}{3}$$

$$x = \sqrt{\frac{13}{3}} \quad \text{or} \quad x = -\sqrt{\frac{13}{3}}$$

$$x = \sqrt{\frac{13}{3}} \cdot \frac{\sqrt{3}}{\sqrt{3}} \qquad x = -\sqrt{\frac{13}{3}} \cdot \frac{\sqrt{3}}{\sqrt{3}}$$

$$x = \frac{\sqrt{39}}{3} \qquad\qquad x = -\frac{\sqrt{39}}{3}$$

The solutions are $\pm \dfrac{\sqrt{39}}{3}$.

21. $7x^2 = 4$

$$x^2 = \frac{4}{7}$$

$$x = \sqrt{\frac{4}{7}} \quad \text{or} \quad x = -\sqrt{\frac{4}{7}}$$

$$x = \frac{2}{\sqrt{7}} \cdot \frac{\sqrt{7}}{\sqrt{7}} \qquad x = -\frac{2}{\sqrt{7}} \cdot \frac{\sqrt{7}}{\sqrt{7}}$$

$$x = \frac{2\sqrt{7}}{7} \qquad\qquad x = -\frac{2\sqrt{7}}{7}$$

The solutions are $\pm \dfrac{2\sqrt{7}}{7}$.

23. $x^2 - 2 = 0$

$$x^2 = 2$$

$$x = \sqrt{2} \quad \text{or} \quad x = -\sqrt{2}$$

The solutions are $\pm \sqrt{2}$.

25. Answers may vary.

27. $(x-5)^2 = 49$

$$x - 5 = \sqrt{49} \quad \text{or} \quad x - 5 = -\sqrt{49}$$

$$x - 5 = 7 \qquad\qquad x - 5 = -7$$

$$x = 5 + 7 = 12 \qquad x = 5 - 7 = -2$$

The solutions are -2 and 12.

29. $(x+2)^2 = 7$

$$x + 2 = \sqrt{7} \quad \text{or} \quad x + 2 = -\sqrt{7}$$

$$x = -2 + \sqrt{7} \qquad\quad x = -2 - \sqrt{7}$$

The solutions are $-2 \pm \sqrt{7}$.

31. $\left(m - \dfrac{1}{2}\right)^2 = \dfrac{1}{4}$

$$m - \frac{1}{2} = \sqrt{\frac{1}{4}} \quad \text{or} \quad m - \frac{1}{2} = -\sqrt{\frac{1}{4}}$$

$$m - \frac{1}{2} = \frac{1}{2} \qquad\qquad m - \frac{1}{2} = -\frac{1}{2}$$

$$m = \frac{1}{2} + \frac{1}{2} = 1 \qquad m = \frac{1}{2} - \frac{1}{2} = 0$$

The solutions are 0 and 1.

33. $(p+2)^2 = 10$

$$p + 2 = \sqrt{10} \quad \text{or} \quad p + 2 = -\sqrt{10}$$

$$p = -2 + \sqrt{10} \qquad p = -2 - \sqrt{10}$$

The solutions are $-2 \pm \sqrt{10}$.

35. $(3y+2)^2 = 100$

$$3y+2 = \sqrt{100} \quad \text{or} \quad 3y+2 = -\sqrt{100}$$
$$3y+2 = 10 \qquad\qquad 3y+2 = -10$$
$$3y = -2+10 \qquad\qquad 3y = -2-10$$
$$y = \frac{-2+10}{3} \qquad y = \frac{-2-10}{3}$$
$$y = \frac{8}{3} \qquad\qquad y = -4$$

The solutions are -4 and $\dfrac{8}{3}$.

37. $(z-4)^2 = -9$

This equation has no real solution because $\sqrt{-9}$ is not a real number.

39. $(2x-11)^2 = 50$

$$2x-11 = \sqrt{50} \quad \text{or} \quad 2x-11 = -\sqrt{50}$$
$$2x-11 = 5\sqrt{2} \qquad\qquad 2x-11 = -5\sqrt{2}$$
$$2x = 11+5\sqrt{2} \qquad\qquad 2x = 11-5\sqrt{2}$$
$$x = \frac{11+5\sqrt{2}}{2} \qquad x = \frac{11-5\sqrt{2}}{2}$$

The solutions are $\dfrac{11\pm5\sqrt{2}}{2}$.

41. $(3x-7)^2 = 32$

$$3x-7 = \sqrt{32} \quad \text{or} \quad 3x-7 = -\sqrt{32}$$
$$3x-7 = 4\sqrt{2} \qquad\qquad 3x-7 = -4\sqrt{2}$$
$$3x = 7+4\sqrt{2} \qquad\qquad 3x = 7-4\sqrt{2}$$
$$x = \frac{7+4\sqrt{2}}{3} \qquad x = \frac{7-4\sqrt{2}}{3}$$

The solutions are $\dfrac{7\pm4\sqrt{2}}{3}$.

43. Let $h = 87.6$

$$h = 16t^2$$
$$87.6 = 16t^2$$
$$\frac{87.6}{16} = t^2$$
$$5.475 = t^2$$
$$\sqrt{5.475} = t \quad \text{or} \quad -\sqrt{5.475} = t$$
$$2.3 \approx t \qquad\qquad -2.3 \approx t$$

The length of the dive is not a negative number so the dive lasted approximately 2.3 seconds.

45. $16 \text{ mi} = 16 \text{ mi} \cdot \dfrac{5280 \text{ ft}}{1 \text{ mi}} = 84,480 \text{ ft}$

Let $h = 84,480$

$$h = 16t^2$$
$$84,480 = 16t^2$$
$$\frac{84,480}{16} = t^2$$
$$5280 = t^2$$
$$\sqrt{5280} = t \quad \text{or} \quad -\sqrt{5280} = t$$
$$72.7 \approx t \qquad\qquad -72.7 \approx t$$

The length of the fall is not a negative number so the fall lasted approximately 72.7 seconds.

47. Let $A = 20$

$$A = s^2$$
$$20 = s^2$$
$$\sqrt{20} = s \quad \text{or} \quad -\sqrt{20} = s$$
$$4.47 \approx s \qquad\qquad -4.47 \approx s$$

The length of a side is not a negative number so the length is approximately 4.47 inches.

49. Let $A = 20$

$$A = s^2$$

$$3039 = s^2$$

$$\sqrt{3039} = s \quad \text{or} \quad -\sqrt{3039} = s$$

$$55.13 \approx s \qquad\qquad -55.13 \approx s$$

The length of a side is not a negative number so the length is approximately 55.13 feet.

51. $x^2 + 6x + 9 = (x)^2 + 2(3)x + (3)^2$

$$= (x+3)^2$$

53. $x^2 - 4x + 4 = (x)^2 - 2(2)x + (2)^2$

$$= (x-2)^2$$

55. $x^2 + 4x + 4 = 16$

$$(x+2)^2 = 16$$

$$x+2 = \sqrt{16} \quad \text{or} \quad x+2 = -\sqrt{16}$$

$$x+2 = 4 \qquad\qquad x+2 = -4$$

$$x = 2 \qquad\qquad\quad x = -6$$

The solutions are -6 and 2

57. Let $A = 36\pi$

$$A = \pi r^2$$

$$36\pi = \pi r^2$$

$$36 = r^2$$

$$\sqrt{36} = r \quad \text{or} \quad -\sqrt{36} = r$$

$$6 = r \qquad\qquad -6 = r$$

The radius of a circle is not a negative number so the radius is 6 inches.

59. Let $d = 400$

$$d = 16t^2$$

$$400 = 16t^2$$

$$\frac{400}{16} = t^2$$

$$25 = t^2$$

$$\sqrt{25} = t \quad \text{or} \quad -\sqrt{25} = t$$

$$5 = t \qquad\qquad -5 = t$$

The length of time is not a negative number so the fall lasted 5 seconds.

61. $(x - 1.37)^2 = 5.71$

$$x - 1.37 = \sqrt{5.71} \quad \text{or} \quad x - 1.37 = -\sqrt{5.71}$$

$$x - 1.37 = 2.39 \qquad\qquad x - 1.37 = -2.39$$

$$x = 3.76 \qquad\qquad\qquad x = -1.02$$

63.

$$y = 1944(x - 0.914)^2 + 19{,}143$$

$$30{,}000 = 1944(x - 0.914)^2 + 19{,}143$$

$$30{,}000 - 19{,}143 = 1944(x - 0.914)^2$$

$$10{,}857 = 1944(x - 0.914)^2$$

$$\frac{10{,}857}{1944} = (x - 0.914)^2$$

$$\sqrt{\frac{10{,}857}{1944}} = \sqrt{(x - 0.914)^2}$$

$$2.36 \approx x - 0.914$$

$$2.36 + 0.914 = x$$

$$3 \approx x$$

$$2001 + x = 2001 + 3 = 2004$$

In 2004 there will be 30,000 thousand metric tons.

Practice Problems 16.2

1. $x^2 + 8x + 1 = 0$

$$x^2 + 8x = -1$$
$$x^2 + 8x + 16 = -1 + 16$$
$$(x+4)^2 = 15$$
$$x + 4 = \pm\sqrt{15}$$
$$x = -4 \pm \sqrt{15}$$

The solutions are $-4 \pm \sqrt{15}$.

2. $x^2 - 14x = -32$

$$x^2 - 14x + 49 = -32 + 49$$
$$(x-7)^2 = 17$$
$$x - 7 = \pm\sqrt{17}$$
$$x = 7 \pm \sqrt{17}$$

The solutions are $7 \pm \sqrt{17}$.

3. $4x^2 - 16x - 9 = 0$

$$4x^2 - 16x = 9$$
$$x^2 - 4x = \frac{9}{4}$$
$$x^2 - 4x + 4 = \frac{9}{4} + 4$$
$$(x-2)^2 = \frac{25}{4}$$
$$x - 2 = \pm\sqrt{\frac{25}{4}}$$
$$x = 2 + \frac{5}{2} \quad \text{or} \quad x = 2 - \frac{5}{2}$$
$$x = \frac{9}{2} \qquad\qquad x = -\frac{1}{2}$$

The solutions are $-\frac{1}{2}$ and $\frac{9}{2}$.

4. $2x^2 + 10x = -13$

$$x^2 + 5x = -\frac{13}{2}$$
$$x^2 + 5x + \frac{25}{4} = -\frac{13}{2} + \frac{25}{4}$$
$$(x+5)^2 = -\frac{1}{4}$$

This equation has no real solution because $\sqrt{-\frac{1}{4}}$ is not a real number.

5. $2x^2 = -3x + 2$

$$x^2 = -\frac{3}{2}x + 1$$
$$x^2 + \frac{3}{2}x = 1$$
$$x^2 + \frac{3}{2}x + \frac{9}{16} = 1 + \frac{9}{16}$$
$$\left(x + \frac{3}{4}\right)^2 = \frac{25}{16}$$
$$x + \frac{3}{4} = \pm\sqrt{\frac{25}{16}}$$
$$x = -\frac{3}{4} \pm \frac{5}{4}$$
$$x = -\frac{3}{4} + \frac{5}{4} \quad \text{or} \quad x = -\frac{3}{4} - \frac{5}{4}$$
$$x = \frac{1}{2} \qquad\qquad x = -2$$

The solutions are -2 and $\frac{1}{2}$.

Mental Math 16.2

1. $p^2 + 8p$

$$\left(\frac{8}{2}\right)^2 = 4^2 = 16$$

2. $p^2 + 6p$

$$\left(\frac{6}{2}\right)^2 = 3^2 = 9$$

3. $x^2 + 20x$

$$\left(\frac{20}{2}\right)^2 = 10^2 = 100$$

4. $x^2 + 18x$

$$\left(\frac{18}{2}\right)^2 = 9^2 = 81$$

5. $y^2 + 14y$

$$\left(\frac{14}{2}\right)^2 = 7^2 = 49$$

6. $y^2 + 2y$

$$\left(\frac{2}{2}\right)^2 = 1^2 = 1$$

Exercise Set 16.2

1.
$$x^2 + 8x = -12$$
$$x^2 + 8x + 16 = -12 + 16$$
$$(x+4)^2 = 4$$
$$x + 4 = \pm\sqrt{4}$$
$$x = -4 \pm 2$$
$$x = -4 + 2 \quad \text{or} \quad x = -4 - 2$$
$$x = -2 \qquad\qquad x = -6$$

The solutions are -6 and -2.

3.
$$x^2 + 2x - 5 = 0$$
$$x^2 + 2x = 5$$
$$x^2 + 2x + 1 = 5 + 1$$
$$(x+1)^2 = 6$$
$$x + 1 = \pm\sqrt{6}$$
$$x = -1 \pm \sqrt{6}$$

The solutions are $-1 \pm \sqrt{6}$.

5.
$$x^2 - 6x = 0$$
$$x^2 - 6x + 9 = 0 + 9$$
$$(x-3)^2 = 9$$
$$x - 3 = \pm\sqrt{9}$$
$$x = 3 \pm 3$$
$$x = 3 + 3 \quad \text{or} \quad x = 3 - 3$$
$$x = 6 \qquad\qquad x = 0$$

The solutions are 0 and 6.

7. $z^2 + 5z = 7$

$$z^2 + 5z + \frac{25}{4} = 7 + \frac{25}{4}$$

$$\left(z + \frac{5}{2}\right)^2 = \frac{53}{4}$$

$$z + \frac{5}{2} = \pm\sqrt{\frac{53}{4}}$$

$$z = -\frac{5}{2} \pm \frac{\sqrt{53}}{2}$$

$$z = \frac{-5 \pm \sqrt{53}}{2}$$

The solutions are $\dfrac{-5 \pm \sqrt{53}}{2}$.

9. $x^2 - 2x - 1 = 0$

$$x^2 - 2x = 1$$

$$x^2 - 2x + 1 = 1 + 1$$

$$(x - 1)^2 = 2$$

$$x - 1 = \pm\sqrt{2}$$

$$x = 1 \pm \sqrt{2}$$

The solutions are $1 \pm \sqrt{2}$.

11. $y^2 + 5y + 4 = 0$

$$y^2 + 5y = -4$$

$$y^2 + 5y + \frac{25}{4} = -4 + \frac{25}{4}$$

$$\left(y + \frac{5}{2}\right)^2 = \frac{9}{4}$$

$$y + \frac{5}{2} = \pm\sqrt{\frac{9}{4}}$$

$$y = -\frac{5}{2} \pm \frac{3}{2}$$

$$y = -\frac{5}{2} + \frac{3}{2} \quad \text{or} \quad y = -\frac{5}{2} - \frac{3}{2}$$

$$y = -1 \qquad\qquad y = -4$$

The solutions are -4 and -1.

13. $x^2 + 6x - 25 = 0$

$$x^2 + 6x = 25$$

$$x^2 + 6x + 9 = 25 + 9$$

$$(x + 3)^2 = 34$$

$$x + 3 = \pm\sqrt{34}$$

$$x = -3 \pm \sqrt{34}$$

The solutions are $-3 \pm \sqrt{34}$.

15. $x^2 - 3x - 3 = 0$

$$x^2 - 3x = 3$$

$$x^2 - 3x + \frac{9}{4} = 3 + \frac{9}{4}$$

$$\left(x - \frac{3}{2}\right)^2 = \frac{21}{4}$$

$$x - \frac{3}{2} = \pm\sqrt{\frac{21}{4}}$$

$$x = \frac{3}{2} \pm \frac{\sqrt{21}}{2}$$

$$x = \frac{3 \pm \sqrt{21}}{2}$$

The solutions are $\dfrac{3 \pm \sqrt{21}}{2}$.

17.
$$x(x+3) = 18$$
$$x^2 + 3x = 18$$
$$x^2 + 3x + \frac{9}{4} = 18 + \frac{9}{4}$$
$$\left(x + \frac{3}{2}\right)^2 = \frac{81}{4}$$
$$x + \frac{3}{2} = \pm\sqrt{\frac{81}{4}}$$
$$x = -\frac{3}{2} \pm \frac{9}{2}$$
$$x = -\frac{3}{2} + \frac{9}{2} \quad \text{or} \quad x = -\frac{3}{2} - \frac{9}{2}$$
$$x = 3 \qquad\qquad x = -6$$

The solutions are -6 and 3.

19.
$$3x^2 - 6x = 24$$
$$x^2 - 2x = 8$$
$$x^2 - 2x + 1 = 8 + 1$$
$$(x-1)^2 = 9$$
$$x - 1 = \pm\sqrt{9}$$
$$x = 1 \pm 3$$
$$x = 1 + 3 \quad \text{or} \quad x = 1 - 3$$
$$x = 4 \qquad\qquad x = -2$$

The solutions are -2 and 4.

21. $5x^2 + 10x + 6 = 0$
$$5x^2 + 10x = -6$$
$$x^2 + 2x = -\frac{6}{5}$$
$$x^2 + 2x + 1 = -\frac{6}{5} + 1$$
$$(x+1)^2 = -\frac{1}{5}$$

This equation has no real solution

because $\sqrt{-\dfrac{1}{5}}$ is not a real number.

23.
$$2x^2 = 6x + 5$$
$$2x^2 - 6x = 5$$
$$x^2 - 3x = \frac{5}{2}$$
$$x^2 - 3x + \frac{9}{4} = \frac{5}{2} + \frac{9}{4}$$
$$\left(x - \frac{3}{2}\right)^2 = \frac{19}{4}$$
$$x - \frac{3}{2} = \pm\sqrt{\frac{19}{4}}$$

$$x = \frac{3}{2} \pm \frac{\sqrt{19}}{2}$$

The solutions are $\dfrac{3 \pm \sqrt{19}}{2}$.

25. $2y^2 + 8y + 5 = 0$
$$2y^2 + 8y = -5$$
$$y^2 + 4y = -\frac{5}{2}$$
$$y^2 + 4y + 4 = -\frac{5}{2} + 4$$

$$\left(y+2\right)^{2}=\frac{3}{2}$$

$$y+2=\pm\sqrt{\frac{3}{2}}$$

$$y=-2\pm\sqrt{\frac{3}{2}}$$

$$y=-2\pm\sqrt{\frac{3}{2}}\cdot\sqrt{\frac{2}{2}}$$

$$y=-2\pm\frac{\sqrt{6}}{2}$$

The solutions are $-2\pm\dfrac{\sqrt{6}}{2}$.

27. $2y^{2}-3y+1=0$

$$2y^{2}-3y=-1$$

$$y^{2}-\frac{3}{2}y=-\frac{1}{2}$$

$$y^{2}-\frac{3}{2}y+\frac{9}{16}=-\frac{1}{2}+\frac{9}{16}$$

$$\left(y-\frac{3}{4}\right)^{2}=\frac{1}{16}$$

$$y-\frac{3}{4}=\pm\sqrt{\frac{1}{16}}$$

$$y=\frac{3}{4}\pm\frac{1}{4}$$

$$y=\frac{3}{4}+\frac{1}{4}\quad\text{or}\quad y=\frac{3}{4}-\frac{1}{4}$$

$$y=1\qquad\qquad y=\frac{1}{2}$$

The solutions are $\dfrac{1}{2}$ and 1.

29. Answers may vary.

31. $\dfrac{3}{4}-\sqrt{\dfrac{25}{16}}=\dfrac{3}{4}-\dfrac{5}{4}=-\dfrac{2}{4}=-\dfrac{1}{2}$

33. $\dfrac{1}{2}-\sqrt{\dfrac{9}{4}}=\dfrac{1}{2}-\dfrac{3}{2}=-\dfrac{2}{2}=-1$

35. $\dfrac{6+4\sqrt{5}}{2}=\dfrac{2\left(3+2\sqrt{5}\right)}{2}=3+2\sqrt{5}$

37. $\dfrac{3-9\sqrt{2}}{6}=\dfrac{3\left(1-3\sqrt{2}\right)}{3\cdot2}=\dfrac{1-3\sqrt{2}}{2}$

39. $x^{2}+kx+16$

$$\left(\frac{k}{2}\right)^{2}=16$$

$$\frac{k^{2}}{4}=16$$

$$k^{2}=64$$

$$k=\pm\sqrt{64}$$

$$k=\pm8$$

41.

$$y = -195x^2 + 602x + 15{,}375$$
$$12{,}500 = -195x^2 + 602x + 15{,}375$$
$$195x^2 - 602x = 15{,}375 - 12{,}500$$
$$\frac{195x^2}{195} - \frac{602x}{195} = \frac{2875}{195}$$
$$x^2 - 3.09x = 14.74$$
$$x^2 - 3.09x + 2.39 = 14.74 + 2.39$$
$$\frac{(x-1.55)^2}{\sqrt{(x-1.55)^2}} = \frac{17.13}{\sqrt{17.13}}$$
$$x - 1.55 = 4.14$$
$$x = 4.14 + 1.55$$
$$x \approx 6$$

$2000 + x = 2000 + 6 = 2006$

In 2006 the retail sales for U.S. bookstores will be 12,500 million.

43. $x^2 + 8x = -12$

$y_1 = x^2 + 8x$

$y_2 = -12$

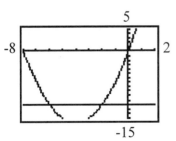

The *x*-coordinates of the intersections, -6 and -2, are the solutions.

45. $2x^2 = 6x + 5$

$y_1 = 2x^2$

$y_2 = 6x + 5$

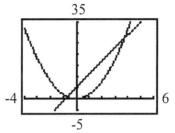

The *x*-coordinates of the intersections, -0.68 and 3.68, are the solutions.

Practice Problems 16.3

1.

$$2x^2 - x - 5 = 0$$
$$a = 2, b = -1, \text{ and } c = -5$$
$$x = \frac{-b \pm \sqrt{b^2 - 4ac}}{2a}$$
$$x = \frac{-(-1) \pm \sqrt{(-1)^2 - 4(2)(-5)}}{2(2)}$$
$$= \frac{1 \pm \sqrt{1 + 40}}{4} = \frac{1 \pm \sqrt{41}}{4}$$

The solutions are $\dfrac{1 \pm \sqrt{41}}{4}$.

2. $3x^2 + 8x = 3$

$3x^2 + 8x - 3 = 0$

$a = 3, b = 8,$ and $c = -3$

$$x = \frac{-b \pm \sqrt{b^2 - 4ac}}{2a}$$

$$x = \frac{-(8) \pm \sqrt{(8)^2 - 4(3)(-3)}}{2(3)}$$

$$x = \frac{-8 \pm \sqrt{64 + 36}}{6}$$

$$x = \frac{-8 \pm \sqrt{100}}{6}$$

$$x = \frac{-8 \pm 10}{6}$$

$$x = \frac{-8 + 10}{6} = \frac{1}{3} \quad \text{or} \quad x = \frac{-8 - 10}{6} = -3$$

The solutions are -3 and $\dfrac{1}{3}$.

3. $5x^2 = 2$

$5x^2 - 2 = 0$

$a = 5, b = 0,$ and $c = -2$

$$x = \frac{-b \pm \sqrt{b^2 - 4ac}}{2a}$$

$$x = \frac{-(0) \pm \sqrt{(0)^2 - 4(5)(-2)}}{2(5)}$$

$$= \frac{\pm \sqrt{40}}{10} = \frac{\pm 2\sqrt{10}}{10} = \pm \frac{\sqrt{10}}{5}$$

The solutions are $\pm \dfrac{\sqrt{10}}{5}$.

4. $x^2 = -2x - 3$

$x^2 + 2x + 3 = 0$

$a = 1, b = 2,$ and $c = 3$

$$x = \frac{-b \pm \sqrt{b^2 - 4ac}}{2a}$$

$$x = \frac{-(2) \pm \sqrt{(2)^2 - 4(1)(3)}}{2(1)}$$

$$x = \frac{-2 \pm \sqrt{-8}}{2}$$

This equation has no real solution because $\sqrt{-8}$ is not a real number.

5. $\dfrac{1}{3}x^2 - x = 1$

$\dfrac{1}{3}x^2 - x - 1 = 0$

$x^2 - 3x - 3 = 0$

$a = 1, b = -3,$ and $c = -3$

$$x = \frac{-b \pm \sqrt{b^2 - 4ac}}{2a}$$

$$x = \frac{-(-3) \pm \sqrt{(-3)^2 - 4(1)(-3)}}{2(1)}$$

$$= \frac{3 \pm \sqrt{9 + 12}}{2} = \frac{3 \pm \sqrt{21}}{2}$$

The solutions are $\dfrac{3 \pm \sqrt{21}}{2}$.

Mental Math 16.3

1. $2x^2 + 5x + 3 = 0$

    $a = 2,\ b = 5,\ c = 3$

2. $5x^2 - 7x + 1 = 0$

    $a = 5,\ b = -7,\ c = 1$

3. $10x^2 - 13x - 2 = 0$

    $a = 10,\ b = -13,\ c = -2$

4. $x^2 + 3x - 7 = 0$

    $a = 1,\ b = 3,\ c = -7$

5. $x^2 - 6 = 0$

    $a = 1,\ b = 0,\ c = -6$

6. $9x^2 - 4 = 0$

    $a = 9,\ b = 0,\ c = -4$

Exercise Set 16.3

1. $x^2 - 3x + 2 = 0$

    $a = 1, b = -3,$ and $c = 2$

$$x = \frac{-b \pm \sqrt{b^2 - 4ac}}{2a}$$

$$x = \frac{-(-3) \pm \sqrt{(-3)^2 - 4(1)(2)}}{2(1)}$$

$$= \frac{3 \pm \sqrt{9 - 8}}{2} = \frac{3 \pm \sqrt{1}}{2} = \frac{3 \pm 1}{2}$$

$$x = \frac{3+1}{2} = 2 \quad \text{or} \quad x = \frac{3-1}{2} = 1$$

The solutions are 1 and 2.

3. $3k^2 + 7k + 1 = 0$

    $a = 3, b = 7,$ and $c = 1$

$$k = \frac{-b \pm \sqrt{b^2 - 4ac}}{2a}$$

$$k = \frac{-(7) \pm \sqrt{(7)^2 - 4(3)(1)}}{2(3)}$$

$$= \frac{-7 \pm \sqrt{49 - 12}}{6} = \frac{-7 \pm \sqrt{37}}{6}$$

The solutions are $\dfrac{-7 \pm \sqrt{37}}{6}$.

5. $49x^2 - 4 = 0$

    $a = 49, b = 0,$ and $c = -4$

$$x = \frac{-b \pm \sqrt{b^2 - 4ac}}{2a}$$

$$x = \frac{-(0) \pm \sqrt{(0)^2 - 4(49)(-4)}}{2(49)}$$

$$= \frac{\pm\sqrt{784}}{98} = \frac{\pm 28}{98} = \pm\frac{2}{7}$$

The solutions are $\pm\dfrac{2}{7}$.

7. $5z^2 - 4z + 3 = 0$

    $a = 5, b = -4,$ and $c = 3$

$$z = \frac{-(-4) \pm \sqrt{(-4)^2 - 4(5)(3)}}{2(5)}$$

$$= \frac{4 \pm \sqrt{16 - 60}}{10} = \frac{4 \pm \sqrt{-44}}{10}$$

There is no real solution because $\sqrt{-44}$ is not a real number.

9. $y^2 = 7y + 30$

$y^2 - 7y - 30 = 0$

$a = 1, b = -7, $ and $c = -30$

$$y = \frac{-(-7) \pm \sqrt{(-7)^2 - 4(1)(-30)}}{2(1)}$$

$$= \frac{7 \pm \sqrt{49 + 120}}{2} = \frac{7 \pm \sqrt{169}}{2}$$

$$= \frac{7 \pm 13}{2}$$

$$y = \frac{7 + 13}{2} = 10 \quad \text{or} \quad y = \frac{7 - 13}{2} = -3$$

The solutions are -3 and 10.

11. $2x^2 = 10$

$2x^2 - 10 = 0$

$a = 2, b = 0, $ and $c = -10$

$$x = \frac{-(0) \pm \sqrt{(0)^2 - 4(2)(-10)}}{2(2)}$$

$$= \frac{\pm\sqrt{80}}{4} = \frac{\pm 4\sqrt{5}}{4} = \pm\sqrt{5}$$

The solutions are $\pm\sqrt{5}$.

13. $m^2 - 12 = m$

$m^2 - m - 12 = 0$

$a = 1, b = -1, $ and $c = -12$

$$m = \frac{-(-1) \pm \sqrt{(-1)^2 - 4(1)(-12)}}{2(1)}$$

$$= \frac{1 \pm \sqrt{1 + 48}}{2} = \frac{1 \pm \sqrt{49}}{2} = \frac{1 \pm 7}{2}$$

$$m = \frac{1 + 7}{2} = 4 \quad \text{or} \quad m = \frac{1 - 7}{2} = -3$$

The solutions are -3 and 4.

15. $3 - x^2 = 4x$

$-x^2 - 4x + 3 = 0$

$a = -1, b = -4, $ and $c = 3$

$$x = \frac{-(-4) \pm \sqrt{(-4)^2 - 4(-1)(3)}}{2(-1)}$$

$$= \frac{4 \pm \sqrt{16 + 12}}{-2} = \frac{4 \pm \sqrt{28}}{-2}$$

$$= \frac{4 \pm 2\sqrt{7}}{-2} = -2 \pm \sqrt{7}$$

The solutions are $-2 \pm \sqrt{7}$.

17. $6x^2 + 9x = 2$

$6x^2 + 9x - 2 = 0$

$a = 6, b = 9, $ and $c = -2$

$$x = \frac{-(9) \pm \sqrt{(9)^2 - 4(6)(-2)}}{2(6)}$$

$$= \frac{-9 \pm \sqrt{81 + 48}}{12} = \frac{-9 \pm \sqrt{129}}{12}$$

The solutions are $\dfrac{-9 \pm \sqrt{129}}{12}$.

19. $7p^2 + 2 = 8p$

$7p^2 - 8p + 2 = 0$

$a = 7, b = -8, $ and $c = 2$

$$p = \frac{-(-8) \pm \sqrt{(-8)^2 - 4(7)(2)}}{2(7)}$$

$$= \frac{8 \pm \sqrt{64 - 56}}{14} = \frac{8 \pm \sqrt{8}}{14}$$

$$= \frac{8 \pm 2\sqrt{2}}{14} = \frac{4 \pm \sqrt{2}}{7}$$

The solutions are $\dfrac{4 \pm \sqrt{2}}{7}$.

21. $a^2 - 6a + 2 = 0$

$a = 1, b = -6,$ and $c = 2$

$$a = \frac{-(-6) \pm \sqrt{(-6)^2 - 4(1)(2)}}{2(1)}$$

$$= \frac{6 \pm \sqrt{36 - 8}}{2} = \frac{6 \pm \sqrt{28}}{2}$$

$$= \frac{6 \pm 2\sqrt{7}}{2} = 3 \pm \sqrt{7}$$

The solutions are $3 \pm \sqrt{7}$.

23. $2x^2 - 6x + 3 = 0$

$a = 2, b = -6,$ and $c = 3$

$$x = \frac{-(-6) \pm \sqrt{(-6)^2 - 4(2)(3)}}{2(2)}$$

$$= \frac{6 \pm \sqrt{36 - 24}}{4} = \frac{6 \pm \sqrt{12}}{4}$$

$$= \frac{6 \pm 2\sqrt{3}}{4} = \frac{3 \pm \sqrt{3}}{2}$$

The solutions are $\dfrac{3 \pm \sqrt{3}}{2}$.

25. $3x^2 = 1 - 2x$

$3x^2 + 2x - 1 = 0$

$a = 3, b = 2,$ and $c = -1$

$$x = \frac{-(2) \pm \sqrt{(2)^2 - 4(3)(-1)}}{2(3)}$$

$$= \frac{-2 \pm \sqrt{4 + 12}}{6} = \frac{-2 \pm \sqrt{16}}{6} = \frac{-2 \pm 4}{6}$$

$$x = \frac{-2 + 4}{6} = \frac{1}{3} \quad \text{or} \quad x = \frac{-2 - 4}{6} = -1$$

The solutions are -1 and $\dfrac{1}{3}$.

27. $4y^2 = 6y + 1$

$4y^2 - 6y - 1 = 0$

$a = 4, b = -6,$ and $c = -1$

$$y = \frac{-(-6) \pm \sqrt{(-6)^2 - 4(4)(-1)}}{2(4)}$$

$$= \frac{6 \pm \sqrt{36 + 16}}{8} = \frac{6 \pm \sqrt{52}}{8}$$

$$= \frac{6 \pm 2\sqrt{13}}{8} = \frac{3 \pm \sqrt{13}}{4}$$

The solutions are $\dfrac{3 \pm \sqrt{13}}{4}$.

29. $20y^2 = 3 - 11y$

$20y^2 + 11y - 3 = 0$

$a = 20, b = 11,$ and $c = -3$

$$y = \frac{-(11) \pm \sqrt{(11)^2 - 4(20)(-3)}}{2(20)}$$

$$= \frac{-11 \pm \sqrt{121 + 240}}{40} = \frac{-11 \pm \sqrt{361}}{40}$$

$$= \frac{-11 \pm 19}{40}$$

$$y = \frac{-11 + 19}{40} = \frac{1}{5} \quad \text{or} \quad y = \frac{-11 - 19}{40} = -\frac{3}{4}$$

The solutions are $-\dfrac{3}{4}$ and $\dfrac{1}{5}$.

31. $x^2 + x + 2 = 0$

$a = 1, b = 1,$ and $c = 2$

$$x = \frac{-(1) \pm \sqrt{(1)^2 - 4(1)(2)}}{2(1)}$$

$$= \frac{-1 \pm \sqrt{1 - 8}}{2} = \frac{-1 \pm \sqrt{-7}}{2}$$

There is no real solution because $\sqrt{-7}$ is not a real number.

33. $3p^2 - \frac{2}{3}p + 1 = 0$

$9p^2 - 2p + 3 = 0$

$a = 9, b = -2,$ and $c = 3$

$$p = \frac{-(-2) \pm \sqrt{(-2)^2 - 4(9)(3)}}{2(9)}$$

$$= \frac{2 \pm \sqrt{4 - 108}}{18} = \frac{2 \pm \sqrt{-104}}{18}$$

There is no real solution because $\sqrt{-104}$ is not a real number.

35. $\frac{m^2}{2} = m + \frac{1}{2}$

$m^2 = 2m + 1$

$m^2 - 2m - 1 = 0$

$a = 1, b = -2,$ and $c = -1$

$$m = \frac{-(-2) \pm \sqrt{(-2)^2 - 4(1)(-1)}}{2(1)}$$

$$= \frac{2 \pm \sqrt{4 + 4}}{2} = \frac{2 \pm \sqrt{8}}{2}$$

$$= \frac{2 \pm 2\sqrt{2}}{2} = 1 \pm \sqrt{2}$$

The solutions are $1 \pm \sqrt{2}$.

37. $4p^2 + \frac{3}{2} = -5p$

$8p^2 + 3 = -10p$

$8p^2 + 10p + 3 = 0$

$a = 8, b = 10,$ and $c = 3$

$$p = \frac{-(10) \pm \sqrt{(10)^2 - 4(8)(3)}}{2(8)}$$

$$= \frac{-10 \pm \sqrt{100 - 96}}{16} = \frac{-10 \pm \sqrt{4}}{16}$$

$$= \frac{-10 \pm 2}{16}$$

$p = \frac{-10 + 2}{16} = -\frac{1}{2}$ or $p = \frac{-10 - 2}{16} = -\frac{3}{4}$

The solutions are $-\frac{3}{4}$ and $-\frac{1}{2}$.

39. $5x^2 = \frac{7}{2}x + 1$

$10x^2 = 7x + 2$

$10x^2 - 7x - 2 = 0$

$a = 10, b = -7,$ and $c = -2$

$$x = \frac{-(-7) \pm \sqrt{(-7)^2 - 4(10)(-2)}}{2(10)}$$

$$= \frac{7 \pm \sqrt{49 + 80}}{20} = \frac{7 \pm \sqrt{129}}{20}$$

The solutions are $\frac{7 \pm \sqrt{129}}{20}$.

41. $28x^2 + 5x + \dfrac{11}{4} = 0$

$112x^2 + 20x + 11 = 0$

$a = 112, b = 20,$ and $c = 11$

$p = \dfrac{-(20) \pm \sqrt{(20)^2 - 4(112)(11)}}{2(112)}$

$= \dfrac{-20 \pm \sqrt{400 - 4928}}{224} = \dfrac{-20 \pm \sqrt{-4528}}{224}$

There is no real solution because

$\sqrt{-4528}$ is not a real number.

43. $5z^2 - 2z = \dfrac{1}{5}$

$25z^2 - 10z = 1$

$25z^2 - 10z - 1 = 0$

$a = 25, b = -10,$ and $c = -1$

$x = \dfrac{-(-10) \pm \sqrt{(-10)^2 - 4(25)(-1)}}{2(25)}$

$= \dfrac{10 \pm \sqrt{100 + 100}}{50} = \dfrac{10 \pm \sqrt{200}}{50}$

$= \dfrac{10 \pm 10\sqrt{2}}{50} = \dfrac{1 \pm \sqrt{2}}{5}$

The solutions are $\dfrac{1 \pm \sqrt{2}}{5}$.

45. $y = -3$

for all values of x.

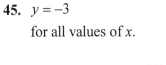
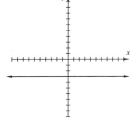

47. $y = 3x - 2$

x	y
3	7
0	-2

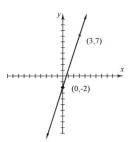

49. $a^2 + b^2 = c^2$

$x^2 + 7^2 = 10^2$

$x^2 + 49 = 100$

$x^2 = 51$

$x = \sqrt{51}$

The length is $\sqrt{51}$ meters

51. Let $x =$ the width then, $x + 5 =$ the length.

$A = lw$

$35 = x(x+5)$

$35 = x^2 + 5x$

$0 = x^2 + 5x - 35$

$a = 1, b = 5, c = -35$

$x = \dfrac{-(5) \pm \sqrt{(5)^2 - 4(1)(-35)}}{2(1)}$

$= \dfrac{-5 \pm \sqrt{25 + 140}}{2} = \dfrac{-5 \pm \sqrt{165}}{2}$

Because the width cannot be negative,

$x = \dfrac{-5 + \sqrt{165}}{2} \approx 3.9$

$x + 5 \approx 3.9 + 5 = 8.9$

Length $= 8.9$ ft., width $= 3.9$ ft.

53. $x^2 + 3\sqrt{2}\,x - 5 = 0$

$a = 1, b = 3\sqrt{2},$ and $c = -5$

$$x = \frac{-\left(3\sqrt{2}\right) \pm \sqrt{\left(3\sqrt{2}\right)^2 - 4(1)(-5)}}{2(1)}$$

$$= \frac{-3\sqrt{2} \pm \sqrt{18 + 20}}{2} = \frac{-3\sqrt{2} \pm \sqrt{38}}{2}$$

The solutions are $\dfrac{-3\sqrt{2} \pm \sqrt{38}}{2}$.

55. Answers may vary.

57. $y^2 - y = 11$

$y^2 - y - 11 = 0$

$a = 1, b = -1,$ and $c = -11$

$$y = \frac{-(-1) \pm \sqrt{(-1)^2 - 4(1)(-11)}}{2(1)}$$

$$= \frac{1 \pm \sqrt{1 + 44}}{2} = \frac{1 \pm \sqrt{45}}{2}$$

$y = \dfrac{1 + \sqrt{45}}{2} \approx 3.9$ or $y = \dfrac{1 - \sqrt{45}}{2} \approx -2.9$

The solutions are -2.9 and 3.9.

59. $7.3z^2 + 5.4z - 1.1 = 0$

$a = 7.3, b = 5.4,$ and $c = -1.1$

$$z = \frac{-(5.4) \pm \sqrt{(5.4)^2 - 4(7.3)(-1.1)}}{2(7.3)}$$

$$= \frac{-5.4 \pm \sqrt{29.16 + 32.12}}{14.6}$$

$$= \frac{-5.4 \pm \sqrt{61.28}}{14.6}$$

$$z = \frac{-5.4 + \sqrt{61.28}}{14.6} \approx 0.2 \quad \text{or}$$

$$z = \frac{-5.4 - \sqrt{61.28}}{14.6} \approx -0.9$$

The solutions are -0.9 and 0.2.

61. Let $h = 0$

$h = -16t^2 + 120t + 80$

$0 = -16t^2 + 120t + 80$

$a = -16, b = 120,$ and $c = 80$

$$t = \frac{-(120) \pm \sqrt{(120)^2 - 4(-16)(80)}}{2(-16)}$$

$$= \frac{-120 \pm \sqrt{14,400 + 5120}}{-32}$$

$$= \frac{-120 \pm \sqrt{19,520}}{-32}$$

Since the time cannot be negative,

$$t = \frac{-120 - \sqrt{19,520}}{-32} \approx 8.1$$

It strikes the ground after 8.1 seconds.

63. Let $y = 3,695,000$

$y = 57,000x^2 - 14,000x + 1,000,000$

$3,695,000 = 57,000x^2 - 14,000x + 1,000,000$

$0 = 57,000x^2 - 14,000x - 2,695,000$

$a = 57,000, b = -14,000,$

and $c = -2,695,000$

$\sqrt{b^2 - 4ac}$

$= \sqrt{(-14,000)^2 - 4(57,000)(-2,695,000)}$

$= 784,000$

$$x = \frac{-(-14,000) \pm 784,000}{2(57,000)}$$

$$= \frac{14,000 \pm 784,000}{114,000}$$

Since time cannot be negative,

$$t = \frac{14,000 + 784,000}{114,000} = 7$$

It will be the year $1998 + 7 = 2005$.

Integrated Review 16.3

1. $5x^2 - 11x + 2 = 0$

$(5x - 1)(x - 2) = 0$

$5x - 1 = 0 \quad \text{or} \quad x - 2 = 0$

$5x = 1 \qquad\qquad x = 2$

$x = \dfrac{1}{5}$

The solutions are $\dfrac{1}{5}$ and 2.

2. $5x^2 + 13x - 6 = 0$

$(5x - 2)(x + 3) = 0$

$5x - 2 = 0 \quad \text{or} \quad x + 3 = 0$

$5x = 2 \qquad\qquad x = -3$

$x = \dfrac{2}{5}$

The solutions are $\dfrac{2}{5}$ and -3.

3. $\quad x^2 - 1 = 2x$

$x^2 - 2x = 1$

$x^2 - 2x + 1 = 1 + 1$

$(x - 1)^2 = 2$

$x - 1 = \pm\sqrt{2}$

$x = 1 \pm \sqrt{2}$

The solutions are $1 \pm \sqrt{2}$.

4. $\quad x^2 + 7 = 6x$

$x^2 - 6x = -7$

$x^2 - 6x + 9 = -7 + 9$

$(x - 3)^2 = 2$

$x - 3 = \pm\sqrt{2}$

$x = 3 \pm \sqrt{2}$

The solutions are $3 \pm \sqrt{2}$.

5. $a^2 = 20$

$a = \pm\sqrt{20}$

$ = \pm 2\sqrt{5}$

The solutions are $\pm 2\sqrt{5}$.

6. $a^2 = 72$

$a = \pm\sqrt{72}$

$ = \pm 6\sqrt{2}$

The solutions are $\pm 6\sqrt{2}$.

7. $\quad x^2 - x + 4 = 0$

$x^2 - x = -4$

$x^2 - x + \dfrac{1}{4} = -4 + \dfrac{1}{4}$

$\left(x - \dfrac{1}{2}\right)^2 = -\dfrac{15}{4}$

There is no real solution.

8. $x^2 - 2x + 7 = 0$

$\quad x^2 - 2x = -7$

$\quad x^2 - 2x + 1 = -7 + 1$

$\quad (x-1)^2 = -6$

There is no real solution.

9. $3x^2 - 12x + 12 = 0$

$\quad x^2 - 4x + 4 = 0$

$\quad (x-2)^2 = 0$

$\quad\quad x - 2 = 0$

$\quad\quad\quad x = 2$

The solution is 2.

10. $5x^2 - 30x + 45 = 0$

$\quad x^2 - 6x + 9 = 0$

$\quad (x-3)^2 = 0$

$\quad\quad x - 3 = 0$

$\quad\quad\quad x = 3$

The solution is 3.

11. $\quad 9 - 6p + p^2 = 0$

$\quad\quad (p-3)^2 = 0$

$\quad\quad\quad p - 3 = 0$

$\quad\quad\quad\quad p = 3$

The solution is 3.

12. $49 - 28p + 4p^2 = 0$

$\quad\quad (2p-7)^2 = 0$

$\quad\quad\quad 2p - 7 = 0$

$\quad\quad\quad\quad 2p = 7$

$\quad\quad\quad\quad p = \dfrac{7}{2}$

The solution is $\dfrac{7}{2}$.

13. $\quad 4y^2 - 16 = 0$

$\quad\quad 4y^2 = 16$

$\quad\quad y^2 = 4$

$\quad\quad y = \pm\sqrt{4}$

$\quad\quad y = \pm 2$

The solutions are ± 2.

14. $\quad 3y^2 - 27 = 0$

$\quad\quad 3y^2 = 27$

$\quad\quad y^2 = 9$

$\quad\quad y = \pm\sqrt{9}$

$\quad\quad y = \pm 3$

The solutions are ± 3.

15. $\quad x^4 - 3x^3 + 2x^2 = 0$

$\quad x^2\left(x^2 - 3x + 2\right) = 0$

$\quad x^2(x-1)(x-2) = 0$

$\quad x^2 = 0 \quad$ or $\quad x-1 = 0 \quad$ or $\quad x-2 = 0$

$\quad\quad x = 0 \quad\quad\quad\quad x = 1 \quad\quad\quad\quad x = 2$

The solutions are 0, 1, and 2.

16. $\quad x^3 + 7x^2 + 12x = 0$

$\quad x\left(x^2 + 7x + 12\right) = 0$

$\quad x(x+4)(x+3) = 0$

$\quad x = 0 \quad$ or $\quad x+4 = 0 \quad$ or $\quad x+3 = 0$

$\quad\quad x = 0 \quad\quad\quad\quad x = -4 \quad\quad\quad\quad x = -3$

The solutions are -4, -3, and 0.

17. $(2z+5)^2 = 25$

$$2z+5 = \pm\sqrt{25}$$

$$2z = -5 \pm 5$$

$$z = \frac{-5 \pm 5}{2}$$

$$z = \frac{-5-5}{2} = -5 \quad \text{or} \quad z = \frac{-5+5}{2} = 0$$

The solutions are 0 and -5.

18. $(3z-4)^2 = 16$

$$3z-4 = \pm\sqrt{16}$$

$$3z = 4 \pm 4$$

$$z = \frac{4 \pm 4}{3}$$

$$z = \frac{4-4}{3} = 0 \quad \text{or} \quad z = \frac{4+4}{3} = \frac{8}{3}$$

The solutions are 0 and $\frac{8}{3}$.

19. $\qquad 30x = 25x^2 + 2$

$$0 = 25x^2 - 30x + 2 = 0$$

$$a = 25, b = -30, \text{ and } c = 2$$

$$x = \frac{-(-30) \pm \sqrt{(-30)^2 - 4(25)(2)}}{2(25)}$$

$$= \frac{30 \pm \sqrt{900 - 200}}{50} = \frac{30 \pm \sqrt{700}}{50}$$

$$= \frac{30 \pm 10\sqrt{7}}{50} = \frac{3 \pm \sqrt{7}}{5}$$

The solutions are $\frac{3 \pm \sqrt{7}}{5}$.

20. $\qquad 12x = 4x^2 + 4$

$$0 = 4x^2 - 12x + 4$$

$$0 = x^2 - 3x + 1$$

$$a = 1, b = -3, \text{ and } c = 1$$

$$x = \frac{-(-3) \pm \sqrt{(-3)^2 - 4(1)(1)}}{2(1)}$$

$$= \frac{3 \pm \sqrt{9-4}}{2} = \frac{3 \pm \sqrt{5}}{2}$$

The solutions are $\frac{3 \pm \sqrt{5}}{2}$.

21. $\frac{2}{3}m^2 - \frac{1}{3}m - 1 = 0$

$$2m^2 - m - 3 = 0$$

$$(2m-3)(m+1) = 0$$

$$2m-3 = 0 \quad \text{or} \quad m+1 = 0$$

$$2m = 3 \qquad\qquad m = -1$$

$$m = \frac{3}{2}$$

The solutions are -1 and $\frac{3}{2}$.

22. $\frac{5}{8}m^2 + m - \frac{1}{2} = 0$

$$5m^2 + 8m - 4 = 0$$

$$(5m-2)(m+2) = 0$$

$$5m-2 = 0 \quad \text{or} \quad m+2 = 0$$

$$5m = 2 \qquad\qquad m = -2$$

$$m = \frac{2}{5}$$

The solutions are -2 and $\frac{2}{5}$.

23. $x^2 - \frac{1}{2}x - \frac{1}{5} = 0$

$10x^2 - 5x - 2 = 0$

$a = 10, b = -5,$ and $c = -2$

$x = \frac{-(-5) \pm \sqrt{(-5)^2 - 4(10)(-2)}}{2(10)}$

$= \frac{5 \pm \sqrt{25 + 80}}{20} = \frac{5 \pm \sqrt{105}}{20}$

The solutions are $\frac{5 \pm \sqrt{105}}{20}$.

24. $x^2 + \frac{1}{2}x - \frac{1}{8} = 0$

$8x^2 + 4x - 1 = 0$

$a = 8, b = 4,$ and $c = -1$

$x = \frac{-(4) \pm \sqrt{(4)^2 - 4(8)(-1)}}{2(8)}$

$= \frac{-4 \pm \sqrt{16 + 32}}{16} = \frac{-4 \pm \sqrt{48}}{16}$

$= \frac{-4 \pm 4\sqrt{3}}{16} = \frac{-1 \pm \sqrt{3}}{4}$

The solutions are $\frac{-1 \pm \sqrt{3}}{4}$.

25. $4x^2 - 27x + 35 = 0$

$(4x - 7)(x - 5) = 0$

$4x - 7 = 0$ or $x - 5 = 0$

$4x = 7$ $x = 5$

$x = \frac{7}{4}$

The solutions are $\frac{7}{4}$ and 5.

26. $9x^2 - 16x + 7 = 0$

$(9x - 7)(x - 1) = 0$

$9x - 7 = 0$ or $x - 1 = 0$

$9x = 7$ $x = 1$

$x = \frac{7}{9}$

The solutions are $\frac{7}{9}$ and 1.

27. $(7 - 5x)^2 = 18$

$7 - 5x = \pm\sqrt{18}$

$7 - 5x = \pm 3\sqrt{2}$

$-5x = -7 \pm 3\sqrt{2}$

$\frac{-5x}{-5} = \frac{-7 \pm 3\sqrt{2}}{-5}$

$x = \frac{7 \pm 3\sqrt{2}}{5}$

The solutions are $\frac{7 \pm 3\sqrt{2}}{5}$.

28. $(5 - 4x)^2 = 75$

$5 - 4x = \pm\sqrt{75}$

$5 - 4x = \pm 5\sqrt{3}$

$-4x = -5 \pm 5\sqrt{3}$

$\frac{-4x}{-4} = \frac{-5 \pm 5\sqrt{3}}{-5}$

$x = \frac{5 \pm 5\sqrt{3}}{4}$

The solutions are $\frac{5 \pm 5\sqrt{3}}{4}$.

29. $3z^2 - 7z = 12$

$3z^2 - 7z - 12 = 0$

$a = 3, b = -7,$ and $c = -12$

$z = \dfrac{-(-7) \pm \sqrt{(-7)^2 - 4(3)(-12)}}{2(3)}$

$= \dfrac{7 \pm \sqrt{49 + 144}}{6} = \dfrac{7 \pm \sqrt{193}}{6}$

The solutions are $\dfrac{7 \pm \sqrt{193}}{6}$.

30. $6z^2 + 7z = 6$

$6z^2 + 7z - 6 = 0$

$a = 6, b = 7,$ and $c = -6$

$z = \dfrac{-(7) \pm \sqrt{(7)^2 - 4(6)(-6)}}{2(6)}$

$= \dfrac{-7 \pm \sqrt{49 + 144}}{12} = \dfrac{-7 \pm \sqrt{193}}{12}$

The solutions are $\dfrac{-7 \pm \sqrt{193}}{12}$.

31. $x = x^2 - 110$

$0 = x^2 - x - 110$

$0 = (x + 10)(x - 11)$

$x + 10 = 0$ or $x - 11 = 0$

     $x = -10$ $x = 11$

The solutions are -10 and 11.

32. $x = 56 - x^2$

$x^2 + x - 56 = 0$

$(x + 8)(x - 7) = 0$

$x + 8 = 0$ or $x - 7 = 0$

    $x = -8$ $x = 7$

The solutions are -8 and 7.

33. $\dfrac{3}{4}x^2 - \dfrac{5}{2}x - 2 = 0$

$3x^2 - 10x - 8 = 0$

$(3x + 2)(x - 4) = 0$

$3x + 2 = 0$ or $x - 4 = 0$

     $3x = -2$ $x = 4$

      $x = -\dfrac{2}{3}$

The solutions are $-\dfrac{2}{3}$ and 4.

34. $x^2 - \dfrac{6}{5}x - \dfrac{8}{5} = 0$

$5x^2 - 6x - 8 = 0$

$(5x + 4)(x - 2) = 0$

$5x + 4 = 0$ or $x - 2 = 0$

     $5x = -4$ $x = 2$

      $x = -\dfrac{4}{5}$

The solutions are $-\dfrac{4}{5}$ and 2.

35. $x^2 - 0.6x + 0.05 = 0$

$100x^2 - 60x + 5 = 0$

$20x^2 - 12x + 1 = 0$

$(10x - 1)(2x - 1) = 0$

$10x - 1 = 0$ or $2x - 1 = 0$

     $10x = 1$ $2x = 1$

$x = \dfrac{1}{10} = 0.1$ $x = \dfrac{1}{2} = 0.5$

The solutions are 0.1 and 0.5.

36. $x^2 - 0.1x + 0.06 = 0$

$100x^2 - 10x + 6 = 0$

$50x^2 - 5x + 3 = 0$

$(5x + 1)(10x - 3) = 0$

$5x + 1 = 0$ or $10x - 3 = 0$

$5x = -1$ $10x = 3$

$x = -\dfrac{1}{5} = -0.2$ $x = \dfrac{3}{10} = 0.3$

The solutions are -0.2 and 0.3.

37. $10x^2 - 11x + 2 = 0$

$a = 10, b = -11,$ and $c = 2$

$x = \dfrac{-(-11) \pm \sqrt{(-11)^2 - 4(10)(2)}}{2(10)}$

$= \dfrac{11 \pm \sqrt{121 - 80}}{20} = \dfrac{11 \pm \sqrt{41}}{20}$

The solutions are $\dfrac{11 \pm \sqrt{41}}{20}$.

38. $20x^2 - 11x + 1 = 0$

$a = 20, b = -11,$ and $c = 1$

$x = \dfrac{-(-11) \pm \sqrt{(-11)^2 - 4(20)(1)}}{2(20)}$

$= \dfrac{11 \pm \sqrt{121 - 80}}{40} = \dfrac{11 \pm \sqrt{41}}{40}$

The solutions are $\dfrac{11 \pm \sqrt{41}}{40}$.

39. $\dfrac{1}{2}z^2 - 2z + \dfrac{3}{4} = 0$

$z^2 - 4z = -\dfrac{3}{2}$

$z^2 - 4z + 4 = -\dfrac{3}{2} + 4$

$(z - 2)^2 = \dfrac{5}{2}$

$z - 2 = \pm\sqrt{\dfrac{5}{2}}$

$z = 2 \pm \sqrt{\dfrac{5}{2}} = 2 \pm \dfrac{\sqrt{10}}{2}$

$= \dfrac{4 \pm \sqrt{10}}{2}$

The solutions are $\dfrac{4 \pm \sqrt{10}}{2}$.

40. $\dfrac{1}{5}z^2 - \dfrac{1}{2}z - 2 = 0$

$2z^2 - 5z - 20 = 0$

$a = 2, b = -5,$ and $c = -20$

$z = \dfrac{-(-5) \pm \sqrt{(-5)^2 - 4(2)(-20)}}{2(2)}$

$= \dfrac{5 \pm \sqrt{25 + 160}}{4} = \dfrac{5 \pm \sqrt{185}}{4}$

The solutions are $\dfrac{5 \pm \sqrt{185}}{4}$.

41. Answers may vary.

Practice Problems 16.4

1. $y = -3x^2$

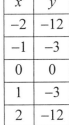

x	y
-2	-12
-1	-3
0	0
1	-3
2	-12

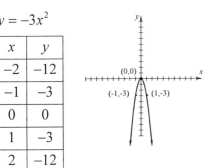

2. $y = x^2 - 9$

y-intercept: $x = 0$, $y = 0^2 - 9 = -9$, $(0, -9)$

x-intercepts: $y = 0$,

$0 = x^2 - 9$

$0 = (x + 3)(x - 3)$

$x + 3 = 0$ or $x - 3 = 0$

$\quad x = -3 \qquad x = 3$

$(-3, 0)$ and $(3, 0)$

x	y
-4	7
-3	0
0	-9
3	0
4	7

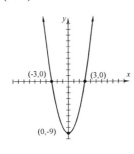

3. $y = x^2 - 2x - 3$

vertex: $x = -\dfrac{b}{2a} = -\dfrac{-2}{2(1)} = 1$ $\Big\}(1, 4)$

$\qquad y = (1)^2 - 2(1) - 3 = -4$

y-intercept: $x = 0$, $y = 0^2 - 2(0) - 3 = -3$,

$\qquad (0, -9)$

x-intercepts: $y = 0$,

$0 = x^2 - 2x - 3$

$0 = (x + 1)(x - 3)$

$x = -1$ or $x = 3$

$(-1, 0)$ and $(3, 0)$

x	y
-1	0
0	-3
1	-4
2	-3
3	0

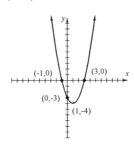

4. $y = x^2 - 3x + 1$

vertex: $x = -\dfrac{b}{2a} = -\dfrac{-3}{2(1)} = \dfrac{3}{2}$ $\Big\}\left(\dfrac{3}{2}, -\dfrac{5}{4}\right)$

$\qquad y = \left(\dfrac{3}{2}\right)^2 - 3\left(\dfrac{3}{2}\right) + 1 = -\dfrac{5}{4}$

y-intercept: $x = 0$, $y = 0^2 - 3(0) + 1 = 1$,

$\qquad (0, 1)$

x-intercepts: $y = 0$,

$0 = x^2 - 3x + 1$

$x = \dfrac{-(-3) \pm \sqrt{(-3)^2 - 4(1)(1)}}{2(1)} = \dfrac{3 \pm \sqrt{5}}{2}$

$x = \dfrac{3 - \sqrt{5}}{2} \approx 0.4$ or $x = \dfrac{3 + \sqrt{5}}{2} \approx 2.6$

$\left(\dfrac{3 - \sqrt{5}}{2}, 0\right)$ and $\left(\dfrac{3 + \sqrt{5}}{2}, 0\right)$

x	y
0	1
0.4	0
3/2	$-5/4$
2.6	0
3	1

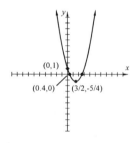

Graphing Calculator Explorations 16.4

1. $x^2 - 7x - 3 = 0$

$y_1 = x^2 - 7x - 3$

$y_2 = 0$

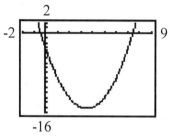

The x-coordinates of the intersections, -0.41 and 7.41, are the solutions.

2. $2x^2 - 11x - 1 = 0$

$y_1 = 2x^2 - 11x - 1$

$y_2 = 0$

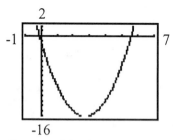

The x-coordinates of the intersections, -0.09 and 5.59, are the solutions.

3. $-1.7x^2 + 5.6x - 3.7 = 0$

$y_1 = -1.7x^2 + 5.6x - 3.7$

$y_2 = 0$

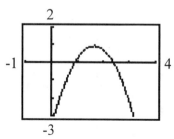

The x-coordinates of the intersections, 0.91 and 2.38, are the solutions.

4. $-5.8x^2 + 2.3x - 3.9 = 0$

$y_1 = -5.8x^2 + 2.3x - 3.9$

$y_2 = 0$

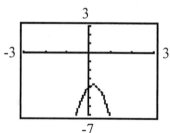

There are no x-intercepts so there are no real solutions.

5. $5.8x^2 - 2.6x - 1.9 = 0$

$y_1 = 5.8x^2 - 2.6x - 1.9$

$y_2 = 0$

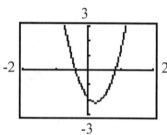

The x-coordinates of the intersections, -0.39 and $0.84,$ are the solutions.

6. $7.5x^2 - 3.7x - 1.1 = 0$

$y_1 = 7.5x^2 - 3.7x - 1.1$

$y_2 = -12$

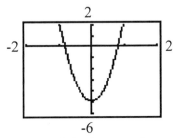

The x-coordinates of the intersections, -0.21 and $0.70,$ are the solutions.

Exercise Set 16.4

1. $y = 2x^2$

x	y
-2	8
-1	2
0	0
1	2
2	8

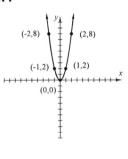

3. $y = -x^2$

x	y
-2	-4
-1	-1
0	0
1	-1
2	-4

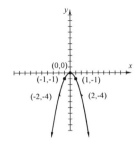

5. $y = \dfrac{1}{3}x^2$

x	y
-6	12
-3	3
0	0
3	3
6	12

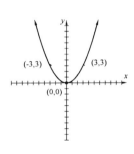

7. $y = x^2 - 1$

y-intercept: $x = 0,\ y = 0^2 - 1 = -1,\ (0, -1)$

vertex: $(0, -1)$

x-intercepts: $y = 0,$

$0 = x^2 - 1$

$0 = (x + 1)(x - 1)$

$x + 1 = 0\ $ or $\ x - 1 = 0$

$\qquad x = -1 \qquad\qquad x = 1$

$(-1, 0)\ $ and $\ (1, 0)$

x	y
-2	3
-1	0
0	-1
1	0
2	3

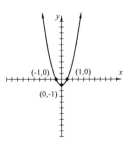

9. $y = x^2 + 4$

y-intercept: $x = 0$, $y = 0^2 + 4 = 4$, $(0, 4)$

vertex: $(0, 4)$

x-intercepts: $y = 0$,

$0 = x^2 + 4$

$-4 = x^2$

There are no x-intercepts because there is no real solution to this equation.

x	y
-2	8
-1	5
0	4
1	5
2	8

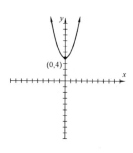

11. $y = x^2 + 6x$

vertex: $x = -\dfrac{b}{2a} = -\dfrac{6}{2(1)} = -3$ $\left.\right\}(-3, -9)$

$y = (-3)^2 + 6(-3) = -9$

y-intercept: $x = 0$, $y = 0^2 + 6(0) = 0$,

$(0, 0)$

x-intercepts: $y = 0$,

$0 = x^2 + 6x$

$0 = x(x + 6)$

$x = -6$ or $x = 0$

$(-6, 0)$ and $(0, 0)$

x	y
-7	7
-6	0
-3	-9
0	0
1	7

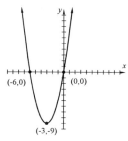

13. $y = x^2 + 2x - 8$

vertex: $x = -\dfrac{b}{2a} = -\dfrac{2}{2(1)} = -1$ $\left.\right\}(-1, -9)$

$y = (-1)^2 + 2(-1) - 8 = -9$

y-intercept: $x = 0$, $y = 0^2 + 2(0) - 8 = -8$,

$(0, -8)$

x-intercepts: $y = 0$,

$0 = x^2 + 2x - 8$

$0 = (x + 4)(x - 2)$

$x = -4$ or $x = 2$

$(-4, 0)$ and $(2, 0)$

x	y
-4	0
-2	-8
-1	-9
0	-8
2	0

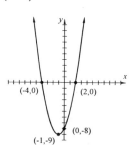

15. $y = -x^2 + x + 2$

vertex: $x = -\dfrac{b}{2a} = -\dfrac{1}{2(-1)} = \dfrac{1}{2}$ $\left.\right\}\left(\dfrac{1}{2}, \dfrac{9}{4}\right)$

$y = -\left(\dfrac{1}{2}\right)^2 + \left(\dfrac{1}{2}\right) + 2 = \dfrac{9}{4}$

y-intercept: $x = 0,\ y = -0^2 + (0) + 2 = 2,$

$$(0,2)$$

x-intercepts: $y = 0,$

$$0 = -x^2 + x + 2$$

$$0 = x^2 - x - 2$$

$$0 = (x+1)(x-2)$$

$$x = -1 \quad \text{or} \quad x = 2$$

$$(-1,0) \text{ and } (2,0)$$

x	y
−1	0
0	2
1/2	9/4
1	2
2	0

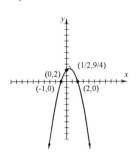

17. $y = x^2 + 5x + 4$

vertex: $x = -\dfrac{b}{2a} = -\dfrac{5}{2(1)} = -\dfrac{5}{2}$

$$y = \left(-\frac{5}{2}\right)^2 + 5\left(-\frac{5}{2}\right) + 4 = -\frac{9}{4}$$

$$\left(-\frac{5}{2}, -\frac{9}{4}\right)$$

y-intercept: $x = 0,\ y = 0^2 + 5(0) + 4 = 4,$

$$(0,4)$$

x-intercepts: $y = 0,$

$$0 = x^2 + 5x + 4$$

$$0 = (x+4)(x+1)$$

$$x = -4 \quad \text{or} \quad x = -1$$

$$(-4,0) \text{ and } (-1,0)$$

x	y
−5	4
−4	0
−5/2	−9/4
−1	0
0	4

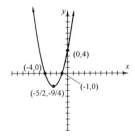

19. $y = x^2 - 4x + 5$

vertex: $x = -\dfrac{b}{2a} = -\dfrac{-4}{2(1)} = 2$
$\left.\begin{array}{l}\\[2mm]\\\end{array}\right\}(2,1)$

$$y = (2)^2 - 4(2) + 5 = 1$$

y-intercept: $x = 0,\ y = 0^2 - 4(0) + 5 = 5,$

$$(0,5)$$

x-intercepts: $y = 0,$

$$0 = x^2 - 4x + 5$$

$$x = \frac{-(-4) \pm \sqrt{(-4)^2 - 4(1)(5)}}{2(1)}$$

$$= \frac{4 \pm \sqrt{-4}}{2}$$

There are no *x*-intercepts because there is no real solution to the equation.

x	y
0	5
1	2
2	1
3	2
4	5

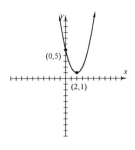

21. $y = 2 - x^2$

y-intercept: $x = 0$, $y = 2 - 0^2 = 2$, $(0, 2)$

vertex: $(0, 2)$

x-intercepts: $y = 0$,

$0 = 2 - x^2$

$x^2 = 2$

$x = \pm\sqrt{2} \approx \pm 1.4$

$\left(-\sqrt{2}, 0\right)$ and $\left(\sqrt{2}, 0\right)$

x	y
-3	-7
-1.4	0
0	2
1.4	0
3	-7

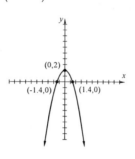

23. $y = 2x^2 - 11x + 5$

vertex: $x = -\dfrac{b}{2a} = -\dfrac{-11}{2(2)} = \dfrac{11}{4}$

$y = 2\left(\dfrac{11}{4}\right)^2 - 11\left(\dfrac{11}{4}\right) + 5 = -\dfrac{81}{8}$

$\left(\dfrac{11}{4}, -\dfrac{81}{8}\right)$

y-intercept: $x = 0$,

$y = 2(0)^2 - 11(0) + 5 = 5$,

$(0, 5)$

x-intercepts: $y = 0$,

$0 = 2x^2 - 11x + 5$

$0 = (2x - 1)(x - 5)$

$x = \dfrac{1}{2}$ or $x = 5$

$\left(\dfrac{1}{2}, 0\right)$ and $(5, 0)$

x	y
0	5
$1/2$	0
$11/4$	$-81/8$
5	0
$11/2$	5

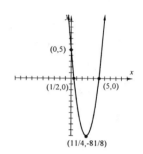

25. $y = -x^2 + 4x - 3$

$\left.\begin{array}{l} \text{vertex: } x = -\dfrac{b}{2a} = -\dfrac{4}{2(-1)} = 2 \\[4pt] y = -(2)^2 + 4(2) - 3 = 1 \end{array}\right\} (2, 1)$

y-intercept: $x = 0$, $y = -0^2 + 4(0) - 3 = -3$,

$(0, -3)$

x-intercepts: $y = 0$,

$0 = -x^2 + 4x - 3$

$0 = x^2 - 4x + 3$

$0 = (x - 1)(x - 3)$

$x = 1$ or $x = 3$

$(1, 0)$ and $(3, 0)$

x	y
0	-3
1	0
2	1
3	0
4	-3

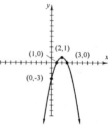

27. $\dfrac{\frac{1}{7}}{\frac{2}{5}} = \dfrac{1}{7} \cdot \dfrac{5}{2} = \dfrac{5}{14}$

29. $\dfrac{\frac{1}{x}}{\frac{2}{x^2}} = \dfrac{1}{x} \cdot \dfrac{x^2}{2} = \dfrac{x}{2}$

31. $\dfrac{2x}{1-\frac{1}{x}} = \dfrac{2x}{\frac{x-1}{x}} = \dfrac{2x}{1} \cdot \dfrac{x}{x-1} = \dfrac{2x^2}{x-1}$

33. $\dfrac{\frac{a-b}{2b}}{\frac{b-a}{8b^2}} = \dfrac{a-b}{2b} \cdot \dfrac{8b^2}{b-a} = \dfrac{a-b}{2b} \cdot \dfrac{8b^2}{-1(a-b)} = -4b$

35. a. 256 feet

    b. 4 seconds

    c. 8 seconds

37. $a < 0$, one x-intercept

    E

39. $a > 0$, no x-intercept

    C

41. $a < 0$, two x-intercepts

    B

Chapter 16 Review

1. $(x-4)(5x+3) = 0$

$$5x+3 = 0 \quad \text{or} \quad x-4 = 0$$
$$x = -\dfrac{3}{5} \qquad x = 4$$

The solutions are $-\dfrac{3}{5}$ and 4.

2. $(x+7)(3x+4) = 0$

$$3x+4 = 0 \quad \text{or} \quad x+7 = 0$$
$$x = -\dfrac{4}{3} \qquad x = -7$$

The solutions are $-\dfrac{4}{3}$ and -7.

3. $\quad 3m^2 - 5m = 2$

$$3m^2 - 5m - 2 = 0$$
$$(m-2)(3m+1) = 0$$
$$m-2 = 0 \quad \text{or} \quad 3m+1 = 0$$
$$m = 2 \qquad\qquad m = -\dfrac{1}{3}$$

The solutions are $-\dfrac{1}{3}$ and 2.

4. $\quad 7m^2 + 2m = 5$

$$7m^2 + 2m - 5 = 0$$
$$(m+1)(7m-5) = 0$$
$$m+1 = 0 \quad \text{or} \quad 7m-5 = 0$$
$$m = -1 \qquad\qquad m = \dfrac{5}{7}$$

The solutions are $\dfrac{5}{7}$ and -1.

5. $\quad 6x^3 - 54x = 0$

$$6x\left(x^2 - 9\right) = 0$$
$$6x(x+3)(x-3) = 0$$
$$6x = 0 \quad \text{or} \quad x+3 = 0 \quad \text{or} \quad x-3 = 0$$
$$x = 0 \qquad\qquad x = -3 \qquad\qquad x = 3$$

The solutions are 0, -3, and 3.

6. $\quad 2x^2 - 8 = 0$

$$2\left(x^2 - 4\right) = 0$$
$$2(x+2)(x-2) = 0$$
$$x+2 = 0 \quad \text{or} \quad x-2 = 0$$
$$x = -2 \qquad\qquad x = 2$$

The solutions are -2 and 2.

7. $x^2 = 36$

$x = \pm\sqrt{36}$

$= \pm 6$

The solutions are ± 6.

8. $x^2 = 81$

$x = \pm\sqrt{81}$

$= \pm 9$

The solutions are ± 9.

9. $k^2 = 50$

$k = \pm\sqrt{50}$

$= \pm 5\sqrt{2}$

The solutions are $\pm 5\sqrt{2}$.

10. $k^2 = 45$

$k = \pm\sqrt{45}$

$= \pm 3\sqrt{5}$

The solutions are $\pm 3\sqrt{5}$.

11. $(x-11)^2 = 49$

$x - 11 = \pm\sqrt{49}$

$x - 11 = \pm 7$

$x = 11 \pm 7$

$x = 11 - 7 = 4$ or $x = 11 + 7 = 18$

The solutions are 4 and 18.

12. $(x+3)^2 = 100$

$x + 3 = \pm\sqrt{100}$

$x + 3 = \pm 10$

$x = -3 \pm 10$

$x = -3 - 10 = -13$ or $x = -3 + 10 = 7$

The solutions are -13 and 7.

13. $(4p+2)^2 = 100$

$4p + 2 = \pm\sqrt{100}$

$4p + 2 = \pm 10$

$4p = -2 \pm 10$

$p = \dfrac{-2 \pm 10}{4}$

$p = \dfrac{-2-10}{4} = -3$ or $p = \dfrac{-2+10}{4} = 2$

The solutions are -3 and 2.

14. $(3p+6)^2 = 81$

$3p + 6 = \pm\sqrt{81}$

$3p + 6 = \pm 9$

$3p = -6 \pm 9$

$p = \dfrac{-6 \pm 9}{3}$

$p = \dfrac{-6-9}{3} = -5$ or $p = \dfrac{-6+9}{3} = 1$

The solutions are -5 and 1.

15. Let $h = 100$

$h = 16t^2$

$16t^2 = h$

$16t^2 = 100$

$t^2 = \dfrac{100}{16}$

$t = \pm\sqrt{\dfrac{100}{16}} = \pm\dfrac{10}{4} = \pm 2.5$

The length of time is not a negative number so the dive lasted 2.5 seconds.

16. Let $h = 5 \cdot 5280 = 26,400$

$$h = 16t^2$$
$$16t^2 = h$$
$$16t^2 = 26,400$$
$$t^2 = \frac{26,400}{16} = 1650$$
$$t = \pm\sqrt{1650} = \pm 40.6$$

The length of time is not a negative number so the fall lasted 40.6 seconds.

17.
$$x^2 + 4x = 1$$
$$x^2 + 4x + 4 = 1 + 4$$
$$(x + 2)^2 = 5$$
$$x + 2 = \pm\sqrt{5}$$
$$x = -2 \pm \sqrt{5}$$

The solutions are $-2 \pm \sqrt{5}$.

18.
$$x^2 - 8x = 3$$
$$x^2 - 8x + 16 = 3 + 16$$
$$(x - 4)^2 = 19$$
$$x - 4 = \pm\sqrt{19}$$
$$x = 4 \pm \sqrt{19}$$

The solutions are $4 \pm \sqrt{19}$.

19.
$$x^2 - 6x + 7 = 0$$
$$x^2 - 6x = -7$$
$$x^2 - 6x + 9 = -7 + 9$$
$$(x - 3)^2 = 2$$
$$x - 3 = \pm\sqrt{2}$$
$$x = 3 \pm \sqrt{2}$$

The solutions are $3 \pm \sqrt{2}$.

20.
$$x^2 + 6x + 7 = 0$$
$$x^2 + 6x = -7$$
$$x^2 + 6x + 9 = -7 + 9$$
$$(x + 3)^2 = 2$$
$$x + 3 = \pm\sqrt{2}$$
$$x = -3 \pm \sqrt{2}$$

The solutions are $-3 \pm \sqrt{2}$.

21.
$$2y^2 + y - 1 = 0$$
$$y^2 + \frac{1}{2}y - \frac{1}{2} = 0$$
$$y^2 + \frac{1}{2}y = \frac{1}{2}$$
$$y^2 + \frac{1}{2}y + \frac{1}{16} = \frac{1}{2} + \frac{1}{16}$$
$$\left(y + \frac{1}{4}\right)^2 = \frac{9}{16}$$
$$y + \frac{1}{4} = \pm\sqrt{\frac{9}{16}}$$
$$y = -\frac{1}{4} \pm \frac{3}{4}$$
$$y = -\frac{1}{4} + \frac{3}{4} \quad \text{or} \quad y = -\frac{1}{4} - \frac{3}{4}$$
$$y = \frac{1}{2} \qquad\qquad y = -1$$

The solutions are $\frac{1}{2}$ and -1.

22.
$$y^2 + 3y - 1 = 0$$
$$y^2 + 3y = 1$$
$$y^2 + 3y + \frac{9}{4} = 1 + \frac{9}{4}$$

$$\left(y+\frac{3}{2}\right)^2 = \frac{13}{4}$$

$$y+\frac{3}{2} = \pm\sqrt{\frac{13}{4}}$$

$$y = -\frac{3}{2} \pm \frac{\sqrt{13}}{2}$$

$$y = \frac{-3\pm\sqrt{13}}{2}$$

The solutions are $\dfrac{-3\pm\sqrt{13}}{2}$.

23. $x^2 - 10x + 7 = 0$

$a = 1, b = -10,$ and $c = 7$

$$x = \frac{-(-10)\pm\sqrt{(-10)^2 - 4(1)(7)}}{2(1)}$$

$$= \frac{10\pm\sqrt{100-28}}{2} = \frac{10\pm\sqrt{72}}{2}$$

$$= \frac{10\pm6\sqrt{2}}{2} = 5\pm3\sqrt{2}$$

The solutions are $5\pm3\sqrt{2}$.

24. $x^2 + 4x - 7 = 0$

$a = 1, b = 4,$ and $c = -7$

$$x = \frac{-(4)\pm\sqrt{(4)^2 - 4(1)(-7)}}{2(1)}$$

$$= \frac{-4\pm\sqrt{16+28}}{2} = \frac{-4\pm\sqrt{44}}{2}$$

$$= \frac{-4\pm2\sqrt{11}}{2} = -2\pm\sqrt{11}$$

The solutions are $-2\pm\sqrt{11}$.

25. $2x^2 + x - 1 = 0$

$a = 2, b = 1,$ and $c = -1$

$$x = \frac{-(1)\pm\sqrt{(1)^2 - 4(2)(-1)}}{2(2)}$$

$$= \frac{-1\pm\sqrt{1+8}}{4} = \frac{-1\pm\sqrt{9}}{4} = \frac{-1\pm3}{4}$$

$$x = \frac{-1+3}{4} = \frac{1}{2} \quad \text{or} \quad x = \frac{-1-3}{4} = -1$$

The solutions are -1 and $\dfrac{1}{2}$.

26. $x^2 + 3x - 1 = 0$

$a = 1, b = 3,$ and $c = -1$

$$x = \frac{-(3)\pm\sqrt{(3)^2 - 4(1)(-1)}}{2(1)}$$

$$= \frac{-3\pm\sqrt{9+4}}{2} = \frac{-3\pm\sqrt{13}}{2}$$

The solutions are $\dfrac{-3\pm\sqrt{13}}{2}$.

27. $9x^2 + 30x + 25 = 0$

$a = 9, b = 30,$ and $c = 25$

$$x = \frac{-(30)\pm\sqrt{(30)^2 - 4(9)(25)}}{2(9)}$$

$$= \frac{-30\pm\sqrt{900-900}}{18} = \frac{-30\pm\sqrt{0}}{18} = -\frac{5}{3}$$

The solution is $-\dfrac{5}{3}$.

28. $16x^2 - 72x + 81 = 0$

$a = 16, b = -72,$ and $c = 81$

$$x = \frac{-(-72) \pm \sqrt{(-72)^2 - 4(16)(81)}}{2(16)}$$

$$= \frac{72 \pm \sqrt{5184 - 5184}}{32} = \frac{72 \pm \sqrt{0}}{32} = \frac{9}{4}$$

The solution is $\dfrac{9}{4}$.

29. $15x^2 + 2 = 11x$

$15x^2 - 11x + 2 = 0$

$a = 15, b = -11,$ and $c = 2$

$$x = \frac{-(-11) \pm \sqrt{(-11)^2 - 4(15)(2)}}{2(15)}$$

$$= \frac{11 \pm \sqrt{121 - 120}}{30} = \frac{11 \pm \sqrt{1}}{30} = \frac{11 \pm 1}{30}$$

$$x = \frac{11 + 1}{30} = \frac{2}{5} \quad \text{or} \quad x = \frac{11 - 1}{30} = \frac{1}{3}$$

The solutions are $\dfrac{2}{5}$ and $\dfrac{1}{3}$.

30. $15x^2 + 2 = 13x$

$15x^2 - 13x + 2 = 0$

$a = 15, b = -13,$ and $c = 2$

$$x = \frac{-(-13) \pm \sqrt{(-13)^2 - 4(15)(2)}}{2(15)}$$

$$= \frac{13 \pm \sqrt{169 - 120}}{30} = \frac{13 \pm \sqrt{49}}{30} = \frac{13 \pm 7}{30}$$

$$x = \frac{13 + 7}{30} = \frac{2}{3} \quad \text{or} \quad x = \frac{13 - 7}{30} = \frac{1}{5}$$

The solutions are $\dfrac{2}{3}$ and $\dfrac{1}{5}$.

31. $2x^2 + x + 5 = 0$

$a = 2, b = 1,$ and $c = 5$

$$x = \frac{-(1) \pm \sqrt{(1)^2 - 4(2)(5)}}{2(2)}$$

$$= \frac{-1 \pm \sqrt{1 - 40}}{4} = \frac{-1 \pm \sqrt{-39}}{4}$$

There is no real solution because

$\sqrt{-39}$ is not a real number.

32. $7x^2 - 3x + 1 = 0$

$a = 7, b = -3,$ and $c = 1$

$$x = \frac{-(-3) \pm \sqrt{(-3)^2 - 4(7)(1)}}{2(7)}$$

$$= \frac{3 \pm \sqrt{9 - 28}}{14} = \frac{3 \pm \sqrt{-19}}{14}$$

There is no real solution because

$\sqrt{-19}$ is not a real number.

33. $y = -8x^2 - 13x + 552$

$180 = -8x^2 - 13x + 552$

$8x^2 + 13x - 552 + 180 = 0$

$8x^2 + 13x - 372 = 0$

Using the quadratic formula:

$a = 8, b = 13, c = 372$

$$x = \frac{-13 \pm \sqrt{(13)^2 - 4(8)(-372)}}{2(8)}$$

$$x = \frac{-13 + \sqrt{12,073}}{16}$$

$x \approx 6$

$1998 + x = 1998 + 6 = 2004$

In 2004 the price of silver

will be 180 cents per ounce.

34. $y = -5x^2 + 79.4x + 357.4$

$450 = -5x^2 + 79.4x + 357.4$

$5x^2 - 79.4x - 357.4 + 450 = 0$

$5x^2 - 79.4x + 92.6 = 0$

Using the quadratic formula:

$a = 5,\ b = -79.4,\ c = 92.6$

$$x = \frac{-(-79.4) + \sqrt{(-79.4)^2 - 4(5)(92.6)}}{2(5)}$$

$$x = \frac{79.4 + \sqrt{4452.36}}{10}$$

$x \approx 14.6$

$1998 + x = 1998 + 14.6 = 2012.6$

Between 2012 and 2013 the price of platinum will be \$450 per ounce.

35. $y = 3x^2$

$$\text{vertex: } x = -\frac{0}{2(3)} = 0 \left.\begin{array}{c} \\ \\ \end{array}\right\} (0,0)$$
$$y = 3(0)^2 = 0$$

x	y
-2	12
-1	3
0	0
1	3
2	12

36. $y = -\frac{1}{2}x^2$

$$\text{vertex: } x = -\frac{0}{2(-1/2)} = 0 \left.\begin{array}{c} \\ \\ \end{array}\right\} (0,0)$$
$$y = -\frac{1}{2}(0)^2 = 0$$

x	y
-4	-8
-2	-2
0	0
2	-2
4	-8

37. $y = x^2 - 25$

$$\text{vertex: } x = -\frac{b}{2a} = -\frac{0}{2(1)} = 0 \left.\begin{array}{c} \\ \\ \end{array}\right\} (0,-25)$$
$$y = (0)^2 - 25 = -25$$

y-intercept: $x = 0,\ y = -25,\ (0,-25)$

x-intercepts: $y = 0,$

$0 = x^2 - 25$

$0 = (x+5)(x-5)$

$x = -5 \quad \text{or} \quad x = 5$

$(-5,0)$ and $(5,0)$

x	y
-7	24
-5	0
0	-25
5	0
7	24

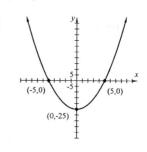

38. $y = x^2 - 36$

$$\text{vertex: } x = -\frac{b}{2a} = -\frac{0}{2(1)} = 0 \left.\begin{array}{c} \\ \\ \end{array}\right\} (0,-36)$$
$$y = (0)^2 - 36 = -36$$

y-intercept: $x = 0,\ y = -36,\ (0,-36)$

x-intercepts: $y = 0$,

$0 = x^2 - 36$

$0 = (x+6)(x-6)$

$x = -6$ or $x = 6$

$(-6, 0)$ and $(6, 0)$

x	*y*
-8	28
-6	0
0	-36
6	0
8	28

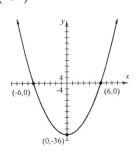

39. $y = x^2 + 3$

$\left. \begin{array}{l} \text{vertex: } x = -\dfrac{b}{2a} = -\dfrac{0}{2(1)} = 0 \\[2mm] \qquad y = (0)^2 + 3 = 3 \end{array} \right\} (0, 3)$

y-intercept: $x = 0$, $y = 0^2 + 3 = 3$, $(0, 3)$

x-intercepts: $y = 0$,

$0 = x^2 + 3$

$-3 = x^2$

There are no *x*-intercepts because there is no real solution to this equation.

x	*y*
-2	7
-1	4
0	3
1	4
2	7

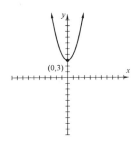

40. $y = x^2 + 8$

$\left. \begin{array}{l} \text{vertex: } x = -\dfrac{b}{2a} = -\dfrac{0}{2(1)} = 0 \\[2mm] \qquad y = (0)^2 + 8 = 8 \end{array} \right\} (0, 8)$

y-intercept: $x = 0$, $y = 0^2 + 8 = 8$, $(0, 8)$

x-intercepts: $y = 0$,

$0 = x^2 + 8$

$-8 = x^2$

There are no *x*-intercepts because there is no real solution to this equation.

x	*y*
-2	12
-1	9
0	8
1	9
2	12

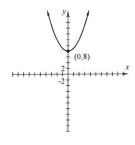

41. $y = -4x^2 + 8$

y-intercept: $x = 0$, $y = -4(0)^2 + 8 = 8$,

$\qquad (0, 8)$

vertex: $(0, 8)$

x-intercepts: $y = 0$,

$0 = -4x^2 + 8$

$4x^2 = 8$

$x^2 = 2$

$x = \pm\sqrt{2} \approx \pm 1.4$

$\left(-\sqrt{2}, 0 \right)$ and $\left(\sqrt{2}, 0 \right)$

x	y
-2	-8
-1.4	0
0	8
1.4	0
2	-8

42. $y = -3x^2 + 9$

y-intercept: $x = 0$, $y = -3(0)^2 + 9 = 9$,

$$(0, 9)$$

vertex: $(0, 9)$

x-intercepts: $y = 0$,

$$0 = -3x^2 + 9$$
$$3x^2 = 9$$
$$x^2 = 3$$
$$x = \pm\sqrt{3} \approx \pm 1.7$$
$$\left(-\sqrt{3}, 0\right) \text{ and } \left(\sqrt{3}, 0\right)$$

x	y
-2	-3
-1.7	0
0	9
1.7	0
2	-3

43. $y = x^2 + 3x - 10$

vertex: $x = -\dfrac{b}{2a} = -\dfrac{3}{2(1)} = -\dfrac{3}{2}$

$$y = \left(-\frac{3}{2}\right)^2 + 3\left(-\frac{3}{2}\right) - 10 = -\frac{49}{4}$$

$$\left(-\frac{3}{2}, -\frac{49}{4}\right)$$

y-intercept: $x = 0$, $y = 0^2 + 3(0) - 10$
$$= -10, \ (0, -10)$$

x-intercepts: $y = 0$, $0 = x^2 + 3x - 10$
$$0 = (x + 5)(x - 2)$$
$$x = -5 \ \text{ or } \ x = 2$$
$$(-5, 0) \text{ and } (2, 0)$$

x	y
-5	0
-3	-10
$-3/2$	$-49/4$
0	-10
2	0

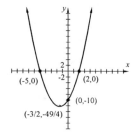

44. $y = x^2 + 3x - 4$

vertex: $x = -\dfrac{b}{2a} = -\dfrac{3}{2(1)} = -\dfrac{3}{2}$

$$y = \left(-\frac{3}{2}\right)^2 + 3\left(-\frac{3}{2}\right) - 4 = -\frac{25}{4}$$

$$\left(-\frac{3}{2}, -\frac{25}{4}\right)$$

y-intercept: $x = 0$, $y = 0^2 + 3(0) - 4$
$$= -4, \ (0, -4)$$

x-intercepts: $y = 0$,

$$0 = x^2 + 3x - 4$$

$$0 = (x+4)(x-1)$$

$$x = -4 \quad \text{or} \quad x = 1$$

$$(-4, 0) \quad \text{and} \quad (1, 0)$$

x	y
-4	0
-3	-4
$-3/2$	$-25/4$
0	-4
1	0

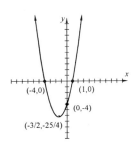

45. $y = -x^2 - 5x - 6$

vertex: $x = -\dfrac{b}{2a} = -\dfrac{-5}{2(-1)} = -\dfrac{5}{2}$

$$y = -\left(-\frac{5}{2}\right)^2 - 5\left(-\frac{5}{2}\right) - 6 = \frac{1}{4}$$

$$\left(-\frac{5}{2}, \frac{1}{4}\right)$$

y-intercept: $x = 0$, $y = -0^2 - 5(0) - 6$

$$= -6, \ (0, -6)$$

x-intercepts: $y = 0$,

$$0 = -x^2 - 5x - 6$$

$$0 = x^2 + 5x + 6$$

$$0 = (x+3)(x+2)$$

$$x = -3 \quad \text{or} \quad x = -2$$

$$(-3, 0) \quad \text{and} \quad (-2, 0)$$

x	y
-5	-6
-3	0
$-5/2$	$1/4$
-2	0
0	-6

46. $y = -x^2 + 4x + 8$

vertex: $x = -\dfrac{b}{2a} = -\dfrac{4}{2(-1)} = 2$ $\left.\begin{array}{c} \\ \\ \end{array}\right\} (2, 12)$

$$y = -(2)^2 + 4(2) + 8 = 12$$

y-intercept: $x = 0$, $y = 8$, $(0, 8)$

x-intercepts: $y = 0$,

$$0 = -x^2 + 4x + 8$$

$$x = \frac{-(4) \pm \sqrt{(4)^2 - 4(-1)(8)}}{2(-1)}$$

$$= \frac{-4 \pm \sqrt{48}}{-2} = \frac{-4 \pm 4\sqrt{3}}{-2} = 2 \pm 2\sqrt{3}$$

$$x = 2 + 2\sqrt{3} \approx 5.5 \quad \text{or} \quad x = 2 - 2\sqrt{3} \approx -1.5$$

$$\left(2 - 2\sqrt{3}, 0\right) \quad \text{and} \quad \left(2 + 2\sqrt{3}, 0\right)$$

x	y
-1.5	0
0	8
2	12
4	8
5.5	0

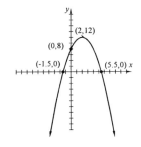

47. $y = 2x^2 - 11x - 6$

vertex: $x = -\dfrac{b}{2a} = -\dfrac{-11}{2(2)} = \dfrac{11}{4}$

$y = 2\left(\dfrac{11}{4}\right)^2 - 11\left(\dfrac{11}{4}\right) - 6 = -\dfrac{169}{8}$

$\left(\dfrac{11}{4}, -\dfrac{169}{8}\right)$

y-intercept: $x = 0$, $y = -6$, $(0, -6)$

x-intercepts: $y = 0$,

$0 = 2x^2 - 11x - 6$

$0 = (2x + 1)(x - 6)$

$x = -\dfrac{1}{2}$ or $x = 6$

$\left(-\dfrac{1}{2}, 0\right)$ and $(6, 0)$

x	y
$-1/2$	0
0	-6
$11/4$	$-169/8$
$11/2$	-6
6	0

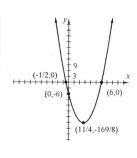

48. $y = 3x^2 - x - 2$

vertex: $x = -\dfrac{b}{2a} = -\dfrac{-1}{2(3)} = \dfrac{1}{6}$

$y = 3\left(\dfrac{1}{6}\right)^2 - \left(\dfrac{1}{6}\right) - 2 = -\dfrac{25}{12}$

$\left(\dfrac{1}{6}, -\dfrac{25}{12}\right)$

y-intercept: $x = 0$, $y = -2$, $(0, -2)$

x-intercepts: $y = 0$,

$0 = 3x^2 - x - 2$

$0 = (3x + 2)(x - 1)$

$x = -\dfrac{2}{3}$ or $x = 1$

$\left(-\dfrac{2}{3}, 0\right)$ and $(1, 0)$

x	y
$-2/3$	0
0	-2
$1/6$	$-25/12$
1	0

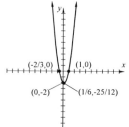

49. The equation has one solution because the graph intersects the x-axis at one point $(-2, 0)$.

50. The equation has two solutions because the graph intersects the x-axis at two points: $\left(-\dfrac{3}{2}, 0\right)$ and $(3, 0)$.

51. The equation has no real solution because the graph does not intersect the x-axis.

52. The equation has two solutions because the graph intersects the x-axis at two points: $(-2, 0)$ and $(2, 0)$.

53. $y = 2x^2$

A

54. $y = -x^2$

D

55. $y = x^2 + 4x + 4$

B

56. $y = x^2 + 5x + 4$

C

Chapter 16 Test

1.
$$5k^2 = 80$$
$$k^2 = 16$$
$$k = \pm\sqrt{16}$$
$$k = \pm 4$$
The solutions are ± 4.

2. $(3m - 5)^2 = 8$
$$3m - 5 = \pm\sqrt{8}$$
$$3m - 5 = \pm 2\sqrt{2}$$
$$3m = 5 \pm 2\sqrt{2}$$
$$m = \frac{5 \pm 2\sqrt{2}}{3}$$
The solutions are $\dfrac{5 \pm 2\sqrt{2}}{3}$.

3. $x^2 - 26x + 160 = 0$
$$x^2 - 26x = -160$$
$$x^2 - 26x + 169 = -160 + 169$$
$$(x - 13)^2 = 9$$
$$x - 13 = \pm\sqrt{9}$$
$$x = 13 \pm 3$$
$$x = 13 - 3 \quad \text{or} \quad x = 13 + 3$$
$$x = 10 \qquad\qquad x = 16$$
The solutions are -6 and -2.

4. $3x^2 + 12x - 4 = 0$
$$\frac{3x^2}{3} + \frac{12x}{3} = \frac{4}{3}$$
$$x^2 + 4x = \frac{4}{3}$$
$$x^2 + 4x + 4 = \frac{4}{3} + 4$$
$$(x + 2)^2 = \frac{16}{3}$$
$$\sqrt{(x + 2)^2} = \pm\sqrt{\frac{16}{3}}$$
$$x + 2 = \pm\frac{4}{\sqrt{3}}$$
$$x = -2 \pm \frac{4\sqrt{3}}{3}$$
$$x = -\frac{6}{3} \pm \frac{4\sqrt{3}}{3}$$
$$x = \frac{-6 \pm 4\sqrt{3}}{3}$$

5. $x^2 - 3x - 10 = 0$

$a = 1, b = -3,$ and $c = -10$

$$x = \frac{-(-3) \pm \sqrt{(-3)^2 - 4(1)(-10)}}{2(1)}$$

$$= \frac{3 \pm \sqrt{9 + 40}}{2} = \frac{3 \pm \sqrt{49}}{2} = \frac{3 \pm 7}{2}$$

$$x = \frac{3 - 7}{2} = -2 \quad \text{or} \quad x = \frac{3 + 7}{2} = 5$$

The solutions are -2 and 5.

6. $p^2 - \frac{5}{3}p - \frac{1}{3} = 0$

$3p^2 - 5p - 1 = 0$

$a = 3, b = -5,$ and $c = -1$

$$p = \frac{-(-5) \pm \sqrt{(-5)^2 - 4(3)(-1)}}{2(3)}$$

$$= \frac{5 \pm \sqrt{25 + 12}}{6} = \frac{5 \pm \sqrt{37}}{6}$$

The solutions are $\dfrac{5 \pm \sqrt{37}}{6}$.

7. $(3x - 5)(x + 2) = -6$

$3x^2 + x - 10 = -6$

$3x^2 + x - 4 = 0$

$(3x + 4)(x - 1) = 0$

$\qquad 3x + 4 = 0 \quad \text{or} \quad x - 1 = 0$

$\qquad\qquad x = -\frac{4}{3} \qquad\qquad x = 1$

The solutions are $-\dfrac{4}{3}$ and 1.

8. $(3x - 1)^2 = 16$

$3x - 1 = \pm\sqrt{16}$

$3x = 1 \pm 4$

$x = \dfrac{1 \pm 4}{3}$

$x = \dfrac{1 - 4}{3} = -1 \quad \text{or} \quad x = \dfrac{1 + 4}{3} = \dfrac{5}{3}$

The solutions are -1 and $\dfrac{5}{3}$.

9. $3x^2 - 7x - 2 = 0$

$a = 3, b = -7,$ and $c = -2$

$$z = \frac{-(-7) \pm \sqrt{(-7)^2 - 4(3)(-2)}}{2(3)}$$

$$= \frac{7 \pm \sqrt{49 + 24}}{6} = \frac{7 \pm \sqrt{73}}{6}$$

The solutions are $\dfrac{7 \pm \sqrt{73}}{6}$.

10. $\qquad x(x + 6) = 7$

$x^2 + 6x - 7 = 0$

$(x + 7)(x - 1) = 0$

$\qquad x + 7 = 0 \quad \text{or} \quad x - 1 = 0$

$\qquad\qquad x = -7 \qquad\qquad x = 1$

The solutions are -7 and 1.

11. $\qquad 3x^2 - 7x + 2 = 0$

$(3x - 1)(x - 2) = 0$

$\qquad 3x - 1 = 0 \quad \text{or} \quad x - 2 = 0$

$\qquad\qquad x = \dfrac{1}{3} \qquad\qquad x = 2$

The solutions are $\dfrac{1}{3}$ and 2.

12. $2x^2 - 6x + 1 = 0$

$a = 2, b = -6,$ and $c = 1$

$$x = \frac{-(-6) \pm \sqrt{(-6)^2 - 4(2)(1)}}{2(2)}$$

$$= \frac{6 \pm \sqrt{36-8}}{4} = \frac{6 \pm \sqrt{28}}{4}$$

$$= \frac{6 \pm 2\sqrt{7}}{4} = \frac{3 \pm \sqrt{7}}{2}$$

The solutions are $\dfrac{3 \pm \sqrt{7}}{2}$.

13.
$$9x^3 = x$$
$$9x^3 - x = 0$$
$$x(9x^2 - 1) = 0$$
$$x(3x+1)(3x-1) = 0$$

$x = 0, \quad 3x+1 = 0, \quad 3x-1 = 0$
$$3x = -1 \qquad 3x = 1$$
$$x = -\frac{1}{3} \qquad x = \frac{1}{3}$$

$x = -\dfrac{1}{3}, 0, \dfrac{1}{3}$

14. $y = -3x^2$

Vertex:

$$x = -\frac{b}{2a} = \frac{0}{2(-3)} = 0$$

$$y = -3(0)^2 = 0$$

Vertex $(0, 0)$; also intercepts

Use table for other points

x	y
-1	-3
1	-3

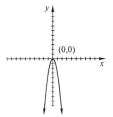

15. $y = x^2 - 7x + 10$

vertex: $x = -\dfrac{b}{2a} = -\dfrac{-7}{2(1)} = \dfrac{7}{2}$

$$y = \left(\frac{7}{2}\right)^2 - 7\left(\frac{7}{2}\right) + 10 = -\frac{9}{4}$$

$\left(\dfrac{7}{2}, -\dfrac{9}{4}\right)$

y-intercept: $x = 0$, $y = 10$, $(0,10)$

x-intercepts: $y = 0$,
$$0 = x^2 - 7x + 10$$
$$0 = (x-2)(x-5)$$
$$x = 2 \quad \text{or} \quad x = 5$$
$(2,0)$ and $(5,0)$

x	y
0	10
2	0
7/2	$-9/45$
5	0
7	10

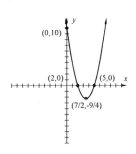

16. Let $h = 120.75$

$$h = 16t^2$$
$$16t^2 = h$$
$$16t^2 = 120.75$$
$$t^2 = \frac{120.75}{16}$$
$$t = \pm\sqrt{\frac{120.75}{16}} \approx \pm 2.7$$

The length of time is not a negative number so the dive lasted 2.7 seconds.

Cumulative Review Chapter 16

1. $\dfrac{786}{10,000} = 10,000\overline{)786.0000}^{\,0.0786} = 0.0786$

2. $\dfrac{818}{1000} = 1000\overline{)818.000}^{\,0.818} = 0.818$

3. $\dfrac{0.12}{10} = 10\overline{)0.120}^{\,0.012} = 0.012$

4. $\dfrac{5.03}{100} = 100\overline{)5.0300}^{\,0.0503} = 0.0503$

5. One + Two + Three + Four or more
$= 47\% + 15\% + 6\% + 3\%$
$= 71\%$

6. Zero + One + Two
$= 29\% + 47\% + 15\%$
$= 91\%$

7. $P = 2L + 2W$
$P = 2(11\text{ inches}) + 2(3\text{ inches})$
$P = 22\text{ inches} + 6\text{ inches}$
$P = 28\text{ inches}$

8. $P = a + b + c$
$P = 6\text{ feet} + 8\text{ feet} + 11\text{ feet}$
$P = 25\text{ feet}$

9. $A = bh$
$A = (3.4\text{ miles})(1.5\text{ miles})$
$A = 5.1\text{ square miles}$

10. $A = \dfrac{1}{2}bh$
$A = \dfrac{1}{2}(17\text{ inches})(8\text{ inches})$
$A = 68\text{ square inches}$

11. $3210\text{ ml} = \dfrac{3210\text{ ml}}{1} \cdot \dfrac{1\text{ L}}{1000\text{ ml}} = 3.21\text{ L}$

12. $4321\text{ cl} = \dfrac{4321\text{ cl}}{1} \cdot \dfrac{1\text{ L}}{100\text{ cl}} = 43.21\text{ L}$

13. $8(2 - t) = -5t$
$16 - 8t = -5t$
$-8t + 5t = -16$
$\dfrac{-3t}{-3} = \dfrac{-16}{-3}$
$t = \dfrac{16}{3}$

14.
$$\frac{5}{2}x - 1 = x + \frac{1}{4}$$
$$4\left(\frac{5}{2}x - 1\right) = 4\left(x + \frac{1}{4}\right)$$
$$2(5x) - 4(1) = 4(x) + 1(1)$$
$$10x - 4 = 4x + 1$$
$$10x - 4x = 1 + 4$$
$$\frac{6x}{6} = \frac{5}{6}$$

15. $3^0 = 1$

16. $-2^\circ = -\left(2^\circ\right) = -1$

17. $r^2 - r - 42 = (r - 7)(r + 6)$

18. $y^2 + 3y - 70 = (y - 7)(y + 10)$

19. $10x^2 - 13xy - 3y^2 = (2x - 3y)(5x + y)$

20. $72x^2 - 35xy + 3y^2 = (8x - 3y)(9x - y)$

21. $8x^2 - 14x + 5 = 8x^2 - 10x - 4x + 5$
$$= 2x(4x - 5) - (4x - 5)$$
$$= (2x - 1)(4x - 5)$$

22. $15x^2 - 4x - 4$
$$= 15x^2 - 10x + 6x - 4$$
$$= \left(15x^2 - 10x\right) + (6x - 4)$$
$$= 5x(3x - 2) + 2(3x - 2)$$
$$= (3x - 2)(5x + 2)$$

23. a. $4x^3 - 49x = x\left(4x^2 - 49\right)$
$$= x\left[(2x)^2 - (7)^2\right]$$
$$= x(2x + 7)(2x - 7)$$

b. $162x^4 - 2 = 2\left(81x^4 - 1\right)$
$$= 2\left[\left(9x^2\right)^2 - (1)^2\right]$$
$$= 2\left(9x^2 + 1\right)\left(9x^2 - 1\right)$$
$$= 2\left(9x^2 + 1\right)\left[(3x)^2 - (1)^2\right]$$
$$= 2\left(9x^2 + 1\right)(3x + 1)(3x - 1)$$

24. a. $9x^3 - x$
$$= x\left(9x^2 - 1\right)$$
$$= x(3x + 1)(3x - 1)$$

b. $5x^4 - 5$
$$= 5\left(x^4 - 1\right)$$
$$= 5\left(x^2 + 1\right)\left(x^2 - 1\right)$$
$$= 5\left(x^2 + 1\right)(x + 1)(x - 1)$$

25. $(5x - 1)\left(2x^2 + 15x + 18\right) = 0$
$$(5x - 1)(2x + 3)(x + 6) = 0$$
$$5x - 1 = 0 \quad \text{or} \quad 2x + 3 = 0 \quad \text{or} \quad x + 6 = 0$$
$$x = \frac{1}{5} \qquad\qquad x = -\frac{3}{2} \qquad\qquad x = -6$$

The solutions are -6, $-\dfrac{3}{2}$, and $\dfrac{1}{5}$.

26. $(x+4)(40x^2-34x+3)=0$

$(x+4)(4x-3)(10x-1)=0$

$x+4=0; \quad 4x-3=0; \quad 10x-1=0$

$x=-4 \qquad \dfrac{4x}{4}=\dfrac{3}{4} \qquad \dfrac{10x}{10}=\dfrac{1}{10}$

$\qquad\qquad\qquad x=\dfrac{3}{4}; \qquad x=\dfrac{1}{10}$

$x=-4, \dfrac{1}{10}, \dfrac{3}{4}$

27. $\dfrac{x^2+8x+7}{x^2-4x-5}=\dfrac{(x+7)(x+1)}{(x-5)(x+1)}=\dfrac{x+7}{x-5}$

28. $\dfrac{x^2-6x+5}{x^2+6x-7}=\dfrac{(x-1)(x-5)}{(x-1)(x+7)}=\dfrac{x-5}{x+7}$

29. Let x = the unknown number.

$\dfrac{x}{6}-\dfrac{5}{3}=\dfrac{x}{2}$

$6\left(\dfrac{x}{6}-\dfrac{5}{3}\right)=6\left(\dfrac{x}{2}\right)$

$x-10=3x$

$-10=2x$

$-5=x$

The number is -5.

30. Let x = a number

$\dfrac{5+4x}{6}=\dfrac{7}{2}$

$2(5+4x)=7(6)$

$10+8x=42$

$8x=42-10$

$\dfrac{8x}{8}=\dfrac{32}{8}$

$x=4$

31.

	x	y
a.	-1	-3
b.	0	0
c.	-3	-9

32. a. $y = -2x + 7$

$y = -2(0) + 7$

$y = 0 + 7$

$y = 7$

$(0, 7)$

b. $y = -2x + 7$

$0 = -2x + 7$

$\dfrac{2x}{2} = \dfrac{7}{2}$

$x = \dfrac{7}{2}$

$\left(\dfrac{7}{2}, 0\right)$

c. $y = -2x + 7$

$y = -2(5) + 7$

$y = -10 + 7$

$y = -3$

$(5, -3)$

33. 17.a $y = -\dfrac{1}{5}x + 1,\ m_1 = -\dfrac{1}{5}$

$2x + 10y = 3,\ 10y = -2x + 3,$

$y = -\dfrac{2}{10}x + \dfrac{3}{10},\ m_2 = -\dfrac{2}{10} = \dfrac{1}{5}$

$m_1 = m_2$, parallel

b. $x + y = 3,\ y = -x + 3,\ m_1 = -1$

$-x + y = 4,\ y = x + 4,\ m_2 = 1$

$m_1 m_2 = (-1)(1) = -1$, perpendicular

c. $3x + y = 5,\ y = -3x + 5,\ m_1 = -3$

$2x + 3y = 6,\ 3y = -2x + 6,$

$y = -\dfrac{2}{3}x + 2,\ m_2 = -\dfrac{2}{3}$

$m_1 \neq m_2$ and $m_1 m_2 \neq -1$, neither

34. a. $y = -2x + 3$

$y = -2x + 5$

These lines are parallel since their slopes are equal.

b. $-2x + y = 3$ in slope-intercept form is

$y = 2 + 3$

$x + 2y = 9$ in slope-intercept form is

$y = -\dfrac{1}{2}x + 9$

These lines are perpendicular since their slopes are opposite reciprocals.

c. $3x - 2y = -8$ in slope-intercept form is

$y = \dfrac{3}{2}x + 4$

$3x + 2y = 1$ in slope-intercept form is

$y = -\dfrac{3}{2}x + \dfrac{1}{2}$

These lines are neither parallel nor perpendicular.

35. a. Every point has a unique x-value: it is a function.

b. Two points have the same x-value: it is not a function.

36. a. function; one x value for each y value

b. not a function; one x with two y values

37. $\begin{cases} 2x+y=10 \\ x=y+2 \end{cases}$

Substitute $y+2$ for x in the first equation.

$2(y+2)+y=10$

$2y+4+y=10$

$3y=6$

$y=2$

Let $y=2$ in the second equation.

$x=2+2$

$x=4$

The solution is $(4,2)$.

38. $\begin{cases} 8x-3y=-4 \\ y=7x-3 \end{cases}$

Using substitution:

$8x-3(7x-3)=-4$

$8x-21x+9=-4$

$-13x+9=-4$

$-13x=-4-9$

$\dfrac{-13x}{-13}=\dfrac{-13}{-13}$

$x=1$

$y=7(1)-3$

$y=7-3$

$y=4$

Solution: $(1,4)$

39. $\sqrt{36}=6$

40. $\sqrt{81}=\sqrt{9\cdot 9}=9$

41. $\sqrt{\dfrac{9}{100}}=\dfrac{3}{10}$

42. $\sqrt{\dfrac{16}{25}}=\sqrt{\dfrac{4\cdot 4}{5\cdot 5}}=\dfrac{4}{5}$

43. $\dfrac{2}{1+\sqrt{3}}=\dfrac{2(1-\sqrt{3})}{(1+\sqrt{3})(1-\sqrt{3})}=\dfrac{2(1-\sqrt{3})}{1^2-(\sqrt{3})^2}$

$=\dfrac{2(1-\sqrt{3})}{1-3}=\dfrac{2(1-\sqrt{3})}{-2}$

$=-1+\sqrt{3}$

44. $\dfrac{7}{\sqrt{5}-2}=\dfrac{7}{(\sqrt{5}-2)}\cdot\dfrac{(\sqrt{5}+2)}{(\sqrt{5}+2)}$

$=\dfrac{7\sqrt{5}+7(2)}{\sqrt{25}+2\sqrt{5}-2\sqrt{5}-4}$

$=\dfrac{7\sqrt{5}+14}{5-4}$

$=\dfrac{7\sqrt{5}+14}{1}$

$=7\sqrt{5}+14$

45. $(x-3)^2=16$

$x-3=\pm\sqrt{16}$

$x=3\pm 4$

$x=3-4=-1$ or $x=3+4=7$

The solutions are -1 and 7.

46. $(x+4)^2 = 9$

$\sqrt{(x+4)^2} = \pm\sqrt{9}$

$x+4 = \pm 3$

$x+4 = -3; \quad x+4 = 3$

$x = -3-4; \quad x = 3-4$

$x = -7; \qquad x = -1$

$x = -7, -1$

47. $\dfrac{1}{2}x^2 - x = 2$

$x^2 - 2x = 4$

$x^2 - 2x - 4 = 0$

$a = 1, b = -2, \text{ and } c = -4$

$x = \dfrac{-(-2) \pm \sqrt{(-2)^2 - 4(1)(-4)}}{2(1)}$

$= \dfrac{2 \pm \sqrt{4+16}}{2} = \dfrac{2 \pm \sqrt{20}}{2}$

$= \dfrac{2 \pm 2\sqrt{5}}{2} = 1 \pm \sqrt{5}$

The solutions are $1 \pm \sqrt{5}$.

48. $2x^2 = \dfrac{5}{2}x + \dfrac{7}{2}$

$2(2x^2) = 2\left(\dfrac{5}{2}x + \dfrac{7}{2}\right)$

$4x^2 = 5x + 7$

$4x^2 - 5x - 7 = 0$

$a = 4; b = -5, c = -7$

$x = \dfrac{-(-5) \pm \sqrt{(5)^2 - 4(4)(-7)}}{2(4)}$

$= \dfrac{5 \pm \sqrt{25+112}}{8}$

$= \dfrac{5 \pm \sqrt{137}}{8}$